Literature Criticism from 1400 to 1800

Guide to Gale Literary Criticism Series

For criticism on	Consult these Gale series
Authors now living or who died after December 31, 1999	**CONTEMPORARY LITERARY CRITICISM (CLC)**
Authors who died between 1900 and 1999	**TWENTIETH-CENTURY LITERARY CRITICISM (TCLC)**
Authors who died between 1800 and 1899	**NINETEENTH-CENTURY LITERATURE CRITICISM (NCLC)**
Authors who died between 1400 and 1799	**LITERATURE CRITICISM FROM 1400 TO 1800 (LC)** **SHAKESPEAREAN CRITICISM (SC)**
Authors who died before 1400	**CLASSICAL AND MEDIEVAL LITERATURE CRITICISM (CMLC)**
Authors of books for children and young adults	**CHILDREN'S LITERATURE REVIEW (CLR)**
Dramatists	**DRAMA CRITICISM (DC)**
Poets	**POETRY CRITICISM (PC)**
Short story writers	**SHORT STORY CRITICISM (SSC)**
Literary topics and movements	**HARLEM RENAISSANCE: A GALE CRITICAL COMPANION (HR)** **THE BEAT GENERATION: A GALE CRITICAL COMPANION (BG)**
Asian American writers of the last two hundred years	**ASIAN AMERICAN LITERATURE (AAL)**
Black writers of the past two hundred years	**BLACK LITERATURE CRITICISM (BLC)** **BLACK LITERATURE CRITICISM SUPPLEMENT (BLCS)**
Hispanic writers of the late nineteenth and twentieth centuries	**HISPANIC LITERATURE CRITICISM (HLC)** **HISPANIC LITERATURE CRITICISM SUPPLEMENT (HLCS)**
Native North American writers and orators of the eighteenth, nineteenth, and twentieth centuries	**NATIVE NORTH AMERICAN LITERATURE (NNAL)**
Major authors from the Renaissance to the present	**WORLD LITERATURE CRITICISM, 1500 TO THE PRESENT (WLC)** **WORLD LITERATURE CRITICISM SUPPLEMENT (WLCS)**

ISSN 0740-2880

Volume 123

Literature Criticism from 1400 to 1800

Critical Discussion of the Works of Fifteenth-, Sixteenth-, Seventeenth-, and Eighteenth-Century Novelists, Poets, Playwrights, Philosophers, and Other Creative Writers

Thomas J. Schoenberg
Lawrence J. Trudeau
Project Editors

Detroit • New York • San Francisco • San Diego • New Haven, Conn. • Waterville, Maine • London • Munich

Literature Criticism from 1400 to 1800, Vol. 123

Project Editors
Thomas J. Schoenberg and Lawrence J. Trudeau

Editorial
Jessica Bomarito, Kathy D. Darrow, Jeffrey W. Hunter, Jelena O. Krstović, Michelle Lee, Rachelle Mucha, Russel Whitaker

Data Capture
Francis Monroe, Gwen Tucker

Indexing Services
Laurie Andriot

Rights and Acquisitions
Emma Hull, Jackie Jones, Lisa Kincade

Imaging and Multimedia
Dean Dauphinais, Leitha Etheridge-Sims, Lezlie Light, Mike Logusz, Dan Newell, Christine O'Bryan, Kelly A. Quin, Denay Wilding, Robyn Young

Composition and Electronic Capture
Amy Darga

Manufacturing
Rhonda Dover

Associate Product Manager
Marc Cormier

LIBRARY OF CONGRESS CATALOG CARD NUMBER 94-29718

ISBN 0-7876-8740-5
ISSN 0740-2880

Printed in the United States of America
10 9 8 7 6 5 4 3 2 1

Contents

Preface vii

Acknowledgments xi

Literary Criticism Series Advisory Board xiii

Preface

*L*iterature Criticism from 1400 to 1800 (*LC*) presents critical discussion of world literature from the fifteenth through the eighteenth centuries. The literature of this period is especially vital: the years 1400 to 1800 saw the rise of modern European drama, the birth of the novel and personal essay forms, the emergence of newspapers and periodicals, and major achievements in poetry and philosophy. *LC* provides valuable insight into the art, life, thought, and cultural transformations that took place during these centuries.

Scope of the Series

LC provides an introduction to the great poets, dramatists, novelists, essayists, and philosophers of the fifteenth through eighteenth centuries, and to the most significant interpretations of these authors' works. Because criticism of this literature spans nearly six hundred years, an overwhelming amount of scholarship confronts the student. *LC* organizes this material concisely and logically. Every attempt is made to reprint the most noteworthy, relevant, and educationally valuable essays available.

A separate Thomson Gale reference series, *Shakespearean Criticism,* is devoted exclusively to Shakespearean studies. Although properly belonging to the period covered in *LC,* William Shakespeare has inspired such a tremendous and ever-growing body of secondary material that a separate series was deemed essential.

Each entry in *LC* presents a representative selection of critical response to an author, a literary topic, or to a single important work of literature. Early commentary is offered to indicate initial responses, later selections document changes in literary reputations, and retrospective analyses provide the reader with modern views. The size of each author entry is a relative reflection of the scope of the criticism available in English. Every attempt has been made to identify and include the seminal essays on each author's work and to include recent commentary providing modern perspectives.

Volumes 1 through 12 of the series feature author entries arranged alphabetically by author. Volumes 13-47 of the series feature a thematic arrangement. Each volume includes an entry devoted to the general study of a specific literary or philosophical movement, writings surrounding important political and historical events, the philosophy and art associated with eras of cultural transformation, or the literature of specific social or ethnic groups. Each of these volumes also includes several author entries devoted to major representatives of the featured period, genre, or national literature. With volume 48, the series returns to a standard author approach, with some entries devoted to a single important work of world literature and others devoted to literary topics.

Organization of the Book

An *LC* entry consists of the following elements:

- The **Author Heading** cites the name under which the author most commonly wrote, followed by birth and death dates. Also located here are any name variations under which an author wrote, including transliterated forms for authors whose native languages use nonroman alphabets. If the author wrote consistently under a pseudonym, the pseudonym will be listed in the author heading and the author's actual name given in parenthesis on the first line of the biographical and critical information. Uncertain birth or death dates are indicated by question marks. Topic entries are preceded by a **Thematic Heading,** which simply states the subject of the entry. Single-work entries are preceded by the title of the work and its date of publication.

- The **Introduction** contains background information that introduces the reader to the author, work, or topic that is the subject of the entry.

- A **Portrait of the Author** is included, when available.

- The list of **Principal Works** is ordered chronologically by date of first publication and lists the most important works by the author. The genre and publication date of each work is given. In the case of foreign authors whose works have been translated into English, the title and date (if available) of the first English-language edition is given in brackets following the original title. Unless otherwise indicated, dramas are dated by first performance, not first publication. Lists of **Representative Works** by different authors appear with topic entries.

- Reprinted **Criticism** is arranged chronologically in each entry to provide a useful perspective on changes in critical evaluation over time. The critic's name and the date of composition or publication of the critical work are given at the beginning of each piece of criticism. Unsigned criticism is preceded by the title of the source in which it appeared. All titles by the author featured in the text are printed in boldface type. Footnotes are reprinted at the end of each essay or excerpt. In the case of excerpted criticism, only those footnotes that pertain to the excerpted texts are included. Criticism in topic entries is arranged chronologically under a variety of subheadings to facilitate the study of different aspects of the topic.

- Critical essays are prefaced by brief **Annotations** explicating each piece.

- A complete **Bibliographical Citation** of the original essay or book precedes each piece of criticism. Source citations in the Literary Criticism Series follow University of Chicago Press style, as outlined in *The Chicago Manual of Style,* 14th ed. (Chicago: The University of Chicago Press, 1993).

- An annotated bibliography of **Further Reading** appears at the end of each entry and suggests resources for additional study. In some cases, significant essays for which the editors could not obtain reprint rights are included here. Boxed material following the further reading list provides references to other biographical and critical sources on the author in series published by Thomson Gale.

Indexes

A **Cumulative Author Index** lists all of the authors that appear in a wide variety of reference sources published by Thomson Gale, including *LC.* A complete list of these sources is found facing the first page of the Author Index. The index also includes birth and death dates and cross references between pseudonyms and actual names.

A **Cumulative Nationality Index** lists all authors featured in *LC* by nationality, followed by the number of the *LC* volume in which their entry appears.

A **Cumulative Topic Index** lists the literary themes and topics treated in the series as well as in *Nineteenth-Century Literature Criticism, Twentieth-Century Literary Criticism,* and the *Contemporary Literature Criticism* Yearbook, which was discontinued in 1998.

An alphabetical **Title Index** accompanies each volume of *LC.* Listings of titles by authors covered in the given volume are followed by the author's name and the corresponding page numbers on which the titles are discussed. English translations of foreign titles and variations of titles are cross-referenced to the title under which a work was originally published. Titles of novels, dramas, nonfiction books, and poetry, short story, or essay collections are printed in italics, while individual poems, short stories, and essays are printed in roman type within quotation marks.

In response to numerous suggestions from librarians, Thomson Gale also produces an annual paperbound edition of the LC cumulative title index. This annual cumulation, which alphabetically lists all titles reviewed in the series, is available to all customers. Additional copies of this index are available upon request. Librarians and patrons will welcome this separate index; it saves shelf space, is easy to use, and is recyclable upon receipt of the next edition.

Citing *Literature Criticism from 1400 to 1800*

When citing criticism reprinted in the Literary Criticism Series, students should provide complete bibliographic information so that the cited essay can be located in the original print or electronic source. Students who quote directly from reprinted criticism may use any accepted bibliographic format, such as University of Chicago Press style or Modern Language Association (MLA) style. Both the MLA and the University of Chicago formats are acceptable and recognized as being the current standards for citations. It is important, however, to choose one format for all citations; do not mix the two formats within a list of citations.

The examples below follow recommendations for preparing a bibliography set forth in *The Chicago Manual of Style,* 14th ed. (Chicago: The University of Chicago Press, 1993); the first example pertains to material drawn from periodicals, the second to material reprinted from books:

Morrison, Jago. "Narration and Unease in Ian McEwan's Later Fiction." *Critique* 42, no. 3 (spring 2001): 253-68. Reprinted in *Literary Criticism from 1400-1800.* Vol. 76, edited by Michael L. LaBlanc, 212-20. Detroit: Gale, 2003.

Brossard, Nicole. "Poetic Politics." In *The Politics of Poetic Form: Poetry and Public Policy,* edited by Charles Bernstein, 73-82. New York: Roof Books, 1990. Reprinted in *Literary Criticism from 1400-1800.* Vol. 82, edited by Michael L. La-Blanc, 3-8. Detroit: Gale, 2003.

The examples below follow recommendations for preparing a works cited list set forth in the *MLA Handbook for Writers of Research Papers,* 5th ed. (New York: The Modern Language Association of America, 1999); the first example pertains to material drawn from periodicals, the second to material reprinted from books:

Morrison, Jago. "Narration and Unease in Ian McEwan's Later Fiction." *Critique* 42. 3 (spring 2001): 253-68. Reprinted in *Literary Criticism from 1400-1800.* Ed. Michael L. LaBlanc. Vol. 76. Detroit: Gale, 2003. 212-20.

Brossard, Nicole. "Poetic Politics." *The Politics of Poetic Form: Poetry and Public Policy.* Ed. Charles Bernstein. New York: Roof Books, 1990. 73-82. Reprinted in *Contemporary Literary Criticism.* Ed. Michael L. LaBlanc. Vol. 82. Detroit: Gale, 2003. 3-8.

Suggestions are Welcome

Readers who wish to suggest new features, topics, or authors to appear in future volumes, or who have other suggestions or comments are cordially invited to call, write, or fax the Associate Product Manager:

Associate Product Manager, Literary Criticism Series
Thomson Gale
27500 Drake Road
Farmington Hills, MI 48331-3535
1-800-347-4253 (GALE)
Fax: 248-699-8054

Acknowledgments

The editors wish to thank the copyright holders of the excerpted criticism included in this volume and the permissions managers of many book and magazine publishing companies for assisting us in securing reproduction rights. Following is a list of the copyright holders who have granted us permission to reproduce material in this volume of *LC*. Every effort has been made to trace copyright, but if omissions have been made, please let us know.

COPYRIGHTED MATERIAL IN *LC*, VOLUME 123, WAS REPRODUCED FROM THE FOLLOWING PERIODICALS:

Comparative Drama, v. 9, spring, 1975. Copyright © 1975, by the Editors of Comparative Drama. Reproduced by permission.—*Early Theatre: A Journal Associated with the Records of Early English Drama,* v. 5, 2002. Reproduced by permission.—*ELH,* v. 62, 1995. Copyright © 1995 The Johns Hopkins University Press. Reproduced by permission.—*English Literary Renaissance,* v. 3, winter, 1973; v. 14, autumn, 1984; v. 20, spring, 1990. Copyright © 1973, 1984, 1990 by *English Literary Renaissance.* All reproduced by permission of the editors.—*English Studies in Africa,* v. 12, September, 1969 for "The 'Finger' Image and Relationship of Character in *The Changeling*" by Normand Berlin. Copyright © Witwatersrand University Press 1969. Reproduced by permission of the publisher and the author.—*English Studies in Canada,* v. 9, March, 1983. Copyright © Association of Canadian University Teachers of English. Reproduced by permission of the publisher.—*Essays in Criticism,* v. 38, January, 1988 for "Folly and Madness in *The Changeling*" by Joost Daalder. Copyright © 1988 Oxford University Press. Reproduced by permission of Oxford University Press and the author.—*Essays in French Literature,* November, 1990. Copyright © Department of French Studies University of Western Australia. Reproduced by permission.—*Fifteenth-Century Studies,* v. 19, 1992. © Copyright 1992 Edelgard E. DeBruck and William C. McDonald. All rights reserved. Reproduced by permission.—*French Forum,* v. 5, January, 1980. Copyright © 1980 by French Form Publishers, Inc. All rights reserved. Reproduced by permission of the University of Nebraska Press.—*French Review,* v. 42, October, 1968; v. 55, March, 1982. Copyright © 1968, 1982 by the American Association of Teachers of French. Both reproduced by permission.—*French Studies,* v. 39, January, 1985. Copyright © 1985 Oxford University Press. Reproduced by permission of the Oxford University Press and the author.—*Humanities Association Bulletin,* v. 20, winter, 1969. Reproduced by permission.—*Journal of English and Germanic Philology,* v. 63, October, 1964. Copyright © 1964 by the Board of Trustees of the University of Illinois. Reproduced by permission of the University of Illinois Press.—*Kentucky Romance Quarterly,* v. 14, 1967. Copyright © 1967 by Helen Dwight Reid Educational Foundation. Reproduced with permission of the Helen Dwight Reid Educational Foundation, published by Heldref Publications, 1319 18th Street, NW, Washington, DC 20036-1802.—*Modern Language Studies,* v. 11, spring, 1981 for "The Five Structures of *The Changeling*" by A. L. Kistner, and M. K. Kistner. Copyright, Northeast Modern Language Association 1981. Reproduced by permission of the publisher and the author.—*Neophilologus,* v. 56, January, 1972. Reproduced by permission.—*Renaissance Drama,* v. 3, 1970. Reproduced by permission.—*Renaissance Drama,* n.s. v. 11, 1980. Reproduced by permission.—*Renaissance Papers,* 1969. Reproduced by permission.—*Romance Languages Annual,* v. 6, 1994. Copyright © 1995 by Purdue Research Foundation. Reproduced by permission.—*Romance Quarterly,* v. 38, August, 1991. Copyright © 1991 by Helen Dwight Reid Educational Foundation. Reproduced with permission of the Helen Dwight Reid Educational Foundation, published by Heldref Publications, 1319 18th Street, NW, Washington, DC 20036-1802.—*Romanic Review,* v. 74, March, 1983. Copyright © 1983 by the Trustees of Columbia University in the City of New York. Reproduced by permission.—*Sixteenth Century Journal,* v. 18, autumn, 1987. Copyright © 1987 by the Sixteenth Century Journal Publishers, Inc., Kirksville, Missouri 63501-0828 U.S.A. All rights reserved. Reproduced by permission.—*Theatre Journal,* October, 1984. Copyright © 1984 The Johns Hopkins University Press. Reproduced by permission.—*Tulane Studies in English,* v. 20, 1972. Copyright © 1972 by Tulane University. Reproduced by permission.

COPYRIGHTED MATERIAL IN *LC*, VOLUME 123, WAS REPRODUCED FROM THE FOLLOWING BOOKS:

Boureau, Alain. From "Joan the Catholic: Thirteenth-Fifteenth Centuries," in *The Myth of Pope Joan.* Translated by Lydia G. Cochrane. The University of Chicago Press, 2001. Copyright © 2001 by The University of Chicago. All rights reserved. Reproduced by permission.—Brady, Patrick. From "Chaos, Complexity, Catastrophe and Control in Marivaux's *La Vie de Marianne*," in *Disrupted Patterns: On Chaos and Order in the Enlightenment.* Edited by Theodore E. D. Braun

Thomson Gale Literature Product Advisory Board

The members of the Thomson Gale Literary Criticism Series Advisory Board—reference librarians and subject specialists from public, academic, and school library systems—represent a cross-section of our customer base and offer a variety of informed perspectives on both the presentation and content of our literature criticism products. Advisory board members assess and define such quality issues as the relevance, currency, and usefulness of the author coverage, critical content, and literary topics included in our series; evaluate the layout, presentation, and general quality of our printed volumes; provide feedback on the criteria used for selecting authors and topics covered in our series; provide suggestions for potential enhancements to our series; identify any gaps in our coverage of authors or literary topics, recommending authors or topics for inclusion; analyze the appropriateness of our content and presentation for various user audiences, such as high school students, undergraduates, graduate students, librarians, and educators; and offer feedback on any proposed changes/enhancements to our series. We wish to thank the following advisors for their advice throughout the year.

The Legend of Pope Joan

Legend about a female pope who ruled from 855 to 858, which first appeared in European literature in the thirteenth century.

INTRODUCTION

According to medieval legend, in the ninth century a woman reigned as pope. There are several versions of the story, but one of the most common is that a young Englishwoman entered a monastic order in Rome disguised as a man. Because of her capability and intelligence she quickly rose in prominence in the church, and upon Pope Leo IV's death in 853 she was unanimously elected as Pope John VII. "Pope Joan," as she was later known, is said to have held power for two years before her true identity was discovered—as she gave birth during a papal procession through Rome. One version of the legend asserts that the people of Rome killed Joan by tying her feet and dragging her behind a horse, while another has her being sent to a convent to raise her child. The story of Pope Joan is, according to most modern historians, a legend. However, from the mid-thirteenth century until the early seventeenth century, the myth was widely disseminated and held to be true, even by the Catholic Church. Pope Joan has been the subject of numerous works of literature and art from the thirteenth century to the present, with many artists using the story as a metaphor for the suppression of female power. Some critics have also insisted that Joan was an actual historical personage. The literature about Joan from the thirteenth through the eighteenth centuries consists mainly of retellings of the legend and discussions of its veracity in works of history and religious polemic, but the numerous plays about the female prelate across Europe indicate that the legend also captured the popular imagination.

Although Joan is said to have reigned from 853 to 855, her story was not put into writing until the early thirteenth century. The first source suggesting the existence of a female prelate is the *Chronica universalis Mettensis* by Jean de Mailly, probably written between 1240 and 1250. De Mailly does not name the pontiff and suggests a later date than most subsequent sources for her reign, around 1100. His chronicle was used as the basis of the retelling of the tale by Etienne de Bourbon (Stephanus de Borbone) in *Tractatus de diversis materiis praedicabilibus* around 1261. A different version of the legend, the one that would become widely popularized, appeared around 1275 in the chronicle of Martinus

Polonus (Martin of Troppau), a papal chaplain. According to his account, a young English girl was taken in male clothing by her lover to Athens, where she excelled in learning. She went to Rome, where under the name John of Mainz (Johannes Anglicus) she taught science. She enjoyed the greatest respect because of her erudition and rose through the ranks of the Church. She was chosen pope, became pregnant by one of her attendants, and gave birth during a papal procession in Rome. One manuscript of the chronicle says she died in childbirth and was buried immediately, and another asserts that she was deposed and did penance in a convent, where she bore her child.

After Polonus's account appeared, the story of Pope Joan became widespread. Giovanni Boccaccio wrote about her in his *De mulieribus claris* (1362; *On Famous Women*), and a late-fourteenth-century guidebook for pilgrims to Rome tells readers that the female pope's remains are buried at St Peter's. At his trial in 1415, the Czech priest Jan Hus argued that the Church did not necessarily need a pope, because during the reign of the female pope (whom he called Agnes), it had survived without incident; Hus's opponents never disputed this argument. In the early fifteenth century a bust of Pope Joan, called "Johannes VIII, Foemina de Anglia," was placed in the Cathedral at Siena along with busts of other popes, and throughout the 1400s and 1500s the Church permitted the myth to be used in art, literature, and popular culture. It was also widely believed that to ensure that a woman was never again mistakenly elected pope, certain measures had been instituted to test the gender of potential pontiffs: the papal throne at St. John Lateran's had been made with a hole in it, it was thought, in order for the cardinals to inspect the pontiff's genitalia. Most accounts of Pope Joan during the fourteenth and fifteenth centuries portray her in an unflattering light, with the exception of that in Martin Lefranc's *Le champion des dames* (circa 1440). Lefranc's poems in five books argue for the honor of the female gender, and his verses about Joan seek to rehabilitate her character by stressing her virtues and merits as a scholar. Lefranc argues that Joan was the victim of masculine persecution whose crimes could not compare to the impropriety of those of various male clerics.

For most of the fifteenth century, Pope Joan's existence was uncritically accepted, but this began to change with the dawn of the new Renaissance humanism. Bartolomeo Platina (Bartolomeo Saachi), the Prefect of the Vatican library, expressed his doubts about the story in his 1472 history of the popes, *Vitae Pontificum*. The story continued to be popular among ordinary people, but the Catholic establishment and literati soon began to view the story of Pope Joan as an embarrassment, particularly as it was increasingly used by Protestants to criticize Catholicism. In his *Defence of the Apology of the Church of England* (1567), for example, the Protestant Bishop John Jewel defended the existence of the female pope and at the same time satirized and attacked the papacy. Numerous Catholic refutations of the existence of the papess began to appear, notably Florimond de Raemond's *L'Anti-Papesse, ou L'erreur populaire de la papesse Jeanne* (1587), which showed it to be a thirteenth-century invention, and in 1601 Pope Clement VIII declared the legend of Pope Joan to be untrue. The bust of her in Siena was destroyed. The legend of Pope Joan was further discredited in 1647 by the Protestant historian David Blondel, who suggested that tale originated as a satire against Pope John XI.

The Catholic Church had by now firmly rejected the story of Joan as myth, but in the sixteenth and seventeenth centuries the tale continued to be used by Protestants to attack Catholicism, both in polemical tracts and on the stage. In England, Alexander Cooke's *Pope Joan, a dialogue between a Protestant and a Papist proving that a woman called Joane was Pope of Rome against the surmises and to the contrarie objections made by Robert Bellarmine and Caesar Baronius,* first published in 1610 and revised in 1675 as *A Present for a Papist,* was popular until the late 1700s. The first known English play about Joan was staged in 1591 or 1592. Elkanah Settle's *The Female Prelate,* which appeared at the Theatre Royal in 1680, and the French farce *La Papesse Jeanne* (1793) by C. Fauconprèt both poked fun at the institution of the papacy.

According to some historians, the Catholic response to these Protestant attacks was to attempt to destroy the historical records concerning the story of Pope Joan. Hundreds of manuscripts and books were seized by the Vatican. Over the next few centuries, the Church claimed that the legend of Pope Joan was nothing more than a Protestant tactic that had originated during the Reformation. They argued too that the lack of references to Pope Joan in contemporary documents was proof that she did not exist and was a fabrication by later writers. Most historians since the eighteenth century have agreed with the Church that Joan is a mythical figure. However, others have seen the Church's stance as suggesting a cover-up, and the story is not universally accepted as a mere fable. The legend continues to inspire writers and artists, who have depicted Joan even into the nineteenth, twentieth, and twenty-first centuries in novels, plays, and films. Literary scholars who have written about Pope Joan have focused on the retelling of the Joan myth, its permutations over the centuries, and its representation in the

chronicles and fictional accounts from the thirteenth century to modern times. Some critics have used the legend to show how myths are used to explain phenomena that seem to have no historical evidence, while others have shown how the debunking of the legend introduced readers to the problem of historical evidence. Few of the chronicles and plays from the thirteenth through the eighteenth centuries depicting Pope Joan have garnered detailed attention from critics; most are viewed as being of little more than historical interest. Most of the modern notice of the legend of Pope Joan surrounds the evolution of the legend and the debates and controversy it inspired, particularly as it was used as a weapon by Reformation Protestants against the Catholic Church.

REPRESENTATIVE WORKS

Anonymous Works
The History of Pope Joan and the Whores of Rome (nonfiction) 1687
Pope Joan, or, An Account out of Romish Authors before and since Luther . . . that there was a She Pope who sat in the See and Ruled the Same (nonfiction) 1689
The Surprising History of Pope Joan (nonfiction) 1744

Archbishop Antoninus of Florence
Chronica Antonini (nonfiction) c. 1450

Pierre Bayle
Dictionnaire historique et critique [*Historical and Critical Dictionary*] (nonfiction) 1697

David Blondel
Familier esclaircissement de la Question, si une Femme a esté assige au Siè Papal de Rome entre Léon IV et Benoit III (nonfiction) 1647

Giovanni Boccaccio
De mulieribus claris [*On Famous Women*] (biography collection) 1362

Jean Bouchet
Annales d'Aquitaine, vol. 2 (nonfiction) 1541

Etienne de Bourbon (Stephanus de Borbone)
Tractatus de diversis materiis praedicabilibus (nonfiction) c. 1261

Alexander Cooke
Pope Joan, a dialogue between a Protestant and a Papist proving that a woman called Joane was Pope of Rome against the surmises and to the contrarie ob-

jections made by Robert Bellarmine and Caesar Baronius (nonfiction) 1610; revised as *A Present for a Papist, or The Life and Death of Pope Joan* 1675

Alan Cope
Dialogi Sex Contra Pontificatos (nonfiction) 1566

C. Fauconprèt
La Papesse Jeanne: Opéra-Bouffon en Vaudevilles, en Trois Actes (play) 1793

Jacopo Filippo Foresti (Jacopo Filippo of Bergamo)
De plurimis mulieribus claris (nonfiction) 1497

Bernard Guidonis
Catalogus Pontificum Romanorum cum inserta temporum historia (nonfiction; fragment) c. 1315-1325

H. S.
Historia De Donne Famose or The Romaine Iubile which happened in the yeare 855 (nonfiction); date of original unknown, English translation 1599

Ranulph Higden
The Cronykles of Englande with the dedes of popes and emperours (nonfiction) 1528

Jan Hus
De Ecclesia (nonfiction) c. 1412

John Jewel
Defence of the Apology of the Church of England (nonfiction) 1567

Martin Lefranc
Le champion des dames (poetry) c. 1440

Jacques Lenfant
Histoire de la papesse Jeanne, fidèlement tirée de la dissertation latine de Fred. Spanheim [translator, of a work by Friedrich Spanheim] (nonfiction) 1691

I. M.
*The Anatomie of Pope Joan (nonfiction) 1624

Jean de Mailly
Chronica universalis Mettensis (nonfiction) c. 1240-50

John Mayo
An Anatomie of Pope Joan (nonfiction) 1591

Francesco Petrarca
Cronica delle vite de Pontifici et imperatori Romani (nonfiction) c. 1370

Amaury du Peyrat
Chronique (nonfiction; fragment) c. 1399

Martinus Polonus (Martin of Troppau)
Chronica de Romanis Pontificibus et imperatoribus [*Chronicon Pontifcum et Imperatum*] (nonfiction) c. 1275

Bartolomeo Platina (Bartolomeo Saachi)
Vitae Pontificum [*Liber de vita Christi ac omnium Pontificum*] (nonfiction) 1472

Florimond de Raemond
L'Anti-Papesse, ou L'erreur populaire de la papesse Jeanne (nonfiction) 1587

Simon Rosarius
Antithesis Christi et Antichristi (nonfiction) 1578

Hartmann Schedel
Nuremberg Chronicle [*Chronicarum liber*] (nonfiction) 1493

Elknah Settle
The Female Prelate, Being the History of the Life and Death of Pope Joan (nonfiction) 1680

Friedrich Spanheim
Disquitio historica de papa foemina inter Leonem IV et Benedictum III (nonfiction) 1691

Johannes Stella
Vitae Pontificum (nonfiction) 1505

Hermann Witekind
Jesuitas pontificis maximi Romani emissaries, falso et frstra negare papam Joannem VIII fuisse mulierem (nonfiction) 1587

*This work is possibly a reprint of John Mayo, 1591.

OVERVIEWS AND GENERAL STUDIES

J. J. I. von Döllinger (essay date 1863)

SOURCE: Von Döllinger, J. J. I. "Pope Joan." In *Fables Respecting the Popes in the Middle Ages,* translated by Alfred Plummer, pp. 3-74. New York: Dodd & Mead, 1872.

[*In the following essay, originally published in German in 1863, von Döllinger maintains that the myth of Pope Joan was not definitively put into writing before the middle of the thirteenth century, that it came into wide circulation several decades later, and that it was accepted doctrine after the appearance of the chronicle of*

Martinus Polonus, sometime before 1278. The critic goes on to describe some of the later written versions of the story and considers how the legend might have originated.]

The subject of Pope Joan has not yet lost the interest which belongs to it as a fact in the province of historical criticism. The literature respecting her reaches down to the very latest times. As recently as 1843 and 1845 two works on this question appeared from the pens of two Dutch scholars; the one by Professor Kist,[1] to prove the existence of Pope Joan, the other, a very voluminous one, by Professor Wensing, of Warmond, to disprove Kist's position. In Italy Bianchi-Giovini wrote a book on the subject in the same year, 1845, without being aware of the works of the two Dutch writers. In Germany no one—at any rate of those who know anything of history—will easily be induced to entertain a serious belief in the existence of the female pope. To do so, one must do violence to every principle of historical criticism. But with the banishment of the subject to the realm of fable all has not yet been completely accomplished. The riddle—how this strange myth originated— remains still to be solved.

Nothing but the insufficiency and ill-success of all previous attempts at an explanation can account for it that a man like Luden, in his *History of the German People,*[2] does all he can to make the reality of the well-known myth at any rate probable. "It is inconceivable," says he, "how it could ever enter into any man's head to invent such a foolish, insane falsehood. He must either have invented his lie out of sheer wantonness in order to scoff at the papacy, or he must have intended to gain some other object by means of it. But of all the dozens of writers who mention Pope Joan and her mishap, there is not a single one who can be called an enemy of the papacy. They are clergy, monks, guileless people, who notice this phenomenon in the same dry way in which they mention other things, that seem to them to be strange, wonderful, laudable, abominable, or in any way worth mentioning." "And it cannot be imagined," says Luden further on, "what object could seem to any one to be attainable by means of such a falsehood. Moreover, it is inconceivable how people in general could have believed in the story, and that without the slightest doubt, for nearly 500 years from the eleventh century onwards, if it had not been true."

It is here to be noted that Luden makes the myth of Pope Joan a matter of general belief from the *eleventh* century onwards. It would be very much nearer the truth to say that it did not find general belief till the middle of the *fourteenth* century. The author, however, of the article on Pope Joan in the *Nouvelle Biographie Générale,* published at Paris by Dr. Höfer, as lately as 1858, goes much further.[3] "This belief prevailed in the christian world from the *ninth* century to the Renais-

sance." And to crown it all, Hase thinks it, at any rate, credible that the Church, not content with creating facts, annihilated them, also, whenever the knowledge of them seemed critical for the already tottering papacy.[4] According to Hase and Kist, then, we must state the matter thus: that soon after the year 855 an edict issued from Rome to this effect: "Let no one presume to say a word about the fact of a female pope," for at that time Rome did not feel her position to be as yet very secure. About the middle of the thirteenth century, however, a counter order issued from the same place: "Henceforth it is lawful to discuss history; we now consider our position safe, and can venture to let the narrative appear in historical works."

The judgment of Kurtz is, at any rate, more sober and free from prejudice.[5] "The evidence before us," he says, "forbids us to assign to the myth any historical value whatever. We must, however, (quite apart from the falsification of the acts, which, in some cases, is manifest, in others is a matter of suspicion,) characterize the myth as a riddle, which criticism has as yet not solved, and *probably never will.*"

That the riddle has not yet been solved, that all attempts at explanation which have been made up to the present time, must be held to have miscarried, is true enough; that a solution which may satisfy the historian is, nevertheless, possible, it will be the object of the following pages to show.

Let us first glance for a moment at the explanations which have been set forth up to this time. Baronius considers the myth to be a satire on John VIII., "ob nimiam ejus animi facilitatem et mollitudinem," qualities which he exhibited more especially in the affair of Photius. Others, Aventine to begin with, and after him Heumann and Schröckh, prefer to reckon the supposed satire as one on the period of female rule in Rome, the reign of Theodora and Marozia under certain popes, some of whom were called John; in which case, however, it would have to be transferred from the middle of the ninth century to the tenth. The opinion published by the Jesuit Secchi in Rome, that it is a calumny originating with the Greeks, namely with Photius, is eqally inadmissible. The first Greek who mentions the circumstance is the monk Barlaam in the fourteenth century. Pagi's assertion also, which Eckhart supports, that the myth was an invention of the Waldenses, is pure imagination. The myth evidently originated in Rome itself, and the first to give it circulation were not the Waldenses, but their most deadly enemies—the Dominicans and Minorites.

Leo Allatius thought that a false prophetess called Thiota, in the ninth century, gave occasion to this myth. The explanation invented by Leibnitz[6] is also a forced attempt to meet the exigencies of the case. There might very well, he thinks, have been a foreign *bishop* (pontifex *i.e.,* episcopus), really a woman in disguise, who gave birth to a child during a procession at Rome, and thus gave occasion to the story.

Blasco and Henke supposed that the myth about the female pope was a satirical allegory on the origin and circulation of the false decretals of Isidore. This interpretation, however, is entirely at variance with the genius of that century, an age in which men had no sense for satirical allegories; and then too it refutes itself, for the story of Pope Joan originated at a time when no one doubted the genuineness of the false decretals of Isidore. Nevertheless, Gfrörer has lately taken up this idea, and worked it out in a still more artificial manner.[7] "The whole force of the fable," he says, "resides in these two points, that the woman was a native of Mayence, and that she came from Greece (Athens), and ascended the papal chair. In the first particular I recognise a condemnation directed against the canons of the pseudo-Isidore, in the second an allegorical censure of the alliance which Leo IV. wished to make with the Byzantines . . . It is said that in the later days of Leo IV. the papal power in Mayence and Greece was abused, or to make use of a metaphor, of which the Italians are very fond in such cases, was at that time *prostituted.*" Side by side with this explanation, which can scarcely fail to provoke a smile from any one who is acquainted with the Middle Ages, stands the extraordinary circumstance, that there is no authority whatever for this intention of Leo IV. to compromise himself more than was right with the Byzantines. It is purely an hypothesis of Gfrörer's. But the myth about Pope Joan, as thus interpreted, is in turn made to do further service as a proof of the correctness of this hypothesis, as well as for his assumption that the false decretals originated in Mayence.

In short, all the attempts at explanation, which have hitherto been made, split on this rock—that the myth had its origin in a much later age; when the remembrance of the events and circumstances of the ninth and tenth centuries had long ago faded away, or at most existed only in the case of individual scholars, and, therefore, could not form material for the construction of a myth. That is to say, I believe, that I can without difficulty produce convincing evidence, that the myth about the female-pope, though it may possibly have had somewhat earlier circulation in the mouth of the people, was not definitively put into writing before the middle of the thirteenth century. This evidence could not have been given with anything like certainty before the present time. For it is only during the last forty[8] years that all the stores of mediæval manuscripts in the whole of Europe have been hunted through with a care such as was never known before. Every library corner has been searched, and an astounding quantity of historical documents, hitherto unknown (what a mass of new material exists in the Pertz collection alone, for instance!), has been brought to light. Nevertheless, not a single notice of the myth about Pope Joan has been discovered, which is earlier than the close, or, at the very most, the middle of the thirteenth century. We can now say quite positively, that in the collected literature, whether western or Byzantine, of the four centuries between 850 and 1250, there is not the faintest reference to the circumstance of a female pope.

For a long time it was supposed that the myth, though certainly not to be found in any author of the ninth or tenth century, appeared as already in existence in the eleventh and twelfth centuries. Marianus Scotus[9] is said to have been the first to mention the female pope, and he certainly does mention her in the text as given by Pistorius. Now, however, that the text in the great Pertz collection has been edited by Waitz[10] according to the most ancient manuscripts, the fact has come to light, that Marianus knew nothing whatever of Pope Joan. In his case, as in the case of so many other authors, the short mention of the female pope has been interpolated at a later period. In the chronicle of Sigebert of Gemblours, and the supplements of the monks of Orcamp (*Auctarium Ursicampinum*), the notice of the papess is wanting in all original manuscripts. She was first inserted by the first editor in the year 1513.[11] Kurtz has lately appealed again to the supposed evidence of Otto of Freysingen.[12] In the list of the popes, continued down to the year 1513, which is printed with his historical work,[13] Pope John VII. (in the year 705) is marked as a woman, without one single word of explanation. And in the edition of the *Pantheon,* as given by Pistorius, we find in the list of the popes these words, "the Papess Johanna is not reckoned."

Meanwhile a close investigation of the oldest and best manuscripts of Gottfried's *Pantheon* and of Otto's chronicle have brought it to light, that originally neither the word "fœmina" was placed in Otto's chronicle against the name of John VII., nor the gloss "Johanna Papissa non numeratur" in the *Pantheon* between Leo IV. and Benedict III.; both of which insertions are given in the printed editions.[14]

In the chronicle of Otto the addition to the name of John VII. is manifestly the work of a later copyist or reader, who inserted the word quite at random, because he was bound to have a female John somewhere among the popes. The fact that this John comes as early as the year 705 was the less likely to puzzle him, because the list of popes in this chronicle does not give the dates.[15]

The first who really took up the myth is the author of a chronicle, to which Stephen de Bourbon appeals without giving any more exact quotation.[16] That is to say, Stephen, a French Dominican, born towards the close of the twelfth century, died in the year 1261, in his work on the Seven Gifts of the Holy Spirit.[17] which was written just about the middle of the thirteenth century, makes the first mention of Pope Joan, whom he asserts he has discovered in a chronicle. Now seeing that he refers with exactness to all the sources from which he has gathered together the collection of passages which contribute to his practical homiletic object, we can, at least with great probability, show from what chronicle he has obtained this mention of Pope Joan. Among chroniclers he names Eusebius, Jerome, Bede, Odo, Hugo of St. Victor, the "Roman Cardinal," and John de Mailly, a Dominican. We may set aside all but the two last. The "Roman Cardinal" (or Cardinal Romanus (?)—there were several of this name, but none of them wrote a chronicle) is probably none other than the author of the *Historia Miscella,* or continuation of Eutropius, whom the Dominican, Tolomeo of Lucca, also quotes later on among his authorities as Paulus Diaconus Cardinalis;[18] but he cannot be distinguished with certainty. It remains then that the lost, or as yet undiscovered, chronicle of the Dominican Jean de Mailly,[19] who, moreover, must have been a contemporary of Stephen, is the only source to which the latter can have been indebted for his account of Pope Joan. And Jean de Mailly, we may be tolerably certain, got it from popular report.

We can, therefore, consider it as established—that not until the year 1240 or 1250, was the myth about the woman-pope put into writing and transferred to works of history. Several decades more passed, however, before it came actually into circulation and became really wide-spread. The chronicle of Jean de Mailly seems to have remained in obscurity, for no one, with the exception of his brother Dominican, Stephen, notices it; and even Stephen's large work—great as was its value, especially to preachers, on account of the quantity of examples which it contained, was not possessed by very many, as is proved by the scarcity of existing manuscripts of it. The *Speculum Morale,* which bears the name of Vincent of Beauvais, was the chief cause of this. For this work appropriated most of the examples and instances given by Stephen, but was superior to Stephen's books both in convenience of arrangement and fulness of matter, and eclipsed it so completely, that the narrative about Pope Joan, in the form in which it appears in Stephen's work, is to be found nowhere else.

The chronicle of Martinus Polonus has been the principal means of giving circulation to the myth. This book, which gives a synchronistic history of the popes and emperors in the form of a dry, mechanical, and utterly uncritical collection of biographical notes, exercised a most extraordinary influence on the chroniclers and historians from the beginning of the fourteenth century onwards, especially on their ways of thinking in the latter part of the Middle Ages. Wattenbach's[20] statement, that Martinus Polonus became almost the exclusive histori-

cal instructor of the catholic world, is not an exaggeration. Of no other historical book is there such an inexhaustible number of manuscripts in existence as of this. All volumes of the *Archiv für deutsche Geschichtskunde* show this. And indeed the book was held in estimation in almost all countries alike, was translated into all languages, was continued over and over again, and still more frequently copied by later chroniclers. That the effect of such a book, utterly unhistorical and stuffed with fables, was to the last degree mischievous, so that (as Wattenbach says) the careful, thorough, and critical investigation of the history of the early Middle Ages, prosecuted with so much zeal during the twelfth century, was completely choked, or nearly so, by Martin's chronicle, cannot be denied.

The position of the author could not fail to win for his history of the popes an amount of authority such as no other similar writing obtained. Troppau was his birthplace, the Dominican order his profession. He was for a long time the chaplain and penitentiary of the popes; as such lived naturally at the papal court, followed, everywhere, the Curia, which was then constantly on the move, and died [A.D. 1278] as archbishop designate of Gnesen. His book, therefore, was considered to a certain extent to be the official history of the popes, issuing from the Curia itself. And hence people accepted the history of Pope Joan also, which they found in Martinus Polonus, all the more readily and unsuspectingly. The form in which he gives the myth became the prevailing one; and most authors have contented themselves with copying the passage from his chronicle word for word. Nevertheless, Martin himself, as can be proved, knew nothing about Pope Joan, or, at any rate, said nothing about her. Not until several years after his death did attempts begin to be made to insert the myth into his book. It is no doubt correct that Martin himself prepared a second and later edition of his work, which reaches down to Nicolas III., 1277, while the first edition only goes down to Clement IV. (died 1268). But the second is exactly like the first in arrangement. Each pope, and each emperor on the opposite page, had as many lines assigned to him as he reigned years, and each page contained fifty lines, that is, embraced half a century. Hence, in the copies which kept to the original arrangement of the author, additions or insertions could only be made in those places where the account of a pope or emperor did not fill all the lines assigned to him, owing to the short period of his reign. But the insertion of a pope had been rendered impossible by Martin himself and all the copyists who kept to the plan of the book, by means of the detailed chronology, according to which every line had a date, and in the case of each pope and emperor the length of his reign was exactly stated. But for this same reason Pope Joan also, if she had originally had a place in his book, could not have been *effaced,* nor have been omitted from the copies which held fast to the arrangement of the original.

Pope Joan then does not occur in the eldest manuscripts of Martinus. She is wanting especially in those which have kept to the exact chronological method of the author. Nor is the opinion tenable, that Martinus brought her into the latest edition of his book prepared by himself. That theory is contradicted by manuscripts, which come down to the time of Nicolas III., and, nevertheless, contain no trace of Pope Joan. Echard[21] has already noticed several such manuscripts. The exquisite Aldersbach[22] manuscript, now in the Royal Library at Munich, gives the same evidence. There are, however, manuscripts in which her history is written in the margin at the bottom of the sheet, or as a gloss at the side.[23] It was thence gradually, and one may add very violently, thrust in the text. This was done in various ways: either Benedict III., the successor of Leo, was struck out, and Pope Joan put in his place, as is the case in a Hamburg[24] codex reaching down to the year 1302. Or she is placed, usually by some later hand, without any date being given, as an addition or mere legend in the vacant space left after Leo IV. Or, lastly—merely in order to gain the necessary two years and a half for her reign—the whole chronological reckoning of the author is thrown into confusion; either by assigning an earlier date than is correct to several of Leo's predecessors, and that as far back as the year 800; or by giving to individual popes fewer years than belong to them. This eagerness to interpolate the female pope in the book at all hazards—so to speak,—without shrinking from the most arbitrary alterations in the chronology in order to attain this object, is certainly somewhat astonishing. Just the very circumstance which above all others conferred on Martin's book a certain amount of value, viz. the painstaking and continuous chronological reckoning line by line, has been sacrificed in several manuscripts,[25] merely in order to make the insertion of Pope Joan possible; or else only one year has been placed against the name of each pope, either in the margin or in the text, in order to conceal the disagreement between the insertion of Pope Joan and the chronological plan of the author.

It was in the period between 1278 and 1312 that the interpolation took place; for Tolomeo of Lucca, who completed his historical work in the year 1312, remarks[26] that all the authorities which he had read placed Benedict III. next after Leo IV.; Martinus Polonus was the only one who put Johannes Anglicus in between. By this means two facts are established; first, the industrious collector Tolomeo knew of no writing in which a mention of Pope Joan was to be found, except the chronicle of Martinus; secondly, the copy of Martinus with which he was acquainted was one which had her *already* inserted, and that in the *text.* Had the account

of her merely been written alongside in the margin, this would undoubtedly have aroused Tolomeo's suspicions, and he would have noticed the fact in his own work.

Another main vehicle for circulating the myth about the papess was the chronicle *Flores Temporum,* which exists in numerous manuscripts under the names of Martinus Minorita, Herrmannus Januensis, and Herrmannus Gigas. It was printed by Eccard, and, in another form, by Meuschen; and after that of Martinus Polonus, was the most widely circulated of all the later chronicles. Unlike Martinus Polonus, however, it appears to have come into general use only in Germany. It reaches down to 1290, and is in the main not much more than a compilation from the chronicle of Martinus Polonus, as the author himself states. According to the conjecture of Eccard and others, Martinus Minorita is the original author,[27] and Herrmannus Januensis or Gigas the continuer[28] of the chronicle down to the year 1349. Pertz,[29] on the other hand, is of opinion that what is printed under the name of Martinus Minorita is only a poor extract from the work of Herrmannus Gigas, who brought his chronicle down to the year 1290, and died in 1336.

The relation between the Minorite Martin and the Wilhelmite Herrmann of Genoa appears meanwhile to be this:—that the latter has copied the Minorite, with[30] many omissions and additions, but without mentioning him. Martin the Penitentiary—that is Martinus Polonus—is given as the main authority. It was from him, then, beyond all doubt, that the story about Pope Joan passed (embellished with additions) into chronicles of considerably later date; for manuscripts in which it is wanting have not come within my knowledge.

The story of Pope Joan has also been inserted in the so-called Anastasius[31] (the most ancient collection known of biographies of the popes), and in precisely the same form as that in which it exists in Martinus Polonus. The literal wording of the text does not allow the possibility that the story really formed any part of the original text. The interpolation must have been made with the most foolish wantonness, or just as has been done in the Heidelberg manuscripts, by striking out Benedict III., and then inserting Joan in his place. In other copies she has been added by a later hand in the margin, at the side, or quite at the bottom of the page.

The most natural supposition, and the one which Gabler[32] also follows, seems then to be, that the papess passed from Martinus Polonus into the few, and very much later, manuscripts of Anastasius which contain it. Nevertheless, I am driven to the conjecture that the myth was in the first instance added at the end of some copy of the collection of biographies of the popes which bears the name of Anastasius. For it has long ago been remarked[33] that the life of Benedict III. in this collection is the work of a different author from that of the lives immediately preceding it, especially of the very detailed life of Leo IV. There must, therefore, beyond all doubt, have been copies which came to an end with Leo IV., whose biographer was obviously a contemporary. The notice of Pope Joan might then have been added at the end by a later hand, and from thence have passed into the manuscripts of Martinus Polonus.

One sees this from the catalogue of manuscripts which Vignoli gives at the beginning of his edition. The Cod. Vatic. 3764 reaches down to Hadrian II., the Cod. Vatic. 5869 only down to Gregory II.; the Cod. 629 to Hadrian I.; others to John VIII., Nicolas I., Leo III., and so forth. In Cod. 3762, which comes down to the year 1142, the fable of the papess is added in later and smaller handwriting underneath in the margin.

This conjecture, one must allow, is by no means easy to prove. But supposing it correct, we have then the simplest of all explanations for the interpolation of Pope Joan between Leo IV. and Benedict III., where she certainly has not the[34] slightest connection with the history of the time. Meanwhile, I find in Martinus himself reasons for this place being assigned to her, and the following two in particular. The first is a mere matter of chance, arising out of the mechanical arrangement; for Martinus did not know how to fill up the eight lines which he was obliged to devote to the eight years of Leo's pontificate, so that the first lines of the page which contained the second half of the ninth century remained empty. Here, therefore, the interpolation could be managed without the slightest trouble. But there was a further reason in the nature of the story itself. For the extreme improbability that a woman should be promoted to the highest ecclesiastical office, and be chosen by all as pope, was explained in the myth by her great intellectual attainments. She surpassed every one in Rome, so it was said, in learning. Naturally then, as soon as a definite historical place had to be assigned to her (the *popular* form of the myth had not troubled itself with fixed dates), a tolerably early period—at any rate, one anterior to the time of Gregory VII.—had to be chosen for her. For this, however, they were obliged to fall back on a period in which there was only a single instance known of a man being elected to the papacy on account of his preeminent knowledge. Since Gregory the Great there had been no pope who was really very remarkable for learning. In the four centuries between John VI., 701, and Gregory VII., this very Leo IV. is the only one whom Martinus notices in particular as a man who "divinarum scripturarum extitit ferventissimus scrutator," one who already, in the monastery [of St. Martin] to which his parents had sent him for purposes of study, became remarkable for his learning no less than for his mode of life, and on this account also was unanimously[35] elected pope by the Romans after the death of Sergius. On that occasion, then, it was intellectual attainment which influenced the votes of the Romans; and therefore it might happen that a woman, whose sex was not known, could be chosen as pope by the Romans, because of her intellectual superiority. Now the interpolated Martinus speaks of Joan in much the same terms as of Leo; "in diversis scientiis ita profecit, ut nullus sibi par inveniretur;" and, "quum in urbe vita et scientia magnæ opinionis esset, in papam concorditer eligitur." And hence in Martinus Polonus, who speaks in this manner of no other[36] pope in that century, the place assigned to Pope Joan was that immediately after Leo IV., whom she resembled in this particular. And since every one took the work of Martinus as their authority, she retained this position.

It is at the stage when the myth was just beginning to gain circulation, and was still received with suspicion on many sides, that the passages on the subject in the *Historical Mirror* of Van Maerlant and in Tolomeo of Lucca come in. Maerlant's Dutch chronicle is in verse, and is mainly taken from Vincent of Beauvais, but with additions from other sources. Maerlant says moreover (about the year 1283), "I do not[37] feel clear or certain whether it is fable or fact; but in the chronicles of the popes it is not usually found." So also a manuscript list of the popes down to John XXII. (13): "Et[38] in paucis chronicis invenitur."

One of the first who took the story of Pope Joan from the interpolated Martinus Polonus was Geoffroi de Courlon, a Benedictine of the Abbey of St. Pierre le Vif at Sens, whose chronicle,[39] a somewhat rough compilation, reaches down to 1295.

Next comes the Dominican Bernard Guidonis, in his unprinted *Flores Chronicorum,* and also (in the year 1311) in his now printed history[40] of the popes. He inserts Johannes Teutonicus (not Anglicus, therefore, according to him) natione Maguntinus, together with the whole fable about Pope Joan, keeping faithfully to his authority, Martinus Polonus.

About the same period another Dominican, Leo of Orvieto, contributed to the circulation of the fable, by receiving it into his history of the popes and emperors, which reached down to Clement V. [1305]. In his case also, Martinus Polonus is the source from which he draws in this particular, as also in his whole book.[41]

Now follow in the first half of the fourteenth century the Dominican John of Paris, Siffrid of Meissen, Occam the Minorite (who turned the story of Pope Joan to account in his controversy with John XXII.), the Greek Barlaam, the English Benedictine Ranulph Higden, the Augustine Amalrich Augerii, Boccaccio, and Petrarch.[42]

A chronicle of the popes by Aimery of Peyrat, Abbot of Moissac, written in the year 1399, has Johannes Anglicus in the list of popes, with the remark: "Some[43] say that this pope was a woman."

The Dominican Jacobe de Acqui,[44] who wrote about the year 1370, inserts the name without this remark, but with the extraordinary statement that this pontificate lasted *nineteen years.*

Of course people in general regarded the circumstance as to the last degree disgraceful to the Roman See, and, indeed, to the whole Church. The woman-pope had reigned for two years and a half, had performed a vast number of functions, all of which were now null and void; and, added to all this, there was the scandal of her giving birth to a child in the open street. It was scarcely possible to conceive anything more to the dishonor of the chair of the Apostle, or, indeed, of the whole of Christendom. What mockery must not this story excite among the Mohammedans!

As early as the close of the thirteenth, or beginning of the fourteenth century, Geoffroi de Courlon introduces the story with the heading *Deceptio Ecclesiæ Romanæ.*

Maerlant[45] says sorrowfully:—

> "Alse die paves Leo was doot—
> Ghesciede der Kerken grote scame."

"Johanne la Papesse," says[46] Jean le Maire, in the year 1511, "fist un grand esclandre à la Papalité."

All state that since that time the popes always avoid that street, so as not to look upon the scene of the scandal.

Now, when we consider that, according to the declaration of the Dominican Tolomeo of Lucca, down to the year 1312, the story was extant nowhere, except in certain copies of Martinus Polonus; that already innumerable lists of the popes, in their chronological order, were in existence, in none of which was there any trace of the female pope to be found,—the eagerness, which suddenly meets us at the close of the thirteenth century, to make the fable pass muster as history, and to smuggle it into the manuscripts, is certainly very astonishing. The author of the *Histoire Lit. de France* has good reason for saying, "Nous[47] ne saurions nous expliquer comment il se fait que ce soit précisément dans les rangs de cette fidèle milice du saint-siège que se rencontrent les propagateurs les plus naïfs, et peut-être les inventeurs, d'une histoire si injurieuse à la papauté." Undoubtedly the thing emanated principally from those otherwise most devoted servants of the Roman See, the Dominicans[48] and the Minorites. It was certainly they, especially the former of the two, who were the first to multiply the copies of Martinus Polonus to such an extent, and thus spread the fable everywhere. The time at which this took place meanwhile solves the enigma. It was in the reign of Boniface VIII., who was not favourably disposed to the two orders, and whose whole policy[49]

displeased them. We see this in the unfavourable judgments which the Dominican historians formed respecting him, and in the attitude which they assumed at the outbreak of the strife between him and Philip the Fair. We notice that from this time, which was in general a crisis for the waning power of the popes, historians among the monastic orders mention and describe with a sort of relish scandals in the history of the popes.

In the fifteenth century scarcely a doubt is suggested. Quite at the beginning of the century the bust of Pope Joan was placed in the cathedral at Sienna along with the busts of the other popes, and no one took offence at it. The church of Sienna in the time that followed gave three popes to the Roman See,—Pius II., Pius III., and Marcellus II. Not one of them ever thought of having the scandal removed. It was not till two centuries later, that, at the pressing demand of pope Clement VIII., 1592-1605, Joan was metamorphosed into pope Zacharias.[50] When Huss at the council of Constance supported[51] his doctrine by appealing to the case of Agnes, who became Pope Joan, he met with no contradiction from either side. Even the Chancellor Gerson himself turned to account the circumstance of the woman-pope as a proof that the Church could err[52] in matters of fact. On the other hand the Minorite Johann de Rocha, in a treatise written at the Council of Constance, uses the case of Johannes Maguntinus to show how dangerous it is to make the duty of obedience to the Church depend upon the personal character of the pope.[53]

Heinrich Korner, a Dominican of Lubeck, 1402 to 1437, not only himself received the story about the woman-pope in its usual form into his chronicle, but stated in addition that his predecessor, the Dominican Henry of Herford (about 1350), whom he had often copied, had purposely concealed the circumstance, in order that the laity might not be scandalised by reading that such an error had taken place in the Church, which assuredly, as the clergy taught, was guided by the Holy Spirit.[54]

The matter was now generally set forth as an indubitable fact, and the scholastic theologians endeavoured to accommodate themselves to it, and to arrange their church system and the position of the popes in the Church in accordance with it. Æneas Sylvius, afterwards pope Pius II., had however replied to the Taborites, that the story was nevertheless not certain. But his contemporary, the great upholder of papal despotism, cardinal Torrecremata,[55] accepts it as notorious, that a woman was once regarded by all Catholics as pope, and thence draws the following conclusion: that, whereas God had allowed this to happen, without the whole constitution of the Church being thrown into confusion, so it might also come to pass, that a heretic or an infidel should be recognised as pope; and, in comparison with the fact of a female pope, that would be the smaller difficulty of the two.

St. Antoninus, belonging, like Torrecremata, to the middle of the fifteenth century, and like him a Dominican,[56] avails himself of the Apostle's words respecting the inscrutability of the divine counsels in connection with the supposed fact of a female pope, and declares that the Church was even then not without a Head, namely Christ, but that bishops and priests ordained by the woman must certainly be re-ordained.

The Dominican order, whose members chiefly contributed to spread the fable everywhere, possessed in their strict organization and their numerous libraries the means of discovering the truth. The General of the order had merely to command that the copies of Martinus Polonus, and the more ancient lists of the popes, of which there were quantities in existence in the monasteries of the order, should once for all be examined and compared together. But people preferred to believe what was most incredible and most monstrous. Not one of these men, of course, had ever seen, or heard, that a woman had for years been public teacher, priest, and bishop, without being detected, or that the birth of a child had ever taken place in the public street. But that in Rome these two things once took place *together,* in order to disgrace the papal dignity—this people believed with readiness.

Martin le Franc, provost of Lausanne, about 1450, and secretary to the popes Felix V. and Nicholas V., in his great French poem, *Le Champion des Dames,* celebrated Pope Joan at length. First we have his astonishment, that such a thing should have been permitted to take place.

> "Comment endura Dieu, comment
> Que femme ribaulde et prestresse
> Eut l'Eglise en gouvernement?"

It would have been no wonder had God come down to judgment, when a woman ruled the world. But now the defender steps forward and makes apology—

> "Or laissons les péchés, disans,
> Qu'elle étoit clergesse lettrée,
> Quand devant les plus suffisants
> De Rome eut l'issue et l'entrée.
> Encore te peut être montrée
> Mainte Préface que dicta,
> Bien et saintement accoustrée
> Où en la foy point n'hésita."[57]

She had, therefore, composed many quite orthodox prefaces for the mass.

It was not until the second half of the fifteenth century that the story came into the hands of the Greeks. Welcome as the occurrence of such a thing would have been to a Cerularius and like-minded opponents of the papal chair in Constantinople, no one had as yet mentioned it, until Chalcocondylas, in the history of his time, in which he describes the mode of electing a pope, mentions also the fiction of an examination as to sex, and apropos of that relates the catastrophe of Pope Joan; an occurrence which, as he remarks, could only have taken place in the West, where the clergy do not allow their beard to grow.[58] It is in him that we get the outrageous feature added to the story, that the child was born just as the woman was celebrating High Mass, and was seen by the assembled congregation.[59]

In the fifteenth and sixteenth centuries, says the Roman writer Cancellieri, the romance about Pope Joan circulated widely in all chronicles which were written and copied in Italy, and even under the very eyes of Rome.[60] Thus it appears in print in Ricobaldo's Italian chronicle of the popes, which Filippo de Lignamine dedicated to pope Sixtus IV. in 1474. So also in the history of the popes by the Venetian priest Stella.[61] For a long time, and even as late as 1548 and 1550, it found a place in numerous Roman editions of the *Mirabilia Urbis Romæ,*[62] which was a sort of guide for pilgrims and strangers.

Felix Hemmerlin, Trithemius, Nauclerus, Albert Krantz, Coccius Sabellicus, Raphael of Volterra, Joh. Fr. Pico di Mirandola, the Augustine Foresti of Bergamo, Cardinal Domenico Jacobazzi, Hadrian of Utrecht, afterwards pope Hadrian VI.,—Germans, French, Italians, Spaniards, all appeal to the story, and interweave it with their theological disquisitions; or, like Heinrich Cornelius Agrippa, rejoice that the tenets of the canonists about the inerrancy of the Church had come to such glaring shame in the deception of the woman-pope, and that this woman, in the two years and a half of her reign, had ordained priests and bishops, administered sacraments, and performed all the other functions of a pope; and that all this had, nevertheless, remained as valid in the Church. Even John, Bishop of Chiemsee, introduces Agnes and her catastrophe as a proof that the popes were sometimes under the influence of evil spirits.[63] Platina, who thought the story rather suspicious, nevertheless would not omit it from his history of the popes (about 1460), because nearly every one maintained its truth.[64] Aventin in Germany, and Onufrio Panvinio in Italy, were the first to shake the general infatuation. But still in the year 1575 the Minorite Rioche, in his chronicle, opposes the certainty of the collected Church to the hesitating statements of Platina and Carranza.[65]

In order to arrive at the causes of the origin and development of the myth, let us now proceed to dissect it.

Originally the woman-pope was nameless. The first accounts of her, in Stephen de Bourbon, and in the *Compilatio Chronologica* in Pistorius' collection, know nothing as yet of a Joan. In the latter authority we read:

"fuit et alius pseudo papa, cujus nomen et anni ignorantur, nam mulier erat." Her *own* name was not discovered till somewhat late—about the end of the fourteenth century. She was called Agnes, under which name she was a very important and useful personage, especially with John Huss; or Gilberta,[66] as others would have it. For the *pope* a name was found at an early stage; people took the most common one—John. There had already been seven of this name before 855, and in the period during which the myth was spreading, the number reached one and twenty.

Much the same thing happened as to the *time* at which she was supposed to have lived. The myth while still in its popular form of course did not touch upon this question. But the first authority who relates it at once gives it a date also. The event, says Stephen de Bourbon, took place about the year 1100. He places it therefore (and this is very remarkable) at the very time in which we have the first mention of the use of the pierced chair at the enthronement of the new pope. How people in general came afterwards to assign the year 855 as her date, has been already explained.

Stephen de Bourbon knows nothing up to his time of England, Mayence, or Athens. The woman is as yet no great scholar or public teacher, but only a clever scribe or secretary (artem notandi edocta), who thus becomes the notary of the Curia, then cardinal, and then pope. A century later, in Amalricus Augerii[67] all this is fantastically enlarged upon and coloured. At Athens she becomes by careful study a very subtle reasoner. While there she hears of the condition and fame of the city of Rome, goes thither and becomes, not a notary, as Stephen says, but a professor,[68] attracts many and noble pupils, lives at the same time in the greatest honour, is celebrated everywhere for her mode of life no less than for her learning, and hence is unanimously elected pope. She continued some time longer in her honourable and pious mode of life; but later on, too much good living made her voluptuous, she yielded to the temptations of the Evil One, and was seduced by one of her confidants.

Particularly astonishing is the disagreement as to the way in which the catastrophe took place. Three or four versions of it exist. According to the first, as we find it in Stephen de Bourbon, it appears that she was with child at the time of her election to the papacy, and the dénouement took place during the procession as she was going up to the Lateran palace.[69] The Roman tribunal condemned her at once to be tied by the feet to the feet of a horse, and dragged out of the city, whereupon the populace stoned her to death. In this version of the story, however, Stephen stands quite alone. The usual narrative, as it has passed from the interpolated Martinus Polonus into later authors, makes her, after a quiet reign of more than two years, give birth to a child

in the street during a procession, die at once, and forthwith be buried on the very spot. Boccaccio is quite different from this again. According to him all takes place tolerably quietly; there is no death, the enthroned priestess merely sheds a few tears, and then retires into private life. "Ex apice pontificatus dejecta se in misellam evasisse mulierculam querebatur." And again: "A patribus in tenebras exteriores abjecta cum fletu misella abiit."[70]

The attitude which Boccaccio assumed with regard to the episode of the female pope, which was just the kind of thing to please a man of his turn of mind, is particularly remarkable. In his *Zibaldone,* which he wrote about the year 1350, he included a short chronicle of the popes, which according to his own confession, was entirely borrowed from the *Chronica Martiniana.* In this the female pope is not mentioned; without doubt because he did not find her in his copy of Martinus Polonus. On the other hand, he has inserted her in two later writings,[71] *De casibus virorum et feminarum illustrium,* and *De mulieribus claris,* and has pictured the whole with the enjoyment which was to be expected from the author of the *Decamerone.* His narrative, however, differs essentially from the usual version according to Martinus; and seeing that it agrees with no other known version, it would appear that Boccaccio has taken it directly from popular tradition (where it would naturally assume very various forms), and worked it up. He knows the length of her pontificate with the greatest exactitude: two years, seven months, and a day or two. Her original name he does not know: "Quod proprium fuerit nomen vix cognitum est. Esto sunt, qui dicant fuisse Gilibertam."

These fourteenth century witnesses are of no very great importance, for they one and all of them merely copied the interpolated passage in Martinus Polonus, often with scarcely the alteration of a word. On the other hand the recently published *Eulogium Historiarum* of a monk of Malmesbury, of the year 1366, has a peculiar form of the story to be found nowhere else, although the author in other places borrows freely from Martinus Polonus. The girl is born in Mayence, and sent by her parents to male teachers to receive instruction in the sciences. With one of these, who was a very learned man, she falls in love, and goes with him in man's attire to Rome. Here, because she surpassed every one in knowledge, she was made cardinal by pope Leo. When, as pope, she gives birth to a child during the procession, she is merely deposed. This version, therefore, would come nearest to the description given by Boccaccio. It knows nothing of the journey to Athens.[72]

The catastrophe appears somewhat further spun out in a manuscript chronicle of the abbots of Kempten. There we are told that "the Evil Spirit came to this Pope John, who was a woman, and afterwards was with child, and said, 'Thou pope, who wouldest be a Father with the other Fathers here, thou shalt show publicly when thou bringest forth that thou art a woman-pope; therefore will I take thee body and soul to myself and to my company.'"[73]

Another less severe and uncompromising finale was however attempted. By a revelation or an angel she was allowed to choose, whether she would suffer shame on earth or eternal damnation hereafter. She chose the former, and the birth of her child and her own death in the open street was the consequence.[74]

The story of the papess once believed, many other fables attached themselves to it. It was through the special aid of the devil, we are told, that she rose to the dignity of pope, and thereupon wrote a book on necromancy.[75] Formerly there was a greater number of Prefaces in the missal. The reduction in number which took place afterwards with regard to those whose author and purpose were unknown, was explained by the supposition, that Pope Joan had composed those which were struck out.[76]

Now, how is the first origin of the myth to be explained? Four circumstances have contributed to the production and elaboration of the fable:—1. The use of a pierced seat at the institution of a newly elected pope. 2. A stone with an inscription on it, which people supposed to be a tombstone. 3. A statue found on the same spot, in long robes, which were supposed to be those of a woman. 4. The custom of making a circuit in processions, whereby a street which was directly in the way was avoided.

In one street in Rome stood two objects, which were very naturally supposed to be connected,—a statue with the figure of a child or small boy, and a monumental stone with an inscription. In addition to this came the circumstance, that solemn and state processions made a circuit round this street. The statue is said to have had masculine rather than feminine features; but certain information on this point is wanting, for Sixtus V. had it removed. The figure carried a palm-branch, and was supposed to represent a priest with a serving boy, or some heathen divinity. But the long robes and the addition of the figure of the boy to the group, created a notion among the people that it was a mother with her child. The inscription was then made use of to explain the statue, and the statue to explain the inscription, the pierced chair and the avoiding of the street served to confirm the explanation. This piece of sculpture was not (as has been maintained) first mentioned by Dietrich von Niem in the fifteenth century; but Mærlant says, as early as 1283, i.e., at the time of the first circulation of the myth:—

> "En daer leget soe, als wyt lesen
> Noch also up ten Steen ghehouwen,
> Dat men ane daer mag scouwen."

The myth now sought, and soon found, further circumstances with which to connect itself. The enigmatical inscription on a monumental stone which stood on the spot, and which hitherto no one had been able to interpret, became all at once clear to the Romans. It referred to the female pope and the catastrophe of the dénouement.

The stone was set up by one of those priests of Mithras who bore the title "Pater Patrum," apparently as a memorial of some specially solemn sacrifice; for the worship of Mithras from the third century of the Christian era onwards was a very favourite one in Rome and very prevalent, until in the year 378 the worship was forbidden and the grotto of Mithras destroyed.

The earliest notice of the stone with the inscription, which was supposed to be the tombstone of the female pope, is to be found in Stephen de Bourbon. According to him the inscription ran thus,—

> "Parce Pater Patrum papissæ prodere partum."

Now without doubt it did not stand so in as many words. But "Pap." or "Parc. Pater Patrum" followed by "P. P. P." was certainly the reading; an abbreviation for "propria pecunia posuit."

"Pater Patrum" appears constantly on monuments as the title of a priest of the Mithras[77] mysteries. In this case, probably, the name of the priest of Mithras was Papirius.[78] The remaining letters may have become illegible.

The problem therefore now was to interpret the three "P's."

One reading was,

> "Parce Pater Patrum papissæ prodere partum;"[79]

or as others supposed,

> "Papa Pater Patrum papissæ pandito partum;"

or, according to another explanation still better,

> "Papa Pater Patrum peperit papissa papellum."

Thus was the riddle of the inscription solved, and the myth confirmed in connection with the statue and the pierced chair. The stone had turned out to be the tombstone of the unhappy Pope Joan.[80]

The verse, however, especially in its first and second form, was altogether a most extraordinary one for an epitaph. There must be something more to account for it, and, accordingly, the myth was soon enlarged. It was reported that Satan, who of course knew the secret of the papess, had addressed her in the words of the verse in a full consistory.[81] That, however, did not seem a very satisfactory explanation; and so the supposed epitaph was altered and enlarged,—and the story at last ran thus:—that the papess, while exorcising a man possessed by a devil, had asked him when the unclean spirit that dwelt in him would leave him, and it had mockingly answered—

"Papa Pater Patrum papissæ pandito partum,

Et tibi nunc edam (or dicam) de corpore quando recedam."[82]

Other instances have occurred of an unintelligible inscription being explained by a story[83] being attached to it. Thus the chronicles, since the time of Beda, declare that an inscription had been found at Rome with the six letters:—

"R. R. R. F. F. F."

According to other instances of abbreviations in inscriptions, this can at any rate mean—

"Ruderibus rejectis Rufus Festus fieri fecit."

But people constructed out of it the prophecy of an ancient Sibyl respecting the destruction of Rome, and interpreted—

"Roma Ruet Romuli Ferro Flammaque Fameque."

While the inscription on the stone occupied more especially the clergy and the more educated among the laity, and stimulated them to attempt explanations of it, the imaginative powers of the populace were chiefly excited by the seat which stood in a public place, and was always to be seen by every one, on which every newly-elected pope, in accordance with traditional custom, took his seat.

From the time of Paschal II. in the year 1099, we find mention of the custom that, at the solemn procession to the Lateran palace, the new pope should sit down on two ancient pierced seats made of stone. They were called *"porphyreticæ,"* because the stone of which they were made was of a bright red kind. They dated from the times of ancient Rome, and had formerly, it appears, stood in one of the public baths; and had thence come into the oratory of S. Sylvester near the Lateran.[84] Here then it was usual for the pope first to sit on the right-hand seat, while a girdle from which hung seven keys and seven seals was put round him.[85] At the same time a staff was placed in his hand, which he then, sitting on the left-hand seat, placed along with the keys in the hands of the prior of St. Lawrence. Hereupon another ornamented garb, made after the pattern of the

Jewish ephod, was placed on him. This sitting down was meant to symbolise taking possession; for Pandulf goes on to say: "per cetera Palatii loca solis Pontificibus destinata, jam dominus vel sedens vel transiens electionis modum implevit."

It was therefore a mere matter of accident that these stone seats were pierced. They had been selected on account of their antique form and the beautiful colour of the stone. Every stranger who visited Rome could not fail to be struck with their unusual shape. That they had formerly been intended to be used in a bath had passed out of every one's knowledge; and the idea of such a use would be one of the last to occur to people in the middle ages. They were aware that the new pope sat, and on this occasion only in his whole life, on this seat, and this was the only use to which the seat was ever put. The symbolical meaning of the act and of the ceremonies connected with it was unknown and foreign to the popular mind. It accordingly invented an explanation of its own, just such a one as popular fancy is wont to give. The seat is hollow and pierced, they said, because they wanted to make sure that the pope was a man. The further question, what need there was to make sure of this, produced the explanation:—because, in one instance certainly, a woman was made pope. Here at once a field was opened for the development of a myth. The deception, the catastrophe of the discovery; all that was forthwith sketched out in popular talk. Myth delights in the most glaring contrasts. Hence we have the highest sacerdotal office, and together with it its most shameful prostitution by sudden travail during a solemn procession, followed by childbirth in the open street. This done, the woman-pope has fulfilled her mission. The myth accordingly at once withdraws her from the scene. She dies in childbirth on the spot; or, according to an older version, is stoned to death by the enraged populace.

The story that the newly-elected pope sat down on the pierced seat in order to give a proof of his sex is first found in the Visions of the Dominican, Robert d'Usez,[86] who died in Metz in the year 1296. He relates that in the year 1291, while he was staying at Orange, he was taken in the spirit to Rome, to the Lateran palace, and placed before the porphyry seat, "ubi dicitur probari papa an sit homo."[87] After him Jacobo d'Agnolo di Scarperia in the year 1405 declares respecting it, in a letter to the celebrated Greek, Emanuel Chrysoloras, in which he describes the enthronisation of Gregory XII. as an eye-witness, that it is a senseless popular fable.[88] It is consequently not correct to say, what has been frequently maintained, that the English writer, William Brevin,[89] about 1470, was the first to make mention of the supposed investigation as to the sex of the pope.[90]

Of later witnesses it is worth mentioning, that the Swede Lawrence Banck, who minutely described the solemnities which accompanied the elevation of Innocent X. to the papacy [Sept. 1644], declares, with all earnestness, that it certainly was the case, that an investigation into the sex of the pope was the object of the ceremony.[91] At that time, however, the custom of sitting on the two stone seats, along with several other ceremonies, had long since disappeared, namely, since the death of Leo X. And, moreover, Banck does not state that he himself had seen the ceremony,[92] but only that he had often seen the *seat,* and by way of proof that it took place, and with this particular object, *appeals to writers of the fifteenth and sixteenth centuries.* Cancellieri, therefore, had good reason for expressing astonishment at the shamelessness of a man, who speaks on other things as an eye-witness, and who had only to inquire of any educated Roman to learn that the custom in question had been given up for more than a hundred years.

But the strongest case of all is that of Giampetro Valeriano Bolzani, one of the literary courtiers of Leo X., and loaded with benefices,[93] according to the immoral custom of the time. This man, in a speech addressed to cardinal Hippolytus dei Medici, printed at Rome with papal privilege, did not scruple to decorate the fiction about the investigation into the sex of each newly-elected pope with new and fabulous circumstances. The ceremony takes places, he declares, quite openly in the gallery of the Lateran church before the eyes of the assembled multitude, and is then most unnecessarily proclaimed by one of the clergy and entered in the register.[94] Thus the wanton frivolity of Italian literati, and the stupid indifference of ecclesiastical dignitaries, worked together to spread this delusion, damaging as it was to the otherwise jealously guarded authority of the papal see, right through the whole mass of the populace. At the same time one could hardly have a more striking instance of the irresistible power which a universally-circulated story exercises over men, even over those of superior intellect. Any one could learn without trouble from a cardinal, or from one of the clergy taking part in the ceremony, what really took place there. But people never asked, or else imagined that the answer meant no more than a refusal to vouch for the fact. They heard this examination of the newly-elected pope spoken of everywhere, in the streets and in private houses, as a notorious fact.

Did, then, the meaning assigned to the pierced seat influence the explanation of the inscription and of the statue; or did, contrariwise, these two objects give origin to the myth about the ceremonies connected with the seat? That point it is now, of course, out of our power to determine. We can only see that the explanation of the three objects is as old as the myth about the woman-pope.

A further confirmation of the whole was soon found in a circumstance of no importance in itself, and for which a perfectly natural explanation was ready at hand. It was remarked that the popes in processions between the Lateran and the Vatican did not enter a street which lay in the way, but made a circuit through other streets. The reason was simply the narrowness of the street. But in Rome, where the papess was already haunting the imagination of the masses, it was now discovered that this was done to remind men how the woman had given birth to a child as she was going through this street, and to express horror at the catastrophe which had taken place just at that spot. In the first version of the fable, as we find it in the interpolated Martinus Polonus, it is said: *"creditur omnino a quibusdam, quod ob detestationem facti hoc faciat."* With[95] later writers the thing is thoroughly established as a notorious fact.

It may now be worth while to show by a few examples, how easily a popular myth, or a mythical explanation, may be called into existence by a circumstance, so soon as anything is perceived in it, which seems in the eyes of the people to be astonishing, or which excites their imagination.

The bigamy of the Count of Gleichen plays an important part in our literature, and is still believed to be true by numberless people. A count of Gleichen is said to have gone to Palestine in the year 1227, in company with the Landgrave of Thuringia, and there to have been captured by the Saracens and thrown into prison. Through the daughter of the Sultan he obtained his liberty; and the story goes that, although his wife was living, he obtained a dispensation from pope Gregory IX. in the year 1240 or 1241, and married the princess; and the three lived together in undisturbed peace for many years afterwards. It is a well-known fact that the very bed itself (an unusually broad one) of the count and his two wives, was shown for a long time afterwards.

This story is told for the first time in the year 1584, that is to say, three centuries and a half later.[96] But from that time onwards it is related in numerous writings, and in the next century became a matter of popular belief, so that henceforth it was printed in all histories of Thuringia, and is to be found in particular in Jovius, Sagittarius, Orlearius, Packenstein. etc. In this case, also, it was a *tombstone* which gave occasion to the story. On it was represented a knight with two[97] female figures, one of whom had a peculiar head dress decorated with a star. No sooner had the myth which fastened on to this figure begun to weave its web, than relics and signs began to multiply. Not only was the bedstead shown, but a jewel which the pope had presented to the Turkish princess, and which she wore in her turban; a "Turk's road," was pointed out, leading to the castle, and a "Turk's room" within it. And not a word about all this until the seventeenth century. In earlier times no one had ever heard a syllable about the story or the relics.[98]

Another instance is afforded by the Püstrich at Sondershausen, a bronze figure, hollow inside, with an opening in the head. It was found in the year 1550, in a subterranean chapel of the castle of Rothenburg, near Nordhausen, and was brought to Sondershausen in the year 1576, where it still exists in the cabinet of curiosities. Thirty or forty years had scarcely passed before a legend had grown up, which quite harmonised with a time immediately succeeding the great religious contest of the Reformation, and with a country in which the old religion was vanquished. The Püstrich was said to have stood in a niche in a pilgrimage church, and by monkish jugglery to have been filled with water, and made to vomit flames of fire, in order to terrify the people, and induce them to make large offerings. Frederick Succus, preacher in the cathedral of Magdeburg, from 1567 to 1576, relates all this, with many details as to the way in which the deception was managed, adding the remark, "that no one could do the like now-a-days, so as to make the image vomit flames, and that many thought it was perhaps brought about by magic and witchcraft."[99]

Again, every one knows the story of Archbishop Hatto, of Mayence, who had a strong tower built in the middle of the Rhine, in order to protect himself from the mice; but in spite of that was devoured by them. This event, which would have fallen within the year 970, had it happened *at all,* is mentioned for the first time at the beginning of the fourteenth century, in Siffrid's chronicle. Before that there is not a trace of it. The Mäusethurm, or Muusthurm[100] (that is, Arsenal), as Bodmann explains, was not built till the beginning of the thirteenth[101] century. Its name with the people slipped from Muusthurm to Mäusethurm, and thus, according to all appearance, gave rise to the whole story. In all that is historically known of Hatto II. there is not a feature with which the legend could connect itself. The story of a prince or great man, who tried to save himself from the pursuit of mice in a tower surrounded by water, is to be found in several other places. It appears in the mountains of Bavaria; it occurs among the myths of primitive Polish history. In[102] the latter case King Popiel, his wife, and two sons, are followed and killed by mice in a tower in the Goplosee, which to this day bears the name of Mouse-tower. Wherever a tower on an island was to be seen, the object of which could no longer be explained, there sprang up the story of the blood-thirsty mice.[103]

If an unusual hollow was remarked in a stone, a hole of extraordinary shape, anything which the imagination could take for the impress of a hand or a foot, there at once a myth found lodgment. A stone in the wall of a church at Schlottau in Saxony, which is thought to look like the face of a monk without ever having been carved by the hand of man, has given occasion to a legend of attempted sacrilege, and marvellous punishment.[104]

On the Riesenthor (Giant-Porch) of St. Stephen's Cathedral at Vienna, a youth is introduced in the carving of the upper part, who appears to rest a wounded foot on the other knee. A legend has been spun out of that. The architect, Pilgram,[105] is said to have thrown his pupil, Puchsprunn, from the scaffolding, out of jealousy, because the execution of the second tower had been transferred to the latter while still under Pilgram.[106]

The fable of the papess belongs to the local myths of Rome, of which a whole cycle existed in the Middle Ages. Hence it may be worth while to compare the birth of such a myth with a Roman example. The legend about the origin of the house of Colonna, whose power and greatness afforded material for the imagination of the people, is so far similar in its origin to that about Pope Joan, as it was a piece of sculpture, viz., the arms of the house with a column, which the legend endeavoured to explain. Just as the lozenge of Saxony, the wheel of Mayence, and the virgin of the Osnabruck arms, have called forth legends of their own to explain them.

A smith in Rome notices that his cow, every day, goes of her own accord in the same direction. He follows her, creeps after her through a narrow opening, and finds a meadow with a building in it. In the building stands a stone column, and on the top of it a brazen vessel full of money. He is about to take some of the money, when a voice calls out to him, "It is not thine; take three denarii, and thou wilt find on the Forum to whom the money belongs." The smith does so, and flings the three pieces of money to three different parts of the Forum. A poor neglected lad finds them all three, becomes the smith's son-in-law, buys great possessions with the money on the column, and so founds the house of Colonna.[107]

This, perhaps, is sufficient illustration of the way in which the legend of Pope Joan arose. Two circumstances, however, require special discussion, the statements that the woman came from Mayence, and that she had studied in Athens.

The first mention that we find respecting the original home of the female pope, namely, in the passage interpolated into Martinus Polonus, combines two contradictory statements. It makes her an Englishwoman, and, at the same time, a native of Mayence: "Johannes Anglus, natione Moguntinus." Probably two stories were extant, of which one made the impostor come from the British Isles, the other from Germany. The reason for one story making her a native of England may have been this. It was a common thing for Englishwomen to go on pilgrimages to Rome: we find St. Boniface even in his day complaining of the number of them, and their dubious character. Or it may have been that the birth, and first spreading of the myth, fell just within that long period of the violent struggle between Innocent III. and King John, while England was accounted in Rome as the power which above all others was hostile to the Roman see. For, from the very beginning, the fictitious event was considered as a deep disgrace, a heavy blow struck at the authority of the Roman see; and the myth expressed that by making a country which was considered as hostile to Rome, to be the home of the papess, a woman-pope. In like manner the mythical king Popiel, who was devoured by mice, on account of the wrong done to his father's brothers, is represented in the Polish myth as having married the daughter of a German prince, in order that the guilt of instigating him to the crime might fall on a woman of a foreign nation, and one always hostile to the Sclaves.[108]

It is not difficult to explain how the other version of the story, which became the prevalent one, came to assign Mayence as the native place of the papess.

The rise of the myth falls into the period of the great contest between the papacy and the empire, a time when the Germans often appeared in arms before Rome, and in Rome broke down the walls of the city, took the popes prisoners, or compelled them to take to flight. "Omne malum ab Aquilone," was the feeling at that time in Rome. Germany had then no special capital; no recognised royal or imperial place of residence. No city but Mayence could be called the most important city in the realm. It was the seat of the first prince of the empire,[109] and the centre of government. "Moguntia, ubi maxima vis regni esse noscitur," says Otto of Freysingen.[110] In the *Ligurinus* of the Pseudo-Gunther, it is said of Mayence: "Pene fuit toto sedes notissima regno."

In the cycle of myths which cluster round Charlemagne, and which Italy also appropriated (e.g. in the *Reali di Francia,* which was extant as early as the fourteenth century, and in other productions belonging to the same cycle of myths), Roman aversion to the German metropolis, Mayence, is glaringly prominent. Mayence is the seat and home of the malicious scheme of treachery against Charles the Great and his house. Ganelo, the arch-traitor, is count of Mayence. All his party, and his associates in treachery, are called "Maganzesi." They and Ganelo, or the men of Mayence, represent the treacherous usurpation of the empire by the Germans, in violation of the birthright of Rome.

So again in Pulci's *Morgante,* and in Ariosto's *Cinque Canti* or *Ganeloni.* The poem, *Doolin of Mayence,* is, to a certain extent, a German rejoinder to the polemics of Rome, as shown in the Carolingian myths. Here Doolin, son of Guido, count of Mayence, steps forward as the rival of Charlemagne, first fights with him, then after an indecisive battle is reconciled to him, with him goes to Vauclere, the city of Aubigeant (Wittekind), king of Saxony, marries Flandrine, the daughter of the latter, and ends by joining with Charles in the subjugation of Saxony.

Ganelo of Mayence, the treacherous founder of the first German kingdom by separation from the West Frank kingdom, is supplemented in the Italian myth (which thus represents the great contest and opposition between Guelf and Ghibelline) by another native of Mayence, Ghibello. The story is to be found in Bogardo's Italian version of the *Pomarium* of Riccobaldo of Ferrara.[111] King Conrad II. (it is Conrad III. who is meant) nominates Gibello Maguntino to be administrator of the kingdom in Lombardy in opposition to Welfo, whom the Church had set up as regent of Lombardy. Gibello is of noble but poor family, had studied for awhile in Italy, acquires then great eminence in his native city, Mayence, becomes chancellor of Bohemia, but is publicly convicted of "baratteria," i.e., of political fraud or treason. He and Welfo now have a contest together, which ends in Gibello dying at Bergamo, and Welfo at Milan. Gibello of Maganza is, as one sees, a repetition of Gano or Ganelo of Maganza. But it is also evident why Johannes or Johanna must be made to come from Mayence, and why "Maguntinus" or "Magantinus" must be called "Margantinus."[112]

In later times the story, now romancing with an object, endeavoured to harmonise the two statements, that the female pope was "Anglicus," and also "natione Maguntinus." The parents of Joan were made to migrate from England to Mayence; or she was called "Anglicus," it was said, because an English monk in Fulda had been her paramour.[113]

In Germany, however, people began now to be ashamed of the German origin of Pope Joan. She was thrown in the teeth of the Germans, we are told in the chronicle of the bishops of Verden, because she is said to have come from Mayence.[114] Indeed some went so far as to say that this circumstance of the German woman-pope was the reason why no more Germans were elected popes, as Werner Rolevink mentions, adding at the same time that this was not the true reason.[115] In order to conceal the circumstance, we find in the German manuscripts of Martinus Polonus "Margantinus" constantly instead of "Magantinus;" and the *Compilatio Chronica* in Leibnitz[116] knows only of Johannes Anglicus. This feeling that the nationality of the papess was a thing of which Germany must be ashamed even produced a new romance, the object of which was manifestly nothing else than to transfer the home of the female pope and her paramour from Germany to Greece.[117]

The other feature in the myth, that the woman studied in Athens, and then came and turned her knowledge to account in Rome as a teacher of great repute, is thoroughly in accordance with the spirit of mediæval legends. As a matter of fact, no one for a thousand years had gone from the West to Athens for purposes of study; for the very best of reasons, because there was nothing more to be found there. But that was no obstacle to the myth, according to which Athens in ancient times (that means perhaps before the rise of the University of Paris) was accounted as the one great seat of education and learning. For that there was, and ought to be, only one "Studium," just as there was, and ought to be, only one Empire and one Popedom, was the prevailing sentiment of that age. "The Church has need of three powers or institutions," we read in the *Chronica Jordanis,* "the Priesthood, the Empire, and the University. And as the Priesthood has only one seat, namely Rome, so the University has and needs only one seat, namely Paris. Of the three leading nations each possesses one of these institutions. The Romans or Italians have the Priesthood, the Germans have the Empire, and the French have the University."[118]

This University was originally in Athens, thence it was transported to Rome, and from Rome Charlemagne (or his son) transplanted it to Paris. The very year of this transfer was stated. Thus we find in the *Chronicon Tielense,*[119] "Anno D. 830, Romanum studium, quod prius Athenis exstitit, est translatum Parisios."

Hence in ancient times, according to the prevalent notion, the University was at Athens; and whoever would rise to great eminence in the sphere of knowledge must go there. There were only two ways in which a foreign adventurer could attain to the highest office in the Church—piety, or learning. The legend could not make the girl from Mayence become eminent through piety; this would not agree with her subsequent seduction and the birth of the child in the open street. Therefore it was through her learning that she won for herself universal admiration, and, at the election to the papacy, a unanimous vote. And this learning she could only have attained in Athens. For the University, as Amalricus Augerii says, was at that time in Greece.[120]

Notes

1. [*A Woman in the Chair of S. Peter.* Another edition of this has lately appeared; Gütersloh, 1866. Professor Kist thinks that Pope Joan was possibly the widow of Leo IV.]

   [Kist's Essay was first published in the *Nederlandsch Archief voor Kerkelijke Geschiedenis,* iii, 27. See Gieseler's *Church History,* New York edition, vol. ii, pp. 30-1,—a long note, summing up all the data in the case.]

2. *Geschichte des deutschen Volkes,* vi., 513-517.

3. Vol. xxvi., p. 569.

4. *Kirchengeschichte,* 7. Aufl. s. 213.

5. *Handbuch der Kirchengeschichte,* 1856, ii. Band, 1. Abtheilung s. 225.

6. *Flores sparsi in Tumulum Papissæ,* ap. Scheid, Biblioth. His. Goetting., p. 367.

7. *Kirchengeschichte,* III., iii., 978.

8. [This was written in 1863.]

9. [Born, probably in Ireland, about 1028; died at Mayence, 1086, not to be confounded with Marianus, the Franciscan, a Florentine writer of the fifteenth century. In 1056 Marianus Scotus entered the abbey of S. Martin at Cologne; in 1059 he moved to the abbey of Fulda, and thence in 1069 to Mayence. He passed for the most learned man of his age, being a mathematician and theologian as well as historian. His *Chronicon Universale* is based on Cassiodorus, augmented from Eusebius and Bede, and the chronicles of Hildesheim and Würzburg, and extends down to the year 1083; published at Basle by Hérold, 1559.]

10. *Monumenta German, Hist.* viii., 550. [v. 551. vi. 340, 470.]

11. "In nullo quem noverimus Sigeberti codice occurrit locus famous de Johanna papissa, quem hoc loco editio princeps exhibet," says the latest editor, Bethmann, ap. Pertz, viii., 340. Compare the remark, p. 470, where Bethmann says decisively, "nemo igitur restat (as interpolater of the passage) nisi primus editor, sive is Antonius Rufus fuerit, sive Henricus Stephanus." It is a mistake when Kurtz elsewhere (p. 228) says with regard to Sigebert and Marianus: "The oldest editors would scarcely have added the passages in question out of their own heads; and therefore it is probable that the passages were purposely omitted in the codices which they had before them." There are no signs whatever of anything being intentionally omitted or effaced; in many of the manuscripts, on the other hand, there are many signs of subsequent insertions and additions in the margin. [Sigebert was born about 1030, and died 1112. His chronicle extends from 381, where Eusebius ended, to 1112.]

12. *Kirchengeschichte,* ii., 226

13. [Otto, Bishop of Freysingen, went with his brother, Conrad III., on his crusade to the Holy Land, resuming his diocese on his return. He died in September 1158, having held the see twenty years. His chronicle in seven books extends down to 1146. The first four books are a mere compilation from Orosius, Eusebius, Isidore, Bede, & c.; the last three are of great value. He also wrote two books *De Gestis Friderici I. Ænobarbi,* which come down to the year 1157.]

14. [That confusion prevailed in some of the lists of the popes precisely at this point is shown by an annalist, who apparently wrote in Halberstadt 854: "Benedictus papa, ut quidam volunt, hoc anno factus est, et post hunc Paulus (!), post eum Stephanus per annos quatuor sedisse inveniuntur."—Baxmann, *Politik der Päpste*, i., p. 361, note.]

15. In the good original manuscripts of the *Pantheon* in the royal library at Munich the addition about Pope Joan is wanting. These are:—Cod. Lat. 43 (from Hartmann Schedel's collection) f. 118, b. Cod. Windberg. 37, or Cod. Lat. 22,237, f. 168 b. Similarly in the oldest manuscripts of the chronicle of Otto in the Munich library the addition to the name of John VII. does not appear. These are Cod. Weihensteph. 61, or Lat. 21,561, which is of about the same date. Cod. Frising. 177, or Lat. 6,517. Cod. Scheftlarn. Lat. 17,124, in which the list of popes comes to an end with Hadrian IV., and therefore is also of the same date.

16. [He merely says] "dicitur in chronicis." He means no more than *one* chronicle; Chronica is constantly used in the plural as a title. Otherwise Stephen would naturally have added "variis" or "pluribus."

17. It has never been printed. The whole, or portions of it, exist in the French libraries, one portion of it in the Munich library. Echard was the first to cite it at great length in his work, *Sancti Thomæ Summa Suo Auctori Vindicata*, Paris, 1708; and again in the *Scriptores Ordinis Prædicatorum*, pt. i.

[The passage from Stephen de Bourbon as cited by Gieseler (ii. 31) from Quetif and Echard, Scriptores Ordinis Pradicatorum, i. 367, reads: Accidit autem, mirabilis audacia, imo insana, circa ann. Dom MC. [CM?] ut dicitur in chronicis. Quaedam mulier literata, et in arte nondi (notandi?) edocta, adsunto virili habitu, et virum sefingens, venit Romam, et tam industria, quam literatura accepta, facta est notarius curiae, post diabolo procurante cardinalis, postea Papa. Haec impraegnata cum ascenderet peperit. Quod cum novisset Romana justitia, ligatis pedibus ejus ad pedes equi distracta est extra urbem, et ad dimidiam leucam a populo lapidata, et ubi fuit mortua, ibi fuit sepulta, et super lapidem super ea positum scriptus est versiculus: "Parce pater patrum papissae edere partum." The same story appears in an enlarged form in Martini Poloni († 1278), Chron., and here the passage is perhaps genuine, although it is also wanting in several MSS. H. B. S.]

18. Cf. Quetif et Echard *Scriptores Ordinis Prædicatorum*, i., 544.

19. On him see the *Histoire littéraire de la France*, xviii., 532.

20. *Deutschlands Geschichtsquellen*, s. 426.

21. On this point see Quetif et Echard. *Scriptores Ordinis Prædicatorum*, 1. 367; and Lequien *Oriens Chr.* iii., 385.

22. Aldersp. 161, fol. Pergam.

23. In the *Archiv fur altere deutsche Geschichtskunde* quotations from several of these are given, e.g., vii., 657.

24. Archiv vi., 230.

25. "Nulla chronologia, sed adest fabula," says Echard of several manuscripts of Martinus which he had seen, p. 369.

26. *Hist. Eccles.*, 16, 8.

27. *Archiv der Gesellschaft fur deutsche Geschichtskunde*, viii., 835.

28. Archiv i., 402 ff.

29. Achiv vii., 115.

30. Bruns, in Gabler's *Journal für theolog. Lit.* 1811, vol. vi., p. 88, etc. Bruns had a manuscript before him in Helmstadt, which was marked as a work of Herrmannus Minorita. But at the end of the document the author was correctly styled Herrmannus Ordinis S. Wilhelmi.

31. [Anastasius, the Librarian of the Vatican, took part in A.D. 869 in the eighth General Council at Constantinople, where his learning and knowledge of Latin and Greek were of great service to the papal legates. His celebrated *Liber Pontificalis* is a compilation of lives of the popes from S. Peter down to Nicolas I., first printed at Mayence in 1602. Only the lives of some of the popes of his own times can be regarded as his own composition.]

32. Gabler's *Kleinere theology. Schriften*, vol. i., p. 446.

33. See Bahr, *Geschichte der Rom. Literatur im Karoling. Zeitalter*, p. 269.

34. Leo IV. died July 11th, 855. Benedict was forthwith [the same month] elected; and, after the emperor had given his consent, was consecrated on 29th of September in the same year, the very day after the Emperor Lothair died. It is notorious that contemporaries, such as Prudentius and Hinemar, notice that Benedict was Leo's immediate successor, and a diploma of Benedict's dated as early as October 7th, 855 (Mansi *Concill.* xv., 113) is still extant.

35. [Sergius died Jan. 27th. Leo IV. was forthwith elected, and consecrated on April 10th, without waiting even for the leave of the sovereign, not as denying his authority, but because of the pressing fear of the Saracens, who had ventured up the Tiber, and plundered the Basilica of St. Peter at the end of 846. See Baxmann, *Politik der Päpste,* vol. i., p. 352. This fear of the Saracens may have had something to do with the unanimity of the electors.]

36. For Gerbert (Sylvester II.) owed his promotion, 999-1003, according to Martinus, not to his great learning, but to the devil.

37. *Spiegel Historical,* uitgeg. door de Maatschappij der nederl, letterk. Leyden, 1857, iii., 220.

38. This is appended to the manuscript of the *Otia Imperialia* by Gervasius in Leyden. Wensing, *de Pausin Johanna,* p. 9.

39. *Notices et Extraits,* ii., 16. He adds, moreover, "Unde dicitur quod Romani in consuetudinem traxerunt probare sexus electi per foramen cathedræ lapideæ."—See *Hist. Lit. de France,* xxi., 10.

40. Maii *Spicil.* Rom. vi., 202.

41. In the third volume of Lami's *Deliciæ Eruditorum,* Florent, 1732, p, 143.

42. *Chronica delle Vite de' Pontefici,* & c., Venetia, 1507, f. LV. He is here called Giovanni d'Anglia, and the dates are advanced two years, so that Benedict III. is placed in the year 857 (instead of 855), and Nicolas I. in 859 (instead of 858). [Benedict III. died early in 858—April 7th; so that the difference between that and the end of 859 would not be far short of two years.]

43. *Notices et Extraits* vi., 82.

44. *Monum. Hist. Patriæ, Scriptores,* iii., 1524.

45. ["Als der Papst Leo war todt—
Geschah der Kirche grosse Schame—"
After Pope Leo was dead
A great scandal rose in the church.]

46. In the *Traité de la Différence des Schismes et des Conciles de l'Eglise,* part iii., f. 2.

47. xxi., p. 10.

48. [A serious rupture between Rome and the friars took place under Innocent IV. The University of Paris, alarmed at the hold which the monks were getting, especially on the professorship, decreed that no religious order should hold more than one of the theological chairs. The Dominicans appealed to the pope. Innocent decided against them, and within a few days died. His death was openly attributed to their prayers—"quia impossible erat multorum preces non audiri." Hence the well-known saying, "From the litanies of the friars, good Lord, deliver us."]

49. [This treatment of the English Franciscans made this not unnatural. The Franciscans, in direct contradiction to their vow of mendicancy, had gradually become very wealthy. The pope alone could free them from their rule. The English Minorites offered to deposit forty thousand ducats with certain bankers, as the price of permission to hold property. Boniface played with the monks till the money was paid, then absolved the bankers from their obligation to pay back money which mendicants ought never to have owned, and appropriated it as "res nullius" to his own uses. He thus made implacable enemies of the most popular and intellectual order in Europe. When Philip appealed severally to all the monastic orders in France, all the Franciscans, and with them the Dominicans, Hospitallers, and Templars, took their stand by him against the pope.]

50. Lequien, *Oriens Christianus,* iii., 392.

51. That is to say, he tried to prove that the Church could get on very well for a long time without any pope at all, because during the whole reign of Agnes, namely, two years and a half, it had had no real pope.—L'Enfant, *Histoire du Concile de Constance,* ii., 334. In his work *De Ecclesia* also, Huss comes back with delight to the woman-pope, whose name was Agnes, and who was called Johannes Anglicus. She is to him a striking proof that the Roman Church has in no way remained spotless: "Quomodo ergo illa Romana Ecclesia, illa Agnes, Johannes Papa cum collegio semper immaculata permansit, qui peperit?"

52. In the speech which he made at Tarascon before Benedict XIII. in the year 1403. Opera, ed. Dupin, ii., 71.

53. In Dupin's edition of the writings of Gerson, v. 456.

54. Ap. Eccard, ii., 442

55. "Quum ergo constet quod aliquando mulier a cunctis Catholicis putabatur Papa, non est incredibile quod aliquando hæreticus habeatur pro Papa, licet verus Papa non sit.'—*Summa de Ecclesia,* edit. Venet., p. 394.

56. *Summa Hist.,* lib. 16, p. 2, c. 1, § 7.

57. Ap. Oudin, *Comm. de Scr. Eccl.,* iii. 2466.

58. *De Rebus Turcicis,* ed. Bekker, Bonn, 1843, p. 303.

59. Ὡς εἰς τὴν θυσίαν ἀφίκετο, γεννῆσαί τε τὸ παιδίον κατὰ τὴν θυσίαν καὶ ὀφθῆναι ὑπὸ τοῦ λαοῦ.

The cleric, who examines the sex of the newly-elected, cries out with a loud voice: ἄρρην ἡμῖν ἐστὶν ὁ δεσπότης, I. c., p. 303. Barlaam, who had mentioned the fable as early as the fourteenth century, lived in Italy.

60. *Storia de' solenni possessi.* Rome, 1802, p. 238.

61. *Vita Paparum,* R. Basil, 1507, f. E. 2.

62. Other old editions of this strangers' guide to Rome have the title—*Indulgentiæ Ecclesiarum Urbis Romæ.* The circumstance about the woman-pope is found in all of them; and for well-nigh eighty years no one in Rome ever thought of having the scandal expurgated from a work, which was constantly reprinted, and was put into the hands of every new-comer. [A reprint has lately been published at Berlin, 1869, edited by Parthey.]

63. *Onus Ecclesiæ,* 1531, cap. 19, § 4.

64. "Ne obstinate nimium et pertinaciter omisisse videar, quod fere omnes affirmant."

65. *Chronique.* Paris, 1576, f. 230.

66. [Besides Agnes, Gilberta, or Gerberta and Joanna, she is also called in various authors Margaret, Isabel, Dorothy, and Jutta.]

67. Ap. Eccard, ii., 1607.

68. Even great teachers, says Jakob von Konigshofen (Chronicle, p. 179), were eager to become her pupils, for she had the chief of the schools in Rome. The papal secretary, Dietrich von Niem (about A.D. 1413), professes to give the very school in which she taught, viz., that of the Greeks, in which St. Augustine also taught.

69. "Quum ascenderet," i.e., palatium, as we have it in the description of the coronation of Paschal II.;—"ascendensque palatium." Ap. Murator. *SS. Ital.* iii., i. 354.

70. In the *Fragmentum Hist. Autoris Incerti* in Urstis. P. ii., p. 82, which says that King Theodoric killed "Johanna Papa" at Rome along with Boethius and Symmachus, Johanna is merely a mistake of some copyist for Johanne. [No version of the myth of Pope Joan places her as early as this—524, 525. John I. was pope precisely at this period 523 to 526.]

71. To speak more exactly, he has related the story twice over in the same work, for the two writings mentioned really make up only one work.

72. *Eulogium, Chronicon ab orbe condito usque ad annum* 1366; edited by Frank Scott Haydon. Lond. 1858, t. I.

73. Ap. Wolf, *Lection. Memorab.,* ed. 1671, p. 177.

74. So in the *Urbis Romæ Mirabilia,* a work frequently printed in Rome during the fifteenth and sixteenth centuries. Then in Hemmerlin, pp. 1597, f. 99, and in a German chronicle of Cologne.

75. Tiraquell, *de Leg. Matrim. ed. Basil.,* 1561, p. 298.

76. Thus, in an Oxford manuscript of Martinus Polonus we read:—"Hic (Johannes Anglicus) primus post Ambrosium multas prefationes missarum dicitur composuisse, quæ modo omnes sunt interdictæ." Ap. Maresium, *Johanna Papissa Restit.,* p. 19. So also the above-mentioned Martin le Franc.

77. Conf. Orelli, *Inscriptionum Latinarum Ampl. Coll.* 1848, 1933, 2343, 2344, 2352.

78. For several inscriptions with the abbreviation P. a P., see Orelli, ii., 25.

79. This is the oldest interpretation as given by Stephen de Bourbon; *see* Echard, *S. Thomx Summa suo Auctori Vindicata,* p. 568.

80. Hence the most ancient witness, Stephen de Bourbon, says expressly: "Ubi fuit mortua, ibi fuit sepulta, et super lapidem super ea positum scriptus est versiculus, etc."—Ap. Echard., I c., p. 568.

81. So the *Chronica S. Ægidii,* ap. Leibnitz SS. Brunsvic., iii., 580. The Chronicon of Engelhusius (Leibnitz, ii., 1065) makes the evil spirit in the air shout out the verse at the birth of the child during the procession.

82. So, for instance, the Chronicle of Hermannus Gygas, p. 94.

83. [Compare the famous verse about Pope Sylvester II.—"Scandit "ab R. Gerbertus in R, post papa viget R," p. 268.]

84. Montfaucon, *Diar. Ital.,* p. 137.

85. "Ascendens palatium," we read in the Roman sub-deacon, Pandulfus Pisanus, "ad duas curules devenit. Hic baltheo succingitur, cum septem ex eo pendentibus clavibus septemque sigillis. Et locatus in utrisque curulibus data sibi ferula in manu, etc."—Ap. Murator. *SS. Ital.,* P. iii., P. i., p. 354.

86. *Hist. Litt. de France,* xx. 501.

87. *Liber trium Virorum et trium Spirit. Virginum,* ed. Lefebre, Paris, 1513, f. 25.

88. Juxta hoc (sacellum Sylvestri) geminæ sunt fixæ sedes porphiretico incisæ lapide, in quibus, quod perforatæ sint, insanam loquitur vulgus fabulam, quod Pontifex attractetur, an vir sit. Ap. Cancellieri, p. 37.

89. In a work *De Septem Principalibus Ecclesiis Urbis Romæ.*

90. According to Hemmerlin (*Dialog. de Nobil. et Rusticis*), the investigation was made by two of the clergy: "et dum invenirentur illæsi (testiculi), clamabant tangentes alta voce; testiculos habet. Et reclamabant clerus et populus: Deo gratias." According to Chalcocondylas the words were:— ἄρρην ἡμῖν ἐστὶν ὁ δεσπότης. [De rebus Turcicis, ed. Bekker, Bonn., 1843, p. 303.] How readily the popular story was believed is shown by Bernardino Corio, of Milan, who describes in his historical work the coronation of pope Alexander VI. in the year 1492, when Corio himself was in Rome. There we read, "Finalmente essendo finite le solite solemnitati in *Sancta Sanctorum* et dimesticamente toccatogli li testicoli, ritorno al palacio." *Patria Historia,* P. vii., fol. Riv. Milano, 1503. In the later editions the passage is omitted. Corio, however, says himself, that he was not in the church where it took place, but was standing outside.

91. In the book *Roma Triumphans,* Franecker, 1645. Cancellieri has quoted his long account entire.

92. Cancellieri, p. 236.

93. For the long list of his benefices, see Marini, *Archiatri Pontificij,* i., 291.

94. Resque ipsa sacri præconis voce palam promulgata in acta mox refertur, legitimumque tum demum Pontificem nos habere arbitramur, quum habere illum quod habere decet oculata fide fuerit contestatum.

95. The chroniclers copy one from another to such a slavish extent in this narrative, that the incorrect expression of the interpolater, "Dominus Papa, quum vadit ad Lateranum, eandem viam semper *obliquat*" (instead of *declinat*) has been retained by all his followers. The avoided street was, moreover, pulled down by Sixtus V., *on account of its narrowness.* [The spot where the catastrophe was said to have taken place is between the Colosseum and St. Clement's.]

96. In Dresseri *Rhetorica,* Lips., p. 76, squ.

97. It is, as Placidus Muth, of Erfurt, has conjectured with much probability, the monument of a count of Gleichen, who died in 1494, and his two wives.

98. See *Hallesche Encycl.* Bd. 69.

99. Rabe, *Der Püstrich zu Sondershausen,* Berlin, 1852, p. 58. He shows how absurd the story is, although repeated in the seventeenth century by Walther, Titus, and Röser. Even in the year 1782 Galetti, and in 1830 the preacher Quehl, related

the ridiculous story. Rabe conjectures with probability that the Püstrich is nothing more than the support of a font. [Others have supposed it to be an idol of the Sorbic-Wends.]

100. Ap. Pistor. SS., Germ., i., 10.

101. [By a bishop named Siegfried, together with the opposite castle of Ehrenfels, as a watch tower and toll-house for collecting duties on all goods which passed up or down the river. Maus is possibly only another form of Mauth, toll or excise. Archbishop Hatto died in 970.]

102. Ropell's *Geschichte Polens,* i., 74.

103. Liebrecht's explanation in Wolf's *Zeitschrift für deutsche Mythologie,* ii., 408, seems to be erroneous. He says, that "at the root of legends on this subject lies the primitive custom of hanging the chiefs of the nation as an offering to appease the gods, on the occurrence of any national calamity, such as famine through the ravages of mice, for instance." In the first place, human sacrifice by means of hanging is almost, if not quite, unknown; secondly, it is not usually a tree, but a tower on an island, to which the legend attaches itself; and, lastly, the legend places the event, as in the case of Hatto, very much later—quite in Christian times. [But may we not give up the hanging, and even the tree, and still retain the idea of propitiatory sacrifice?]

104. See Grasse's *Sagenschatz des Konigreichs Sachsn.* Dresden, 1855.

105. [Pilgram was one of the later architects, successor of Jörg Œchsel about 1510. The church was founded in 1144. The Riesenthor seems to belong to a period subsequent to the fire of 1258; but it and the Heidenthürme are almost the oldest parts of the present building, and therefore existed long before Pilgram's time.]

106. Hormayr. *Wien, seine Geschichte, u. s. w.,* 27, 46.

107. Fr. Jacobi de Acqui *Chronicon Imaginis Mundi,* in the *Monumenta Hist. Patriæ, Script.,* Vol. iii., p. 1603.

108. Röpell, *Geschichte Polens,* p. 77.

109. [The electoral archbishops of Mayence were the premier princes of the empire; they presided at diets, and at the election of the emperor. Even in Roman times the Castellum Moguntiacum was the most important of the chain of fortresses which Drusus built along the Rhine, and which in like manner became the germs of large towns.]

110. *De Gestis Friderici I.,* c. 12.

111. In Muratori, *SS.* Ital ix, 360, 57.

112. Both in manuscripts and printed copies we repeatedly find Margantinus instead of Marguntinus. It would appear that Margan, a famous abbey in Glamorganshire, is here indicated, where the *Annales de Margan,* with which the second volume of Gale's *Historiæ Anglic. Scriptores* commences, were composed. People could not reconcile the appellation Anglicus with the distinctive name Maguntinus, and accordingly changed the German birthplace into an English one. Bernard Guidonis came to the rescue in a different way; instead of Anglicus, he wrote Johannes Teutonicus natione Maguntinus. *Vitæ Pontificum,* ap. Maii *Spicil. Rom.* vi., 202. Among the amusing attempts which have been made to reconcile the two adjectives Anglicus and Maguntinus, may be mentioned the version of Amalricus Augerii (*Historia Pontificum,* ap. Eccard, ii., 1706). Here the woman-pope is called Johannes, Anglicus natione, dictus *Magnanimus* (instead of Maguntinus). The author would intimate that the boldness and strength of character, without which such a course of life, involving the concealment of her sex for so many years, would not have been possible, had won for her the distinctive title of "magnanimous."

113. Compare Maresii *Johanna Papissa Restituta,* p. 18.

114. Ap. Leibnitz, *SS. Brunsvic.,* ii., 212.

115. *Fascic. Temp. æt.* vi., f. 66. So also in the Dutch *Divisie-Chronyk,* printed at Leyden in the year 1517. "Om dat dese Paeus wt duytslant rus van ments opten ryn, so menen sommige, dat dit die sake is, dat men genen geboren duytsche meer tat paeus settet."

116. *SS. Brunsvic.,* ii., 63.

117. It is to be found in a manuscript from Tergernsee, now in the royal library at Munich, of the fifteenth century, *Codex lat. Tegerns.,* 781. [See Appendix A.]

118. In Schard. *De Jurisd. Imperiali ac Potest. Eccles. Variorum Authorum Scripta.,* Basil., 1566, p. 307.

119. Ed. van Lecuwen, Trajecti, 1789, p. 37. So also Gobelinus Persona. The anonymous writer in Vincent of Beauvais had previously stated, "Alcuinus studium de Roma Parisios transtulit, quod illuc a Græcia translatum fuerat a Romanis."

120. See Eccard., ii., 1707.

C. A. Patrides (essay date 1982)

SOURCE: Patrides, C. A. "'A Palpable Hieroglyphick': The Fable of Pope Joan." In *Premises and Motifs in Re-* naissance Thought and Literature, pp. 152-81. Princeton, N.J.: Princeton University Press, 1982.

[*In the following excerpt, Patrides chronicles the history of the legend of Pope Joan, from its establishment in the late twelfth century to its debunking in the mid-sixteenth century to the discussion of the female pope's existence in fictional and scholarly works of the seventeenth and eighteenth centuries.*]

> Truely, there are some passages in the Legend of Pope *Joan,* which I am not very apt to believe; yet, it is shrewd evidence, that in so many hundreds of years, six or seven, no man in that Church should say any thing against it: I would they had been pleas'd to have said something, somewhat sooner: for if there were slander mingled in the story, (and if there be, it must be their own Authors that have mingled it) yet slander it self should not be neglected.
>
> —John Donne

I

Pope Joan is not a historical figure. But she is part of history in that her existence has been so persistently believed in that at times belief threatened to create the thing it contemplated.

To meander through the vast literature devoted to Pope Joan might readily make us suspect that judgment had fled to brutish beasts, and men had lost their reason. On the other hand, her frequent appearance during the Middle Ages and the Renaissance shows, it could be said, "the very age and body of the time his form and pressure." So far, indeed, a study of Pope Joan's advent and progress through history is justified; for, even if our sense of the suspension of men's reason is thereby confirmed, the motives to this particular lunacy might delineate for us the nature of the ages under consideration. Though a byway in the popular literature of the Middle Ages and the Renaissance, the legend merged in due course with the highway traversed by illustrious authorities and obscure figures, enlightened humanists and "enthusiastic" partisans.[1]

The story of Pope Joan—"the stupid story of Pope Joan," as an irate scholar would have it[2]—involves details which, all too often mutually exclusive, have been debated at far greater length than they ever merited. Even the champions of her existence, for instance, were by no means agreed about her place of birth or her original name. Most frequently, it was alleged that she was born in Moguntia or Maguntia, the city of Mainz (Mayence) in Hesse, which in some accounts was confused with the city of Metz in Lorraine. Yet several writers also believed her to have been Dutch, while John Lydgate, displaying in *The Fall of Princes* a rather exceptional talent for the rearrangement of the map of Europe, asserted that she was a native of "Mayence, a cite stondyng in Itaille, / Vpon the Reen"! (IX, 979-80). Moreover, by virtue of Joan's common appellation as "Joannes Anglicus," it was often claimed that legitimately she can only be fathered upon the English. Such a claim—ventured, needless to say, solely by Continental writers—was not welcomed in England with any noticeable enthusiasm. The English normally argued, as did Bishop John Jewel, that ". . . shee was not called *Iohane Englishe* by the name of the Countrie, for that she was an English Wooman, borne in *England* . . . but onely by the Surname of her Father. So are there many knowen this daie by the names of *Scot, Irishe, Frenche,* . . . : and yet not borne in any of al these Countries, but onely in *Englande*."[3] Much the same disaccord pervades the claims about her name prior to the assumption of the papal crown. One possibility was, of course, Joan or Joanna; but most writers appear to have favored Gilberta, still others Agnes—perhaps an intentionally assonant echo of "Joannes Anglicus"—and a few others Margaret or Isabella, even Glaucia, and finally Tutta or Jutta. A characteristic feature of the legend is, clearly, its variety.

No surviving account disputes our heroine's formidable intellectual abilities, even where we are informed that "it is said"—by those who denounced her as satanic, no doubt—that "she writ a Booke of *Necromancie,* of the power and strenth of deuils."[4] From Western Europe, at any rate, she is reported to have pursued her studies all the way to Athens. But another controversy promptly arose. Was medieval Athens the proper place to have advanced one's knowledge? Thomas Harding, in opposition to Bishop Jewel's contention that Athens was still highly respectable, predictably argued that "at that time neither any Athenes stoode, neither was there any place of learning there any lenger: but al the countrie of Attica became Barbarous, and vtterly void of learninge."[5] "This tale," Bishop Jewel responded impatiently, "is your owne." One is led to suppose that to have determined the state of medieval Athens was also to have determined the existence of Pope Joan. Another characteristic feature of the legend, in short, is its impressive lack of logic.

From Athens the future Pope proceeded to a confrontation with her destiny in Rome. The court of the Roman pontiff must have been devoid no less of well-educated individuals than of perceptive ones, for, while the recognition of her intellectual abilities was immediate, that of her disguise was deferred until a more dramatic moment. In due course made a cardinal, Joan—to use one of her many aliases—was finally elected Pope. The actual date of her election, however, invited several hypotheses of scant relationship to each other. Pope Joan was diversely said to lurk behind one or the other of four "real" popes: John VII (705-707), John VIII (878-882), John IX (898-900), or John XIV (983-984). But according to a fifth theory of even greater popularity,

she is said to have reigned as either John VII or John VIII for nearly two and a half years from 855, thereby intervening between the officially recognized reigns of Leo IV (847-855) and Benedict III (855-858). Once elected, at any rate, Joan gained a lover too. She was widely said to have had one earlier, a young monk from the Benedictine abbey of Fulda in Hesse-Nassau, who accompanied her to Athens and eventually died there, cruelly abandoned. In Rome her paramour was a servant or, according to authors more favorably disposed, a chamberlain and possibly even a cardinal. In the event, the Pope was big with child.

The end came swiftly and, it must be granted, most theatrically. Joan's child—the "popit or little Pope," as an aggressive Protestant rather unkindly called him[6]—was born at an embarrassingly inopportune moment, during a formal procession to the Lateran Basilica (the Pope's official residence until the Avignon interlude). Soon after this epiphany, evidently, Joan died; but her manner of death, like her place of birth, is reported in a number of different ways. Most commentators simply record that she and her son died immediately; others claim that she was torn apart by the raging mob; still others rather nastily assert that she was tied to the tail of a wild horse and dragged to a most painful death. At least one generous soul, however, decided to spare her life; for it is also said that Pope Joan was merely deposed, that she retired to a monastery by way of penance, and that in time she died and was buried at Ostia where her "popit" had acceded to the bishopric.[7]

Partisans of the legend also add that, in acknowledgment of the Church's shame, the street that witnessed the revelation of Joan's secret was thereafter avoided by all papal processions; while opponents of the legend maintain that the diversion was in fact dictated by the street's inability to accommodate any substantial pageant. The spot where Joan died, moreover, is alleged to have been marked by a statue; but its reputed inscription was debated with such passion, and had such an impact on the course of the controversy, that the evidence—such as it is—must be considered later. So must the most nefarious detail of all, centered on a ceremony said to have been introduced in order to prevent a woman from ascending St. Peter's throne ever again.

II

The *Liber Pontificalis,* the unofficially official list of Popes compiled in the ninth century, reported the reign of Joan in no uncertain terms. Two centuries later, in the eleventh, the frequently cited chronicler Marianus Scotus (d. 1082?) provided an entry under A.D. 854 to the effect that Leo IV was succeeded by Joan—"Joanna, mulier"—for two years, five months, and four days.[8] Early in the following century, a chronicler of a like reputation, Sigebert of Gembloux (d. 1112), ventured a fuller entry on "Ioãnes papa Anglicus" and expressly reported the "rumor" that she was a woman.[9] Three sources—one of them contemporary—constitute sufficiently respectable proof, especially for a legend.

Unfortunately for the champions of the legend, however, all three entries are interpolations made sometime in the thirteenth century and, in the case of the item in the *Liber Pontificalis,* in the fourteenth.[10] The first authentic relations of the legend, in fact, do not occur much before the thirteenth century. They include the accounts by the Dominican Étienne de Bourbon (d. 1261), by an anonymous Franciscan friar at Erfurt, and especially by the official chronicler at Metz, who alike assign Joan's pontificate to the years 1099-1101.[11] As already noted, however, it was still another account that in time proved most popular; and here Joan's reign was assigned to the years 855-857. Its author was the chronicler Martin of Troppau—usually referred to as Martinus Polonus (d. 1278)—whose credentials include service first as penitentiary under Pope Nicholas III and later as Archbishop of Gniezno (Gnesen). His influential account deserves to be quoted in full:

> After this Leo [IV], John an Englishman by nation Margantinus, held the see two years, five months, and four days. And the pontificate was vacant one month. He died at Rome. He, it is asserted, was a woman [*hic, vt asseritur, fœmina fuit*]. And having been, in youth, taken by her lover to Athens in man's clothes, she made such progress in various sciences, that there was nobody equal to her. So that afterwards lecturing on the Trivium at Rome, she had great masters for her disciples and hearers. And forasmuch as she was in great esteem in the city, both for her life and her learning, she was unanimously elected pope. But while pope, she became pregnant by the person with whom she was intimate. But not knowing the time of her delivery, while going from St. Peter's to the Lateran, being taken in labour, she brought forth a child between the Coliseum and St. Clement's church. And afterwards dying, she was, it is said, buried in that place. And because the Lord Pope always turns aside from that way, there are some who are fully persuaded that it is done in detestation of the fact. Nor is she put in the Catalogue of the Holy Popes, as well on account of her female sex as on account of the foul nature of the transaction.[12]

The first chronicler promptly to adapt this account to his purposes was another Martin, a Minorite;[13] but interpolations also drew on the same source, witness the report on Pope Joan inaccurately attributed to the English Benedictine chronicler Ranulph Higden.[14] Thus at any rate began a tradition that was to extend over the centuries ahead, not exclusive of our own.

In time, Pope Joan passed from chronicles into literature. The most celebrated literary adaptation of the legend during the fourteenth century assuredly belongs if not to Petrarch then to Boccaccio, whose *De claris mulieribus* (Ch. 99) recounts Joan's rise—"spurred by the devil"—in an evident effort to convert her into an exemplar of lust.[15] John Lydgate's versification of Boccaccio's tales in the next century also related Joan's fortunes, as we have noted. Given the outrages she committed, however, Lydgate vowed to restrain himself. "I wil," he wrote, "on hire spende no more labour"—and, amazingly for such a garrulous poet, he did not.[16] The chronicles, in the meantime, continued to reiterate the story. The most popular version during the fifteenth century formed part of the universal history by Philip of Bergamo (Jacobus Philippus Foresti), whose account in Latin and its translation into Italian were alike reprinted several times.[17] Of other important versions during the later half of the same century, five in particular deserve to be mentioned: the accounts in the highly respected chronicle of St. Antoninus, Archbishop of Florence (d. 1459), and in the enormously popular *Fasciculus temporum* of Wernerus Rolewinckius de Laer; the entry in the annals of the historian Palmieri (d. 1475); the relation in the popular collection of miscellanies by Battista Fregoso (Fulgosus), sometime Doge of Genoa (d. 1502); and especially the details provided by the German humanist Hartmann Schedel in his famous *Nuremberg Chronicle* of 1493.[18] It may be added that this same period also witnessed the advent of several eloquent illustrations. One occurs in the *Nuremburg Chronicle,* where Joan is designated John VII and depicted in the line of succession immediately after Leo IV, moreover clearly sporting not her predecessors' staff but the "popit." An even more sensational illustration, setting forth the moment of Joan's childbirth during the formal procession to the Lateran, was first provided by *Der kurcz sin von etlichen frowen* (Ulm, 1473), which is to say the German version of Boccaccio's *De claris mulieribus*; but soon the plate began to be reproduced in editions of the original Latin—for example, *De claris mulieribus* (Berne, 1539), fol. 73v—and was eventually adapted by Protestants like "H. S." Well might one exclaim, as did St. Antoninus, "O the depth of the riches both of the wisdom and knowledge of God: how unsearchable are his judgments, and his ways past finding out!"[19]

We pause in astonishment, of course. Why was it that such a legend arose at all and, having arisen, how could it have been endorsed by reputable members of the Church's hierarchy like Martinus Polonus or St. Antoninus? Efforts to account for this phenomenon are not wanting, however inadequate each may be. It has been suggested, for instance, that the origins of the legend should be sought in the protests heard not infrequently during the Middle Ages that one or another of the popes was, as it were, weak "like a woman"; and that eventually the popular imagination endowed the given protest with flesh and bones. This interpretation usually focuses on the pontificate of the "real" John VIII (878-882), whose attitude toward the Patriarch Photius of Constantinople was so conciliatory that

"John" was by way of derision transmuted into "Joan."[20] The great Catholic historian Baronius, while endorsing this theory, endorsed also another one, according to which Pope Leo IX (1048-1054) protested to the Patriarch Michael Cerularius over a rumor that eunuchs had been elected to the See at Constantinople and that even a woman had been elevated to the priesthood; whereupon the Eastern Church is said to have retaliated by fabricating the legend of the female pope. However, no Eastern document even remotely confirms Baronius' dark suspicions. On the contrary, we are now in possession of a Western document, written in the tenth century, that purports to relate the election to the patriarchate at Constantinople of a woman who reigned for a year and a half—a deception, it is said, discovered through the intercession of an evil spirit in a dream.[21] Might it be that this unlikely report was in time transferred to the West by imaginative Western chroniclers? If so, however, the larger question of its endorsement by far more responsible historians lingers still. It lingers even where it is asserted, according to yet another theory, that the legend was first disseminated by Franciscans in revenge of Boniface VIII's adverse attitude toward them. And it lingers, too, when we are tempted to attribute the legend merely to the fondness of friars for a "spicy incident" by virtue of their "gossipy habit of mind."[22] No such habit, of course, is even remotely discernible in Martinus Polonus or St. Antoninus.

It is even less discernible in the authorities who in the sixteenth century likewise credited the existence of Pope Joan. These include, we should remind ourselves, the widely respected philologist and historian Marcantonio Coccio surnamed Sabellicus, "one of the famousest men in his time for all manner of good learning"; the poet Baptista Spagnuoli surnamed Mantuanus, whose ecclesiastical credentials include service as general of the Carmelites; the polymaths Joannes Nauclerus, Abbot Joannes Trithemius of Sponheim, Archbishop Bartolomé Carranza of Toledo, Paulus Constantinus Phrygio, and especially Raffaele Maffei surnamed Volaterranus, whose encyclopedic compilation was dedicated to Pope Julius II; the antiquary Richard de Wassebourg; the historians Giovanni Lucido, Christian Masseeuw, Marco Guazzo, and Francisco Vicente de Tornamira; and lastly the Spanish "universal man" Pedro Mexía, whose lengthy account of Pope Joan was translated into English as part of the vast compilation collected by Thomas Milles.[23] "I make no doubt," wrote Mexía in a spectacular understatement, "but that many have heard of a Woman, who was made Pope of *Rome*." So they had; and because they had, a militant Protestant could triumphantly yet justly remark of the legend: ". . . where I pray began the historie of her first? In Rome. From what place was it first published abroad into the world? Frō Rome. What be they that have written & declared it? The trustie friends of Rome: yea the

great authenticall Doctors & commissioners of the Pope. . . ."[24] Somewhat less hysterically but much to the same purpose, John Donne maintained in 1626 that while he was "not very apt to believe" a number of the legend's aspects, it was rather odd that "no man" within the Catholic Church had ventured to correct the "slander."[25] In fact, however, Donne must have been fully aware that the counter-movement had begun well before his time, in the fifteenth century, by Platina.

One of Italy's great humanists, Bartolomeo de' Sacchi called Platina (1421-1481), was the means to the end eventually attained by an even more illustrious humanist. Platina completed his exhaustively researched biographies of the popes after his appointment by Sixtus IV as librarian of the Vatican. Published in 1479 as *Liber de vita Christi ac de vitis summorum pontificum omnium,* and thereafter translated into Italian and French as well as English, it includes an account of Pope Joan under the pontificate devoted to John VIII.[26] The basic details, duplicated largely from Martinus Polonus but encompassing the relations of other chroniclers too, were disposed after such a strictly scholarly fashion that the legend's glaring inconsistencies drew attention to themselves. Thus alerted, two scholars in the next century advanced to the only conclusion possible. One was the Bavarian historiographer Johann Turmair surnamed Aventinus (d. 1534), who in his *Annales* dismissed the "fabula de papa muliere" with utter contempt; the other was the Italian antiquary Onofrio Panvinio (d. 1568), who in his *Chronicon* bypassed Pope Joan silently even as in his annotations on Platina's *Lives of the Popes* argued his case against her authenticity with exemplary scholarship.[27] Without Panvinio, Platina could be made to appear what he may have been, the legend's defender; but with Panvinio, he was transformed into its opponent.

So effective were Panvinio's annotations, and so venomous the fury they aroused among the partisans of Joan's existence, that he was tellingly denounced by some of the more livid Protestants as "one of the Popes Parasites."[28] Panvinio's influence was certainly formidable; and thereafter the attacks on the authenticity of the legend proliferate greatly. On the Continent Florimond de Raemond, Georg Scherer, and Leone Allacci penned elaborately detailed treatises; Robert Cardinal Bellarmine and Caesar Cardinal Baronius argued against the legend more briefly but no less effectually; while still others—the French Jesuits Denis Pétau and Philippe Labbé among them—dismissed Pope Joan with eloquent brevity.[29] In England, at the same time, Thomas Harding was as we have seen controverting the legend with Bishop Jewel; and soon the ever-embattled Robert Parsons, S.J., endeavored to cope with John Foxe's lurid account of Pope Joan in the widely read *Book of Martyrs.* Parsons and Foxe were decidedly well matched in that both were journalists of the last order.

Among the weapons in Parson's armory were shells fired indiscriminately on all exponents of the legend beginning with Martinus Polonus ("a very simple man"); a barrage of rhetoric intended to undermine confidence in a story replete with "incongruityes, simplicityes, absurdityes, varietyes and contrarietyes"; and a ruthless endeavor to deflect the enemy through the report, already noted, that a woman was elected not pope in Rome but patriarch in Constantinople ("so abhominable a thing, as the horror thereof doth not permitt vs to beleeue it").[30]

Thus spokesmen for the Catholic Church had—*pace* John Donne—argued extensively against the fable of Pope Joan. Frequently, indeed, they were joined by Protestants. As Parsons for once accurately maintained, "the very truth is, that this whole story of Pope Ioane is a meere fable, and so knowen to the learneder sort of Protestants themselues."[31]

III

As if by anticipation of the common Protestant response to the legend of Pope Joan, the Bohemian reformer John Huss both during the formal investigation of his opinions and in the course of his treatise on the Church accused the Catholic hierarchy of being "soiled with wicked, deceitful depravity and sin, as at the time of Pope Joanna, the Englishwoman, who was called Agnes."[32] The legend, clearly, seemed but to wait for the advent of Protestantism in order to become a powerful enough weapon to vex Catholics into nightmares. The tenor of predictable account after predictable account changed but slightly; only our heroine's name altered, as if to remind us that we had moved from one writer to another. Heinrich Bullinger's exceptionally brief remarks condense what others expanded into countless pages of abuse: "What will you saye that through the wonderfull prouidence of God it came to passe, that a woman fayning her selfe a manne, dyd clyme vp to the See of Rome, was created Bisshoppe, and called *Iohn* the 8. whyche was one *Gylberta,* a great whore, borne at *Mentz.* For thus woulde God declare, that the Bysshoppe of Rome sitteth a whore vpon the beaste."[33]

In England there was in the first instance a play on Pope Joan ("poope Jone"), already old when Philip Henslowe first saw it in March 1591. We are not aware of the play's burden; but we are only too well aware of how another influential writer, John Foxe, treated its subject. "And here," Foxe proclaimed with evident glee after an account of several popes culminating in Leo IV:

"And here next now followeth & commeth in, the whore of Babylon (rightly in her true colours by the permission of God and manifestly without all tergiuersation) to appeare to the whole world: and that not onely after the spiritual sense, but after the very letter, and the right forme of an whore in deed. For after this *Leo* aboue mentioned, the Cardinals proceeding to their ordinary electiō (after a solemne Masse of the holy Ghost, to the perpetuall shame of them & of that sea) in stead of a mā Pope, elected an whore in deed to minister Sacraments, to say masses, to geue orders, to constitute Deacons, Priests, and bishops, to promote Prelates, to make Abbots, to consecrate Churches and altars, to haue the raigne and rule of Emperors and kings. . . ."[34]

The passage continues with an account of Pope Joan's pontificate and death, appropriately embellished to coincide with Foxe's usual tone of unmitigated sensationalism. True, Parsons protested that Foxe's details are "as follish and blasphemous, as they are wont [to be] in such cases";[35] but, considering the source, the protest could readily misfire—and did. Other Protestants were in any case already preparing whole treatises, alike improbable, and alike splenetic. They include Simon Rosarius, who installed the hapless Joan at the very center of his scurrilous *Antithesis Christi et Antichristi* (1578); "H. S."—often assumed to be the German philologist Hermann Witekind—whose vitriolic tract, *Iesvitas, Pontificvm, Romanorvm emissarios, falso et frvstra negare Papam Ioannem VIII. fvisse mvlierem* (1588), was deemed worthy to be translated into both German (1596) and English (1599); and "I. M.," an Englishman, who in *The Anatomie of Pope Ioane . . . : Necessarie for all those that . . . abhore the sottish illusions of Romish Antichrist* (1624) demonstrated that he was as capable as "H. S." to prove that the Catholic Church was "a sinke of wickedness." Such histrionic tracts were often accompanied by equally histrionic illustrations, even if in some cases—notably the title page of the Latin tract by "H. S."—the plate was not devised by Protestants but, as already noted, was first ventured by Catholics for Boccaccio's *De claris mulieribus.*

Not every Protestant monomanically espoused abuse, however. A few aspired to some semblance of scholarly detachment, like the German polymaths Matthias Flacius surnamed Illyricus and Sethus Calvisius, the one reiterating the legend in the massive compilation known as "the Centuries of Magdeburg," the other endorsing it in his outline of chronology.[36] England could also pride herself on the relatively inoffensive discussions of the fable by Gabriel Powel and especially by Alexander Cooke, who managed to overcome his evident anti-Catholic bias long enough to review the evidence as fairly as his ill-starred age could tolerate;[37] nor can it be held against Cooke that a posthumous adaptation of his work—*A Present for a Papist: or the Life and Death of Pope Joan* (1675)—carried opposite the title page yet another illustration of the inopportune birth of Joan's child. The event is annotated in appropriately horrendous verses:

A Woman Pope (as History doth tell)
In *High Procession* Shee in Labour fell,
And was *Deliuer'd* of a *Bastard* Son;
Thence *Rome* some call *The Whore of Babylon.*

It is all the same disconcerting to find among Joan's defenders four individuals one had assumed were far less partisan: Bishop John Jewel, "a iuell rare indeed," as a contemporary epigram called him; John White, the liberal Anglican theologian; John Donne; and, lastly, Henry More, the Cambridge Platonist, whose acceptance of the fable was dictated by the common obsession to discern in Pope Joan "a palpable Hieroglyphick . . . that *Rome* was indeed the Seat of that great Apocalyptick Strumpet." For More, in fact, Joan's pontificate was not merely a demonstration of God's intervention in history but a particular example of God's odd playfulness, one of those "notorious *Specimens* of *Festivity,* as I may so speak, that is sometimes observable in Divine Providence, answerable to that Lidibundness in Nature in her *Gamaieu*'s and such like sportful and ludicrous Productions."[38] More's tortuous grammar and pretentious vocabulary are perfectly commensurate to his objectives.

Nevertheless, Parsons quite properly suggested that "the learneder sort of Protestants" were persuaded that the story of Pope Joan is "a meere fable." Earnestly questioned by Protestants in the sixteenth century, the fable was to be demolished in the seventeenth century again by Protestants—or, to be more exact, by one reputable Protestant in particular. The attempt was mounted by the Huguenot David Blondel (1590-1655), who had initially pleased his fellow-Protestants mightily by proving that the Isidorian decretals, until then regarded as genuine letters of the early popes, were in fact forgeries of the ninth century.[39] But those same Protestants were less than pleased when Blondel argued with equal impartiality against the legend of Pope Joan in *Familier Éclaircissement de la question si une femme a été assise au siège papal de Rome* (Amsterdam, 1647), later translated by himself into Latin as *De Ioanna Papissa: sive Famosæ Quæstionis, an fœmina ulla inter Leonem IV, & Benedictum III, Romanos Pontifices, media sederit.* ἀνάκρισις (Amsterdam, 1657). Exhaustively detailed, the treatise displays its author's credentials in its impressive scholarly apparatus and especially in its tone, untouched as it is by the scorching fire of partisanship. Replies were not long in materializing, notably by Pierre Congnard and Samuel Desmarets;[40] but Blondel's treatise withstood such onslaughts to remain the definitive scholarly confirmation that the fable of Pope Joan is indeed but a fable.

IV

While Joan's existence engaged Catholics as well as Protestants and aroused the passions of both equally, two particular aspects of the legend appear to have exercized nearly everyone involved. Through these aspects one can appreciate the inflammable nature of the controverted legend and the alarming dimensions that it often assumed.

The first of these aspects involves the report by Adam of Usk in the early fifteenth century that an "image [of Pope Joan] with her son stands in stone in the direct road near St. Clement's"—i.e., the street between the Coliseum and the Lateran where Joan's son was born and where both of them died.[41] The report was soon confirmed by John Capgrave, who remarked in his description of Rome (c. 1450) that the Church "was decayued ones in a woman whech deyied on processioun grete with child for a image is sette up in memorie of her as we go to laterane."[42] The question thereafter debated *ad nauseam* centered not on the actual existence of the statue, nor even on whether it was a representation of Joan and her son or—as a modern scholar has argued rather ingeniously—of Juno suckling Hercules.[43] What concerned the combatants from the fifteenth century on was an inscription which other accounts claimed to have been carved on the statue: *P.P.P.P.P.P.* Disregarding the obvious possibility that the six *P*'s are of classical origin in accordance with a standard monumental inscription—i.e., the formula "*P* (designating any given praenomen so beginning) *pater patrum* (title of the priests of Mithra) *propria pecunia posuit* ('has put up at his own expense')"—four other theories were proposed: *Petre pater patrum papisse prodito partum* ("O Peter, father of fathers, betray the giving birth of a popess"); *Parce pater patrum papisse edere partum* ("Spare, O father of fathers, that a popess should give birth"); *Papa, pater patrum, papisse pandito partum* ("O Pope, father of fathers, reveal the giving birth of a popess"); and *Papa pater patrum peperit papissa papellum* ("O Pope, father of fathers, a pope has given birth to a baby pope"). The first theory was often said to have been the inscription's intended meaning; the second was, evidently, a *cri de cœur*; the third was attributed to the devil; while the fourth was normally favored by the least forgiving Protestants.[44] In the light of such convolutions, one can readily imagine the treatment reserved for a report on yet another statue of Pope Joan, said to have formed part of a sequence of statues of popes in the very cathedral of Siena![45]

The other aspect worthy of attention is the incredible ceremony said to have been introduced in order to preclude the election of another female pope. It appears that newly elected popes were wont to sit during their inauguration on a marble chair or throne as the choir chanted, "suscitans de terra inopem et de stercore elevat pauperem";[46] and the chair was in consequence termed the *sedes stercorata.* Somehow, however, the purpose of the ceremony and the nature of the chair were amended after the fashion reported by the Byzantine historian Laonikos Chalcocondylas (d. 1464?):

καθίζουσι δὲ ἐπὶ σκίμποδος ὀπὴν ἔχοντος, ὥστε
καὶ τῶν ὄρχεων αὐτοῦ ἐπικρεμαμένων ἅπτεσθαί
τινα τῶν προσαχθέντων, ὥστε καταφανῆ εἶναι
ἄνδρα εἶναι τοῦτον. δοκοῦσι γὰρ τὸ παλαιὸν
γυναῖκα ἐπὶ τὴν Ρώμης ἀρχιερατείαν ὠφικέσθαι.[47]
Even the most frenetic of anti-Catholics understandably
hesitated to translate Chalcocondylas' precise words.
The English version of the vitriolic tract by "H. S.," for
example, tactfully renders the passage thus: ". . . they
place him who is chosen [pope] vpon a sell [i.e., cell]
hauing an open hole, by which his golden fleeces, hanging downe, of some one deputie to this office, they are
handled, that it may be knowne whether he is a man:
for they perceiue that in times past, a woman crept into
the See of Rome."[48]

A number of Catholic reports to the same effect—notably those by Platina and Sabellicus—strenuously asserted that the ceremony had a different purpose, that
"he who is plac'd in so great authority may be minded
that he is not a God but a man, and obnoxious to neces-
sities of Nature, as of easing his body."[49] But the more
belligerent Protestants continued to sneer at what one of
them called the "groping" of successive popes.[50] It
hardly helped that prominent scholars like the French
antiquary Jean Chifflet provided illustrations of the *sedes
stercorata*. These but assisted the visualization of a ceremony already insistently described by Catholics themselves—and in one case described with an explicitness
that attests to some mental derangement:

> ". . . when any one comes to bee enstaulled Pope,
> they [the cardinals *et al.*] haue a Chaire purposely made
> open, like a Close-stoole, and by their passage
> vnderneath it, it is secretly and assuredly knowne, if
> *Habet testiculos*, hee bee a Man or Woman."[51]

The Catholic Church suffered some wounds during the
controversy; but this one, in its essential premises
largely self-inflicted, was by far the worst.

V

Blondel's definitive treatise on Pope Joan marks the
end of an epoch. In the latter half of the seventeenth
century attitudes began visibly to shift. On the Continent, the learned Friedrich Spanheim the Younger attempted belatedly to resuscitate the legend but failed;
and his tone—like the illustration provided in one edition—was in any case dramatically different from the
emotional outbursts of the increasingly more distant
past.[52] In England an interesting representative of the
new outlook was an erstwhile associate of the old, Thomas Fuller. He removed the legendary Joan from his
list of English popes for rather novel reasons, not because he wished to eschew her at all costs. "Pope *John-
Joan* is wholly omitted," he explained, "partly because
we need not charge that See with suspicious and doubtful crimes, whose notorious faults are too apparent;

partly because this *He-She,* though allowed of *English*
extraction, is generally believed born at *Ments* in *Germany.*"[53]

Yet Pope Joan survived, no longer indeed because any
theological issues were involved, but because her fable
could be made to carry a variety of other burdens. Thus
the years of the Popish Plot in England (1678-1682) released anti-Catholic prejudices which displayed themselves most lucidly in Elkanah Settle's politically motivated play, *The Female Pope* (1680). Settle's heroine is
a vastly ambitious, utterly egocentric woman who experiences her first defeat when she falls in love with the
bombastic Duke of Saxony. "I die for the Duke," she
proclaims; but he is so far from responding that he
rouses the multitude against her. By the end of the
"tragedy" order is fully restored; but Settle, bent on
confirming the political argument of his play, went on
to provide an explicitly anti-Catholic tract on *The Character of a Popish Successour* (1681).[54] As John Wilkes
in conversation with Dr. Johnson was to say, "*Elkanah
Settle* sounds so *queer,* who can expect much from that
name?"[55]

Pope Joan's presence in the eighteenth century was
minimal. Curiosity on the popular level was but spas-
modically lively, in spite of the sensational accounts
still furnished by persistent individuals like Maximilien
Misson. The period's intellectuals, certainly, were la-
conic to the point of total indifference. The lexicogra-
pher Pierre Bayle, for example, rejected the legend outright, paying due tribute to Blondel's momentous labors;
and Gibbon confined himself to a single scornful reference to "the fable of a female Pope."[56]

But in the second half of the nineteenth century Pope
Joan revived in the very different setting of a re-
emergent Greece. The delightful novel of which she is
the protagonist, Emmanuel Rhoïdes' *Pope Joan* (1866),
was established in time as a classic of modern Greek
literature. It gained an international audience too, in
that it was translated thrice into French and twice into
German and English; it appeared in Italian, Danish, and
Russian; and, more recently, it was adapted by Lawrence
Durrell (1954, revised 1960). Rhoïdes' Joan is a
picaresque figure in the Byronic vein; and if one is also
reminded of *Tom Jones,* it is in order to mark Rhoïdes'
similarly "epic" range as well as the zest of his considerably more vulpine heroine. In a long "historical" introduction, Rhoïdes dutifully listed all the spokesmen in
favor of the legend and somberly declared that his intention was "the delineation of the state of religion as
well as of the customs and traditions in the ninth century." In fact, however, the novel is a caustic satire on
ecclesiastical abuses everywhere: the ignorance, the il-
literacy, the presumption, the commercialism of the
Church whether East or West. The Holy Synod of the
Greek Orthodox Church, not amused, promptly anath-

ematized the novel as "anti-christian and maleficent." But Rhoïdes characteristically responded by suggesting that the Holy Synod was actually in collusion with himself since the anathema increased his sales thousandfold! He also added that his attack was directed against "the laughable ecclesiastics, not the Christian faith itself." "If my work has generated laughter," he wrote, "it was the result of the absurdity of things as they are."[57] Therefore the details of his account of Joan—her cohabitation at Fulda with her first lover Frumentius, their years in Athens, her departure for Rome, her election to the papacy, her love affair with Florus the son (*sic*) of Leo IV, her childbearing, her death—are but the framework that sustains a remonstrance against the perverse traditions, practices, and attitudes openly endorsed by the Church. Often serious in the extreme, Rhoïdes protested with fiery indignation that hagiographers should recount the experiences of Christian martyrs but neglect those "charred by the flames of Christian injustice." Far more typical of his normal tone, however, is his conflation of the serious and the comic in the manner of Horace and Juvenal or the ethically oriented irony of Pascal's *Les Provinciales*.[58] The degree of the monks' dedication at Fulda, for example, is stated thus: "All submitted to the blessing on the Sabbath, but since it is not known for certain on which day God rested after the creation of the world, and they being fearful of falling into error, they remained idle the whole week long." The articulation of Charlemagne's proselytizing tactics is even more delectable: "No other missionary succeeded in so short a time in christianising so many unbelievers. The eloquence of the Gallic emperor was invincible. 'Believe or die,' he told the Saxon prisoner, in whose eyes the glitter of the executioner's sword shone with the light of persuasive argument. The mob jammed the fonts as geese do ditches after rain."[59]

Our own century has so far provided no comparable contribution. It began most inauspiciously, indeed, with a hysterical tract[60] reminiscent in its excessive zeal of the sensationalism of John Foxe or "H. S." Its title: "The End of the Papacy . . . never to rise again into political power over the nations of the earth. A brief review of the over-ruling providence of God in history. . . . With an appendix, including the history of the Woman Popess Joan." Far worse, however, was the legend's adaptation for the cinema. Produced in 1972, it featured two major stars but also a screenplay whose monotony—as a film critic remarked at the time—was "occasionally varied by a religious gathering or a rape."[61] The film's foreword proclaimed that the legend is one of "the most enduring." True enough; but it was interred at long last by the film's prodigious vulgarity.

Was it the ultimate manifestation of Providence, perhaps?

Notes

1. The legend's primary sources—such as they are—will be mentioned selectively below. They were frequently cited during the Renaissance, for example by "H. S." (see note 4), "I. M." (note 24), Powel (note 37), White (note 38) *et al.* Modern studies of major importance include in particular: Johann J. I. von Döllinger, "Die Päpstin Johanna," in his *Die Papst-Fabeln des Mittelalters* (Munich, 1863), pp. 1-45, trans. Alfred Plummer, *Fables respecting the Popes of the Middle Ages* (1871), pp. 1-67; Félix Vernet, "Jeanne (la Papesse)," in *Dictionnaire apologétique de la foi catholique*, ed. A. d'Alês (Paris, 1911), II, 1254-70; Herbert Thurston, S.J., *Pope Joan* (1929; originally published in 1917); and Elphège Vacandard, "La Papesse Jean," in his *Études de critique et d'histoire religieuse*, 4th series (Paris, 1923), pp. 15-39. One should not neglect Pierre Bayle's entries in the *Dictionary Historical and Critical*, trans. Pierre Des Maizeaux, 2nd ed. (1735), II, 24-25 [apropos David Blondel], IV, 708-709 [apropos Martinus Polonus] and 725-40 [on Pope Joan]. See also Otto Andreae, *Ein Weib auf dem Stuhle Petri oder das wieder geöffnete Grab de Päpstin Johanna* (Gütersloh, 1866), which quotes from most of the primary sources; and Francisco Mateos Gago y Fernandez, *Juana la Papisa* (Seville, 1878), as well as its French version, *La Fable de la Papesse Jeanne* (Geneva, 1880), which alike contain full bibliographies. More recent efforts include Cesare d'Onofrio, *Mille anni di leggenda: una donna sul trono di Pietro* (Rome, 1978), and Mario Praz, "La leggenda della papessa Giovanna," *Belfagor,* XXXIV (1979), pp. 435-42. There are any number of other studies, often lengthy but just as often of slight consequence, such as Aurelio Bianchi-Giovini, *Esame critico degli atti e documenti relativi alla favola della papessa Giovanna* (Milan, 1845). Still other efforts may safely be avoided, for example the "popular" account by Angelo S. Rappoport, *The Love Affairs of the Vatican or the Favourites of the Popes* (1918), Ch. III.

2. Horace K. Mann, *The Lives of the Popes,* 2nd ed. (1925), II, 307.

3. *A Defense of the Apologie of the Churche of Englande. Conteininge an Answeare to . . . M. Hardinge* (1570), p. 429. For a typical Continental claim, see the assertion by Philip of Bergamo (in the editions cited below, note 17) that Joan was of "natiõe anglicus"—or, as his Italian version more amply avers, "nato nella prouincia ouero Isola de Anglia." Pedro Mexía (below, note 23) just as firmly calls her "vna muger natural de Ingalaterra."

4. "H. S.," *Historia de donne famose. Or the Romaine Ivbile which happened in the yeare 855* (1599), sig. C2v. This work is the English version of the Latin tract attributed to Witekind (below, §3; also Pl. 3). A particular dimension of its diverse versions is discussed by Sarah Lawson, "From Latin Pun to English Puzzle: An Elizabethan Translation Problem," *Sixteenth-Century Journal,* IX (1978), iii, 27-34.

5. *Op.cit.* (note 3), p. 428.

6. "H. S." (as above, note 4), sig. C4v.

7. The episode involving the wild horse is mentioned by H. Daniel-Rops, *The Catholic Reformation,* trans. John Warrington (1962), p. 339; and the more auspicious turn of events, by Thurston (as above, note 1), p. 7n. The former is detailed in the Metz chronicle (as below, note 11).

8. "Leo papa obiit cal. Aug. Huic successit Joanna, mulier, annis 2, mensibus 5, diebus 4" (*Chronicon,* in *Rerum Germanicarum Scriptores,* ed. Joannes Pistorius [Regensburg, 1726], I, 639).

9. "Fama est hunc Ioannẽ fœminam fuisse: & vni soli familiari tantum cognitam: qui eã complexus est / et grauis facta peperit / papa existens. quare eam inter pontifices non numerant quidam: ideo nomini numerum nõ facit" (Sigebertus Gemblacensis, *Chronicon,* ed. A. Rufus [Paris, 1513], fol. 66v).

10. L. Duchesne, ed., *Le Liber Pontificalis* (Paris, 1892), II, p. xxvi, where the entry is cited and its authenticity disputed. Editions of the other chronicles no longer even bother to include the interpolations. In Sigebert's case, for example, the *Patrologia latina* sidesteps the "locus famosus de Johanna papissa" (CLX, 162n). Yet another early authority, Anastasius Bibliothecarius (fl. 869), was strictly silent: the edition I consulted of his *Historia, de vitis Romanorvm Pontificvm* (Mainz, 1602), expressly disclaims his mention of "Ioannes 8. Fœmina."

11. For Étienne's account, see: *Scriptores ordinis praedicatorum,* ed. J. Quetif and J. Echard (Paris, 1719), I, 367; and for the other two accounts: the anonymous *Chronica* and the *Chronica Universalis Mettensis,* alike in *Monumenta Germaniae Historiae: Scriptorum tomus XXIV* (Hannover, 1879), pp. 184 and 514, respectively. The first and the third of these are translated by Thurston (as above, note 1), pp. 3-4.

12. *Chronicon* (Antwerp, 1574), pp. 316-19; trans. S. R. Maitland in *The British Magazine,* XXII (1842), pp. 42-43.

13. Martinus Minorita, *Flores temporum,* in *Monumenta Germaniae Historiae* (as above, note 11), p. 243. Another late thirteenth century adapta-

tion from Martinus Polonus was made by Gaufridus de Collone: see *Monumenta* etc. (Hannover, 1882), XXVI, 614.

14. *The Cronykles of Englonde with the dedes of popes and emperours,* trans. John Trevisa (1528), fol. 75. Higden's *Polycronicon* is also available in an anonymous fifteenth-century translation: see the edition by Joseph R. Lumby (Rolls Series, 1876), VI, 333, which also provides the original Latin and the version by Trevisa.

15. Petrarch (attr.), *Chronica delle vite de Pontefici et Imperatori Romani* (Venice, 1507), fol. 55v, and Boccaccio, *Concerning Famous Women,* trans. Guido A. Guarino (1964), pp. 231-33. The latter work was written and revised in 1355-1359.

16. *The Fall of Princes,* IX, 967-1015 ("Off pope Iohn a woman with a child and put doun"); ed. Henry Bergen (Washington, D.C., 1923), III, 946-47.

17. The Latin is found in *Supplementvm* (Venice, 1513), fol. 193v-94, and the Italian in *Cronycha de tuto el mondo vulgare* (Venice, 1491), fol. 198v.

18. St. Antoninus, *Chronicorvm secvnda pars* (Lyon, 1586), pp. 568-69; Rolewinckius, *Chronica* (Basle, 1482), fol. 66v; Matthias Palmerius, *Evsebii . . . Chronicõ . . . Ad quẽ & Prosper & Matthaeus Palmerius . . . addidere* (Paris, 1518), fol. 126; Fulgosus, *Factorvm dictorvmqve memorabilivm libri IX* (Paris, 1587), fol. 254; and Schedel, *Registrum huius operis liber cronicarum* (Nuremberg, 1493), fol. 169v. Leonard E. Boyle, O.P., of the Pontifical Institute of Mediaeval Studies in Toronto, alerted me to the occurrence of the fable in an equally unexpected place, the *Sanctorale* of Bernard Gui, O.P., a copy of which was presented to Pope John XII in 1329.

19. *Ibid.*; quoting, of course, Romans 11.33.

20. The interpretation was later to be endorsed even by Lenglet du Fresnoy (as below, note 56). On the relations between John VIII and Photius, consult Francis Dvornik, *The Photian Schism: History and Legend* (Cambridge, 1948), *passim.*

21. *Chronicon Salernitatum,* XVI; in *Monumenta Germaniae Historia: Scriptores* (Hannover, 1839), III, 481; trans. Thurston (as above, note 1), p. 16. This document was first noted by E. Bernheim, "Zur Sage von der Päpstin Johanna," *Deutsche Zeitschrift für Geschichtswissenschaft,* III (1890), 412.

22. Thurston (as above, note 1), pp. 12, 13.

23. *Seriatim:* Sabellicus, *Rhapsodiae historiarvm enneadvm* (Lyon, 1535), II, 325 [the quoted phrase is by Cooke (as below, note 37: *A Dialogve,* pp.

19-20]; Mantuanus, *Alfonsus* (Deventer, 1506), sig. G5; Nauclerus, *Chronica* (Cologne, 1579), pp. 712-13; Trithemius, *Chronicon* (Basle, 1559), p. 17; Carranza, *Svmma conciliorvm et pontificvm* (Salamanca, 1549), p. 529; Phrygio, *Chronicvm regvm* (Basle, 1534), p. 402; Volaterranus, *Commentariorvm vrbanorvm Raphaelis Volaterrani* (Basle, 1559), p. 503; Wassebourg, *Des antiquitez de la Gaule Belgicque* (Paris, 1549), fol. 162 and 167v; Lucidus, *Chronicon* (Venice, 1575), fol. 62 [also available in several earlier editions]: Massaeus, *Chronicorum . . . libri viginti* (Amsterdam, 1540), sig. flv; Guazzo, *Cronica* (Venice, 1553), fol. 176; Tornamira, *Chronographia, y Repertorio de los Tiempos* (Pamplona, 1585), p. 237; and Mexía, *Silua de varia lection* (Valladolid, 1551), fol. 9-9v [Part I, Ch. IX], trans. Milles, *The Treasvrie of Avncient and Moderne Times* (1613), I, 47-49 [Bk. I, Ch. XXI].

24. "I. M.," *The Anatomie of Pope Ioane* (1624), sig. A8v.

25. Quoted more fully in the headnote, above, from his *Sermons*, VII, 153.

26. I consulted the Latin version in *Historia de Vitis Pontificum Romanorum* (Venice, 1562), fol. 101v-102. I also checked one of the editions in Italian (Venice, 1563), pp. 118 ff. ["Giovanni Femina"], as well as the translation into English by P. Rycault, *The Lives of the Popes* (1685), p. 165.

27. Aventinus, *Annalivm Boiorvm libri septem* (Ingolstadt, 1554), p. 474; and Panvinio, *Chronicon ecclesiasticvm* (Cologne, 1568), sig. H4, and—for his annotations on Platina—the edition in Latin cited in the previous note: fol. 102-104v.

28. "I. M." (as above, note 24), sig. A7.

29. *Seriatim*: Raemond, *Errevr popvlaire de la Papesse Ieanne* (n.p., 1588), also available in several editions and in a Latin translation; Georg Scherer, *Ob es war sey Das auff ein zeit ein Papst zu Rom Schwanger gewesen vnd ein Kindt geboren babe* (Vienna, 1584); Allacci, *Confvtatio Fabvlæ de Ioanna Papissa* (Amsterdam? 1645); Bellarmine, *De Romano Pontifice*, Bk. III, Ch. XXIV, in *Bibliotheca Maxima Pontificia*, ed. J. T. Rocaberti (Rome, 1698), XVIII, 624-26; Baronius, *Annales ecclesiastici* (Mainz, 1603), X, 124 ff.; Pétau [Petavius], *Rationarivm temporum* (Mainz, 1646), I, 498; and Labbé, *Epitome historiæ sacræ ac profanæ* (Paris, 1654), p. 10.

30. *A Treatise of the Three Conversions of England*, trans. from the Latin (n.p., 1603), I, 387-404 [Part II, Ch. V, §§ 17-36]. For another Catholic effort to

establish that "Pope *Iohn* the Woman is a fable," see "Michael Christopherson"—i.e., Michael Walpole, S.J.—*A Treatise of Antichrist* ([St. Omer], 1613), pp. 415-20.

31. *Ibid.*, p. 391.

32. *De Ecclesia*, Ch. VII and XIII; trans. David S. Schaff (1915), pp. 62, 127, 133-34. See also *John Hus at the Council of Constance*, trans. Matthew Spilka (1965), pp. 192 and 209.

33. *A Hvndred Sermons vpõ the Apocalips*, trans. John Daws (1561), p. 507. Bullinger added, with the hyperbole characteristic of all partisans: "herein I follow the constant consent of al Historiographers."

34. *Actes and Monuments*, rev. ed. (1583), p. 137. The lost play on "poope Jone" is recorded in *Henslowe's Diary*, ed. Walter W. Greg (1904), I, 13.

35. *Op.cit.* (above, note 30), p. 387.

36. Illyricus, *Ecclesiastica historia* (Basle, 1559-1574), IX, 332-33, 337, and 500-502; Calvisius, *Chronologia* (Leipzig, 1605), p. 733.

37. Powel, *Dispvtationvm theologicarvm & scholasticarvm de Antichristo & eius Ecclesia, libri II* (London, 1605), pp. 274-76; Cooke, *Pope Joane* (1610), translated into both Latin (Oppenheim, 1619) and French (Sedan, 1633), re-issued in English as *A Dialogve betweene a Protestant and a Papist. Manifestly prouing, that a woman called Ioane was Pope of Rome* (1625), and adapted after Cooke's death as *A Present for a Papist* (1675; 1740; 1785). It may be noted that the Tudor antiquary John Leland also credited Joan's existence; but then he also defended the historicity of the Trojan Brutus and of King Arthur, and accepted the British origins of St. Helen, the discoverer of the Cross (T. D. Kendrick, *British Antiquity* [1950], p. 58).

38. *Seriatim*: Jewel, "Dame Iohane Pope," *op.cit.* (as above, note 3), pp. 427-34, and *The Apologie of the Church of England*, trans. Anne Lady Bacon, (1600), p. 111 [the epigram is quoted from William Gamage, *Linsi-Woolsie* (Oxford, 1613), §42]; White, *The Way to the Trve Church*, 4th impr. (1616), pp. 416-18; Donne, *op.cit.* (as above, note 25), as well as VI, 249, and X, 146; and More, *A Modest Enquiry into the Mystery of Iniquity* (1664), p. 316.

39. Owen Chadwick, *The Reformation* (1964), p. 218.

40. Congnard, *Traité contre l'eclarcissement donné par M. Blondel, en la question, Si vne femme a esté assise au Siège Papal de Rome, entre Leon IV. & Benoist III* (Saumur, 1655); Desmarets [Maresius], *Joanna Papissa Restituta* (Groningen, 1658).

41. *Chronicon,* ed. and trans. Edward M. Thompson (1876), pp. 88 and 215.

42. *Ye Solace of Pilgrimes,* ed. C. A. Milles (1911), p. 74.

43. G. Tomassetti, "La statua della papessa Giovanna," *Bollettino della Commissione Archeologica Comunale di Roma,* XXXV (1907), pp. 82-95. Some sources refer not to a statue, however, but to a monument in stone.

44. I have depended for this paragraph on both Daniel-Rops and Thurston (as above, note 7), but especially on the useful annotation provided by Mr. C. B. L. Barr of the York Minster Library.

45. The statue, Cooke reported excitedly, "is to be seene there [Siena] at this day" (as above, note 37: *A Dialogve,* p. 3); and so, too, claimed the controversialist Thomas Bell in *The Suruey of Popery* (1596), p. 191. Later in the seventeenth century, Jean Mabillon and Michael Germain confirmed the statue's existence (*Museum Italicum* [Paris, 1687], I, 159); but numerous others denied it.

46. Psalm 112.7 (Vulgate): "[He] rais[es] up the needy from the earth, and lift[s] up the poor out of the dunghill" (Douay version). The last word also occurs in the King James Version (Psalm 113.7).

47. *Historiarum libri decem,* Bk. VI; ed. I. Bekker, in *Corpus Scriptorum historiae byzantinae* (Bonn, 1843), XXXI, 303.

48. *Op.cit.* (above, note 4), sigs. C1-C1v.

49. Platina, *The Lives of the Popes* (as above, note 26). See also Sabellicus (above, note 23); and among a number of similar reports, the one by Johannes Stella, *De vitis ac gestis summorum pontificum* (Amsterdam? 1650), pp. 112-13. For a scholarly explanation of the import of the ceremony, see the extensive footnote—a learned essay in itself—by Francesco Cancellieri, *Storia de' solenni possessi de' sommi Pontefici* (Rome, 1802), pp. 236 ff.

50. "R. W.," *Pope Joan* (1689), p. 21.

51. Pedro Mexía, in the version by Thomas Milles (as above, note 23).

52. Spanheim, *De Papa foemina* (Leyden, 1691), with translations into French (Cologne, 1694; 3rd ed., 1736) and German (Frankfurt, 1737). Cf. Fridericus Montanus' scholarly *Disquisitio historica de Papa Foemina* (Leyden, 1690).

53. *The History of the Worthies of England* (1662), p. 13.

54. *The Female Pope: being the History of the Life & Death of Pope Joan. A Tragedy* (1680). Settle's 1681 tract was reprinted in 1689 and again in *State Tracts* (London, 1693), pp. 148-64—the same collection that included a reprint of Marvell's *Account of the Growth of Popery.* To the same general period belong the reissue of Cooke's adapted account (above, p. 171) together with its sensational illustration (Pl. 4), and the account by "R. W." already quoted (note 50).

55. Boswell, *Life of Johnson,* ed. G. B. Hill (Oxford, 1934), III, 76.

56. Bayle, *op.cit.* (above, note 1); and Gibbon, *The History of the Decline and Fall of the Roman Empire,* ed. J. B. Bury (London, 1898), V, 298. Among the other responsible scholars who also rejected the fable was Pierre Nicolas Lenglet du Fresnoy, *A New Method of Studying History,* trans. Anon. (1728), I, 317. For Misson's sensational account, on the other hand, see his *A New Voyage to Italy,* 4th ed. (London, 1714), II, 82 ff. and 111 ff.

57. 'Η Ἱστορία τῆς Πάπισσας Ἰωάννας . . . Πρόλογος—'Επιμέλεια-σχόλια, ed. Aghisilaos Tselalis (Athens, 1963), p. 255.

58. These works are cited as precedents by Rhoïdes himself in his pseudonymous—and devastatingly ironic—"Letters of a Man from Agrini" (*ibid.,* pp. 262, 267).

59. *Pope Joan: A Romantic Biography,* trans. Lawrence Durrell (1960), p. 19; the other quotations from the novel are from pp. 65 and 106. Like others before him, Rhoïdes did not escape "responses"—as by Charles Buet, *Études historiques: La Papesse Jeanne. Réponse a M. Emmanuel Rhoïdis* (Paris and Brussels, 1878).

60. By Edward Poulson (1901).

61. *Pope Joan,* with Liv Ullmann in the title role, Trevor Howard as her predecessor Leo IV, and Franco Nero as the Emperor Louis II; directed by Michael Anderson, screenplay by John Briley; Columbia Pictures, 1972. The film critic quoted is Dilys Powell in *The Sunday Times* (London) for October 29, 1972.

Barbara Sher Tinsley (essay date autumn 1987)

SOURCE: Tinsley, Barbara Sher. "Pope Joan Polemic in Early Modern France: The Use and Disabuse of Myth." *Sixteenth Century Journal* 18, no. 3 (autumn 1987): 381-98.

[*In the following essay, Tinsley argues that Florimond de Raemond's debunking of the fable of Pope Joan in 1578 was a defense of papal infallibility, freed religious controversy from a dependence on fictitious evidence, and introduced ordinary readers to the problems of historical research.*]

The thirteenth century literary tradition that a female had once reigned as pope was frequently retold in sixteenth-century Europe by Protestants anxious to destroy the validity of the papacy. They attempted to do that by insisting that her reign had made an irreparable breech in the heretofore uninterrupted (and male) apostolic succession from Saint Peter. This Protestant campaign was answered by Catholic Counter-Reformation writers, the last of whom before the seventeenth century was Florimond de Raemond (1540-1601), a magistrate in the Bordeaux *Parlement* and an amateur archaeologist. He put the finishing touches on the exposure of the popess myth in his best-selling book, *Erreur Populaire*[1] which appeared anonymously in Bordeaux in 1587, and was a short forty-four-page essay. The next year's edition was three times as long, and the third edition (1594), no longer anonymous, was over three hundred pages. This exposé, which went through fifteen editions between its first and its last appearance (1691), made it difficult to resurrect this Pope Joan without offending against the rules of humanist literary criticism, historical accuracy, and plain logic.

Given the problems posed by religious schism during the seventeenth century, it cannot be said that Raemond's book dissolved old tensions. It can be demonstrated, however, that the legend had been put to good use, for Joan was a hard worker even if she were a figment of the medieval imagination. The best use to which Joan, with Raemond's help, was put was that she aided in establishing a firmer, more historically accurate foundation under ecclesiastical history. This involved a more deliberate analysis of old medieval documents, especially of medieval chronicles which had been altered since the thirteenth century to include Joan's story.

In the process of this analysis, Europe's serious, but not formally educated, readers were initiated into the mysteries of historical methodology. Even before the efforts of Raemond and his Counter-Reformation predecessors, the myth had been used to vent the frustration of reform-minded Catholics. After their efforts, Catholics possessed polemical works with which to defend their doctrine against Protestant polemic. Exposed as myth, Joan became a Defender of her Faith, Roman Catholicism, rather than the defence of Protestantism against Catholicism. While Joan's exposure was used to teach Catholics not to apologize for their faith, this same exposure had ecumenical potential—it freed Protestants from the trammels of myth, enabling them to use the new history and reason in their own defence.

The fable had all the makings of soap opera. A girl of twelve named Joan, Agnes, Jane, Marguerite, or Geliberte, had run off from home in Mainz,[2] having quarreled with her folks. She may have been seduced by the monk or servant who accompanied her to an English university, or to a convent in Fulda, so that Joan,

in male disguise, could be educated. That English universities did not yet exist—Oxford, England's oldest, dates from the thirteenth, not the ninth century[3]—seems not to have troubled medieval chroniclers. Having earned her *baccalarius,* another thirteenth-century invention, Joan and friend went to Athens to study science and philosophy. Not until the sixteenth century did the Augustinian friar, Onofrio Panvinio (Panvinius),[4] object that ninth-century Athens was not yet equipped with schools which could provide such instruction. Athens was still in barbarian hands; Joan could not have furthered her education in such hostile surroundings. Panvinius's work was only five pages long, but upon it Raemond, and everyone else who wrote to refute the popess myth, could build. After Joan's lover died, presumably of natural causes, Joan went to Rome. Employed there as a Lecturer, or reader of Scripture in the church, she made a rapid rise up the clerical ladder. Some sources say she became a cardinal; all agree she was soon elected pope. The Roman mob had elected her by public acclamation because of her learning and piety. Unfortunately for Joan, one of her staff members had seen through her disguise. Whether this staff member was a cardinal or a mere clerk in the Curia was always a matter of conjecture. The result, however, was plain to see: Joan delivered her child while officiating at Mass, or on horseback, or while marching in a Corpus Christi Day procession. Raemond objected that the latter supposition was impossible. Corpus Christi was not in existence during the ninth century. Pope Urban IV had instructed its observance only in 1264.[5] In any event, Joan's delivery was also her public humiliation, and it proved fatal—not to her, but to her reign. Deposed, Joan was variously dealt with.

Although Protestants would try to fasten Joan's story to the eleventh-century *Chronicon* (1082) of Marianus Scotus, Joan really made her debut in Jean de Mailly's chronicle of 1250.[6] She appeared in other chronicles afterwards, each time with changes which Raemond felt made her reign improbable.[7] One detail of her career never changed: She was always deposed for her adultery. Giovanni Boccaccio (1313-75) was the earliest Renaissance man of letters to re-tell her story. His *De Claris Mulieribus* (1353) cited Joan and other women famed for their prowess in the literary or martial arts. It has been remarked that Boccaccio, who seemed to admire his unique female subjects, carefully recorded the gross humiliations most suffered for their uniqueness.[8] His feelings toward bold and learned women were not unmixed. In the next century, John Hus referred to Joan at the Council of Constance shortly before he was burned there for heresy. Before his condemnation, he had urged the church to clarify its position regarding the status of the primacy after, and because of, Joan's interruptive reign.[9] Joan was a weapon in Hus's effort to question papal authority. Since no one at the Council objected to his having raised the issue, it seems likely that conciliarists found Joan a convenient means for strengthening their case, hoping to substitute an ecumenical church council for what they believed was damaged papal authority.

The first doubts raised about Joan's authenticity were those of the fifteenth-century humanist, Aeneas Sylvius Piccolomini, later Pope Pius II (1458-64). In a letter to one of his bishops, Juan de Carvajal, Aeneas recounted an interview that he had had with Nicholas, bishop of the Taborites. He had told Nicholas that he did not believe Joan's reign was an error on Rome's part; that it did not break any tenet of faith or of law. It was only a sign of the church's ignorance of the real status of Joan. He thought the whole story was far from certain.[10] Aeneas did not publish his doubts, nor did he reproduce the story in any of his historical works. Nevertheless, the early seventeenth-century Lutheran theologian and polemicist, Johann Gerhard (1582-1637), said he had seen such a work, published in 1493 in Nuremberg. What he had really seen was Hartman Schedel's illustrated *Chronica Universalis* or *Nuremberg Chronicle* (1493) which contained generous portions of Aeneas's *Historia Bohemica* (1475) and his manuscript *Europa*; both works were used by Schedel for contemporary reference. But he did not get his popess information from Aeneas. Gerhard's memory betrayed him, perhaps because the prestige of Aeneas as an historian was greater than Schedel's, whose profession was medicine, not history. There are two sources from which Schedel may have drawn for his brief paragraph on Joan. One was Giacomo Filippo of Bergamo (Bergomensis, d. 1520), whose *Supplementum Chronicarum* (1493) was a prime source for Schedel and which contained a reference to the popess.[11] Another was the account of Platina.

Bartolomeo de' Sacchi (Platina) (1421-81) had personal reasons for disliking papal authoritarianism. Pope Paul II had abolished the Roman Academy, and Platina had led a protest movement against the closure. The protest was against a loss of income, but Paul believed that Platina and his colleagues were conspirators. Platina was imprisoned twice on charges of conspiracy and heresy. He disavowed heretical ideas, saying that he had lived as a Christian and had gone to confession and to communion once each year.[12] Platina took his revenge on Paul by incorporating anti-papal polemic, including the popess story, into his popular *Lives of the Popes* (1474).[13]

The French theologian and humanist, Jacques Lefèvre d'Etaples (1455-1537), a Catholic reformer whose piety was attested by practical deeds of church reform as well as by scholarship, edited a work by a medieval friar named Robert of Uzès. This book, *Liber Trium Virorum et Trium Spiritualium Virginum,* published in Paris in 1513, concerned a dream which Robert said had permitted him to visit Rome. There he had seen the object

that would become the most notorious reminder of Joan's reign—the perforated porphyry chair on which the *probatio sexus* was said to have been administered immediately after a papal election.[14]

On the eve of the Reformation several of the uses of the myth had already made their appearance. The story had been told to entertain. Misogyny permeated western culture, and the notion that women might achieve power or intellectual distinction made monkish chroniclers laugh. If their humor was barbed, hiding clerical resentment of papal power, their brief entries offer little certain evidence. During the Renaissance, Joan's tale was used by men of letters to indicate, albeit tentatively, that new standards for civility rendered ignorance in either sex less than desirable.[15] Civility offered new standards of social conduct, and new interest in sexual misconduct. The story was alluring for its pornographic aspects. Raemond believed Boccaccio had capitalized on the grossness of the story for the sole purpose of expanding his readership.[16] The fact that Joan's story always ended in her public humiliation or punishment offered a justification for reading unsavoury material.

If Renaissance literature was sometimes ribald, the late fifteenth and early sixteenth centuries seethed with spiritual unrest. Many people longed for reforms of a church grown worldly and an administration grown insensitive to that longing. Joan became a symbol of papal immorality and also of papal fallibility. Conciliarists, who wished to substitute ecumenical councils for papal leadership, used Joan as an example of papal misconduct. Her story was a reproach to popes and their curial officials, but was not commonly viewed (except by Hussites) as a wholesale condemnation of the Roman church. Some pious Catholics mentioned her so casually they seemed not to have been disturbed by the possibility of the story's most dangerous use—the denial of spiritual validity to the church hierarchy.

With the onset of the Reformation, that use of Joan became common. The Protestants charged that Rome was not merely error-prone (fallible), but totally bankrupt spiritually. Joan's reign was a case in point, and they insisted it had fatally interrupted whatever claims to legitimacy it once had. Martin Luther said that in 1510 he had seen a monument to the popess (Agnes) in the form of a stone tablet on which she appeared in papal garb, holding a child by the hand.[17] He concluded that the papacy had become so callous it had not bothered to destroy the incriminating monument. John Calvin said that it would be impossible to "leap over Popess Joan" even if one could exclude the male heretic popes who had similarly interrupted the apostolic succession.[18] Joan's crime was unique: she was a woman.

Once the Reformation was well under way, the pursuit and exposure of the female pontiff became for Catholic historians a political necessity and a religious obligation. Although the basic refutation was composed by Panvinius, it was Florimond de Raemond who proved to be Joan's real nemesis. He transformed Panvinius's brief outline of debating points into a lively yet systematic book over three hundred pages long. Since he wrote in French, the literate but not learned among his countrymen could profit by the scholarship of the Counter-Reformation. Latin and Dutch translations appeared in the course of time.[19] Raemond surveyed much of the medieval literature, soliciting friends and booksellers for examples of rare manuscripts and printed works. Though he was handicapped by the limitations imposed by a provincial city, he nevertheless examined an impressive number of sources. To forestall criticism of his conclusion, he cited the work of the "all knowing Pithou,"[20] whose diligence in documentary research had not yielded any reference to the popess.

Chronicles which mentioned Joan varied. Although researchers like Raemond knew this, not many of his contemporaries did. Raemond aired difficulties with which scholars were familiar, but which ordinary readers must have found surprising. Even after the printing press made standardized copies of medieval manuscripts available, the amount of misinformation was not reduced. It probably increased, because many printers set in type chronicles which they did not carefully edit. Raemond knew that not all the additions to original manuscripts were of Protestant manufacture. Along with Panvinius, he cited the case of the chronicle of Sigebert of Gembloux (d. 1112). Panvinius had attributed its alteration to include the popess to an English monk, Galphridus of Oxfordshire who died (1356) over two hundred years after Sigebert.[21] Panvinius's judgment has been borne out by a nineteenth century scholar.[22] But while Raemond knew that Catholics had altered many such chronicles, he vented his wrath principally upon Protestant printers and editors who failed to exercise adequate caution in their work:

> So if afterwards, these annotated books fall into the hands of some printer, he does not fail to make what the commentator has added appear the work of the first master's hand even though innocent of all errors.[23]

In Raemond's haste to condemn Protestant printers, he made some errors. For example, the same Sigebert replete with the Joan reference had been printed in 1513 by the Estienne press. He attributed this edition to Robert Estienne, the reformed printer who in 1550 fled from Paris, where he was printer to Francis I, to Geneva. Robert had been the victim of Catholic attacks. But in 1513 Robert was still a child. It was not until 1526 that he assumed the business which his father, Henri (d. 1520), had founded. Henri was no Protestant. In attributing the edition of Sigebert to the reformed son, Raemond's passion seems to have got the better of him, even though he warned his readers against the violence of emotions which distort truth.[24]

His suspicion of Protestant printers led him to villify Johann Herold of Basel, a Protestant with Erasmian views who continued to hope for religious unity between all Christians. A pastor for some years, Herold satisfied neither his parishioners nor his superiors, all of whom seemed to consider him a covert Catholic backslider.[25] Herold was obliged to turn from pastoral work and to rely solely on printing for his living. Among his printed works are the two medieval chronicles of Marianus Scotus and Martin of Troppau, or Polonus. Raemond said he had deliberately falsified Polonus by omitting the term *dicitur* (it is said) used by Polonus to indicate that he doubted the story of the popess.[26] Herold's 1549 edition was followed in 1574 by one from a Catholic printer, Suffridis Petri of Louvain, and Petri's edition contained the persistent popess. Whatever Raemond felt was the case, the religious preference of printers was not the determining factor in the reiteration of this myth. Not until the next century was an edition of Polonus, who larded his chronicle with many fables, to appear minus the popess.[27]

Although Raemond was harsh on Herold, whom a modern critic has excused from altering Scotus,[28] he was right to say that "Jean Oporin Lutherien" (Johann Herbster, or Oporinus) of Basel had printed an inaccurate edition of the fifteenth century Greek scholar, Calcondile. The original had not mentioned Joan, but Clauser, the German who translated it, had. Oporinus said he knew no Greek, but he was disingenuous, for he had taught Greek at the university in Basel and Latin in the local Latin school there. Oporinus, formerly the employer of young Johann Herold, was not, however, Lutheran, but a Zwinglian.[29]

The acceleration of religious unrest, in part a result of the revolution caused by printing, was also a cause of its success. The availability of copies shaped public opinion. If "typographical fixity" perpetuated positions once taken, it did not slow down the invention of new positions.[30]

The sixteenth century was beginning to interest itself in the discovery of antiquities.[31] Often, its enthusiasm outstripped its expertise. Luther's "identification" of the stone tablet was no unusual case. A statue of another woman and child, rediscovered around the time of the *Erreur Populaire*'s first appearance, and now thought to represent Juno nursing Hercules, seems to have been described in a fourteenth-century book as the statue of the popess.[32] Raemond ordered a sketch of this statue to be forwarded to him. He agreed with the verdict already rendered by Panvinius that the subject was classical, not Christian.

The sculpted bust of Joan could be found in the sixteenth century, together with those of other popes, along an interior cornice frieze in the Cathedral of Siena.

Raemond included (Chap. 21 of *Erreur Populaire*) an appeal to Clement VIII to have this offending sculpture removed. He must have been very pleased when he received (1600) a letter from Cardinal Baronius, the same man who had lavished fulsome praise on Raemond's book on the popess in his *Annales Ecclesiastici*.[33] The Cardinal was writing to tell him that the Grand Duke of Tuscany had ordered the bust removed. It was later to be transformed into the likeness of Pope Zacharias and replaced on the cornice in that guise.[34]

More troubling than the sculpture, which only a few could actually see in the cathedral, was the story of the porphyry chair with the hole in its seat, a rumor everyone who knew about Joan was likely to repeat. This perforated chair had first been described, as we have seen, in the thirteenth century. Platina had included the first reference in his *Lives of the Popes,* but gave his readers another interpretation of the use of the chair. He said that rather than the means for performing the *probatio sexus,* the chair was simply a toilet seat, or *stercoria sedes.* Its use during papal installation ceremonies was simply as a reminder that God, who had elevated the candidate to such high office, left him subject to all the ordinary vicissitudes of human nature.[35] Raemond thought the whole business of the perforated chair of porhyry was "so gross" that the only possible response for Catholics was to laugh at the Protestants' folly in repeating it. The mystery of this chair has only recently been solved. In fact it was a *sella obstetrica,* or parturition chair, used by women in antiquity during childbirth, and in papal installations to symbolize *Mater Ecclesia,* or Mother Church.[36] Although no explicit comments to my knowledge were made by reformers linking this maternal concept of the church to Joan, the mother of an illegitimate child, it is certainly possible that sixteenth-century readers made such inferences themselves. Apparently, Pope Urban VIII (1623-44) took steps to restore the nobility of this concept to the church by commissioning Bernini to depict labor pains on four female faces which decorate the Bernini baldaquin in St. Peter's. He also hired two historians to write repudiations of the popess myth.[37]

One of the many lamentable features of the popess myth to Raemond's mind was its acceptance by Catholics as well as by Protestants. Raemond knew a Franciscan friar who had used the story of Joan as sermon material until he had disabused him of the story.[38] Since friars were not frequently well educated, Raemond found it more disturbing when an acquaintance of unimpeachable cultivation perpetrated the same error. This was the case of Etienne Pasquier, eminent jurisconsult and prolific historian, and like Raemond, a friend of Montaigne, the essayist. Pasquier had several times referred to Joan in his popular *Recherches de la France* which began appearing in 1560. Raemond reproached him for this. In the *Erreur Populaire* he wrote that "he who had

given France his *Recherches* ought to have searched more carefully for the truth, and not to have sullied his lovely pages with such filthy stuff."[39] Pasquier, in a letter to a friend years later, said that he was much obliged to Raemond for having lifted the seals from his eyes.[40]

In the process of disabusing his readers of their belief in Joan, Raemond undertook to analyze certain aspects of early medieval history. He used Joan to expose the tactics of his Protestant opposition. He said the Protestants had made heroes of the Eastern emperors and saints of their patriarchs in order to put the papacy in the poorest light. Three popes, Nicholas I (858-67), Hadrian II (867-72) and John VIII (872-882), were cast as villains for refusing to give their blessing to one of the emperor's men, Photius, a candidate for the patriarchate of Constantinople. Although John VIII[41] did eventually recognize Photius and give him his blessing, he was no more popular with Protestant historians than his predecessors. As for Catholics, John VIII was an embarrassment for having given in on the Photius issue, thus weakening (so they believed) papal authority in the East still further. Cardinal Baronius believed that John's critics (who eventually bludgeoned him to death) gave rise to the myth by their portrayal of this pope as a weak, womanish creature.

Although Raemond frequently followed the lead of more famous Catholic writers, he could display independence on other occasions. He rejected Baronius's theory about John's character. Photius had simply been adopted by Protestants because he was perverse and, though a learned man, had "spit up a thousand insults at the Roman church."[42] That was why, according to Raemond, he was the idol of Lutheran writers. But Photius had not mentioned the popess while petitioning Rome for its blessing. His failure to do so proved Joan's non-existence. For, mused Raemond, why would Photius—who could have made his own qualifications for high church office glitter by comparison with Joan—have failed to mention her disgrace? Although this kind of argument (from silence) is generally regarded as a logical fallacy, in this case it was not unconvincing. The significance of the controversy over Photius is meaningful when we learn that it was mixed with the growing tendency of the Roman church to insist on spiritual as well as political primacy throughout the Christian world. A matter of spiritual tension between East and West was the exact manner in which the Holy Spirit was believed to operate. The West claimed that it proceeded through the Father and the Son (the so-called *filioque* clause), the East did not. Political tension derived from Rome's contention that it should have the direct jurisdiction over Illyricum, when in fact Photius believed that jurisdiction belonged only to Constantinople.[43] In championing Photius, Protestant writers believed they were demonstrating their dissatisfaction with the extent of Rome's claim to total authority over all spiritual and temporal matters, with that kind of caesaro-papism which was so inimical to reformers such as Luther. The irony of the sixteenth-century debate over Photius was that John VIII's eventual recognition of him was conciliarist in nature, and conciliatory in spirit; for it was given in a council at which papal legates met with representatives from the patriarchates of Jerusalem, Antioch, and Alexandria.[44]

Raemond used the myth to appeal to French chauvinism, largely anti-German. Germans were presented as immoderate by their very nature, preferring strong drink and weak women.[45] He said they had invented Joan because they preferred secular to spiritual leadership, because their kings were often heretics, and because their bishops imitated their monarchs' religious heterodoxy.[46] He did not mention the Gallican Liberties which gave the French church immunity from some of the inconveniences of papal monarchy, and gave French kings some of the powers German ones hoped to obtain. He did not mention spiritual discontent on the eve of the Reformation either, except in connection with heresy. Raemond claimed that Germans had used Joan to symbolise their detestation of chastity. She was the symbol of temptations which inevitably befell celibate clergymen, a kind of occupational hazard which resulted from inappropriate vows. Raemond was an admirer of the controversial works of Cardinal Robert Bellarmine, among which was a discussion of celibacy. This the Cardinal regarded as apostolic law.[47] In fact, celibacy had been a matter of debate as late as the Council of Constance (1415) and that of Basel (1432). The subject was interesting not only to Germans, as Raemond's readers might have been led to conclude. But celibacy was a subject more distressing in German-speaking lands than elsewhere, and early in the Reformation treatises on the problem were written by Andreas Carlstadt (1521)[48] and by Luther, too (1521, 1522).[49]

Against those German historians, the Centuriators,[50] whose *Septima Centuria* had contained the popess myth they claimed had damned all subsequent popes, Raemond made a serious accusation. He said that these writers, concerned more with the defense of Lutheranism than with historical truth, had invented a correspondance between Nicholas I and a German monk named Hildaric who opposed celibacy. The correspondance was impossible on several grounds, Raemond said.[51] First of all, the two men were not contemporaries. Furthermore, the letter purported to have been written by Hildaric never mentioned Joan, whose adultery might have given him support for his case, i.e., the renunciation of a policy (celibacy) which had produced such a notorious lapse.

Apart from the theological issues of apostolic succession, primacy, infallibility and celibacy—and apart, too, from any consideration of historiographical method—

the popess was used to reinforce Renaissance misogyny, a theme which appeared in this and in Raemond's last great work, his history of the Reformation.[52] That the myth was not intended by its monkish creators to invite commentary on the role of women in society is obvious. Raemond thought the story was intended merely to amuse. After all, there were no learned women to speak of in the thirteenth century, and of female philosophers, there were none at all. A few women in the Middle Ages achieved clerical prominence within their own orders,[53] but none attained Joan's universal authority.

Research into feminine history indicates that medieval attitudes towards women were predominantly misogynist, but that a softening of opinion occurred during the Renaissance and persisted into the Reformation.[54] Still, women remained under the stigma of a supposed inferiority to men.[55] There were few acceptable outlets to which educated women in the sixteenth century could turn in order to justify the expense of their education. The patronage formerly given by great ladies to authors of poetry or romance had long since become unobtainable. Religious struggle replaced the artificial struggles on tournament grounds, once the focus of romance. Humanists turned their talents to more pious uses. Learned ladies turned theirs as well, but found religion at least as restrictive as it was liberating. The scope which noblewomen had for patronizing serious scholarship, and even on occasion engaging in it themselves, was not unlimited. A Marguerite of Navarre could, it is true, exercise both her pen as well as her patronage; but there were risks she ran which only the services of a king (her brother, Francis I) could obviate.[56] While the involvement of women in religion—a role pioneered by our Joan—has frequently been studied in terms of the stimulus given by Protestantism to feminine education and liberation,[57] recent research has taken the opposite direction, indicating that Catholicism offered more educational opportunity than was formerly thought.[58] Women's history seems to attract a growing number of historians, and the subject certainly bears further exploration.[59]

The questions that concern us with respect to feminine roles in the Reformation are of a more restricted nature, limited by the subject of the popess. To what degree might it be said that Joan influenced feminine advance or was influenced by it? Was popess polemic useful in advancing the cause not only of women, but of humankind in general?

If the *Erreur Populaire* of Florimond de Raemond was representative of late sixteenth-century opinion, and its brisk sale indicates that it was, it could not help but reinforce misogynist opinion at a time when misogyny was being threatened by feminine assertiveness and increased female involvement in political and in religious life.[60] Raemond reminded his contemporaries that feminine achievement, however possible, was always undesirable. The real popess, he wrote, was Elizabeth I of England, to whom he devoted two chapters. While he admired her diplomatic skill and her authoritative style—he especially liked the decisive way in which she dealt with Puritans—he was appalled by the active role she took in the Anglican church:

> That certainly is unnatural to see one who was created for obedience, wilfully command; and one who by Scripture is excluded from any performance and administration of ecclesiastical things, bind and loose the most holy and sacred mysteries of religion as she pleases. . . .[61]

Joan probably did little if anything to encourage women to go into religion or to challenge the prevailing prejudice against their sex.[62] She may, however, have reminded her readers that some real women had overcome hierarchical limitations and in this way fed the fires of feminist dialogue.[63]

Despite her charisma, or maybe because of it, Joan could not prevent a number of Protestant writers from refusing to abjure their belief in her. Pierre Bayle recorded a number of such die-hards[64] who refused to follow the lead of more rational members of their faith. Pierre Bayle was not one of Raemond's ardent admirers, but he was able to say that on the whole Raemond's *Erreur Populaire* was the best refutation of Joan that had ever been written.[65]

Though Joan could not disabuse all sixteenth- and seventeenth-century folk of the inferiority of women, nor even of her own historicity, she had nevertheless performed several outstanding services in the course of the late Renaissance and during the Reformation period. These made her story serviceable. In the earlier period, Joan provided some solace to reform-minded Catholics who tried, by means of ridicule (next to revolution the most powerful of social tools), to promote change within the Roman church. During the Counter-Reformation Rome did change, taking upon itself the investigation of its own ecclesiastical history. Such research taught Catholics not to apologize for the major tenets of their faith, and Protestants not to devalue theirs by resorting to myths of less scrupulous centuries. Joan's hands were raised over everyone. By the time David Blondel's refutation was published in the first half of the seventeenth century, fair-minded Protestants could accept what he proffered by way of consolation: that the popess had not, after all, been a Protestant myth, but a Catholic one.[66]

In sum, Joan was herself a reformer, a charismatic personality who stimulated many people to think and reason their way to new intellectual and spiritual positions. Though she could not teach everyone to read history more carefully, she could justifiably claim, along with

Florimond de Raemond, that she had been used to instruct Catholics and Protestants in one great truth: that men do not have to defame another religious establishment in order to justify their own. In the Enlightenment, Protestantism no longer needed Joan to survive, and Catholics were no longer embarrassed by her. Even if Joan were only a fictitious popess, she was, in addition to being a great reformer, a great ecumenicist. She distributed even-handedly blessings to Protestants and Catholics alike, encouraging them to investigate their common historical roots and to subject written history to rigorous analysis. From readers of this new history, Joan anticipated great works: an end to religious polemic and freedom from the unproductive postures of religious discrimination and sexism.

Notes

1. The first edition was entitled *Erreur Populaire de la Papesse Jane* (Bordeaux: S. Millanges, 1587). After 1599 it was frequently entitled *L'Anti-Papesse ou l'Erreur Populaire de la Papesse Jane* having appeared in the same edition with Raemond's second original work, *L'Anti-Christ*, (1st ed. 1597). All references are to (*AP*) *L'Anti-Papesse* in the combined edition, *L'Anti-Christ et L'Anti-Papesse*, (Paris: Abel l'Angelier, 1599).

2. Despite her birthplace, her nickname was frequently given as John the Englishman (Jean l'Anglois). Said Raemond: "these people cannot agree where in fact she came from. . . ." *AP*: 363.

3. Charles Homer Haskins, *The Rise of Universities*, (New York: Holt, 1923), 4.

4. Panvinius (1520-68), a Vatican librarian, had as his ambition the re-writing of all Roman and Christian antiquity from reliable sources. His work ran to sixty-eight volumes, seventeen on the history of the papacy. F. Roth, *The New Catholic Encyclopedia*, s.v. "Panvinio, Onofrio."

5. Kenneth Scott Latourette, *A History of Christianity* (New York: Harper and Row, 1975), 1:466; Raemond, *AP*: 429-30.

6. August Potthast, *Bibliotheca Historica Medii Aevi*, (Berlin: 1896), 1: 241. Mailly's work was the *Chronica Universalis*.

7. Mailly put her reign between Urban II (d. 1099) and Paschall II (1099-1118); Stephen of Bourbon (1262), after Sergius III (d. 911), and before Anastasius III, who succeeded immediately. Some versions of Polonus lodged Joan after Leo IV (d. 855), and before Benedict III. In fact, there was no interval between these two, but 855-57 became the most-cited dates for Joan.

8. Margaret King, "Book Lined Cells," in *Beyond Their Sex*, ed. Patricia Labalme (New York: New York University Press), 79-80.

9. Frantisek Palacky, *Documenta Mag. Joannis Hus Vitam,* etc. (Osnabruck: Biblio-Verlag, 1966), 59-61.

10. ". . . neque certa historia est . . ." was Aeneas's phrase, in Rudolf Wolkan, ed., *Der Briefwechsel des Eneas Silvius Piccolomini* (Vienna: Hölder, 1918), 68: 40.

11. On Gerhard, see Robert D. Preus, *The Theology of Post-Reformation Lutheranism* (Saint Louis: Concordia, 1970), 52-53. Preus calls him "The third preeminent Lutheran theologian after Luther and Chemnitz." He was a professor at Jena from 1616 until his death (1637), and was known for his orthodoxy. His reference is to what he imagined to have been Aeneas's work rather than Schedel's: "Aeneas Sylvius, Pontifex ipsemet tandem factus, hanc Historiam excripsit in sexta mundi aetate p. 170 operis Historici [sic] impressi Norinberg. anno 1493 per Kobergerum." (Gerhard, *Locorum Theologicorum* (Jena: 1620), 5: 1004). It is on that very page (170) in the *Nuremberg Chronicle* that one reads the major facts of Joan's story and sees her figured as John VII, a female, crowned, and holding an infant. On Schedel, see Adrian Wilson, *The Making of the Nuremberg Chronicle,* (Amsterdam: Nico Israel, 1976), 20, 28. Foresti numbered Joan Johannes VIII.

12. Quoted in Denis Hay, *The Italian Renaissance* (Cambridge: Cambridge University Press, 1970), 143 n.2.

13. In Platina's book Joan is assigned the number VII, a number very rarely given to her. Schedel thus appears to have followed Platina's text.

14. This test was "performed" by a young cleric probing beneath the hole in the chair to determine if the newly elected pope had male genitalia.

15. Natalie Zemon Davis, *Society and Culture in Early Modern France* (Stanford: Stanford University Press, 1965), 72-73, finds that many women in the late Renaissance were still illiterate, with well-born women literate in the vernacular rather than in the classical languages. She notes (134) that Pope Joan had "limited potential" for criticism of the hierarchical social structure because her arrogance had caused her to sin.

16. Raemond, *AP,* 367.

17. Martin Luther, *WA, Tischreden,* no. 6447: 667.

18. "Verum his omissis, Joannam papissam transsiliant oportet, si continuare suam ab apostolisseriem volent." from J. Calvin, "Vera Christianae Pacificationis et Ecclesiae Reformandae Ratio" (1549) in *Joannis Calvini Opera Quae Supersunt Omnia* VII, (Brunswick, 1868), 633.

19. Raemond's son Charles made the first Latin translation in 1601. The first Dutch edition appeared in 1614.

20. Pierre Pithou (1539-96), respected legist and historian, published works from original manuscript sources.

21. O. Panvinius, *Annotationi,* appended to *Battista [sic] Platina Cremonese Delle Vite De' Pontefici,* (Venice: 1650), 228. The first edition of Panvinius's correction of Platina appeared in 1562.

22. Ludwig Bethman, *Mon. Germ. Hist. Script.* (Hanover: 1844), 6: 340, said that a monk altered Sigebert to contain the popess tale.

23. Raemond, *AP,* 387.

24. Raemond, *AP,* 378.

25. Andreas Burckhardt, *Johannes Basilius Herold* (Basel: Verlag von Helbing & Lichtenhahn, 1967), 126ff; 134-40.

26. Raemond, *AP,* 367, charged Herold with having "adjusted" Polonus, but Joh. Jos. Ign. v. Döllinger, *Die Papst-Fabeln des Mittelalters* (Munich: 1863), 9, said that Polonus was altered several years after his death (1278) to include this myth.

27. L. Weiland, *Mon. Germ. Hist. Script.,* 22: 386, said that the first useful edition of Polonus dates from 1616.

28. G. Waitz, *Mon. Ger. Hist. Script.,* 5: 493, found that while Herold's Scotus was a flawed work, Herold was not guilty of falsification. (Also found in *Patrologia Latina,* ed. Migne (Paris: 1879) 142: 619-20).

29. Josef Benzing, *Die Buchdrucker des 16. und 17. Jahrhunderts In Deutschen Sprachgebiet* (Wiesbaden: Harrassowitz, 1963), 36; Martin Steinmann, *Johannes Oporinus* (Basel: Verlag von Helbing & Lichtenhahn, 1967), 2 n. 15.

30. "Typographical fixity" is a term used by Elizabeth Eisenstein, "The Advent of Printing and the Protestant Revolt," in *Transition and Revolution,* ed. Robert M. Kingdon (Minneapolis: Burgess, 1974), 244. However valid in other contexts, such fixity did not prevent the permutation of the popess myth in the post-print era. Raemond took umbrage at Protestant authors—John Bale, Johann Turmair (Aventinus), Johann Funck (Funcius)—and at four Centuriators (M. Flacius Illyricus, J. Wigand, M. Judex, and J. Faber) who had produced innovations on the popess story. All these were either reformed Christians or Lutherans.

31. Raemond's own Roman art collection was a regular garden museum. A young German tourist urged travellers in 1627 to visit it. (Justus Zinzerling, *Voyage Dans la Vieille France,* trans. T. Bernard [Paris: 1859], 23. [1st. ed., 1627].)

32. A picture of this statue (now in the Vatican Museum) appears in Cesare D'Onofrio, *Mille Anni de Leggenda: Una Donna Sul Trono di Pietro* (Rome: Romana Società Editrice, 1978)—the best book on the popess legend.

33. Baronius described Raemond as a pious, learned man whose book on Joan left the Protestants defenseless. (*Annales Ecclesisastici,* ed. Augustus Theiner, (Rome: 1868), 14: 407.

34. D'Onofrio, 82 and fig. 60.

35. Bartolomeo de'Sacchi (Platina), *Hystoria de Vitis Pontificum Periucunda* (Venice: 1504), lvii.

36. D'Onofrio, 138-44. (Illustrations of the *sella.*)

37. D'Onofrio, 215 n. 45.

38. Raemond, *AP,* 411.

39. Raemond, *AP,* 373.

40. Étienne Pasquier, *Oeuvres* (Amsterdam: 1723) 2: 354.

41. Joan was often called John VIII, although more circumspect writers omitted the VIII.

42. Raemond, *AP,* 383.

43. Kenneth Scott Latourette, *A History of Christianity* (rev. ed.) (New York: Harper and Row, 1975), 302.

44. Ibid., p. 304.

45. Raemond, *AP,* 409: "_____A German can no more leave women alone than he can wine. . . ."

46. Raemond, *AP,* 407.

47. Robert Bellarmine, "Coelibatum Jure Apostolico Rectissime Annexum Ordinibus Sacris," in *Opera Omnia,* ed. Justinus Fèvre, (Frankfurt: Minerva G. M. B. H., 1965), 2: 454-60.

48. *Super Coelibatu Monachatu, etc.* (1521).

49. *On Monastic Vows* (1521); *On the Married Life* (1522).

50. These men (see n. 30 above) helped write the *Magdeburg Centuries,* printed in Oporinus's shop 1559-1574. Raemond despised them.

51. Raemond, *AP,* 409: "_____a letter falsely published under the name Hildaric_____" was his exact phrase.

52. Raemond, *L'Hitoire de la Naissance, Progrèz et Decadence de l'Hérésie de ce Siecle* (Paris: 1605). Subsequently printed twenty times between 1605 and 1746 in Latin, German, and Dutch, translations.

53. See Joan Morris, *The Lady Was a Bishop* (New York: Macmillan, 1973).

54. Émile Telle, *L'Oeuvre de Marguerite d'Angoulême Reine de Navarre et la Querelle des Femmes* (Geneva: Slatkine Reprints, 1960), 39. (1st ed., 1937).

55. Maité Albistur and Daniel Armogathe, *Histoire du Feminisme Français du Moyen Age à Nos Jours* (Paris: Éditions des Femmes, 1977), ch. 4.

56. Marguerite's book, *Le Miroir de l'Âme Pécheresse* (1531), was condemned by the Faculty of Theology of the University of Paris for subversive ideas. Francis got this condemnation lifted.

57. Sherrin Marshall Wyntjes, "Women in the Reformation Era," in *Becoming Visible: Women in European History* eds. R. Bridenthal and C. Koonz (Boston: Houghton Mifflin), 1977.

58. Retha M. Warnicke, *Women in the English Renaissance & Reformation* (Westport, Conn.: Greenwood Press, 1983) has upset the traditional view, which accords more credit to Protestantism in this regard.

59. See Merry E. Wiesner, *Women in Sixteenth-Century Europe: A Bibliography,* (Saint Louis: Center for Reformation Research, 1983).

60. Roland Bainton's *Women of the Reformation in Germany and Italy,* (Minneapolis: Augsburg, 1971; _____In France and England* (1973); and _____From Spain to Scandinavia* (1977); and Nancy Lyman Roelker, "The Appeal of Calvinism to French Noblewomen in the Sixteenth Century," in *The Journal of Interdisciplinary History,* (1971/72) 2: 391-418, and "The Role of Noblewomen in the French Reformation," in *Archiv für Reformationsgeschichte* 63 (1972), 168-95, are examples of such research.

61. Raemond, *AP,* 397.

62. Joan was a repugnant symbol to Protestants and to Catholics alike, and could hardly have been a role model for women. The scope which the sixteenth century did offer women in religious life is reviewed in Joyce Irwin's "Society and the Sexes," a bibliographical essay of broad dimensions in Steven Ozment, ed., *Reformation Europe: A Guide to Research* (Saint Louis: Center for Reformation Research, 1982). However, Irwin notes that at the end of the sixteenth century a marked rigidity vis-à-vis the role of women set in (345).

63. An example of one female, Marie de Gournay, author of a work (1622) on the equality of men and women, deserves mention here. Marie was the protegé of Raemond's friend, Montaigne. She was

known by Raemond and, as an associate of his literary circle, must have read his book on the popess. Nevertheless, neither its misogynist message nor Montaigne's own reticence on the subject of female education discouraged her from taking an aggressive position on the nature of women.

64. Pierre Bayle, *Dictionnaire Historique et Critique* (Paris: 1820) s.v. "Papesse," remark F. A few twentieth-century writers have clung to the belief that Joan was historical. In this connection see Clement Wood, *The Woman Who Was Pope* (New York: W. Faro, 1931). Wood, writing from a rabid anti-Catholic point of view, concluded that "_____Joan was as historical as Charlemagne" (56).

65. Pierre Bayle, 11: 373.

66. Blondel was a Protestant clergyman whose book, *Familier Esclaircissement de la Question si une Femme A Esté Assise au Siège Papal de Rome Entre Léon IV & Benoist III* (Amsterdam: 1647), was a vindication of Raemond's conclusion that the popess was imaginary.

Alain Boureau (essay date 1988)

SOURCE: Boureau, Alain. "Joan the Catholic: Thirteenth-Fifteenth Centuries." In *The Myth of Pope Joan,* translated by Lydia G. Cochrane, pp. 107-64. Chicago: The University of Chicago Press, 2001.

[*In the following essay, originally published in French in 1988, Boureau traces the evolution of the Pope Joan legend from the thirteenth to the fifteenth centuries, focusing on how she was used in clerical discourse, first as an exemplar and then as a historical case.*]

> To be verified: There is supposed to have been a certain pope, or, rather, a popess, for it was a woman; disguised as a man, he became, thanks to the honesty of his character, a notary of the Curia, then cardinal, and finally pope. One day when he was riding on horseback, he gave birth to a child, and immediately Roman justice tied his feet together and had him dragged, attached to the tail of a horse; he was stoned by the people over half a league and was buried where he died; at that place was inscribed: "Petre, Pater Patrum, Papisse Prodito Partum" (Peter, Father of the Fathers, Publish the Parturition of the Popess). Under his papacy the Fast of the Four Times, called the Fast of the Popess, was instituted.[1]

FIRST VERSION: AN ITEM IN A CHRONICLE

This first known version of the story of Joan comes from a brief *Universal Chronicle* written in a monastery in Metz around 1255.

At the risk of anachronism, we might call this entry in the Metz chronicle a news item. The author seizes on a bizarre, astonishing encounter between an individual and a milieu that ought to be mutually exclusive. "Hoax in Rome: A Woman Becomes Pope." An intruder creates an anecdote, but fails to make the institution totter; the event changes the course of the history of the papacy, only slightly, but enough to cause scandal, which calls for an investigation. The change is limited to a rectification and the invention of a new term: "a pope, or, rather, a popess *(vel potius papissa),* for it was a woman." Papal history absorbs the anecdote, enfolding its singularity within regularity. The acts of a woman are reported as if the subject were male (or, more accurately, neuter animated, which amounts to the masculine): *factus; tractus; lapidatus.* The real subject exists only in the revelation of the hoax ("one day when he was riding on horseback"); the real subject has no name and no individual history, given that he/she exists only as long as the scandal lasts. We do not know the reason for the cross-dressing ("disguised as a man . . . he became a notary of the Curia"). We know nothing about how the pregnancy originated: childbirth is not given as the result of immoral behavior, but simply permits the strange event to come to light. The story of the popess, in short, is a Church story: in a typical rise justified by the "honesty of his character," a desirable quality in a cleric, he/she becomes a papal notary, then a cardinal. When the transgression is discovered, it is immediately pursued by "Roman justice" and punishment is completed by the Roman people and noted in an inscription attesting to the serenity of the Church: "Peter, Father of the Fathers, Publish the Parturition of the Popess." The institution continued to function during this singular papacy, however: "Under his papacy the Fast of the Four Times . . . was instituted." As in a news item, the individual, the pinch of salt in the narration and the grain of sand in the machine, does not really trouble the institution. When the story appeared in Metz around 1255, it surprised and piqued people's curiosity, but it did not produce meaning. Meaning was born later, from a different narrative.

Joan had entered into a new existence, however: far from Rome and its festivals and rites, she left the limbo of rumor, both jocose and tearful, to create a sensation in texts all over Europe.

THE ENIGMA OF JOAN

Thus far the enigma of Joan has resided in a silence; henceforth there was a surprising amount of chatter about her. Between 1250 and 1450 dozens of clerical texts transmitted the story related in the Metz chronicle. These texts never cast doubt on the popess's existence; no author tries to dissimulate her, twist her story, or omit her. The popes themselves lent credence to the fable by following the processional detour commemorating the event. Until the Reformation (or at least until the Hussite revolution), the Church believed and presented as worthy of belief an event that seemed to compromise its reputation and that it would later present as a vile, base, Protestant, or anticlerical invention.

That paradox (which will require explanation) will perhaps protect us from the determinist temptation to ask "who benefits" from the story. The implicit notion of "ideological profit" is a variant of a vapid theory of reflection that often governs cultural history, and recent scholarship has been all too quick to reduce the motivation for writing a life of Joan to a desire to harm the papacy. The facts prove that this view is anachronistic: until around 1450 Joan belonged to no party and was used by all parties.

The abundance of versions, however, offers the danger of a false objectivity. It is tempting to become fascinated by the series itself, to hold it up as a pseudoreality, and to treat the Joan narrative as a "legend" or a "motif," those ersatz substitutes for the phenomenon in the narrative order. The existence of the series is contested, however, both de facto and de jure. By fact: an omission may conceal the loss of a manuscript; a particular density of mentions may result from the hazards of conservation. By right: the texts about Joan are, first and foremost, words. In medieval clerical discourse Joan's story is told gravely, seriously, dramatically; it does not shift key as a simple literary or historiographical theme might do.

The way seems narrow, then, between an ad hoc analysis of specific occurrences and a historiographical description of an anecdote often repeated and varied. Nonetheless, in her place between the happenstance of the event and the constraint of cultural usages, Joan embraces a large portion of truth and reality concerning the Middle Ages. This means that we will have to approach her person prudently, considering first her attractions and her ambience, her forms and forces, as she moved along the path that the Church of the Middle Ages laid out for her.

A Chronicle in Search of an Author

The inaugural text is our first stop. Thanks to the powers of deduction of Ludwig Weiland (in 1874) and Antoine Dondaine (in 1946), the Metz *Universal Chronicle* found an author: Jean de Mailly, a Dominican.[2] Another Dominican, Etienne de Bourbon (Stephanus de Borbone), repeated the story of Joan several years later in a collection of anecdotal exempla left uncompleted at his death in 1260. In his prologue Etienne cites among his general sources "the chronicle of Jean de Mailly of the Order of Preachers."[3] In the body of the text the source of the anecdote is simply given as "a chronicle." Etienne uses no other contem-

porary chronicle, however, which means that the story of the popess could only have come from the work of this "Jean de Mailly." The most obvious candidate is a preacher of that name who completed the first Dominican universal collection of legends, the *Abrégé des gestes et miracles des saints* (ca. 1243).[4] These two works, the legendary and the chronicle, contain at least two episodes rarely given elsewhere, the apparition of St. Michael at Monte Gargano and Pope Cyriacus's renunciation of the papacy so that he could follow St. Ursula and her eleven thousand virgins. Moreover, both texts confuse Gerbert of Aurillac (Pope Sylvester II) with Guibert of Ravenna (antipope Clement III).

Unfortunately, our knowledge of Jean de Mailly is limited to these two attributions. One biographical inference is perhaps justifiable: because a Burgundian sanctorale is included in the legendary, the "Mailly" attached to Jean's name may be a village of that name near Auxerre. The Dominican house at Auxerre was founded late (in 1241), which would explain Jean's choice of Metz.

These wisps of Lorraine and Burgundy mist make the rapid mention of the popess in the chronicle even more enigmatic. The autograph copy of this work (Bibliothèque National, Paris, Latin 14 593) presents what seem to be a draft and a clean copy, written one after the other by the same hand. Jean de Mailly enters this vague, already ancient news item at the bottom of a folio of the draft dedicated to the late eleventh century, adding a touching note that shows the historian at work: *Require* (To be verified).

Apparently, what we see here is rumor pushing its way into a text: a medieval author, especially if he is relating an event unknown to him or that he is unsure of, seldom fails to note his source, oral or written, provided that it offers the least guarantee or credibility, or at least to note a vague *legitur* (we read somewhere). The lack of any sign of a source in Jean de Mailly's report of the Joan episode is a clear sign of a rumor "to be verified." How, and why, did Jean de Mailly pick up that rumor? We will probably never know. Nothing in the text permits us to assign any intention to Jean, and the mention of "bad" popes in his chronicle (Gerbert, Leo VIII) was a common occurrence in both earlier and later texts, as we shall see.

The Dominican Network

The near anonymity of Jean de Mailly, whom we know only by his works, shows the power of the Order of Preachers' system for the diffusion of Christian narratives and dogmas throughout Europe. It is amusing to note that Jean, an unknown preacher, was both the first to report the story of Joan and the first in a long line of Dominicans who compiled collections of legends, a genre that produced and popularized a steady stream of saints' lives. After Jean de Mailly's anthology (1234) there came the *Epilogue on the Lives of the Saints* of Bartholomew of Trent (1245),[5] the *Miroir historial* of Vincent of Beauvais (ca. 1260), and the famous *Golden Legend* of Jacopo da Voragine (ca. 1265), a medieval best-seller with over a thousand known extant manuscripts.[6] The Preachers' passion for popularizing and compiling soon led them to include the legend of the popess in their chronicles (for example, in Martinus Polonus's *Chronicle of the Popes and the Emperors* and Jacopo da Voragine's *Chronicle of Genoa*) and in anthologies of exempla (such as those of Etienne de Bourbon and Arnoldus of Liège). The rapid pace of Dominican narrative production can perhaps be explained more by a cultural logic than by any political or religious orientation: thirteenth-century Dominicans offered constant and loyal support to the papacy.

The story of Joan might have been told elsewhere (and indeed it was, as we shall see). Its entry into the Dominican corpus made its circulation inevitable: whereas a monastic manuscript was copied only by chance or by individual decision, a Dominican text traveled rapidly. The Order of Preachers was in fact famous for its far-reaching network, for the mobility of its members, and for its production of easily transported intellectual tools. By definition, a preacher moved from one friary to another; whether a simple preacher or a preacher general, he covered the vast area of a Dominican province (the province of France covered the entire northern half of the country from Lyon to Metz). Etienne de Bourbon had probably read Jean de Mailly in the friary at Metz. If a brother became a reader or a prior, which were more stable responsibilities, the Order would still move him regularly from house to house.[7] Regular and frequent provincial chapters and general assemblies brought together large crowds of Dominicans. Moreover, itinerant preaching encouraged the production of easily transportable manuscripts: the legendaries of Jean de Mailly and Bartholomew of Trent were circulated in closely written, small-format manuscripts. This explains how the legendary of the obscure Jean de Mailly could have enjoyed an honorable career (to date, at least ten manuscripts have been located) and could have been copied, in part, as far away from Lorraine as Italy. Bartholomew of Trent's legendary, which was used by Jacopo da Voragine, survives in thirty manuscripts.

Thus, if the first vehicles for the legend of Joan seem fairly modest (the Metz *Universal Chronicle* and Etienne de Bourbon's *Traité des sept dons du Saint Esprit*), they nonetheless paved the way for the inclusion of the anecdote in the most widely propagated historical memoir of the Middle Ages, the *Chronicle* of Martinus Polonus. In fewer than twenty-five years (1255-79), Joan's fortune had been made.

TELLING ALL

If speculation about Jean de Mailly's motivations as the receiver and transcriber of a rumor seems an exercise in vanity, it should be noted that a mental attitude widespread in Dominican circles (and beyond) excluded censoriousness. A solid confidence in the powers of faith and knowledge permitted a compiler to consider any assertion and any narrative. Still, Jean de Mailly's notation, *Require* (to be verified), has to be taken seriously: if Jean had lived long enough to complete his text, he would undoubtedly have reviewed his chronicle with a critical eye and added some indication of the credibility of this item. Admittedly, such a critical review would have been made with the methods of the times. It would have been founded primarily on the authorities, and only secondarily on a more general chronological concordance. Still, critical review permitted repetition of any statement, provided that the acceptable critical apparatus of evaluation had been applied. When Jacopo da Voragine relates the legend of St. George (for the first time in the West), he prefaces his narration with a warning: "At the council of Nicaea his legend was included among the apocryphal writings because there is no sure record of his martyrdom."[8] Any anecdote, any "news item," any legend could be related without danger, because the narrator had available ways to modalize, neutralize, and suspend the question of truth. The intellectual revolution of the twelfth century gave the Church the means for this universal absorption of meaning: biblical exegesis, techniques of meditation, and a mastery of allegorical and figural decipherment made it possible to transform everything into Christian truth.

THE CHURCH CONQUERS THE REALM OF THE IMAGINATION

If everything can be told, everything must be told. The Church in the thirteenth century, at the height of its cultural monopoly, held a position of total, global power, and it claimed that it could account for everything. That desire to say everything perhaps explains the paradox of the reduction to folklore of thirteenth-century religious culture described by Jacques Le Goff.[9] Jacopo da Voragine gives an explicit description of this process of commandeering extraneous meaning *ad majorem Dei gloriam*. In his chapter in the *Golden Legend* on the purification of the Virgin, Jacopo explicitly presents the Church's tactic when he deals with the ancestral custom of carrying lighted candles on Candlemas, the Feast of the Presentation in the Temple and the Purification of the Virgin, 2 February:

> The Church established this usage for four reasons. The first is to do away with an erroneous custom. On the calends of February the Romans honored Februa, the mother of Mars the god of war, by lighting the city with candles and torches throughout the night of that

day. This they did every fifth year (that span of years being called a *lustrum*) in order to obtain victory over their enemies from the son whose mother they so solemnly celebrated. . . . Since it is hard to relinquish such customs and the Christians, converted from paganism, had difficulty giving them up, Pope Sergius transmuted them, decreeing that the faithful should honor the holy mother of the Lord on this day by lighting up the whole world with lamps and candles. Thus the Roman celebration survived but with an altered meaning.[10]

The clerical talent for absorbing and assimilating customs explains why medieval texts are so seldom watered down, unlike the texts of the post-Tridentine era. Another Dominican, Hermann Korner of Lübeck, who has already been mentioned in connection with the rite of verification of the pope's manhood, relates the story of Joan (as do many of his confrères), following the common version of Martinus Polonus. Korner expresses surprise, however, at not finding any trace of Joan in the chronicle of yet another Dominican, Henry of Herford (ca. 1350), which he used as a secondary source. Korner implicitly blames his fellow Dominican's timidity for his rejection of the precedent: "However, Henry of Herford makes no mention of that woman who so fraudulently invaded the papacy, perhaps out of fear of scandalizing the laity who know how to read by making it known that such an error was produced in the Church of God, which professed to be guided by the Holy Spirit but is directed by clerics and priests."[11] Henry's timidity, which was not widely shared, given that few universal chronicles omitted Joan, nonetheless testifies to an interesting awareness of the dangers of literacy. Individual reading of the Bible was cause for fear that was much more intense and more frequently expressed,[12] precisely because legendary or historical narration was usually completely smothered by clerical interpretation, whereas with individual reading there was always a risk that the divine Word might pierce through the ecclesiastical ornamentation surrounding it.

Platina gave a particular meaning (and a slightly perverse slant) to his decision to relate the life of the popess in the chronicle that he wrote at the command of Sixtus IX (1472), but he perpetuated the thirteenth-century intention of "telling all." For Platina it was communitarian concern that made telling all important:

> These events [the verification of the pope's virility] that I have indicated are commonly related, even though the guarantees for them are uncertain and obscure. I have decided to give them, nakedly and briefly, so as not to seem to omit too obstinately and tenaciously what almost everyone affirms, at the risk of erring with the commonality in this matter, although it appeared that these events that I have reported belong to the class of what can in all likelihood occur.[13]

Beginning in the twelfth century, legendary themes were gradually assimilated into the lore of the Church, but this process reached its height with Dominican compilations of the thirteenth century. Nothing illustrates this Dominican conquest of people's imaginations better than a comparison between the legendaries of Jean de Mailly and Bartholomew of Trent. As Antoine Dondaine convincingly demonstrates,[14] Jean de Mailly wrote a first version of his *Abrégé* for the sheer pleasure of argument when he was a cleric but not yet a Dominican (probably around 1230). He was at the time loathe to state that the legends he was relating were untrue. He says about certain marvelous aspects of the lives of Cyricus and Julitta: "If we report these things, it is in order to refute the apocryphal writings by means of authoritative works, for if they were true the historians would surely not have kept silent about them."[15]

Jean de Mailly is equally firm regarding another apocryphal episode (mentioned above): when he deals with the Nativity of Christ, Jean drew upon an ancient tradition derived from a Greek apocryphal text of the second century, the Gospel of James, translated into Latin in the sixth century under the name of "Pseudo-Matthew." According to this text, two midwives, Zebel and Salome, assisted the Virgin Mary at the birth of Jesus. Zebel immediately proclaimed Mary's miraculous virginity, but Salome was skeptical, and when she attempted to verify Mary's virginal state manually, she paid for her incredulity with a withered arm. St. Jerome, one of the highest patristic authorities in the West, had strongly condemned this version of the Nativity, citing the Gospel of St. Luke, according to which Mary herself, unaided, brought forth and swaddled the divine newborn. The suspect version of the story nonetheless circulated in the West, as attested in iconography, but it was never dignified with a text version (except for a metric adaptation by Abbess Hrothsvitha in the tenth century).

Jean de Mailly was sufficiently confident of his mastery of veracity to relate this episode, then reject it: "Neither were there midwives to assist her, no matter what certain books or old wives' tales say."[16]

Several years later Bartholomew of Trent, who was better versed in the Dominicans' techniques of integration, offered a clever compromise version in which Joseph calls in the midwives only because it was customary to do so: "Although Joseph was not unaware that it was the Lord who was to be born of the Virgin, nonetheless he followed the custom of his land and sent for midwives."[17] The minute Bartholomew could justify Joseph's move without impinging on the dogma of the Incarnation (which was the nub of Jerome's criticism), he was free to relate the episode, which served as the paradigm for many miracles in medieval hagiography in which skeptics are punished. Jacopo da Voragine makes constant use of such clever devices, which permit reconciliation of the irreconcilable and bring together scattered traditions for the greater profit of the Christian story. In the thirteenth century the legendary narrative thus seems to have been the essential element in an ideological mastery that presented, simultaneously, a symbolic object, its valorization, its use, and its subjection to control. Everything could be said within the Church, because nothing should be said outside of it.

Moreover, the permanence of narration seemed a doctrinal duty. The profound originality of Christianity lies in the Incarnation: God manifested himself on earth, among humankind and in the middle of its history, not at the time of origins. He returned; He announced a Last Judgment at the end of terrestrial time, the end of the history of the world. The sacred thus is related and must be related, for it manifests itself (or can do so) suddenly, in proximity to humankind. The grand evangelical model is first a narrative: legend, the historical anecdote, or a banal news item can arrive like a meteor, bearing the sacred. Thus in March 1429, when Joan of Arc went to Chinon to proclaim her divine mission, a commission of clerics presided by the archbishop of Reims examined her closely. They concluded, very prudently, that events would have to confirm the divinity of Joan's inspiration. She pointed out, however, that it would be impious to let pass an opportunity to witness a celestial manifestation: "For to doubt of it or neglect it with no appearance of evil would be repugnant to the Holy Spirit and would make oneself unworthy of the aid of God, as Gamaliel said to a council of Jews [the Sanhedrin] regarding the Apostles."[18] The Incarnation gives an ontological foundation to narrative: because narrative has an essence of the sacred at its disposal, it brings together and reveals what informs the being of the terrestrial world. Everything must be said in the Church, because everything may possibly bear significance.

This means that in the thirteenth century the Church methodically aspired to universal narration. Churchmen took over the oral tradition regarding the popess, possibly discernible in Rome beginning in the mid-twelfth century, within a centripetal whirl (*vorago*, which it is tempting to see as an imaginary etymology for "Voragine").

When the history of the popess fell within the Dominican network, it had an excellent chance of being infused with meaning, developed, and circulated. The medium created the message, thanks to an exemplary combination of chance (who knows? someone in Metz made a note of a rumor; a traveler passed that way; a pilgrim related the latest news from Rome) and necessity (the Dominican system converted all raw data into reproducible discourse).

CHANCE AND NECESSITY: ENIKEL AND VAN MAERLANT

Necessity seems to have played a major role in establishing Joan, precisely because the beginning of her story among the Dominicans was not its origin. The anecdote had quite certainly been related elsewhere and earlier (between 1150 and 1250), but within the realm of contingency and without the mediations necessary for it to spread. Perhaps as forgotten texts continue to be discovered, would-be popesses will be found in chronicles predating Jean de Mailly's. It is true that the "Johannists" (those who have believed in the real existence of the popess) have tried in vain to move the date of the tale's narration closer to the events it narrates by finding pertinent texts written before 1250. Some read the story of Joan into the *Liber pontificalis,* but only before the critical edition of Louis Duchesne, who clearly demonstrated, with facsimiles to back up his argument, that the twelfth-century manuscript that the Johannists had used as a source (Vaticanus latinus 3762) mentions the story of the popess only in a fourteenth-century marginal note that repeats the Martinus Polonus version word for word. Nor was Marianus Scotus (1086) aware of Joan: the edition of Scotus prepared by Johann Pistorius in 1583, which has misled even such scholars as Cesare D'Onofrio, is in fact based on a fourteenth-century manuscript. The same editorial mechanism pertains regarding Sigebert von Gembloux (1112), Otto of Freising (1158), Richard of Poitiers (1174), Geoffroy of Viterbo (1191), and Gervase of Tilbury (1211), but they may have copied the mention from one another.[19]

Still, the dam constructed by scholars and philologists since the late nineteenth century does not exclude the possibility that narrative streams may have flowed into the current of the Joan story upstream, without reaching the Dominican pool. For example, there is a mention written slightly later than Jean de Mailly's (around 1280), but certainly not dependent on Jean's version, in a lengthy rhymed chronicle in Old High German by one Jansen Enikel, a Vienna burgher. The episode, told in a rough, uncertain style, runs thus:

> There was in Rome a woman who had a beautiful body and who disguised herself as a man. No one could guess that she was a woman. One day, she was elected pope, for she was held to be a hero agreeable to God. She was very versatile, for, a woman, she wanted to be a man; and thus, she became pope. What she did that was extraordinary while she was pope I cannot say, so I must remain silent on the question. But about her there is one thing that I must say: she was not spared, and what they did to her, that I know well, for she had to suffer a misunderstanding aimed at her honor and was obliged to leave Rome. She harmed people by the horrible misdeed that her body did.[20]

With Jansen Enikel we are within a hair's breadth of rumor: the narrator knows nothing and says as much several times ("des kan ich niht gar gesagen / dâ von sô muoz ich stille dagen"). Briefly stated, a woman succeeded in becoming pope by cross-dressing, and the adventure ended badly. At roughly the same time (1283) but at the other end of Europe, another burgher, Jacob van Maerlant, reported a similar anecdote in a rhymed chronicle written in Flemish, the *Speigel historiael*.[21] Van Maerlant, too, knows almost nothing, but he states that he has heard about a commemorative statue (whose existence is confirmed by the oral tradition) and that he sought in vain to authenticate the story of the popess in the pontifical chronicles. Enikel and van Maerlant note and repeat the rumor, but they are incapable of drawing any conclusions from the anecdote. They lack the Dominicans' mechanisms for creating meaning.

SECOND: FROM NEWS ITEM TO EXEMPLUM: ETIENNE DE BOURBON

Around 1260, only a few years after Jean de Mailly's account, Etienne de Bourbon pressed Joan into his service. He took the anecdote, handily extracted from the Metz *Chronicle*, moralized it, and set it up as an exemplum.

We know a bit more about Etienne de Bourbon than about Jean de Mailly, but not much. He was born in Belleville-sur-Saône, not far from Lyon, around 1190-95. He attended the chapter school at Mâcon, then the University of Paris, and he entered the Dominican house in Lyon in 1223, hence in the very early years of the Order of Preachers. For some thirty years he led the itinerant life of a preacher general, traveling in the vast Dominican province of France from Savoy to Lorraine. We find him at Vézelay in 1226, preaching the crusade against the Albigensians; he later became diocesan inquisitor (a post usually filled by a Dominican) at Clermont, then at Lyon. At the end of a long and laborious life he retired to the Dominican house in Lyon, where he died around 1261.[22] Etienne was primarily a preacher. The only work he left behind (unfinished) had a practical purpose: in his retirement in Lyon, between 1250 and 1261, he wrote a thick treatise on sermon topics, *Tractatus de diversis materiis praedicabilibus*, a work more commonly known as *Traité des sept dons du Saint-Esprit* because its contents were divided into seven books, each one devoted to one of the seven virtues that the Spirit breathes into the faithful. The book offered preachers an organized summa of citations from authorities *(auctoritates)*, scholastic arguments *(rationes)*, and exempla, the three major components of the medieval sermon. An exemplum was a brief narrative used within a sermon to illustrate a doctrinal or moral truth.[23] The prodigious preaching campaigns of the thirteenth century, especially on the part of the mendicant orders, created a demand for large numbers of exempla, and a skilled and active practitioner like Etienne de Bourbon would quite understandably dip into all the available written sources as well as into real

life and reported experiences. It was natural that the anecdote that a fellow Dominican in Metz had noted down should find a place in Etienne's anthology.

The story is lodged in one small niche of one subdivision of Etienne's weighty, hierarchically constructed treatise: we find it in book 5, "On the Gift of Counsel"; title, "On Prudence"; division, "On the precautions to be taken in the election of prelates"; chapter, "That the election must be pure"; paragraph 10, "Which shows that the election must be sheltered from all usurpation." The text states:

> An astonishing stroke of audacity, or, rather, insanity, took place around the year 1100, according to what is said in the chronicles. A well-educated woman, learned in the art of writing, dressed in men's clothing and was taken for a man. She came to Rome, where she was well received for her energy and her culture; she was named a notary of the Curia, then, with the devil's help, cardinal, and finally pope. Pregnant, she gave birth during a cavalcade. Roman justice having learned of these events, her feet were bound and she was attached to the hoofs of a horse, which dragged her out of the City, and she was stoned by the people for half a league. She was buried at the very place of her death, and on the stone that covered her body were written these words: "Beware, Father of the Fathers, of Publishing the Parturition of the Popess." See to what a detestable end such bold audacity leads![24]

The narrative no longer relates an event in papal history (as it did with Jean de Mailly), but rather a crime of a scope that augments its gravity and broadens its import. The moral lesson to be drawn from the event is forcefully presented in introduction to the narrative and in conclusion to it: "An astonishing stroke of audacity, or, rather insanity. . . . See to what a detestable end such bold audacity leads!" This time a genuine subject stands at the center of the story. Etienne calls her "a woman," using the word *mulier*, in contrast to the *femina* used by Jean de Mailly, a term that designates a social and moral category in the literature of exempla, an often misogynous genre. Moreover, the female subject governs a narration in the feminine: *facta est notarius . . . distracta*. Here the popess is clearly responsible for her acts, as seen by her premeditation and the fact that they begin before her arrival in Rome. The Curia and the papacy are simply echo chambers here, seemingly not engaged in the event. Nothing is said of the popess's official acts. Above all, Etienne differs from Jean de Mailly by deliberately situating both the preparation of the crime and its punishment outside of Rome: "She came to Rome"; she was "dragged out of the city *(extra Urbem)*." This is clearly Etienne's interpretation, given that he does not modify the facts as reported in Jean de Mailly: in both narratives the popess is dragged "for half a league" from the place where the scandalous birth took place. What is more, in his desire to preserve the papacy, Etienne reverses the thrust of the formula with the six Ps, giving: "Beware . . . of publishing" rather than "Publish." We shall return to the question. The popess's female deceptiveness and the devil's aid exonerate the Curia: "She was well received for her energy and her culture; she was named a notary of the Curia, then, with the devil's help, cardinal, and finally pope." The means used (deception and an appeal to the devil) and the motivation for the crime (insane presumption) win our heroine a place in the literature of exempla within the category of unscrupulous women.

Jacopo da Voragine Provides a Moral

The traits of the exemplum also appear in the version of the Joan story given by Jacopo da Voragine, a Dominican and archbishop of Genoa, in his *Chronicle of Genoa* (completed around 1297). The story of Joan, as it is inserted in this chronicle, speaks to our interests because it reflects a free, undetermined use of the episode before it became fixed in the historical and juridical mold imposed on it by writers who had read Martinus Polonus.

Jacopo da Voragine was born in Liguria around 1230, probably in Varazze, on the Italian Riviera west of Genoa. He entered the Order of Preachers at a very early age, where he carved out a career much more brilliant than those of Jean de Mailly and Etienne de Bourbon: he was in turn a preacher general, reader, and prior before moving on to the highest administrative ranks of the Order as provincial prior for the province of Lombardy (1267-77 and 1281-86) and even as master general of the Order when that post was temporarily vacant. Around 1265, just before taking on those high functions, he wrote the famous *Golden Legend* that won him lasting fame. He never abandoned his literary activities, however, and he composed several collections of model sermons in 1270 and 1290. In 1292, when he was archbishop of Genoa, he undertook the task of writing a brief history of his city "for the instruction of his readers and for the edification of his auditors," but also to give its due to a city that the historians had unjustly neglected: "We are astonished that so little has been said about this city of Genoa, so illustrious, so noble, and so powerful."[25] The rhetoric of prefaces was not the only reason for the dual aim that Jacopo set himself; the composition of the work sets it apart from the common sort of city annals. The first five parts treat the city as a collective religious subject, created (parts 1 and 2), named (part 3), converted (part 4), and striving constantly toward moral perfection (part 5). Parts 6 through 9 present a short treatise on Christian political morality. It is not until the final three parts that Jacopo discusses the history of Genoa, following the chronological succession of bishops and archbishops. A grasp of the doctrinal construction of the *Chronicle of Genoa* helps for an understanding of the exemplum that Jacopo makes of the story of Joan.

Joan's story is told in part 9 of Jacopo's *Chronicle* ("Genoa in the Age of the Bishops"), chapter 8, when he writes about the eighth bishop, Sigebert. Jacopo did his utmost to present the bishops of Genoa in an unbroken line of succession, but for the early times he had only a list of names with no knowledge of contemporary events in the city. This led him to insert episodes pertaining to the age that he had found in universal chronicles but that had no bearing on Genoa. Thus the chapter on Sigebert includes the story of the woman pope; a passage on Pope Sergius IV, who initiated the custom of a pope taking a papal name (perhaps because the name he was known by, Os Porci, had unfortunate connotations as "pig bones" or "pig head"); the episode of a false accusation made against Theodulf, the bishop of Orléans in the reign of Louis the Pious; and an account of a prodigy (a rain of blood on Brescia). The last three episodes had already been included in the brief universal chronicle that Jacopo placed in the chapter on Pope Pelagius in the *Golden Legend,* which indicates that in 1265, despite his fondness for collecting stories and legends, he was unaware of Joan.

The narratives in the *Chronicle* aim at the same comprehensiveness that Jacopo gave to the *Golden Legend,*[26] offering in turn historical instruction (on the institution of papal names; on Theodulf's creation of the liturgical response when he used liturgical dialogue to communicate with the outside world from his prison cell); eschatological instruction (the prodigy of Brescia); or moral instruction (the story of the popess). Joan's story is followed by a moral commentary as long as the narrative itself. I will not reproduce the text itself, as it offers little that does not appear in Martinus Polonus's version (given below). It has not been proven that Jacopo da Voragine based his text on Martinus's, and he uses none of Martinus's phraseology (which was copied incessantly in the fourteenth and fifteenth centuries), but both authors place Joan's papacy around the same time (864, which may be a faulty reading for 854), and both note the existence of a lover before her election to the papacy and speak of a ritual detour taken by later Roman processions. Finally, it seems improbable that in 1297 a reader as subject to cultural bulimia as Jacopo da Voragine could have been unaware of Martinus's versions of the story, which were rapidly known after 1280. Nonetheless, details that all later readers of Martinus mentioned (the popess's identity as "John the Englishman," the fact that she was born in Mainz, the length of her papacy), are not given in Jacopo's version. Perhaps it was Jacopo da Voragine's moralistic perspective and his penchant for exempla that made him prefer a more generic description: "a woman *(quedam mulier)*." Two new details surface, however: Jacopo da Voragine was the first (after Jacob van Maerlant, who was not part of the Dominican network) to speak of "a marble effigy that signals this event." He also states that when the popess felt the onset of labor, she entered "into a little house situated on the street; she gave birth there, died of the pains of childbirth, and was buried there." This detail confirms the topographical hypothesis of Cesare D'Onofrio, who, as we have seen, identified the places whose odd configuration may have given rise to the legendary event. D'Onofrio, who does not mention Jacopo da Voragine's *Chronicle of Genoa,* bases his conclusions on a much later mention in the *Itinerary of the City of Rome* (1517) of Mariano da Firenze, a Franciscan.[27] No other medieval version of the story contains this detail, which fits well with the Roman legends discussed in part I. The clerical inscription of the episode may have briefly crystalized oral traditions that had spread from Rome, but the force of the canonical narrative obliterated the Roman circumstances of the event from memory.

Jacopo da Voragine adds to his narrative a weighty moral commentary close in inspiration to that of Etienne de Bourbon, but with a more scholastic insistence on demonstration. He hammers in his point:

> That woman (*ista mulier*) undertook with presumption, pursued with falsity and stupidity, and ended in shame. That is indeed the nature of women (*natura mulieris*), who, before an action to be undertaken, have presumption and audacity at the start, stupidity in the middle, and meet with shame at the end. Woman, therefore, begins to act with presumption and audacity, but fails to take into consideration the end of the action and what accompanies it; she thinks she has already done great things; if she can begin something grand, she is no longer able, after the beginning and during the course of the action, to pursue with sagacity what has been begun, and this is because of a lack of discernment. Thus she must end in shame and ignominy what has been undertaken with presumption and audacity and pursued with stupidity. And thus it appears clearly that woman begins with presumption, continues with silliness, and ends with ignominy.[28]

We can note that beyond a solid misogyny common to men of the age and a wholly scholastic delight in tripartite structures, Jacopo da Voragine seems to have a curiously Machiavellian view of the popess's acts. He seems almost to regret her lack of firmness: she might have gotten away with it. Should we interpret this as an early emergence of the fascination with the adventure of transgression that appears in Boccaccio half a century later? This question will be discussed in the next chapter.

THE POPESS IN THE ALPHABET: ARNOLDUS OF LIÈGE

The story of Joan might have become a permanent fixture in the genre of moral tales, but that literary mode did not last long, whereas the corpus of exempla continued to grow until the fifteenth century, thanks to copyings and borrowings, and Etienne de Bourbon's anthology continued to meet with success and was reproduced in other broadly circulated collections. The only other instance of Joan's story as an exemplum occurs in the *Alphabet of Tales (Alphabetum narrationum)* that another Dominican, Arnoldus of Liège, wrote around 1307.[29] This large collection of 819 exempla was highly successful (there are 98 extant manuscripts), probably thanks to its alphabetical classification of themes and its ingenious system of cross-references. It was translated into English and Catalan, and I might note in passing that although the English translation was quite literal, a Catalan adaptation, *Recull de eximplis e miracles, gestes et faules e altres ligendes ordenades per ABC,*[30] adds a detail not found in the canonical version by Martinus that Arnoldus summarizes: during the procession, Joan arrives before an image of the Virgin Mary, who asks her if she would prefer to expiate her sin throughout eternity or in this world; Joan chooses immediate purgation and dies in childbirth.

MARTINUS'S METHOD

Another way of relating the episode of the popess arose very early (around 1260) but embryonically in the *Chronica minor* of an anonymous Franciscan in Erfurt, which states: "There was yet another pseudopope (*pseudo-papa*) whose name and dates in office are unknown. It was a woman, according to what the Romans say."[31] The term *pseudopapa* returns us to the institution of the papacy, whereas Jean de Mailly used the more picturesque term *papissa* and Etienne de Bourbon and Jacopo da Voragine omitted any reference to the papacy (except in the formula with the six Ps). The version of Joan's story by Martinus Polonus integrates it even more markedly into the history of the papacy (in contrast to pure anecdote).

Born Martin Strebsky in Troppau, in Bohemia, Martinus entered the Dominican house in Prague, which depended from the vast province of Poland, which means that "Polonus" was more administrative in origin than geographical. Martinus had a brilliant career, to the point of becoming chaplain and penitentiary to Pope Clement IV in 1265. He was retained in these functions under Clement's successors; in 1278 Nicholas III named him bishop of Gnesen (now Gniezno) in Poland, consecrating him personally. Gnesen was an important diocese, whose bishop became primate of Poland in the fifteenth century, but Martinus never took up his episcopal duties because he died in Bologna as he was making his way there. His works include a slim alphabetical index to Gratian's *Decretals,* in the purest Dominican tradition of aids for the divulgation of Christian doctrine, and the *Margarita Decreti,* which contained the article on "woman" mentioned in chapter 1. In a similar spirit, he wrote a brief universal chronicle, the *Chronicle of Roman Popes and Emperors,* several hundred manuscript copies of which are extant, as well as translations into

English, Armenian, Czech, Spanish, French, German, Greek, and Italian. The success of this chronicle was perhaps due to its concision, as well as to a clever page layout that permitted rapid consultation: in the copies made from the original manuscript, each page was made up of fifty lines and covered fifty years of history.

Joan's story does not appear in the earliest extant manuscripts of Martinus's *Chronicle*. According to Ludwig Weiland,[32] Martinus wrote three versions of his chronicle, first under Clement IV (1265-68), then in 1268, and finally around 1277. The note on the popess was presumably inserted into the third version. It is also possible that the addition was made by another hand in a posthumous version circulated after Martinus's death or by someone who continued his chronicle. In any event, the episode figures in all the manuscripts that appeared after 1280 under Martinus's name and bearing his authority. This short text deserves to be read in its entirety; by fixing the form of the Joan story, giving it broad circulation, and granting it reliability, it closed a phase in her history. Martinus states:

> After that Leo [Pope Leo IV], John, English of nation, born in Mainz, reigned for two years, seven months, and four days. He died in Rome and the papacy was vacant for a month. According to what is said, he was a woman; in her adolescence she was taken to Athens, dressed as a man by the man who was her lover; she made so much progress in the various branches of knowledge that no one equal to her could be found; it was for that reason that she next taught the trivium [the literary arts] in Rome and had high officials as her disciples and auditors. And because her conduct and her learning were held in high repute in the City, she was elected pope by unanimous vote. But during the course of her papacy her companion made her pregnant. But she/he was unaware of the time of her delivery, and, while making her way toward the Lateran coming from St. Peter's, seized with the pains of childbirth between the Coliseum and the church of St. Clement, she gave birth, then died right at the precise spot where she was buried. And as the lord pope always takes a detour on this route, it is generally believed that he does so out of detestation of that event. He has not been inscribed in the catalogue of holy pontiffs by reason of the nonconformity that the female sex involves in this matter.[33]

The story begins to take on the colors of truth, because Martinus indicates a date and a rank in papal succession. He wards off scholarly contestation by explaining that no list of popes contains Joan's name. Moreover, he gives the episode a certain coherence: Joan's actions are motivated by love; her meteoric career is due to her extraordinary talent. When gifted with an identity (name, date, acts), Joan finally begins to live as an individual.

We can never know where Martinus found the indispensable details that give Joan a durable life in the realm of the imagination. Her romance might just as easily have been constructed on the basis of the raw event, as reported by Jean de Mailly, with the addition of responses to questions of why and how the popess acted as she did.

In Martinus, Joan begins her career with general teaching (the trivium), rather than as a notary. This correction may be based on likelihood. The notary's position was no longer as prestigious after the invention of the *cursus,* the pontifical style of redaction, as it had been in the eleventh and twelfth centuries. In the autobiography of Guido Faba, as deciphered by Ernst Kantorowicz, the notary (in Faba's case, a civil notary) is compared to a tanner because he works with dog feces (to whiten parchment) and an awl (to sew and stretch his working materials).[34] Martinus was the first to give an emotional reason (following a lover) for Joan's decision to dress as a man.

It seems more difficult to trace the formation of Joan's identity. Martinus calls her John, not Joan. The name "John" was chosen by many popes of the ninth and tenth centuries, from John VIII (882) to John XVII (1003). Thanks to the tumultuous vicissitudes of the papacy (depositions and returns to the papal throne) the numbering of popes who shared the same name became confused. The bad reputation of John XI and John XII, the "pornocracy" popes, may have influenced Martinus's choice (or that of his unknown source).

Martinus's odd indication of Joan's origins ("English of nation, born in Mainz") is even harder to explain. I shall propose a few summary associations, but without suggesting they be given the dignity of causes: spare us from the demon of endless analogy!

Anglicus, the Englishman. The only English pope in history was Adrian IV (1154-59), whom we have already met in the context of his conflict with Frederick Barbarossa. If we admit that the Joan legend circulated for the most part in Germanic lands (which would include the Empire, plus Lorraine and Burgundy, which were culturally oriented toward the Germanic sphere), we can imagine—though the hypothesis is admittedly feeble—that the intense Germanic production of antipapal materials in the eleventh and twelfth centuries might have charged that English pope with a thousand sins and oddities. The sudden appearance of a pope from a distant nordic realm surprised Christianity: a *Cronica pontificum et imperatorum sancti Bartholomaei in insula romani* (Chronicle of St. Bartholomew, ca. 1256) includes an account of Adrian's life and meteoric career that may have some relation to Joan. The *Chronicle* states: "His English father, come to Avignon, earned his living there with his own hands, and at his death his son, who was still young, was placed as a servant in the hospital of Saint-Ruf; then he became a canon, then abbot, and finally pope."[35] Legend transposes the facts of a life that was in fact a truly astonishing example of social promotion. Nicholas Breakspear, the son of a humble cleric, wanted to enter the monastery of Saint-Alban; while waiting to be received there, he went to Paris, where he lived on charity before putting himself in the service of the chapter of Saint-Ruf in Avignon, where he became a canon, then a prior, before he caught the notice of Eugenius III (when Breakspear and his canons had been brought to Rome by a suit) and the pope made him bishop of Albano. Even if the life of Adrian IV has only a remote connection with Martinus's elaboration of the Joan story, it sheds light on one important aspect of that story: the papacy, the supreme power on earth, might be offered to anyone, grace and merit aiding. In a strongly hierarchical world, the assumption of someone who would normally be excluded—a pauper or a woman—gives one pause.

There is only one vowel separating "Anglicus" (the Englishman) from "Angelicus" (the angelic): even less, given that medieval scribes regularly abbreviated an interconsonantal "e." Plays on words involving the two terms had an ancient and noble pedigree, beginning with Gregory the Great, who was supposed to have exclaimed, on catching sight of the handsome blond slaves for sale in Rome, that they should be called angels rather than Angles. The strong impression they made on him is reputed to have kindled in him a desire to convert the people of the British Isles.[36]

While we are taking a break from causality, let us indulge in a few paragraphs of free association. The idea of the imminent arrival of an angelic pope *(angelicus papa)* was in fact a notion that circulated in people's minds in the late thirteenth century, as we shall see in connection with Joachimite and Franciscan expectations. We shall also see traces of it in heretical circles in Milan, but that, too, is for a later chapter. For the moment it is enough to remark that clerics were used to wordplay and appreciated it. We might imagine a clerical discourse that evokes Joan as a response to Joachimite prophecy and insists that nothing in it announces an angelic pope, but rather an English pope who is female. An ironic *reductio ad absurdum* of the sort had proven its worth in euhemerism: in his *Sacred History* (third century B.C.E.), Euhemerus rationalized Greek myths by showing that the gods were men, deified by fear or admiration. Christian apologetics made constant use of derisive euhemerism in their struggle against paganism and heresy.

The plot thickens in Mainz, as does the mystery. From the whirl of analogies we might also pull out St. Ursula and the eleven thousand virgins in the Rhineland, escorted by Pope Cyriacus, who (according to the twelfth-century visionary, Elizabeth of Schönau) was dropped from the list of popes (like Joan) because he had abandoned the papal throne. There is also Hildegard of Bingen, who was active in the twelfth century not far from Mainz. We shall return to Hildegard, a woman of inspired knowledge and high, almost pontifical, spiritual stature, in the next chapter. None of these connections is convincing.

And what if Martinus had moved from one association to another with no intention of signifying anything? In that case, we can image the learned Dominican leafing through the chronicles of his times, trying to find in accounts that related to the end of the reign of Pope Leo IV (854) passages that marked or masked the presence of Joan. He might have found, for example, in the *Book of the Times (Liber de temporibus)* of Alberto Milioli, a notary in Reggio Emilia, that in 854, in a parish in Mainz, an evil spirit possessed priests and citizens. Chased away by aspersions of holy water, the spirit took refuge "under the cape of a priest, as if it were his familiar" *(familiaris* is the word Martinus applies to Joan's clerical lover).[37]

Where did Martinus get the date 854? Jean de Mailly made a note of the rumor concerning the popess at the bottom of a folio regarding the late eleventh century, perhaps only because he found free space there, intending to verify the story and date it more accurately when he could. Etienne de Bourbon may have taken the date given in Jean's notation ("around 1100") without close chronological inspection, given that the exemplum is a form that does not imply temporality. If we allow Martinus a similarly cavalier attitude toward methodology, we might imagine that in his page layout he might have had eight lines to use up for the reign of Leo IV, a pope little known to history about whom he knew nothing. His painstaking calculations, what is more, leave a gap of more than two years. But this reductive and lazy hypothesis fails to take into account the chronological intuition of the Franciscan from Erfurt, who wrote before Martinus, and who places the history of the pseudopope in the ninth century, without adding further precisions. Are we to imagine that Joan, a figure of disorder, might have been placed in the interdynastic gap between the Carolingian and Ottonian emperors as a sign of disintegration and an appeal to a return to Germanic order?

Enough of this series of analogies, which are endless and perhaps senseless. To continue on this path is to risk finding all the reasons in the world to situate John, the Englishman from Mainz, in 854, thanks to a cancerous proliferation of microcausal cells that coagulate without any articulation among them. Contextual causality, that peril to historiography, begins here. Its ravages are obvious to anyone who cares to peruse school textbooks for the "causes" of the French Revolution in 1789 or of World War I in 1914: everything converges, hence nothing is explained. The event disappears under layers of a context that exists only by reason of the event.

This means that we need to return to more rational certitudes by examining the reality of Martinus Polonus's text and the historical uses to which it was put. Martinus was not content to give the popess an identity and a coherence: he also assigned a function to the story of her life that (once again) neutralized its venom.

THIRD: FROM EXEMPLUM TO
JURIDICAL-HISTORICAL CASE: MARTINUS
POLONUS (CA. 1279)

Martinus treats the episode of the woman pope as a historical case, as we can see by its subtle interplay of genders. As pseudopope (mentioned with no ordinal number in Petrine succession), the subject of the passage governs the masculine (*Iohannes Anglicus, mortus est)*; when Martinus speaks of Joan as an individual, it governs the feminine (*ducta, sepulta*). In short, the narrative presents a case of nonlegitimacy within pontifical history, signaled here by the feminine subject and elsewhere by other means. This juridical and historical orientation of the text can be seen just as clearly in Martinus's exoneration of the Curia. Etienne de Bourbon was intent on protecting the purity of the Roman site; here Martinus seems instead to emphasize early premeditation: Joan is seduced as an adolescent (*in aetate puellari),* and far from Rome (her lover takes her from Mainz to Athens); after her election to the papacy, the father of her child is the same lover, not a Roman. The election itself seems perfectly regular and sincere: "Because her conduct and her learning were held in high repute . . . she was elected pope by unanimous vote (*concorditer*)." The final portion of Martinus's entry no longer centers on morality (as in Etienne de Bourbon and Jean de Mailly), but on the question of papal legitimacy. After noting the detour taken by the papal processions (a positive and institutional reading), Martinus concludes that the reign was invalid (a reading in applied canon law): "He has not been inscribed in the catalogue of holy pontiffs by reason of the nonconformity that the female sex involves in this matter (*propter mulierus sexus quantum ad hoc deformitatem*)." Martinus's vocabulary is patently juridical. He resolves a case: an ineligible individual, even when elected legally, does not benefit from any legitimacy. The conclusion was to bear a great deal of weight a century later, with the Great Schism.

Geoffroy de Courlon, one of the first chroniclers to follow Martinus Polonus, relates the episode of the popess in comparable terms in his chronicle of the Abbey of Saint-Pierre-le-Vif in Sens (completed ca. 1290). The heading he gives to the episode is characteristic of the juridical-historical approach: "Deception directed at the Roman Church" (*Deceptio Ecclesiae Romanae*).[38] Geoffroy's version of the case is the first to mention the use of the pierced chair to verify the manhood of the pope as a preventive measure made necessary by such a break in trust (see chapter 1).

Thus at the turn of the fourteenth century, the narrative mode of the case history shifted the story of Joan toward a juridical and historical usage that, in contrast to its use as an exemplum, confined it within the world of the Church, or at least did so as long as debate on papal authority remained internal to the Church of Rome.

SHOULD WE BELIEVE IN JOAN?

The story of Joan, as told within Church discourse, could stop here: from Martinus Polonus to 1450, the canonical narrative was repeated, paraphrased, and summarized, with no notable changes, in innumerable chronicles. The existence of the popess was never questioned; the nearly juridical presentation of Joan's case threw her into the controversies of the fourteenth and fifteenth centuries with no contestation of her strange papacy. This general acceptance seems simple and clear; it derived from a solid cultural logic. The disquieting and obscure event reported to the laity by Jansen Enikel and Jacob van Maerlant had no hope of taking on meaning or prestige; within the Dominican network, however, where nothing was lost and everything bore meaning, the anecdote grew and multiplied. All the story needed was to pass through the hands of a great transformer, and in 1280 he was Martinus Polonus. Twenty years earlier, he would have been Jacopo da Voragine. To cite just one example: the legend of St. Christopher, the Christ-Bearer, which had arrived in mysterious ways from the far reaches of Mozarabic liturgy in Spain, appeared in the *Golden Legend*; it then invaded the entire West and continued to be believed until our own times, when Pope John XXIII brutally struck St. Christopher from the calendar of saints. This process of diffusion, as we have seen, cannot be reduced to automatic reproduction: in the Dominican laboratory, the story, pruned of disturbing elements, had undergone a first transformation into an exemplum. Martinus's text removed the story from a possibly dangerous contact with the faithful (as an exemplum set with a sermon) and gave it a place in ecclesiastical history, a genre primarily reserved to clergy. In short, a collective subject, the Dominican Order, served as *auctor* (in Latin, originator and warrant as well as author) of the episode, and once it had been cast into a form that lent itself to broad diffusion, eminent secondary and locally identified figures (Jean de Mailly, Etienne de Bourbon, Jacopo da Voragine, Martinus Polonus) fixed the form of the anecdote, addressing another collective subject, the Church. Around 1450 interest in the story declined as those two collective subjects gradually weakened under such pre-Reformation assaults as the Hussite revolution.

An inescapable and essential question remains, however: did people of the Middle Ages—that is, churchmen between 1280 and 1450—believe the story of Joan? Thus far, our analysis provides only ambiguous answers.

On the one hand: the question of belief does not arise. Jean de Mailly registers a rumor and defers the question of truth with *Require*, "to be verified." Etienne de Bourbon places the story within a moral world in which signification is more important than truth. Along with anecdotes that he presents as true, he includes several of Aesop's fables, and when he retells the story of the lion, the wolf, and the fox, he is well aware that the fable is not true referentially but metaphorically.[39] It is of course probable that the story of Joan's presumption may have had more reality for Etienne than the tale of the lion taking advantage of the other animals, but in the long view of veracity in the exemplum, his belief or that of his reader is not pertinent. In Martinus's treatment of the story, as we have seen, the jurisprudential aspect of the narrative neutralizes the question of belief.

On the other hand: ecclesiastical history claims to relate what is true, and the precision of the details given by Martinus (Joan's name, date, place within papal succession; her place of birth; the location of the spot where the scandal took place; the reasons for her absence of lists of popes) all engender a "reality effect." We return here to the binary choices we have attempted to avoid: in 854, Joan/John either reigned or did not reign. Until 1450, no one claimed that she had not reigned. Neutralizing belief in her existence simply reflects an attempt to acclimatize her; it is a trick played with belief.

In reality the question is more complex. We will undoubtedly never know what people believed between 1280 and 1350; it is difficult enough to discern what they were given to believe. Do we ourselves know what we believe? When we are confronted with direct or indirect knowledge ("The cat is on the mat," or "Water boils at 100 degrees Celsius"), what weight should be assigned to belief, tastes and aesthetic certitudes, moral and social conventions, or habits of thought and language, which are so easily shaken and so easily reconstituted? Something as viscous as tar flows in to close the gaps in reality, often taking the place of the living mortar of belief.

Nonetheless, let us try to define the question of belief in the Middle Ages.

MEDIEVAL BELIEF: A LONG BUT NECESSARY EXCURSUS

Assigning strict veracity to history (in this case, Martinus Polonus's chronicle of the popes and emperors) seems anachronistic. History, like anecdote or legend, tells one truth that is plausible, optional, and open to permutations. To take a simple example from within papal history: Sylvester II (Gerbert of Aurillac), who was pope at the turn of the first millennium, has a well-established, historical existence. Medieval chronicles (regardless of exact chronology; their mo-

ment of redaction is not pertinent) regularly present two opposing versions of his life. In the first, Sylvester was a good pope, learned, and attentive to the possessions of the Church. He shaped the careers of two great sovereigns (Robert the Pious, king of France, and Otto III of Germany), teaching them to respect the Holy Mother Church. In the second view, Sylvester was a diabolical pope who made a pact with Satan, gave his soul to the Evil One in exchange for mastery of the malefic arts, and did his utmost to weaken the venerable structure of the Church. His punishment shows the defeat of the devil: the impious Gerbert had been told that he would die in Jerusalem, so he took care not to go in holy pilgrimage to that city, but he died suffocated under the rubble of the Roman church of San Giovanni di Gerusalemma when it collapsed, struck by divine providence.

Both of these versions speak of facts, not judgments or evaluations: we are indeed in the realm of the binary nature of truth and falsehood. Polemics do not enter into these divided opinions, as they did in the case of Pope Gregory VII (Hildebrand, called Brandellus or Merdellus), whom his imperial adversaries charged with all possible sins. Moreover, the choice between one version and the other happens almost by chance, even when each chronicler has both versions available to him. Nothing proves this better than the chronicle of the popes written by the Dominican Leone da Orvieto (ca. 1315). Leone himself states that his principal source was Martinus Polonus; his chapter on Joan copies Martinus word for word; his continuation of Martinus's chronicle (1278-1315) seems fairly critical of the papacy since, as well shall see, his chapter on Boniface VIII is downright ferocious. Thus he has every reason to copy or summarize Martinus's version of the life of an evil Sylvester II. He chooses to praise him, however, with no further explanation. We will never penetrate the mind of Leone da Orvieto, a fairly obscure Dominican whom we know only from a few brief remarks on his career in the Order of Preachers and this one work, which has come down to us in only one, probably autograph manuscript.[40] It seems certain, however, that Leone, like many others, saw history as a reservoir of narratives that did not involve truth, imposed or proved.

The narrative tradition (both historical and legendary) is not a closed and delimited corpus of the true, or even of the probable: it offers an indeterminate raw material that takes on the color of truth through a series of operations that produce significance and of contracts that lend veracity.

The simplest form of those operations, as we have seen, links a writer and a reader or auditor who receives elements to be evaluated. Jacopo da Voragine did not hesitate to relate a fabulous or apocryphal episode, and he pointed them out to the reader as such. A century later (around 1340) Pietro Calo da Barletta (also a Dominican) gives a version of the birth of St. Stephen that does not figure in the canonical texts. He adds: "I wanted to mention this apocryphal story here, leaving it up to the reader to judge."[41]

The compiler creates an index of truth for himself by placing a narrative on a dual scale of evaluation, in relation to its source (the scale of guarantee) and in relation to the use that he makes of the text (the scale of implication).

The apex of the scale of guarantee is the revealed. Revelation is limited to Scripture, but the question of apocryphal texts sets up uncertain boundaries to this domain. Next come what might be called the authorized. These texts are the writings of the Fathers of the Church, whose authority is incontestable. Here, too, the outside limits of the category are difficult to ascertain. A time-honored custom, confirmed by Jacques-Paul Migne, has patrology stop with St. Bernard, but if one defines patrology by the absolute refusal to contest an author, the last Father of the Church would be the Venerable Bede. The next level is the authenticated. In this case, the authenticity of an episode proceeds from a contract of belief renegotiated in each instance. This means that it is the narrator himself who offers the guarantee and who invokes either his own credibility (stating, "I have seen," "I have remarked") or the credibility of a live witness or a text that he interrogates. When Guibert de Nogent, in *De vita sua* (1115), authenticates the legend of the British king who took the name Quilius on his conversion, he confirms an oral tradition (*historia*) by citing inscriptions in the church in Nogent.[42] The moral and religious value of the witness is worth at least as much as confirmation by texts. An early-fourteenth-century English Franciscan, John Lathbury, expresses this idea in connection with his account of a miracle of the Virgin, declaring that he had heard of it from a "certain trustworthy man to whose word I hold (*adhereo*) as I would to his book (*quaterno*)." Elsewhere John says about another legend: "A venerable knight, whose holy life gave credence to his words, devoutly related this to me."[43] It is significant that in both of these instances the anecdote related was in fact extremely old (but did John Lathbury know that?). The medium was more important than the tradition. There is another essential clause in the contract of belief that deserves mention: signification, too, gives authenticity. The intention of the knight, who speaks "devoutly" (*devote*), is as important as his holy life. Similarly, in the history of King Quilius, a pagan who, alone and unassisted (as Guibert claims to be), found faith even before he knew of Christ's Passion, Guibert's projection of himself into the narrative provides a signification that lends it authenticity. We must respect Guibert's ambivalence when he states that the texts of the inscriptions merit belief (*roborant fidem*). Simulta-

neously, they confirm the reader's confidence (*fidem*) in their existence and fortify his faith (*fidem*). What is being authenticated in this contract between the witness and the compiler (or the redacter) is chosen out of the immense, unstable mass of what is alleged (*dicitur; fertur*), which is the same position that Pietro Calo and Jacopo da Voragine take when they establish a contract with the reader. What is alleged—given without guarantee, but nonetheless given—is not excluded from the field of legend, unlike the fabulous. The alleged governs an obscure zone of strong belief, the zone of history that is basically true (that is, that lies beyond formal veracity, at the bottom of things, where everything must be taken as true). At this point, history approaches rumor, the oral and unstable form of the alleged, where guarantees are insinuated ("Of course, naturally," the speaker says, with a wink), which makes them all the more forceful. Here the contract privileges the reader who understands subtleties. The legend of Judas in the twelfth century, for example, clearly demonstrates how close a connection there is among rumor, the alleged, and the authenticated. When the Church wanted to dissipate a rumor, it made use of a counter-authentification. This was what occurred in 1247 when Pope Innocent IV sent the bishops of the Rhineland a letter stating that the rumor about Jews who had supposedly performed a ritual cutting up of the heart of a Christian child was totally untrue.[44]

A second, parallel scale ranks narratives according to the nature of their use. At the top of the scale is liturgy or paraliturgy (for example, texts for monastic collations or reading at table), and the list continues, in descending order, with devotional reading (matter for oral reading judged worthy of being put into writing, thus that enjoyed great prestige); sermons (and here the freer oral form must be distinguished from notes on sermons and rewritten sermons); celebrations of an institution (including ecclesiastical chronicles); and, finally, controversy or moral discussion (including the nontheological exempla). The lower degrees on the scale of narrative usage neutralize the question of the authenticity and signification of legend. The history of the popess belongs in the lowest categories of this double scale of truth, in alleged historical narrative. It is not contested because it is not presented as incontestable. Narrative, in medieval clerical discourse, was evaluated by its effects and its causes. In turn true, significant, or illustrative, it might be compared with the case in psychoanalysis, where the narrative, ceaselessly reiterated and reinterpreted, bears a truth that is neither literal or original (in the sense of going back to origins), but rather is secondary and constructed. The transitive and transitional narrative acts more than it represents.

This plasticity of truth is not an inconsistency that might lead to a generalized relativism. It came, as has been said, from the particular conditions of Revelation within

Christianity: the truth is not crystalized in a text, given that God came to earth in order to revise the ancient contract. That is both the drama and the grandeur of the Christian Incarnation. Truth became mingled with history and with time, without preceding them or dominating them. At the time of Christ, truth became meteoric, and one cannot determine exactly what are its fragments and its luminous traces. It was only in the sixth century that the Gelasian Decree attempted to separate the corpus of revealed, canonical texts from apocryphal ones. To be sure, a mystical and spiritual tradition guided the popes and the doctors of the Church in the wake of that meteor, but nothing seemed sure in that domain, as shown by the debate over papal infallibility, which started in the thirteenth century and concluded only in 1870! I may perhaps be reproached for slipping from narrative truth to doctrinal truth here, but the two domains are not easy to distinguish in a universe whose founding text is the narrative of a life.

The Incarnation multiplied the possible sources of truth. The uncertainty and the tolerance of the medieval Church (a florilegium, narrative and doctrinal, of the orthodox doctors of the Church would confirm this apparently provocative phrase) were the result of an overproduction of truth. Scholars have all too often confused the ardor (at times violent or literally incandescent) of conviction with doctrinal closed-mindedness; the mind truly closed to the spirit of truth is found instead in the indifference that followed post-Tridentine dogmatism.

Medieval belief thus should be represented as a series of contracts drawn up between a subject (individual or collective) and a guarantor who can be of infinite extension (God the author). Scripture is the only indispensable part of this contract, which can also include the Fathers, Tradition, the papacy, and the Holy Spirit (which blows where it wants).

The truth of Joan is thus not a deposed truth, but one ceaselessly included, adjusted, and modulated, though not rejected. It moves through a clerical discourse that is indefinitely flexible and conjunctive, full of restrictive terms (most of the narrators relate the story to the accompaniment of "according to what is said": *dicitur; fatentur*), and segmented—that is, fragmented and recomposed according to the meaning that the writer wants to give it. Nothing shows that characteristic better than the second version of the story attributed to Martinus Polonus, in which the popess does not die of her treatment by Roman justice, but is deposed and repents; her son becomes bishop of Ostia. After her pious death, miracles occur at her tomb. Here Joan's story is grafted into the great hagiographic tradition of repentant female sinners.[45] This sort of clerical discourse could embrace everything, assimilate everything. In Hegelian terms, it was a discourse without negativity, an observe with no reverse, as long as it did not en-counter the contrary discourse of a strong rival institution—that is, until it clashed with the Reformation.

The thirteenth century found even greater possibilities for a new manifestation of the truth as it went through alternating movements of expansion and contraction. Beginning in the late twelfth century the Spirit had been breathing harder. This is not the place to draw up the vast and impressive inventory of the various prophetical movements of the central Middle Ages that André Vauchez dubbed "informal powers,"[46] but mention must be made of the enormous repercussions of the prophetical work of Joachim of Fiore (ca. 1140-1202), a Calabrian Cistercian with whom medieval minds were obsessed. Joachim announced that the Last Times and the final revelation would arrive in the year 1260. After the book of the Father (the Old Testament) and the book of the Son (the New Testament), the book of the Holy Spirit would have to be written, and it was that Eternal Gospel that a Franciscan, Gerardo da Borgo San Donnino, thought he was redacting in 1254. In the prophetic tradition, Christian truth spread by successive, dovetailed advances. The popess was to find her place in that tradition, as we shall see.

The domain of guaranteed truth could also contract, however. From the twelfth century on, as Marie-Dominique Chenu has shown, theology was considered a science.[47] Where the prophetic spirit added, the science of theology pared away. It even threatened the venerable text of Revelation, as Bernard Guenée remarks in connection with Roger Bacon and Pierre d'Ailly. Roger Bacon (1210-92), a Franciscan, "gave numerous proofs that in Jerome's Latin translation of the Bible, the Vulgate, which the Church adopted as its official version of Holy Scripture, the illustrious doctor had made mistakes or had not said everything or had added to the text."[48] Roger Bacon's minimal contract bound him only to the Author of the Hebrew or Greek text, excluding the venerable translator. It would obviously be absurd to make the illustrious and subtle-minded Bacon into a reforming fundamentalist: his great learning honored the doctors of the Church, but it also commanded him to anchor his belief to new connections. Bernard Guenée has noted the response that Pierre d'Ailly (1351-1420), a prudent and orthodox theologian, gave to Bacon a century later in his *Epistola ad novos Hebraeos* (Letter to the New Hebrews):

> The obligation to believe a human authority is not absolute. Salvation does not hinge on such a belief: "Nulla auctoritas humana firmiter est credenda de necessitate salutis." . . . It was absolutely necessary, in order to be saved, to believe in the authority of the Christian Church *(auctoritas ecclesiae christianae a quolibet firmiter credenda est de necessitate salutis).*[49]

Pierre d'Ailly's position permitted him to rescue Jerome, whose translation of the Bible was guaranteed by the Church, but it did little to define the realm of truth: Where, in what texts, did the authority of the Church reside? (In the ancient councils? In the present councils? In the pope? The Curia? The Fathers?) The question was not vain; it was to rend the Church asunder in the fourteenth century.

Pierre d'Ailly's formulation confirms the concept of a systematic scale of veracity in the Middle Ages, discussed above. Jerome's truth, Pierre d'Ailly tells us, is probable in itself, but absolute within the Church system of verity. Belief in the Middle Ages was not brought to bear analytically on one object or another, which is why acceptance of Joan can be found in systems of truth as mutually exclusive as those of William of Ockham, John Wycliffe, Jan Hus, and Dietrich of Nieheim. Moreover, Pierre d'Ailly defines firm belief as a necessary component of salvation: there is no salvation without just and good belief. The originality of that concept lay in its combination of the possible and the necessary. By twisting a fine phrase of Daniel Milo's, one might posit that medieval religious belief became established when "the possible aspires to the necessary in order to escape the aleatory."[50]

The Fortunes of Joan

This long excursus into the domain of medieval belief helps us to understand the immense success of the story of Joan, which Martinus Polonus situated at a low level of the scale of belief, but among a segmented body of materials (ecclesiastical history) that were ceaselessly manipulated to serve as the foundation for systems of salvation. This gave Martinus's version of the Joan story a very wide circulation within Church discourse until around 1450, a threshold that corresponds, as we shall see, with a profound break in the organization of Catholicism. Joan will help us grasp that turning point. Still, old mental habits remained strong, and the life of the popess continued to be repeated here and there within the Catholic Church until the late sixteenth century, even in the face of a growing number of refutations and even when the various Reformations had co-opted the story and used it to attack Rome. Around 1550 the Dominican Bartolomé Carranza (†1576) mentions Joan in his *Summa omnium conciliorum* (Summa of All the Councils). Although his comments clearly devalue the story—he states: "The thing is currently told, but under the guarantee of uncertain and obscure authors"[51] (a phrase that he borrows from Platina but transfers from the rite of verification to the life of Joan)—he nonetheless repeats it. In 1576 Jean Rioche, a Franciscan from the friary of Saint-Brieuc in Brittany, not only repeats the episode but gives it credence: "Although Platina and the *Somme des Conciles* [Carranza's work] affirm that one should scarcely believe in it, the universal Church nonetheless gives witness to this event."[52]

Accommodations

It would be tedious to analyze all the occurrences of the life of Joan in clerical writings between 1280 and 1450 (or 1500), given that they make up a repetitive corpus of indefinite size. A rapid glance at the major lines of diffusion of Martinus Polonus's text will have to do.

Some chroniclers were content to give a literal copy of the canonical text. This was the practice of the Dominican Leone da Orvieto (ca. 1315), the English Benedictine Ranulf Higden in his *Polychronicon* (ca. 1330),[53] the anonymous authors of interpolations to the *Liber pontificalis* (early fourteenth century), and the chronicle of Richard of Poitiers.[54]

Such authors quite often limit themselves to condensing Martinus's narrative into a rapid mention of Joan. This was the procedure of the fourteenth-century interpolators who copied the ancient chronicles (Marianus Scotus, Sigebert von Gembloux, Otto of Freising, Geoffroy of Viterbo, Gervase of Tilbury, etc.). Vast numbers of summaries of this sort can be found up to the sixteenth century (the *Chronicle* of the monastery of Hirsau by the German Benedictine Johannes Trithemius, 1462-1516, or the *Enneades* of the Venetian Marco Antonio Coccio, known as Sabellico, 1436-1506).

There were also a large number of vernacular adaptations of Martinus, particularly in Germanic lands. These are arid stuff, however, for which the reader is referred to the chronological bibliography of works regarding Joan.

Finally, there were other chroniclers who paraphrased Martinus without changing the broad outlines of his narrative. The paraphrasers produced only a few significant variants that deserve mention, and we shall pass over copyists' distortions and errors, although at times these could be sizable. For example, Jacopo d'Acqui (ca. 1370) has Joan reigning for nineteen years. Neither will we mention stylistic improvements: Platina's 1472 version adds nothing to Martinus, but he writes in an elegant humanistic Latin.

Some of Martinus's readers attempted to rationalize Joan's identity, given the geographically contradictory indications that Joan was both English and from Mainz. In the list of popes that Bernard Gui, an illustrious Dominican, appended to his great *Flores chronicarum* (probably ca. 1315), he copied Martinus but substituted *Teutonicus* (the German) for *Anglicus* (the Englishman). This rationalization met with little success, however, thanks to the authority of Martinus's text (or perhaps because writers thought it risky to Germanize the popess!).[55] Later, many authors resolved the contradiction by respecting Martinus's terminology but eliminating one geographical indication or the other: Joan was

English for Tolomeo da Lucca, Antoninus of Florence, and Jean Rioche; she was from Mainz in the *Eulogium historiarum* and for Dietrich of Nieheim.

The precise date ascribed to Joan in Martinus called for her inclusion, with name and number, among the popes, but Martinus himself stated that the popess did not figure in the catalog of popes (which was what explained her absence in earlier documents). Martinus calls her "Johannes" (John), a name that corresponds to the institutional, masculine-neuter nature of the personage. Catholic tradition retained that name, and it was feminized as "Johanna" or "Johanessa" only in the lay and romanesque versions of her story that we will turn to in chapter 5. The only writers who were exceptions to this rule were Wycliffe, who speaks of "Anna," and Jan Hus, who calls the popess "Agnes." These exceptions reflect a pre-Reformation rejection of the Catholic model. We shall return to the topic. Let me note in passing a comment made by Robert-Henri Bautier: "If there are texts that call [the popess] Anna or Agnes, this should be seen in relation to the deformation that occurred, under similar conditions, concerning Anne of Kiev, queen of France: for certain chroniclers of the eleventh century 'Anna' became 'Agnès,' and for others 'Johanna.'"[56] For Catholic chroniclers, however, Joan remained Johannes, the woman pope.

Joan was soon promoted to full nominal status: Tolomeo da Lucca, a Dominican, a late disciple and continuator of St. Thomas Aquinas, and a respected scholar, wrote of her in his *Ecclesiastical History* (ca. 1312), giving her the title of "John VIII" and placing her 107th in the papal succession. He gives a close paraphrase of the narrative of his fellow Dominican, Martinus.[57] Bartolomé Carranza and Jean Rioche retained "John VIII," but another tradition preferred "John VII" for the popess. She is presented thus in the *Eulogium historiarum* (1366), an anonymous English chronicle, and in Platina's *History of the Popes* (1472). Placing Joan among the "Johns" did not pose any great historiographical problem: all that was needed was to conflate two previous Johns (stating that the return of an exiled pope had created the confusion), or to eliminate a doubtful or schismatic John. Even now, although contemporary scholarship is categorical about the Johns, it hesitates over the Stephens, giving dual numbers such as "Stephen III/IV." Joan's integration into the list of popes was not universally recognized, and there were many authors who refused to assign her a name or a number. For instance, in his *Chronik* (1340) Johannes of Winterthur, a Franciscan, lists 197 popes who preceded Gregory X, "Linus and Cletus excepted, as well as a woman who is not counted."[58]

This effort to achieve historical coherence was accompanied by a search for confirmation through supporting references. Martinus showed the way (if the pun may be pardoned) by presenting the detour taken by papal processions through Rome as a lasting trace of Joan. Chroniclers constantly repeated this information, and it was confirmed in ritual until the reconfiguration of the streets that lead to the Lateran. When Urban V attempted (unsuccessfully) to return the papacy to Rome from Avignon in 1368, he quite naturally refused to take the detour, not so much to deny Joan's reality, but rather to deny the need to commemorate her in Rome, which he wanted to reestablish in its primitive purity after the many years in Avignon. The *Life of Urban* states:

> From there [the Lateran], he returned to the palace [of the Vatican] peacefully and tranquilly, riding through the city and following the most direct route, without changing direction here and there, even in relation to that mad woman who is said to have occupied the papacy one day and to have given birth to her runt in that same street; such a detour, it is said, was sometimes taken by some of his predecessors.[59]

In reality, Martinus's text did as much to establish the detour as did physical disposition of the streets around San Clemente. The papal Master of Ceremonies, Johann Burchard, states in his journal that in 1486 he attempted to eliminate the commemorative detour for a procession led by Innocent VIII. He had the support of the bishop of Pienza, but he met with a vehement, angry reaction from Rinaldo Orsini, the archbishop of Florence.[60]

Martinus's readers complemented his account by noting the existence of the marble statue (Jacopo da Voragine around 1295, Siegfried of Balhusen around 1304, etc.); Dietrich of Nieheim noted that the statue was still standing in his day *(adhuc),* and Martin Luther claimed (in his *Tischreden*) that he saw it during his trip to Rome in 1510. Dietrich of Nieheim offers an additional referential proof, stating in his *Chronicle of the German Emperors* that the story of Joan was a gloss on the Greek school of Rome, where St. Augustine and Joan were supposed to have taught.[61]

THE SIX Ps AND NEGLECT OF THE FRANCISCAN TRADITION

Supporting references disappear fairly quickly from the literature on Joan. This absence deserves careful examination, because it will put us on the track of a total reinterpretation of the clerical history of Joan.

First Jean de Mailly, then Etienne de Bourbon, who had read Jean, mentioned a stone that bore an inscription with six initial Ps commemorating the popess's childbirth. Martinus, who had in turn read Etienne, did not choose to include this memorial in his narrative, which means that the detail had every chance of disappearing, given that Martinus "replaced" and perfected Etienne's version within the Dominican network. As we have seen, the detail reappeared around 1260 in a Franciscan version of the popess's story (hence independent of the Dominican tradition) in an anonymous chronicle written in Erfurt:

> There was still another pseudopope, whose name and dates of rule are unknown. In fact it was a woman, according to what the Romans say, of great beauty and considerable learning and, beneath a deceitful appearance, of perfect conduct. She hid under a male habit until she had been elected pope. And during her papacy she conceived, and when she was pregnant, the demon revealed the fact to everyone publicly in a consistory by launching at the pope the phrase: *Papa, Pater Patrum, Papisse Pandito Partum* (Pope, Father of the Fathers, Publish the Parturition of the Popess).[62]

Although this version of the episode was roughly as fully elaborated as Jean de Mailly's account, its chances for wide diffusion were less. The Dominicans, whose network circulated the versions of Etienne de Bourbon and Martinus Polonus (1260, 1280), soon outstripped the Franciscans, who were less well equipped for the diffusion of texts.

The only known repetition of the Erfurt version of the story of Joan occurred in the *Compendium historiarum* of Siegfried of Balhusen (or of Meissen), who copied the Erfurt passage around 1304, adding a mention of the marble statue that gives fuller detail than in Jacopo da Voragine: "Since then, they show in Rome, on a square in the city, a figure *(symulacrum)* in pontifical robes sculpted on a marble slab, with an image of a child."[63] Siegfried, a fairly obscure author, was a priest, not a Franciscan, and he probably borrowed from the Erfurt text because he was unaware of Martinus Polonus's chronicle. Moreover, Erfurt, in Thuringia, was not far from his natal Meissen, and the two areas had both been part of the margravate of the Wettin family in the thirteenth century, which may have had something to do with his choice of source.

The Dominicans did not totally obliterate the Franciscan tradition, however. In 1290 a Franciscan chronicle, the *Flores temporum* (Flowers of the Times), widely circulated in Germany and continued by several hands,[64] reproduced Martinus's narrative almost textually. Ten years earlier, the *Flores* might have played the same role as Martinus in circulating the Joan story; after Martinus, writers felt obliged to follow the tradition that had become canonical. The anonymous author of the *Flores* adds to his borrowed passage on Joan a quotation of the phrase with six Ps, following the Erfurt version but completing and refining it. He repeats the passage, including the devil's challenge, but he gives it a different setting: "She was made pregnant by the lover of whom we have spoken; she then interrogated the demoniacal one, begging him to say when it would please the demon to withdraw from her. The devil answered in these words: 'Pope, father of the fathers, publish the parturition of the popess / And I will tell you when I will withdraw from your body.'"[65]

Beyond the problem of textual filiation, this episode is interesting because it brings us back to the mysterious six Ps that accompanied Joan from her first appearance in the world of texts. We need to pause over it for a moment, calling on the definition of the three levels of the existence of a text proposed by Jean Molino and Jean-Jacques Nattiez:[66] the neutral level (the level of the immanent existence of the text); the level of poetics (the level of the fabrication of the text); and the aesthetic level (the level of the reception of the text).

THE FORMULARY TEXT

In itself, the phrase with six Ps is presented as a mnemonic device: the listener retains the forceful phonic pattern and the overall theme associated with it (a pope gave birth). We are close to the model analyzed by Albert Bates Lord and Jean Rychner in connection with the oral epic narrative, in which a rhythmic and phonic matrix is transmitted without establishing any lexical or semantic detail.[67] Our authors are sensitive to rhythm; what is more: they speak of lines of verse, verses (in the biblical sense), or versification *(versiculus; versus; versifice)*. Thus two concomitant texts (ca. 1255; 1260) that appeared in Metz and in Erfurt find different ways *(Petre/Papa; Prodito/Pandito)* to render the same phonetic and thematic pattern, which had probably been transmitted orally from Rome to the far reaches of Europe. The formula then became associated with a cry of alarm: *Require* (to be verified); *Fuit et alius pseudopapa* (there was yet another pseudopope). But the continuators went beyond the stage of astonishment to moralization: Etienne de Bourbon, by charging the phrase with conjuring away danger rather than denouncing misdeeds, and the *Flores*, by revealing an implicit pact made with the devil. At a third stage (with Martinus), the formula disappears. When the story is integrated into history, its terrifying auditory recall is no longer needed. The cry becomes text; memory attaches to chronology rather than to a phonic and thematic structure.

FABRICATING THE FORMULA

Let us attempt (following Nattiez's level of poetics) to return to the source of the fabrication of the six-P phrase that appeared here and there in Lorraine and Thuringia. There is no direct documentary evidence of how it first arose. Ignaz von Döllinger applied his ingeniously philological mind to the problem and proposed a possible reconstitution of the process. His point of departure is a model attested in a medieval chronicle, which states that an inscription was found in Rome that read "R.R.R.F.F.F.," deciphered by modern scholarship as

Ruderibus Rejectis Rufus Festus Fieri Fecit (After having swept away some ruins, Rufus Festus had [this construction] built). The medieval inhabitants of Rome, sensitive to prophetic signs, interpreted the initials as a terrible pronouncement of the ancient Sibyl: *Roma Ruet Romuli Ferro Flammaque Fameque* (Rome will collapse by the sword of Romulus [and by] flame and famine). This model, applied to the six-P inscription, suggests a possible primitive text from late antiquity: a worshiper of Mithra commemorated a donation with a stone inscription: *Propria Pecunia Posuit* (with his own money has offered) *Patri Patrum* (to the Father of Fathers [a title for the officiant of the mysteries of Mithra]) *P* (the initial of the unknown donor's name).[68]

Döllinger's reconstruction seems fairly convincing, although we might reproach him with designating as the "author" of the formula regarding the event in 1250 (?) a subject (the people of Rome?) incapable of reading an authentic text and being fooled by it. Döllinger is anticipating Cesare D'Onofrio here. When D'Onofrio speaks of the rite of verification, he supposes the existence of both a primitive "text" (in which the pope is the mother of the community of the faithful) and an ignorant and literal-minded decipherer who draws the conclusion that the pope has given birth. The philological spirit implies a general entropy of meaning, which can only degenerate.

The explanation proposed in the preceding chapter is perhaps not very different from Döllinger's. It suggested a satirical reading of an ancient inscription that was infused with the spirit of a carnivalesque challenge to the papacy when it dealt with a solemn reuse of ancient materials and inscriptions, vehicles of an overwhelming opacity. That same explanation also leads to rejecting a timeless binary scheme (primitive and authentic text; naive decipherment) in favor of the model proposed by Christian Jouhaud of contemporary, partial, and hierarchical but convergent readings that include an initial text, learned reuse, authoritarian nonscholarly reuse, satirical scholarly decipherment, satirical nonscholarly decipherment, and erroneous reading.[69] Such concurrent readings would operate together to construct a symbolic system figured by the popess.

If we look at the narrative content of the formula rather than its form as an epigraph, we can hope to return it to other possible places of production. We have seen that Franciscan versions place the formula in the mouth of the devil: in the Erfurt chronicle as in later chronicles (the *Chronicle of Saint-Gilles* and Engelhusen's *Chronicon*),[70] the phrase was a cry of triumph from the devil. This is even clearer in the *Chronicle* of the Abbey of Kempten, in Bavaria, where the formula is translated into German without any attempt to respect the phonetic repetition of the six Ps: "O du papst der du solt senn ein Vater unter allen andern Vatern nie du wirst offenbahren in deiner Geburt dass . . ." (O you, Pope, who should be a father above all other fathers, you will reveal by your childbirth), and the text continues: "that you are a popess, and that thus I am going to carry you away with your soul and your body and take you home with me and into my society."[71]

The supernatural interpretation of the event attaches to the Virgin in the chronicle of Heinrich von München. Here Joan, passing before the church of San Clemente, addresses an *Ave Maria* to an effigy of the Virgin Mary painted on the outside wall of the church. The painting responds, telling Joan that because she has put herself above women, her body and its fruit will be accursed: "Du pist gesegen ueber allens weib de sprach daz pild so sei dein Leib verfluocht under allen weiben die suend solt du niht mer treiben."[72] Heinrich von München, an author who is unfortunately unknown, uses the Franciscan *Flores* (as can be seen from the duration of Joan's papacy, three years, five months, and two days, as in the *Flores*), but he introduces a new source for the sanction against Joan (the Virgin) and a new definition of her crime (raising herself above the female condition). This sort of supernatural punishment, signaled by a miraculous utterance, may mark the emergence within clerical discourse of fragments of "popular" culture. The fact that the Franciscans gave a more "popular," less "Roman" treatment of the narrative than the Dominicans had done might thus reflect the genuinely popular orientation of the Order founded by St. Francis. This hypothesis finds confirmation in the development of the narrative itself: in the 1290 *Flores* the six-P formula draws meaning from an implicit pact between Joan and Satan in which Joan wins salvation in exchange for public exposure of her misdeed. In this interpretation the childbirth simultaneously signifies the devil's triumph (in public exposure of her fault) and his loss of a hold on Joan. In the Catalan version of the *Alphabet of Tales* of Arnoldus of Liège (and the Franciscans had an enormous influence in Catalonia), the image of the Virgin gives Joan a choice between immediate punishment (public exposure of her sin, followed by death) and celestial punishment (eternal damnation). The universe of tales contains countless examples of this schema of a choice between immediate but temporary suffering and delayed but irrevocable damnation, which was a narrative transcription of choices to be made among the major categories of existential investments.[73] This would explain the exceptional success of the Joan narrative in southern Germany: in theory, this episode in Church history coincided with and absorbed a current form of popular narration that centered on the theme of the unlimited ambition of women (Heinrich von München) and that used the device of a choice between immediate danger and a promising future.

Although we cannot totally exclude this hypothesis, it has limitations. Like philology, folklore postulates a collective and intemporal subject (the people, who are no longer ignorant and serve as narrator) by a simple reversal of the mechanism of diffusion in which it is the Church that becomes the unwitting and distorting mirror of an authentic primitive text.

The odd particularity of the Franciscan tradition, however, incites us to move from the production of the formula to its reception and to give up the uncertain quest for the "original" meaning of the formula in favor of its adventitious, historically identifiable meaning. This means that the detour of a methodical analysis of the six-P formula has brought us back to the principle of ideological profit that we rejected at the beginning of this chapter. We are constrained to do so by the limitations of a strictly immanent and cultural analysis of the diffusion of the Joan narrative. That sort of analysis told us how, by means of what narrative modes, and by what combination of chance and necessity *a* legend could spread within clerical discourse, but it fails to tell us why this legend spread.

The Franciscans and the Pseudopope

A rereading of what the Franciscan chronicle from Erfurt tells us about Joan shows that its author had no more information available to him than Jean de Mailly had at the same period (1255-60), but also that the Erfurt chronicler lacked Jean's dominating curiosity and his insistence on verification *(Require)*. The Franciscan author is moved by fear: the devil, who pronounces the six-P formula, has appeared within the Curia and speaks to the pope. The phonic structure of the formula signals the satanic nature of its message, recalling the repeated Rs that, according to St. Louis, rasp the throat of the Christian and "stand for the devil's rakes."[74] The Erfurt chronicler, unlike Jean de Mailly, confidently proclaims, "There was yet another pseudopope." This is an astonishing statement: for Martinus Polonus, Joan was not a pseudopope, but a pope illegitimately elected; it was up to the jurists to determine her status. Indeed, even at the end of the Middle Ages it was a delicate problem that Cardinal Domenico Giacobazzi found it impossible to resolve, as we have seen. The chroniclers who followed Tolomeo da Lucca in calling the popess John VII or John VIII decided that Joan had been a real pope.

For a Franciscan in 1260 the term "pseudopope" had a weighty and specific meaning. It needs to be clarified, even at the cost of yet another detour (but Joan is the Roman patron of detours!).

In the early thirteenth century Francis had no intention of creating a new institution; rather, he wanted to convert the whole of society to the authentic message of the poor Christ. His *Testament* demanded that his initial intent be respected: he required of the Friars Minor absolute obedience to the Rule, which meant strict observance of poverty and rejection of all privilege. Until his fall from papal grace in 1239, Brother Elias of Cortona also insisted on respect of the spirit of Francis's *Testament*. From Gregory IX to John XXII, however, the papacy repeatedly attempted to integrate this anomic Order into the Church structure by encouraging tendencies within the Order that favored compromise (like-minded friars were called Conventual Franciscans). It is important to appreciate fully the broad attraction that the "fundamentalist" segment of the Franciscans (at first called *zelanti*; later known as Spiritual Franciscans) exerted over Christendom. By affirming its loyalty to Francis and to the poverty of Christ, that "zealous" fraction crystalized the immense eschatological and reformist aspirations of the faithful. Papal policy from 1230 to 1330 seems to have fluctuated regarding the Franciscans, not only because policy varied with the spiritual choices of each pope, but also because political and ecclesiological shifts within the Church brought to prominence configurations that also changed constantly. The Franciscan purists, the *zelanti,* represented a threat to the institution of the Church because they encouraged a simmering urban heresy. On the other hand, the Franciscan Order, by its discipline, by its centralization, and by its direct dependence on Rome (reinforced by the bull *Ordinem vestrum* of Innocent IV in 1245 and the bull *Quanto Studiosius* of Alexander IV in 1247) offered the Church a precious ally in its struggle against the centrifugal claims of national churches, the bishops, the university masters, and the cardinals of the Curia. It is understandable that the popes' shifting policies aroused genuine perplexity among the Spirituals, who were inclined to see changeable papal policies as dictated either by the Holy Spirit or by the Evil One. Defending their "state" (which amounted to a defense of Francis's *Testament*) became an obsession with them, because they were totally persuaded that they were defending the salvation of the Church and that their "state" embodied Christian perfection. One Spiritual Franciscan declared in a eulogy of "the perfection of the state of the Friars Minor" that "this state" was "more arduous, more perfect, and more essential to the existence and perfection of the church" than that of the bishops; it was "more perfect and more meritorious" than even the papal "state."[75]

Between 1254 and 1260 (when Joan's story was elaborated in clerical discourse), the tension between the papacy and the mendicant Orders was at its height. The papacy had constantly supported the Orders' independence from the bishops concerning preaching and hearing confession (which were considerable sources of prestige, authority, and revenues), but pressure from the bishops obliged Innocent IV to restrict that liberty in a bull, *Etsi animarum* (1254). Innocent died only a few days after the promulgation of the bull, which some

Franciscans viewed as proof of heaven's wrath or of satanic influence over the pontiff. Innocent IV's successor, Alexander IV, annulled the bull, but the Franciscans continued to live under a threat. The Council of Lyon (1274) suppressed all the new Orders except the Franciscans and the Dominicans, with the Carmelites and the Augustinians obtaining only a provisory continuance. The papacy continued to be a genuine threat.

During that same year, 1254, the mendicant Orders (that is, the Franciscans and the Dominicans) were attacked from another quarter: the secular masters of the University of Paris, who chafed at the favorable position accorded to mendicant masters who enjoyed the freedom of regular clergy, privileges as university scholars, and the prestige attached to the great doctors of the age, Thomas Aquinas, Bonaventura, and Albertus Magnus.

The details of that skirmish would not concern us if William of Saint-Amour, the Paris master who headed the attack, had not singled out the Spiritual Franciscan Gerardo da Borgo San Donnino, the author (in 1254, decidedly a year of coincidences for the Friars Minor) of an *Introduction to the Eternal Gospel.* This work was a systematic rearrangement of the prophecies of Joachim of Fiore predicting the end of time in the year 1260. The Middle Ages had known many other eschatological deadlines, both before and after the thirteenth century,[76] but no prophetic author had made as strong an impression on the faithful as Joachim. His work, which the Franciscans circulated massively, completed, and commented on, was part of a complex and coherent exegetical system that Joachim based in his vast theological culture. His perception of the immanence of the Last Times took on a special meaning in an age whose best minds were imbued with the principles of a historical economy of salvation that had been put in place, as Father Chenu has shown, in the twelfth century.[77] Brian Tierney notes that around 1250 historical ecclesiology became an integral part of theology.[78] Gerardo da Borgo San Donnino's treatise presented the Franciscans as the apostles of the imminent reign of the Holy Spirit; the writings and the Rule of Francis constituted a third Testament, the Testament of the Holy Spirit; Francis took on the role of the Angel of the sixth seal of the Apocalypse.

William of Saint-Amour responded to Gerardo's treatise in 1254, the very year of its publication. His *De periculis novissimorum temporum* (On the Dangers of Urgent Times) mocked the Franciscans' fears and eschatological enthusiasm, presenting these as the real dangers of the age. The attacks of the masters of Paris came to naught in 1257, thanks to Alexander IV's energetic support of the Franciscans and his reinforcement of their position at the University with the bull *Quasi lignum vitae,* but the decisive year of 1254 had shown

the Spirituals that the external Church could be headed by a malevolent pope (Innocent IV) just as easily as by a spiritual one (Alexander IV). That distinction fitted in with Joachimite-Franciscan prophecies that declared that the arrival of the Last Times would be preceded by the reigns of a pseudopope and an angelic pope. Somewhat later, Peter of John Olivi (1248-98), with Angelo Clareno and Ubertino da Casale, among the prime movers of the Spiritual movement, connected the eschatological announcement with current ecclesiology: A mystical Antichrist would appear, and when he did, "a prince of the house of Frederick" would "establish as pseudopope a certain false religious who will plot against the evangelical rule" and impose a false *(dolosam)* dispensation.[79] "Dispensation" refers to the Franciscans' vow of absolute poverty, constantly eroded by the popes since the bull *Quam elongati* promulgated by Gregory IX in 1231.

The Erfurt chronicle (ca. 1260) thus appears to transcribe a genuine fear that a pseudopope might usurp the Holy See. The narrator does not doubt the existence of the female pseudopope, questioning only the accuracy of her date of reign, which affected eschatological computation. The brief note in the Franciscan text insists on an opposition between appearances and reality (*latuit,* "he hid," as opposed to *publice,* "publicly"; *in ypocrisi magne vite,* "and under the deceptive appearance of perfect conduct"). The six-P formula crystalizes that opposition; it commands the pope (*papa,* the neuter, institutional form) to reveal the childbirth of the popess (*papessa,* the same individual, but a satanic, female reality). In this terror-stricken version, the devil denounces more than he mocks; he splits the pseudopope into two, a pope and a popess, as a way to contaminate the one by the other. The version of the *Flores temporum,* interpreted above as folklore, also (and especially) develops the message of the triumph of Satan within the Church: the diabolical possession of Joan's body is part of the devil's plan; the Evil One has invaded her body in order to publicize his triumph.

This interpretation differs notably from the Dominican version: the stone inscription (which is not satanic) is addressed to St. Peter, who is taken as a motherlike, eternal figure; like a rock he cannot be shaken by one deplorable incident. The inscription urgently invites to vigilance, as Etienne de Bourbon makes clear. The formulaic text, written on stone and in Peter (following the play on the words *petra* and *Petros* that Jesus himself initiated) asserts the solidity of the papacy, come what may.

Still, in spite of the strength of the Dominicans' network of preachers and their efforts to neutralize the story of Joan, they failed to obliterate one capital aspect of the secret life of the popess, and Joan's adventure, as it was told around 1260, served as a dress rehearsal for the great shadow play of the Franciscans, which was promised a great future and lasted until the 1330s.

THE ANGELIC POPE AND THE PSEUDOPOPE: THINGS COALESCE IN 1294

An extremely important event occurred in 1294, giving a new meaning to Joan's case after Martinus Polonus's juristic interpretation, but also giving a new shape to the pairing of the pseudopope and the angelic pope.

In 1294 the Holy See had remained vacant for twenty-seven months. The cardinals, gathered in conclave, were unable to agree on a pope from among their number, so they elected the eighty-five-year-old Pietro da Morrone, a Benedictine from the Abruzzi, the founder of a hermit colony, and a man who had lived in retirement from the world for eight years. Christendom, after years of debate about poverty, put at its head Celestine V, the man who best embodied a return to the letter of Christ's message, but also the least skilled administrator imaginable. The crafty, somewhat devious Cardinal Benedetto Caetani swiftly obtained the pope's abdication, and on 13 December of the same year he himself succeeded Celestine, taking the name Boniface VIII. The event aroused intense anxiety within Christianity: could a pope, designated by the Holy Spirit, abdicate? What was one to do about a pope who proved inadequate to the task but had been elected following all the proper canonical procedures (also the case with Joan)? Celestine V soon came to be called "the angelic pope," which ineluctably led to Boniface VIII being identified as the "pseudo-pope" of prophecy who used trickery to dislodge the angelic pope. Jacopone da Todi did in fact call Boniface *pseudopresul.*[80]

The tumultuous succession of two such opposite popes provided a concrete paradigm (the prelate *vs.* the hermit; authority *vs.* humility, etc.) that forced many to take sides. To be sure, there were also many of the faithful who did not participate in this search for the "bad" pope (be he Celestine or Boniface). Jacopo da Voragine, in his *Chronicle of Genoa,* a work written not long after the event, takes an institutional position, recognizing both the merits and the inadequacies of Celestine V.[81] Bohemond, bishop of Trier, illustrates that same position in his episcopal *Gesta* by comparing the paired popes, Celestine and Boniface, first to Mary and Martha, then to Rachel and Leah. Pairs of biblical women were often cited in the Middle Ages to demonstrate that industrious activity (Martha, Leah), which was ungrateful but necessary, formed the essential complement to illuminated but inactive meditation.[82] We cannot but admire, in passing, Bohemond's subtle and intricate use of the biblical narrative. In Genesis, Jacob wants to marry the beautiful Rachel, not her sister Leah, but Laban, the father of the two sisters, substitutes Leah for Rachel by trickery. Thus the role of Boniface-Leah

(the fertile servant without grace) is justified, but the comparison also suggests that trickery was used to harm Celestine-Rachel. On the one hand, the substitution of one woman for another was part of the divine plan; on the other hand, it did not prevent Jacob from eventually marrying Rachel, a union that proved belatedly fertile and brought new hopes. Bohemond's dizzying "dialogic" virtuosity should dissuade us from any pronouncements on the claimed sterility of the commonplace in the Middle Ages.[83]

The Franciscan idea of the pseudopope had made sufficient headway in the Church to induce commentators to classify popes into the good and the bad. Arnoldus of Liège, in the compact style of an author of exempla, notes *bonus papa* (good pope) in preface to an episode in the life of Gregory the Great. Evaluating the popes had become part of ecclesiastical mores.

By an odd twist of history, however, the most eminent of the Spiritual Franciscans, Peter of John Olivi, supported Boniface VIII as a true pope.[84] This support, which ran counter to the Spirituals' principles, can probably be explained by a radical conception of papal infallibility, to which we shall return. Olivi might also have been moved by tactical considerations, because at the beginning of his pontificate Boniface VIII had championed the Spirituals' cause; in 1290, before he himself became pope, Nicholas IV, the Franciscan pope, had delegated the then Cardinal Caetani to defend the cause of the friars in Paris. Most of the Dominicans were ranged against Boniface VIII, however. Influential Preachers such as Jean Quidort (Jean de Paris), the author of a formidable treatise attacking Boniface VIII and the hierocratic claims that he pressed against the king of France, Philip IV (Philippe le Bel),[85] were more apt to back limitations on the growing power of a papacy that they needed less than the Franciscans did. The Dominicans of the house of Saint-Jacques in Paris supported Philip in his fulminations against Boniface. The nearly spiritualist (or at least reformist) tendencies of certain Dominicans (tendencies that were less pronounced than among the Franciscans, however) had not been the target of papal attacks, and this group displayed a certain sensitivity toward the austere image of the hermit-pope from the Abruzzi. Robert d'Uzès, one of the first witnesses to the rite of the verification of the pope's manhood, connected his terrible visions to the events of 1294. In his thirty-second vision, "On the carrying off and despoilment of a sovereign pope," he gives an interpretation of somber scenes of violence and adds, "After that, and after several days had passed, we learned that the lord pope Celestine had renounced the papacy and had once again become a hermit; several days later, we learned that Benedetto had been elected pope."[86]

The possible parallel between Joan and Boniface, two clever usurpers, appears in Leone da Orvieto as well.

We know little about Leone apart from his modest career in the Order of Preachers as reader and subprior at Orvieto from 1287 to 1295, visitor of the Dominican houses of Tuscany in 1304, and prior at Tivoli, Cortona, and Arezzo (where he died in 1315). He probably took little part in the struggles in Italy between Boniface and the Colonna cardinals, but in his *Chronicle of the Times and Acts of the Roman Pontiffs,* into which he copied Martinus's entry on Joan, he relates the papacy of Celestine thus:

> He attempted to reduce the cardinals to their former status; all the cardinals were to ride simple donkeys. That is why one of the cardinals, who was named master Benedetto Caetani, a man artful in all domains and filled with malice, sent children up to the roof of the house in which the pope was sleeping. They called to the pope and said to him that he was in a dangerous state, about to lose his soul, and that the only way he could save it was by abdicating. The pontiff, hearing these voices, thought they came from angels, and after having consulted with the cardinals, he abdicated, and master Benedetto Caetani, the inventor of this trick, was elected to the supreme papacy.[87]

This anecdote combines the angelic, innocent character of the good Pope Celestine and the ambitious, deceitful ruse of the man who, thanks to angelic disguise, obtained the papacy.

Beyond the antagonism between the Franciscans and the Dominicans, and beyond the struggles between priesthood and royalty, the pressure put on Celestine V and the imprisonment of Boniface VIII at Anagni in 1303 that brought his papacy to a violent end seriously shook the papacy. On both sides, the Bonifacian and the Celestinian, the argument of guaranteeing the salvation of the Church was used to justify putting an end to a papacy. Whether Joan was seen as the prototype of a pope illegitimately installed through ambitious trickery or as an example of a pope harmful to the good administration of the Church, she served all causes. The gap through which Joan slipped was to broaden into a full-fledged schism some seventy-five years later.

JOAN, PATRONESS OF PAPAL INFALLIBILITY

Joan's career does not stop here, and by a prodigious paradox, the popess contributed to creating the notion of papal infallibility. Brian Tierney has brilliantly analyzed the mechanism of that ideological construction, and we shall follow him, but still keeping an eye on Joan.[88]

The Spiritual Franciscans believed, above all else, in Francis's insistence on absolute poverty, the key to their eschatological role. Beginning in 1231, they had been obliged to resist accommodations gradually imposed on them by the papacy and by the Conventual branch of the Order. St. Bonaventura (1221-74) attempted to rec-

oncile the *zelanti* and the Conventuals by writing a watered-down *Life of Francis,* freely glossing his Rule and persuading the chapter at Narbonne (1260) to approve the *usus pauper,* or moderate use of possessions. This compromise position proved impossible to maintain after Bonaventura's death in 1274, when the Conventuals challenged the doctrine of poverty itself.

In reaction, Nicholas III (1277-80) promulgated the bull *Exiit qui seminat* (1279), which imposed a return to both the spirit and the letter of Francis's *Testament.* The Spirituals were deeply grateful to him, perceiving his act as the result of divine inspiration. Peter of John Olivi attempted to place Nicholas's text within an untouchable, sacred tradition by asserting that the pope, as the heir of Jesus and of Peter, could not err in matters of faith. Thus Olivi brought a radical solution to the old, ceaselessly debated problem of defining the limits of matters of faith: Should the Christian consider that matters of faith resided only in Scripture, or in Scripture and Tradition? In the latter case, what should be included in Tradition? Was it made up of the writings of the Fathers and/or the early conciliar texts? And/or papal doctrine? The Spiritual Franciscans resolutely added the doctrinal work of the popes to this list, thus producing the first affirmation of papal infallibility. The bull *Exiit qui seminat* was not merely a praiseworthy text; it was absolutely sanctified by infallibility. But if this were the case, how could one condemn the positions of the successors of Nicholas III who challenged (or who might challenge) either the bull or the status of the Order? The way out of this dilemma was to return to the eschatology of the 1250s: any pope hostile to that status declared himself a pseudopope, *ipso dicto.* By divine right, the universal Church and its leader, the pope, could never be mistaken. In fact, however, a pseudopope, a pseudocouncil, a pseudo-Curia, or a pseudo-Church could obliterate the sanctified life of the true Church, which, according to Peter of John Olivi, could never disappear, though it could be reduced to a handful of the faithful, even to a few women and children.

This startling theological and ecclesiological construction (which should not be taken as a mere trick of argumentation) clearly appears, and in relation to Joan, in the work of William of Ockham. Ockham, arguably the greatest philosopher of the fourteenth century, was born at the end of the thirteenth century in Surrey. He entered the Franciscan Order at an early age and studied at Oxford in 1312 and again in 1318. His commentary at Oxford on Peter Lombard's *Sentences* (1318-20) caused him difficulties that gave his career a new direction: the Curia called him to Avignon to explain himself on some theological positions that seemed suspect. He went there in 1324, and stayed for four years. There he met Michael of Cesena, the general of the Franciscan Order, who had also been summoned on suspicion of heresy. The question of poverty had, in fact, reemerged in dramatic fashion. Although Clement V (1305-14) supported Ubertino da Casale, he had attempted to update Bonaventura's gestures of reconciliation by justifying a moderate use of possessions in his bull *Exivi de paradisio* (1312). John XXII, elected in 1316, was a strict canonist with mystical tendencies who at first seemed moderately favorable to the Spirituals, but he soon became irritated by their extremism, and in 1317 he demanded, in the bull *Quorumdam exigit,* that they submit to the Conventuals. Four Spiritual Franciscans were burned in 1318. Ubertino da Casale left the order, and Angelo Clareno and his disciples, the *fraticelli,* took refuge in the mountains of central Italy. Resistance continued, however, and the general administrator of the Order, Michael of Cesena, who had started out as a Conventual, passed over to the Spirituals. John XXII decided to have done with this cycle of compromise and condemnation, and he put an end to the debate in 1322 with the bull *Quia nonnumquam,* in which he demonstrated that Christ and the apostles had had personal possessions. The Franciscans, gathered in a chapter general at Perugia that same year, explicitly contradicted John XXII, who, like a good administrator, replied with the bull *Ad conditorum canonum* (1322), in which he eliminated the juridical fiction of papal ownership of the Franciscans' possessions. Henceforth the Order was, de facto, the possessor of such goods. The pope then delivered a statement on the theological basis of the debate with the bull *Cum inter nonnulos* (1323). Michael of Cesena, who had come to Avignon to explain his conduct, accused the pope of heresy and fled from there with William of Ockham on 26 March 1328. The two Franciscans then went to Munich to the court of Louis of Bavaria, where they met Marsilius of Padua, a resolute opponent of the Avignon pope. While he was in Munich Ockham write a series of libels against John XXII, and he died in that city in 1350.[89]

In 1332 Ockham wrote the *Opus nonaginta dierum* (or Work of Ninety Days, so called because it took him ninety days to write it). This treatise is an immense commentary (more than a thousand printed pages in modern editions) on the bull *Quia vir reprobus* (1329), aimed at Michael of Cesena and his companions. In the 124th and last chapter of his treatise, Ockham finally arrives at a discussion of the bull that declared the Spirituals to be heretics. Ockham turns the accusation back against the pope, painstakingly defining the crime of heresy as explicit, manifest, and repeated error. The pope's faults corresponded precisely to all those criteria. Thus it was necessary to appeal to Christianity at large and to avoid any contact with the pope, because any Christian who considered John XXII to be pope would himself be open to the accusation of heresy. William states:

> And concerning what precedes, the accusers [*impugnatores,* the assailants, that is, the true Christians; the Spirituals] conclude that the accused [*impugnatus*; John XXII, who is never referred to in other terms throughout the treatise] must be avoided *(vitandus)* for the necessity of salvation, by all those who know that he is a heretic. But those who do not know that he is a heretic, even if they suffer from a crass and lazy ignorance, are in no way excused from the gravest moral sin. Those who are unaware that he is a heretic, if they suffer from a reasonable and invincible ignorance by reason of ignorance of that fact, seem excused from communicating with the accused and from obeying him. As to the question of avoiding him or not, it is the same for the accused and for the woman who was thought to have been a man and who was raised to the papacy. Indeed, those who, afterward, knew that she was a woman should not in any fashion hold her to be pope. But those who did not know, and who suffered from an invincible ignorance, who presented her as pope, were excused by their ignorance for holding her as a pope. The same is true of the accused, for he has no more true authority than had that woman who, as the chronicles say, was venerated as pope by the universal Church for two years, seven months, and three days.[90]

Ockham thus enrolled Joan as a prototype for John XXII and as an image of a pseudopope capable of deluding people. John's lack of existence in the Church (the true Church) was just as real and just as concealed as Joan's existence. But this factual illusion, this confusion in meanings, by no means leads to any certitude that the universal Church and the pope (the true pope) could ever be mistaken:

> And what if someone should say that such a thing [the real inexistence of John XXII] could not happen because the universal Church cannot err, the accusers respond that in the domain of faith and custom, the Church cannot be mistaken, but in the domain of fact, the Church militant can err and can be mistaken. It was in this manner that it erred in venerating a woman as pope.[91]

Ockham goes on to give other examples: Anastasius II, Sylvester II, and in all twenty-seven popes had criminally deceived the Church. Joan was his first and principal reference because, in her case, de facto ignorance could be proven very clearly, with no need to refer to any scale of crimes or faults.

Ockham returned to the question ten years later, in his *Octo quaestiones de potestate Pape* (Eight Questions on the Power of the Pope; 1340-42). In chapter 17 of this work he shows that it is legitimate to bring the pope before justice and to appeal his decisions if he is guilty of heresy, because at that point the "pope" would no longer be part of the body of the Church: "Thus no heretic is the true head of the Church, even if it is thought that he is; similarly, the woman who was thought to be the pontiff for two years was not the true head of the Church, even though everyone thought that she was."[92]

Franciscan argumentation bore fruit well beyond the realm of spiritual subversion. The founding concept that gave structure to infallibility and imposture (and that can be found in a totally different context in czarist Russia of the sixteenth to the eighteenth centuries, brilliantly analyzed by Claudio Sergio Ingerflom)[93] found an immediate, pro-papal, and absolutist application in Guido Terreni, a Carmelite. A century later, in spite of the great shock of the Schism, two pillars of the monarchical papacy of the fifteenth century, Torquemada and Antoninus of Florence, picked up the Franciscan argument and used Joan to illustrate their point.

The famous Dominican cardinal, Tomás de Torquemada (1420-98) uses terms in his *Summa de Ecclesia* (Summa on the Church) that closely resemble the ones that Ockham had used in his *Eight Questions*: "Since it is established that one day a woman was held to be pope by the generality of the Catholics, it is not incredible that one day a heretic could be held to be pope, even though he is not the true pope *(verus papa)*."[94]

A bit earlier, at the beginning of the fifteenth century, St. Antoninus, the Dominican archbishop of Florence, had related the story of the popess in his *Chronica,* closely following the version of Martinus Polonus. Commenting on the popess according to the Ockhamite distinction between fact and faith, a distinction that had become of capital importance in the diffusion of the story of Joan, Antoninus states:

> But if the story is true, it bears no prejudice for salvation, for the Church in those times was not deprived of its head, which is Christ; He held it in the river of grace, and the ultimate effects of the sacraments that she [the popess] conferred were not lacking to those who accepted them devoutly from her, that is to say, from grace. To be sure, this woman, no more than other women, was not capable of bearing the mark of any sacred order, nor of conferring the eucharist; certainly she could not, de facto, perform ordination, nor absolve sins, therefore the faithful received nothing from her. Nonetheless, Christ compensated for grace in the sacraments for those who received them worthily, and ignorance of the facts *(ignorantia facti)* excused them from sin.[95]

This distinction between fact and faith could lead to a separation between a work (which was inspired by the Holy Spirit) and its author (an individual usurper who was physically present, but whose role was fulfilled by the Holy Spirit or by Christ). Thus Leone da Orvieto, after depicting Boniface VIII as a usurper and noting that he was malevolent, wily, full of pride, avarice, and greed, could still declare that "he made the sixth book of the *Decretals,* which contains many good and useful things."[96] This suggests that Jean de Mailly's remark concerning the Fast of the Four Times (a custom initiated by the popess and maintained in Catholic liturgy) is perhaps a good illustration of this duality. Other au-

thors attributed prefaces to the Mass to Joan: Martin Lefranc, the prevost of Lausanne around 1450 and secretary to Popes Felix V (that is, the antipope, Amadeus VIII of Savoy) and Nicholas V, mentions Joan's liturgical activities with approval in his poem *Le champion des dames.* Martin says:

> So let us leave the sins, saying
> That she was a learned clergywoman
> When before the most prideful
> Of Rome [she] had issue and entry.
> Moreover, there can be shown to you
> Many a preface that [she] dictated,
> Well ordered and in saintly fashion,
> Where in matters of faith she did not hesitate.[97]

JOAN AT THE FRONTIERS

Ockham and the Spirituals made no distinction between orthodoxy and heresy, but instead offered the specter of continual evaluation. The most ardent supporters of the papacy reduced errors of fact to a few isolated incidents, but for the Spirituals, such errors became increasingly frequent with the approach of the Last Times. In the long run, all it took to turn impostures into history, and to arrive at the heretical conclusion that the apparent Church was a permanent lie and an obliteration of the true Church, was to link those impostures. There was only a step from the Bavarian schism to heretical secession, a step that Wycliffe took, dragging the unfortunate Joan with him as a hostage.

Thirty years after Ockham, John Wycliffe (1330-84) had a destiny similar to Ockham's, though with the essential difference that Wycliffe did not enter the Franciscan Order. Both were trained at Oxford; both received protection from an antipapal monarch (the king of England); both were condemned. Their ecclesiologies present traits in common: both were founded on an opposition between the apparent Church (Wycliffe called it the "visible" Church) and the real Church. But whereas for Ockham that opposition occurred within time and could be reduced to the period when the Church was headed by a pope like Nicholas III, for Wycliffe the two Churches were a perennial, hard reality. Above all, predestination made the role of the institution completely secondary. Where Ockham's nominalism permitted him to build a fine Catholic construction in which various planes of Church reality could be shifted to cover one another, integrating all Christian dogmas into them, Wycliffe's rough and summary realism led him, unhesitatingly, to separation, secession, a rejection of transubstantiation, and the harsh Reformation tautology that the Elect are the Elect. From Wycliffe on, the popess, whom he calls "Anna," stood as proof of the continuing decadence of the Roman Church. In 1382, in a brief work titled *Cruciata,* written to protest the crusade launched by Urban VI at the beginning of the Great Schism, Wycliffe relates the episode of the popess as a way of denying the Curia any spiritual power: "In the apocryphal chronicles it is commonly reported that the assembly of the cardinals was deceived concerning the sex of a pope when they elected as pope Anna, who was pregnant; whatever the case, it is certain that the assembled cardinals could be mistaken, to the point of electing as pope a demon who hated the memory of Christ and troubled the Church."[98] Wycliffe concludes, after citing the precedent of Judas, that only a man's acts authorize a "probable supposition" about his spiritual power. Ockham's Joan floated on the buoy of "fact," and Ockham, a fortunate Franciscan swimmer borne along by the current of the grace of Christ and the Church, could simply avoid her, as he "avoided" John XXII. Wycliffe's Anna attached her satanic ballast to the Church and sank it.

Jan Hus (1369-1415) further radicalized Wycliffe's position, completing the job of compromising our popess. He used the story of Joan, whom he calls Agnes, on several occasions. The last and most dramatic of these occurred in his defense, during his trial at Constance in 1415, according to the moving account of his disciple, Peter of Mladoňovice.[99] On 8 June 1415 the court examined the authenticity of certain propositions drawn from Hus's treatise *De Ecclesia*; according to the fourteenth article of accusation bearing on chapter 13 of that work, Hus was accused of claiming that the pope was simply the head of a particular church, unless he was predestined by God. Hus confirmed this stand, and supported it with this argument: "This is clear because otherwise the Christian faith would be perverted and a Christian would have to believe a lie. For the church was deceived in the case of Agnes." On the same day, when the first article of his treatise against Stanislas of Znojmo was being examined, Hus repeated his argument. Next he added, in response to questions about the fourth article:

> Nor is the doctor able to give a reason why the Church at the time of Agnes had been without a head for two years and five months, living on the part of many members in Christ's grace. Why cannot it in the same way be without a head for many years, when Christ without such monstrous heads, through His true disciples scattered over the circumference of the earth, would rule His Church better?

Hus made similar statements during the hearing of 18 June. On 6 July 1415, Jan Hus was burned at the stake.

The dangerous development of the Franciscan machinery, which contributed both to the installation of the notion of papal infallibility and to radical contestation of the sacred legitimacy of Rome, brings us to the crucial moment of the Great Schism (1378-1415). This was, however, when Joan played her role as a Catholic for the last time, a more modest role than she had played in the great Franciscan drama, for Joan the Catholic was

content with the juridical (rather than ecclesiological) role that Martinus Polonus had created for her. At that time, when opposing camps of jurists competed to display their demonstrative virtuosity, the case of Joan had become valuable only as an illustration. In 1399, when the University of Paris suggested to the Oxford masters that they withdraw their obedience from the pope, basing their arguments on the cases of Anastasius II and Calixtus II, the Oxford masters replied that the law says what should be, not what is.[100] Let us follow Joan in this last stage in her clerical career.

JOAN IN THE SCHISM

On 7 April 1378, Bartolomeo Prignano was elected pope and took the name Urban VI. The conclave, divided, had long hesitated. The Roman people grew impatient; worried that the papal court might depart for Avignon, they demanded an Italian pope. They became threatening, and riots broke out. The conclave was terrified, to the point that the cardinals disguised the aged Cardinal Tebaldeschi as pope to gain time. Urban VI, elected in a climate of division and haste and in the absence of the powerful French cardinal, Jean de la Grange, displayed a rigor that soon alienated the Curia, which yearned to be rid of him and demanded that he step down. Urban refused. After Jean de la Grange had returned to Rome, he had Robert of Geneva elected pope under the name Clement VII. Since Clement was unable to occupy the Roman see, he moved to Avignon, thus bringing about the Great Schism. The Christian nations were divided between obedience to Urban or Clement, Rome or Avignon, but the shock seems to have been profound within Christian consciences as well. From 1378 to 1415, all Christendom endlessly debated questions of papal legitimacy and power. Joan was used in support of a variety of arguments: a popess served all the imaginable solutions to resolve an unbearable schism. Three ways, three means were suggested for achieving that end.

The first of these was the *via facti,* or the way of fact. At first, each faction thought that it could crush the other. That name for their war (the "fact" involved) by implication cited Joan's adventure in its Ockhamite version: an illegitimate pope was a matter of fact, not a matter of faith or mores. Before Martinus Polonus had Joan die in childbirth, Jean de Mailly and Etienne de Bourbon had presented her lapidation, without benefit of judgment by the people or the Church of Rome, as normal procedure.

The second way to resolve the schism was the *via cessionis,* cession, or persuading one or both popes to resign. In 1394 the court of France, which had imposed obedience to Pope Clement VII on the University of Paris, was persuaded by the University to seek a resolution of the crisis by withdrawing its support of the

Avignon popes (Clement and his successor, Benedict XIII). This *subtractio obedience* (and Bernard Guenée suggests that the full import of the Latin term would be better rendered as a "refusal" of obedience)[101] resulted, on the practical level, in the deposition of popes who could not be persuaded to abdicate. This option claimed to be juridical.

The story of the woman pope bore two warnings: first, an election stained with illegality could be annulled; second, it was in the interest of the Church to take the lead and authorize deposition in case of scandal. The first argument had been raised as early as 1378, when the French cardinals stated that the election of Urban VI was invalid since it had been imposed by pressure from the Roman people and voted under the grip of fear (*timor* was a canonical case for annulling a decision).

Some years later (and before France abandoned the Avignon popes), Philippe de Mézières invoked Joan in *Le songe du Vieil Pèlerin* (ca. 1386) to support just that sort of argument. Philippe, formerly a councilor of Charles V and chancellor of Cyprus, devoted the last years of his life to piety and to writing that great work, which preached a general reform of Christianity, a revival of the crusades, and putting an end to the Schism. In book 1 of his *Songe,* the "Old Pilgrim," Ardent Desire, sets off under the escort of Good Hope to find Queen Truth in the farthest reaches of the Egyptian desert so as to persuade her to return and remain among humanity. The queen agrees to test Christendom by traveling through the world to search for a place worthy of her lasting presence. This immense and vain quest carries her and her escort from the Indies to the Low Countries. Rome offers the travelers the spectacle of a parade of men with the heads of animals. Truth cannot imagine remaining very long in the company of Ambition, Simony, and Avarice, the divinities honored in Rome. Soon after, they arrive in Avignon just as a consistory is being held in which Pride, Avarice, and Lust play major roles. In describing the hold she enjoys over the papal court, Lust tells Truth: "Lady Queen, as lieutenant to your Father [God] in this court of Rome I caused to reign a woman, who was of England."[102] Somewhat later Ardent Desire seizes on this allusion to suggest a plan for resolving the schism, "in order to put an end to the great doubts and perils of the said division and to the subtle arguments of the Italians and others of the adverse party." The cardinals could, in fact, undo a papal election in cases of deception or physical pressure. Ardent Desire explains:

> They have such power that if in electing the sovereign shepherd they have been deceived in any fashion, for they are men, by ignorance, as they were by the woman who was pope, or out of reasonable fear and manifest oppression, as it happened in our case, or by simony and several other cases written about in decrees and di-

vine Scripture, the said cardinals have full power to renegotiate their difficulty, without the authority of others, and to make a new election or elections valid according to both divine and positive law.[103]

In a different context, far from the affairs of France and Avignon, the same sort of argument was put forth in favor of rejecting another supernumerary pope. Dietrich of Nieheim, who occupied a high post in the Church and who relates the story of Joan in his *History of the Acts of the Roman Emperors,*[104] discusses the right to undo a papal election. Addressing his remarks to John XXIII (1410-15), who had succeeded Alexander V as a "third pope," and who had been elected to remedy the untenable situation of obedience to two popes but had refused to abdicate when the operation failed, Dietrich states:

> And if the lord pope says "There was at Pisa a true council, holy and just; what was decided there is holy and just, and the two who were rejected there [Gregory XII, the Roman pope, and Benedict XIII, the Avignon pope] must not be heard." (Response): "The council can be holy and just, but the election that results from it can be null for many reasons, for a defect in the person or in the form, if the elect is incapable, insufficient in his learning, or even criminal."[105]

Dietrich's final phrase corresponds exactly to Martinus Polonus's juridical disqualification of Joan. Moreover, one of Martinus's versions of the story of Joan states that she was deposed. The *Eulogium historiarum* (ca. 1366) confirmed that juridical outcome (*ipsa deposita est).*[106] Even in this legal debate, the Franciscan version of Joan retained its grip: when in 1399 the masters of the University of Cambridge refused to withdraw their allegiance to the Roman pope, they spoke of Urban VI in the ecclesiological language of the Spirituals rather than in the juridical vocabulary of the canonists. Walter Ullmann remarks: "One could not easily presume that such eminent men [the cardinals] would have suggested *toti christianismo* a false (*falsum*) vicar of Christ."[107]

Jean Gerson (1363-1429), a major figure in the French Church of the late fourteenth century, developed a second justification for a pope's withdrawal that took into consideration the primacy of the peace of the Church in cases of scandal. On the Feast of the Circumcision in 1403, Gerson preached at Tarascon before Benedict XIII, Clement VII's successor, who had been sequestered at Avignon since 1398 by the French court, under the influence of the University of Paris and its two great Doctors, Gerson himself and Pierre d'Ailly. In his sermon Gerson made another attempt to move the pope to abdicate:

> Second consideration. All power, in the ecclesiastical hierarchy, is oriented toward a salutary peace. . . . It appears that the salutary peace can be broken by the persistence of an ecclesiastical power, in the case of

John, for example, whereas the destitution of that power would bring back peace: in that case, rejecting that power is to use [power] well; its maintenance becomes an abuse. Moreover, there is no power that is not subject to the law, divine and natural, that is not liable to sin, to suppression of suspension, and to abdication.[108]

The "John" mentioned by Gerson has traditionally been seen as our popess, but the identification is not certain. Gerson might also have been thinking of John XII, deposed by Otto I of Germany in 964, although that identification is not totally persuasive either. Whatever the case, the brevity of the allusion reflects at least a passing thought of Joan.[109]

Later in his sermon, Gerson's reference to Joan illustrates an error of fact, not of doctrine, thus an error that should be resolved by a simple "retreat": "Moreover, these circumstance that bring dissension in the present schism consist essentially in questions of fact, in which not only one individual or another may err without risk to his salvation, but also the Church has been or can be (as is said) deceived, as when, long ago, it honored a woman as pope."[110]

But Joan, with her typical agility, also served as an argument against the antihierarchical fideism of Gerson, who contributed to weakening the papacy (even if he did not hold the "pre-Gallican" opinions of the French prelate Simon de Cramaud in his 1396 treatise, *Sur la soustraction d'obédience*).[111] Jean Roques, a Franciscan who had come to the Council of Constance as vicar of the minister general of the Franciscans of the Observance (the latter-day heirs of the Spirituals), argued against Gerson's position in the session of 24 October 1415, where he praised the idea of the absolute necessity of the ecclesiastical hierarchy, independent of the personal qualities of the popes. Here Joan no longer represented error or deceit, but another, more considerable evil, the suspension of order. Jean Roques states: "First, the hierarchical status of the Church loses all certitude and all surety if there is no pope; and that status was also uncertain when John of Mainz reigned as pope."[112]

A third way to resolve the schism was the *via conventionis,* or by the convocation of a general council. From the outset of the Great Schism, theologians on both sides had urged that the schism be resolved in that manner (Vincent Ferrer and Nicolas Eymeric among the supporters of Clement VII; Konrad von Gelnhausen and Heinrich von Langenstein in support of Urban VI). Around 1408 a number of cardinals and prelates, weary of the schism, formed a third, conciliar party, and in 1415 they succeeded in calling the Council of Constance. The idea of a council was not new in the fifteenth century, but the schism gave it a high priority among theories concerning limitations on the power of the popes, replacing the oligarchical ideology that had been developed in the eleventh to the thirteenth centuries by the great canonists who gravitated to the Sacred College of Cardinals. William of Ockham was by no means a conciliarist, but his ecclesiological dialectic influenced theorists of the council of the time of the Schism. These theorists made a distinction between *potestas habitualis* (habitual, subsistent power) and *potestas actualis* (actual power); the community of the faithful or the Church held the first; the pope could only dispose of "actual" power, which meant the Church, represented by the council, could dispossess him of that power. We return here to Ockham's distinction between fact (and *factum* is close to *actus,* the act to which papal power is reduced) and faith; between the individual who had been invested (and, at times, "transvested") and the sacred institution. In a new irony of history, the operative scheme here was an exact inverse of the theory of the sovereign's two bodies (which, as a theory, hence indefinitely reversible, is not a thing, but rather a vocabulary ceaselessly made into discourse). Joan, a woman and a pope, was an excellent figure for the duality of that power, and Dietrich of Nieheim, the most resolute conciliarist of his time, was also the most prolix of the biographers of the popess and the one most convinced of her existence.

JOAN AND THE DOGS OF GOD

Between 1250 and 1450 Joan was a faithful servant of the Church, which she served and followed, with her agile dialectics, through the sinuous twists and turns of a Catholic discourse gripped in the claws of time and necessity. The Dominicans (Jean de Mailly, Etienne de Bourbon, Martinus Polonus, Jacopo da Voragine, Arnoldus of Liège, Bernard Gui, Tolomeo da Lucca, and others) had been fond of the popess, the mother of paradoxes and reversals, but it was their rivals, the Franciscans, mere stammerers in promoting Joan in comparison to the skilled Dominican preachers, who armed Joan with a trenchant argument and gave her the poignancy of a suspicion. One might even stretch the hypothesis to another domain and see a dramatic Franciscan orchestration of Dominican themes.

On the other hand, this opposition between the two mendicant Orders might require revision, correcting some of what has been said above about the efficiency of the Dominican network. Cultural continuity probably masks some gaps. There is no common measure between the transcription of a rumor in a cloistered community in Metz or Lyon and its inscription in a history of the popes written by a papal chaplain. We have neglected an important detail: the pope who protected Martinus Polonus, personally ordaining him bishop in 1278 (the probable moment of the third[?] redaction of his *Chronicle,* the version that contains the story of Joan), was Nicholas III, whom the Franciscans considered the most authentic of the popes, as we have seen.

At the same time that the pope laid down rules for authenticity (in the bull *Exiit qui seminat*) the Dominican wrote his narrative on imposture that provided the matrix for many other accounts. This chronological proximity weakens the image of the Dominicans as sage mediators, particularly if we look at the conjunction of events in 1278. Martinus, who occupied a position close to the angelic pope, was telling that angelic pope how close supreme dignity was to its total subversion. He was playing the role of the pope's fool, evoking a possible inversion (Ockham would say, of fact: "The pope is a woman") in order to exalt a necessary inversion (Ockham would say, of faith: folly in Christ; Peter of John Olivi said that if the Church should fail, a woman might also be the final depository of grace). Martin recalls to mind the figure of the fool Ramón in the romance *Blanquerna* of the Franciscan Ramon Llull (1233-1315): "A man with shaven head and clothed in the garb of a fool" arrives at the papal court, accompanied by a sparrowhawk and leading a dog. He announces that "in praise of God and to reprove the vices of the Court of Rome Ramón the Sage has taken the office of fool." Ramón's dog (and the dog was the traditional attribute of God's fools)[113] reminds us that the Franciscans were not alone in playing the fool or being *joculatores Dei*: the Dominicans carefully conserved the etymology of the name that they gave themselves in honor of their founder, St. Dominic, *Domini Canis*, or "the dog of God."

The crucial event in this chronicle of Joan the Catholic becomes opaque at this point: was the 1278 narrative a product of the cultural necessity of Dominican transmission, hence quantitatively established, or does it instead arise from an ideological choice of a "spiritual" history (both Dominican and Franciscan) that is significant qualitatively? The serial presentation of the various Joan narratives given at the beginning of this chapter privileges the first hypothesis, whereas the contextualization of the moments of conjunction in 1254, 1278, 1294, and 1378 that wound its way through this narrative sequence leads instead to the second hypothesis. We are right back to the dilemma with which we began, and we have not resolved it. Yet the meaning of Joan depends on resolution.

Only with the end of Joan's Catholic career, after 1450, could these recurrent cycles of appearances and hypotheses come to a stopping point. Nonetheless, before the popess's expulsion from the tense but captivating clerical discourse in which Joan, a woman of passion, was quite at home, she found a way to slip out of the Church and insist that she was a woman, not just a pseudopope.

Notes

1. Jean de Mailly, *Chronica universalis Mettensis*, in *MGH, Scriptores*, vol. 24 (Hannover, 1879), 502-26, esp. p. 514.

2. See Ludwig Weiland, "Die Chronik des Predigermönches Johannes von Mailly," *Archiv der Gesellschaft für alter deutschen Geschichtkunde* 11 (1874): 419-73, and Antoine Dondaine, "Le dominicain français Jean de Mailly et la Légende dorée," *Archives d'Histoire Dominicaine* 1 (1946): 53-102.

3. Etienne de Bourbon, quoted in Dondaine, "Le dominicain français Jean de Mailly."

4. Jean de Mailly, *L'Abrégé des gestes et miracles des saints*, trans. Antoine Dondaine (Paris: Cerf, 1947).

5. On Bartholomew of Trent and his *Liber epilogarum*, see Alain Boureau, "Les vignes de Bolzano: Edition de l'Epilogus de Barthélémy de Trente sur la Nativité du Seigneur," in *Contributi alla Storia della Regione Trentino-Alto Adige, Civis: Studi e Testi*, supplement 2 (Trent, 1986), 91-104. For a more general presentation, see Boureau, "Barthélémy de Trente et l'invention de la 'Legenda nova,'" in *Raccolte di Vite di Santi dal XIII al XVIII secolo: Strutture, messaggi, fruizioni*, the Acts of a colloquy, Rome, May 1985, ed. Sofia Boesch Gajano (Fasano di Brindisi: Schena, 1990), 23-39.

6. See Alain Boureau, *La Légende dorée: Le système narratif de Jacques de Voragine (†1298)* (Paris: Cerf, 1984), and Barbara Fleith, *Studien zur Überlieferungsgeschichte des lateinischen Legenda aurea*, a dissertation on the manuscript tradition of the *Golden Legend*, University of Geneva, 1986 (Brussels: Société des Bollandistes, 1991).

7. For a concrete illustration of this mobility, see the biography of Bernard Gui in Bernard Guenée, "Bernard Gui (1261-1331)," in Guenée, *Entre l'Eglise et l'Etat; Quatre vies de prélats français à la fin du Moyen Age, XIIIe-XVe siècle* (Paris: Gallimard, 1987), 49-85, available in English translation as *Between Church and State: The Lives of Four French Prelates in the Late Middle Ages*, trans. Arthur Goldhammer (Chicago: University of Chicago Press, 1991), 37-70.

8. Jacopo da Voragine, *Legenda aurea*, ed. Theodor Graesse, 3d ed. (Dresden, 1890), 260, quoted from *The Golden Legend: Readings on the Saints*, trans. William Granger Ryan, 2 vols. (Princeton, N.J.: Princeton University Press, 1993), 1: 238.

9. Jacques Le Goff, "Culture ecclésiastique et culture folklorique au Moyen Age: Saint Marcel de Paris et le dragon," in Le Goff, *Pour un autre Moyen Age: Temps, travail et culture en Occident: 18 essais* (Paris: Gallimard, 1977), 236-79, available in English translation as "Ecclesiastical Culture

and Folklore in the Middle Ages: Saint Marcellus of Paris and the Dragon," in *Time, Work and Culture in the Middle Ages,* trans. Arthur Goldhammer (Chicago: University of Chicago Press, 1980), 159-88.

10. Jacopo da Voragine, *Legenda aurea,* 164; *Golden Legend,* 1: 148.

11. Hermann Korner, *Chronica novella,* ed. Johann Georg von Eckhart, *Corpus historicum Medii Aevi* (Leipzig, 1723), 2: 442.

12. See Vittorio Coletti, *Parole dal pulpito: Chiesa e movimenti religiosi tra latino e volgare* (Genoa: Marietti, 1983), in French translation as *L'éloquence de la chaire: Victoires et défaites du latin entre Moyen Age et Renaissance,* trans. Silvano Serventi (Paris: Cerf, 1987).

13. Bartolomeo Platina, *Platynae historici Liber de vita Christi ac omnium Pontificum (aa. 1-1474),* ed. Giacinto Gaida (1913), new enlarged ed. (Città di Castello: S. Lapi, 1932), 152.

14. Dondaine, "Le dominicain français Jean de Mailly."

15. Ibid.

16. Jean de Mailly, *Abrégé des gestes et miracles des saints,* 93.

17. See Boureau, "Les vignes de Bolzano," 100.

18. Quoted from Georges and Andrée Duby, *Les procès de Jeanne d'Arc* (Paris: Gallimard, 1973), 15.

19. See *Dictionnaire apologétique de la foi catholique,* (1911), s.v. "Jeanne (la papesse)" (Félix Vernet).

20. Jansen Enikel, *Weltcronik,* ed. Philipp Strauch, in *MGH, Scriptores qui vernacula lingue usi sunt,* vol. 3, *Deutsche Chroniken,* vol. 3 (Hannover and Leipzig, 1900), p. 434 (verses 22, 295-22, 520). My thanks to Jean-Marie Moeglin for calling this text to my attention.

21. Jacob van Maerlant, *Spiegel historiael,* vol. 3 (Leiden, 1857), 220.

22. Jacques Berlioz and others are preparing a critical edition of Etienne de Bourbon, *Traité de divers matériaux de la prédication (Tractatus de diversis materiis praedicabilibus).*

23. I am paraphrasing here the definition given by Claude Bremond, Jacques Le Goff, and Jean-Claude Schmitt in *L'exemplum* (Turnhout: Brepols, 1982), 37-38, omitting one term of their definition, "donné comme véridique." Fables in the spirit of Aesop are never given as truthful, but rather as signifying. See below, on the development of belief in the Middle Ages.

24. Etienne de Bourbon, *Tractatus de diversis materiis,* MS Bibliothèque Nationale, Paris, Latin 15970, fol. 574r.

25. Jacopo da Voragine, *Chronica Januensis,* in a modern edition as *Iacopo de Varagine e la sua Cronaca di Genova: Dalle origini al MCCXVII,* ed. Giovanni Monleone, 3 vols. (Rome: Tipografia del Senato, 1941), 2: 4.

26. See Boureau, *Légende dorée,* 45-63.

27. Mariano da Firenze, *Itinerarium urbis Romae,* ed. Enrico Bulletti (Rome: Pontificio Istituto di Archeologia Cristiana, 1931), 169, quoted in Cesare D'Onofrio, *La Papessa Giovanna: Roma e papato tra storia e leggenda* (Rome: Romana Società Editrice, 1979), 213-14.

28. Jacopo de Voragine, *Iacopo de Varagine e la sua Cronaca di Genoa,* 2: 268-69.

29. There is a critical edition of the Latin text of Arnoldus of Liège: *L'Alphabetum narrationum: Un receuil d'exempla compilé au début du XIVe siècle,* ed. Colette Ribeaucourt, *thèse* defense, Ecole des Hautes Etudes en Sciences Sociales, Paris 1985.

30. Arnoldus of Liège, *Recull de eximplis e miracles, gestes et faules e altres ligendes ordenades per ABC,* ed. A. Verdaguer (Barcelona, 1881), 147.

31. *Chronica minor auctore minorita Erphordiensi,* ed. Oswald Holder-Egger, *MGH, Scriptores,* vol. 24 (Hannover, 1897), 172-204, esp. p. 184.

32. Ludwig Weiland, "Die Chronik des Predigermönches Johannes von Mailly," *Archiv der Gesellschaft für alter deutschen Geschichtkunde,* 12 (1875): 1-78.

33. Martinus Polonus, *Chronica de Romanis Pontificibus et imperatoribus,* in *MGH, Scriptorum,* vol. 22, ed. Georg Heinrich Pertz (Hannover, 1872), 428.

34. See Ernst H. Kantorowicz, "An 'Autobiography' of Guido Faba," reprinted in Kantorowicz, *Selected Studies* (Locust Valley, N.Y.: J. J. Augustin, 1965), 194-212.

35. *Cronica pontificum et imperatorum sancti Bartholomaei in insula romani,* ed. Oswald Holder-Egger, *MGH, Scriptorum,* vol. 31 (Hannover: Hahn, 1903), 218.

36. Jacopo de Voragine, *Legenda aurea,* 190; *Golden Legend,* 1: 172. The source of the pun is older, however (John Hymmonides).

37. Alberto Milioli, *Liber de temporibus,* ed. Oswald Holder-Egger, *MGH, Scriptores,* vol. 31 (Hannover: Hahn, 1903), 353-668, esp. p. 420.

38. Geoffroy de Courlon, *Chronique de l'abbaye de Saint-Pierre-le-Vif de Sens,* ed. Gustave Julliot (Sens, 1876), 296-99.

39. This exemplum is translated in Albert Lecoy de la Marche, *Anecdotes historiques, légendes et apologues tirés du receuil inédit d'Etienne de Bourbon, Dominicain du XIIIe siècle* (Paris, 1877), anecdote 376.

40. Leone da Orvieto, *Chronica de temporibus et gestis Romanorum Pontificum,* Biblioteca Riccardiana, Florence, 338, fols. 99-163. The manuscript was published by Giovanni Lami in *Deliciae eruditorum, seu Veterum ΑΝΕΚΔΟΤΩΝ opusculorum collectanea* (Florence, 1736-), vol. 3 (1736), 337.

41. Pietro Calo da Barletta, quoted in Baudouin de Gaiffier, "La nativité de saint Etienne: A propos des fresques de Tivoli," *Atti e Memorie della Società Tiburtina di Storia e d'Arte* 41 (1968): 105-112.

42. Guibert de Nogent, *De vita sua,* consulted as *Autobiographie,* ed. and trans. Edmond-René Labande (Paris: Belles Lettres, 1981), 213-25, available in English as *Self and Society in Medieval France: The Memoirs of Abbot Guibert of Nogent,* ed. John F. Benton (Toronto and Buffalo: University of Toronto Press in association with the Medieval Academy of America, 1984).

43. John Lathbury, quoted in Beryl Smalley, *English Friars and Antiquity in the Early Fourteenth Century* (New York: Barnes and Noble, 1960), 225.

44. Innocent IV's letter is quoted in Solomon Grayzel, *The Church and the Iews in the XIIIth Century* (Philadelphia: Dropsie College for Hebrew and Cognate Learning, 1933), 268-71.

45. Martinus Polonus, *Chronica,* 428.

46. See "Les pouvoirs informels dans l'Eglise," special issue, ed. André Vauchez, *Mélanges de l'Ecole française de Rome* 98, 1 (1986).

47. Marie-Dominique Chenu, *La théologie comme science au XIIIe siècle,* 3d ed. rev. and enlarged (Paris: J. Vrin, 1969).

48. Guenée, *Entre l'Eglise et l'Etat,* 141, quoted from *Between Church and State,* 116.

49. Guenée, *Entre l'Eglise et l'Etat,* 141; *Between Church and State,* 117.

50. Daniel Milo, "Laboratoire temporel grandeur naturelle: Le calendrier révolutionnaire," in Milo, *Trahir le temps (histoire)* (Paris: Belles Lettres, 1991), 193-224.

51. Bartolomé Carranza, *Summa omnium Conciliorum et Pontificum* (1546) (Rome, 1665), 734.

52. Jean Rioche, *Compendium temporum et historiarum ecclesiasticarum . . .* (Paris, 1576), fol. 230v.

53. Ranulf Higden, *Polychronicon . . . ,* ed. Churchill Babington and Joseph Rawson Lumby, 9 vols. (London, 1865-86), vol. 6 (1876), 330.

54. See *Histoire littéraire de la France,* vol. 12 (Paris, 1869), 479, and vol. 13 (1870), 330.

55. Bernard Gui (Bernardus Guidonis), *Catalogus Pontificum Romanorum cum inserta temporum historia,* in Angelo Mai, *Spicilegium Romanum,* vol. 6 (Rome, 1841), 202-3.

56. See the report of a discussion given after Alain Boureau, "La papesse Jeanne: Formes et fonctions d'une légende au Moyen Age," *Comptes-Rendus de l'Académie des Inscriptions et des Belles-Lettres* (1984): 446-64; esp. p. 464.

57. Tolomeo da Lucca, *Historia ecclesiastica,* published in Ludovico Antonio Muratori, *Rerum Italicarum Scriptores* (Milan, 1723-51), XI, 2: 1013-14.

58. *Chronik Johanns von Winterthur (Cronica Iohannis Vidodurani)* in *MGH, Scriptores rerum germanicarum, Nova Series,* vol. 3 (Berlin: Weidmann, 1924), 33.

59. *Vita Urbani V,* ed. G[uillaume] Mollat, in *Vitae Paparum avenionnensium,* 4 vols. (Paris: Letouzey et Ané, 1914-27), 1: 366.

60. Johann Burchard, *Liber notarum,* ed. Enrico Celani (Città di Castello: Lapi, 1907-10), 1: 82-83.

61. Dietrich of Nieheim, *Historia de gestis Romanorum Principum,* ed. Katharina Colberg and Joachim Leuschner, in *MGH,* Staatsschriften des späteren Mittelalters (Stuttgart: Hiersemann, 1980), 27-28.

62. *Chronica minor autore minorita Erphordiensi,* 184.

63. Siegfried of Balhusen (or of Meissen), *Compendium historiarum,* in *MGH, Scriptorum,* ed. Oswald Holder-Egger, vol. 25 (Hannover, 1880), 679-718, esp. p. 684.

64. See Jean-Marie Moeglin, *Les ancêtres du Prince: Propagande politique et naissance d'une histoire nationale en Bavière au Moyen Age (1180-1500)* (Geneva: Droz, 1985), 59-61.

65. *Flores temporum,* in *MGH, Scriptores,* ed. Oswald Holder-Egger, vol. 24 (Hannover, 1847), 228-50, esp. p. 248.

66. See Jean-Jacques Nattiez, *Fondements d'une sémiologie de la musique* (Paris: UGE, 1975, 1978).

67. See Jean Rychner, *La chanson de geste: Essai sur l'art épique des jongleurs* (Geneva and Lucca: Droz, 1955), which refers to Lord's works. See also Marcel Jousse, *Etudes de psychologie linguistique: Le style oral rythmique et mnémotechnique chez les verbo-moteurs* (Paris: 1925), available in English translation as *The Oral Style,* trans. Edgard Sienaert and Richard Whitaker (New York: Garland, 1990).

68. Johann Joseph Ignaz von Döllinger, *Die Papst-Fabeln des Mittelalters: Ein Betrag zur Kirchengeschichte (1863),* 2d ed. (Stuttgart, 1890), in English translation of the first edition, *Fables Respecting the Popes of the Middle Ages,* trans. Alfred Plummer (London, Oxford, and Cambridge, 1871), 44-47.

69. Christian Jouhaud, "Lisibilité et persuasion: Les placards politiques," in *Les usages de l'imprimé (XVe-XIXe siècle),* ed. Roger Chartier (Paris: Fayard, 1984), 309-42, in English translation as "Readability and Persuasion: Political Handbills," in *The Culture of Print,* trans. Lydia G. Cochrane (Oxford; Polity Press/Blackwell, 1989), 235-60.

70. *Chronica S. Ægidii in Brunswig* and *Chronicon Theodorici Engelhusii,* in *Scriptores Brunsvicienses,* ed. Gottfried Wilhelm von Leibniz (Hannover, 1707-11), 3: 580, 2: 1065, respectively.

71. The text of this chronicle is apparently lost, but the fragment pertaining to Joan is published in Johann Wolf, *Lectiones memorabiles et reconditae* (1600), 2d ed. (Frankfurt, 1671), 1: 177.

72. Heinrich von München, *Weltchronik,* is unpublished. Extracts (which include the passage concerning Joan) appear in Paul Gichtel, *Die Weltchronik Heinrichs von München in der Runkelsteiner Handschrift des Heinz Sentlinger* (Munich: C. H. Beck, 1937), 391-92, for the passage on Joan. My thanks to Jean-Marie Moeglin for calling this text to my attention.

73. This is one of the themes of the legend of St. Eustace and of the constellation of tales from which that legend was drawn. See *Les avatars d'un conte,* ed. Claude Bremond, special issue on narrations of *Communications* 39 (1984).

74. Joinville, *Histoire de Saint Louis,* ed. Francisque Michel (Paris, 1830), 23, quoted from *The Life of St. Louis,* trans. René Hague from the text edited by Natalis de Wailly (New York: Sheed and Ward, 1955), 30.

75. *De perfectione statuum ordinis fratrum minorum,* quoted in Brian Tierney, *The Origins of Papal Infallibility, 1150-1350; A Study on the Concepts of Infallibility, Sovereignty and Tradition in the Middle Ages* (Leiden: E. J. Brill, 1972), 166-68.

76. See Marjory Reeves, *The Influence of Prophecy in the Later Middle Ages: A Study in Joachimism* (Oxford: Clarendon Press, 1969).

77. See, in particular, Marie-Dominique Chenu, "Conscience de l'histoire et théologie," in Chenu, *La théologie au XIIe siècle* (1957) (Paris: J. Vrin, 1976), 62-89.

78. Tierney, *Origins of Papal Infallibility,* 76.

79. Peter of John Olivi, *Lectura super Apocalypsim,* quoted in Tierney, *Origins of Papal Infallibility,* 107.

80. Jacopone da Todi, in Brian Tierney, *The Foundations of the Conciliar Theory: The Contributions of the Medieval Canonists from Gratian to the Great Schism* (Cambridge: Cambridge University Press, 1955), 159.

81. Jacopo da Voragine, *Iacopo de Varagine e la sua Cronaca di Genova,* 2: 409-10.

82. On the pairing of Martha and Mary and its polemical currency, see Jean-Claude Schmitt, *Mort d'une hérésie: L'Eglise et les clercs face aux béguines et aux bégards du Rhin supérieur du XIVe au XVe siècle* (Paris, The Hague, and New York: Mouton, 1978), 101-4.

83. *Gesta Boemundi archiepiscopi Treverensis,* in *MGH, Scriptores,* vol. 24 (Hannover, 1879), 476. The term "dialogic" is used in the sense given to it by Mikhail Bakhtin.

84. Olivi, *De renuntiatione,* as mentioned in Tierney, *Origins of Papal Infallibility,* 102.

85. Jean de Paris (Jean Quidort), *De regia potestate et papali,* ed. Fritz Bleiestein (Stuttgart: Klett, 1969), available in English translation as *On Royal and Papal Power,* trans. Arthur P. Monahan (New York: Columbia University Press, 1974).

86. Robert d'Uzès, in Jeanne Bignami Odier, "Les Visions de Robert d'Uzès," *Archivum Fratrum Praedicatorum* 25 (1955): 258-320, esp. pp. 285-86.

87. Leone da Orvieto, *Chronica,* in Lami, *Deliciae eruditorum,* 3: 335. See also Arturo Graf, "Il rifiuto di Celestino V," in Graf, *Miti, leggende e superstizioni del Medio Evo,* 2 vols. (Turin, 1892-93), reprint (Milan, 1894), 287-92. Graf's brief but penetrating analysis does not mention Leone da Orvieto's version of these events, however.

88. Tierney, *Origins of Papal Infallibility.*

89. See Wilhelm Kölmel, *Wilhelm Ockham und seine kirchenpolitischen Schriften* (Essen: Ludgerus, 1962).

90. William of Ockham, *Opus nonaginta dierum,* ed. J. G. Sykes and H. S. Offler, in *Guillelmi de Ockam Opera politica,* ed. R. F. Bennett and H. S. Offler, 4 vols. (Manchester: University of Manchester Press, 1940-97), vol. 2 (1963), 854. The first part of the *Opus nonaginta dierum* appears at the end of vol. 1, ed. J. G. Sykes (1940).

91. See ibid.

92. Ibid., vol. 1.

93. Claudio Sergio Ingerflom, "De l'inversion au despotisme et à l'imposture: Quelques réflexions sur les représentations du pouvoir dans la Russie des XIVe et XVIIe siècles."

94. Tomás de Torquemada, *Summa de Ecclesia* (Venice, 1561), 394.

95. Antoninus, *Chronica Antonini* (Lyon, 1543), fol. 148.

96. Leone da Orvieto, in Lami, *Deliciae eruditorum,* 337.

97. Martin Lefranc, *Le champion des dames* (ca. 1430) (Paris, 1530), fol. 335; in Casimir Oudin, ed., *Commentarius de scriptoribus ecclesiae antiquis,* 3 vols. (Leipzig, 1722), 3: 2466.

98. John Wycliffe, *Cruciata,* in *John Wiclif's Polemical Works in Latin,* ed. Rudolf Buddensieg, 2 vols. (London, 1883), 2: 619.

99. Here and below, quotations regarding Hus are taken from Matthew Spinka, *John Hus at the Council of Constance* (New York: Columbia University Press, 1965), 192, 209, 212.

100. See Walter Ullmann, "The University of Cambridge and the Great Schism," *Journal of Theological Studies,* n.s., 9 (1958): 53-77.

101. Guenée, *Entre l'Eglise et l'Etat,* 153.

102. Philippe de Mézières, *Le songe du Vieil Pèlerin,* ed. George William Coopland, 2 vols. (Cambridge: Cambridge University Press, 1969), 1: 338.

103. Ibid., 370.

104. Dietrich of Nieheim, *Historia de gestis Romanorum Principum.*

105. Dietrich of Nieheim, *De modis uniendi et reformandi ecclesiam in concilio universale,* ed. Hermann Heimpel (Leipzig: Tübner, 1933), 55-56.

106. *Eulogium historiarum sive temporum,* ed. Frank Scott Haydon, 3 vols. (London, 1858-63), 1: 243.

107. Ullmann, "The University of Cambridge and the Great Schism," 60.

108. Jean Gerson, Sermon, "Apparuit" ("De Pace"), in *Oeuvres complètes,* ed. Palémon Glorieux (Paris and New York: Desclée, 1960-), 5: 64-90.

109. John XII was deposed by Otto, the emperor, not by the Church. He returned to power and was assassinated. The absence of a number after "John" in Gerson's text might seem to point to Joan, in Martinus's version. The text seems to infer that "John" was deposed. This was true of Joan in only two versions, which we have seen.

110. Jean Gerson, "Apparuit," 87.

111. See Howard Kaminsky, "Cession, Substraction, Deposition; Simon de Cramaud's Formulation of the French Solution to the Schism," in *Post Scripta: Essays on Medieval Law and the Emergence of the European State, in Honor of Gaines Post,* ed. Josephus Forchielli and Alphonsus M. Strickler, Studia Gratiana, 15 (Rome: Studia Gratiana, 1972), 295-318.

112. Jean Roques (de Rocha), *Contra evasiones Johannis de Gersono super suis assertionibus erroneis,* in Gerson, *Opera omnia,* ed. Louis Ellies Du Pin (Antwerp, 1706), 5: 456. It is probable that Joan appears in many other places in the immense polemical literature (still largely unpublished) that developed around the Great Schism. For example, Honoré Bonet speaks of Joan in a juridico-apocalytical context in *Arbre des batailles* (ca. 1386). For this passage, see *Arbre des batailles,* ed. Ernest Nys (Brussels and Leipzig, 1883), 21-22, available in English translation as *The Tree of Battles,* ed. and trans. George William Coopland (Liverpool: University Press, 1949).

113. See John Saward, *Perfect Fools: Folly for Christ's Sake in Catholic and Orthodox Spirituality* (Oxford and New York: Oxford University Press, 1980), 91, in French translation as *Dieu à la folie; Histoire des saints fous pour le Christ* (Paris: Seuil, 1983).

Steven M. Taylor (essay date 1992)

Taylor, Steven M. "Martin Le Franc's Rehabilitation of Notorious Women: The Case of Pope Joan." *Fifteenth Century Studies* 19 (1992): 261-78.

[*In the following essay, Taylor offers an account of Martin Lefranc's effort to salvage Pope Joan's reputation in his mid-fifteenth-century work* Le champion des dames.]

Martin Le Franc, unlike Boccaccio and Chaucer, adduces notorious women with a didactic rather than an ironic intent. I would argue that the French poet's strategy is to confute misogynistic false induction of female turpitude by a vigorous defense of such controversial individuals as Cleopatra and Pope Joan. Le Franc found an unflattering portrait of the latter in his Florentine predecessor's fourteenth-century text, *De Claris Mulieribus,* which he knew extremely well.[1] He considered this Latin collection of women's lives a valuable source of information. However, he also found it to be a work whose equivocal attitude toward certain notorious women demanded rectification, a task that he undertook in his *Le Champion des Dames* (1440-42). Boccaccio began his collection of 104 women's biographies by stating his intention to include some individuals with "very strong but destructive characters" (xxxvii). His preface goes on to explain:

> For it is not my intention to give the word "famous" so strict a meaning that it will always seem to signify "virtuous," but rather to give it a wider sense, if the reader will forgive me, and to consider as famous those women whom I know to have become renowned to the world through any sort of deed.
>
> (xxxvii-xxxviii)

In other words, Boccaccio presented the famous and the notorious together, juxtaposing Medea, Flora, and Sempronia with Penelope, Lucretia, and Sulpicia.

It is in chapter 99 of *De Claris Mulieribus* that Boccaccio relates what he considers to be the scandalous life of Pope Joan. He explains that she was seduced as a young girl by a student who subsequently made her wear masculine apparel, so that she could accompany him incognito. She followed him to England, where people took her to be a cleric. After her lover's death, she led a celibate life as she continued to study, eventually going to Rome, where her fame and wisdom led the cardinals to elect her pope. Boccaccio then claims to be scandalized that the formerly chaste woman, once pope, again took a lover and became pregnant, revealing her sex and imposture when giving birth to her child during a solemn procession.

In the case of Boccaccio's work, we can posit that the Florentine author included this legend as part of a rhetorical program intended to discredit women as a class. Such a tactic would in theory preclude them from usurping masculine prerogatives in the public arena. But why would Martin Le Franc, a wholehearted and unambiguous defender of women's virtues and abilities, include a version of the life of the female pope in his vindication of womankind entitled *Le Champion des Dames*?[2] In this essay I will address this paradox by clarifying the strategies and techniques which Le Franc uses to rehabilitate Pope Joan in particular and infamous women in general.

Martin Le Franc composed his monumental defense of women, *Le Champion des Dames,* toward the middle of the fifteenth century. Its more than 24,000 octosyllabic verses are grouped in octaves with the rhyme scheme ababbcbc. In each of the work's five books, Franc Vouloir, also known as "Le Champion des Dames," debates a different misogynous opponent: Brief Conseil (Book I, 539 octaves), Vilain Penser (Book II, 851 octaves), Trop Cuidier (Book III, 457 octaves), Lourt Entendement (Book IV, 707 octaves), and Faulx Semblant (Book V, 488 octaves). Unlike his most obvious French sources, *Le Roman de la Rose* (Jean de Meun's continuation), *Les Lamentations de Mathéolus* (the French translation by Jean Le Fèvre, c.1371-72), and *La Cité des Dames* (Christine de Pizan, 1404-05), Martin Le Franc presents his refutation of attacks on women throughout history in the form of an allegorical debate. Like Jean Brisebarre de Douai, an early fourteenth-century *trouvère* who chose a courtroom setting for a debate between Droit, the personification of law, and Mensonge, Simonie, and Faux Semblant, the legal hirelings of a venal bishop,[3] Martin Le Franc adopts an adversarial context in which opposing attorneys present arguments for or against a defendant, in this case, womankind. Such an expedient avoids the cumbersome procedure used by Jean Le Fèvre in his palinode, *Le Livre de Leësce* (c.1374), where the author laboriously cites lengthy passages of his French translation of Matheolus in order to be certain that the reader is following his refutation.[4] However, the livelier debate format entails certain drawbacks. In spite of due care on the part of the author, a direct confrontation between the opposing sides risks making the "devil's advocates" and their reasoning too attractive, thus causing readers to resist the conversional rhetoric of Franc Vouloir.

In light of the text, I would argue that Martin Le Franc weighed the liabilities of the debate model and successfully took on the challenge. First, by letting the misogynous camp have some say, he avoids the appearance of an endless paean of praise. Martin introduces *chiaroscuro* and humor in his discussion of women by letting Vilain Penser and Lourt Entendement, like the *diables* in the *Mystères,* interrupt lengthy enumerations of worthy women scholars or rulers with flagrant aberrations such as Messalina, Cleopatra, Calfurnia, and, indeed, the female pope, Joan. Unlike Christine de Pizan, who sought to present her readers with an unsullied female society in her *Cité des Dames,* Martin includes notorious women precisely because they did have an historical or literary existence and were already familiar to the intelligentsia of his time. In *La Cité des Dames,* Christine de Pizan has Lady Reason explain that the City of Ladies is one "where no one will reside except all ladies of fame and women worthy of praise, for the walls of the city will be closed to those women who lack virtue."[5] Such a stance is ethically and structurally defensible, since Christine wishes to offer flawless role models and to restore a sense of self-worth and empowerment to women who, like herself, were made to feel somehow condemned to "inhabit a female body in this world" (*City*, I.1.2). However, Martin Le Franc, seeking a universal audience but targeting his male readers in particular, could not risk his credibility by presenting an enumeration of exclusively virtuous women.

Furthermore, by allowing allegorical traducers of women such as Vilain Penser and Lourt Entendement to allege a few exceptions to each category of outstanding women, Martin could proceed to rehabilitate at least partially the character of those whom society had considered infamous for centuries. Unlike Boccaccio, who includes notorious women to create ambiguity, and Christine, who excludes them as unworthy, Martin elects to show that these women are: (1) more virtuous than they appear, (2) victimized by masculine machinations, and (3) less corrupt than men, for even if a woman has been lascivious, frivolous, or otherwise unworthy, her excesses pale in comparison with those of her far more numerous male counterparts.

Martin Le Franc applies this strategy at length to Pope Joan, but first he establishes it as a paradigm in the earlier part of his work. Thus, in Book II of *Le Champion des Dames*, Franc Vouloir vaunts women's fidelity to their husbands or lovers, even under the most difficult circumstances. He cites Penelope, Dido, Lucretia, Julia, and others as evidence of wives faithful unto death. Vilain Penser then attempts to vitiate these examples by adding two "*ad feminam*" arguments of his own: the cases of Cleopatra and Messalina. He alleges that Cleopatra was a power-hungry, lustful opportunist who married her son, had her sister killed, seduced the already-married Anthony into marrying her, and committed suicide after his death only because Octavian would not succumb to her wiles. Similarly, he impugns Messalina as a nymphomaniac who drugged her husband so she could roam all night in the brothels of Rome. These scurrilous attacks trigger the rehabilitation process we have described.

Franc Vouloir begins his defense of Cleopatra with a proverbial palliative: "Moult est sage qui ne folye" (*Champion*, II, 815). Whatever Cleopatra's errors during her life may have been, Franc Vouloir finds her manner of dying a worthy one: he argues that she committed suicide either because of sincere grief for Anthony or because of her desire to defy Octavian. If it was for the second reason, is she not as worthy of praise as Cato, who chose to die rather than honor Caesar? As for Messalina, even if her lechery were as Vilain Penser asserts, there are worse and more numerous cases of masculine perversion and excess. Franc Vouloir cites Midas, Gaius Caligula, Claudius, Nero, and Tiberius. The latter shamelessly defiled the day with his perversions, whereas Messalina hid her excesses under the cover of darkness. Messalina put her husband to sleep with drugs so she could sin, but Tiberius fell asleep himself after his exertions in the arms of two or three

lovers. Messalina had the excuse of youthful passion, whereas the geriatric lust of Tiberius was totally unseemly. But rather than prolong the argument with endless examples of male turpitude, Franc Vouloir concludes his rebuttal with the axiomatic statement that no matter how vile a woman one adduces, a worse man can be found:

> Et suis content de dire en somme
> Que tu ne trouveras jamais
> Male femme sans peieur homme.
>
> (*Champion*, II, 829)

The technique of refuting aspersions against women by showing that the pot is calling the kettle black occurs earlier, in Christine de Pizan's *Cité des Dames*, where Lady Rectitude also lists the names of Roman emperors, such as Claudius, Nero, and Tiberius, to show that men's behavior is far more shameful than that of the women they criticize (*City*, II.47.1-49.3). As we have seen, Martin Le Franc adopts both the process and the actual examples.

The poet returns to this rebuttal device in Book IV, where he applies it to other infamous women, including Pope Joan. Book IV of *Le Champion des Dames* appears to be patterned closely after Christine de Pizan's *Cité des Dames*. It consists of a listing of extraordinary women in various roles throughout history. Franc Vouloir begins by attributing, as does Christine, the development of the basic elements of human civilization to women: agriculture and language were created by Ceres, Isis, and Opis. Women have been equally illustrious in the realms of government and warfare. Franc Vouloir cites a number of Amazon queens, as well as queens of pagan and biblical antiquity, and concludes this list with Joan of Arc. He then discusses women's contributions to the arts, from Minerva to painters such as Irene and Marcia. Next, he cites women's achievements in literature and scholarship, listing numerous characters, ranging from the Nine Muses to the Queen of Sheba. At this juncture, Lourt Entendement interrupts his opponent to interject the two most embarrassing examples of aberrant female intellectuals he can muster, namely, the legal shrew Calfurnia and Pope Joan. The former was banned from Roman courts for "mooning" the judge, an act which, according to the legal legends of the Middle Ages, was the reason for the subsequent exclusion of all women from pleading in court. It is this detail which Martin Le Franc stresses in Lourt Entendement's comical character assassination of learned women:

> Diras tu de Calfurnie
> Qui son cul au juge monstra?
> Dit l'autre plein de vilenie.
> Pourquoi puis la femme n'entra
> En jugement pro ne contra?
> Ne scay s'elle avoit plaisan dis

Mais si mal sa robe escoutra
Que monstra son *de profundis*.

(*Champion*, IV, 490)

Here, Martin seems to give more license than necessary to Lourt Entendement, actually enhancing the crude humor of the gesture by his blasphemous macaronic word play. Franc Vouloir, in this instance, does not deign to honor such vulgarity with a response.

In the case of Pope Joan, however, Franc Vouloir displays all his rhetorical wares. On his part, Lourt Entendement, borrowing from the accounts of Martinus Polonus and Boccaccio, taunts Franc Vouloir with the scandal of a woman who, while disguised as a man, dared to accept the papacy, thus profaning the most sacred mysteries. Franc Vouloir, indignant, retaliates by making full use of the strategies explained earlier; namely, that Pope Joan, like Cleopatra and Messalina, possessed mitigating virtues. Furthermore, she was the victim of masculine treachery, and, finally, as scandalous as her case may have been, some male popes were even less worthy than she of the papal see.

Masculine perfidy plays a key role in the defense of Pope Joan. Like Jean Le Fèvre before him, Martin Le Franc attributes any sin in women to man's nefarious influence, a direct reversal of the stereotypical view of woman as temptress. In *Le Livre de Leësce,* referring in particular to witchcraft but also to any vice in women, Le Fèvre explains that man is the real culprit:

Se les vieilles font sorceries,
Karaudes ou maquelries
Ou choses qui vers Dieu leur nuisent,
Les hommes a ce les induisent
Et leur ennortent et conseillent
Et, pour mal faire, se traveillent
Nuit et jour pour femmes frauder.
Les hommes veulent ribauder,
Ja femme n'y fera meffait
Se moyennant homme n'est fait.

(*Leësce,* 2967-76)

Franc Parler reiterates this accusation in Book IV of *Le Champion des Dames,* using a comparison which heightens man's culpability: "Femme seroit comme lait / Blanche et nette se n'estoit homme" (*Champion,* IV, 424). As he explains, it was a male cleric who seduced Joan at an early age, forcing her at the same time to assume a male identity. Her bad habits, in all senses, were induced by masculine interference:

Sy luy dit: L'escolier ribault
Lui bailla le commencement
Jeunesse ce que de prin sault
Prent, elle tient moult longuement
Prendre il luy fist s'abillement
D'omme en sa petite jeunesse

Que par vergongne ou aultrement
Continua en sa viellesse.

(*Champion*, IV, 501)

Disregarding her alleged sexual indiscretions, Franc Vouloir praises her extraordinary merits as a scholar. As "clergesse lettrée," she was the most respected individual in the Rome of her day. To bolster Joan's reputation further, Franc Vouloir cites the numerous canonical prefaces for the Mass which she was supposed to have written (*Champion,* IV, 502). In other words, Franc Vouloir argues that, *qua* scholar, the putative Joan was far superior to her contemporaries, to say nothing of her predecessors or successors.

It is the third step of the rehabilitation process, namely, the vindication of an infamous woman by comparison with even more infamous men, that permits Martin Le Franc to, as it were, kill two birds with one stone. He was, as Piaget explains, a resolute supporter of the Council of Basle against Pope Eugenius IV (1431-47), being as well an appointee of the anti-pope Felix V.[6] Therefore, by allowing Lourt Entendement to impugn Pope Joan, Le Franc was creating a context in which he could embarrass an inveterate opponent of the conciliar movement. Franc Vouloir points out that no written records indicate that Pope Joan ever practiced simony or indulged in the other excesses of Nicholas III, the Orsini pope who ruled from 1277-80 (*Champion,* IV, 504). Neither did she purge her predecessor and indulge in the abuse of power of Boniface VIII (1294-1303). Nor did she ever gainsay the power of councils, as did the contemporaneous pope, Eugenius IV: "Qui affin que l'esglise bale / Donne et fait tant d'empeschement / Au tres sainct concile de Bale" (*Champion,* IV, 505). Finally, Franc Vouloir recalls that Pope Joan's disguise was foisted upon her and that the resulting confusion concerning her gender did not detract from her character and scholarship. Using a rhetorical commonplace of the period, he states that, in the case of male clerics, the imposture is worse, for while they dress as shepherds, they are in fact predatory beasts. Le Franc implies that this misrepresentation is a far greater scandal than having a basically worthy woman celebrate Mass. As octave 506 puts it:

La papesse, ne scay comment,
Mussa son sexe femenin.
Mais plusieurs papes vrayement
Soubz miel ont couvert le venin
Et cuer de volpe ou de monnin
Dessus peau d'aignel plus doulcette
Que ne soit le mon (*sic*) Appennin
Quant vestu est de sa moussette.

(*Champion*, IV, 506)

As the proverb states, Franc Vouloir prefers the lesser of two evils, particularly since the deception involved in the case of Pope Joan was not malicious. As in Book

II, where the scandalous behavior of emperors is contrasted with the lesser crimes of their feminine counterparts in order to put the latter in a more positive light, Martin Le Franc uses certain popes as the standard of impropriety by which to judge Pope Joan's relative blamelessness. Of course, as we indicated earlier, Le Franc, as provost of Lausanne, may well have had a political ulterior motive.

In any event, whether or not Franc Vouloir's refutation of the charges against Pope Joan was totally successful, Martin Le Franc, like Jean Le Fèvre before him, had an irrefutable final argument to prevent misogynists from reaching a false global induction; namely, that one wicked or notorious woman cannot be presented as proof that all women are corrupt. Franc Vouloir metaphorically explains:

> Doit on tout ung champ de froment
> Blasmer pour quelque herbette pire?
> Et se vous trouves a redire
> En aulcune qui a mespris,
> Esse droit et raison, Beau Sire,
> Que toutes mettes a ce pris?

> (*Champion,* IV, 622)

The author thus reveals how untenable is the attempt to create a type of gender-based guilt by association, or to seek to discredit the superior numbers of virtuous women by asserting that they all possess the vices of a few individuals.

In summation, what answers can we claim to have found to our initial question as to why Martin Le Franc would include the case of Pope Joan in his work, *Le Champion des Dames*? I would first argue that he discusses such an infamous woman because one of his major sources and predecessors, Giovanni Boccaccio, had done so with an obviously hostile intent. Furthermore, since Christine de Pizan, another of Le Franc's sources, had not refuted this particular attack on learned women in *La Cité des Dames* because of restraints imposed by propriety and her own decision to include only virtuous ladies in the pages of her literary city, Le Franc acted to correct this omission. As I have shown, the debate format which Le Franc adopts in *Le Champion des Dames* itself necessitates the inclusion of "evidence" on both sides of the question. The decision to use Vilain Penser, Lourt Entendement, and their associates as foils for Franc Vouloir made it incumbent on them to use the most embarrassing cases of infamous women known at the time. Martin was not reluctant to undertake the latters' defence for the reasons which we have explained: (1) he felt that each notorious woman had some redeeming traits, which Franc Vouloir highlights while he understates or ignores their flaws; (2) whatever vices women had, Martin alleged, men were responsible for instigating and abetting them; and (3) if a woman in a given category had serious character flaws, there were innumerable men who had the same weaknesses, but to a much greater degree. The case of Pope Joan provides an excellent synopsis of Martin Le Franc's strategy for the rehabilitation of the individuals cited by misogynists in an effort to discredit all women: after praising Pope Joan's great achievements, the poet stresses that her defects and downfall were due to the influence of men, and that her crime or scandal was insignificant in comparison to that of her male counterparts. Rather than simply excuse one woman, Le Franc indicts all men. Embroiled in the controversy surrounding the Council of Basle and active in the entourage of the anti-pope, Felix V, Martin Le Franc used his defense of Pope Joan as polemic in several senses. However, the opportunity to attack Eugenius IV was simply an ancillary benefit. By rehabilitating Joan and other "notorious" women, Le Franc undertook the creation of a truly "universal" history and vindication of womankind, in which the term "*Dames*" applies to all women, rather than to only the most virtuous ones.

APPENDIX

Le Champion des Dames, Book IV, Octaves 490-507

[L'Adversaire par truffe parle de Calfurnie et de Dame Jehanne la papesse.]

490

> Diras tu de Calfurnie
> Qui son cul au juge monstra,
> Dit l'autre plein de vilenie,
> Pourquoi puis la femme n'entra
> En jugement pro ne contra?
> Ne scay s'elle avoit plaisans dis
> Mais si mal sa robe escoutra
> Que monstra son *de profundis.*

491

> Or, se Jhesucrist te doint joye,
> Fait l'Adversaire, qui se moque,
> Franc Vouloir, tu portes bon foie,
> Or dis, je te requier ne joque,
> Fais nous icy la niquenoque
> De quelque aultre bonne clergess.
> Et se mainte as larde en broque
> Mes apres Jenne la papesse.

492

> Tu scez qu'elle sceut tant de lettres
> Que pour son sens on la crea
> Papesse et prestresse des prestres.
> O, comme bien estudia,
> O, grande louenge y a!
> Femme se dissimula homme
> Et sa nature regnia
> Pour devenir pape de Romme.

493

> O benoit Dieu, comme osa femme
> Vestir chasuble et chanter messe?

O femme outrageuse et infame!
Comment eut elle la hardiesse
De se faire pape et papesse?
Comment endura Dieu, comment,
Que femme ribaulde prestresse
Eust l'esglise en gouvernement?

494

Bien deust elle au siege sainct Pierre
Seoir se les clercs y debvoient soir.
En Allemaigne et en Angleterre
Avoit estudié main et soir
Sans qu l'on puist appercepvoir
Quelles estoient ses derrees.
De son amy ne dis je voir
Car pas ne luy furent serrees.

495

Lors le monde estoit bien nouvel,
Dire on peut qu'il ne tenoit
Sinon a la queue d'ung vel
Puis que femme le gouvernoit.
Merveille estoit que ne tournoit
Le ciel et que pour vengement
Dieu sur la terre ne venoit
Tenir son cruel jugement.

496

Mais il est tardif a pugnir
En attendant que l'on s'amende.
Et quant on ne veult revenir
A raison, combien qu'il attende,
Certes c'est force qu'il entende
A donner sa pugnicion
Et qu'a justice son droit rende
Sans plus longue remission.

497

Ainsi tousjours pas n'endura
Que l'Esglise fut abusee
De celle qui trop y dura
Car sa fraude fut encusee,
O vengence bien advisee,
La saincte papesse enfanta!
N'onques puis la putain rusee
A l'autel sainct Pierre chanta.

498

Entre le moustier sainct Clement
Et Colisee chescun vit
Le feminin enchantement.
Si fut tantost fait ung edict
Que jamais pape ne se fist
Tant eust il de science au nas
S'il ne monstroit le doit petit
Enharnechié de son harnas.

499

O dames, dames, couronnes
Vostre pape et vostre papesse
Dessus les quatre couronnes.

Elle accreut moult vostre noblesse!
Alors le Champion se dresse
Et en jectant le dextre bras
Dit: Temps est que ce parler cesse,
De ceste mal te remembras.

[Le Champion excuse Jehanne la papesse et sur ce parle d'aucuns papes.]

500

Ainsi que Liladan entroit
Lors en sa force grandement
Quant ses ennemis rencontroit,
Le Champion pareillement
Tant plus chevalereusement
Ou champ de bataille sailloit
Quant plus impetueusement
Son adversaire l'assailloit.

501

Sy luy dit: L'escolier ribault
Luy bailla le commencement.
Jeunesse ce que de prin sault
Prent, elle tient moult longuemnent.
Prendre il luy first l'abillement
D'omme en sa prime jeunesse
Que par vergogne ou autrement
Continua en sa vieillesse.

502

Or, laissons les pechez, disans
Qu'elle estoit clergesse lettree
Quant devant les plus souffisans
De Romme eust l'issue et l'entree.
Encor te peut estre monstree
Mainte preface que dicta
Bien et sainctement accoutree
Ou en la foy point n'herita.

503

En la chaiere du pescheur
A qui Dieu laissa le papat
Assist on ung glouton lescheur
Qu'on appeloit frere Juppart
Car forment pis qu'ung agrappart
Il fist en sa papalite
Contre la papaliste part
Et l'ecclesiastre unite.

504

Je n'ay pas leu en escripture
Que la papesse gouvernast
Ou par symoniaque ordure
Ou heresie machinast
Et la saincte esglise minast
En tresors, chappes et coussins
Ne que jamais tant forsennast
Comme le pape des Ursins.

505

Ou comme cil faulx palatin
Cardinal qui tant faussement

Trompa le pape Celestin
Dont puis regna crueusement.
Ou comme cil presentement
Qui affin que l'Esglise bale
Donne et fait tant d'empeschement
Au tres sainct concile de Bale.

506

La papesse, ne scay comment,
Mussa son sexe femenin,
Mais plusieurs papes vrayement
Soubz miel ont couvert le venin
Et cuer de voulpe ou de monnin
Dessous peau d'aignel plus doulcette
Que ne soit le mon[t] Appennin
Quant vestu est de sa moussette.

507

Je n'en dis plus: le remenant
Est tenebreux, obscur et noir
Comme les oulles de Dinant.
Vous scavez bien se je dy voir
Si laissons le propos manoir
Et parlons des dames jolies
Desquelles pour le grant scavoir
Les louanges ne sont faillies.

Notes

1. Giovanni Boccaccio, *Concerning Famous Women,* trans. Guido A. Guarino (New Brunswick, NJ: Rutgers University Press, 1963): xxxvii-xxxviii. Subsequent references to this work are made within parentheses in the text. In *De Claris Mulieribus* (c.1355-59) Boccaccio was the first medieval author to present a lengthy series of women's "biographies." Geoffrey Chaucer, in *The Legend of Good Women* (c.1385-86), ostensibly sought to stress feminine steadfastness and masculine treachery, presenting Cleopatra as a noble queen. In both cases, the inclusion of notorious women was disingenuous, despite the authors' disclaimers to the contrary, and subverted rather than supported women's cause.

2. Martin Le Franc, *Le Champion des Dames* (Lyons: Printer of The *"Complainte de l'âme damnée,"* c.1488). This edition, found in the Newberry Library, Chicago, Illinois, is attributed also to the fifteenth-century printer Guillaume Le Roy. In addition, I have used the MS. Paris Bibliothèque de l'Arsenal, n° 3121, to emend and complete the incunabulum text. It is important to note that *Le Champion des Dames,* despite its historical significance and poetic interest, has never been presented in a modern edition in its entirety. Book I and part of Book II were edited by Arthur Piaget and published posthumously in 1968 (Lausanne: Librairie Payot). Subsequently, under the guidance of Harry Williams of Florida State University, two American scholars published other parts of this massive work: Don Arthur Fischer prepared an edition of Book III as his doctoral dissertation, "Edition and Study of Martin Le Franc's *Le Champion des Dames*" (Tallahassee, 1981), and J. Carroll Brooks edited the last fifty-nine octaves of Book V as part of his dissertation, "La Filiation des manuscrits du *Champion des Dames* de Martin Le Franc" (Tallahassee, 1976). Book IV, in which Le Franc undertakes a defense of talented women even more comprehensive than that of Christine de Pizan in *La Cité des Dames,* has been hitherto almost untouched, with only odd verses or octaves cited by Piaget, Gaston Paris, and even Pierre Bayle, who was delighted to include the scandal of Pope Joan in his *Dictionnaire historique et critique,* article on "Franc, Martin" (Geneva: Slatkine Reprints, 1969, repr. Paris ed. 1820-1824): 538-39. I include the full excerpt dealing with Pope Joan in the Appendix of this article as a prelude to an edition and translation of all of Book IV. Because there is no definitive edition with cumulative numbering of verses, I have chosen to identify citations with the Book number in Roman numerals and the octave/s with cardinal numbers, rather than to provide verse numbers. With regard to the historical controversy concerning the apocryphal female pope and other literary depictions of her, see J. J. I. Von Döllinger, *Fables Respecting the Popes in the Middle Ages,* trans. Alfred Plummer (New York: Dodd & Mead, 1872), and Rosemary and Darroll Pardoe, *The Female Pope: The Mystery of Pope Joan* (Wellingborough, England: The Aquarian Press, 1988).

3. See Steven M. Taylor, "The Virtues and Vices in Court: A Fourteenth-Century French *Psychomachia,*" *Ball State Forum* 22/1 (Winter 1981): 3-8.

4. Jean Le Fèvre, *Les Lamentations de Matheolus et Le Livre de Leësce,* ed. A.-G. Van Hamel, 2 vols. (Paris: Emile Bouillon, 1892, 1905).

5. Christine de Pizan, *The Book of the City of Ladies,* trans. Earl Jeffrey Richards (New York: Persea Books, 1982): 11.

6. Arthur Piaget, *Martin Le Franc, prévot de Lausanne* (Lausanne: Librairie F. Payot, 1888): 217-31.

Peter Stanford (essay date 1998)

SOURCE: Stanford, Peter. "Chapter Two." In *The Legend of Pope Joan: In Search of the Truth,* pp. 16-34. New York: Henry Holt and Company, 1998.

[In the following essay, Stanford asserts that Pope Joan was not, as has been frequently alleged by the Catholic church, the creation of post-Reformation Protestant forgers.]

'When could they say, till now, that talked of Rome,
That her wide walls encompassed but one man?
Now is it Rome indeed and room enough,
When there is in it but one only man.'

William Shakespeare, *Julius Caesar*

I quickly discovered that, whatever gloss Father Boyle put on it, the standard response of the Catholic church to talk of Pope Joan has been to damn it as a Protestant forgery. The scenario is simple. After the Reformation, dedicated followers of Luther, Calvin and Henry VIII tampered with ancient manuscripts and inserted fictitious references to a woman pope so as to make the papacy look foolish and hence belittle its claim to universal, God-given authority. These references were often so cunningly disguised that subsequent generations of readers could not tell the original from the interpolations and hence assumed that for much of the Middle Ages, Joan's existence was a truth universally acknowledged.

The She-Pope's story is recorded by some 500 chroniclers[1] of the papacy and matters Catholic, writing from early medieval times until the end of the seventeenth century. Among the phalanx of authors who testify unambiguously to her existence are papal servants, several bishops and some of the most distinguished and respected medieval chroniclers, writers whose accounts are the bedrock of current historical and church orthodoxy about their period. Yet in the matter of Joan, it is suggested that those manuscripts which date back to before the Reformation were subsequently altered.

At first glance, this official version is plausible. Joan's literary heyday—between 1200 and 1600—belongs largely to the age before the mass production of books. What texts do still exist are often in later versions, opening the door to the possibility that the originals may have been amended to include references to Joan. If my investigation was not to be stillborn, my time in the library would have to show that this explanation did not stand up to scrutiny.

The first printed texts appeared in the middle of the fifteenth century with Johann Gutenberg of Mainz, credited as the earliest European to use movable type, closely followed by William Caxton. Before that—and indeed with all but a handful of the most popular books for some 200 years afterwards—texts were handwritten. Each new copy had to be transcribed word for word on to parchment. In the early medieval period—up to 1200—the scribes were mostly monks and nuns, and more often male religious than female. They were the only group with both the time to spend laboriously producing, illuminating and illustrating manuscripts, and the learning—literacy remained the domain of a privileged few—to master the complexities of the task.

The great monasteries had libraries that grew to become treasure houses of texts. Monks from smaller foundations would visit, write out a new version of one of the books they found in the library and travel back with the result of their labours to their own house. Then others would visit them for the same purpose, passing the text down a chain. It was a torturously slow process, made slightly less taxing by having its own language of abbreviations. 'PP', for example, stood for pope.

However, mistakes in transcription would inevitably creep in. Often, too, there was the temptation to add interpolations to the original as a means of showing superior learning or adapting it to local circumstances. In that way a text could be altered over the years as amended copies were made of already amended copies of an unseen—and too often lost, given the turbulence of the times—original.

It is not surprising that in the pre-1200 period there was not a great range of texts. Most were on religious and ecclesiastical themes: versions of the Bible, lives of pontiffs and emperors, accounts of papal or ecclesiastical happenings, hagiographies of venerable saints who sent the devil packing.

However, in the post-1200 era, the monopoly of the monasteries on books was broken, allowing a greater experimentation with formats, subjects and styles. A new generation of professional scribes and artists grew up in towns, many of them educated by monks and some of them graduates of the newly-founded ecclesiastical universities of Paris, Bologna and Oxford. These lay craftsmen were the first flourishing of the book trade. Their customers were the university libraries, whose demand for illustrated books could not be satisfied by the monasteries. Increasingly, too, the rich and powerful wanted manuscripts to celebrate their own families and achievements. 'Books of Hours' were among the most popular manifestations of this trade, collections of prayers and readings handwritten to the orders of a particular nobleman or his lady.

The greater part of these early manuscripts and books, however, is composed of ecclesiastical chronicles, written by monks and clerics, circulated and copied many times over. Most monasteries where writing was undertaken would keep a chronicle of local events, but the bigger institutions specialised in overviews of church history.

For the time when Joan is said to have held the papal throne, and for almost four hundred years afterwards, these vast, all-embracing accounts are historians' principal source of insight. This was after all the Dark Ages, so named because of the lack of information about what happened. Hovering indistinct but not undetected in the gloom of this shadowy landscape is the figure of Pope Joan.

If Pope Joan can be counted as having an early champion, a biographer in today's terms, it was the Dominican Martin Polonus—or Martin of Poland as Father

Boyle had referred to him. Any attempt to trace a kind of family tree back through the various versions of her life inevitably ends up at him. Many subsequent writers reproduce his details and phrases verbatim.

Martin and Joan were not contemporaries. His chronicle first appeared in 1265, almost 400 years after the dates he gave for her reign. It was as if a current-day biographer were writing about the reign of Elizabeth I or the achievements of Sir Walter Raleigh.

Martin was a senior churchman at a time when the papacy was at the height of its powers and much of the turmoil, gloom and insecurity that characterised the Dark Ages had lifted. His writings celebrated that church hegemony. He was one of the most esteemed chroniclers of an age of outstanding scribes, with a reputation for seriousness and scholarship. His writings have endured because, unlike his rivals, he seldom fell victim to embroidering fanciful notions on to the facts that he was reporting.

Born in Troppeau, Poland, in the early years of the thirteenth century, he joined the Dominican order as a young man and was sent to Rome, where he rose steadily through the ranks, reaching the exalted post of papal chaplain under Clement IV (1265-8). His legal skills were well used in the Church's already burgeoning bureaucracy, but his passion was history and so he took up the popular medieval cleric's pastime of compiling chronicles.

Given the favour he enjoyed under several popes, and his access to all papal documents, his writings have come to be regarded by later generations as the quasi-official line of the Vatican. In his own time, too, they attracted admiration. Most of the major monastic libraries would have kept a copy of his chronicles. The first *Chronicon Pontificum et Imperatum* ended in 1265. He subsequently amended this detailed and by all accounts dispassionate account of popes and emperors to extend its reach until 1277.

Soon afterwards, he was named Archbishop of Gneisen in Poland by Pope Nicholas III (1277-80). It was a curious appointment since Martin Polonus had already reached the ripe old age—by the standards of his contemporaries—of seventy. Perhaps it was homesickness that made him accept, or just obedience to the pope. On the long journey to his new diocese, he took ill and died in Bologna, in central Italy.

His *Chronicon Pontificum et Imperatum,* however, outlived him. In both the first and the updated versions, popes are listed on the left side of the page, with emperors on the right. The originals of both editions of the chronicle are now lost, but a fourteenth-century copy, held in Berlin's Staatsbibliothek, is thought to be the oldest still in existence[2]. It tells the following story after an account of the death of Pope Leo IV in 855:

> After the aforesaid Leo, John, an Englishman by descent, who came from Mainz, held the see two years, five months and four days, and the pontificate was vacant one month. He died at Rome. He, it is asserted, was a woman. And having been in youth taken by her lover to Athens in man's clothes, she made such progress in various sciences that there was nobody equal to her. So that afterwards lecturing on the Trivium at Rome she had great masters for her disciples and hearers. And for as much as she was in great esteem in the city, both for her life and her learning, she was unanimously elected pope. But when pope she became pregnant by the person with whom she was intimate. But not knowing the time of her delivery, while going from Saint Peter's to the Lateran, taken in labour, she brought forth a child between the Colosseum and Saint Clement's Church. And afterwards dying, she was, it is said, buried in that place. And because the Lord Pope always turns aside from that way, there are some who are fully persuaded that it is done in detestation of the fact. Nor is she put in the Catalogue of the Holy Popes, as well on account of her female sex as on account of the foul nature of the transaction.

Alongside the account quoted above, the Berlin manuscript contains an additional page. It is of a later date than the rest of the text and makes no attempt to integrate itself. The addenda retells the same story but embellishes it with new and shocking details: that Joan's lover was a secretary-deacon, that the street where she was disgraced was forthwith known as the 'Vicus Papissa'—Georgina Masson's description of the thoroughfare outside the window of my Roman flat—and that she was not killed after her deception was revealed but rather deposed and banished to a convent where she lived in penance to see her son become Bishop of Ostia, a coastal town at the mouth of the Tiber near Rome.

This effort at embroidering on the 'facts' as Martin Polonus recorded them was the first of many down the ages that added details to the skeleton of the story, names, places, emotions, motivations. It was Martin Polonus's basic text, however, that subsequently became the standard by which the story of Pope Joan was judged true or false. Supporters of the She-Pope tried to prove its authenticity, explaining away the gaps in some surviving versions of it as the work of Catholic librarians anxious to cover up an embarrassing tale, while detractors argued that talk of a female pontiff in drag had been added later by Protestants who tampered with originals held in various libraries around Europe in a concerted attempt to discredit the papacy. It brings to mind a picture of libraries as the battleground of the Reformation.

This 'official' version of history which rejects Joan's pontificate as a Protestant plot depends on the idea that Martin Polonus's was the first chronicle to mention it.

This 'school' has channelled most of its energy into proving that all remaining early copies of the manuscript have been tampered with. Yet, as my trawl through the various mentions of Joan on the card index was showing, Martin Polonus was not the first to talk of the She-Pope. He can certainly claim to have furnished the most detail, but the family tree has deeper roots.

The German historian, Frederick Spanheim, a Protestant professor of philosophy at the University of Leyden at the end of the seventeenth century, tracked down some 500 references to Joan in manuscripts many of which have subsequently been lost. Given his denominational background and the climate of the times, Spanheim may well have taken pleasure in the discomfiture his study caused the Vatican. His *de Papa Foemina,* first published in 1691 in Latin, was so much in demand in French translation as *Histoire de la Papesse Jeanne* that there were three separate reprintings before 1736.[3]

Yet however popular his writings, and however much they pandered to anti-papal sentiments, they cannot be dismissed as lightweight; his scholarship was careful and precise, with lists showing every reference had been double-checked. Spanheim ascribed the first recorded references to Joan to Anastasius, the papal librarian and her contemporary, and to a monk called Rudulphus, five years later. Neither original source still exists and both have to be discounted today through lack of corroboration. Some sceptics have suggested that Rudulphus did not live until the eleventh century,[4] though it could be that Spanheim was referring to a now lost document from Rudulphius of Fulda.

Spanheim's quotes from Anastasius are likewise open to question, since they cannot now be traced back to the originals that he examined. Anastasius was papal librarian in the ninth century, with many of the same responsibilities as Father Boyle. He is a key figure in the riddle of Pope Joan, principally because it was part of his official responsibilities to update the Church's own, official *Liber Pontificalis*—or *Book of Popes*—with details of contemporary incumbents in the latter part of the ninth century. The various versions of this text are the principal and indeed often the only source of information for historians of the papacy in the Dark Ages.

The earliest version of Anastasius's chronicle that survives today is a 1602 edition, published in Mainz after the Reformation. It contains references to Joan's story but at that time her tale was well enough known from other sources to make forgery or interpolation on the ninth-century original a possibility.

Though Spanheim has him down as endorsing the history of the She-Pope, another possibility is that Anastasius was the historian responsible for the 400-year gap between Joan's life and Martin of Poland's account. For if he had decided—or been ordered—to remove all trace of her deception from the *Liber Pontificalis,* then the centuries of official silence are more easily understood. The details of Joan's reign would have been expunged from the authorised version and could live on only in the oral tradition and unofficial texts.

This theory fits better with the Anastasius known to later historians.[5] He was a decidedly unsavoury character who tried in 855—the year, according to Martin of Poland's record, when Joan died—to seize the papal throne. Though he had the backing of the Emperor Louis II, grandson of Charlemagne, Anastasius was blocked by a popular revolt in Rome in favour of Benedict III. He was neither well liked nor well respected. His reputation was as a schemer and hedonist, with little time for piety and less still for the moral constraints of Christianity.

With Benedict on Saint Peter's throne, Anastasius was excommunicated but later rehabilitated by Benedict's successor, Nicholas I (858-67) and subsequently put in charge of the papal library by Hadrian II (867-72). There he is said to have shown a talent for rewriting history to his own and his master's advantage. As J. N. D. Kelly comments in his *Oxford Dictionary of Popes,*[6] Anastasius 'did not hesitate to get rid of documents incriminating himself'.

Did he also delete any mention of Joan from the papal chronicle? Out of loyalty to the popes who rehabilitated him he might have felt he had no choice. The precedents for such lack of scruple among more godly figures than Anastasius are strong. His contemporary and another still studied chronicler, Hincmar, Archbishop of Rheims (845-82), frequently suppressed information damaging to the Church in his letters and other writings. Even the theologian and monk Alcuin of York, right-hand man to Charlemagne, was not above being economical with the truth. In one of his letters he owns up to destroying a report on Pope Leo III (795-816), detailing his adultery and his corrupt administration of church offices.[7]

And if Anastasius did delete Joan on orders from above, then perhaps he recorded this act of omission in a diary or a letter and it is to that that Spanheim referred. But with Anastasius there is surely another factor to be taken into account—his enormous sense of grudge and disappointment. The nephew of Arsenius, an immensely powerful figure in Rome who purchased for himself the title of Bishop of Orte, Anastasius came to regard the papacy as his birthright, the appropriate setting for his undoubted intelligence and good connections. His failure to hold the papal throne for more than three days and his immediate and subsequent consignment to the ranks of 'anti-pope' must have rankled, particularly compared with the success of an upstart foreigner from Mainz who turned out to be a woman. There is no evidence for this, but the possibility that such a crucial and malevolent figure corrupted the records of the papacy in the centuries after Joan's death to make her disappear cannot be discounted.

Seeing Anastasius as central to the riddle of Pope Joan, some later writers have presented him as her sworn enemy, others as the father of her misbegotten child. Noting that Joan and Anastasius shared a knowledge of Greek, historian Joan Morris has speculated rather unconvincingly that he may have been her lover: 'Anastasius fits the picture perfectly. He was a few years older than Joan, he was of a Germanic family, so that he may well have studied at Fulda for a while'.[8]

Morris's reference to Fulda raises an important question about Pope Joan's origins. Martin Polonus had already cleared up any confusion in my mind as to whether Joan came from England or Germany. She was, he wrote 'of English' descent, but came from Mainz in Germany. Along with Inghilhem and Fulda, Mainz was one of the principal centres of Christianity in Germany in the Dark Ages and a base for English missionaries who came in the eighth and ninth centuries to bring the word of God to the pagan people of this region. In the connection with the English missionaries lay, I was sure, the possibility of an explanation for the description of Joan as 'of English descent'. It simply needed further investigation.

But another confusion had now appeared: between Mainz, mentioned by Martin Polonus as Joan's birthplace, and Fulda, the town most associated with her by the historians who have subsequently championed her cause. The two are less than 100 miles apart—though in the ninth century this would have counted as some distance—and were closely linked, with Inghilhem, as the cultural centres of Charlemagne's empire.

Each of the three had its distinct but inter-connected role, as can be seen in the life of Saint Boniface, known to this day as the 'Apostle of the Germans' who in the eighth century led the English efforts to convert the Germans. At Inghilhem he would visit the palace of Charlemagne, while Mainz was Boniface's own administrative centre, where he chose to establish his cathedral. He was later appointed Archbishop of Mainz by the Pope. At Fulda, by contrast, he founded a monastery and would retreat there for periods of prayer, reflection and study. The library at Fulda's monastery was one of the most celebrated in Europe and the town had a reputation as a centre of scholarship across the continent. After Boniface's death, the ongoing link between Fulda and Mainz was reinforced with the head of the monastery also serving as Archbishop of Mainz. Hrabanus Mauras in the ninth century went from one

post to the second, while Rabanus, in the tenth century, held both simultaneously.

The young Joan, according to both Martin Polonus and many of the chroniclers quoted by Spanheim, was an outstandingly bright child. Fulda, with its books and air of scholarship, would have acted as a magnet to her and her parents who, by all accounts, sought to encourage her to exercise her mind. Though born in Mainz, Joan would have visited Fulda, spent time there in its rarified atmosphere, though once she reached the age of twelve the doors of its monastery and any further access to education would have closed on her as a woman.

If the *Liber Pontificalis* omitted Joan, others between 855 and Martin of Poland 410 years later dared to break the silence. Foremost among them was the theologian Marianus Scotus who had close links with both Fulda and Mainz. An Irish monk with a taste for severe hardship characteristic of the times, he lived between 1028 and 1082. As a twenty-four-year-old he entered a monastery in Ireland—then renowned for its ascetic Christian scholarship and learning, rather than the often unthinking and showy piety with which it is sometimes popularly associated today. Like many Irish monks of the period, he later travelled to Germany as a missionary with the aim of converting the pagan peoples. His chosen method of evangelisation was to retire to an abbey cell, first at Fulda and later at Mainz, where he was walled in and lived as a recluse. He converted by example and by the power of his prayers.

Marianus gives the impression in his writings that Joan's story was still remembered in Fulda and Mainz. *Historiographi,* his chronicle, which is fiercely loyal to the papacy in the face of the claims of its secular detractors, tells of the year 854: 'Leo the Pope died in the kalends of August. After him succeeded Joan the woman who sat two years, five months and four days.'[9]

The duration he quotes is identical to that later mentioned by Martin Polonus. So if Martin Polonus's credibility can be brought into question by the Catholic authorities, then Marianus Scotus may likewise be sidelined. The earliest version of his work still in existence to mention Joan comes from 1559, allowing plenty of time either for forgers or for a more measured rewrite in the light of versions of Martin of Poland's chronicle then circulating. Furthermore, since an earlier edition of Marianus Scotus, held in the British Museum, contains no reference to Joan, his worth as a witness for the defence of the She-Pope is questionable.

The brevity of Marianus Scotus's remarks on Joan have also led many doubters to suspect a trick, but it should be borne in mind that these chroniclers would not have repeated the story with any relish. It was, they imply and Martin Polonus states, a black mark in the history of the papacy, one which should be acknowledged briskly and honestly rather than covered up.

Marianus Scotus did not mention Joan having a child. The first reference to that came in the chronicle of Sigebert, a Benedictine monk from the Abbey of Gembloux in Belgium. A contemporary of Marianus, he outlived him by many years and Sigebert's list of popes continues through to 1112 when he died. Indeed, given that Sigebert spent part of his life at Metz—close to Mainz—he may well have encountered Marianus, if only through a wall.

Deemed by the medievalist Joseph Strayer 'one of the most prolific, multi-faceted and important authors of the eleventh century',[10] Sigebert headed an abbey with a reputation for scholarship and a library of international importance. He may have been consulting some texts now lost but then available in that library when he wrote in his *Chronographia* of Pope John: 'It is rumoured that this John was a woman and that only a single person knew about it who was her lover, and caused her to become pregnant and she gave birth to a child whilst pope, for which reason she is not counted among the popes and is not given a number.' This account, however, is not in all the early editions of Sigebert's writings,[11] and where it is, it is often in the margin. It cannot therefore be taken as an unimpeachable source.

In a sixteenth-century edition, Sigebert records a prophetess of Moguntia, another name for Mainz, who succeeded in persuading her archbishop to ordain her to the priesthood. This may or may not be an alternative reference to Joan, though the lack of disguise of her womanhood could rule this out. Equally—if one bears in mind the distorting effect of transferring oral history down the generations into written testaments—it may be that the story of this earlier 'prophetess' was transformed into the tale of Pope Joan.

Sigebert casts one other beam of light—albeit through a glass darkly—on the She-Pope with a reference to the Bishop of Ostia. Martin Polonus later was to claim that Joan's son went on to be Bishop of Ostia. Sigebert reports that it was a particular privilege of the bishops of Ostia—from the third century until an unspecified date—to crown popes. In recounting the tale of a pope many of his contemporaries would have preferred to forget, Martin Polonus's mention of the see of Ostia therefore takes on a special significance. It is rather like mentioning a friend's name to get yourself an introduction to a powerful man or woman. The friend's name acts as a sign that you are bona fide. The mention of Ostia symbolically gives added weight to accounts of Pope Joan.

Sigebert was the first of a run of chroniclers, some of them very considerable figures, who tell of Pope Joan. All come one after the other in quick succession and all

were writing before Martin Polonus. The connections between them and the degree to which one influenced the other is impossible to judge at so great a distance and with so little supporting material. Yet while questions can be raised about the dating of various of the editions that contain these chroniclers' records, overall their effect is to reduce the time slip between the dates given for Pope Joan and Martin Polonus's first mention of her.

Otto of Freising was one of the most important of this group, a man of his time with interests in both the secular and ecclesiastical domains. He has been described as 'the greatest medieval historical thinker'.[12] Grandson of the Holy Roman Emperor Henry IV (1050-1106) and a Crusader in the army of his half-brother Conrad in 1147, Otto was also a Cistercian monk, a scholar and Bishop of Freising in Germany until his death in 1158. His treatise *The History of Two Cities* mentions 'Pope John VII, a woman', but puts her back at the start of the eighth century. The original version of this work—completed, it is thought, between 1143 and 1146—has been lost, and surviving copies containing mentions of Joan were completed after the time of Martin Polonus.[13]

Godfrey of Viterbo, an Italian chronicler, in his *Pantheon* of 1191 maintains the dominant view on dates—between Leo IV and Benedict III—but urges that 'the popess Joan is not counted' on account of her decemption. His book is dedicated to Pope Urban III (1185-7) whom he served as chaplain and secretary. It may have been taboo to praise Joan in such company, but Godfrey's example would suggest it was not taboo to mention her. Again, though, there are no originals of Godfrey's chronicle.[14]

Gervase of Tilbury, an English writer who spent much of his life in France, adds another element to the picture, building up to the narrative presented by Martin Polonus. In his *Otiis Imperialibus* of 1211—of which an original copy is available—Gervase states under his entry for the year 849: 'John the English, Pope, was a woman and gave birth between the Colosseum and Saint Clement.'[15]

Sigebert's reference to a child is now fleshed out, though some opponents of the story of the She-Pope have raised question marks over the veracity of Gervase's observations. With the next figure in this chain of information, however, there can be no doubting historical accuracy. The French Dominican Jean de Mailly wrote his *Chronica universalis* in 1225. Original copies survive with the following entry for 1099:

> It is known of a certain pope, or rather popess who was female. She pretended to be a man. By her intellect she became a curial secretary, then a cardinal and went on to become pope. One day, while she was getting off her

horse, she gave birth to a child. Immediately the Roman justices tied the feet to the tail of the horse, but meanwhile the people stoned her for half a league. At the point where she died and was buried, it was written: *Petre, Pater Patrum, Papisse Prodito Partum* (O Peter, father of fathers, betray the child-bearing of the woman pope).[16]

The Roman historian Cesare D'Onofrio believes that it was de Mailly who created the story of Joan and who was later copied—though he moved the dates—by Martin Polonus.[17] De Mailly lived in Metz near the German border with France and is principally remembered as a hagiographer of saints. He was largely responsible, too, for the *Chronica Universalis Mettensis* of 1250 which repeats word for word his earlier account of Joan.[18]

In this latter chronicle, Joan's papacy is again put at 1099, but explained away against the more conventional record by stating that Paschal II, who according to the official roll of honour ascended to the papal throne in that year, did not actually begin his reign until 1106, leaving seven years for Joan. If Martin Polonus knew of de Mailly's writings—and there is no evidence that he did, de Mailly being a comparatively minor scribe—he evidently decided that he had most of the details regarding timing and length of service wrong.

The French Dominican Stephen de Bourbon acknowledged de Mailly as the source for his *De diversis materiis praedicabilibus,* written shortly before his death in 1261. De Bourbon moves the date forward a year and expresses his outrage.

> But an occurrence of wonderful audacity or rather insanity happened around 1100, as is related in chronicles. A certain woman, learned and well-versed in the notary's art, assuming male clothing and pretending to be a man, came to Rome. Through her diligence as well as her learning in letters, she was appointed as a curial secretary. Afterwards, under the devil's direction, she was made a cardinal and finally pope. Having become pregnant she gave birth while mounting (a horse). But when Roman justice was informed of it, she was dragged outside the city, bound by her feet to the hooves of a horse, and for half a league she was stoned by people. And where she died, there she was buried, and upon a stone placed above her, this line was written: *Parce, Pater Patrum, Papisse Prodere Partum* (Forbear, father of fathers, to betray the child-bearing of the female pope). Behold how such rash presumptiousness leads to so vile an end.[19]

Though he claimed de Mailly as his source, de Bourbon was already changing details—most notably the tombstone inscription—either through the shortcomings of his copying or for some grander design now lost. This account is notable, too, in that it explicitly links Joan to the devil for the first time. In the fearful, introspective and image-laden world of medieval Christianity, Satan was an omnipresent figure, looming larger even than

God. All who offended the Church in any way—be they pagans who resisted attempts to convert them, Jews who bankrolled Christian expansionism and then demanded their money back, Moslems who invaded Spain, Knights Templar who grew too independent or Cathars and Waldensians who objected to the worldly goods of Rome—were damned as cohorts of the devil, demonised and cast out into darkness.[20]

The devil crops up again in the account of Joan, dated 1261, by an anonymous Dominican of Erfurt, near to Joan's alleged birthplace in Germany. Returning the story of the She-Pope to the Dark Ages, the writer of *Chronica Minor* gives a new slant on the inscription mentioned by de Mailly and de Bourbon.

> There was another false pope, whose name and year are unknown. For she was a woman, as is acknowledged by the Romans, and of refined appearance, great learning and hypocritically of high conduct. She disguised herself in the clothes of a man, and eventually was elected to the papacy. While pope, she became pregnant, and when she was carrying, a demon openly published the fact to all in the public court by crying this verse to the pope: *Papa, Pater Patrum, Papisse Pandito Partum* (O Pope, father of fathers, disclose the child-bearing of the woman pope).[21]

It is an odd turn-about for the story, since the demon is not in league with Joan and she appears to be its enemy. However, the account does demonstrate that the phrase beginning *Papa, Pater Patrum* was a minor riddle within the wider riddle of Joan's existence. A final twist was given by another German chronicle—the *Flores Temporum*—written by an anonymous author or authors around 1290. This came after Martin Polonus's first chronicle in 1265 and copied his basic narrative, but inserted an episode with a woman possessed by the devil.

> She (Pope Joan) was made pregnant . . . At this time a demoniac was questioned on oath as to the time the demon would depart. The devil responded in verse: *Papa, Pater Patrum, Pandito Partum. Et tibi tunc edam, de corpore quando recedam* (O Pope, father of fathers, disclose the child-bearing of the woman pope. And then I will make known to you the time I will depart from the body).[22]

Again the story was changing shape, fitting more easily into the existing fears and conventions of the devil-obsessed medieval period. But behind such tampering, the riddle of Joan had clearly developed a fascination. The Dominicans—as Father Boyle had already suggested, and as revealed by this run-through of the main figures in the literary drama taken from the library shelves—played a crucial part in promoting the tale.

Though hedged with question marks over provenance—and confused by the existence only of later editions of earlier works which cannot therefore be verified against the Protestant forgers so demonised by a later generation of official Catholic scholars—there is enough manuscript evidence from all over Europe and from a variety of otherwise respected sources to suggest that Joan was more than a whim of the Dominican Martin Polonus. He may have given her story the stamp of authenticity and authority, but others, no less venerable, had written of her earlier.

While the Vatican Library contained manuscripts which sketched the outline of Joan's story, it was nearer to home that I found conclusive proof that she was not, as has constantly been alleged, the creation of post-Reformation Protestant forgers. The standard contention of the Church down the ages that the She-Pope had been invented and inserted into old history books by zealots anxious to do down the Church of Rome can conclusively be shown to be bunkum.

There are a handful of libraries around the world that stand head and shoulders above the rest. The Vatican is one. The British Museum Library is another. Paris's Bibliothèque Nationale is a third. One step down are the great collections. Among their number is Oxford's Bodleian Library. Its medieval manuscripts can be counted in tens of thousands—not hundreds of thousands as is the case with Father Boyle's library—but among its collection is a rare copy of Martin Polonus's chronicle.

The Duke Humfrey Library is on the second floor of the Old Bodleian and has been there since 1488, when it was established in memory of Duke Humfrey of Gloucester, the younger brother of Henry V and a Renaissance man who handed over his collection of books to the newly-founded School of Divinity at the university. A creaking wooden staircase leads up to the enquiries desk where two ancient manuscripts—as arranged in advance by post—were waiting. My real interest was Martin Polonus's *Chronicon Summorum Pontificum et Imperatorum Romanorum,* known to the Bodleian simply as Manuscript 452. But a helpful librarian had directed me to another text on Pope Joan held at the Bodleian, a seventeenth-century French work.

I was issued with a foam reading mat—two triangles lying on a rectangle so you don't strain the spines of these venerable old manuscripts—and directed to the seating area. Scholars bent over their manuscripts in the prayerful silence of medieval monks. I found a place under an extraordinary portrait of a Bishop of Lincoln. He appeared every inch a woman down to his pursed lips. But perhaps my quest for Pope Joan was beginning to make me to look askance at everyone in ecclesiastical garb.

Since my French is marginally better than my shaky Latin, I opted for the younger of the two volumes first.[23] Written by hand in the second half of the seventeenth

century, it rehearses the usual account of Pope Joan and then stands up and knocks down arguments for and against. The library label announced that the manuscript was 'very neatly written'—which I assumed to mean easy to decipher. As I quickly found out, you can be neat without being clear. The brown ink had seeped through the thin parchment and marked the next page, so the echo of already-read words disguised their successors.

Having for three-quarters of the text reviewed in a brusque sort of way the various writers who had chronicled Joan, the anonymous author suddenly revealed his or her hand and returned to the damning line first taken in the introduction on this 'inept and malicious fable'. Quite how so many documentary sources could be dismissed so lightly the writer never bothered to address. This was polemics, and legitimate doubts were swept aside with confident talk of a Protestant plot and of the wantonness of women.

With the main business of reducing Joan to a fairy-story thereby concluded, the last quarter of this book consisted of an index, mainly of writers already known to me, who had mentioned the She-Pope in their outpourings but also, strangely, of some, plucked at random from the annals of history, who should have. If the story had been true, the argument went, then the following might have been expected to mention her . . . Since they did not, she could not have existed, two negatives making a positive.

The high rhetoric of the whole piece was its most revealing feature. Evidently Joan had been a subject of fevered debate in the seventeenth century between clerics—given the sermon-like feel of the text, my instinct was that its author was a man or woman of the cloth—and those who would damn the Church.

The Bodleian cannot be specific about the origin of its copy of Martin Polonus.[24] It is believed to be English and was given to the library by the dean and canons of Windsor in 1612. However, it can be clear on the date—fourteenth century, before the Reformation. I had imagined that establishing the vintage of ancient books, rather like finding out if the Turin Shroud is Christ's burial wrap, was done by carbon-dating techniques. The librarians at Duke Humfrey greeted my assumption with polite mirth. Why bother with gadgets when their own expertise was sufficient? Between them they could spot every style of script and illustration and date it to within a couple of decades. After all, they pointed out, you would not mistake a Degas for a Hockney, or a letter written by your grandparents at the start of this century for one written today.

So with the Martin Polonus manuscript, they would start with the date of the final entry—the last pontiff mentioned is John XXII who in 1316 became the second of the Avignon popes—and work forward from that point in time. The style of the script—high Gothic, with arches, pointed minims and adornments—is as distinctive to the trained eye as the Gothic façade of Chartres Cathedral is to an architectural historian. The decorated letters, at the start of each section, give further clues. Their colouring and shape have their own chronology as in the parallel world of art history.

If, then, as the Bodleian has established, the references to Joan in Martin Polonus are from the fourteenth century, and not later additions in the margins or on a fly-sheet, then the allegation that Protestant forgers were responsible for the story of Joan can be conclusively proved false.

Inside a worm-eaten leather binding attached to a wooden backing were the sheets of parchment. Early pages began with coloured capitals written in a big flowing hand. Later a modest letter would start the litany of popes on the left-hand page, and a similarly discreet flourish the emperors on the right. The hand was small and scrawling with grand swirls, the ink after all these years a pale brown.

On folio 31 was John VIII, nestling in his/her usual place between Leo IV and Benedict III. It took a few minutes to get used to the handwriting. The first three or four words were a struggle, but then they came more easily. Like getting the hang of reading music, suddenly your eye is in and you are tripping along. *Joannes* 8. *Cognomento Anglicis natione Maguntinus* (John VII, known as the English, born in Moguntia). Before moving on to the version quoted earlier from the Berlin copy, this edition of Polonus told that John VIII was the first since Saint Ambrose to write so many prefaces to masses. A fourth-century bishop of Milan, Ambrose was a great preacher and hymn-writer. The compliment to John/Joan was a significant one but was followed by an explanation that, since John had been a woman, these prefaces were no longer used. So there it was in the text, well before the Reformation and its allegedly cunning raids on libraries.

The strangest touch was a note in the margin—scribbled in black in a different hand with a large arrow at some later date by an astonished reader—*ffemina fuit pp.* In the shorthand language of medieval manuscripts, double 'F' signifies a capital and for 'pp' read *'papa'*. So 'the Pope was a Woman'. Perhaps it was a would-be Protestant forger, surprised to find Joan's femininity already in the text, but making doubly sure that no one missed this damning incident in the history of the papacy. Or was it a seminarian, poring over the manuscript in all seriousness as part of his studies when he came upon this remarkable reference. He had been as taken aback as I was when I discovered her on my Roman holiday. Unable to contain himself, but forbidden in the semi-

nary library to speak, he had scribbled a note in the margin and passed it to his friend sitting alongside.

The main text states that this John VIII could not be included in the catalogue of popes on account of her sex. And so the next John listed—in 872—is referred to again as John VIII, but the same interfering hand in black has crossed this out and put instead IX. And each John thereafter has been tampered with in like fashion.

Perhaps I have a pessimistic and suspicious turn of mind, but it was hard to believe that the time-honoured retort of the Catholic church to the story of Pope Joan—that it was a Reformation forgery—could so easily be dismissed. What, I asked the librarians, if a seventeenth-century forger had set out to imitate the written and illustrative style of the fourteenth century in producing a new version of Martin Polonus with the story of Joan in the main text? The answer was simple. They would not have had the expertise. The detailed knowledge of styles and dates that is today available in abundance at the Duke Humfrey is a decidedly modern development. As late as the nineteenth century, for instance, the Bodleian was buying manuscripts that were deemed by experts to be fourteenth century, only for subsequent experts to find out that they came from Anglo-Saxon times. Any later attempt to reproduce the Gothic style of the fourteenth century would be spotted, I was reassured. It would be as unmistakable and over-the-top as a Victorian copy of a medieval building.

Here, then, was the conclusive evidence which gave the lie to any talk of post-Reformation forgers inventing Joan. What had not been changed in the fourteenth-century manuscript was the central assertion that there was a Pope Joan who ruled for two years, five months and four days before she gave birth to a child and was killed. Well before the Reformation Joan was accepted as fact. True or false, the story of Pope Joan had a source other than malicious forgery.

I was hooked, but there was one other matter arising from my trip to Rome that I had to clear up. Was there any evidence that the strange seat I had seen in Rome and read about in skimpy guidebooks was what it was alleged to be?

Bernardino Coreo, a Milanese writer and historian offers an eyewitness account of the coronation of Pope Alexander VI in 1492 in his *Patria Historia* of 1503. He concludes: 'Finally, when the usual solemnities of the "sancta sanctorum" ended and the touching of testicles was done, I returned to the palace.'[25] Alexander VI was, of course, the most notorious of the Borgia popes and a certain irony is added to Coreo's account by the fact that the pontiff's four grown-up sons were in the audience when their father was so rudely frisked.

Another eyewitness was the Welsh late-medieval chronicler, Adam of Usk, an Oxford-educated cleric who travelled across the continent to Rome and in 1404 witnessed the election of Innocent VII. He recounts Innocent's triumphal procession through the streets of Rome from the Vatican to the Lateran:

> Then, after turning aside out of abhorrence of Pope Joan whose image with her son stands near Saint Clement's, the pope, dismounting from his horse, enters the Lateran for his enthronement. And there he is seated in a chair of porphyry, which is pierced beneath for this purpose, that one of the younger cardinals may make proof of his sex; and then while a *Te Deum* is chanted, he is borne to the high altar.[26]

As late as September 1644 the Swedish writer Lawrence Banck is recording a similar spectacle at the elevation of Innocent X.[27] Bartolomeo Platina, keeper of the Vatican library under Pope Sixtus IV (1471-84), is another who mentions the ceremony in his *Lives of the Popes.* Moreover, this venerable and well-placed scholar links it explicitly with Pope Joan. He includes his reference at the end of an entry on Pope John VIII who reigned, according to Platina, in the middle of the ninth century. John was a woman, this insider records, who disguised herself as a man and tricked her way to the papal throne. Once she was discovered, the practice of touching the testicles was introduced as part of the enthronement ceremony to ensure that no such treachery should ever be allowed again.[28]

Notes

1. Figure quoted by Frederick Spanheim in *Histoire de La Papesse Jeanne,* vols 1 and 2 (Paris, 1720). See later in chapter for more detail

2. *Berlin Lat. qu. 70,* folio 196r in the Staatsbibliothek. See also *MGH Scriptorum* edited by G. H. Pertz (Basle, 1872)

3. See note 1 above

4. See Dollinger's *Fables Respecting Popes of the Middle Ages* translated by Alfred Plummer (London, 1871)

5. See Leonardi Claudio's *Anastasio Bibliotecario* (Studii Medievali, 1967)

6. See chapter 1, note 4

7. See L. Wallach, 'The Genuine and the Forged Oath of Leo III' in *Traditio* (vol. 11, 1955)

8. Joan Morris includes a whole section on historians' views on the relationship between Joan and Anastasius in her *Pope John VIII, an English Woman, Alias Pope Joan* (London, 1985)

9. *Marianus Scotus Chronica*; Heroldt edition (Basle, 1559)

10. *Dictionary of the Middle Ages* edited by Joseph Strayer (New York, 1985)

11. Sigebert's *Chronicon* is in *Germanicarum Rerum Quator Celebriores Vetusque* edited by Lamberti (Frankfurt, 1566)

12. See note 10 above

13. Otto of Freising's *Chronica* edited by A. Hofmeister (Hanover, 1912)

14. Godfrey of Viterbo's *Pantheon* in *Rerum Germanicarum Scriptores aliquot insignes* edited by J. Pistorius (1726)

15. Gervase of Tilbury's *Otiis Imperialis* can be found in Rolls Series no. 66 edited by W. H. Stevenson (London, 1875)

16. Jean de Mailly's *Chronica universalis* was translated into French by A. Dondaine (Paris, 1947)

17. *La Papessa Giovanna* by Cesare D'Onofrio (Rome, 1979)

18. See note 16 above

19. Stephen de Bourbon's *De Diversis materiis praedicabilibus* is found in *Scriptores Ordinis Praedicatorium* edited by J. Eccard (Lipsae, 1723)

20. See Peter Stanford's *The Devil: A Biography* (London and New York, 1996)

21. Found in the collection *Monumenta Germaniae Historica: Scriptores*

22. See note 21 above

23. Manuscript 179 in the Bodleian Library, Oxford

24. Manuscript 452(A) in the Bodleian Library, Oxford

25. Bernardino Coreo, *Historia continente la storia di Milano* (Milan, 1503)

26. *The Chronicle of Adam of Usk* edited by Edward Manude Thompson (London, 1876)

27. Lawrence Banck, *Roma triumphans seu actus inaugurationum* (Frankfurt, 1645)

28. Platina, *Storia delle vite di pontifici* (Venice, 1761)

FURTHER READING

Criticism

Boureau, Alain. "The Popess and Her Sisters." In *The Myth of Pope Joan,* translated by Lydia G. Cochrane, pp. 165-218. Chicago: The University of Chicago Press, 2001.

Provides an overview of the evolution of the myth of Pope Joan over the centuries.

Cross, Donna. *Pope Joan: A Novel.* New York: Ballantine Books, 1996, 448 p.

Work of historical fiction that portrays Joan as intelligent, imaginative, and determined.

Pardoe, Rosemary and Darroll. *The Female Pope: The Mystery of Pope Joan. The First Complete Documentation of the Facts behind the Legend.* London: Crucible Press, 1988, 112 p.

Historical analysis of all aspects of the Pope Joan legend; the authors debunk the fourteenth- and fifteenth-century references usually cited as proof of Joan's existence.

Roydis, Emmanual. *Pope Joan,* translated by Lawrence Durrell. London: Overlook, 1984, 160 p.

Humorous retelling of the Pope Joan legend originally published in Greek in 1886.

Shuttleworth, Humphrey. "The Life and Death of Pope Joan." In *A Present for a Papist, or the History of the Life of Pope Joan from her Birth to her Death,* pp. 5-25. London: J. F. and C. Rivington, 1785.

Provides a biography of Joan, arguing in favor of her existence.

Stanford, Peter. *The Legend of Pope Joan: In Search of the Truth.* New York: Henry Holt and Company, 1998, 207 p.

Chronicles the author's personal search for the truth behind the stories of Pope Joan.

Wright, Stephen K. "Joseph as Mother, Jutta as Pope: Gender and Transgression in Medieval German Drama." *Theatre Journal* 51 (May 1999): 109-66.

Discusses Pope Joan's evolution into a character in a fifteenth-century miracle play.

Pierre Carlet de Chamblain de Marivaux
1688-1763

French playwright, novelist, journalist, essayist, and poet.

The following entry presents an overview of Marivaux's life and works. For additional information on his career, see *LC,* Volume 4.

INTRODUCTION

Marivaux is considered one of the most important playwrights and novelists of eighteenth-century France. In addition to composing a number of successful stage comedies, he also produced two important contributions to the emerging novel genre, *La vie de Marianne* (1731-42; *The Virtuous Orphan*) and *Le paysan parvenu* (1734-35; *The Fortunate Peasant*). Marivaux's penchant for minute analysis in his works is termed "marivaudage," which until recently was often used pejoratively to describe an elaboration of apparently trivial details and a convoluted expression of ideas.

BIOGRAPHICAL INFORMATION

Biographical details on Marivaux are scarce; however, it is known that he was born Pierre Carlet in Paris on February 4, 1688, and that sometime during his early childhood his father took a position as director of the Royal Mint and moved the family to Riom. Marivaux returned to Paris in 1710 at the age of twenty-two to study at the Faculty of Law; while there, he decided to pursue a literary career. He became a regular at the salons of Madame de Lambert and Madame de Tencin, where he encountered other members of the literary community who encouraged his writing. He joined a group led by Houdar de la Motte, called the Moderns, who criticized and abandoned the classical aesthetic tradition in favor of a more progressive approach to literature. Sometime before 1716 Marivaux added "de Chamblain" to his name, possibly borrowed from his cousin Bullet de Chamblain, an architect. In 1719 he married Colomb Bollogne and signed the marriage contract "Carlet de Marivaux." The couple had one daughter. In 1720 Marivaux lost most of his fortune in the collapse of the Law Bank, but he was by this time producing plays. Although financial success did not come immediately, he was eventually able to support himself with his writing, thanks in large part to the journals he

founded. Marivaux's wife died in 1723. In 1742 he was elected to the Académie Française and served as its Chancellor in 1750 and its Director in 1759. Marivaux died on February 12, 1763, in Paris.

MAJOR WORKS

Marivaux began his writing career with a one-act play, *Le père prudent et equitable,* which was written sometime between 1709 and 1711, produced privately, and published in 1712. In 1720 he began what would be a long and profitable association with the Théâtre Italien in Paris with the production of his comedy *Arlequin poli par l'amour* (*Harlequin Polished By Love*), which proved popular with both critics and audiences. He produced a number of highly successful plays for the group, including his theatrical masterpiece, *Le jeu de l'amour et du hasard* (1730; *The Game of Love and Chance*), *Le legs* (1736; *The Legacy*), *Les fausses confidences* (1737; *False Confidences*), and *L'epreuve* (1740;

The Test). Marivaux's association with the Théâtre Français was less successful; his only tragedy, *Annibal* (1720; *Hannibal*), was the first of many unpopular productions with the group, whose style did not well suit Marivaux's innovative dramatic style.

While Marivaux continued to write for the theaters, he began publishing periodicals as a means of supporting himself. *Le spectateur Français* was his first independent effort; it appeared from 1721 to 1724 and was loosely modeled on Addison and Steele's *Spectator.* This was followed by *L'indigent philosophe* from 1726 to 1727, and *Le cabinet du philosophe* in 1734. All were highly successful and provided Marivaux with a forum for articulating his innovative theories and techniques.

Marivaux's first novel, *Les effets surprenants de la sympathie* (1713-14), adhered to the conventions of the seventeenth-century romance. After its publication, however, Marivaux began to distance himself from the classical tradition and satirized himself, along with classical authors such as Homer, in *Pharsamon,* which was written around 1714 but not published until 1737. During the 1730s Marivaux firmly established a reputation as a novelist with his innovations in first-person narratives. His best-known novel, *La vie de Marianne,* consisting of the reminiscences of an impoverished orphan who becomes a countess, continues to attract critical attention, and is considered his non-dramatic masterpiece. Closely associated with this work is *Le paysan parvenu,* which some critics consider the companion piece to *Marianne.* The novel features a male narrator, also from humble origins, who looks back on his life and rise through the ranks of society.

CRITICAL RECEPTION

Marivaux wrote at a time when traditional views were being challenged by progressive writers experimenting with both form and content. Many critics have explored how Marivaux's works often deal with the relationships between the classes and the emerging issue of social mobility. Derek F. Connon has contended that Marivaux's fiction far outpaced the actual possibilities for class rise in contemporary reality. Both of Marivaux's two memoir-novels deal with the desire of members of the lower classes to advance themselves through marriage. Shawncey Webb, in a study of sexual differences in *La vie de Marianne* and *Le paysan parvenu,* has suggested that both are stereotypical "rags to riches" narratives, like those that would characterize many novels of the later eighteenth and nineteenth centuries. Chavarche Tchalekian has commented on Marivaux's use of social criticism in his dramatic works, contending that, unlike Molière who satirized

the actions of individuals, Marivaux's target was more often groups of people with common customs, particularly members of the nobility and the bourgeoisie. Oscar Haac has responded to critics such as Voltaire, who accused Marivaux of "excessive delicacy," by documenting the elements of social commentary in Marivaux's work.

Scholars have also examined Marivaux's formal innovations, including his rejection of the well-established five-act form for in favor of one- and three-act plays. His nondramatic works often take on hybrid forms: *La vie de Marianne* is a memoir-novel and *L'indigent philosophe* is a memoir-journal. Both works feature narrators whose reliability is called into question—in the novel, by Marianne's selective memory and attempts at self-justification, and in the journal by the philosopher's claim that his writing is completely "natural," devoid of any authorial intent. Felicia Sturzer has maintained that "by his denial of formality," the indigent philosopher in the journal "manages to ingratiate himself with the reader," a strategy that lends credibility to the narrative. Frank Abetti has suggested that in *La vie de Marianne,* "we should be wary not only of Marianne's claim that she doesn't have the first idea what style is, but also of her claim that there is some substance to her story, which, if we look closely, is mostly finesse, or style."

Critics have devoted much attention to the details of Marivaux's other stylistic innovations. Haac has studied the author's realistic treatment of violence as a departure from the conventions of earlier Romanesque fiction, maintaining that Marivaux portrayed human suffering with no illusions, but without the picturesque descriptions of physical violence common to the earlier style. Ruth P. Thomas has explored Marivaux's use of the literary portrait, particularly in his two most famous novels. She has claimed that his lengthy descriptions of characters—sometimes running to several pages—were designed to offer the reader clues to the inner nature of characters based on exterior appearances.

Scholars disagree when assessing Marivaux's representations of women. Arthur Robbins has claimed that Marivaux was acutely aware of the dangers of living in a world filled with artifice, particularly for women. Marivaux saw, according to Robbins, "that it was the woman who was the most vulnerable in these circumstances and that she would have to resort to role-playing in order to achieve her aims in life and not be victimized." Valentini Papadopoulou Brady has argued, however, that "there is no 'victim' type woman in Marivaux's world," and that "no matter how soft, gentle, innocent and obedient his heroines may be, when it comes to protecting their happiness they always have something to say." Sturzer, in her study of *La vie de Marianne,* has asserted that the novel "is not a revolutionary feminist statement" despite the fact that it involves a female narrator writing to another woman and questioning the social system, the laws, and the stereotypes that govern their lives. Ultimately, according to Sturzer, Marianne's discourse is not transgressive since it becomes "integrated into and accepted by the established patriarchal structure." H. T. Mason has arrived at similar conclusions, contending that although the author apparently accepted women as intellectual equals and was aware of the problems associated with gender inequality, he "can scarcely be termed a leading feminist of his day." He was, according to Mason, more concerned with the human condition in general rather than the condition of women specifically.

PRINCIPAL WORKS

Le père prudent et equitable; ou, Crispin l'heureux forbe (play) 1712

Les effets surprenants de la sympathie; ou, Les aventures de *** (novel) 1713-14

L'Homère travesti; ou, L'Iliade en vers burlesques. 2 vols. (poetry) 1716

Lettres sur les habitants de Paris (essays) 1717

L'amour et la verité (play) 1720

Annibal [*Hannibal*] (play) 1720

Arlequin poli par l'amour [*Harlequin Polished By Love*] (play) 1720

Le spectateur Français [*The French Spectator*] (journal) 1721-24

La surprise de l'amour [*The Surprise of Love*] (play) 1722

Le dénouement imprévu [*The Unforeseen Solution*] (play) 1723

La double inconstance [*Two Cases of Infidelity*] (play) 1723

Le prince travesti [*The Prince in Disguise*] (play) 1723

La fausse suivante [*The False Servant*] (play) 1724

L'héritier du village [*The Farmer Inherits a Fortune*] (play) 1725

L'ile des esclaves [*The Island of Slaves*] (play) 1725

L'indigent philosophe [*The Indigent Philosopher*] (journal) 1726-27

L'ile de la raison; ou, Les petits hommes [*The Island of Reason*] (play) 1727

La [seconde] surprise de l'amour [*The [Second] Surprise of Love*] (play) 1727

Le jeu de l'amour et du hasard [*The Game of Love and Chance*] (play) 1730

La réunion des amours (play) 1731

La vie de Marianne; ou, Les aventures de Mmd. La Comtesse de ***. 11 vols. [*The Virtuous Orphan; or, The Life of Marianne, Countess of ******] (novel) 1731-42

Les serments indiscrets (play) 1732

Le cabinet du philosophe (journal) 1734

Le paysan parvenu. 5 vols. [*Le Paysan Parvenu: or, The Fortunate Peasant, Being Memoirs of the Late Mr.———*] (novel) 1734-35

La mère confidente (play) 1735

Le petit maître corrigé (play) 1735

Le legs [*The Legacy; or, The Fortune-hunter*] (play) 1736

Le télémaque travesti (novel) 1736

Les fausses confidences [*False Confidences*] (play) 1737

**Pharsamon; ou, Les nouvelles folies romanesques* [*Pharsamon; ou, Le Don Quichotte moderne*] (novel) 1737

L'epreuve [*The Test*] (play) 1740

Les sincères (play) 1740

La dispute (play) 1744

La colonie (play) 1750

La provinciale (play) 1761

Oeuvres complètes de M, de Marivaux. 12 vols. (novels, plays, essays, short stories, poetry) 1781

---

*This work was written around 1714 but not published until 1737.

CRITICISM

Oscar Haac (essay date 1967)

SOURCE: Haac, Oscar. "Violence in Marivaux." *Kentucky Romance Quarterly* 14, no. 3 (1967): 191-99.

[*In the following essay, Haac examines a passage from* La Vie de Marianne *as an example of Marivaux's treatment of violence in his work.*]

Marivaux' concern for violence will seem paradoxical only if one clings to Voltaire's view of him as the author of spiderwebs, one who knew all about the byways of the human heart and nothing about its great passions. Violence may not seem an essential concern of eighteenth century authors, if we continue to think of them as confirmed optimists.

While it is true that Marivaux, after the first products of his youthful inexperience, two long novels entitled ***Les Effets surprenants de la sympathie*** and ***Pharsamon,*** turned from the traditional resources of romanesque fiction and, after 1720, gave up descriptions of fury, murder, cloak and dagger romances, his newly found realism presents violence in a different form. There is still cruelty and suffering. We propose to illustrate this with a passage from ***La Vie de Marianne.*** Since its literary sources have not before been analyzed, the present paper has two purposes: to study the sources of an episode in the life of Tervire, the nun who recounts the last three sections of ***Marianne,*** and to analyze it as an example of violence in Marivaux. The comparison between Marivaux' account and its sources caracterizes his style and illustrates his technique of internalizing the battles of cloak and dagger romance, his realism, irony, and "modern" sensibility.

Frédéric Deloffre, the editor of **La Vie de Marianne** in the Classiques Garnier, comments as follows on the adventures of Tervire, the baron de Sercourt, and the abbé, his nephew: "Tout cet épisode du baron de Sercourt paraît de l'invention de Marivaux. La scène qui le termine est particulièrement audacieuse. Il faudra attendre *Jacques le fataliste* ou *Les Liaisons dangereuses* pour en trouver de semblables. L'abbé est un des premiers personnages pervers de notre littérature. Il sera suivi de Cléon, le 'méchant' de Gresset (1747) et de Damis, 'l'indiscret' de Desmahis (1750)."[1]

Bitterness and cruelty are the attributes of the abbé, whose ambitious schemes threaten Tervire. Marianne, who listens to her story, is hardly more fortunate: Valville has tired of her at the very moment when her arduous battle for recognition (Marianne was a foundling) had been won and Valville's haughty relatives were ready to accept her. Tervire hopes that her example will enable Marianne to decide whether or not to withdraw form the world and enter a convent.

Tervire's story is one of rejection. Her mother had been as unacceptable to her father-in-law, as Marianne to Valville's family. Tervire's mother had been finally accepted by the family only to face the death of her father-in-law who left her without financial resources (435-436). Tervire's father joined the army in despair and was killed in the first battle. Her mother, tired of being the victim of society, made use of her beauty and married a nobleman at the court (437); Tervire was sent to the country as an obstacle to her mother's glamorous career. Fate was to punish this misdeed, for Tervire was later to find her mother destitute, having lost her second husband, and forsaken by her son (Tervire's half-brother), and his pleasure-seeking wife (552). Tervire's mother thus suffers the fate of Père Goriot but she lacks the redeeming virtues which might have made her a tragic heroine.

In the episode which concerns us, we find Tervire in the country living with simple peasants, the Villot family. She is under the not disinterested tutelage of Mme de Ste Hermières who acts as the agent of Tervire's mother and tries to convince Tervire to choose convent life (455). Tervire vigorously resists this suggestion (462), all the more because a nun reveals her unhappiness and tells of her tragic love for the abbé whose nefarious schemes will soon undo Tervire herself.

Mme de Ste Hermières would therefore like to rid herself of her charge some other way. Tervire's marriage to the baron de Sercourt seems an excellent solution. The baron is wealthy, forty years old, infirm, unlikely to live for long. Tervire, hardly an idealist, is prompted by "reason" (469, 474) to accept the proposal: she sees herself as a wealthy widow in the near future. Soon, however, the villainy of the abbé upsets these plans; he reduces her to such misery that, by comparison to him, she appears a virtuous lamb!

The abbé happens to be the nephew and potential heir of the baron de Sercourt and stands to lose a fortune should Tervire marry his uncle. He tries to forestall this by having Mme de Ste Hermières impress on Tervire how unappealing such a marriage would be, how much better she would feel in a convent. When this argument proves ineffective, the abbé gives Mme de Ste Hermières a rather expensive ring (480) in payment for more drastic measures. She asks Tervire to write a note requesting a rendez-vous (Mme de Ste Hermières pretends her hands hurt); then, at night, the abbé hides in Tervire's closet while Mme de Ste Hermières brings Sercourt and another guest with drawn sword, supposedly to pursue thieves. Tervire is hopelessly compromised by the presence of the abbé and the note she is presumed to have sent, inviting him to her room. The baron de Sercourt cancels the marriage while Tervire redeems herself in the mind of the reader by shedding copious tears.

Once more fate intervenes. Soon after the frame-up, Mme de Ste Hermières confesses the blackmail on her deathbed. The abbé is forced to leave; his misdeeds will confine him to prison. Sercourt finally renews his offer of marriage, but Tervire has been too deeply hurt and will not reconsider.

It is interesting to note Marivaux' restrained language in describing the abbé. He is called nothing worse than "malhonnête, pas bon, un tartufe, un perverti." When the disillusioned nun hands Tervire an unopened note from the abbé, Tervire comments: "Je me doutais . . . qu'il ne s'était pas agi de moins que d'un enlèvement, et il n'y avait guère qu'un *malhonnête* homme qui eût pu en avoir fait la proposition" (463-464). The nun hands Tervire the note because she has decided to remain in the convent. "Quant à l'abbé, cette aventure ne le rendait *pas meilleur*" (464). The abbé is described as "ce jeune *tartufe*, avec sa mine dévote" (463). "La religieuse n'était qu'une égarée; l'abbé était *un perverti, un faux dévot* en un mot, et Dieu, qui distingue nos faiblesses de nos crimes, ne lui fit pas la même *grâce* qu'à elle" (464). Later, the abbé shows his hypocrisy when he sarcastically tells Tervire "avec un sourire assez forcé . . . : 'Puisque j'avais à perdre le bien de mon oncle . . . j'aime mieux que vous l'ayez qu'une autre'" (472). Tervire knows there is nothing sincere in him: "la tranquilité m'avait semblé si *fausse*" (472).

It must be understood that "malhonnête" is a serious reproach in the speech of Marivaux who usually confines himself to joking about the kind of gentleman ("honnête homme") who is not truly that honorable ("honnête").[2] Furthermore, as Frédéric Deloffre points out, the reference to grace is equally serious; it must be taken in its theological sense like the attribute, "perverti," and the comment on the death-bed confession of Mme de Ste Hermière: "Il restait encore une coupable à qui Dieu, dans sa miséricorde, voulait accorder le repentir de son crime." Deloffre (481) notes the Christian terminology, and cites parallel passages from the *Spectateur,* the *Cabinet du philosophe,* and the commentary of Lesbros de la Versane.

A style in which the terms "malhonnête" and "un tartufe" are powerful condemnations and in which religious terms carry grave implications may seem surprising. Earlier, Marivaux had interrupted publication of *La Vie de Marianne* after book 2, from January 1734 to November 1735, because the strong language he had put into the mouth of the laundress, Mme Dutour, had provoked an outcry among his readers. In 1741, the date of the Tervire episode, he is more careful in his choice of words, although he is still far from optimistic about human nature: indeed, the villainous abbé is only one of the portraits which betray the author's bitterness. There is a great deal of unfeeling cruelty and violence in the scene.

The primary inspiration for the scene of the frame-up comes from *La Comtesse de Savoie,* a novel by Mme de Fontaines. She had found the theme in Ariosto's *Orlando furioso.* She, in turn, passed it on to Voltaire, to the Italian players, and to Marivaux. Let us briefly summarize the plots of each of the critical episodes.

In book V of the *Orlando furioso,* Palinesso, the unsuccessful rival of Ariodant for the love of Ginevra, plans his revenge. He makes Dalinda disguise herself as Ginevra and kisses her on Ginevra's balcony, in plain sight of the public and of Ariodant. In this manner Ginevra is dishonored and must be put to death unless a knight defends her reputation. Rinaldo appears just in time to defeat the sly Palinesso; then Ariodant and Ginevra can marry.

In the novel of Mme de Fontaines, the heroine, the Comtesse, remains faithful to her husband, the count of Savoy, even though she secretly loves Mendoce who is in exile. Like Zaïde of Mme de Lafayette, the Comtesse had fallen in love with the portrait of Mendoce and then found him the realization of the image. It so happens that the prime minister, Pancallier, and his nephew also love the Comtesse. Rejected, Pancallier seeks revenge. He engages his nephew to hide in her apartment, then escorts an official party there. This enables him to ruin her reputation and to stab his nephew for being an inopportune rival. Justice now requires that the Comtesse be put to death unless a knight defends her honor. Mendoce like Rinaldo arrives just in time. The

people in revolt kill the defeated Pancallier. Soon the count of Savoy dies and the Comtesse is free to marry Mendoce.

La Comtesse de Savoie furnishes the closest parallel to the story of Tervire because, in both cases, uncle and nephew are rivals. Characteristically, the nephew is not killed in **La Vie de Marianne.** Marivaux's account is less bloody but no more optimistic about human nature: Mme de Ste Hermières reconciles uncle and nephew in her self-interested way: she wants to preserve her friendships with all her wealthy friends. Mme de Fontaines wrote her novel as early as 1713, for that year Voltaire expressed his admiration for it in a poem. Before the novel was published (1726), he used its theme in his tragedy, *Artémire* (1720),[3] a moderate success, performed eight times, until the Italian players produced a parody of it (March 10).[4] *Artémire* and its parody are parallel in most respects. We shall use the names of characters in the parody because it is more directly related to Marivaux. Furthermore, Voltaire's play is preserved only in fragments and the essential scene of the frame-up is lost. Let us note the following equivalence of names in the two plays:

Artémire	*Parody*
Artémire, the queen	Artémire
Cassandre, the king, her husband	Pantalon
Philotas her love since childhood	Philotas
Pallante, the king's favorite	Trivelin
Ménas, his relative and confident	Arlequin

Artémire loved Philotas as a young girl, but was forced by her father to marry Pantalon, a choleric and jealous man. Pantalon soon killed her father and threatened Artémire's life as well. After Philotas returns, Pantalon takes measures to have Artémire killed by Trivelin who also happens to love her. Wishing only for death, she remains faithful to Pantalon, while Trivelin is only too willing to carry out Pantalon's death sentence. In the last minute Pantalon realizes she is true to him and saves her life. Trivelin still bent on revenge now resorts to deceit. He engages Arlequin to declare his love for Artémire so he can surprise him in her company. When Arlequin refuses, Trivelin convinces Pantalon that Arlequin embraced her knees (in Voltaire's melodrama, Ménas is killed, as was the nephew in the *Comtesse*). Again Pantalon is sure Artémire has betrayed him: "Je suis cocu, vous dis-je!" Voltaire's tragedy is slightly less grotesque, but in both plays Artémire pathetically states that her only crime is that she cannot love her husband. Finally a popular uprising saves Artémire's life, Philotas kills the villain (Trivelin) and Pantalon, wounded and dying, cedes Artémire to the man she loves (Philotas). In Voltaire's tragedy, the king laments like Othello that he has been the victim of an imposter.[5]

Marivaux borrowed one scene of the parody in his **Prince travesti** (1724) where, like Trivelin, Frédéric tries to corrupt Arlequin with money and promises. Frédéric is the most despicable character in any of Marivaux' comedies, a true successor to the villains, Palinesso, Pancallier, and Pallante.

The scene of the frame-up occurs in each of these sources as it does in *La Vie de Marianne*. Each time the villain would ruin the reputation of the heroine by having her seemingly "caught in the act"; in reality, the heroine has done nothing to compromise herself. The villain's success is only temporary; in all cases he is eventually defeated or killed.

In Marivaux the overt violence of the sources is dimished but the nefarious schemes of Frédéric and the abbé are evident. The violence of his sources has been internalized; Marivaux presents cruelty in a more realistic setting. The effect is even more powerful, at least for the modern reader unconvinced by the melodrama of romanesque fiction.

Only in the earliest works did Marivaux portray the excesses of passion and unreason in the romanesque tradition. In *Les Effets surprenants de la sympathie,* rejected lovers are willing to go to any extremes and resort to rape and murder; slaves are abused and whipped in mines.[6] In his second novel, *Pharsamon,* Marivaux began to free himself from this style by presenting similar scenes in a burlesque context. Then, in the *La Voiture embourbée* (1714), the examples of bloody violence, told in the style of the *Arabian Nights,* are fantasies of travellers, invented to pass the time. They reflect on the frustrations of each story teller. Bastille is raped by the Sophi; her lover, Créor, takes revenge by hanging him while Bastille perforates the Sophi's body with a dagger.[7] Such scenes, even presented as imaginary episodes, still reflect the spirit of the novels of La Calprenède. When the theme of rape by an all-powerful prince recurs in *La Double inconstance* (1724), Marivaux masks the cynical plot by Silvia's voluntary surrender and the appealing charm of the prince. This is Marivaux' definitive style. Cruelty is transformed by a new realism, but it is no less present. Jean Anouilh, in *La Répétition,* interprets *La Double inconstance* as pessimistically as Marivaux conceived it, when he transposed Bastille's fate into a setting in fairy land.

We see how Marivaux changed his style between 1714 and 1724. His *Télémaque travesti,* of 1715-16, still pictures physical violence, the dragonnades, a local baron who persecutes Protestant subjects and ravishes their daughters,[8] the Camisard wars and miscarriages of justice. Marivaux' grotesque and comic tone foreshadows *Candide.* After this novel. Marivaux renounced the picturesque popular language of the *Télémaque travesti* along with its kind of realism; the *Spectateur français* furnishes examples in a more tragic mood[9] and in the

style of the society toward which Marivaux was aspiring. He banned the picturesque popular humor of the *Télémaque* as well as the traditional romanesque image of violence. As Marivaux developed his definitive style, he abandoned the tradition of melodrama and outrage. Murder is banished from his stage but self-interest and evil are still man's nature. He describes them without illusions, even in the plays of fantasy set on imaginary islands.

We conclude that Marivaux became more, rather than less conscious of the inhumanity and bitterness which pervade so many of his later plays and which he dramatically expressed in the final scene of Tervire's story, in book XI of *La Vie de Marianne.* Seeing how her unfeeling sister-in-law has acted toward her mother, Tervire upbraids her sharply, even though she knows this will be to no avail:

> Ma mère qui ne s'ent rien réservé, et
> que vous et son fils avez tous deux
> abandonnée aux plus affreuses extrémités;
> qui a été forcée de vendre jusqu'aux
> meubles de rebut que vous lui avez
> envoyés, et qui n'étaient point ceux
> qu'elle avait gardés; enfin cette mère
> qui n'a cru ni son fils, ni vous, madame,
> capables de manquer de reconnaissance;
> qui, moyennant une pension très médiocre
> dont on est convenu, a bien voulu renoncer
> à tous ses droits par la bonne opinion
> qu'elle avait de son coeur et du vôtre;
> elle que vous aviez tous deux engagée à
> venir chez vous pour y être servie,
> aimée, respectée autant qu'elle le
> devait être; qui n'y a cependant essuyé
> que des affronts, qui s'y est rebutée,
> méprisée et insultée, et que par là vous
> avez forcée d'en sortir pour aller vivre
> ailleurs d'une petite pension qu'on ne
> lui paye point, qu'elle n'avait eu garde
> d'envisager comme une ressource, qui
> est cependant le seul bien qui lui reste,
> et dont la médiocrité même est une si
> grande preuve de sa confiance; cette belle-
> mère infortunée, si punie d'en avoir
> cru sa tendresse, et dont les intérêts
> vous importunent si peu; je viens vous
> dire, madame, que tout lui manquait
> hier, qu'elle était dans les derniers
> besoins, qu'on l'a trouvée ne sachant ni
> où se retirer, ni où aller vivre; qu'elle
> est actuellement malade et logée dans
> une misérable auberge. . . .

(578-579)

Tervire talks on while her sister-in-law remains silent. Earlier she had interjected: "Vous feriez vraiment d'excellents sermons" (578). Eventually Tervire can say no more. She bids: "Adieu madame," without eliciting a response. Within his chosen framework, Marivaux portrays human suffering. Indeed, in the scene we have quoted he came dangerously close to expressing his own indignations and giving a moral lesson; this violates his own precept against didactic literature. Knowing that readers will not stand for sermons and that Tervire had overstepped the bounds, he judges it best not to continue the novel. Thus he leaves Tervire and Marianne to their quanderies and speculations.

The subtle, treacherous, and self-satisfied attitudes of the abbé, or of Tervire's sister-in-law, illustrate man's inhumanity to man more forcefully than rape and murder! Furthermore, the cruelty or suffering we find in *Marianne* is also implied in most of plays, often where we least suspect it.[10] When, in the *Jeu de l'amour* Silvia refuses to reveal her identity even when Dorante has shown who he is and forces him to humiliate himself by asking for the hand of a servant girl, she not only makes him suffer, she knows it and, at the end, asks him if he is angry at her for it. With love and marriage assured, Dorante only thanks her for putting him to this test. It was Mamade de Lambert, in whose salon Marivaux met Paris society, not Laclos, who wrote: "Il y a toujours une sorte de cruauté dans l'amour. Les plaisirs de l'amant ne se prennent que sur les douleurs de l'amante. L'amour se nourrit de larmes."[11]

Notes

1. P. 478, with reference to the *Petit-maître corrigé* (Droz, 1955), pp. 35-37, 71-72. All references will be to the Garnier edition of *La Vie de Marianne* (Paris, 1957), with page numbers in parentheses in our text. The Tervire episode can be found pp. 457-483.

2. Cf. my "Marivaux and the Honnête homme," *Romanic Review* 50: 255-267, 1959, and "honnête" in the "Glossaire" of the Garnier ed.

3. *La Comtesse de Savoie*, pp. 3-61 in the *Oeuvres de Mmes de Fontaines et de Tencin*. Bibliothèque amusante (Garnier, s. d.); for the frame-up see pp. 43-46. A reference to Mendoce travelling to Sicily with "Les Tancrède," the famous warriors, p. 41, will furnish the link to Voltaire's later tragedy, *Tancrède* (1759, performed 1760) where the situation of the frame-up will be repeated against a background of Normans fighting saracens. Thus Voltaire adopted the theme twice, in *Artémire* and in *Tancrède*. For the detail concerning *Artémire*, cf. Voltaire, *Oeuvres*, ed Moland, II, 121, sq. Other instances of novels influencing plots of Marivaux, see F. Deloffre in *Mélanges . . . Dimoff, Annales Universitatis Saraviensis* 3: 59-66, 1965, also the prefaces to the Garnier eds. of *La Vie de Marianne* and *Le Paysan parvenu*.

4. Published in the *Parodies du nouveau théâtre italien*, 4 vols.

5. Cf. *Marianne*, Voltaire's next tragedy with Herod in a similar role.

6. *Œuvres* (Paris, 1781) VI, 98. Cf. Tarmiane's story at the end of *Pharsamon* picturing rape, abduction by corsairs, XI, 523.

7. Marivaux, *Romans*, ed. Pléiade, pp. 47-67.

8. Actions of Omenée, in the Deloffre edition, Droz 1956, pp. 207-221, especially 209, 212, 218; cf. 131, 196, 261, 269, all scenes of violence.

9. Feuilles 4 (girl asking for help), 9-11 (Mirski episode).

10. Haydn T. Mason, "Cruelty in Marivaux' Theater," *The Modern Language Review*, 62: 238-247, 1967, commenting on *La Double inconstance*, *L'Epreuve*, etc.

11. *Avis d'une mère*, cited by Deloffre in *Revue des Sciences humaines*, 1958, p. 564.

Ruth P. Thomas (essay date October 1968)

SOURCE: Thomas, Ruth P. "The Art of the Portrait in the Novels of Marivaux." *French Review* 42, no. 1 (October 1968): 23-31.

[*In the following essay, Thomas comments on Marivaux's use of the literary portrait as a means of revealing the inner nature of characters.*]

The modern reader of *Le Paysan parvenu* and *La Vie de Marianne* is immediately struck by the number, the variety, and the length of the portraits in the novels. Almost every character, regardless of his importance, receives a portrait of some sort, and while brief one or two line sketches are not uncommon, more often the portrait is a full-scale description averaging one or two pages. Occasionally, even, they are very developed indeed: that of Marianne's benefactress, Mme de Miran, is four pages long, and the portrait of Mme Dorsin, her friend, reaches the quite extraordinary length of twelve pages.

But his initial surprise over, the reader is likely to dismiss the portraits summarily. After all, since the middle of the seventeenth century, the portrait has been an independent literary genre, a set piece to be exploited in its own right, and, the reader can conclude, Marivaux is merely continuing a literary tradition. The portraits of living persons, which came into vogue in the salons of the "précieux," whose members found amusement in depicting themselves and one another verbally, greatly influenced the literature of the period, particularly the novel. There they replaced the portraits of imaginary characters, and the practice was so popular that novels such as *Le Grand Cyrus* and *Clélie* were little more than galleries of portraits in which, under the thinnest of disguises, were painted the contemporaries of Mlle de Scudéry. According to René Bray: "Le public du XVIIᵉ siècle, féru de morale et de psychologie, se plut beaucoup à s'arrêter ainsi, au cours d'une oeuvre plus ample, pour considérer avec attention une figure connue. Le goût de l'indiscrétion et parfois du scandale s'ajouta à cette disposition naturelle du Français. On s'habitua à chercher derrière les personnages historiques ou fictifs d'un roman ou d'une autre oeuvre la réalité d'un contemporain."[1] The conclusion that Marivaux is simply following a conventional literary tradition seems all the more justified since, as Deloffre has shown, many of the portraits in *La Vie de Marianne* depict real people, the author's contemporaries.[2]

There is little doubt that Marivaux was in fact inspired by the seventeenth century portrait. But to determine the actual extent of his debt, let us consider for a moment these portraits themselves. The portrait, Lanson points out in *L'Art de la prose,* is "laudatif ou satirique," and its object is not to "*faire voir* la personne," but rather to "mêler si intimement l'exercice de l'esprit du peintre à la description des caractères du modèle, que l'on ne sache pas ce qui intéresse ou amuse le plus, le modèle étudié, ou le tour donné à cette étude." The portrait, he adds, "n'est pas une peinture, c'est une dissertation: le commentaire élogieux ou satirique enveloppe et obscurcit l'image."[3] Nor is this all. An examination of what are, perhaps, the two most famous portraits of the period, that of Julie d'Angennes in *Le Grand Cyrus,* and that of Mlle de Scudéry herself in the same work, reveals that the portraits of the era are so completely uniform in tone and in style as to be almost indistinguishable from one another. The descriptions are extremely vague, the vocabulary and images highly stylized, and the attention of the writer most often fixed on the same qualities. Hyperbole abounds, and the point of view is always predetermined, bearing no relationship to the author's attitude towards the person portrayed. It is clear that such portraits do not individualize, nor are they devices of characterization. They are merely highly stylized, conventional literary forms.

Such was the form that the seventeenth century bequeathed to the eighteenth, and it is little wonder that its popularity diminished accordingly. Prévost, for example, did not use the portrait at all in *Manon Lescaut,* and those of Lesage in *Gil Blas* are modeled after the social types of La Bruyère's *Caractères.*[4] It was Marivaux who took the portrait in its primitive state, imposed his own personality upon it, and made it an actual device of characterization.

In the psychological novels of Marivaux, the technique of the portrait is determined not by some fixed and rigid moral standard, as it was in the seventeenth century, but rather by the narrator's own impression of the person being described. The length, the nature and form,

the tone, the very presence or absence of the portrait in the novel, all reflect the narrator's own personality and his attitude towards the person before him. The portrait has become for Marivaux still another means of revealing the psychology of the protagonist. Jacob, the hero of *Le Paysan parvenu,* views the persons he encounters with a certain detachment; Marianne is emotionally involved with those she describes. Thus does the technique of the portrait vary from one novel to the other.

The different perspectives of the two narrators may be clearly seen in the brief sketches which both offer of other characters. For Jacob, who views characters at a distance, such sketches often point up a few objective, realistic, physical qualities which are then comically linked to the personality itself. Thus the lawyer whom Jacob meets on his way to Versailles is "un grand homme sec et décharné, qui avait l'air inquiet et les yeux petits, noirs et ardents." "Ce métier," adds the narrator, "vu la mine du personnage, lui convenait on ne peut pas mieux."[5] Catherine, the Habert cook, is characterized in a similar fashion.[6] Or the narrator may develop his sketches a little more and in a less purely colorful and comic manner may point up the mannerisms, affectations and tics of those he describes. So in his short description of the financier, M. Bono, he draws attention to the tooth pick and the speech mannerisms of the financier "qui avait la parole si rapide, que de quatre mots qu'il disait, il en culbutait la moitié" (p. 211).[7] Jacob's sketches thus become concrete images of the person.

Marianne also uses brief sketches but for a very different effect. While in *Le Paysan parvenu* short sketches are employed to characterize only minor figures, in *La Vie de Marianne* they are used for the portrayal of major characters as well. M. de Climal, Marianne's hypocritical benefactor, and the middle-aged officer who seeks Marianne's hand in marriage are characterized in this way, and contrary to what one might expect, Valville, who is so central to the plot, receives no portrait at all. This happens because the heroine must pretend that her own attitude towards such personages has not yet been formed. In addition, too extended a characterization would destroy the suspense necessary to the melodramatic effect of the novel.

Marianne's brief sketches differ from Jacob's in their method as well. Her emotional involvement with the persons painted does not permit her to reduce characters to a few significant physical traits or to insist merely on their mannerisms and affectations. Her sketches, while as concise as Jacob's, give a much broader, overall impression of the person, and are of a much more immediately subjective nature. They are also a great deal more vague visually. Thus Mme Dutour, the linen merchant, is described as "une grosse réjouie qui, à vue d'œil, paraissait la meilleure femme du monde; aussi l'était-elle" (p. 31). Or again, in a sketch which completely fails to give a precise notion as to what the person is like, Marianne's first guardian, the sister of the village priest, is depicted as "une personne pleine de raison et de politesse, qui joignait à cela beaucoup de vertu" (p. 14). The "aussi l'était-elle" with which Marianne concludes the description of Mme Dutour reveals at once the narrator's orientation towards the character; while the sketch of Marianne's guardian is expressly given so as to remove the reader's prejudices and dispose him favorably towards the character for "ordinairement, qui dit nièce ou sœur de curé de village dit quelque chose de bien grossier et d'approchant d'une paysanne" (p. 14).[8] Marianne's descriptions are judgments.

The different attitudes of the two narrators are brought into even sharper focus in the full-scale portraits. In *Le Paysan parvenu,* where such portraits are reserved for major or at least prominent characters, the hero's detachment is revealed through his presentation of the character in objective, realistic terms. For the less important figures, the narrator may insist on a particular weakness or a few unfavorable moral traits. Agathe, the daughter of Jacob's landlady, is characterized in this way. The young woman is hypocritical and unscrupulous, and her portrait is almost entirely focused on these unappealing features. Agathe, the narrator advises the reader, "à vue de pays, avait du penchant à l'amour; on lui sentait plus de disposition à être amoureuse que tendre, plus d'hypocrisie que de mœurs, plus d'attention pour ce qu'on dirait d'elle que pour ce qu'elle serait dans le fond; c'était la plus intrépide menteuse que j'aie connue" (p. 88). Jacob's matter-of-fact, impersonal tone here is interesting. In spite of her unattractive qualities, the narrator is not without sympathy for the landlady's daughter. The reason, however, is clear, for adds Jacob on completing the portrait: "il est certain qu'elle me trouva à son gré." With his personal point of view, Jacob determines the reader's attitude towards the character.

To describe Mme d'Alain, the landlady, the narrator again uses the technique of objective, realistic characterization, but in a more intricate fashion. The portrait centers on the landlady's tendency to chatter incessantly. The narrator, however, does not describe Mme d'Alain's comic weakness: he transcribes in indirect discourse the speech patterns themselves. Once again Jacob's attitude towards the character is clear. He views the landlady with sympathetic detachment. She has "l'innocente faiblesse d'aimer à parler, et comme qui dirait une bonté de cœur babillarde" (p. 78).

With the major characters, characterization is usually fuller, but the emphasis on the realistic and objective is always the same. The portrait focuses on the concrete aspects of a character, those which can be perceived through the senses or known directly. The portrait of Mlle Habert, at first Jacob's employer and then his wife, is a description of her physical appearance. Her round face "qui avait l'air d'être succulemment nourrie, et qui, à vue de pays, avait coutume d'être vermeille quand quelque indisposition ne la ternissait pas," first fixes the narrator's attention, which is then drawn to her clothing and her general air. The "écharpe de gros taffetas sans façon, une cornette unie, un habit d'une couleur à l'avenant, et je ne sais quelle réforme dévote répandue sur toute cette figure" are noted by Jacob, and enable the reader to visualize easily the character (p. 42). In addition they permit the narrator to know the personality of the person described. Following the tradition of the seventeenth century which linked the physical and the moral, and which in the nineteenth century will become a scientific study, Marivaux makes the exterior the sign of the nature within. Mlle Habert's face shows her leanings towards gourmandise and sensuality. Her clothing and air permit Jacob to know at a glance that there is "une femme à directeur." The reader will now view the character from a certain angle and be amused by her interest in Jacob.

Although the portraits in *Le Paysan parvenu* are frequently based on physical appearance,[9] concrete images may be drawn without insistence on the physique. The mistress of the household in which Jacob is first employed spends her time in pursuit of worldly pleasures, and she is characterized in terms of these "dissipations" themselves. Her portrait is largely a little catalogue of the activities which constitute her daily existence. Madame is a person who "allait aux spectacles, soupait en ville, se couchait à quatre heures du matin, se levait à une heure après-midi; qui avait des amants, qui les recevait à sa toilette, qui y lisait les billets doux qu'on lui envoyait, et puis les laissait traîner partout" (p. 10). The quick succession of verbs of action in the imperfect is a particularly effective device, for it conveys an impression of mechanical movement which corresponds to the instinctive behavior of Madame, who was a coquette "sans réflexion, sans le savoir."

Marianne's full-scale portraits are of quite another nature. Almost always longer than Jacob's, they are not necessarily reserved for major characters but are utilized for minor ones as well. Mme de Miran, a central figure, receives a long portrait, but so too does the very minor Mlle de Fare, who is Valville's cousin, and the minister at Marianne's trial. The portrait of Mme Dorsin, who has no real part in the action, is the most developed of any in the novel. Deloffre points out this technical shortcoming, viewing it as a consequence of the author's personal intervention in *La Vie de Marianne.* The portraits are modeled after those of Marivaux's contemporaries, and Deloffre identifies the persons portrayed.[10] Thus while in *Le Paysan parvenu* Marivaux is guided in his creation of the portrait by the technical exigencies of the novel, in _La Vie de Marianne_ he returns to the seventeenth century tradition of the "portraits à clef." Nevertheless, Marivaux does not merely follow an outdated literary convention; he changes the portrait by giving it a definite not simply stylized point of view which the reader is made to feel through Marianne's attitude towards the person portrayed. Marianne's attitude towards specific people is linked to her own general personality. Thus the "portrait à clef" becomes an integral part of the psychological novel.

Marianne's greater emotional involvement is revealed in her different perspective on the persons she draws. She approaches people indirectly through her intuition, rather than directly through her senses; she interprets rather than sees physically, going so far as to insist: "je connais bien mieux les gens avec qui je vis que je ne les définirais; il y a des choses en eux que je ne saisis point assez pour les dire, et que je n'aperçois que pour moi, et non pas pour les autres; ou si je les disais, je les dirais mal" (p. 166). Initially, then, her portraits will contain a great deal of judgment based on vague impressions and will be built on abstract notions rather than concrete images.

Marianne's different point of view can be particularly well observed in the portrait of the minister, whose real life counterpart is Cardinal Fleury. The portrait begins with a brief and totally subjective description of the physique. The physical features are not depicted and the moral character extracted from them, as is Jacob's habit, but the physical is described in moral terms. Thus the minister has "une physionomie qui vous rassurait en la voyant, qui vous calmait, qui vous remplissait de confiance, et qui était comme un gage de la bonté qu'il aurait pour vous, et de la justice qu'il allait vous rendre." His healthy appearance is even depicted in moral terms. It is described as "encore moins l'effet du tempérament que le fruit de la sagesse, de la sérénité et de la tranquillité de l'âme" (p. 314). The reader cannot visualize the minister precisely, but he does have a feeling for the personage.

The portrait continues in an equally subjective and moral fashion. The minister, whose counterpart in real life Marivaux admired as a kind, just and wise legislator, is praised by Marianne in terms almost identical to those which Marivaux will himself use when paying tribute to the Cardinal in his **"Discours de Réception à l'Académie Française."** Both portrait and speech bring to light the Cardinal's ability to act without attempting to surround himself with an air of mystery, as did his predecessors. Both also reveal his desire to work not for his own glory, but for the public good. The two testimonials show, in addition, his amiable relationship with the subjects. As in _Le Paysan parvenu,_ the portraits in _La Vie de Marianne_ reveal the narrator's reaction to the character. They have the added interest of showing Marivaux's own response to his contemporaries.

In Mme Dorsin's portrait, the technique is even more intricate, for the real life model is not merely a public figure whom Marivaux would have the reader admire and respect, but a benefactress and close personal friend whom the author looks upon with affection and whom he would have the reader view in the same light. She is "une dame que j'ai bien aimée, que vous aimerez aussi sur le portrait que je vous en ferai" (p. 161). The portrait must, moreover, not merely bring to light the virtues of Mme de Tencin; it must disguise her faults, most especially the "genre d'esprit caustique, parfois dénigrant, que l'on redoutait chez Mme de Tencin."[11] Marivaux, however, does not return to the stylized, almost meaningless eulogies of the seventeenth century. The point of view is a personal one.

In creating Mme Dorsin's portrait, Marivaux compiles, in a more or less systematic fashion, his own subjective impressions of his friend. The narrator begins the portrait with a short, flattering view of the physique, again described in moral terms, and again lacking in precision. She then passes to a discussion of Mme Dorsin's "âme." Mme Dorsin is next compared to other women with "beaucoup d'esprit" so that Marivaux can point out the absence of coquetry in his friend. The "cœur" of Mme Dorsin is then described, with the portrait continuing as a testimonial to the "esprit" and "cœur" of Mme Dorsin. Praise of her salon follows, and the portrait concludes with a discussion of the "âme" of Mme Dorsin, the author citing instances and examples of this "âme forte, courageuse et résolue; de ces âmes supérieures à tout événement, dont la hauteur et la dignité ne plient sous aucun accident humain" (p. 227).

Thus in _La Vie de Marianne_ the author angles the portrait completely so that the reader can view the subject in only one way. Details are selected, qualities are described, not because they explain the character's role in the action, as in _Le Paysan parvenu,_ but simply to make the reader share the author's sentiments towards a real person. The portraits have an interest in themselves. They are sufficiently concrete and detailed enough to awaken the reader's interest in the character as a person.

Occasionally, nevertheless, both novels show similar techniques. Jacob and Marianne both use caricature for personages they wish to put in an unfavorable light. They select one or a few physical features, and focus on them rather than on the person as a whole. A close analysis of the physique reveals much about the inner nature of the character. The eyes of Mme de Fare, who is responsible for revealing Marianne's identity, are the object of a portrait of this type.[12] The stoutness of the prioress at whose convent Marianne seeks refuge is exploited in a similar manner. The nun's obesity, Marianne finds on close examination, is "l'ouvrage d'une délicate, d'une amoureuse et d'une dévote complaisance qu'on a pour le bien et pour l'aise de son corps" (p. 148). In Jacob's adventures, the Habert confessor is treated in much the same fashion. The complexion, the eyes, the face, the hair, the lips, the teeth of M. Doucin are examined piecemeal, until the narrator concludes that the spiritual director "contre son intention sans doute, avait été jusqu'à l'ajustement" (p. 60). But even when the basic technique of caricature is identical in the two cases, there are differences in the portraits which reflect the differences in the narrators themselves. Jacob's portrait is drawn with a biting irony which Marianne's lacks. In **La Vie de Marianne,** moreover, the author does not consider distorted caricature the equivalent of an actual portrait. Having concluded the description of the prioress, Marianne adds, "j'en ferai peut-être le portrait quelque part" (p. 149).

Marivaux has clearly made a significant contribution to the genre of the portrait. He has taken a conventional, highly stylized, almost meaningless literary form, and made it an actual representation of fictional and real personages. The reader can see Mlle Habert, he can know Mme Dorsin, as he could not see or know Mlle de Scudéry or Julie d'Angennes. In addition, Marivaux has understood that the portrait must have a clearly definable, not morally simplistic, point of view. The narrator's sympathy for or detachment from the characters enables the reader to share the narrator's view of the personage and see him from the same angle. The characters, moreover, become more human, for they are seen from the point of view of another human being.[13] Thus Marivaux is able to integrate the portrait into two different psychological novels. That he is successful can, perhaps, be seen in the works of Diderot and others, who use some of the same devices to make their characters living and vital.

Notes

1. René Bray, *La Préciosité et les précieux de Thibaut de Champagne à Jean Giraudoux* (Paris: Albin Michel, 1948), pp. 189-190.

2. Frédéric Deloffre, ed. *La Vie de Marianne,* by Marivaux (Paris: Garnier Frères, 1957), Introduction, pp. xxxiii-xxxiv. All references to *La Vie de Marianne* are taken from this edition.

3. Gustave Lanson, *L'Art de la prose* (Paris: Librairie des Annales, 1911), pp. 127-8.

4. See Vivienne Mylne, *The Eighteenth Century French Novel: Techniques of Illusion* (New York, 1965), p. 118.

5. Marivaux, *Le Paysan parvenu,* ed. Frédéric Deloffre (Paris: Garnier Frères, 1959), p. 190. All references to *Le Paysan parvenu* are taken from this edition.

6. p. 47.

7. M. de Fécour, the financier whom Jacob visits at Versailles, also receives a sketch of this type (pp. 202-3).

8. The description of Marianne's middle-aged suitor is slightly more concrete but equally as subjective. He is "un homme d'environ cinquante ans tout au plus, de bonne mine, d'un air distingué, très bien mis, quoique simplement, et de la physionomie du monde la plus franche et la plus ouverte" (p. 420).

9. See the portraits of Mme de Ferval (pp. 141-3) and Mme de Fécour (pp. 179-81), the two middle-aged women who find Jacob so attractive.

10. *La Vie de Marianne,* Introduction, pp. xxxiii-xxxiv.

11. Gustave Larroumet, *Marivaux: Sa Vie et ses œuvres* (Paris: Librairie Hachette et Cie, 1894) p. 344n.

12. pp. 253-4.

13. For a discussion bearing on this problem, see Herbert Dieckmann, "The Presentation of Reality in Diderot's Tales," *Diderot Studies* III, ed. Otis Fellows and Gita May (Geneva: Librairie E. Droz, 1961), pp. 101-28.

Chavarche Tchalekian (essay date winter 1969)

SOURCE: Tchalekian, Chavarche. "Social Criticism in Marivaux's Plays." *Humanities Association Bulletin* 20, no. 1 (winter 1969): 20-6.

[*In the following essay, Tchalekian discusses Marivaux's criticism of the behavior of his contemporaries among the nobility and bourgeoisie.*]

Marivaux himself dated the awakening of his critical and analytical spirit from a seemingly rather minor event which occurred in 1705 when he was seventeen and a law student at Paris. At this time, a year before he wrote his first play, **Le Père prudent et équitable,** he was acquainted with a young lady, of whom he says (**Le Spectateur Français,** Première Feuille, pp. 38-40):

Je lui trouvais d'ailleurs tant d'indifférence pour ces charmes que j'aurais juré qu'elle les ignorait. Que j'étais simple dans ce temps-là! Quel plaisir, disais-je en moi-même! si je puis me faire aimer d'une fille qui ne souhaite pas d'avoir des amants, puisqu'elle est belle sans y prendre garde, et que, par conséquent, elle n'est pas coquette. . . . Il me semblait toujours qu'elle n'y entendait point finesse, et qu'elle ne songeait à rien moins qu'à être ce qu'elle était.

Un jour qu'à la campagne, je venais de la quitter, un gant que j'avais oublié, fit que je retournai sur mes pas pour l'aller chercher: j'aperçus la belle de loin, qui se regardait dans un miroir, et je remarquai, à mon grand étonnement, qu'elle s'y représentait à elle-même dans tous les sens où, durant notre entretien, j'avais vu son visage; et il se trouvait que ses airs de physionomie, que j'avais cru si naïfs, n'étaient, à les bien nommer, que des tours de gibécière: je jugeais de loin que sa vanité en adoptait quelques-uns, qu'elle en réformait d'autres: c'était de petites façons qu'on aurait pu noter, et qu'une femme aurait pu apprendre comme un air de musique. Je tremblai du péril que j'aurais couru si j'avais eu le malheur d'essayer encore de bonne foi ses friponneries, au point de perfection où son habilité les portait, mais je l'avais crue naturelle, et ne l'avais aimée que sur ce pied-là; de sorte que mon amour cessa tout d'un coup, comme si mon coeur ne s'était attendri que sous condition. Elle m'aperçut à son tour dans son miroir et rougit. Pour moi, j'entrai en riant, et ramassant mon gant: "Ah, mademoiselle, je vous demande pardon, lui dis-je, d'avoir mis jusqu'ici sur le compte de la nature des appas dont tout l'honneur n'est dû qu'à votre industrie."—"Qu'est-ce que c'est que signifie ce discours?" me répondit-elle.—"Vous parlerai-je plus franchement, lui dis-je. Je viens de voir les machines de l'Opéra. Il me divertira toujours, mais il me touchera moins." Je sortis là-dessus, et c'est de cette aventure que naquit en moi cette misanthropie qui ne m'a point quittée, et qui m'a fait passer ma vie à examiner les hommes, et à m'amuser de mes réflexions.

Although here Marivaux describes as misanthropy his dislike of sham and hypocrisy and his preoccupation with *la vérité,* he certainly is not an Alceste, for he is not a reformer in his social criticism. Nor does he consider man innately wicked. On the contrary, he is open-minded and indulgent toward weaknesses and presents man as he finds him in the society of which he is a part, not only in the salons which he frequented, such as those of Mme. de Lambert and Mme. de Tencin, but also in the everyday occupations of the bourgeoisie.

One critic has compared Marivaux's ideas about the theatre's effect on society as expressed in *L'Ile de la Raison* to Rousseau's "La Lettre à d'Alembert," written some thirty years later.[1] It is true that in a certain passage of *L'Ile de la Raison* (Act I, scene x) where the poet is describing contemporary theatre to Blectrue and defining tragedy and comedy for him, he says:

LE POÈTE:

Et puis il y a des comédies où je représentais les vices et les ridicules des hommes.

BLECTRUE:

Ah! je leur pardonne de pleurer là.

LE POÈTE:

Point du tout; cela les faisait rire.

BLECTRUE:

Hein?

LE POÈTE:

Je vous dis qu'ils riaient.

BLECTRUE:

Pleurer où l'on doit rire, et rire où l'on doit pleurer! les monstrueuses créatures.

Taken alone, this passage may lead one to believe that Marivaux, like Rousseau, is attacking the theatre as it was, in the sense that the theatre presented vices as agreeable and virtues as ridiculous. But, if we take into account Marivaux's complete theatre, we realize that this is not so. Marivaux continues in the tradition of Molière, but Marivaux's satire is usually directly at certain aspects of society rather than the foibles of particular individuals. His ridiculous characters, unlike Molière's, always see their shortcomings in the end and understand their mistakes. They are more flexible. Molière's characters never achieve self-criticism. A real Alceste could not have written *Les Sincères,* a play in which the two protagonists, Ergaste and La Marquise, who pride themselves on being sincere and on always telling the truth, realize at the end that they cannot in every circumstance do this, but must at times come to terms with society. At one point the Marquise says: "La sotte chose que l'humanité! qu'elle est ridicule! que de vanité! que de duperies! que de petitesse! et tout cela, faute de sincérité de part et d'autre." (Act I, scene iv). An Alceste would have maintained this attitude, but Marivaux here, as always, though a champion of sincerity, realizes and makes allowances for man as he is in society.

The basis of much of Marivaux's criticism of society is found in one of his very early plays, *L'Amour et la Vérité* (1720). Here L'Amour complains that true love no longer exists, but that love now inspires men to debauchery and greed rather than to modesty and tenderness. La Vérité replies by complaining that truth has also been driven out of the hearts of men by falsehood and flattery. Marivaux continues this criticism of the contemporary concept of love in *Arlequin poli par l'Amour.* In this play, Sylvia, who is in love with Arlequin, asks her cousin for advice on love. The cousin replies (Act I, scene ix):

Garde-t'en bien, ma cousine; sois bien sévère; cela entretient l'amour d'un amant.

SYLVIA:

Quoi! il n'y a point de moyen plus aisé que cela pour l'entretenir?

LA COUSINE:

Non; il ne faut point aussi lui dire tant que tu l'aimes.

THE COUSIN LEAVES AND SYLVIA MUSES:

> J'aimerais autant ne point aimer que d'être obligée
> d'être sévère; cependant elle dit que cela entretient
> l'amour. Voilà qui est étrange; on devrait bien changer
> une manière si incommode; ceux qui l'ont inventée
> n'aimaient pas tant que moi.

Thus, according to Marivaux, if love is sincere, modest
and tender, it should not be hidden away by coquetry.
Marivaux often blames the affectation and hypocrisy of
society on the sort of moral training prevalent. In ***L'Ile
des Esclaves*** the servant Cléanthis says of her mistress:

> . . . car vous verrez aussi comme quoi Madame entre
> dans une loge au spectacle, avec quelle emphase, avec
> quel air imposant, quoique d'un air distrait et sans y
> penser; car c'est la belle éducation qui donne cet
> orgueil-là.

> (Act I, scene iii)

In this same play Marivaux lists the characteristics
which he finds admirable in a person: "Il faut avoir le
coeur bon, de la vertu et de la raison; voilà ce qu'il
faut, voilà ce qui fait qu'un homme est plus qu'un
autre." (Act I, scene ix). He objects to the lack of these
qualities, to the superficiality of everyday life and the
behavior of the rich and noble. He recognizes and ridicules the innate human weakness in their desire for flattery. For example, Cléanthis, again speaking of her mistress, relates: "Un jour qu'elle pouvait m'entendre, et
qu'elle croyait que je ne m'en doutais pas, je parlais
d'elle, et je dis: 'Oh! pour cela il faut l'avouer, Madame est une des plus belles femmes du monde.' Que
de bontés pendant huit jours, ce petit mot ne me valut-il
pas!" (Act I, scene iii).

Marivaux often speaks through his more naive characters who see and measure things by their own values
and who, because of their simplicity and innocence,
give an ingenuous and often entirely unexpected interpretation to what they are told. For instance, nobility of
birth was not important to Marivaux. What gave value
to a person's character was the possession of such virtues as sincerity, modesty and tenderness. He satirizes
those who possess only nobility of birth in ***Le
Dénouement Imprévu***. Maître Pierre cannot undertand
the importance of being "d'un sang noble" and says:
"Que guiable d'invention d'avoir fait comme ça du
sang de deux façons, pendant qu'il vient du même
ruisseau. . . ." Somewhat later he tells his master:
"Monsieur Dorante, vous avez du sang noble, c'est moi
qui vous le dis; ça se connait aux pistoles que vous me
pourmettez . . ." (Act I, scene i). Thus, to this simple
man, nobility is only a matter of money.

Marivaux continues this sort of criticism in ***La Double
Inconstance***. Here the prince has fallen in love with
Sylvia and tries to bribe Arlequin with *lettres de no-*
blesse to give up his claims to her. Arlequin replies to
the persuasion used to make him accept the letters that
they would make him more feared and respected by his
neighbors:

ARLEQUIN:

> Jai opinion que cela les empêcherait de m'aimer de
> bon coeur; car quand je respecte les gens, moi, et que
> je les crains, je ne les aime pas de si bon courage; je ne
> saurais faire tant de choses à la fois.

LE SEIGNEUR:

> Vous m'étonnez!

ARLEQUIN:

> Voilà comme je suis bâti; d'ailleurs, voyez-vous, je suis
> le meilleur enfant du monde, je ne fais de mal à
> personne; mais quand je voudrais nuire, je n'en ai pas
> le pouvoir. Eh bien! si j'avais ce pouvoir, si j'étais
> noble, diable emporte si je voudrais gager d'être
> toujours brave homme: je ferais parfois comme le
> gentilhomme de chez nous, qui n'épargne pas les coups
> de bâton à cause qu'on n'oserait les lui rendre.

LE SEIGNEUR:

> Oh! Comme les hommes sont quelquefois méchants,
> mettez-vous en état de faire du mal, seulement afin
> qu'on n'ose pas vous en faire, et pour cet effet prenez
> vos lettres de noblesse.

> (Act III, scene iv)

In this passage the lord's cruelty to his serfs comes out,
as well as the idea that man in general will be cruel if
he possesses power and knows that he can exercise this
power with impunity.

In another passage of the same play Marivaux satirizes
the customs of the court, using the *procédé* which
Montesquieu had used in his *Lettres Persanes,* which
had appeared two years earlier in 1721. Arelequin has
been taken through the prince's palace, and here is his
reaction to what he saw:

FLAMINIA:

> Benjour, Arlequin. Dites-moi donc de quoi vous riez,
> afin que j'en rie aussi.

ARLEQUIN:

> C'est que mon valet Trivelin, que je ne paye point, m'a
> mené par toutes les chambres de la maison, où l'on
> trotte comme dans les rues, où l'on jase comme dans
> notre halle, sans que le maître de la maison
> s'embarrasse de tous ces visages-là et qui viennent
> chez lui sans donner le bonjour, qui vont le voir man-
> ger sans qu'il dise: "Voulez-vous boire un coup?" Je
> me divertissais de ces originaux-là en revenant, quand
> j'ai vu un grand coquin qui a levé l'habit d'une dame
> par derrière. Moi, j'ai cru qu'il lui faisait quelque niche,
> et je lui ai dit bonnement: "Arrêtez-vous, polisson,
> vous badinez, malhonnêtement." Elle, qui m'a entendu,

s'est retournée et m'a dit: "Ne voyez-vous pas bien qu'il me porte la queue?"—"Et pourquoi vous la laissez-vous porter, cette queue?" ai-je repris. Sur cela le polisson s'est mis à rire; la dame riait, Trivelin riait, tout le monde riait; par compagnie je me suis mis à rire aussi. A cette heure je vous demande pourquoi nous avons tous ri.

FLAMINIA:

D'une bagatelle. C'est que vous ne savez pas que ce que vous avez vu faire à ce laquais est un usage parmi les dames.

(Act II, scene v)

Throughout this play Marivaux attacks the customs of the rich bourgeois and the nobility. He implies his disapproval of their extravagant and wasteful life that is of no benefit to society as a whole. The simple Arlequin cannot understand why one should need both a country and a city house. He says:

Il ne me faut qu'une chambre; je n'aime point à nourrir des fainéants. . . . Eh bien! avec un bon lit, une bonne table, une douzaine de chaises de paille, ne suis-je pas bien meublé? . . . Oh! mais je n'ai point de carrosse! . . . (En montrant ses jambes.) Ne voilà-t-il pas un équipage que ma mère m'a donné? n'est-ce pas de bonnes jambes? Eh! morbleu, il n'y a pas de raison à vous d'avoir une autre voiture que la mienne. Alerte, alerte, paresseux; laissez vos chevaux à tant d'honnêtes laboureurs, qui n'en ont point; cela nous fera du pain; vous marcherez, et vous n'aurez pas les gouttes.

(Act I, scene iv)

In another scene of *La Double Inconstance* Marivaux's criticism is even sharper. Sylvia, one of Marivaux's ingenuous characters, sees through the affectations of the palace residents, who are sophisticated and polite on the surface, but basically shallow and hypocritical:

C'est quelque chose d'épouvantable que ce pays-ci! Je n'ai jamais vu de femmes si civiles, d'hommes si honnêtes. Ce sont des manières si douces, tant de révérances, tant de compliments, tant de signes d'amitié! Vous diriez que ce sont les meilleures gens du monde, qu'ils sont plein de coeur et de conscience. Point du tout! De tous ces gens-là, il n'y en a pas un qui ne vienne me dire d'un air prudent: "Mademoiselle, croyez-moi, je vous conseille d'abandonner Arlequin et d'épouser le Prince"; mais ils me conseillent cela, tout naturellement, sans avoir honte, non plus que s'ils m'exhortaient à quelque bonne action. "Mais, leur dis-je, j'ai promis à Arlequin; où est la fidélité, la probité, la bonne foi?" Ils ne m'entendent pas; ils ne savent ce que c'est que tout cela; c'est tout comme si je leur parlai grec. Ils me rient au nez, me disent que je fais l'enfant, qu'une grande fille doit avoir de la raison; eh! cela n'est-il pas joli? Ne valoir rien, tromper son prochain, lui manquer de parole, être fourbe et mensonger; voilà le devoir des grandes personnes ce ce maudit endroit-ci. Qu'est que ces gens-là? D'où sortent-ils? De quelle pâte sont-ils?

(Act II, scene i)

Not only does Marivaux condemn the people described above by Sylvia, but all those who take marriage lightly, including husbands who have fallen out of love. Like Molière, he criticizes parents who force young women into marriages which are against their inclinations. However, Molière's criticism in *Tartuffe* and *L'Avare,* for example, differs from Marivaux's. Molière's parents are usually obstinate; Marivaux's are liberal-minded. Molière makes his point by ridiculing the parents. On the other hand, Marivaux's parents leave the final choice to their children.

Marriage in the Parisian society of the eighteenth century was often regarded as an unpleasant necessity and was usually arranged by the parents without the consent of the parties involved. Conjugal fidelity was not the usual thing. This is why many of Marivaux's lovers go to extremes to prove that they are sincerely loved. (*Le Jeux de l'Amour et du Hasard* is a good example.) In *La Réunion des Amours,* an allegorical fantasy, Love is depicted as the god of sentiment, while Cupid is the god of passion and voluptuousness, representing the loose morality of the eighteenth century. Mercure tells Cupidon that he is responsible for infidelity: "Vous mettez toujours après leurs femmes quelque chasseur qui les attrape." Cupidon replies: ". . . mes chasseurs ne poursuivent que ce qui se presente . . . La plupart sont des coquettes, qui en demeurent là, ou bien ne se retirent que pour agacer . . . la coquetterie les a déjà bien étourdies avant qu'on les tire" (Act I, scene iii). Here Marivaux places the blame for infidelity on the coquetry of women.

The subject of fidelity in marriage occurs again in *Le Petit-Maître Corrigé.* In this play, Dorimène has come from Paris in order to marry Rosimond. However, Rosimond is beginning to fall in love with Hortense, whom his father wanted him to marry, and he tries to put off Dorimène.

ROSIMOND:

Mais vous ressouvenez-vous que vous êtes en province, où il y a des règles, des maximes de décence qu'il ne faut point choquer?

DORIMÈNE:

Plaisantes maximes. . . . Ah! il y a des puérilités qui ne doivent pas arrêter. Je vous épouserai, Monsieur; j'ai du bien, de la naissance, qu'on nous marie; c'est peut-être le vrai moyen de me guérir d'un amour que vous ne méritez pas que je conserve.

ROSIMOND:

Nous marier? Des gens qui s'aiment!

(Act II, scene vi)

This is the concept of love and marriage which Marivaux observed and satirized. From this play it seems that marriage is an antidote to love, that love and marriage are incompatible. But then in *Les Serments Indiscrets* Damis, who is afraid of the consequences of marriage, says: "Dans le mariage pour bien vivre ensemble, il faut que la volonté d'un mari s'accorde avec celle de sa femme, et cela est difficile; car de ces deux volontés-là, il y en a toujours une qui va de travers . . ." (Act I, scene v). Here Marivaux tells us how a marriage can succeed, though he admits that it is difficult.

Another factor in arranged marriages which Marivaux criticizes is the great consideration given to money. In *Les Fausses Confidences,* Monsieur Rémy, Dorante's uncle is trying to persuade him to marry:

Monsieur Rémy:

Hum! Quoi? Entendez-vous ce que je vous dis, qu'elle a quinze mille livres de rente, entendez-vous?

Dorante:

Oui monsieur; mais en eut-elle vingt fois davantage, je ne l'épouserais pas; nous ne serions pas heureux ni l'un ni l'autre: j'ai le coeur pris; j'aime ailleurs.

(Act II, scene ii)

Then Marivaux adds a comment on the consideration of social rank when Madame Argante, Araminte's mother, who is beginning to fear that her daughter may refuse to marry the Count Dorimont and who is herself a snob, says: "Le beau nom de Dorimont et le rang de Comtesse ne la touchent pas assez; elle ne sent pas le désagrément qu'il y a de n'être qu'une bourgeoise. Elle s'endort dans cet état, malgré le bien qu'elle a." (Act I, scene x).

Marivaux was criticizing a society in which marriage was considered less as a romantic union of two people in love with each other than as an outgrowth and an extension of the more commercial and snobbish aspects of that society. To Marivaux, mutual agreement, mutual love and understanding were the important constituents in a marriage. This seems to have been Marivaux's own situation. He himself waited until he was over thirty before he married, but when he married, his union was a very happy one and lasted until the death of his wife.

From the preceding examples it seems evident that Marivaux can be accurately classed with the social satirists. His characters, unlike those of Molière who never realize their shortcomings nor recognize their faults, may appear ridiculous for a time, but in the end gain the sympathy of the audience. Yet if Marivaux satirizes, he certainly does not preach, for in most of his plays the satire is incidental. He noted and sketched with humor and accuracy the superficiality and hypocrisy of his society, elements possibly not observable to the insensitive, but which Marivaux's powers of psychological penetration brought to the surface. No segment of society escaped his satirical pen from the rich and powerful to the bourgeoisie. As a social satirist he exposed the affectation and hypocrisy of the men and women of his age, viewing them as if they were "les machines de l'Opéra," and in doing so amused not only himself with his reflections but posterity as well.

Note

1. Kenneth N. McKee, *The Theatre of Marivaux* (New York: New York University Press, 1958), p. 93.

Valentini Papadopoulou Brady (essay date 1970)

SOURCE: Brady, Valentini Papadopoulou. "The Concept of Love in Marivaux." In *Love in the Theatre of Marivaux: A Study of the Factors Influencing Its Birth, Development, and Expression*, pp. 13-43. Geneva: Librairie Droz, 1970.

[*In the following excerpt, Brady examines Marivaux's representations of love in his plays, contending that, although the playwright distinguishes between erotic love and spiritual love, the two are combined in his concept of ideal love.*]

Numerous critics have defined the nature of the love experienced by Marivaux's characters. Some are strongly critical of it—Alain, for example, sees it as "une conception d'amour bien frivole", and wonders what will come of it in marriage: "Ce qui en résulte dans les ménages, Marivaux ne l'a point dit. Mais je devine d'étranges époux unis par ces souvenirs de carnaval."[1] Others, more tolerant, admit a certain lack of spontaneity and depth but emphasize its gallant, delicate, and subtly complex nature: Gustave Larroumet, for example, seems to regret that it is "plutôt une galanterie aiguisée de sentiment qu'un vif entraînement, encore moins la passion telle que nous l'entendons aujourd'hui",[2] but goes on to describe it as "un mélange de sensibilité et d'ironie, de sincérité et de feinte, de discrétion et de hardiesse".[3] He sees the protagonists as distinguished, well-bred and refined by experience in the salons; they are gallant, even tender, but avoid exaltation because they are afraid of appearing ridiculous.[4] In a similar tone, G. Brereton defines the love portrayed by Marivaux as "a delicately pleasurable sensation filling the characters with the same delight they would find in a fine summer morning or a properly-ordered party among congenial friends in the right surroundings".[5] In other words, a pleasant experience but certainly not unique in its kind.

The 19th century was, in general, rather unkind to Marivaux: Charles Lenient, for, example, deplores not only the mildly "pleasant" nature of Marivaux's version of love ("l'amour ne doit être à ses yeux ni une chaîne ni un supplice, mais un état agréable où chacun trouve son compte")[6] but also its superficiality: "L'amour . . . est un doux passe-temps plutôt qu'une folle ivresse ou un tourment douloureux."[7] Naturally, the notion of the romantic hero and romantic love has something to do with this attitude towards Marivaux. The twentieth century has been, as a whole, kinder to our author and his portrayal of love. Maurice Donnay, writing in 1929, may admit the superficial nature of the main elements of this love, at least in its birth ("la curiosité, le goût, l'amour-propre, le désir d'approbation", and "des qualités extérieures: le plumage et le ramage"), but affirms that "cet amour-là n'est souvent qu'une première étape vers un amour plus sincère, plus profond et même vers une passion véritable qui peut venir assez vite".[8] A. Feugère, writing in 1935, stresses the non-fatalistic nature of this love, and more particularly its dependence on pride and reason:

> L'amour que peint Marivaux n'est pas l'impulsion presque irrésistible qui entraîne les amoureux bon gré mal gré au bien ou au mal; il est représenté comme une inclination naissante, qui se plaît à rester sous le contrôle de la raison, et qui, pour grandir, a besoin du consentement de la volonté; or la volonté met longtemps à consentir, car une force rivale de l'amour intervient: l'amour-propre, jaloux de son indépendance menacée.[9]

Marcel Arland sees the whole of Marivaux's theatrical world as "le monde de l'homme et de la femme dans le pur climat de l'amour et de la poésie".[10] As for the kind of love that Marivaux portrays, Arland distinguishes it from passion but recognises its importance in the life of the characters: "Il ne s'agit point d'une passion effrénée qui fonde sur eux et d'eux-mêmes les arrache . . . Pourtant ils ne seraient rien sans cet amour; . . . c'est leur seule aventure."[11] Kibédi Varga defines not the nature but the stage of love portrayed by Marivaux: ". . . seuls les présages, les premières inquiétudes l'intéressent et non pas l'Amour, le sentiment à l'état pur . . . Il s'est choisi le moment de l'éveil de l'amour, le seul moment précisément dans la vie humaine où coquetterie et sincérité, préciosité et gravité coïncident tout naturellement."[12]

R. Niklaus prefers to define love in Marivaux by saying what it is *not* rather than what it *is*; "It is not cerebral, nor romanesque, nor libertine", he says in 1959,[13] and in 1963: "Il ne s'agit évidemment pas du grand amour romantique, ni de l'amour passion des classiques; il ne s'agit pas vraiment non plus de l'amour littéraire ou romanesque du siècle précédent; à plus forte raison, et malgré une sensualité sous-jacente, nous n'avons pas affaire à l'amour grossier des premiers zannis ou de leurs maîtres."[14] Marlyse Meyer starts with a similarly negative definition: "Ce sentiment qui attire l'un vers l'autre les amoureux de Marivaux n'a rien de la passion foudroyante qui écrase les héros raciniens: on ne meurt

jamais d'amour ici, et on peut assez facilement passer d'un amour à un autre."[15] And: ". . . ces amoureux . . . ne vont guère sombrer dans ces abîmes de passion où, vers la même époque, Des Grieux ou Cleveland seront entraînés. Ce n'est pas non plus un sentiment édulcoré, purement livresque, héritier de l'amour galant ou précieux."[16] But then the critic moves on to a more positive statement: it is simply "le coup de foudre", étincelle qui jaillit brusquement entre deux êtres, qui brusquement se plaisent, se désirent",[17] ". . . cet amour 'quotidien', né du désir, qui, brusquement, jaillit entre un homme et une femme . . . et qui peut, ou non, se transformer en tendresse".[18]

Mme Meyer's contention that Marivaux's theatre is a "comédie du désir"[19] brings us to the question of the "sensuality" which some critics see in the author's conception of love. The best-known advocate of this interpretation is Paul Gazagne, whose work dates back to 1954.[20] Gazagne's theory has already been discussed by E. J. H. Greene[21] but, for the sake of completeness, we shall briefly indicate its main point: the centre of Marivaux's theatrical world is sensuality and the main preoccupation of his characters, desire. For him, the four main plays (*La Surprise de l'amour, La seconde Surprise de l'amour, Le Jeu de l'amour et du hasard, Les fausses Confidences*), which are generally considered "des surprises de l'amour", are really "des surprises du désir et non des surprises de la tendresse".[22] The critic explains the difference by referring to Marivaux's usage of the term *amour* and the verb *épouser* with two distinct meanings,[23] and by pointing out that when Marivaux wants to speak of *sentiment* he uses the word *tendresse* and not the word *amour.*[24]

Many critics, both before and after Gazagne, have taken a view opposed to that of this critic: Käthy Lüthi,[25] Claude Roy,[26] Xavier de Courville,[27] Jacques Scherer,[28] and even Renée Papin, who is, on the whole, glad of Gazagne's vigorous defense of Marivaux's realism, question the critic's contention that sensuality is the centre of his theatre.[29]

Is Marivaux, then, sensual or not? There are critics who hesitate between the two and are inclined to see him as combining both. R. Niklaus speaks of a "sensualité sous-jacente",[30] and affirms that the love Marivaux portrays is not essentially sensual "although the awakening of sensuality attends its birth".[31] For Lionel Gossman, the "ambiguity" of Marivaux's plays lies in the possibility of taking them both as "configurations of erotic adventures" or as "configurations of sentimental ones".[32] Jean Maquet believes that it is not the notion of eroticism which will clarify Marivaux's work but Marivaux who can reveal to us the meaning of eroticism.[33] *Eros* or *Agapè*? asks Maquet. "Je me demande", he says, "si le secret de Marivaux n'est pas d'avoir pressenti et peut-être même touché de quelque manière un point d'où

Eros et Agapè sont aperçus comme une seule et même divinité."[34] This Greek dichotomy between two basic types of love is, however, not very useful for our purposes, as the second term strictly represents brotherly love or charity. A more useful pair of opposed conceptions is that which opposes the Platonic and Ovidian conceptions of love. The latter is realistic, and correponds to *Eros,* physical desire, with an admixture of cynicism; the former is idealistic and spiritual. The corresponding Marivaudian terms, in this case, would be *amour* and *tendresse.* Occasionally, Marivaux makes the distinction between these two terms,[35] but the two concepts are not consistently separated in the author's mind; in fact, they are usually found together in his idea of real love. For example, in a passage which Gazagne himself quotes,[36] Marivaux speaks of *amour-désir* and *amour-tendresse* without excluding desire from the latter. And in his description of a young girl at the beginning of **La Voiture embourbée,** he declares as "véritable tendresse" a combination of *amour-désir* and *amour-tendresse.*[37]

In the plays, the first indication of an opposition between two kinds of love is in **L'Amour et la Vérité.** Tender love has gone out of fashion, supplanted by libertine love. The former, characterized by "tendres et tremblants aveux", "dépits délicats", "air de vivacité tendre et modeste", "yeux qui apprivoisaient la vertu même, qui ne demandaient que le cœur", "transports d'amour d'après les plus innocentes faveurs, d'après mille petits riens précieux", began to bore people: "J'ennuyais, je glaçais; on me regardait comme un innocent qui manquait d'expérience, et je ne fus plus célébré que par les poètes et les romanciers". The latter ("l'amour libertin")—the fruit of a moment's weakness on the part of Venus, who, tempted by *Débauche* and *Avarice,* gave in to Plutus' desire—has, according to his rival, "des airs grossiers", "un caractère brutal". But people gradually accepted him and soon he took over completely: ". . . ce maudit Amour fut insensiblement souffert; bientôt on le trouva plus badin que moi; moins gênant, moins formaliste, plus expéditif . . ."

To which kind of love does Marivaux give his preference? On this point we may refer to his play **La Réunion des amours.** Produced at the Théâtre Français on the 5th November 1731, between **Le Jeu de l'amour et du hasard** (23rd January 1730) and **La Vie de Marianne** (1731-1741), **La Réunion** derives its significance partly from the fact that it is a production of the author's "peak period",[38] when Marivaux was at the height of his powers. Its importance owes even more, however, to the explicit character of its theoretical comments: as several writers such as René de Planhol[39] and Paul Gazagne[40] have pointed out, Marivaux here presents a fundamental opposition between two types of love: Amour—tender, sentimental, discreet; and Cupidon—sensual, passionate, physical.

It may well be that the many different forms taken by love through the ages are related to the dialectic between two such basic conceptions. These two basic conceptions however, vary somewhat in nature. This variation is certainly less obvious in the case of physical, sexual love, and indeed it may be argued that the nature of the fundamental biological urge for sexual possession remains the stable element in this dialectic: Cupidon is, if not identical with, at least the direct descendant of *Eros* (desire), through Ovid's *Ars Amatoria* (where it is mixed with irony and sentimental strategy) and that medieval strain we now term *amour gaulois* (where it is treated with frankness and bawdy humour).[41]

But if Cupidon corresponds roughly with *Eros,* Amour (tender, sentimental, discreet love) is not *Agapè* (brotherly love, charity), and in fact the gap between them is such that several other fundamental conceptions fit into this gap. Somewhat after *Agapè* we have the spiritual love admired by Plato, and further on again (closer now to *Amour*) we find *l'amour courtois.* *L'amour courtois* and *Amour* oppose physical love by merely de-emphasizing, *Agapè* and Plato's ideal love oppose it by actually excluding; the opposition to sexual desire is thus much more radical in the latter.

Having already claimed that when Marivaux writes "je vous aime" he invariably means "je vous désire", Gazagne consequently affirms that in **La Réunion des amours** it is not sentimental Amour but sensual Cupidon who represents the author's own preference. For this critic, Marivaux's play criticizes excessive sentimentality, which pretends to ignore and even condemn physical manifestations of love. He draws this conclusion because he says that Marivaux gives to Amour "un rôle effacé et un comportement si terne que ses interlocuteurs en bâillent", whereas Cupidon is presented as "brillant, enjoué, entreprenant et séduisant",[42] in other words more attractive. However, the ending of the play contradicts this thesis: Minerve reprimands Cupidon and demands a compromise between Cupidon and Amour.[43]

MINERVE:

> Cupidon, la Vertu décidait contre vous; et moi-même j'allais être de son sentiment, si Jupiter n'avait pas jugé à propos de vous réunir, en vous corrigeant, pour former le cœur du prince. Avec votre confrère, l'âme est trop tendre, il est vrai; mais avec vous, elle est trop libertine. Il fait souvent des cœurs ridicules; vous n'en faites que de méprisables. Il égare l'esprit; mais vous ruinez les mœurs. Il n'a que des défauts; vous n'avez que des vices. Unissez-vous tous deux: rendez-le plus vif et plus passionné, et qu'il vous rende plus tendre et plus raisonnable; . . .

(Scene 14)

Furthermore, the passage in Marivaux upon which Gazagne bases his chief argument presents us with a criticism of Cupidon rather than a justification: ". . .

les sentiments n'étaient plus à la mode, il n'y avait plus d'amants, ce n'était plus que libertins qui tâchaient de faire des libertines. On disait bien encore à une femme, je vous aime, mais c'était une manière polie de lui dire, je vous désire . . ."[44] In fact, Marivaux deplores this situation.

In our examination of **La Réunion,** we take the following as a key passage:

Cupidon:

> . . . Mais, dites-vous, vous êtes le dieu du vice. Cela n'est pas vrai; je donne de l'amour, voilà tout: le reste vient du cœur des hommes. Les uns y perdent, les autres y gagnent, je ne m'en embarrasse pas. J'allume le feu; c'est à la raison à le conduire . . .

(Scene 10)

We take *vice* here to mean sexual libertinism, *amour* to mean something different, something less—the initial spark of attraction that brings a man and a woman together. If this initial spark becomes a cause of corruption, says Cupidon, it is not my fault but that of man himself (*cœur des hommes*). Some lose by it, some gain; in other words, in some people, this love causes corruption in the form of libertinism, whereas in others it generates virtues in the form of *tendresse*. Thus, since "les uns y perdent, les autres y gagnent" is preceded by considerations of a moral nature and followed by "c'est à la raison à le conduire", we take it to mean not win or lose in the game of love (as Greene implies in the case of *Le Triomphe de l'amour*), but in the sense of gaining virtues or losing them according to the way love will develop in each individual: it will become discreet, restrained, delicate, through *raison,* or it will become *vice* through the predominance of the instincts.

There are three structural aspects in the passage quoted above which must be considered in its elucidation: firstly the equation *amour* plus [*ce qui*] *vient du cœur des hommes* equals *vice*; secondly, the symmetry and contrast between "je donne de l'amour . . . le reste vient du cœur des hommes" and "j'allume le feu, c'est à la raison à le conduire"; and thirdly, the pivotal function of "les uns y perdent, les autres y gagnent": its first part ("les uns y perdent") links the two contrasted elements just mentioned by referring backward, and then forward ("les autres y gagnent"). It is, of course, disconcerting to find *cœur* here used almost pejoratively in contrast with reason, to mean "instincts", especially from the pen of the man who wrote many a passage on the superiority of *cœur* over *esprit* or *raison*.[45] But Marivaux is notorious for his extremely varied usage of the word *cœur,* as Leo Spitzer has pointed out.[46] Thus the main idea is that *amour,* if it is not to become libertinism, needs the help of reason (or *sagesse*), and must not be guided by man's instincts alone.

What is then the nature of love as portrayed by Marivaux in his theatre? It is not tragic, nor violent or romanesque, but elegant and sophisticated. Its birth depends largely on a first impression created by appearance and personality. Its aim is always marriage. As we shall see later (Chapter 6, physical qualities), in most of the plays, as well as in the novels, love is born at the first glance: "Comment avez-vous fait pour m'aimer, vous?" Silvia asks the lovesick *berger* (**Arlequin poli par l'amour**). "Moi! je vous ai vue; voilà tout" (scene 4), he replies. Silvia cannot understand, but she too will fall in love with Arlequin as soon as she sees him. Ergaste (**La Méprise**) is struck by a sudden "coup de foudre"[47] after only a few seconds of seeing Clarice's face. Mlle Argante (**Le Dénouement imprévu**) takes scarcely longer upon seeing Eraste. The same reaction is to be found in the case of the two couples in **La Dispute,** and, although much more subtly implied, the first attraction is there in the more sophisticated plays. We are told that this is exactly how the hero of **Les fausses Confidences** fell in love with Araminte, and although they will not admit it, this is also how the protagonists of **Les Serments indiscrets, La Surprise, La seconde Surprise, Le Jeu** and so on fell in love.

A second important characteristic is that love cannot be explained rationally: it follows its own rules and it is beyond the characters' power to change the way they feel. Young Lina in **La Colonie** says of love: ". . . je ne l'ai pas pris; c'est lui qui m'a prise . . ." (scene 5). Lucile (**Les Serments indiscrets**) cannot understand why she loves Damis,[48] and another young girl, Constance (**La Joie imprévue**), recognises love's independence from her will.[49] Dorante of **L'heureux Stratagème,** although exclaiming "Que nous étions mal assortis" and wishing he could love the Marquise instead of the frivolous Countess, cannot help loving the latter. The Prince of **La double Inconstance** is convinced, and he also convinces Silvia, that "on n'est pas le maître de son cœur" (III, 9), and the heroine of **Le Jeu** falls in love with "Bourguignon" in spite of all the defences provided by her reason and her social conscience. Dorante himself admits: ". . . je n'ai pu me défendre de t'aimer" (II, 12). The fact that the protagonists' preconceived ideas about marriage and love, their experience of the world (sometimes theoretical, sometimes based on observation), do not protect them from falling in love in the same instinctive way is another proof of the inexplicable and nonrational nature of this love.[50] We may distinguish one exception: Hortense of **Le Petit-Maître corrigé,** who refuses to marry Rosimond and, to a certain extent, stops herself from becoming involved with him until she sees evidence of a change in his attitude towards love and marriage.

Several critics have questioned the depth, the intensity and the spontaneity of this love. Charles Lenient deplores the lack of strongly-felt emotions in Marivaux's characters, who are content with "une sensibilité tempérée et modérée, qui effleure l'âme et la chatouille légèrement sans la déchirer".[51] He sees Marivaux's world as situated "dans la zone des passions tempérées par l'intérêt et le bon sens".[52] He accuses Marivaux of frivolity,[53] lack of depth. He reproaches him with the portrayal of "les petits riens du beaumonde, saupoudrés de réflexions philosophiques, les petits jeux de cachecache et de colin-maillard".[54] This is, with a few exceptions, the attitude of the 19th century. Even Gustave Larroumet, who was the first scholar to take Marivaux seriously enough to devote a voluminous doctoral thesis to him, admits that "le grand défaut des plus aimables [amoureux], c'est qu'ils ont moins de sentiment que de raison, moins de cœur que d'esprit".[55] Käthy Lüthi defines the love Marivaux's heroines feel as *amour de tête* and says that they are satisfied with "un peu de sentiment".[56] To support this she quotes as an example the Marquise of *Les Sincères,* who is suspicious of and laughs at Dorante's "exaggerated" passionate expressions. What the critic omits is that, at the end of the play, the Marquise is glad to return to Dorante, his "emphases", and his "apostrophes galantes".

It is not true that Marivaux's heroines are as easily satisfied as Käthy Lüthi claims, and we can give numerous examples to support our contention. For instance, one of the main reasons why Silvia (*La double Inconstance*) cannot finally resist the young "officer" 's courting is because he represents the ideal Courtly Lover with his total submission, his silent suffering, his continuous adoration for her, and a love which, he claims, will only end with his death. Similarly, the Countess of *La fausse Suivante* is influenced in favour of the "Chevalier" because of the ardent and eloquent nature of "his" love.[57] Hortense (*Le Prince travesti*) was delighted with the kind of love Count Rodrigue showed for her before their marriage,[58] and cannot stress enough what this love means to a woman and what a catastrophe it is to lose it.[59] Having had a taste of it, Hortense cannot be satisfied with anything less, and the only man who may reconcile her with love again is the man who gave evidence of this kind of love: Lélio, the young hero who saved her life, followed her for two days and left at her request but not without "quelque sorte de douleur". His love for Hortense subsequently proves to be ardent and impetuous, yet full of "sentiments de tendresse qui ne finiront qu'avec [sa] vie" (I, 8): it survives her feigned refusal ("je pars dans l'instant, et je ne vous oublierai jamais", II, 7), defies danger ("j'aime autant mourir que de ne vous plus voir", II, 7), resists temptations of wealth and power.

In *La seconde Surprise,* one of the first things about the Chevalier that impresses the Marquise is his capacity for love, the intensity with which he can love, as is shown by his despair at losing Angélique ("Je me meurs, je voudrais mourir, et je ne sais comment je vis

encore", I, 7). The extent of this love as well as his determination to obey Angélique's wishes—never to try and see her again—make the Marquise comment that he is "un honnête homme", that he has "un fonds de probité qui la charme" and that he is, like her, "né sensible". If Lucile in *Les Serments indiscrets* is against marrying someone unknown to her, it is because she believes that a marriage arranged according to the customs of the day would not give her the kind of relationship she wants, that is "un amour tendre"; "J'ai l'âme tendre", she says, and "une âme tendre et douce a des sentiments, elle en demande; elle a besoin d'être aimée parce qu'elle aime" (I, 1). She will not be happy with less, and is convinced that a sensitive heart "entre les mains d'un mari n'a jamais son nécessaire" (*ibid.*).[60] Hortense (*Le Petit-Maître corrigé*) has decided not to marry Rosimond unless he not only loves her but also is prepared to express his love openly. "Un peu de sentiment" is not enough for her; she expects a lot more from the man she will marry:

> Je n'accorderai mon cœur qu'aux soins les plus tendres, qu'à tout ce que l'amour a de plus respectueux, de soumis; il faudra qu'on me dise mille fois 'je vous aime', avant que je le croie et que je m'en soucie; qu'on se fasse une affaire de la dernière importance de me le persuader; qu'on ait la modestie de craindre d'aimer en vain, et qu'on me demande enfin mon cœur comme une grâce qu'on sera trop heureux d'obtenir. Voilà à quel prix j'aimerai . . . et je n'en rabattrai rien.
>
> (II, 8)

And, in fact, it is not until she is convinced that Rosimond loves her in this way, not until she hears him say it and repeat it himself, that she agrees to marry him. Eraste's despair at the thought of losing Angélique (*L'Ecole des mères*) ("je ne me soucie plus de la vie . . . je me meurs"; scene 7), his efforts to see her (which lead him to disguise himself as a servant), exhorting her to refuse the marriage arranged by her mother, everything indicates that what he feels is much more than "un peu de sentiment".

Dorante (*La Mère confidente*) displays even more passion, even more despair at the thought of losing Angélique, partly because his lack of fortune presents a greater obstacle than M. Damis (Orgon) did for Eraste. Angélique is moved by Dorante's expressions of love ("je n'ai que mon cœur à vous offrir, il est vrai; mais du moins n'en fut-il jamais de plus pénétré ni de plus tendre"; I, 3), by his despair when she sends him away pretending to be indifferent to his love (II, 3), by his continuous affirmations of love, even by the extremes to which he goes when he proposes elopement and a secret marriage, a proposition which shocks Angélique but which is another confirmation of the intensity of his feelings. She forgives him and tries to justify him to her mother by saying that his great love for her, his despair at the thought of losing her made him lose his head (II,

12). If Angélique forgives him, justifies him, deceives her mother and even criticises her in spite of their close relationship, it is partly because she feels that Dorante's love for her is quite unique ("il m'adore, on n'en peut douter"; II, 12), exceptional, well above "un peu de sentiment". Her mother realises this too, and when she sees that Dorante is also capable of self-sacrifice she consents to his union with her daughter.

The Countess of **Le Legs** is, in general, pre-disposed unfavourably towards men who use a certain vocabulary (*passion, brûler, adorer, flamme, appas,* and so on). In this, she resembles the Marquise of **Les Sincères,** who is suspicious of "adulateurs" and "visionnaires". The Countess has the reputation of a woman who is matter-of-fact and "raisonnable"; but when she hears from Lisette that the Marquis is in love with her (with all the *passion* and *flamme* he is capable of), all her attitudes change. What she despises, she says, is not those who are capable of sincere and deep love but all those "étourdis" for whom love is only a pose and who pretend to feel great passion when they do not (scene 6). Not only is she not scornful towards the Marquis, she is moved, and is certainly happy to marry a man who is in love with her—a man she might not have married if he only thought of her as a "good friend", or if he only had "un peu de sentiment" for her. The Countess may want to give the impression that she is marrying him for the good reasons carefully set out by Lisette, but this is partly because she likes to retain her image of a woman who is "raisonnable", not influenced by emotions. We feel that what decides her is her knowledge of the Marquis' love for her. There is no doubt, says Lisette, "c'est de l'amour qui regarde vos appas; il en a prononcé le mot sans bredouiller comme à l'ordinaire. C'est de la flamme. Il languit, il soupire" (scene 6).

Araminte's decision to marry Dorante (**Les fausses Confidences**) as well as her falling in love with him, are closely dependent on the fact that she knows his love for her has thrown him into the state so vividly described by Dubois (I, 14), into a life concerned wholly with her every move. She is deeply touched by his anxiety, by his despair, even by his acceptance of and complicity in an elaborate plan of deceit to win her. If she defies her mother and social opinion it is because she is convinced that Dorante's love is exceptional in its intensity, different from the usual kind of feeling that she would get from other men. It is Dorante's desperate attempt to win her, the nature and extent of his love, that distinguish him from other men. We feel that these examples should suffice to prove our point.

What is the effect of love on the characters? For Georges Poulet, the Marivaudian hero or heroine is in a state of nothingness or "vacuum"[61] until, through the experience of love, he is thrown into existence. The critic illustrates his idea of this "état de néant

psychologique, semblable à la paralysie et au sommeil" with a quotation from **La Surprise de l'amour** (I, 2), one of Lélio's speeches: "Sans l'aiguillon de l'amour et du plaisir, notre cœur à nous autres, est un vrai paralytique: nous restons là comme des eaux dormantes, qui attendent qu'on les remue pour se remuer . . ." The obvious objection is, of course, that Lélio speaks only of men, not of women (he goes on to make the distinction and comparison immediately after).[62] There are other passages quoted by Poulet which are taken out of their context: for example, the one he uses from **Le Dénouement imprévu** (scene 4) in order to illustrate that there is nothing fixed, nothing immutable, even when one continues to love the same person. One can be inconstant, the critic implies, even within the bounds of faithfulness, since it is impossible to love someone in the same way for different consecutive moments. This idea may be valid in a general way, but the particular example chosen does not prove the point since it is obvious in the original context that Mlle Argante is not in love with Dorante. She may think she is, and she says "je l'aime", but the swiftness with which she decides to marry Eraste, whom she has seen for a few minutes, instead of Dorante (a four-year-old acquaintance), is proof of the opposite. Her "mais oui, je l'aime; car je ne connais que lui depuis quatre ans" is sufficient to make us doubt the nature of her feelings towards Dorante.

It would be beyond the scope of our task to examine in detail all of Poulet's ideas. Let us say, though, as a general objection, that it is possible to take a completely different stand to his key idea[63] (that the Marivaudian character moves from a state of nothingness to a state of existence): it is possible to suggest that, from a state of stability and continuity in his existence, from an awareness of his entity as an individual, the Marivaudian character is thrown, through the experience of love which implies a loss of identity (a loss which Poulet himself admits),[64] into a state of confusion, of chaos,[65] a kind of non-existence in so far as he can no longer live happily until his union with the object of his love. Once this union takes place (often the equivalent of a mutual avowal in the theatre), the character regains his stability and is able to join the continuity of his existence. Were we to quote Poulet in the same way as he quotes Marivaux, we would find ample support for our point of view. For example: "Or, telle est l'aventure du personnage marivaudien. Il a perdu le fil de sa propre existence. Il voudrait le reprendre, le renouer, retrouver sa continuité de vie. Il ne le peut."[66] This passage strongly implies that the Marivaudian character *had* existence (with continuity) before love breaks the thread. We suggest that he cannot make contact again with this continuity until he admits his love and is united with the person he loves.

The critic suggests that the state of astonishment (and almost stupor) brought about by love results in the inability on the part of the character to distinguish himself from what is happening to him,[67] in other words to separate his existence from his sensations and feelings. We question the validity of this statement for the theatre: the fact that the protagonists, without necessarily seeing the truth, realize they are no longer the same, do not recognise themselves in their actions and reactions,[68] indicates an awareness of a certain division within themselves, a certain dichotomy.[69]

A good number of critics (most of them writing before 1950) insist that Marivaux's protagonists are too much in control of themselves to give in to their emotions.[70] However, a careful examination of the plays may provide us with numerous examples of the contrary. The Countess of *La Surprise* shows signs of bad temper and confusion from the moment she meets Lélio (see II, 1, 7; III, 2) until her clever servant Colombine helps her to admit she is in love (III, 2). From that moment her anger subsides. Lélio's emotions follow the same pattern: he is bad-tempered with Arlequin (II, 5; III, 6), confused about his own feelings (II, 4, 5), but his rancour and his upset will disappear as soon as he admits he loves. Arlequin is certain of the change that will take place in his master when he says to the Countess: ". . . Madame vous me feriez bien du plaisir de l'obliger à vous dire qu'il vous aime; il n'aura pas plus tôt avoué cela, qu'il me pardonnera" (III, 6).

The main characters of *La seconde Surprise* experience similar emotions of bewilderment and anger. Four consecutive scenes of Act II (4, 5, 6, 7) show a Marquise losing her temper with Lubin (scene 5), Lisette (scene 6), Hortensius (scene 6), and the Chevalier himself (scene 7). During this last scene, the temperature of the conversation rises continuously on both sides: the Marquise is so upset and confused that she has forgotten what she wanted to say: "Je reviens . . . laissez-moi finir . . . je ne sais où j'en suis." In the third Act, their bad temper subsides to give place to an unhappiness which they cannot explain:

La Marquise:

> Ah! je ne sais où j'en suis; respirons; d'où vient que je soupire? les larmes me coulent des yeux; je me sens saisie de la tristesse la plus profonde, et je ne sais pourquoi. . . .
>
> (III, 11)

And to Lisette: ". . . je ne sais plus où j'en suis, je ne saurais me démêler; je me meurs! Qu'est-ce que c'est donc que cet état-là" (III, 12). As for the Chevalier, he is "dans un état à faire compassion" reports Lubin: "Je crois que le bon sens s'en va; tantôt il s'arrête; il regarde le ciel, comme s'il ne l'avait jamais vu; il dit un mot, il en bredouille un autre . . ." (III, 13).

In *Le Jeu,* the first indication of the loss of the protagonists' self-control is evident in their first encounter (I, 7): struck by each other's appearance and personality, in the midst of their still jokingly amorous battle, they forget their original aim. Soon Dorante will begin to feel the impact of this first encounter: he is lost and confused, afraid of the way things may develop, uncertain of his next move: "Je ne sais plus où j'en suis; cette aventure-ci m'étourdit: que faut-il que je fasse?" (I, 9.) He is angry with Arlequin's clumsiness, and by the time he finds himself alone with Silvia again (II, 9) he is no longer only confused but already positively unhappy. At this stage, they are both aware of a certain strangeness in their state of mind, associated with a possible loss of reason. In a later scene (scene 12), Dorante looks back at his state of mind, recalls his emotional waverings and his inabilty to control his feelings with reason. Reason, then, appears as a force set in motion against love, a weapon of lucidity representing order and stability, which man's rational part uses against the chaos and confusion created by love.

This is how we see the progress of love and the mechanism of self-protection in the case of the Marivaudian character in general: the first phase sees the progression of *encounter—emotion—confusion.* Awareness of confusion causes a retreat and subsequently a call for help from his rational self: reason (and/or pride) comes to the rescue, temporarily slowing down the progress of love. This awareness of the confusion and the intervention of reason constitute the second phase. The third begins with their defeat, followed sometimes by another stage of confusion and unhappiness, thus leading to an impasse. In order to cross the gap from unhappiness to happiness and stability, the Marivaudian character is forced to take a leap: avowal. This leads him back to his original state of peace and stability, thus completing the circle of the love process.

We have already followed Silvia's progress through the first stages of encounter, emotion, confusion, and awareness of this confusion (II, 9), intensified in Act II scene 11 through the intervention of M. Orgon and Mario. This marks her final stage of bewilderment, of chaos, of conflict within herself and with the rest of the world. The storm is over: Silvia is now left alone. Her outburst of anger in the presence of others subsides, leaving behind it a deep sadness: "Ah! que j'ai le cœur serré! Je ne sais ce qui se mêle à l'embarras où je me trouve: toute cette aventure-ci m'afflige; je me défie de tous les visages; je ne suis contente de personne: je ne le suis pas de moi-même." (II, 12.) Here ends Silvia's struggle. Fortunately for her, Dorante has been preceding her all the way, always one step ahead; and, by revealing his true identity to her, he extends a helping hand. So they both reach their destination: happiness in love, peace and stability which come from having seen the end of a conflict. Dorante has completed the cycle, taking with him Silvia, whose success in reaching this goal depends almost entirely on him. In this sense, and from the moment of his unmasking, Dorante has become the star of the play: it is *his* progress that we follow.

In *Les fausses Confidences,* we hear a lot about Dorante's emotions. One of the main differences between this play and the three we have already examined is that one of the protagonists, Dorante, is already in love. When we see him for the first time, when we hear him speak to Dubois, we find him already in a state of emotion and confusion. From Dubois' account (I, 14), we know that Dorante's love for Araminte was a clear case of love at first sight. No hesitations, no reason or pride prevented the sudden surge of emotion; it was a complete surrender from the beginning. Dorante was left motionless and in a kind of ecstasy under the impact of Araminte's appearance. Again love is associated with the loss of reason: "Dubois: Hélas! Madame ce fut un jour que vous sortîtes de l'opéra, qu'il perdit la raison." According to Dubois, this love has altered Dorante's character to an unbelievable degree: first, it is so powerful that it is ruining his life and his future; Dorante is no longer interested in any other woman. Then, it affects his temperament: his common sense, his jovial spirit, his charming nature have all disappeared. Finally, this love has undermined his health, because he would often stay out late in the cold, hiding and waiting to see her for a few seconds (I, 14).

These details we are given by Dubois. As we see Dorante in the second scene of the first Act, he is seized by worry, fear of failure and ridicule, anxiety as he is about to begin the battle. And, in spite of moments of apparent calm and *sang-froid,* Dorante seems to be in the grip of these emotions throughout the play. Tears are a not uncommon manifestation of Dorante's emotions: in Dubois' story (I, 14), he is reported to have "la larme à l'œil" when he speaks of his love. In Act II scene 12, again according to Dubois, he pleaded with him on his knees, then, on Dubois' insistence that he must leave the house, fell "dans des gémissements, dans des pleurs, dans le plus triste état du monde". He is supposed to have been seen "plus mort que vif", "pâle", "triste" (II, 9), and Arlequin comes sobbing to tell Araminte that Dorante "demande à genoux" to come and see her, and that he is waiting outside the door "où il pleure" (III, 11). All this information comes from other people—Dubois in the first three examples, and Arlequin in the last one. We do not actually see Dorante cry, but we do see him in the grip of emotion, particularly in scene 13 of Act II, when Araminte pretends she has decided to marry the Count and asks Dorante to write the letter of acceptance to his rival. Dorante is so upset that he cannot hear what Araminte is asking him to do; he changes colour, his hand is shaking and he is so changed that Araminte notices it: "Je crois que la main vous tremble; vous paraissez changé. Qu'est-ce

que cela signifie? Vous trouvez-vous mal?" Then looking at the letter: "Voilà qui est écrit tout de travers! Cette adresse-là n'est presque pas lisible". Finally, the climax of his anxiety can be seen in Act III scene 12, when, still not knowing Araminte's feelings, he enters to face her, trembling at the idea that he will never see her again.[71]

Araminte's emotions follow a slightly different pattern from those of the three heroines we have already examined. At times she becomes like the others, emotional and confused, but to a much lesser degree; she generally shows more calm and maturity. She is not presented as an emotional person; in fact, she is described by Dubois as "extrêmement raisonnable" (I, 2), and she will continue to appear rational even when she is already in love with Dorante. All her self-deception, the reasons and excuses she gives to herself and to the others for keeping Dorante are expressed in the name of reason (I, 14; II, 12). Reason does not stand in the way of Araminte's love; it is not an obstacle, an instrument used against love as in the previous cases. She adapts it and uses it sub-consciously as a means to attain love.[72]

At first, she is pre-disposed in his favour by his graceful manner and his appearance; in her first conversation with him (I, 7), there is no indication of confusion or emotion on her part, but it is obvious that she likes him. However, she has not been confronted with the real Dorante yet; she has seen the young and likeable *intendant* but not the man desperately in love with her. When this revelation comes from Dubois, Araminte begins to feel a little disturbed, and a slight apprehension like a shadow of premonition marks her following words: ". . . voici une confidence dont je me serais passée moi-même" (I, 15). Faced with Dorante and with the task of telling him she may not be able to keep him, she weakens and hesitates because he becomes upset (I, 15). She leaves, moved, realizing that she cannot even look at him: "Je n'oserais presque le regarder". In their next meeting (II, 1), she seems more self-assured; she can even pretend that her marriage with the Count is not impossible. In that case, she continues, she will find him a better position. But her self-assurance, her confidence does not last very long; faced with Dorante's sadness, she weakens again:

DORANTE (TRISTEMENT):

> Non, Madame; si j'ai le malheur de perdre celle-ci, je ne serai plus à personne; et apparemment que je la perdrai; je m'y attends.

ARAMINTE:

> Je crois pourtant que je plaiderai; nous verrons.

Weakness is then the first result of her encounter with Dorante. Also a tendency to become moved by his unhappiness, an indication that she is sensitive to the way he feels. Already on two occasions she has had to leave in order to hide her emotion (I, 15 and II, 2). The second occasion marks the point of awareness. It is also from this moment that the development of Araminte's feelings takes a different turn from that of the other three heroines: Araminte does not fight against her feelings as much as the others, perhaps partly because she practises more self-deception, partly because she is a more mature person and does not have as much pride as the others. Also, and this is important, the whole situation is different: firstly, she has the security of Dorante's continuously affirmed and proclaimed love; there are no doubts in her mind regarding his feelings, no uncertainty and therefore no anxiety. She has little reason to fight against her feelings: she is a young, attractive and mature woman, a widow but not a recent one like the heroine of *La seconde Surprise.* Nor is she as unconsolable as the Marquise, who had married for love after two years of perfect courtship. We may presume that Araminte had married someone quite a lot older than herself—since her husband is referred to as a highly successful financier, which would normally imply age and experience—and that she felt neither love nor hate for her husband. She is not altogether removed from the idea of a second marriage; furthermore she is not presented as a man-hater like the Comtesse of the first *Surprise*: we hear her admit quite openly in a conversation about Dorante that she likes "les gens de bonne mine". Neither is she in Silvia's predicament, which demands a much greater social sacrifice and which creates a more serious problem for the heroine.

All in all, Araminte is in an easier situation; she does not claim indifference towards men like the Comtesse of the first *Surprise,* and therefore has no reputation to live up to; unlike the Marquise of the *Seconde Surprise,* she has not been a widow for only six months and is not presented as heartbroken or as still deeply in love with her dead husband. Finally, the social problem which she will have to face if she marries Dorante is of a minor nature compared to that of Silvia, and can be overcome. She is rich enough and the mistress of her own life—which Silvia is not. All these facts make Araminte's progression towards love more smooth, without extremes of emotion resulting in unhappiness, anger and bewilderment. But it would be incorrect to think of her as lacking in complexity. Araminte may well be of a more calm and even temperament than the previous three heroines, she is nonetheless a woman of many moods: full of humour and irony when she tries to cover up for Dorante by laughing at her mother's insinuations (II, 10, 11); gently reproachful to Dubois when he puts her in an embarrassing situation by the attention he brings to the incidents of the portraits (II, 12); distantly cool with Marton who has come to take leave of her, yet soft and sympathetic a few seconds later when the young girl, showing the extent of the wound, cries out: "Pourquoi avez-vous eu la cruauté de

m'abandonner au hasard d'aimer un homme qui n'est pas fait pour moi . . ." (III, 10); full of compassionate understanding and concern when Dubois reveals to her Dorante's love (I, 14), or when she hears of his despair after the incident of the letter (III, 9) (". . . Mais qu'on aille donc voir. Quelqu'un l'a-t-il suivi? Que ne le secourez-vous? Faut-il tuer cet homme?"); protective in an almost motherly way towards Dorante, reassuring him about his position (II, 13), defending him against the others (II, 6, 7), yet only moments later cruelly determined in her effort to make him declare himself, almost enjoying his suffering (II, 13); gently probing the secret of his heart, warm, understanding, encouraging, then suddenly, realizing that he has been seen on his knees, abrupt, authoritarian (". . . Laissez-moi; allez-vous-en; vous m'êtes insupportable . . .") (II, 15); angry and bad-tempered with Marton, her mother and even the Count (III, 8), furious with Dubois, who reveals to her that he is behind the incident of the interception of Dorante's letter (III, 9); finally hesitating, not knowing what decision to make (II, 12), confused and disturbed about her own feelings, uncertain of the way things will eventuate, especially when she realizes that she is losing control of the situation.[73] From all these instances, Araminte emerges as a character with all the emotional complexity of a real human being, but measured and without extremes.

Lucile (*Les Serments indiscrets*) has the reputation of being "d'un esprit raisonnable" (I, 5). Cool-headed and calm, she decides against marriage, and begins by taking the necessary steps to avoid it. However, her theories about marriage and men begin to break down when she sees Damis. From that moment, the young girl will be torn between her emotions and her pride, her desire to break her word and marry Damis, and her unwillingness to lose face, especially as at certain moments she doubts Damis' feelings. Before they meet, they are both calm, they know exactly what they want; at the end of their first encounter, they are unhappy and confused.[74] Awareness of their emotion has come to both of them immediately, although Lucile will be more anxious to hide it than Damis. Like most of Marivaux's heroines, she is inclined to get angry. Lisette becomes her first target in Act II scene 5, when the servant tells her that her sister Phénice is falling in love with Damis. Lucile's bad mood does not escape Lisette, and she makes a remark on it which makes things worse. Finally, after Lisette has reported her conversation with Phénice and how the latter left with her feminine pride hurt, Lucile cannot control her anger any longer. The result is the familiar "je ne sais où j'en suis". Lisette's worst mistake is to say that she thinks Damis loves Phénice and that he seems to be more attracted to her than to Lucile. This is too much for the young girl: "Vous êtes donc aveugle, impertinente que vous êtes? Du moins mentez sans me manquer de respect." (II, 5.) Lucile's tone of voice must have risen to the point of shouting, because

Lisette retreats: "Oh! il est inutile de tant crier; je ne m'en mêlerai plus; accommodez-vous, ce n'est pas moi qu'on menace de marier . . ." Alone for a few moments, Lucile sighs and lets us see how unhappy she is, how much she suffers: "Hélas! tu ne sais pas ce que je souffre, ni toute la douleur et le penchant dont je suis agitée!" (II, 6.) She has now openly admitted to herself that she is attracted to Damis; but it will take her a long time to admit it to anyone else. Torn by two conflicting sentiments, Lucile's nerves, always taut, are ready to break. All their meetings are permeated by an electric atmosphere, ready to explode. As a result of her emotion, all her replies to Damis are cutting, sharp, full of impatience, and even sarcastic (II, 8). At every moment, because of misunderstandings which occur continually, they are ready to separate, before they have even started a conversation. The constant state of insecurity in which she keeps Damis by her bad temper and sharp replies makes him very hesitant. This exasperates Lucile: "Si vous saviez l'envie que j'ai de vous laisser là!" (III, 7) After Lisette's intervention (*ibid.*), the protagonists are soon back at their arguing (III, 8).

The third meeting ends like the others; they separate hurt, upset and unhappy. Lucile's anger will next be directed to Phénice (IV, 7) and she certainly does not sound like the Lucile "d'esprit raisonnable" of the beginning. She becomes angry, emotional, almost hates her sister, goes to extremes by threatening to leave and never forgive Phénice if she marries Damis. And in all this turmoil of the emotions, she is also confused about her own feelings: is she in love or is she not?[75]

Damis himself is in a state of extreme unhappiness after his last conversation with Lucile (III, 8). In a last effort to discover her feelings, he spoils everything by pretending to accept his marriage with Phénice. Lucile leaves him coldly, and Damis can only lament in bewilderment: "Je me meurs, et je ne sais plus ce que je deviendrai" (IV, 11). We know from Frontin that he is desperate and that he can think only of running away. Frontin sums up Damis' state of mind and concludes with the remark that, in cases like these, intelligence and sensitivity make things worse (V, 1). What he means is that people in love cannot reason, cannot see things clearly: confusion, a certain blindness appear as the inseparable companions of love.

From the way they react to each other and to their own feelings, the protagonists, and particularly Lucile, emerge as two people in whom the shock of love creates emotion and confusion which they cannot control; they cannot, in fact, solve their problem without the help of others.

In *L'heureux Stratagème,* as in the previous plays, the characters are shaken, in the course of the action, by emotions such as jealousy and unhappiness. Confusion,

which is the result of a secret conflict between the characters' inner desire and their pride, naturally plays an important part here too.

At the beginning of the play, we are immediately shown Dorante's unhappiness: the Countess forgets him and neglects his love for the sake of the Chevalier. We hear Dorante firstly tell his grief to Maître Blaise (I, 1), painfully interrogate Arlequin on what he has seen of the Chevalier and the Countess (I, 2), then despair before the others and Lisette when the latter confirms his fears ("Je me meurs de douleur") (I, 3). He is not only unhappy but also at a loss, not knowing what line of action to adopt. The scene with the Countess (I, 5) shows a man still in love although hurt in his feelings, in fact in despair.[76] But he also is a man with temperament, and the Countess' cruel treatment exasperates him to the point of anger: "J'ai besoin de tout mon respect pour ne pas éclater de colère." He has progressed from a resigned and rather passive unhappiness to despair, then to anger and finally rage: "La perfide!" he cries out as the Countess leaves him. "Ah! je suis outré!" His conversation with the Countess, followed by a discussion with Lisette, leaves both Dorante and Arlequin in a state of turmoil which they express in terms of physical suffering:

DORANTE:

J'ai le cœur saisi!

ARLEQUIN:

Je perds la respiration!

The Marquise's arrival makes them even more eloquent:

DORANTE:

On me trahit, Madame, on m'assassine, on me plonge le poignard dans le sein.

And Arlequin, in slightly less dignified terms: "On m'étouffe, Madame, on m'égorge, on me distingue!" But soon anger subsides and as he calms down Dorante returns to his original state of sadness and passive lamentation: ". . . je ne vois plus rien à tenter: on nous quitte sans retour . . ." (I, 8).

During Frontin's account (scene 12), Dorante wants to appear indifferent but he suffers. Frequent sighs, exclamations such as "je me meurs", "quel récit, Marquise" indicate his emotion. Halfway through the scene he tries to stop Frontin from giving any more details. Finally he feels his emotion is taking over and pleads with the Marquise to make Frontin stop: "Faites-le finir; je n'y tiendrais pas". When the servant leaves he confesses to the Marquise: "J'avoue que ses récits m'ont fait souffrir"; but he promises not to allow his emotion to take over again (". . . je me soutiendrai mieux dans la suite"), and in fact, from that point on, apart from a moment's hesitation (III, 4), Dorante will control his emotions while the Countess will gradually lose control of hers.

The first weakening in the Countess' self-confidence comes with the Marquise's covert threat: her conquest of Dorante. She is not given much time to think about it and dismiss the possibility: Dorante arrives immediately after the Marquise's exit and his behaviour does nothing to restore her faith in her power over him: "Je ne reconnais point Dorante à cette sortie-là", reflects the Countess. A more serious blow comes with Frontin's report regarding Dorante's reaction, or rather his lack of reaction (II, 7). Things are beginning to take on a disturbing aspect, but by the end of the scene, the Countess manages to overcome her growing anxiety. She is even preparing an attack herself: cancel the marriage of Lisette to Arlequin and give her to Frontin. She is certain this will upset Dorante and therefore prove that he is still in love with her. But the Marquise has preceded her: under her instructions, Dorante had forced Arlequin to pretend he is no longer in love with Lisette. The young girl comes with her father to cry in front of her mistress (II, 10). This is an unexpected turn for the Countess: she takes it upon herself to conclude Lisette's marriage with Arlequin in order to prove to herself and to the others that she still has a hold on Dorante. She does not know that she is preparing a disappointment for herself. Dorante acts quite differently from the way she had expected. Infuriated with the way he defends the Marquise, she makes it clear she expects him to obey her (II, 11). Dorante's answer leaves her almost speechless. She cannot believe her ears. It is now her turn to become indignant: "Ah! l'indigne homme!" This is the real beginning of her bewilderment and unhappiness. The realization of the loss of her power over Dorante—loss which indicates the end of his love, at least in her eyes—throws her off balance. The Countess now enters the first phase in the cycle of emotions: from now on she will be at their mercy and will not attain happiness until the moment she admits her love for Dorante by conquering her pride and by no longer hiding her despair. The first thing she does after the shock caused by Dorante's behaviour (II, 11, 12) is to dismiss the Chevalier (II, 13). She is confused, she does not know exactly what she will do (II, 13). In a moment of weakness, she sends Lisette with a message to Dorante (III, 5). Already she is harkening less to her pride. When Lisette reports Dorante's answer, the Countess yields more and more to her emotions. With Lisette's help she is now ready to face the fact that she loves Dorante and that the whole situation is her fault (III, 6). But she is in such a confused state of mind that, a few seconds after she has admitted her guilt, her pride reverses the verdict and throws the blame on Dorante. She speaks in short sentences, probably pacing up and down. She is so agitated, so obviously unhappy that Lisette is worried about her and tries to calm her down: ". . . Calmez-vous donc, Madame; vous êtes dans une désolation qui m'afflige . . ." (III, 6). During the whole of this scene the Countess is shaken by emotions. She falls in turn from surprise to distress, regret, self-accusation, then returns to an accusation of Dorante and to a hatred for the Chevalier. But she is still not completely out of action; she has, it seems, some plan in mind when she instructs Lisette to go and fetch the Chevalier. In the meantime however the final blow has been prepared by the Marquise: it is the arrival of the *notaire*. This throws our heroine completely off balance. She feels lost and turns to Lisette for advice: "Lisette, parle donc! Tu ne me conseilles rien. Je suis accablée! Ils vont s'épouser ici, si je n'y mets ordre." (III, 7.) What are the Countess' feelings towards Dorante? She detests him. But as soon as Lisette suggests that she should let them go ahead, she contradicts herself. Of course she hates him, but that does not stop her from loving him! In any case, it is all her fault, she admits for the second time. Now there is no way out: she must look for him and tell him the truth. Anxious and agitated, the Countess waits for Dorante's answer to her letter, but instead he comes to see her with the Marquise, asking for her permission to get married in her house. The Countess makes a last attempt but she fails and finds herself obliged to witness what she thinks is a marriage certificate between Dorante and the Marquise. The strain is too great for the Countess: she signs but immediately falls into Lisette's arms crying: "Ah! perfide!" This is the surrender of pride and the victory of the emotions. As soon as she has done this, the Countess is rewarded by a return to peace and stability, through love.

In *L'Epreuve* it is not the actual falling in love that arouses emotions such as anger and confusion in the heroine. Angélique, not complicated by society and its rules of "musts" and "must-nots", falls in love simply, naturally, without fighting against it: the experience of love is for her a source of happiness. Emotional upset, anger, unhappiness, bewilderment, all come when her illusions of love are destroyed, at least temporarily, by Lucidor's test. What we see then is not so much the Angélique presented by Lucidor in the first scene, not the Angélique of scene 8 ("un cœur simple, honnête et vrai", "un caractère distingué", "aimable", with "innocence", "honneur", "vertu" and so on). We see an angry young girl who, after an initial weakness which makes her run to her room to hide her unhappiness, after an initial hesitation caused by her mother's presence, recovers her pride and her fighting spirit and shows that she will not let herself be pushed into anything. Her tongue is loosened by her mother's absence, and, after dealing with Lisette and Frontin with perfect control of the situation, she turns to Lucidor, and tells him exactly what she thinks:

. . . Il ne faut pas croire, à cause de vos rares bontés, qu'on soit obligée vite et vite, de se donner au premier venu que vous attirerez de je ne sais où, et qui arrivera tout botté pour m'épouser sur votre parole; il ne faut pas croire cela. Je suis fort reconnaissante, mais je ne suis pas idiote.

(Scene 17)

She seizes upon Lucidor's suggestion that her refusal of his rich friend is motivated by some secret love, to show once again that she will do as she pleases.[77] And when Lisette so much as hints at the idea that she knows why Angélique is so bad-tempered towards Lucidor, the young girl promises her "de la rancune pour mille ans". Those critics who are worried about Angélique's fate after her marriage with Lucidor have obviously not noticed the sharpness of her words, which indicates that she is quite capable of protecting herself.

All this proves that Angélique is capable of hitting back, but only to be overcome again at the end and resort to the final expression of frustration in a woman, and perhaps her last weapon, tears. From our earlier impression of Angélique, we may have thought that she would be the soft, gentle, silently suffering and self-sacrificing young girl, who, having fallen in love with someone above her station, would simply live with the memory of such a love. But there is no "victim" type woman in Marivaux's world. No matter how soft, gentle, innocent and obedient his heroines may be, when it comes to protecting their happiness they always have something to say. They all have, more or less, the same instinct for self-preservation—except perhaps for the Angélique of *La Mère confidente.*

As soon as Silvia (*La double Inconstance*) begins to fall in love with the young "officer", she is (partly through Flaminia's machinations) in an almost continuous state of bewilderment: "Je ne puis que dire; il me passe tant de oui et de non par la tête, que je ne sais auquel entendre" (II, 11). She does not even know what she wants, what will make her happy: "Oh! ce que je veux! j'attends qu'on me le dise; j'en suis encore plus ignorante que vous" (II, 12). And: "Mais mon plaisir, où est-il? Il n'est ni là, ni là; je le cherche" (II, 11). All she knows is that everything is confused in her mind and everything makes her unhappy: "Je rêve à moi, et je n'y entends rien"; ". . . je suis bien malheureuse d'avoir tout ce tracas-là dans la tête" (II, 12). This state continues until the moment she decides that she is in love with the Prince.

In *Le Prince travesti,* love makes the Princess suspicious, jealous and violent. She herself attributes the turmoil in her heart to her love for Lélio: ". . . j'ai de l'amour, en un mot, voilà mon excuse" (II, 5). As for Hortense, the emotions created by her love for Lélio are of a different kind: generosity, self-sacrifice, fear for his life, pathos.

In *Le Petit-Maître corrigé,* we know, from the servants who report to Hortense, that Rosimond is involved in a struggle against his heart and his emotions, and this proves to them that he is in love.[78] Frontin says that Rosimond does not know what he wants, but a certain force makes him want to see Hortense: ". . . c'est par force qu'il demande à vous voir; il ne saurait faire autrement; il n'y a pas moyen qu'il s'en passe; il faut qu'il vienne" (III, 1). Marton explains it further: "C'est son cœur qui le mène en dépit qu'il en est, voilà ce que c'est" (*ibid.*).

Hortense is quite an exception among Marivaux's heroines: she does not display emotions, always retains her self-assuredness and does not become confused, but this is because she remains relatively uninvolved. Rosimond's charm has not had very much effect on her, probably because she finds him ridiculous. Her servant does say that ". . . il est sûr que vous auriez plu à Hortense si vous ne l'aviez pas fait rire; mais ce qui fait rire n'attendrit plus . . ." (II, 5).

It is interesting to note that Rosimond's main fault is described as that of not being *raisonnable.* This word occurs frequently during the play and we should like to examine the way it is being used. First of all Hortense is referred to by Marton as being *raisonnable* on two occasions (I, 6; III, 9), and reason seems to be an important quality which, unfortunately, Rosimond appears not to possess.[79] Hortense's "est-ce que la raison même n'exige pas un autre procédé que le sien?" may be taken to mean that even if feelings did not exist, reason would still not justify Rosimond's behaviour.[80] Marton's answer enlightens us a little as to the nature of reason, or at least the way it is regarded by "les jeunes gens du bel air": "il n'y a rien de si bourgeois que d'être raisonnable" (I, 1). The term *bourgeois,* associated with *raisonnable,* may be considered a derogatory adjective by Rosimond's friends, but for Hortense it is the thing that would make the young man dear to her: "il me sera cher s'il devient raisonnable" (I, 1). Rosimond himself uses the same expression at the end: "Oui, Monsieur, c'est Rosimond devenu raisonnable, et qui ne voit rien d'égal au bonheur de son sort" (III, 12).

We must, however, distinguish the meaning that this word has here from that attributed to it in other plays. For instance, when the Marquis of *Le Legs* says that the Countess is *raisonnable,* he means rational, as opposed to emotional. When the Silvia of *Le Jeu,* the Countess and Lélio of *La Surprise,* and others speak of *raison,* they oppose it to *cœur,* that is emotions, love, and so on. This is not the kind of *raison* that Hortense wishes Rosimond to have. For her, *raisonnable* would mean not rational but reasonable, or *sensé* as the Marquise puts it. She does not want Rosimond's reason to fight against his love, but to make him realize he is being ridiculous in hiding his feelings and affecting indifference.

In *Le Triomphe de l'amour,* the rise of the emotions as a result of falling in love can be seen mainly in the case of Hermocrate and Léontine. Unlike the plays we have already examined, *Le Triomphe* presents the heroine's love as a *fait accompli,* and she remains cool-headed, clear-thinking and self-confident right through the action, always in control of the situation. Léonide (not taking into account the heroine of *La fausse Suivante,* since she does not fall in love at all) is an exception (much more so than Hortense) in Marivaux's theatre: no hesitation, no confusion, no self-deception on her part; she has seen Agis, she has fallen in love with him at first sight, she has decided he will love her, she sets out to make his conquest and marry him. A very simple process, too simple perhaps, compared to the labyrinth of contrasting emotions, to the interminable meandering of feelings of a Lucile in *Les Serments indiscrets.*

Agis' journey towards love is also a comparatively short one: he responds immediately, first with an instinctive and spontaneous offer of friendship towards "Phocion", then, after he is told she is a woman, with a timid attraction which he still calls "amitié" and which soon develops into love easily admitted and openly expressed. A fairly straight-forward process too when compared to that of Lélio (*La Surprise*), the Chevalier (*La seconde Surprise*), and Damis (*Les Serments indiscrets*). He does, however, go through a stage of confusion when he knows he feels something and cannot determine the nature of his feelings. But "Aspasie" is there to help him, very gladly too, in understanding himself, and this only takes a very short scene (II, 11). He also goes through a moment of despair and unhappiness when he thinks he has been deceived (III, 8), but the misunderstanding is soon cleared up (III, 9) and Agis' suffering only lasts a few minutes.

We can say then that for the protagonists the process of falling in love has not been a bewildering and painful experience. This is much less the case with Hermocrate and Léontine. The latter, for instance, is shaken, from the very moment of "Phocion" 's passionate declaration, by conflicting emotions: the desire to believe what she hears is at the beginning fought back by her reason, which tells her that love is no longer for her. Her surprise is soon replaced by bewilderment and the fear that her heart may prove stronger than her reason. In her mind, the heart, love, emotions are all associated with a loss of reason: they are the enemies of reason, whose function is to protect her from the "égarements du cœur" (". . . voulez-vous que mon cœur s'égare? . . . Faudra-t-il que ma raison y périsse? . . ." I, 6). Away from "Phocion" 's dangerous presence, her reason gains strength, especially since her brother has refused his permission for the young traveller's stay: ". . . Tes refus me rappellent moi-même à la raison" (II, 5). But only a few moments later, "Phocion" 's eloquence and Arlequin's intervention (II, 6) throw her back to her previous state of mind: "où suis-je? tout ceci me paraît un rêve". But "Phocion" has not finished his attack yet; the portrait is produced, and Léontine is thrown deeper and deeper into a state of emotion which annihilates any will she might have left to fight: "Je me sens dans une émotion de cœur où je ne veux pas qu'on me voie." She leaves, assuring "Phocion" of her brother's approval, feverishly prepares for her secret marriage, all eager and excited, until the painful moment of truth: "Phocion", her beloved, the man whom she was going to marry, is a woman! How can one describe what she feels? Bitter disappointment, frustration, a feeling of emptiness . . . Léontine herself does not say very much . . . "Juste ciel! où en suis-je?" (III, 8) Fortunately, in a way, she takes refuge in anger: "Je suis outrée, je l'avoue." But will anger, and the meagre satisfaction of calling Léonide "fourbe", compensate for her lost dream of love?

Hermocrate becomes not less than his sister a prey to the emotions which are part of the process of falling in love. They are both equally vulnerable because of their sheltered life, their isolation, their age. He too is disturbed immediately after "Aspasie" 's declaration: ". . . [je] ne reviens point du trouble où ce discours me jette . . ." (I, 8). He too seeks help from reason ("la raison me défend d'en entendre davantage") but "Aspasie" 's passionate expressions disturb him so much that he cannot continue to listen: "Je ne saurais plus supporter ce récit. Au nom de cette vertu que vous chérissez, Aspasie, laissons-là ce discours, abrégeons; . . ." (I, 8). But Léonide has no intention of letting him escape, and she continues until he admits: "Vous me troublez, je vous réponds mal, et je me tais."

Alone and confused, he realizes how close he came to losing his reason: "J'ai pensé m'égarer dans cet entretien" (I, 9). And lost he soon is, poor Hermocrate, for whom Léonide is carefully planning and will masterfully deliver a series of blows: Dimas' report moves him; a second *tête-à-tête* with "Aspasie", in which he, by confessing his weaknesses,[81] by threatening to expose her, desperately tries to resist the temptation, leaves him exhausted from her persistence and open to the impact which the discovery of his portrait will cause in him: the portrait is an uncontested proof of love; Hermocrate can no longer resist any of "Aspasie" 's wishes, however much they damage his dignity. He is so willing to please her, so weak, that even Léonide feels, for a moment, sorry for him. But pity must be discarded if she is to get what she wants. Hermocrate is sent off to prepare for his secret marriage with her, still agitated and torn between his reason and his emotions, until the moment he is forced to face the truth: "Aspasie" has deceived him. As a man involved in political machinations, his instinct for survival prevails; he does not seem hurt or disappointed. But can we believe, after the emotions of which we know he is capable, that his reason will now help him to appease his heart?

To summarise these introductory pages: after having reviewed the various critics' attitudes towards the nature of love as portrayed by Marivaux, we have attempted to define it ourselves by pointing out its main characteristics and by examining the effects of love on the characters. We have tried to show, by means of concrete examples, that not all Marivaudian characters are as self-controlled and calculating as they have been represented by traditional criticism, and that they often go through a cycle of emotions before the moment of avowal, the latter presaging the passage from an emotional state of being to a state of stability, thus marking the end of a psychological conflict.

Notes

1. Alain, "Marivaux", *Mercure de France* ("Extraits du *Journal* d'Alain", septembre 1943), vol. 308 (1950), p. 579.

2. Gustave Larroumet, *Marivaux, sa vie et ses œuvres* (Paris, 1894), p. 166.

3. *Ibid.,* p. 167.

4. *Ibid.,* p. 185.

5. G. Brereton, *A Short History of French Literature* (Middlesex, 1954), p. 168.

6. Charles Lenient, *La comédie en France au XVIIIᵉ siècle* (Paris, 1888), vol. I, ch. 14 ("Marivaux"), p. 362.

7. *Ibid.,* p. 348.

8. Maurice Donnay, "Marivaux, ou l'amour au XVIIIᵉ siècle", *La Revue des Vivants,* n° 6 (juin 1929), p. 848.

9. A. Feugère, "Rousseau et son temps: la littérature du sentiment au XVIIIᵉ siècle; le théâtre de Marivaux", *Revue des Cours et Conférences,* 36ᵉ année (première série), n° 4 (30 janvier 1935), p. 336.

10. Marcel Arland, *Marivaux* (Paris, 1950), p. 182.

11. *Ibid., loc. cit.*

12. Kibédi Varga, "Note sur Marivaux", *Neophilologus,* XLI-XLII (1957-1958), p. 255. See also *ibid.,* p. 253. Other critics who have pointed out that Marivaux is only interested in the birth of love are: Jean Fleury, *Marivaux et le marivaudage* (Paris, 1881), p. 148; T. S. Eliot, "Marivaux", *Art and Letters,* II, n° 2 (Spring 1919), p. 84; R. Niklaus, *Arlequin poli par l'Amour* (ed., London, 1959), p. 35; H. T. Mason, *Les fausses Confidences* (ed., Oxford, 1964), p. 10; and many others.

13. Robert Niklaus, *Arlequin poli par l'Amour* (ed.), p. 34.

14. Robert Niklaus, "La comédie italienne et Marivaux", *Studi in onore di C. Pellegrini* (Torino, 1963), p. 284.

15. Marlyse Meyer, *La Convention dans le théâtre d'amour de Marivaux* (São Paulo, 1961), p. 17.

16. *Ibid.,* p. 71.

17. *Ibid.,* p. 17.

18. *Ibid.,* p. 71.

19. *Ibid.,* p. 69.

20. Paul Gazagne, *Marivaux par lui-même* (Paris, 1954). He has, since then, written several articles (1956, 1957, 1958) to support his original idea. See our bibliography.

21. E. J. H. Greene, *Marivaux* (Toronto, 1965). See particularly pp. 60, 107, 109, 213. Although in general Greene finds Gazagne's interpretation extreme, just before he discusses *Le Triomphe de l'amour* (and in order to show that Marivaux was not really concerned with the moral issues that arose from the situation) he finds himself obliged, for a moment, to adopt the idea that it is Cupidon and not Amour that represents Marivaux's idea of love in *La Réunion des amours.* Thus he says: "Now that Gazagne's contention is generally accepted, the preceding sentence is seen to take on a wider interest, for here we have the creative artist speaking through the mouth of Cupid: 'Les uns y perdent, les autres y gagnent; je ne m'en embarrasse pas.' This is precisely the point of view of a writer who has several masterpieces on the way, masterpieces which baffle those who have their moral judgment all ready to apply to works of art." (*Op. cit.,* p. 137.) It is true that the modern reader or spectator no longer thinks of the attraction felt by Marivaux's characters as entirely devoid of any physical element, but even if Gazagne's contention is accepted to some extent, it does not necessarily follow that it is Marivaux who speaks through Cupidon when the latter says: "Les uns y perdent, les autres y gagnent; je ne m'en embarrasse pas". When speaking of *Le Triomphe de l'amour,* Greene takes this to mean, then, that Léonide and Agis win, Hermocrate and Léontine lose, and that Marivaux "ne [s]'en embarrasse pas". In fact, as we shall see later (Part IV: *The Mask,* ch. 10, p. 274), Marivaux makes a point of justifying his heroine.

22. Gazagne, *op. cit.,* p. 85. In 1957 he adds to this list *Les Serments indiscrets.*

23. ". . . l'une charnelle, amour étant le synonyme édulcoré de désir, épouser étant une expression mondaine mise à la place de s'accoupler; l'autre

plus conventionnelle,—l'amour s'y limitant à un pur sentiment, et les épousailles à la signature d'un contrat." (*Ibid.*, p. 44.)

24. *Ibid.*, p. 44.

25. Käthy Lüthi denies the sensual aspect in Marivaux: "Il y a une période où l'amour est encore tout sentimental; c'est celle où, troublés d'inquiétudes secrètes, les jeunes gens se sentent attirés l'un vers l'autre sans nullement songer au plaisir des sens. Se croyant complètement détachés des joies terrestres, ils se perdent dans des rêveries et des extases qui suffisent à leur félicité. C'est le moment de 'l'aube' de l'amour, dont Marivaux a, le premier, analysé le charme; . . . Chez ses héroïnes l'amour n'a donc rien de sensuel." (*Les Femmes dans l'œuvre de Marivaux* (Bienne, 1943), p. 32.) This critic's comments, however, are subject to caution, because of the high proportion of unacknowledged quotations from critics such as Deschamps and Jaloux.

26. Claude Roy, *Lire Marivaux* (Paris, 1947), p. 58.

27. Xavier de Courville's attitude was evident in a lecture he gave at the Sorbonne in 1962, where we heard him criticise Gazagne's interpretation.

28. Jacques Scherer objects to Roger Planchon's "sensual" interpretation of *La seconde Surprise,* which coincides with that of Gazagne, in his article "Marivaux et Planchon", *Les Lettres Nouvelles,* n° 18 (1er juillet 1959), pp. 36-39. See also our article: "Producing and Interpreting Marivaux", *Australian Journal of French Studies,* IV, n° 1 (1967), pp. 44-61 (particularly pp. 57-59).

29. Renée Papin, "Marivaux, les femmes, l'amour et la lutte des classes . . .", *Nouvelle Critique,* n° 125, (1960-1961), p. 89.

30. "La comédie italienne et Marivaux", (*art. cit.*), p. 284.

31. *Arlequin poli par l'amour* (ed.), p. 34.

32. Lionel Gossman, "Literature and Society in the Early Enlightenment: the Case of Marivaux", *Modern Language Notes,* LXXXII, n° 3 (May 1967), p. 331. He says that the plays "offer a coherent structure which can be diversely interpreted according to the audience's wish . . . the initial desire may be the anonymous desire of a body or it may be 'l'amour naissant', the desire of a real individual; the marriages at the end may be taken as the culmination of erotic encounters or as the true meeting of subjects in love. The 'aristocratic' reading and the 'bourgeois' one both fit. Yet many of the plays would be destroyed if we plumped for one or the other, for they depend on nothing so much as the bracketing of any single 'real meaning'."

Our application of the terms "aristocratic" and "bourgeois" differs slightly from that of Gossman. The critic is right when he says both readings fit, but he means *either* the one *or* the other. We would like to change the *or* to *and,* in the sense that these two elements co-exist in the plays. In other words, the content is "bourgeois" (there is love, but a love that leads to marriage, and, what is more, a marriage with all the practical aspects of financial security, class suitability and so on, no "living on love alone" about it), and the form is "aristocratic", in the sense that the protagonists' language and behaviour belong to the same tradition as the *préciosité* of the seventeenth century and the *amour courtois* of the Middle Ages, a tradition dependent on leisure and refinement.

33. ". . . ainsi pourrait-il nous faire apercevoir que l'érotisme n'est pas autre chose que ce désir de reconnaissance, désir essentiellement supra-animal, que Hegel tenait pour fondamental en l'homme, pour spécifiquement humain. Et de même nous montrerait-il qu'ainsi qu'il va dans son théâtre l'amour ne saurait trouver sa satisfaction dans la possession physique—qui lui est au contraire fatale. Mais seulement dans une sorte de danse quasi extatique, de viol spirituel, qui est paradoxalement un viol réciproque, un *viol* sans *violence.*" (*Art. cit.,* p. 372.)

34. *Ibid., loc. cit.*

35. In *Le Chemin de la fortune ou le Saut du fossé* (1734), a young widow, Clarice, complains that the rich men who pursue her "n'ont que de l'amour pour elle". She further explains that "ils ne sont qu'amoureux et point tendres", meaning that they only desire her (scene 4) and do not want to marry her. Thus Marivaux associates *tendresse* with marriage.

36. "C'est un vilain amant qu'un homme qui vous désire plus qu'il ne vous aime: non pas que l'amant le plus délicat ne désire à sa manière, mais du moins c'est que chez lui les sentiments du cœur se mêlent avec les sens; tout cela se fond ensemble: ce qui fait un amour tendre, et non pas vicieux, quoiqu'à la vérité capable de vice." (Gazagne, *op. cit.,* p. 93.)

37. ". . . il me paraissait . . . qu'elle n'eût point été tendre sans être amoureuse, et voilà justement la véritable tendresse; et, n'en déplaise aux héritières du sentiment des antiques héroïnes, le reste est simplement imagination." (*Les Romans de Marivaux.* (Éd. Pléiade, Paris, 1949), p. 7.)

38. Term used by Greene, *op. cit.,* p. 166, for the period 1733-1735; we extend it to 1730-1735, to include *Le Jeu.*

39. René de Planhol, *Les Utopistes de l'amour* (Paris, 1921), pp. 120-123.

40. Paul Gazagne, "Réflexions sur *la Réunion des amours*", *L'Illustre Théâtre,* IV, n° 10 (1958), p. 28.

41. Marivaux, on the other hand, identifies *amour gaulois* with his character Amour ("Cupidon: Ne serait-ce pas cet Amour gaulois, ce dieu de la fade tendresse . . . ?"), who is apparently a latter-day variation on *amour courtois.*

42. "Réflexions sur *la Réunion des amours*", p. 28.

43. See also Planhol, *op. cit.,* "Marivaux ou la tentative de conciliation", pp. 121-123.

44. *Le Spectateur Français* (17ᵉ feuille), ed. William Wrage (unpublished Ph. D. thesis, Wisconsin, 1964), p. 188.

45. See *Le Cabinet du Philosophe* (3ᵉ feuille), *Œuvres Complètes de Marivaux,* éd. Duviquet (Paris, 1830), IX, p. 388.

46. For a list of the many different ways in which *cœur* is used by Marivaux see Leo Spitzer, "A propos de *la Vie de Marianne* (lettre à M. Georges Poulet)", *Romanic Review* XLIV (1953), p. 105.

47. When we use this expression, we do not refer to the intensity of Ergaste's feelings but to their suddenness. Indeed, Maurice Donnay makes the following distinction: Marivaux's characters, he says, "ne ressentent jamais le coup de foudre; ce n'est jamais entre eux, pour commencer, l'éblouissant éclair, mais la jolie étincelle bleue . . ." (*art. cit.,* p. 850). To this, however, we may oppose examples such as Hortense and Lélio in *Le Prince travesti,* or even Donrante of *Les fausses Confidences,* whose feelings are presented as something more than that.

48. "Il faut avouer qu'on a quelquefois des inclinations bien bizarres. D'où vient que j'en ai pour cet homme-là, qui n'est point aimable?" (II, 11.)

49. ". . . Celui que vous me destinez feindra peut-être plus d'amour qu'il n'en aura; je n'en aurai peut-être point pour lui, quelque envie que j'aie d'en avoir: *cela ne dépend pas de nous . . .*" (scene 13). (Our italics.)

50. On this point, Robert Mauzi says that "Marivaux est le peintre de l'amour-mystère. Pour ses personnages, l'amour est toujours une surprise. Jamais la conscience ne peut prévoir un sentiment, en deviner l'éclosion ou l'approche". (*L'Idée du bonheur dans la littérature et la pensée françaises au XVIIIᵉ siècle* (Paris, 1960), p. 466.)

51. *Op. cit.,* p. 348.

52. *Ibid.,* p. 360. Speaking of *Les fausses Confidences,* Lenient says: "De passion violente, il n'en est guère trace. Tous ces gens-là sont à la température moyenne, que marque d'ordinaire le thermomètre de Marivaux" (*ibid.,* p. 371). And: "L'exaltation intense et aveugle leur est inconnue" (*ibid.,* p. 361).

53. Michel Braspart, however, attests the lack of frivolity in Marivaux's theatre as seen in the characters' preoccupation with choosing their partner. The way he sees it is that they prefer "le choix et le mérite" to "une inclination aveugle". ("Marivaux ou le poids de la légèreté", *La Nef,* 4ᵉ année, n° 34 (septembre 1947), p. 61.) This statement is, however, misleading because it implies that Marivaux's characters sometimes have to make a choice between the two. This is not true, as this "inclination" happens mostly to be directed to a deserving partner who has all the necessary "mérite". We can even produce one example to show that the critic's statement is not only misleading but wrong: Dorante (*L'heureux Stratagème*), abandoned by the coquettish Countess in favour of the Chevalier, regrets not being able to love the Marquise, who, he feels, deserves it: "Pourquoi n'est-ce pas vous que j'aime?" (I, 8.) (Note also the juxtaposition of "la perfide que j'adore", *ibid.*) This seems to be a clear case of "inclination aveugle" being stronger than "mérite".

54. Lenient, *op. cit.,* p. 357.

55. Larroumet, *op. cit.,* p. 190.

56. Lüthi, *op. cit.,* p. 34.

57. *Vide infra,* Part IV: *The Mask,* ch. 10, pp. 284-285.

58. "Hortense: . . . Avant que le comte Rodrigue m'épousât, il n'y avait amour ancien ni moderne qui pût figurer auprès du sien. Les autres amants auprès de lui rampaient comme de mauvaises copies d'un excellent original; c'était une chose admirable, c'était une passion formée de tout ce qu'on peut imaginer en sentiments, langueurs, soupirs, transports, délicatesses, douce impatience, et le tout ensemble; pleurs de joie au moindre regard favorable, torrent de larmes au moindre coup d'œil un peu froid; m'adorant aujourd'hui, m'idolâtrant demain; plus qu'idolâtre ensuite, se livrant à des hommages toujours nouveaux; enfin, si l'on avait partagé sa passion entre un million de cœurs, la part de chacun d'eux aurait été fort raisonnable. J'étais enchantée. Deux siècles, si nous les passions ensemble, n'épuiseraient pas cette tendresse-là, disais-je en moi-même; en voilà pour plus que je n'en userai. Je ne craignais qu'une chose, c'est qu'il ne mourût de tant d'amour avant que d'arriver au jour de notre union. . . ." (I, 2.)

59. ". . . Imaginez-vous ce que c'est que d'être humiliée, rebutée, abandonnée, et vous aurez quelque légère idée de tout ce qui compose la douleur d'une femme alors. Etre aimée d'un homme autant que je l'étais, c'est faire son bonheur et ses délices; c'est être l'objet de toutes ses complaisances, c'est régner sur lui, disposer de son âme; c'est voir sa vie consacrée à vos désirs, à vos caprices, c'est passer la vôtre dans la flatteuse conviction de vos charmes; c'est voir sans cesse qu'on est aimable: ah! que cela est doux à voir! le charmant point de vue pour une femme! En vérité, tout est perdu quand vous perdez cela. Eh bien! . . . cet homme dont vous étiez l'idole, concevez qu'il ne vous aime plus, et mettez-vous vis-à-vis de lui; la jolie figure que vous y ferez! Quel opprobre! Lui parlez-vous, toutes ses réponses sont des monosyllabes, oui, non, car le dégoût est laconique. L'approchez-vous, il fuit; vous plaignez-vous, il querelle; quelle vie! quelle chute! quelle fin tragique! Cela fait frémir l'amour-propre . . ." (I, 2.)

60. Lucile would also like the external manifestations that go with love. She does not want a man who hides his feelings. Lisette speaks for her when she says: "Eh! où est-il donc, cet amour qu'il a? Nous avons regardé dans ses yeux, il n'y a rien; dans ses paroles, elles ne disent mot; dans le son de sa voix, rien ne marque, dans ses procédés, rien ne sort; de mouvements de cœur, il n'en perce aucun." (II, 1.)

61. "Avant donc que rien ne s'y passe . . . , rien encore ne s'y trouve, sinon un état de vacance et de paresse, cet état de néant préalable qui est celui de l'être qui, n'existant que par ses sensations, n'a pas encore de sensation." (G. Poulet, *Etudes sur le temps humain*, t. II: *La Distance intérieure* (Paris, 1952), p. 1.)

62. This has already been pointed out by Leo Spitzer, *art. cit.*, p. 123.

63. An idea which is accepted by Mauzi (*op. cit.*, pp. 123, 275).

64. *Op. cit.*, p. 12.

65. H. T. Mason recognises this confusion, this loss of identity of the character when he falls in love. The critic describes this as ". . . the miracle whereby a human being, quite literally surprised by love, loses his autonomy of judgment and action, and falls under the influence of another so completely that his whole outlook is altered and his freedom of manœuvre is destroyed". (*Op. cit.*, p. 9.) This is also expressed by Marivaux in *La Vie de Marianne* when the heroine says: ". . . un mélange de trouble, de plaisir et de peur; oui, de peur, car une fille qui en est là-dessus à son apprentissage ne sait point où tout cela la mène: ce sont des mouvements inconnus qui l'enveloppent, qui disposent d'elle, qu'elle ne possède point, qui la possèdent; et la nouveauté de cet état l'alarme . . . il y a quelque chose qui la menace, qui l'étourdit, et qui prend déjà sur elle . . . L'âme, avec lui [l'amour], sent la présence d'un maître qui la flatte, mais avec une autorité déclarée qui ne la consulte pas . . ." (Ed. Deloffre (Paris, 1963), p. 66.)

66. Poulet, *op. cit.*, pp. 10-11.

67. "Cet événement qui m'arrive, je ne sais encore rien de lui, sinon qu'il m'arrive, que je ne puis le distinguer de moi, qu'il fait partie de ma propre existence." (Poulet, p. 5.)

68. Silvia in *Le Jeu*, the Marquise in *La seconde Surprise*, the Countess in *La Surprise*, and so on.

69. In *La Vie de Marianne*, the heroine can distinguish between *être* and *vivre* (in other words, *sentiments* and *existence*) when she says: ". . . on dirait que pour être, il n'est pas nécessaire de *vivre*, que ce n'est que par *accident* que nous vivons; mais que c'est naturellement que nous sommes." (Ed. Deloffre, p. 129.) Even though in love with Valville, Marianne *can* say: "Cette situation ne regardait que *ma vie*; ce qui m'occupait me regardait moi." (*Ibid., loc. cit.*) There is therefore, in her mind, a difference between her *life* and her *self,* which she equates in the following sentence with her emotions: ". . . notre vie, pour ainsi dire, nous est moins chère que nous, que nos passions." (*Ibid., loc. cit.*)

70. Lenient says that Marivaux's characters are "trop égoïstes, et surtout trop maîtres d'eux-mêmes, pour s'abandonner . . . aux émotions" (*op. cit.*, p. 348); "ils discutent, spéculent et jouent avec leurs sentiments" (p. 361). For Gustave Larroumet's attitude, *vide supra*, p. 23. Käthy Lüthi affirms that "elles ne s'oublient jamais", "elles sont trop maîtresses d'elles-mêmes" (*op. cit.*, p. 34); "Quelques-unes . . . , en particulier la Silvia du *Jeu de l'amour et du hasard,* semblent un peu trop raisonnables, trop décidées, trop clairvoyantes pour des jeunes filles de dix-huit ans, chez qui l'esprit devrait être, au moins quelquefois, la dupe du cœur" (*ibid.*, p. 55). This is not entirely correct. Silvia may have thought quite objectively about marriage, its dangers and its problems, and the kind of man who would or would not make a good husband, but all this is rather theoretical. Silvia, when faced with Dorante's charm and personality, almost forgets everything, at least her emotional self does. The critic herself has to admit that "néanmoins, l'auteur a soin de nous

représenter Silvia cédant à une émotion qu'il ne dépend pas d'elle de maîtriser . . ." (*ibid.*, p. 73).

71. There are other examples: Act I scene 15, when Araminte, having just heard Dubois' revelation, shows some hesitation at keeping him; Act III scene 1, when Dubois urges him to send the prepared letter; scene 7 of the same Act, when, convinced by Marton that he will be dismissed in less than an hour, he comes to Araminte for support.

72. Bernard Dort very perceptively remarks: ". . . l'égarement d'Araminte est peutêtre plus profond que celui de la plupart des héroïnes de Marivaux, dans la mesure où il est le produit de sa raison, où il coïncide avec la transformation de cette raison active en déraison." (*Théâtre*, IV, pp. 170.)

73. "Dorante: Je n'ose presque paraître devant vous.

Araminte (à part): Ah! Je n'ai guère plus d'assurance que lui. . . .

Araminte (à part, avec émotion): Ah! que je crains la fin de tout ceci!"

And after a few lines of an attempt at conversation, aware of her emotion: "Je ne sais ce que je lui réponds." (III, 12.)

74. "Damis (à part, en sortant): Je suis au désespoir." (I, 6.)

"Lucile (seule): Ah! il faut que je soupire, et ce ne sera pas pour la dernière fois. Quelle aventure pour mon cœur! Cette misérable Lisette, où a-t-elle été imaginer tout ce qu'elle vient de nous faire dire?" (I, 7.)

75. "Lucile: . . . dans la confusion d'idées que tout cela me donne à moi, il arrive, en vérité, que je me perds de vue. Non je ne suis pas sûre de mon état. . . ." (V, 2.)

76. "Faut-il que je vous aime encore, après d'aussi cruelles réponses que celles que vous me faites!"

"Que je suis malheureux! Qu'êtes-vous devenue pour moi? Vous me désespérez."

77. "Lucidor: . . . il y a quelque amour secret dont vous me faites mystère.

Angélique: . . . oui, Monsieur; voilà ce que c'est; j'en ai pour un homme d'ici; et quand je n'en aurais pas, j'en prendrais tout exprès demain pour avoir un mari à ma fantaisie." (Scene 17.)

78. "Marton: Il est, dit-on, dans une extrême agitation: il se fâche, il fait l'indifférent, à ce que dit Frontin; il va trouver Dorimène, il la quitte; quelquefois il soupire; . . ." (III, 1.)

79. Even his mother is beginning to suspect, by Act II, that Rosimond is not very "raisonnable". Speaking to Dorante she says: "Il n'est pas aussi raisonnable que vous me paraissez l'être, et je voudrais bien que vous m'aidassiez à le rendre plus sensé dans les circonstances où il se trouve." (II, 1.)

80. Another example, in which this time "raison" seems to be identified with common sense:

"Hortense: . . . votre petit jargon de galanterie me choque, me révolte; il soulève la raison"(III, 5.)

81. He is so desperate that he even admits all the torments love has given him: ". . . M'avez-vous cru susceptible de tous les ravages que l'amour fait dans le cœur des autres hommes? Eh bien! l'âme la plus vile, les amants les plus vulgaires, la jeunesse la plus folle, n'éprouvent point d'agitations que je n'en aie senties: inquiétudes, jalousies, transports, m'ont agité tour à tour. . . ." (II, 12.)

Works Consulted

EDITIONS OF MARIVAUX

Œuvres complètes de Marivaux, édition par M. Duviquet (Paris, Dauthereau, 1830).

Marivaux: Théâtre, présenté et annoté par Bernard Dort (Paris, Le Club français du livre, 1961-1962), 4 vols.

Marivaux: Théâtre complet, préface de Jacques Scherer, présentation et notes de Bernard Dort (Paris, Les Editions du Seuil, 1964).

Marivaux: Romans, suivis de Récits, Contes et Nouvelles, extraits des Essais et des Journaux de Marivaux, texte présenté et préfacé par Marcel Arland (Bibliothèque de la Pléïade, Paris, Gallimard, 1949).

La Vie de Marianne, éd. Frédéric Deloffre (Paris, Garnier, 1963).

Arlequin poli par l'amour, ed. Robert Niklaus and Thelma Niklaus (London, University of London Press, 1959).

Les fausses Confidences, ed. H. T. Mason (London, Oxford University Press, 1964).

WORKS ON MARIVAUX

Alain: "Marivaux-Musset" (Extraits du Journal d'Alain, septembre 1943), *Mercure de France,* vol. 308, n° 1040 (1er avril 1950), 577-583.

Arland, Marcel: *Marivaux* (Paris, Gallimard, 1950).

Braspart, Michel: "Marivaux ou le poids de la légèreté", *La nef,* 4e année, n° 34 (septembre 1947), 58-63.

Donnay, Maurice: "Marivaux, ou l'amour au XVIIIe siècle", *La Revue des vivants,* n° 6 (juin 1929), 843-867.

Dort, Bernard: "*Le Triomphe de l'amour* de Marivaux (régie de Jean Vilar, au T.N.P.)", *Théâtre populaire,* n° 17 (1er mars 1956), 71-73.

————"*La seconde Surprise* de Marivaux (mise en scène d'Hélène Perdrière, à la *Comédie-Française*)", *Théâtre populaire,* n° 24 (mai 1957), 89-91.

Eliot, Thomas S.: "Marivaux", *Art and Letters,* II, n° 2 (Spring 1919), 80-85.

Feugère, A.: "Rousseau et son temps: la littérature du sentiment au XVIIIe siècle: le théâtre de Marivaux", *Revue des cours et conférences,* 36e année (première série), I, n° 4 (le 30 janvier 1935), 333-345.

Fleury, Jean: *Marivaux et le marivaudage* (Paris, Plon, 1881).

Gazagne, Paul: *Marivaux par lui-même* (Paris, Editions du Seuil, 1954). (Reviewed by F. Deloffre in *Revue des sciences humaines,* fasc. 80 (octobre-décembre 1955), pp. 523-527.)

————"Réflexions sur *La Réunion des amours*", *L'Illustre Théâtre,* IV (1958), n° 10, 27-31.

Gossman, Lionel: "Literature and Society in the Early Enlightenment: the Case of Marivaux", *Modern Language Notes,* LXXXII (May 1967), n° 3, 306-333.

Greene, Edward J.H.: *Marivaux* (Toronto, University of Toronto Press, 1965). (Reviewed by Fr. Deloffre in *Revue d'histoire littéraire de la France* (67e année), LXVII (1967), 144-146.)

Larroumet, Gustave: *Marivaux, sa vie et ses œuvres* (Parish, Hachette, 1894).

Lenient, Charles: *La comédie au XVIIIe siècle* (Paris, Hachette, 1888). (See especially vol. I, ch. 14.)

Luthi, Käthy: *Les Femmes dans l'œuvre de Marivaux* (Bienne (Suisse), Les Editions du Chandelier, 1943).

Niklaus, Robert: "La comédie italienne et Marivaux", *Studi in onore di C. Pellegrini* (Torino, 1963), pp. 279-287.

Papin, Renée: "Marivaux, les femmes, l'amour et la lutte des classes . . .", *Nouvelle Critique,* n° 125 (1960-1961), 88-99.

Poulet, Georges: *Etudes sur le temps humain.* Tome II: *La Distance intérieure* (Paris, Plon, 1952). (See especially ch. 1, "Marivaux", pp. 1-34.)

Roy, Claude: *Lire Marivaux* (Paris, Editions du Seuil, 1947).

Scherer, Jacques: "Marivaux et Planchon", *Les Lettres nouvelles,* n° 18 (1er juillet 1959), 36-39.

Spitzer, Leo: "A propos de la *Vie de Marianne* (Lettre à M. Georges Poulet)", *Romanic Review,* XLIV (1953), 102-126.

Varga, Kibédi: "Note sur Marivaux", *Neophilologus,* XLI-XLII (1957-1958), n° 4, 252-257.

Wrage, William: *A Critical Edition of "Le Spectateur Français" of Marivaux* (unpublished Ph.D. thesis, University of Wisconsin, 1964).

GENERAL WORKS

Mauzi, Robert: *L'idée du bonheur dans la littérature et la pensée françaises au XVIIIe siècle* (Paris, A. Colin, 1960).

Planhol, René de: *Les Utopistes de l'amour* (Paris, Garnier, 1921).

Ronald C. Rosbottom (essay date January 1972)

SOURCE: Rosbottom, Ronald C. "Marivaux and the Possibilities of the Memoir-Novel." *Neophilologus* 56, no. 1 (January 1972): 43-9.

[*In the following essay, Rosbottom examines Marivaux's early experiments with the memoir form that would figure so prominently in his later works.*]

The most prevalent novelistic form of the first third of the eighteenth century in France was the memoir-novel, and one of its most successful practitioners was Marivaux[1]. First with **La Vie de Marianne, ou les mémoires de la comtesse de * * *,** then with **Le Paysan parvenu, ou les mémoires de * * *,** Marivaux explored all the formal and thematic aspects of the genre[2]. Yet these two great novels, published rather late in Marivaux's literary life, were not the first efforts he had made in analyzing the literary possibilities of the memoir format. In this study, we shall look at two other prose works of Marivaux, almost unknown, which reveal an early preoccupation with fictional autobiography, both formally as well as thematically. In these short pieces, Marivaux treats many of the themes—*coquetterie, amour-propre,* the refractive process of memory, autojustification—that will figure so prominently in **La Vie de Marianne** and **Le Paysan parvenu.** We will see how, in his search for psychological realism, Marivaux evolved thematic reasons as to why Marianne and Jacob decided to write their life stories.

The first of these pieces was written five years before Marivaux began work on **La Vie de Marianne**[3]. Entitled **"Mémoire de ce que j'ai fait et vu pendant ma vie",** it appeared in his **Spectateur français** in 1723[4]. It is in this story that Marivaux examines for the first time the psychological reasons that cause a person, and especially a woman, to compose her memoirs. The memorialist is a seventy-four-year-old woman who begins her story with a discussion on growing old. At first she rationalizes that age is only a state of mind, and being seventy-four is not as bad as one would think (pp. 207-208). Yet she cannot admit to her readers, nor to herself, that she has lost all those charms that had once made her the center of so much gallant attention. At the same time that she starkly admits "je suis vieille", she tells us that she is still a woman, "et qu'on ne peut être femme sans être coquette" (pp. 208, 209)[5]. This dichotomy between the old woman trying to come to grips with advancing age and the coquette whose memories are still vivid forms the tension which gives life to this short piece, and which will reappear even more forcefully in *La Vie de Marianne.*

As Marivaux's narrator continues her story, she recounts her education in *coquetterie*. There emerges from this account the portrait of a delicate art of mask-wearing of which Marivaux believes every woman capable. On its simplest level, it is only "une coquetterie machinale" (or automatic). As the old lady explains: "Et qu'on n'aille pas dire que c'est là une grande coquetterie, car c'est la moindre de toutes celles qu'une femme peut avoir . . . ; vraiment, quand la réflexion s'en mêle, c'est bien autre chose" (p. 209). She continues to relate how she gradually became a consummate actress, successful at duping others, equally successful in not being duped. The memory of her beauty and amorous successes reaches a climax when she exults: "Je recevais tous les jours tant de preuves que j'étais aimable, et ces preuves-là me faisaient tant de plaisir, que je n'oubliais rien pour en recevoir toujours de nouvelles" (p. 213). Thus is the portrait of a coquette deftly sketched by Marivaux's elderly memorialist. At the same time, by means of his heroine's obvious enjoyment at reliving and recounting her past, Marivaux shows that although her beauty is gone, her *coquetterie* remains intact.

As she continues her story, the memorialist tells of how the advancing years began to affect her: "D'ailleurs mes années commençaient à m'inquiéter; leur course me semblait plus rapide qu'à l'ordinaire. J'étais jeune encore, mais je ne me voyais pas loin de ce terme où la jeunesse d'une femme devient équivoque" (p. 214); "l'âge enfin me gagnait, il n'était plus question de jeunesse, ni d'aucun artifice pour paraître jeune: mon visage là-dessus n'était plus disciplinable, et il fallait me résoudre à l'abandonner" (p. 219); and finally, "je n'étais plus jeune" (p. 220). Confronted with the imminent loss of her physical charms, she decides that the only recourse left open to her is to convince others of her *past* beauty:

> Me voilà donc vieille, et reconnue par moi pour telle, et avec ces débris de beauté qui font connaître aux autres qu'on a été belle. Eh bien, puisqu'il faut le dire, ces débrislà me flattaient encore, *je m'intéressais* à *ce qu'on en pensait.* Cela est bien fou, j'en conviens; mais aussi c'est l'histoire d'une femme que je rapporte: coquettes quand nous sommes aimables, coquettes quand nous ne le sommes plus; dans le premier cas, nous

> travaillons à être aimées, dans le second, *nous travaillons à montrer que nous avons mérité de l'être.*
>
> (p. 220, my italics)

But there is a danger in this strategy, namely that one will leave oneself open to ridicule. And Marivaux's heroine soon learns (p. 221) that she has been the victim of snide comments and gossip because of her efforts to convince others of her past beauty. At this juncture, she goes into a convent to retire from the world. Here the story ends, but it is while in the convent, ostensibly in retirement, that Marivaux's heroine decides to write her memoirs. The memory of the past is still vivid, and her reconstruction of it is a final effort to persuade, at least literarily, another generation that she was once worthy of more attention than she now receives. Five years later, Marivaux was to augment this situation, through a sophistication of the memoir technique, and create his *two* Mariannes: the young, carefree coquette, and the older, more experienced, "retired" memorialist. But, as he begins *La Vie de Marianne,* Marivaux will compose one more short work which examines yet another aspect of the relationship between a memorialist and the past, and thereby gives us another insight into the meaning of his best novel.

This later piece, published in another of Marivaux's journalistic works, *Le Cabinet du philosophe* (pp. 419-426), tells the story of a coquette who finds herself confronted by middle age. The text has no title, nor is it in the memoir form, but it does provide us with a metaphorical replacement for memoirs: a magic mirror which can see into the past. In his story, Marivaux depicts a widow, about forty-five or fifty years old, who finds herself in a liaison with a man a few years younger than she. They are having a successful affair, but the difference in years cannot be overlooked, and Marivaux's heroine soon discovers that her lover is showing less interest in her. Since the story is in the third person, we soon learn from Marivaux that in fact the gentleman has fallen in love with a young girl half the age of his present mistress. Unable to admit that another woman is capable of stealing her lover from her, the widow determines to discover who her rival is. She goes to a local magician, renowned for solving problems of the heart. At the magician's she tells her story, lies about her age somewhat, and asks to know for whom her lover has left her. The magician slyly asks: "Vous lui pardonneriez donc . . . s'il n'était infidèle qu'en faveur de quelque dame qui vous valût?" The answer: "Du moins serait-il plus excusable, dit-elle la larme à l'oeil; mais c'est une excuse que personne ne peut lui fournir ici" (p. 424). Here, the magician brings out his magic mirror and tells his client that she is about to see the face of her rival in it. The face of a pretty young girl suddenly appears, and the widow immediately begins to berate her young challenger. She criticizes every aspect of her rival's physical appearance, concluding: ". . . Il n'est pas possible que mon perfide n'ouvre les yeux, et ne revienne à moi; ou bien vous me trompez, et vous ne me montrez pas ma rivale" (p. 425).

Following this outburst, the magician tells the widow that she is correct; the young lady who first appeared in his mirror was not her true rival. He warns her that now "c'est votre rivale, c'est la véritable qui vous allez voir: regardez et considérez attentivement . . ." (p. 425). Her interest is immediately aroused, but when she looks into the mirror and sees yet another young woman, she continues her vicious attacks, criticizing the portrait point by point. It is here that the magician drops his bombshell: "C'est vous que vous voyez dans la glace; vous-même, telle que vous étiez à l'âge de vingt ans: regardez-vous bien, vous ne pouvez pas manquer de vous reconnaître; et je n'osais pas espérer que vous vous méconnussiez" (p. 425). And to prove what he says, the magician asks the widow to look at a portrait made of her when she was in her early twenties. But the widow still refuses to understand the moral of the magician's deception, and the story ends as she leaves, affirming "vous pouvez me convaincre que j'ai tort, mais vous ne m'en persuaderez jamais" (p. 425).

In this short apologue, Marivaux has deftly underlined another of his favorite themes. As the magician says, the widow's true rival is not the young mistress of her lover, but rather the *memory* of her own lost charms. The past cannot be recaptured, although, through the processes of memory, its appearance is always attainable. It was the "remembrance of things past" that had duped the widow, preventing her from making the necessary adjustments that advancing age demands. Her own mirrors had lied to her. Only a magic mirror could lift off her mask of self-deception, no matter how briefly, and show her who her true rival was. Like the old lady in our first example, like Marianne, Marivaux's widowed coquette finds herself imprisoned by her past.

It is of course in **La Vie de Marianne** that Marivaux will successfully combine the major themes of these stories—*coquetterie*, self-deception and the harshly therapeutic nature of memory—and the memoir form. The texts which we have analyzed help significantly in elucidating the function that Marivaux intended for the narrator of his most famous memoir-novel. Apparently, he had planned to give a more active role to Marianne the narrator than she actually has. Unfortunately, after Part I, the portrait of the authoress becomes less clear as the younger Marianne's adventures take on more importance, and only infrequently does Marivaux choose to mention the problems and personality of the memorialist[6]. Yet the tantalizing glimpses that we have of the older Marianne are significant, and are essential to the understanding of **La Vie de Marianne** as a whole.

From the beginning, we have the fascinating *dédoublement* of the initial naïveté of the younger Marianne and the pretended naïveté of the older countess who demurs about writing her memoirs: "Il est vrai que l'histoire [de ma vie] est particulière, mais je la gâterai, si je l'écris; car où voulez-vous que je prenne un style? Il est vrai que dans le monde on m'a trouvé de l'esprit; mais, ma chère, je crois que cet esprit-là n'est bon qu'à être dit, et qu'il ne vaudra rien à être lu."[7]. The hesitancy, more apparent than real, to rely on her charms that we find in the younger Marianne is reflected in the affected modesty of the older narrator, aware of her ability to write well, but quick to pretend an innocence of purpose in presenting her life to the public. This "coquetterie de style" has replaced the "coquetterie machinale" that the younger Marianne had practiced so well.

In these first few pages of his novel, Marivaux uses a hackneyed technique, common to almost all "serious" novels of the early eighteenth century, which ostensibly gives an impression of verisimilitude to the story and an innocence of intention to the writer. But even by the 1730's this ploy had become transparent, and it is safe to assume that Marivaux uses Marianne's demure denials for other, essentially thematic purposes. There are other examples of Marianne's stylistic coquettishness throughout the novel: "Au reste, je parlais tout à l'heure de style, je ne sais pas seulement ce que c'est. Comment fait-on pour en avoir un? . . . Celui de mes lettres vous paraît-il passable? J'écrirai ceci de même" (p. 9); "Mais peut-être que j'écris mal" (p. 57); "Cette réflexion a coulé de ma plume sans que j'y prisse garde" (p. 209); "Je n'écris que pour vous amuser" (p. 271); etc. All of these passages exemplify the *coquetterie* of the older narrator, i.e., her desire to influence her reader(s), to gain their sympathy, yet at the same time not appear to do so.

We have already seen that the elderly lady who wrote her **"Mémoire de ce que j'ai fait et vu"** was nostalgic about a lost past, and aware of the difficulties of old age in a society where appearances counted for so much. The problem is treated somewhat differently in **La Vie de Marianne**: this is the story of a middle-aged woman, not unlike the widow in the story of the magic mirror, who has to accept suddenly the fact that she is losing her charms. The older Marianne tells a brief anecdote in the first few paragraphs of her story which graphically illustrates her problem. A beautiful young woman had been considered witty and charming by society, but she had contracted smallpox and had seemingly lost her wit. She became a "babillarde incommode." Marianne tells her reader: "Voyez combien auparavant elle avait emprunté d'esprit de son visage! Il se pourrait bien faire que le mien m'en eût prêté aussi dans le temps qu'on m'en trouvait beaucoup. *Je me souviens* de mes yeux de ce temps-là, et je crois qu'ils avaient plus d'esprit que moi" (p. 8, my italics). "Je me souviens": this is the key to Marianne's reasons for reliving her life through the composition of her memoirs. Ill at ease in the present, she searches for happiness in the past. In fact, the book she writes becomes her past. But the reconstruction of her life is inevitably influenced by her present nostalgic state. As a result, Marianne's story must be seen not only as the adventures of a young orphan who wants to arrive, but also as a justification, on the part of the middle-aged narrator, of her claims that she was once more beautiful and witty than she is now.

There are other instances where Marianne's nostalgia penetrates her mask of disinterestedness. Referring to the young woman afflicted with smallpox, she reminisces on how she herself used to charm others more with her physical beauty than through any natural wit she may have had. "Tout me réussissait, et je vous assure que dans la bouche d'une laide, mes folies auraient paru dignes des Petites-Maisons . . ." (p. 9). But realization of her present situation suddenly returns to the middle-aged narrator, and she admits that "à cette heure que mes agréments sont passés, je vois qu'on me trouve un esprit assez ordinaire, et cependant je suis plus contente de moi que je ne l'ai jamais été" (p. 9). This final remark, reminiscent of a similar one by the elderly narrator of our first example, is belied by subsequent references to her advancing age: "J'ai eu un petit minois qui ne m'a pas mal coûté de folies, quoiqu'il ne paraisse guère les avoir méritées à la mine qu'il fait aujourd'hui: aussi il me fait pitié quand je le regarde, et je ne le regarde que par hasard; je ne lui fais presque plus cet honneur-là exprès" (p. 51). It is through passages such as these that Marivaux insinuates that there is a psychological reason as well as a practical one (her friend asked for her life story) for Marianne's taking the time and effort to reconstruct her past. Despite her protestations, Marivaux's narrator is constantly aware of her vanishing charms, and of the effect this will have on her existence in a society whose values are predicated on appearances. She is unhappy at the prospect of growing old, and wants to arrest the process if only through concretizing her existence on the printed page.

Finally, another, and more subtle consequence of Marianne's nostalgia, which the story of the magic mirror helps to illuminate, is the corollary theme of Marianne the narrator's jealousy of Marianne the young coquette. We have seen how Marivaux had recognized that as a coquette grows older, she becomes more and more a prisoner of the memory of herself as a young and beautiful woman. The old lady who wrote **"Mémoire de ce que j'ai fait et vu"** felt compelled to justify herself, to remind others of her past glories. And the haughty widow in the story of the magic mirror is shown to be jealous of all beautiful women, even of herself as a young girl. In **La Vie de Marianne,** the memoir form may be seen to serve as a magic mirror

for the older Marianne as she comes to realize that the young girl she has resuscitated is in fact her most potent rival. In most successful memoir-novels, there is a tendency on the memorialist's part to smile knowingly at the naïve and sometimes humorous actions of himself as a youth. But in Marivaux's novel, this understandable feeling of superiority takes on added significance when we recall the points made by Marivaux in his earlier pieces, and when we study closely the portrait of the narrator that he so carefully delineates in the first part of Marianne's story. The narrator finds herself in the ironic and unenviable position of using the memory of the younger Marianne as a psychological crutch, while at the same time slyly insinuating that the young girl was often not as she appeared to be.

After years of experimentation and fascination with the literary possibilities of memory, Marivaux had arrived at the complexity and originality of **La Vie de Marianne**[8]. He sketches for us a personality in conflict with itself as it undergoes the refractive process of memory. Marianne's narration of her life, although ostensibly truthful, is tinged with the regret of a middle-aged coquette who cannot quite bring herself to admit that the past is irretrievable. Her sincerity as a memorialist is tarnished by those very qualities which made the younger Marianne so charming: coyness, an *espritr evendicateur,* and a strongly felt need to present to the public a persona which would hide the true Marianne.

Notes

1. For detailed studies of the memoir-novel and its significance in the development of the modern novel, see Moses Ratner's *Theory and Criticism of the Novel in France, from l'Astrée to 1750* (New York, 1938); Georges May's *Le Dilemme du roman au XVIIIe siècle: Etude sur les rapports du roman et de la critique (1715-1761)* (Paris 1963); and the more recent study of Philip R. Stewart, *Imitation and Illusion in the French Memoir-Novel, 1700-1750: The Art of Make-Believe* (New Haven, 1969). Also of interest is May's article "L'histoire a-t-elle engendré le roman?" *RHLF* [*Revue d'Histoire Littéraire de la France*], LV (1955), 155-176.

2. Jean Rousset has also studied this aspect of Marivaux's work, with especial reference to *La Vie de Marianne,* in "Marivaux, ou la structure du double registre", *Studi Francesi,* I (1957), p. 58, and in "Emploi de la première personne chez Chasles et Marivaux", *CAIEF* [*Cahiers de l'Association Internationale des Etudes Françaises*], no. 19 (1967), p. 110.

3. An even earlier piece (published in the *Mercure* in 1719-1720) entitled "Lettres contenant une aventure", tells the story of a young man who

overhears two women discussing love and *coquetterie*. One of the women recounts her life to the other, and thereby creates an oral memoir. We see then that at the beginning of his literary career, Marivaux was aware of the possibilities afforded by literary autobiography.

4. Marivaux, *Journaux et Oeuvres diverses,* édition de F. Deloffre et M. Gilot (Paris, 1969), pp. 206-224. Subsequent references will pertain to this edition and will appear in the text.

5. This recalls an earlier passage where Marivaux affirms that "une femme qui n'est plus coquette, c'est une femme qui a cessé d'être" (*Journaux,* p. 28).

6. The same is true of Marivaux's depiction of Jacob, the narrator of *Le Paysan parvenu* (1734-1735). Jacob's nostalgia for his youth is less evident than Marianne's, but nonetheless present. In Part I, he briefly explains why he is composing his memoirs: "Je cherche . . . à m'amuser moi-même. Je vis dans une campagne où je me suis retiré, et où mon loisir m'inspire un esprit de réflexion que je vais exercer sur les événements de ma vie. Je les écrirai du mieux que je pourrai; chacun a sa façon de s'exprimer, qui vient de sa façon de sentir . . . Ce n'est point ici une histoire forgée à plaisir, et je crois qu'on le verra bien" (p. 6 of F. Deloffre's edition, Paris, 1959). Again, we glimpse a narrator who has retired from an active life, and who wants to recreate his past in order to instruct others, but especially to satisfy his own psychological needs.

7. Marivaux, *La Vie de Marianne, ou les mémoires de la comtesse de * * **, édition de F. Deloffre (Paris, 1957), p. 8. Subsequent references will pertain to this edition and will appear in the text.

8. F. Deloffre, in the introduction to his edition of *La Vie de Marianne,* would put as early as 1712-1713 Marivaux's preoccupation with this theme of "retour sur soi" (p. xi). The example that he makes reference to is found in Marivaux's first novel, *Les Effets surprenants de la sympathie.*

Oscar A. Haac (essay date 1973)

SOURCE: Haac, Oscar A. "Success on the Stage." In *Marivaux,* pp. 40-66. New York: Twayne, 1973.

[*In the following excerpt, Haac offers an overview of Marivaux's early dramatic successes between 1720 and 1728.*]

I ARLEQUIN POLI PAR L'AMOUR (HARLEQUIN POLISHED BY LOVE), COMEDY IN ONE ACT, T.I., 1720.

Marivaux' first comedy independently written for the Italian players is justly famous. The stage directions that happen to be unusually complete show how care-

fully he planned for pantomime and used the actor's skills. The meeting of Silvia and Arlequin is notable. Arlequin enters playing with a shuttlecock, like a child. It falls down, and as he picks it up, he perceives Silvia; he is so struck by her beauty that he can only gradually recover his upright position. Their naïve manners are hilarious. Greedily Arlequin kisses her fingers: "I never tasted goodies that good" (*de bonbon si bon*), *T* [*Théâtre Complet*] I, 94.

Their love threatens the plans of the Fairy Queen who wanted Arlequin for herself. She justifies her desire for the attractive boy who is much younger than she, by saying: "Nothing is so natural as loving what is loveable" (*T* I, 87), but she is unwilling to let the maxim apply to others. Her desire for Arlequin seems grotesque, her use of power seems unjust and barbarous. It is a characteristic paradox that in this fairy world only the Fairy Queen is unattractive.

Trivelin, the Queen's prime minister, defects from her cause; he tells Arlequin how to cope with her: "Swear that you love her, then cleverly and playfully try to get hold of her wand!" (*T* I, 106) The trick works and the Fairy Queen becomes his prisoner. She is furious. Arlequin admonishes: "Quiet now, I am the master, look sweetly at me!" Silvia, in what may seem like a pun on the "usefulness" and appeal of virtue, suggests they release her: "Let us be generous; compassion is a great quality!" (*T* I, 109), and so Arlequin sets her free but keeps Silvia. Love has indeed "polished him," i.e., made him not only polite (*poli*) but knowing in the ways of the world, and powerful!

A number of sources for the play have been identified, plays by Autreau and Fuzelier, a short story by Mme Durand-Bédacier, entitled *The Miracle of Love*; a parallel in *Persiles and Sigismunda* by Cervantes has been mentioned. They show that Marivaux, much like Shakespeare, is not an inventor of plots and that his originality lies in his form, style, and the magic of his characterizations. One comparison is particularly interesting, the parallel between **Arlequin Poli** and Racine's *Phèdre*. Phèdre loves Hyppolite just as the Fairy Queen loves Arlequin; in each case the young man foils the Queen; Hyppolite loves Aricie and goes to his death before Phèdre can claim him. Of course Marivaux wrote no tragedy, but the touching quality of young love is common to both plays and Arlequin stands closer to Hyppolite than to Agnès in Molière's *Ecole des Femmes* (*School for Women*), though Agnès, like Arlequin, finds ways to outwit age and experience. Marivaux' admiration for Classical tragedy is ever present and the example bears out the theoretical statements of 1719.

II ANNIBAL (HANNIBAL), TRAGEDY IN 5 ACTS IN VERSE. T.F., 1720.

Marivaux hoped to establish himself on the French stage as well, but somehow the Comédie Française never brought him satisfaction. His one and only complete tragedy was particularly poorly received. It convinced him that he could do better in the natural prose style of comedy.[1]

Annibal is an antiheroic tragedy with an heroic ending! The hero is pictured in his old age, a defeated warrior who has found refuge at the court of Prusias and has been promised his daughter, Laodice, in marriage; only it so happens that the Roman ambassador, Flaminius, has loved her in times past and now returns to claim her for himself. Besides, Flaminius wants to break up the alliance which seems dangerous for Rome. A remarkable passage describes how Laodice first met Flaminius. As she recalls the birth of love, we are reminded of Arlequin setting eyes on Silvia: "My eyes were proud. They met his and his easily conquered mine. I was moved from the depth of my heart. I could neither escape nor sustain his look" (*T* I, 124).

Under such circumstances, it is clear that Laodice will prefer Flaminius, but she feels sympathy for Annibal; she wants to protect him from her father, Prusias, a weak and cowardly king, who has withdrawn his support from Annibal in favor of the more powerful Romans. For this reason, Laodice sets a condition to her marriage to Flaminius. She will become his wife if he will protect Annibal, i.e., violate his instructions from Rome and his professional ethics. "Would you accept a suitor who preferred you to faith and honor?" Flaminius asks Laodice. She replies: "Why not give up your exalted idea of honor?" (*T* I, 160). A heroine in a traditional tragedy would have given the opposite response. The spirit of compromise fits Marivaux' attitude as a "Modern," but is ill-suited to this tragedy which suddenly shifts to the heroic mold in which the author must have felt most uncomfortable.

Prusias has treacherously urged Annibal to flee and let the Romans capture him. Thus compromise becomes impossible. Annibal rises to his former glory and poisons himself, exclaiming: "I die but lose only my life!" (*T* I, 172). Laodice is theoretically free to marry Flaminius now the obstacle has been removed, but, like the Princesse de Clèves (in the novel of Mme de Lafayette), she rejects her lover with violence. After all, he has broken her trust and left Annibal no choice but suicide or an ignominious death in Rome.

Thus, after four acts of a new kind of tragedy, with suggestions of ambiguous compromises, a fifth, heroic act provides solutions clearly at odds with Marivaux' philosophy. One confirmation: only two years after he portrayed Annibal's suicide, he criticizes Montesquieu for defending the right to take one's life (*OD,* [*Journaux et Oeuvres Diverses*] 154 of 1722). Besides, Marivaux must have felt out of his element drawing on Livy and Plutarch and on *Nicomède* by Corneille in order to evoke antiquity like the "Ancients" he made fun of.

III *Le Spectateur Français* (*The French Spectator*), periodical in 25 issues (feuilles), 1721-24, issued as a volume in 1728.

The *Spectator* of Addison and Steele had been an outstanding success; imitations were numerous and known to Marivaux, especially those of Van Effen; translations of the *Spectator* had begun to appear in 1714, but the perplexing fact is that Marivaux at times imitated passages that had not as yet appeared in French; they must have been discussed in salons for, in spite of the monumental thesis of Lucette Desvignes-Parent, it is not proven he knew English. The pattern of Addison and Steele fitted him perfectly. He adopted a tone, purposely whimsical, a method of random comments in great variety without imitating particulars too closely.

Thus he set out to "capture the thoughts chance inspires" (*OD,* 114-17), frivolous, fortuitous, but also pertinent, forceful, and concise (*OD,* 114-16, 139), an "orgy of ideas" (*libertinage d'idées, OD,* 132), gathered at random. To amuse the reader, he changes topic frequently and excuses his apparent lack of plan and method by claiming they are the result of laziness (*OD,* 117, 252). The term must not mislead us, for beside the twenty-five issues of the *Spectateur,* Marivaux composed three comedies during the same period. His *Lettre sur la Paresse,* 1740 (*Letter on Laziness, OD,* 443-44), credits laziness with enabling him to write without interruptions and other concerns. Laziness refers to the reluctance to formulate ideas unless carefully conceived or to continue writing when he has said enough.

To stake out his claim to wisdom, Marivaux assumes the age of Madame de Lambert; he poses as an old man of seventy-four (*OD* 207). Madame de Lambert's conversations, and also her published work, inspired many passages; for instance, the theory of man's natural infidelity (*OD,* 203) is found in her *Treatise on Friendship,*[2] and her books giving *Advice to a Son* and *to a Daughter* provided other ideas like the suffering that naturally accompanies love.

An important theme, here as elsewhere, is sentiment. We cannot resist passions; indeed, the passions furnish us insights inaccessible to reason, i.e., to traditional, systematic philosophy (*OD,* 227, 232). Marivaux admits that he likes to savor his emotions in order not to "lose a single part of grief and compassion for those who suffer" (*OD,* 129). It is their emotional impact that makes him sing the praises of *Romulus* and *Inez de Castro,* two tragedies by his friend, La Motte, that today leave us cold (*OD,* 123, 227).

Love is no dream of peaceful happiness. Two girls complain that they were undone because they believed their lovers to be gentlemen (*OD,* 155, 165). A wife who wants to remain faithful to her husband appeals to the honor of her lover and miraculously gets him to leave and thus preserves her innocence, but she admits how much his attentions had flattered her; "an ugly woman would have been respected with less trouble" (*OD,* 212, cf. 122-23). The virtuous wife whose very virtue makes her so attractive, better be on her guard (*OD,* 162). Like Saint-Evremont, Marivaux is an Epicurean who regards virtue as infinitely attractive (*OD,* 162-63, 217, 260) and speaks of the "voluptuous satisfaction" of doing good (*OD,* 132).

Since innocence and virtue are in constant danger, none of this expresses an easy optimism. A good example is the story of his return to the home of a girl with whom he was much taken, because he had forgotten a glove. He finds her sitting in front of a mirror, practicing the wiles that entranced him. This shock, he tells us, makes him break with her for good: "Now I know the machines of the opera, it interests me less" (*OD,* 118). And thus, he pretends that he became an unalterable misanthrope.

This account is no more autobiographical than its companion piece which provides a contrary view. He tells us that a woman without makeup and artifice is not truly herself. Love requires means to entice (*piquer, OD* 201). Besides, Marivaux is no misanthrope. He is not at all like Hermocrate, whom he pictures ready to withdraw to a desert as a hermit because he has found that kindness leaves him powerless and little respected (*OD,* 179-86). Marivaux is no Alceste; he remains in the world, he is a realist; he is not shocked by artifice and ambiguity; he describes marriage as fraught with constant dangers. The marriage partners must continuously find ways to reawaken love (*OD,* 201-2), for being accustomed to one another is insufficient for happiness. He also reports the dream of a Spaniard, a kind of "topography" of love with a warning that there is a "monster" inside Love's palace (*OD,* 142).

Marivaux strikes a balance. He calls virtue infinitely attractive, but feels that this very appeal breeds danger. The generous Hermocrate makes everyone jealous (*OD,* 180-85) while flatterers succeed (*OD,* 199, 252). The tone of these descriptions is humorous, but there are moments when Marivaux turns into an intransigent and pessimistic idealist. The evil, he tells us, are shamed by the righteous (*OD,* 260); the rewards of vice are too brutish to be satisfying (*OD,* 206, 260); atheists (*esprits forts* as in La Bruyère) "brazenly walk in darkness" and are themselves the best argument for religion (*OD,* 197). In essays of 1751 and 1754, he speaks of the impotence of the honest man (*honnête homme*), the most valuable subject of his prince, the one to be trusted before all others. Such statements break with the dominant humor and lighthearted acceptance of man's ambiguity, but Marivaux does not remain entrenched for long in his

extreme position. The strong attack on atheists, for instance, is matched by a comment that many sermons express the priest's vanity (*OD,* 195) and that ever so many pious ladies are really in love with their confessors (*OD,* 224).

Still, some moments of extreme bitterness stand out. They concern the abuses of wealth. Having lost his modest fortune, Marivaux speaks from experience. The wealthy fear those who seek their aid; they humiliate them (*OD,* 116). Wealth corrupts. An unfeeling son neglects his father after inheriting all his money (*OD,* 186-88, cf. *Marianne,* Pt. XI). Gaudy clothing is a hateful show of wealth; to escape such a display when the Spanish Infanta arrived in Paris (March, 1722), Marivaux takes refuge in a barrelmaker's shop (*OD,* 133). He speaks of a girl who would have been ruined by the offensive propositions of a wealthy libertine, had he not given her all the money he carried on him and enabled her to resist (*OD,* 129).

Around 1723-24 there are further attacks on the abuses of wealth, on the humiliation of the poor (*OD* 256-67). In one disillusioned scene, autobiography is barely camouflaged. A woman (actually Marivaux himself) comes to see a lady; as she steps up to embrace her, she finds that this friend just died of a heart attack (*OD,* 222). Marivaux' wife must have died this way. The story speaks of a son, ten years old, while Marivaux' daughter was only four, but the parallel is evident and gives special meaning to the plea to seize the happiness of every moment, for it may have eternal consequences (*OD,* 208). This statement made Georges Poulet present Marivaux as a precursor of Existentialism (*Etudes sur le Temps Humain*), but this may be an inopportune extension of Marivaux' pessimism. The fact remains that he was greatly affected by his limited social condition and by the loss of his wife. This was the time when he composed several comedies without happy endings, like ***La Fausse Suivante***.

Basically, Marivaux attempts to remain impersonal and humorous. He inserts a burlesque letter from a husband whose wife is a miser. To get even with her, he has embarked on ruinous expenses and hopes the shock of finding this out will kill her; yet he regrets his course; she is too pretty to die! (*OD,* 172-76) Most of the time, Marivaux dissociates himself from categorical positions in defense of virtue or opposition to vice, for he is resolutely "Modern," and associates moralizing literature with an outmoded past. In this connection he returns several times to his party position opposing the "Ancients." The worshipers of antiquity deny the merit of contemporary literature; to make fun of them, he tells us that he found groceries wrapped in a sheet of the *Iliad*; Homer must be turning in his grave! (*OD,* 146-49, 159). He laughs at those who judge a work by its number of pages; the thicker it is, the more philosophical it is supposed to be (*OD,* 137-39). He affirms that he is writing for his own times and therefore must not emulate the past (*OD,* 148). He is proud of the wit and intelligence (*esprit*) of his own day; without pursuing it for its own sake, he wants to remain natural and express himself in terms characteristically his own (*rester dans la singularité d'esprit qui nous est échue,* **OD,** 144-49).

This remarkable formulation of his literary objective seemed so absurd to his critic, the abbé Desfontaines, that he quoted it to make fun of Marivaux and did not even feel the need to explain why it was inadequate (in the *Dictionnaire Néologique*). Marivaux felt that Desfontaines' comments were too personal and, therefore, offensive (*OD,* 137, 246). He became so angry that he suspended the **Spectateur** for four months (*OD,* 143). Then he counterattacked: critics, he says, are like women unable to bear the beauty of a rival (*OD,* 150-55); they rarely recognize talent (*OD,* 134) while he would give credit where credit is due, e.g., to Montesquieu and his *Lettres Persanes* (*Persian Letters,* **OD,** 153-54).

Once again we find a rather stark expression of personal feelings. Marivaux aims at a witty tone but often cannot hide his position. He wants to "penetrate the minds of men" (*OD,* 127), but he also establishes a doctrine, and shows a passionate humanism that is barely concealed. The difficulty is to define a code of conduct, toward critics, toward other authors, and his neighbors in general, when he knows that didactic tracts will be discarded by the modern reader. He must sweeten the pill:

> Let us be good and virtuous. . . . What I can reasonably want another to do for me, even though he may fail to act that way, shows me what I must do for him. . . . We may be born evil, but we bear our evil like a monster we must fight. . . . As soon as we become members of society, we are forced to observe an order that shields us from our evil impulses. Reason which reveals this need to us, is itself the corrective of our iniquity.
>
> (*OD,* 233-34)

This attitude implies a kind of psychology. "We are the object, or rather the subject of this science we should like to possess" (*OD,* 232). Just as in 1749-50, before the French Academy, he proposes a "science of the human heart," in the **Spectateur,** he attempts to formulate it as amusingly as possible; he presents serious considerations not as his own, but as those submitted by an unknown reader (*OD,* 231-32). In the **Spectateur** and other journals to follow, he sets forth many of the principles which his plays and novels illustrate.

IV *LA SURPRISE DE L'AMOUR* (*THE SURPRISE OF LOVE*), COMEDY IN 3 ACTS, T.I., 1722.

The three comedies produced while he edited the **Spectateur** rank among Marivaux' best. These are im-

portant years in his career, during which he turned into a major dramatist. Meanwhile Silvia played an ever more important role in the Italian troupe, second only to that of Lelio in **La Surprise**; she played the lead in **La Fausse Suivante.** Lesbros de la Versane tells an anecdote that took place during the rehearsals of **La Surprise.** One day Marivaux came to watch, incognito; he volunteered to read part of her role. "You read so well, you are the author of the devil!" she exclaimed. He indicated that he was not the devil (*L'Esprit de Marivaux,* p. 16). Nothing is known to confirm or deny that this meeting took place; we are not informed about their actual relations. Paul Gazagne (in *Marivaux par lui-même*) indulges in pure fantasy when he sees them as lovers; he also goes too far when he asserts that, in Marivaux' plays, marriage is an euphemism for surrender, and love for sensual desire.

La Surprise de l'Amour inverts the plot of the early novels. It begins with two disappointed lovers who foreswear love like Alceste at the end of the *Misanthrope.* They will withdraw from the world like Hermocrate in the **Spectateur.** Obviously they have drawn the wrong conclusion from past experience but they will be the last to know it. As a dutiful servant, Arlequin attempts to adopt his master's pessimism. The spectator will smile as Arlequin finds temptation all around him. He wants to step across the way in order not to see two birds in a tree. "I swore to forego love but when I see it, I almost feel like violating my resolve" (*T* I, 190). Lelio tells him women are vipers. "But they are such pretty animals," replies Arlequin, "such lovely kittens. What a shame they have so many claws" (*T* I, 192). Here he is upholding Lelio's position to Colombine, the maid of the Countess:

COLOMBINE:

Why are you and your master such misanthropes?

ARLEQUIN:

Because the proverb says, a scalded cat fears the water.

COLOMBINE:

Explain! Why is Lelio avoiding my mistress?

ARLEQUIN:

Because we know love and what it is worth.

(*T* I, 197)

Unencumbered by the rules of etiquette and conceptions of honor, less subject to resentments, the servants will recognize their desire to marry long before their masters but stage conventions require that they wait until their masters are ready for the ceremony. This makes them like their masters' alter egos. Once they understand the situation, the servants can do much to hasten the conclusion.

In this manner, Colombine helps Arlequin to see the light:

COLOMBINE:

This fellow is fighting his own desires as if he were a gentleman.

ARLEQUIN:

Aren't you ashamed of being so pretty?

(*T* I, 206)

Very soon Arlequin gives up the battle against love, but Lelio takes to the end of the play to come to the same conclusion: "Today I have no taste for the role of a gentleman. I am tired of that little matter" (*T* I, 231). Just how much self-deception he had to overcome is clear when he tells the Countess before the final conversion: "If I loved you, I would be the most humiliated, the most ridiculed and pitiful of all men who might conceivably love you" (*T* I, 220). He even imagined that he was carrying the Countess' portrait on his person only because it resembled a friend of his (*T* I, 230).

Love is presented on three levels: (1) Jacqueline, a maid, and Pierre, the gardener, are ready to marry from the start. Arrangements for them become a pretext for meetings between Lelio and the Countess. Pierre philosophizes: "No harm in loving one's neighbor, especially if she is pretty" (*T* I, 188), and Jacqueline likes his advances. They are so much children of nature that there is only one danger: Pierre might fall for Thomas' daughter if there is much of a delay. (2) Arlequin and Colombine, beset by their masters' hesitations, struggle until the second act. (3) Lelio and the Countess battle until the end of the third.

When Colombine tells Lelio that all of his actions betray love, he replies: "But how was I to know?" Arlequin adds: "It isn't my fault, I warned you!" (*T* I, 232). Finally, Lelio must choose between the yoke (*tyrannie*) of marriage and the insult (*grossièreté*) of saying "no" (*T* I, 231). "You are the master," says the Countess.—"Of what?"—"To love or not to love" (*T* I, 235). He says "yes" and Arlequin can marry Colombine "without ceremony," i.e., without further ado, but there is a pun: Repeatedly Marivaux expresses the idea that the ceremony adds nothing if there is love. Love had already stated this in *L'Amour et la Vérité*; but had it not taken three acts of "ceremony" in *La Surprise* to come to this conclusion?

Of the fairy world in *Arlequin Poli*, there remains only the circle the Baron draws around Lelio and the Countess to tie them together as by enchantment. The atmosphere has become mundane, with practical matters like Pierre's marriage serving to draw the two misanthropes into each other's trap. It is characteristic of Marivaux to find two such persons who are forced to give up their foolish principles, for principles or gems of wisdom, like proverbs, grandly enunciated are generally misconceived or misunderstood. Marivaux' "maxims," like those of La Rochefoucauld, merely emphasize the ambiguity of truth and man's illusions.

To compose his play, Marivaux turned to the repertoire of the first and second Italian troupes, including plays by Riccoboni and Autreau (and thus, indirectly to Moreto); while disillusioned lovers are common also in Molière, his situations are different. Marivaux avoids following him as a model!

V *LA DOUBLE INCONSTANCE* (*TWO CASES OF INFIDELITY*), COMEDY IN 3 ACTS, T.I., 1723.

Marivaux' preferred play retells, in comic form for the stage, the tale of the rape of Bastille, in *La Voiture Embourbée* (R, 47-68), and there are parallels to another melodramatic episode in the *Spectateur*, the story of Eléonore who mortified Mirski by substituting her maid for herself because she foresaw that Mirski would abandon her (*OD*, 163-72). Marivaux must have been particularly proud of the way he was able to camouflage the tragic theme of seduction. The technique is inspired by the conventions of Classical tragedy which, e.g., proscribes death from the stage but does not hide the fact violence occurs. Thus the inherent cruelty of the story remains even in the fairy kingdom of *La Double Inconstance* where a charming Prince is committed, by the law of the land, to marry one of his subjects without doing violence to her feelings.

When the play begins, Arlequin and Silvia love each other; when it ends, they both marry another partner. Their estrangement is gradual, the alienation of affection almost imperceptible, and yet it is carefully planned by the Prince who uses a disguise and a number of assistants to succeed. The rape of Bastille lurks in the background. Jean Anouilh, perhaps unaware of the parallel, sensed the tragic theme when he interpreted the action, in his play, (*La Répétition The Rehearsal*), as a plan for seduction.

This does not inhibit comedy. Arlequin is funny when he protests against the abuse of wealth and power. From the start he distrusts the "honor" of having the Prince provide him with a servant, i.e., of seeing the spy, Trivelin, assigned to follow him about (*T* I, 262). Later on the Prince offers patents of nobility in exchange for Silvia. Arlequin wonders whether an edict can make him into a gentleman (*honnête homme*); it seems that often such patents dispense their holders from honorable conduct (*honnêteté*), for the "honor" of noblemen seems frequently as dubious as their motives (*T* I, 305). "The Prince," says Arlequin, "is a gentleman. If he had not stolen my mistress, I might like him a lot" (*T* I,

280). Eventually Arlequin succumbs. He has rejected the advances of Lisette (sent by the Prince) who was all too forward, but when Flaminia comes to sympathize, serves good food and excellent wine and displays charm and kindness, he falls in love with her; Flaminia effectively supports the plans of the Prince without Arlequin noticing it.

Silvia's fate is similar, and here too the action provides a great deal of humor. At the outset, she rejects the very idea of being courted by the Prince: "A decent girl must love her husband, and I could never love you" (*T* I, 256). At that, she does not know to whom she is talking to, for the Prince is disguised as one of his own officers. "Better a commoner content in her little village than a princess weeping in a luxurious apartment" (*T* I, 257). At the end of the play she will be only too happy to marry the Prince and she won't be weeping in his luxurious apartment! The Prince is very clever. He will not reveal his identity until he is sure of Silvia's love. She would never have yielded to the advantages of rank, she had too noble a soul for that. Indeed, it is her sensitive, noble soul that makes her discover a special kinship in the Prince and repells her from Arlequin who seems vulgar when he leaves her to taste Flaminia's good food and wine. Silvia seems born to be noble and to marry the Prince; her very delicacy makes the seduction succeed so easily. Meanwhile, Lisette, Flaminia, Trivelin, all paid assistants of the Prince, have unobtrusively advanced his cause; disguise, along with rapid, witty dialogue have done much to camouflage the plans that propel the action.

A reviewer in the *Mercure* finds there is too much analysis of delicate feelings; he objects to Marivaux' "metaphysics of the heart" (*T* I, 247), a reproach used by Voltaire and others, who disliked psychological comedy. They overlooked that there is considerable social comment in Marivaux' play. The setting in a fairy kingdom has not infringed on the understanding, and portrayal of political and social reality.

VI *Le Prince Travesti* (*The Prince in Disguise*), comedy in 3 acts, T.I., 1724.

The underlying pessimism of the years 1723-24, which we discovered in the *Spectateur* and in *La Double Inconstance,* becomes even more manifest in the following plays. In *Le Prince Travesti* we find, for the first time, a character who is fundamentally evil, Frédéric, the despicable counselor of the Princess, always ready for a deal and for a bribe. To him we can apply the following comment from the *Spectateur*:

> An evil man is always evil . . . only, when he is surrounded by honors and has high rank with important functions . . . things look different . . . , evil is masked . . . , even its excesses are embellished. . . .

> That is why . . . in high stations disrepute usually brings honor, whereas ordinary people like ourselves are reduced to shame for the slightest fault.

(*OD*, 242-43)

In *La Double Inconstance,* deceit was justified in the name of love; in the next two plays it makes an even bolder appearance though the comic tone is preserved.

The Classical triangle, Lelio, The Princess, Hortense, corresponds to a large extent to Racine's *Bajazet,* Roxane, Atalide, and Frédéric can be compared with Acomat. The Princess who becomes the rival in love of her own confidente, Hortense, also appears in Corneille's *Cid,* but, more to the point, there is a parallel situation in *Les Effets Surprenants* where Frédélingue, before he can marry Parménie, finds himself pursued by a princess who resents Parménie as her rival. Frédélingue has won the love of Parménie by an heroic rescue just as Lelio has rescued Hortense. Enough is said to show that the noble deeds of tragedy and romance are very much present in Marivaux' comedy. He has, in fact, created a new genre which combines sentiment with heroic comedy of the type of Molière's *Dom Garcie de Navarre*. *Le Prince Travesti* goes further in this direction than other plays of Marivaux. It is not surprising to find that he also produced a version in 5 acts (*T* I, 330).

The Princess of Barcelona is negotiating her marriage to the King of Castille. She does not know that the ambassador she is talking to is the King himself in disguise. She would proceed immediately, had she not fallen in love with Lelio whom she has appointed to be her prime minister, much to the displeasure of Frédéric who wants the post for himself. Now Frédéric needs Lelio to support his cause. He offers him his daughter as a reward. When he is refused on both counts, he becomes furious. Lelio, actually the King of Leon, also in disguise, does not reciprocate the feelings of the Princess because he fell in love with her confidante, Hortense, when he rescued her some time ago from highway robbers. Both recall the event as the most significant of their lives. It occurred before the death of the husband of Hortense. Hers has been an unhappy marriage which left her as disillusioned as the Countess in *La Surprise.*

Frédéric schemes to defeat the power of Lelio, but he accomplishes little. He attempts to bribe Lelio's valet, Arlequin, but is powerless in the face of Arlequin's lack of discretion, which is one of the main resources of comedy in the play. Frédéric offers him money, a ring, even a pretty girl, if he will spy on his master. Arlequin is impressed with the gifts and ready to accept them, but he will tell all to Lelio and the Princess:

FRÉDÉRIC:

You miserable fellow, you are bent on dishonoring me.

ARLEQUIN:

Eh! When one isn't honorable, why does one need the reputation of having honor?

FRÉDÉRIC:

If you tell them, you scoundrel, my vengeance will be terrifying. . . . But someone might approach . . . , let's get on with it. I shall pay the price you ask for your silence. How much do you want?

ARLEQUIN:

Watch it! It won't be cheap!

FREDERIC:

Let's hear what you want. Your finagling is killing me!

ARLEQUIN:

Look, the idea of being a gentleman appeals to me. . . . Why don't you present your request in a more formal style and call me "Sir" for a while? Let me be Frédéric and you be Arlequin.

(**T** I, 356-57)

The scene is hilarious. It resembles Scene 4 of a parody of Voltaire's *Artémire,* composed by the Italian troupe, which shows that Marivaux adopted dialogue from many sources. In any event, Arlequin accepts the money and the ring, but tells all. Unwittingly he helps Frédéric, for Hortense has also confided in him and asked him to deliver her love letter to Lelio. Arlequin delivers it to the Princess who becomes so upset and jealous that she jails Lelio. It looks as if Frédéric might yet win out.

But now the King of Castille enters heroically into action. He may be Lelio's rival, or so he thinks, for the love of the Princess, but he will not let the honorable Lelio be defeated by a vile creature like Frédéric; indeed, he tells Lelio, when he later finds out that he is the King of Leon: "Your rank does not surprise me; it corresponds to the sentiments you have shown!" (**T** I, 394). The King of Castille pleads for Lelio with the Princess, and she, in turn, is eventually reconciled with Hortense, and this is a touching scene. Frédéric, on the other hand, is put in his place by Hortense: "We will have to kill you to deliver you from the sad fate of being hateful to everyone; that is the best we can do for you!" (**T** I, 381). And later: "I am no longer seeking your aid. You are too wicked to be feared. Your evil spirit is so manifest that you cannot hurt anyone but yourself!" (**T** I, 392). Is this comedy? The tone varies; humor alternates with heroic action, fury, tenderness, moral apostrophe, much as in a novel or in the *Spectateur.* The Princess will marry the King of Castille because his intervention on Lelio's behalf was so noble; virtue, as we read in the *Spectateur,* is infinitely attractive.

So love is born, and this leaves Lelio free to marry Hortense. The disguise of the two kings enables them to observe the person they hope to marry; as in the *Jeu*

de L'Amour, the mask provides perspective. Virtue wins out just as it will in Marivaux' major novels, perhaps because he knew reality to be different. It is a characteristic paradox. Broad laughter is provided primarily by Arlequin. Thus comedy has come to include a great number of moods, some quite tragic and bitter, and some tender, like the victory of friendship in the reconciliation of the Princess with Hortense. *Le Prince Travesti* is a complex play and an interesting one.

VII *LA FAUSSE SUIVANTE (THE FALSE SERVANT),* COMEDY IN 3 ACTS, T.I., 1724.

This time it is Silvia who wears the disguise. Her marriage to Lelio is being discussed; she wants to observe her intended husband. Dressed as the Chevalier (a small nobleman), she becomes Lelio's valet and finds him interested only in her money. He had first planned to marry a Countess with the annual income of six thousand francs; now he has set his mind on Silvia who is twice as rich! He knows her only as a girl from Paris whom he has not met. There is one complication. If he breaks with the Countess, he owes her thirty thousand francs, but not if she breaks with him. For this reason Lelio asks the Chevalier to court the Countess. He wants her to fall in love with him (her):

CHEVALIER:

I don't have much inclination for this kind of marriage.

LELIO:

Why not?

CHEVALIER:

For ever so many reasons. For one, I could never love the Countess.

LELIO:

Who is asking you to love her? Must one love one's wife? If you don't love her, that's just too bad for her; that's her business, not yours.

CHEVALIER:

Oh, I thought one had to love one's wife, for if one doesn't, one lives on bad terms with her.

LELIO:

Well, so much the better. If you are on bad terms with her, you don't have to see her, and that's all to the good.

CHEVALIER:

You win! I am ready to do as you wish and marry the Countess. I can always count on my good friend, Lelio, to strengthen my conviction that one owes one's wife nothing but disdain.

LELIO:

There I shall set you an excellent example! You don't by any chance think that I'm going to love that girl from Paris? A couple of weeks, at most; after that I shall be completely tired of her . . .

CHEVALIER:

Did they tell you that she is pretty?

LELIO:

The letter says that she is, but the way I feel, that won't do her much good. If she is not ugly now, she will surely become ugly being my wife. It can't fail?

(*T* I, 424-25)

Under such circumstances, all Silvia can think of is to ruin his vile schemes. She makes sure that he must pay the thirty thousand francs and lose both chances to marry. That is no happy ending! The undertone is one of bitterness, and of resolve to avenge the victims of such scoundrels as Lelio, or Frédéric in the preceding play. The *Spectateur* expresses Marivaux' disillusionment of this period in these terms:

If I stated earlier that my stories could be of some profit to my readers, I no longer lay claim to such grand results, for I know men read only to be amused, and the pleasure of amusing them no longer tempts me.

(*OD,* 253)

This is a half-truth, for the *Spectateur* as well as *La Fausse Suivante* do amuse, but the sadness of 1723-24 is barely hidden.

The play was written for Silvia; she was a great success in the role of the Chevalier. Her greatest scene is when she wins the love of the Countess. Another hilarious moment is Trivelin's discovery, from Frontin, that the Chevalier is a girl in disguise; so Trivelin tells her: "I shall be your valet on the stage and your lover behind the scenery" (*T* I, 420). Trivelin has an interesting part in the first act. He appears as a true *picaro* with his meager bundle of possessions, and tells of his stormy career, "sometimes master, sometimes servant" (*T* I, 412). His explanations to Frontin of two gangs, the "Ancients" whose captain is Homer, and the "Moderns who do not go back four thousand years," are very funny (*T* I, 414) and represent a humorous restatement of Marivaux' position. However, the role of Trivelin becomes insignificant later on and he is no Figaro. The revolutionary, if there is one in this play (cf. Arlequin in *La Double Inconstance*), is the Chevalier: Silvia fights injustice, i.e., Lelio's plan; she defends women's rights, her own!

Gustave Lanson has shown how frequently the girl disguised as a man, following her lover, occurs in literature,[3] but the most interesting parallel occurs in Shakespeare. In *Twelfth Night,* Viola becomes the valet of the man she loves just like Silvia, and like her is asked to court a Countess (Olivia) who then falls in love with her. The difference in tone is great, for the Chevalier stages a seduction scene while Viola goes to Olivia much against her will; her devotion to Duke Orsino is infinite. Shakespeare portrays the victory of sweet love, Marivaux, vengeance against a Don Juan. Besides, Shakespeare's range of emotions is far greater, from the outrageous jokes directed against Malvoglio and rough humor unthinkable in eighteenth-century France, to lyrical love. It is not a case of influence, but of a common source, Bandello, that explains the parallel. The story of Bandello reached Marivaux through the repertoire of the Italian troupe and Shakespeare through the Belleforest translation. It provides an instructive comparison, for *La Fausse Suivante* shows Marivaux at his best.

VIII *LE DÉNOUEMENT IMPRÉVU* (*THE UNFORESEEN SOLUTION*), COMEDY IN ONE ACT, T.F., 1724.

Finally Marivaux succeeds in having a comedy accepted by the Comédie Française. It was a fair success, but soon the play disappeared from the repertoire. Marivaux did not come into his own on this stage until well after his death; still, he never ceased submitting plays. *Le Dénouement Imprévu* is brief, excellent, and, according to Lessing, Marivaux' best work.

The title is a typical paradox. Mademoiselle Argante marries the suitor chosen by her father, but only after making determined efforts to foil his plan, and pretending to be mad, not like Lucinde in *Le Médecin Malgré Lui* (Molière's *Doctor in Spite of Himself*) who claimed to have lost her speech, but most articulately so. Later, her haste to marry the man chosen for her and the precipitous ending are hilarious.

Eraste, the young man whom her father has invited, arrives much like Dorante in the *Jeu de l'Amour*: His servant, Crispin, announces in his inane way: "We have come to marry her . . . my master to take her to be his wife, I to have her as my mistress" (*T* I, 498). With Monsieur Argante's consent, Eraste will pretend to be a friend of his, so that he can give Mademoiselle Argante her full freedom of choice. In this manner he finds out that she plans to play the idiot to preserve her freedom. Love at first sight triumphs before Eraste's identity is clear to her.

The scenes where Mademoiselle Argante falls in love with Eraste are tender and delicate; in opposing her father she shows herself forthright and resolute: "One does not force a heart! That is the law! If you want to force mine, you break the law!" (*T* I, 497). She will not have a husband imposed on her and expresses herself in strong and picturesque terms. The young nobleman who is to come from the country, she calls "a nasty faun . . . an uncouth bear emerging from his den," and asks her father whether he takes her to be a "stupid monkey" (*T* I, 496-97).

To this hearty humor Master Pierre adds his bit. He claims "to govern" Monsieur Argante (*T* I, 484). First he sympathizes with Dorante whom Mademoiselle

Argante thought she loved before she met Eraste; later he is all in favor of Eraste who pays him well. Master Pierre takes the place of Arlequin in the plays for the Italian troupe and does much to sustain the fun. He upbraids Monsieur Argante because he wants to marry his daughter to a nobleman (Eraste is noble, Dorante is not): "Noble blood? What the devil of an invention is that? How can blood flow in two ways when it all comes from the same river?" (*T* I, 484), but for all that, he will be happy to accept Eraste, once he has seen him. And then there is Crispin, naïve and funny. When Monsieur Argante asks whether the women can overhear them, he replies: "Gosh, Sir, you don't know women's ears. You see, those ears hear what one says half a mile away, and what one is going to say a quarter mile away" (*T* I, 498).

As compared to Molière, Dancourt, or Regnard, Marivaux' originality lies in the "surprise of love" which brings about the solution. Sentiment wins out: It leaves the audience almost stunned. What could be less unforeseen than the marriage that was long planned and that everyone expected?

IX *L'ILE DES ESCLAVES* (*THE ISLAND OF SLAVES*), COMEDY IN ONE ACT, T.I., 1725.

Three island plays, **The Island of Slaves, The Island of Reason** (1727), and **The New Colony** (1729, published as **La Colonie,** 1750), continue the series of allegories that began with **L'Amour et la Vérité.** Delisle de la Drévetière had popularized the style through his *Arlequin Sauvage* (*Wild Harlequin*), 1721, a play that made daring attacks against injustice.

On the island of slaves, masters must trade places with their servants and undergo a course in humility (*T* I, 509). They are to gain perspective on the duties which accompany the privileges of rank and education. Arlequin says: "I shall be a bit insolent now I am the master" (*T* I, 530), and reminds Iphicrate that he used to call him "Hey, there!" as if he had no name (*T* I, 520). "Once you have suffered a little, you will become more reasonable and realize what suffering you may inflict on others!" (*T* I, 519). It is similar to **La Double Inconstance,** where Arlequin protests: "Dishonorable men are unworthy of being honored" with respect (*T* I, 272).

Euphrosine is subjected by Cléanthis, her maid, to the same reeducation, but the lesson is tempered, since a "naturally weaker sex" cannot avoid certain foibles (*T* I, 523, 531, cf. *OD,* 344). Marivaux has been called an outstanding spokesman for the equality of the sexes, but there are limitations to what equality he would recognize. Thus, Euphrosine is naturally flirtatious and vain. She loves beautiful clothes and the alluring négligées (*T* I, 527).[4] Cléanthis and Arlequin treat their masters with great kindness. They condemn overbearing and injustice, but sympathy takes the upper hand as soon as they have overcome their resentment (*T* I, 521). They do all they can to achieve a reconciliation. This makes the play both moving and effective.

Arlequin suggests that he revert to the service of his master (*T* I, 539), while Cléanthis feels for her mistress: In her servitude, "she has only her despair to keep her company" (*T* I, 537). Cléanthis started out by asserting her rights: "It is evil to base your merit on gold, silver, and rank alone" (*T* I, 540), but the plight of Euphrosine moves her to tears.

Marivaux is no revolutionary! Once the rights of the "slaves" have been clarified, they resume their former functions, while the noble Athenians are pardoned and may return home. Henceforth they will be aware of the demands of humanity; their natural goodness transcends their faults.

X *L'HÉRITIER DU VILLAGE* (*THE FARMER INHERITS A FORTUNE*), COMEDY IN ONE ACT, T.I., 1725.

Marivaux had portrayed peasants before, in **Pharsamon**; the **Télémaque Travesti**; Master Pierre is important in **Le Dénouement Imprévu**; soon Dimas, the gardener in **Le Triomphe de l'Amour,** will be added. However, in **L'Héritier du Village,** for the first time a character like Blaise, a farmer-would-be-gentleman, plays the main role. His good humor in wealth and poverty make for the success of the play.

Blaise has inherited a fortune, though it remains in the hands of a banker in the capital. Blaise aims to convert his family into high society. He will no longer be so foolish as to love his wife. His son, Colin, and his daughter, Colette, are to marry into nobility. Blaise is about to accept two penniless scoundrels as his children-in-law, Madame Damis and the Chevalier. Under these circumstances, news from Paris that bankruptcy has ruined him and wiped out his inheritance, is a blessing. It makes the two swindlers withdraw in haste. Colin and Colette will be all the happier and Blaise can settle down to enjoy the wine he ordered for the marriage feast.

Like **La Fausse Suivante,** the play does not end with happy marriages. On the contrary, here two very bad ones have been avoided. Like Silvia in **La Fausse Suivante,** Colin and Colette have escaped unhappiness, while Blaise can return to normalcy. Definitely, surprises of love do not triumph every time in Marivaux. Common sense wins out. Behind the gaiety, there is the realization that honor, nobility, and respectability can be shams. This is the theme on which Marivaux elaborates in his next journal, presenting the "indigent philosopher," his "philosophical bum."

Humor in *L'Héritier du Village* is rather sparse. There are few funny scenes besides one reminiscent of the *Spectateur*. As an aspiring member of the aristocracy, Blaise refuses to pay a bill; the tax collector has to fool him and make him believe that he is borrowing money, in order to get Blaise to settle his account (*T* I, 569). Marivaux must have noticed that gaiety was leaving him; the *Indigent Philosophe* seems like a determined effort to recapture it.

XI *L'INDIGENT PHILOSOPHE* (*THE INDIGENT PHILOSOPHER*), PERIODICAL IN 7 ISSUES, 1727.

A modern Diogenes except for his barrel, far from Paris and its hypocrisy, is drinking with a friend, the son of a drunken musician, and listens to his life story, a varied career which eventually turned him into a tragic actor, not a good one, but a good-looking one. As such he became the prize for whom vie two ladies of provincial society, two *précieuses ridicules*; he stands between "two vanities" (*OD,* 300). He derives great satisfaction from being desired even by such supercilious creatures. The story of this friend takes up somewhat less than half the periodical; his attitudes coincide closely with those of the philosophical bum himself. They share the haphazard view of life. After praising the virtues of wine, the friend says: "Your hat off, please, in spite of my ragged clothing" (*OD,* 295); the main character, in an analogous passage, significantly placed at the very end of the text, explains: I may be good, generous, easily forgiving, "but don't humiliate me" (*OD,* 323). A proud independence, a fierce individualism, a self-righteous insistence on their fundamental honesty qualifies the image of the two easy-going drinking companions significantly.

Our indigent philosopher is poor because he has spent the money he inherited; he dislikes his restricted means but he prefers the "ruinous follies" that have brought him there to the "sad follies" of those who think they are wise (*OD,* 280). He would gladly live his youth over again and reduce himself once again to poverty. If he had more money, he would spend it all. Worldly possessions hardly matter to him, only the enjoyment of life.

Another issue he seeks to make quite clear. He is fundamentally opposed to the reasonable attitudes of those who are considered serious, good citizens. He will have nothing to do with pedants, and let us recall that Marivaux repeatedly portrays *philosophes* as pedants. We shall find them described that way in the next two plays, *L'Ile de la Raison* and *La Seconde Surprise de l'Amour* and, for that matter, all the "Ancients" pictured in the previous works have similar traits. This sets "the philosophical bum" at opposite poles not only from rationalists of the traditional mold, but also from those who will eventually form around the *Encyclopédie*. It is

characteristic that our philosopher admits he always was favorable to religion (*OD,* 318), though he also protests against excesses of "tender spirituality" (*OD,* 296-97) and laughs with a farmer who doubts that there is a soul because he never saw one (*OD,* 318). Yes, life must be laughter and he will drink water only if wine is not available (*OD,* 278), but there are fascinating aspects to this double opposition to the old-style and new-style *philosophes*. Marivaux seems to anticipate Carl Becker's *Heavenly City of Eighteenth Century Philosophers,* (Yale University Press, 1932), for he rejects the intransigent rationalism of many contemporaries, be they Aristotelians, orthodox "Ancients," or modern materialists. Becker felt that Voltaire and medieval philosophers shared a systematic intransigence. Marivaux condemns it at every step, most effectively perhaps in the most unsystematic *Indigent Philosophe.*

Our hero is naturally opposed to the show of wealth. He protests, as had the *Spectateur,* against resplendent clothes. The suit of one rich gentleman can provide the dowry of half a dozen orphans (*OD,* 307). He tells how a suitor was rejected because he was too simply dressed; when he came into money, he haughtily rejected the girl who now was anxious to marry him (*OD,* 319). Even more biting is the account of the young girl who married an old man for his wealth. She found the union ever so disappointing; she had never considered the natural failures of age (*OD,* 320).

There are bitter words, perhaps too bitter to suit the tone of the periodical, against evil persons (*les méchants*) who abuse their prerogatives (*OD,* 304-5), those who succeed because of family connections which should give them no rights other than to be known as the children of their parents (*OD,* 303). "How I hate them, how I detest them," he exclaims, though realizing that "we must live with everyone" and "pretend not to notice the impositions" of vanity (*OD,* 315). As elsewhere, Marivaux comes close to revolt but acquiesces: The reasonable man will feel only pity for false pride (*OD,* 309). Individuals and nations yearn for freedom, and are ready to die for it, but they would renounce complete independence were it granted because they would feel deprived of guidance and accuse those relinquishing control of being unconcerned with the welfare of the people (*OD,* 321); what attitude could be more conservative?

The indigent philosopher keeps coming back to the issue of vanity. He pretends to be happy without means just like Blaise, in *L'Héritier du Village,* after he lost his fortune. Our philosopher pretends to be content with the simple life and claims, "those who love joy have no vanity" (*OD,* 276), but later he contradicts all this: "Is there anything as malicious and lacking in humanity as vanity offended" (*OD,* 323). Men may act like children when they play with polite manners as with a hobby horse (*OD,* 323) but all men have their vanity, even those who hide it playfully:

> We are all spirits of contradiction. As long as we can choose, we manifest no great desires. As soon as we have chosen our course, we want everything! If we made a good choice, we tire of it. What to do? If we are badly off, we want something better. When we obtain it, are we satisfied? Of course not! What is the solution? Everyone must search for it on his own."

> (*OD,* 321)

So he wants more than his humble existence! Our philosopher ends his account with the shrill warning: "Don't humiliate me!" (*OD,* 323).

When he pretended that his only objective in writing was "to be amusing" (*OD,* 317), was he not discounting his fierce pride? And how amusing is it to attack wealth, vanity and vain-glory, and to accuse evil persons of not even being human, because they are not humane and kind! (*OD,* 304). We sense a great deal of disillusionment and pessimism when we read: The good man, the gentleman, is "that creature you always want to deal with and would like to find in all parts, though you do not wish to be like him," the implication being that the good man always loses out (*OD,* 309). If we examine the text closely, we find the same accents of bitterness that qualify the previous works and made Marivaux create a character like Frédéric in **Le Prince Travesti.** The philosophical bum is lighthearted, he drinks; does he choose this front because he is so disillusioned?

XII *L'ILE DE LA RAISON* (*THE ISLAND OF REASON*), COMEDY IN 3 ACTS, T.F., 1727

Gulliver's Travels had just been translated by the abbé Desfontaines when Marivaux staged his "little men" at the *Théâtre Français.* Obviously they had something to do with Swift. The translation had created a wave of interest. Marivaux was taking advantage of it, but even so these characters who change size one or several times were hard to put across. The play did not succeed.

A group of shipwrecked Europeans is reduced to diminutive size until they recover their reason, which means, until they understand their overbearing attitudes and are able to correct them. Marivaux insists his play is original (*T* I, 593) and he is right. His interpretation of reason is quite novel, his imitation of Swift is remote. We readily understand that he was not anxious to advertise a translation by his most biased critic. Marivaux' theme is that "one needs a great deal of judgment to realize one lacks judgment" (*T* I, 594). This implies that there is some hope of reform, a hope not germane to Swift's black pessimism. Marivaux' "animals" are nowhere as degenerate as those in Swift and his attack is more limited; it is directed against

vanity and pride which prevent men from respecting the feelings of others. The humaneness demanded in the **Indigent Philosophe** is central also here.

The Europeans are all reduced in size upon landing; they recover their original size, i.e., their human greatness and dignity, at very different speeds. As in the Scriptures, the last shall be first. The servants, less tied to social prejudice, less in need to justify privilege, are first to become "reasonable." There is Blaise who will be a great help to Blectrue, the islander in charge of re-educating the group;[5] then comes Lisette who will also assist Blectrue; she guides her mistress, the Countess, toward seeing the light. The Countess has spent all too much time on "the architecture of her hair," and on related foibles of vanity (*T* I, 627-28). Frontignac, the Gascon secretary (cf. **Le Petit-Maître Corrigé**) of the Courtier, also makes rapid progress and then can be a model for his master.

The greatest difficulty is experienced by the three intellectuals in the group. The Doctor must work hard to realize that he has considered only his own enrichment. The Poet understands his faults, but soon finds that he derives so much joy from attacking others by writing poisonous little poems, that he relapses to small size. The Philosophe is worse. He seems entirely incapable of becoming "great," so sure is he of himself, so vain, so adamant. He will not concede anything. Blectrue and the islanders will leave nothing undone to further the progress of the Poet and the Philosophe (*T* I, 648). While this shows a fundamental belief in human goodness, in man's capacity for regeneration, nothing is said about how long it might take. It is interesting to note that Voltaire could be designated in both cases; the two problem cases are left under guard like Voltaire in the Bastille before he left for England. There is nothing to confirm this association, but it is clear that Marivaux advocates a kind of "reason" which is diametrically opposed to the thought of Voltaire, a "reason of the heart" which makes him a forerunner of Rousseau.

As on the island of slaves, the humanitarian ideal applies equally to servants and to masters. To emphasize that the new society lacks all prejudice, two islanders, Parmenès and Floris, the son and daughter of the Governor, will marry two of the Europeans. The third marriage will be that of Blaise and Lisette. Blaise continues to be the center of things and has the most important part.

There are two revolutionary aspects to marriage on the island: Women, recognized to be the weaker sex, are required to be first to declare their love—this for their own protection (*T* I, 652-53)—and marriage contracts are unnecessary since, once love is declared, "reasonable" persons are in accord (*T* I, 648). These provisions scandalized some readers. They are much in line with earlier statements of Marivaux on these matters. In the last scene, the three marriages are consecrated without contract, but in a formal ceremony before the Governor.

One passage, the confession of the Poet, is important because it elucidates, amusingly, Marivaux' theory of drama. The Poet tells that he wrote both tragedies and comedies, and when Blectrue asks him to explain what these genres represent, he says: In tragedy, the heroes

> are so tender, alternately so admirably virtuous and so passionate, noble criminals with such astonishing pride, whose crimes betray such greatness and whose self-accusations are so magnanimous, men, in short, with such respectable weaknesses, whom we admire for killing themselves at times in so noble a manner, that we cannot watch them without emotion and weeping for pleasure.
>
> (*T* I, 610)

Blectrue would prefer to see men weep over their faults, not over their virtues. The faults, the Poet explains, are pictured in the comedies, but they cause the spectators to laugh. This upsets Blectrue even more: "They laugh where they should weep?" Marivaux calls for a new genre which combines the serious with the burlesque, nobility of sentiment with the realism of traditional comedy.

The play failed. It was withdrawn after four performances. Only in 1950 did a director think of a simple device, a lift behind a bush, which could raise the Europeans, or lower them, from one stage to another, so as to simulate the large and the small stature. That performance, by the amateur troupe, L'Equipe, was the first successful one for this comedy.[6] Marivaux was evidently discouraged, and commented that he had been carried away by a unique situation incapable of staging (*T* I, 590); he was merely ahead of his time.

The Italian troupe honored the play with a parody, *L'Ile de la Folie* (*The Island of Folly*) by Dominique and Romagnesi (1727). It echoes Marivaux' themes. Reason is defined as that "little nothing" (*bagatelle*) which we acquire by simply giving away wealth, ridding ourselves of pride, prejudice, and malice, and by replacing these faults by candor, docility, and wisdom (*Parodies* IV, 147). Folly announces that Reason is threatened by a usurper, True Reason. We also find erotic fantasies. An island girl will first marry a Frenchman, then Gulliver the next day, because she knows Frenchmen are unfaithful; her plan will enable her "to enjoy all the pleasures of infidelity" (*Parodies,* IV, 171). The parody is no more of an attack on Marivaux than his own *Télémaque Travesti* was an attack on Fénelon. The Italian troupe remained on the best of terms with Marivaux. On April 22, 1728, they will perform his *Triomphe de Plutus.*

XIII *La (Seconde) Surprise de l'Amour* (*The (Second) Surprise of Love*), comedy in 3 acts, T.F., 1727.

The "indigent philosopher" was above all anxious to free himself from the fetters of society and give himself over to his subjective sensibility. In a somewhat more somber mood, this applies also to the two principal characters of Marivaux' new *Surprise de l'Amour,* written so that the *Théâtre Français* would also have a play on this theme in its repertoire; as usual there were difficulties and a considerable delay between submission of the script and performance.

The Chevalier formerly loved Angélique; she was forced to join a convent in order not to accept the husband her parents wanted to impose on her. The Marquise is recently widowed and as disillusioned with marriage and society as the Chevalier. They have foresworn the world for six months and quite literally buried themselves in their grief. The Chevalier will "steep himself in sorrow until death"; the Marquise agrees that this has been her very thought. They are ever so sensitive (*T* I, 683) and realize that their meeting is a unique experience, "the only tolerable moment in these difficult times" (*T* I, 684).

They understand their plight and each other, but they are utterly deluded in believing that their meeting of minds can limit itself to a mere "friendship" (*amitié*), to a feeling of solidarity between two persons disappointed in love (*T* I, 686). In her treatise on friendship, Mme de Lambert had stressed how difficult it was to establish such a relationship between members of the opposite sex. In view of this, it is most amusing to find the Marquise mention this *Traité de l'Amitié* to Hortensius as a book she has enjoyed (*T* I, 698). Hortensius is the pedant she has engaged to edify her and bring her the consolation of philosophy. He spouts useless syllogisms and tries to seduce Lisette; he is the very image of the ridiculous *philosophe.*

It will take three acts and a plan for the Marquise to marry the Count (it almost entraps her) to make her love for the Chevalier apparent. They engage in self-pity and much sentiment. The scenes with Hortensius are hilarious and make up for this. They are determined to go their separate ways, but when they meet "a last time" to say goodbye, the "surprising effects of sympathy" bring them just that much closer to each other; their case is unique, and a unique love must lead to marriage (*T* I, 683, n. 14).

In this play obstacles are internal, for the Chevalier is free to make his decisions and the Marquise is a young widow with the enviable advantage of being able to arrange her future as only widows could. The plot draws on sources not only in Marivaux' own work, but on some of the oldest and most traditional like the *Matron of Ephesus* (who set out to mourn her dead husband and before long was willing to abandon even his corpse to save the soldier she loved and kept from guarding a hanged man), recently restaged by La Motte. *La Surprise* is an excellent play, less successful than it should have been because the French troupe did not have the actors to do it justice; there was no one like Thomassin-Arlequin of the Italian players; for the same reason Blaise, in *L'Ile de la Raison*, had not appeared as comic as he was intended to be. To make the meeting of two disappointed persons, isolated in their loneliness, a subject for comedy, requires resources of superior sensitiveness and talent. Modern performances have been most successful.

XIV LE TRIOMPHE DE PLUTUS (*PLUTUS TRIUMPHANT*), COMEDY IN 1 ACT, T.I., 1728.

This farce of "bourgeois mythology" (Jean Fabre) comes to life through the character of Plutus. He appears as Monsieur Richard (Rich Man) and resolves to win the girl whom Apollo-Ergaste is courting with his good looks and delicate sentiments. The victory of Plutus is complete. He captures the love of Aminte, he obtains the cooperation of her uncle, Armidas, of Spinette, her maid, and even of Arlequin, the valet of Ergaste, for Plutus has money at his disposal, not just pretty words; those of Ergaste seem quite shopworn at that. Plutus' final triumph comes when he takes over the musicians whom Ergaste has hired. The audience is all for him, as well, since Apollo's initial self-confidence was full of conceit. Apollo grasps none of his mistakes and bitterly accuses the fate which permitted that the God of wealth should take precedence over the God of merit.

The play furnishes one of the most eloquent proofs that Marivaux is not to be identified—as all too often he has been—with the unworldly, abstract, and hopeless *bel-esprit* Apollo represents. The plays without happy endings, like *La Fausse Suivante, L'Héritier du Village,* and characterizations in other plays and essays from the earliest to the ***Indigent Philosophe*** have caused us to speak of Marivaux' realism. Allegorical setting, the use of stock characters, and other self-imposed restrictions never infringe on the individuality of his portrayals. They involve desire, sensuality, vanity, greed, love of rank and power, and every other fault unreconcilable with the excessive delicacy that many critics attributed to him. Ever since Marivaux showed Truth taking refuge in a well to poison its waters (***L'Amour et la Vérité***), he has expressed his conviction that the forces of life win out over the kind of spirituality which makes one yawn (***OD,*** 296). Plutus is the life-force; one must cope with him. There may have been times when Marivaux wished that he were more like him!

Notes

1. A second tragedy, *Mahomet Second,* remained incomplete; the fragment will be included in a new edition of the *Théâtre Complet* (ed. Deloffre). Written about 1726, when Voltaire argued with La Motte over the need for verse in tragedy, the fragment first appeared in the *Mercure* of March, 1747. It was discovered by Henri Lagrave.

2. *Traité de l'Amitié* in *Oeuvres* I, 435.

3. *Nivelle de la Chaussee* (Paris, 1887), pp. 67-68. There are instances in the repertoire of the old Italian troupe, in the theater of Regnard and Dufresny (cf. T I, 397-98), also in Book 4, Chs. 4-5 of *Gil Blas* by Lesage (1724), where Aurore de Guzman is disguised as Félix de Mendoce.

4. In the *Lettres sur les Habitants de Paris,* the negligee is called a subterfuge for nudity (OD 28); in *Le Dénouement Imprévu,* Mademoiselle Argante would wear a negligee to reveal herself to Eraste, just to convince her father she is mad: "So that he will see only me and that will be all to the good" (T I, 494).

5. The name, Blectrue, seems to stem from *blictri,* taken to mean a rational idea of God by John Toland; this shows the influence of deism on Marivaux. Cf. Haac, "Deism in Marivaux."

6. There is an illustration showing the stage in Paul Gazagne, *Marivaux par Lui-Même,* p. 15.

Selected Bibliography

Our abbreviations in the text refer to the *Oeuvres Complètes* and the Deloffre editions and Deloffre's *Marivaux et la Marivaudage;* the reference letters D, M, OD, OJ, P, T, and X appear in parentheses after the listing of the respective titles below.

PRIMARY SOURCES

Dates of original editions are generally those of our *Chronology;* more exact indications are given in the critical editions by Deloffre where manuscript sources are also listed. Very few manuscripts remain.

1A. COMPLETE WORKS:

Oeuvres Complètes de Marivaux. Paris: Veuve Duchesne, 1781. Vol. X (Ref: X) contains the complete *Homère Travesti* (only half in OJ); all other texts are available in the Deloffre editions.

2B. CRITICAL EDITIONS:

Marivaux, *Oeuvres de Jeunesse* (Ref: OJ), ed. Deloffre and Rigault, Paris: Gallimard, 1972.

Marivaux, *Journaux et Oeuvres Diverses* (Ref: OD), ed. Deloffre and Gillot. Paris: Garnier, 1969.

Marivaux, *Théâtre Complet* (Ref: T I, T II), ed. Deloffre. Paris: Garnier, 1968, vols. I and II.

Marivaux, *La Vie de Marianne* (Ref: M), ed. Deloffre. Paris: Garnier, 2nd ed., 1963.

Marivaux, *Le Paysan Parvenu* (Ref: P), ed. Deloffre. Paris: Garnier, 2nd ed., 1965.

Other critical editions with notable commentary (incorporated partly into those above): *Le Télémaque Travesti*, ed. Deloffre. Geneva: Droz, 1956; *Le Petit-Maître Corrigé*, ed. Deloffre. Geneva: Droz, 1955; *La Commère*, ed. Sylvie Chevalley. Paris: Hachette, 1966; *Le Miroir*, ed. Matucci. Naples: Ed. Scientifiche, 1958; cf. the latter's anthology, *Marivaux Narratore e Moralista*, *ibid.*, 1958.

3. TRANSLATIONS

Bentley, Eric, *The Classic Theatre*, IV: *Six French Plays*. Garden City: Doubleday Anchor Books, 1961. A good rendition of *Les Fausses Confidences*.

Conlon, Pierre and Lotte, *Marivaux, Two Plays*. Ontario: McAllister University Library, 1967. Good renditions of *La Double Inconstance, Les Fausses Confidences*.

Mandel, Oscar, *Seven Comedies by Marivaux, English by Oscar and Adrienne S. Mandel*. Ithaca: Cornell University Press, 1968. Renditions, partly faithful, partly fanciful, of *Arlequin Poli par l'Amour, La Double Inconstance, Le Triomphe de Plutus, Le Jeu, L'Heureux Stratagème, Les Fausses Confidences, L'Epreuve.*

Translations from Marivaux' time are listed in Séguin, J. A. R., *French Works in Translation*. Jersey City: Ross Paxton, 1966, for novels in vol. II (1731-40) and III (1741-50), for plays not rendered until 1762, in vol. V. Most were faithful but not one by Mary Collyer, cf. note 2, Chapter 5 above.

SECONDARY SOURCES

Brooks, Peter, *The Novel of Wordliness*. Princeton: Princeton University Press, 1969. Sensitive study of *Marianne*.

Haac, Oscar A., "Deism in Marivaux, *Blictri* and Blecture," *Romantic Review* 63: 5-19, 1972.

Poulet, Georges, *Etudes sur le Temps Humain*, II, *La Distance Intérieure*. Paris: Plon, 1953. Existentialist view, cf. Spitzer.

H. T. Mason (essay date 1979)

SOURCE: Mason, H. T. "Women in Marivaux: Journalist to Dramatist." In *Women and Society in Eighteenth-Century France: Essays in Honour of John Stephenson Spink*, edited by Eva Jacobs, et al., pp. 42-54. London: The Athlone Press, 1979.

[*In the following excerpt, Mason explores Marivaux's various representations of women, some informed by sympathy, others by cynicism.*]

'Aucun auteur n'a cru plus fermement à l'éternel féminin', says a recent author, with justice, of Marivaux.[1] Many a critic has laboured to define the 'féminin marivaudien' with all its equivocations; the task is endless. In the plays and novels, we can never be sure how far his self-avowed 'misanthropie' established in his adolescent years[2] is held at bay by benevolence and sympathy. The Journals offer a rather better basis for confidence (though here too we must beware of taking the narrator as simply Marivaux's mouthpiece) because of their more direct approach. It may be useful to consider some of the aspects of the feminine condition upon which the essayist lays emphasis, proceeding thereafter to see how those attitudes are exemplified in his drama.

With the appearance of his **Lettres sur les habitants de Paris** in the pages of the *Mercure* (1717-18), Marivaux may be said to come of age as a prose writer, the sharpness of his observation as he describes the Parisian scene giving promise of what is to come. In this loosely-linked, almost random, series of topics he characteristically devotes an important section to women. There is an amusing vignette of the clever saleswoman overwhelming the raw provincial customer so completely by her courteous attentions that he cannot escape without buying something (p. 16). Marivaux dwells on the moral dangers to which such a woman is exposed, constantly living in the public gaze and acquiring from her environment a boldness which is transmitted from eyes to speech and eventually to actions.

If coquetry were to disappear, says Marivaux, it would be rediscovered amongst women shopkeepers. For the dominant passion of *bourgeoises* is vanity, which is seen in their love of pleasure, finery, good food and in their back-biting. Marivaux has already announced the *leit-motif* of his views on feminine attitudes: *coquetterie*. Equally significant, he does not pursue the theme among bourgeois company but switches to 'femmes de qualité'. For the aristocratic woman is the summit of refinement and therefore of affectation: 'Grâces ridicules aux gens raisonnables . . . inimitables aux bourgeoises . . . peut-être le chef-d'œuvre de l'orgueil' (pp. 26-7). Everything is studiedly artificial: l'habillement, la marche, le geste et le ton' (p. 26)—developed by parental vanity and the examples set by other gracious ladies, and consummated through personal study in this particular domain. Marivaux is struck by the magnificence of the paradox: so much effort and style, all deployed to serve the ends of folly. He sees clearly how fundamental is the play-element to this code of behaviour: 'tout est jeu pour elles; jusqu'à leur réputation' (p. 27). It is a striking observation for the light it throws on a refined class imprisoned by their gratuitousness and irresponsibility (one thinks, for instance, of Mathilde de la Mole in *Le Rouge et le noir*, striving to escape from frivolity into the perils and joys of commitment).

Everything for these women is ritual, courtship above all; and the garment most proudly worn is the slightest, the *négligé,* because it is the equivalent of nakedness, pretending to do without extra charms but pretending falsely. It is 'une abjuration simulée de coquetterie; mais en même temps le chef-d'œuvre de l'envie de plaire' (p. 28). It has the simplicity of modest clothes, but it is itself immodest, the product of the lubricious vanity that invented it. Not that the unchastity is itself deliberate, adds Marivaux, for the motive force is a feeling of complaisance for one's own charms; but the end result is the same. Women dressed in a *négligé* exclaim: 'Laissez-moi . . . je me sauve, je suis faite comme une folle.' But in reality they are thinking the very opposite: 'Regardez-moi, je ne suis point parée comme les femmes doivent l'être . . . tout naît de moi, c'est moi qui donne la forme à mon habit, et non mon habit qui me la donne . . .' (p. 29). The apparent rejection of coquettish aids proves to be the highest form of coquetry; the female form, barely clad and accessible to furtive glances in the boudoir, is at its most erotic. It is the world of Fragonard.

Here then, as Marivaux enters into his true domain, the observation of man in his contemporary reality, and discovers within himself 'ses dons, ses pouvoirs et ses armes',[3] the basic elements of his attitude to women are being set down. His fascination with feminine coquetry will henceforth be constant. The fundamental marvel of womankind is that it must, out of necessity, set out to please men. Coquetry is of the essence of being feminine: 'c'est en un mot le mouvement perpétuel de leur âme, c'est le feu sacré qui ne s'éteint jamais; de sorte qu'une femme veut toujours plaire, sans le vouloir par une réflexion expresse. . . . Une femme qui n'est plus coquette, c'est une femme qui a cessé d'être' (p. 28). Here Marivaux is manifestly not speaking only of titled ladies. These latter may represent the crowning glory of feminine charms, because education and leisure have allowed the opportunity of perfectibility, but all women possess this motivation, which forms the ground of their being, as instilled by nature itself. The coquette is a wearer of masks, instinctively equivocating, and disguising the dross of reality; she will provide the dramatist with a lifetime's reservoir of ironic situations.

By the time Marivaux begins editing **Le Spectateur français** a few years later, these attitudes have been confirmed and augmented. The **Spectateur** period (1721-4) coincides with the appearance of some of his most penetrating comedies, including **La Surprise de l'amour** and **La Double Inconstance**;[4] the dramatist is fully fledged. Looking at **Le Spectateur,** we find an insistence upon the essentiality of cosmetic devices as an inherent part of the feminine personality. Marivaux calls upon a beautiful woman and catches her unprepared. She is indeed wearing a *négligé,* but it is not one meant for show: 'un négligé des plus négligés, tranchons le mot . . . un négligé malpropre'. The author goes on to portray most evocatively the embarrassed actions of the poor woman, and concludes with the shrewd observation: 'une belle femme qui n'a point encore disposé ses attraits, qui n'a rien de préparé pour plaire, quand on la surprend alors, on ne peut pas dire que ce soit véritablement elle' (16e feuille, p. 200). Well might we anticipate Voltaire's famous paradox of the 1730s on luxury: 'Le superflu, chose très nécessaire' (*Le Mondain,* v. 22). Marivaux may have had in mind Dufresny's similar observation in the *Amusemens sérieux et comiques* (1699): 'telle qui a besoin de toute la matinée pour perfectionner ses charmes, seroit plus fâchée d'être surprise à sa toilette, que d'être surprise avec un galant'.[5] But the unsurprising if witty comment by Dufresny has been transformed by Marivaux into a more universal point: the very selfhood of such women depends upon external graces.

For, as Marivaux sees it in **Le Spectateur,** women have no choice but to be *coquettes.* To cite one of the most famous passages in the essays, given to a female narrator: 'on ne peut être femme sans être coquette. Il n'y a que dans les romans qu'on en voit d'autres, mais dans la nature c'est chimère, et les véritables sont toutes comme j'étais' (p. 209). But there is a darker side to this for women. They must flirt, but they must also lose. A virtuous woman resists advances by her lover; 'mais en résistant, elle entre insensiblement dans un goût d'aventure; elle se complaît dans les sentiments vertueux qu'elle oppose' (10e feuille, p. 162). There follows a detailed description of the way in which she connives at her own ineluctable defeat, a passage which, as the editors of the *Journaux* point out (pp. 595-6, nn. 197, 199), is highly characteristic of a Marivaux manner that inspired Crébillon fils. Trivelin puts it with epigrammatic brevity in **Arlequin poli par l'amour:** 'Femme tentée, et femme vaincue, c'est tout un'.[6] This sense of fatalism had been implicit in the **Lettres sur les habitants de Paris**; now Marivaux has given it explicit articulation. There is scarcely any way of remaining virtuous if one is a young and attractive woman in society. Marivaux chooses to make the point with hyperbolic emphasis at the very outset of the second number of **Le Spectateur**: 'Les austérités des fameux anachorètes de la Thébaïde, les supplices ingénieux qu'ils inventaient contre eux-mêmes pour tourmenter la nature; cette mort toujours nouvelle, toujours douloureuse qu'ils donnaient à leurs sens; tout cela, joint à l'horreur de leurs déserts, ne composait peut-être pas la valeur des peines que peut éprouver une femme du monde jeune, aimable, aimée, et qui veut être vertueuse' (pp. 118-19). For the architect of a woman's downfall is not simply her seducer; he is aided by her willingness to believe his false words, she like him has 'le transport au cerveau' (11e feuille, p. 170). Otherwise, her complaisance is inexplicable, as every rational inclination urges her to refrain. Women are self-deceived, not just about their beauty (as for instance the third number of *Le Spectateur* makes clear) but about all their desires in life. In a striking prefiguration of 'bovarysme' Marivaux has a woman write, as she looks back on her life: 'avec de la passion . . . nous ne voyons plus les objets comme ils sont, ils deviennent ce que nous souhaitons qu'ils soient, ils se moulent sur nos désirs' (19e feuille, p. 219).

Marivaux is also becoming interested in the social circumstances under which women are placed at a disadvantage. In the last two issues of *Le Spectateur* the narrator tells of being left at the age of eighteen a poor orphan with his sister. He can make his way in the world, but she is utterly defenceless, without any honest means of advancement. Only the convent is open to her, and this is where she flees, despite her grief at parting from her brother, after an experience in which her poverty exposes her to moral danger. The incident serves to remind us that social structures work in harmony with a desire to please men and aid in her seduction. To remain chaste, flight is the only answer.

We shall return presently to Marivaux's sociological observations on women in *Le Cabinet du philosophe* (1734). Before that he had published seven numbers of *L'Indigent Philosophe* (1727), where a more provocative, even cynical attitude appears towards life. Women too fall under this mocking gaze. It is fortunate, says the narrator, that nature has made women necessary, for seen from one particular angle 'elles paraîtraient trop risibles pour avoir rien à démêler avec notre coeur, elles cesseraient d'être aimables . . .' (7e feuille, p. 319). Though we should not forget that the 'Indigent Philosophe' is a more colourful personality than the 'Spectateur' and that he himself is one of the characters in the world he is portraying rather than just Marivaux's mouthpiece, it is as well to set passages like the above alongside the more sympathetic views which generally emerge from *Le Spectateur*. Woman for Marivaux is Other in her endlessly fascinating persona.

To this statement a rider must be added which can be clearly exemplified also in *L'Indigent Philosophe.* The narrator's supercilious attitude easily accommodates a story he tells about a young girl married to a very old man. Virtuous and sensible, she was confident of a happy marriage: but 'c'était compter sans son hôte . . . ; et cet hôte, c'est le diable, ou nous' (7e feuille, p. 320). The bride's awakening to the truth is melancholy. This tale typifies Marivaux's naturalist materialism about human instincts. But then a still more interesting aspect of Marivaux's thinking emerges. For, having made the point about women, he goes straight on to generalize, not about women but about the whole of human nature: 'C'est que nous sommes des esprits de contradiction: pendant qu'on peut choisir ce qu'on veut, on n'a envie de rien; quand on a fait son choix, on a envie de tout; fût-il bon, on s'en lasse, comment donc faire? Est-on mal, on veut être bien; cela est naturel; mais est-on bien, on veut être mieux; et quand on a ce mieux, est-on content? oh que non! Quel remède à cela? Sauve qui peut (ibid., p. 321). The crucial conclusion is about mankind in general; women serve only as a means to that end.

Woman, then, wears a dual aspect. She has manners and attitudes quite foreign to men, almost enough to make her a race apart. Feminine vanity may be a source of derision; but by her vanity, woman rejoins men: 'Les hommes sont plus vains que méchants; mais je dis mal: ils sont tous méchants, parce qu'ils sont vains' (ibid., p. 323). Women serve Marivaux's purpose admirably, because they are by far the more complex and interesting half of the human race; but their special characteristics are ultimately of interest because they enlighten our understanding of ourselves, whichever our sex.

The *Cabinet du philosophe* retraces much of the same ground, often with new perspectives. Marivaux's fascination with coquettish ways ever finds new objects for its delight, as when he describes a lady removing her gloves, ostensibly to work on embroidery but in reality to show off her pretty hands: 'les femmes, et même les plus sages, ont tant de ces petites industries-là! (8e feuille, p. 403). He returns to the more general question of women's desire to be seduced. In one of the boldest passages in his essays he points out that a suitor who says: 'Je vous aime, madame, vous avez mille charmes à mes yeux' is really saying: 'Madame, je vous désire beaucoup, vous me ferez grand plaisir de m'accorder vos faveurs'. What is more, the lady, far from being deceived by the complaint, fully understands its explicit sexual reference and indeed is delighted by the flattery which it contains, whereas a platonic declaration of love would have been of no interest: 'toute femme entend qu'on la désire, quand on lui dit: Je vous aime; et ne vous sait gré du: *Je vous aime,* qu'à cause qu'il signifie: *Je vous désire* (1ère feuille, p. 337). It is because of passages such as this that Paul Gazagne was right to stress the sensual aspect of love in Marivaux;[7] and though Gazagne goes too far in suggesting that the key to Marivaux's characters is sexual desire,[8] his thesis served a useful contribution in providing a corrective to the view that love in Marivaux was purely cerebral.

So the essayist reiterates his opinion, asserted in *Le Spectateur,* that a lover can hardly fail to win as he presses his suit with a lady, even if 'le tout finit par une banqueroute qui la déshonore' (5e feuille, p. 379). While Marivaux recommends prudence, and suggests that the best way of maintaining a partner's passion is to keep him anxious and uncertain, he is sceptical that reason can dominate the heart to this extent. The cause of such unfortunate human weaknesses lies in natural necessity: 'Si l'amour se menait bien, on n'aurait qu'un amant, ou qu'une maîtresse en dix ans; et il est de l'intérêt de la nature qu'on en ait vingt, et davantage.

'Et voilà, sans doute, pourquoi la nature n'a eu garde de rendre les amants susceptibles de prudence; ils s'aimeraient trop, et cela ne ferait pas son compte' (2e feuille, p. 344). If love is fragile and lovers inconstant, our biological condition provides the *raison d'être*.

As in *Le Spectateur,* we see that social circumstances reinforce the biological in tending to the same end. One of the most compassionate sections in the *Cabinet* deals with the situation of the married woman. If she finds herself with a brutish husband, she has scarcely any choice open to her but patience and resignation unto death.[9] For if she takes a lover, 'Point de quartier pour elle: on l'enferme, on la séquestre, on la réduit à une vie dure et frugale, on la déshonore . . .' (5e feuille, p. 376). Marivaux is not particularly sympathetic to her plight, adding 'et elle la mérite'. But he is exercised by the double standard which prevails concerning conjugal infidelity. A man, far from suffering any punishment, does not even need to conceal his libertinage. Indeed, his *galanterie* makes him a hero: 'on se le montre au spectacle' (ibid., p. 377); one thinks of Prévan at the end of *Les Liaisons dangereuses*.[10]

From this Marivaux moves on to the old theme of co-quetry; this time he lays the blame for it squarely upon men. Giving women the right to speak for themselves, he has them assert that they have no other resource than 'le misérable emploi de vous plaire'. Men are their jail-ers. 'Dans cet état, que nous reste-t-il, que la ruse? . . . Notre coquetterie fait tout notre bien. Nous n'avons point d'autre fortune que de trouver grâce devant vos yeux.' Otherwise, single girls will never escape from the seclusion of their own family: 'nous ne sortons du néant, nous ne saurions vous tenir en respect, faire fig-ure, être quelque chose, qu'en faisant l'affront de substituer une industrie humiliante, et quelquefois des vices, à la place des qualités, des vertus que nous avons, dont vous ne faites rien, et que vous tenez captives' (ibid., p. 378). Nowhere in his essays does Marivaux use more eloquent words in defence of women, sharing the view of his friend Mme de Lambert that the whole of civilized society, through its educational system, cus-toms, laws, is set up to ensure male hegemony.[11]

It is then a particular blend of sympathy, fascination, and condescension regarding women that Marivaux car-ries over into his plays. An oft-quoted passage in *Le Spectateur,* describing the moment when he had sur-prised a young girl affecting her apparent naturalness before a mirror, explains, he says, the source of his 'misanthropy': 'c'est de cette aventure que naquit en moi cette misanthropie qui ne m'a point quitté, et qui m'a fait passer ma vie à examiner les hommes, et à m'amuser de mes réflexions' (1ère feuille, p. 118). But

the author is over-simplifying; misanthropy unmitigated could not have produced the insights of his *œuvre*. More significant is it perhaps to note that here again he uses woman as the springboard for conclusions about 'les hommes'. The otherness of the female sex is subsumed, in classical manner, beneath the universality of human nature.

It is possible to trace, in Marivaux's plays as in his es-says, a steadily growing concern about feminine in-equality;[12] in the space of this article, however, one can do no more than touch on some of the more significant plays in this regard. *L'Ile des esclaves* (1725) addresses itself essentially to class differences between masters and servants; but the dramatist does not fail to comment on the caprices of 'femmes de qualité'. On this island, slaves and servants (no clear distinction is made) wish to destroy the barbarism in their masters' hearts and re-store them to the ranks of humanity. Candour being one means to this end, Arlequin and Cléanthis recount their masters' faults with great enthusiasm and no small pen-etration. Cléanthis reminds her mistress Euphrosine of an evening when the latter had used all the tricks of co-quetry to conquer her *cavalier*. Having damned a rival with faint praise, Euphrosine had pretended not to no-tice when her lover 'offrit son cœur'. 'Continuez, folâtre, continuez, dites-vous, en ôtant vos gants sous prétexte de m'en demander d'autres. Mais vous avez la main belle; il la vit, il la prit, il la baisa . . .' (Sc. 3). This picture, which strikingly resembles one of Sartre's most famous examples of *mauvaise foi* in *L'Etre et le néant*,[13] anticipates the description we have already noted above in the *Cabinet du philosophe*. In the same scene Euphrosine reiterates Marivaux's views on the *négligé*: 'Regardez mes grâces, elles sont à moi, celles-là. . . . Voyez comme je m'habille, quelle simplicité! il n'y a point de coquetterie dans mon fait.' But before the play is over Euphrosine, her pretensions now shat-tered, wins Arlequin's pity by her heartfelt cry for mercy. The servants' revolt is not pushed to the point of total ascendancy. The radicalism of the play is moral and religious rather than social and political. Once the masters have acquired a degree of self-knowledge and contrition it is time to call a halt. The attitude which emerges is that of a Christian moralist. Feminine vanity, like human vanity in general, can never be erased but only, at best, abated through the workings of charity and greater understanding.

L'Ile de la raison (1727) dwells too on the marvels of coquetry (II, 6), but adds a different aspect of the femi-nine situation: on the Island of Reason only women may make declarations of love. Men become the pas-sive element, sought out only when the women want them, and obliged to play the reluctant role until the al-liance is assumed. Blectrue, one of the islanders, is hor-rified at European courtship customs (II, 3: 'Que deviendra la faiblesse si la force l'attaque') which he argues are the consequence of men's vicious inclinations. By contrast, on the Island of Reason men help to save women from themselves. 'L'homme ici, c'est le garde-fou de la femme' (II, 7). This feminist paradox presumably owes something to Mme de Lambert's *Réflexions sur les femmes* (1727), but probably represents too the dramatist's desire to see what the 'pure' woman is like when the need for coquetry is removed.[14]

If so, the exploration of woman *in esse* is more arrestingly carried out in *La Dispute* (1744). Marivaux organises an enquiry into which of the sexes first proved unfaithful, and in typical eighteenth-century manner[15] constructs a situation where two boys and two girls are brought up in isolation from the world. The first heterosexual encounters are idyllic; each looks on the other and loves. The first meeting between the two girls is quite other. The mental universe is Hobbesian; jealousy, suspicion, hostility are the instinctive reactions on each side. By contrast, the two men are initially well-disposed towards each other, so long as no sexual conflict comes between them. Why this essential difference? Because, in Marivaux's view women, being obliged to please others, are immediately moved to jealousy in the presence of another attractive member of their sex. So it is that the girls take the first step in arranging infidelities; it springs almost simultaneously from the inclination in each to prove that she can assert her superiority by winning the other's lover. As Deloffre points out in his 'Notice' to the play (p. 597), if it were transposed into a tone less naïve and more libertine, these attitudes would be appropriate to *Les Liaisons dangereuses*.

Significantly, the dramatist presents the meeting of the two girls before that of their lovers; their reactions are so much richer for psychological portraiture. Whereas the men drift along more amiably, but also duller of sense, the girls' state of mind is complex to the point of being incomprehensible even to themselves. Eglé, for instance, is upset with herself, upset with her lover Azor: 'je ne sais ce qui m'arrive . . . je ne sais à qui j'en ai'. The real reason for her discontent emerges: she has found Mesrin to be more attractive than Azor. But Mesrin's only advantage is novelty—'d'être nouveau venu'. Even so, Eglé is unhappily divided within herself: 'Je ne suis contente de rien, d'un côté, le changement me fait peine, de l'autre, il me fait plaisir' (Sc. 15). She is able to resolve the dilemma only when she learns that Mesrin is the lover of the other girl, Adine; at that point jealousy impels swift action.

The conclusions of *La Dispute* are therefore sombre ones. Inconstancy, it would appear, is well-nigh inevitable; woman designs, man consents. Though one should not interpret a fable such as this with undue literalism, it seems that for Marivaux the urge to please is deeply ingrained in womankind. Social conditions may,

as he shows in the essays, confirm this inclination, but in the uncorrupted environment of *La Dispute* the female sex is just as bent on ruthless demonstration of its capacity to attract the male.

But the women do not emerge as villains from the play. The judicious conclusion of the Prince, who had arranged the whole experiment, is that virtues and vices are equal between the two sexes. Hermiane protests at this: 'votre sexe est d'une perfidie horrible, il change à propos de rien, sans chercher même de prétexte'. The Prince agrees: 'Le procédé du vôtre est du moins plus hypocrite, et par là plus décent, il fait plus de façon avec sa conscience que le nôtre' (Sc. 20). This observation, striking in its disillusioned detachment, seems to sum up Marivaux's whole attitude to women. They are more 'civilized'. More complex psychologically, more committed to the desire they feel to attract the opposite sex, they are more alive in their sensibilities, more aware of a moral order; they do not drift into falsity as do men. Paradox though it is, they show greater integrity in coming to terms with the human predicament.

These attitudes are therefore probably more far-reaching than those emerging from the comedy which one immediately thinks of as most involved with the female question, *La Colonie* (1750). In this play Marivaux's views are sharply developed and dramatically rich; but the subject is narrower. Here the dramatist is mainly concerned with the social question. In *La Colonie* the feminist leaders seek for equality with men, and especially within the state of marriage. Men, however, treat women as 'à n'être . . . que la première de toutes les bagatelles' (Sc. 9). As in the 5e feuille of the *Cabinet du philosophe,* coquetry is a response to male domination, in a world where, says Arthénice to the men, 'c'est votre justice et non pas la nôtre' (Sc. 13). Women are brainwashed into submission and self-denigration. Madame Sorbin finds herself unconsciously saying 'je ne suis qu'une femme' until Arthénice points out to her how deep the conditioning has gone (Sc. 9). Coquetry therefore becomes the only answer. But what a waste of talent and energy go into it; 'plus de profondeur d'esprit qu'il n'en faudrait pour governer deux mondes comme le nôtre, et tant d'esprit est en pure perte' (ibid.).

The women ask for equality in all realms: finance, judiciary, the army. The claims seem utopian, and besides there is near-revolt in the ranks when the leaders urge their followers to make themselves ugly; in addition, young lovers like Lina will always follow the spontaneous promptings of the heart. So it is hardly a surprise when the feminist cause collapses at the end. Marivaux's attitude towards the women protagonists appears sympathetic; but it is also equivocal.

In *La Colonie* and elsewhere Marivaux seems concerned about the rights of women. But though he indicts men for their tyrannous ways, he feels that the problem goes to the roots of human nature and is not to be solved by social reform. Improvements are however possible. One of the pleas most eloquently expressed in *La Colonie* harks back to the *Cabinet du philosophe.* Both of the women leaders want equality between husband and wife: 'le mariage qui se fait entre les hommes et nous', says Arthénice, 'devrait aussi se faire entre leurs pensées et les nôtres' (Sc. 13). Here at least is a practical way forward, though it depends more on improving the moral climate than on the institution of new laws.

In Marivaux subsists a deep-rooted pessimism about ever effecting wholesale changes in man's, and therefore woman's, lot. The picture is however not black. The essayist, like the dramatist, is presenting a human comedy. Women suffer many disadvantages, but they have consolations. Not only are they prettier, they are more interesting. Besides, if men rule the earth, women rule men:

> Si les lois des hommes dépendent,
> Ne vous en plaignez pas, trop aimables objets:
> Vous imposez des fers à ceux qui vous commandent,
> Et vos maîtres sont vos sujets.

('Divertissement', *La Nouvelle Colonie,* I, p, 771)

Marivaux can scarcely be termed a leading feminist of his day. He is alive to feminine inequality, but he deals relatively little with the disabilities facing eighteenth-century women: the economic and legal limitations, the right to divorce, educational reform. Not that he was unaware of these problems. By choosing for instance a widow as heroine of **Les Fausses Confidences** he recognized the greater degree of liberty she enjoyed as compared with a single girl. But these details were of interest to him in serving the ends of psychological enquiry. If Marivaux can be termed a feminist at all, it is surely in his acceptance, as in **La Colonie,** that women are men's equals intellectually. Indeed, as we have seen and as almost any one of his comedies makes clear, women's minds are far more interesting. They are the more colourful part of the species. Ultimately, they are of value for what they tell us about the human race as a whole; for they are the quintessence of humanity. When in **La Dispute** Adine, who has never seen another young girl, meets Eglé she asks ingenuously: 'Etes-vous une personne?' Eglé retorts: 'Oui assurément, et très personne' (Sc. 9). It is the reply that, about womankind, Marivaux himself might have made.

Notes

1. P. Stewart, *Le Masque et la parole: le langage de l'amour au XVIIIe siècle* (Paris 1973), p. 140.

2. *Le Spectateur français,* 1ère feuille, *Journaux et œuvres diverses,* ed. F. Deloffre and M. Gilot (Paris 1969), p. 118. All subsequent references to the *Journaux* will be to this edition.

3. M. Gilot, *Les Journaux de Marivaux: Itinéraire moral et accomplissement esthétique* (Paris/Lille 1975), 2 vols., i, 127.

4. Gilot, op. cit., persuasively argues that irregularities in the appearance of issues of *Le Spectateur* can be directly related to the periods when Marivaux was composing his plays (i, 250-1).

5. ed. J. Dunkley (Exeter 1976), p. 19.

6. Sc. I, *Théâtre complet,* ed. F. Deloffre (Paris 1968), 2 vols., i, 89. All subsequent references to Marivaux's plays will be to this edition.

7. *Marivaux par lui-même* (Paris 1954).

8. A judicious survey, with sensible conclusions, is conducted by V. P. Brady, *Love in the Theatre of Marivaux* (Geneva 1970), pp. 15-21.

9. Divorce was impossible, but most of the leading *philosophes* claimed it as a human right: cf. L. Abensour, *La Femme et le féminisme avant la Révolution* (Paris 1923), pp. 402-5.

10. The editors of the *Journaux* document the inequality of treatment accorded to the sexes, p. 652, n. 130.

11. p. 653, n. 139; cf. Gilot, op. cit., pp. 653-4.

12. L. Desvignes-Parent argues this persuasively in *Marivaux et l'Angleterre* (Paris 1970), pp. 317-24, though she surprisingly makes no reference to *L'Ile de la raison* in this particular survey.

13. The woman in Sartre's scene, ardently pursued by her suitor, enjoys the situation because she can temporarily put off any decision and pretend to a belief in platonic love. When he takes her hand, 'la jeune femme abandonne sa main, mais *ne s'aperçoit pas* qu'elle l'abandonne' (Paris 1943, p. 95; author's italics). Marivaux is more indulgent in his comment but no less observant.

14. cf. Deloffre's comments, p. 1087, n. 43; p. 584.

15. cf. W. H. Trapnell, 'The "Philosophical" implications of Marivaux's *Dispute*', *Studies on Voltaire and the Eighteenth Century,* lxxiii (1970), 193-219, which fascinatingly relates the play to contemporary social philosophy.

Herbert Josephs (essay date January 1980)

SOURCE: Josephs, Herbert. "*Le Paysan Parvenu*: Satire and the Fiction of Innocence." *French Forum* 5, no. 1 (January 1980): 22-9.

[*In the following essay, Josephs maintains that Marivaux employed the conventions of satire as well as those of the memoir-novel in* Le paysan parvenu.]

Though we often acknowledge the critical premise that no pure example of a fictional form can be discovered in any given work, some of the problems, formal and thematic, raised by *Le Paysan parvenu* have proved to be especially stubborn precisely because of a tendency to preserve a novel-centered conception of fiction. The memoir-novel of Marivaux needs to be reexamined in terms of its own hybrid nature, from the vantage point, that is, of the literary conventions selected by the author. The conventions informing *Le Paysan parvenu,* which was, for Marivaux, somewhat of an experiment in narrative modes, are heterogeneous, alternating between those of satire and those of the memoir-novel. The author organized his fiction according to the shifting principles of a picaresque, satiric narrative form whose tentative quality remains tenaciously resistant to readers nourished on the more coherent, albeit misleading view of the novel as a distinct literary medium. While satire generally accommodates itself without strain to other genres, its persistence throughout the narration of Jacob's rise to respectability creates the impression of conflicting artistic objectives and it remains questionable whether these divergent goals were susceptible of adequate resolution within the boundaries of Marivaux's mixed form.

On the evidence provided by his earlier works, it is clear that Marivaux had been experimenting with satiric narrative. For *Le Paysan parvenu,* he selected as his protagonist, from the literary baggage of his own time, a figure of stylized innocence who, as a consequence of his suitability for exposing self-deceit, necessarily appears empty, on occasion, of moral and psychological dimension. In other words, Jacob's usefulness to the author for the observation of manners altered his value as a fictional character of interest; his realistic potential and problematic human appeal nonetheless provided a focus for the examination of those themes dearest to the author, who, from the start of his career, had been dedicated to probing and pitting against each other the private self and the social self.

It is upon these shifting values and voices of a peculiarly unstable form that our ambivalent experience of *Le Paysan parvenu* depends. The formal and rhetorical hesitations that are apparent intermittently in the work mirror faithfully the novel's ethical uncertainties: occasionally the memoirs proclaim a world of fixed and certain values which are, if not untarnished by the vagaries of surface change and circumstantial realism, at least still intact. But almost simultaneously we cannot fail to discern, as we are offered an intimate view of Jacob's destiny, the unsubstantial nature of the self and the fragility of identities constructed upon incantations and acquired forms. The reader has been promised, even with the title, the narration of a successful career, the transformation of Jacob, narrator and protagonist, from peasant to *parvenu*; the memoirs tell of an engaging and virile rustic youth who is destined by the novel's logic to become, in his more advanced years, a settled and respected financier and, by inference, the self-contemplative author of the memoirs in question. He will achieve, ostensibly, this social ascension above all through the generosity of flattered and desiring women whose influence he secures for himself by exploiting his natural attributes of simplicity and quickness of wit. The expectations initially raised by the title and increased by the memoirs themselves are not, however, satisfied at the conclusion of the fifth part, where Marivaux interrupted his story definitively. We are left, instead, with a burlesque image of Jacob at the Comédie Française, humiliated and still the country bumpkin; he has remained, it would seem, essentially unchanged in character, if not entirely in manner. While Jacob's climb to success, though interrupted, has been throughout the narrative a foregone conclusion, the actual conclusion of the novel, the abrupt and indecisive termination of Jacob's adventures, fails to resolve either the thematic inconsistencies of Marivaux's innovative tale or the exigencies of plot governing the memoirs—that is, the hero's social, moral, and intellectual evolution. If there has been any genuine moral growth in Jacob, we must assume, with the novel's most persuasive critic, Henri Coulet, that it has taken place some time during the period about which we know nothing[1]. And is it, then, by means of new learned gestures of decorum or through an accumulative process of acceptance and self-acceptance, of deception and self-deception, that Jacob eventually comes to merit his title of M. de la Vallée?

Towards the end of the novel, we are offered a momentary glance at an episodic character, M. d'Orville, weak with sickness and living in the near squalor that Chance has reserved for him, but possessing the undiminished and immediately perceptible air of a gentleman, his manner and his style. Gentility, this brief encounter seems to reveal, is a matter of provenance. *Le Paysan parvenu* proclaims, at least for a moment, that not even the caprices of fortune redirected by a most effective picaresque wit can undo what Nature has decreed:

> En effet, ces choses-là se sentent; il en est de ce que je dis là-dessus comme d'un homme d'une certaine condition à qui vous donneriez un habit de paysan; en faites-vous un paysan pour cela? Non, vous voyez qu'il n'en porte que l'habit; sa personne est vêtue, et point habillée, pour ainsi dire; il y a des attitudes, des mouvements et des gestes dans cette personne, qui font qu'elle est étrangère au vêtement qui la couvre.[2]

This crucial and explicit pronouncement that seems to capsulize the novel's ethical position on falsehood and essential identity echoes, in fact, the wisdom announced in the prologue, where we are advised by Jacob of the folly of attempting to dissimulate one's lower-class origins. By a logical extension of the novel's own criteria, then, we must accept the impossibility of outwitting our own deepest personal truths:

On a beau déguiser la vérité . . . elle se venge tôt ou tard des mensonges dont on a voulu la couvrir, et l'on est toujours trahi par une infinité d'événements qu'on ne saurait ni parer ni prévoir; jamais je ne vis, en pareille matière, de vanité qui fît une bonne fin.[3]

But Marivaux equivocates in his treatment of the novel's central thematic concern; he offers his reader a mass of conflicting evidence on the subject of appearances as he traces the history of Jacob's entry into dizzying circles of mundanity, the gradual expansion of his consciousness, and his superficial acquisition of impressive manners and finer forms. But whether or not *Le Paysan parvenu* was designed to test a wavering hypothesis concerning the dynamics of growth in the age of progress, its explicit observations on appearances and the implications of its plot are often inconsistent and finally at odds.

Marivaux's novel, then, is essentially duplicitous and its ethical clarities ultimately obliterated. Nowhere is the ambiguity of Jacob's story more in evidence than in the quality of innocence that is one of his principal attributes and that Marivaux might have encountered everywhere about him in the evolving Enlightenment literature of satire, of memoir fiction, and especially in the narratives of worldliness and initiation. It is the sensationalist epistemology of the Enlightenment, reducing the ideal and the abstract to the hard and fast realities of experience, that bridges the distance between these literary modes and that facilitated the occasional merging of satire with the still experimental genre of the novel. And satire, as Northrup Frye has suggested, while offering its own style of mock oracular wisdom, has represented, in some of its most celebrated examples, the feeling that experience itself is finally larger than any set of beliefs that can be constructed *about* experience[4]. One has only to survey the major literary expressions of the period to recognize generic affinities within both satire and the novel that led eventually to the integration of their conventions Fielding's puncturing of virtuous stances, Defoe's consistent muting of any nonmercantile moral voice, Voltaire's assault on philosophical idealism and Johnson's on Rasselas's quest for life's meaning; finally, in a paradoxical culmination of this quest for a new humanist style, there is the subversion in Sade's fiction of soul, spirit, and intellect by the brutal realities of the flesh, betraying a compulsive dynamics of reduction that has led one critic to observe in both satire and in the fiction of Sadism the same rhetoric in operation[5]. The novel and satire, then, nourished each other, absorbed each other's functions, and offered the possibilities of both intellectual renewal and of tradition preserved.

Among the conventions transformed by the blending of old and new in the early Enlightenment, none served the purposes of the age's critical spirit more diversely than the literary metaphor of innocence. For an intelligence in quest of its own processes, the invention of a state of mind analogous to the philosophical blank slate and embedded within the stuff of fiction was a courageous initial step outside of the self. Locke's essay on the origins of human understanding had been translated into a satiric mask that blended a pre-cultural simplicity with curiosity and a thirst for experience. The increasingly popular literary innocents of the time were the result of a sophisticated effort on the part of culture to release critical energy by uncluttering the intelligence of inherited beliefs; simplicity could at least be feigned in order to restore to the human psyche its original creative forces from beyond the provincialism of lifeless symbolic forms. Wisdom, it was apparent, unlike Athena from the head of Zeus, did not burst forth already shaped. Throughout the century, we encounter diverse figures of intellectual naïveté which, however restricted their human dimensions, provided fictional shape to the dawning of reason; the neutral state of literalmindedness that characterized the age's many bewildered travelers, conventional primitives, and literate peasants, was an urbane way of playing dumb; it provided a penetrating heuristic weapon to the critical intelligence whose struggle for survival had to be renewed persistently because this was a struggle that could never permanently be won.

"Il faut se défaire des yeux de l'habitude," then, was virtually a battle cry, sounded first by Bayle and Fontenelle, echoing everywhere in the polemic literature of the *philosophes,* and still reverberating in the opposing sonorities of Rousseau and Sade. And of the several voices traditionally available to the satirist, it was that of the *ingénu* figure, endowed principally with unpretentious origins, a figure of fancy divested of custom, that provided Marivaux with the free-moving intelligence necessary for the unmasking function he made it serve. In *Le Voyageur dans le Nouveau Monde,* Marivaux offered his most explicit statement of the educative task performed by characters constructed solely upon the uncommon naïveté with which they express what they feel and think: "Ainsi donc, en vous peignant ces hommes que j'ai trouvés, je vais vous donner le portrait des hommes faux avec qui vous vivez, je vais lever le masque qu'ils portent"[6]. And like Voltaire's Ingénu, like Diderot's Tahitians and poets, originals and fools, Jacob's directness and freedom from restraint have the effect of exposing, by the dynamics of contrast, the paralyzed institutions of the mind. He forces us, as Maynard Mack has said of the muse of satire, to see the ulcer where we are accustomed to see the rouge[7]. His initial value resided in the antics of borrowed simplicity and spontaneity which he performed for the author: "Je disais hardiment mon sentiment sur tout ce qui s'offrait à mes yeux"[8]. Artificial surfaces abound in Marivaux's gallery of social masks, but Jacob peers crudely through keyholes while the author casts the refracted light of satiric vision on scenes of strained gallantry and false piety, on the vanity of class pretensions and on the irresistible forces of self-deception.

Many episodes in *Le Paysan parvenu* appear to have as their sole esthetic justification the opportunity they provide for Marivaux to focus the lens of his satiric perspective. For the purpose of the satirist, everything, of course, is susceptible to serving as illustration and example. However, as Peter Brooks has noted, "Marivaux's essayism is marked by a repeated need to violate the form he has set for himself, to let his narrative penchant take control and to carry what was supposed to be illustrative incident, exemplary anecdote, to a length where characters and situations begin to exist in their own right"[9]. It is surely not Jacob's satiric effectiveness that grasps and holds the attention of his reader, but rather the complexity that his character assumes as he journeys towards comfort and respectability. Though his satiric versatility is reduced as a consequence of an increased psychic fullness, he acquires in its place that virtue which is endemic to the novel, the quality of inner depth, and with it a temporal density that is likewise an adjunct of the novel. The handsome and hypocritical peasant, whose nature is as tantalizingly hybrid as the ethical values of his memoirs, is perverse, but with innocence, according to one reader[10], and to another he is impulsive and prudent, naïve and full of art, existing simultaneously in several modes and at several levels[11].

For the satiric mode alone, clearly, does not provide the coherent organizing principle for *Le Paysan parvenu.* The concerns of the satirist, with regard to the component of character, are substantially different from those of the novelist; inconsistencies of character, like those of Gulliver, for example, simply demonstrate the adaptability required of the satiric mask. They do *not* testify to the presence of internal motivation within a satiric agent created rather as a filter of naïveté for the self-confident voice of the author. The character whose function is to assume whatever stance is required to lift the masks of social ritual cannot be of a piece psychologically. That is, unless incoherence and adaptability are the structuring principles of his literary identity, as in the case of Rameau's Nephew, who represents the most consummate fusion within a single character of function and inner life—the disturbing fool and the disturbed wretch. Analogously, Jacob's personal simplicity is not merely surrounded by the empty shell of a satiric function; his innocence is spoiled by artifice, and like many a contemporary *ingénu,* he aspires to a condition the opposite of his own. The simplicity which is so basic a component of his nature becomes his most effective pose, struck for its tested value in surroundings barren of even the semblances of candor. His ingenuousness is rarely unaffected; his directness is stylized

and self-conscious: "A travers l'épaisseur de mon ignorance," the older narrator acknowledges with regard to his earlier indelicacies, "je voyais qu'elles ne nuisaient jamais à un homme qui n'était pas obligé d'en savoir davantage . . ."[12]. Jacob ultimately barters the clear-sightedness of the peasant for the clouded wisdom of mundanity: "Voyez que de choses capables de débrouiller mon esprit et mon cœur. . . . Voyez quelle école de corruption, et par conséquent de sentiment; car l'âme se raffine à mesure qu'elle se gâte"[13]. His worldly lessons, summarized in M. Bono's mockery of the values of romance, finally alter, in the direction of the cynical, the novel's perspective on the merits of its protagonist's original simplicity. When not a vehicle of satire, innocence becomes once again the stuff of romance and the object of satire. It is menaced by the intellectual impulse, by the will to encounter and to know the real, and by what Foucault has called "un si cruel savoir"[14]. We nowhere encounter in Marivaux, as we do in Richardson, Rousseau, and again in Sade, indomitable though perverted, that figure of innocence which is the image of a metaphysical entity, some essential moral force residing in man, untarnished by the effects of experience, and resisting in this respect the direction that the novel generically followed. There is little more than a trace, in *Le Paysan parvenu,* of a utopian moral innocence that would become the object, during the declining years of the century, of both a sentimental nostalgia and a violence born of frustration.

However, to complete the portrait of Jacob's curiously mixed literary nature, appealingly simple, but obdurately realistic, we must turn to still another narrative tradition, the mode of the picaresque. It is finally neither Jacob's mobility nor his will to survive nor his amoral probity that reveals in Marivaux's novel the legacy of the picaresque and that locates it at the frontiers of satire. The peregrinations of an outsider are preserved in the spirit of formal idiosyncrasy to which the narrator of *Le Paysan parvenu* conforms tenaciously in the several pages of his prologue. "Chacun a sa façon de s'exprimer qui vient de sa façon de sentir"[15], he tells us; and later,

> Il faut qu'on s'accoutume de bonne heure à mes digressions; je ne sais pas pourtant si j'en ferai de fréquentes; peut-être que oui, peut-être que non, je ne réponds de rien; je ne me gênerai point, je conterai toute ma vie, et si j'y mêle autre chose, c'est que cela se présentera sans que je le cherche.[16]

Jacob, the narrator, arrogates to himself a freedom of narrative movement that guarantees the versatility of the whimsical satiric stylist; he is simply an amateur craftsman working amidst shifting conventions in an innovative medium. He will sacrifice consistency of belief and coherence of statement in exchange for the picaro's privilege of seizing chance opportunities for comic interludes and set pieces of literary portraiture;

he will offer us satiric *hors d'œuvre* on the subject of spiritual directors, on piety and devotion, on gluttony and on gossips, all of which are loosely bound together in a novel that purports to relate a single destiny.

Still, most of the elements of the novel do gravitate around a fixed thematic center—the changing modes of the self and the interplay between borrowed clothes, simulated postures, mimicked linguistic forms, and an emerging identity. But the conclusion of the novel also belongs to the satirist who is bound by neither the convention of completion nor that of final resolution. We are left to contemplate a last comic image of an *almost* successful picaro reduced to the behavior of a mechanism, reversing, as in an earlier scene of interrupted gallantry, the direction once taken by Harlequin, who had gradually blossomed forth into life, "poli par l'amour." While we have been made to share concern over the fate of this unusually complex peasant, and while we have been made witness to Jacob's intricately traced progress towards moral depth, he exists in the guise of the buffoon rather than of the *parvenu.* We discover in the last paragraphs of the novel that our interest has been focused on changes that have occurred predominantly in Jacob's external condition. And precisely at the crucial moment, when his reader might justifiably wonder about the internal reverberations of this most recent humiliation of the hero, Marivaux turns away from Jacob, blending tones of kindness and contempt, to open yet another digression, the development of which, this time, would never occur. Marivaux does not really end his novel at all, he merely breaks off, underscoring the tainted integrity of his narrative. When we remember to ask how, indeed, the burlesque peasant could ever become the articulate and refined author, we are assuming still another convention, the inevitability of action promised by the title, and of cause-and-effect relationship, a convention which is, however, not entirely germane to the dynamics of *Le Paysan parvenu.*

The beliefs embodied in Marivaux's novel are as difficult to discern with clarity as their form is uncertain. The author traffics in duplicity, the indeterminacy of his ethical criteria reflecting his hesitations between the voice of the satirist and that of the memorialist. The central focus of the plot, furthermore, the rise of Jacob to respectability, is everywhere nuanced by an underlying satiric presence that invites us to perceive the texture of social existence as constituted by the dexterous manipulation of forms. The satire finally must turn on Jacob himself; his individualism, originating in his innocence and so affectionately offered as a refreshing contrast to a ritualistic society, has been fated to dissolution by his own aspirations and is neutralized in the end by the irresistible, shaping force of the same social structure that he has been created to expose.

Satiric art flourishes, Scholes and Kellogg have reminded us, in a world in transition from an ideally oriented moral scheme of the cosmos to an empirically oriented non-moral scheme, and "the values of the satirist himself, since he is striking out against a present society that has fallen away from an ideal past, and *against* the ideal past *itself* for having so little relevance to the real world, are therefore notoriously difficult to locate"[17]. Marivaux's memoir-fiction, furthermore, reveals a certain incompatibility which the author apparently experienced between the satirist's and the novelist's conception of their narrative art. *Le Paysan parvenu* depends upon a weak principle of coherence and upon a sliding purpose that, whatever the cost in terms of blurred perceptions, offers experiences of intellectual renewal and esthetic continuity that help define the early Enlightenment. They are experiences that are conditioned in literature by the unstable modulations of narrative voices which succeed each other, eclipse each other, and occasionally fuse.

Notes

1. *Marivaux romancier* (Paris: Colin, 1975), p. 193.

2. *Romans,* ed. M. Arland (Paris: Gallimard, 1949), p. 780.

3. *Ibid.,* p. 567.

4. *Anatomy of Criticism* (Princeton: Princeton Univ. Press, 1957), p. 229.

5. Joseph Bentley, "Satire and the Rhetoric of Sadism," in *The Perverse Imagination,* ed. Irving Buchen (New York: New York Univ. Press, 1970), pp. 57-73.

6. *Romans,* p. 927.

7. "The Muse of Satire," in *Studies in the Literature of the Augustan Age,* ed. R. C. Boys (Ann Arbor: George Wahr Publishing Co., 1952), p. 230.

8. *Romans,* p. 570.

9. *The Novel of Worldliness* (Princeton: Princeton Univ. Press, 1969), p. 95.

10. Coulet, *Marivaux romancier,* p. 195.

11. Emita Hill, "Sincerity and Self-Awareness in the *Paysan parvenu,*" *Studies in Voltaire and the Eighteenth Century,* 88 (1972), 747.

12. *Romans,* p. 572.

13. *Ibid.,* p. 722.

14. *Critique,* No. 182 (1962), pp. 597-611.

15. *Romans,* p. 568.

16. *Ibid.,* p. 570.

17. Robert Scholes and Robert Kellogg, *The Nature of Narrative* (New York: Oxford Univ. Press, 1966), p. 112.

Felicia Sturzer (essay date March 1982)

SOURCE: Sturzer, Felicia. "Exclusion and Coquetterie: First-Person Narrative in Marivaux's 'L'Indigent Philosophe.'" *French Review* 55, no. 4 (March 1982): 471-77.

[*In the following essay, Sturzer examines the first-person narrator of Marivaux's memoir-journal, who, like the narrator of* La vie de Marianne, *professes no knowledge of writing style and claims, therefore, to be producing a "natural" account of his life.*]

Marivaux's *L'Indigent Philosophe,* which focuses on a philosophical pauper, first appeared in 1727. A memoir-journal, it is similar in form and content to *Le Spectateur français,* which precedes it, and *Le Cabinet du Philosophe,* which follows it in 1734. Critics such as Frédéric Deloffre and Oscar Haac have linked the impoverished philosopher to the picaresque tradition of the clever hero, gay in spite of adversity. In this context, the pauper is a logical outgrowth of Cliton in Marivaux's early novel, *Pharsamon ou Les Folies romanesques,* as well as a precursor of Jacob in Marivaux's later work, *Le Paysan parvenu* (1734-35). In his critical self-analysis and his dialogue with the reader, the philosopher is kindred in spirit to Rameau's nephew and Diderot's determined fatalist. Pierre Jacoebée, E. J. H. Greene, Ronald Rosbottom, and others have emphasized the disconnected narrative content and chronology of *L'Indigent Philosophe*; but the relationship of such discontinuity to the philosopher's emergence as a successful "Marivaudian" character is virtually ignored. Above all, the poverty-stricken narrator is characterized by his exclusion from society, more specifically Parisian society, and the deceitful game-playing it entails. In order to assert himself in spite of exclusion, the narrator needs a vehicle, and the text of his memoir-journal becomes this vehicle. By means of the text, the social outcast is transformed into a philosopher whose witty dialogue with the reader parallels the ambiguous "coquetterie" of Marivaux's most successful characters. This essay traces the circuitous path of this transformation.

At the outset, the narrator presents himself as a prodigal, penniless being, forced to become a spectator of the social scene. His stated purpose in writing is self-knowledge: "je viens d'acheter quelques feuilles de papier pour me mettre par écrit, autrement dit pour montrer ce que je suis, et comment je pense, et j'espère qu'on ne sera pas fâché de me connaître."[1] Accompanying this statement of purpose is a denial of any authorial intent or presence in his text and an insistence on the "natural," unembellished style of his thoughts. This, he claims, justifies the lack of temporal and narrative chronology in his memoir: "Pour moi, je ne sais pas comment j'écrirai: ce qui me viendra, nous l'aurons sans autre cérémonie; car je n'en sais pas d'autre que d'écrire tout couramment mes pensées; et si mon livre ne vaut rien, je ne perdrai pas tout" (*IP,* [*L'Indigent Philosophe,* in *Journaux et Œuvres diverses,*] première feuille, p. 276). The narrator wants to establish his being by means of a text that avoids the artificiality of "style" and thus becomes a crystallization of himself. This desire to define one's being, to become both subject and object of a quest, is a distinguishing trait of the successful Marivaudian character.

In the comedies, a character's being exists in a timeless void, a chaos from which it emerges only in stages, jolted into awareness by such shocks as love and death. Once a character defines the source of his being, he spends all his energy maintaining the *amour-propre* he needs in order to survive in a competitive society. Therefore, Marivaux's characters cannot admit they love, for doing so would entail giving up a part of their "être." Ultimately, love entails a bitter linguistic struggle and is the reward for a well-fought battle of the intellect. Thus, in *Le Jeu de L'Amour et du Hasard* (1730), Silvia and Dorante are engaged in a game that neither can win without surrendering pride. Disguised as servants, each tries to avoid the inevitable admission of love. When Dorante finally declares himself, Silvia continues wearing her mask until Dorante makes a total and unequivocal commitment of his being. Only when she knows that she will lose nothing can Silvia accept love. The same struggle for equilibrium is evident in the novels. Marianne, the narrator of *La Vie de Marianne* (1731-42), engages in a psychological game-playing that is incorporated into the memoirs she is writing. Preoccupied with justifying her motivations not only to others but to herself, Marianne's bad faith results in self-deception as well as deception of the careless reader. Exemplifying bad faith, she succeeds in satisfying her desires as well as establishing the social worth of her "being." Both Marianne and Silvia exemplify successful Marivaudian heroines who achieve their goals using deceit, hypocrisy, and "coquetterie."

For the indigent philosopher, the "unembellished" text serves the same function as Silvia's disguise or Marianne's ambiguous self-justifications. By his denial of formality, the narrator manages to ingratiate himself with the reader and to establish the conversational tone that characterizes the entire journal. Repeatedly, the narrator emphasizes that he is by nature "babillard" and that he is speaking to the reader directly, transcending the written word. The use of the first-person "je" emphasizes the directness of the narrator-reader relationship, and gives the narrator a psychological depth that enhances his credibility.[2] This is further reinforced by the rambling nature of the discourse. Without quite knowing why or how, the reader is suddenly seduced, drawn into the text, bewitched by its charm and fleeting grace: "Dans cette absence de toute symétrie, de tout ordre apparent qui caractérise la composition naturelle, il nous faut finalement reconnaître la présence du 'Je ne sais quoi' qui est grâce, ce mouvement perpétuel qui trouve son unité dans le varié et qui, apparemment désordonné, parce que vivant, demeure essentiellement inachevé. Par son caractère fuyant, le gracieux se fait insidieux, fascinant et attachant" (Jacoebée, p. 85). By establishing such intimacy with his reader, the philosopher achieves a degree of literary sophistication that enables him to transform his exclusion into inclusion. As a member of a small but literate group, the narrator becomes both object and subject of an evolving narration: "l'identité du personnage et de son histoire par l'exclusion de ce médiateur qu'est le romancier comme conteur externe, c'est l'intimité du narrateur avec les sentiments qui font la narration, cette narration qui est lui-même, qui est sa propre vie" (Rousset, "L'Emploi," p. 104).

The narrator uses his intimacy with the reader to accomplish three things. First, by denying his own literary talents, he forces the reader to engage in a dialogue that questions the latter's critical judgment as well as the intellectual capabilities of so-called "authors." Our narrator distinguishes himself from ordinary writers whom he describes as follows:

> Il a un sujet fixe sur lequel il va travailler . . . il a une demi-douzaine de pensées dans la tête sur lesquelles il fonde tout l'ouvrage; elles naissent les unes des autres, elles sont conséquentes, à ce qu'il croit du moins; comme si le plus souvent il ne les devait pas à la seule envie de les avoir. . . . Car il s'imagine que le bon sens a tout fait, ce bon sens si difficile à avoir, ce bon sens qui rendrait les livres si courts, qui en ferait si peu, s'il les composait tous. . . .
>
> (*IP,* sixième feuille, p. 311)

Throughout the essay, the philosopher turned literary critic states his views on what authors and books should be, to the detriment of what he finds around him. It soon becomes evident that the narrator's repeated claims that he is not an author constitute false modesty. This same tactic is used by the older narrator of *La Vie de Marianne* when recounting the adventures of the young and supposedly innocent heroine. The older woman, now a countess, also claims that she cannot write, that she has no "style," and that she is certainly no author. She is quite aware, of course, that she has a very engaging style and her claims of "innocence" are merely what Rosbottom calls a "coquetterie de style."[3] Too old to flirt with prospective lovers, Marianne, like our indigent philosopher, flirts with her reader.

As further proof that he possesses the philosopher's wit as well as an author's style, our narrator gives particular attention to the meaning of words, to the relationship between signs and what they represent. His text evolves into a synthesis of assertions, denials, and psy-chological justifications. This typical aspect of a Marivaux text has been labelled "marivaudage" by his detractors. But within the framework of a specific text, "marivaudage" has a self-representational function and constitutes a practical effort at self-expression.[4] Thus, it releases the tension created by the Marivaudian character's attempt to define himself in relation to those around him. In *L'Indigent Philosophe,* "marivaudage" becomes a form of stylistic flirtation, particularly when the narrator assumes the role of moralizer and arbiter of social values. Exploiting his position of outsider looking in, he satirizes human vanity as it is revealed in social "types" such as the rich man, the clever man, or the falsely humble one. Thus the rich man turned pauper loses his vanity with his material goods:

> Un homme était riche, il devient pauvre . . . il aimera le pain comme il aimait la perdrix, l'eau fraîche comme il aimait le bon vin, et le vin comme il aimait la plus exquise des liqueurs; en un mot, ses besoins s'humanisent, ils demandent peu, parce qu'ils ne peuvent avoir beaucoup, et le peu qu'ils ont les satisfait mieux cent fois, que le beaucoup quand ils l'avaient.
>
> (*IP,* première feuille, p. 278)

In a single sentence, past and present merge as wealth is transformed into poverty. Further on in the essay, the careful analysis of "gens d'esprit" who turn virtue into a "précieuse" is another example of the philosopher's stylistic "coquetterie" teasing the reader, challenging him to participate in an intellectual tug of war.

The second function of the intimacy resulting from the use of first-person narrative is to make the reader see the narrator, especially the positive aspects of his personality. Throughout the text seeing ("voir") is identified with knowing ("savoir"), which results in understanding. This is explained in the comparison between the evil and the virtuous man:

> L'homme d'esprit vertueux peut voir tout ce que voit le méchant, peut se dire tout ce que celui-ci se dit, et peut-être plus; car le vertueux a plus de dignité dans l'âme, il porte plus haut le sentiment de son excellence que nous avons tous: car c'est même l'abus de ce sentiment qui fait que nous sommes tous orgueilleux; en un mot, ce sentiment nous est naturel, et celui qui le consulte le plus peut en apprendre bien des choses inconnues à celui qui le néglige, il peut en tirer bien des pressentiments d'une haute destinée.
>
> (*IP,* cinquième feuille, pp. 305-6)

The theme of seeing is extended by the introduction of a second narration into the indigent philosopher's initial one. Up to that point, the details we have concerning the philosopher's early life are sparse. We know he was once wealthy, socially sought-after, and popular with women. If we are to judge by his easy-going manner, we can state that he has a pleasing personality. These characteristics also describe the philosopher's drinking companion, who is the second narrator. The latter's narration becomes a mirror image of the first one, revealing the social "coquetterie" of the worldly Marivaudian character whom the indigent philosopher admires. The second narrator combines the wit of Rameau's nephew with the physical sensuality of a Jacob. The son of an unsuccessful musician, he joins a troupe of traveling actors and becomes the star of the show. This is accomplished by a combination of personal charm, native wit, and fortuitous circumstance.

Like the philosopher, the actor-narrator wants the reader to "know" him, to sympathize with his situation, and to accept him. Consequently, he resorts to first-person narrative. But while the philosopher's narration is inward-oriented, and attempts to delineate his moral and psychological constitution, the actor's narration is outward-oriented, concentrating on the physical trait easily perceived by the senses. He describes himself in the following terms: "Je n'étais pas laid au moins, je suis bien aisé que vous le sachiez; j'étais gros et gras, et j'avais l'air espiègle; de l'esprit, je n'en manquais pas, de l'effronterie encore moins" (*IP,* deuxième feuille, p. 286). Even during his apprenticeship as a servant for the troupe, the narrator refers to his sexual instincts by informing us that he seduces several maids. Once he becomes an actor, his talent joined to his good looks inflates his already overabundant supply of vanity: "Ajoutez que j'étais frais et potelé, ce qui est considérable auprès des femmes: cela fait grand bien à l'esprit qu'on a avec elles; aussi me regardaient-elles comme un objet fort intéressant" (*IP,* troisième feuille, p. 290). The stylistic "je ne sais quoi" of the first narration is thus replaced by the tactile seductiveness of a narrator who appeals to his reader's sensuous instincts. Unlike the philosopher's narration, the second text is characterized by temporal continuity. Just as Jacob's new name in *Le Paysan parvenu* transforms him from peasant to bourgeois, so our actor's new profession thrusts him from insignificance to importance: "Nous quittâmes la ville: il y avait bien de la différence entre moi qui en sortais, et moi qui y étais venu; j'en sortais en héros, et j'y étais entré en moucheur de chandelles. Et voilà le monde: aujourd'hui petit, demain grand" (*IP,* troisième feuille, p. 291). From the seduction of servant girls, the self-satisfied narrator proceeds to the seduction of a "femme bourgeoise," including one who spent some time in Paris! Suddenly, at the height of his success, the narrator's discourse stops and the text reverts to the philosopher's original narration.

Characteristically, as in *La Vie de Marianne* and *Le Paysan parvenu,* Marivaux ends the story unexpectedly. For him a character is only interesting while he is in the process of becoming, struggling to assert himself. Once he is successful, Marivaux's interest in him wanes. As in his dramatic works, the action is developed only to the point where the characters become aware of their true feelings, and then the play ends. It is the surprise of love, for example, that challenges the playwright, not the consequences of passion. Similarly, the second narration stops when the narrator is at the peak of his popularity and power over others. The two narrations demonstrate distinctly different forms of first-person narrative. Intimacy with the reader is attained by both the atemporal, fragmented text of the pauper as well as the chronologically orthodox narration of the actor. By a contrived appeal to the reader's intellect, the first narration emphasizes the moral and ethical aspects of human nature whereas the second one calls attention to the physical and the erotic. Ending abruptly, the actor's narrative voice is replaced by that of the philosopher, who continues his journal by commenting on what he has just heard: "c'est un gaillard qui me fera rire, mais je le lui rendrai bien, ma vie vaut bien la sienne" (*IP,* quatrième feuille, p. 301). Although he admires his friend's worldly success, he also criticizes the state of social "inclusion" because it breeds hypocrisy. The reader must not conclude from this, however, that the human condition is categorically condemned. The philosopher continues his memoir by seeking an answer to the question "qu'est-ce qu'un homme? Est-ce la naissance qui le fait?" (*IP,* cinquième feuille, p. 303). The narrator's attempt to resolve this problem reveals the third consequence of his intimacy with the reader—the latter's realization that in his quest for self-knowledge lies man's humanity.

Ultimately, *L'Indigent Philosophe* focuses on one's potential for self-fulfillment in society. This assertion is important, for it contrasts with the interpretation that this text is a misanthropic condemnation of worldliness. A case in point is Pierre Jacoebée's study of this essay (see note 2). He divides Marivaux's journalistic works into fictional frameworks revealing two moral orders—charity and God's kingdom as opposed to ignorance and worldly pride. The philosopher-pauper, physically and spiritually removed from society, is therefore viewed as seeking to enter the order of "Charité" (Jacoebée, pp. 44-70, 120-40, *passim*). Jacoebée, it seems, has fallen into the trap the narrator has set for the unwary reader. Just because his economic situation forces him to withdraw from society does not mean that his memoir is a negation or condemnation of the world. Precisely the opposite is true—in order to assert himself and remain a successful Marivaudian character, the narrator must maintain his link with society. Critics who see in Marivaux's works the seeds of social reform or metaphysical escapism are misreading him. The idea that man cannot hope to penetrate the mysteries of God as long as he remains a mystery to himself is further elaborated in *Le Cabinet du Philosophe.*[5] Through his intimacy with the reader, the narrator gains his support for the assertion that worldliness is not only preferable but superior to social exclusion. Thus, the narrator emphasizes that his own situation is a result of unfortunate circumstances rather than a desire to attain a higher moral order:

> pour avoir du plaisir, il n'est pas nécessaire de se ruiner, de devenir pauvre: la pauvreté est une cérémonie qu'on peut retrancher, ce n'est pas elle qui m'a rendu joyeux et content comme je le suis; je l'étais avant que d'avoir tout mangé; mais si j'avais à recommencer, si on me remettait dans mon premier état, j'aimerais mieux faire des folies ruineuses, qui seraient du moins gaies pendant qu'elles dureraient, que de faire de ces folies tristes, dures et meurtrières; j'aimerais mieux avoir le plaisir d'être fou, que d'avoir la douleur de faire le sage, avec tout l'honneur qui m'en reviendrait.
>
> (*IP*, première feuille, p. 280)

This is a rather remarkable affirmation of the pleasure principle! With its inherent potential for individual self-gratification, society must be worth maintaining. By seeking to define a "man," the narrator is seeking to affirm those humanistic values that are opposed to ignorance. It is within the context of "le monde" and life on earth that the philosopher pursues his quest: "Ce qui est en cause, c'est non de vivre selon la vérité, mais de vivre la vérité en société."[6]

The narrator, nevertheless, has a great deal of difficulty defining the true man he is seeking. Instead of the expected affirmations, one finds a series of negations: "Ce n'est ni la naissance ni les richesses qui le font, ce n'est pas non plus celui qui a de l'esprit, ce n'est pas la créature qui pense" (*IP*, cinquième feuille, p. 309). Although these are qualities of "man" they do not adequately define a Man. At best, they are instruments to be used in the formation of the final product. Just when the reader expects the philosopher's search to end with a definition of a "man," he receives only the following elusive answer:

> Un homme c'est cette créature avec qui vous voudriez toujours avoir affaire, que vous voudriez trouver partout, quoique vous ne vouliez jamais lui ressembler. Voilà ce que c'est: vous n'avez qu'à étendre ce que je dis là; tous les hommes la cherchent, cette créature, et par là tous les hommes se font leur procès, s'ils ne sont là pas tous comme elle. Adieu, l'homme sans souci n'y voit plus goutte.
>
> (*IP*, cinquième feuille, p. 309)

In typical Marivaux fashion, the reader is deceived by the coquettish nature of this "marivaudage." The balance between negations and affirmation results in the emptiness of no statement at all. The deeper he searches, the less the narrator sees, and in effect he ends his investigation with the words "l'homme sans souci n'y voit plus goutte" and goes on to a different topic.

The narrative focal point of *L'Indigent Philosophe* is where the social and non-social, inclusion and exclusion, meet. Suspended between these two states, the philosopher searches for equilibrium. In his effort to define the social fabric, he transforms his solitude into a positive force. Using the written word as his link to the world and to posterity, "se dire" becomes synonymous with "être." The reader, enticed by the narrator's stylistic "coquetterie," becomes a catalyst in the transformation of pauper into philosopher and ultimately into a "man." The pauper's memoir-journal affirms not only his own vitality, but that of the human condition as well. By seeking to define what is truly human, the text reaffirms the universality of the narrative "je."

Notes

1. Pierre Carlet de Chamblain de Marivaux, "L'Indigent Philosophe," in *Journaux et Œuvres diverses,* ed. F. Deloffre and M. Gilot (Paris: Garnier, 1969), première feuille, p. 276. Subsequent references are to this edition and will be represented by IP.

2. For a study of first-person narrative, see Jean Rousset, "L'Emploi de la première personne chez Chasles et Marivaux," *Cahiers de l'Association Internationale des Etudes Françaises,* 19 (1967), 101-14. See also Jean Rousset, *Forme et Signification: Essai sur les structures littéraires de Corneille à Claudel* (Paris: Librairie José Corti, 1962). Particularly relevant to this study is W. Pierre Jacoebée, *La Persuasion de la Charité—Thèmes, Formes et Structures dans les Journaux et Œuvres diverses de Marivaux* (Amsterdam: Rodopi, 1976).

3. Ronald C. Rosbottom, "Marivaux and the Possibilities of the Memoir-Novel," *Neophilologus,* 56 (1972), 43-49.

4. See Felicia Sturzer, "'Marivaudage' as Self-Representation," *French Review,* 49 (1975), for an elaboration of this concept.

5. Pierre Carlet de Chamblain de Marivaux, "Le Cabinet du Philosophe," in *Journaux et Œuvres diverses,* ed. F. Deloffre and M. Gilot (Paris: Garnier, 1969), troisième feuille, pp. 353-54.

6. Bernard Dort, "A la recherche de l'amour et de la vérité: Esquisse d'un système marivaudien," *Les Temps Modernes,* 189 (1962), 1058-87.

Marie-Paule Laden (essay date March 1983)

SOURCE: Laden, Marie-Paule. "The Pitfalls of Success: Jacob's Evolution in Marivaux's *Le paysan parvenu.*" *Romanic Review* 74, no. 2 (March 1983): 170-82.

[*In the following essay, Laden discusses issues of transparency and reliability associated with the first-person narration of* Le paysan parvenu.]

If the third-person discourse of an omniscient narrator carries a presumption of truth, especially when it is the voice of an author anonymous save on the title page, first-person narration invites suspicion. Although even with a narration in the third person the reader must form conclusions as to the veracity, consistency, and scope of the narrator's vision, first-person narrative, whatever its claims of forthrightness, cannot shed its veil of subjectivity. It is, if not a lie, at least a puzzle. As the discourse of the narrator infiltrates and colors the story told, we have to sift through clues to reach our own idea of what the narrator and characters are like. Discourse purporting to be transparent, a vehicle, acquires a curious thickness or opacity we must pierce; perhaps this situation appealed to Marivaux as much by its irony as by its extension to the literary medium itself of a problematic of masks and truth which so often furnished the theme of eighteenth-century literature. With characteristic sophistication Marivaux complicated what seemed a clear opposition of surface to depth, of apparent to real identity. The intuited identity on which *La Vie de Marianne* turns is identical to neither; this gap (the non-identity of identities) and its convergence propel both the story and its telling, ultimately joining them. At first glance *Le Paysan parvenu* may seem simpler, a lesson in deception worthy of its picaresque forerunners. Yet when we consider Jacob—a peasant, crude, *épais,* but possessing insight into his own *épaisseur* and the knack of seeing through worldly façades—and when we try to account for the book's lack of conclusion (an abrupt end which is more conclusive than it might first appear),[1] it is by no means clear who Jacob really is.

Jacob himself does not seem to suffer from any problem of identity.[2] He knows and proclaims who he is: a peasant. The narrator insists on the importance of his origins from the start: "Le titre que je donne à mes mémoires annonce ma naissance; je ne l'ai jamais dissimulée à qui me l'a demandée, et il me semble qu'en tout temps Dieu ait récompensé ma franchise là-dessus."[3] And indeed, together with his "bonne mine" (p. 29), his peasant origin is his main asset at first. Males as well as females are taken with his rustic ingenuousness, which amuses the sophisticated high society as well as the servants: "Les domestiques m'affectionèrent tout d'un coup; je disais hardiment mon sentiment sur tout ce qui s'offrait à mes yeux; et ce sentiment avait souvent un bon sens villageois qui faisait qu'on aimait à m'interroger" (p. 28).

This refreshing spontaneity, however, is a quality that Jacob promptly turns to his advantage: "Je n'étais pas honteux des bêtises que je disais pourvu qu'elles fussent plaisantes; car à travers l'épaisseur de mon ignorance, je voyais qu'elles ne nuisaient jamais à un homme qui n'était pas obligé d'en savoir davantage" (p. 30). What the narrator is telling us here is that Jacob acts and speaks according to his audience's preconceived idea of what can be expected from a peasant. In other words, Jacob plays a role from the start; he already detaches himself from himself to fit a part assigned to him from the outside. For Jacob the self becomes a wondrous object to be admired: "Mon séjour à Paris m'avait éclairci le teint et, ma foi! quand je fus équipé, Jacob avait fort bonne façon" (p. 32).

The first part of this sentence is clearly the narrator's utterance; but the second part is more problematic. The switch from first to third person shows that the dissociation is not between the narrator and the protagonist, separated by a gap of many years, but exists also at the level of the protagonist, who objectifies himself in order to contemplate himself. Such a structure in which "Jacob" occupies the position of complement is not an isolated example, as witness the sentence "Avant le dîner j'eus la joie de voir Jacob tranformé en cavalier" (p. 155).[4]

This notion of progress, of gradation, is central to the understanding of Jacob's character, and it is by introducing into the self a dialectical movement that he can gauge his success. No total repudiation of the old self is possible, nor even the union of an antithesis, but rather a combination of identity and difference. As the narrator points out, without his former self he could not enjoy the new one fully: "Car c'était comme Jacob que j'étais si délicieusement étonné de me voir dans cet équipage, c'était de Jacob que M. de La Vallée empruntait toute sa joie. Ce moment-là n'était doux qu'à cause du petit paysan" (p. 226). The existential singularity of this split but cumulative identity is underlined when Jacob chooses a name to fit his new condition on marrying Mlle Habert. Retaining his peasant name of "Jacob" ("Il est beau ce nom-là . . . je m'y tiens," p. 85), he adds to it "de La Vallée." Although M. de La Vallée needs his peasant personality to measure his progress, he similarly uses others as yardsticks: "Je vécus là deux jours avec des voituriers qui me parurent très grossiers; et c'est que je ne l'étais plus tant, moi" (p. 53; cf. also p. 175).

Hence the compulsion to move on continually. He abandons Geneviève as soon as he feels superior to her. And it is evident that Mlle Habert would have known the same fate had Marivaux finished his novel (her forthcoming death is already hinted at, p. 225) "parce que," as Jacob puts it, "ce ne serait pas ma pareille que j'aimerais. Je ne m'en soucierais pas, ce serait quelque personne qui serait plus que moi; il n'y a que cela qui me ferait envie" (p. 133). The epitome of this superiority is someone of a rank so lofty that the distance from Jacob seems unbridgeably great. "C'était de cette distance qu'on venait à moi, ou que je me trouvais tout d'un coup porté jusqu'à une personne qui n'aurait pas seulement dû savoir que j'étais au monde" (p. 135).

Paradoxically, it is precisely when distance becomes impossibly great that Jacob can cease to be a non-entity. The person who should be unaware of his existence but knows him, creates him. Mme de Ferval's attentions in a sense give him birth: Mme de Ferval "était une ces femmes enfin qui nous tiraient, mon orgueil et moi, du néant où nous étions encore: car avant ce temps-là m'étais-je estimé quelque chose? avais-je senti ce qu'était qu'amour-propre?" (ibid.). Distance, too, is recursive: the distance of difference between distance and lack of distance. Characteristically, the protagonist cannot help comparing his relationship with Mme de Ferval to that he has with Mlle Habert, "qui avait débuté par me dire que j'étais autant qu'elle, qui ne m'avait pas donné le temps de m'enorgueillir de sa conquête, et qu'à son bien près, je regardais comme mon égale: N'avais-je pas été son cousin? Le moyen après cela, de voir une distance sensible entre elle et moi?" (ibid.).

If Jacob can only love someone above his station, "quelque personne qui serait plus que moi," it means that the object of his desire is never attainable, that he conceives of life as an ever-receding future. Under these circumstances the notion of desire itself becomes a paradox. When Jacob's desire is spurred by an image of satisfaction projected into the future, it becomes a suicidal force foreseeing and laboring toward its own extinction. When it is a desire for misalliance, a protension toward a tension, the object pales into insignificance beside the mere fact of its position, its otherness. Since the desired object disappears as such—either once secured (because no longer desired) or from the beginning (because what is desired is not the object in its essence but simply its prestige)—desire turns into the pursuit of illusions, if not the illusion of pursuit. Pursuit or flight? Jacob's peasant self is essential for him, since it is the starting-point from which he measures his progress in this *fuite en avant,* but the more his peasant self becomes a reference point rather than the crude, vital energy of a real being, the more Jacob risks being left without any identity. If Jacob's desire is a force of nature (the aggressiveness of the peasant), the more Jacob succeeds in distancing himself from his natural essence, the more the entire movement is imperilled, risks losing its mainspring and collapsing. The logic of desire is in either case one of sudden reversal, of failure through success. Its pendular menace hangs over Jacob's whole ascension, preparing the structure of the catastrophic scene upon which the novel closes. Such a vision of Jacob's desire need not blind us to the overreaching comic spirit of the novel. Sudden reversals typify the structured commonality of many comic and tragic situations. Comedy is usually predicated on catastrophes, and its twists are all the more elegant as they are crushing. A characterization of the final scene as catastrophic does not constitute a claim that Marivaux intended us to read his novel as a tragedy, nor is it fundamentally at odds with an appreciation of those comic elements that pervade the novel (so undeniable that the work is often labelled a masculine, broader, and more comic version of *La Vie de Marianne*).[5] To assert a tragic intention would be to make a claim not only improbable, but also unjustifiable and irrelevant. As regards Jacob's desire, at issue is not an esthetic framework which makes us see a situation as tragic or comic, but rather a mechanism which structures the narrative so that it can become either.

Jacob's ascent, therefore, flirts with paradox, since the person who rises is not the same one who wanted to rise. In Jacob's behavior, the means of his ascension are also evidence of a fundamental change in him. For instance, the subversion of nature and Jacob's need for distance vis-à-vis himself and others emerge in his use and abuse of language. Taking language as a social mask, Jacob modifies his according to his audience. The sign for him has no intrinsic truth; as a formal means of exchange with others, it is utterly pliant to his aims. Even for others in Jacob's world the sign and the referent are totally independent. The narrator's remark about Mme de Fécour illustrates this dichotomy: "lui disiez-vous: j'ai du chagrin ou de la joie . . . elle n'entrait dans votre situation qu'à cause du *mot* et non pas de la *chose*" (p. 169, my emphasis). Jacob's relation of his story to Mlle Habert when he first meets her features a studied application of this dominance of form over facts:

> Je conçus aussi que mon histoire était très bonne à lui raconter et très convenable.
>
> J'avais refusé d'épouser une belle fille que j'aimais, qui m'aimait et qui m'offrait ma fortune, et cela par un dégoût fier et pudique qui ne pouvait avoir frappé qu'une âme de bien et d'honneur. N'était-ce pas là un récit bien avantageux à lui faire? Et je le fis de mon mieux, d'une manière naïve, et comme on dit la vérité. Il me réussit, mon histoire lui plut tout à fait.
>
> (p. 56)

This version of the affair with Geneviève evidently clashes with that given by the narrator a few pages before, and he himself ironically acknowledges as much ("et comme on dit la vérité"). But the contradiction is irrelevant, since what counts is the manner in which the story is told. Because Mlle Habert believes it, the story becomes true and Jacob becomes what he says he is. The performative value which the sign derives from its place in socio-literary codes of style and behavior has totally supplanted its primary referential content.

Jacob's relationships with others are entirely based on his conscious handling of language. He plays up his peasant side with Mlle Habert, who shares his origins: "Je n'avais conservé cette tournure avec Mlle Habert que parce qu'elle me réussissait auprès d'elle, et que je lui avais dit *tout ce qui m'avait plu* à la faveur de ce langage rustique; mais il est certain que je parlais meilleur français quand je voulais" (p. 90; my emphasis). He also exaggerates his peasant demeanor with noble ladies (e.g., his first mistress and Mme de Ferval) in order that his sexual aggressiveness may be expressed more openly without their taking offense or feeling threatened. (This is also evident in the under-lined part of Jacob's sentence regarding Mlle Habert.) Here the communication is double; the exchange be-tween peasant and noble—a relation of inferior to supe-rior—masks a sexual dialogue between hunter and prey, between superior and inferior. This double level of com-munication might be compared to those two levels, nonsense façade and aggressive intention, which Freud finds in jokes, and Jacob's license resembles that of a court jester. In dealing with his first mistress Jacob uses the two levels instinctively, but with Mme de Ferval he is quite aware of what he is doing; and so is she, ac-cording to the narrator: "et je vis que, toute réflexion faite, elle était bien aise de cette grossièreté qui m'était échappée; c'était une marque que je comprenais ses sentiments, et cela lui épargnait les détours qu'elle aurait été obligée de prendre une autre fois pour me les dire" (pp. 134-5).

In his relationships with men, however, Jacob downplays his peasant origins. On his way to Versailles he travels with three men, and Jacob is less voluble than usual: "Je m'observai beaucoup sur mon langage, et tâchai de ne rien dire qui sentît le fils du fermier de campagne" (p. 177). Jacob is as careful during his con-frontation with the elder Habert sister at the Presi-dent's—"Je m'observai un peu sur le langage, soit dit en passant" (p. 123)—and he adopts the language of a petit bourgeois in order to win over the President. It is by his versatility of language, by his brilliance in ma-nipulating it—as his eloquent and skillful play on the words "domestique" and "serviteur" demonstrate in the trial scene[6]—that Jacob outwits society's system of signs and makes his way in the world. His conception of language is not just stylistic: it does not consist sim-ply in finding the right equivalents for things, of show-ing the self off to best possible advantage, although this he also does. Jacob knows that the self is always many things and that mastery of language implies not only the use of the best system for the circumstances, but even recourse to two simultaneous systems.

Visual language is, of course, also represented in Jacob's multiplicity of language. He always resorts to it along with words, but he never uses it as brilliantly as during the trial scene, as he wins over most of the audi-ence before he starts speaking: "J'avais dit des yeux à l'une: il y a plaisir à vous voir, et elle m'avait cru; à l'autre: Protégez moi, et elle me l'avait promis. . . . Monsieur l'abbé même avait eu quelque part à mes in-tentions . . . de sorte que j'avais dejà les deux tiers de mes juges pour moi, quand je commençai à parler" (p. 126).

Freed from the burden of intrinsic truth, language ac-quires a demiurgical power that escapes the speaker. In-stead of representing a preexisting concept, language creates it. Discourse comes first, and truth limps along after. For instance, when Jacob starts courting Mlle Habert, he has no feelings for her, yet he literally talks himself into "loving" her: "J'avoue pourtant que je tâchai d'avoir l'air et le ton touchant, le ton d'un homme qui pleure, et que je voulus orner un peu la vérité; et ce qui est singulier, c'est que mon intention *me gagna tout le premier*. Je fis si bien que j'en fus *la dupe moi-même*, et que je n'eus plus qu'à *me laisser aller* sans m'embarrasser de rien ajouter à ce que je sentais" (p. 96; my emphasis). Jacob's discourse has the same magic in his courtship of Mme de Fécour and Mme de Ferval, convincing himself as well as the ladies in question.

If words hold the power to create and transform, so do objects in **Le Paysan parvenu.** Jacob's outfits are not the sign of his present condition, they herald a future one. For instance, after changing his name, he explains to his wife that he needs a sword "pour être M. de La Vallée à forfait" (p. 155). The sword, however, soon be-comes much more than Jacob intends it to be. Like his words, it is at first a sign without substance, but then communicates to him a courage of which he was un-aware, as he draws his brand-new sword to rescue the comte d'Orsan: "Sans hésiter et sans aucune reflexion, me sentant une épée au côté, je la tire . . . et je vole comme un lion au secours du jeune homme" (pp. 227-8). Again the narrator (who relives the scene, as is indi-cated by his use of the present tense) insists on the lack of premeditation on the protagonist's part; rather than acting deliberately, he reacts spontaneously to forces beyond his control. When Jacob talks himself into lov-ing Mlle Habert or rescues the count, the usual distinc-tion between appearances and reality makes no sense. In light of such instances, critical disputations as to whether Jacob, M. de La Vallée, and the narrator are sincere or hypocritical are inevitably fruitless: they ig-nore what we must perforce call, in such illustrations, appearing reality or real appearances.

What is remarkable in this scene is that after his bout of heroism, M. de La Vallée no longer needs Jacob to de-light in his identity; it seems that his action has helped him unite his two selves. As Jacob affects a cool mod-esty, "un air de héros tranquille," the narrator observes: "je me regardais moi-même moins familièrement et avec plus de distinction qu'à l'ordinaire; et je n'étais plus ce petit polisson surpris de son bonheur, et qui trouvait tant de disproportion entre son aventure et lui. Ma foi! j'étais un *homme de mérite*, à qui la fortune *commençait à rendre justice*" (p. 229, my emphasis). This discarding of the peasant self has already been foreshadowed in a similar scene in which Jacob sponta-neously gives up the job he has been offered for the benefit of Mme d'Orville's ailing husband. After this first generous act, the narrator remarks: "ce discours quoique fort simple, n'était plus d'un paysan, comme vous voyez; on n'en sentait plus le jeune homme de village, mais seulement le jeune homme naïf et bon" (p. 193). These virtuous and heroic acts (prompted, as we have seen, by exterior forces) enable Jacob, or rather M. de La Vallée, to live up to the image of his worth which he projects to others. When the comte d'Orsan invites him to the theater, Jacob is acutely aware of this: "Il faut prendre garde à vous, M. de La Vallée, et tâcher de parler bon français; vous êtes vêtu en enfant de famille, soutenez l'honneur du justaucorps, et que votre entretien réponde à votre figure, qui est passable" (p. 236). It is evident, however, that if Jacob feels the need to address himself in the third person, the fusion between his two selves is not completed. It is not sufficient to discard the peasant to become M. de La Vallée. In spite of his recent self-promotion to the status of "homme de mérite," Jacob is not really at one with his new identity, as his devastating experience at the theater demonstrates.

Jacob gets carried away as he drives to the *Comédie* in the comte d'Orsan's luxurious carriage: "Jusqu'ici je m'étais assez possédé, je ne m'étais pas tout à fait *perdu de vue*; mais ceci fut plus fort que moi, et la proposition d'être ainsi mené gaillardement à la Comédie me tourna entièrement la tête" (p. 237). Up to this moment Jacob has never "lost sight" of himself; with a scrupulous detachment, he has always remained aware of his various selves and of what distance separates them. This distance has been the source of his delight. Ironically, when the distance between Jacob and M. de La Vallée, and between Jacob and the comte d'Orsan and his friends increases, Jacob loses his nerve: "Nous étions arrivés à la Comédie . . . Ici se dissipèrent toutes ces enflures de coeur dont je vous ai parlé, toutes ces fumées de vanité qui m'avaient monté à tête" (p. 239). Jacob is overwhelmed by the dazzling world before him, and dismayed by the disparity between its grandeur (as he perceives it) and what he sees as his own appearance and behavior. He is so bewildered and self-conscious that he cannot think and respond naturally to the demands of his situation. As with a tightrope walker who panics, stiffens, and falls, his fear increases his awkwardness and makes him seem even more hopelessly out of place than might otherwise be the case.

The supreme irony, of course, lies in the fact that it is at the theater, that temple of illusions, that Jacob's previously successful mask fails utterly; he loses control, gets lost in his various selves. There is no doing away with Jacob now; he comes back to the surface, not as the usual source of pleasure for M. de La Vallée, but as an embarrassment, as the peasant deprived of all his past charm and ingenuity: "Mes yeux m'embarrassaient, je ne savais sur qui les arrêter; je n'osais prendre la liberté de regarder les autres de peur qu'on ne démêlât dans mon peu d'assurance que ce n'était pas à moi à avoir l'honneur d'être avec de si honnêtes gens, et que

j'étais une figure de contrebande . . . et je tremblais qu'on ne connût à ma mine que ce monsieur-là avait été Jacob" (p. 240).

What had been Jacob's main weapon is turned against him in this short scene. Whereas Jacob's gaze has heretofore mesmerized others, making them mirrors for his narcissistic contemplation of his image, now he does not know where to look. His self-assurance is shattered; his "mine," which had opened all the doors and all the hearts before, now becomes a threat to himself. Jacob suddenly becomes a fraud in his own eyes, a "figure de contrebande"; the narrator has never used such a derogatory metaphor to describe the protagonist before. The magnificent outfit lined with red silk, in which he had gloried so much (p. 157), suddenly shrinks into "mon petit habit de soie" (p. 240). Jacob's world of metamorphoses (the narrator uses the word frequently) is completely shattered, deflated. He finally takes refuge in the darkness of the theater; on the stage, in fact. "C'était une tragédie qu'on jouait, *Mithridate,* s'il m'en souvient" (p. 241).

Did Marivaux need to finish his novel after this line? Whether we consider this scene a proper conclusion depends on our understanding of its relationship to Jacob's story until this point. The scene is a paradigm of the entire novel, built on a dialectic between inside and outside; yet it stands in curious opposition to it, almost as its comic reversal or burlesque. Jacob has relied all along on what was exterior to him: either his physical appearance, or a language conditioned by what was expected of him by others. Here, on the contrary, his impression of being inadequate seems to come from inside ("le comte d'Orsan continuait de parler sans s'apercevoir de ce qui se passait sur mon compte," p. 241), and it shatters the façade.

How is all this possible? Why does this final scene undo all of Jacob's laborious climb in one precipitous slide into nothingness ("acheva de m'anéantir," p. 241)? Either the owner of the "bonne mine," the wearer of the mask, becomes faceless—"de ma contenance, je n'en parlerai pas, attendu que je n'en avais point" (p. 239)—or else the versatility of the joker, formerly Jacob's strength in adapting to diverse circumstances, now returns to mortify him as "mon hétéroclite figure," of which he says "je pense qu'il n'y avait rien de si sot que moi, ni de si plaisant à voir" (p. 240). Where he is normally natural, self-assured, charming, full of "bon sens villageois," Jacob now appears foolish and bumbling; even his gestures are awkward ("si gauche"), constrained, mechanical "courbettes de corps courtes et fréquentes" which others laugh at and elicit as if playing with a toy. If Jacob was ever aware of how others viewed him, it was to manipulate and exploit their image of him. Here, on the contrary, Jacob's desperate self-consciousness only plunges him deeper into humiliation, and he is more the victim of appearances than their master.

Strangest, perhaps, is that the confident upstart, the energetic impostor, should suddenly yield to total panic ("me confondirent et m'épouvantèrent," "je tremblais"), should become "un homme qui se sauve" (pp. 239-41). Jacob's reaction is not just a loss of nerve. As he pointedly explains, the novelty of the experience is not responsible: "Pour étonné . . . ce n'aurait été que signe que je n'avais jamais été à la Comédie, et il n'y aurait pas eu grand mal" (ibid.). Jacob's panic stems from shame, from moral considerations heretofore extraneous: "c'était une confusion secrète de me trouver là, un certain sentiment de mon *indignité*" (my emphasis). Twice the narrator uses the word "honteux," and his language translates his shame by its deliberate self-depreciation in imagery and style (the contrast between the "honnêtes gens" and his "figure de contrebande," and the loss of self-worth he insists on by calling attention to "cette expression qui n'est pas trop noble"). The whole tone of the narration becomes as moralizing as a sermon, lapsing almost into the triteness of the maxim: "Il y en a qui, à ma place auraient eu le front de soutenir cela, c'est-à-dire qui auraient payé d'effronterie; mais qu'est-ce qu'on y gagne? Rien. Ne voit-on pas bien alors qu'un homme n'est effronté que parce qu'il devrait être honteux?" (ibid.). Jacob's recantation goes with the shame that prompts the excessive self-mockery of the narrator's description, the references to himself as "un si petit compagnon," "si sot," "si plaisant à voir."

This extraordinary palinode is hard to account for. Must we consider it illogical, a betrayal of the character as delineated, or does this violent reversal somehow fit the pattern of Jacob's behavior despite its seeming violation of *vraisemblance*? Our answer to this question is critical: it determines our understanding of who Jacob is, of the relationship between Jacob and M. de La Vallée, and ultimately our interpretation of the entire book. It is possible to argue that this scene is no departure at all from the story so far but rather the reemergence of Jacob's real nature, and that we should see in it a return to the origin or true course after a detour through society by Jacob's false persona, La Vallée. Such is the position taken by Marie-Hélène Huet, in one of the densest and most thought-provoking articles on Marivaux published to date: "c'est du côté de Jacob qu'il faut chercher l'authenticité dans une aventure parallèle à l'ascension de La Vallée . . . Jacob, fidèle à lui-même, coexiste avec l'intrigant La Vallée, et il faut croire que la brillante aventure de son double est aussi superficielle que la société qu'il fréquente, car jamais cette société n'oblige Jacob à oublier ses origines."[7] Huet adds later, "Au terme de la conquête, le héros se retire à la campagne; son rôle joué, l'ombre de La Vallée s'estompe, et le paysan entreprend alors de le ressusciter dans l'acte d'écrire" (ibid., p. 48). La Vallée in this view is thus a passport or disguise that lets Jacob the peasant see society as a tourist; but he is both afraid and unwilling to stray too far from his rightful place.

Huet's explanation as applied to the final scene echoes the platitudinous tone of the narrator: *chasser le naturel, il revient au galop.* After all, behind the mask of La Vallée the hero is just a peasant, and we cannot expect him to carry off his impersonation in the more discerning high society found at the theater. Huet's interpretation has troubling elements. For one thing, the final scene is anything but a "conquête"; though Jacob is initially giddy with triumph and anticipation at the thought of riding to the Comédie in a carriage, the disaster that ensues makes his pride seem so hollow that its emotional impact stretches beyond this last episode and undermines his entire previous ascension. Still, we could extend Huet's argument and attribute this failure to La Vallée, with Jacob emerging essentially unscathed. In fact, we could see in the protagonist a battle between Jacob and La Vallée, with La Vallée's discomfiture attributable to and confirming Jacob's victory. Such would seem to be Huet's view: "contre La Vallée, au fond, Jacob a gagné" (p. 44). The panic of the final scene might then be a form of neurotic phobia or paralysis prompted by the return of the repressed.

What complicates this boomerang hypothesis is that Jacob does not seem to be present at all in the final scene: i.e., even the character who threatens La Vallée, and who is identified with Jacob—je tremblais qu'on ne connût à ma mine que ce monsieur-là avait été Jacob"— does not have much to do with the Jacob we encounter at the outset of the story. La Vallée is not rejected like a failed graft; Jacob does not glance around, decide that high society is not all it is cracked up to be, and head back to till the fields in a Rousseauistic paradise. His somewhat concupiscent awe at the sight of "tant d'habits magnifiques" is the reaction of the parvenu more than of the peasant (strange that the master of signs should here take the superficial glories of society at face value), and it is difficult to see in this passage a renunciation of ambition, of the same becoming the other. Nor is this scene Jacob's "crise de conscience," as Huet maintains (p. 50), during which the "ordre naturel" overcomes and throws off the "ordre social" (p. 49).

Huet's claim is understandable, given the mixture of voices and ideas in the narration. On the one hand we do indeed find a plea for authenticity, couched in the disillusioned wisdom of ironic proverbs: "Quand on manque d'éducation, il n'y paraît jamais tant que lorsqu'on veut en montrer" (p. 239); feeling "on n'en voyait que mieux, parce que je m'efforçais de les cacher" (p. 240); "Ne voit-on pas bien alors qu'un homme n'est effronté que parce qu'il devrait être honteux?" (ibid.). We might feel justified in following the structure of these rhetorical reversals and considering the scene, as Huet implicitly does, an example of what one calls in French *qui perd gagne,* with the defeat of imposture ensuring the victory of authenticity.

And yet what authenticity, what natural order wins out here? Does the natural order include shame and snobbery, or is not the triumph of shame instead that of culture over the nature to which the peasent belongs? It is hard to see in these maxims of resignation what we are shown of Jacob's true nature: his boldness, his native peasant shrewdness. Rather than portraying an unbridgeable opposition between authenticity or self-identity, on the one hand, and the masquerade on the other, the narrator implies that transformation is possible, as long as it is progressive. La Vallée's difficulty simply comes from going too far too fast: "je n'avais pas passé par assez de *degrés* d'instruction et d'accroissements de fortune pour pouvoir me tenir au milieu de ce monde avec la hardiesse requise. J'y avais sauté *trop vite*" (p. 240, my emphasis). Although La Vallée cannot yet cut as fine a figure as he would have to were he to move in high society, he is at bottom no longer Jacob. He does not say "je tremblais qu'on ne connût à ma mine que ce monsieur-là *était* Jacob," but rather "que ce monsieur-là *avait été* Jacob." Furthermore, it is conceivable that La Vallée would fare better had he retained more of Jacob, and that his panic is evidence that he has lost what used to be his nature. The abject figure we see in this passage, skulking toward the protection of the crowd ("il me mena sur le théâtre, où la quantité de monde me mit à l'abri de pareils affronts, et où je me plaçai avec lui comme un homme qui se sauve," p. 241), is hardly Jacob: he has none of Jacob's natural energy, his charm, or his self-assurance.

If La Vallée fails here, it is perhaps because he has succeeded too well in distancing himself from the peasant Jacob. His story is akin to the tragedy of the *colonisé*, of the formerly noble savage in a frock coat who can no more go home again than he can be at home in his new world. Rather than Jacob's "prise de conscience," we should find here the hero taking another's point of view: he finally sees himself through society's eyes, but has lost the gift of manipulating that vision. If his panic is neurotic, it is not the triumph of the repressed (Jacob) but the triumph of repression.

Whereas the *colonisé* is an innocent victim, Jacob-La Vallée has contrived his own fate. Initially he distanced himself from himself in order to observe his progress, to gauge with reference to the peasant how far he had advanced. When the distance becomes too great the yardstick is too short to measure it, or the observer cannot focus on the beginning and the end at the same time. The protagonist cannot measure in "degrés" the success of his impersonation; losing his reference points, he panics. Without the union of extremes, without measure and distance mastered, his mind swings wildly between the peasant he has left behind and the dazzling world still beyond his reach. The problem for the hero is that the peasant is no longer a source of authenticity; he has been preserved only as a reference, and as such is inauthentic: he has the exterior qualities of the peasant without the life and strength inside. We can trace the hero's alienation, from the initial affirmation that he has never sought to hide his origins to his efforts to shroud them in vagueness or conceal them. (E.g., asked who he is, Jacob declares himself to be "le fils d'un honnête homme qui demeure à la campagne," pp. 199, 239; his wife "eût bien vu que c'était ce petit valet, ce petit paysan, ce petit misérable qui se trouvait si heureux d'avoir changé d'état, et il m'aurait été déplaisant (Jacob is speaking) qu'elle m'eût envisagé sous ces faces-là," p. 226.) The more La Vallée succeeds in hiding Jacob, the more the vitality of the peasant is eroded: as if, by a paradoxical reversal similar to the Marivaldian ironies strewn throughout this passage, the mask had devoured the face wearing it, until with nothing left to support it, the mask drops away to reveal the emptiness staring out behind.

Such an erosion of Jacob makes it impossible to accept Huet's contention, mentioned earlier, that the narrative is the peasant's attempt to resurect La Vallée ("le paysan entreprend alors de le ressusciter dans l'acte d'écrire"). Questions of who or what remains at the end of the final scene, what we can deduce about what happens afterward, and what the book itself represents go beyond the evidence of the narrative into a realm of speculation: the logic they must satisfy is one of the formal unity of an interpretation. Huet's idea seems to be that Jacob's impersonation fooled no one, and the book is Jacob's effort to redress the failure and restore the illusion in the person of La Vallée. Without our going over here an overly familiar problematics of writing—writing as the quest for an origin, as the product and translation of a fundamental gap or breach, as a means of suture—the loss of Jacob's vitality would require a different conclusion. The disappearance of Jacob's energy and of the bond between Jacob and La Vallée (i.e., of that projection or forward movement of the self which constitutes part of Jacob's identity) may be taken as a profoundly traumatic event, compulsively relieved in the act of narration. But rather than substituting success for failure, rather than dealing with what is a symptom or apparent problem, the stretch of the narrative retraces the entire development and deeper cause of the situation as the distance between La Vallée and Jacob increases and the initial character of Jacob is suppressed.

The notion of excessive distance, a transgression of some possible or permissible radius of action, or of too rapid a change—a transgression of some immanent measure or pace of ascension—can be made to fit the usual view of Marivaux's fondness for circumscribed experiments and limited challenges to the social order. The final predicament of Jacob-La Vallée is an insoluble problem, inscribed in the givens of Jacob's character. It is important, however, not to confuse the mechanism of this necessity with a notion that so much and no more can be expected from a peasant. If there is a fundamental conservatism behind the story, it derives perhaps from another source. The macabre image of the mask consuming the face behind it is a way of expressing the draining of life—its transformation into the mechanical—which is, according to Bergson, the mainspring of comedy. My feeling is that Jacob's humiliation is not simply comic, but draws on a darker and more brutal satire discernible beneath the exquisite ironies of Marivaux's writing. In his novels as well as his plays, Marivaux flirts with a violation of tone, with a comedy that plays on excess and transgression, on bared outrage and emotional discomfort. Here and there, and notably in this ultimate scene of *Le Paysan parvenu,* we see traces of the heterogeneous satire Bakhtin describes so well, as the viewpoint shifts and victimizes the hero.

The cyclism implicit in such "dialogical" reversals itself would arrest change: the inflation of an illusion leads inescapably to its deflation. In the case of Jacob's plight at the *Comédie,* however, it is not that the mask is lifted and reveals the reality beneath (Huet's authenticity of Jacob); the fact that nothing remains beneath suggests that what counts for Marivaux is the movement of reversal and paradox as such, a delight in the formal at the expense of the essential.

Notes

1. It is impossible to divine Marivaux's intent, and I do not presume here to provide an answer to the troubling question of why he left his best novels unfinished. The interested reader might glance at the hypotheses entertained by W. H. Trapnell, in "Marivaux's Unfinished Narratives," *French Studies* XXIV (July 1970), pp. 237-253. My essay deliberately sets aside the psychological speculations of literary history, looking instead at whatever consistency or internal logic the text itself may offer.

2. Unlike Marianne, whose memoirs are a search for identity both retrospective and prospective: her origins and her ultimate place in society. Remarks such as "Il valait mieux qu'une fille comme moi mourût d'indigence que de vivre aussi déplacée que je l'étais," or "Mais en vérité j'étais déplacée et je n'étais pas faite pour être là," are typical expressions of this problem in *La Vie de Marianne* (ed. Frédéric Deloffre (Paris: Garnier, 1963), pp. 45, 32).

3. Marivaux, *Le Paysan parvenu,* edited by Michel Gilot (Paris: Garnier-Flammarion, 1965), p. 26. Reference will be to this edition.

4. Related passages are found on p. 208 ("ce nom de Jacob . . ." et seq.), p. 219 ("Ce n'était que pour éviter une scène . . ." et seq.), and p. 226 ("Car c'était en me regardant comme Jacob . . .").

5. See especially Ruth Thomas, "The Critical Narrators of Marivaux's Unfinished Novels," *Forum of Modern Language Studies* (1973), pp. 363-69, and "The Role of the Narrator in the Comic Tone of *Le Paysan parvenu,*" *Romance Notes* 12, N° 1 (1970), pp. 134-41.

6. Pourquoi, reprit le président, me dis-tu que tu n'as été qu'un moment son domestique, puisque tu es actuellement à son service?

    Oui, Monsieur, à son service comme au vôtre, je suis fort son serviteur, son ami, et son prétendu, et puis c'est tout.

    (p. 124)

7. In *Le Héros et son double* (Paris: José Corti, 1975), p. 42.

Frank Abetti (essay date March 1983)

SOURCE: Abetti, Frank. "'La Honteuse Nécessité de Devenir Finesse': The Pathos of Style in *La Vie de Marianne.*" *Romanic Review* 74, no. 2 (March 1983): 183-201.

[*In the following essay, Abetti explores the relationship between pathos and realism in* La vie de Marianne.]

The new importance of the role of objects in the eighteenth-century novel and the greater concreteness of its language both suggest that, for a change, the novel means to convey a sense of physical reality. To give the change its due, we will remember that in the first half of the seventeenth century physical details had all but been banished from pastoral and heroic novels on the ground that they sullied the emotions of the inhabitants of "La Haute Romancie." A change in taste, however, tolled the death of the long novels of La Calprenède and Scudéry, although they were, in fact, an improvement over those of Gomberville, and brought these cerulean inhabitants back to earth. And as a result of the new air they breathed, the novel acquired a new density and richness.

The first novelist to lead his characters from the ideal world of emotions into the shadowy world of objects no doubt took a step forward in the direction of realism, although some felt that it was a step backwards for the novel. Du Plaisir's dislike for writers who have an eye for detail is characteristic of the period.

> Outre que ce détail de nez, de bouche, de cheveux, de jambes, ne souffre point de termes assez nobles, pour faire une expression heureuse, il rend l'Historien suspect de peu de vérité. Les Lecteurs sçavent que tous ces traits ne consistent que dans son imagination. . . . Enfin ce sortes de peintures ne plaisent point universellement; s'il est des Personnes qui aiment dans

les Hommes une taille fine, il en est qui aimeront davantage une taille pleine; et ainsi l'Autheur pêche contre le dessein qu'il a de faire aimer de tout le monde, ceux dont il parle.[1]

"At its most extreme," notes English Showalter, "this vision of truth leads to allegory."[2] However, the growing number of realistic details in the novel proves that the trend was away from allegory, towards greater literalism.

Now the realistic detail, whose importance for the eighteenth century can scarcely be exaggerated, "ne sert à rien," writes Genette,

> qu'à faire entendre que le récit [le] mentionne seulement parce qu'[il] est là, et que le narrateur, abdiquant sa fonction de choix et de direction du récit, se laisse gouverner par la "réalité," par la présence de ce qui est là et qui exige d'être "montré." Détail inutile et contingent, c'est le medium par excellence de l'illusion référentielle, et donc de l'effet mimétique: c'est un connotateur de mimésis.[3]

Critics consider a more literal use of language a sign of the times, symptomatic of the changing nature of fiction. In fact, the history of the novel is, to some extent, synonymous with the attempt of its language to become entirely literal.

To support this claim, one may bring to attention, as Philip Stewart has recently done, the variety of historical techniques used to create literal illusion.[4] Although the imitation of historical genres constitutes a formal strategy, readers historically determined content as well, literalizing what is only, in the words of Genette, a "connotateur de mimésis." Bayle, for example, charged Mme de Villedieu with inciting literal belief in her "nouvelles historiques" simply by including a few well known facts.[5]

Bayle's strictures came too late, however, for the attempt to pass fiction off as historical fact, while certainly an important factor in giving birth to the novel, had already lost its drive in the waning years of the seventeenth century, precisely when Bayle wrote his article for the *Dictionnaire historique et critique.*

René Démoris even goes so far as to call the years between 1680 and 1728—the period of most intense production of pseudo-memoirs—a period of crisis precisely because a break with history took place then.[6] Indeed, many novelists ceased paying homage to history and, after the fashion of Courtilz de Sandras, admitted the active part they played, as editors, in the compilation of memoirs.[7]

It would seem, then, that Stewart's argument for the use, or rather pillage, of history in the first half of the eighteenth century stands in need of revision. We might beneficially quote Frédéric Deloffre who gives, to my mind, a more accurate historical picture.

Ainsi, la recherche de la vraisemblance n'est pas le propre de la génération 1700-1715. Exigée des théoriciens du roman vers 1660-1670, elle inspire dans les vingt années qui suivent un renouvellement des genres et des techniques romanesques, grâce surtout à l'utilisation de l'histoire mise au service de l'illusion. Mais si le roman de cette période 1700-1715 rend, comme il le semble bien, un son nouveau, ne serait-ce que parce que le problème de la vraisemblance y est, non pas résolu—il l'était—mais remis en cause et finalement dépassé?[8]

Deloffre puts the use of history in its proper place, that is, in the twenty years following the first "nouvelles historiques." In addition, he maintains that already by 1715, if not earlier, representing reality was no longer the major concern of such important and influential writers as Hamilton, Lesage, Challes and Marivaux who, by that time, had all experimented with modes of writing inconsistent with realism.

These novelists developed a new mode of the novel, which I call pathos, deriving my terminology from Northrop Frye's *Anatomy of Criticism.* Pathos arises from a conflict between objective reality and the hero's experience of that reality or, to quote Frye, "between imaginative reality and the sort of reality which is established by a social consensus."[9] It would be a mistake, however, to assume that pathos replaced realism as the mode of the novel at a given moment in time. Both modes coexist in the novel in a dialectical relationship; and while the ratio of one mode to another may vary, their interaction remains a constant feature of the memoir-novel.

I propose to test this theory of modes against *La Vie de Marianne,* chosen as a typical example of the kind of novel which flourished between 1731 and 1761. On the one hand, by increasing the number of realistic details and the importance of the role of objects, Marivaux gives a material foundation to the world of the novel. On the other hand, Marivaux endows his heroine with a pathetic sensibility. Even the most "realistic" descriptions, I wish to argue, metaphorically refer to an inner state of consciousness. Thus the representation of objects—traditionally the privileged function of the novel—loses ground to the representation of emotions, accounting for, in Démoris' formulation, "la différence radicale que présentent les créations de Marivaux et de Prévost avec les oeuvres immédiatement antérieures."[10]

Jacques Derrida neatly sums up the change with reference to Rousseau, whose *La Nouvelle Héloïse* represents the summa of the pathetic novel's development. "En un mot, il rend à l'expression des émotions une propriété qu'il accepte de perdre, dès l'origine, dans la désignation des objets."[11]

This important change, wrought a whole generation before Rousseau's novel, has correctly been described as a turn inward, but has, for the most part, wrongly been interpreted. The memoir-novel does not make use of a pathetic mode to fill the void left by the loss of the material presence of objects, as might hastily be concluded from Derrida's statement. The novel only puts emotions into play in order to reveal their emptiness, which adds yet another dimension to its already complex structure, namely irony.

Irony erodes the sympathy won by a pathetic mode, just as pathos destroys the credibility gained by a realistic mode. Thus, if we may make a fanciful comparison, the novel's chances of coming into contact with empirical reality are doubly jeopardized, or about as good as d'Artagnan's chances of duelling with Aramis, considering the two formidable antagonists, irony and pathos, standing between them. D'Artagnan's apology runs as follows: "It is impossible that I shall be able to pay my debt to all three: for M. Athos has the right to kill me first, which greatly decreases the value of your bill, M. Porthos, whilst it renders yours, M. Aramis, of scarcely the slightest value."[12]

Yet literary criticism has labeled *La Vie de Marianne* realistic, unmindful of the presence of other modes and their disruptive effect on referential discourse. The translation of a text into explicit, assertive statements by obliterating its figurative dimension leaves a residue, and raises precisely the question of the "literary overflow."[13] Marianne's style fits the description of such an overflow, and so we will now address the question of the narrator and her style.

Already in the first paragraph, Marianne recognizes the importance of style to her story: "Il est vrai que l'histoire en est particulière, mais je la gâterai, si je l'écris; car où voulez-vous que je prenne un style?"[14] Marianne fears losing the appeal of her story by setting it down in writing because she doesn't know how to go about acquiring a style which would do justice to her wittiness in the salon: "Il est vrai que dans le monde on m'a trouvé de l'esprit; mais, ma chère, je crois que cet esprit-là n'est bon qu'à être dit, et qu'il ne vaudra rien à être lu." Marianne reveals, however, that women are considered brilliant conversationalists only because they make themselves, and consequently what they say, appear in the best possible light: "Nous autres femmes, car j'ai été de ce nombre, personne n'a plus d'esprit que nous, quand nous en avons un peu; les hommes ne savent plus alors la valeur de ce que nous disons; en nous écoutant parler, ils nous regardent, et ce que nous disons profite de ce qu'ils voient." In the next paragraph, Marianne illustrates this general reflection with an example, proving that style is not all that foreign to her.

> J'ai vu une jolie femme dont la conversation passait pour un enchantement, personne au monde ne s'exprimait comme elle; c'était la vivacité, c'était la fi-

nesse même qui parlait: les connaisseurs n'y pouvaient tenir de plaisir. La petite vérole lui vint, et elle en resta extrêmement marquée: quand la pauvre femme reparut, ce n'était qu'une babillarde incommode. Voyez combien auparavant elle avait emprunté d'esprit de son visage!

The example shows that even the dullest topic of conversation might be rendered agreeable by the charm of the speaker, and perhaps unwisely lays Marianne open to the same criticism. Indeed, it turns out that Marianne too owed her reputation of a wit to her visual appeal. When she was young and pleasing to the eye, she had no trouble in captivating an entire audience. Nor does Marianne gloss over the reason for her success:

> Combien de fois me suis-je surprise à dire des choses qui auraient eu de la peine à passer toutes seules! Sans le jeu d'une physionomie friponne qui les accompagnait, on ne m'aurait pas applaudie comme on faisait, et si une petite vérole était venue réduire cela à ce que cela valait, franchement, je crois que j'aurais perdu beaucoup.

Following her discovery of how easily men are duped by a pretty face, Marianne admits having frequently used it to her advantage; she even goes so far as to warn the reader against the seductive charms of the spoken word, confident that in her old age she is forever absolved from such a charge.

> Il n'y a pas plus d'un mois, par exemple, que vous me parliez d'un certain jour (et il y a douze ans que ce jour est passé) où, dans un repas, on se récria tant sur ma vivacité; eh bien! en conscience, je n'étais qu'une étourdie. Croiriez-vous que je l'ai été souvent exprès, pour voir jusqu'où va la duperie des hommes avec nous? Tout me réussissait, et je vous assure que dans la bouche d'une laide, mes folies auraient paru dignes des Petites-Maisons: et peut-être que j'avais besoin d'être aimable dans tout ce que je disais de mieux. Car à cette heure que mes agréments sont passés, je vois qu'on me trouve un esprit assez ordinaire. . . .

Now few readers find Marianne ordinary, even though her story scarcely contains unprecedented misfortunes. What, we may well ask, causes readers to look twice at her oft-told tale of misfortune? What sets it apart from so many others on the same theme, including Mlle de Tervire's, which reveal the plight of abandoned (but always virtuous!) orphans succored by unscrupulous villains? Obviously her story does not rely on seductive visual impressions for its popularity since what we have before us is a written document.

The freshness and originality of Marianne's style compensates for the bloom that has faded from her cheeks, and deputizes as well for "le jeu d'une physionomie friponne" which she considers vital to arouse interest in her story. Accordingly, Marianne's warning against seductive visual impressions accompanying spoken words applies equally to style in writing since both serve the same purpose. Both offer themselves as substitutes for an absence of meaning.

Consequently, we should be wary not only of Marianne's claim that she doesn't have the first idea what style is, but also of her claim that there is some substance to her story, which, if we look closely, is mostly finesse, or style.

Yet, for all its stylistic excesses, Marianne's story more successfully evokes pity than Mlle de Tervire's more stream-lined version of similar misfortunes. In fact, Marivaux himself underscored the inability of rapid narration to elicit a pathetic response: "Je trouve à mon gré qu'on a retranché des romans tout ce qui pouvait les rendre utiles et souvent même intéressants. Ceux qu'on compose à présent ne sont que de simples aventures racontées avec une hâte qui amuse le lecteur à la vérité, mais qui ne l'attendrit, ni ne le touche."[15] This remark provides us with a valuable insight into the nature of pity and how it is awakened. It is precisely Marianne's style, or the figurative dimension of her language, that accounts for the pathos of her story. Marianne's prose does not restrict itself to a "descriptive and denotative use of language"[16] the way Mlle de Tervire's does. Her language, although deceptively concrete, thereby giving the illusion of reality, corresponds in fact to Rousseau's "langage passionné," which displaces referential meaning inward.[17]

We find a number of examples of language being used metaphorically in this way in *La Vie de Marianne*. Consider, for example, Marianne's arrival in Paris. Although the novel pays some attention to the outside world, its main drive is unmistakably inward. "Il y avait une douce sympathie entre mon imagination et les objets que je voyais" (p. 17), says Marianne, showing signs of a precocious romantic sensibility, and perhaps even initiating what has become, thanks to romantic nature poetry, a familiar pattern of continuity—or "douce sympathie"—between imagination and perception, described as follows by one critic: "Souvent le monde extérieur et le monde intérieur se mêlent si profondément que rien ne discerne plus les images que perçoivent les sens et les chimères de l'imagination."[18]

Marianne's semi-comatic state clarifies, I think, the role imagination plays in perception and the tricks it plays on memory. From what Marianne says, she was in no condition to observe anything at all: "je ne saurai vous dire ce que je sentis en voyant cette grande ville, et son fracas, et son peuple, et ses rues . . . je n'étais plus à moi, je ne me ressouvenais plus de rien; j'allais, j'ouvrais les yeux, j'étais étonnée, et voilà tout" (p. 17). And even upon regaining consciousness, Marianne clearly imagined more than she saw, or so the following reflection leads us to believe.

> Il y a des âmes perçantes à qui il n'en faut pas beaucoup montrer pour les instruire, et qui, sur le peu qu'elles voient, soupçonnent tout d'un coup tout ce qu'elles pourraient voir.

> La mienne avait le sentiment bien subtil, je vous assure, surtout dans les choses de sa vocation, comme était le monde. Je ne connaissais personne à Paris, je n'en avais vu que les rues, mais dans ces rues il y avait des carrosses, et dans ces carrosses un monde qui m'était très nouveau, mais point étranger. Et sans doute, il y avait en moi un goût naturel qui n'attendait que ces choses-là pour s'y prendre, de sorte que, quand je les voyais, c'était comme si j'avais rencontré ce que je cherchais.

The movement of the description, from Paris to the streets, from the streets to the carriages in them, and from the carriages to the people in them, duplicates the conversion of outward, visible properties into an inner feeling, which is precisely the action of metaphor.[19]

First we feel the bustle and movement of the capital because Marianne is elated at the prospect of living there. The quickening tempo of the narration ("et son fracas, et son peuple, et ses rues") helps convey this feeling. The suspicion we may have that Marianne owed her first impression of Paris to her ebullience rather than to anything she actually observed is reinforced when just a short while after her arrival the situation changes drastically: her protectress lies dying and Marianne, afraid of what is to become of her, calls the world a desert. "La frayeur alors s'empara de moi, et ce fut une frayeur qui vint de la certitude de la perdre: je tombai dans l'égarement; je n'ai de ma vie rien senti de si terrible; il me sembla que tout l'univers était un désert où j'allais rester seule" (p. 21). Marianne's feeling of solitude, the referent of the metaphor, stands in sharp contrast to the thickly populated streets she had traversed earlier in the day. We can be sure that language is being used metaphorically because Paris cannot be at once a desert and a busy metropolis. The patent falsity of the statement when taken literally invites us to accept it as a metaphor.[20]

In the next scene, Marianne gives free rein to her imagination out of fear for her safety, and this new emotion peoples the streets of Paris once more, this time with no-good villains.

> Je ne saurais pourtant vous dire précisément quel était l'objet de ma peur, et voilà pourquoi elle était si vive: tout ce que je sais, c'est que je me représentais la physionomie de mon hôte, que je n'avais jamais trop remarquée jusque là; et dans cette physionomie alors, j'y trouvais des choses terribles; celle de sa femme me paraissait sombre, ténébreuse; les domestiques avaient la mine de ne valoir rien. Enfin tous ces visages-là me faisaient frémir, je n'y pouvais tenir; je voyais des épées, des poignards, des assassinats, des vols, des insultes; mon sang se glaçait aux périls que je me figurais: car quand une fois l'imagination est en train, malheur à l'esprit qu'elle gouverne.

> (p. 26)

This description hardly gives a realistic portrayal of Marianne's actual situation: there are no assassins lurking around the corner imperiling her life. Again, the truth lies in the passion, not in the hostile world Marianne pictures herself in. We come to this reassuring conclusion by interpreting what Marianne says metaphorically, an interpretation authorized by the literal falsity of her statement.

The question of metaphorical truth raises an issue central to the rest of my remarks on language and style. Metaphor has been denied ontological significance until recently on two counts: either it says nothing beyond what ordinary language says, and thus is a mere ornament; or, worse still, it masquerades as literal language and the fiction it purveys passes for truth. For this reason, many philosophers consider figurative language a powerful instrument of error and deceit.[21]

The absence of a rigorous distinction between a malicious lie and a harmless metaphor raises an important question regarding literary texts, in which metaphor is common currency. How do we deal with a metaphor that is not patently false, and therefore does not call attention to its metaphorical status? I think we would agree that such an obvious example of metaphor as the one Marianne made in the grip of fear is not meant to deceive. It is an innocent metaphor that harms no one. But such a special case must not leave the impression that metaphorical discourse can so easily be distinguished from literal discourse.

The danger of confusing the two, slight at first, increases as the novel progresses, calling into question Marianne's claim that her story contains "faits" rather than "aventures d'imagination" (p. 376). Such a claim is valid only when the reader can distinguish for certain between literal and metaphorical discourse. Otherwise the danger looms of taking a metaphorical statement literally and accepting the fiction it purveys as fact.

The story Marianne tells to father St. Vincent of her ride home in M. de Climal's carriage illustrates that metaphor can be far from a harmless activity. The scene captures, in addition, the full intricacy of the relationship of language to truth and reality by managing to shift, by the end of the interview, each of the characters' faith in what is real.

Marianne's story does not limit itself to recording objective data. It includes confessions of inner feelings as well as data available to the senses. Thus, for example, Marianne's acceptance of the underclothes given to her by M. de Climal comes to our ears with the feeling of guilt at having accepted more than Climal's presents, or, what is the same thing, his desire. "Je vous avoue que je me trouvais bien embarrassée, car je voyais qu'il était sûr qu'il m'aimait, qu'il me donnait à cause de cela, qu'il espérait me gagner par là, et qu'en prenant ce qu'il me donnait, moi je rendais ses espérances assez bien fondées" (p. 39). It might be objected that

Marianne cannot take for granted the link, necessary to establish her guilt, between Climal's presents and his desire. Indeed, in all fairness to Marianne, the link between an act and its intention can never be established for certain. She cannot be as certain of his desire as of his presents, for which the evidence is referential. Intentions can only be suspected, never proven, which is in fact the excuse Marianne gives for having accepted the presents: "On m'a menée à lui comme à un homme charitable et pieux, il me fait du bien: tant pis pour lui si ce n'est pas dans de bonnes vues, je ne suis point obligée de lire dans sa conscience, et je ne serai complice de rien tant qu'il ne s'expliquera pas; ainsi j'attendrai qu'il me parle sans équivoque" (p. 40).

In saying this, Marianne expresses faith that there is such a thing as an unequivocal, i.e., entirely literal, language of passion—for example, a kiss. Now a kiss is, literally, an act, but is so invariably understood to express an emotion that the metaphorical meaning has well-nigh supplanted the literal meaning.

The interview Marianne has with father St. Vincent illustrates this substitutive process. The kiss becomes, in Marianne's version of her ride home with M. de Climal, a symptom of his ungovernable passion for her. Since she obviously wants to convince the father of M. de Climal's passion, she interprets the kiss metaphorically. The more circumspect father, on the other hand, shies away from anything but a literal interpretation of the kiss. Side by side, then, with the father's literalism runs Marianne's figurative language of passion. Thus we find two different assessments of the same situation, one upholding M. de Climal's charity, the other denouncing his love.

In the matter of M. de Climal's presents, consisting of "habits, linge, argent" (p. 138), the father seems on solid ground. Whereas we only have Marianne's word for M. de Climal's illicit love, the evidence of his charity is referential. The existence of the clothes may be vouched for by touching them, and who would deny the usefulness of clothes for a needy orphan? On the face of things, Marianne's charges seem unfounded.

In view of M. de Climal's charitable works, the father considers Marianne's unkind thoughts a product of her imagination: "Lui jaloux! Lui vous aimer! Dieu vous punira pour cette pensée-là, ma fille; vous ne l'avez prise que dans la malice de votre coeur" (p. 138). He then takes her up sharply on the dishonesty of her behavior: "Quelle conduite! . . . porter la mauvaise humeur et la rancune jusqu'à être ingrate envers un homme si respectable, et à qui vous devez tant. . . . Quel malheur qu'un esprit comme le vôtre! oh! en vérité, votre procédé me scandalise." Marianne's scandalous behavior consists in giving other than a literal meaning, i.e., one predicated on use, to the clothes. For some reason best known to herself she interprets the clothes as a sign of M. de Climal's love.

The construction Marianne puts on his presents is resolutely rejected by father St. Vincent, who insists that M. de Climal acted toward her more like a parent than a lover: "Voyez, vous voilà d'une propreté admirable; qui est-ce qui dirait que vous n'avez point de parents? et quand vous en auriez, et qu'ils seraient riches, seriez-vous mieux accommodée que vous l'êtes?" (pp 138-39).

Marianne, perhaps realizing what a hopelessly literal mind the good father has, speaks in a language he can more readily understand:

> Vous parlez de mes hardes, elles ne sont que trop belles; j'en ai été étonnée, et elles vous surprennent vous-même; tenez, mon père, approchez, considérez la finesse de ce linge; je ne le voulais pas si fin au moins; j'avais de la peine à le prendre, surtout à cause des manières qu'il a eues avec moi auparavant.
>
> (p. 139)

Marianne forces the father to actually touch the under-clothes, so that he may feel their fine texture. Clothes, as well as words, may have a "style" exceeding their utilitarian capacity. Although unquestionably useful objects for a penniless orphan, the clothes may be interpreted differently on account of their "finesse." Indeed, they flatter her vanity as well as fill a specific need. In this connection, M. de Climal bade Marianne look in the mirror to judge the effect of her new finery. According to Marianne, then, M. de Climal did not give her presents out of mere charity, since less fine clothes would have sufficed for that purpose.

Turning now to the kiss, Marianne's case against M. de Climal seems airtight—a respectable gentleman does not go around kissing young girls. "Quand on n'est que pieux, parle-t-on du coeur d'une fille, et lui laisse-t-on le sien? lui donne-t-on des baisers comme il a encore tâché de m'en donner dans ce carrosse?" Marianne asks. In response to Marianne's viperous attacks against his friend's piety, the father first voices incredulity:

> Un baiser, ma fille . . . un baiser! vous n'y songez pas! comment donc! savezvous donc qu'il ne faut jamais dire cela, parce que cela n'est point? Qui est-ce qui vous croira? Allez, ma fille, vous vous trompez, il n'en est rien, il n'est pas possible; un baiser! quelle vision! ce pauvre homme!
>
> (p. 139)

But significantly he does not rule out the actual physical contact, just the motivation behind the kiss: "C'est qu'on est cahoté dans un carrosse, et que quelque mouvement lui aura fait pencher sa tête sur la vôtre; voilà tout ce que cela peut être, et que, dans votre chagrin, vous aurez pris pour un baiser" (pp. 139-40).

In this manner, the father reduces the "kiss" to its basic facticity, thereby neutralizing its meaning. Marianne, however, brings forward more evidence to support her argument that M. de Climal is a sly hypocrite.

> Et puis, si je m'étais trompée sur ce baiser que vous ne croyez point, M. de Climal, dans la suite ne m'aurait pas confirmée dans ma pensée; il n'aurait pas recommencé chez Mme Dutour, ni tant manié, ni tant loué mes cheveux dans ma chambre, où il était toujours à me tenir la main qu'il approchait à chaque instant de sa bouche, en me faisant des compliments dont j'étais toute honteuse.
>
> (p. 140)

Again, after an initial moment of surprise, the father reduces the act to its facticity.

> Des cheveux qu'il touchait, qu'il louait? M. de Climal, lui! je n'y comprends rien; à quoi rêvait-il donc? Il est vrai qu'il aurait pu se passer de ces façons-là; ce sont de ces distractions qui ne sont pas convenables, je l'avoue; on ne touche point aux cheveux d'une fille: il ne savait pas ce qu'il faisait; mais n'importe: c'est un geste qui ne vaut rien.
>
> (p. 140)

Marianne, still unconvinced, asks, "Et ma main qu'il portait à sa bouche . . . mon père, est-ce encore une distraction?" Undaunted, the father defends his friend by writing off that action as a mere gesture, done out of habit: "Il y a mille gens qui vous prennent par la main quand ils vous parlent, et c'est peut-être une habitude qu'il a aussi; je suis sûr qu'à moimême, il m'est arrivé d'en faire autant."

According to the father, then, M. de Climal's actions are completely unmotivated. His arguments have the common strategy of reducing acts to their facticity, which eliminates any meaning they may have.

Marianne, however, reserves a surprise for the father: "A la bonne heure, mon père, mais quand vous prenez la main d'une jeune fille, vous ne la baisez pas je ne sais combien de fois; vous ne lui dites pas qu'elle l'a belle, vous ne vous mettez pas à genoux devant elle, en lui parlant d'amour" (p. 140). Such idolatrous behavior truly shocks the good father—one only gets down on bended knee before God! Indeed, the vision of M. de Climal worshipping Marianne shakes his belief and at last tempts him to examine the meaning of his friend's behavior.

At first, however, he refuses to believe his ears, and even tries to silence Marianne:

> Ah! mon Dieu! s'écria-t-il, ah! mon Dieu! petite langue de serpent que vous êtes, taisez-vous. Ce que vous dites est horrible, c'est le démon qui vous inspire, oui,

le démon; retirez-vous, allez-vous-en, je ne vous écoute
plus; je ne crois plus rien, ni les cheveux, ni la main, ni
les discours: faussetés que tout cela! laissez-moi.

In spite of this apparently firm stand, the father has already begun to weaken. After first refusing to even listen, he next marks incredulity, then only surprise, and
finally resignation at Marianne's further revelations of
M. de Climal's behavior. Marianne, taking advantage of
the father's weakening, continues in the following vein.

Vous voulez que, dans la douleur et dans les extrémités
où je suis, un homme avec qui je n'ai été qu'une heure
par accident, et que je ne verrai jamais, m'ait rendue si
amoureuse de lui et si passionnée, que j'en aie perdu
tout bon sens et toute conscience, et que j'aie le courage et même l'esprit d'inventer des choses qui font
frémir, et de forger des impostures affreuses pour lui,
contre un autre homme qui m'aiderait à vivre, qui
pourrait me faire tant de bien, et que je serais si
intéressée à conserver, si ce n'était pas un libertin qui
fait semblant d'être dévôt, et qui ne me donne rien que
dans l'intention de me rendre en secret une malhonnête
fille!

(p. 142)

The father expresses disbelief of course, but no longer
tries to silence Marianne: "Ah! juste ciel, comme elle
s'emporte! Que dit-elle là? Qui a jamais rien ouï de
pareil? cria-t-il en baissant la tête, mais sans
m'interrompre." And when Marianne, after enumerating
all the advantages she is to have as Climal's mistress,
triumphantly dares the father to say that she has invented everything, he doesn't take her up; his feeble rejoinder, "voilà un furieux récit! Que faut-il que j'en
pense?" opens a further breach in his defenses. This irrecoverable slip marks the shift away from resistance,
towards acceptance. From this point on, he no longer
denies Marianne's evidence in the least. On the contrary, the father's doubts grow stronger and stronger as
Marianne proceeds with her story; in particular, the part
about the "solliciteur de procès" baffles him. "Vous me
tentez, ma fille," he admits: "ce solliciteur de procès
m'embarrasse, il m'étonne, je ne saurais le nier" (p.
143).

Far from silencing her this time, he avidly questions her
for more incriminating details: "C'est un homme de
mauvaise mine, n'est-ce pas? ajouta-t-il." At this point,
he marvels at each new bit of information instead of refusing point-blank to believe Marianne. Even his objections take the form of rhetorical questions; for example,
when he finds out what sort of arrangements M. de
Climal has made for Marianne, he feebly remonstrates:
"Mais, ma fille, voilà qui est étrange; si vous dites vrai,
à qui se fiera-t-on?" And by the end of her story he is
in such a weakened state of mind that he can only respond with a remark expressing pity for human frailty:
"Un homme comme M. de Climal! Que Dieu nous soit
en aide. Mais on ne sait qu'en dire: hélas! la pauvre

humanité, à quoi est-elle sujette? Quelle misère que
l'homme! quelle misère" (p. 144)! This remark signals
the melting of the father's last suspicions and final acceptance of Marianne's story.

In a surprising turnabout, then, the father abandons his
unimaginatively literal interpretation of his friend's actions, and accepts their figurative connotation. In particular, the fact that M. de Climal meant to have
Marianne learn to dance, play the piano and sing, sways
his opinion in her favor, for such accomplishments are
unquestionably frills, which do not come under the
heading of charity since they do not fill needs. At last
convinced of his friend's duplicity, he vociferates:
"Qu'est-ce que ces meubles, et que ces maîtres pour ces
fariboles? Avec qui veut-il que vous dansiez? Plaisante
charité qui apprend aux gens d'aller au bal" (p. 144)!

Thus only when the father discovers that M. de Climal's
"charity" exceeds Marianne's need does he accept
Marianne's interpretation and recognize it as love. This
interpretation of Climal's actions depends on various
forms of excess: the magnificence of the furniture, the
spending money in excess of Marianne's need, the
frivolous lessons and above all the finesse of the clothes.
The presents, then, both stand for love and point to its
figurative mode of representation. On the level of language, it is also style (the choice of a metaphor in place
of a proper expression) that induces belief in M. de
Climal's passion.

Moreover, the father accepts the truth value of metaphor. He accepts M. de Climal's passion on a par with
empirically verifiable phenomena such as the kiss.

Yet even while accepting in the end the consequences
of what he has just learned, the father urges on
Marianne an "innocence de pensée" hardly compatible
with M. de Climal's duplicity. "Tâchez même de croire
que vous avez mal vu, mal entendu; ce sera une disposition d'esprit, une innocence de pensée qui sera
agréable à Dieu, qui vous attirera sa bénédiction" (p.
144). We should note that once the link between outward signs and emotions is established in the father's
mind, he locates the possibility of error in the senses,
not in the correspondance between inside and outside
properties.

A further illustration of the father's change of faith is
provided by the use of the word "tout," which both
opens and closes the interview. In the opening paragraph, it has a substantial referent: "Habits, linge, argent, il vous a fourni de tout," said the father by way of
admonishing Marianne for her base ingratitude. In the
last paragraph, when Marianne finds herself practically
assured of losing M. de Climal's material assistance,
the father's promise of divine assistance fills her with
despair. "Moi! chère enfant! hélas! Seigneur, quelle

pitié! un pauvre religieux comme moi, je ne puis rien; mais Dieu peut tout" (p. 145). Here the word "tout" does not have a referent capable of filling Marianne's need. The father's empty promise testifies to his belief in a providential order beyond the world of the senses. This, of course, is entirely consistent with his belief in M. de Climal's passion, which also escapes sense perception.

With God as her only hope, Marianne finds her situation very bleak indeed.

> Je le saluai sans prononcer un seul mot, et je partis pour le moins aussi triste que je l'avais été en arrivant chez lui: les saintes et pieuses consolations qu'il venait de me donner me rendaient mon état encore plus effrayant qu'il ne me l'avait paru; c'est que je n'étais pas assez dévote, et qu'une âme de dix-huit ans croit tout perdu, tout désespéré, quand on lui dit en pareil cas qu'il n'y a plus que Dieu qui lui reste: c'est une idée grave et sérieuse qui effarouche sa petite conscience. A cet âge, on ne se fie guère qu'à ce qu'on voit, on ne connaît guère que les choses de la terre.
>
> (p. 145)

Marianne's last remark comes as somewhat of a surprise given that just a short while back she just as firmly believed in more than she could see, namely M. de Climal's love for her. Marianne, in turn, fills the position vacated by the father. Thus the reversal of positions is complete: the father believes in super-sensory totalities, and Marianne, on the contrary, in the evidence of her own senses.

The change occurs because of the character's confusion regarding what is real, itself arising precisely to the extent that metaphor contaminates all discourse. The scene shows how metaphorical meaning comes to be accepted as proper meaning, thus giving, in this case, love the same ontological significance as the kiss.

The story does not yet end here. A more literal version also exists, which exposes the metaphorical character of the one Marianne told to father St. Vincent. Originally, to justify keeping the presents, Marianne accepted a blander interpretation of M. de Climal's actions than the one she gave to father St. Vincent. In fact she anticipated the father's considerable feat of reducing acts to their facticity in order to suppress their sexual connotation. Some of her arguments bear an extraordinary likeness to the father's in this respect. Commenting on M. de Climal's affection, she said it was similar to a parent's:

> Quoique je le visse enchanté de moi, rien n'empêchait que ma jeunesse, ma situation, mon esprit et mes grâces ne lui eussent donné pour moi une affection très innocente. On peut se prendre d'une tendre amitié pour les personnes de mon âge dont on veut avoir soin . . . tous les motifs de simple tendresse qu'un bienfaiteur

peut avoir dans ces cas-là, une fille de plus de quinze ans et demi, quoiqu'elle n'ait rien vu, les sent et les devine confusément; elle n'en est pas plus surprise que de voir l'amour de son père et de sa mère pour elle.

> (p. 36)

Equally, with respect to M. de Climal's untoward habit of touching her hair, Marianne fastened on the least compromising explanation: "M. de Climal les regardait, les touchait avec passion, mais cette passion, je la regardais comme un pur badinage" (p. 36). Finally, she too seemed willing to strip such an obvious sign as a kiss of its meaning: "Monsieur, ne vous ai-je pas fait mal? m'écriai-je d'un air naturel, en feignant de prendre le baiser qu'il m'avait donné pour le choc de sa tête avec la mienne. Dans le temps que je disais cela, je descendais de carrosse, et je crois qu'il fut dupe de ma petite finesse, car il me répondit très naturellement que non" (p. 42).

Calling the "choc" a "baiser" constitutes a metaphorical use of language in that it displaces referential meaning from an outward, visible symptom to a definite cause. This of course sheds a different light on what "really happened." It makes love, the referent of the metaphor, as certain as the "choc," even though love is an airy creation of language and style, possessing no more substance than the style which gave it birth. Moreover, Marianne most certainly added some stylistic touches, such as calling the "choc" a "baiser," to the strict narration of events solely in order to persuade the father of M. de Climal's guilt and her own innocence. Marianne's little "finesse" betrays a willingness to use language seductively and misleadingly in order to persuade.

My main point is that persuasion replaces truth in *La Vie de Marianne,* and that the two are mutually exclusive goals because persuasion relies on the rhetorical dimension of language, which does not include proper meaning among its possibilities.

In all of the above examples, Marianne uses language metaphorically to displace referential meaning from objects to emotions, a process Paul Ricoeur calls "la référence dédoublée."[22] But is this second meaning really referential?

In his study, "Métaphore et référence," Ricoeur argues eloquently against Frege's assumption that literature suspends the referential function of language, and therefore has no truth value. His discussion focuses on the referential function of metaphorical language. "C'est dans l'analyse même de l'énoncé métaphorique," writes Ricoeur, "que doit s'enraciner une conception référentielle du langage poétique qui tienne compte de l'abolition de la référence du langage ordinaire et se base sur le concept de référence dédoublée" (p. 289).

Ricoeur explains that the impossibility of taking a statement literally leads to the conclusion that the statement must be metaphorical: "le sens d'un énoncé métaphorique est suscité par l'échec de l'interprétation littérale de l'énoncé; pour une interprétation littérale, le sens se détruit lui-même. Or cette auto-destruction du sens conditionne à son tour l'effondrement de la référence primaire" (p. 289). An example of this in *La Vie de Marianne* would be Marianne's vision of armed robbers which we determined was not literally true. Paul Ricoeur goes on to say that this is only the first phase or "la contre-partie négative d'une stratégie positive." "Ne peut-on pas dire," he then asks, "que l'interprétation métaphorique, en faisant surgir une nouvelle pertinence sémantique sur les ruines du sens littéral, suscite *aussi* une nouvelle visée référentielle, à la faveur même de l'abolition de la référence correspondant à l'interprétation littérale de l'énoncé?"

We have determined on more than one occasion the absurdity of taking Marianne literally, but it does not necessarily follow that the metaphorical meaning, although making more sense, is any more referential.[23] To use Frege's terms, "sense" does not imply "reference." Indeed, that would mean giving a proper meaning to emotions. The portrait of Mme de Miran shows, however, the impossibility of succeeding in the attempt.

The description Marianne gives of her benefactress does not dwell for long on physical details. And even when she does mention them, it is only in the light of some moral trait, before which physical traits pale. This is the case with beauty and goodness. "Quoiqu'elle eût été belle femme, elle avait quelque chose de si bon et de si raisonnable dans sa physionomie, que cela avait pu nuire à ses charmes, et les empêcher d'être aussi piquants qu'ils auraient dû l'être" (p. 167). The presence of beauty in the concessive clause shows its subordinate position to goodness; moreover, beauty is even crowded out of the physical appearance of Mme de Miran in favor of goodness: "Quand on a l'air si bon, on en paraît moins belle; un air de franchise et de bonté si dominant est tout à fait contraire à la coquetterie; il ne fait songer qu'au bon caractère d'une femme, et non pas à ses grâces; il rend la belle personne plus estimable, mais son visage plus indifférent." Even so, Mme de Miran's physical portrait conveys a moral impression. The portrait is the outside version of what is inside Mme de Miran.

However, Marianne can only intuit confusedly what is inside Mme de Miran for herself, not for others. Appropriately, she calls these inside properties "objets de sentiment," and admits to the difficulty she has in expressing them: "Ce sont des objets de sentiment si compliqués et d'une netteté si délicate qu'ils se brouillent dès que ma réflexion s'en mêle; je ne sais plus par où les prendre pour les exprimer: de sorte qu'ils sont en moi, et non pas à moi" (p. 166). Marianne's feelings give such a true picture of Mme de Miran that the portrait promises to be a perfect likeness—that is, if Marianne

could only express her feelings. Marianne's difficulty in expressing what is inside other people is a function of the difficulty she has in expressing what is inside herself.

We can fully understand, therefore, the moment of hesitation before naming Mme de Miran, and beginning the long-awaited portrait. Indeed, before applying the first brushstroke to the portrait, Marianne warns the reader against ever expecting to see it completed: "Quand je dis que je vais faire le portrait de ces deux dames, j'entends que je vous en donnerai quelques traits. On ne saurait rendre en entier ce que sont les personnes" (p. 166).

As Roland Barthes notes, the proper name has an economical function: "Il permet de substituer une unité nominale à une collection de traits."[24] Similarly, the function of the portrait is to sum up a person's character in a word, so to speak, and realize a similar economy of description. But with the words, "Ma bienfaitrice, que je ne vous ai pas encore nommée, s'appelait Mme de Miran," a naming process begins which despairs of ever having an end. Marianne attempts the task of defining Mme de Miran's character, although it escapes definitional language by refusing to be fixed.

Marianne's attempt to define Mme de Miran's character corresponds to her attempt to arrive at a definition of the "bonté" which pervades all aspects of her character. "Mme de Miran ne pensait rien, ne disait rien qui ne se sentît de cette abondance de bonté qui faisait le fond de son caractère" (p. 169). Therefore, defining "bonté" seems to lie at her artistic journey's end. The text gives the impression of progress in its search for the meaning of "bonté," yet leads nowhere. The portrait consists in the very movement to which it is supposed to put an end. "Bonté" most nearly describes the dominant trait of Mme de Miran's character, yet it is subjected to endless revisions, which in turn deprives Mme de Miran of a stable identity.

The goodness which most aptly describes Mme de Miran does not have a definite, proper meaning because Marianne constantly touches up her one essential trait, blurring its outline. "Et n'allez pas croire que ce fût une bonté sotte, aveugle, de ces bontés d'une âme faible et pusillanime, et qui paraissent risibles même aux gens qui en profitent. Non," she continues,

> la sienne était une vertu; c'était le sentiment d'un coeur excellent; c'était cette bonté proprement dite qui tiendrait lieu de lumière, même aux personnes qui n'auraient pas d'esprit, et qui, parce qu'elle est vraie bonté, veut avec scrupule être juste et raisonnable, et n'a plus envie de faire un bien dès qu'il arriverait un mal.

With the ostensible purpose of narrowing down the semantic field of "bonté," Marianne considerably expands it. Where we thought there was only one "bonté," now there are many, which makes it appear that "bonté," at least in its present form, can never be "proprement dite."

Marianne makes yet another distinction, further jeopardizing the metaphor's ability to unify. Mme de Miran's goodness, although closely resembling nobility of soul, nonetheless stands apart from it. "Je ne vous dirai pas même que Mme de Miran eût ce qu'on appelle de la noblesse d'âme, ce serait aussi confondre les idées: la bonne qualité que je lui donne était quelque chose de plus simple, de plus aimable, de moins brillant." Marianne's dissection of "bonté" leads her into a discussion of nobility of soul by means of the familiar figure of preterition, which takes us further and further away from the proper meaning of "bonté"—in the guise of more closely approximating it.

Mme de Miran's generosity, less showy for being real, sets her apart from people who, although they wear coronets, do not have kind hearts: "Souvent ces gens qui ont l'âme si noble, ne sont pas les meilleurs coeurs du monde; ils s'entêtent trop de la gloire et du plaisir d'être généreux, et négligent par là bien des petits devoirs. Ils aiment à être loués, et Mme de Miran ne songeait pas seulement à être louable; jamais elle ne fut généreuse à cause qu'il était beau de l'être, mais à cause que vous aviez besoin qu'elle le fût."

At this point the portrait threatens to shift from a descriptive to a narrative mode. A move in this direction is indicated by the introduction of needs, which acts alone can satisfy. By suiting the action to the word, Mme de Miran exteriorizes her goodness in the world. On the other hand, as Marianne pointed out, goodness remains a benign attitude in most people. Mme de Miran's goodness is not "inside" her, but "outside" her in the world. This breaks down the concept of "bonté" or, in rhetorical terms, shifts it from a metaphorical totality to a metonymic aggregate.[25] And this in turn results in a complete fragmentation of the concept of character itself through this one revealing trait.

In summary, Marianne first attempts to sum up Mme de Miran's character by condensing it into, as Peter Brooks says, a "total metaphor." For this purpose, she chooses "bonté" as common denominator, as all her character traits partake of it. But then the portrait reveals differences which the metaphor had masked, or subsumed into a single unit of meaning. Indeed, we saw how the portrait revealed hidden articulations in seamless metaphorical totalities by distinguishing between qualities that appeared to be one.

Aside from reducing individuals to types, metaphors give the illusion of a stability of meaning not borne out, alas, by temporal existence. For example, Valville's

"love" for Marianne disappointed readers' expectations by not running true. Equally, M. de Climal, originally dubbed a "pious" and "respectable" man on the basis of his previous conduct, failed to live up to his reputation. Neither character can be said to be true to himself, let alone true to type.

The concept of character invites belief in a permanent and stable identity. In reducing "bonté" to "bienfaits" Marivaux helps dispel the myth of character. "Bonté" has no general meaning; that is, it has no meaning independent from reference to a particular action. By the same token, a person does not have some internal essence of character, a soul or a self.

The loss of a stable identity of the self as a result of its temporal mode of existence constitutes the irony of the text. Both realism and pathos, as alternate modes, give the illusion of plenitude, but only to fill the void left by the experience of temporality.

Notes

1. *Sentimens sur les Lettres et sur l'Histoire,* 1683, in Henri Coulet, *Le Roman jusqu'a là Révolution* (Paris: Armand Colin, 1968), Vol. II, p. 91. Quoted by English Showalter, Jr., *The Evolution of the French Novel* (Princeton: Princeton University Press, 1972), p. 30.

2. *The Evolution of the French Novel,* p. 49.

3. *Figures* III (Paris: Seuil, 1972), p. 186.

4. *Imitation and Illusion in the French Memoir-Novel,* 1700-1750 (New Haven and London: Yale University Press, 1969).

5. "Il est fâcheux que Mademoiselle des Jardins ait ouvert la porte à une licence dont on abuse tous les jours de plus en plus; c'est celle de prêter ses inventions, et ses Intrigues Galantes, aux plus grands hommes des derniers siècles, et de les mêler avec des faits qui ont quelque fondement dans l'Histoire. Ce mélange de la vérité et la fable se répand dans une infinité de Livres nouveaux, perd le goût des jeunes gens, et fait que l'on n'ose croire ce qui au fond est croyable" (Quoted by Georges May, "L'Histoire a-t-elle engendré le roman?" *Revue d'Histoire Littéraire de la France* [avril-juin 1955], 160).

6. *Le Roman à la première personne* (Paris: Armand Colin, 1975), pp. 7 and 448.

7. "En effet, si je n'en suis pas le père, j'en ai eu du moins la direction" (*Mémoires de Mr. d'Artagnan . . .* [Cologne: Pierre Marteau, 1700], Avertissement, p. 5. Quoted by Démoris, *Le Roman à la première personne,* p. 206).

8. "Le Problème de l'illusion romanesque et le renouvellement des techniques narratives entre

1700 et 1715," in *La Littérature narrative d'imagination,* Colloque de Strasbourg, 23-25 avril 1959, ed. Albert Henry (Paris: P.U. F., 1961), p. 117.

9. *Anatomy of Criticism* (Princeton: Princeton University Press, 1957), p. 39.

10. *Le Roman à la première personne,* p. 453. I would add that Prévost singled out emotions as the means of distinguishing between the novel and history. In reference to the latter genre, he writes: "Rien n'y est petit et méprisable lorsqu'il peut servir à la connaissance du caractère principal. Ce serait néanmoins abuser de cette règle que de se croire autorisé à s'étendre beaucoup sur les sentiments et sur la peinture des passions. Cette sorte d'ornements, dont l'unique but est d'émouvoir, est propre aux romans; et c'est ainsi que chaque genre a ses règles et ses bornes" (*Histoire de Marguerite d'Anjou,* Preface. Quoted by Stewart, *Imitation and Illusion in the French Memoir Novel,* p. 199).

11. *De la grammatologie* (Paris: Editions de Minuit, 1967), p. 389.

12. Alexandre Dumas, *The Three Musketeers,* trans. William Barrow, ed. Sidney Dark (London and Glasgow: Collins, 1952), p. 71.

13. Shoshana Felman, "Madness and Philosophy or Literature's Reason," *YFS* [*Yale French Studies*], 52 (1975), 224. Felman's article concerns us here in that it explicitly relates pathos to style. See esp. p. 219. Cf. J.-P. Sartre, *L'Idiot de la famille* (Paris: Gallimard, 1971), p. 1616: ". . . le style, d'ailleurs souvent confondu avec la beauté et la hardiesse des images, des métaphores, est le dernier traitement d'une histoire émouvante et pathétique. . . ."

14. *La Vie de Marianne,* ed. Frédéric Deloffre (Paris: Garnier, 1963), p. 9. All references will be to this edition.

15. *Les Effets surprenants de la sympathie,* Preface. Quoted by English Showalter, *The Evolution of the French Novel,* p. 45.

16. Ian Watt, *The Rise of the Novel* (London, 1957; rpt. Berkeley: University of California Press, 1974), p. 29. According to Watt, such a use defines realistic prose.

17. See Paul de Man, "Theory of Metaphor in Rousseau's Second Discourse," in *Romanticism,* ed. David Thorburn and Geoffrey Hartman (Ithaca and London: Cornell University Press, 1972), p. 102 and "The Rhetoric of Blindness: Jacques Derrida's Reading of Rousseau," in *Blindness and Insight* (New York: Oxford University Press, 1971), p. 133. In the latter essay, de Man writes:

"Rousseau no longer locates the literal meaning in the referent of the metaphor as an object, but he interiorizes the object and makes the metaphor refer to an inner state of consciousness, a feeling or a passion."

18. Daniel Mornet, *Le Sentiment de la nature en France de J.-J. Rousseau à Bernardin de Saint Pierre* (Paris, 1907; rpt. New York: Burt Franklin, n.d.), p. 187.

19. See de Man, "Theory of Metaphor in Rousseau's Second Discourse," p. 102.

20. Donald Davidson remarks, "Generally it is only when a sentence is taken to be false that we accept it as a metaphor and start to hunt for the hidden implication. It is probably for this reason that most metaphorical sentences are patently false . . ." ("What Metaphors Mean," in *On Metaphor,* ed. Sheldon Sacks [Chicago and London: The University of Chicago Press, 1979], p. 40).

21. The expression comes from John Locke, *Essay on Human Understanding,* book 3, chap. 10. Thomas Hobbes voices a similar opinion and goes so far as to banish metaphor from serious philosophical discourse. "In . . . all rigorous search for truth . . . metaphors . . . are in this case utterly excluded. For seeing they openly profess deceit, to admit them into counsel, or reasoning, were manifest folly" (*Leviathan,* part 1, chap. 8).

22. *La Métaphore vive* (Paris: Seuil, 1975), pp. 282 and 289. Future page references to this work will be given in parentheses in the text.

23. Ricoeur's theory of "la référence dédoublée" depends on the prior assumption that "le sentiment n'est pas moins ontologique que la représentation" (p. 387).

24. *SZ* (Paris: Seuil, 1970), p. 101.

25. For a discussion of portraiture in terms of "metaphor" and "metonymy" see Peter Brooks, *The Novel of Worldliness* (Princeton: Princeton University Press, 1969), pp. 15-16, 79-80 and 91-92. For an analysis of this portrait in particular, see pp. 103-110.

D. J. Culpin (essay date January 1985)

SOURCE: Culpin, D. J. "Marivaux's Apology for Religion." *French Studies* 39, no. 1 (January 1985): 31-42.

[*In the following essay, Culpin examines Marivaux's ambiguous defense of orthodox religion in his work.*]

In his *Éloge de Marivaux* d'Alembert refers to the sincerity of Marivaux's religious convictions and to their important position in his attitude to life:

Quoique très éloigné d'afficher la dévotion, il l'était encore plus de l'incrédulité: "La religion" disait-il, "est la ressource du malheureux, quelquefois même celle du philosophe; n'enlevons pas à la pauvre espèce humaine cette consolation, que la Providence divine lui a ménagée".[1]

This importance has been emphasized more recently by Pierre Jacoebée who affirms the inadequacy of any critical interpretation of Marivaux's work which takes no account of what he considers to be 'le point de départ nécessaire, inévitable, en même temps que l'aboutissement de toute étude sur Marivaux, son christianisme'.[2] Jacoebée's purpose is to demonstrate that the religious ethic of 'la charité' has a corresponding aesthetic which influences the style and structure of Marivaux's journals, but he does not pretend to offer an analysis of Marivaux's religious beliefs in their own right; as he says himself, 'prouver l'orthodoxie ou l'hétérodoxie de Marivaux n'est pas le but de la présente étude'.[3] Other scholars have pointed out the influence of St Augustine and Malebranche on Marivaux, but there exists no systematic study of the nature of his religious faith.[4]

In spite of the reserve which is so notable a feature of Marivaux's personality, his defence of religious values strikes a combative note. The opening page of *Le Cabinet du philosophe* [*CP,*] announces that the work will contain '[des] réflexions gaies, sérieuses, morales, chrétiennes, beaucoup de ces deux dernières' (*CP,* I, 335).[5] The same conviction is conveyed in an anecdote recounted by d'Alembert who tells of an occasion at the salon of Mme de Tencin when Marivaux openly rebuked a sceptic who, according to the *Almanach littéraire* of 1782, was none other than Bolingbroke.[6] It is at men like Bolingbroke that Marivaux's defence of Christianity is directed, that is, at the *honnêtes gens* whose scepticism is part of their stance as men and women of fashion. As early as the dedicatory letter of the *Lettres sur les habitants de Paris* Marivaux describes a group of people who accept the restraints of traditional morality not out of respect for that moral code but in deference to social *bienséances*:

Cette secte, madame, ne laisse pas que d'être un peu pyrrhonienne; car elle n'a de vertus que par convention; mais vivre bien avec les hommes, et penser autrement qu'eux, est une chose qui paraît si belle, et si distinguée, que dans bien des endroits à Paris vous ne passez pour homme d'esprit, qu'autant qu'on vous croit confirmé dans cette impiété philosophique.

(LSHP, [*Lettres sur les habitants de Paris*] 9)

So frivolous a rejection of religion is condemned by the writer of the *Cabinet du philosophe,* who says: 'Il y a des gens qui se damnent, dans la seule crainte du ridicule qu'il y a dans le monde à vouloir se sauver' (*CP,* I, 341). But Marivaux, like Pascal whose Apology is ad-

dressed to a similar audience, tries to win their assent to his views by adapting his manner to suit their taste. When he arraigns the wealthy man who does not relieve the suffering he sees around him he does not claim to speak from a position of moral superiority but 'en honnête homme, dont le cœur est heureusement forcé, quand il le faut, de ménager les intérêts d'autrui dans les siens' (*SF,* [*Le Spectateur français*] IV, 130).

The sceptic is an *incrédule* or *esprit fort* who justifies his position with the claim that the traditional teachings of revealed religion have been undermined by the progress of reason. The same argument is used by the *déiste* (*CP,* X, 419) and the *athée* (ibid., 426), but, in rejecting their claims, Marivaux maintains that religious truth is inaccessible to human reason:

Il y a des vérités qui ne sont point faites pour être directement présentées à l'esprit. Elles le révoltent quand elles vont à lui en droite ligne; elles blessent sa petite logique; il n'y comprend rien; elles sont des absurdités pour lui.

(CP, III, 352)

Man habitually overvalues his intellect and the writer of the journal reminds us that 'l'orgueilleuse envie de tout savoir fut son premier péché' (ibid., 353). This is one of the criticisms levelled by Marivaux against the *Lettres persanes* in which Montesquieu condemns European laws against suicide: 'De l'air décisif dont il parle, on croirait presque qu'il est entré de moitié dans le secret de cette même création' (*SF,* VIII, 154).[7] The same condemnation extends to all those whom Marivaux describes pejoratively as 'hommes aux systèmes' (*LSHP,* 35) or 'faiseurs de systèmes' (*SF,* XXI, 232). Their attempt to give a rational explanation for everything is a mere pretence, and the Indigent philosophe tells a brief story to demonstrate this:

Je me souviens qu'un jour à la campagne nous disputions, deux de mes amis et moi, sur l'âme. Un bon paysan qui travaillait auprès de nous, entendit notre dispute, et me dit après: Monsieur, vous avez tant parlé de nos âmes: est-ce que vous en avez vu quelqu'une? et il avait raison de me demander cela, et je la demanderais à tous ceux qui en disputent.

(IP, [*L'Indigent philosophe*] VII, 318)

For the Spectateur français the explanations and discoveries of 'ceux que le vulgaire appelle philosophes' are nothing but empty visions: 'A quoi servent leurs méditations là-dessus', he opines, 'qu'à multiplier les preuves que nous avons déjà de notre ignorance invincible?' (*SF,* XXI, 232).

The arguments used by Marivaux against the destructive intrusion of reason into matters of religion resemble those used by the Classical *moralistes* to defend religious orthodoxy against the seventeenth-century *libertins.* For Marivaux religion is not contrary to reason but beyond it, and he echoes Pascal in his appeal to those who would discover the truth: 'Sacrifiez-moi, non votre raison, mais les raisonnements d'un esprit si borné qu'il ne se connaît pas lui-même' (*CP,* I, 342).[8] Elsewhere he recalls La Bruyère for, like him, he doubts that the scepticism of the *esprit fort* is really the product of his reasoning: 'On parle d'une espèce d'incrédules qu'on appelle athées; et s'il y en a, ce que je ne crois pas, ce n'est point à force de raisonner qu'ils le deviennent' (*CP,* X, 426).[9] Rather the contrary is true, for those who call themselves atheists adopt that label either because they have not thoroughly examined the issue and its consequences, or because they lack the ability to control their passions and so take the course of denying those standards which would censure their behaviour. For Marivaux the arguments of a typical sceptic, when critically examined, amount to no more than 'un peu de libertinage, beaucoup de vanité, et force ignorance' (*SF,* XV, 197).

However, on closer examination, Marivaux's religious beliefs are not as orthodox as they might at first appear to be, and they diverge markedly from those of the writers just mentioned. Like Pascal he looks to the heart as the source of religious conviction, and when the heart is won it will in turn convince the mind:

> En fait de religion, ne cherchez point à convaincre les hommes; ne raisonnez que pour leur cœur: quand il est pris, tout est fait. Sa persuasion jette dans l'esprit des lumières intérieures, auxquelles il ne résiste point.
>
> (*CP,* III, 352)

But, unlike Pascal, Marivaux's belief in the heart, or *sentiment,* as the mediator of religious truth does not lead him to an enthusiastic assertion of specific points of Church doctrine such as the Fall, the Incarnation, Redemption and Grace.[10] His only certainty is that the conscience instructs us to act with virtue: 'Le reste de cette religion, ce sont des mystères qu'il faut croire' (*CP,* I, 342). The essence of Marivaux's religion is a number of ideas which he believes are innate in man, including 'celle d'un Dieu, celle de l'Infini, d'Immortalité, d'Éternité' (*CP,* III, 355). D'Alembert confirms that Marivaux's religion was a simple one and that he was content to respect what he could not understand: 'sa philosophie *religieuse* était très simple et très modeste. On lui demandait un jour ce que c'est que l'âme: "Je sais", répondit-il, "qu'elle est spirituelle et immortelle, et n'en sais rien de plus"'.[11] In fact the only doctrinal truths which he affirms are the existence of God, the importance of works of charity (i.e., the practice of virtue), and the immortality of the soul.

That God exists he does not doubt and little space is taken up with the elaboration of this point. The Spectateur says 'il est un Etre supérieur qui préside sur nous' who allows social inequalities to exist as a spur to acts of charity (*SF,* XXV, 266). Emander in Marivaux's first novel, **Les Effets surprenants de la sympathie,** tells the savages that it is the 'Etre souverain' who has created the world and established its norms of morality:

> C'est cet Etre, leur dis-je, qui a fait tout ce que vos yeux vous font voir; il est l'admirable ouvrier de toute la nature, de ce ciel parsemé d'éternelles clartés, et de ce soleil qui réchauffe les entrailles de la terre, et qui donne la vie aux moindres plantes.
>
> (*ESS,* [*Les Effets surprenants de la sympathie*] 286-87)[12]

They are convinced of what he says by the testimony of their own hearts: 'Ils écoutaient ces discours avec un sentiment intérieur qui leur faisait connaître que j'avais raison' (ibid., 287).

It is towards their consciences that Emander turns the savages in order that they learn the precepts of virtue: 'de jour en jour je réveillais dans leurs cœurs ces sentiments de justice et de religion que tous les hommes apportent en naissant' (ibid., 288). The Spectateur echoes these words when he advises men who want to act with justice: 'écoutez la voix de votre conscience!' (*SF,* XXI, 233). The ideas derived from such an intuition are clear in principle if not in detail, for, as Marivaux says in the **Pensées sur différents sujets,** 'l'instinct est à l'âme humaine un sentiment non déployé, qui lui prouve la vérité des choses qu'elle aperçoit nettement' (**PDS,** [**Pensées sur différents sujets**] 71-72). It is the clarity of perception which guarantees for Marivaux, as it does for Descartes, the truth of the ideas perceived. Descartes's belief in the truth of such ideas is momentarily shaken by the supposition that a 'Dieu trompeur' or 'mauvais génie' might be systematically deceiving him, and the extremity of doubt into which this possibility plunges him is resolved only with the realization that: 'il n'y a donc point de doute que je suis, s'il me trompe'.[13] Marivaux develops a very similar argument, asking whether this conscience which he has just proclaimed the ultimate source of moral judgement might not be a 'guide imposteur'. He sees the conscience which should guide a man 'ou comme la règle sacrée de ses actions, ou comme un guide imposteur qui va, s'il le suit, l'égarer à mon avantage et n'en faire qu'un imbécile' (*SF,* XXI, 233-34). If the latter is the case 'l'homme vertueux n'est qu'un sot, qu'une misérable dupe de sa raison' (ibid., 234). It seems preposterous to Marivaux that those values of which we feel ourselves most certain should be mistaken, and he rejects the consequence that follows if his supposition is true, namely that 'il n'y aura donc d'homme sage que celui qui expliquera toutes ses idées de justice à contresens' (ibid.). Like Descartes he adopts an ontological solution, arguing that because we have the idea of virtue, objective virtue must exist. It is no reply to say that man might have invented his own standards of judgement, for Marivaux's response is that man would break for his convenience rules he had made for his convenience. Only innate values corresponding to ultimate realities will conserve, as they do, their effectiveness among men:

> Glissez-leur dans le fond de l'âme, comme Dieu a fait, la connaissance de ce Dieu même: frappez-les d'une impression de la crainte de ce Dieu, d'une impression d'amour pour la vertu; mettez en eux une certaine lumière, qui leur rende le crime aussi horrible, aussi condamnable qu'il est funeste; et l'innocence aussi louable qu'elle est utile et nécessaire: donnez-leur enfin des idées de justice.
>
> (*CP,* IV, 364)

Our ideas of God and morality come from the conscience or the heart, and, in consequence, they are reliable.

Faced with the impotence of the reason to discover eternal truths the Spectateur says simply: 'faisons l'ouvrage qui nous est indiqué, soyons bons et vertueux; on apprend si aisément à le devenir' (*SF,* XXI, 233). Emander therefore instructs the savages not in dogma, but in their duty to love God and their neighbour:

> Le culte que vous lui devez, ajoutais-je, consiste à le remercier des biens dont il vous partage, à ne point murmurer des maux dont souvent sa juste colère vous punit: il vous a faits pour lier ensemble une société; la paix doit en faire le fondement: vous devez, après cet Etre, vous aimer les uns les autres, et éviter surtout les trahisons, les meurtres, et toutes ces actions violentes, dont l'Etre souverain est irrité.
>
> (*ESS,* 287)

In Marivaux's eyes the service of man is a consequence of the service of God.

Through the Spectateur Marivaux says elsewhere: 'il est triste de voir souffrir quelqu'un, quand on n'est point en état de le secourir' (ibid., IV, 129). On this point his words clearly echo the teaching of Scripture. The Spectateur exclaims:

> Quoi! voir les besoins d'un honnête homme, et n'être point en état de les soulager, n'est-ce pas les avoir soi-même? Je serai donc pauvre avec les indigents, ruiné avec ceux qui seront ruinés, et je manquerai de tout ce qui leur manquera
>
> (*SF,* XIII, 181)

recalling Christ's description of those who are truly his disciples:

> Car j'ai eu faim, et vous m'avez donné à manger; j'ai eu soif, et vous m'avez donné à boire; j'étais étranger, et vous m'avez recueilli; j'étais nu, et vous m'avez vêtu; j'étais malade, et vous m'avez visité; j'étais en prison, et vous êtes venu vers moi.[14]

The wealthy, in particular, have a moral obligation to allay the sufferings of the poor, and if they do not, the Spectateur tells them, it will be held against them: 'vous répondez de ses murmures, et de l'iniquité où il se livre, et en périssant il vous condamne' (*SF,* XXV, 266). If this were not so 'Dieu, qui est juste autant que sage, n'en serait-il pas comptable à sa justice . . . ?' (ibid.).

There is no question that man is unable to carry out the actions which he knows to be good. There is basically no difference between the *homme vertueux* and the *incrédule* or *méchant*. Both types partake of the same human nature and are endowed with the same moral conscience to discern between good and evil; both of them are subject to the same temptations and passions, and yet only the former adheres to virtue, which he is able to do in spite of the 'peine qu'il y a à être bon et vertueux' (*IP,* V, 306). The explanation is that he exercises his will to implement the judgement of his conscience, and Marivaux believes that in all matters apart from religious conversion the will remains in our control. This is true of even the most unpromising or vicious individuals, whose particular combination of abilities and characteristics seems to offer little hope of virtue: 'Il faut bien que la formation la plus ingrate et la plus défectueuse ne soit pas irrémédiable, et puisse devenir meilleure et moins maligne, si nous le voulons' (*RSEH,* [*Réflexions sur l'esprit humain*] 488). Our *formation,* however corrupt, cannot resist the 'efforts de notre volonté [. . .] qui la rende encore susceptible de notre part d'une dernière façon, et comme d'un dernier pli qui la corrige, ou qui diminue considérablement ses défauts' (ibid.). While taking care to avoid areas of theological controversy, Marivaux affirms that no man need be the slave of vice and that the world is full of examples of corrupt men who have mended their ways. The 'malhonnête homme' has only to assert his will in order to achieve virtue:

> Je ne parle pas de conversion, c'est une autre affaire; mais d'un changement moral auquel il arrive, ou par des attentions réitérées et victorieuses sur son propre intérêt mieux connu, ou sur la douceur de mener une vie dont le repos et l'innocence lui paraissent préférables aux satisfactions inquiètes, brutales, périlleuses ou criminelles qu'il avait coutume de se permettre, ou sur le plaisir aussi utile que flatteur d'acquérir l'estime et la bienveillance des hommes.
>
> (*RSEH,* 489)

Women no less than men possess this freedom of will, as Emander tells the natives: 'les femmes étaient, comme les hommes, douées d'une âme à qui l'Etre souverain avait donné pour avantage une liberté de se déterminer, qui ne relevait de personne' (*ESS,* 286).

Such a conception of free-will presupposes an optimistic view of man, though Marivaux does not forget the Church's teaching on the fact of human sin.[15] He speaks much of 'le méchant' and acknowledges the evil that can be done by 'les grands' when they are devoid of humanity. Man has a potential for evil but, in Marivaux's eyes, he is not irremediably corrupt. The heartless rich man has 'le penchant au mal' which is common to humanity, but the Spectateur tells him: 'Vous n'êtes que la moitié d'une créature humaine'. He partakes of the evil which is the lot of all men but has 'ni la dignité ni la noblesse' with which they are equally endowed (*SF,* IV, 130). Elsewhere the Spectateur says: 'Il est vrai que nous naissons tous méchants', but man is not unable to remedy his iniquity, and the Spectateur goes on: 'cette méchanceté, nous ne l'apportons que comme un monstre qu'il nous faut combattre'. Man recognizes his potential for evil by the light of his reason: 'et la raison [. . .] est le correctif de notre iniquité même' (*SF,* XXI, 234). Human nature has a certain number of attributes which determine individual knowledge or abilities; these characteristics have a potential for good or evil but no one's *formation* condemns him to evil alone:

> [. . .] car d'iniquité, de bassesse et de petitesse d'âme, de stupidité ou d'infériorité d'esprit positives, primitives, distinctes et proprement dites, il n'y en a point: rien de pareil n'a été créé pour nous.
>
> (*RSEH,* 485)

Marivaux does not favour a Jansenistic interpretation of original sin but neither does he believe that mankind is totally uncorrupted. He reiterates that Pauline distinction between corrupt and regenerate human nature, the 'old man' as typified by Adam and the 'new man' as typified by Christ.[16] Pride is the origin of evil, but according to Marivaux 'l'amour est humble et c'est cette humilité qui expie l'orgueil du premier homme' (*CP,* III, 353). It is through the love of one's neighbour which issues in the practice of virtue that man recovers his lost dignity.

Though a number of Marivaux's plays are set on distant islands and the *insulaire* Trivelin in *L'Ile des esclaves* possesses more natural virtue than the shipwrecked Europeans, Marivaux does not use this device to develop the myth of the noble savage. *La Dispute* most nearly evokes a world of uncorrupted innocence, but it is with a characteristically balanced result. When Eglé is tempted to be unfaithful to Azor, Carise tries to recall her to virtue by advising her to listen to her heart, which will condemn her inconstancy. Eglé mournfully replies: 'mon bon cœur le condamne, mon bon cœur l'approuve, il dit oui, il dit non, il est de deux avis' (Scene 15). The faith of one character in the goodness of human nature is met by another's equally firm experience of the reality of evil. The same mixture of natural goodness and degradation is found in the natives among whom Emander is shipwrecked. When he arrives he does not find them in a state of edenic bliss; rather they are ill-nourished, a prey to sickness, and living in squalid conditions. But goodness is latent within them and has only to be aroused by instruction.

Marivaux, like Pascal, sees greatness and weakness as complementary parts of a duality at the heart of human nature. The writer of the *Cabinet du philosophe* says of 'les mœurs des hommes': 'Quel monstrueux melange de démence et de raison, de dépravation et de justice!' (*CP,* IV, 362). Two contradictory tendencies are present:

> Y a-t-il rien de plus singulier que nous? D'une part, un corps qui occupe si peu de place, qu'on a tant de peine à transporter.
>
> Et de l'autre, un esprit qui va si loin, qui se transporte où il veut, qu'aucun éloignement d'un lieu à un autre n'arrête, qui franchit tous les espaces en un instant, qui mesure les cieux, qui se rend présents l'avenir et le passé.
>
> (*CP,* III, 354)

The explanation of this contradiction is the fact of human sin: man has fallen from the state of perfection for which God destined him. It is sin that is responsible for man's present misery: 'Il n'était fait que pour avoir un maître, qui est Dieu; et le péché lui en a donné mille, dont la supériorité lui est toujours étrangère et douloureuse' (*CP,* IV, 364). In spite of his fall there remain intimations of glory in the human heart: 'Y eut-il jamais d'ouvrage qui annonçât tant de dessein, qui donnât matière à de si grandes conjectures que son âme?' (*CP,* III, 354). The desire to escape from this impasse and recover man's lost grandeur drove Pascal back to the dogmas of revealed religion and to Christ as the Redeemer, 'qui unissant en lui les deux natures, humaine et divine, a retiré les hommes de la corruption du péché pour les réconcilier à Dieu en sa personne divine'.[17] For him, man is impotent to recover his true destiny without the intervention of divine grace. Marivaux, from his more optimistic standpoint, does not stress this necessity, though when, in his discussion of free-will, he says of conversion that it is 'une autre affaire' (*RSEH,* 489) he is making a formal acknowledgement of the sovereignty of God in the work of salvation. But this remark, whether intended sincerely or as a simple disclaimer, does little to mitigate the force of Marivaux's insistence on the possibility of self-amendment. He assents to the traditional teaching of the Church on original sin and salvation through divine grace, but he does not develop these themes in his work and does not hold that human corruption completely eradicates man's dignity and free-will.

The practice of virtue is more important than the idle speculations of reason, but from man's intellectual curiosity a lesson can be learned:

> L'envie que nous avons de nous connaître n'est sans doute qu'un avertissement que nous nous connaîtrons

un jour et que nous n'avons rien à faire ici qu'à tâcher de nous rendre avantageux ce développement futur des mystères de notre existence.

(*SF,* XXI, 232-33)

Belief in immortality comes not from Revelation but from the ontological argument that the surest proof of eternal life is man's ability to conceive of an idea which would be ludicrous were it not true. Man is preoccupied by the fate of his soul: 'notre âme et son avenir sont pour nous une furieuse affaire' (*CP,* III, 353). The elderly coquette who recounts her life of libertinage and subsequent conversion experiences this concern when her friend, who has not lived a strictly moral life, suddenly dies:

> Je savais que, lorsqu'elle mourut, il y avait bien loin des idées qui l'occupaient à l'idée de la mort, et je me demandais ce qu'elle était devenue, par inquiétude pour ce que je pouvais devenir moi-même. Où était-elle alors? ne restait-il rien d'elle que ce corps sans mouvement que j'avais vu emporter? Cette âme subitement enlevée à tant de chimères, quel était son sort? Et moi, je mourrais donc aussi, me disais-je; et j'ai vécu jusqu'ici sans le savoir. Mais qu'est-ce que mourir? Et quelle aventure est-ce que la mort? Qu'elle est terrible, si j'en crois ma religion!

(*SF,* XIX, 222-23)

The fate of the soul is important and depends upon the quality of the actions performed in this life: as the Spectateur put it, by our virtue we can 'rendre avantageux' the life to come. Emander is explicit about the immortality of the soul and its fate beyond death. For the savages, Death is a god who must be worshipped. Emander acknowledges the importance of death, but rectifies their misconceptions:

> Cette vie que vous perdez, cette mort que l'Etre souverain vous envoie, ne borne pas sur vous son pouvoir. Cette âme qui vous anime, qui vous fait maintenant sentir les vérités que je vous apprends; cette âme qui a jugé qu'il y avait une puissance au-dessus de vous, et qui ne s'est trompée que dans le choix; cette âme ne meurt jamais: l'Etre souverain l'a faite immortelle, et capable de jouir de biens infinis, quand elle l'a craint: et capable de souffrir un éternel malheur, quand elle l'a méprisé sur terre.

(*ESS,* 287)

Divine benediction or retribution awaits the soul beyond death, according to the quality of the actions performed in the present.

Marivaux's religious sincerity and devotion to the Christian faith are beyond doubt. For him, faith informs man's actions in the present, consoles him in his miseries, and holds before him the prospect of future bliss. But equally Marivaux was, in his religion, undogmatic and tolerant, like Phocion in *Le Télémaque travesti* who disapproves of attempting to convert the Hugue-

nots to the Catholic faith by force rather than by gentle persuasion (*TT,* [*Le Télémaque travesti*] 832-37). The doctrines which come to us through Revelation are not discussed in Marivaux's work because they are mysteries which can only be accepted and not understood. In their place Marivaux stresses the practice of virtue, and it is significant that, according to Lesbros de la Versane, his first biographer, Marivaux valued the *Pensées* not for their doctrinal and theological content but as 'le meilleur livre de morale qui eût jamais été écrit'.[18] True religion, like true love, is not a furious passion, but is sustained quietly and calmly. The young girl who writes to the Spectateur complains that all pleasure is driven from her life by her mother who, out of zealous piety, tries to make each moment of her daughter's life exude a conscious devotion. She, however, fears that it is more likely to have the opposite effect:

> Quand je vous dis cela, ne croyez pas que je blâme la dévotion; j'en ai moi-même ce qu'il m'en faut; je suis naturellement sage, mais jusqu'ici j'ai plus de vertu que de piété, cela est dans l'ordre; et de cette piété, je vous jure que j'en aurais encore davantage, si ma mère n'exigeait pas que j'en eusse tant. Jamais je ne me sauverais, si je devais vivre toute ma vie avec elle.

(*SF,* XII, 177)

Marivaux's conception of religious devotion can be compared to that of Molière's Cléante who sees no reason why true devotion should not be *humaine* and *traitable.*[19]

These views, which constitute the ethical framework of Marivaux's novels and plays, stand within an optimistic but nevertheless perfectly orthodox tradition of Christian thought.[20] However, by their spirit of toleration and insistence on morality rather than doctrine they are associated with those ideas which lead from free-thought to Deism and natural religion. The ideas themselves are reminiscent of Saint-Evremond's own somewhat sceptical religious faith as expounded in his epistle *A Mr. le maréchal de Créqui,* whilst Marivaux's terminology reminds us of the language of Voltaire and Rousseau, for he speaks of God as an *Etre supérieur* or *souverain,* that is as a distant God who is outside and above his creation, not one who intervenes in transcendence. But Marivaux's position is distinct from that of either Voltaire or Rousseau, for he neither submits doctrine to the critique of reason as does the former nor accepts only those teachings which can be validated by the heart as does the latter. Nevertheless, d'Alembert seems to have recognized the implications of Marivaux's claim to be ignorant of all but the most fundamental aspects of Christian faith, and he attempts to defend him against the imputation of doctrinal laxity by comparing his views with those held by Malebranche:

> Si on était tenté de former quelque soupçon sur l'ignorance de Marivaux à cet égard, celle du pieux oratorien suffirait pour la justifier aux yeux du moins

des hommes sages, qui, déjà trop affligés de voir
l'impiété où elle est, n'ont garde de la chercher encore
où elle n'est pas.[21]

Unfortunately this justification does little to exonerate
Marivaux, for, as Bossuet saw, Malebranche is himself,
in matters of doctrine, equally suspect.

Marivaux reconciles an acceptance of the doctrine of
original sin with an optimistic view of the potentialities
of human nature, creating a blend of faith that has been
called by Pierre Jacoebée 'un humanisme chrétien', and
by Michel Gilot 'une sorte d'humanisme dévot'.[22] In rejecting Deism, atheism and the scepticism of the *esprits
forts* Marivaux's conscious intention was to defend an
orthodoxy that was increasingly under attack, but there
are in his work implications of which he would himself
have disapproved. We can discern in his position an
ambivalence which is also visible in the work of
Fénelon, of whom René Pomeau has said: 'son
optimisme chrétien a ouvert la voie à l'optimisme
déiste, que Fénelon eût répudié'.[23] In Marivaux this ambivalence is a product of that modification of values associated with 'la crise de la conscience européenne'
through which he lived and to which he bears witness.
Consciously he was clinging to the faith which around
him was disintegrating, but unconsciously he was part
of the process which was undermining orthodoxy and
substituting natural for revealed religion.

Notes

1. D'Alembert, *Éloge de Marivaux,* in Marivaux,
   Théâtre complet, edited by Frédéric Deloffre, 2
   vols (Paris, 1968), II, 979-1024 (1001).

2. Pierre Jacoebée, *La Persuasion de la charité:
   thèmes, formes et structures dans les "Journaux et
   œuvres diverses" de Marivaux* (Amsterdam,
   1976), 16.

3. Ibid., 35.

4. On various aspects of Marivaux's religious
   thought see H. Coulet, 'Marivaux et Malebranche',
   *Cahiers de l'Association Internationale des Études
   Françaises,* 25 (1973), 141-60 and the ensuing
   discussion, ibid., 343-52; M. Gilot, *Les Journaux
   de Marivaux,* 2 vols (Paris, 1975), especially Vol.
   1, 685-702; and O. A. Haac, 'Deism and
   Marivaux', *Romanic Review,* 63 (1972), 15-19.

5. Marivaux's Journals and miscellaneous works are
   referred to in the edition of the *Journaux et œuvres
   diverses* edited by Frédéric Deloffre and Michel
   Gilot (Paris, 1969). The titles of individual works
   are abbreviated as follows: *Lettres sur les habitants de Paris* (LSHP), *Pensées sur différents sujets*
   (PDS), *Le Spectateur français* (SF), *L'Indigent
   philosophe* (IP), *Le Cabinet du philosophe* (CP)
   and *Réflexions sur l'esprit humain* (RSEH).

6. D'Alembert, op. cit., 1001. The reference to the
   Almanach littéraire is given by Deloffre and Gilot
   in their edition of the *Journaux et œuvres diverses,*
   606-07, note 315.

7. The reference to the *Lettres persanes* is to Letter
   LXXVI.

8. Cf. Pascal, *Pensées,* Section 1: XIII 'Soumission
   et usage de la raison', nos. 167-88 in Lafuma's
   edition (Paris, 1962).

9. Cf. La Bruyère, *Les Caractères,* XVI, 2 and 16.

10. A study of the meaning of the term *sentiment* in
    Marivaux's novels can be found in Mario Matucci,
    'Sentiment et sensibilité dans l'œuvre romanesque
    de Marivaux', *Cahiers de l'Association
    Internationale des Études Françaises,* 25 (1973),
    127-39. A comparison with the meaning of the
    term as it occurs in the *Pensées* is found in the
    ensuing discussion, 343-52.

11. D'Alembert, op. cit., 1001.

12. Marivaux's early writings are referred to in the
    edition of the *Œuvres de jeunesse* edited by
    Frédéric Deloffre and Claude Rigault (Paris,
    1972). The titles of individual works are abbrevi-
    ated as follows: *Les Aventures de * * * ou les
    effets surprenants de la sympathie* (ESS), and *Le
    Télémaque travesti* (TT).

13. *Œuvres de Descartes,* edited by Charles Adam
    and Paul Tannery, new edition, 13 vols (Paris,
    1965-75), Volume IX-I, *Méditations,* II, 19.

14. Matthew 25. 35-36.

15. For contrasting interpretations of Marivaux's opti-
    mism or pessimism see respectively J. S. Spink,
    'Marivaux: The "Mechanism of the Passions" and
    the "Metaphysic of Sentiment"' (*Modern Lan-
    guage Review,* 73 (1978), 278-90), and Lester G.
    Crocker, 'Le Portrait de l'homme dans le *Paysan
    parvenu*' (*Studies on Voltaire and the Eighteenth
    Century,* 87 (1972), 253-76).

16. 1 Corinthians 15. 45-47.

17. Pascal, *Pensées,* ed. cit., no. 449.

18. Louis Lesbros de la Versane, *Esprit de Marivaux:
    ou analectes de ses ouvrages précédés de la vie
    historique de l'auteur* (Paris, 1769), 38-39.

19. Molière, *Le Tartuffe,* I. 5. 390.

20. For a discussion of the influence of Marivaux's
    religious views on his imaginative writing gener-
    ally and his theatre in particular see my article
    'The religious morality of Marivaux's *comédies
    d'amour*', *Romance Studies,* no. 4, Summer 1984,
    64-78.

21. D'Alembert, op. cit., 1024, note 31.

22. Pierre Jacoebée, op. cit., 32, and Michel Gilot, 'Quelques traits du visage de Marivaux', *Revue d'Histoire Littéraire de la France,* 70 (1970), 391-99 (393). Gilot uses the term when discussing an anonymous writing entitled *Compliment fait à Mlle de Richelieu par les dames religieuses de l'abbaye du Trésor, dont elle avait été quelques mois absente* which appeared in the *Mercure* in 1754 and which he attributes to Marivaux.

23. R. Pomeau, *La Religion de Voltaire* (Paris, 1956), 64.

Felicia Sturzer (essay date November 1990)

SOURCE: Sturzer, Felicia. "Names, Origins and the Female Voice in Marivaux's *La Vie de Marianne.*" *Essays in French Literature,* no. 27 (November 1990): 1-10.

[*In the following essay, Sturzer discusses Marianne's narrative as a somewhat ambiguous challenge to patriarchal authority.*]

The naming of women has been affected by men primarily through control of the social institutions that determine behaviour and attitudes.[1]

A recurring theme, the problem of female identity, remains the subject of critical debate. The focus has been not only on the implications of gender for our readings of various texts, but on the interaction between sexual difference and the power structures which control our social institutions. Among others, Hélène Cixous, Madeleine Therrien, Simone de Beauvoir, Nancy Miller, Carolyn Heilbrun, Annette Kolodny, Gerda Lerner and Charlotte J. Frisbie have discussed various aspects of this topic.[2] Our focus in this paper is on the process which links the literal act of naming to the concept of female self-identity and writing. "'Female identity is a process', and writing by women engages us in this process as the female self seeks to define itself in the experience of creating art."[3] If a woman writer can identify and formulate her "self" through the narratives she creates, then what are the implications for male authors who trace the development of a feminine self? One can ultimately ask if such a literary process is viable or intellectually honest, a question which this essay will address.

In the eighteenth century, Pierre Carlet de Marivaux was one of the few French male authors who discussed these issues in his novels, essays and plays. In his works, the feminine voice appears as Other, as an interplay of opposites, yet a voice demanding to be heard. In order to be accepted within a patriarchal system, the feminine must create a new text which establishes the centrality of woman as subject. In Marivaux's novel, *La Vie de Marianne ou Les Aventures de Madame la Comtesse de* *** (1731-42), the heroine encodes her "self" into a signifying system whose power structure is based on origins and the ability to name, to identify one's place in a stratified, patriarchal social order. As Marianne's story emerges, her marginality is transformed into centrality as object becomes subject. The female voice creates a new text which asserts the power of feminine inscription and challenges the established order's right to nomenclature. With reference to female authors, Tilde Sankovitch views this process as the creation of "empowering myths" which not only subvert male myths, but integrate themselves into existing structures.[4]

For the reader, the title of Marivaux's novel encodes not only the text narrated by "Marianne" but also of the unnamed "Madame la Comtesse de ***". As the title progresses from Marianne to Madame la Comtesse, an orphan with an assumed name is transformed, before our story even begins, into the aristocratic, mature, established Countess. The reasons for this transformation remain ambiguous, but the details of Marianne's mental and social progression are written, "read" and manipulated by a feminine voice seeking legitimacy and the power of textual inscription. The very possibility of such a progression questions the parameters which determine the moral and socio-economic basis of eighteenth-century French society.[5] It can be argued, nevertheless, that Marianne's female voice is *framed* (in both senses of the word) by a masculine source—the author who created it. However, the essential fact remains that, textually, a woman is writing to another woman, questioning the laws and stereotypes of a system into which they are now both integrated and presumably accepted. By challenging the concept of origin within a given socio-economic structure, Marianne/ Marivaux transform an insignificant, nameless orphan into a significant public figure (a countess) with a developed and mature sense of self. Thus, the original male source of the text, rather than falsifying it, strengthens the subversive message which encodes it.[6] The fabric of Marianne's narrative thus consists of a series of multiple discourses which disrupt and negate our traditional concept of origin as beginning or source.

Marianne's text is announced and publicized in the conventional eighteenth-century mode—it is "found" (presumably by a man), and presented as a story written by a woman to a nameless female friend. We are warned that the story has no pre-conceived plan, no particular style, no original source. Denying her role as author and the masculine authority it implies, the writer focuses instead on the act of writing her story, a woman's story which reveals a new set of parameters for human relationships: "N'oubliez pas que vous m'avez promis de ne jamais dire qui je suis; je ne veux être connue que de vous" (p. 9).[7] This initial complicity between women is not based on names made significant by men, but rather maintained and elaborated by the feminine network of support in the narrative which follows. Marianne, like the text she writes, was found, a victim of a crime which robbed her of family, material goods, and most important, of a name. The beginning of "Marianne's" text, like her assumed name, is thus one she selects and determines:

> on ne trouva, dans les habits des personnes qu'ils avaient assassinées, rien qui pût apprendre à qui j'appartenais. On eut beau recourir au registre qui est toujours chargé du nom des voyageurs, cela ne servit de rien; on sut bien par là qui ils étaient tous, à l'exception de deux personnes, d'une dame et d'un cavalier, dont le nom assez étranger n'instruisit de rien, et peut-être qu'ils n'avaient pas dit le véritable [. . .]

> Par tout cela ma naissance devint impénétrable, et je n'appartins plus qu'à la charité de tout le monde.

> (pp. 12-13)

The orphan becomes a devalorized figure, belonging to no one and everyone. Yet the ambiguity and silence surrounding her birth enable Marianne to challenge both the "helpless orphan" motif and the myth of the abandoned female caught in the double bind of whore or virgin. Belonging to no one in particular, Marianne can belong to herself. Her text encompasses multiple narrative possibilities. The orphan, who is also a woman, is doubly a potential victim, seduced, objectified, suppressed and marginalized. But she is also a woman who uses her ambiguous status to reconcile virtue with desire, vanity with modesty and subjectivity with alterity.

Enter the first representative of patriarchal power, the saviour-seducer in the guise of the charitable M. de Climal, whose sexuality is encoded in the discourse of the *dévot.* Marianne *reads* Climal thus: "je trouvais sa conversation singulière; il me semblait que mon homme se mitigeait, qu'il était plus flatteur que zélé, plus généreux que charitable; il me paraissait tout changé" (p. 30). Initially, she refuses to read the gift of fine clothes he gives her as a sign of erotic desire but rather of friendship and religious charity. She tells us, however, that Climal "seems changed" because she correctly deciphers the code of the *faux dévot.* Conscious and unconscious motivations clash as Marianne places Climal within a sexual economy based on possession: "ce fut ce beau linge qu'il voulut que je prisse qui me mit au fait de ses sentiments; je m'étonnai même que l'habit [. . .] m'eût encore laissé quelque doute, car la charité n'est pas galante dans ses présents" (p. 39). Marianne's *reading* of Climal's text becomes subversive. Knowledge of his duplicity gives her the power to write herself out of "his" story. Yet, the code of her new script remains suspended within a system whose

meaning shifts between the interspaces of *mauvaise foi.* Climal may be deceiving others, but he knows the truth of his lie. Marianne, however, is both *trompeuse* and *trompée,* deceiver and deceived, a writer who authenticates her text as she falsifies her story. The sexual significance of Climal's "gift" becomes obscured by the potential pleasure it gives. A sign of guilt is thus transformed into a sign of innocence. How can we characterize the feminine voice—is it vain or virtuous? submissive or domineering? To enhance the interest and possible validity of Marianne's text, meaning must remain equivocal, multiple, elusive. Names must be suppressed, as Climal's "undeclared" declaration of love offers the possibility of meaning deferred. Hence the irony of a discourse based on half truths: ". . . j'avais conclu qu'il fallait que je le visse tout entier pour le reconnaître, sinon il était arrêté que je ne verrais rien" (p. 40). Only total recognition and knowledge, a totality she refuses, can permanently inscribe Marianne's narrative with meaning. Victim desiring to be transformed into heroine, Marianne manipulates and refines her text, anticipating the *dévot's* unmasking and the revelation of *l'homme amoureux.*

The unmasking of the *dévot,* however, simultaneously reveals the subtext of Marianne's bad faith. This subtext emerges through yet another female voice, the laundress Mme Dutour, who sees what Marianne hides, and supplements her system of signification. Climal's gift of fine clothes is thus ultimately "named" for what it is and inscribed into the economy of sexual appropriation: "Mais je vois bien ce que c'est, ajouta-t-elle en tirant l'étoffe de l'habit qui était dessous [. . .] je vois bien ce que c'est; je devine pourquoi on a voulu m'en faire accroire sur ce linge-là, mais je ne suis pas si bête qu'on le croit" (p. 44). Forced to recognize the truth of Dutour's interpretation, the equilibrium of Marianne's discourse is threatened, and the female voice violently shatters the silence of an implied complicity in a system which equates sexual favours with economic gain. "Enfin j'étais comme un petit lion, ma tête s'était démontée, outre que tout ce qui pouvait m'affliger se présentait à moi" (pp. 45-46). However, vanity and virtue are superimposed on the subtext framed by *amour-propre.* Meaning emerges only between the lines of the "si" and the "mais" of Marianne's discourse: "Mais malgré cela, depuis que j'étais sûre que M. de Climal m'aimait, j'avais absolument résolu, s'il m'en parlait, de lui dire qu'il était inutile qu'il m'aimât. Après quoi, je prendrais sans scrupule tout ce qu'il voudrait me donner; c'était là mon petit arrangement" (p. 49). Socio-religious considerations have been reconciled with vanity and the desire for personal gain.

Marianne's self-justifying discourse results in the negation of Climal's moral and religious status. The outcome is unacceptable, since it subverts the system Climal represents. Thus, for the priest who introduced

Marianne to Climal, her revelations are infused with the unholy power of demonic inspiration: "Ce que vous dites est horrible, c'est le démon qui vous inspire, oui, le démon [. . .]; je ne vous écoute plus [. . .] Ah! la dangereuse petite créature! elle me fait frayeur" (pp.140-141). The priest's discourse embodies all the stereotypes historically associated with woman—the evil, unclean seducer, inspired by the devil. Marianne's revelations not only imply Climal's hypocrisy, but by extension, that of all *faux dévots* and the priestly authority they represent. By telling an unacceptable story, Marianne must be rejected and marginalized, punished for daring to speak the unspeakable.

> Ce rôle féminin, celui de la sorcière, celui de l'hystérique, est ambigu, à la fois contestataire et conservateur. *Contestataire,* car les symptômes, les crises, révoltent et secouent ceux pour qui ils sont faits, le public, le groupe, les hommes, les autres . . . Car l'hystérique défait les liens familiaux, introduit la perturbation dans le déroulement réglé de la vie quotidienne . . . Mais *conservateur* en même temps. Car toute sorcière finit par être détruite, et rien ne s'inscrit d'elle que les traces mythiques.[8]

Not only is Marianne dangerous and demonic, but she must be silenced, for her knowledge implies the power to name and condemn unacceptable behaviour, i.e., authority. Her scandalous text must remain unwritten and unheard, erased and thus silenced. "Ne révélez jamais cette étrange aventure à personne; gardons-nous de réjouir le monde par ce scandale, il en triompherait, et en prendrait droit de se moquer des vrais serviteurs de Dieu. Tâchez même de croire que vous avez mal vu, mal entendu . . ." (p.144). Marianne, however, refuses to be silenced, for silence would result in her destruction. When her assertions are ultimately validated and Climal's sin is named, a new text is introduced into a system which must now accept a truth it had sought to falsify. Interestingly, it is only at Climal's death that he reveals the truth of his actions. Marianne is vindicated, but only through Climal's validation—a spokesman for the masculine power structure he represents.

While pride excludes the prostitution of self, it does not prohibit the transformation of the body from an object of erotic desire into a subject of textual inscription. Having deciphered and named Climal's text of seduction and refusing its falsification, Marianne is aware that she still remains both subject and object within a patriarchal system. Still another text must be written, one which maximizes the opportunities for advancement and self-assertion yet subverts the fixed code of familial origin. The possibility for such a text is provided by Valville, an aristocrat with the name and connections necessary for social integration. Marianne attracts Valville's attention through the ambiguous sexual manipulation of coquetterie. Aggressive but appearing passive, she controls a system of exchange which promises more than it gives. Within the setting of a Church, Marianne "innocently" uses her body in an erotic dialogue between virtue and desire. Thus, she raises her head to look at the pictures on the ceiling "parce que cette industrie-là me faisait le plus bel œil du monde". She adjusts her hair, revealing a pretty hand, "qui amenait nécessairement avec elle un bras rond, qu'on voyait pour le moins à demi . . ." (p. 62). As the desire for pleasure mingles with the desire for virtue, cause and effect are interchanged and Marianne is *seen* by the potential lover, Valville. To validate her text, however, to establish herself as Valville's equal, she must also legitimize her name and integrate her "self" into society. For outside the system of family origin, she is suppressed, doomed to remain forever the other, and in her own words, the eternal "grisette, aventurière et petite fille", sacrificial victim "dont on ne se soucierait plus" (p.177). However, in a new twist to the traditional love story, a legitimate origin will not be acquired through Valville, but in spite of him, using a system of feminine values which challenge and ultimately triumph over a hierarchy determined by male-dominated institutions.

As Marianne deciphers the code of social legitimacy, she recognizes that the feminine voice is not only body, the exterior materiality of the text, but also mind, the interior space of spiritual worth. Deprived of a natural mother, Marianne must establish her identity as "daughter" worthy of a name and social status. Mme de Miran, Valville's mother, recognizes Marianne's moral and spiritual value. Serving as her adoptive mother, she confers credibility on Marianne not only as narrating subject, but in her new status as daughter: "dès sa première rencontre avec Valville, Marianne reconnaît aussitôt l'amour, mais cette grande passion perd peu à peu de son importance en face des perspectives d'établissement et de l'affection quasi maternelle de Mme de Miran".[9] The mother-daughter relationship not only links Marianne to an origin, but provides the means to penetrate a socio-economic power structure which excludes that which cannot be named: "je n'ai peut-être pas perdu plus de biens que j'en retrouve; la mère à qui je dois la vie n'aurait peut-être pas été plus tendre que la mère qui m'adopte, et ne m'aurait pas laissé un meilleur nom que celui que je vais porter" (p. 287). Let us note that the women who help Marianne are widows with independent sources of income who in practice, though not in theory, control the status of women within their social circle. It is thus that Marianne's reference is to the name left by the mother, not the father, for it is the spiritual legacy of the former which influences the process of her own development.

But the "name" which Mme de Miran offers Marianne must be legitimized by the social and legal tribunals of family and law. Only then can the potential for Marianne's feminine self-determination be fully realized. Abducted from the supposed safety of her convent, Marianne is forced to undergo a trial, instigated by one of Mme de Miran's female relatives, which questions not only her personal integrity but her claims to aristocratic origins. The central episode in Marianne's narration, the trial scene crystallizes the struggle between two, mutually exclusive power systems. Before a magistrate and a family tribunal, Marianne is accused of seducing Valville for her own personal gain, thereby usurping the social hierarchy to which he belongs. The initial insult to her status is the refusal by Mme de Miran's relative to address Marianne as "mademoiselle". This relegates her to a state of alterity devoid of legitimate rights and privileges. "Mademoiselle! s'écria encore là-dessus, d'un air railleur, cette parente sans nom; mademoiselle! Il me semble avoir entendu dire qu'elle s'appelait Marianne, ou bien qu'elle s'appelle comme on veut, car comme on ne sait d'où elle sort, on n'est sûr de rien avec elle . . ." (p. 327). The argument centres on the power "to name", ironically assumed by the nameless relative who presents Marianne's case before the tribunal. But this time Mme de Miran's role as adoptive mother is to legitimize Marianne by transforming the common *fille* into the noble *demoiselle*. Using Marianne's actions as signs of her inner qualities, she begins a process of textual decoding in which being and seeming merge: "sa figure, qui vous paraît jolie, est en vérité ce qui la distingue le moins; et je puis vous assurer que, par son bon esprit, par les qualités de l'âme, et par la noblesse des procédés, elle est demoiselle autant qu'aucune fille, de quelque rang qu'elle soit, puisse l'être" (p. 329). To validate her discourse, Mme de Miran re-tells and re-creates the story of Marianne's origin, emphasizing the signs which could signify a noble birth. The servants killed with the "distinguished" foreigners, presumably Marianne's parents, the fine clothes the victims were wearing, and the verification of the story by "un saint religieux" all support the legitimate and proper "origin" which Marianne embodies by her words and actions (p. 328).

But Marianne's identity remains supported only by circumstantial evidence. To maintain the established hierarchy, the magistrate decides that she must nevertheless be rendered harmless and prevented from marrying Valville. What better guardian of the *status quo* than another man, a substitute for the one she cannot have. He is offered by the judge in the person of M. Villot, a nonentity Marianne rejects outright.

> Et il lui montrait M. Villot, qui, quoique assez bien fait, avait alors, autant qu'on peut l'avoir, l'air d'un pauvre petit homme sans conséquence, dont le métier était de ramper et d'obéir, à qui même il n'appartenait pas d'avoir du cœur, et à qui on pouvait dire: retirez-vous, sans lui faire d'injure.
>
> (p. 332)

By rejecting Villot, Marianne rejects sexual and economic manipulation. "Jamais, avec ce cœur-là, je ne pourrai aimer le jeune homme qu'on me présente, jamais" (p. 333). Next, Marianne rejects the very thing she is accused of desiring—Valville. Though she loves him, it is not Valville who will be her saviour, but rather the mother and the link she represents between past, present and future. With her judges as witnesses, she tells Mme de Miran: "je ne vivrais point si je vous perdais; je n'aime que vous d'affection; je ne tiens sur la terre qu'à vous qui m'avez recueillie si charitablement, et qui avez la générosité de m'aimer tant" (p. 335). Marianne thus rejects the role of feminine subordination by transforming the text of her potential downfall into one of triumph. Having rejected her judges' proposals, she procedes to challenge the very assumptions upon which their system is based.

The choices Marianne makes are determined by her own sense of justice and ethical standards. But they also reveal the strategy of a female voice which exploits the various possibilities of multiple narrations. In an intertextual twist, Marianne reads the script of a victim's role—a part she never intends to play. Mlle Varthon, Marianne's rival for Valville's affection, appears in the stylized role of weak, helpless femininity. she becomes an "objet [. . .] intéressant" to Valville when she faints, a pathetic creature ready to be saved, nurtured and loved by man, waiting prince and saviour (p. 351). Ironically, however, it is Varthon who has written this script which she, like Marianne, can read and interpret. Fainting, the "romanesque" convention of eighteenth-century heroines, becomes yet another vehicle of feminine control. Varthon confirms what Marianne and the reader already know: "D'où lui est venue cette fantaisie de m'aimer [. . .] Hélas! je vais vous le dire: c'est qu'il m'a vue mourante". In good health Valville would have never noticed her! Varthon thus reads her text: "c'est mon évanouissement qui en a fait un infidèle" (p. 378). Marianne and Varthon know that Woman as object of desire is woman "intacte, éternelle, absolument impuissante. Il ne doute pas qu'elle l'ait attendu depuis toujours . . . Cependant elle respire. Juste assez de vie; et pas trop".[10] Marianne, mistress of her own destiny, no longer fulfils the feminine role of dependent alterity and is unwilling to play the part, even if she must lose Valville. She chooses life, refusing to be the voice singing a song of death yet beckoning with signs of life.

> En voyant cette jeune personne, on eût plutôt dit: Elle ne vit plus, qu'on n'eût dit: Elle est morte. Je ne puis vous représenter l'impression qu'elle faisait, qu'en vous priant de distinguer ces deux façons de parler, qui paraissent signifier la même chose, et qui dans le sentiment pourtant en signifient de différentes.
>
> (p. 350)

Valville, not Marianne, plays the role of inessential Other, while she strengthens her filial bond with the mother and ultimately fulfils the textual destiny promised by the title—Marianne becomes "Mme la Comtesse".[11] By "giving" him Mlle Varthon, Marianne nullifies Valville's masculine authority: "Ma générosité le terrassa, l'anéantit devant moi; je ne vis plus qu'un homme rendu . . ." (p. 406). His humiliation confirms Marianne's superiority and becomes her ultimate vengeance: "cette humiliation que je laissais dans son cœur, cet étonnement où il devait être de la noblesse de mon procédé, enfin cette supériorité que mon âme venait de prendre sur la sienne" (p. 407). The masculine bond is weakened as feminine bonds are strengthened. Socially disgraced and textually superfluous, Valville-the-son's betrayal can only engender misunderstanding and disbelief: "Je n'ai pas voulu le croire" (p. 419). The reader, likewise, is left questioning the patriarchal code.

Closure perceived but never attained, Marianne's narrative remains unfinished, for the Woman's story is still being written. From a postmodern perspective, Marivaux's novel is not a revolutionary feminist statement. In an age when established institutions were just beginning to be challenged and new alternatives proposed, Marianne's voice emerges as a discourse ultimately integrated into and accepted by the established patriarchal structure. In the spectrum of feminine discourses, Marianne's statement is one of differentiation, validation and re-integration rather than complete separation from the masculine. Hence, the occasional ambiguity of its message. As text and intertext mingle in a multiplicity of narratives (Marianne's re-telling, the Comtesse's re-writing, and Mme de Miran's reformulation of the text), the feminine voice renews itself by refusing to be circumscribed and silenced. As each ending implies a new beginning, "Marivaux/Marianne's promise to deliver binds the reader to the pleasure of postponement . . . The enigma of origins remains intact; and the price of Marianne's 'feminine' destiny, like the name of the female *destinataire* of her narrative, remains *en blanc*".[12]

Notes

1. Sheila Ruth, "The 'Naming' of Women—Images of Women in Patriarchy: The Masculist—Defined Woman", in *Issues in Feminism—An Introduction to Women's Studies,* ed. Sheila Ruth (Mountain View, California, 1990), p. 81.

2. Simone de Beauvoir, *Le Deuxième Sexe. I. Les Faits et Les Mythes. II. L'Expérience Vécue* (Paris, Gallimard, 1949); Charlotte J. Frisbie, "Anthropological Perspectives on the Subordination of Women", in *Issues in Feminism—An Introduction to Women's Studies*; Carolyn G. Heilbrun, *Reinventing Womanhood* (New York, Norton, 1979); Annette Kolodny, "Dancing through the Minefield: Some Observations on the Theory, Practice, and Politics of a Feminist Literary Criticism", *Feminist Studies,* 6, 1 (1980), pp.1-25; Gerda Lerner,

"A New Angle of Vision", in *Issues in Feminism—An Introduction to Women's Studies.* See also Gerda Lerner, *The Creation of Patriarchy* (New York, Oxford U.P., 1986); Madeleine Therrien, "La problématique de la féminité dans *La Vie de Marianne", Stanford French Review,* (1987), pp. 51-61.

3. Judith K. Gardiner, "On Female Identity and Writing by Women", *Writing and Sexual Difference,* ed. Elizabeth Abel (University of Chicago Press, 1982), p.191.

4. Tilde A. Sankovitch, *French Women Writers and the Book—Myths of Access and Desire* (Syracuse U.P., 1988).

5. René Démoris, *Le Roman à la première personne—Du Classicisme aux Lumières* (Paris, A. Colin, 1975), pp. 398-99.

6. The question of male authors writing in the female voice is further discussed in my essay, "Text, Reading and Writing in Marivaux's *Pharsamon ou Les Nouvelles Folies Romanesques* and *La Vie de Marianne", Romance Languages Annual,* 1 (1990), pp. 316-21.

7. All page numbers are to the 1963 Editions Garnier edition of *La Vie de Marianne.*

8. Hélène Cixous and Catherine Clément, *La Jeune Née* (Paris, Livre de Poche, 1975), pp.13-14.

9. Démoris, *op. cit.,* p. 401.

10. Cixous and Clément, *op. cit.,* p.120.

11. Nancy K. Miller, *The Heroine's Text—Readings in the French and English Novel 1722-1782* (Columbia U.P., 1980), pp.21-22.

12. *Ibid.,* p. 36.

Jay L. Caplan (essay date August 1991)

SOURCE: Caplan, Jay L. "Love on Credit: Marivaux and Law." *Romance Quarterly* 38, no. 3 (August 1991): 289-99.

[*In the following essay, Caplan offers an interpretation of the play* Le jeu de l'amour et du hasard *based on an examination of the failed economic policies of Marivaux's contemporary, John Law.*]

In 1716, the French regent, Phillippe d'Orléans, chartered John Law's *Banque Générale* (later the *Banque Royale*), and authorized it to issue paper notes. He later placed the Scotsman at the head of the newly consolidated *Compagnie Générale des Indes,* whose notes were guaranteed by the state. The success of these measures was such that in 1720, Law became controller general of finances, and brought the bank and the stock company under his direction. After a frenzied wave of speculation in the so-called "Mississippi bubble," the entire "system" went bankrupt on July 17, 1720.[1]

Law's system was based upon the assumption that the greater the means of payment in a society, the more prosperous that society will become—a position that has been called "Keynesian." He expressed this belief in terms of an analogy with the circulation of the blood, which had been demonstrated in 1628 by William Harvey, in his treatise *Exercitatio anatomica de motu cordis et sanguinis* ["On the Movement of the Heart and Blood in Animals"]. In a 1705 treatise entitled *Money and Trade Considered with a Proposal for Supplying the Nation with Money,* Law asserted that: "When blood does not circulate throughout the body, the body languishes; the same when money does not circulate."[2] Law was doubtless the first influential monetary theorist to think of the economy in terms of physiology and health, and we may owe to him the habit of speaking of a "healthy" or "sick" economy. In order to get money circulating in the Scottish system, Law suggested simply printing it, on paper, while guaranteeing its value in land holdings, rather than in precious metals.

Like many of his contemporaries, Law was an "adventurer," a man who spent his life imagining various schemes in order to become rich or powerful, and yet he never seems to have made any clear distinction between the schemes that had a good chance of working and those that would need a miracle to succeed. For a number of years Law made his living as a gambler, but he was also a rational planner, or "projector." Indeed the first loans and resulting note issued by the "Banque Générale" were perfectly reasonable moves, and they considerably eased the financial position of the French government.[3] In the judgment of John Kenneth Galbraith, "Had Law stopped at this point, he would be remembered for a modest contribution to the history of banking" (pp. 23-24). Of course, he did not stop there[4] and is now remembered primarily for the panic and bankruptcy that ultimately ensued.

In fact there were two successive, and very different versions of the famous "system." Both versions called for the State-owned Company to purchase the leases on tax farms, and offer to reimburse the entire public debt by buying back its paper obligations (an offer that most *rentiers* would presumably have declined). But while the first version was to rely upon a limited note issue (of "actions rentières"), guaranteed by the land holdings of the company, in the version of the system *that was ultimately adopted* there was no limit (beyond permission of the Regent) to the right of the Banque Royale to issue notes, which were guaranteed only by stock in the Company. Edgar Faure has called the first version "the

reasonable plan" ("le plan sage") and the second version, the one finally adopted, "the mad plan" ("le plan fou").[5] Of course, it certainly remains to be seen whether rational planning and irrational risk-taking are not really two sides of the same coin.[6]

When *Money and Trade* was published in 1705, Law had already been in exile for ten years from Scotland, where he was condemned to death for having killed a man in a duel. Throughout his many adventures in foreign lands, Law, who was the son of a goldsmith, would steadfastly maintain his opposition to the power of gold. As late as 1720, when the System was beginning to unravel, he wrote (this time, in French) that: "Il est de l'intérêt du Roi et de son peuple d'assurer la monnaie de banque et d'abolir la monnaie d'or" (Faure, p. 36). By injecting a transfusion of monetary "blood" into the French economic system (that is, by radically increasing the means of payment, while also cutting interest rates drastically), Law's expansionist monetary policy put a temporary end to a prolonged recession. Its long-term effects were less fortunate. According to Charles Kindleberger, "A traumatic experience with paper money under John Law set back the evolution of bank notes [in France] for a century" (p. 60). By seeking to abolish the use of gold as money, and instead printing guaranteed paper notes (in this case, the notes of Law's bank were guaranteed—temporarily as it turned out—by the reality of the land holdings of the Company in Louisiana, and by the promise of gold that the Louisiana subsoil allegedly contained), Law's system effected a separation between money as substance and money as function. More radically, it had the effect of turning money into a form itself insubstantial, a mere *sign* of real value.[7]

This article argues that, despite the failure of the Banque Royale on July 17, 1720 (after which France would return to the use of precious metals as money), Law's attack on gold money may be viewed as symptomatic of more systematic changes in the status and meaning of signs. In order to suggest the nature of this semiotic shift, I should like to compare *Le Jeu de l'amour et du hasard* (1730) of Marivaux (who was bankrupted by the failure of Law's system) with the play that, in Rousseau's view, most forcefully articulated the corrupt values of the *ancien régime,* Molière's *Le Misanthrope* (1666).

At the beginning of act III of *Le Misanthrope,* the two *petits marquis,* Acaste and Clitandre, argue about which of them has more reason to be satisfied with himself generally, and in particular to believe that the coquettish Célimène loves him. Acaste declares: "Mais le gens de mon air, marquis, ne sont pas faits / Pour *aimer à crédit* et faire tous les frais" (*Le Misanthrope,* III, 1).

What does Acaste mean by "aimer à crédit"? According to Furetière's *Dictionnaire universel* (1690), "crédit" refers to the measure of a person's status within a given community, as in its first definition: "Croyance, estime, qu'on s'acquiert *dans le public* par sa vertu, sa probité . . ." (emphasis added). Credit is a value that one acquires in relationship to a certain *public*; it must be openly, publicly known. It is a value that an individual or groups acquire through action in the public sphere. Although his first definition stresses moral values ("sa vertu, sa probité"), Furetière's first example ("Les Grecs se sont mis en *crédit* par leurs sciences") suggests that the meaning of credit is not limited to the moral sphere. "Crédit" refers more generally to what is publicly believed, or credited, about a person or group. In this sense, credit is the result of previous actions, but it is not itself active; it is the measure ("estime") of what a person or group is believed capable of doing. However, Furetière's second definition of "crédit" has a more active sense, which is retained in modern Franch: "CREDIT se dit aussi de la puissance de l'autorité, des richesses qu'on acquiert par le moyen de cette réputation qu'on a acquise. Ce ministre a acquis un grand *crédit* à la cour sur l'esprit du Prince." According to this definition, credit is the publicly recognized value or reputation that a community grants a person, on the basis of his or her previous actions, and which allows that person to exert power over the other members of that same community. This sort of credit leads others to pay attention to one's opinions, or to entrust one with money or goods ("richesses"). Since it makes the past actions of a person or group even more valuable within the community, it is active, or productive credit. In both the virtual and active senses recorded by Furetière in 1690, "credit" refers to an interaction between the value or worth of an individual and the beliefs that are publicly held about that individual. Credit, in other words, is based upon an *economy of public belief.*

The third meaning recorded by Furetière locates this credit economy within a specifically commercial context. In business, credit is "ce *prest* naturel qui se fait d'argent & de marchandises, sur la réputation & solvabilité d'un négociant" (emphasis added). Credit is a loan or *prest* and is therefore something that never actually *belongs* to anyone. We may perhaps infer that not only in business, but in all forms of human commerce, credit is always borrowed, and therefore can always be recalled by the lending community. The beliefs on which one's credit is predicated are always subject to revision, as the following ominous example suggests: "Ce banquier a bon *crédit* sur la place, sa banqueroute n'a guère diminué son *crédit.*"

Returning to Acaste's words, "aimer à crédit," we note that the first meaning of "à crédit" ("without paying cash") has also survived in modern French (and English) and is also associated by Furetière with financial ruin: "On dit, Faire *crédit,* vendre *à crédit,* acheter *à crédit* pour dire, ne payer pas comptant ce qu'on achète. C'est

le *crédit* que font les Marchands aux Grands Seigneurs qui ruine leur fortune, leur négoce." Like Moliere's Acaste, Furetière does not approve of this sort of credit, although not entirely for the same reasons. From his bourgeois perspective, Furetière implicitly condemns buying or selling "à crédit," since the practice works to the sole advantage of the great noblemen to whom credit is given, while condemning their creditors (such as Mr. Dimanche in Molière's *Dom Juan*) to ultimate ruin. As we shall see, the distaste of a petty court nobleman like Acaste for loving "à crédit" is not related to his desire for immediate "payment." However, Furetière suggests another relevant sense of the term. We read: "A CREDIT se dit souvent pour dire, A plaisir, sans utilité, sans fondement. Cet homme s'est ruiné *à crédit,* à plaisir, *sans faire de dépense qui parût*" (emphasis added). In this example, one can still hear the archaic conception of conspicuous, public expenditure ("dépense qui parût") as the measure of a noble's worth. From that perspective, it is useless ("sans utilité") to dilapidate one's resources, unless it is done publicly, in the eyes of the community whose recognition determines an individual's value. A sense of the contemporary meanings of "crédit" and "à crédit" casts new light upon Acaste's speech, which will be quoted here at greater length:

> *Mais les gens de mon air, marquis, ne sont pas faits*
> *Pour aimer à crédit et faire tous les frais.*
> Quelque rare que soit, le mérite des belles,
> Je pense, Dieu merci, qu'*on vaut son prix* comme elles,
> Que, pour se faire honneur d'un cœur comme le mien,
> Ce n'est pas la raison qu'*il ne leur coûte rein,*
> Et qu'*à frais communs* se fassent les avances.
>
> (*Le Misanthrope,* III, 1, 815-22; emphasis added)

The meaning of "aimer à crédit" now appears more clearly. In Acaste's social group, "loving" ("aimer") refers to a form of coded public display, and certainly not to one's feelings about another person. According to the conventions of "politeness" ("politesse"), love—like friendship—is a ritualized behavior that is conventionally performed in a certain public situation. It is elicited, not by interior states, but by specific social relations. For example, in the presence of an attractive young widow like Célimène, any gentleman who has an appropriate sense of his own worth ("[quil] vaut son prix") simply must "make love" to her, for the same reason that she must courteously allow those advances to be made. According to the constraints of this code, which would arouse Rousseau's indignation in his famously brilliant misreading of *Le Misanthrope,* a concern with *feelings* (whether one's own or those of other persons) is not only irrelevant but vulgar.

In any case, what Acaste calls "loving" is behavior elicited by an aristocratic form of self-love ("amour-propre"). This behavior is based, first of all, upon an estimation of his position (or "net worth") in a hierarchy of fixed values: rank, wealth, courage (which has become willingness to defend one's "honor" in a duel); it also depends upon an awareness of his audience, and upon the possession of various social graces, all of which are supposedly *inherited,* rather than acquired, and give effortless expressions to a nobleman's social identity. For Acaste and Clitandre, to love is to expect prompt recognition of one's socially recognized worth, and therefore to have only contempt for "loving on credit" (*aimer à crédit*). They know that a gentleman cannot court a lady without declaring his affections, without spending, not just money, but also other tokens of his love. Regardless of his true feelings, he must make considerable symbolic expenditures, to which Acaste refers ("faire tous les frais," "à frais communs," etc.) in his speech. To love costs; it requires making representations of one's love and thereby diminishing, if only temporarily, one's recognized worth. Since it entails offering tokens of love to a woman without rapid repayment in kind, loving on credit ("aimer à crédit")— that is, without the lady's quickly signifying that she loves him, too—is a risky investment for a gentleman like Acaste or Clitandre. The more one spends without being paid back, the more one's worth is visibly diminished in the eyes of one's peers. Since that necessary reevaluation cannot be postponed without a gentleman's devaluation, for him love on credit amounts to love discredited. As a matter of fact, this belief leads the two *marquis* to require from Célimène a public declaration of her preference, and this demand that will precipitate her eventual discreditation.

Louis Marin has argued that portraits of Louis XIV were believed to have the same value as the king himself, in precisely the same sense that the Eucharist was believed to be the body of Christ.[8] Likewise the presence in coins of a certain quantity of precious metal guaranteed their value, and insured that a *louis d'or,* for example, was worth its weight in gold. In the patriarchal hierarchy of this society the value of persons was a treasure, immediately given in their nature. Rank, in turn, was measured by the standard of the Sun-king, just as currency was measured in silver and gold. Yet rank was always subject to rapid and unpredictable turns of fortune, to the sudden devaluation or revaluation that classical theater represented as the *coup de théâtre.*

Whereas in Molière one's worth must always be shown, publicly and theatrically displayed, in order to be effective—a situation that precludes the granting of credit, characters (at least, upper-class characters) in Marivaux refuse to take anyone, especially themselves, at face value, in terms of a public image, and consequently commit themselves to the risks and pleasures of speculation and credit. "Marivaux," whose real name was Pierre Carlet de Chamblain, lost everything in the wake

of Law's bankruptcy. It is tempting, and probably not entirely fantastic, to view Marivaux's *Le Jeu de l'amour et du hasard* (1730) as an idealized representation of the experiment in credit whose dramatic failure brought on the ruin of so many speculators. It is also worth noting the biographical fact that, starting in 1698, Marivaux's father was Director of the Royal Mint at Riom, a town in Auvergne. In the ideal, or utopian form of the experiment that *Le Jeu de l'amour et du hasard* can be shown to represent (a form that most resembles the first version of Law's system), credit is granted to "instruments" that are themselves worthless, but whose face value and yield are guaranteed, if the pun can be avoided or pardoned, by Law. In that ideal form, value is no longer fixed in the hierarchical order of the *ancien régime,* but rather is *produced* through the interplay of credit and speculation. The result of this *jeu* will be a new order, based on individual performance rather than inherited social position. The upper-class code of *politesse,* in which Voltaire saw the essence of manners under the *ancien régime,* is replaced by a new code of sincerity. Whereas *politesse* implied an aristocratic subordination of the individual's true thoughts and feelings to the smooth functioning of the social group, the code of sincerity would require a constant effort to express and impose subjective truth. In a world governed by sincerity, "forms" would become synonymous with lack of real meaning, while they had previously been consubstantial with meaning. Forms, and signs in general, would ultimately be perceived as empty or "rhetorical," irrelevant (if not fundamentally opposed) to the expression of full, interior truth. With this semiotic shift, the status of social behavior and of signs in general would become analogous to that of banknotes in Law's System: insubstantial as paper money, yet guaranteed by something as reputedly solid and reliable as land, gold, . . . or the human heart. This new code of sincerity was perhaps first articulated in France through the exquisite linguistic practice that has come to be known as *marivaudage.*

In Marivaux, love is a *speculative* activity, in several senses of the word: in the etymological sense, it requires looking at a mirror (Latin *speculum*); it entails economic planning, which the eighteenth century called "speculation"; and love is also "speculative" in a more modern sense, that of requiring a high-risk investment. To fall in love is to plan, to gamble, and to mirror (oneself). Falling in love in a Marivaux play entails taking the risk of losing, and perhaps ultimately finding oneself in a *speculum* or mirror image. His most famous play, *Le Jeu de l'amour et du hasard,* opens with a scene in which Silvia, the heroine, expresses her apprehensions about the marriage that her father has arranged for her. Like other leading ladies in Marivaux's *comédies d'amour,* Silvia believes that she and her ideals are unconventional, different from what one might expect to find in young ladies of her social position.

She believes, or more precisely, she *feels* herself different from what she appears *at face value*. Behind her conventional appearance, she feels unique, singular, maybe even *originale* (that is, "odd": the word still retains a pejorative value in 1730): "Si elle osait, elle m'appelerait une originale," she says to Lisette in act I, scene 1. She senses that her values are unique, that they cannot be represented or reproduced, and therefore fears that the conventionally attractive young man her father has chosen for her, may not turn out to be her type, that he may not be *unique, like her.* Lisette paints a picture of Dorante as he appears to public opinion (the *on dit*): as an ideal match, a young man who leaves nothing to be desired. His moral qualities are summarized by the term "honnête," which abstractly designates everything that makes Dorante socially desirable; that set of moral qualities that, since the ideal of the *honnête homme* was forged in the early seventeenth century, have depended less and less upon noble birth, and more and more upon that curious form of cultural capital that the English call "breeding." Physically Dorante is *bien fait, de bonne mine,* in short, *aimable.* In fact, Lisette adds, no young lady would think twice about marrying this young man: for not only is he attractive ("Aimable, bien fait, voilà de quoi vivre pour l'amour"), but he has all the requisite social graces ("sociable et spirituel, voilà pour l'entretien de la société" (I, 1). However, Silvia is more concerned with inner worth, or character than she is with appearances, and she is particularly worried about the habit men seem to have of putting on a public face that is very different from their real selves.

It will turn out, of course, that Dorante has the same apprehensions about Silvia, and the same sense of his own uniqueness. In order to negotiate this discrepancy between face value and real worth, between public facade and domestic reality, Silvia and Dorante independently devise (spontaneously, they think) a theatrical strategy as unique (or as conventional) as themselves: with the complicity of Silvia's family and servants, each will trade roles with his or her servant, in order better to observe the other party, before making any rash commitments. Not only does the perfect symmetry of their desires, duplicated by the apparently symmetrical desires of the chamber maid and valet, underline that Silvia and Dorante are meant for each other; but the subsequent interplay of identities leaves Silvia and Dorante apparently defenseless against a development that they fear even more than marriage: love.

Yet that vulnerability may only be apparent. Since neither imagines that the other could remotely resemble her or him, each appears momentarily to take the other at face value, as the valet Arlequin and the chamber maid Lisette respectively, that is, as beings so clearly unlike their masters, so obviously unworthy of their love, that they need not be feared, either. For a moment, Silvia and Dorante appear, to the audience and even to themselves, to have suspended their prejudices against both love and the servant class, long enough for the damage to be done. It remains to be seen however, whether that typical, fatal moment in Marivaux, when the protagonists first lay eyes upon each other, and love is born, whether this is a moment of vulnerability, or of mirroring "speculation." A moment, that is, when each character sees him- or herself in the other, when he or she sees in the other the mirror image of a superior being, who will not take others at face value. Only the servants can really believe that the person with whom they have fallen in love and who has fallen in love with them, is the master or the mistress, and capable of taking her or him for their equal. Precisely because they credit appearances, the servants have no apprehensions about love and marriage either. In that speculative moment,[9] that moment of reciprocal mirroring of one's ideal self, Silvia and Dorante have the impression (that the audience may share) of putting themselves (their ego) at risk: of *speculating,* in another sense. But it is really *speculation without risk*; the masters never have anything to lose (or the servants anything to gain), because the value they will have at the end of the *Jeu*—their *redemption value,* so to speak—is guaranteed (by their fathers, as we shall see). Thus Silvia's brother Mario argues against letting his sister know that Dorante will also be disguised as his servant, because Mario is confident that the two of them will sense what they are worth anyhow: "Voyons si leur cœur ne les avertiraient pas de ce qu'ils valent" (I, 4). A few moments later, the protagonists find themselves alone together for the first time, each pretending to be a servant, and the first thing that the false Arlequin says to the false Lisette is: "[T]a maîtresse te vaut-elle?" (I, 7). The question already contains its own answer: No, the "mistress" is not worth as much as the false Lisette; no, neither of them should be taken at face value. The question already implies what Dorante feels in his heart but does not yet consciously know: namely, that this chamber maid is really worth more than her mistress, because she really *is* the mistress.

From this speculative moment on, the *Jeu* plays itself out in symmetrical patterns, visibly, in a stylized Italianate performance style, as if to underscore the resemblance of the players to pieces on a game board, as they mirror each other's moves through various stages of amorous development, until a conclusion that was inevitable even before the first exchange of glances. But if the *Jeu* is a game, the ground rules of the game were not written by the young lovers, even though they lay claim to this privilege at the outset of the play. Before the action of the play began, the rules of the game were laid down by M. Orgon and Dorante's (unnamed) father, when they arranged the marriage betwen Silvia and Dorante. But since they are liberal fathers, they have the goodness of heart to allow their children the freedom to choose a partner for themselves. ("[I]l faut être un peu trop bon pour l'être assez," remarks M. Orgon in I, 2.) Of course, their children immediately, spontaneously choose the same person that their fathers had intended for them. In contrast, young lovers in Molière always find themselves in conflict with male authority figures, whether fathers (Argan, the Orgon of *Tartuffe*, et al.) or a guardian like Arnolphe, who always want to marry the poor girl to someone (like themselves) that she is not suited for (because he is too old, too vulgar or both), whom she could not possibly love. In a curious way, as this stock figure of the father who conventionally opposes his children's desires is transformed into a father with a heart of gold, who has only his child's interest at heart, the audience now can notice that even his name ("Orgon") had gold (*or*) in it. Although the name of the father had lost its face value through usage, in Marivaux the play of speculation re-invests "Orgon" with gold, and thereby reaffirms the paternal gold standard.

In Marivaux the obstacle, but also the means, to the realization of the father's desire (the Father's Law) is not another, more appropriate man, but love itself: "love," that is, a determinate form of speculation. In the *Jeu* the well-born heroine does not require any help from the servants to overcome her father's tyrannical desire, since her father is enlightened and good, since he and she ultimately desire the same thing. The strategic objective of the game is to ratify the father's judgment (the "gold standard," speaking anachronistically), to teach the daughter (and the audience) that father (even Marivaux's father, the Director of the Royal Mint) knows best.

In its speculative form then, love is less an obstacle to realization of the father's desire than the ideal means of fulfilling it. As a speculative investment, love is ideal in Marivaux, since it guarantees that everyone (at least everyone "upstairs") will make a profit. M. Orgon gains a worthy son-in-law, while enjoying what for Mario is the sadistic pleasure of staging the *Jeu* ("Je veux me trouver au début et les agacer tous deux," says Mario in I, 4). Silvia and Dorante will not only gain each other, but by overcoming their prejudices they will *prove* themselves worthy of their fathers and transform their trial (*épreuve*) into retrospective pleasure. "Peut-être," suggests Mario, "que Dorante prendra du goût pour ma sœur, toute soubrette qu'elle sera, et cela serait charmant pour elle" (I, 4). Mario does not mean to suggest that his sister will enjoy believing that she has fallen in love with a servant, but that when she learns the truth she will find her error quite *charmant*. At the end of the play, Silvia will look back at herself, and in a final speculative gesture, she will savor the nobility of her real character, of the self that she has revealed to herself.

Dorante, too, has a final moment to discover himself in the speculative mirror. In the very last scene, after having finally become conscious of Silvia's true identity,

he exclaims: "[C]e qui m'enchante le plus, ce sont les preuves que je vous ai données de ma tendresse" (V, 9). At the end of the play then, what Dorante finds most delightful is not the girl he loves but the "proof," the image of an ideal self, that he has produced by overcoming social prejudice and proposing marriage to a chamber maid.

For Silvia and Dorante the yield on this speculative investment in love, this *"jeu de l'amour et du hasard,"* is high self-esteem, based on a knowledge of their personal worth that they could only feel or "credit" at the beginning of the play, but which now has acquired full-blown, objective reality. Their initial gesture of investor confidence in speculation has paid off, in self-esteem and pleasure. That is, their initial sense of each other's worth ("de ce qu'ils valent") has now been confirmed by their own *performance,* in all senses of the word, and retrospectively it has been a delightful experience.

Of course the experience, or experiment, was also meant to be "charmant" (and profitable as well) for Mario and his father, the masters of ceremonies. It would perhaps be more accurate to speak of them as the laboratory assistants in a "test" (*épreuve*) called ***Le Jeu de l'amour et du hasard,*** that they perform for an audience that, like M. Orgon, liked to think of itself as fundamentally good and liberal in the classical sense. The audience was also meant to know the pleasure of seeing an idealized image of itself, of viewing liberal humanity on stage. The importance of these tests or *épreuves* in Marivaux has led critics to emphasize the "scientific" dimension of his theater, its way of constituting the audience as a detached observer of the human heart.[10] But like Silvia and Dorante, the audience sees only its ideal self in the experiment, the intellectual and sentimental *preuves* of its worth.

In this play, value appears in two forms: the real or ideal form, that is, the form in which it appears to the masters, and the illusory, potentially catastrophic form in which it appears to the servants. In the form presented as real or ideal, value is no longer a treasure, determined or guaranteed by the reality of its public representation; it depends instead upon a reality that is hidden from public view (e.g., money depends on land holdings, personal worth on the "heart," etc.). And whereas value in the *ancien régime* depended upon a systematic dilapidation of resources whose emblem was the Sun, in the utopian economic order of the *Jeu,* the granting of credit ensures a play of speculation, in which the face value at risk is not only realized at the end, but increased. In this theatrical facsmile of Law's system, planning and gambling work together toward the same end.

Servants, however, do not see things this way, and they do not profit from the *Jeu* in the same way, either. Arlequin and Lisette actually believe in the *credibility* of their disguises and that they really can increase their value in a spectacular way, by marrying the master or mistress. For them, the paper is real. Unlike their masters, they *believe* in the bourgeois values of love and marriage. For Lisette and Arlequin, it is as if nothing, no regulation or law, determined their value, or that of paper money, nothing except the willingness of investors to credit it. For them it is as if the paternal gold standard—all the implicit paternal controls over money, persons, language, and love—had magically been abolished, simply by trading roles with their masters. Yet the symmetry between masters and servants is only apparent: for at the end of the play Lisette and Arlequin are worth no more than they were at the beginning. Speculation and *marivaudage* do not concern them, although their labors do make these higher activities possible. Love on credit does not work to the servants' advantage.

Despite the existence of this double standard, both masters and servants in Marivaux repudiate the value of appearances; they all refuse to credit face value or "forms." Either they believe, like the masters, that value is guaranteed by something more substantial than forms or they believe that it is a pure convention, grounded in nothing more than public belief. In Marivaux's play, all of the characters willingly commit themselves to a credit economy that could have been prescribed by Law. Whereas lovers in *Le Misanthrope*—not just Acaste and Clitandre, but also Alceste and Célimène, Philinte and Eliante—refuse to credit anything beyond appearances, and therefore remain alone at the end, in love with their own images. In the credit economy of **Le Jeu de l'amour et du hasard,** love and chance are allowed to interact through speculation, that combination of self-mirroring, planning, and gambling without risk. Thanks to this speculative investment, Silvia and Dorante are saved from emotional bankruptcy.[11]

Notes

1. According to the Littré dictionary, the word "millionaire" was created to describe people whose fortunes, thanks to Law, numbered in the millions of francs.

2. Paul Harsin, *Les Doctrines monétaires et financières en France du XVIè XVIIIè siècle* (Paris: Alcan, 1928), p. 146. Quoted in Charles Kindleberger, *A Financial History of Western Europe* (London: George Allen & Unwin, 1984), p. 96.

3. John Kenneth Galbraith, *Money: Whence it Came, Where it Went* (Boston: Houghton Mifflin Company, 1975), p. 23.

4. "It is possible that no man, having made such a promising start, could have stopped" (Galbraith, p. 24).

5. Edgar Faure, *La Banqueroute de Law: 17 Juillet 1720* (Paris: Gallimard, 1977), pp. 219*ff.*

6. We have inherited from the Enlightenment the belief that taking risks without concern for the outcome is incompatible with planning and rational calculation. Yet the recent work by Thomas Kavanagh (*Enlightenment and the Shadow of Chance,* forthcoming) suggests that gambling and planning may in fact be intimately related.

7. Strictly speaking, of course, the notes issued by Law's banks were not *money* (that is, in the "general-equivalent form"). They were used primarily in payment of government expenses, and declared legal for the payment of taxes. The distinction of issuing the first paper money belongs to the Massachusetts Bay Colony in 1690. See Galbraith, pp. 51*ff.*

8. Louis Marin, *Le Portrait du roi* (Paris: Editions du Seuil, 1981), pp. 251*ff.*

9. In *Fragments d'un discours amoureux* (Paris: Editions du Seuil, 1977), Roland Barthes calls this the moment of "enamoration."

10. *Cf.* Pierre Voltz, *La Comédie* (Paris: A. Colin, 1964), pp. 108-20; Henri Coulet and Michel Gilot, *Marivaux: un humanisme expérimental* (Paris: Larousse, 1973).

11. This article forms part of a larger project, which will also deal with Saint-Simon, Watteau, and Casanova, among others.

D. J. Culpin (essay date 1993)

SOURCE: Culpin, D. J. "Morality: The Good Life." In *Marivaux and Reason: A Study in Early Enlightenment Thought,* pp. 31-51. New York: Peter Lang, 1993.

[In the following excerpt, Culpin discusses Marivaux's work in the context of early eighteenth-century debates on the moral teachings of Stoicism versus those of Epicureanism.]

The metaphysical distinction between Rationalists and Empiricists examined in the last chapter resides in their respective allegiance to what La Mettrie described as the spiritualist and materialist conceptions of man. That distinction had its counterpart on the moral plane. In general, Rationalists were broadly sympathetic to a number of precepts inherited from Stoicism while Epicureanism exercised an important influence on the development of materialist thought. The antithetical nature of the moral teaching emanating from Stoicism and Epicureanism was pinpointed by Malebranche who noted, in the *Recherche de la vérité,* that 'Les stoïciens

. . . mettaient le bonheur dans la vertu', whereas 'Les épicuriens le mettaient dans le plaisir'.[1] In broad terms, Stoics assert that happiness is independent of sensual or emotional gratification and is to be found in following the precepts of universal reason. For Epicureans there can be no happiness which does not take account of man's physical nature.

Epicureanism enjoyed a considerable renewal of interest in France from the mid-seventeenth century onwards. It penetrated learned circles as a result of the sustained attempt made by the philosopher Gassendi to rehabilitate Epicurus, whose doctrines had long been anathema to the Christian Church. Cultivated but less specialist readers, like those in the salon of Madame de Sablé, were offered a more easily digestible introduction to Epicureanism by Bernier in his *Abrégé de la philosophie de Gassendi* (1678) and by Saint-Evremond whose essays preach a discreet but mildly self-indulgent form of *bonheur* as a corner-stone of the good life. Gradually a less austere and inflexible morality replaced the Stoic ideal preached by Seneca and embodied in the first half of the seventeenth century by Corneille and Descartes. La Rochefoucauld's *Maximes* (1665) carry a frontispiece showing a bust of Seneca from whom a false mask of impassivity is being stripped to reveal a face that has been marked by the reality of suffering; Montesquieu's *Lettres persanes* make unflattering reference to the misguided austerity of 'un philosophe qu'on appelle *Sénèque*';[2] while La Mettrie himself wrote a treatise entitled *L'Anti-Sénèque* (1750). Whether and to what extent the opinions of these writers were moulded by Epicureanism is a matter of dispute, but all were agreed that Stoicism ignores the emotional and psychological realities of human nature. Happiness, for those of their persuasion, cannot be found solely in the life of the mind or completely divorced from the pleasures of the flesh.

By the early eighteenth century these values had permeated even those *milieux,* like the salon of Madame de Lambert frequented by Marivaux, which were not particularly open to the spirit of philosophy or sympathetic to the materialist implications of Epicureanism. The Marquise herself, though a disciple of Descartes and Fénelon, was an admirer of Saint-Evremond's undogmatic *honnêteté* and she numbered among her guests Fontenelle and the poet Chaulieu who were both well known for their Epicurean sympathies. In these circumstances it is not surprising to find Marivaux's thought tinged by the moral precepts of a system which is fundamentally at odds with his metaphysical presuppositions.

Marivaux joins in the criticism levelled against the moral austerity of Stoicism. The pedant Hortensius in *La Seconde Surprise de l'amour* recommends a Stoic imperviousness to grief, asserting 'que le chagrin est toujours inutile, parce qu'il ne remédie à rien, et que la raison doit être notre règle dans tous les états' (I.xiv). He cites Seneca as the authority for his opinions but the Chevalier is not convinced, and sends Hortensius into an apoplexy of indignation by responding that 'Sénèque ne sait ce qu'il dit' (II.viii). The narrator of the *Indigent philosophe* recounts the story of a *seigneur* who tries to follow this sort of advice when, Job-like, he simultaneously loses his only son and half his worldly goods. Driven by the perversity of his philosophical creed he dons a mask of *fermeté* pretending, in public, to be emotionally invulnerable but unable, in private, to restrain his tears (*JOD* [*Journaux et œuvres diverses,*] 281). The Indigent views him with a mixture of sadness and contempt as a *comédien* playing out a painful rôle, whose plight is both tragic and bitterly comic. Not only is he attempting to suppress emotions that cannot be denied but he has not understood that the central feature of human nature is not *fermeté* but *inconstance*. This is the experience of many of Marivaux's lovers including Silvia in *La Double Inconstance* who naively laments that since her love for Arlequin both came and went without her permission she cannot be blamed for inconstancy (III.viii). And Marivaux does not blame her. He does not write tragedies castigating culpable weakness but comedies relishing the contradictions of human nature. His attitude towards the foibles of humanity recalls Philinte's advice to Alceste in Molière's play *Le Misanthrope*: indignation is pointless, 'car il faut vivre avec tout le monde' (*JOD* 315). Since there is an inevitable capriciousness about human nature infidelity need not be lamented nor pleasure shunned, but enjoyed where it is found.

Marivaux acknowledges the existence of carnal appetites and, unlike the Stoics, is prepared to admit that sensual satisfaction is central to human experience, particularly the experience of love. He satirises the concept of heroic or gallant love portrayed in seventeenth-century novels like those written by Madeleine de Scudéry, and focuses on the comic unreality of the Platonic psychology which it implies. The heroes of these tales protest an eternal though ever-unrequited devotion to their beloved which, according to the *Cabinet du philosophe,* is neither *vrai* nor *vraisemblable* (*JOD* 375). When Dorante employs extravagantly gallant terminology to woo the Comtesse in *L'Heureux Stratagème* she is unimpressed, merely observing with amusement that he would have made 'un excellent héros de roman' (I.v). In Marivaux's plays the badinage of sophisticated lovers who inhabit the world of the *honnêtes gens* is simply a vehicle by which to reconcile the sensual piquancy of Cupidon with the moral decorum of Amour, two characters representing the twin aspects of love who are united at the end of *La Réunion des amours.* Trivelin's description of himself in *La Fausse Suivante* as 'libertin dans le fond, réglé dans la forme' (I.i) is, in reality, more widely applicable to

Marivaux's conception of human nature. It signals a moral vision closer in substance to the voluptuousness of Epicureanism than to the austerity of Stoicism. In this it reflects the moral ambivalence, the subtle eroticism beneath a veneer of innocence, typical of Rococo art and the paintings of Watteau with which Marivaux's work has been compared.[3]

From among the characters of Marivaux's fictional universe, those usually cited as examples of a more indulgent form of pleasure-seeking are the eponymous hero of *L'Indigent Philosophe* and Jacob, his spiritual counterpart in *Le Paysan parvenu.* They share a lively good humour, a thinly-disguised sensuality and a gourmet's delight in food and drink. Neither of them has the social sophistication or the restraint in manners and speech that is usually associated with Marivaux's principal characters, but they are not otherwise unique in his work. As a tramp and a peasant they are freed from the constraints governing their social betters, sharing the spontaneity and frankness traditionally allowed to the *valets* of comic drama. They possess the characteristics of the traditional Arlequin inherited by Marivaux from the Italian theatre, the gluttony by which he is tempted to forget Silvia in *La Double Inconstance* and the forthright sensuality shown at the end of *Les Fausses Confidences* when he remarks that after love and marriage comes procreation. The unique feature of *L'Indigent Philosophe* and *Le Paysan parvenu* is that the peasant or valet, whose social origins allow him to display the substance of human sensuality without the veneer which renders it culturally acceptable, has here become the hero.

Nevertheless, in spite of their freedom of expression, both characters, though particularly the Indigent Philosophe, exercise a degree of restraint over their natural appetites. Of itself such restraint is not incompatible with Epicureanism, which does not teach the unfettered pursuit of pleasure with which it is associated in the popular imagination. Epicurus found solid happiness in simplicity and equanimity rather than in wealth or excess, for riches are subject to the vicissitudes of fate and surfeit gives way to regret. This is the sort of moderation which, in his so-called *Lettre sur la paresse* (1740), Marivaux takes as the measure of happiness. This letter is assumed to refer to the collapse, in 1720, of Law's bank and commercial enterprises in which Marivaux had apparently been induced to speculate. In it he laments the momentary desire for gain which brought about his financial ruin. *Paresse,* he suggests, is not the vice it is thought to be: had he resisted the temptations of greed he would have preserved that untroubled *repos* much prized by the Epicureans.

It is important, however, not to be misled by Marivaux's terminology or to overemphasize the self-indulgence and freedom traditionally allowed to the peasants and valets of literature. To do so would be to misconstrue Marivaux's moral standpoint which, though overlain with a patina of Epicureanism, remains fundamentally compatible with his Rationalist metaphysics. In particular he remained a consistently outspoken critic of the two extreme forms of Epicurean indulgence which most characterised contemporary society: sexual licence and extravagant luxury.

Although Marivaux recognised that sensuality and inconstancy are inherent features of human nature, he refused to sanction the sexual *libertinage* that flourished in French literature following the death of Louis XIV. It is a notorious critical perversity to suggest, as Paul Gazagne has done, that Marivaux equates love solely with the desire for sexual fulfilment.[4] In the fourth part of *Le Paysan parvenu* (1734) he specifically reproaches Crébillon *fils* for the overt licentiousness of his novel *L'Ecumoire* (1734) which panders unnecessarily to the debauched taste of his readers (*PP* [*Le Paysan parvenu,*] 200). According to Marivaux, even the most upright of men and women cling only tenuously to their moral standards, and the imaginative impact of salacious literature may all too readily subvert the strength of will by which they persevere in virtue. The forthright spontaneity attributed to the Indigent and Jacob stops short of scurrility and, as in the case of Arlequin on stage, is largely exploited for its comic potential. Textual similarities between *L'Indigent philosophe* and the *Lives of Eminent Philosophers* by Diogenes Laertius suggest that Marivaux modelled his amiable vagrant on the personality of Diogenes the Cynic who despised the gratifications upon which the happiness of others depends.[5] The Indigent, like Diogenes, finds the demands of the sexual appetite unacceptably insistent, and he rejoices that, though nature dictates that women are necessary, his poverty puts them beyond his reach (*JOD* 320). Jacob enjoys for a time the piquancy of mild flirtation with Madame de Ferval and Madame de Fécour; but the novel closes upon a picture of domestic bliss in which he cites his sense of duty towards his wife, formerly the younger Mademoiselle Habert, as the means which will secure the continued happiness of his marriage (*PP* 247).

The Indigent lives a Bohemian existence on the margins of society and Jacob remains at heart a peasant who has acceded to the *petite bourgeoisie;* but Marivaux expects the *honnêtes gens* to exercise greater control over their latent sensuality than their social inferiors are able to do. Very early in his career he condemns as 'l'équivalent de la nudité même' the fashionable *négligé* which a woman might wear even when receiving male guests (*JOD* 28). Nearly two decades later, in *Le Petit-Maître corrigé* (1734), he pointedly rejects the Parisian notion of fidelity 'qui se permet toutes les petites commodités du savoir-vivre' (I.iii). In circumstances of such moral depravity the very language of love has become debased, and Marivaux notes with regret that, beneath the linguistic codes of polite society, 'Je vous aime' means simply 'Je vous désire' (*JOD* 206, 337). Viewed from this perspective the *métaphysique du cœur* of which Voltaire complained in Marivaux's plays constitutes not a refusal to engage with the issues of the real world but a rejection of the widespread contempt for marriage and fidelity known among his contemporaries as *l'amour à la mode*.⁶ In contrast with such depravity, the concept of gallant love enshrined within the seventeenth-century novel offers a spiritualised ideal which, in spite of its ridiculous excesses, is described in both the **Indigent Philosophe** and the **Cabinet du philosophe** as 'beau' (*JOD* 296, 375). Unlike *libertinage*, which seeks only sensual delight, the heroic ideal embodies a Platonic concept of love which is synonymous with virtue and originates not in the senses but in the soul. The lover takes pride in containing those baser instincts which he, like others, possesses, in order to attain his fullest moral stature (*JOD* 207). Ultimately, too, such love remains Platonic in the commonest sense now given to that word. It seeks no consummation, for Marivaux knows that, given the inconstancy of passion, 'De toutes les façons de faire cesser l'amour, la plus sûre, c'est de le satisfaire' (*JOD* 338).

Marivaux's criticism of luxury, like his condemnation of *libertinage*, is directed against a prominent aspect of contemporary society which he considered a moral defect. The century's greatest publishing achievement, the *Encyclopédie* (1751-72), is not only a store-house of intellectual achievement, it also celebrates, as its full title reveals, the latest developments in craft and technology which had made possible the vastly increased production of luxury goods. The article on luxury presents a balanced discussion of the subject, but the writer maintains that those moralists who, since the beginning of time, have condemned luxury have been spurred on more by bad temper than insight. Voltaire makes less effort at impartiality, and in the article on luxury in his *Dictionnaire philosophique* (1764) proclaims that Spartan austerity brought no advantage to ancient Greece. Luxury, on the other hand, according to his poem *Le Mondain* (1736), is the 'Mère des arts et des heureux travaux'. It is therefore socially useful.

Marivaux takes an opposite view. Voltaire's poem praises luxury for stimulating need, but those needs are, for the Spectateur français, 'besoins imposteurs' which serve only to create a spirit of envy (*JOD* 130). The unscrupulous rich man, in particular, may exploit them to ensnare the virtue of the innocent. Marivaux offers his readers the contrasting example of a humble shoe-maker who, on the day of the Infanta's arrival in Paris in 1722, works calmly on in his shop while crowds throng to watch the spectacle of the passing procession. 'Ce brute Socrate', as he is called, knows that if he witnessed a parade of such oppulence it would serve only to make

him dissatisfied with his lot (*JOD* 133). This danger is forestalled by Frédelingue in **Les Effets surprenants de la sympathie** who, in legislating to create an ideal society, abolishes private wealth with the result that 'L'envie et ses noirs chagrins étaient ignorés' (*OJ* [*Œuvres de jeunesse,*] 288). During the late 1720s and 1730s Marivaux wrote a series of plays, including **Le Triomphe de Plutus, Le Legs, Les Fausses Confidences, La Joie imprévue** and **L'Epreuve,** in which he openly criticises the subordination of moral values to financial gain. Worth, in his eyes, is more important than wealth. The Indigent denounces the heartless rich man whose clothes are worth 'une mine du Pérou' (*JOD* 307). That same value is the price placed by Dubois, in **Les Fausses Confidences,** upon the appearance and moral qualities of the impecunious Dorante (I.ii).

Virtue and happiness are rarely compatible with wealth and power, a unique exception being Fleury, Louis XV's minister, who is praised specifically because he lived 'sans faste et sans ostentation' (*JOD* 451). More usually contentment is associated with *médiocrité*, which implies a modest social station and moderate financial means. The *bourgeois* who occupies this intermediate position in society is often tainted by the characteristic vices of the two social classes between which he is placed: the greed of *les grands* and the vulgarity of *le peuple*. But, says Marivaux, if he could be freed from these defects, 'cet homme serait mon sage' (*JOD* 15).

The simplicity necessary for the stimulation of virtue is best cultivated away from the corruption of city life. The immorality of *l'amour à la mode* is associated with Paris in **L'Héritier de village** and **Le Petit-Maître corrigé,** whilst courses in moral rehabilitation take place on distant islands in **L'Ile de la raison, L'Ile des esclaves** and **La Colonie.** The *philosophe* Hermocrate, described in **Le Spectateur français,** has fled from the iniquities of men and come to live 'dans ce désert' where he survives on the produce of a modest plot of land which he cultivates himself (*JOD* 186). His namesake in **Le Triomphe de l'amour** has followed a similar path. Of course Marivaux's rejection of civilised society is only relative. He, like Marianne, was most at home in the Parisian *salons,* and the country houses which are the setting for some of his plays stand in well-tended gardens. Like Molière he pokes fun at unsophisticated rusticity and his castaways all return to civilisation.

Marivaux's advocacy of moderation draws upon a variety of sources, including biblical injunction.⁷ But the single most important factor shaping the formulation of his thought was almost certainly the idealised simplicity of pastoral literature. Although the genre had flourished on stage and page in the seventeenth century, much influenced by the success of d'Urfé's novel *L'Astrée* (1607-27), it continued to find favour in those *milieux,* notably the salons, which inherited the ethical ideals of preciosity. In particular, Fénelon's *Télémaque* (1699) provided Marivaux not just with the model for his *Télémaque travesti* (*c.* 1714) but with an influential and widely-read statement of his own political, religious and moral opinions, expressed with a linguistic graciousness that parallels his own literary style. One episode tells of a dream in which Venus invites Télémaque to enjoy the pleasures of love. He almost succumbs to her blandishments but is saved by Mentor, from whom he learns to distrust voluptuousness as the greatest of all dangers to morality. Mentor, like Marivaux, identifies a direct link between superfluity and moral corruption, so when he is invited to reform the laws and institutions of Salente his first major concern is to remove 'le faste inutile qui corrompait les mœurs'.[8]

But Fénelon was swimming against the tide of social change. In the new climate of eighteenth-century France the pursuit of pleasure became not only an active ingredient in social life but also the basis for a theory of moral action. Moralists no longer accepted that ethical codes exist simply to re-direct man's basically corrupt instincts towards more socially acceptable ends. Instead they argued that the pursuit of pleasure is fundamental to human action and that morality is assured precisely because it proceeds from the operation of this same basic instinct.[9] Individuals, it is said, derive pleasure from acting in accordance with those precepts which are necessary for the maintenance of social cohesion. This theory, known as eudaemonism, was particularly favoured by the materialists who, being unable to derive ethics from innate values, sought a means of reconciling morality with pleasure or self-interest. It gained widespread currency and was more popularly known as *bienfaisance,* a term apparently coined by the abbé de Saint-Pierre to describe the obligation to act charitably towards one's neighbours. It defines an ideal endorsed by La Mettrie who himself said that 'il y a tant de plaisir à faire du bien . . . tant de contentement à pratiquer la vertu'.[10]

In this context pleasure or self-interest can be understood in two ways, either altruistically or egotistically. Christ's commandment to love our neighbour as ourself may be read either as call to lay aside self-interest in the service of others or as a recognition of self-love as the legitimate basis of morality.[11] Diderot opts for the altruistic version, understanding virtue as a spontaneous *élan* which demonstrates a disinterested concern for the welfare of others. In his *Eloge de Richardson* he praises the English writer for the moral utility of his novels which, he says, carry the reader irresistibly towards the practice of virtue 'avec une impétuosité qu'on ne se connaissait pas'.[12] Helvétius takes a more utilitarian view from which self-interest is not banished, for he claims that it is quite simply impossible to 'faire le bonheur particulier sans faire le bien public'.[13] Both

versions of the theory assume an optimistic understanding of human nature which is a product of the revolution in thinking concerning *amour-propre* that had taken place during the previous century.[14] For Pascal, writing from a Jansenist perspective, self-love is, by definition, a reprehensible instinct. But Voltaire, specifically refuting Pascal, takes an opposite view. According to him, 'C'est l'amour de nous-mêmes qui assiste l'amour des autres'.[15]

Marivaux is the spokesman of his times in the prominence he gives to *bienfaisance* and the association which he makes between virtue and happiness. Monsieur Orgon's famous affirmation in *Le Jeu de l'amour et du hasard* that 'dans ce monde il faut être un peu trop bon pour l'être assez' (I.ii) was, according to Lesbros de la Versane, a maxim by which Marivaux guided his private life.[16] The Spectateur français rejects the uncertainties of metaphysical speculation in favour of a moral code which is based on a simple principle reminiscent of the Gospel injunction to love one's neighbour as oneself (*JOD* 233). But Marivaux understands this duty altruistically, not egotistically. The virtuous man must respect the self-interest of others in his own search for pleasure and 'ménager les intérêts d'autrui dans les siens' (*JOD* 130). D'Alembert records how the sight of suffering distressed Marivaux and moved him to innumerable acts of charity which, in his own reduced circumstances, he was little able to afford.[17] Even Arlequin in *L'Ile des esclaves* recognises the link between happiness and virtue. When given the opportunity to take vengeance on his former master he refuses to do so because, as he tells him, 'je n'aurais point le courage d'être heureux à tes dépens' (ix).

Because the sight of suffering brings misery to the virtuous observer, *bienfaisance* can at times be identified with a form of sentiment which implies the presence of emotion. A charitable deed is 'une œuvre de sentiment' (*VM* [*La Vie de Marianne*,] 30) and men of wealth who do not respond to the needs of the poor are described by the Spectateur français as 'des hommes sans sentiment' (*JOD* 129). Madame de Miran is spurred to help Marianne because her heart is touched by the young girl's affliction (*VM* 147), whereas M. de Fécour is impervious to a young woman's plea for assistance because his heart is 'naturellement dur' (*PP* 207). Scenes of virtue are accompanied by an emotional *attendrissement* reminiscent of Nivelle de la Chaussée's *comédies larmoyantes* and Diderot's *drames bourgeois.* Those of Marivaux's works in which emotion is given its most unrestrained expression, *La Vie de Marianne, L'Ecole des mères* and the fourteenth issue of the *Spectateur français,* are precisely the ones singled out for praise by d'Alembert in his *Eloge de Marivaux* (1785).

But Marivaux was not able to make a wholehearted association between emotion and virtue because he did not share that belief in the intrinsic goodness of self-love or *amour-propre* on which it is based. Like the Spectateur français he subscribes to an intermediate view, believing that 'la nature a le pour et le contre' (***JOD*** 227). He does not accept a polarised view of self-love but believes that the same instinct can manifest itself in either of the two forms that Descartes called 'l'amour de bienveillance' and 'l'amour de concupiscence'.[18] This view looks back to the distinction made by St Augustine in *The City of God* between two loves, love of self and love of God, which are respectively the foundations of the earthly and heavenly cities. But these loves are not radically disunited, for one may be purified and lead to the other.[19] Augustine's view is a Christianisation of Plato, who interpreted human love as a subconscious desire for union with an ideal concept of beauty gradually realised through a process of enlightenment.

Malebranche and Fénelon both subscribe to the intermediate position. They affirm the Christian doctrine of original sin but take issue with Arnauld and the Jansenists for overstating Augustine's emphasis on man's depravity. Malebranche accepts that 'l'amour de nous-mêmes', implanted by God, is the source of brotherly love and human society. It should lead in an upward progression from selfishness, through altruism, and ultimately to love of God. But such *charité,* or pure love, is no longer possible unless God, by an act of grace, enlightens the understanding of fallen man, replacing his sinful inclinations with 'un amour clair'[20] In the 'Avertissement' preceding his *Explication des maximes des saints* Fénelon sets out, in an ascending scale, five types of love which man may have for God, ranging from complete self-interest to unalloyed charity. In the middle categories, where self-interest is progressively replaced by disinterested love, Fénelon accepts that although 'l'intérêt propre' is still present it is not entirely vitiated and may produce acts of virtue.

Marivaux's own understanding of self-love conforms to this pattern. Like Pascal and La Rochefoucauld he recognises that *amour-propre* is inseparable from human life itself. It is, he says, 'à peu près à l'esprit ce qu'est la forme à la matière. L'un suppose l'autre' (***JOD*** 35). But he is not pessimistic about the intrinsic nature of *amour-propre.* It is an instinct which, as he explains in the ***Réflexions sur l'esprit humain,*** can be a reliable guide to life and happiness but which may lead us into pleasures which are brutal, dangerous or criminal. In its purest form *amour-propre* is equivalent to a sense of self-respect or pride which the Indigent philosophe calls 'le sentiment de son excellence que nous avons tous'. The virtuous man is more clear-sighted than the villain and from this instinct gleans presentiments of a higher destiny of which the wicked man is unaware (***JOD*** 305-6). *Le méchant,* whose moral vision is limited, possesses only the 'penchant au mal' which is the common

lot of humanity without the 'dignité' or 'noblesse' by which it should be counterbalanced. Marivaux follows the Platonic tradition in equating virtue with knowledge and wickedness with error. He insists that people tell lies not through love of lying but because of some short-term, and possibly frivolous, desire for gain which has blunted their perception (***JOD*** 484). It is, however, always possible by will-power and perseverence, to rediscover 'son propre intérêt mieux connu' (***JOD*** 489).

For Marivaux, *amour-propre* is synonymous with pride and is the source of all actions, from the debased to the morally elevated. In its most purified form it is known as *fierté* and stimulates truly disinterested action. According to ***Le Cabinet du philosophe,*** 'L'homme fier veut être intérieurement content de lui' and so pursues virtue rather than selfish pleasure. Those who are 'les plus fiers et les plus superbes' are also the most humble. They know God and serve him as they serve their fellow men, to whom God has made them subject (***JOD*** 364-5). Theirs is a degree of enlightenment that can be achieved only on the wings of love, and it provokes in Marivaux a response of respectful admiration (***JOD*** 353).

At a less exalted level, in the world of mundane reality, human behaviour is characterised by a relatively innocuous vanity. According to the Indigent philosophe men are both wicked and vain though, more precisely, they are wicked because they are vain (***JOD*** 323). In the everyday lives of ordinary people self-interest and altruism combine to form what Marivaux calls an assortment of comic vices and estimable virtues (***JOD*** 192). He has Pascal's vision of the *grandeur* and *misère* which constitute the human predicament, but without the tragic dimension by which that vision is overshadowed. Mankind's commonest vices are venial sins and minor follies which Marivaux regards with amused detachment. Though he does not condone vice he adopts a tolerant attitude towards the petty vanity of authors, pedants, lovers and coquettes whose failings are essentially harmless and provide an inexhaustible source of amusement for the dispassionate observer.[21] Vanity transforms people into *comédiens* and, for the Indigent who likes to laugh, 'Paris est de tous les théâtres du monde celui où il y a la meilleure comédie' (***JOD*** 304).

At the lower end of the moral spectrum is *le glorieux* who, unlike *l'homme fier,* pursues unalloyed self-interest rather than virtue. He is essentially a hypocrite: 'Il ne tient pas à la probité, il tient à l'honneur qu'elle procure' (***JOD*** 380). He is motivated by a manifestation of pride called *orgueil* which is found notably in people like Monsieur de Climal and Monsieur de Fécour who possess the wealth or position in society which permits them to damage the lives of those whose well-being they should promote. Indignation replaces Marivaux's tone of benevolent detachment when he addresses *les* *grands* whose insensitivity and perverted *orgueil* consititute an attack on 'la généreuse fierté de l'honnête homme' who stands in need of their compassion (*JOD* 116, 243).

Marivaux considered *amour-propre* to be potentially capable of both virtue and vice, though enlightened self-interest reveals an indissoluble link between happiness and a dedicated commitment to the common good. But, if this is true, some explanation must be found for the errors of judgement which produce selfishness and evil. Stoic and Christian moralists, in spite of the differences between them, were united in attributing error to a clouding of the judgement for which they blamed the passions. On this point Descartes adopted a cautious attitude, stating that the passions themselves are inherently good: it is only when they are excessive or mismanaged that evil ensues.[22] Malebranche is more forthright in his condemnation. As he puts it in the *Conversations chrétiennes,* 'nos passions nous éloignent du vrai bien'.[23] They obscure our vision and deafen our ears to the sound of God's instruction. But by the early eighteenth century such a view was already something of a moral anachronism. The rejection of Stoicism, the revaluation of *amour-propre,* and the influence of Epicureanism all fostered the development of a more favourable attitude towards the passions. Fontenelle's *Nouveaux Dialogues des morts* (1683) provide an early example of this transition. In the dialogue between Hérostrate and Démétrius de Phalère, Hérostrate elavates passion over reason as the motive force of action, comparing it with the wind that is necessary to drive a ship at sea. The ship's captain recognises the dangers of a gale but fears that danger less than the flat calm which robs his vessel of movement.[24] Half a century later, while still claiming to be aware of the dangers of excess, Diderot asserts in his *Pensées philosophiques* (1746) that 'il n'y a que les passions, et les grandes passions, qui puissent élever l'âme aux grandes choses'.[25]

On occasion Marivaux appears not unsympathetic to the new climate, and defends the passions in terms very similar to those employed by Fontenelle. He describes the domestic lives of the common people as a perpetual turmoil of conflicting passions very unlike the disciplined existences of the *honnêtes gens*; but, says Marivaux in the **Lettres sur les habitants de Paris,** 'la mer agitée me paraît préférable à la mer calme' (*JOD* 12). Similarly, in the preface to **Les Effets surprenants de la sympathie** he claims to have been guided by nature in the writing of his book, adding that though nature may lead one astray such *égarements* are of no importance if they are *vrais* (*OJ* 3). Although a certain amount of youthful enthusiasm may be detected in these judgements, Marivaux continues, even in his later work, to recognise the importance of passion. The **Spectateur français** contains a critique of La Motte's tragedy *Inès*

de Castro which was enormously successful in 1723, largely due to the unprecedented emotional impact which it had on the audience. Marivaux claims that its success derives from the author's readiness to be guided by passion, which in turn allowed him to cast off the restraining hand of dramatic convention. Passion, he concludes, provides insights which are irresistible even if they are foolish. According to the **Réflexions sur les hommes** the same lesson may be learned from the achievements of Cromwell, towards whom Marivaux had ambivalent feelings: though he is suspicious of political usurpation and describes Cromwell pejoratively as an *enthousiaste* and an *inspiré,* he is prepared to concede that there are certain occasions when 'il faut des fous d'un puissant esprit' (*JOD* 511).

Nevertheless, Marivaux remains equivocal about the reliability of passion: a note of caution modifies his youthful approbation when the reality of unbridled passion conjures up the spectre of immorality. Young girls should remember, when tempted to succumb to their lovers' entreaties, that 'Les passions sont farouches; il faut les ménager d'abord . . . pour les mieux combattre' (*JOD* 168). It is all very well to say that nature's excesses are acceptable if they are true, but what if they are false? Nature can be deceptive: 'elle a de quoi tromper celui qui la veut voir mal, comme elle a de quoi éclairer celui qui la veut voir bien' (*JOD* 306). These reservations surface in **La Mère confidente** where Dorante suggests to Angélique that they elope, justifying himself by the strength of his passion. When Angélique's mother learns of the plan she exclaims in alarm: 'Les passions seraient bien à leur aise, si leur emportement rendait tout légitime' (III.xi). The danger is that passion can overpower the counterbalancing force of intuitive reason which is the source of moral knowledge. This point is made in the **Spectateur français** when a father warns his son that the soundness of his judgement would be quickly undermined 'si un peu d'extravagance humaine . . . égarait ta raison, et mitigeait tes principes de vertu' (*JOD* 242). It is because of Marivaux's suspicions about the potentially corrupting force of passion that sensibility plays so small a part in his work. Though by no means hostile to the display of emotion Marivaux did not elaborate a morality of sentiment. Contrary to what Pierre Trahard has claimed, his journals do not contain 'une théorie, originale à sa date, qui fonde la morale sur la sensibilité'.[26]

Marivaux's writing is filled with stratagems whose sole purpose is to act as a bulwark against the changeability of human nature and the corrupting force of passion. Among them is the institution of marriage. In Marivaux's opinion the relationship between a man and a woman is neither more holy nor legitimate simply because certain legal or religious obligations have been satisfied (*JOD* 165). In **L'Ile de la raison,** where reason governs action, the islanders practise only a simple but public exhange of vows that serves to reinforce the mutual commitment of the contracting partners (III.ix). But Marivaux makes clear in *Félicie,* as in *La Mère confidente,* that some external formality is necessary to encourage the formation of a binding agreement. The only effective difference brought about by marriage is that the erstwhile lovers, now contractually united, 'ne doivent point s'attacher ailleurs' (*JOD* 201).

But Marivaux looks beyond the planned wedding by which stage comedies are traditionally concluded. He believes as little in the inevitability of uninterrupted marital bliss as he does in the durability of gallant fidelity. Passion becomes as easily wayward after marriage as it does before. Its excesses are to be prevented by the love test, found conspicuously in *Les Fausses Confidences* and *L'Epreuve,* which has seemed to some critics to smack of gratuitous cruelty.[27] Araminte and Angélique are manipulated and driven to extremes of emotional distress by suitors who appear simply to seek the gratification of knowing that the beloved's devotion is total. And when their machinations are revealed those who have suffered are quick to pardon the deception that has been practised on them. In *Le Jeu de l'amour et du hasard* the explanation is given by Silvia who, having reduced Dorante to the extremity of confessing his love for a woman he believes to be a servant, proclaims that 'Il ne pourra jamais se rappeler notre histoire sans m'aimer, je n'y songerai jamais que je ne l'aime' (III.iv). Marivaux follows Descartes in his understanding of the relationship between the will and the passions. Actions should be determined by the will, but when the will is irresolute its functions may be duplicated by a deliberate manipulation of the passions.[28] In this case, the memory of the love-test will stir in the mind images of devotion which will be of sufficient strength to counter-balance the mirage of false delights so easily stimulated by the passions.

Other stratagems may help to *entretenir* or *ménager l'amour* but, in the last resort, morality can be maintained and duty performed only through the exercise of individual free-will. Marivaux is ready to concede that ultimately the heart remains largely beyond our control, but he insists that 'nous sommes les maîtres de nos actions' (*JOD* 201). On this point he does not subscribe to the determinism favoured by Diderot and the materialists. While prudently setting aside the religious domain in which, according to orthodox doctrine, divine grace must intervene to bring about spiritual conversion, the *Réflexions sur l'esprit humain* affirm that man retains the free exercise of his will to bring about moral amendment (*JOD* 489). Marivaux's condemnation of the *méchant* is founded upon the premise that the villain remains responsible for his actions. There is nothing fore-ordained about moral choice, and the Jansenist doctrine of predestination is without appeal

for Marivaux. His plays almost all illustrate a process of personal education, and there is no one, not even the *philosophe* in *L'Ile de la raison,* who is not ultimately amenable to a *cours d'humanité.* Prejudice and passion are mastered by the imposition of the will which constitutes an act of *générosité.* The *généreux* who acts in this way will therefore, as Descartes put it, be able to perform 'toutes les choses qu'il jugera être les meilleures'.[29]

By the mid-eighteenth century the term *générosité* had taken on something of its modern sense, meaning emotional responsiveness and sensitivity to the needs of others. Vauvenargues, for example, writes in his *Réflexions et maximes* (1746) that 'La générosité souffre des maux d'autrui comme si elle en était responsable'.[30] Marivaux's usage is marked by this semantic evolution, though for him the term continues to carry something of the meaning which it had in the seventeenth century, implying nobleness of soul and a readiness to subordinate self-interest to a higher moral motive. Silvia for example, in *Le Jeu de l'amour et du hasard,* suggests that Dorante, like Corneille's Rodrigue in his attitude to Chimène, should, by an act of *générosité,* conceal the love which he has for her (III.viii). Such self-control is not expected of the *peuple* who are subject to their passions, but Marivaux consistently assumes *générosité* to be a basic characteristic of the *honnêtes gens.* When the Comtesse imprisoned on the *île de la raison* greets Parmenès with the words 'Vous me paraissez généreux, Seigneur' (I.iii), she is saying not only that he appears to be a person of education and breeding, but is also implying a capacity for moral rectitude. This is equally true in *La Double Inconstance* when Arlequin criticises the *seigneur* who, having been corrupted by life at court, proposes a definition of *honnêteté* which requires the *honnête homme* to be neither *honnête* nor *généreux* (III.iv). True morality therefore depends upon the interrelationship of reason, by which virtue is perceived, and *générosité,* by which its precepts are enacted. The process of reeducation to which the castaways are subjected in *L'Ile des esclaves* seeks to bring about the realisation of this ideal, enlightening their understanding and strengthening their will so that they become both 'raisonnables et généreux' (ii).

Marivaux's writings accurately reflect the evolution in eighteenth-century moral thought which took place as a result of what has been called the rehabilitation of human nature. Like many contemporaries of various philosophical persuasions, he rejected the austere emotional detachment of the Stoics and associated pleasure with the practice of virtue. But Marivaux was an outspoken critic of the sensuality and luxury which were the hallmark of the years following the death of Louis XIV, and he rejected the naively optimistic endorsement of passion on which such social *mores* were based. Instead he interprets *amour-propre* in the light of the Platonic and Augustinian tradition which identifies virtue with enlightened self-interest and invests man with the free-will necessary to determine his own course of action. Marivaux, like other contemporaries, used Seneca as a conventional target for the criticisms he directed against an impossible philosophic idealism, but the emphasis that he places on *générosité* and the control of the passions reveals his sympathy for a more moderate form of Stoicism. In this he agrees with Fontenelle who, though critical of 'les Philosophes rigides', admits that the equation made by the Stoics between happiness and moderation has much to recommend it. In fact, he concludes, 'le plus qu'on en pourra conserver, ce sera le mieux'.[31]

Notes

1. Malebranche, *Recherche de la vérité*, I, XVII, iii.

2. Montesquieu, *Lettres persanes*, XXXIII.

3. See Patrick Brady, 'Rococo and Neo-Classicism', and 'French Rococo Poetry'; G. Poe, *The Rococo and Eighteenth-Century French Literature: A Study through Marivaux's Theater*; Robert Tomlinson, *La Fête galante: Watteau et Marivaux*; and my article, 'The Religious Morality of Marivaux's *comédies d'amour*'.

4. Paul Gazagne, *Marivaux par lui-même*.

5. See Diogenes Laertius, 'Diogenes the Cynic', in *Lives of Eminent Philosophers*. The Indigent cries out: 'Je cherche un homme, c'est-à-dire quelqu'un qui mérite ce nom' (*JOD*.306), while, according to Laertius, Diogenes 'shouted out for men, and when people collected, hit out at them with his stick, saying, "It was men I called for, not scoundrels"' (VI, 32). Diogenes and the Indigent also express a disillusionment with human follies which is more pronounced in this journal than anywhere else in Marivaux's work.

6. See James S. Munro, 'The Moral Significance of Marivaux's *comédies d'amour*'.

7. For example, 'Keep your life free from the love of money and be content with what you have', Hebrews 13. 5.

8. Fénelon, *Télémaque*, IV, p. 131; X, p. 279.

9. See Robert Mauzi, *L'Idée du bonheur dans la littérature et la pensée française au XVIIIe siècle*.

10. La Mettrie, *L'Homme-Machine*, p. 124.

11. Matthew 22. 37-39.

12. Diderot, *Eloge de Richardson*, in *Œuvres*, p. 1061.

13. Helvétius, *De l'esprit*, II, xxii.

14. See Roger Mercier, *La Réhabilitation de la nature humaine 1700-1750*.

15. Pascal, *Pensées*, 617; Voltaire, *Lettres philosophiques*, 25, 'Sur les Pensées de M. Pascal', XI.

16. Lesbros de la Versane, *Esprit de Marivaux, ou analectes de ses ouvrages, précédé de la vie historique de l'auteur*, p. 35.

17. D'Alembert, *Eloge de Marivaux*, in *TC*, II, p. 999. Some further details of Marivaux's charitable acts are given by Michel Gilot in 'Quelques traits du visage de Marivaux'.

18. Descartes, *Traité des passions*, 81.

19. Augustine, *De Trinitate*, VIII, 12. For background on the debate concerning *amour-propre* see A. Levi, '*Amour-propre*: the Rise of an Ethical Concept'.

20. Malebranche, *Recherche de la vérité*, IV, V; IV, XIII; IV, X.

21. Marivaux's detachment should not be construed as a sign of amorality (as it is by William Trapnell in the conclusion to *Eavesdropping in Marivaux*). His moral stance is too firmly grounded in universal reason for this to be the case.

22. Descartes, *Traité des passions*, 211.

23. Malebranche, *Conversations chrétiennes*, VII.

24. Fontenelle, 'Hérostrate et Démétrius de Phalère', in *Nouveaux Dialogues des morts*.

25. Diderot, *Pensées philosophiques*, 1.

26. See Pierre Trahard, *Les Maîtres de la sensibilité française au dix-huitième siècle*, I, p. 73.

27. See H. T. Mason, 'Cruelty in Marivaux's Theatre'; and D. J. Culpin, 'Marivaux and the *conte merveilleux*', p. 104.

28. Descartes, *Traité des passions*, 48.

29. Descartes, *Traité des passions*, 153.

30. Vauvenargues, *Réflexions et maximes*, CLXXIII.

31. Fontenelle, *Du Bonheur*, in *Œuvres complètes*, III, p. 212.

Bibliography

This bibliography contains only works which are referred to in the text or which are directly relevant to Marivaux's ideas and their intellectual context. It is divided into four sections: 1) Editions of Marivaux's Works, 2) Primary Sources, 3) Critical Works on Marivaux, and 4) The Intellectual Context.

I) EDITIONS OF MARIVAUX'S WORKS

La Vie de Marianne, edited by Frédéric Deloffre, revised edition (Paris, Bordas, 1990)

Le Paysan parvenu, edited by Frédric Deloffre (Paris, Garnier, 1959)

Théâtre complet, edited by Frédéric Deloffre, 2 vols (Paris, Garnier, 1968)

Journaux et œuvres diverses, edited by Frédéric Deloffre and Michel Gilot (Paris, Bordas, 1969)

Œuvres de jeunesse, edited by Frédéric Deloffre and Claude Rigault (Paris, Gallimard, 1972)

II) Primary Sources

Augustine, St, *Augustine of Hippo: Selected Writings,* translation and introduction by Mary T. Clark (London, SPCK, 1984)

Descartes, René, *Œuvres et lettres* (Paris, Gallimard, 1953)

Diderot, Denis, *Œuvres philosophiques* (Paris, Garnier, 1961)

————*Œuvres* (Paris, Gallimard, 1951)

Diogenes Laertius, *Lives of Eminent Philosophers,* 2 vols (London, Heinemann, 1925)

Fénelon, François de Salignac de La Mothe-,

————*Les Aventures de Télémaque* (Paris, Garnier-Flammarion, 1968)

Fontenelle, Bernard Le Bovier, Sieur de, *Nouveaux Dialogues des morts* (Paris, Didier, 1971)

————*Œuvres complètes,* III (Paris, Fayard, 1989)

Helvétius, Claude-Adrien, *De l'Esprit* (Paris, Fayard, 1988)

La Mettrie, Julien Offroy de, *L'Homme-Machine* (Paris Denoël/Gonthier, 1981)

Malebranche, Nicolas, *Œuvres,* I (Paris, Gallimard, 1979)

Montesquieu, Charles de Secondat, Baron de, *Lettres persanes* (Paris, Garnier, 1975)

Pascal, Blaise, *Pensées* (Paris, Editions du Seuil, 1962)

Vauvenargues, Luc de Clapiers, Marquis de, *Introduction à la connaissance de l'esprit humain et autres œuvres,* etc., (Paris, Flammarion, 1981)

Voltaire, *Œuvres complètes,* ed. Louis Moland (Kraus Reprint Ltd., Nendeln, Liechtenstein, 1967)

III) Critical Works on Marivaux

Alembert, Jean Le Rond d', *Eloge de Marivaux,* in Marivaux, *Théâtre complet* (Paris, Garnier, 1968), II, 979-1024

Culpin, D. J., 'The Religious Morality of Marivaux's *comédies d'amour',* *Romance Studies,* 4 (1984), 65-78

Gazagne, Paul, *Marivaux par lui-même* (Paris, Editions du Seuil, 1954)

Gilot, Michel, 'Quelques traits du visage de Marivaux', *Revue d'Histoire Littéraire de la France,* 70 (1970), 391-399

Lesbros de La Versane, *Esprit de Marivaux: ou analectes de ses ouvrages précédé de la vie historique de l'auteur* (Paris, Veuve Pierres, 1769)

Mason, H. T., 'Cruelty in Marivaux's Theatre', *Modern Language Review,* 62 (1967), 238-247

Munro, James S, 'The Moral Significance of Marivaux's *comédies d'amour',* *Forum for Modern Language Studies,* 14 (1978), 116-128

Poe, G., *The Rococo and Eighteenth-Century French Literature: A Study through Marivaux's Theater* (New York, Peter Lang, 1987)

Tomlinson, Robert, *La Fête galante: Watteau et Marivaux* (Geneva, Droz, 1981)

Trapnell, W. H., *Eavesdropping in Marivaux* (Geveva, Droz, 1987)

————'The "Philosophical" Implications of Marivaux's *Dispute',* *Studies on Voltaire and the Eighteenth Century,* 73 (1970), 193-219

IV) The Intellectual Context

Brady, Patrick, 'Rococo and Neo-Classicism', *Studi Francesi,* 22, (1964), 34-49

Levi, A., '*Amour-propre*: the Rise of an Ethical Concept', *The Month,* 21 (1959), 283-294

Mauzi, Robert, *L'Idée du bonheur dans la littérature et la pensée française au XVIIIᵉ siècle,* fourth edition (Paris, Armand Colin, 1969)

Mercier, Roger, *La Réhabilitation de la nature humaine 1700-1750* (Villemomble, Editions La Balance, 1960)

Trahard, Pierre, *Les Maîtres de la sensibilité française au dixhuitième siècle,* 4 vols (Paris, Boivin et Cie, 1931-33)

Derek F. Connon (essay date 1993)

SOURCE: Connon, Derek F. "The Servant as Master: Disguise, Role-Reversal and Social Comment in Three Plays of Marivaux." In *Studies in the Commedia Dell'Arte,* edited by David J. George and Christopher J. Gossip, pp. 121-37. Cardiff: University of Wales Press, 1993.

[*In the following excerpt, Connon discusses the importance of costume in representations of class and social status in Marivaux's comedies.*]

As is pointed out by Norbert Jonard in his study of the *commedia dell'arte,* disguise is one of the principal devices employed in the scenarios of the form.[1] Mel Gordon, in his study of *lazzi,* draws attention to a more specific use of disguise, one which involves not only pretence about the character's identity, but also about his social class: 'Often, the humour grows out of a class reversal, the servant acts like a master and the master becomes confused.'[2] Given the importance of the *théâtre italien* in Marivaux's career, the frequency of his use of the topos of disguise in his plays is hardly surprising, but in only one does he relate it specifically to the notion of social role- or class-reversal, doing so in a context where the device is clearly underlined by the stylized symmetry of the plot: that is to say *Le Jeu de l'amour et du hasard* (1730), where the duplication of the reversal in both male and female characters produces a quartet of individuals all parodying with more or less success their social opposites. Although there is no true use of disguise in the earlier play *L'Ile des esclaves* (1725), since the identity of the various characters is never in doubt either for the audience or for each other, a similarly symmetrical use of role-reversal backed up by costume changes relates it strongly to *Le Jeu,* and in this briefer play the social burden of the device is much more clearly underlined.

Although these are the only plays to use such a symmetrical structure, in a number of others one or other side of the equation is found in isolation. She (or he) stoops to conquer in works like *La Double Inconstance* (1723), *Le Prince travesti* (1724) and *Le Triomphe de l'amour* (1732), and in *La Fausse Suivante* (1724) the result of the trial is the more surprising rejection of the original beloved. But in only one other is there an important use of the situation described by Gordon, in which it is the servant who pretends to be of the class of his master: that is *L'Epreuve* (1740). It is this depiction of the servant as master in these three plays, *L'Ile des esclaves, Le Jeu de l'amour et du hasard* and *L'Epreuve* that it is my intention to examine here. Whilst there seems little doubt that the Italian theatre was a fundamental influence in Marivaux's frequent use of disguise in his plays, it is a device which is by no means unique to that tradition. By focusing on this one particular aspect, on the other hand, we will be led to a consideration of a much more specifically Italianate aspect of Marivaux's theatre, the development of one facet of his treatment of his most persistently archetypal character, Arlequin.

That costume is an important icon of social status in these plays is in no doubt, otherwise there would be no point in the swapping of clothing specified in *L'Ile des esclaves* when the nobles are cast down to servitude and the servants (or, even more pointedly for the philosophical message, slaves, as they are here) are elevated to higher rank, for here there is no deception involved.

Even on this island, where the slaves have realized the injustice and artificiality of social inequality, the symbol of the outward trappings of costume will be one of the most important indicators of the masters' fall from grace and the slaves' elevation.

One anomaly should, however, be noted: the swapping of costumes is specified by Trivelin for both couples: '(*Aux esclaves*) Quant à vous, mes enfants, qui devenez libres et citoyens, Iphicrate habitera cette case avec le nouvel Arlequin, et cette belle fille demeurera dans l'autre; vous aurez soin de changer d'habit ensemble, c'est l'ordre' ('[*To the slaves*] As for you, my children, who are now free citizens, Iphicrate will live in this cabin with the new Arlequin, and this beautiful young lady will live in the other; you will make sure to exchange clothing, that is the rule'), (430-1).[3] Arlequin and Iphicrate exit immediately after this, and at their subsequent re-entry the scene heading specifies 'ARLEQUIN, IPHICRATE, *qui ont changé d'habits*' ('ARLEQUIN, IPHICRATE, *who have exchanged clothing*'), (438). The absence of any similar indication with regard to the female characters, the fact that the continuity of the action prevents them from leaving the stage until after Cléanthis's denunciation of Euphrosine, by which time the exchange has become almost redundant, and the absence of any opportunity for them to resume their original costumes before the final reinstatement of the status quo all point to the fact that Marivaux did not actually envisage any exchange taking place between them in performance. The scene in which the men resume their original clothing (scene ix) is one of the emotional highpoints of the play, and, although the fact that this latter exchange takes place in full view of the audience suggests that it was only some sort of over-costume which was exchanged, with Arlequin retaining his traditional motley, it seems fair to assume that much comic effect would be derived from his inappropriate dress. A remark by Silvia in *Le Jeu de l'amour et du hasard* concerning her disguise as a servant—'Il ne me faut presque qu'un tablier' ('Virtually all I need is an apron'), (680)—suggests that, on the other hand, as a result of the habitual over-dressing of actors of the time, the costumes of Euphrosine and Cléanthis would have been so similar that the exchange would have made little visual impact;[4] accordingly Marivaux sacrifices it to the fluency of his action. This suggests that, even in *Le Jeu de l'amour et du hasard,* where the women clearly do adopt disguises, the sartorial impression given by Lisette will be both less striking and less inappropriate than that of Arlequin.

The characters' behaviour, though, does not always live up to the costume, and so, in its superficiality, the disguise is shown to have no profound effect on their essence, and it is in the case of Arlequin, where the visual disguise is at its least effective, undermined as it would have been by his traditional trappings of mask and slap-stick as well as clear evidence of his suit of shreds and patches under his assumed garb, that the character also proves least able effectively to fulfil his new role. For if we compare him not only with his female counterparts, but also with Frontin his successor in *L'Epreuve,* who, unencumbered by Arlequin's traditional acessories, would have cut a much more dashing figure in his disguise as master, we will find that it is Arlequin who is least able to provide a convincing impersonation of the ruling classes, and who is in consequence the source of the most broadly parodic humour.

Cléanthis, for example, although not totally devoid of vulgarity—even Trivelin becomes exasperated by her inability to know when to stop at the end of scene iii of *L'Ile des esclaves*—displays a rather subtle sense of satire and observation; indeed, as Haydn Mason has shown,[5] her satirical *tour de force* of scene iii is very closely related to a passage which appears later in *Le Cabinet du philosophe* (1734). And it is she who becomes most obviously exasperated by Arlequin's inability to adjust his behaviour to either his new role or costume:

CLÉANTHIS

Il fait le plus beau temps du monde; on appelle cela un jour tendre.

ARLEQUIN

Un jour tendre? Je ressemble donc au jour, Madame.

CLÉANTHIS

Comment! vous lui ressemblez?

ARLEQUIN

Eh palsambleu! le moyen de n'être pas tendre, quand on se trouve tête à tête avec vos grâces? (*A ce mot il saute de joie.*) Oh! oh! oh! oh!

CLÉANTHIS

Qu'avez-vous donc? vous défigurez notre conversation!

ARLEQUIN

Oh! ce n'est rien; c'est que je m'applaudis.

CLÉANTHIS

Rayez ces applaudissements, ils nous dérangent.

(442)

CLÉANTHIS

The weather is as beautiful as can be; people call this a tender [i.e., gentle] day.

ARLEQUIN

A tender day? In that case I am like the day, Madam.

CLÉANTHIS

What do you mean, you are like the day?

ARLEQUIN

Sblood! how could I not be tender [i.e., loving], when I am in the company of your charms? (*At this witticism he jumps for joy.*) Ho! ho! ho! ho!

CLÉANTHIS

What is the matter? you are spoiling our conversation!

ARLEQUIN

Oh! it is nothing; I am just applauding myself.

CLÉANTHIS

Cut the applause, it disturbs us.

It is true that the parody of the poetic lover's conceit at the beginning of this extract is almost subtle, but it is clearly only present to permit the inappropriate oath and the naively childlike ebullience, which are much more typical both of the humour produced by Arlequin elsewhere in this particular play and of his usual archetypal self.

Such internal commentaries by the characters on their own and each other's actions as that found in the above extract are of course impossible in *Le Jeu de l'amour et du hasard,* where the disguises must be sustained, but the comedy of Arlequin's role still resides in the inappropriateness of his behaviour:

ARLEQUIN

Un domestique là-bas m'a dit d'entrer ici, et qu'on allait avertir mon beau-père qui était avec ma femme.

SILVIA

Vous voulez dire Monsieur Orgon et sa fille, sans doute, Monsieur!

ARLEQUIN

Eh! oui, mon beau-père et ma femme, autant vaut; je viens pour épouser, et ils m'attendent pour être mariés; cela est convenu; il ne manque plus que la cérémonie, qui est une bagatelle.

SILVIA

C'est une bagatelle qui vaut bien la peine qu'on y pense.

ARLEQUIN

Oui; mais quand on y a pensé, on n'y pense plus.

(688)

ARLEQUIN

A servant down there told me to come in here, and that my father-in-law would be informed that I was with my wife.

SILVIA

No doubt you mean Monsieur Orgon and his daughter, Monsieur!

ARLEQUIN

Yes, my father-in-law and my wife, same difference; marriage is what I am here for, and what they are waiting for; it is all agreed; all we need now is the ceremony, which is a mere trifle.

SILVIA

It is a trifle which it is worth making the effort to remember.

ARLEQUIN

Yes; but once you have remembered it, you do not give it another thought.

Lisette, on the other hand, is used so much by Marivaux as a sort of 'straight-man' for Arlequin's excesses that she provides little humour of her own. As with Cléanthis, her sense of *savoir faire* is sufficiently superior to that of Arlequin for her to react with surprise at his excessive behaviour, as the following extract shows, but it is not developed enough for her ultimately to see through his disguise.

MONSIEUR ORGON

Adieu, mes enfants: je vous laisse ensemble; il est bon que vous vous aimiez un peu avant que de vous marier.

ARLEQUIN

Je ferais bien ces deux besognes-là à la fois, moi.

MONSIEUR ORGON

Point d'impatience; adieu. [*Il sort*].

ARLEQUIN

Madame, il dit que je ne m'impatiente pas; il en parle bien à son aise, le bonhomme!

LISETTE

J'ai de la peine à croire qu'il vous en coûte tant d'attendre, Monsieur; c'est par galanterie que vous faites l'impatient: à peine êtes-vous arrivé! Votre amour ne saurait être bien fort; ce n'est tout au plus qu'un amour naissant.

(693)

MONSIEUR ORGON

Goodbye my children: I will leave you together; it is right that you should have the chance to fall in love a little before you get married.

ARLEQUIN

I would just as soon do the two things at the same time.

MONSIEUR ORGON

Be patient; goodbye. [*He leaves*].

ARLEQUIN

Madam, he tells me to be patient; it is all very well for him to say that, the old dodderer!

LISETTE

It is hard to believe that you find it quite so difficult to wait, Monsieur; it is through pure gallantry that you pretend to be impatient: you have only just arrived! Your love cannot really be very strong; it is no more than beginning.

And again, in the Frontin of ***L'Epreuve***, we find that we have almost left the ineptitude of Arlequin behind. True, there is enough Arlequinesque conceit and whimsicality to give away his origins in a comment like 'On s'accoutume aisément à me voir, j'en ai l'expérience' ('I know from experience that people very easily get used to seeing me'), (1326), and his silencing of Madame Argante is much too peremptory to be that of the true master: 'Point de ton d'autorité, sinon je reprends mes bottes et monte à cheval' ('Do not take that authoritarian tone or I will put my boots back on and get back on my horse'), (1331). In general though, Marivaux allows his servant character in this play to achieve an impersonation which is almost credible.

So the costume changes nothing: Silvia and Dorante, Lisette and Arlequin are instinctively drawn to their social equals despite the multiple disguises. Convincing as Frontin's acting may be, he still lacks the nobility which will cause Angélique to love him instead of Lucidor (although in this late play Marivaux again weakens the case against Frontin by the strength of Angélique's fidelity: even a real master, he suggests, would still have failed to win her from Lucidor). Perhaps most interesting is the situation presented in ***L'Ile des esclaves***, in which the two slaves, rather than being attracted to each other, are unable to resist the attraction of the nobles, despite the fact that on the island of slaves the latter have become technically their social inferiors. The slaves' sense of their masters' superiority will not easily be modified by mere changes in clothing or arbitrary reversals of the power structure.

The social comment in ***L'Ile des esclaves*** is quite explicit, although critics who have compared Arlequin's remarks to those of Figaro are perhaps understimating the significant extent to which the subversive character of comments like the following is mitigated by the tone of reconciliation in which they are spoken: 'Tu veux que je partage ton affliction, et jamais tu n'as partagé la mienne. Eh bien! va, je dois avoir le cœur meilleur que toi; car il y a plus longtemps que je souffre, et que je sais ce que c'est que la peine. Tu m'as battu par amitié: puisque tu le dis, je te le pardonne; je t'ai raillé par bonne humeur, prends-le en bonne part, et fais-en ton profit' ('You want me to share your affliction, and you have never shared mine. Go on then! I must be softer-hearted than you, for I have suffered for longer, and I know what pain is. You beat me out of friendship: because you say so, I forgive you; I mocked you out of good humour, take it in the way it was intended, and learn from it'), (448). Ultimately the play calls for humanity rather than social upheaval.

Similarly, although we may be led by the plight of Silvia and Dorante in *Le Jeu de l'amour et du hasard,* in the most emotional moments of the struggle between love and the reason which tells them they cannot cross the social divide, to question the humanity of a society in which Silvia the mistress would not be allowed to wed Dorante if he really were Bourguignon, and although we may have an amused sympathy for the fact that the plans of Lisette and Arlequin to better themselves socially by marriage are doomed to failure, the play leaves us in no doubt that the mutual attraction of the characters comes not from costume, but from a deeper inherent sense of class and the different outlook on life and love which goes with it, neither of which can be so easily donned or doffed. I have discussed elsewhere, in relation to *La Colonie,* the fact that this situation may be more complex than Marivaux's merely negating his social comment by stressing stereotype and reasserting the status quo, and that the traditional elements provide for the audience a familiar framework through which the philosophical point can be made the more effectively.[6] The main point for the present argument is, however, the way in which all of these plots contain elements of social climbing: the character who assumes the clothing of his social superior begins to think seriously of aspiring to the rank which would usually go with it.

For the two slaves in *L'Ile des esclaves* social elevation is a reality, but only within the mythic confines of the island, a fact which they seem to understand as well as we do, given their disastrous attempts to woo their social superiors from the real world. And, although Cléanthis is admittedly less convinced than Arlequin, their reversion to their original lowly status is self-willed; they realize that their natures are determined by their original roles and that they cannot cope with their new-found responsibility. When Cléanthis asks Arlequin why he has resumed his original costume, the symbol of his servitude, he replies in terms which can be understood on either the literal or the symbolic plane: 'C'est qu'il est trop petit pour mon cher ami, et que le sien est trop grand pour moi' ('It is because it is too small for my dear friend, and his is too big for me'), (449).

The symmetries of *Le Jeu de l'amour et du hasard* make it clear that this is no more an attempt at realistic theatre than *L'Ile des esclaves.* We are a very long way here from the illusionism of Diderot's dramatic theory, or even the specific references to Paris found in *Les Fausses Confidences.* Neither, however, does Marivaux introduce anything like the distancing effect of the Greek setting of *L'Ile des esclaves:* the period is contemporary, and the location sufficiently anonymous to allow Marivaux's audience to identify it with their own milieu. The fact that the costume changes of this play have become true disguise, rather than mere symbolism, means that, despite the title of the play, for Lisette and Arlequin the attempt at social elevation through matrimony is much less of a game than it was for their predecessors in the earlier philosophical piece. Their failure too, although the audience shares with Monsieur Orgon and Mario the knowledge that it is inevitable, is a result of the given circumstances rather than of choice. So in this play we have moved a step closer to social climbing as a true possibility. But only a step: whilst Lisette and Arlequin here lack the self-knowledge of the Arlequin of *L'Ile des esclaves,* which allows him to understand and express the fact that he is happier in his old position, Marivaux shows, through the ease of their acceptance of their disillusionment, that he wishes us to understand that subconsciously they have come to a similar realization, and our sympathy for them is as short-lived as their disappointment:

LISETTE

    Venons au fait. M'aimes-tu?

ARLEQUIN

    Pardi! oui: en changeant de nom tu n'as pas changé de visage, et tu sais bien que nous nous sommes promis fidélité en dépit de toutes les fautes d'orthographe.

LISETTE

    Va, le mal n'est pas grand, consolons-nous.

                                (719)

LISETTE

    Get to the point. Do you love me?

ARLEQUIN

    Good God, yes: by changing your name you have not changed your face, and you know very well that we promised to be faithful to each other despite all spelling mistakes.

LISETTE

    Come on, it is no great pity, we will get over it together.

By the time Marivaux came to write *L'Epreuve,* he had already completed *Les Fausses Confidences,* a play in which the crossing of the social divide by marriage becomes a reality, for in marrying Dorante, Araminte weds her own servant, as *intendant* a very high-class servant, it is true, but a servant nonetheless. Dorante may have become *intendant* to Araminte as part of Dubois's stratagem to bring about their marriage, but there is no sense in which he has disguised himself as a social inferior, as does the Dorante of *Le Jeu de l'amour et du hasard*: he really has taken the job as Araminte's servant, and such a post is seen to be compatible with the reduced status brought about by the loss of his fortune. His uncle, Monsieur Remy, certainly sees no shame in this position, and even believes the servant Marton to be a fitting bride for his nephew. Araminte, on the other hand, learns from Dubois of Dorante's condition as impoverished son of a good family as early as the first act of the play, but this high social status certainly does not override his position as servant in her house; it is this which makes the psychological struggle so acute as she gradually falls in love with him and is forced to admit her affection both to herself and to her household. And for Madame Argante, her delightfully odious mother, the status of servant negates all other considerations, preventing her ever accepting Dorante as son-in-law; indeed, she is still affirming this at the final curtain: 'Ah! la belle chute! Ah! ce maudit intendant! Qu'il soit votre mari tant qu'il vous plaira; mais il ne sera jamais mon gendre' ('What an unhappy ending! Ah, that confounded steward! He can be your husband as much as you like; but he will never be my son-in-law'), (1235). Despite the mitigating factors of Dorante's high status in both social and domestic terms, Araminte has still taken the very significant step of breaking through the barrier separating her from her servants.

From here we move on to *L'Epreuve*, which is full of the crossing of social barriers, although across a social distance less extreme than that dividing master from servant seen in the earlier plays. Angélique is of a lower class than Lucidor, but they wed. Maître Blaise aspires, however half-heartedly, to his social superior Angélique, and his wealth will eventually represent a step up the social ladder to Lisette, who finally accepts his proposal of marriage.

But what of the disguised character Frontin? Given that the whole point of the plot of this play is that Angélique passes the test which is set for her, perhaps the best measure of Marivaux's intentions concerning the competence of Frontin's impersonation is not his rejection by her, but rather the treatment he receives from Lisette. Whilst her namesake in *Le Jeu de l'amour et du hasard,* although convinced of the social superiority of the disguised Arlequin, is still emboldened to woo him, Frontin, despite being both recognized and loved by his Lisette, nonetheless manages not only to convince her that she is mistaken about his true identity, but also to put any notion that he would be accessible to her out of her mind. So Frontin's disguise succeeds, and we are more inclined to believe his warnings that he may win Angélique away from Lucidor than we are that Arlequin

could ever win a true member of the ruling class. But if the servant Dorante is able to win his mistress in *Les Fausses Confidences,* the daring of this conclusion is, as we have seen, at least mitigated not only by his being *intendant* rather than valet, but also by the fact that he is a man who has had both rank and fortune and has been ruined. In *L'Epreuve,* even in a world where both Lucidor and Maître Blaise marry beneath them, the true servant cannot be permitted to find a wife who is of either the nobility or the *haute bourgeoisie*. And the symmetry of the fantasy of the earlier plots has also disappeared, with the result that in this more realistic world there are victims as well as winners: the role he is playing for Lucidor deprives Frontin of Lisette, just as the Marton of *Les Fausses Confidences* is deprived of the servant who, according to traditional plot-structure, is rightfully hers.

There is a clear development here: as Marivaux moves away from the stock characters and symmetries of traditional *commedia* models, social mobility becomes more of a possibility. And this development is even more pronounced if compared with a well-known seventeenth-century model: the nobles in *Le Bourgeois Gentilhomme* are prepared to trick Monsieur Jourdain out of his money by promises of marriage and of favours, but that these should ever actually be granted is never their intention. In Marivaux's *L'Héritier de village,* on the other hand, the nobles are quite prepared to marry Blaise's children in order to get at his money, the follies and dishonesty of such an alliance being avoided only by the revelations of the *dénouement*.

Clearly this modification has its roots in social reality. It seems likely that contemporary audiences would assume that the Dorante of *Les Fausses Confidences* was ruined in exactly the same way as Marivaux himself, that is in the financial crash caused by John Law. John Lough comments as follows:

> The immediate economic consequences of the *Système* were mixed. On the one hand thousands of people were ruined (it is perhaps to the *Système* that we owe the plays and novels of Marivaux who was driven by his losses in it to seek a living with his pen), and the violent inflation which caused a steep rise in the cost of living brought suffering to the lower classes, especially in the towns . . . Enormous fortunes were made almost overnight; the lackeys of yesterday became the masters of today.[7]

But such social mobility does not imply that members of the ruling class suddenly began forming marital alliances with servants: far from it. Elinor Barber points out that nobles were only likely to marry beneath their status for considerable financial gain, and that even this compromise was far from being universal:

> The poverty-stricken provincial nobility continued to disdain any alliance with the rich bourgeoisie, even though they might be reduced to the status of

hobereaux. The acceptance by the Court nobility of these marriages may, therefore, be one more indication of its defection from a genuine noble ideology and of its espousal of a way of life no longer congruent with its older functions as a political and military aristocracy.[8]

So the aspirations of Cléanthis and Arlequin in *L'Ile des esclaves* and of Lisette and Arlequin in *Le Jeu de l'amour et du hasard* are unrealistic, and, whilst rightly belonging to the fantasy worlds of these two plays, are, even in that context, inevitably doomed to failure. The slight social mismatch of the marriage of Lucidor to Angélique, on the other hand, may lack some of the fairy-tale extravagance of the earlier plays, but it is perfectly justified in the more realistic atmosphere of *L'Epreuve,* since in terms of contemporary social reality it was actually possible. It is for the same reason that Lisette, although attracted to Frontin, makes no attempt to aspire to the conquest of the master she thinks him to be. Unlike her namesake in *Le Jeu de l'amour et du hasard,* she knows the attempt to be pointless, for she, like the play in which she figures, is more in touch with social reality.

Lionel Gossman comments, however: 'The plain truth seems to be that works of literature do not "reflect" social reality, at least not immediately, so that the relation between the social background and the work of literature is never a simple causal one.'[9] This is certainly true of *Le Jeu de l'amour et du hasard*: there is a degree of reflection of the increased social mobility of the period in the servants' attempts to marry above themselves, but whilst they are not unaware of the difficulty of the attempt, in the real world of the time it would surely have been impossible. Similarly in relation to the masters: although much of the emotional tension of their roles comes from their reluctance even to consider a *mésalliance*, Silvia's eventual manipulation of Dorante to the point that he proposes marriage to a girl whom he believes to be a servant is again the stuff on which dreams and romantic comedies are made, but is not representative of contemporary reality. It is not just, therefore, the symmetricality of this play or the tidiness of its *dénouement* which have an almost fairy-tale quality; the exaggerated aspirations of the servant characters and the extent to which Dorante's love triumphs over the demands of commonsense and social reality come into a similar category. The characters themselves may not feel that they are involved in a game, but through his title Marivaux signals to his audience that the content of this play should be taken none too seriously.

By the time we reach *Les Fausses Confidences* we are in much more plausible territory, for, despite the daring conclusion in which mistress marries not only a servant, but actually her own servant, we can see that the situation is much more closely analogous to that described by Lough and Barber: Araminte is the rich bourgeoise, and Dorante, although ruined, has a social rank which makes him an acceptable partner; Marton too, is quite justified in seeing Dorante as her legitimate partner, since both belong to the servant class. And then, in Marivaux's final play for the Italians, we move ever further from *commedia dell'arte* fantasy, for, as we have seen, *L'Epreuve* depicts a situation which, on the social level at least, is more or less uncontroversial.[10]

But the collapse of Law's system dates from 1720, *L'Ile des esclaves* from 1725, *Le Jeu de l'amour et du hasard* from 1730, *Les Fausses Confidences* from 1737 and *L'Epreuve* from 1740. The plays certainly inhabit post-Law society, but, given this time-scale, they can scarcely be seen as a specific response to the collapse of the *Système*. Should we seek other reasons for the development in Marivaux's approach seen in these plays?

The naming of the characters is not without significance. In *L'Ile des esclaves* names chosen for their relevance to the Greek setting (Iphicrate, Euphrosine, Cléanthis) rub shoulders with the Italianate (Trivelin and Arlequin). It is, of course, the Arlequin archetype who is the most persistently Italian element of Marivaux's theatre, and we note that when he swaps roles and costumes with Iphicrate, even though, as I have suggested, it seems unlikely that the actor playing the part of the noble took over the traditional elements of the costume (the stylized patchwork suit, the mask and the slap-stick), his master does take over his name. This is part of his humiliation: 'Arlequin', as we are told in this play, is little better as an appellation than 'Hé' (428), and we will learn in *Le Jeu de l'amour et du hasard* that one of its principal features is that it rhymes with 'coquin' ('rascal') and 'faquin' ('wretch') (718). In *Le Jeu de l'amour et du hasard,* on the other hand, whilst Silvia in her disguise becomes Lisette and Lisette Silvia, Arlequin even becoming Dorante, Dorante is spared not only Arlequin's traditional costume, but also his name: he becomes Bourguignon. In Marivaux's first important play for the Italians, *Arlequin poli par l'amour,*[11] Silvia had been a fitting partner for Arlequin, but by the time we reach *Le Jeu de l'amour et du hasard* her suitor cannot be expected even to assume his name. Whilst the name Lisette is a traditional enough name for a *soubrette,* it does not have enough archetypal significance to compromise either the dignity or the nature of Silvia's performance as a servant.

Arlequin is another matter: in *L'Ile des esclaves* Iphicrate makes no pretence of actually being Arlequin; all he needs to do is appear offended whenever he is called by this name, and, indeed, the role is so sketchy in the central part of the work that this is virtually all he does do. Dorante, on the other hand, is in disguise, and, in terms of her social status, Silvia has come a long way since her first appearance in a play by Marivaux; there is a sense in which the mere fact of calling himself Arlequin would completely compromise Dorante's wooing of her, for the archetypal force of the name is such that it would be completely inappropriate to the refined servant played by Dorante: 'le galant Bourguignon' (704). The archetypal force of the name also causes it to demand of the actor playing the part, even in disguise, the *lazzi* which are typical of it, and these were not only counter to Marivaux's purpose, they were also, as it were, the property of Thomassin, who was playing the 'real' Arlequin, and not of Luigi (often known as Louis) Riccoboni, who was in the role of Dorante. So the swapping of names demanded by the role-reversal in *L'Ile des esclaves* has disappeared: here roles are still reversed, master pretends to be servant and servant master, but whilst Arlequin still pretends to be Dorante, Dorante emphatically does not pretend to be Arlequin. Arlequin has, in consequence, been marginalized: in *Arlequin poli par l'amour* he is central to the plot. In *L'Ile des esclaves* the servant characters dominate the action and his presence is also, as it were, duplicated by the fact that Iphicrate is given his name. In *Le Jeu de l'amour et du hasard* it is the action involving the masters which is paramount, and when they are on stage we are not even reminded of Arlequin by the disguised Dorante's using his name. And when we reach *L'Epreuve*, Marivaux's last play for the Italians, he has disappeared completely.

When Marivaux calls his female lead in *Les Fausses Confidences* Araminte and in *L'Epreuve* Angélique, it is true that these changes denote a certain change in the type of character, for the former is a rather more emotionally mature woman than the Silvias of the earlier plays, and the latter a little more modest and passive; but these modifications are subtle, the type remains broadly similar and the parts were still played by the actress Silvia. Much the same is true of Riccoboni's Lélios, Dorantes and Lucidor; and if the Marton of *Les Fausses Confidences* is a slightly more serious character than our two Lisettes, the emphasis is surely on 'slightly'. In the case of Arlequin, however, the situation is completely different, for with the name goes the archetype. Indeed, so strong is the archetypal force of the name, that in the scene in *Le Jeu de l'amour et du hasard* in which Arlequin reveals his true identity to Lisette (III. vii) an interesting situation arises: Arlequin confesses to being the servant of Dorante, but does not give his name. Logically, given the symmetry of the plot, Lisette should assume that he is called Bourguignon. But no: a few lines further on, without needing to be told, she calls him Arlequin. That this should occur without causing any sense of incongruity, without giving rise to the feeling that here we have an authorial error, is entirely attributable to the impossibility of dissociating the name from the character-type. The one implies the other, so it would be superfluous

for the character to identify himself by name. And so the different name given to Frontin implies a significant difference in character: not for him the traditional trappings of Arlequin's costume. Yves Moraud comments, for instance: 'Arlequin est à peu près le seul personnage qui continue, à la fin du XVII siècle, à porter régulièrement le masque' ('Arlequin is virtually the only character who, at the end of the seventeenth century, still regularly wears a mask').[12] In order to permit the much more convincing portrayal of the master by the disguised Frontin, Marivaux had to make use of such an alternative servant figure: an actor playing Arlequin would have provided the conventional *lazzi*, which the audience would have expected. Not only would the use of the archetypal character without his tomfoolery have disappointed the audience, but the expectations of his name and the conventional trappings of his costume would in any case have ensured that any attempt on Marivaux's part to make the servant's impersonation of the master convincing with him in the role was doomed to failure from the outset.

Kenneth McKee remarks of *L'Epreuve*:

> With its felicitous role for Silvia, *L'Epreuve* was a fitting climax to Marivaux's career as purveyor to the Italian actors. Yet, strangely, the play shows no trace of the old Italian influences. In the twenty years since Marivaux submitted *Arlequin poli par l'amour* to Riccoboni, he drew less and less on the *commedia dell'arte,* and his writing evolved to such a point that none of his last eight plays, except *Les Fausses Confidences,* contain even a minor part for Arlequin.[13]

And that role in *Les Fausses Confidences* has been even more marginalized than the relegation from central character to servant figure that we noted between *Arlequin poli par l'amour* and *Le Jeu de l'amour et du hasard,* for in this play he has even become a secondary servant, the dolt who amuses us with his *lazzi* in a few cameo-like scenes, and has but minor importance for the plot; the main function is reserved for the Machiavellian first servant and *meneur du jeu*, Dubois.

Arlequin was for Marivaux, to a large extent, not merely an archetype, but an actor: Tommaso Visenti, known as Thomassin. There seems no doubt that, at the height of his powers, he played the part very well, but, in the few years before his death in 1739, 'après une longue maladie' ('after a long illness') as the *Mercure* stated,[14] his failing health must have made him a less acrobatic and lively *zanni* and possibly even a less reliable colleague. After his death, the Italians replaced him with Carlo Bertaggi, but Marivaux had already written his final Arlequin; his loss of interest in the role coincides with Thomassin's decline. But is the playwright being controlled by the archetype, or the archetype by the playwright? Does Marivaux stop writing roles for Arlequin because he loses Thomassin, or is it through loyalty for the actor that he goes on writing them for as long as he does? Is the development in Marivaux's theatre a result of the disappearance of Arlequin, or is he dropped because he is incompatible with the new direction that Marivaux is pursuing?

There is no clear or certain answer to these questions, and it would be misguided to claim that one alternative were true to the exclusion of the other, but certain trends related to the concerns we have already examined suggest that the second of each pair of alternatives may represent the dominant force in Marivaux's development. We have seen that Arlequin dominates the plot in *Arlequin poli par l'amour. La Double Inconstance* (1723) has a similarly artificial symmetricality to our first two comedies of role-reversal, but the work is constructed in such a way that in each part of the plot one of the *commedia* characters (Arlequin and Silvia, who at this point is still seen as his legitimate partner) is paired with one of the courtly characters, thus spreading the *commedia* influence evenly through the texture of the play. By the time of *L'Ile des esclaves* and *Le Jeu de l'amour et du hasard* the servants are paired together as are the masters, but if in the former the servants dominate the plot, in the latter it is the masters who hold centre stage. In *Les Fausses Confidences* and *L'Epreuve* the symmetry has disappeared and it is the masters who are at the centre of the plot-line, the *commedia* archetypes having been first marginalized and then banished. This development marks a gradual abandonment of the *commedia dell'arte* models which Marivaux adopted at the beginning of his career, in favour of a more emotional and sentimental form of drama represented by the dominance of the higher-born characters, a form which is more typical of later currents in eighteenth-century French theatre.[15] And along with this move towards the dominance of a more serious form of comedy we find a tendency for both settings and social attitudes to become more realistic; the latter trend we have already examined, the former can be seen in the move from the fantasy worlds of *Arlequin poli par l'amour* and *L'Ile des esclaves* to the anonymously contemporary setting of *Le Jeu de l'amour et du hasard* and further to the specific references to Paris found in *Les Fausses Confidences* and *L'Epreuve*; the Madame Dorman for whom Frontin has worked, for instance, lives, 'du côté de la place Maubert, chez un marchand de café, au second' ('by the Place Maubert, at a coffee merchant's, on the second floor'), (1327). There are certainly exceptions to this trend, *La Dispute* (1744), for example, which, although written after *L'Epreuve,* inhabits a world every bit as fantastic as the three island comedies,[16] but the general trend seems clear enough. Indeed, *Les Fausses Confidences* and *L'Epreuve* inhabit very similar milieux to Marivaux's two great novels, *La Vie de Marianne* and *Le Paysan parvenu,* both of which were undertaken during the period between *Le Jeu de l'amour et du hasard* and *Les*

Fausses Confidences, and both of which are much concerned with the theme of social climbing which we have also observed in our comedies of disguise and role-reversal.

So the issue of disguise and role-reversal and Arlequin's relationship to this theme turn out to be related to the central development of Marivaux's theatre away from its *commedia dell'arte* origins. Arlequin's inability to change his nature is central to the philosophy of *L'Ile des esclaves,* and adds to the comedy in a play like *Le Jeu de l'amour et du hasard,* where the basic artificiality of the plot structure makes it clear that we should not take lapses in credibility too seriously. A play like *L'Epreuve,* in which our response to Angélique's emotional crisis depends on our ability to believe that she is taken in by Frontin's disguise, would be impossible with Arlequin in the role of disguised servant. For Arlequin cannot ever truly be disguised; Marivaux may polish him, he may become Sauvage, Deucalion or Roi de Serendib,[17] but fundamentally he is always immutably himself.

Notes

1. *La Commedia dell'arte* (Lyon, L'Hermès, 1982), 71.

2. 'Lazzi': The comic routines of the 'Commedia dell'Arte' (New York, Performing Arts Journal Publications, 1983), 37.

3. All references to Marivaux's plays are from *Théâtre complet,* ed. Marcel Arland (Paris, Gallimard, 1949).

4. Jean Emelina comments too: 'Les frontispices de l'edition de 1701 [du *Théâtre italien* de Gherardi] en six volumes ne permettent pratiquement pas de distinguer d'après l'habit, Colombine de sa maîtresse' ('The frontispieces of the six-volume 1701 edition [of Gherardi's *Italian Theatre*] hardly allow us, in terms of costume, to distinguish at all between Colombine and her mistress'), *Les Valets et les servantes dans le théâtre comique en France de 1610 à 1700* (Grenoble, PUG, 1975), 398.

5. 'Women in Marivaux: Journalist to Dramatist', in *Women and Society in Eighteenth-Century France: Essays in Honour of J. S. Spink,* ed. E. Jacobs, et al. (London, Athlone Press, 1979), 42-54, (49-50).

6. 'Old dogs and new tricks: Tradition and revolt in Marivaux's *La Colonie*', in *The British Journal for Eighteenth-Century Studies,* XI (1988), 173-84.

7. *An Introduction to Eighteenth-Century France* (London, Longmans, Green, 1960), 146.

8. *The Bourgeoisie in 18th-Century France* (Princeton University Press, 1955), 102.

9. French Society and Culture: Background for 18th-Century Literature (New Jersey, Prentice-Hall, 1972), 113.

10. There is, of course, Frontin's suggestion in the first scene that he may win Angélique from Lucidor, but, in the event, this comes to nothing. The controversial aspects of this play reside rather in the morality of Lucidor's treatment of Angélique, and perhaps also the fact that Lucidor's manipulations lose for Frontin his rightful bride.

11. The brief allegorical *L'Amour et la Vérité* had been given by the Italians on 3 March 1720. *Arlequin poli par l'amour* followed on 17 October of the same year.

12. *Masques et jeux dans le théâtre comique en France entre 1685 et 1730* (Lille, Atelier Reproduction des Thèses, Université de Lille III, 1977), 393, n. 22.

13. *The Theater of Marivaux* (New York University Press, 1958), 231.

14. See *Théâtre complet,* ed. F. Deloffre, 2 vols. (Paris, Garnier Frères, 1968), II, 341.

15. Although, mercifully, even in his most sentimental plays, *La Mère Confidente.* (1735) and *La Femme fidèle* (1755), Marivaux never approaches the humourlessness of Nivelle de La Chaussée at his most larmoyant, of Madame de Graffigny or of Diderot's *drame.* Arlequin may have disappeared from *L'Epreuve* and Frontin's role may be quite restricted, but Maître Blaise is the source of much low comedy. However, whilst the figure of the dialect-speaking peasant may have his roots in similar *commedia dell'arte* characters, Maître Blaise is so French in both his attitudes and accent that he has left any hint of the Italian far behind.

16. *L'Ile des esclaves, L'Ile de la raison* and *La Colonie.*

17. See the plays by Delisle de La Drevetière, Piron and Lesage.

Shawncey Webb (essay date 1994)

SOURCE: Webb, Shawncey. "The Role of Fidelity and Infidelity in *Le Paysan Parvenu* and *La Vie de Marianne*: Sexual Difference and Narrative." *Romance Languages Annual* 6 (1994): 198-202.

[*In the following essay, Webb examines the double standard for sexual behavior represented in Marivaux's two first-person novels.*]

The concept of fidelity/infidelity plays an important role in Marivaux's two first-person novels *Le Paysan parvenu* (1734) and *La Vie de Marianne* (1731). The concept serves to emphasize the importance of sexual difference in eighteenth-century France. It also has a significant effect upon the following aspects of the narrative in the two works:

(1) narrator expectations: what reactions to their sexual conduct and to the sexual conduct of other characters in the story do the narrators expect from their implied readers?

(2) narrator as narrator and as character: are they one and the same or does the narrator present a contrast to him(her)self as character?

(3) events of the narrative: are they affected by the sex of the narrator? Does the narrator/character present him(her)self as an active or passive element in these events?

(4) other characters: what is the attitude of the narrator in each novel toward the other characters? Is he (she) concerned about them or is the focus totally egocentric?

The concept of fidelity/infidelity is also important in regard to the titles of the two novels: *Le Paysan parvenu* in contrast to *La Vie de Marianne* and serves to make them companion novels, but one definitely masculine, the other feminine, given the mores of the society depicted by Marivaux and shared by his contemporary readers.

In *Le Paysan parvenu* and in *La Vie de Marianne,* Marivaux recounts typical "rags to riches" stories. Each novel is purported to be the memoirs of an individual who was originally without wealth or social standing and who has at the time of writing gained a certain position in society. Marianne, who was once an impoverished orphan, has become a countess. Jacob, a peasant by origin, has apparently risen to at least the highest ranks of the bourgeoisie. Although Jacob does not state precisely his social status, he does give sufficient information to allow the reader to assume that he has achieved such social position. The two novels, often viewed as companion works, thus present the life available to a man and to a woman of similar circumstances in eighteenth-century France.

In spite of its characterization as the Age of Enlightenment, the eighteenth century remained a male dominated period and maintained a sharp distinction between men and women, between what was masculine and what was feminine, and between acceptable conduct for one and for the other. In *A History of Their Own,* Anderson and Zinsser state

> there was no Enlightenment for women. . . . Instead, often at great cost to their own logic and rationality, they [Enlightenment thinkers] continued to reaffirm the most ancient inherited traditions about women. . . . In

philosophy and in art, men of the Enlightenment upheld the traditional ideal of woman: silent, obedient, subvervient, modest and chaste.

(2: 113)

While this accusation against the century may be somewhat severe and oversimplified, there was a vast difference between the life afforded to a man and to a woman during the century. On almost any social level, the eighteenth century adhered to a different standard of opportunity, of duty and of morality for the two sexes: "Le rôle de la femme est d'aimer, la loi de l'homme est d'ambitionner" (Etienne 106). "Une vie de femme peut être abruptement terminée quand l'homme l'abandonne pour vivre sa vie d'homme—c'est s'avancer, effacer les autres et parvenir" (Etienne 105-06). Women were born to love and to suffer for that love, while men were to seek success.

In his article "De Marianne à Jacob: Les deux sexes du roman chez Marivaux," Frédéric Deloffre discusses the way in which the choice of narrator, masculine or feminine, gives predominance to *sensibilité* or *sensualité* in the novel. We should like now to consider how the concept of fidelity and infidelity serves to emphasize this contrasting predominance and sexual difference and how it affects the narratives, in particular how it restricts Marianne's and how it frees that of Jacob. During the eighteenth century, particularly in the early part, a woman's infidelity was decried as "le plus grand crime qu'une femme puisse commettre" (Chasles 2: 383). In contrast, a man's infidelity or infidelities were viewed as being of little consequence. Women were divided into two categories: *femmes vertueuses* and *femmes perdues de réputation,* while men were free to be faithful or unfaithful according to their needs and whims.

Based upon these facts, one can develop a set of equations of acceptability which represent the sexual mores of the period. Man + unfaithful = acceptable to society as does Man + faithful (although the number of unfaithful men far outnumbers the faithful) while Woman + faithful = acceptable to society, but Woman + unfaithful = unacceptable to society. In Marivaux's novels, the two major equations of acceptability which equate male and infidelity, female and fidelity serve as basic premises which are accepted by both the narrators and the implied readers to whom they address themselves. The memoirs are addressed to contemporaries of Jacob and of Marianne. Therefore, the narrators expect certain reactions from their implied readers. Jacob can with a certain amount of confidence speak of his infidelities because he anticipates indulgence from his implied readers. He sees his memoirs as a lesson, an educational tract, something from which the readers can profit and benefit because they illustrate how a man of little standing and insignificant ancestry can succeed in the world. Jacob begins his narrative with a series of six paragraphs in which he extols his honesty about his ancestry and the good fortune that has accrued to him because of it.

> Le tître que je donne à mes Mémoires annonce ma naissance; je ne l'ai jamais dissimulée à qui me l'a demandée, et il me semble qu'en tout temps Dieu ait récompensé ma franchise là-dessus; car je n'ai jamais remarqué qu'en aucune occasion on en ait eu moins d'égard et moins d'estime pour moi.
>
> (Marivaux, *Le Paysan parvenu* 5)

He then proceeds to assure the reader that

> le récit de [ses] aventures ne sera pas inutile à ceux qui aiment à s'instruire. Voilà en partie ce qui fait que je le donne; je cherche aussi à m'amuser moi-même.
>
> (*Paysan* 6)

Jacob is confident; he is familiar with his readers. They belong to the same social system and hold the same basic beliefs. Thus Jacob writes for what Eco has termed the model reader—that is he describes by his references and assumptions the characteristics of his reader. Jacob is authoritative and leaves little or no room to his reader to take issue with his beliefs. Jacob then proceeds to recount his life, a series of events, which all deal in one way or another with his relationships with women, and which all turn out to be infidelities. Confident in the shared belief of his readers that a man's infidelities are excusable, he describes them with a certain pleasure and lends a comical tone with such euphemisms as "une femme de chambre d'un monsieur" in reference to the unfortunate Geniève who is exploited by both Jacob and the master.

Jacob's story is one of "how I succeeded in life." Jacob (narrator) is the same individual as Jacob (character); he writes to show himself off, to brag about himself and declare what a fine job he has done in attaining his present position. Jacob's story is composed of a series of incidents of encounters with women of various social classes. He grants himself the privilege of playing the role of judge in each instance. He is a very active character, who remains the dominant and controlling force at every moment of his narrative.

Upon arriving in his master's household, Jacob is attracted to Geneviève, a maid in the household. This attraction soon passes when he discovers that she is willing to be the master's mistress. The fact that Geneviève apparently believed that thus acquiring a fortune would enable her to marry Jacob sooner, that is the fact that she did it for him, has little effect. Jacob has nothing but contempt for unfaithful women. Secure in the belief that his reader shares his contempt for such women, Jacob is able to joke about the poor abandonned Geneviève. He recounts how he has refused his master's suggestion that he marry her by saying:

dans notre village, c'est notre coutume de n'épouser que des filles, et s'il y en avait une qui eût été femme de chambre d'un monsieur, il faudrait qu'elle se contentât d'avoir un amant; mais pour de mari, néant; il en pleurrait, qu'il n'en tomberait pas un pour elle; c'est notre régime et surtout dans notre famille.

(*Paysan* 29)

His contempt for licentious women appears once again when the chevalier discovers Mme de Ferval with him at Mme de Remy's house. Jacob has been overjoyed at his good fortune in becoming the intended lover of two women of the nobility—Mme de Ferval and Mme de Fecour. He keeps gloating over the fact that Jacob, a peasant, is now wearing silks and velvets and being fawned over by women of the aristocracy. However, Jacob tells the reader that when he overhears Mme de Ferval playing the same coy game of allowing herself to be seduced with the chevalier that she had just been playing with him, he has "beaucoup de mépris pour Mme de Ferval, mais beaucoup d'estime pour sa figure" (*Paysan* 241). Jacob is very practical about women and philosophizes that "Ce n'est pas du coeur d'une femme dont on est en peine, c'est de sa personne; on ne songe point à ses sentiments, mais à ses actions" (*Paysan* 231). Jacob divides women into two classes: those worthy of being wives and those relegated to the status of momentary amusements.

The most important quality for a wife, of course, is fidelity. And it is this quality in Mlle Habert which makes her such an excellent choice for Jacob and one of which he can be proud. Fifty, *dévote* and absolutely infatuated with Jacob, she is not about to look elsewhere for sexual fulfillment. She brings to Jacob financial security, a superior position in society, and a faithful and honorable wife. While Jacob is pleased to enjoy the security of a faithful bourgeois wife, he does not let his marriage restrict him in any way. And, once again, given the shared attitudes of Jacob and his implied reader, he can wittily and good-naturedly excuse his would-be infidelities to Mlle Habert by his "masculine" vanity:

En fait d'amour, tout engagé qu'on est déjà, la vanité de plaire ailleurs vous rend l'âme si infidèle, et vous donne en pareilles occasions de si lâches complaisances!

(*Paysan* 136)

And besides, what harm is he doing? None at all; he assures his readers: that "rien dans [son] esprit n'a changé pour elle [sa femme], et [il allait] la revoir aussi tendrement qu'à l'ordinaire" (*Paysan* 230). Moreover, Mme de la Vallée (Mlle Habert) is not jealous and never suspects a thing. Jacob takes advantage of the morality of his time and remains free to indulge in extra-marital affairs in which "nature" not "sentiment" is the stimulus, for fidelity remains a feminine virtue. Jacob is the center of his narrative; the other characters, primarily

women, exist to enable him to show off, to display himself and his cleverness. Jacob moves through his story with all eyes focused on him. He has an amusing tale of success to relate. He recounts this story to a reader who shares his beliefs and attitudes and is ready and willing to excuse his infidelities and smugly laugh with him at the unfaithful women he encounters along the way.

For Marianne, the situation is different. Her story is not one of "how I succeeded" but rather "how I bore up under the dreadful experience of being abandoned." While Marianne's narrative, like Jacob's, is written in the first person, Marianne's is immediately distanced from the reader. This is not a story written to instruct others or to flaunt success. It is private and personal, veiled and protected. Marianne's story is introduced by an *avertissement* in which the reader is informed that it is a true story and was not written "exprès pour amuser le public" (*Marianne* 5) but rather "à une amie" (*Marianne* 5). In Part One, the origins of the manuscript are further obscured and surrounded with mystery as the reader is told that it was found in a wardrobe located in an alcove in a country house near Rennes and that this house had been owned by five or six different persons. (*Marianne* 7). The handwriting is that of a woman who first calls herself Marianne and later countess and addresses herself to a female friend.

The story that Marianne tells is that of her life, primarily of her love affair with Valville. Marianne's perspective as narrator is very different from that of Jacob. Marianne (narrator) contrasts significantly with Marianne (character). Marianne (character) is the young emotional woman loved by and then abandonned by Valville, while Marianne (narrator) is older, wiser, and possessed of a degree of reasonableness and detachment impossible for Marianne (character). It is Marianne (narrator) who can be described as "le contraire d'un idéaliste" (Mauzi 466). "Elle concilie fort bien la tendresse et la souci d'elle-même. Surtout elle est sans illusion et ce n'est pas d'elle qu'il faut attendre de grands désespoirs" (Mauzi 466). But before achieving this serenity of being without illusions, Marianne has experienced all of the heights and depths of emotion which, in Marivaux's eyes and in the eyes of the century, make up a woman's life—"la vie d'une femme ne comporte . . . que la joie d'être aimée et de souffrir pour ce qu'elle aime" (*Marianne* xxxviii). Marianne has undergone significant changes; Jacob, on the other hand, has the same beliefs and ideas at the time he is writing as he had when he entered his master's house. So Jacob remains very much intact, while Marianne has experienced considerable metamorphosis.

Jacob's story may be representative of the ascendency of any young man of little means in society, but it remains Jacob's story. Jacob is very visible in his narrative. Marianne, although she also is an overt narrator addressing comments on her life to her friend, dominates neither her life nor her narrative as does Jacob. Marianne's narrative is severely restricted by her passivity, and her role in her own story is made static and reduced to a fixed point around which the action takes place. The theme of fidelity or rather more accurately of infidelity has this effect. Without question, Marianne is the faithful, virtuous female acceptable to the century. The story that she tells turns out to be that of an unfaithful man and the momentarily devastating effects of that faithlessness upon her. Her dreadful experience is brought about by her obscure background; she is not suitable to become the wife of Valville. The intrigue is simple. Valville sees her and falls in love with her. Subsequently, he encounters strong opposition from his family and extricates himself from a difficult situation by committing "une infidelité de coeur." He encounters Mlle de Varthon, a young woman acceptable to his family; and fortunately for him, the same *coup de foudre* effect as had taken place when he saw Marianne, occurs again and he is saved. He can have a wife of his choice and still respect the wishes of his family. Marianne never has an opportunity to be unfaithful nor does she have a reason to be. Her fidelity is primarily a fidelity of inertia. Although she narrates her own life, she curiously enough does not seem to play the major role in it. Perhaps before her meeting with Valville, Marianne shows a certain amount of initiative and self-direction. In her relationship with M de Climal, she refuses to accept a position as a domestic in the home of his sister-in-law, a situation far below the station in life which she believes is rightfully hers (***Marianne*** 27-28) and at the church it is her naïve *coquetterie* which results in her meeting with Valville. There, she seats herself in the most advantageous of positions to attract the attention of the crowd, particularly the men. Nancy Miller in *The Heroine's Text* (25) sees this action on Marianne's part as an indication of her ability to manipulate her life. And to this point in her story Marianne has appeared to be working toward a certain goal. But at this point, Marianne is victimized by the *coup de foudre* and becomes a character to whom things happen. Once she meets Valville's mother Mme de Miran, it is no longer Marianne who directs her life, but rather this surrogate mother, who eventually is as concerned for Marianne as for her own son. Thus, Marianne is a passive character.

Nor does she have the freedom to comment and judge that Jacob has. He excuses himself, but he has little tolerance for the other characters in his story. His opinions are set and he scoffs at those who do not share them or who do not live up to his expectations. Marianne, on the other hand, does neither. She is a very serious narrator. The subject of a man's infidelity and the abandonment of a woman is no laughing matter, as she portrays it. However, she never condemns Valville; she even defends him when her friend speaks ill of him.

Eventually, she assumes much of the responsibility for her despair. Marianne often turns the voice of her narrative over to another character. Jacob never lets anyone else speak at any length. There are two major incidents of this phenomenon in Marianne's story. One is the somewhat sudden appearance of a nobleman of about fifty who offers her a marriage based solely upon reason. His discourse to her forms a tirade against love (passion) as a basis of marriage, trust or security. The concept of love as physical attraction is at the base of his reasoning. He attributes love to a *coup de foudre* which takes hold of people upon their first seeing each other and is dispelled as easily as it was born. Marianne's self-esteem is re-awakened by this man's interest. And this perhaps helps her to absolve Valville of any wrong doing. Valville is after all "un homme fort ordinaire" (***Marianne*** 376). Marianne refers to Valville as such when she reproaches her friend for expecting from him conduct befitting "un héros de roman." Marianne has come to understand the world in which she lives. The second incident of interrupted narrative is the inclusion of the nun's story which occupies the final three parts of the novel. The story corroborates the precariousness of a woman's fate in life. It contains other examples of women abandoned by their lovers for social and financial reasons. Thus, it repeats the same ideas and opinions expressed in Marianne's own story. Consequently, Marianne as narrator is abandoned much as she was abandoned by Valville. Marianne loses her function as narrator. Marivaux as author is unfaithful to Marianne as narrator just as Valville character was unfaithful to her as character. Another woman takes up the narration of the story which can be told by almost any woman of her class. Marianne becomes "une femme fort ordinaire" and a narrator of little importance as the task of narration passes to another woman who recounts more episodes of abandonment. Marianne, narrator and character, has served her purpose and been cast aside for a new and more interesting narrator just as she was cast aside for the more acceptable Mlle Varthon? Who can say? But this change of narrators does perhaps serve to emphasize Marianne's passivity and fidelity as the reader expects her to be there to continue once the nun has finished her story. Unfortunately, such is not the case, since the novel remains unfinished. *Le Paysan parvenu* is unfinished as well, but Jacob is still the narrator and concludes the fifth part with the promise of more to come.

Both Jacob and Marianne can be described as typical eighteenth-century narrators who, according to Chatman, served to strengthen the versimilitude of the novels.

> Eighteenth-century authors took another view [did not try to minimize the narration]. Their overt narrators were orators of sorts, though they persuaded their readers not to practical action but to accepting the legitimacy of their mimesis. They portrayed characters and scenes consistent with "the ordinary way of the world";

troublesome questions could be answered by explanatory generalizations.

(Chatman 227)

Thus Marianne and Jacob speak in a straightforward fashion to their implied readers who share their beliefs and standards. The novels are written for readers who agree with the narrators. Jacob expects his reader to be amused with him and to be impressed by him. Marianne, for all of her humility, has confidence that the reader will understand and see her as having done the best she could. Given what was acceptable for men and for women in matters of fidelity in love or marriage, given the equation of male with action, ascendency and control and of female with passivity, stasis and submission, both Jacob and Marianne have narrated appropriate stories, believable and worth the reading in eighteenth-century France.

The importance of the complicity between these narrators and their implied or contemporary readers causes considerable problems for them with readers of the twentieth century. It is difficult not to condemn Jacob and Valville. Lester Crocker defines Valville as "a thoughtless petit-maître" (*An Age of Crisis* 146). Jacob's casual attitude toward his own fidelity or lack thereof has resulted in his being called a "sexual opportunist" (Mylne 123). Marianne, while she may be believable and trustworthy to her contemporaries, may be difficult for the present-day reader to believe. Her complacency, her acceptance of Valville's conduct are possibly annoying to the modern reader. Surely, she is mocking Valville, "cet homme fort ordinaire," and the whole system. But she is not. In the eighteenth century her conduct is plausible and correct. Marianne is the ideal woman, passive and submissive. Her only fault is perhaps writing down her life. In this way she breaks silence, but she must for Marivaux to write the novel and her narrative is intended for another woman, a close friend. So Marianne writes **La Vie de Marianne,** the story of her experience of love and of the unfaithfulness of the man she loved. Jacob, as inexcusable as he may be to us today, is acceptable in his own world. The century's continuing sense of male dominance and superiority is always present with Jacob; he lives in a male world, and this world is his oyster. For Jacob, there are women with whom he will be seen in public, others whom he reserves for more secret meetings. And he himself is free to advance however he can. Thus he writes not *La Vie de Jacob,* not even *La Vie amoureuse de Jacob* but **Le Paysan parvenu,** because what matters most for him is to advance, to succeed; and love (actually infidelity in love) functions to help him attain this goal. Each narrator has depicted the life of a person of his (her) sex in the social climate of eighteenth-century France.

Works Cited

Anderson, Bonnie S., and Judith P. Zinsser. *A History of Their Own: Women in Europe from Prehistory to the Present.* 2 vols. New York: Harper, 1985.

Chasles, Robert. *Les Illustres Françaises.* Ed. F. Deloffre. 2 vols. Paris: Les Belles Lettres, 1967.

Chatman, Seymour. *Story and Discourse: Narrative Structure in Fiction and Film.* Ithaca: Cornell UP, 1978.

Crocker, Lester. *An Age of Crisis: Man and the World in Eighteenth-Century French Thought.* Baltimore: Johns Hopkins UP, 1959.

Deloffre, Frédéric. "De Marianne à Jacob: les deux sexes du roman chez Marivaux." *L'Information littéraire* 5 (1959): 185-92.

Eco, Umberto. *The Role of the Reader: Explorations in the Semantics of Texts.* Bloomington: Indiana UP, 1979.

Etienne, Servais. *Le Genre romanesque en France depuis l'apparition de la "Nouvelle Héloïse" jusqu'aux approches de la Révolution.* Paris: Armand Colin, 1922.

Marivaux, Pierre Carlet. *Le Paysan parvenu.* Ed. F. Deloffre. Paris: Garnier, 1965.

———. *La Vie de Marianne.* Ed. F. Deloffre. Paris: Garnier, 1963.

Mauzi, Robert. *L'Idée du bonheur dans la littérature et la pensée française au XVIIIe siècle.* 2 éd. Paris: Armand Colin, 1965.

Miller, Nancy K. *The Heroine's Text: Readings in the French and English Novel, 1722-1782.* New York: Columbia UP, 1980.

Mylne, Vivienne. *The Eighteenth-Century French Novel: Techniques of Illusion.* Manchester: Manchester UP, 1965.

Patrick Brady (essay date 2000)

SOURCE: Brady, Patrick. "Chaos, Complexity, Catastrophe and Control in Marivaux's *La Vie de Marianne.*" In *Disrupted Patterns: On Chaos and Order in the Enlightenment,* edited by Theodore E. D. Braun and John A. McCarthy, pp. 65-77. Amsterdam: Rodopi, 2000.

[*In the following excerpt, Brady applies the principles of emerging theories—chaos, catastrophe, complexity, and control—to* La vie de Marianne, *while still taking into account the more conventional critical analyses of Marivaux's novel based on aesthetics.*]

La Vie de Marianne (1731-41), the most important novel of the French playwright Marivaux, has provoked the admiration and elicited the analysis of such brilliant twentieth-century critics as Leo Spitzer (1953) and René Girard (1963), who gave interpretations of it that were essentially psychological.[1] Next, its aesthetic character was shown to illustrate the rococo style that dominated in the early eighteenth century.[2]

Our novel was subjected to a dozen different modes of structuralism, drawn from theorists as diverse as Claude Lévi-Strauss, Roland Barthes, Jacques Lacan and Lucien Goldmann, in a series of articles in the 1970s, collected in volume form in 1978.[3] In that same volume (pp. 81-82), use is also made of a cousin of structuralism named catastrophe theory, a new perspective derived from topology, a branch of mathematics; the year before there had appeared the first article to apply catastrophe theory to literary studies.[4] The founder of this new theory, René Thom, had found in the work of Lévi-Strauss "corroboration for his growing belief that thought and language are shaped by deep principles of structural stability just as surely as physical processes."[5]

Catastrophe theory competed with bifurcation theory for recognition as the key to the analysis of discontinuity. Bifurcation equations served to describe phenomena such as "the onset of turbulence in a smoothly flowing fluid" (*ibid.*, 76), while catastrophe theory utilized "strange attractors [to] describe the chaotic behaviour of systems caught by these attractors" (*ibid.*, *loc. cit.*). David Fowler "proposed one of the elementary catastrophes as a qualitative model for phase transition in physics" (*ibid.*, 36). Alexander Woodcock and Monte Davis speculated in 1978 "that in the long run one of the two theories will be absorbed by the other, or that both will become part of some wider theory as yet unnamed" (*ibid.*, 75-76). The result was chaos theory.

Several of the names connected with catastrophe theory by Woodcock and Davis reappear later in the works on chaos by James Gleick (1987) and on complexity by Roger Lewin and Mitchell Waldrop (1992), including those of René Thom,[6] John Guckenheimer,[7] Steven Smale,[8] Brian Goodwin,[9] and Jack Cowan.[10] In 1988, the first paper applying chaos theory to the analysis of literature and culture was read at the annual meeting of the Modern Language Association.[11]

In 1990 and 1991 there appeared the seminal and henceforth indispensable volumes by Katherine Hayles.[12]

The publication of research applying chaos theory to *Marianne* had already begun, however, with a section entitled "Chaos theory and Marivaux" in an article published in Australia in 1989. This was followed by a section entitled "A *La Vie de Marianne* et l'ordre subverti: structure rococo et effet papillon" in an article published in Canada in 1991.[13]

The pages just mentioned represent mere fragments of larger theses. The present essay explores more fully and systematically the application to our novel of these new perspectives. It seeks to throw new light on the rococo character of *La Vie de Marianne* both by combining the existing aesthetic analysis of the novel with specific insights provided by chaos, complexity and catastrophe theories and by bringing to bear certain other insights provided by control theory.

Compared to chaos theory and its more recent branch, complexity theory, which focuses primarily on the emergence of order (spontaneous self-organization), catastrophe theory has attracted even less attention from literary critics, and in fact its exploitation appears to have been limited so far to sections of two essays published in 1994 and 1995.[14] Indeed, it appears that the only literary text to which catastrophe theory has been applied is Proust's *A la recherche du temps perdu*, so that its application here to Marivaux's chief novel will be only the second such application.

Control theory was inspired by dissatisfaction with Lévi-Strauss's notion (drawn from Rousseau) that *Ecriture* is inferior to *parole* and with Derrida's declaration that it is comparable to masturbation. Like chaos theory, it deals with the issue of order versus disorder, but, being drawn not from science but from psychoanalysis, it replaces description by interpretation. It postulates a disorder neurosis for which the perception of order represents a necessary therapy and which inspires a drive to control one's environment that may, in extreme cases, take the form of what Alfred Alder called *libido dominandi*. Indeed, the question of perception is one that has yet to be taken into account by the theoreticians of chaos.

While there have been chaos theory studies on Balzac,[15] Zola,[16] and Proust,[17] chaos research on the eighteenth century has been primarily devoted to Marivaux and the rococo (Brady),[18] Voltaire (Braun),[19] and Diderot (De la Carrera, Cohen).[20] Theodore Braun's choice of Voltaire would seem particularly pertinent, given the famous summing-up of the latter's work as "un chaos d'idées claires," and Braun's scrupulously thorough analyses of the Voltairean texts represent a major contribution to this emerging field.

Chaos Theory

Chaos theory is characterized by four primary tendencies: concealed order (order so complex as to be perceived as disorder), non-linearity (disproportion between cause and effect), self-similarity (irregular shapes that are repeated on varying scales), and constrained randomness (random behaviour within set boundaries). This theory also possesses two secondary characteristics: feed-back loops or mechanisms and holism.[21]

The principle of concealed order has a dual aspect: an appearance of disorder on the most obvious, superficial level, caused by the degree of complexity of the order actually present on a deeper level. This is true of the rococo, which represents apparent disorder (atectonicity) by comparison with Classical order, as reflected in the rococo's dispensing both with the orders of columns typical of Classical façades and with the internal columns which, blocking the light streaming in from the clerestory of the Baroque cupola, threw dramatic shadow upon the church floor. The result, however, was not disorder but a different, and perhaps at the time imperceptible, order, made up of a newly austere façade and a delightful compensatory prettiness of interior decoration full of fantasy and frivolity. In painting, this austerity took the form of the eschewing of subjects from history, mythology and religion, while the gaiety was manifested in formal elements such as the swirling, "chaotic" movement that was one of Boucher's most characteristic contributions to the rococo.[22] The apparent disorder of the rococo is simply a more complex mode of order with a dual message of reduction and compensation, expressed in a form that in non-linear, unpredictable but constrained in its spontaneity, studied in its negligence.

Furthermore, this highly organized disorder may be viewed as papering over the fundamentally disorderly society that led to the French Revolution. To make such a connection, such an interpretation, does of course involve a leap from form to content—the sort of leap that Lévi-Strauss, a convinced formalist, was reluctant to make in the heyday of structuralism, which, so he liked to insist, was merely a method. However, that method involved certain conceptions of the very nature of Man (Man is not free: Man is not the free-choosing subject of processes such as language but the structured object of them) that go well beyond methods and formalism. In the case of rococo society, the arts are symptoms of the state of mind (or of decay) of the culture, so that the deduction from aesthetic form to psychological and moral tenor is logical and justified.

In rococo literature, we find spontaneity and unpredictability (the kiss—a whim or caprice—in Goethe's *Die Laune des Verliebten*)—an appearance of chance. But chaos theory has shown that many phenomena that appear to be ruled by chance in the sense of pure randomness are not purely random but merely chaotic. That is, beneath the appearance of random occurrence, as in the throwing of dice, there eventually emerges a concealed order at a deeper level, as ascertained by computer simulation. The key to any in-depth understanding of rococo culture, of which the various arts are symptoms, is the coexistence of metonymic reduction and a compensatory euphemization. That is, a loss of all transcendental values and, with them, the disappearance of tragedy, comedy, the lyric, the epic, and the loss or at least weakening of the basic metaphorical signifiers in the various arts: verse and rhyme, line and colour, melody and harmony. The result is what I have

termed "the mask of pleasure and the muting of pain." What appears to be a frantic and disorderly search for pleasure amounts to, beneath this shiny surface, a systematic rejection of beliefs. Concealed beneath the rococo hedonism of Voltaire's *Le Mondain* is the existential papering over of a rent or tear in the fabric of Western civilisation; anguish of a culture without faith.[23]

This order/disorder duality is illustrated in **La Vie de Marianne.** On the surface level, we have an appearance of inconsistency or incoherence created by the *mélange de tons,* consisting of *réflexions ennuyeuses, éléments ignobles,* and *préciosité et métaphysique,* to use the Abbé Desfontaines' words. On a deeper level, however, we have the very real order or coherence provided by the first-person point of view. Because of the latter, which filters all the elements of the story, however disparate they may seem, we know that the *mélange de tons* is produced by the fictional narrator's creative imagination. Not her memory, in spite of her claims that she is reporting certain conversations nearly word for word: we must not fall into the fallacy of assuming the reliability of the narrator.

Non-linearity (disproportion between cause and effect), as embodied in the Butterfly Effect (sensitive dependence on initial conditions), is represented in the rococo in various ways. One example is the tremendous role played in the development of this style by a mere marginal notation from Louis XIV to the royal architect Mansart regarding the decoration of the apartment of the young Duchesse de Bourbon: "de l'enfance répandue partout." (*Ibid.*)

Early in the emergence of rococo literature, we have Pope's *The Rape of the Lock,* where a trivial incident inspires a long mock-heroic masterpiece which, in turn, inspires rococo poetry throughout Europe, from its direct translation into Italian verse to Uz's *Sieg des Liebesgottes,* explicitly subtitled: *Nachahmung des Lockenraubs.* Fifty years later, at the style's decline, Parini's superb poem *Il Giorno,* which is even longer, doesn't even involve an incident, but simply recounts, in sumptuous detail, a day in the life of a spoiled young aristocrat. The nonlinearity of this magnificent treatment of a trivial topic is directly contrary to the neo-Classicism of a writer like Montesquieu, for whom it is "comme de l'or que vous mettriez sur l'habit d'un mendiant." (*Ibid.,* 188.)

Such nonlinearity is also visible in **La Vie de Marianne,** on several different levels. On that of plot, events that appear to be quite insignificant turn out to have tremendous consequences. Thus it is the fact that the protagonist sprains her ankle on leaving the church which is the occasion of her meeting Valville, who will be the great love of her young life (always excepting, of course, her love for her adoptive mother), and a similarly trivial incident results in her losing him later to Mlle Varthon. (The question of whether such events are purely coincidental or, on the contrary, significant examples of synchronicity cannot be dealt with here.) On the level of style, we have, for example, the passage on *l'art de mettre un ruban,* where the most trivial preoccupation is cited to illustrate an entire philosophy of female psychology and of its subtlety and profundity, a philosophy so elaborate that next to it "Aristote ne paraîtrait plus qu'un petit garçon."

Self-similarity is evident in the rococo in the shape of the *rocaille* ornament, which constitutes what Mandelbrot christened a "fractal" in the sense of an irregular shape repeating itself on varying scales. It is to be found everywhere, from an endlessly repeated motif high in a great rococo church in Bavaria (e.g. the Wieskirche) or Franconia (Vierzehnheiligen) or a garden ornament in a Boucher scene of lovers' rendezvous to the back of a delicate, exquisitely upholstered piece of furniture or the smallest element of a small pictureframe. The very name of the style, "rococo," comes from the name of this ornament.

In **La Vie de Marianne,** self-similarity is represented by two episodes. One is the Varthon episode just mentioned, inserted within the Marianne story, and the fractal character of its relationship to the main plot is obvious. It starts with a very similar incident, in which Valville takes advantage of helping a young lady in distress to examine her body, first Marianne's leg and then Varthon's bosom, and as a result falls in love with the lovely victim. However, this similar episode occurs on a smaller scale to the extent that it is told more briefly and not by the protagonist, as is Marianne's story, but by her rival, Marianne. Varthon thus remains merely an episode in the story of Marianne and Valville; an example of self-similarity that is much more drastic on the level of formal structure is the Tervire story that totally replaces the Marianne/Valville/Varthon plot. This is an astonishing development, since it prevents Marianne from finishing her own story; and then Tervire does not finish hers either, so that the whole work remains unfinished, making the fractal relationship even clearer.

In chaos theory, the principle of constrained randomness is expressed in strange attractors, which are described thus by David Ruelle: "These systems of curves, these clouds of points suggest sometimes fireworks or galaxies, sometimes strange and disquieting vegetal proliferations" (Gleick, 153). Compare this with the analysis of *rocaille* ornament by Nicholas Pevsner: "The forms in detail seem to be incessantly changing, splashing up and sinking back. What are they? Do they represent anything? Sometimes they look like shells, sometimes like froth, sometimes like gristle, sometimes like flames."[24] Both are characterized by an appearance of

radical indeterminacy, but one thing about them is certain: they are derived not from the static, rationalistic straight lines and fractions of circles so typical of Classicism in all its modes, but rather from the dynamic, organic forms, whether animal or vegetable, found in nature. This source relates the rococo to such previous styles as Gothic, Mannerism and Baroque, with their rejection of the strait-jacket of *la raison raisonnante* in favour of intuition and imagination.

The "constrained randomness" of a chaotic system finds its counterpart in the "studied negligence" of the rococo: such a negligence, like the randomness, is genuine and spontaneous but not totally free, since the one is really as studied as the other is constrained. In plays like Marivaux's **Le Jeu de l'amour et du hasard** (again the theme of chance), and Goldsmith's *She Stoops to Conquer,* we see the experimental introduction of a perturbance of the social order (the Ancien Régime) that is pathologically rigid, but this is not a genuine challenging of the social order, merely a playful toying with possibilities.

In our novel, constrained randomness is detectable in the narrating Marianne's toying with the absurdity of class distinctions: she appears to allow herself complete freedom, but in reality she does so only within the boundaries set by the conventions of the time—she is by no means a social revolutionary, as we know from other comments she makes on servants and their faults: "Ces gens-là sont plus moqueurs que d'autres; c'est le régal de leur bassesse, que de mépriser ce qu'ils ont respecté par méprise" (92).

Chaos theory also possesses two secondary characteristics: feed-back loops or mechanisms and holism or interconnectedness.

The "daisy world" postulated by James Lovelock, originator of the Gaia hypothesis, provides a simple illustration of a feedback loop. White daisies reflect light, making the planet cooler, while black daisies absorb light, thus making the planet warmer, the result being biological homeostasis—a self-sustaining process of dynamical feedback (Gleick, 279). Hayles remarks that "both the literary and scientific manifestations of chaotics are involved in feedback loops with the culture. They help to create the context that energizes the questions they ask; at the same time, they also ask questions energized by the context" (Hayles, *Chaos and Order,* 27).

In the rococo, feed-back loops take the form of the rococo arabesque, a feature almost as ubiquitous as the rocaille ornament, which constantly turns back upon itself with a flourish and a curtsey before continuing on its dancy, serpentine way. Beyond its frequent use in all kinds of decoration, this dynamic is detectable in a painting like Watteau's masterpiece *L'Embarquement pour Cythère,* in which the forward movement (towards the lower left of the canvas, where the boat is waiting) is interrupted by a reluctant, regretful, nostalgic turning back before resuming its progress. Because in the West we read from left to right, so that to our left is the past we have just left behind, the very fact that the movement is towards the lower left corner is full of suggestions of remembrance and nostalgia.[25]

Feed-back loops are represented in *La Vie de Marianne* by the reprise of a word already used, often at the end of a thought-sequence, this end-word serving in turn as a catalyst for the production of another thought (supplementary proposition). This reprise resembles the motion of the waves of the incoming tide as they fold under themselves upon a stretch of beach before surging further up the sand. Such a technique represents a stylistic version of the feed-back loop, in which output is processed again as input.

As for holism (unification, interconnectedness), this is provided in art and architecture by the subordination of all elements to supporting roles as parts of an ensemble.[26] Thus freestanding columns and pillars are reduced to mere decorative pilasters embedded into the walls, leaving the centre occupied by the characteristic central space-void of the rococo. Freestanding tables are often reduced to two-legged versions attached to the walls—again, little more than decorative elements surrounding the central space.

A similar effect is obtained in literature by the unifying first-person point of view, that of a narrator relating her own memoirs in her narcissistic *parole vide.* The narrator's personality thus comes to colour all actions, events, portraits, and of course comments and reflections: we are faced with the impossibility for the narrator to free herself of that particular personality which is her own, in which she is imprisoned, and which colours and flavours reality (if such exists), so that to the blue eyes of her mind all phenomena appear blue, as if perceived through some tinted veil.

Ultimately, the essential character of first-person narration resides in the fact that it presents us not with a reality, not even a veiled reality, but merely with layer upon layer of veils; and the task of criticism must be to focus on these veils and to analyse them with a delicate scepticism which leaves them intact—if we tear them asunder to find the Truth, we shall find nothing, for the Veil is the Truth: there is no Truth or Reality beyond the Veil.[27]

The majority of novels are couched in this mode in the eighteenth century, in direct opposition to the dominance of the third person, with its omniscient implied author, in the seventeenth and nineteenth centuries.[28]

The fragmentation alleged by Paul de Man to be universal[29] not only flies in the face of the New Physics (relativity theory and quantum mechanics) but also is easily discredited by a sensitive reading of such a text as *Marianne,* where even the *mélange de tons* denounced by the Classicizing Desfontaines (see above) becomes merely a feature of the capricious playfulness of the narrating protagonist, and thus a stylistic elaboration of the psychological portrait that is always the crucial, because only knowable, dimension of any first-person narration.

COMPLEXITY THEORY

The key features of complexity theory are firstly emergence (the phenomenon of spontaneous self-organization) and secondly negentropy,[30] which are even more intimately related than concealed order and constrained randomness. It is perhaps not surprising to find these manifested in a domain such as biology, but Nobel laureate chemist Ilya Prigogine has demonstrated the occurrence of emergence among even inert substances (Waldrop, 32-35).

What emerges from an experience of rococo architecture is a realization of the two-sidedness of this style. The naked austerity of the façade is followed by the exquisitely fanciful raiment of carving and stucco that clothes the interior. This experience is then, in a sense, reversed, as we realize that the reduction of furniture and columns to symbiotic parts of an ensemble creates a new space that dominates the centre of the interior—a void expressive of the loss of which the naked façade was the first symbolic expression. Such is the desperately empty heart of the rococo.

In *La Vie de Marianne,* the central principle of self-organisation is female vanity and coquettry, as embodied in and illustrated by Marianne herself. As we read this story, with its paucity of incident (and those incidents which do occur are trivial), what gradually emerges is a certain tone. As indicated above in our discussion of concealed order and holism, it is not the *unité de ton* observed in the contemporary novel *Manon Lescaut* (1731) and demanded by Classical critics such as Abbé Desfontaines, who was offended by the *mélange de tons.* What emerges is less purely linguistic than psychological, since it derives from the use of first-person point of view.

The notion of emergence provides us with a less static, more dynamic interpretation of this stylistic feature of our text. What, then, emerges from this filtering of incident through the first-person point of view? It is a certain conception of female psychology as irreducibly vain, narcissistic, coquettish. The dominance of this dimension of the work is indicated by the fact that both of its dominant stylistic characteristics, namely the *réflexions ennuyeuses* and the *préciosité et métaphysique,* serve mainly to nourish this conception of female psychology, almost overwhelming the narrative (both action and dialogue) in the process. The reader gradually realizes that it is this conception rather than any plot line that constitutes the essential substance of the novel. (This is quite revolutionary, as evidenced by the fact that the other key novels of the first half of the eighteenth century are *Gil Blas, Lettres persanes,* and *Manon Lescaut,* in all of which the role given to plot is much greater, even where, as in *Gil Blas,* it is only the serial plot of the picaresque tradition, or where, as in *Lettres persanes,* plot is menaced by thematic embroidery in the later half of the work.)

The gradual emergence of this understanding in the mind of the reader produces an ordered grasp of the message of the novel. This narcissism is the worm ensconced at the heart of the succulent rococo apple, or, to change metaphors, this empty female chatter is the void at the centre of the rococo room, reminding us of the loss for which it seeks desperately to compensate.

This brings us to our second but closely-related criterion, negentropy: like a ship emerging from a fog, this order materializes negentropically from the mists of entropy.

Once we turn from the point of view of our novel to the plot line, at first glance we seem to be faced with something very different, something that evokes rather a gradual dissipation into entropy through the eight Parts devoted to Marianne. However, the notion of *structure opératoire* proposed by Jean Piaget may help us to integrate into our analysis the sudden substitution of the story of Tervire, which may be seen as replacing entropy with negentropy. Piaget sees a *structure opératoire* as being relational, transformational, and self-adjusting: it "self-adjusts" until a point is reached where it can no longer handle the tensions and stresses within by means of this self-adjustment (*autoréglage*)— and what happens then is transformation, reminiscent of the last straw that breaks the camel's back.[31]

Most narratives end not with a whimper but with a bang, in the form of death of the protagonist, or at least with a whimper, in the form of marriage. Here, however, the narrative voice simply ceases to be heard. There are various levels on which the reason for this can be discussed, the two most obvious being that of purely internal textual analysis on the one hand and that of authorial options and strategy on the other.

Rather than seeing the story line of Marianne entropically "petering out," as one may under the influence of chaos theory, I propose to draw on complexity theory to suggest that Marivaux had written himself into a corner and that the negentropic substitution of

Tervire, while radical, may well have seemed the only way out. Marivaux was a master of comedy, in which the plot ends in marriage (just as in tragedy the plot ends in death). However, in *La Vie de Marianne* he has reached a point where our heroine either has to marry or be shut up in a convent. If she marries, whether Valville or another suitor, that is traditionally the ending: he cannot continue the novel, which apparently he wants to do. If she is shut up in a convent, there remains little opportunity for Marivaux to study the subtle struggles for and against love and its acknowledgement that constitute the very essence of his art. Because of this dilemma, we have a build-up of tensions over Valville's choice between Marianne and Varthon, on the one hand, and Marianne's choice between Valville and his mother on the other, not to mention other suitors. Marivaux explores these issues, but self-adjustment can keep things going only so long, and he reaches a point where the only solution is to abandon the story of Marianne altogether and begin another story, that of Tervire, in a radical transformation of what the novel is about.

This appears to correspond to the kind of radical shift categorized as "transformation" by Piaget, the catastrophic change analysed by catastrophe theory, and the edge-of-chaos phase transition (self-organised criticality) studied by complexity theory. If such an example does indeed correspond to aspects of each of these different theories, it holds out the promise of bridging the gap between them and ultimately of contributing to the construction of a unified theory of catastrophic change.

It may be objected that the analogy between the negentropic substitution of the voice and story of Tervire for those of Marianne is limited by the fact that this negentropy represents only a brief reprieve, and entropy triumphs in the end in the silence that follows the cessation of narrative, whereas in the domain of biology the negentropy of increasing complexity apparently goes on indefinitely. However, life will not go on forever: although predictions as to the future of the universe do vary, all foresee an Earth on which life will be impossible, followed almost certainly by its disappearance, perhaps into a black hole. Thus the increasing complexity of the last several eons will prove to have been, in fact, a brief reprieve, followed by silence, as in *La Vie de Marianne.*

CATASTROPHE THEORY

As pointed out in the 1994 article on Proust mentioned above,[32] catastrophe theory was developed by René Thom.[33] It is an aspect of topology, which Ian Stewart refers to as "rubber sheet geometry."[34] Alexander Woodcock, a disciple of Thom, classes the elementary versions as fold, cusp, swallowtail, and butterfly catastrophes.[35] While "the fold catastrophe has little to tell us" (p. 55), and the swallowtail and butterfly catastrophes cannot be represented adequately by a drawing (p. 61), the cusp catastrophe proves applicable to many domains, occurring as it does in systems whose behaviour depends on two control factors (pp. 56, 58, 60); it is the model used here. The idea is that, instead of moving continuously down over the surface, one suddenly finds oneself to have fallen over a fold and onto a distant part of the surface without having traversed the area in between. The effect is thus sudden, discontinuous, "catastrophic," reminiscent of Foucault's *ruptures arbitraires* between *épistèmes* and Piaget's *transformation* of *structures opératoires,* already mentioned.[36]

In principle, such a theory should be applicable to any narrative construct in which there is a dramatic change at some point in the evolution of the plot. The first attempt at such an application was inspired by the strange change in the depiction of Dr Cottard at the beginning of the second volume of *A la recherche du temps perdu.*[37] Another might be the point quite late in *The French Lieutenant's Woman* when the protagonist first makes love to the heroine and discovers that, contrary to the impression she had deliberately given to everyone, an impression on which she had built her whole persona ("Tragedy") and her entire notoriety, and from which the novel derives its very title, she had remained a virgin until that moment. However, not every novel possesses events sufficiently cataclysmic to warrant the application of these parameters.

In *La Vie de Marianne,* a truly extraordinary break in the plot line takes place after eight episodes starring herself: she is evicted both as narrator and as protagonist and replaced by Tervire, who sets out to tell her own story to Marianne much as Marianne has been telling hers to a woman friend. Not only that, but we never return to Marianne. In *La Vie de Marianne,* the two control factors are the point of view and the role of narrator-heroine. We continue to hear the voice of a female first-person narrator, but instead of the voice of Marianne that voice is now that of Tervire. The person addressed, with whom we identify, is also no longer Marianne's friend but Marianne herself. It is this sudden and surprising substitution—a radical example of plot discontinuity—that constitutes the catastrophe.

The catastrophic change that takes place after Part Eight is mirrored in that, even more catastrophic (because definitive), which occurs after Part Eleven. The latter change, however, is one shared with every work of literature or music (because of the very nature of narrative linearity), namely from activity to stasis, from sound to silence, from life to death of the narrative. We should not normally see it as a form of catastrophic change, because it is not internal to the narrative. In the present case, however, the analogy between the end of

the whole novel and the end of Part Eight is so striking that it has to be viewed differently. Moreover, whereas it seems that the first change occurs because the author has "written himself into a corner," resulting in a "transformative" catastrophe, the second change appears rather to represent the inevitable ultimate triumph of the principle of entropy over negentropy.

. . . I have plotted the evolution of the role of narrator-protagonist in terms of two control factors (two-factor processes require the use of the "cusp" model). These factors are point of view (which is unchangingly first-person and female) and action/narration (which changes from Marianne to Tervire). The major discontinuity clearly occurs in the strictest parallel both in the action and in the narration. In the action, we have the passage from one protagonist (a) to the other (c), via point (b), where the plot line involving Marianne encounters the lip of the fold and abruptly falls over the edge to where the new protagonist is Tervire. In the narration, we have the passage from one narrator (d) to the other (f), via point (e), where the narration by Marianne encounters the lip of the same fold and abruptly falls over the edge to where the new narrator is Tervire. While there are still two control factors, the parallelism of the present case required a modification of the diagram used to plot the transformation of Cottard in the 1994 article, where there was no such parallelism.

CONTROL THEORY

The issue of order versus disorder is central to the three theories we have applied so far, but their interest is limited to the description of phenomena in terms of such categories. Two further dimensions of this issue need to be addressed, the one philosophical and the other psychological.

The philosophical question is this: are we capable of actually perceiving disorder, or only of failing to perceive the order imposed by our organs of perception (which operate through templates that mould the phenomenal and divorce it from the noumenal), so that the "perception" of disorder merely represents an overload of our organs of perception? The psychological question is the following: what is the cause of the "rage for order" that is a distinguishing characteristic of humankind?

It is the latter question that control theory seeks to answer, leaving the former for a later time.

Control theory postulates a disorder neurosis caused primarily by the trauma of birth: the mother's body expels the infant from the warm, dark, silent, liquid passivity of the nurturing womb through a passage of life-threatening compression and out into the cold, blinding, noisy, dry air and the necessity to breathe—such is the child's first experience of rejection, of Otherness and of the environment outside the womb. In a word, this external reality is alien, hostile, incomprehensible, unpredictable, uncontrollable. The resulting disorder neurosis in turn spawns a drive to achieve order by controlling one's environment.

In *La Vie de Marianne,* the heroine is convinced that she was born into an order, namely that provided by an aristocratic lineage. She was born "somebody" (to adapt Des Grieux's phrase about himself, "elle était née quelque chose"), and because of the accidental death of her parents she became a "nobody," without name, pedigree or rank. She was thus expelled from her exalted social rank as from a Garden of Eden, itself an analogon for expulsion from the womb.

This expulsion condemns her to spend her early life among the mediocre things, insignificant people, and trivial incidents that constitute provincial life. Life in Paris is hardly an improvement: she despises the chaotic and demeaning squalor of the working classes, to which she feels superior, and she is sure that she is not supposed to live in such surroundings.

She is determined to reassert control over her life by rejoining the nobility. Marianne strives constantly to return to the upper classes, to which she is convinced she belongs. Marriage with a young aristocrat like Valville is the obvious solution, but adoption by Mme de Miran is also a solution, given that social rank, rather than transsexual love, is the over-riding goal. And this goal is dictated by the need to regain control over the circumstance of her life by regaining access to the order into which she was originally born.

Conclusion

Katherine Hayles was recently reported as opining that chaos theory had been rendered *passé* by the emergence of complexity theory (sometimes called "emergence theory").[38] However, just as structuralism and deconstructionism have not been discredited by these new theories, merely dislodged by them as the avantgarde of the moment, neither has chaos theory been rendered less valid by complexity theory. In fact, chaos and complexity are intimately related, as Katherine Hayles herself argues at some length in her excellent books on chaos, where she classifies emergence theory as one of the two main branches of chaos theory.[39]

Methods of analysis and interpretation constantly go out of fashion, but none that was ever valid has ever become invalid, merely absorbed. The parameters provided by chaos theory are simply different from those provided by complexity theory, and the same is true of catastrophe theory, partly because they all draw on different sciences. They all have the potential to enrich our understanding of the formal features of works of literature. Indeed, the exploitation of chaos theory has in a sense only just begun, and its features remain more numerous, more promising and less nebulous that those of emergence theory for the analysis of culture and literature, while the application of catastrophe theory is even more embryonic. Finally, control theory adds to these methods of formal analysis the dimension of interpretation and explanation, thus making a very different, complementary contribution.

The four new perspectives used here provoke a new exploration of our Marivaux novel that sometimes draws attention to aspects of the work hitherto neglected (e.g., the fractal relationship between certain episodes), sometimes enables us to see familiar aspects of the work in a new light and even make sense of them for the first time as structural elements (e.g., the catastrophic and negentropic replacement of Marianne by Tervire as narrator and protagonist at the beginning of Part Nine), and sometimes enables us to grasp the psychological sources of Marianne's driving social ambition (she is driven by the need to control her environment by integrating herself into an order that calms her insecurities and shaky self-esteem, evident in the overcompensation of her overt narcissism).

Each perspective thus makes its modest contribution to the elaboration of the cumulative interpretation of Marivaux's *La Vie de Marianne.*

Notes

1. Leo Spitzer, "A propos de *La Vie de Marianne, The Romanic Review,* 44 (1953), 102-126; René Girard, "Marivaudage and Hypocrisy," *American Society Legion of Honor Magazine,* 34 (1963), 163-174.

2. Patrick Brady, "Rococo Style in the Novel: *La Vie de Marianne,*" *Studi francesi,* 19 (1975), 25-43, reprinted in *Rococo Style versus Enlightenment Novel.* Geneva: Slatkine 1984, 199-220 and 267-270.

3. Patrick Brady: *Structuralist Perspectives in Criticism of Fiction: Essays on* Manon Lescaut *and* La Vie de Marianne. Bern: Lang 1978.

4. Patrick Brady, "Period Style in the Light of Structuralism, Semiotics and Catastrophe Theory," *French Literature Series,* 4 (1977), 119-130, reprinted in *Structuralist Perspectives, op.cit.,* 77-83 and in Henry Freeman, ed.: *Twenty Years of French Literary Criticism.* Mobile AL: Summa 1994.

5. Alexander Woodcock & Monte Davis: *Catastrophe Theory.* London: Penguin 1978, p. 29.

6. M. Mitchell Waldrop: *Complexity.* N.Y.: Simon & Schuster 1992, p. 116; Roger Lewin, *Complexity.* N.Y.: Macmillan 1992, Collier 1994, p. 185.

7. Woodcock and Davis, 71, 76, 83, 99; James Gleick: *Chaos.* N.Y.: Viking-Penguin 1987, p. 182.

8. Woodcock and Davis, 75; Gleick, 4, 45-53, 61, 70, 76, 89, 118, 132, 171, 182, 208, 247.

9. Woodcock and Davis, 37-38, 70-71, 72, 99; Lewin, 28-29, 32-43, 72-74, 166, 176, 180-182; Waldrop, 116.

10. Woodcock and Davis, 37, 78; Lewin, 185; Waldrop, 85, 87, 116, 134.

11. Patrick Brady, "From Catastrophe and Chaos to Control." Science and Literature Section of the Annual Meeting of the Modern Language Association, December 1988, published in less truncated form as "Chaos Theory, Control Theory, and Literary Theory or: A Story of Three Butterflies," *Modern Language Studies,* 20 (1990), 65-79.

12. N. Katherine Hayles: *Chaos Bound.* Ithaca NY: Cornell University Press 1990 and *Chaos and Order.* Chicago: University of Chicago Press 1991.

13. Patrick Brady, "From Transactional Analysis to Chaos Theory: New Critical Perspectives," *Australian Journal of French Studies,* 26 (1989), 176-193 [see 184-188] and "Théorie du chaos et structure narrative," *Eighteenth-Century Fiction,* 4 (1991), 43-51 [see 44-46].

14. Patrick Brady, "Does God Play Dice? Deterministic Chaos and Stochastic Chance in Proust's *Recherche,*" *Michigan Romance Studies,* 14 (1994), 133-149 [see 136-138 and 145-146], and Simon Simonse, "Mimesis, Schismogenesis, Catastrophe Theory: Gregory Bateson as Forerunner of Mimetic Theory," *Synthesis,* 1 (1995), 147-172 [see 157-164].

15. Maria Assad, essay on Balzac's *Le Chef-d'oeuvre inconnu* entitled "Michel Serres: In Search of a Tropography," in Hayles, *Chaos and Order,* 278-298.

16. Patrick Brady, "Chaos and Revolution: Zola's *L'Oeuvre,*" *Nineteenth-Century French Studies,* 20 (1991-1992), 196-202; "La théorie du chaos et *L'Oeuvre*: peinture, structure, thématique," *Les Cahiers Naturalistes,* 66 (1992), 105-112; "Zola's Other Shoe: From Chaos Theory to Control Theory," in M. Fol, ed.: *Emile Zola 1991: Un Nouvel Engagement: Le Cri de ma chair.* Berkeley: Nouvelles Presses Universitaires Weslof 1992, pp. 112-115; etc.

17. See above, note 14.

18. See above, and note 16, etc.

19. Theodore Braun, "Chaos, Determinism and Free Will in *Zadig,*" *Studies on Voltaire and the Eighteenth Century* 347 (1996),634-637; "Chaos, Contingency, and *Candide,*" *1650-1850,* 5 (1999); "Voltaire, *Zadig, Candide,* and Chaos," *Studies on Voltaire and the Eighteenth Century* 358 (1998), 1-20; "Voltaire's *Zadig,* Chaos Theory, and the Problem of Determinism vs. Free Will," *Studies in Eighteenth-Century Culture,* 27 (1998), 195-207.

20. Rosalina De La Carrera: *Success in Circuit Lies: Diderot's Communicational Practice.* Stanford: Stanford University Press, 1991; Huguette Cohen, "Diderot's Cosmic Games: Revisiting a Dilemma," *Diderot Studies* 26 (1995), 71-87; reprinted in this volume.

21. See Patrick Brady, ed.: *Chaos in the Humanities.* Knoxville: New Paradigm Press 1995, 5-17: "Chaos and Emergence Theory in the Humanities."

22. Brady 1989 (above, note 14), 187.

23. See Brady, *Structuralist Perspectives,* 105-114.

24. N. Pevsner: *An Outline of European Architecture.* London: Penguin 4th ed. (1953), p. 195.

25. Patrick Brady, "Psychological Indeterminacy, Semiotic Monosemy: A Rococo Interpretation of *L'Embarquement pour Cythère,*" *Eighteenth-Century Life,* 11 (1987), 1-11.

26. Patrick Brady, "Rococo and Neo-Classicism," *Studi Francesi,* 8 (1964), 34-49.

27. Brady, *Structuralist Perspectives,* 55, 74.

28. One popular form that uses the first-person mode exclusively does not illustrate the holistic, blending effect of the single first-person narrator: this is the epistolary novel (*Lettres persanes, La Nouvelle Héloïse, Les Liaisons dangereuses,* etc.), in which every statement is made in the first person but there is a multiplicity of narrators and a consequent fragmenting of the point of view so that the interconnectedness is not such as to justify recourse to the holism characteristic of chaos theory.

29. "Nothing, whether deed, word, thought or text, ever happens in relation, positive or negative, to anything that precedes, follows or exists elsewhere, but only as a random event whose power . . . is due to the randomness of its occurrence." Paul de Man: *Allegories of Reading.* New Haven: Yale University Ppress 1979, p. 69.

30. See above, note 24.

31. Patrick Brady, "From Traditional Fallacies to Structural Hypotheses: Old and New Conceptions in Period Style Research," *Neophilologus,* 56 (1972), 1-11.

32. See above, note 17.

33. René Thom: *Structural Stability and Morphogenesis: An Outline of a General Theory of Models.* Reading: Benjamin 1972. See my article "Period Style in the Light of [. . .] Catastrophe Theory," cited above, note 4.

34. Ian Stewart: *Does God Play Dice? The New Mathematics of Chaos.* Oxford: Blackwell 1988; London: Penguin 1989, p. 63.

35. Woodcock and Davis, 54-64.

36. See my article cited above, note 4.

37. See above, note 17.

38. Thad Camp and Karen Piper, "Literature and Science," *Bulletin of the American Comparative Literature Association,* 1995-96, pp. 36-37.

39. Hayles, *Chaos Bound,* 93 *et seq.* and *passim,* and especially *Chaos and Order,* 12 *et seq.* and *passim.*

FURTHER READING

Criticism

Conroy Jr., Peter V. "Marivaux's Feminist Polemic: *La Colonie.*" *Eighteenth-Century Life* n.s. 6, no. 1 (October 1980): 43-66.

Praises Marivaux as the eighteenth-century writer most sympathetic to women's problems, evidenced especially in his 1750 one-act play, *La colonie.*

Greene, E. J. H. *Marivaux.* Toronto: University of Toronto Press, 1965, 361 p.

Detailed analysis of Marivaux's life and works that considers whether or not his place is secure among the great writers.

McBurney, William Harlin and Michael Francis Shugrue. Introduction to *The Virtuous Orphan or, The Life of Marianne Countess of * * * * *,* translated by Mrs. Mary Mitchell Collyer, pp. xi-xliv. Carbondale: Southern Illinois University Press, 1965.

Twentieth-century critical introduction of an eighteenth-century translation of Marivaux's most famous novel.

McKee, Kenneth N. *The Theater of Marivaux.* New York: New York University Press, 1958, 267 p.

Collection of brief analyses of individual plays by Marivaux.

Munro, James S. "The Moral Significance of Marivaux's 'Comédies d'Amour.'" *Forum for Modern Language Studies* 14, no. 2 (April 1978): 116-28.

Examines the gradual unfolding of the love relationships in Marivaux's romantic comedies, including *Le jeu de l'amour et du hazard, La double inconstance,* and *Les fausses confidences.*

Robbins, Arthur. "Marianne and Moral Expediency." *Revue des Langues Vivantes* 36 (1970): 258-65.

Contends that the title character of *La vie de Marianne* is more concerned with presenting the appearance of a high-principled, virtuous woman than with actually living as one.

Russo, Elena. "Libidinal Economy and Gender Trouble in Marivaux's *La fausse suivante.*" *MLN* 115, no. 4 (September 2000): 690-713.

Explores Marivaux's use of transvestism and its implications for gender identity in his play *La fausse suivante.*

Sturzer, Felicia. "'Marivaudage' as Self-Representation." *French Review* 49, no. 2 (December 1975): 212-21.

Explanation of the infamous label attached to Marivaux's style by contemporary critics.

Trapnell, W. H. "Marivaux's Unfinished Narratives." *French Studies* 24 (July 1970): 237-53.

Considers why Marivaux left his best novels unfinished.

Wyngaard, Amy. "Switching Codes: Class, Clothing, and Cultural Change in the Works of Marivaux and Watteau." *Eighteenth-Century Studies* 33, no. 4 (summer 2000): 523-42.

Explores connections between Marivaux's plays and Watteau's art, particularly with regard to the use of clothing as a marker of class and social standing.

The Changeling

Thomas Middleton and William Rowley

The following entry presents criticism of Thomas Middleton and William Rowley's tragedy *The Changeling* (1622). For discussion of Middleton's complete career, see *LC,* Volume 33, and for discussion of Rowley's complete career, see *LC,* Volume 100.

INTRODUCTION

With its scenes of sensational horror, intricate plot, allusions to Christian morality, and melding of comedy and tragedy, *The Changeling* is widely acknowledged to be among the best Jacobean tragedies, and it appeals to modern audiences because it presents chilling psychological studies of sexuality, madness, and corruption. A collaborative effort between Thomas Middleton and William Rowley, the play has two distinct plots that are linked thematically. The main action of the play concerns Beatrice-Joanna, a woman betrothed to one man but in love with another. She has her father's servant De Flores kill her intended husband, which sets in motion a series of events that she is too weak to control. The subplot, which takes place in a madhouse, presents the love-struck Antonio trying to seduce Isabella, the chaste wife of an older man. *The Changeling* was extremely successful during its own time and for some decades after, but then ceased to be staged for almost three hundred years, despite recognition by critics of its tragic force and power. Since the 1960s, however, there has been renewed interest in the play by directors, both of live theater and film. Critical commentary on the work has flourished as well, with scholars discussing, among other issues, the work's moral structure, its characterization and treatment of women, its status as a collaboration, its focus on the female body, its religious and political concerns, and its attitudes toward sexuality.

TEXTUAL HISTORY

Most scholars believe that Rowley wrote the beginning and end of *The Changeling* and its comic subplot, and that Middleton was responsible for the main action of the work. Middleton likely found the story for the main plot in a 1621 book by John Reynolds entitled *The Triumphs of God's Revenge against the Crying and Ex-*

ecrable Sin of Wilful and Premeditated Murder, as well as a 1622 translation by Leonard Digges of a Spanish story called *Gerardo, the Unfortunate Spaniard.* No definite source for the subplot has been identified.

Middleton and Rowley had previously collaborated on several works, and had enjoyed success with *A Fair Quarrel* in 1617. By 1622, when *The Changeling* was first staged, both were veterans of the London stage. Middleton had written and had produced a number of highly successful comedies and tragedies beginning in 1604. He was often commissioned to write and produce Lord Mayor's pageants and other civic entertainments, and in 1620 had been appointed city chronologer. Rowley's career had not been as distinguished; from approximately 1607 he had worked as an actor in what would eventually become known as Prince Charles' company, the least favored and least profitable of the acting companies in London at the time. He often had financial difficulties, perhaps because he sought out roles and projects that were critical of the authorities and the status quo. Because of his girth, Rowley was known for playing fat clowns.

After the success of *The Changeling* Middleton and Rowley continued to collaborate, co-writing *The Spanish Gypsy* in 1623. Both Rowley and Middleton worked in the London theaters until the end of their lives. Rowley died in 1626 and Middleton in 1627.

PLOT AND MAJOR CHARACTERS

The Changeling has a two-plot structure, with the action alternating between a castle fortress in Alicante, Spain, and the town's madhouse. The main plot concerns Beatrice-Joanna, the spoiled and capricious daughter of Vermandero, the governor of the castle and the most powerful man in Alicante. Vermandero has betrothed his daughter to Alonzo De Piracquo; they are to be married within the week. However, unbeknownst to her father, Beatrice-Joanna has fallen in love with another nobleman, Alsemero, a merchant and man of action. In addition, Vermandero's servant, the hideously disfigured and villainous De Flores, is obsessively in love with Beatrice-Joanna, although she loathes him and treats him with contempt. Beatrice-Joanna persuades De Flores to murder Alonzo. De Flores arranges to show Alonzo Vermandero's castle so that he can kill him in secret; he then cuts off Alonzo's finger with its ring, and presents them to Beatrice-Joanna. When Beatrice-Joanna tries to pay De Flores with gold, he says that his reward will not be money but her virginity, and he rapes her.

Vermandero puzzles over the disappearance of Alonzo but permits Beatrice-Joanna to marry Alsemero. However, she has been noticed talking secretly to De Flores, and their complicity is rumored. Alsemero, an amateur scientist, plans to use a chemical potion to test his wife's virginity. Worried that he will discover that she is not chaste, Beatrice-Joanna tests her maidservant and confidante, Diaphanta, and then fakes the necessary reactions to convince her husband of her chastity. However, she cannot fake the real test on their wedding night, so she sends Diaphanta to him in the dark. But then, because Diaphanta now knows of their deceit, De Flores and Beatrice stage a fire and burn the maid in it. Eventually Alsemero becomes convinced that Beatrice-Joanna has not only been unfaithful to him with De Flores but is a murderer. In the meantime, Beatrice-Joanna falls in love with De Flores. Guilt-ridden, she confesses her crimes to her husband and is locked in a closet with De Flores. When her father comes upon the scene, Alsemero tells him the truth and opens the closet to reveal De Flores and Beatrice-Joanna—both now fatally wounded by De Flores's hand.

The play's comic subplot takes place is a madhouse run by Alibius and Lollio. Vermandero's clerks Antonio and Franciscus both pretend to be mad in order to gain access to Isabella, the chaste young wife of Alibius. She rejects them both. They emerge from the madhouse and are charged with Alonzo's murder, which took place just as they vanished. However, it is eventually found out that Beatrice-Joanna is responsible for the crime.

MAJOR THEMES

The themes of the play are developed in quite different ways in the main plot and subplot; the comic subplot serves to heighten and comment on the issues explored with more seriousness in the main action. The title of the play points to its most obvious theme: that of inconstancy and change. A "changeling" is a changeable, fickle person, and in the play many of the characters qualify as such; indeed the main action of the play moves forward because Beatrice-Joanna changes her affections for Alonzo to Alsemero to De Flores. But another definition of the word "changeling" is a person of deficient intelligence. In the madhouse subplot, Antonio takes on this role, and indeed it is he who is often regarded as the changeling of the play's title. The love-struck Antonio's actions of imitating a fool reinforce

the interrelatedness of the two plots and underscore the themes of madness and psychological weakness that permeate the entire play.

Another key theme of the play, again developed in both plots, is that of chastity or virginity. In the main action, De Flores rapes his mistress, and Beatrice-Joanna will do anything to hide this dishonor from her husband, including sending another woman to his bed—and then sending the woman to her death. In the subplot, Isabella, wife of Alibius, protects her virginity from Antonio by disguising herself as a madwoman. Another important theme in the play is appearance and reality, which once again is handled with great complexity, as characters of beauty (Beatrice-Joanna), ugliness (De Flores), weakness (Antonio), and moral superiority (Isabella) all hide the truth and pretend to be what they are not.

CRITICAL RECEPTION

When it was first staged in 1622, *The Changeling* appears to have been an immediate success, as it was soon performed at court. The play remained popular until the closing of the theaters during the Puritan Interregnum, and then once again after the reopening of the theaters during the Restoration. In 1661 Samuel Pepys remarked that he had seen *The Changeling* at the Playhouse, noting that "it takes exceedingly." However, from all indications, after about 1668 it disappeared from the stage and was not revived professionally until the 1960s. This is not to say that the play was not read, and many critics viewed it as among the most important Jacobean dramas and a work of tragic force that rivals those of Shakespeare. T. S. Eliot, writing in the 1920s, declared the play to have a moral universality and "more than any other play except those of Shakespeare . . . has a profound and permanent moral value and horror."

Criticism on *The Changeling* in the twentieth and twenty-first centuries has been vast. Scholars have covered a range of general issues, including the collaboration of Rowley and Middleton, the moral force of the work, and the themes of inconstancy, madness, and chastity. More detailed studies have also been undertaken of the play's narrative structure, the careful integration of plot and subplot, the relationship between Christian ideals and morality, and its fusing of comedy and tragedy. Many critics have pointed out that Middleton's restrained use of language (there are few poetic flourishes in the main plot) adds a powerfully realistic dimension to the play. The use of recurrent words to emphasize themes and emotions has also been analyzed. Feminist scholars have paid particular attention to the development of the female characters in the play and commented on the attitudes toward rape and honor as shown in the work.

Because of its psychological elements and its concern with horrible people and events, *The Changeling* is seen as particularly suited to modern tastes, and it is has been successful in film and television adaptations as well as on the stage. Critics concur that *The Changeling* is an extremely rich piece of theater that, because of its originality, intelligence, superb characterization, and psychological acuity, must be regarded as one of the most important works of Jacobean drama and perhaps the greatest seventeenth-century play apart from those of Shakespeare.

PRINCIPAL WORKS

Thomas Middleton

The Wisdom of Solomon Paraphrased (poetry) 1597

Micro-Cynicon: Six Snarling Satires (satire) 1599

The Ghost of Lucrece (poetry) 1600

Caesar's Fall, or The Two Shapes [with Anthony Munday, John Webster, and Michael Drayton] (play) 1602

Randall, Earl of Chester (play) 1602

The Phoenix (play) c. 1604

The Ant and the Nightingale, or Father Hubbard's Tales (pamphlet) 1604

The Black Book (pamphlet) 1604

The Magnificent Entertainment Given to King James upon his Passage Through London [contributor, to an entertainment by Thomas Dekker] 1604

The Honest Whore, Part I [with Dekker] (play) 1604

Timon of Athens [with William Shakespeare] (play) c. 1605

A Trick to Catch the Old One (play) c. 1605

Your Five Gallants (play) c. 1605

A Mad World My Masters (play) c. 1606

Michaelmas Term (play) c. 1606

The Puritan, or The Widow of Watling Street (play) c. 1606

The Revenger's Tragedy [attributed to Middleton] (play) c. 1606

A Yorkshire Tragedy (play) c. 1606

The Viper and Her Brood (play) 1606

No Wit, No Help Like a Woman's (play) c. 1611

The Roaring Girl, or Moll Cutpurse [with Dekker] (play) 1611

The Second Maiden's Tragedy (play) 1611

A Chaste Maid in Cheapside (play) c. 1613

The New River Entertainment (entertainment) 1613

The Triumphs of Truth, a Solemnity (pageant) 1613

Wit at Several Weapons [with William Rowley] (play) c. 1613-15

The Witch (play) c. 1614

The Masque of Cupid (masque) 1614

The Nice Valour, or the Passionate Madman (play) c. 1616

The Widow (play) c. 1616

Civitatis Amor, The City's Love; an Entertainment (entertainment) 1616

A Fair Quarrel [with Rowley] (play) c. 1617

The Triumphs of Honor and Industry, A Solemnity (pageant) 1617

The Old Law, or A New Way to Please You [with Rowley] (play) c. 1618

The Mayor of Queenborough, or Hengist, King of Kent (play) 1618

More Dissemblers Besides Women (play) c. 1619

The Inner Temple Masque, or Masque of Heroes (masque) 1619

The Triumphs of Love and Antiquity, A Noble Solemnity (pageant) 1619

A Courtly Masque: The Device Called the World Tossed at Tennis [with Rowley] (masque) 1620

Anything for a Quiet Life [with Webster] (play) c. 1621

Women Beware Women (play) c. 1621

The Sun in Aries, A Noble Solemnity [with Munday] (pageant) 1621

The Changeling [with Rowley] (play) 1622

An Invention for the Service of Edward Barkham (play) 1622

The Triumphs of Honor and Virtue, A Noble Solemnity (pageant) 1622

The Puritan Maid, Modest Wife, and Wanton Widow (play) c. 1623

The Spanish Gypsy [with Rowley; revised by Dekker and John Ford] (play) 1623

The Triumphs of Integrity, A Noble Solemnity (pageant) 1623

A Game at Chess (play) 1624

The Conqueror's Custom (play) c. 1626

The Triumphs of Health and Prosperity (pageant) 1626

William Rowley

The Travels of the Three English Brothers [with John Day and George Wilkins] (play) 1607

A Shoemaker a Gentleman (play) c. 1608

Fortune by Land and Sea [with Thomas Heywood] (play) c. 1609

A Search for Money, or The Lamentable Complaint for the Losse of Mounsieur l'Argent (pamphlet) 1609

A New Wonder, A Woman Never Vexed (play) c. 1611-14

Hymen's Holiday, or Cupid's Vagaries (play) c. 1612

Great Britain, All in Black. For the Incomparable Losse of Henry, Our Late Worthy Prince, 2nd Edition [contributor, to a volume edited by John Taylor] (poetry) 1612

The Fool Without Book (play) c. 1613

A Knave in Print or One for Another (play) c. 1613

The Birth of Merlin [possibly with William Shakespeare] c. 1613-15

Wit at Several Weapons [with Thomas Middleton] (play) c. 1613-15

A Fair Quarrel [with Middleton] c. 1617

The Old Law, or A New Way to Please You [with Middleton] (play) c. 1618

All's Lost by Lust (play) c. 1619

A Courtly Masque: The Device Called the World Tossed at Tennis [with Middleton] (masque) 1620

For a Funeral Elegy on the Death of Hugh Atwell, Servant to Prince Charles (poetry) 1621

The Witch of Edmonton [with John Ford and Thomas Dekker] (play) 1621

A Match at Midnight (play) c. 1622

The Changeling [with Middleton] (play) 1622

The Four Honourable Loves (play) c. 1623

The Nonesuch (play) c. 1623

The Maid in the Mill [with John Fletcher] (play) 1623

The Spanish Gypsy [with Middleton; revised by Dekker and Ford] (play) 1623

The Late Murder in Whitechapel, or Keep the Widow Waking (play) 1624

A Match or No Match (play) 1624

A Cure for a Cuckold [with Webster] (play) c. 1624-25

CRITICISM

T. B. Tomlinson (essay date October 1964)

SOURCE: Tomlinson, T. B. "Poetic Naturalism in *The Changeling*." *Journal of English and Germanic Philology* 63, no. 4 (October 1964): 648-59.

[*In the following essay, Tomlinson discusses the naturalism of the verse dialogue in* The Changeling *and explores the power of the play's dominating image: Vermadero's castle.*]

The Changeling has an importance beyond itself much greater, I think, than that of any other Jacobean play, or, if it comes to that, than any other play in English outside Shakespeare. Indeed with the exception of Shakespeare and Tourneur, Middleton seems to me incomparably the most powerful dramatist we have in English, and if we can grant this dogmatic assertion for the moment, two things follow. First, the unique texture and fabric of Middleton's writing in *The Changeling* represent something which is so unlike the usual run of Jacobean tragedy that the play, and Middleton's work generally, virtually stand on their own in the period.[1] Second, it is probable that the virtual collapse of English drama after the second decade of the seventeenth century is related to the fact that nobody could—or would—recognise the fresh directions being taken in Middleton's plays. Consciously or unconsciously, Middleton recognised that fresh experience was at hand and that a dramatic form and texture different from the richly proliferating imagery of a Webster or a Tourneur would have to come into being to deal with it. The Shakespearean age, Middleton knew, was over; and in **Women Beware Women,** with its concentration on "factorship" in love and business, and its ability to bring alive the world of "merchandising" which dominates modern life (cf. Leantio's opening speeches seeing love and marriage in terms of contracts and mercantile prudence, ". . . when the long warehouse cracks"), he prefigured the forms drama should have taken two centuries and more before Ibsen. *The Changeling* deals with the same area of experience but from a more richly metaphorical point of view.[2]

In the analysis of *The Changeling* that follows I shall attempt to show the kind of thinking, and the kind of imagination, which dominates what is probably Middleton's greatest play. Rowley, of course, may have been in part responsible for the power of this play, but it seems to me sufficiently characteristic of Middleton to be grouped with his other work (especially **Women Beware Women**) and hence set apart from most, if not all, Jacobean and Caroline plays. Certainly the clarity of outline that it has, the reliance on spareness and understatement in its approach to deeply imaginative concerns, puts it far apart from Webster's operatic brilliance. Indeed, only in the conventionally "Revenge" holocausts at the end of many of his plays does Middleton even begin to resemble Webster. His name has, of course, been linked with Tourneur's,[3] but personally I can see no justification for this. Once again, the Middleton dialogue seems exceptionally spare, and far removed from the brilliant, figured ironies of a Vendice. In Tourneur, conceits and near "metaphysical" poetry proliferate, and the characteristic vision of **The Revenger's Tragedy** could be summed up in terms of the compressed, telescoped ironies of the silkworm "undoing" herself (in the double sense of spinning to create silk and spinning to no valuable end) and "yon fellow" falsifying highways, putting himself "between the judge's lips. . . ." For all the incidental similarities of phrase noted by Oliphant, Barker, Schoenbaum, and others, Middleton as a whole seems to me to stand apart from this (as from Webster and the Jacobean age generally) and to rely on dialogue which is as subtle as Tourneur's, but which is also consistently sparer and more clear-cut. He also concentrates more specifically on the "bourgeois" world of reason and judgment (disturbed by irrational forces of the kind that in part motivate Beatrice-Joanna); and on the gap between a controlled, sensible world of the kind Vermandero would take to be essentially normal and the disruptive passions which (little though Vermandero realises it) govern people *in* the normal world. Certainly Vermandero's world is sane, ordered, reasonable in a sense that the world facing Vittoria, the Duchess, Vendice, and most other Jacobean or Caroline characters is not. Middleton's distinction is to see the importance of the concern Vermandero and Beatrice show for normal, sane living, and at the same time the significance of the forces (e.g., those within Beatrice herself) which threaten this.

The originality of *The Changeling* is seen best in the power of its dominating, and very unusual, image: Vermandero's castle. By this I do not mean that "imagery" alone can make a play good or bad, but that, in the case of *The Changeling,* the play's deepest resources can most readily be tapped through the gathering momentum of this one image. The process is radically different from the rich proliferation of suggestion in, say, Shakespeare. For in the first place it is dependent on that apparently naturalistic surface to Middleton's writing which others have noticed and likened to Ibsen. And furthermore, as the action traces the unfolding of Beatrice-Joanna's real love (i.e., her passion for that "wondrous necessary man," De Flores), Middleton repeats the *same* basic image, until naturalistic dialogue builds up into something beyond naturalism—the powerfully concentrated metaphor of Vermandero's castle. It is this metaphor which both focuses and expands Middleton's concerns. The early dialogue which, as Miss Bradbrook has pointed out,[4] is so intensely concerned with questions of seeing and not seeing, of rational processes *versus* the disturbing irrationality of love—all this links and expands in the gathering momentum and depth of that image, seen through, or in, the calmly naturalistic surface of the dialogue.

First, and early in Act I, the significantly pointed entrance given to De Flores prefigures the essence of the drama. Beatrice has advised "judgment" in love—more seriously than she at first intended—and it must be pointed on Middleton's part to bring in then, within the space of a few lines, the very thing that removes her judgment entirely:

DE F.:

> (*announcing Vermandero*)
> Your eye shall instantly instruct you, lady;
> He's coming hitherward.

BEA.:

> 　　　　　What need then
> Your duteous preface? I had rather
> He had come unexpected; you must stall
> A good presence with unnecessary blabbing:
> And how welcome for your part you are,
> I'm sure you know.

> 　　　　　　　　(I.i.93-99)

De Flores' statement about the eye "instructing" is an unwitting but sharp mockery of Beatrice's late advice to her new lover, Alsemero:

> Be better advis'd, sir;
> Our eyes are sentinels unto our judgments,
> And should give certain judgment what they see;
> But they are rash sometimes. . . .

> 　　　　　　　　(I.i.71 ff.)

In this context, the unsettling presence of De Flores—from the first *so* unsettling that it is never surprising Beatrice's hate "changes" to love—points the drama's true concerns. Alsemero, Beatrice—all the characters in the *Changeling* world, in fact—are convinced that they are living and acting in a world dominated by the virtues of clarity and good sense. Everything they say, in that finely controlled naturalistic dialogue, hints that they are drastically mistaken in this belief. There is, we are continually being reminded, too wide and too sudden a gap between the talk of reason and the presence of passion; and this, simply, is what the play is about. The bewildering irrationality and power of passion in a world otherwise dominated by reason yields a concept in some ways similar to Racine's. Love is a "possession" in the Racinian sense ("C'est Vénus tout entière à sa proie attachée . . ."). Indeed the form of the play as a whole is reminiscent more of Racinian tragedy than of anything in English literature. Middleton's concerns with a world of bourgeois naturalism are far removed from Racine's, but the dominating image of Vermandero's castle (with, as we shall see, its "labyrinths" of sex and passion) is, in structure and significance, very like the palace-labyrinths of *Phèdre* and *Andromaque.*[5]

The beginning of *The Changeling,* then, presents a calmly reasoned, civilised world in which every remark betrays the power of the *un*civilised, unreasonable world of passion and lust.[6] It is the developing image of Vermandero's "castle" which gives this simple opposition imaginative depth and power. The fact that Middleton builds up this image and concept without forsaking, except in some sections of the sub-plot, his naturalistic frame of reference is a clue to his true originality and insight. Nobody else in English drama has seen so clearly the nature of the deadly opposition between the power of civilisation and reason on the one hand, and passion on the other.

The image of the castle is rather like that of the temple mentioned in the opening scenes. (Alsemero swears by this, and will not "change" from it, but Beatrice fears she may.) The castle, owned by Beatrice's father, stands for something which looks, and in a sense perhaps is, firmly irreproachable. In a limited way there is a stability behind Alsemero's worshipping at the temple and, also, behind Vermandero's concept of a stronghold ("castle") which must be jealously guarded, simply because it is a position of strength and order. But Middleton sees these images *both* as admirable in themselves *and* as modified, even endangered, by the fact that their nature, like Beatrice's own, is to exist by ignoring what is going on around them. The first important mention of the castle image is in I.i.155 ff. It comes in the middle of an admirably controlled dialogue between Alsemero, Vermandero, and Beatrice which culminates in the beautifully naturalistic maunderings of the old man about his youth with Alsemero's father. The surface—again as in certain important Ibsen passages—is unruffled, and this reinforces Vermandero's estimate of himself and his household; but the reinforcement is ironically twisted because Vermandero has not the faintest conception of how far his remarks really reach into the depths of the circumstances that even now surround him. The key speech is in answer to Beatrice's request that Alsemero be shown over the castle; Vermandero is terribly proud, and terribly cautious of his castle:

> With all my heart, sir.
> Yet there's an article between; I must know
> Your country; we use not to give survey
> Of our chief strengths to strangers; our citadels
> Are plac'd conspicuous to outward view,
> On promonts' tops; but within are secrets. . . .
>
> (I.i.161 ff.)

"Within are secrets" indeed. A little later, after the talk of Alsemero's father, the same note of curious foreboding returns, this time firmly based on one of the equivocations of "changed." Alsemero, realising that Beatrice is lost to him because contracted to Piracquo, suddenly decides to leave and is rebuked by Vermandero:

> How, sir? By no means;
> Not chang'd so soon, I hope! You must see my castle,
> And her best entertainment, e'er we part.
>
> (I.i.200-202)

The exchange concludes with an aside from Alsemero, who, alone with Beatrice, has recognised the likely implications of Vermandero's innocent insistence on his daughter's marriage and the arrival of Piracquo:

> How shall I dare to venture in his castle,
> When he discharges murderers at the gate?

"Murderers" is of course a pun, the primary meaning of which is "cannon." But at this stage nobody has the faintest conception of what the "best entertainment" will turn out to be, and the dramatic irony is doubly enhanced by the wonderfully real heartiness and insensitivity of Vermandero, completely unconscious alike of what his castle is about to provide in the way of entertainment and of what his daughter is thinking, indeed of what *she* is really like inside. The sort of slightly blunted or stupid calm of mind that Vermandero is given here is one of the best examples of Middleton's ability to introduce the naturalistic solidity of common life into tragedy which reaches beyond naturalism to a poetic ordering of experience.

From this point in the play onwards, with a gathering intensity which is marred but not crippled by the sillier of the "asylum" scenes in the sub-plot, the "castle" image supports and governs the play. I think it is not too much to say that, right up to the end, the plan of the action in a general way is that the main plot takes place on or near the "outward view" of the castle, either in the open or in rooms like Alsemero's apartments recognised, by the ethos of the play, as having an official status in the well-ordered living of the household; the sub-plot, on the other hand, is deliberately placed in the asylum kept, at Vermandero's pleasure, by Alibius. This may or may not be specifically placed in some remote part of the castle, but the point is that, by the character of the dialogue, especially Isabella's, the asylum takes on the character of a labyrinth of sex, a section within Vermandero's apparently straightforward "castle" which will have a comment to make on the quality and worth of the outside:

Isabella:

> Stand up, thou son of Cretan Dedalus,
> And let us tread the lower labyrinth;
> I'll bring thee to the clue.

In terms of the staging of the play there are, admittedly, difficulties in the way of seeing the "asylum" scenes as part of the gathering image of Vermandero's castle. For one thing, some passages in the asylum scenes are feeble writing (cf. the variations on the all too familiar "we three" joke and the farcical tinge to the writing generally in I.ii). Also, the physical limitations of any Jacobean stage-setting—even one which included an upper stage for the madmen, as in III.iii—might present obstacles to the rapid juxtaposition of plot and sub-plot essential if Middleton's point is to be established. On the other hand, there is clearly a very strong thematic relation between plot and sub-plot,[7] and I think that most of the writing in the asylum scenes is good enough, and pointed enough, to make them imaginatively part of Vermandero's world.

Indeed the progress of the play generally is best summarised as a syncopated exchange between events on the outside and events on the inside of Vermandero's "castle." First of all, in I.ii, the perfectly well-meant remarks of Vermandero about his castle spring back to mind when we begin to see what is in fact "within." This scene presents us with the first display of madmen and, more particularly, introduces Antonio, disguised as an idiot (love is a "tame madness") so he can win Alibius' young wife. This fills out considerably the fairly simple statement of the castle image in I.i, because, though no direct comparisons have yet been made, this *is* the inside of the castle (figuratively at least), and it is given over to the frank pursuit of lust, accompanied by the lewd chorus of madmen "Cat

whore, cat whore! her permasant, her permasant!"
Beatrice has earlier been specifically connected with the
fair outward view of the castle, and though she has
done nothing yet beyond disobeying her father in the
matter of marriage, or wanting to, the parallel between
her actions and Antonio's (and hence the inside of the
castle) is the more significant. A hint of relationships
not yet fully worked out can be far more telling than a
direct statement.

Parallels of this kind continue as the action develops.
Beatrice talks of "judgment" and De Flores, again, is
given an entrance which immediately removes all shred
of control and judgment from her (II.i). And in all the
scenes where "judgment" is shown as being radically
disturbed, the irony depends as much on the unruffled
naturalism of the dialogue as on any other single aspect
of the writing. In such a context, the absolute irrationality of Beatrice's loathing for De Flores is doubly alarming and significant. Beatrice shares her father's vein of
complacent reasoning and rationalisation, but Middleton,
right from the beginning, couples this fairly consistently
with language reserved for De Flores: "This ominous
ill-faced fellow more disturbs me / Than all my other
passions." In context I think it is fair to suggest that the
phrase "all my other passions" implies that De Flores—
and all he comes to stand for in connection with the inner forces of Vermandero's world—disturbs Beatrice
more even than her accepted lover, Alsemero. In fact
the energy of the play consistently comes from the *un*-
reasonable and the irrational, which therefore appears
as twisted and destructive not because it is in essence
evil, but because somehow the gap between reason and
passion has grown too large. The energetic forces of the
play are the "secrets within": the focus of Middleton's
dramatic structure allows them to contribute depth and
strength to the poetic image (the castle), even while
they are presented as inevitably destroying the people
in their power.

The twisted labyrinths where De Flores, at Beatrice's
command, murders Piracquo, the man Beatrice no
longer wants, deepen our insight into Vermandero's
"castle" further still. These scenes, too, are cast in
calmly naturalistic dialogue—

De F.:

> All this is nothing; you shall see anon
> A place you little dream on. . . .
> My lord, I'll place you at a casement here
> Will show you the full strength of all the castle.
> Look, spend your eye awhile upon that object.

Alon.:

> Here's rich variety, De Flores . . .

(III.ii.1 ff.)

—but they reach forward to a further uncovering of the
irrational as they link with later scenes from the mad-

men of the asylum and with the growing bond between
Beatrice and De Flores.

The best and most important of the asylum scenes is
IV.iii, where Isabella (at this point clearly acting as
Beatrice's *alter ego*) dresses up as a madwoman in order to meet Antonio (also disguised) and, possibly, submit to his proposals.[8] The castle image itself is here,
and finally, defined in terms of the Greek myths that
Isabella and Franciscus refer to from time to time. Most
of the dialogue is in phallic terms, and includes a bid
for Isabella by Lollio: ". . . if I find you minister once,
and set up in the trade, I put in for my thirds; I shall be
mad or fool else." This is of course another version of
De Flores' point to Beatrice, and Isabella's reply differs
from Beatrice's only in being more clear-sighted: "The
first place is thine, believe it, Lollio / If I do fall." In
this world of *actual* madmen, lust is a sordid business
deal, but it is also more frankly recognised for what it
is than in the world where society and "reason" dominate. The two planes of action combine in Isabella's
important speech after her entry as a madwoman,
frankly tempting her lover:

> Hey, how he treads the air! Shough, shough, t'other
>   way!
> He burns his wings else; here's wax enough below,
>   Icarus,
> more than will be cancelled these eighteen moons;
> He's down, he's down, what a terrible fall he had!
> Stand up, thou son of Cretan Dedalus,
> And let us tread the lower labyrinth;
> I'll bring thee to the clue.

(IV.iii.102-108)

The sense beneath the nonsense is evidently telescoping
the fall of Icarus (a plain invitation to Antonio) and the
business of facing and destroying the Minotaur in the
Dedalus-Theseus-Ariadne myth. The phallic suggestions clearly start with the evocation of Pasiphae's
monster of lust, the beast born of her union with the
bull and then confined by Minos in the labyrinth; link
at this point with the idea of Dedalus, the fabulous arti-
ficer, containing unrestrained lust by the intelligence
and artifice of his labyrinth; and take in also the cunning of Theseus and Ariadne, with their clue of thread,
and the "fall" of Icarus. Here in this scene is the final
enactment of the character of Vermandero's castle and
the powerful labyrinths which its rational, civilised surface attempts to ignore or suppress. The paradox,
Middleton is saying, lies in the fact that the public, accepted way of life and the outward appearance of people
like Beatrice can remain so apparently secure, when obviously they cannot be taken at face value in view of
the powerful, uncontrollable forces at work underneath.

The end of the play brings to a halt at last the intricate
juggling of different worlds, different values. Most significantly, the obvious change of tone in Beatrice's last

speech (and it does not matter from this point of view whether Middleton or Rowley was responsible) marks the end of her fatal single-mindedness and of the separation of the public and private worlds in Vermandero's castle:

> O, come not near me, sir, I shall defile you!
> I am that of your blood was taken from you
> For your better health; look no more upon't,
> But cast it to the ground regardlessly:
> Let the common sewer take it from distinction.
> Beneath the stars, upon yon meteor
> Ever hung my fate, 'mongst things corruptible. . . .
>
> (V.iii.149 ff.)

The change here towards a richer note in the verse seems to me to mark a just and necessary conclusion to the play. It is a speech collating complex ideas and relationships (e.g., the relationship of honour to whoredom, of reason and logic to passion and lust), and it is also the moment in the play when Beatrice at last, and with virtually no further prevarication, sees truly.

Finally, the tone of Beatrice's last speech points in another way the uniqueness, and the significance, of the dramatic texture and thinking developed by Middleton in this play. Vermandero's castle is the dominating image and issue throughout, and it is the key which opens for us the play's fullest meaning. On the other hand, the concentration of this developing image is directed towards a view of the *human* dilemma. The play is not—as far too many Jacobean plays are—a mere imagistic fantasy where people do not matter. The controlled emotion and sympathy in that last speech of Beatrice's are a clear demonstration of the way Middleton builds on the imagistic level and on the level of human action and emotion at once. This speech is the natural extension of the view we have seen developing all along of Beatrice and her lover-accomplice De Flores, the key figures in the drama. The public and the private emotions of Vermandero's world, as well as being imagistically extended by the castle image, are securely founded in these two people. De Flores' uncompromising directness ("Push! you forget yourself; / A woman dipp'd in blood, and talk of modesty!") constantly pushes Beatrice to the point where she speaks in more heartfelt terms, dropping the tone of frightened self-justification in which for the most part she attempts to shrug off complicity in murder and adultery. There is a very pointed contrast, for instance, between the primness of the murderess who dare not admit complicity—

> Thy language is so bold and vicious,
> I cannot see which way I can forgive it
> With any modesty.
>
> (III.iv.123-25)

—and the same woman pushed by De Flores' remorseless bargaining to the point where submerged terror and guilt break through:

De F.:

> Justice invites your blood to understand me.

Bea.:

> I dare not.

De F.:

> Quickly!

Bea.:

> Oh, I never shall!
> Speak it yet further off, that I may lose
> What has been spoken, and no sound remain on't;
> I would not hear so much offence again
> For such another deed.
>
> (III.iv.100-105)

It is quite clear here that Honour is no mere empty word to Beatrice, any more than it is when she arranges for her maid to take her place on the wedding-night lest Alsemero find out that she is not a virgin. This is a Jacobean play which works with an unusual and startling directness on the human level.

This is why a term like "poetic naturalism" seems inevitable for this play and for Middleton's work generally. What we have been observing in *The Changeling* is a depth of focus unique in Jacobean (and probably any other) drama. The play is not to be placed in the richly evocative line of Shakespearean development; its meaning and significance are the result of a fresh start in Jacobean enquiry and one which depends a good deal on unswervingly naturalistic attitudes in the verse and dialogue. Yet a term like "naturalism" is after all wrong or inadequate for Middleton's work as a whole and certainly for this play. Here as nowhere else we are presented, not with a flat, naturalistic surface, but with the spectacle of a single complex image—Vermandero's "castle"—dominating a whole drama. Not only do we look at and admire the progress of the action; at the same time we, as it were, look down through the surface of this dominant image into the complexity of its internal structure. Where in other plays—Tourneur's, some of Marlowe's, Shakespeare's—we watch and participate in the growth of a network of inter-connected images, in *The Changeling* we are presented with something which is much more clearly a single complex image, a product of the whole play which grows in depth like a gradually expanding sphere, the surface of which is firm but also clear enough for us to gaze into the complex, disturbed centre. The play is therefore unique, though linked with *Women Beware Women* in obvious ways. Together with the rest of Middleton's work it separates itself from Jacobean drama generally.

As it turned out, the separation was indeed all too complete. There is no subsequent development of Middleton's insights in English drama. Indeed, for 250 years or more there are virtually no significant developments on the English stage—certainly there is no great tragedy. Tragedy after Middleton tends more and more to substitute a sentimental idealism for his hard-headed recognition of the facts of life. The works of Ford, for instance, and the Heroic writers, betray their inability to recognise the real business of drama—that is, to see the difficulty, toughness, and vulgarity of life as a source of spiritual and intellectual food.⁹ Thus both Ford's quietism ("They are the silent griefs which cut the heartstrings: / Let me die smiling") and the soft lyricism with which he endows Giovanni's desperate praise of incest ("Go thou, white soul, to fill a Throne / Of innocence and sanctity in Heaven") are suspect. Like the inflated rhetoric of much Heroic drama, Ford's writing assumes too readily that the ordinary business of living is intolerable; it looks, therefore, towards a sentimentally conceived ideal where all impurities shall be purged by lyric grace or burning passion.

In late Jacobean and Caroline drama, only Middleton's great plays stand out firmly against prevailing tendencies. *The Changeling* is I think the richest of his plays, but even it embraces, far more readily than do plays by Middleton's contemporaries, the hard-headed world of commerce in love and marriage signified by, for instance, the tough bargaining of Beatrice, De Flores, Lollio, and Isabella. Middleton's distinction is to realise, in a social context which has obviously changed radically from Elizabethan times, that drama can never flourish if it isolates love and passion from the nourishing substantiality of common social and personal relations. After Middleton, however, the few signs that remain of his toughness of mind about problems of modern living are rapidly submerged in a growing, and sentimentally conceived, idealism.

Notes

1. See M. C. Bradbrook, *Themes and Conventions of Elizabethan Tragedy,* 2nd ed. (Cambridge, 1952), and J. D. Jump, "Middleton's Tragedies," in the Pedican Guide No. 2, *The Age of Shakespeare* (London, 1955). On the "bourgeois" world of Middleton, see also R. B. Parker, "Middleton's Experiments with Comedy and Judgement," *Jacobean Theatre: Stratford-upon-Avon Studies I* (London, 1960).

2. The dates of the two plays are in dispute: G. E. Bentley assigns *The Changeling* to 1622, *Women Beware Women* to 1625?-27 (*The Jacobean and Caroline Stage* [Oxford, 1941-56], IV, 861, 905-907). Some put *Women Beware Women* before 1622 (see Bentley, p. 906).

3. The evidence is summarised by R. H. Barker, *Thomas Middleton* (New York, 1958), pp. 165-69. For a full account see P. B. Murray, "The Author-

ship of The Revenger's Tragedy," *PBSA,* LVI (1962), 195-218. On the question of collaboration with Rowley, see *The Changeling,* ed. N. W. Bawcutt (London, 1958), pp. xxxix-xliv.

4. Bradbrook, *op. cit.,* pp. 214 ff.

5. See Martin Turnell's study of Racine in *The Classical Moment* (London, 1947).

6. On the hidden, punning references to sex, see C. Ricks, "The Moral and Poetic Structure of *The Changeling,*" *Essays in Criticism,* X (1960), 290-306.

7. See Bradbrook, *op. cit.,* pp. 221 ff. However, she has not convinced others: see Barker, *op. cit.,* pp. 129-30, and R. Ornstein, *The Moral Vision of Jacobean Tragedy* (Madison, 1960), pp. 180-81.

8. For a contrary view on Isabella's willingness to grant her lovers' demands, see Bradbrook, *op. cit.,* p. 222; Jump, *op. cit.,* p. 367; W. Empson, *Some Versions of Pastoral* (London, 1935), pp. 49-51; and I. Ribner, *Jacobean Tragedy* (London, 1962), esp. p. 129.

9. For a contrary view on Ford see Ornstein, *op. cit.,* pp. 200-21: and H. J. Oliver, *The Problem of John Ford* (Melbourne, 1955).

Normand Berlin (essay date September 1969)

SOURCE: Berlin, Normand. "The 'Finger' Image and Relationship of Character in *The Changeling.*" *English Studies in Africa* 12, no. 2 (September 1969): 162-66.

[*In the following essay, Berlin examines the finger-ring-hand-glove group of images in* The Changeling, *whose effectiveness, the critic asserts, stems from its illumination of the relationships in the play.*]

The Changeling, one of the most discussed and highly regarded of Jacobean plays, continues to display qualities of brilliance that have not been fully examined. Fine studies of the play have appeared,¹ some discussing the play's imagery, but not one has given attention to a group of images that seems so compelling that it is difficult to understand its neglect—the finger-ring-hand-glove group. I suspect that the neglect is based on the critics' examinations of the play as a work to be read rather than performed, so that the important idea-images tend to overshadow what could be called images *in action,* images that are theatrically alive, to be heard *and* seen.

The effectiveness of Middleton's "finger" group stems not from its reflection on individual character or its reenforcement of theme or evocation of atmosphere—the usual functions of images—but from its illumination of the actual *relationship* of character. It verbally and visually links Beatrice-Joanna and DeFlores, and effectively indicates the progress toward oneness of the two egotists.

By the end of I. i. the intense hatred of Beatrice for the ugly DeFlores has already been firmly established, as has his passion for her. By then, too, the themes of "change" and "appearance *vs.* reality" and the pregnant words "judgment" and "will" have been presented. "Will" is especially important in connection with the Beatrice-DeFlores relationship, because it has sexual connotations which influence from the beginning the audience's attitude toward the two main characters. When DeFlores attributes Beatrice's hatred for him to "a peevish will", we have a glimpse of his awareness of the full meaning of the word, and an indication of her ignorance of the inverted infatuation which she feels for him. Then, at the end of the scene, Beatrice drops her glove. DeFlores picks it up and offers it to her, but she is so filled with disgust for him, that she takes off her other glove and throws it down, rather than have what he touched touch her. DeFlores happily accepts this "present" with these words:

> Here's a favour come, with a mischief! Now I know
> She had rather wear my pelt tann'd in a pair
> Of dancing pumps, than I should thrust my fingers
> Into her sockets here; I know she hates me,
> Yet cannot choose but love her:
> No matter, if but to vex her, I'll haunt her still;
> Though I get nothing else, I'll have my will.
>
> (I. i. 231-237)

This piece of stage action is both dramatically effective and symbolically significant. DeFlores sees the sexual symbolism connected with Beatrice's act, and expresses himself in sexual terms. The word "thrust" suggests the kind of sexual force he will display in his relations with Beatrice and as he utters the word, surely the audience must *see* him plunging his fingers into the glove's sockets. The gesture carries great weight; it is itself sexual, and is re-enforced by the phallic significance of the words "fingers" and "sockets". And DeFlores's speech, ending the scene, concludes with the word "will". Here, in the play's beginning, a stage action and the words of DeFlores effectively and concretely indicate the kind of relationship DeFlores and Beatrice will have when they later literally achieve the oneness of fingers in a glove.

Immediately this action is verbally re-enforced in the sub-plot when Alibius, worried that his young wife will find another man, tells Lollio, "I would wear my ring on my own fingers; / Whilst it is borrowed, it is none of mine, / But his that useth it." To this, Lollio replies, "You must keep it on still then; if it but lie by, one or other will be thrusting into't." Here we have the first

reference to a "ring", a word and object which attains great importance in the main plot, and which is a natural outgrowth of the glove-socket idea. Also we have a reference to the sexual "finger" after this it is no longer found in the sub-plot—but it also suggests, by its very obviousness, the importance of the image to Middleton.

The image next appears in the crucial exchange between Beatrice and DeFlores (II. ii.), when Beatrice asks "the ugliest creature" to be of "use" to her. The asides effectively indicate the thoughts of the two egotists—Beatrice dwelling upon DeFlores's service to her, DeFlores enraptured because of her attention to him and her changed attitude. She praises him and actually touches his face—visually producing a stunning effect because of her previous aversion. His aside—"Her fingers touch'd me!"—indicates his momentary rapture *and* it calls to mind the "fingers" that we encountered before. The rapture stems from the touch which DeFlores already sees as an embrace after he has performed his "service" to her of killing Alonzo.

> Oh my blood!
> Methinks I feel her in mine arms already,
> Her wanton fingers combing out this beard,
> And being pleased, praising this bad face.
> Hunger and pleasure, they'll commend sometimes
> Slovenly dishes, and feed heartily on 'em.
> Nay, which is stranger, refuse daintier for 'em.
> Some women are odd feeders.
>
> (II. ii. 146-153)

The words themselves ravish. "Blood", like "will", has a sexual meaning as well as the ordinary one. Her fingers, which before touched him, are now "wanton fingers" combing his beard. This leads to the idea of "Hunger and pleasure" and reference to dishes and feeding. DeFlores sees himself as the man who will feed on that dish, Beatrice, and she will feed on him. (The food-sex idea in Shakespeare's *Troilus and Cressida* and *Antony and Cleopatra* is strongly echoed here.) When Alonzo comes on stage, DeFlores states, "Here comes a man goes supperless to bed", for Alonzo will soon be killed before he tastes Beatrice, and DeFlores will be the man who comes to dinner. At a crucial moment in the play, therefore, the sexual "finger" image becomes bound up with the sexual "feeding" image, and the combination stunningly reveals the nature of the DeFlores-Beatrice relationship.

When DeFlores stabs Alonzo, the ring on Alonzo's finger sparkles in DeFlores's eyes. He decides to bring the ring to Beatrice to prove that he performed his service. However, the ring and finger will "not part in death", so he cuts off the finger. In III. iv., surely one of the most powerful scenes in Elizabethan drama, the finger is brought to Beatrice. She is horrified at the sight—"Bless me, what thou done?" His answer:

> Why, is that more
> Than killing the whole man? I cut his heart-strings.
> A greedy hand thrust in a dish at court,
> In a mistake hath had as much as this.
>
> (III. iv. 29-32)

Here the finger-dish association, present when he declared his service to her, reappears when the service is performed. It carries forward a dramatic thread, and it reaffirms the notions of sexuality held by DeFlores. But this is not all. For the image of the ring-finger, discussed further by DeFlores, pinpoints at the play's most exciting moment the *exact* nature of the relationship of the two characters.

> I was loath to leave it,
> And I'm sure dead men have no use of jewels.
> He was as loath to part with't, for it stuck
> As if the flesh and it were both one substance.
>
> (III. iv. 35-38)

For just as the ring and finger "will not part in death", will stick together, so too will DeFlores and Beatrice. The ring is *her* diamond, given as a gift to her husband-to-be Alonzo, whose finger is displayed. (We must never forget that we *see* it.) Now she offers the ring to her partner-in-crime DeFlores. His finger will now be "thrust" in it. They have symbolically wedded, for the crime has made them one as man and wife. When Beatrice seems shocked with his behaviour, DeFlores must say: "Why are you not guilty? In, I'm sure, / As deep as I; and we should stick together." He is, of course, telling her that she must now live in a new world of values produced by their joint guilt, and in this new world he is her partner.

> Y'are the deed's creature; by that name
> You lost your first condition, and I challenge you,
> As peace and innocency has turn'd you out,
> And made you one with me.
>
> (III. iv. 137-140)

His finger will forever occupy her ring, just as his fingers had previously occupied the sockets of her glove. The "finger" image vividly indicates DeFlores's sexual possession of Beatrice, but the sexual possession is at the same time a spiritual possession, for the sexual, the physiological, has been operating *along with* the psychological. The "sticking" applies to both ring and finger *and* to the perpetual togetherness of the sinful creatures of the deed. It is this fusion which charges the image with a special vibrancy. As the scene ends, DeFlores tenderly raises the kneeling Beatrice, and they leave the stage—surely, hand in hand, fingers clasped. They are one. The dumb show, immediately following, portrays the ghost of Alonzo showing his hand *sans* finger, perfectly accentuating the importance of the finger in the love triangle. The dead Alonzo has lost not only his ring (Beatrice) but his finger (phallic) to DeFlores, who is now sexually and spiritually wed to Beatrice.

Many critics feel that after III. iv. the play deteriorates, since it progresses now not on a psychological level but on the level of intrigue. Once DeFlores and Beatrice are joined, once their progress toward oneness is completed, the rest of the play seems less exciting. The group of images I have been discussing stops with the joining of Beatrice and DeFlores—a perfect example of the complete interdependence of image and relationship of character in drama.

Although the image is dropped when DeFlores and Beatrice become one, it provides an effective back-drop to the last scene of the play, indicating the rich suggestiveness of Middleton's art. After Beatrice openly admits her corruption to the court, DeFlores turns to Alsemero and happily relates: "I coupled with your mate / At barley-brake; now we are left in hell." Vermandero adds: "We are all there, it circumscribes here." Barley-brake is a game played by pairs of men and women, who *hold hands* and are not allowed to separate while they are in a marked circular space, a chalk *ring,* called "hell". The allusion is a common one in Elizabethan drama, but it achieves a special brilliance here, for it calls to mind the hands and rings that Middleton exploited in the progress toward oneness of DeFlores and Beatrice. No director could miss the opportunity of having DeFlores and Beatrice die holding hands. In this final clasp, we are reminded of the gloves into which fingers are thrust, of the sticking together of ring and finger, of the spiritual partnership that has, indeed, led to hell. The ring on a dead man's finger has grown to become the circle circumscribing all the participants in a tragedy of blood and will.

Note

1. Especially the discussions in Richard Barker, *Thomas Middleton* (New York, 1958), M. C. Bradbrook, *Themes and Conventions of Elizabethan Tragedy* (Cambridge, 1935), Una Ellis-Fermor, *The Jacobean Drama* (London, 1936), Samuel Schoenbaum, *Middleton's Tragedies* (New York, 1955), and in N. W. Bawcutt's introduction to the Revels Plays edition (London, 1958). All quotations are taken from the Revels Plays edition.

Thomas L. Berger (essay date 1969)

SOURCE: Berger, Thomas L. "The Petrarchan Fortress of *The Changeling*." *Renaissance Papers* (1969), pp. 37-46.

[*In the following essay, Berger analyzes how* The Changeling *dissects the Petrarchan convention of comparing the beloved to a fortress and the lover to its besieger, and how in doing so the play uncovers the madness and tragedy at the base of the conceit.*]

Although the methaphor or simile equating or comparing the beloved one to a fortress or fortified castle and the lover to a besieger of that castle is by no means the most popular conceit of the Elizabethan sonneteers and love poets, it is nonetheless commonplace. In many of the poems of the period does the lover look on his mistress as a castle or fortress, a fortress which must be attacked and conquered before the mistress yields up her heart, and thence her honor, to him.[1]

It is the purpose of this essay to investigate Middleton and Rowley's *The Changeling* (1623/24) in the light of this convention.[2] Just as Shakespeare probed many of the Petrarchan formulae to employ them ironically ("My mistress' eyes are nothing like the sun") and Donne explored them either literally for the same ironic if not cynical effect ("The Legacy" and "The Message") or metaphorically for devotional purposes ("Batter my heart, three-personed God"), so too does *The Changeling* dissect and anatomize one particular metaphor, both in the main and secondary plots, to expose the ultimate reality and horror at its base. Taking only the barest outlines from their sources, John Reynolds's *God's Revenge Against Murder* (1621) and Leonard Digges's *Gerardo the Unfortunate Spaniard* (1622),[3] Middleton and Rowley create two worlds, each testing the Petrarchan conceit. In the world of Alibius's asylum, the conceit is safe among fools and madmen. In Vermandero's castle it brings dishonor and death.[4] The play takes the conceit at its face value, tests it, and carries it to its furthest extremes. The literal and the metaphorical become tragically enmeshed in such a test, and the horrible reality of the Petrarchan world is defined and exposed.[5]

The fortress metaphor commences with Vermandero's entrance in Act. I. Beatrice-Joanna tells her father that Alsemero wants to see the castle:

> And in discourse I find him much desirous
> To see your castle: he hath deserv'd it, sir,
> If ye please grant it.
>
> (I, i, 159-161)

Whose castle does Alsemero really want to see, Vermandero's or Beatrice-Joanna's? Vermandero's response to his daughter's request continues the image and establishes the parallel between the literal and the metaphorical fortresses:

> With all my heart, sir.
> Yet theres' an article between, I must know
> Your country; we use not to give survey
> Of our chief strengths to strangers; our citadels
> Are plac'd conspicuous to outward view,
> On promonts' tops; but within are secrets.
>
> (I, i, 161-166)[6]

Indeed, there is "an article between," in the person of Alonzo, Beatrice-Joanna's suitor. Beatrice-Joanna will not give survey of her "chief strengths to strangers," for

only De Flores, denizen of the literal castle, will ever take full survey. Her citadels and those of every sonnet lady—golden hair, rose-like lips, marble skin—[7] "are plac'd conspicuous to outward view." Beatrice-Joanna's honor, however, is within, and the secret that she must keep from Alsemero, the loss of her virginity to De Flores, brings about the play's catastrophe in Act V.[8]

Once established, the metaphor highlights incidents at the very beginning of the play. Before the first scene has really gotten underway, Alsemero has declared his love to Beatrice-Joanna. Her reply to him leans toward the fortress metaphor:

> Our eyes are sentinels unto our judgments,
> And should give certain judgment what they see;
> But they are rash sometimes, and tells us wonders
> Of common things, which when our judgments find,
> They can then check the eyes, and call them blind.
>
> (I, i, 72-76)

Beatrice-Joanna's eyes serve as guards, as sentinels, for the fortress that is her body, protecting the treasure that lies therin.[9] Smitten with Alsemero, she declares that her "eyes were mistaken" (I, i, 84) when they chose Alonzo de Piracquo as her intended. With such sentinels, how can her fortress of honor resist attack? The image is extended and reinforced a few lines later with De Flore's entry, as he tells Beatrice-Joanna that her "eyes shall instantly instruct" her as to her father's health (I, i, 94). To round out the image cluster before Vermandero's entry, De Flores says to himself that he will please himself "with sight / Of her at all opportunities" (I, i, 103-104), and Beatrice-Joanna describes her distaste for De Flores:

> Your pardon, sir, 'tis my informity
> Nor can I other reason render you,
> Than his or hers, of some particular thing
> They must abandon as a deadly poison,
> Which to a thousand eyes is that same fellow there,
> The same that report speaks of the basilisk.
>
> (I, i, 109-115)[10]

Even before the fortress metaphor has formally begun, then, have all the lovers been introduced in terms of the reactions they make on Beatrice-Joanna's "sentinel" eyes. Alonzo proves to be a mistake of her eyes, Alsemero is able to penetrate her eys and capture her love, and, ironically, De Flores is loathsome to her eyes.

As soon as Vermandero learns that Alsemero is the son of a friend, he insists that Alsemero see his castle "And her best entertainments, ere we part" (I, i, 202). By his birth Alsemero is qualified to see the literal castle of Vermandero and to become the besieger of the metaphorical fortress of Beatrice-Joanna.[11] Alsemero's aside before his exit from the scene is at once ironic and Petrarchan:

How shall I dare to venture in his castle,
When he discharges murderers at the gate?
But I must on, for back I cannot go.

(I, i, 222-224)

In the first line Alsemero again broaches the castle, both literal and metaphorical. The second line is filled with dramatic irony: first, with the literal meaning of "murderers" (small cannons loaded with shot) and its sexual overtones; second, with De Flores as a murderer, both of Alonzo and of Beatrice-Joanna (first with the murder of her honor, then with her actual murder); and third, with the discharge of Antonio and Franciscus, who intend to murder the honor of Isabella and who are later accused of murdering Alonzo (IV, ii, 1-16). The final line is a summary of the situation in which the Petrarchan lover constantly finds himself, ensnared in an impossible net of passion and possibility. Thus in Act I does the conceit of the lady-fortress become established in terms of the major characters in the main plot. The metaphorical and the literal begin to become mixed, and they will remain so until the deaths of Beatrice-Joanna and De Flores dissolve them.

In Act II the metaphorical and literal fortresses come together again. Here, following Reynolds in terms of plot but not language, Alonzo asks De Flores to show him the "full strength of the castle" (II, ii, 158). Ironically, De Flores, who knows the full strength of the literal castle, will be the only character who will ever know the full strength of Beatrice-Joanna's fortress. De Flores's promise to Alonzo, "if the ways and straits / Of some of the passages be not too tedious for you, / I will assure you, worth your time and sight" (II, ii, 159-161), reinforces the parallel between Beatrice-Joanna and the castle.

As Act III opens Alonzo declares that the literal fortress is "a most spacious and impregnable fort" (III, i, 4). To Alonzo both fortresses, the literal and the metaphorical, are impregnable. To one who, like De Flores, knows the inner workings of the fortress, its secret passages and labyrinthine ways, the question of pregnancy is, ironically, irrelevant. Alonzo marvels at "the rich variety" of the castle's strength (III, ii, 9), and De Flores, who is knowledgeable in the workings of the literal castle and who will become so for Beatrice-Joanna's metaphorical fortress, slays him.[12]

In the fourth scene of this same act, Vermandero again offers to show Alsemero the secrets of his fortress, vowing "you shall see the pleasures / Which my health chiefly joys in" (III, iv, 718). Equally as important are the lines immediately preceding and following his offer, in which the fusion of the literal and metaphorical fortresses works toward its tragic completion. Vermandero wishes he had another daughter for Alsemero (l. 2), Alsemero reports that he has heard of the castle's repu-

tation for beauty (l. 4), and, after their exit, Beatrice-Joanna comments that "I have got him now the liberty of the house: / So wisdom by degrees works out her freedom" (ll. 12-13).

The act concludes with De Flores's demand of Beatrice-Joanna's honor in reward for the deadly task he has undertaken and accomplished. Beatrice-Joanna, despairing because De Flores refuses money, declares that she is "in a labyrinth" (III, iv, 71). Like her metaphorical fortress, it is a labyrinth of her own creation. She is lost, ironically, in her own Petrarchan fortress, and like Alonzo, who is killed in the labyrinthine passages of Vermandero's castle, she too will die. But for the moment she needs someone to guide her through the labyrinth, and she is forced to choose De Flores. The master of the workings of the literal fortress becomes the master of the metaphorical one. Beatrice-Joanna is made to see that Alonzo's death will be the murderer of her honor (III, iv, 122), and it is De Flores, the murderer of Alsemero's rival, who will steal Alsemero's beloved.

Plot and metaphor continue to fuse in Act IV when Jasperino overhears Beatrice-Joanna and De Flores:

'Twas Diaphanta's chance (for to that wench
I pretend honest love, and she deserves it)
To leave me in a back part of the house,
A place we chose for private conference;
She was no sooner gone, but instantly
I heard your bride's voice in the next room to me;
And lending more attention, found De Flores
Louder than she.

(IV, ii, 89-96)

Alsemero is now forced to test Beatrice-Joanna with his chemicals, and Beatrice-Joanna, having already tested Diaphanta, knows well the purpose of such a test. More important is the place of conversation, the "back part of the house," again known only to masters of the fortress.

By Act V the literal and the metaphorical have become one. When De Flores suggests setting Diaphanta's chamber on fire, the literal and the metaphorical fortresses again co-mingle:

DE FLORES:

This is my reach: I'll set some part a-fire
Of Diaphanta's chamber.

BEATRICE-JOANNA:

How? Fire, sir?
That may endanger the whole house.

DE FLORES:

You talk of danger when your fame's on fire?

(V, i, 31-34)[13]

The metaphorical now controls, and the literal must now match the metaphorical, not, as in previous acts, the metaphorical following and being informed by the literal. Vermandero's response to the fire, "oh bless my house and me" (V, i, 87), another echo of his constant concern over fortifications, foreshadows the destruction not of his literal castle but of his daughter's metaphorical one.

When De Flores enters with the wounded Beatrice-Joanna, stabbed, significantly, in Alsemero's closet, a room within a room, the same room of first tested honor, Vermandero's simile ironically captures the essence of the Petrarchan horror to which the main plot has been leading:

> An host of enemies enter'd my citadel
> Could not amaze like this: Joanna! Beatrice! Joanna!
>
> (V, iii, 147-148)

The two worlds, the literal and the metaphorical, having been brought together to a state of co-existence, are now co-extinguished.

In the secondary plot the same Petrarchan conceit is operative.[14] With Alibius and Vermandero, Lollio and De Flores, Antonio and Alonzo, Franciscus and Alsemero, Isabella and Beatrice, and, even, Pedro and Tomazo, the two plots are in terms of character almost exactly parallel. While Vermandero worries about the secrets of his fortress, Alibius is concerned with the protection of his wife's fortress. The metaphorical of the main plot becomes the literal of the secondary plot.[15] Here, however, in the world of the insane, Isabella, unlike Beatrice-Joanna, retains her honor.

On bringing Antonio to the madhouse, Pedro requests that Lollio give his friend "sweet lodging," and Lollio tells him the lodging will be "as good as my mistress lies in, sir" (I, ii, 116-117).[16] Following so closely on Vermandero's invitation to Alsemero to see the chief strengths of his castle, the intimation that Antonio will lodge himself with Isabella at once parallels and supports the main plot.

In Act III Isabella complains that Lollio is keeping her in a prison:

> Why, sirrah? Whence have you commission
> To fetter the doors against me?
> If you keep me in a cage, pray whistle to me,
> Let me be doing something.
>
> (III, iii, 1-4)

De Flores has slain Alonzo in the preceding scene; he has used the literal fortress in order to gain entrance to and conquer the methaporical one. Here Lollio imprisons Isabella in order to protect her metaphorical fortress for Alibius, the master of the mad castle. In this same scene Lollio twice wishes that Alibius were at home (ll. 166-167 and l. 201), for he cannot govern the madmen and fools alone, much less look after Isabella's honor. Isabella's comment on home and honor a few lines later becomes ironic in terms of the main plot:

> . . . would a woman stray,
> She would not gad abroad ot seek her sin,
> It would be brought home one ways or other.
>
> (III, iii, 213-215)

Only De Flores knows the ways and passages of Vermandero's castle, not Alonzo or Alsemero. Beatrice-Joanna, finally, does not "gad abroad to seek her sin." She finds it not with the aliens Alonzo or Alsemero but, fully and tragically, at home with De Flores.

The letter from Franciscus, the "lunatic lover," that Lollio and Isabella read in Act IV is filled with the figures of the standard Elizabethan distressed lover:

> 'If any fault you find, chide those perfections
> in you, which have made me imperfect; 'tis the
> same sun that causeth to grow, and enforceth
> to wither—'
>
> (IV, iii, 17-19)

Franciscus's love has not, ironically, driven him to madness. Rather, it has driven him to the pretense of madness. Like the Petrarchan lover, Franciscus will remain "'mad till I speak with you, from whom I expect my cure'" (IV, iii, 27-28). The real madness and the feigned, the sickness and the cure, the literal and the metaphorical, all become entangled, like Beatrice-Joanna, in the Petrarchan web. Antonio also reveals himself in this act, and Lollio offers them both the prize of Isabella's honor. Just as De Flores, a trusted servant, is the guide to Vermandero's fortress, so too does Lollio, a trusted servant, become the guide to Isabella's honor.

When Isabella appears like a madwoman in the same scene, she invites Antonio to "tread the lower labyrinth" (IV, iii, 107), an ironic reminder of the Petrarchan labyrinth which Beatrice-Joanna has created for herself (III, iv, 72) and from which only De Flores can free her.[17] Isabella, however, preserves her honor, for she can recognize feigned madness and feigned foolishness within the total madness and folly of her world. In her fortress, the madhouse, the conceit is safe; it is as harmless as the fools, madmen, and counterfeit fools and madmen that inhabit the fortress. In the actual world of Vermandero's literal castle and Beatrice-Joanna's metaphorical fortress, the conceit, as twisted and circuitous as the passageways only De Flores knows, is transformed into a tragic device at once informing Beatrice-Joanna's passion and De Flores's love. Middleton and Rowley have taken the Petrarchan conceit to its logical extremes in order to uncover the madness, the folly, and the horribly tragic reality at its base.

Notes

1. Examples of and variations on the conceit of the besieger and the besieged can be found in the following sonnet sequences: Sir Philip Sidney, *Astrophel and Stella* (1591, 1598), sonnets 9, 12, 29, 36, 61, 79, and song 2; Samuel Daniel, *Delia* (1592, 1594), sonnets 42 and 51; Giles Fletcher, *Licia* (1953), sonnets 28 and 48; Thomas Lodge, *Phyllis* (1593), sonnets 23 and 24; Michael Drayton, *Idea* (1594, 1599, 1602, 1065, 1619), sonnet 63; William Percy, *Coelia* (1594), sonnet 10; the anonymous *Zepheria* (1594), sonnet 25; Edmund Spenser, *Amoretti* (1595), sonnet 14; and Bartholomew Griffin, *Fidessa* (1596), sonnet 4. All number references are to Sidney Lee, ed., *Elizabethan Sonnets,* 2 vols. (London, n.d.). See also the several seductions and attempted seductions in *The Faerie Queene*: I,ii,25; I,vi,1-5; and III,x,10. In Petrarch, where an abstract and personified Love plays a more active role, it is often the lover who is besieged, as in sonnets 2, 39, 132, 274, and 327; this also is the case in *Idea,* sonnet 29 and Richard Lynch, *Diella* (1596), sonnet 7. The lover besieging and the loved one besieged obtains in Petrarch's sonnets 45, 125, and 170. All number references are to G. Carducci and S. Ferrari, eds., *Le Rime di Francesco Petrarcha* (Florence, 1899).

2. N. W. Bawcutt, ed. (London, 1958). Subsequent references will appear in text.

3. Bawcutt reprints the pertinent parts of both sources in his edition, pp. 113-129.

4. Robert Ornstein, in his discussion of the play in *The Moral Vision of Jacobean Tragedy* (Madison, 1960), pp. 179-190, points out certain Petrarchan parallels with *The Maid's Tragedy* and *Romeo and Juliet* and ironic Petrarchan inversions in the play. His discussion centers in terms of plot, not metaphor. In Christopher Ricks's study of the play's imagery, such words as "honour," "performance," "service," "act," and "deed" are traced in terms of sexual innuendo. See "The Moral and Poetic Structure of *The Changeling*," *EIC,* X (1960), 290-306.

5. In his chapter on *The Changeling* in *A Study of Elizabethan and Jacobean Tragedy* (Cambridge, 1964), pp. 185-212, T. B. Tomlinson sees the castle as "the really important focal point which both widens and sharpens Middleton's investigation of his theme" (p. 192). Tomlinson suggests that Beatrice-Joanna is very like the castle is more concerned with the outer stability of the castle and its inner weakness (appearance-reality, public-private, sanity-madness). What I hope to demonstrate is that as the play progresses metaphor becomes reality, Beatrice-Joanna and the castle *are* one as appearance-reality, public-private, and sanity-insanity become ironically reversed.

6. In Reynolds the incident is barely mentioned: "We will purposely omit the conference which Alsemero and Beatrice-Ioana had in the Coach, and allow them by this time arrived to the Castle; where first her selfe, then the Captaine her father, thanke him for his honour and courtesie: in requitall whereof, he shewed him the rarities and strengths of his Castle" (Bawcutt, p. 117).

7. For full descriptions, see L. C. John, *The Elizabethan Sonnet Sequences* (New York, 1938), p. 198; L. E. Pearson, *Elizabethan Love Conventions* (Berkeley, 1933), pp. 325-326; Bartholomew Griffin, *Fidessa* (1596), sonnet 39; and Richard Lynch, *Diella* (1596), sonnet 3.

8. In Reynolds, Beatrice-Joanna marries Alsemero, *then* engages in adultery. The difference is important.

9. The fact that, according to most Elizabethan psychologists, love enters through the eyes adds a touch of irony. For a full discussion, see Lawrence Babb, "The Physiological Conception of Love in the Elizabethan and Early Stuart Drama," *PMLA,* LVI (1941), 1020-1035. Edward Engelberg describes the main action of *The Changeling* as one which stems from Beatrice-Joanna's faulty eyesight. See his article, "Tragic Blindness in *The Changeling* and *Women Beware Women*," *MLQ,* XXIII (1962), 20-28.

10. The irony of the basilisk, a beast who can kill by a glance, is important. It is not De Flores who is the basilisk; rather, in Petrarchan terms, it is the lady, in this case Beatrice-Joanna, whose eyes will bring about murder.

11. We learn of his acceptability in Act III: "Valencia speaks so nobly of you, sir, / I wish I had a daughter now for you" (III,iv,1-2).

12. The sexual symbolism here, Alonzo without a sword, De Flores with one, cannot be overlooked in terms of dramatic foreshadowing.

13. The method De Flores uses does not appear in Digges and is sexually symbolic. De Flores will use "a piece high-charg'd, / As 'twere to cleanse the chimney" (V,i,45-46).

14. Defenses of the secondary plot can be found in Bawcutt's edition, pp. lxii-lxviii, and in the edition of George Walton Williams (Lincoln, Nebraska, 1966), pp. xiii-xxiv, as well as in William Empson, *Some Versions of Pastoral* (London, 1935), pp. 48-52; Muriel C. Bradbrook, *Themes and Conventions of Elizabethan Tragedy*

(Cambridge, 1935), pp. 213-224; Karl Holzknecht, "The Dramatic Structure of *The Changeling*," *Renaissance Papers 1954*, pp. 77-87; Robert Ornstein, *The Moral Vision of Jacobean Tragedy*, p. 180; and Irving Ribner, *Jacobean Tragedy* (New York, 1962), pp. 134-137.

15. Bawcutt states the relationship succinctly: ". . . what is implied in the main plot becomes literal in the sub-plot. The deceptive appearances which are suggested by imagery in the main plot become actual disguises in the sub-plot, and the madness of love which is no more than hinted at in the main plot moves much closer to real madness in the sub-plot" (p. lxvi).

16. It is tempting to equate Lollio with Chaucer's Lollius (Petrarch?).

17. In *Middleton's Tragedies* (New York, 1955), Samuel Schoenbaum remarks on the irony of "the amoral girl in a moral labyrinth from which she never can escape" (p. 142).

Robert Jordan (essay date 1970)

SOURCE: Jordan, Robert. "Myth and Psychology in *The Changeling*." *Renaissance Drama* 3 (1970): 157-65.

[*In the following essay, Jordan asserts that what many critics have viewed as psychological complexity of character in* The Changeling *is in fact a presentation of mythic patterns and types.*]

Commentators on Middleton and Rowley's **The Changeling** seem to be close to agreement on at least one point, the psychological subtlety of the play.[1] Critic after critic comments on this feature, and many of them concentrate their energies on a depth analysis of the characters. In the present article I would like to challenge this standard critical perspective by suggesting that in the very place where so many critics see complexity of character there can also be found operating something vastly different—a mythic and poetic pattern that may do more to build the play's haunting power than any amount of psychology.

Talk of the play's richness of character inevitably concentrates on two figures. Apart from Beatrice and De Flores the persons in the play are the palest of stock types, most of them having no more character than the walking gentlemen of Victorian melodrama. In Beatrice and De Flores, however, we have an intensity of emotion coupled with a perversity of behavior that has normally been construed as psychological complexity rather than as the maladroit inconsistency of character

to which so many Jacobean playwrights (notably Fletcher) are prone. It is true, of course, that the love felt by De Flores is so brooding that it often seems a morbid obsession, and the selfishness shown by Beatrice is so total that it sometimes appears pathological, but this is usually interpreted not as evidence that Middleton is clumsy but rather as proof that he is sophisticated enough to handle abnormal psychological states.

But Beatrice and De Flores can be looked at from another point of view. We are all familiar with the way in which many studies of the Othello-Iago relationship have moved away from Bradley or Leavis-like character analyses of the two men towards a view of the relationship as the struggle between opposed instinctive forces or fundamental values. The best known example of this is probably G. Wilson Knight's reading of Othello as a symbolization of heroic idealism and Iago as an embodiment of cynicism,[2] but an even more striking, though related, example is provided by J. I. M. Stewart's view of the relationship as expressive of the conflict that exists in any human mind between idealizing and cynical impulses.[3] Othello and Iago, that is, are facets of the one consciousness. Now **The Changeling** is a play that is in some ways similar to *Othello*—in its concentration on the two-person struggle and in the simple clear line of action which leads remorselessly on from a first weakness to a final catastrophe. I would suggest that it is also like *Othello* in that the central characterizations are likewise susceptible to an analysis in abstract terms, though in this case the terms are those of myth or folklore rather than those of differing value systems.

Thus, if De Flores can be regarded as a figure of great psychological sophistication he can also be seen as an extremely simple character construct. Basically he is composed of two qualities, each realized so intensely as to take on monolithic proportions. These two qualities, moreover, are so incongruous that their enforced conjunction generates even more the sense of forces that are both stark and massive. On the one hand, there is the softness of love, a romantic infatuation which is so emphasized as to appear an obsession. On the other hand, equally emphasized, is the brutishness of the man, a brutishness that is not only a matter of coarseness and savagery of spirit but also a matter of physical repulsiveness. There are frequent and striking references to the hideousness of De Flores, a hideousness conveyed through references to his hairiness and roughness of skin[4] and also through the use of gross animal images—serpent, toad, dog.[5] This animal baseness is further reinforced by the emphasis on his menial position, and the whole picture is given an extra intensity by the contrast with his partner, Beatrice-Joanna, who is presented in terms of an antithetical set of simple, stark qualities—aristocratic where he is lowly, beautiful where he is gross, hysterically repelled where he is morbidly doting. In the center of the play, then, standing out all the more because of the pallid quality of the other characters, are two figures locked in a relationship, figures simplified down to a few qualities apiece so that the relationship itself takes on a monumental simplicity—brutishness and love at the feet of beauty and revulsion. With the animality of De Flores emphasized not only through his coarse and savage nature but also through his physical appearance, and through the animal imagery that clusters about him, it seems to me that Middleton is here hovering on the verge of one of the more potent of mythic confrontations, that of beauty and the beast, the princess and the frog. I believe that the dramatic power that the De Flores-Beatrice relationship undoubtedly generates owes much to the way it reverberates with the echoes of this traditional pattern.

Claims of the kind I have just made for a mythic substratum to a dramatic situation usually face an enormous difficulty. The presence of the myth can be asserted but not in any sense demonstrated. What makes the example in *The Changeling* especially interesting, however, is that one can trace the situation in the play back to earlier literary models which actually overlap the primitive forms of this myth.

A starting point for this analysis is a feature of the play that has been noted by Professor Ornstein.[6] In the first three acts of *The Changeling* the De Flores-Beatrice relationship is quite consciously and systematically developed as a perverted and mordantly ironic variant on a courtly love relationship. Every significant step in this phase of the story seems conceived in these terms. Thus the opening situation is a travesty of the doting lovesick knight being spurned by his cruel and haughty mistress. This is followed by the first sign of grace—the lady drops a glove which the ever attentive knight recovers for her and which the lady allows him to keep as a favor. After this comes the longed-for occasion when the lady, in peril, needs a champion to defend her. And so we find De Flores literally kneeling before Beatrice, begging the service and being granted it. He becomes her champion, kills the threatening enemy, is given a further token (the ring) as a sign of favor, presses his suit, and wins the lady. As an example of the way the travesty works and of the savagery of it, one has only to consider one of these incidents, one not noted by Professor Ornstein. De Flores may actually speak of the dropped glove as a favor (I.i.231), but if the lady allows him to keep it it is not out of a nascent affection but out of revulsion. Once he has touched it she is so disgusted by the object that she refuses to have anything to do with it. As if this were not a sufficient degradation of the romantic image of the glove, it receives a further defilement when De Flores, talking of it, turns it into an image of gross sexuality:

> Here's a favour come, with a mischief! Now I know
> She had rather wear my pelt tann'd in a pair

> Of dancing pumps, than I should thrust my fingers
> Into her sockets here. . . .

> (I.i.231-234)

The same sexual defilement, incidentally, is involved in the other love token, the ring, in Act III, scene iv. It is a ghastly enough perversion of elegant romance that this ring should have the murdered owner's finger still in it. It is an extra twist that the finger in the ring is a very sleazy sexual image—one that occurs, moreover, in the subplot (I.ii.27).

But it is more than the broad pattern of incident that reflects the courtly conventions. Much of the detailing of the story is similarly conceived in terms of the inverted or travestied courtly affair. Thus the killing of the villain knight who threatens the lady here becomes the murder of the innocent Piraquo. This murder is presented on stage with a striking amount of circumstantial detail, and to the casual glance this might look like the accumulation of small facts to give an air of solid realism to the events. Actually these details seem to have been selected to stress the nature of the action as a complete reversal of the courtly contest. In this contest what one normally has is an open challenge and then the face-to-face armed combat, something that by Middleton's time had ossified into the code of the duel, complete with seconds. But instead of the formal challenge and the fight with equal weapons, we are shown De Flores presenting himself to Piraquo as a friend, tricking him into putting aside his weapons, luring him into a deserted part of the fortress, persuading him to admire the view through an embrasure, and then, while he looks out, stabbing him, presumably in the back. The choice of words and many of the turns of language are similarly inspired by the courtly code (for example, II.i.26-35).

Professor Ornstein, as I have said, makes the basic point that there is inversion of the courtly love convention in the Beatrice-De Flores relationship. Nevertheless, he continues to speak of the psychological reality of these characters[7] and to concentrate on the analysis of motive and personality. It would seem to me that where characters are so systematically conceived in terms of a literary convention, albeit one turned on its head, there are at least some grounds for being cautious in one's psychological analyses and some possibilities that the relationship may operate on levels other than the psychological.

But there is more to be said than that. Professor Ornstein finds the inspiration for the courtly love travesty in the use of such techniques in *The Maid's Tragedy*.[8] Perhaps Fletcher's play may have given Middleton the idea, but it seems to me that in choosing to present his travesty suitor as a coarse brute (unlike Fletcher) he may in fact be harking back to a much earlier and more widespread variation on the normal courtly love relationship. What I am suggesting is an echo of that very popular medieval and Renaissance motif, the wild man and the maiden. And if on one side this motif impinges on the courtly love relationship, on the other side it merges into the legendary pattern I spoke of earlier—beauty and the beast.

The wild man, or wodewose, who has been described in great detail by Professor R. Bernheimer,[9] is a shaggy and uncouth creature who lives the life of a primitive huntsman in the depths of the woods. He is a standard figure of European folk tales and folk rituals and from there has moved across into the iconography of late medieval and Renaissance art, literature, and ceremonial, where he is often merged with the classical satyr. More than anything else he is an embodiment of the bestial side of man's nature—man as the savage creature without culture giving free rein to his brute appetites. A figure such as this, of course, is the complete antithesis of the chivalrous ideal, and so he sometimes appears among the evil creatures overcome by questing knights on their peregrinations.[10] However, as a figure of folklore and of sophisticated iconography the wild man is capable of all sorts of subtle modifications, and it is with some of these that I am chiefly concerned. Thus the primary role of the wild man in relation to woman would seem to be that of the ravisher and kidnapper who bears her off into the forests. But even in some of the folk rituals the pattern one finds is that of the woman "capturing" the wild man—leading him on a ribbon or luring him with a ring[11]—and the same reversal of roles can occur in the courtly use of the material. The wild man can be "tamed" by the highborn lady and can even become her servant. When this tendency is exploited to the full, what we seem to have is an icon for the traditional power of the beauteous lady, the power of taming the savage impulses in man and bringing him to gentleness and civility—one of the central motifs of the courtly code.[12]

Elizabethan and Jacobean dramatic entertainments provide a few examples of such wild-man-lady relationships. In *Mucedorus* Bremo the wild man first views the heroine simply as a good meal but is suddenly smitten by her beauty:

> I cannot wield my weapons in my hand;
> Methinks I should not strike so fair a one,
> I think her beauty hath bewitch'd my force,
> Or else within me altered nature's course.
> Ay, woman, wilt thou live in woods with me?[13]

Thereafter he dotes on the lady, while remaining in every other respect the cannibal savage, a De Flores of the woods. Similarly transfigured in an instant of time is the satyr in Fletcher's *The Faithful Shepherdess,*

though in this case it is the radiant chastity of the lady rather than her beauty that effects the change.[14] The satyr, moreover, seems less savage than Bremo to begin with, and in his case the lady's powers seem to have led to a general reformation of manners. Many decades earlier George Gascoigne had turned this idea to a courtly compliment in *The Princely Pleasures at Kenelworth Castle* where he has his Savage Man transfigured by the sight of the beautiful and highborn female guests at the entertainment, and particularly by the Queen, whom he begs to serve:

> . . . I, which live at large,
>   a wilde and savadge man:
> And have ronne out a wilfull race,
>   since first my lyfe began:
> Doe here submit my selfe,
>   beseeching you to serve:
> And that you take in worth my will,
>   which can but well deserve.[15]

In this transformation by love, and in this desire to serve, the wild man is beginning to impinge on the functions of the courtly knight, and part of Professor Bernheimer's concern in Chapter Five of his book is to demonstrate the ways in which the wild man develops as parody, subversion or outright replacement of the traditional courtly lover. Earlier in his book (pp. 18-19) he has remarked on a number of occasions on which the savage man appears as a full-fledged courtly knight. The best example of this in Renaissance England is provided by that happy hunting ground for wild men, Spenser's *The Faerie Queene,* where Sir Satyrane, who "ever lov'd to fight for Ladies right" (I.vi.20) rescues Una from his less cultivated brethren, the satyrs.

There are grounds, then, for seeing De Flores as a shadowy evocation of the wild man tradition in the area where that tradition interpenetrates with the courtly love convention. The matter could be left at that point, but I would like to argue the further extension, that through the wild man and the lady pattern the De Flores-Beatrice relationship impinges on the even more potent beauty-and-the-beast legends. The relationship is, in fact, a very simple one. In folklore there is plenty of evidence for confusions between the shaggy wild man and the brute beast. Thus a ritual pattern that in one part of the countryside calls for a wild man in another area will make use of a bear.[16] Similarly, in the courtly love stories the beauty and virtue of the woman is often shown as taming not only wild men but also wild beasts—Una's lion, for example, in *The Faerie Queene,* I.iii.5-6. Into the context I have been describing then, the beauty-and-the-beast story pattern fits without difficulty. Some of the folk tales based on the beauty-and-the-beast motif, moreover, involve not only the basic beauty-beast opposition that is my main concern but also details of narrative and character that are analogous to those in the type of courtly love story that lies behind *The Changeling.* In the version of "The Princess and The Frog" given by the brothers Grimm[17] the frog certainly lacks the threatening power of a bear or other shaggy beast, but on the other hand the tale contains the haughty lady, the service performed, and the efforts to evade payment. In this folk tale, of course, the climactic event is the transformation of the beast into a handsome prince, and it is easy enough to see this as symbolic of savagery transformed by the lady's kindness into gentleness and civility, a parallel with the "taming" of the wild man.

In my analysis I have concentrated on the primary image that the De Flores-Beatrice relationship generates—that of the shaggy beast fawning on the beautiful lady. But of course the outcome of the relationship as it is shown in the play is hardly the conventional one. De Flores may observe the formal stages of the courtly wooing, but the forms are hollow ones. They are drained of idealism, purity, and selflessness and exist only as the vehicles for gross lust, brutal selfishness, and crude cynicism. The wild man may do obeisance before the fair lady but this lady's glance does not purify. The wild man is a wild man still. Indeed, with this lady it could not be otherwise, for in her also one has only the forms of the courtly mode and not the essence—the beauty, the birth, the virginity, but not the inner purity. The fairy-tale ending is subject to a bitter reversal. Instead of the beast being revealed as a prince, the process of this story is to reveal that the princess is in fact a beast.

Notes

1. For example, Richard Hindry Barker, *Thomas Middleton* (New York, 1958), p. 124; Una Ellis-Fermor, *The Jacobean Drama* (London, 1961), p. 149; and Samuel Schoenbaum, *Middleton's Tragedies* (New York, 1955), pp. 137-140. Even critics whose interest lies in other aspects of the play frequently begin by acknowledging this strength of characterization—for example, Muriel Bradbrook, *Themes and Conventions of Elizabethan Tragedy* (Cambridge, Eng., 1960), pp. 213-214; and T. B. Tomlinson, *A Study of Elizabethan and Jacobean Tragedy* (Cambridge, Eng., 1964), pp. 185-188.

2. G. Wilson Knight, *The Wheel of Fire* (London, 1960), pp. 97-119.

3. J. I. M. Stewart, *Character and Motive in Shakespeare* (London, 1949), pp. 107-110.

4. Thomas Middleton and William Rowley, *The Changeling*, ed. N. W. Bawcutt, The Revels Plays (London, 1958), pp. 27 (ll. 35-45), 35 (ll. 43-45), 37 (ll. 73-75), 40 (ll. 147-150). All references in the text are to this edition.

5. *Ibid.*, pp. 9 (l. 115), 14 (l. 225), 29 (l. 80), 40 (l. 146).

6. Robert Ornstein, *The Moral Vision of Jacobean Tragedy* (Madison and Milwaukee, Wis., 1965), pp. 179-190.

7. *Ibid.*, p. 181.

8. *Ibid.*, p. 179.

9. Richard Bernheimer, *Wild Men in the Middle Ages* (Cambridge, Mass., 1952).

10. *Ibid.*, pp. 121-122.

11. *Ibid.*, p. 136.

12. *Ibid.*, pp. 124-125, 135-136.

13. *A Select Collection of Old English Plays,* ed. W. Carew Hazlitt, comp. Robert Dodsley, 4th ed., 15 vols. (London, 1874-1876), VII, 233.

14. *The Works of Francis Beaumont and John Fletcher,* ed. Arnold Glover and A. R. Waller, 10 vols. (Cambridge, Eng., 1906), II, 373-375.

15. *The Complete Works of George Gascoigne,* ed. John W. Cunliffe, 2 vols. (Cambridge, Eng., 1910), II, 100.

16. Bernheimer, *Wild Men in the Middle Ages,* pp. 53-55.

17. "The Frog King, or Iron Henry," in *The Grimms' German Folk Tales,* trans. Francis P. Magoun, Jr., and Alexander H. Krappe (Carbondale, Ill., 1960), pp. 3-6.

J. Chesley Taylor (essay date 1972)

SOURCE: Taylor, J. Chesley. "Metaphors of the Moral World: Structure in *The Changeling.*" *Tulane Studies in English* 20 (1972): 41-56.

[*In the following essay, Taylor maintains that* The Changeling *is unified by the Renaissance concept of moral perfection, which, the critic states, offers an alternative to the inconstancy and failures of the play's characters.*]

Since 1935, when William Empson and M. C. Bradbrook first pointed out the parallels between the play's main action and its subplot,[1] critical analysis of *The Changeling* has been almost exclusively concerned with its dramatic unity. There has not been much debate over the subplot's artistry; response has varied little from Karl J. Holzknecht's refusal "to defend the doubtful artistry of madhouse scenes intended to be comic," to Samuel Schoenbaum's assessment of the subplot as "stupid and tedious" and Richard H. Barker's remark that "it would be nice, in fact, if we could forget that the play has a comic story at all."[2] It is precisely this artistic failure, however, that has spurred examination of the thematic links between the two levels of the play's action, for a secondary plot becomes a severe liability if it is, as Professor Barker calls it, "completely contemptible."[3] Both Barker and Schoenbaum argue that dramatic artistry and thematic unity are inseparable; the failure of technique leads inevitably to the failure of the play's controlling idea.[4] Nevertheless, Empson, Bradbrook, and Holzknecht have yet acknowledged the fact that the subplot, even with its artistic inadequacies, does reinforce the play's major themes and in so doing heightens the dramatic intensity of the central conflict. In addition, Christopher Ricks has argued persuasively for the play's unity through a detailed study of its language, and George W. Williams has demonstrated not only its thematic unity but its structural, tonal, and metaphoric unity as well.[5]

It seems clear, as Williams suggests, that the "concept of transformation" (p. xiv) is the unifying concept on which the dramatic action of the play as a whole is predicated. It is equally clear that the changes which the characters undergo are essentially moral changes (although physical, psychological, and intellectual transformations are to be seen as well). The path taken by Beatrice and De Flores is a descent into a moral labyrinth, the central metaphor of which is the child's game of barley-brake, with its image of hell at the center. The moral implications of this metaphor are established by references in both the main plot and the subplot. In the main plot, for example, we find De Flores explicitly linking the barley-brake game with the idea of damnation: "Yes, and the while I coupled with your mate / At barley-brake; now we are left in hell" (V.iii.163-64). In the subplot, the association is reinforced when Isabella refuses to dismiss Antonio (thus placing herself in moral jeopardy) and the madmen cry out, "Catch there, catch the last couple in hell" (III.iii.162).

But the play is unified in a more subtle fashion as well by the Renaissance concept of moral perfection, a concept which offers an implicit alternative to the moral failures of the characters and to the inconstancy which makes them changelings. It is this ideal which we find at the heart of Sir Philip Sidney's *An Apology for Poetry*: "This purifying of wit, this enriching of memory, enabling of judgment, and enlarging of conceit, which commonly we call learning, under what name soever it come forth, or to what immediate end soever it be directed, the final end is, to lead and draw us to as high a perfection, as our degenerate souls, made worse by their clayey lodgings, can be capable of." Richard Hooker differentiates man from the lower orders by the impulse toward perfection which he exhibits. Directed by the force of reason, this striving is one of the "grand mandates, which . . . must be obeyed by the will of man" (*Of the Laws of Ecclesiastical Polity* I.viii). This

same vision informs *Macbeth,* and against it Macbeth and Lady Macbeth work out their tragic destinies. The pattern of action in *The Changeling* reflects a similar dramatic design. In Middleton and Rowley's play, three central metaphors of this vision of perfection—the temple, the madhouse, and the castle—along with the image patterns that evolve from them, combine to present a unified vision of human nature and of the moral world in which man pursues his fate.

Alsemero, in the opening lines of Act I, introduces the concept of perfection by equating his love for Beatrice with the holiness and perfection of the temple in which he has twice seen her:

> 'Twas in the temple where I first beheld her,
> And now again the same; what omen yet
> Follows of that? None but imaginary.
> Why should my hopes or fate be timorous?
> The place is holy, so is my intent;
> I love her beauties to the holy purpose
> And that, methinks, admits comparison
> With man's first creation, the place blest,
> And is his right home back, if he achieve it.
> The church hath first begun our interview
> And that's the place must join us into one;
> So there's beginning and perfection too.

> (I.i.1-12)

The idea of perfection is implicit in two allusions: the reference to the Garden of Eden, "the place blest," and the image of the circle in the final line, "So there's beginning and perfection too." Alsemero uses the circle, the traditional symbol of perfection, to suggest the perfection of the union with Beatrice which he desires. The line also returns us to the image of the Garden of Eden, man's "beginning and perfection" in Paradise; Alsemero clearly thinks of himself and Beatrice as Adam and Eve.[6] That these analogies are suspect, however, is underscored by the scene's constant references to eyes and sight, suggesting the limitations of his perceptions.

These images of Paradise and of perfection are linked with both the castle and the madhouse through a wide variety of metaphors, all of which remind us of the characters' moral imperfection and of the moral ideals from which they fall. Thus, while the play begins on a reference to the Garden of Eden, it concludes with an image of a fallen world. Jasperino opens V.iii by revealing that he has given Alsemero the ocular proof of Beatrice's true character: "the prospect from the garden has show'd / Enough for deep suspicion." They have seen the unsuspecting lovers together; and Alsemero's new knowledge, like that of Adam and Eve, is indeed of evil. The "prospect" in this scene also provides an ironic finale to the motif of sight established in Act I.[7] The connotations of "garden" are reinforced by De Flores' description of Beatrice as "that broken rib of mankind" (l. 147). Vermandero can equate their revelation only with the fall of his castle—"An host of enemies enter'd my citadel / Could not amaze like this" (ll. 148-49)—while Beatrice reminds us that man, like all the things of the world, is created mutable and may fall: "upon yon meteor / Ever hung my fate, 'mongst things corruptible" (ll. 155-56). The difference is that man is mutable in the moral as well as the physical sense; for the broad thematic implications of the play, it is a crucial distinction.

The circle as image of perfection is even more pervasive. It recurs in the madhouse scene in which Alibius asks Lollio to keep a watchful eye on his wife:

ALIBIUS:

> There's the fear, man;
> I would wear my ring on my own finger;
> Whilst it is borrowed it is none of mine
> But his that useth it.

LOLLIO:

> You must keep it on still then; if it
> but lie by, one or other will be thrusting into't.

(I.ii.26-31)

The ring is the symbol of the perfect union of man and wife in the sacrament of marriage, a union that Alsemero intends when he says, "The church hath first begun our interview / And that's the place must join us into one" (I.i.10-11). Alibius' extended metaphor reflects his possessiveness: the ring is Isabella. Lollio takes his words in their sexual sense—"one or other will be thrusting into't"—thus effectively linking the scene with the one immediately preceding, in which De Flores, holding Beatrice's gloves, speaks of "Thrust-[ing] my fingers into her sockets here" (I.i.230). But the ring as symbol of perfection plays its most significant role in the death of Alonzo. De Flores wishes to have the diamond from Alonzo's hand,[8] but, as he tells Beatrice, he was forced to cut off the entire finger, for the ring "stuck / As if the flesh and it were both one substance" (III.iv.38-39). The matter is particularly horrifying, not only because of the grisly fashion in which De Flores presents to Beatrice the proof of his deed (foreshadowing the later sensationalism of Ford's 'Tis Pity She's a Whore), but also because the act reflects De Flores' cool willingness to desecrate the body of the man he has just murdered, a final, devastating violence to universally accepted moral values. It is a demonstration of the true profundity of De Flores' evil and leaves him fully revealed to us. Thereafter, the fascination lies in watching Beatrice succumb to his insistent desires—"Can you weep fate from its determin'd purpose?" (III.iv.162) asks De Flores irresistibly—while the mask is stripped from her real nature.[9]

By the conclusion of the play, the metaphoric meaning of ring and circle has been inverted: it is evil that seems to surround man and to order his existence. In testing Diaphanta's virginity with the "glass M," Beatrice reflects aside:

> Just in all things and in order
> As if 'twere circumscrib'd, one accident
> Gives way unto another.

(IV.i.110-12)

The lines suggest the inevitability of the course of events, primarily through the word "circumscrib'd," with its overtones of determinism. But the word is also important for its prefiguring of the final scene. After Beatrice and De Flores admit their guilt, Vermandero cries out, "We are all there, it circumscribes here" (V.iii.165). The reference is to the circle which represents hell in the game of barley-brake; it also suggests the extent of the characters' moral journey from the "beginning and perfection" of the play's first lines. Alsemero concludes the play with a reaffirmation of divine justice—"innocence is quit / By proclamation and may joy again" (ll. 187-88)—but cannot alter the tragic nature of that journey nor lighten the burden of its dark revelations.

Two other complex image patterns emerge in the play in relation to the temple metaphor, and both develop more fully the motif of a journey. The first of these patterns involves images of water. Alsemero, we learn in I.i, is on a sea voyage and has put in at the port of Alicant; his departure has apparently been delayed until wind and tide are right. Moreover, he is an inveterate voyager, one "in continual prayers for fair winds" (l. 33) about whom Jasperino, bewildered by Alsemero's sudden change of heart, remarks:

> I never knew
> Your inclinations to travels at a pause
> With any cause to hinder it, till now.

(ll. 26-28)

The voyage becomes a metaphor of the moral voyage the characters in *The Changeling* undertake, and of their journey of self-discovery. Once Jasperino sees that Alsemero will not be moved, he undertakes his own voyage, the seduction of Diaphanta, maintaining the nautical language of the metaphor: "Methinks I should do something too; I meant to be a venturer in this voyage. Yonder's another vessel, I'll board her; if she be lawful prize, down goes her topsail" (I.i.85-88). The difference between the two men is central to the unifying concept of moral transformations and the self-knowledge those transformations effect. Alsemero sets out knowing neither himself nor the woman he loves "at first sight" (l. 64); the double failure leads him into the labyrinth of evil which opposes the vision of perfection voiced by his opening speech. Jasperino, on the other hand, knows precisely what he is about; there is no elaborate process of rationalization and certainly no indication at this point that love has anything to do with his desires. His actions are no less immoral for being more open; rather, his contrast with Alsemero suggests that the latter is not necessarily more moral, simply a good deal less candid. As we shall see when we examine the character of Alsemero more closely, his idealism masks a shallow and mechanical understanding of moral values.

The metaphor of a voyage is continued in the scenes dealing with the murder of Alonzo. In offering to show Alonzo the "full strength of the castle," De Flores promises:

> And if the ways and straits of some of the
> Passages be not too tedious for you,
> I will assure you worth your time and sight,
> My Lord.
>
> (II.ii.162-65)

"Straits" is used here in both its senses: a narrow space, and a narrow waterway between two large bodies of water. The narrowness of the passageway forces Alonzo to discard his weapon, leaving him defenseless. De Flores has the second meaning in mind when he says, "you shall see anon / A place you little dream on" (III.ii.1-2). The narrow passageway is a "strait" which leads Alonzo from earth to heaven.[10] The unsuspecting Alonzo provides the final irony with his own reference to a voyage, a reference that also gives De Flores the alibi he needs:

> I am glad
> I have this leisure; all your master's house
> Imagine I ha' taken a gondola.
>
> (III.iii.2-4)

The humor in the remark is at best macabre. Alonzo's casual comment gives De Flores knowledge which he sees "makes up my safety" (l. 5). With that reassurance he turns to the business at hand.

The last use of the "voyage" metaphor occurs in IV.ii.123-24, where Beatrice comments on the plan to substitute Diaphanta in the marriage bed: "My woman's preparing yonder / For her sweet voyage which grieves me to lose." The remark brings the minor plot of Jasperino and Diaphanta's affair full circle, completing the parallel with the scene in which they met. There it was Jasperino who spoke of his intentions as a venture at sea. Diaphanta is equally aware of the moral implications of what she is about to do, and she dismisses those implications as readily as did Jasperino. One significant fact has altered, however. Jasperino is no longer merely intent upon seducing her; he offers her "honest love." That he also believes "she deserves it" (IV.ii.91) reveals his own blindness. Just as Jasperino has come

to resemble Alsemero, so we recognize that Diaphanta is no better than her mistress. The thousand ducats she is to be paid lead her to reject Jasperino with contempt: "I'm for a justice now, / I bring a portion with me, I scorn small fools" (IV.i.126-27). There is even a dramatic irony in her choice of a justice, for, as Alsemero points out at the play's conclusion, it is justice she finally gets. But as voyages must have ports, so acts inevitably have consequences; Diaphanta, like Beatrice, has little thought what port her voyage is likely to bring her to.

Related to the metaphor of a voyage is the pattern of images involving water. The first scene initiates this pattern; the play's final scene concludes it. The Christian connotations of water are traditional and familiar: water is associated with the ideas of spiritual life, redemption, and the cleansing of original sin through baptism. It is appropriate, therefore, that the metaphors of water and a sea voyage should originate in the scene which is dominated by the image of the temple. Jasperino, trying to convince Alsemero to continue his voyage, offers his final and most telling argument: the zodiacal sign is in Aquarius, the Water Bearer, a good omen for a journey by sea, and one carrying all the force of astrological science. Alsemero rejects the omen outright, though in his first speech he had reflected on the temple as an omen of success in his pursuit of Beatrice.[11] It is more than a curious coincidence that the sign of Aquarius lies between the signs of Pisces (the Fish) and Capricorn (the Goat). In addition to their astrological significance, the two signs are readily recognizable as the symbols of Christianity and, for the Renaissance audience, the horned beast of lust and cuckoldry. One thinks of Othello's fierce and despairing cry, "Goats and monkeys," when faced with the subtle insinuations of Iago.

But the two signs are not allegorical in function; they merely suggest the moral alternatives which the characters face. Of greater importance is the sign of Aquarius; out of it evolves one of the central ironies of the play. For we discover in IV.i. that Alsemero is himself a "water bearer," a would-be physician who attempts to test Beatrice's virtue by chemical means, using the "water in the glass M" (IV.i.47). The absurdity of such a test is apparent, for it equates virginity, a physical state, with virtue, a moral condition. De Flores has already seized upon the distinction between the two, when he points out to Beatrice that she is "the deed's creature" (III.iv.138). Alsemero's test, long considered an absurd incident, is instead a dramatic demonstration of the failure of his reason and judgment.[12] The metaphoric use of water and his role as a physician who "does practice physic for his own use" (IV.i.22) link Alsemero with Beatrice, who promises to be De Flores' physician: "I'll make a water for you shall cleanse this / Within a fortnight" (II.ii.83-84). The pattern extends to the subplot, when Lollio agrees to let Isabella be physician to Franciscus' desire: "she shall cast your water next," he promises Franciscus. The images of both voyages and water are brought together in the final scene, when Alsemero urges Beatrice and De Flores to "rehearse again / Your scene of lust" so that they may be "perfect"; the howls of the damned will be their "music," lust their "pilot . . . to the Mare Mortuum, / Where you shall sink to fathoms bottomless" (V.iii.115-21). The image of the Sea of Death fuses the metaphors of water and voyage, and completes the reversal of Alsemero's vision of perfect and holy love.

Such images as these consistently involve the three central metaphors of temple, madhouse, and castle, suggesting through them the metaphoric structure of the play. But the madhouse is perhaps the most specific metaphor of the three: it functions as a parodic emblem of man's rational capacity. The inmates of the madhouse may be fools and madmen, but so are their keeper and the two would-be lovers. Antonio at the end of the play admits that he was changed "from a little ass as I was to a great fool as I am," Franciscus sees that he "was chang'd from a little wit to be stark mad," and Alibius promises that he will "never keep / Scholars that shall be wiser than myself." Like the lunatics, Beatrice acts out her desires without restraint. Isabella observes that the madmen

> act their fantasies in any shapes
> Suiting their present thoughts; if sad, they cry;
> If mirth be their conceit, they laugh again.
> Sometimes they imitate the beasts and birds,
> Singing or howling, braying, barking; all
> As their wild fancies prompt 'em.

(III.iii.190-95)

Beatrice shifts her loyalties in similarly uninhibited fashion, from Alonzo to Alsemero to De Flores, disposing of such obstacles as fiancé and servant with little hesitation.

That the madmen should sometimes act like "beasts and birds" is appropriate, for the natural world lacks both the power of reason and the concept of chastity which is a part of that impulse toward perfection which Sidney and Hooker so graphically describe. In this sense the madmen are little different from the others. Beatrice, De Flores, Diaphanta, Jasperino, Antonio, Franciscus, Lollio—these characters are hardly chaste in their actions, and none use the powers of right reason to guide them. They are directed instead by the forces of passion and will. Like Alsemero, Beatrice believes that "Our eyes are sentinels unto our judgments" (I.i.69); nevertheless, we cannot help but feel the incredibly ingenuous and irrational nature of a woman who can order the death of her intended and then plead with the murderer to "Let me go poor unto my bed with honor" (III.iv.158).

Her final protest to De Flores blames heredity for her plight, not the failure of reason or moral conviction: "Was my creation in the womb so curs'd / It must engender with a viper first?" (ll. 165-66). And the initial encounter between Jasperino and Diaphanta, in addition to establishing a thematic link with the subplot, reflects upon the unbalanced condition of all the characters. If Jasperino is a "mad wag" who knows "what physic is best for the state of mine own body," it is Diaphanta who sees that it is "scarce a well-govern'd state" (I.i.133-38). As Worcester points out to Hotspur in Shakespeare's *1 Henry IV*, the supremacy of passion and will often results in "want of government" (III.i.182). Diaphanta's own "voyage" to take her mistress' place on the wedding night is an ironic commentary on her inability to apply this perception to herself. It is this theme of man's irrationality of which the madhouse is emblematic.

An important figure in relation to this theme is Alsemero, who begins the play on the note of self-deception and the misuse of reason. Adopting the stance of the romantic idealist, Alsemero, in his opening speech, identifies himself and Beatrice with Adam and Eve before the Fall, and sees their love as "perfection," despite the fact that he has not even met her. His evidence is that of his eyes and his emotions, though he calls it "judgment." In the process he has conveniently forgotten that man lives in a postlapsarian world and is imperfect. He touches unwittingly on this human condition when he reassures Jasperino that he is not ill, "Unless there be some hidden malady / Within me, that I understand not" (I.i.24-25). The "hidden malady" is a metaphor of man's imperfect state brought about by the Fall, a conventional Renaissance view of human nature yet one that Alsemero, through the lover's willingness to deceive himself, cannot accept. Thus the most telling irony in Alsemero's self-deception is in his explanation of Beatrice's feelings for De Flores:

> This is a frequent frailty in our nature.
> There's scarce a man amongst a thousand found
> But hath his imperfection: one distastes
> The scent of roses, which to infinites
> Most pleasing is and odoriferous;
> One oil, the enemy of poison;
> Another wine, the cheerer of the heart
> And lively refresher of the countenance.
> Indeed this fault, if so it be, is general;
> There's scarce a thing but is both lov'd and loath'd.
> Myself, I must confess, have the same frailty.

(I.i.112-22)

The entire speech explains man's "imperfection" in terms of sense perception and his subjective responses to what his senses tell him. He omits completely any reference to the imperfect state of man's moral and rational nature. Thus the pseudo-philosophic observation about man becomes an ironic commentary on his imperceptiveness.

Despite his own admission that man's sense perceptions are imperfect, he consistently bases his judgment on them. Throughout the scene he allows his senses to tell him what he wants to see and hear, rather than subordinating them to rational perception. As a result, his lines are filled with ironic meanings. When Jasperino informs him that the wind is "fair" and promises "a swift and pleasant passage," Alsemero replies, "Sure y'are deceived, friend; 'tis contrary / In my best judgment." He adds:

> Even now I observ'd
> The temple's vane to turn full in my face;
> I know 'tis against me.
>
> (I.i.19-21)

It is an omen that he again mishandles because it opposes his desires. He even refuses to admit that he is no longer the avid voyager "in continual prayers for fair winds": when Jasperino asks if he has changed his "orisons," Alsemero claims, "No, friend, / I keep the same church, same devotion" (ll. 34-35). His self-deception in this scene reaches its climactic point with his metaphor of the "houses" to describe the agreement of reason with the senses:

> . . . yesterday
> Was mine eyes' employment, and hither now
> They brought my judgment where are both agreed.
> Both houses then consenting, 'tis agreed.
>
> (ll. 74-77)

But the senses can tell nothing about moral character; thus his "judgment" is unreliable. The lovers make the mistake of identifying the eyes with the rational soul seated in the brain, where it controls both reason and will. Sight is a wholly external sense, capable of limited understanding of the images it perceives and tending to emphasize "qualities agreeable to sense rather than to the general welfare of man."[13] It is separated from the rational soul and cannot understand the workings of reason and imagination; like will, it is subordinate to reason. Thus, when the characters act upon will (as does Beatrice at I.i.223) or upon "the eyes of judgment," they deceive themselves about the rational basis of their acts.

Despite his claim of a holy and rational love, Alsemero proposes to solve the problem of Beatrice's engagement by sending a challenge to Alonzo (II.ii.28). Such intentions contradict his earlier avowals. Now his values are entirely different: they are the values of a warrior whose father died in "fight with those rebellious Hollanders" (I.i.178) and whose death he would have revenged had not political circumstances intervened. Like Tomazo, then, Alsemero is associated with the figure of the revenger, whose values, as *Hamlet* illustrates, conflict with Christian ideals. It is not moral conduct which

concerns him in this role, but the warrior's reputation: for Alsemero "the honorablest piece 'bout man" is "valor" (II.ii.27). He is stopped from rendering this "service" by Beatrice, whose protests are based not on moral principle but on the simple fear that Alsemero might be killed. In the desire to challenge Alonzo he thus becomes little different from De Flores. Both men wish to kill Alonzo, performing a "service" for Beatrice that each hopes will permit him to possess her.

The play's constant emphasis on wit, reason, and judgment, and its reiteration of the metaphors of Paradise, circle, water, voyage, and labyrinth, lead us into one of its major themes, that of true and false liberty, a theme conveyed by a new set of images—images of flight, of falling, and of confinement. These images serve to remind us that moral action is the product of right reason, and that the only true freedom lies in the pursuit of divine perfection. After the patent distortion of reason and judgment in I.i, the characters continue to follow will instead of reason, and lust instead of love, and they constantly seek a false freedom based on escape, not on understanding. The subplot contains an image of their progress in Pedro's remark to Lollio that he will be satisfied if Antonio can be taught "to creep but on all four / Towards the chair of wit" (I.ii.106-107). In Act II, De Flores hears Beatrice sigh and urges her to give voice to her discontent: "'las, how it labors / For liberty" (ii. 105-106). Her response is to wish she were a man, for then she would not have to marry Alonzo: in such a change lies "the soul of freedom" (l. 109). For Beatrice, this moment is the crucial turning point in the play: she agrees to let De Flores remove the obstacle for her. The decision dooms her, for at precisely that moment she becomes "the deed's creature." She does not, of course, understand what she has done, or how the deed reveals her true nature. Rather, she thinks joyfully that Alsemero now has "the liberty of the house; / So wisdom by degree works out her freedom" and that, with the death of Alonzo, he shall "shine glorious" in her father's favor through the "refulgent virtue of my love" (III.iv.12-17). The images of light are in stark contrast with the darkness of her soul, while the reality she has created for herself is the reverse of the freedom she envisions.

Thus when De Flores claims his due, she can only tell him to "take thy flight"; with unerring logic he replies, "You must fly too, then" (III.iv.82). When she tries to take refuge in her superior "blood," he cuts her off: "Push, fly not to your birth" (III.iv.135). And as the plot moves inexorably toward its conclusion, Vermandero calls for "winged warrants" (IV:ii.16) to apprehend Antonio and Franciscus, though he cannot believe the accusation of murder. He prefers to think Alonzo has simply broken the engagement and fled: "Oh, 'twas most ignoble / To take his flight so unexpectedly," a line whose ironic second meaning the audience can grasp.

In Isabella's description of Antonio's dancing, the motif of flight reaches its climax, linking the subplot with the main plot and with the broad theme of man's imperfect nature and his fall:

> Hey, how he treads the air; shoo, shoo, t'other way, he burns his wings else; here's wax enough below, Icarus, more than will be canceled these eighteen moons.
>
> [*Antonio falls.*]
> He's down, he's down; what a terrible fall he had.
> Stand up, thou son of Cretan Daedalus,
> And let us tread the lower labyrinth;
> I'll bring thee to the clue.
>
> (IV.iii.100 ff.)

"Flight," "fall," and "labyrinth" sum up the course of all the lovers in the play. Rather than freeing themselves, they have all become the prisoners of their moral blindness. Alsemero, refusing to believe her unchaste, embraces Beatrice with the words, "thus my love encloses thee" (IV.ii.151). His obtuseness underscored by the attempt to define virtue in physical terms, relying to the end upon his senses, not his reason, he is at last forced to shut Beatrice in his closet: "I'll be your keeper yet," he says (V.iii.88). His is an understanding of morality not far removed from that of Alibius, who cages his wife in an attempt to force a fugitive and cloistered virtue upon her. Finally, the immoral purposes of Antonio and Franciscus lead them to a willing imprisonment in the madhouse, while very nearly making them victims of Tomazo's vengeance.

The concept of the ideal moral state from which the characters fall is suggested also in early references to angels, "those heavenly and divine creatures" for whom there is "no shadow of matter for tears, discontentments, griefs, [or] uncomfortable passions," and who reflect "the perfect idea of that which we are to pray and wish for on earth."[14] Beatrice alludes to this vision when she sends Jasperino with a message for Alsemero, though the conventional nature of the phrasing suggests there is little real meaning in it for her: "Good angels and this conduct be your guide" (II.i.3), she tells him. She then rhapsodizes in his choice of Jasperino as a friend, calling it a "sign" of his good judgment, while praising her own judgment in selecting Jasperino as her messenger. But the irrational behavior of Alsemero and Beatrice, and the immoral intentions of Jasperino in I.i have already led us to suspect their judgment; those suspicions are reinforced by her next use of the word "angel," when she links this image of perfection with gold in the hiring of De Flores to murder Alonzo— "Belikes his wants are greedy, and to such / Gold tastes like angels' food" (II.ii.125-26)—after which she gives him money to encourage him. Her judgment, of course, is entirely wrong; it is not gold that De Flores is after. Nevertheless, the incident is important as one of a series of incidents involving the exchange of money:

Beatrice offers more money to De Flores in III.iv; Diaphanta is to be paid a thousand ducats for her role in the plot to deceive Alsemero; Pedro pays Lollio for keeping Antonio in the madhouse; Franciscus pays Lollio for help in seducing Isabella; and Alibius is to be paid by Vermandero for having his madmen perform a dance at the wedding festivities. All but the last involve payment for immoral purposes; the dance of the madmen would have been a fitting comment on the irrational and immoral behavior of the lovers.

The emphasis of the action on money, coupled with the references to "Good angels" and "angels' food," plays on the Renaissance audience's familiarity with a particular coin of the time, the gold "angel," so called because it had as its device the archangel Michael piercing the dragon. It was first coined in 1465 by Edward IV and last minted by Charles I, and was copied from the French *angelot* or *ange,* a gold coin struck by Louis XI. More importantly, it was the coin always presented to a patient "touched" for the King's Evil (see *OED*). The King's Evil was scrofula, a disease of the lymph glands which left the skin, particularly around the neck and face, ulcerated, scarred, and draining. It is probably the disease from which De Flores suffers. Beatrice refers to him in terms of "poison," "basilisk," "ill-faced," and "standing toad-pool." De Flores himself admits that his face is "bad enough" (II.i.37) and mentions his "foul chops" (l. 84) and "scurvy" appearance (II.ii.77). He is clearly diseased, for Beatrice, in II.ii, touches him and, calling the illness "but the heat of the liver," promises to cure him: "I'll make a water for you shall cleanse this / Within a fortnight." De Flores exclaims in disbelief, "With your own hands, lady?" Beatrice replies, "Yes, mine own, sir; in a work of cure, / I'll trust no other" (ll. 80-86). Immediately after this, Beatrice speaks of "angels' food" and gives De Flores money. The scene is an extended metaphor bringing together the conflict between the ideas of perfection on the one hand and moral evil on the other which lies at the heart of the play's dramatic action, while the scene's thematic complexity is increased by the ironic strains that run throughout its pattern of images.

The play's action, its characters, and the patterns of metaphor all move steadily toward the castle.[15] It is from the castle, for example, that Antonio and Franciscus set out in their plan to seduce the wife of Alibius, and it is the castle to which they return. The castle is filled with labyrinths, reflecting the tortuous moral route of the lovers and their internal imperfections. Thus, though the castle is built to withstand physical assault from outside, it is hardly the "most spacious and impregnable fort" (III.i.4) Alonzo declares it to be, a mistake that costs him his life. This same misapprehension causes Vermandero to cry out, "An host of enemies enter'd my citadel / Could not amaze like this" (V.iii.148-49), when he sees his daughter with De

Flores. It is in the castle that the motifs of confinement-liberation, water and voyages, illusion and reality, and perfection and failure culminate. The final vision, despite Alsemero's claim that justice has triumphed, is of a fallen world, a hell that "circumscribes" the characters "here."

Two characters stand out as dramatic embodiments of that vision. One is Tomazo, who repudiates the evidence of the senses entirely, going to the other extreme from Alsemero. Tomazo is reduced to trusting no one; life is a mask which neither reason nor the senses can penetrate:

> All league with mankind I renounce forever
> Till I find this murderer. Not so much
> As common courtesy but I'll lock up,
> For in the state of ignorance I live in
> A brother may salute his brother's murderer
> And wish good speed to th' villain in a greeting.
>
> (V.ii.43-48)

But the more dramatic exponent of that vision is De Flores, a wholly amoral figure who pursues an unwavering course of nihilistic sensualism from beginning to end. He is the one character who never even considers changing, for nothing is of value to him but physical pleasure. With complete conviction he tells Beatrice:

> Thy peace is wrought forever in this yielding.
> 'Las, how the turtle pants! Thou'lt love anon
> What thou so fear'st and faint'st to venture on.
>
> (III.iv.169-71)

He is right; she does "love anon" what she so fears "to venture on." But her peace is not "wrought forever" as he promises; instead, she is led ever deeper into the labyrinth of moral evil, and even death brings images of "howls and gnashings" (V.iii.118) and "wraths / Deeper than mine . . . about 'em" (ll. 195-96). Even De Flores' last words communicate a vision of a world that is meaningless beyond physical pleasure:

> . . . her honor's prize
> Was my reward. I thank life for nothing
> But that pleasure; it was so sweet to me
> That I have drunk up all, left none behind
> For any man to pledge me.

At play's end it is not even certain that Alsemero, who voices conventional wisdom about the triumph of justice and innocence, understands fully his own role in the events. The tragedy concludes on this juxtaposition of the vision of perfection and the triumph of goodness on the one hand, and the reality of pain, death, degradation, evil, and human imperfection on the other, reflected in the complex metaphors of temple, madhouse, and castle.

Notes

1. William Empson, *Some Versions of Pastoral* (London: Chatto & Windus, 1935), pp. 48-52; M.

C. Bradbrook, *Themes and Conventions of Elizabethan Tragedy* (Cambridge: Cambridge Univ. Press, 1935), pp. 213-24.

2. Karl J. Holzknecht, "The Dramatic Structure of *The Changeling,*" *Renaissance Papers,* ed. Albert H. Gilbert (Southeastern Renaissance Conference, 1954), p. 77; Samuel Schoenbaum, *Middleton's Tragedies: A Critical Study* (New York: Columbia Univ. Press, 1955), p. 147; Richard Hindry Barker, *Thomas Middleton* (New York: Columbia Univ. Press, 1958), p. 129.

3. Barker, p. 130.

4. Thus Schoenbaum, who finds both *The Changeling* and *Women Beware Women* "marred by tedious, almost irrelevant subplots involving tiresome and offensive clowns" (p. 103), calls Bradbrook's argument "ingenious rather than convincing" (p. 236, n. 3). Barker agrees, saying that "there is nowhere a suggestion of parallelism that can be described as fundamental or significant" and that "no real unity can be expected from a play in which the tragedy is as brilliant and the comedy as completely contemptible as in this one" (p. 130). Even Empson suggests a contradiction between Swinburne's claim that *The Changeling* is one of the great plays of the age and his conclusion that the subplot is "very stupid, rather coarse, and almost vulgar." Empson, p. 48; A. C. Swinburne, "Introduction," *Thomas Middleton,* ed. Havelock Ellis (New York: Scribner's, 1887), I, xxxv.

5. Christopher Ricks, "The Moral and Poetic Structure of *The Changeling,*" *Essays in Criticism,* 10 (1960), 290-306; George W. Williams, ed., *The Changeling* (Lincoln: University of Nebraska Press, 1966), pp. ix-xxiv. The latter is the edition used for this article.

6. In the face of such a conventional delusion, one cannot help but recall the ideal love expressed in Donne's "A Valediction: Forbidding Mourning," particularly in relation to the image of the circle:

> Such wilt thou be to me, who must
>   Like th' other foot, obliquely run;
> Thy firmness makes my circle just,
>   And makes me end where I begun.

7. See Bradbrook, Ricks, and Williams for more detailed discussions of this motif.

8. The diamond is another of the play's metaphors of perfection; see also II.i.15, where Beatrice speaks of Alsemero as "A true deserver [who] like a diamond sparkles."

9. The mask is an obvious metaphor for deception and disguise and forms a recurrent pattern in the play, as various critics have noted. Ruth Leila

Anderson points out in her early study, *Elizabethan Psychology and Shakespeare's Plays*, Univ. of Iowa Humanistic Studies, Vol. 3, No. 4 (Iowa City: Univ. of Iowa Press, 1927): "According to an important doctrine inherited by the Renaissance from Plato and the medieval psychologists, there should be correspondence between outer lineaments of the body and the nature of the soul: fair features presage a noble mind" (p. 114). Middleton and Rowley's use of this belief is richly ambiguous: though De Flores' features are an index to his soul, the beautiful Beatrice's appearance is wholly deceiving. She appears to understand this concept, for when Alsemero accuses her of being unfaithful, she cries out, "It blasts a beauty to deformity; / Upon what face soever that breath falls / It strikes it ugly" (V.iii.32-34), to which Alsemero replies, "There was a visor / O'er that cunning face and that became you" (ll. 45-46). The passage suggests that Beatrice's violent antipathy toward De Flores is a reaction to her instinctive recognition that his physical appearance is the true mirror of her moral nature.

10. The familiarity of such metaphoric meaning is reflected in, for example, Donne's "Hymn to God my God, in my Sickness."

11. Ironically, Alsemero turns to another "science," music, to woo Beatrice (I.i.62-64). The most telling comment on such romantic word-play is offered by Antonio, who sees that reason and emotion, science and romance, are polar opposites, in his speech beginning "Love has an intellect that runs through all / The scrutinous sciences" (III.iii.122-27). The play's other reference to zodiacal signs, "the sign of Scorpio," occurs at IV.iii.9, in a letter from Franciscus to Isabella charged with metaphors of change, of growth and decay, of creation and destruction.

12. Schoenbaum, for example, calls the test "a ridiculous episode" (p. 147).

13. Anderson, p. 13.

14. Hooker, *Of the Laws of Ecclesiastical Polity*, I.iv.

15. For other interpretations of the thematic function of the castle, see Thomas L. Berger, "The Petrarchan Fortress of *The Changeling*," *Renaissance Papers 1969*, ed. George W. Williams (Southeastern Renaissance Conference, 1970), pp. 37-46; and T. B. Tomlinson, "Poetic Naturalism— *The Changeling*," *JEGP*, 63 (1964), 648-59.

Penelope B. R. Doob (essay date winter 1973)

SOURCE: Doob, Penelope B. R. "A Reading of *The Changeling*." *English Literary Renaissance* 3, no. 1 (winter 1973): 183-206.

[*In the following essay, Doob discusses the theme of madness in* The Changeling, *exploring the issue in the play itself as well as in its cultural context, noting how it is linked to the question of Christian morality.*]

One of the more remarkable features of Jacobean drama is its fascination with every conceivable kind of mental aberration, from the humor-defined characters of Jonson and Ford to the mad morrises of Webster and the Bedlam scenes of Dekker and Middleton. Too often, however, this preoccupation with madness is explained by generalizations about the Jacobean love of spectacle as constituting "the chief motive and the chief characteristic of most of the mad-folk scenes," while the mad characters themselves are seen as "symbolic expressions of human disillusionment" which "both illustrate and reflect the evident skepticism that marked the intellectual thought of the period."[1] Statistically such explanations may be valid, but they tell us little or nothing about the function of madness in a specific play, especially when the play is as brilliant as *The Changeling*.

Although the role of madness in *The Changeling* has often been discussed, its full significance and importance have not been understood. Most critics consider the theme of madness solely in order to attack or defend the subplot: some find it "stupid and tedious," characterized by a "treatment of insanity . . . offensive to the modern reader,"[2] while others view love-madness as an important link between the plots and as a justification of sorts for the horseplay in the asylum.[3] A much broader examination is called for, in which the theme of madness is considered not only throughout the play as a whole but also in its cultural context. Both in the play and in Jacobean thought, madness is intimately linked to a cluster of ideas including bestiality, blindness, deformity, lust, and the dominance of will over reason. Only when madness is properly seen in relation to these other ideas can the play be fully understood; and only an appreciation of the traditional symbolism of madness and related concepts can illuminate many aspects of the play—the imitation of the Fall in the main plot, the role of the subplot, the significance of the virginity test, and the meaning of the diamond ring given to Alonzo and then to De Flores. Seen from this point of view, *The Changeling* is a symbolic morality play at least as much as it is a naturalistic tragedy, and its psychological concerns are those of the moralist rather than of the unbiased observer of human nature.

Many critics have noted the play's dependence on key words (e.g., blood, eyesight) and images (the castle, transformation).[4] What has not been discussed, however, is the fact that many key words and images— blindness, deformity, bestiality, lust, madness, reason, will, judgment—form a large and important lexical set that dominates both poetic and visual aspects of the play. Specific examples of these words and concepts are unnecessary here; they can be found on virtually any page of the play, and many will be discussed later. What is important now is the concept that unites this lexical set, a concept crucial to the meaning of the play: it is the idea of sin—its causes, mechanisms, and consequences. It is my contention that madness, deformity, bestiality, and related ideas are important in ***The Changeling*** primarily in that they illustrate, literally or metaphorically, the workings of sin, and that the play is about the terrible madness of sin, not merely the madness of love.

The relationship of each idea to others in this cluster will be discussed, implicitly or explicitly, throughout this essay; but a brief explanation of the theoretical interrelationships is desirable before we look at specifics. Traditionally, sin consists in turning away from God, in violating divine order by desiring something that God has forbidden but that seems good to the sinner.[5] Psychologically, the sinner's will and passions overrule his reason or, even worse, pervert reason so that both will and reason assent to sin. As a result, the due order and hierarchy of the mental faculties are overturned, as Chaucer notes: "God sholde have lordshipe over resoun, and resoun over sensualitee [will and/or the sensitive appetite], and sensualitee over the body of man. But soothly, when man synneth, al this ordre or ordinaunce is turned up-so-doun."[6] In other words, passion or will rules reason or judgment; the sinner ceases (temporarily, at least) to be reasonable; and consequently he may be considered mad, for madness too is a state in which reason does not function and passions dominate. Robert Burton, like most Renaissance moral psychologists, describes all sins as forms of madness which render the sinner akin to unreasonable beasts: "All men are carried away with passion, discontent, lust, pleasures, etc.; they generally hate the virtues they should love, and love such vices they should hate. Therefore more than melancholy, quite mad, brute beasts, and void of reason. . . ."[7] The sinner's madness, then, is real, not metaphorical, although it may last only so long as the act of sin, after which reason may again assert itself. But persistence in unreason and sin leads almost inevitably to permanent madness, bestiality, and disease: "we, as long as we are ruled by reason, correct our inordinate appetite, and conform ourselves to God's word, are as so many living saints: but if we give reins to lust, anger, ambition, pride, and follow our own ways, we degenerate into beasts, transform ourselves, overthrow our constitutions, provoke God to anger, and heap upon us this [affliction] of *Melancholy,* and all kinds of incurable diseases, as a just and deserved punishment of our sins" (Burton, pp. 118-19). Madness is not only one way of describing the psychological state of the sinner, it is also a devastating and appropriate punishment for continual sin. And, taken metaphorically or literally, it describes us all, whether we seem mad to observers or not: "Ask not with him in the Poet, What madness ghosts this old man, but what madness ghosts us all? For we are all mad, not once, but always so, & ever and altogether as bad as he . . ." (Burton, p. 36). Thus

sin leads to madness and bestiality, states that share the rule of passion and will and the subjugation or loss of reason. In this state of sin and madness, a man is blind in understanding if not in physical eyesight, for "that vision of eternal things is withdrawn . . . so that the light of his eyes is gone from him."[8] And he is also deformed in the etymological sense of that word: man was made in the image or form of God in that his soul had three faculties (understanding, will, memory) echoing the Trinity; but in sin the understanding or reason is suppressed or perverted and will usurps the rule, so that man is changed from the image of God and deformed.[9] Thus the cluster of ideas dominant in ***The Changeling***—madness, blindness, deformity, bestiality, will, reason—may all be related to the process and consequences of sin. That they are so related in the play will be demonstrated throughout the rest of this essay, which follows Helen Gardner's lead in considering ***The Changeling*** as a play set firmly in the context of orthodox Christianity, as a "tragedy of damnation."[10]

I. The Main Plot: Madness, Will, and the Imitation of the Fall

Although images of madness in the play are most flagrantly present in the subplot, Middleton places considerable emphasis on unreason, sin, and even madness in the main plot, which is, as Bawcutt has noted, "basically a study in sin and retribution, expressed in terms of sexual relationships" (p. xlv). All the characters are shown to have dominant and often unreasonable wills;[11] every action in the play that leads to tragedy is the product of a will that has mastered reason. Thus Alsemero's desire for Beatrice keeps him in Alicante despite favorable winds for Malta (in the source, Reynolds' *God's Revenge Against Murder,* bad winds force Alsemero to stay), and he describes his "eyes" (senses, passions) as having influenced his decision (I.i.76-77). Jasperino's overtly sexual desire for Diaphanta leads to that friendship which will prove so fatal to Beatrice. It is Beatrice's "peevish will" that makes her hate De Flores, although she has no "other reason" for it (I.i.107, 110), and that irrational hatred inspires her to employ him in the murder of Alonzo. Alsemero's similar "frailty" (I.i.116) causes him to hate cherries for little more reason than he loves Beatrice. Vermandero insists that Beatrice obey his "will" (I.i.220) and wed Alonzo, while Alonzo's desire for Beatrice prevents him from seeing the dislike his more clear-sighted brother Tomazo notices. These examples could be multiplied many times over, but it should be clear that the unfettered will is the cause of strife in every character and in every phase of the action. The vocabulary of the play does not let us forget the conflict between will and reason for a minute, and the significance of this conflict can be measured by the possible outcomes. If reason wins, one has acted virtuously; if will is victor, temporary madness results; but if the perverted reason assents to the evil desires of the will, one has committed mortal sin. Since Isabella is the only person whose will and passions are completely governed by reason, all save her are sinners, temporarily mad, irrational, deprived of the image of God, blind.[12]

But some characters are worse than others; although almost everyone is moved by passion rather than reason, only Beatrice and De Flores give conscious assent to their passions' perversion of their reason and plan crime after crime to further the demands of their sensuality. Joined together initially by passion—by De Flores' hopeless lust and Beatrice's violent and unreasonable aversion to him—the two grow together in coldblooded and voluntary sin, and in that perversion of reason and exaltation of passion lies their downfall and their moral insanity.

Ironically, the willful and imperious Beatrice, in choosing to murder Alonzo, also chooses to lose much of her freedom of action, and therein lies much of her tragedy. As T. S. Eliot noted, "what constitutes the essence of the tragedy is something which has not been sufficiently remarked; it is the *habituation* of Beatrice to her sin; it becomes no longer merely sin but custom."[13] Habituation is the third step in Beatrice's degradation: the first was her tendency to permit will to dominate reason by convincing herself that her desires were reasonable, and the second was instigating Alonzo's death. Now, since "a sin that is not quickly blotted out by repentance is both a sin and a cause of sin,"[14] she is a slave to further sin—fornication, adultery, deception, another murder. One thing leads to another in devious but seemingly inevitable ways, and it is hard for us at any point to remember that she, like Faustus, could presumably stop the process by confessing her sins. The habit is too deeply entrenched for that, as De Flores notes in a grossly sexual image: once a woman sins, "She spreads and mounts then like arithmetic" (II.ii.62), and Alsemero, hearing of her adultery after the murder, comments, "It could not choose but follow" (V.iii.108). By her sins, then, Beatrice submits to the power of fate and the logic of sin. When she substitutes Diaphanta for herself, she claims, "Necessity compels it; I lose all else" (IV.ii.124). And at her death, she complains,

> Beneath the stars, upon yon meteor
> Ever hung my fate, 'mongst things corruptible;
> I ne'er could pluck it from him: my loathing
> Was prophet to the rest, but ne'er believed. . . .
>
> (V.iii.154-57)

Such, it would seem, is tragic inevitability, but we must not be wholly taken in by it. Just as Beatrice could have stopped the spiral into degradation by repenting, so she could have kept herself out of the grip of fate: "*The wise man is stronger than the stars,* inasmuch as, namely, he conquers his passions."[15] But even here

Beatrice is blind, her flair for tragic gesture overcoming reason. She alone is responsible for her downfall, but even in death, when she clearly sees her own corruption, she does not recognize that responsibility. The independent spirit who initially prides herself on the excellence of her reason, on seeing "with the eyes of judgment" (II.i.13), finally prefers to see herself as the victim of circumstances, and this lack of true vision is the most pitiful thing about her. She has chosen sin, unreason, entanglement; even with all exposed, she denies her freedom of action and refuses to accept full blame for her deeds. She fails even at being a tragic heroine, and at last she is seen in her true spiritual depravity: her sin "blasts a beauty to deformity" (V.iii.32). She has been spiritually akin to De Flores all along, and at last her spiritual ugliness matches De Flores' physical repulsiveness. It is a measure of Alsemero's and Vermandero's relative sanity that they can at last see her as she is; their reason finally triumphs, permitting them to see accurately, to denounce her as a monster, to realize that denial of the image of God by sinning can result only in deformity and a kind of madness.

The fall of Beatrice is terrible enough in its own right, but Middleton is not content to let us rest with this specific instance of sin and retribution. So that we may fully understand the dreadful consequences of unreason in the fallen world, he expands her fall metaphorically to include us all in two ways: he juxtaposes her degradation and moral insanity to the follies of the madhouse in the subplot, as we shall see shortly; and he introduces a range of imagery which places her fall in the context of the Fall of Man, thereby suggesting that the action is, in a limited sense, a reenactment of that archetypal fall which first brought sin and madness into the world.[16] The significant parallels to the Fall story lie in two areas: first, Alsemero's quest for ideal love in marriage is compared to an attempt to regain Paradise; second, the relationship between Beatrice and De Flores is shown as analogous to that of Eve and the serpent. I should like to examine some of these parallels and their meaning in the play.[17]

In the first act, and indeed throughout much of the play, Alsemero appears as a moon-struck lover in the Petrarchan mode, a man who believes that marriage "admits comparison / With man's first creation, the place blest, / And is his right home back, if he achieve it" (I.i.7-9). In his quest for Paradise, Alsemero goes to the castle, described by Vermandero in terms somewhat reminiscent of Eden:

> we use not to give survey
> Of our chief strengths to strangers; our citadels
> Are plac'd conspicuous to outward view,
> On promonts' tops; but within are secrets.
>
> (I.i.163-66)

A walled enclosure on a mountain top, its contents secret, barred to strangers—this is Eden from the outside, from the point of view of postlapsarian man. If Alsemero can get in, the castle cannot be Eden, and the marriage he can find there will not be paradisal. Alsemero's idealism, as revealed in the first scene, is folly. Burton acknowledges the possibility of "honest love," a special kind of matrimonial love that is "a blessed calling, appointed by God himself in Paradise" (p. 654); but he knows that such love is extremely rare: usually "this love of ours is immoderate, inordinate, and not to be comprehended in any bounds . . ." (p. 655), "this mad and beastly passion" (p. 657). Thanks to the Fall, most love now is lust, "mad and beastly," and it is this sort of love that Alsemero will find despite his idealism, despite the fact that he is too deluded by love to see its danger until the end.[18]

Eventually Alsemero becomes suspicious of Beatrice's relationship to De Flores, and Jasperino suggests her fall in significant terms: "The prospect from the garden has show'd / Enough for deep suspicion" (V.iii.2-3). Alsemero is furious, exclaiming as Adam might have done, "Did my fate wait for this unhappy stroke / At my first sight of woman?" (V.iii.12-13). But unlike Adam, he is not again seduced by Eve; although Beatrice claims that her crimes have been for him, even to the extent of kissing poison and stroking a serpent (V.iii.66), he denounces both the murder of Alonzo and her later crimes. The emergent reason of Adam casts off the sin of Eve, thereby preparing us for a partially happy ending. In words that bring to mind the banishment of Adam and Eve from the ground of Eden and God's words to the serpent that Eve's heel should bruise his head (see Gen. 3.15 and 17), Alsemero responds to Beatrice's query "Show me the ground whereon you lost your love,"

> Unanswerable!
> A ground you cannot stand on: you fall down
> Beneath all grace and goodness, when you set
> Your ticklish heel on't. . . .
>
> (V.iii.43-46)

Despite his temporary blindness of love for Beatrice, Alsemero's reason conquers and he damns Beatrice and De Flores utterly. He learns that lust is not love, that his Beatrice is not Dante's, that marriage is not Paradise regained. Although the play starts with reminiscences of Eden, it ends in hell (V.iii.163-64), and the marriage which was to re-create Paradise is a mockery.[19]

If Alsemero's experience teaches us to overcome the consequences of the Fall by avoiding the delusion that lust is love and by asserting the power of reason, the relationship of Beatrice and De Flores provides a negative example by demonstrating how, thanks to Eve, Beatrice and all the rest of us can reenact the Fall in

our own lives. In the first scene, Beatrice refers to De Flores as poison, a basilisk, a serpent—all images associated with the devil; in later scenes, she experiences the truth behind those images and indeed becomes a sort of basilisk and poison herself (III.iv.152-53 and V.iii.149-51). Although she realizes that "the ugliest creature / Creation fram'd for some use" (II.ii.43-44), she fails to draw the obvious conclusion—that even the devil serves God's purpose in tempting—and prefers instead to use De Flores for her own purpose as "poison, / . . . one to expel another" (II.ii.46-47). When the deed is done, she learns that bloody instructions return to plague the inventor; she claims immunity by chastity and birth, but De Flores reminds her that one is what one has done:

BEATRICE:

> Think but upon the distance that creation
> Set 'twixt thy blood and mine, and keep thee there.

DE FLORES:

> Look but in your conscience, read me there,
> 'Tis a true book, you'll find me there your equal:
> Push, fly not to your birth, but settle you
> In what the act has made you, y'are no more now;
> You must forget your parentage to me:
> Y'are the deed's creature; by that name
> You lost your first condition, and I challenge you,
> As peace and innocency has turn'd you out,
> And made you one with me.
>
> (III.iv.130-39)

The speech could have been made by Satan to Eve. The imagery is loaded: by his first parentage, man is the fallen child of Adam and Eve, and his first conscious sin confirms that identity beyond all denial; saintliness and nobility come from deeds, not from birth, and by her deeds Beatrice has made herself De Flores' equal. His desire for her is no longer presumption, nor can he be accused of pulling her down from her former (rather tenuous) elevation. She has fallen of her own free will, and she must pay the price: virginity, symbol of a spiritual purity she has never had in the play. The action here mimics that of Jewish legend: Eve must copulate with the serpent.[20] And that act perverts her beyond all reckoning. Although she continues to give lip service to her love for Alsemero, she has once again changed her saint, and her avowed love for him is really fear: she dreads what she supposes to be his clear judgment, she spies on him, she tries to hide her loss of virginity just as Eve tried to hide her nakedness from God. She has tasted the apple poisoned by lust, and she now loves De Flores: "His face loathes one, / But look upon his care, who would not love him? / The east is not more beauteous than his service" (V.i.70-72). If the East may be associated with sunrise, Christ, and Eden, Beatrice has come a long way. The serpent-devil whom she shunned at the start has become an angel of light, a kind of Lucifer, ironically at the very moment when he is setting fire to the castle in an act symbolic of arousing lust and passion. In her perversion of values, Beatrice is like Faustus, another whom sin had reduced to utter depravity, to whom the pageant of the Seven Deadly Sins was "as pleasing vnto me, / As paradise was to *Adam,* the first day / Of his creation."[21]

Yet she betrays De Flores in the end, as one might expect from Chaucer's comments on the lustful: "And the lovynge children, that whilom loveden so flesshly everich oother, wolden everich of hem eten oother if they myghte. . . . For truste wel, hir flesshly love was deedly hate . . ." (CT x. 201, 203). The love that is lust cannot last in hell, and hell is precisely where we are in the last scene. Beatrice's betrayal and shifting of blame to De Flores (V.iii.154-57, cited above), of course, echoes Eve's blaming the serpent. Like Eve, Beatrice is not denying that she has sinned, but she is trying to reject the punishment due her, and this is the traditional ninth and greatest folly of Eve: "But it is a worse and more damnable pride which casts about for the shelter of an excuse even in manifest sins. . . . Here there is no word of begging pardon, no word of entreaty for healing. For though they [Adam and Eve] do not, like Cain, deny that they have perpetrated the deed, yet their pride seeks to refer its wickedness to another—the woman's pride to the serpent, the man's to the woman."[22] In the moments before her death, Beatrice is one of those who "telle it not in as foule wise as they do it, and ar shamed to saye it, but thei be not shamed to do it; and therfor thei be lyke Eue that wolde haue excused her."[23]

There is, of course, one very important difference between Eve and Beatrice: a willful and selfish girl, Beatrice is hardly an innocent at the start of the play, and De Flores is no devil, although many critics seem to think he is. Thus Barker finds him a "monster," Schoenbaum describes him as "a study in abnormal sexuality," and even Bradbrook thinks that he arouses a "natural antipathy" among the good people in the play.[24] Yet it is De Flores who has a conscience, who appreciates the enormity of murder for pay (III.iv.64-67), who feels his own guilt and who is willing to accept blame at the end. It is almost always Beatrice who casts him as poison, the serpent, the basilisk, the viper (see, for example, I.i.112, 115, 225; III.iv.166; V.iii.66). And her judgment is hardly objective. She seems to see herself as Eve, as the tragic victim of diabolical evil, and she does quite a good job of convincing readers to see her in the same light and to forget that in reality she leads De Flores into murder, that he does not tempt her. Beatrice shirks the issue of responsibility, but I think that Middleton does not; surely Alsemero feels no pity for the woman who led herself into temptation.

These reminiscences of the Fall pattern in the play serve a number of important functions. I have already suggested that Alsemero's role as a kind of Adam points both to the absurdity of sexual idealism and to the possibility of qualified optimism in a postlapsarian world where, no matter what Beatrice thinks, we are not doomed to repeat Adam's mistakes. The lesson we learn from Beatrice is less hopeful, for she falls even lower than Eve in that she herself is the instrument of her own temptation and fall. In placing her fall so firmly in the context of the Fall of Man, Middleton is reminding us that we too are changelings, fallen substitutes for what man should have been, and he is warning us against enacting a similar fall in our own lives. Finally, the Fall pattern of the play seems to me to serve an aesthetic as well as a moral function. As Robert Jordan has suggested, we should perhaps look for a "mythic and poetic pattern that may do more to build the play's haunting power than any amount of psychology" (p. 157). But where he would find the most important pattern to be an ironic reversal of the "Beauty and the Beast" pattern—"Instead of the beast being revealed as a prince, the process of this story is to reveal that the princess is in fact a beast" (p. 165)—I would argue that the pattern which gives so much power and vitality to the play is that of the Fall, a pattern which undergoes a double reversal in order to give the play its oddly optimistic/pessimistic ending.

II. THE MORAL SETTING: MADNESS

Beatrice seems to see her own fall as tragic, but her vision is not to be trusted. Lest she take us in completely, her potentially tragic stature must be reduced, and we must see the stupidity and grotesqueness of her actions clearly. We must also be forced to see that Beatrice is not alone, that there are many of us just as sinful, and that there are some who can withstand temptation. The main plot, largely tragic and serious, nevertheless has occasional comic and optimistic overtones; and these overtones are reinforced in the subplot.[25] The madhouse is the very picture of what the world has become since the Fall, and the contrast between castle and asylum emphasizes Beatrice's degradation by showing that even the maddest people are not so fatally mad as she and that a woman with much less theoretical nobility to fall back on can be much more successful in avoiding disaster.

The subplot is one of the most maligned parts of the play, yet many critics have found important connections between the plots, both in theme and action.[26] Empson rightly comments that "the madhouse dominates every scene; every irony refers back to it" (p. 49). He and others consider the subplot a kind of antimasque to the main plot, and Bradbrook adds that the subplot shows the relationship between love and madness which is only implied in the main plot (p. 214). According to Bawcutt, "one of the functions of the sub-plot is to enable the audience to grasp the essential themes of the main plot—the madness of love, the deceptiveness of appearances, the transformations men and women undergo through love—by isolating and enlarging them to the point of literalness" (p. lxvii). I think all these observations are valid, but I would like to go a little farther and be a little more explicit.

Ekeblad has said that the masque in *The Duchess of Malfi,* unlike most antimasques which are intended to show the coherence of the masque proper, "acts as an ideograph of the *dis*-unity, the *in*-coherence, of the Duchess's world."[27] Similarly, the subplot in **The Changeling** is an extension of the confusion of the main plot on the literal level, but on the moral level it is an equivalent to the world of the main plot—or rather, it is not a strict equivalent, for the morality of the subplot characters is preferable to that of Beatrice and De Flores. In one sense, too, the madhouse is the product of the world of the castle when the castle is taken as a parody of Eden, for original sin, reenacted by Beatrice, caused all earthly madness and disease. As Burton notes, "the impulsive cause of these miseries in man, this privation or destruction of God's image, the cause of death and diseases, of all temporal and eternal punishments, was the sin of our first parent Adam" (p. 114). Madness and folly are always the product of original or actual sin, and the sinner, to the extent that he has forfeited his reason, is as bestial and mad as any of Alibius' inmates. Again according to Burton, "last of all, that which crucifies us most, is our own folly, madness (Whom Jupiter would destroy, he first drives mad; by subtraction of his assisting grace God permits it), weakness, want of government, our facility and proneness in yielding to several lusts, in giving way to every passion and perturbation of the mind: by which means we metamorphose ourselves, and degenerate into beasts" (p. 118). And as for folly—for in the long run folly is equated with madness—

MANKIND:

    Folly! What thing callest thou folly?

CONSCIENCE:

    Sir, it is pride, wrath, and envy,
    Sloth, covetise, and gluttony,
    Lechery the seventh is:
    Those seven sins I call folly.[28]

Folly and madness, then, are ideal metaphors for sin and its effects. Yet there is a difference between literal madness and sin, and here the madhouse shows its superiority. As we have seen, mortal sin demands that reason be perverted by and consent to the will and its desires. In true madmen and fools, however, reason is so deficient or passion so very strong that all use of reason is impossible; although the passionate madman is responsible for having become mad—he let passion get the better of him—neither madmen nor fools are responsible for acts committed in their state of unreason.[29] To put it another way, all sinners are mad, but all madmen are not sinners. We cannot determine the moral status of the truly mad, but clearly the feigned madmen, Antonio and Franciscus, leave something to be desired. Yet they are finally cured by Isabella's good sense, which frees them from their debilitating lust and allows them once more to be reasonable and even to gain considerable self-knowledge. The real fool is Beatrice— "For what can be more mad, than for a little worldly pleasure to procure unto themselves eternal punishment?"[30]

A Jacobean audience, confronted with the many literal and metaphorical uses of folly in the play, might recall familiar biblical passages that both illuminate the moral significance of Beatrice's folly within the Christian framework and hint that some degree of folly is almost inevitable (although not therefore excusable) in this world. Considering Beatrice's willfulness, a spectator might remember Prov. 12.15, "The way of a fool is right in his own eyes; but he that hearkeneth unto counsel is wise." Her disobedience to her father might suggest Prov. 15.5, "A fool despiseth his father's instructions: but he that regardeth reproof is prudent." As for the probability that one sin will lead to another, "As a dog returneth to his vomit, so a fool returneth to his folly" (Prov. 26.11). Beatrice's spiritual deformity, linking her with the mad chorus, would call to mind Psal. 73.22, "So foolish was I, and ignorant: I was as a beast before thee"; and her presumption that she can disregard the strictures of conventional morality to get what she wants allies her with the fool in Psal. 14.1 who "hath said in his heart, There is no God. They are corrupt, they have done abominable works, there is none that doeth good." Such behavior has appropriate consequences in the Bible: Deut. 28.28 threatens the disobedient, "The Lord shall smite thee with madness, and blindness, and astonishment of heart." In this cultural context, Beatrice's folly would be seen clearly as mortal sin, and it would be obvious that Lollio's pronouncement, which includes us as well as Beatrice, is more than a joke:

ISABELLA:

    Why, here's none but fools and madmen.

LOLLIO:

    Very well: and where will you find any other, if
    you should go abroad?

                   (III.iii.15-17)

Middleton and Burton would probably agree on the aim of their depictions of madness: "To conclude, this being granted, that all the world is melancholy, or mad, dotes, and every member of it, I have ended my task, and sufficiently illustrated that which I took upon me to demonstrate at first" (Burton, p. 101).

Many of the moral characteristics of the sinner become visible in the subplot. In the main plot, will and sensuality dominate reason; here, will becomes explicitly sexual desire, and lust, traditionally the most irrational and bestial mental state, is overtly the mainspring of the action. And the central episode, iconographically speaking, is the chorus of madmen as birds and beasts. Pedro diagnoses the ills of the whole establishment—indeed of the whole play-world—when he mentions that Antonio's reason is the "sick and weak part of nature in him" (I.ii.87-88). The deformity and bestiality of sin is vividly imaged: Franciscus stoops to be ridden before being sent back to his "kennel," and the chorus and morris of madmen as beasts could be singularly effective when staged. Other parallels between the workings of sin and the workings of folly suggest themselves: the lies and stratagems of Beatrice are echoed by the plots of the lustful Antonio and Franciscus, and Beatrice's feigning of virtue and virginity for evil ends is contrasted with Isabella's feigning of madness for good ends (to rid herself of Antonio). Antonio claims that "This shape of folly shrouds your dearest love" (III.iii.119), while Beatrice hides her folly under the appearance of love for Alsemero. Antonio is terrified by the apparent madness of Isabella (IV.iii) but Beatrice is not sufficiently terrified of moral depravity when she sees its outward deformity in De Flores.

The most important comment the subplot makes on the main plot, as several critics have recognized, is the spontaneous appearance of the madmen as birds and beasts. Isabella describes them pointedly:

> Yet are they but our school of lunatics,
> That act their fantasies in any shapes
> Suiting their present thoughts; if sad, they cry;
> If mirth be their conceit, they laugh again;
> Sometimes they imitate the beasts and birds,
> Singing, or howling, braying, barking; all
> As their wild fancies prompt 'em.
>
> (III.iii.192-98)

This is, certainly, "a symbolic presentation of the bestiality that is released when human actions cease to be governed by reason and sanity," as Bawcutt says (p. lxvii). But, more important, as *reductio ad bestiam,* it is a portrait of man not in God's image, of what men do to their souls when they sin, as Thomas Nashe points out in a different context:

> If wee had the witte to conceiue the basenesse of sinne . . . we would hate it as a Toade, and flye from it as an Adder. Not without reason haue manie learned Wryters called it Bestiall, for it is all deriued & borrowed from Beastes. Pride and inflamation of hart we borrow from the Lyon, auarice from the Hedghog. . . . So that as wee apparraile our selues in Beastes skinnes, in selfe same sorte we clothe our soules in theyr sinnes. . . . Let vs not glory that wee are men, who haue put on the shapes of Beastes. . . . Woe vnto vs,

we shall, if wee appeare to God in the image of beastes, and soone redeeme not from sathan the image of our creation he hath stolne from vs.[31]

Isabella knows enough to fly from such beasts, to maintain her "image of creation," but Beatrice, lacking in moral wit, embraces De Flores even though she sees him as toad and adder. The beasts are controlled in the madhouse, but the sinners they represent roam at large in the main plot. As Empson notes, Isabella is sane compared to the tragic characters (or indeed to anyone else in the play): "living among madmen she sees the need to be" (p. 50). Beatrice may feel controlled by fate, but Isabella knows the necessity of choice, and therein lies her superiority.

Superficially, the world of the madhouse is alien to ours, while the castle is more realistic. But the fact that all the main characters in the madhouse plot are capable of being reformed suggests that we would do better to think of the madhouse as our world, or rather to see our world as a madhouse, if only so that *we* see the need to be sane. And perhaps that is why the mad morris is never performed in the castle: the world has become so much madder in a moral sense than the asylum that there is no need for a traditional antimasque. The antimasque might seem astonishingly coherent beside the wedding it is to celebrate.

III. Iconography: The Virginity Test

If anything in **The Changeling** causes critics more problems than the subplot, surely it is the virginity test in IV.ii. Schoenbaum speaks for the majority in finding it "preposterous" (p. 145), but Bradbrook feels that it is "not out of place, for it belongs with the 'omens' and other irrational elements rather than with the naturalism of character" (p. 220); and Thomson thinks it shows the inadequacy of the relationship between Beatrice and Alsemero (p. xxv). Although Bawcutt assumes that "the fantastic nature of the virginity test makes us wonder whether Middleton himself took it very seriously," he pardons it "as symbolic of the kind of problem Beatrice has constantly to face now that she has committed herself to evil" (p. lvii). Even Jasperino is puzzled: he finds it "the strangest trick to know a maid by" (IV.ii.142), and it seems likely that a Jacobean audience would have agreed with him. What, then, is the virginity test doing in the play? Like the subplot, it was added to the bones of the plot taken from Reynolds, and thus its inclusion should have some importance.[32]

It is understandable that most critics, like Jasperino, have been troubled by the virginity test when it is considered realistically in the context of what many people see as a highly naturalistic psychological drama. But our examination of madness, bestiality, and related concepts in the play has shown that Middleton often uses moral symbolism, and he may be doing so here as well. Seen emblematically, the scene loses many of its difficulties and achieves marked significance. Two aspects of the scene are striking: first, the actions that Beatrice must feign—gaping, sneezing, and violent laughter—are extremely grotesque and ugly; second, they are potentially quite comic. That her actions should be grotesque is peculiarly appropriate. If all human dignity comes from the imitation of God and the maintenance of his image, such grotesquerie reminds us that although Beatrice may try to be a tragic and heroic figure, she is a sinner, and moral deformity traditionally makes itself evident physically. As for the comedy (a comedy admittedly qualified somewhat by the dramatic tension of the scene), it lies partly in the inherently ridiculous nature of the normally involuntary actions she imitates. Modern readers and audiences perhaps find such comedy of deformity tasteless; with our romantic visions of evil and our predilection for uniformly tragic or uniformly comic characters, we posit a hack's hand in the scenes where Faustus is degraded and comic, and we sympathize with Satan in *Paradise Lost,* failing to appreciate the comedy of the "sense of injur'd merit" and of Satan's transformation into a serpent.[33] Just so we are offended by the indignity that Beatrice suffers in the virginity test. But the Middle Ages and Renaissance had quite different notions, as the abundance of absurd vice figures, devils, and madmen on the stage testify. In many cases, vice and the deformity it causes in a figure or action seem to have been favorite butts of laughter.[34] Following the precedent of his namesake Democritus, Burton claims, "Never so much cause of laughter as now, never so many fools and mad-men" (p. 42). The point is not that incapacity is funny or that evil is ridiculous, but that madmen and fools who are what they are through their own sins are absurd. The assumption is that, had they lived better lives, they would be less deformed, less incapacitated, less comic. One may justly laugh at the perpetrators of both human follies and crimes to the extent that the doer's own deeds reduce his stature and make him ridiculous. To appreciate *The Changeling,* we must accept the ideas that self-induced deformity is funny and that comedy and tragedy can coexist in the same plot, let alone in the same play. The virginity test then, is appropriately funny, partly because of the nature of the actions themselves and partly because Beatrice *wills* to imitate them—in fact, she studies them so that she can mimic them the better. The actions and her imitation of them are involuntary, mechanical; and this is fitting because she is trapped in the habit of sin, she chooses to submit to the rule of necessity, as we have seen.

The virginity test is a fitting come-down for a woman of so imperious a will, but it is also sad and ironic: deprived of the image of God in her soul, she is forced to feign absurd actions as mad as any in the subplot to delude others into thinking she has retained her purity.

She feigns sanity and wholesomeness as Franciscus and Antonio feign madness. This is another link between subplot and main plot, but here the main plot comes out the madder; the two plots are initially widely separated on a scale of seriousness, morality, and sanity, but by Act IV the plots have come together with the main plot about to sink below the subplot. Beatrice's actions are for an evil purpose, and they are both funnier and more horrible than, say, the masque of birds and beasts. And Alsemero's blindness in believing Beatrice's feigning—for many Jacobeans would have thought his trust in the test to be ludicrous[35]—is emphasized in the following scene by Isabella's first words: "O heaven! Is this the waiting moon? / Does love turn fool, run mad, and all at once?" (IV.iii.1-2). The audience would surely have applied her lines to what they had just witnessed. In the following madhouse scene, the madness of love is a major subject, and we are certainly tempted to apply all Isabella's sane comments to the main plot and particularly to the scene just ended. The parallels between the scenes become even more obvious when Isabella disguises herself as a madwoman, recapitulating Beatrice's antic feigning of virginity (in which the gaping and violent laughter are, after all, not far removed from the asylum). Yet while Beatrice tries to deceive her lover, Isabella tries to cure hers by teaching that lust is madness and lovers are notoriously shortsighted. Antonio loves Isabella's raiment, not Isabella; Alsemero loves Beatrice for feigning virginity, not for what she is.

The virginity test, then, functions on a symbolic and moral level. It is particularly appropriate to an orthodox tragedy of sin, for it recapitulates in the main plot what the madmen's chorus of beasts signifies in the subplot, that lust and irrationality are sin and deformity. And it serves the dramatic function of alienating our sympathies from Beatrice, whom we should view here with some degree of comic detachment; we are thus prepared for the emergence of Isabella as the example of excellence and for the moderately happy ending.

IV. ICONOGRAPHY: THE DIAMOND RING

If we think of *The Changeling* as a play *to be staged,* several events would clearly have an exceptional visual impact—the double appearance of the madmen as beasts and birds, the twice-repeated virginity test, and the moments when De Flores chops off Alonzo's finger, when he presents the finger to Beatrice with the diamond ring she had given still on it, and when the ghost of Alonzo appears to De Flores at the beginning of Act IV, accusingly showing his mutilated hand. Several critics have commented on the importance of the finger-ring-glove images in the play, pointing particularly to the sexual symbolism involved and to the frequency of jewel lexis in the play.[36] But more remains to be said on the function of the ring and especially on the significance of the diamond set in it. Like the virginity test and the subplot, the incident of the ring is not found in the sources of the play, and it was added for good reason.

An examination of the significance of the diamond as a precious gem should help to clarify that reason. Of course, it must be admitted that few specific properties are mentioned in the text, but lapidary lore was popular in the period and it seems quite likely that Middleton was familiar with the stone's better-known qualities. In any case, a reading of the lapidaries adds irony upon irony to the play.[37] For instance, the diamond was supposed to protect its wearer from poison, devils, serpents, wild beasts, strife, and sorrow; but such powers are of little help to Alonzo against the poisonous viper De Flores. Diamonds were thought to keep a man's limbs whole, but the very finger wearing this diamond is not protected. As for the stone's vaunted powers against lechery, illusion, and madness, here too it fails: Alonzo is an exceptionally foolish victim of "love's tame madness" (II.i.154). Burton notes that some say "a Diamond hath excellent virtue, to reconcile men and wives, to maintain unity and love" (p. 865)—another property that applies only ironically to Alonzo and Beatrice, though it might fit the relationship of Beatrice and De Flores more accurately. Alonzo's problem may be his own fault, however: the North Midland Lapidary notes that "Hym behoues for to be of holy lyfe that so vertus a ston wyll ber," that only the chaste owner, the man with "gud belefe" (presumably in God), benefits from the powers of the diamond. And Mandeville comments, "it befalleth often tyme that the gode dyamand leseth his vertue be synne and for incontynence of him that bereth it, and thanne is it nedfulle to make it recoueren his vertue ayen, or elles it is of litille value." A fifteenth-century English manuscript explains the stone's potential loss of power still more significantly: with the Fall, all gems lost much of their virtue, and those owned by sinners lose all unless restored by a special ritual that cleanses jewels as penance cleanses souls.[38] Perhaps Alonzo's diamond is of little value not only because of his own faults but also because of the woman who gave it. Both gem and lady appear to be of far greater worth than they are; both may be tainted by sin and in need of restoration.

Perhaps we are on surer ground in examining the significance of the diamond in contemporary drama. In *The Jew of Malta,* Abigail is compared to a diamond, never foiled; the stone here clearly signifies chastity, purity, and excellence which does not need artificial aid (a foil) to make it seem better than it is. In *The White Devil,* Vittoria, defending her chastity, states that her innocence will appear in the house of convertites: "Through darkenesse Diamonds spred their ritchest light."[39] The reference is to the legend that diamonds are found in India at night by their brilliance in darkness, and the traditional symbolic interpretation of this observation is that the diamond signifies moral excel-

Thomas Middleton

lence shining among sinners or even that it represents Christ.[40] Most important is the evidence from *Cymbeline,* I.iv: Posthumus compares Imogen to his diamond ring, stating that she is more valuable than it because she is won by grace rather than by money or merit. His wager with Iachimo risks his ring against Imogen's chastity; the diamond clearly signifies chastity and virtue, and the ring itself has the sexual connotations found also in *The Changeling.* All these meanings of the diamond function in *The Changeling,* where the stone symbolizes Beatrice's chastity and apparent worth until these are undercut by her deeds and by her gift of the ring to De Flores.

As for the development of the diamond ring's significance in the play, the first act suggests the sexual symbolism of the ring (I.ii.27-31) and the second act establishes the equation of the diamond with virtue as Beatrice cites the proverb Vittoria had used: "A true deserver like a diamond sparkles, / In darkness you may see him, that's in absence . . ." (II.i.15-16). In the third act, the sexual connotations of the ring are fused with the ethical connotations of the diamond, and the result is the grotesque image of the severed phallus-finger joined to the ring whose stone signifies chastity. The diamond, like the "true deserver," sparkles in the darkness (III.ii.20-22), and the result is that the once-favored deserver is mutilated; if the diamond fails to protect him, perhaps its symbolism of chastity and worth is questionable. In any case, the sacred bonds of betrothal are violated, the gift of chastity to Beatrice's future husband has been denied, and both finger and life are sacrificed so that Beatrice may bestow her chastity on the latest true deserver, Alsemero. At this point, Thomas Fuller's comment on marriage is applicable: "Some hold it unhappy to be married with a diamond ring, perchance (if there be so much reason in their folly) because the diamond hinders the roundnesse of the ring, ending the infinitenesse thereof, and seems to presage some termination in their love. . . ."[41] Whatever the reason, the diamond ring involves termination of both marriage and life for Alonzo.

Given the symbolism of the diamond ring as Beatrice's chastity, it is shocking for her to give the ring to De Flores; as both he and we know, whoever has the ring is entitled to Beatrice's virginity. The ironies set up by the gift of the ring echo throughout the scene, for Beatrice—ever concerned with her immediate wants and never with the implications of her deeds—is blissfully ignorant of what the gift betokens. "The stone / you may make use on shortly" (III.iv.41-42), she says, and De Flores does just that. But first Beatrice must be made to realize what her gift conveys. De Flores tries to make her understand by using language derived from the image palpably present on stage, the finger stuck to its ring: "Why, are you not as guilty, in (I'm sure) / As deep as I? And we should stick together" (83-84); "Nor is it fit we two, engag'd so jointly, / Should part and live asunder" (88-89). When she finally sees, she unconsciously uses the same imagery:

> Oh misery of sin! Would I had been bound
> Perpetually unto my living hate
> In that Piracquo, than to hear these words.

>   (127-29)

The grounds of her objection to De Flores are her noble blood, her chastity, her modesty—all of which may be symbolized by the diamond she has already given. But De Flores knows that the diamond, like the lady, is worth less than it seems or than she thinks. He comments: "'Twill hardly buy a capcase for one's conscience, though, / To keep it from the worm, as fine as 'tis" (44-45). We have seen that exposure to sin was thought to diminish the diamond's value just as it degrades the sinner, so De Flores' scorn for the gem is proper, although he seems to overvalue the chastity it signifies. But he appraises the woman justly and harshly: "Push, you forget yourself! / A woman dipp'd in blood, and talk of modesty?" (125-26). For those familiar with lapidary lore, the phrase is doubly striking:

the only way to break a diamond was to dip it in "new hot blood," as Batman claims. In sin and blood the diamond loses any power and integrity it once had, and so with Beatrice.

The ring, then, ties many of the play's themes together. It emphasizes the sexual implications of Beatrice's love for her various suitors; it points to her unchastity, her fickleness (if one is free with the symbol, one is free with the thing). It suggests her blindness (she never seems to understand what the ring means), and, on the dead finger of Alonzo, it signifies the wages of sin and lust: far from being good for witless men to look upon, as the Peterborough Lapidary describes it, it leads to madness and death. In its contrast between physical beauty and actual lack of virtue, it reminds us of Beatrice's moral deformity. Finally, it brings to mind the futility of sin. As Gardner notes (though not in connection with the ring), Beatrice, like Macbeth, has given her "eternal jewel . . . to the common enemy of man," and all for nought.[42]

Ring, virginity test, subplot, main plot—all point the moral provided by Burton: "All sorts, sects, ages, conditions, are out of tune . . . they are intoxicated by error's cup, from the highest to the lowest have need of physick, and those particular actions in Seneca, where father & son prove one another mad, may be general. . . . For indeed who is not a fool, melancholy, mad?—Who attempts nothing foolish, who is not brainsick? Folly, melancholy, and madness, are but one disease, *delirium* is a common name to all" (p. 31). There are numerous kinds of madness in **The Changeling**—clinical idiocy and frenzy, feigned madness, normal human folly, the spiritual insanity of crime. Ironically, the most serious kind is also the least spectacular—the appalling madness of mortal sin.

Notes

1. Robert Rentoul Reed Jr., *Bedlam on the Jacobean Stage* (Cambridge, Mass., 1952), pp. 64, 82.

2. Samuel Schoenbaum, *Middleton's Tragedies: A Critical Study* (New York, 1955), p. 147.

3. E.g., William Empson, *Some Versions of Pastoral* (London, 1935), p. 50; M. C. Bradbrook, *Themes and Conventions of Elizabethan Tragedy* (Cambridge, Eng., 1935, rpt. 1952), pp. 214-15; Dorothy M. Farr, "The Changeling," *MLR*, 62 (1967), 586-97; Karl L. Holzknecht, "The Dramatic Structure of *The Changeling*," *RenP*, 1954, 77-87; and N. W. Bawcutt, ed., Thomas Middleton and William Rowley, *The Changeling*, Revels Plays (London, 1961), p. lxiii. All citations from *The Changeling* are to this ed.; refs. to editorial apparatus will be identified by "Bawcutt" and page no. For convenience, in my text I refer to

Middleton as the author of the play, but I accept the traditional attribution of certain scenes to Rowley (Bawcutt, p. xxxix).

4. See Bawcutt, pp. xlv-xlviii; Thomas Berger, "The Petrarchan Fortress of *The Changeling*," *RenP,* 1969, 37-46; Normand Berlin, "The 'Finger' Image and Relationship of Character in *The Changeling*," *ESA,* 12 (1969), 162-66; Bradbrook, pp. 214-18; Edward Engelberg, "Tragic Blindness in *The Changeling* and *Women Beware Women*," *MLQ,* 23 (1962), 20-28; Catherine A. Hébert, "A Note on the Significance of the Title of Middleton's *The Changeling*," *CLAJ,* 12 (1968-69), 66-69; Holzknecht, "Dramatic Structure"; Robert Jordan, "Myth and Psychology in *The Changeling*," *RenD,* 3 (1970), 157-65; Irving Ribner, *Jacobean Tragedy: The Quest for Moral Order* (London, 1962), pp. 126-39; Christopher Ricks, *EIC,* 10 (1960), 290-306; T. B. Tomlinson, *A Study of Elizabethan and Jacobean Tragedy* (Cambridge, Eng., 1964), pp. 185-208; and George Walton Williams, ed., *The Changeling,* Regents Renaissance Drama (Lincoln, Neb., 1966), pp. xv-xxiv.

As is almost inevitable in discussing *The Changeling,* I will often treat images and passages the importance of which has been noted elsewhere, but I hope to present them in a new light whenever possible. Unfortunately limitations of space preclude both my indulgence in explicit critical controversy and continual annotation of other discussions of topics considered here.

5. For the definition, process, and results of sin, see Thomas Aquinas, *Summa Theologica,* I.II, Questions 6-17 and 74-77, in *Basic Writings,* ed. Anton C. Pegis, 2 vols. (New York, 1945). For later sources, see Lily B. Campbell, *Shakespeare's Tragic Heroes: Slaves of Passion* (Cambridge, Eng., 1930), pp. 93-102; Lawrence Babb, *The Elizabethan Malady* (East Lansing, Mich., 1951); and J. B. Bamborough, *The Little World of Man* (London, 1952).

These modern discussions emphasize the continuity of medieval and Renaissance psychology and stress the inseparability of ethics, theology, psychology, and physiology in the period.

6. *Canterbury Tales* X. 261-62, in *Works,* ed. F. N. Robinson, 2nd ed. (Boston, 1957). Additional refs. will be given in the text.

7. *The Anatomy of Melancholy,* ed. Floyd Dell and Paul Jordan-Smith (New York, 1927), p. 61. Additional refs. will be given in the text.

Possibly Middleton was familiar with Burton's work: the highly popular *Anatomy* was first published in 1621, in time for it to influence *The Changeling,* and Middleton may have been interested in the work of an Oxford contemporary. Certainly both men share the idea that all men are sinners and to that extent mad; and perhaps Lollio's mention of Lipsius (III.iii.179) is indebted to Burton's frequent citation of him. Dyce's conjecture that Lipsius is important chiefly for the first syllable of his name (Bawcutt, p. 53, n. 179) may be valid, but it is also worth noting that Burton cites Lipsius as an authority on the deflowering of virgins by devils (p. 650), and as such he would be appropriate reading for the lecherous and superficially deformed Antonio.

8. Augustine, *On the Trinity* 12.8, in *Basic Writings,* ed. Whitney J. Oates, 2 vols. (New York, 1948).

9. A commonplace; see, for instance, John Donne, *Sermons,* ed. George R. Potter and Evelyn M. Simpson, II (Berkeley, 1955), pp. 72-73.

10. "The Tragedy of Damnation," originally published as "Milton's Satan and the Theme of Damnation in Elizabethan Tragedy," *E & S,* I (1948), 46-66, rpt. with new title in *Elizabethan Drama: Modern Essays in Criticism,* ed. Ralph J. Kauffman (New York, 1961), pp. 320-41.

11. Bradbrook (pp. 214-16) notes the importance of "will" as a key word in the first scene.

12. The point is controversial. Many critics, like Bradbrook (p. 220), find Alsemero exemplary; others, like Holzknecht (p. 82), think that Isabella intends to commit adultery but is forestalled by Antonio's disgust.

13. *Elizabethan Essays* (London, 1934), p. 92.

14. *Summa Theologica,* I.II, Q. 75, A. 4.

15. *Summa Theologica,* I, Q. 115, A. 4.

16. Allusions to the Fall are made in both Rowley's and Middleton's contributions to the play: most parallels appear in I.i (Rowley), III.iv (Middleton), and V.iii (Rowley). If both authors consciously collaborated in shaping Beatrice's story to resemble Eve's, the Fall may fairly be taken as a major thematic concern of the play.

17. Several critics have noted some of the Fall parallels: Ribner sees Beatrice as Eve, whose "first condition" of innocence in Eden was lost when she became "the deed's creature" by sharing in original sin; De Flores in the devil (pp. 130, 134). Bawcutt gives a fuller discussion: "Alsemero thinks of marriage in terms of the creation (I.i.7-9); Beatrice is 'that broken rib of mankind' (V.iii.146) and she loses her 'first condition' and is turned out by 'peace and innocency' (III.iv.138-39) just as Eve loses her innocence. . . . De

Flores is . . . the 'serpent' (I.i.225), and Alsemero's remark towards the end of the play: 'Did my fate wait for this unhappy stroke / At my first sight of woman?' (V.iii.12-13) might be said to contain a hint of Adam's experience: his attempt to create a paradise on earth by means of marriage has been frustrated by Beatrice's discovery of evil" (p. lvi).

Although Bawcutt thus begins to consider the importance of the Alsemero-Adam parallel (and I agree with him as far as he goes), there has been no full discussion of the great range and thematic function of Fall imagery.

18. According to Augustine and many later theologians, a major consequence of original sin was that men became subject to lust and that sexual intercourse, which would have been governed by reason in Eden, became irrational (*City of God* 14.15-26), in *Basic Writings,* II.

19. There are several interesting discussions of anti-Petrarchanism as a major theme in both plots: see Berger, "The Petrarchan Fortress"; Jordan, "Myth and Psychology"; and Robert Ornstein, *The Moral Vision of Jacobean Tragedy* (Madison, Wisc., 1960), pp. 179-80.

20. Both pseudepigraphal Books of Enoch describe the seduction of Eve by the devil after the Fall—Enoch 69.6 and 2 Enoch 31.6, in *The Apocrypha and Pseudepigrapha of the Old Testament,* ed. R. H. Charles (Oxford, 1913), II, 233 and 451. See also J. M. Evans, *'Paradise Lost' and the Genesis Tradition* (Oxford, 1968), pp. 33, 46-47, 64-65, and 73; and John Block Friedman, *Orpheus in the Middle Ages* (Cambridge, Mass., 1970), p. 185.

21. Ll.716-18, in *The Works of Christopher Marlowe,* ed. C. F. Tucker Brooke (Oxford, 1910).

22. Augustine, *City of God* 14.14.

23. *Book of the Knight of La Tour Landry,* ed. Thomas Wright, EETS, o.s. 33 (London, 1906), 61-62.

24. Richard Hindry Barker, *Thomas Middleton* (New York, 1958), p. 125; Schoenbaum, p. 140; Bradbrook, p. 234. Bawcutt (pp. liv-lvi) and Patricia Thomson (ed., *The Changeling,* New Mermaid ed. [London, 1964], pp. xi-xiii) agree in finding that Beatrice, far from being corrupted by De Flores, corrupts herself.

25. On comedy in the main plot, which will be discussed here in regard to the virginity test, see also Ornstein, p. 186; G. R. Hibbard, "The Tragedies of Thomas Middleton and the Decadence of the Drama," *RMS,* 1 (1957), 35-64; and Farr, "*The Changeling.*" Una Ellis-Fermor comments that in

Middleton's comedies he, like Chaucer, has a "sense of the relations of the comic and the pathetic and, latterly, of the comic and the grim"— *The Jacobean Drama: An Interpretation,* 4th ed. (London, 1958), p. 133. This observation might well be extended to *The Changeling.*

26. For representative attacks on the subplot, see Schoenbaum, p. 103, and Barker, pp. 129-30; for a good recent defense, see Richard Levin, *The Multiple Plot in English Renaissance Drama* (Chicago, 1971), pp. 34-48. Most critics acknowledge some thematic and dramatic parallels between the plots but still find the subplot markedly inferior: see Hibbard, pp. 62-63, and Thomson, pp. xxvi-xxvii. I do not plan to defend the artistic merits of the subplot, but I suspect that it might be very successful when staged.

27. "The 'Impure Art' of John Webster," *RES,* n.s. 9 (1958), 253-67.

28. *Mundus et Infans,* in *A Select Collection of Old English Plays, Originally Published by Robert Dodsley,* ed. W. Carew Hazlitt, 4th ed., 1 (London, 1874), 258.

29. See *Summa Theologica,* I.II, Q. 76, A. 3, 4, and Q. 77.

30. Burton, p. 34.

31. *Christs Teares ouer Ierusalem,* in *Works,* ed. R. B. McKerrow, rev. F. P. Wilson (Oxford, 1958), II, 112-13.

32. Farr (p. 587, n. 1) feels that the virginity test is a vestige of Alsemero's extreme jealousy in Reynolds, but Hibbard thinks its inclusion is an example of catering to popular taste (pp. 61-63).

33. See C. S. Lewis, *A Preface to 'Paradise Lost'* (London, 1942), pp. 92-100.

34. See Bernard Spivack, *Shakespeare and the Allegory of Evil* (New York, 1958); for a discussion of the comedy of evil in medieval drama, see V. A. Kolve, *The Play Called Corpus Christi* (Stanford, 1966), ch. 6 *et passim.*

The comedy of evil and of deformity is, of course, also characteristic of satire, and to the extent that works like *The Changeling* are funny, they are also satirical in effect and presumably in purpose. On Middleton as a satirist, see David M. Holmes, *The Art of Thomas Middleton: A Critical Study* (Oxford, 1970), ch. 1 *et passim.*

35. See Bawcutt, pp. 68-69, n. 25.

36. See esp. Berlin's fine study, "The 'Finger' Image," and Dorothea Kehler, "Rings and Jewels in *The Changeling,*" *ELN,* 5 (1967), 15-17. See also

Ricks, "Moral and Poetic Structure" and "The Tragedies of Webster, Tourneur, and Middleton: Symbols, Imagery, and Conventions," in *History of Literature in the English Language,* III, *English Drama to 1710,* ed. Christopher Ricks (London, 1971), 310-11.

37. Most powers of the diamond here discussed can be found in three highly popular works: *Batman uppon Bartholeme his Booke De Proprietatibus Rerum* (London, 1582), Bk. XVI, ch. 9; *Mandeville's Travels,* ed. M. C. Seymour (Oxford, 1967), pp. 115-18; and Burton, pp. 568 and 865. Also important are the North Midland Lapidary of King Philip (pp. 50-51) and the Peterborough Lapidary (pp. 83-84), both fifteenth-century, and the late sixteenth-century Sloane Lapidary (p. 121), all in *English Mediaeval Lapidaries,* ed. Joan Evans and Mary S. Serjeantson, EETS, o.s. 190 (London, 1933).

Given the prominence of the virginity test in *The Changeling,* it is fascinating to note a common property of the diamond as a test of chastity in a wife: "Lay this stone vnder her head & if she be trew she will turne her toward him [her husband], and if not she shall stir as a beast, And make as though she falleth, and cry as if she had feard an vngodly sight" (Sloane Lapidary). Could Middleton possibly have got the idea for both the virginity test and the prominence of the diamond ring from reading a lapidary?

38. Latin text cited by Joan Evans, *Magical Jewels of the Middle Ages and the Renaissance, Particularly in England* (Oxford, 1922), pp. 64-65.

39. *Jew of Malta,* 809-30 (Brooke ed.); *White Devil,* III.ii.305, ed. F. L. Lucas, *Complete Works of John Webster,* I (London, 1927).

40. See, for example, the Alphabetical Lapidary, probably by Philippe de Thaon, in *Anglo-Norman Lapidaries,* ed. Paul Studer and Joan Evans (Paris, 1924), p. 204.

41. *The Holy State and the Profane State,* ed. Maximilian Graff Walten (New York, 1938), II, 213. Fuller is writing in 1642, but presumably the superstition to which he refers was current earlier. It is possible, of course, that *The Changeling* may have been instrumental in creating such a superstition: Fuller's reason for disliking a diamond ring in fact applies to *any* ring, so presumably the superstition is based on other grounds for disliking the diamond in particular, and no such reasons are evident in the lapidaries.

42. "Tragedy of Damnation," p. 330.

Raymond J. Pentzell (essay date spring 1975)

SOURCE: Pentzell, Raymond J. "*The Changeling*: Notes on Mannerism in Dramatic Form." *Comparative Drama* 9, no. 1 (spring 1975): 3-28.

[*In the following essay, Pentzell suggests that, with its use of contrivances and seemingly intentional irresolution,* The Changeling *can be viewed as using the techniques of Mannerism.*]

In the first act of **The Changeling** Beatrice-Joanna enters the stage a light-comic ingenue, as transparent and inconsequential as a spoiled Molière *fille,* and just as self-centered. Near the end of the fifth act she dies, guilty of murder and betrayal, her *amour-propre* having grown to fruition as a selfishness which grotesquely perverts her zeal for her own honor. She lies next to the catalyst of her ripening, the hideous De Flores, her lover and her murderer, now a suicide. Her death brings her as close as she ever comes to an *anagnorisis*; self-satisfaction ebbs from her enough that, finally, she can beg pathetically of her surviving victims, "Forgive me . . . all forgive."

No one does. Her father bemoans his own disgrace. Her traduced husband is attentive only to him, comforting him with the observation, "Justice hath so right / The guilty hit, that innocence is quit / By proclamation, and may joy again." Suddenly there is set in motion a finale which may be the most insane ever written for a play respected as a tragedy: when Alsemero, the aggrieved husband, begins to retail all the "changes" he has gone through, his catalogue of puns must surely have reminded the playgoers of 1622 no less than ourselves of the kind of drawnout wordplay used in comedy as early as the prologue to Gascoigne's *Supposes.* Upon finishing his list, he calls, "Are there any more on's?" And up pops Antonio, a comedian from the subplot, who volunteers his "changes." He is followed in turn by other contributors out of the comic subplot, Franciscus, Isabella, and Alibius. Each patters out more "changes" until the "tragic" Alsemero regains his turn with a moralizing speech which slips promptly into rhymed couplets as the "epilogue." Music up. All bow. Exeunt.

There are two dead bodies left on stage. No provision has been made to carry them off. They have been lying there all through the punning changes rung on "change." Now what? Either they lie in place until the whole audience files out chuckling (a bit of the macabre worthy of *Monsieur Verdoux*), or else they also get up, bow, and walk off, no doubt reminding us of Leslie at the end of Behan's *The Hostage.*[1] Either way, our "tragedy" has ended in a double-take of grisly comedy. Nowhere in the canon of tragedy can there be found another example of such an ending.[2] This scene, in its preternatural absurdity, embodies none of the thematic ironies of, say, a Euripidean epilogue. Its ironies lie almost totally in the sharp clap of suddenly juxtaposed tones—juxtaposed, as it were, for the hell of it.

But if the irony of the finale is, strictly speaking, uninterpretable, it is neither meaningless nor unprepared-for. Its meaning lies in the fact that it *is* prepared for, the culmination of a structural pattern which has been at work throughout the play. Many critics have avoided trying to track down an overall structure in *The Changeling,* for to do so is to risk bringing discussion to a halt by admitting the play is a botch. Everyone's first indigestible question is this: What is the subplot, the madhouse farce, doing there?

At the outset we must chew on a paradox. *The Changeling* was written by two men, each writing in a manifestly different set of styles and each (most would say) possessing a different measure of talent. Modern critics typically think of the play as if it were written by Thomas Middleton "with additions by" William Rowley. Though the nucleus of the Beatrice-De Flores plot is Middleton's most obvious contribution and the farcical subplot Rowley's, it was Rowley who wrote the longish first scene and all or most of the final scene. However unmistakably different in style they are from Middleton's scenes, they are of course part of the main plot.[3]

We can imagine, perhaps, the two writers briefly discussing the subject of the play, outlining its progression only roughly, and then going off to separate garrets each to write his own assigned scenes in his own way, never to meet again until their manuscript pages were collated. But this notion will scarcely do. William Empson, M. C. Bradbrook, and Karl Holzknecht have plotted the many correspondences in imagery, situation, and phrasing between the two lines of action; even the most casual reader or spectator will notice the larger movements of this distorting-mirror game.[4] The most likely hypothesis, then, has Rowley and Middleton working in rather close collaboration: checking up on each other periodically, discussing their plans and progress, and mutually assimilating their separate products *en route.* No other conjecture about their collaborative arrangement fits the evidence nearly so well.[5]

Then why did one man wield flexible, crackling dialogue to thrust his characters into scenes of mordant psychological irony while the other man dawdled his way around them: beginning a Fletcherian tragicomedy (largely in neat, old-fashioned verse at times reminiscent of Spenser and even Lyly); hacking together an unoriginal and difficult-to-follow farce which leads nowhere; constructing a formalized denouement which seems almost a prank?

This is our paradox, and even when (as here) we overstate it, it makes a good question. Unless we can find some sort of satisfactory answer, we will not only (in the good company of T. S. Eliot, Una Ellis-Fermor, and Robert Brustein) have to "ignore the silly subplot contributed by Rowley,"[6] but also, and with greater difficulty, have to conquer our dizziness as we stand at the finale of the play looking back on what went before and trying to suppress an uncomfortable giggle.

Empson, noting parallels between the two stories, leads us to think of their relationship in terms of parody—the irony that comes of viewing the same basic action alternately as serious and funny. The first alternate (riding on the main plot) entails empathy: to the extent that we can regard Beatrice, De Flores, and Alsemero as creatures like ourselves, their version of the story will appear threatening and pitiful, or at least morbidly fascinating. The subplot provokes the second response, which assumes that we will feel superior to its characters in intelligence, or regard them as somehow unreal, or feel that the outcome of their intrigues will not cause them much harm (or all three attitudes together). For Empson the design of such a play lies in the "double view" of a dramatic action which is essentially single, a view made possible by an artfully closed system of figurative check and thematic balance which (like many forms of irony) allows the playwrights to become as hyperbolic as they wish in either direction without altogether losing the audience's trust in the play's ultimate "sensibleness"—its pertinence to reality as the audience is accustomed to perceiving it.

However helpful Empson's reading, his interpretation is not totally successful in accounting for the subplot's function. The madhouse story is just not similar enough in plot and character to the major plot for us to regard it merely as a comic version of the same action; it is certainly no *gracioso-graciosa* parody taking place belowstairs in a serious Spanish *comedia,* but a tale independent enough to go its own way. (Indeed, it wanders far enough afield that the authors evidently believed the developments necessary to resolve it on its own premises would have delayed unforgivably the climax of the main plot.) If Isabella suggests a Beatrice with better moral balance, it is not so clear whether her elderly husband Alibius can be matched parodically with either Vermandero or Alsemero. Likewise, the fool Lollio may buzz around her as De Flores around Beatrice, but the real threat of bloodshed comes ultimately from Antonio and Franciscus, who, as lovestruck outsiders, could logically be expected to correspond in their rivalry to Alsemero and Alonzo—whom Beatrice keeps from fighting. And the ongoing vaudeville relationship of Lollio with Alibius has no parallel in Vermandero's castle. Although the subplot develops comically some themes which appear also in the main action, and despite the ubiquitous re-echoes of imagery and situation, it is hard to believe that a spectator could feel he was witnessing the progression of an integral dramatic action on which he was invited to hold differing viewpoints in alternation. Further, if we look beyond simple parody for a more variegated system of irony arising from juxtaposed lines of action which coherently mirror a single theme, we will probably be equally disappointed. *The Changeling* behaves neither like *A Midsummer Night's Dream* nor like *I Henry IV,* still less like *Lear.* Even so thorough and sympathetic a reader as N. W. Bawcutt, the editor of the Revels edition of the play, finds "a very real difference in tone and intention between the two plots," and concludes that "The total effect of all these kinds of relationship between the two halves of the play is not easily assessed."[7]

Let us put aside for the moment our Empson-inspired concern with the play's characters, plots, and themes, and pick up as clues Bawcutt's words "tone" and "effect." Perhaps the determinant structure of *The Changeling* can be traced not so much in the order of meaning as in the stylistic flux itself. If so, this might suggest that an audience is more likely to "put the play together" (progressively in retrospect) through its organization of affective "tones" than through any counterpoint of plot or character. Metaphorically, we could imagine that the play's structure is more musical than architectonic, and musically post- rather than pre-Wagnerian.

"Tone," though one of the least precise of critical terms, denotes a most important aspect of style. It can be discussed generally only by way of a style's presumable effect on an audience, since it so often depends on a subtle pattern of stylistic predictability and unpredictability. To perceive any point of style (in dramatic structure no less than in dialogue) as predictable or unpredictable is to predicate a shared consciousness of what is and is not conventionally "appropriate" (plausible or familiar) in language and action. Normally, we call tone the effect of those stylistic "notes" or data (provided by author and actor alike) by which we judge *how* a dramatic action is to be regarded. "How we take" any single theatrical incident, of course, is hugely affected by whatever sense of satisfaction or surprise we can derive from its relation to a previous incident and from our recall of data we previously received. But *within* any single step in a dramatic action tone operates most obviously by causing us to locate our response somewhere on a broad continuum which ranges across many varieties of "funny" and "serious," the ultimate pole of seriousness comprising that "arousal of pity and terror" by which we signify our recognition of high tragedy. Often our very notion of "genre" is, at bottom, simply a recognition of general categories of tone. It is well known that any translator or any actor can, with a minimum of effort, make *Oedipus the King* hilarious.[8]

The tone of a scene can also place it for us on a different but not unrelated scale, that by which we perceive (through our relative "engagement" or "estrangement")

a dramatic event as varying from "credible" to "artificial." The former defines the nearest we can come to ignoring our ever-present knowledge that the event and characters are fictitious; the latter, our most pronounced awareness of the playwright or actor as a conscious manipulator of words and actions.[9]

Examined in this light, *The Changeling* is a tonal thrill-show, a roller-coaster ride on hills of many heights and many angles of steepness. As our initial look at its final scene has made clear, far more is involved than the main-plot-serious/subplot-funny coefficient implied in the parody idea. We must notice at once that the Beatrice-De Flores plot, taken *in toto,* progresses on two distinct planes of reality. Surely Robert Brustein (echoing Eliot *et al.*) was not deluding himself when he praised it as "the closest thing to a realistic tragedy in the Stuart canon" and "the most subtle psychological tragedy in English outside of Shakespeare."[10] The twisting development of the relationship between the two principals warms the cockles of any Freudian heart. Yet Robert Jordan is equally on the mark in demonstrating how the anecdote cleverly and consistently follows, while inverting, the normative incidents of a stereotypical courtly-love romance on a "Beauty and the Beast" pattern: surely a dimension that would have been promptly appreciated in the early seventeenth century and one that certainly must complicate the tone of even the "unified" central sections.[11] We must see Middleton's "psychological tragedy" (as Shakespeare's Hermia says upon waking) "with parted eye."

Moreover, whatever psychological credibility Beatrice and De Flores ultimately have for us can hardly be said to emerge until II.i. Rowley's introduction of the characters of the main plot in I.i is handled unremittingly up near the "artificial" end of our tonal scale. The rather old-fashioned verse with its symmetrical turns of antithetical images (72-85, 119-29) and rhetorical or stanzaic "builds" (1-12, 66-72), the dance-like implied movement (139-57), and a technique of character-motivation that veers from bluntly explicit (6, 160-61) to totally veiled (112-18, 243-44) give the opening of the play an opaque sheen not at all promissory of "psychological tragedy." Indeed, it may be observed that the first farcical scene, I.ii, comes not as a sharp tonal shift but as a tonal narrowing: the notes of sexual punning and badinage running through I.i are here focused upon exclusively, picked up and carried further into a scene which is thereby structured like a vaudeville act.

Middleton himself, when he enters with Act II, does not blast the audience out of its seats with a "whole new play"; on the contrary, he preserves a couple of Rowley's stylistic hallmarks until De Flores opens his mouth to speak. Though we cannot mistake Middleton's own style in these opening speeches, the formality of Jasperino's "The joy I shall return rewards my service" and the reversion not only to Beatrice's "eyes vs. judgment" conceit but also to such verse construction as "A true deserver like a diamond sparkles, / In darkness you may see him, that's in absence" (15-16) bespeak an intention to keep the tonal transition from becoming too abrupt. With De Flores, of course, there is no turning back stylistically, and the play moves to new levels of both credibility and seriousness. The "comic" and "tragic" halves of the play have completely separated.

Nevertheless, the new tone of "psychological realism" buoyed up by Middleton's taut, truncated verses does not by any means continue through the rest of the main plot, nor does the vaudevillian atmosphere persist at the madhouse. In preparation for her dreaded wedding night, Beatrice gets elbow-deep in potions right out of Jonson's *Alchemist.* Unless we frankly accept IV.i (Diaphanta used as guinea pig) as essentially farcical, we will never understand why Middleton chose "gaping," "sneezing," and "laughing" as the required "virginity" reactions; when Beatrice herself feigns them (IV.ii) she can resemble nothing so much as the gawking Antonio and the giggling Franciscus rolled into one. (Does "glass M" stand for "maidenhead," "murder," or "madness"?) Yet in the Diaphanta scene itself, any such ironic connections must appear remote; they show up superimposed on the straightforward funniness only when they become significant by Beatrice's *feigning.* Immediately following, in IV.iii, Rowley's subplot itself turns sour; the note of violence introduced in III.iii. 247-48 (when Isabella warns Lollio that unless he keeps silent she will have Antonio cut his throat) begins to infect the "farce" with explicit threat. Lollio grows ugly in his direct echoing (38) of De Flores (II.ii.61); Isabella reacts to abuse by an ostensibly prankish charade (106-39) that may hint as much at genuine hysteria (133, 139) as at revulsion; and before the scene ends a dual murder is plotted.

As late as 1622 that old warhorse of romance, the substitution-in-bed trick, could hardly have been taken as the stuff of realistic psychology. Yet not only is it planned (IV.i), Alsemero actually falls for it (V.i). To that extent, the brilliant character revelations in the latter scene (Beatrice: "I'm forced to love thee now, / 'Cause thou provid'st so carefully for my honor," 47-48) take place against a background of pasteboard plotting conventions. The action becomes generally more pasteboard as Act V proceeds, though not always in ways we can identify as conventional. What is immediately necessary, of course, is that the mare's nest of plot be untangled in the portion that remains of a single act. In order to do so the authors often resort to a kind of dramaturgic shorthand, in which incident itself is detachable from expectations engendered by characterization and preceding events. In IV.ii Tomazo Piracquo saw eye-to-eye with his "honest De Flores"; in V.ii, without preparation, he remarks upon seeing the villain,

> Oh, the fellow that some call honest De Flores;
> But methinks honesty was hard bestead
> To come there for a lodging.
>
> (9-11)

Finding simply "a contrariety in nature / Betwixt that face and me" (12-13), he promptly strikes him, draws his sword, and is prevented from precipitate murder only by De Flores' equally precipitate attack of conscience, which causes the latter to back off:

> I cannot strike, I see his brother's wounds
> Fresh bleeding in his eye, as in a crystal.
>
> (32-33)

De Flores has already seen Alonzo's ghost glide past him twice, once in the dumbshow preceding Act IV and again just before the house-afire ruse in V.i, but even an outright ghost had not kept him from his villainy before. As with the Cardinal in *The Duchess of Malfi,* this sudden, illogical, and vivid burst of "conscience" functions chiefly as a signal to the audience that they should expect him to have no further successes. Both character-reversals in this scene (but particularly Tomazo's) are radical enough to remind one of Fletcher's techniques, whereby a desired twist of event or a theatrical "passion" takes complete precedence over any logic of human motivation and interrelation.[12]

Before V.ii has run its course Alibius, in company with his wife and Vermandero, arrives to reveal the presence in his madhouse of Antonio and Franciscus (on whom suspicion for Alonzo's murder falls), thus short-circuiting once and for all the subplot, which was just beginning to "thicken" when we last looked in on it. As V.iii begins, Jasperino and Alsemero come from spying on De Flores and Beatrice in the "garden"; Alsemero's once-allayed suspicions have been rekindled to the point at which they need only an admission of guilt to become certainties. We must leap over dramaturgic oddities here: we are not told exactly what De Flores was doing in this secret meeting occurring so soon after his attack of "conscience." More importantly, we must forego the presumable treat of watching Alsemero's *anagnorisis* actually take place on stage. One cannot imagine a playwright concerned chiefly with revealing and developing his characters declining to dramatize such a spying-scene. But we have made it to the final scene with no more plot left to accomplish than a confrontation, an admission of guilt, and the disposal of Alibius's red herring.

Here, apparently, Rowley takes over, although possibly in tandem with Middleton, and the tone of the dialogue quickly catches up with that of the events. A gauze of formality gradually lowers between the audience and the figures on stage, lifted only briefly for Beatrice's death-speech. We become conscious of the increase of epigrammatic rhythms, the virtual disappearance of colloquial contractions, and the propensity of the characters to use concise if extravagant metaphors such as "The bed itself's a charnal, the sheets shrouds / For murdered carcasses" (83-84). The incidence of people being addressed as "sir" increases. The dialogue is punctuated with exclamations at each revelation: "Ha!"; "oh cunning devils!"; "Diaphanta!"; "Ha! My brother's murderer!"; "Horrid villain!" When Alsemero presses his questioning, Beatrice smiles, then personifies her "innocence" as the smiler in a short, sentimental speech ending in a rhetorical question (24-27). We at once recognize the diction of I.i. Alsemero's response crouches, springs, and pounces ("You are a whore!" 31) in exactly the same pattern as his first announcement of love (I.i.69-72).

The tone veers from merely formal to an overt suggestion of the comic. De Flores bandies words with his accuser ("'twas quite through him, sure," 104) and readily owns up to both murder and adultery. When both criminals are locked in Alsemero's closet (along with, presumably, all his virginity-test bottles), Vermandero enters with Alibius, Isabella, Tomazo, Antonio, and Franciscus in tow. Vermandero and Alsemero play Cox and Box:

VER.:

    Oh, Alsemero, I have a wonder for you.

ALS.:

    No sir, 'tis I, I have a wonder for you.

VER.:

    I have suspicion near as proof itself
    For Piracquo's murder.

ALS.:

             Sir, I have proof
    Beyond suspicion for Piracquo's murder.

VER.:

    Beseech you hear me, these two have been disguised
    E'er since the deed was done.

ALS.:

             I have two other
    That were more close disguised than your two could
       be,
    E'er since the deed was done.

VER.:

    You'll hear me! These two mine own servants—

ALS.:

    Hear me! Those nearer than your servants,
    That shall acquit them and prove them guiltless.

                         (121-32)

At length even Tomazo objects: "How is my cause bandied through your delays!"[13] This is the kind of unraveling we expect to find in *The Importance of Being Earnest,* and though it is interrupted by the murder-suicide of the captured pair and by Beatrice's affecting plea for forgiveness, one can see that the scene's tone, while it careens madly, is drifting directly toward the farce-style resolution with which we began our questioning. Our brief examination should, I think, make it clear that the finale is in some odd way merely the capstone of a pile of artificialities, distancing (or "estrangement") effects, sudden comic turns, and parodic notes, which has been a-building during much of the seemingly serious play.[14]

On the hypothesis that **The Changeling**'s runaway tonal variety was to some degree intended by its authors and not simply the result of their ineptitude, we must then ask if their intentions were directed to an overall effect of anarchy (a Marx Brothers' "Night at the Castle" or a random burlesque of tragedy itself), or whether there can be found some control on mere variety by which we might perceive a tonal structure or design. Here Empson's reading helps us. Although the many mainplot-subplot correspondences do not add up to coherent parody, we may see them as effective counterbalances to the centrifugal effects of the tone itself. Operatively, these unmistakable hints of correspondence serve to keep the audience in a state of expectation that "real" (plot, character, theme) connections will eventually be made. The fact that many of these expectations are aroused only to be frustrated throws off balance our ordinary way of discerning dramatic structure (as a recognizable pattern of expectations and recollections moving through time)[15] but at the same time keeps us unwilling to throw in the towel and turn from the play as a gabble of unrelated data. We keep waiting, perhaps puzzling, and find our attention skillfully mocked.

The best indication that this *trompe l'oeil* effect is deliberate is, of course, the clear pattern that emerges from the variation in tone itself. The play begins in a never-never land of pure theatricality, no more to be predicted as serious than as funny.[16] As it divides into two plots, it flies apart rapidly to the farthest poles of both the funny-to-tragic scale and the artificial-to-credible scale. Then, as the main plot gets progressively less serious and more conventional, the subplot begins to sprout growths of psychological believability and threatened bloodshed—potentially serious in effect. As the subplot evaporates and its characters join the main plot as hangers-on, the tone of the action returns to the artificiality of I.i and begins to oscillate quickly between the tragedy-of-blood seriousness of, say, III.ii and the vaudeville of I.ii, ultimately withdrawing behind the decorative theatrical frame out of which the play first stepped. If the final image with which we are left is that of a comic tableau, it is there, perhaps, to call our attention to the fun we have been having in trying unsuccessfully to "nail the play down" in terms of a recognizable overall effect.

We may imagine a three-dimensional graph of *The Changeling*'s tonal pattern: tracking the progression of the play down a vertical scale marked off scene by scene, we would localize the overall tone of each scene at the intersection of a horizontal scale marking degrees from "farcical" to "tragic" and a scale-in-depth designating degrees from "artificial" to "credible." If such a model could be made, we would, I believe, end up with an uneven but recognizable spiral, wide at the top, snaking downward in a tightening gyre to a point near the edge where "artificial" crosses "black comic." But a relatively straight line could join the three scenes of the subplot, and another straight line could link the four most memorable scenes of the main plot. Such "straight lines" are what we normally expect of a play; these scenes are the ones concentrated on by most critics, who correspondingly despair of the unity of the "double plot."

Finding our clearest sense of *The Changeling*'s overall design in an aspect of its style—moreover in a quality which stresses the reactions of a hypothetical audience—imputes to the play an essentially "theatrical" or aesthetic mode of composition, but it certainly does not imply that the play is finally meaningless *except* as a device for patterning audience emotions. This can be said of Fletcher's plays, but not of *The Changeling*.[17] Similarly, the fact that the play's action is bracketed (even "matrixed") by scenes inviting complete detachment from the serious implication of the content does not mean that we have witnessed a "camp" on tragedy or a send-up of the play's own material. There may be a suppressed note of truth in this interpretation; still, if it were taken as the summary perception a reader or spectator must have of the play, then we would not, once let in on the joke at the finale, continue to find the play tentative and shifting in its focus at all. On the contrary, the psychological and moral implications of the Beatrice-De Flores story are indeed there. Appraisals such as those of Eliot and Miss Ellis-Fermor, although based on only part of the play, cannot be dismissed as misinterpretations in themselves.

By the same token, we can note that the madhouse scenes are not mere hackwork or filler, but that, as Isabella's character begins to develop, they exhibit in their own way a series of effective comic strokes on some of the moral and psychological themes suggested by the main plot. Though neither an integral action in itself nor a sustained parody of the main plot, the madhouse plot is far from meaningless. We should see in Middleton and Rowley's work, I think, not the intention of mystifying the spectators nor solely of exciting them, but rather a refusal (or inability) to force their commitment to a single kind of stage reality. The play *is* a psy-

chologically believable moral tragedy; it is also a courtly-love parody; it is also a laugh-grabbing farce and a black-comic "revue" on certain themes.

The patterned juxtaposition of one kind of stage reality with another and one range of mood with another is constantly in flux, continuously unpredictable, yet by means of those very qualities the primary unifying dynamic of the play as it is experienced in time. On the basis of this conclusion, its compositional similarities with many early-seventeenth-century plays should become apparent, not least of which are *Measure for Measure* and *All's Well That Ends Well*, "problem plays" not in the Ibsenite sense so much as in their notorious inability to be read by any two critics in anything like the same way.[18]

By the evidence of collaboration it yields, *The Changeling* gives us no warrant for interpretations rooted in the idea that Middleton and Rowley wrote at loggerheads with each other. But it is possible to speculate that both men occasionally found themselves at loggerheads with the story and the themes they had agreed on. If so, the sense of tentativeness and irresolution we derive from the patterned but unsettled tone might reflect the authors' indecision in striving to entertain their audience with enjoyable and comfortably familiar kinds of dramatic action, while simultaneously feeling a conflicting commitment to the unique meanings embodied in the material. Or we might suspect a personal tension between confident and forthright communication of the story, including its thematic stresses, and self-consciousness about the demands of theatrical form itself—a self-consciousness perhaps made all the more acute in a day when Marstonian cynicism and Fletcherian virtuosity had exploited the private-theatre spectator's delight in stylish contrivance and *bizarrerie*. However such a polarity is phrased, it may be no more than a peculiar example of the uneasy relation of style, tone, and content which Jacobean literature, poised on the brink of Eliot's "dissociation of sensibility" since the Metaphysicals, often exhibited. This critical moment in the history of taste has been explored under the rubric "Mannerism" by pan-generic historians of art, such as Wylie Sypher.

At the risk of leading a snipe-hunt, I suggest it may be worth-while to expand our inquiry in that general direction. An attempt to describe the kind of precarious success which *The Changeling* is capable of achieving in performance calls up echoes of several plays which can unsettle a modern reader or audience in ways which seem similar. Shakespeare's "problem plays" have already been mentioned as examples of seemingly intentional tonal irresolution. To them we might add *Pericles, Cymbeline, The Winter's Tale*, Fletcher's plays, and perhaps even Marlowe's *The Jew of Malta*—drama which invites, and refuses to answer, the question, "How am I to take this?" We can have no hope of making "Mannerism" or any other label serve as an answer—arguments still break out about its usefulness in discourse about the visual arts—but some collective term can prove helpful in marking notes on the problem. "Mannerism" strikes me as preferable to any other available generality; its usefulness will, I hope, emerge as we proceed.

Historians have taken three fundamentally distinct approaches in trying to isolate Mannerism as a late-renaissance phenomenon. Walter Friedlaender's pioneer treatment of Mannerist painting stressed its dialectic relationship with its predecessor, the accomplished "classicism" of Italian painters from Da Vinci to Raphael, and with its successor, the early-Baroque paintings of the Carracci family.[19] Thus Mannerist art began as "anti-classicism" and finally vanished in the 1590s under a wave of "anti-mannerism." Examining the paintings of Pontormo, Rosso, and Parmigianino, Friedlaender saw the style's initial impetus as the upwelling of an essentially medieval taste for intensity and variety—multiple focus, unrealistic or puzzling juxtapositions of scale, acknowledgement of the spectator, heightened or distorted movement—in a context in which the high-renaissance masterworks, with their balanced calmness, organized realism, and mastery of visual rhythm, were regarded as oppressively limiting despite the impressive technical sophistication which inescapably made them models of artistic accomplishment. Northern artists like Dürer, who were still in the process of assimilating the lessons of late-quattrocento Italian painting into a consciousness not entirely cut off from medieval habits of perception and composition, were themselves much admired by the "younger generation" of Italian artists. The result was often an oddly unsettling blend of the pseudo-naive and the highly polished, all evidently governed by a high degree of self-awareness and a corresponding interest in the effect to be had on the spectator.

Certain later art historians have abandoned Friedlaender's emphasis on a historical dialectic of action and reaction as too schematic and not sufficiently applicable to the work of many sixteenth-century artists who clearly share some of the stylistic features of Pontormo, Rosso, and Parmigianino. A recent, thorough survey of Mannerism by John Shearman uses a much wider historical compass and a no-nonsense historical approach to defining the fundamental predilections of the style.[20] Shearman finds the common denominator of all sixteenth-century Mannersim in the contemporary importance attached to its root-term, *maniera*—"style," implying both the elegance stressed in Castiglione's descriptive term, *sprezzatura* ("seemingly offhand virtuosity"), and the extreme consciousness of technique evidenced by the importance given to theories of *disegno*. That the painting, sculpture, architecture, and literature which Shearman regards as Manneristic found its patrons, practitioners, and audiences in highly sophisticated—usually courtly—circles is self-explanatory. By emphasizing *maniera* Shearman manages to clarify the stylistic connections between the Italian artists of Pontormo's generation and those following Bronzino (whom Friedlaender considered merely "mannered" in comparison with his earlier anti-classical Mannerists), as well as between the Florentine-Roman schools and late-sixteenth-century artists elsewhere in Europe. Yet he strictly avoids diluting the term to a mere synonym for "sixteenth-century." Thus Bruegel, Tintoretto, and El Greco, who manifest artistic premises essentially unconditioned by admiration of *maniera,* are ruled out, while literary artists of any nationality who exploited styles of elaborate, elegant "conceit" are included: Bembo, Gongora, Lyly. Far from simply compiling a list, however, Shearman stresses more strongly than Friedlaender the fluidity of the borders between Mannerist style and its predecessors, heirs, and contemporary alternatives. He employs "Mannerism" descriptively in a purely historical context (thus subject to the shadings and partial applicability of any historical phenomenon), locking neither the style nor history itself into any idealized critical framework.

Almost at the opposite extreme to the approach represented by Shearman is that first put forward by Max Dvořák in 1920 and developed in various ways by pan-artistic critical historians such as Arnold Hauser and Wylie Sypher.[21] If Shearman attached little importance *per se* to the "subjective," "speculative," and "unearthly" qualities which Friedlaender discerned in Manneristic form, the followers of Dvořák have tended to place their major stress on such psychological determinants. Dvořák saw in Mannerism manifestations of a general "spiritual crisis" in the sixteenth century. Whether one investigates its roots in the crisis itself, in the sociological vein of Hauser, or its stylistic evidences of mental unease, with Sypher, Mannerism emerges principally as an expressive phenomenon rather than as a phase of artistic technique. Close attention is paid to the Mannerists' presentation of "high nervous tension" and their apparent need for incongruity, irresolution, and basic questioning (or abandonment) of the possibility of meaning. Friedlaender's anti-classicists are wedded to El Greco, Cervantes, Shakespeare, and Donne with little intervening but the basilisk stares of Bronzino's portrait figures. The juxtapositions of sunlit classical order with "neo-Gothic" distortion and arbitrariness become a kind of sixteenth-century Surrealism, with much that is thereby implied about twentieth-century-style *Angst,* loss of conviction, and artist-as-ironic-public-performer. Such perceptions of Mannerism have had a lasting effect on criticism and have often proved invaluable in bringing late-renaissance art in focus for twentieth-century eyes.

Though I have not given anything like justice to Friedlaender, Shearman, Dvořák, Hauser, or Sypher in these capsule descriptions, I have tried to isolate three chief areas of emphasis which may allow us to consider Mannerism in more particular senses. Each point of attack is distinct, even in part contradictory, but each can offer help providing we do not make our chief question, "Which is most true historically?" We intend to use the category "Mannerism" critically, as an aid in discussing certain kinds of dramatic structure and effect. If we pick and choose among the salient points of each approach, we may surface with some useful and flexible concepts.

We confront, of course, a historical barrier at the outset in trying to make Mannerism a term for distinguishing kinds of drama *within* the Elizabethan-Jacobean corpus; as a "period" tag "Mannerism" may be used to label all or none of the drama written between 1560 and 1625. If we approach Mannerism as anti-classicism, we must acknowledge that the English dramatic tradition contained no established classicism to be "anti." If we concentrate on *maniera,* we find that Lyly's theatricalist fantasy and costume-jewelry verse at the beginning of the period's crest are at least as stylized as Fletcher's enameled, unmotivated "conversation of gentlemen" at the period's end, as Shearman himself has noted. If we search for a sense of historical crisis, an ambiguity of stage reality, or an attraction to mental anguish, we may choose to find the first as early as *Gorboduc,* the second in *Cambyses,* and the third in *The Spanish Tragedy.* Thus Sypher and Hauser treat Elizabethan drama as *characteristically* Manneristic. Clearly, we must appropriate the art historians' guidelines with some freedom.

From Friedlaender we can derive the idea that, whatever we end up calling "Mannerism" in this context, we should expect it to occur as an aftermath of—if not a reaction to—an artistic synthesis in which evident formal order combines with representational credibility to evoke a sense of "meaningfulness." That is, artistic form in such a synthesis (or "classic" phase) will seem to express the assurance that it is adequate to the artist's and perceiver's common grasp of reality. Any "classic" grasp of reality includes not only observable phenomena but also a fairly clear-cut set of shared values and ideals. Mannerism, then, represents a "decadence" of such a synthesis, the beginnings of an acknowledgement that one's perceptual and conceptual field ("reality") can no longer be adequately expressed by the received norms of formal organization.[22] Friedlaender saw Pontormo and his contemporaries rebelling against an art of focal clarity, idealized proportion, and calm orderliness; *prima facie,* we may suppose that these norms seemed inadequate as well to their felt need for "speculative" risk-taking and heightened, "subjective" spirituality. But if Friedlaender's dialectic is viewed more abstractly, "Mannerism" need not apply only to the particular forms distinguishing his anti-classical painters from their high-renaissance teachers. By the same token, "classic" can be used to define any art which similarly integrates form, meaning, clarity, and a sense of finality, no matter how. Indeed, such a "trans-historical" approach to Manneristic form has been used by German scholars and their pupils: E. R. Curtius, G. R. Hocke, G. Weise. If wrenching Mannerism loose from its anchor in mid-sixteenth-century painting thus subjects the definition to historical criticism, the historical problem of Elizabethan and Jacobean drama, noted above, makes such a step necessary if these concepts are to be helpful to the present discussion.

At least since Una Ellis-Fermor, "Jacobean" (post-1600) drama has been thought of as a decadence of the Elizabethan in precisely the sense used here. Bert O. States, in his wide-ranging, Burkean treatment of irony in drama, explores the underlying notion of decadence succinctly.[23] Unfortunately, "decadence" is an inexact and loaded word (which is one of the reasons why I have chosen to work with "Mannerism" as a term, though it is scarcely more exact). It is to Friedlaender's credit that by rigorous attention to form he freed Mannerism from being thought of as only an entropic corruption of high-renaissance style. An ostensibly decadent phase of artistic form, as Friedlaender saw, can be a period in which artistic frustration, reassessment, and experimentation result in tense but strongly affecting art.

In a decadence thus defined, artists may take one of two postures to cope with the breakdown of formal and perceptual coherence. If their received classic forms, through familiarity and increasing hints of irrelevancy, seem no longer to touch the bedrock of a reality which thereby threatens to become inarticulate, one strategy is to burrow feverishly toward the shock of naked experience. Sometimes extreme, detailed verisimilitude can be prized above any norms of composition, as in some fifteenth-century Northern (decadent Gothic) art. Surface realism aside, the artist may attempt to force the perceiver's engagement (and perhaps his own) by serving up "raw" a teeming, disordered world. The Mannerist painters' "medieval" abandonment of scale and symmetry may partially embody such an attitude. Certainly the Jacobean satirical impulse, whether manifest in the loosely organized "town comedy," Websterian *grand-guignol,* or the wide-spread attention paid to psychological extremes, suggests at least a touch of this "super-realistic" strategy. It is not important in this context what *kind* of intensified reality the artist and his audience prefer to the ordered vision already fixed in classic form: the violent, counterthrusting movement of Rosso; the neon colors of Pontormo; the naked, elemental landscapes of *Macbeth* and *Lear;* the seething stage-Italian "court"; the brothels of *Measure for Measure* and *Pericles*; the grotesque dream-life of the modern surrealist tradition; or the amoral and protean pantheon of Euripides. What is important is that "form" itself, insofar as it is still conceptualized in classic terms, is now seen as an obstacle to genuine involvement in the artwork, so that an experience of relative "chaos" becomes necessary as a breakthrough.[24] The magnifying mirror is replaced by the X-ray machine, the microscope, and the kaleidoscope.

Nor is it essential that the artist presume that the discrepancy between received form and perceived experience is in fact a discrepancy within reality itself: we need not go all the way with Dvořák, Hauser, and Sypher. Our emphasis here is not on the concept that "the time is out of joint" but on a situation in which an artist's available way of expressing such a concept seems itself out of joint. For such a situation to occur, it is obvious that received classic conceptions of form must exert powerful influences as models by virtue of their erstwhile "perfection"; they cannot be regarded by the artist as easily improved-upon, no matter how lacking he subliminally suspects they have become. No Mannerist painter was a premature Frondist intent upon junking the Renaissance; quite the contrary, his conscious models were normally the very high-renaissance masterpieces Friedlaender sees him rebelling against.

At the opposite pole an artist may altogether avoid trying to force empathic or emotional engagement. He may even refuse to allow his audience (or himself) any presupposition of a connection between "art" and "life." Here is a part *maniera* can play. The "stylized style" seems exaggerated when compared to its classical origins, because to some extent the artist expects it to be noticed in and for itself. Style, more than content, becomes the artist's preoccupation irrespective of how egotistic, "mannered," or self-conscious he is, since the possibilities of content, recognizable to him only through the medium of his received forms, have all been "used up." "Content," here, is not the fundamental connection with experience dug for by the super-realists, but the already-formed conceptual possibilities perfected by the classic predecessors through their own developed techniques: the explicit subject-matter of a painting (together with its intended spectator-response), or the plot, characters, themes, and *milieu* of a play.

It must be recognized that *maniera,* with all that it implies about a manipulation of fantasy and artifice, can in fact be a dominant concert of an artist prior to a recognized period of classic synthesis. Botticelli is *manieroso*; he accepts the technical conventions of his predecessors (outlines, frieze-like composition) as given, and proceeds from there to an individual ideal of pure elegance and grace. Lyly, even more than Spenser and Sidney, was usually content to mine the same kind of romance material (whether medieval or "classical" in

explicit subject) as the journeyman authors of romantic drama from the Digby *Mary Magdalene* to *Mucedorus*, without developing it significantly toward greater inclusiveness of theme, character-psychology, or composition. In the context of the choirboys' courtly "entertainment," he put his energy almost totally into stylistic elaboration ("decoration") and in so doing learned to exploit some of the possibilities of disengagement which the naive material would naturally suggest to a clever and ambitious hanger-on at court.[25]

However, when stylistic virtuosity becomes a preoccupation of a post-classical artist, quite different results occur, for "high style" seems somehow to have been "imposed" on a content already made familiar by complex, fully realized classical models. That is, such work often has the effect of seeming to treat its material *as if* it were naive, in the face of the audience's conditioned expectation of the contrary. *The Changeling*'s putative "core" of earnest, moral intrigue-tragedy would not predictably imply Middleton and Rowley's theatrical embroidery. The reverse side of the same coin is the ambiguous effect of a truly naive "content" when treated by an artist of known accomplishment: an audience may well be pre-conditioned to look for far greater subtlety of meaning and effect in *Pericles* than in *Mucedorus* or even in *Alexander and Campasbe.*

Though post-classical experiments in style *per se* may hint at a later formal synthesis (as Fletcher points to Dryden or Rosso to Salviati), such art most frequently appears as a fragmentation of the parent synthesis—a split between style and content in which the former "shows off" and elaborates the technical sophistication absorbed from the classic, while the latter is merely "indicated," presuming upon the spectator's familiarity (or even boredom) with its established articulation. Fletcher's subjects and his notion of what plot and characterization might be all seem to be derived from his predecessors' standard practice. But here they are reduced to interchangeable parts in a machine which has as its *chief* function the display of operatic "passion" by means of rhetorically effective dialogue. The audience is to be "moved" *in vacuo*. Sometimes, at one remove further, a received content is overtly parodied, as in Euripides' *Electra*. Even then, the parody is often inconsistent and without an unequivocal thematic point. The Duke in *Measure for Measure* is obviously an ironically conceived version of the type of satirical, string-pulling "agents of Providence" represented by Marston's Altofronto and, more grandly, by Shakespeare's later Prospero. For all his blundering and impotent machinations, however, he is not clearly a butt of ridicule. Such tentativeness is rarely the case when a clever artist parodies naive material from a pre-classical phase of formal development; what is then parodied (however fondly) is naiveté itself, as in Peele's *Old Wives' Tale* no less than in Beaumont's *Knight of the Burning Pestle.*

We have, then, attempts to *force* engagement and to *curtail* engagement, neither of which is a major concern of artists confidently working in a fully integrated classic mode. Each of these diametrically opposite "strategies" results in a different kind of art (of which Susan Sontag has provided thumbnail sketches in her article, "Notes on Camp"[26]). Rarely, however, does any post-classical artist take such extreme postures *vis à vis* his classical models or the "strategy" opposite the one he elects. The experiments we should focus on as Manner-istic are precisely those which give evidence of an attempt to encompass both poles at once, attempts which indicate the kind of formal (hence tonal) irresolution we first lit upon in **The Changeling.**[27] Indeed, though Pontormo's asymmetry, shocking colors, and crowded, angular space often appear to exhibit the first "strategy" while the smooth, frozen denizens of Bronzino's courtly world suggest the second, neither can be said to represent a "pure" alternative.

Bronzino's *maniera* was suited not only to tense, icy portraits such as those of Eleanor of Toledo, Bartolommeo Panciatichi, and the anonymous, insolent "Young Man" in the Metropolitan Museum (all of whom could be characters from Fletcher). In *Christ in Limbo* and in *Venus, Cupid, Folly, and Time* the same sleek sophistication is applied to the disturbed colloca-tion of thrusting bodies which Rosso had pioneered; what is more, the "elusive air of obscenity" in the latter picture is actually enhanced by Bronzino's detached dexterity.[28] Fletcher again is brought to mind. Pontormo, even when his composition is most "Gothic" (*Joseph in Egypt*) or when his color and mood are most eerie (*Visitation, Deposition*: "crazed . . . as if lit by some monstrous aurora borealis"[29]), still puts enormous care into a complicated but "legible" *disegno* of focus and counter-focus—an evident intellectual deliberateness seemingly at odds with his "expressionistic" notes of hysteria. Parmigianino's famous *Madonna del Collo Lungo,* for all its bursting of the classical boundaries of weight-distribution, proportion, perspective, and visual "common sense," derives its very title from the cool, swan-like elegance into which the painter has forced his central figure.

The function of *contrapposto* in Giovanni Bologna's statuary is another case in point. In itself, exaggerated *contrapposto* ("counter-poise") represents a game-like approach to form: how twisting and multi-faceted, how apparently top-heavy and incapable of balance can I make a statue, without forfeiting gracefulness, move-ment, or support? Yet the most obvious effect of this appreciable virtuosity is to involve the spectator, at some length, in experiencing the object. He must see it from every possible angle, for each vista beckons him to the next, yet each angle of vision offers a surprise: a seemingly different statue, as interesting in its contours as the last. (Perhaps it is not too far-fetched to see this

very *contrapposto,* proceeding ultimately from interwo-ven serpentine spirals in conflicting rhythms, as a con-crete analogue of the serpentine arrangement of tones which our imagined model depicted for **The Changeling.**) Our two "strategies," conscious virtuosity at the possible expense of meaning and engagement, and forced engagement at the possible expense of for-mal coherence, become two ends of the same rubber band. The first keeps the second from ever becoming a Romantic (or expressionistic) anti-classicism; the sec-ond does not allow the first to become an art-for-art's-sake decorativeness.

The point is that the artist, working in the shadow of his classical teachers, cannot escape knowing what he is about. He cannot be naive about form and technique, nor can he afford to allow his spectators to think he is. Having had their own perceptions conditioned by a classic perfection of form, they are likely to give short shrift to an apparently genuine "primitive." He cannot whip up his own engagement with whatever confusing reality he perceives by simply "painting what he sees" or "writing what he feels," because both seeing and feeling have been colossally educated. He must, it seems, demonstrate to himself and his audience that he is a past master of good technique—at the same time that he casts doubt on technique's adequacy by "ex-ploding" the general forms which it was previously de-veloped to realize. This is a large generalization, but it provides a clue to the "heart" of Mannerism: the proto-typical Mannerist painters and the most "Jacobean" of English playwrights are the ones in whose works we recognize an extreme tension between totally manipula-tive artifice (the *terminus ad quem* of *maniera*) and "the shock of recognition." As a result, their works inevita-bly appear "self-conscious." Irony, in its broadest criti-cal senses, is their essential condition.

The best symbol of this ironic consciousness is the *repoussoir* in some Mannerist pictures, the man stand-ing in the foreground glaring at the viewer and beckon-ing him into the "scene." He gestures to include us in the strangely affecting iconic world behind the picture-plane, and by so doing reveals himself as a painted de-vice and the framed world itself a deliberate construc-tion made for us to look at. Sypher has already noted that he corresponds to the *persona* of the satirist in Jacobean drama: Asper's "Macilente" mask, Altofronto's "Malevole." Functionally, the *repoussoir* parallels Gower in *Pericles.* That he should also suggest the Prospero of "Our revels now are ended" and the Epilogue is no wonder.

Mannered artifice and emotional engagement play the same unresolved tug-of-war in the plays as in the paint-ings. It is worth noting that the terms of the tension were familiar to seventeenth-century audiences no less than to ourselves. James Shirley, in his preface to the first folio of Beaumont and Fletcher's collected plays (1647), displays his understanding of how their dramaturgy managed to provoke both empathy and estrangement together. In the course of a typical scene, says Shirley, the spectator's passions are "raised . . . by such insinuating degrees" that he "shall not chuse but consent, and go along with them" to the point where he is in complete empathy with the character onstage: "grown insensibly the very same person." Yet, *"in the same moment"* (my emphasis), he cannot but "stand admiring the subtile Tracks of his engagement."[30]

A purely critical use of these formal concepts may easily transcend historical definition and provide insights into, say, Euripides' drama. It is not difficult to see also in Harold Pinter's *The Homecoming,* for instance, an analogous dramaturgy: his unnerving talent for detaching ostentatiously realistic dialogue from its conventional underpinnings in plot and "motivated" character. We might contrast Edward Albee's *Who's Afraid of Virginia Woolf?* with one of its apparent models, O'Neill's masterpiece of autobiographical realism, *Long Day's Journey Into Night.* In O'Neill, the relations among the characters can be schematized psychologically as a repetitious "game" (formula: "I hate you; no, I hate myself for saying that; therefore I love you; therefore don't hate me"). Yet in Albee, game-playing literally comprises the characters' relationships, a formal condition which leads with some plausibility directly to the revelation of George and Martha's fictitious child: a somewhat arbitrary "symbol." It is not that Albee's play is "unbelievable" (neither are Pinter's[31]), so much as that its patterns of suspense and surprise are so obviously a result of the playwright's conscious concern and (undoubtedly) of his ironic enjoyment in writing the play. Such is his manipulation of the interplay of our estrangement and our empathy, our accustomed sense of the "serious" and of the "funny," that we are never allowed to predict the tone of the next five minutes with any confidence.

We started with *The Changeling* and galloped far afield. Obviously, this exploratory excursus into Manneristic form was not necessary simply to elucidate that play. Rather, some such line of inquiry was suggested by the general problems *The Changeling* introduced. Though these problems of critical approach to a wide variety of late-Elizabethan and Jacobean plays have not by any means been "solved," we have reason, I think, to expect that the qualities of Manneristic form we have singled out for brief examination can continue to be refined as critical tools. If we are to adapt these categorical ideas appropriately (and not merely to "apply" them), we will, in our readings of the drama, have to persist in emphasizing subtleties of tone itself. It must be apparent that this critical route is neither easy nor, after a lapse of three and a half centuries, capable of leading to certainty.[32] But it may be hoped that in the long run a

general approach of this kind will provide us with a fuller understanding of the interrelated modern enthusiasms for Mannerist painting, Euripides, the Jacobeans, and recent "Manneristic" dramatists like Albee and Pinter.

Notes

1. It seems clear that the latter was intended by the authors: "Your only smiles have power to cause re-live/ The dead again . . ." (V.iii.224-25).

2. However, the play was entered in the Stationers' Register (Oct. 19, 1652) as "a Comedie . . . written by Rowley."

3. See N. W. Bawcutt, ed., *The Changeling,* Revels edn. (London 1958), pp. xxxixff. Line for line, Rowley may have written more of the play than Middleton (1073 lines to 1018 lines). Dorothy M. Farr, in *Thomas Middleton and the Drama of Realism* (Edinburgh, 1973), believes Middleton had ultimate control over the entire composition, even over the scenes (including the subplot) which Rowley penned (p. 131n, p. 133n). If this is true, at least it reinforces my argument that we ought not to separate the two authors' work when discussing the play's structure.

4. Empson, *Some Versions of Pastoral* (London, 1935), pp. 48-52; Bradbrook, *Themes and Conventions of Elizabethan Tragedy* (London, 1935), pp. 213-24, and *The Growth and Structure of Elizabethan Comedy* (London, 1955; rpt. Baltimore: Penguin, 1963), p. 165; Holzknecht, "The Dramatic Structure of *The Changeling,*" *Renaissance Papers, A Selection of Papers Presented at the Renaissance Meeting in the Southern States,* ed. Allan H. Gilbert (Orangeburg, S. C., 1954), pp. 77-87. Richard Levin, in *The Multiple Plot in English Renaissance Drama* (Chicago, 1971), proposes a linkage on the basis of Aristotle's four kinds of causality: material (characters of both plots related to each other as friends, kinsmen, or neighbors), effective (characters or events from one action influence happenings in the other), formal (plots separate but related by parallel or contrast), and final (an "affective relationship between plots" is created by their qualities of tone, emotion, and sensibility). Yet for his scheme to work in *The Changeling,* Levin posits a "missing" scene: the wedding-masque brawl logically occurring before Act V.

5. Note also the internal evidence that the part of Franciscus was written to be played by the same actor who played Jasperino. This is not only an indication that Middleton and Rowley worked together but also a contributing factor to the lameness of the subplot. In IV.iii a letter is substituted

for the (preferable) presence of Franciscus, who cannot appear until late in the scene because Jasperino has just exited in costume at the end of IV.ii.

6. Quotation from Brustein, *Seasons of Discontent* (New York, 1967), p. 253. Cf. Eliot, *Essays on Elizabethan Drama* (1932; rpt. New York: Harcourt Brace, 1956), pp. 85-86; Ellis-Fermor, *The Jacobean Drama* (London, 1936), p. 146.

7. Bawcutt, pp. lxv, lxvii. See also Richard Hindry Barker, *Thomas Middleton* (New York: Columbia Univ. Press, 1958), p. 121.

8. Eugene Ionesco has noted, for example, that any tragedy becomes comic simply if it is speeded up. See Susan Sontag, *Against Interpretation and Other Essays* (New York, 1969), p. 123.

9. This polarity corresponds generally to "transparent" vs. "opaque" as used by Bernard Beckerman, *Dynamics of Drama* (New York, 1970), pp. 31-33. Beckerman, when he speaks of "credibility" and "artificiality," uses a narrower focus, the former approaching the notion of stylistic realism, the latter referring to dramatic "conventions" such as the soliloquy. Obviously, a "convention" can be "transparent" (or, in my terms, "credible") to the extent that the audience is accustomed to it and accepts it simply as a way to express the fictive "content" of a dramatic event. Here, as in most such discussions, my judgments about what "engages" and what "estranges" in Jacobean drama are based on my assessment of a Jacobean audience's sensibilities in this regard, although scenes are singled out for comment on the basis of the problems they might have for us today.

10. Brustein, p. 253.

11. Jordan, "Myth and Psychology in *The Changeling*," *Renaissance Drama*, n.s. 3, (1970), 157-66.

12. In this and in all further observations about Fletcher's dramaturgy I am much indebted to Eugene M. Waith, *Patterns of Tragicomedy in Beaumont and Fletcher* (New Haven: Yale Univ. Press, 1952).

13. Alfred Harbage has drawn attention to the obvious parallels between "intrigue" tragedies, beginning with *The Spanish Tragedy,* and their near relatives (and perhaps immediate ancestors), the neo-Plautine comedies: "Intrigue in Elizabethan Tragedy," *Essays on Shakespeare and Elizabethan Drama in Honor of Hardin Craig* (Columbia: Univ. of Missouri Press, 1962), pp. 37-44. *The Changeling,* although unusual in this respect, is not the only "serious" play to take the comic potential inherent in such plotting the one crucial step further, to the emergence of an overt comic tone; cf. *The Jew of Malta.*

14. By far the most interesting topic explored by recent Elizabethan scholars has been this very perception of "Verfremdungseffekten." See, for example, Maynard Mack, "Engagement and Detachment in Shakespeare's Plays," *Essays . . . in Honor of Hardin Craig,* pp. 275-96; Anne Righter, *Shakespeare and the Idea of the Play* (New York, 1962); and Michael Shapiro, "Children's Troupes: Dramatic Illusion and Acting Style," *Comparative Drama,* 3 (1969), 42-53, and "Toward a Reappraisal of the Children's Troupes," *Theatre Survey,* 13, no. ii (Nov. 1972), 1-19. Jackson I. Cope, in *The Theatre and the Dream: From Metaphor to Form in Renaissance Drama* (Baltimore: Johns Hopkins Press, 1973), approaches many of these questions in a different but complementary perspective. His notion of the "Baroque" in drama includes some of the formal notes others have discussed as "Manneristic."

15. My debt to Kenneth Burke in all this should be apparent. See "Lexicon Rhetoricae," *Counter-Statement* (New York, 1931), pp. 157-61. In Burkean terms, the formal principle I find *The Changeling* exploiting (often by inversion) is that of "qualitative progression": a sequence of qualities which evoke audience-responses that seem "appropriately" to follow one another. Madeleine Doran's commentary is excellent: *Endeavors of Art: A Study of Form in Elizabethan Drama* (Madison: Univ. of Wisconsin Press, 1954), pp. 21-23. Burke's "qualitative progression" has much in common with Levin's "final causality"; the "parodic" interpretation of the plot-linkage would, at its simplest, highlight Burke's "repetitive form" and Levin's "formal causality."

16. Alsemero's earlier speeches are full of "forebodings." But heard in the context of the first scene's artificial rhetoric, they can provide no firm expectation that the play will not turn out to be—if not an outright comedy—a tragi-comedy or a romance of the lightest sort; cf. *The Malcontent.*

17. Waith, for example, says flatly (p. 41) that *A King and No King* (in this typical of the corpus of Fletcher's plays) "has no meaning."

18. The extremes of criticism pertaining to these plays, dating back to the eighteenth century, are well known. Only recently have the possibilities of Shakespeare's tonal manipulation (including parody) been concentrated on; see William Empson, *The Structure of Complex Words* (London, 1951), pp. 270-84; Joseph G. Price, *The Unfortunate Comedy: A Study of All's Well That Ends Well and Its Critics* (Toronto, 1968); and Jonathan R. Price, "*Measure for Measure* and the Critics," *Shakespeare Quarterly,* 20 (1969), 179-204.

19. Friedlaender, *Mannerism and Anti-Mannerism in Italian Painting* (New York, 1957). Friedlaender first advanced his views in a lecture at Freiburg in 1914.

20. Shearman, *Mannerism* (Harmondsworth: Penguin, 1967). Shearman's historical care is mirrored in the excellent essays on French literary Mannerism by Marcel Raymond: "La Pléiade et le Maniérisme," *Lumières de la Pléiade* (Paris, 1966); "Aux frontières du Maniérisme et du Baroque," *Etre et dire* (Neuchatel, 1970); *La Poésie française et le maniérisme 1546-1610* (Geneva, 1971).

21. Dvořák, *Geschichte der italienischen Kunst im Zeitalter der Renaissance* (Munich, 1927-29), vol. II; Hauser, *The Social History of Art,* trans. by the author with Stanley Godman (New York, 1951), vol. I; Sypher, *Four Stages of Renaissance Style* (Garden City, N.Y.: Doubleday, 1955). See also Douglas A. Russell, "Mannerism and Shakespearean Costume," *Educational Theatre Journal,* 16 (1964), 324-32; D. B. Rowland, *Mannerism—Style and Mood* (New Haven: Yale Univ. Press, 1964); and Roy Daniells, "The Mannerist Element in English Literature," *University of Toronto Quarterly,* 36 (Oct. 1966), 1-11.

22. My premises about the evolution of artistic forms are derived from George Kubler, *The Shape of Time* (New Haven: Yale Univ. Press, 1962). Kubler's concepts effectively supersede both the "organic" (growth-decay) metaphor and Friedlaender's "action-reaction" pattern. For a finely nuanced discussion of Mannerism in the context of historical "flow," see Blake Lee Spahr, "Baroque and Mannerism: Epoch and Style," *Colloquia Germanica,* 1 (1967), 78-100. Spahr reconciles the "historical" and "trans-historical" approaches to Manneristic style.

23. States, *Irony and Drama: A Poetics* (Ithaca, N.Y., 1971), pp. 126-38.

24. See Morse Peckham, *Man's Rage for Chaos* (Philadelphia, 1965).

25. See Shapiro, op. cit.

26. Sontag, pp. 288-89. Sontag's articles, "On Style," "Marat/Sade/Artaud," "Happenings: an art of radical juxtaposition," "Notes on Camp," and "One Culture and the New Sensibility," all provide remarkable insights into the range of artistic forms we are touching upon here.

27. See Davy A. Carozza, "For a Definition of Mannerism: The Hatzfeldian Thesis," *Colloquia Germanica,* 1 (1967), 66-77.

28. Michael Levey, *A Concise History of Painting from Giotto to Cezanne* (New York, 1962), p. 118.

29. Levey, p. 116.

30. See Maynard Mack, pp. 276-77.

31. The plausibility of Pinter's plays is argued by Martin Esslin, *The Peopled Wound* (Garden City, N.Y.: Doubleday, 1970).

32. See n. 9 above.

J. L. Simmons (essay date 1980)

SOURCE: Simmons, J. L. "Diabolical Realism in *The Changeling*." *Renaissance Drama* n.s. 11 (1980): 135-70.

[*In the following essay, Simmons explores the use of psychology in* The Changeling, *especially in the depiction of sexual matters, noting how for Jacobeans sexuality was intimately tied up with the demonic or diabolical.*]

Middleton's paradoxical genius was affirmed by T. S. Eliot in 1927 in a way that modern criticism tends to vulgarize into simple contradiction. Middleton was, for Eliot, an "impersonal" artist with "no point of view," "no message"; he was "merely a great recorder," his work grounded by "a strain of realism underneath."[1] With those characteristics, however, and perhaps even because of them, he wrote in *The Changeling* a play of "profound and permanent moral value and horror"; here "Middleton is surpassed by one Elizabethan alone, and that is Shakespeare." Eliot apparently saw no dichotomy: in *The Changeling* Middleton objectively exposed "fundamental passions of any time and any place"; he was not distracted from reality by the Elizabethan deduction that God's revenge triumphs over the crying and execrable sin of murder. The playwright's masterpiece exhibited to Eliot the perennial tragedy, beyond historical pieties, of "the immoral nature, suddenly trapped in the inexorable toils of morality—of morality not made by man but by Nature—and forced to take the consequences of an act which it had planned lightheartedly." The horrible discovery of these moral toils, Eliot asserted, reveals a "truth permanent in human nature." With his impersonal genius Middleton recorded the tragic progression, thereby transcending (as Eliot thought Shakespeare had transcended) the inferior thought of his age. One nevertheless discovers in Eliot's criticism the potentiality for apparent contradiction: Middleton's tragedy, even if impersonally observed, surely establishes a point of view and even, one would infer from such horror, a message.

Unwisely we have come to see the temporal and the timeless Middletons as problematically opposed. One of the most reputable critics of Middleton's early comedies speaks of "the struggle between satiric observa-tion and determined moralizing."[2] With the tragic Middleton the dichotomy opposes the historical moral-ist—the author who could bear to read Reynolds's *The Triumphs of God's Revenge* in the first place—against the modern psychological realist who breathed life into the dead weight of his source. Obviously, these opposi-tions are insidious if we must choose between a moral-ized Middleton indistinguishable from contemporary hacks and a Middleton modernized for all time, vaguely, as a realist, a naturalist, or a psychological dramatist.[3] Eliot went too far in isolating Middleton from his age, but historical criticism has had little success in account-ing for the impulse that distinguishes Middleton and Rowley's mutual enterprise from Reynolds's novella. We end up either with the moral vision that every Jacobean playwright can be blindly made to share or with the recording realism that is discomfited by any pressure from beyond the natural or, in a modern sense, the psychological realm. And precisely how Rowley could have adapted himself so completely to Middleton's psychological genius is a mystery that no critic, not even Eliot, has touched.

The word *psychology* should itself beg the question; as Robert West observes, it was not a word or, in our con-ception, a science known to Elizabethans. He continues:

> similarly, perhaps, they lacked our conception of the cleavage between the objective and the subjective. But it was not that they were without a theory of mental process, or neglected to distinguish the forms impinged upon the intellect by the outside world from combina-tions of these forms which the soul itself originated. It was rather that they were not so sure as we of the in-violability of the personality, not sure that alien person-alities could not come into the mind in a manner much more immediate than anything our theories of sugges-tion and hypnotism admit of. The subjective . . . was an uncertain category in a day when authorities held that a percept might indeed be peculiar to a man as shared with no other and having no existence outside his mind, yet originate with and represent a foreign substance.[4]

It is this foreign substance that I intend to investigate, as well as the artifice whereby the two collaborators were able to exhibit and, simultaneously, to incorporate the alien within the violated personality. As J. Leeds Barroll has argued in relation to Shakespeare's charac-terizations, a playwright of another age may very likely have discovered truths of human nature acceptable to modern psychology; but "the structure of ideas by which he sought to account for such phenomena would have been quite importantly different."[5]

In order to reach this conceptual structure, I shall begin with the sexual fantasies of Beatrice-Joanna and De Flores as projections of an alien and demonic order pe-culiarly rationalized in the characters themselves. I shall

proceed to the major sources of the play where we can discover, as did Middleton and Rowley, this connection between demonology and those sexual fantasies. I shall give new consideration to an important topical matter alluded to in the play; indeed I shall urge that the Essex divorce or nullity trial and the scandal following the murder of Sir Thomas Overbury are sufficiently influen-tial for these events to be considered an inspiration for the play and even a source. Finally, I want tentatively to trace in the works of Middleton and of Rowley be-fore 1622 a few signs that these two playwrights would prove uniquely compatible for what may be the greatest of all dramatic collaborations. By going over some old material in a new light, I hope to establish a meeting ground between our preoccupation with the psychologi-cal in sexual matters and the Jacobean preoccupation, in such matters, with the demonic. Perhaps we can thereby get closer to what Eliot saw in the play as fun-damentally true, even if the two centuries approach this truth from different directions.

I

Wherein lies the essential tragedy of *The Changeling*? "The *habituation* of Beatrice to her sin," answers Eliot, emphatically. But that fact, one would have to say, does not in itself distinguish her from a bustling company of impudent Jacobean heroines. Eliot's conclusion is suc-cinct but, for purposes of definition, uncritically reti-cent: "The tragedy of Beatrice is not that she has lost Alsemero, for whose possession she played; it is that she has won De Flores." I think, however, that Eliot considered *The Changeling* to be more than a tragedy of ironic retribution. What tragedy, after all, is not? It is grimly appropriate that Eliot's intelligent modesty would prevent his further specification; for, if the trag-edy has any message, it is that such delicacy in human sexuality, even when proceeding from a morally vacu-ous nature, is in some way self-protective and therefore genuinely ethical. The mask of modesty, facially and linguistically, hides a reality that is death to explore—a bawdy death, but death nevertheless:

> Speak it yet further off that I may lose
> What has been spoken, and no sound remain on't.
> I would not hear so much offence again
> For such another deed.
>   . . . . .
> Why, 'tis impossible thou canst be so wicked,
> Or shelter such a cunning cruelty,
> To make his death the murderer of my honour!
> Thy language is so bold and vicious,
> I cannot see which way I can forgive it
> With any modesty.

(III.iv.102-125)[6]

The tragedy of winning De Flores does not lie merely in the irony of the retribution but in the sexual night-mare of it, a sexual hell both horrible and fascinating.

In this respect the popular wisdom of our day is the same as in Middleton's. One recent critic, inspired by the BBC Television production in 1974, has called the play "the tragedy of an arrogant self-indulgent nature, hell-bent on total appetite, total experience, total destruction." He acknowledges that now more than ever, with our alluring delusions of sexual liberation, we are able to perceive the real focus of the tragic experience: "many young Beatrices of today would recognize, rather more readily than literary scholars, their affinity with the Jacobean teenager,"[7] But we will only convict ourselves once more of the modernist's fallacy unless in the psychological perception we take seriously the literal force of *hell-bent*. The total loss of sexual control, the complete abandonment of the self to eros, leads to eternal death; therefore Beatrice-Joanna justly loathes De Flores "As much as youth and beauty hates a sepulchre" (II.ii.67). Her revulsion is not only "the obverse of a fascination";[8] it also represents a ghost-guessed apprehension of her infinite capacity for damnation when that damnation is perceived, as Beatrice-Joanna perceives everything, sexually.

The Changeling uniquely dramatizes the progression of a diabolically psychosexual nightmare, a progression in which the sexual drive is not tamed, sublimated, and legitimized within the conventions of courtship and marriage. Middleton and Rowley show a yielding to the wild and naked thing itself, a yielding that plunges one into a sexual abyss:

> if a woman
> Fly from one point, from him she makes a husband,
> She spreads and mounts then like arithmetic,
> One, ten, a hundred, a thousand, ten thousand. . . .
>
> (II.ii.60-63)

Arithmetically spreading and mounting, Beatrice physically and psychically conjoins the feminine abandon and masculine aggression that lead toward a grotesque infinity. When she embraces the horror, as dreadful as it is, she is ensnared in the damnable satisfaction of a world-without-end:

> Thy peace is wrought for ever in this yielding.
> 'Las, how the turtle pants! Thou'lt love anon
> What thou so fear'st and faint'st to venture on.
>
> (III.iv.169-171)

The peculiar fascination of the tragedy is not that it shows the wages of sin to be death but that it discloses in Beatrice the whispering allure of being "undone . . . endlessly" (IV.i.1). We see through her the horror that Joseph Conrad's Marlow saw through Kurtz, the result of losing all restraint, of yielding to the diabolic darkness in a voracity for its "unspeakable rites." To look upon that depravity, as to look upon the face of God, is to die; and Beatrice, when she is united with De Flores,

cannot avoid the final obscene *Liebestod*. "I'll be your pander now," says Alsemero, closeting the doomed lovers for their sexual as well as their dramatic catastrophe:

> rehearse again
> Your scene of lust, that you may be perfect
> When you shall come to act it to the black audience
> Where howls and gnashings shall be music to you.
> Clip your adult'ress freely, 'tis the pilot
> Will guide you to the Mare Mortuum,
> Where you shall sink to fathoms bottomless.
>
> (V.iii.114-120)

Beatrice's nature is in both sexual and Calvinistic terms reprobate from the beginning, before the confirmation with De Flores that she is bent on hell. Her change of affection from Alonzo to Alsemero was, as De Flores charges, "a kind / Of whoredom in thy heart" (III.iv.143-144); but her forbidden desires are not to be domesticated by either the civil Alonzo or Alsemero. It is obscenely appropriate that, as she moves toward her deadly satisfaction, De Flores returns to her "the first token" given Alonzo in their courtship, her ring upon his severed phallic digit;[9] and all feeling for the pallid Alsemero is transcended in the erotic and murderous excitement of her pact with De Flores. The Edenic chances for Beatrice are lost in her fascination for the serpent that will deflower her:

> This ominous ill-fac'd fellow more disturbs me
> Than all my other passions.
>
> (II.i.53-54)

The ugly face, which "Blood-guiltiness becomes," represents her destiny, as she is finally able to see when, in his arms, she looks not to heaven but to his prodigious visage:

> Beneath the stars, upon yon meteor
> Ever hung my fate, 'mongst things corruptible;
> I ne'er could pluck it from him: my loathing
> Was prophet to the rest but ne'er believ'd.
>
> (V.iii.154-157)

Beatrice's sexuality, then, has demanded a literal phallic worship, with the meteoric face ultimately adored for all its loathsomeness. In elevating her Florentine admirer to her service, this perverted Petrarchan lady is a witch raising her familiar devil.[10] In metaphor she fondles and arouses the tumescent instrument of her destruction and her desire, though it is the same object she has loathed "to a hair and pimple":

BEATRICE:

> Hardness becomes the visage of a man well,
> It argues service, resolution, manhood,
> If cause were of employment.

DE FLORES:

> 'Twould be soon seen,
> If e'er your ladyship had cause to use it.
> I would but wish the honour of a service
> So happy as that mounts to.

(II.ii.92-97)

The result of raising the turgid face for her service is that it must finally, in exchange, become her god:

> How heartily he serves me! His face loathes one,
> But look upon his care, who would not love him?
> The east is not more beauteous than his service.

(V.i.70-72)

The sadomasochistic alliance rhetorically identifies each of the demonic lovers as both subject and object: "His face loathes one"; "one loathes his face." The rhetoric penetrates the pat explanation Alsemero gives for Beatrice's "infirmity": "There's scarce a thing that is both lov'd and loath'd" (I.i.125). It is this duality in Beatrice—the love in the loathing, the loathing in the love—that is most striking in **The Changeling**: not exactly that she becomes habituated to sin or that, losing Alsemero, she gains De Flores; rather that she comes to acknowledge the love of what she hates at the same time that she is able to see fully her own degradation:

> Oh come not near me, sir, I shall defile you:
> I am that of your blood was taken from you
> For your better health; look no more upon't,
> But cast it to the ground regardlessly:
> Let the common sewer take it from distinction.

(V.iii.149-153)

These lines are among the most terrifying in dramatic literature and the recognition lifts Beatrice—a most unlikely candidate—among the great tragic figures. Her recognition, furthermore, clearly distinguishes this tragedy of damnation from *Macbeth* or *Paradise Lost*—though, as Helen Gardner has shown, the common pattern is clearly present.[11] Beatrice is distinct because her damnation depicts the fascination of evil as it is manifested in forbidden sexual fantasies loathed and loved, fantasies which, pursued to their sadistic and masochistic climax, annihilate the self. In this process, as De Flores insists, there is indeed eternal rest. Beatrice's loss of identity—a tenuous distinction at best—is quintessentially the Jacobean dissolution of personality in the face of erotic evil.

II

Within the period of Middleton and Rowley's inspiration, where could one find an expression of these sexual fantasies mingling eros and evil in an alliance that leads to physical and spiritual death? That a conceptual structure of ideas for such an experience was extant I take to be self-evident from the close collaboration: Rowley contributed not only the subplot that physically reflects the spiritual grotesquerie of Beatrice-Joanna and De Flores; the minor playwright also fashioned the opening and closing scenes, initiating and resolving the tragic main plot. No doubt Middleton's genius was inspiriting; but clearly the two men conceived the tragedy together or at least shared, as a communicable point of reference, a concept of sexual damnation that became a source both for the characterization and for the metaphoric pattern of the tragic experience. This psychological structure was a nightmare that captured the sexual imagination of Europe during the sixteenth and seventeenth centuries—the fascination with witchcraft and demonology. The specific source of the play in fact points to this frame of reference; and, if we take seriously the structural pattern that informs the exemplary tales in *The Triumphs of God's Revenge,* we can discover this more general source of the play.

The tale of Beatrice and her De Flores, like the other stories in the collection, is the tragedy of individuals "seduced partly by sin, but chiefly by Satan, who is the author thereof."[12] In these stories of lust and murder, the absolutes of good and evil exert their force externally upon the tortured psyche; but, while they remain outside the mind, they manifest their power within: "how can wee giue our selues to God, when in the heat of lust and fume of reuenge, we sell our hearts to the deuill?" (p. 106). When Beatrice is plotting to rid herself of Alonzo, Reynolds didactically exposes the supernatural pattern underlying the scene in the play: "And now, after shee had ruminated, and runne ouer many bloody designes: the deuill, who neuer flies from those that follow him, proffers her an inuention as execrable as damnable" (p. 127). At this crucial point Middleton and Rowley diverged from Reynolds's conventional account by their transformation of De Flores. Instead of externalizing the devil's proffered "inuention" as the De Flores who is "a Gallant young Gentleman," they internalized and rationalized the process by creating in their De Flores a demonic creature, "as execrable as damnable," who offers himself to be her instrument. The playwrights nevertheless retained the idea of a pact between a woman, ingenuously evil, and the fiend conjured by her bloody designs.

In the sadomasochistic fantasy of the demonic pact, Middleton and Rowley found the sexual labyrinth into which Beatrice descends. In the English witch-hunts the sexual nature of the alliance was never explored so eagerly as on the Continent; but by the end of Elizabeth's reign the work of Reginald Scot and King James had given notoriety to the erotic elaborations of Continental demonologists.[13] Both Scot and James, whether attacking or supporting the tradition of the *Malleus Maleficarum,* describe the "carnall copulation with *Incubus*" as the chief capital crime of witchcraft, a crime confirming idolatry and apostasy.[14] Since the evidence of **The Witch** argues that Middleton derived his knowledge of witchcraft from the skeptical *Discoverie of Witchcraft*, it is significant to observe that Scot concludes his account "of such abhominable lecheries" with a rationalization: "Thus are lecheries covered with the cloke of *Incubus* and witchcraft."[15] Even when deemed self-serving exculpations, in other words, the diabolic rationale of sexual depravity remained psychologically as well as morally the most persuasive fantasy. The essential characteristic of the diabolic alliance is also that of the unrestrained sexual urge. As Thomas Cooper explained in his *Mystery of Witch-craft* (1617), the witch is motivated to make this "desperate covenant" by "the earnest and unsatiable desire to accomplish our lusts";[16] but the devotee, signaling this insatiability, at once loses the will to act independently and yields to all that was once deemed ugly, degrading, and evil. If the forbidden fruit turns to ashes, it nevertheless remains perpetually compelling. In the fantasy, then, lies the fascination with the horror, the love in the loathing, that Beatrice manifests; and this ambivalence is notable in almost all testimonies. Although Scot simplistically assumes that women have "more pleasure and delight (they say) with *Incubus* that waie, than with anie mortall man," those more intimately associated with the experience report differently. As Henry Charles Lea observes, "while the demonologists tell us that the gratification of lust was one of the leading incentives to witchcraft . . . yet the women with singular unanimity everywhere describe the relation as painful and distasteful."[17] But this masochistic confusion in the accounts of pain and pleasure is of course precisely at the source of the fantasy: "His face loathes one, / But look upon his care, who would not love him?"

Of course if the origins of De Flores were satanic only, the educated might expect the sexual drive of the character to be unimpressive. Cooper describes the archfiend as sexually rather passive, though the physical act of intercourse religiously seals the spiritual union: "Lastly, to gratifie them somewhat for this their dutiful seruice, it pleaseth their new Maister oftentimes to offer himselfe familiarly vnto them, to *dally and lye with them,* in token of their more neere *coniunction,* and as it were *marriage* vnto them." Then follows the orgy of the witches' sabbath, ending with that infamous kiss the witch bestows, kneeling in adoration, upon her master: "The baser and vnseemelier the homage is, the more it binds."[18] But the sexual capacity of Satan need not deter one from indulging in demonic fantasies because lower orders of demons were at hand—incubi, succubi, satyrs—which monomaniacally lusted after humans. Authorities offer little in rigorous definition of these beings, their names and origins; but St. Augustine had affirmed for the Christian era their continued existence as progeny of the fallen angels who shortly after the loss of Paradise began to fornicate with "the daughters of men." The power of love affects "the spirits of the air, and devils of hell themselves," writes Robert Burton, whose *Anatomy of Melancholy* preceded **The Changeling** by only a year and, like the play, scientifically observes a psychophysiological morbidity ultimately satanic in origin: these demons "are as much enamoured and dote (if I may use that word) as any other creatures whatsoever. For if those stories be true that are written of incubus and succubus, of nymphs, lascivious fauns, satyrs, and those heathen gods which were devils . . . or those familiar meetings in our days, and company of witches and devils, there is some probability for it."[19]

Though demonic, De Flores is not portrayed as precisely satanic. With his perpetual "hardness" arguing "service," he is also the jovial and scurvy satyr or incubus.[20] "To a hair and pimple" he is a phallic creature who "dotes" on Beatrice. Suffering from a diabolic satyriasis in his lust for her, De Flores has the potency to undo the nymphomaniac endlessly. In his scientific *Historie of Foure-Footed Beastes,* Edward Topsell assures the reader "that the deuils do many waies delude men in the likeness of Satyres." Because of their all-consuming lust "the auncient Graecians coniecture their name to be deriued as it were of *Stathes,* signifying the yarde or virile member: and it is certain that the deuils haue exercised their praestigious lust, or rather their imagination of lust vpon mankind, whereof commeth that distinction of Fauni, that some are *Incubi* defilers of Women, and some *Succubi* defiled by men." Satyrs abuse their victims "in most odious and filthy manner . . . not onely in that part that nature hath ordained, but ouer the whole body most libidinously."[21] Not only does the sexual nature of De Flores find its origin in the popular idea of this demon; the character's comic powers of satiric observation also reflect the literary concept of the satyr, etymologically confused with *satura.* Rough and crude in the Juvenalian manner, full of sexual envy, De Flores exposes the hypocrisy of the modest world around him and has a moral conscience in his corruption. Satyr figures had been preoccupied with sexuality since their development in the 1590s, first in verse satire, then in the drama; and De Flores is surely in this regard the culmination of the type.

A representation strongly suggesting Beatrice's satyric captivation is in Book III of *The Faerie Queene,* in the episode of Hellenore's rapture. Seduced and deserted by Paridell, the sexually frustrated wife finds satisfaction in the enthrallment of satyrs. Her husband, the impotent Malbecco, witnesses her grotesque ecstasy:

> At night, when all they went to sleep, he vewd,
>   Whereas his louely wife emongst them lay,
>   Embraced of a *Satyre* rough and rude,
>   Who all the night did minde his ioyous play:
>   Nine times he heard him come aloft ere day,
>   That all his hart with gealosie did swell;
>   But yet that nights ensample did bewray,

> That not for nought his wife them loued so well,
> When one so oft a night did ring his matins bell.[22]

Spenser's comedic moralism in this episode is directed toward the aged husband and toward the adulterous courtly love that, stripped of all delusions, leads the lady to this sexual abandon. In addition to the satiric matter, the pastoral setting also encourages Spenser in a mood very close to Ovidian humor: between a *malbecco* and the satyr's virile member there is little contest. Nevertheless, the depiction of Hellenore's bestiality is comically grim. Malbecco has difficulty arousing his wife from her contented sleep and then must plead with her not to alert her protective satyr:

> Tho gan he her perswade, to leaue that lewd
> And loathsome life, of God and man abhord,
> And home returne, where all should be renewed
> With perfect peace, and bandes of fresh accord,
> And she receiu'd againe to bed and bord,
> As if no trespasse euer had bene donne:
> But she it all refused at one word,
> And by no meanes would to his will be wonne,
> But chose emongst the iolly *Satyres* still to wonne
>
> (III.x.li)

Middleton and Rowley keep the satyric joviality of the paganized satyr, but De Flores also becomes demonic—possessed and possessing—in his transformation to a tragic human sphere. And Beatrice, whose name like Hellenore's ironically evokes an idealization of the sexual impulse, must face a metamorphosis far more horrific than anything dreamed of in the Ovidian realm.

Like De Flores, Beatrice has the sexual monomania attributed to demons of the pagan world and its folklore, the world that Christianity incorporated into the infernal. Beatrice is the nymph who, once deflowered, suffers hysterical annihilation. She is an alternate Eve, the Lilith who leaves her Eden to copulate with the serpent and who in a later manifestation as lamia hides her ugliness with the illusion of beauty and lures mortals to their destruction. Edward Topsell, in his account of this infinitely lustful creature, relates the story from Philostratus that in Burton's *Anatomy* was to inspire Keats's poem: Menippus becomes enamored of a beautiful phantasm, and only the wisdom of Apollonius, penetrating the illusion, saves the lover from a serpentine marriage. The word *lamia*, writes Topsell, "hath many significations," one of which is the Lilith of Hebraic tradition. These demons are "wonderfull desirous of copulation with men." They can transform themselves, like witches, into other shapes; or, more precisely, they can give the illusion of transformation, for they have in their beautiful appearance "no matter or substance." If they do not actually exist, they are meaningful as fantastic projections of a diabolical reality:

> These and such like stories and opinions there are of Phairies, which in my iudgement arise from the praestigious apparitions of Deuils, whose delight is to deceiue and beguile the minds of men with errour, contrary to the truth of holye Scripture, which doeth no where make mention of such inchaunting creatures; and therefore if any such be, we will holde them the workes of the Deuill, and not of God, or rather I beleeue, that as Poets call Harlots by the name of *Charibdis,* which deuoureth and swalloweth whole shippes and Nauies, aluding to the insatiable gulph of the Sea, so the *Lamiae* are but beautiful alligories of beautifull Harlottes, who after they haue had their lust by men, doth many times deuour and make them away.

In case a lamia should be more than allegorical, however, Topsell offers an antidote: the best way to expose the true nature of the diabolic creature, as Apollonius knew, is to "rate it with very contumelious and despightfull words."[23] The reality of language dispels the false appearance, and the phantasm either vanishes or reassumes its terrible shape.

This demonic myth underlies the psychic metaphor when Alsemero discovers Beatrice's true nature. When he tells her "You are a whore," she exhibits all the pain of a supernatural being whose passionate world of illusions has been destroyed by a moral and rational voice:

> What a horrid sound it hath!
> It blasts a beauty to deformity;
> Upon what face soever that breath falls,
> It strikes ugly: oh, you have ruin'd
> What you can ne'er repair again.
>
> (V.iii.31-35)

One aspect of Beatrice's characterization that has not been fully appreciated is her truly desperate concern with appearances, with her reputation and honor:

> Let me go poor unto my bed with honour,
> And I am rich in all things.
>
> (III.iv.158-159)

This fear, totally divorced from any genuinely moral awareness, is perhaps the psychological sign of a spoiled child or a limited intelligence; it is also the apprehension of a real changeling—a fairy who, left in place of a human child, has no moral sense except insofar as appearances are concerned. Appearance, for her, is truly the only reality, and we cannot dismiss as merely fatuous her struggle against the exposure that will effectively spell her dissolution.[24] As indicated in her waiting-woman's name, these nymphs—whose virginal nature exists only in the membrane—are diaphanous, without any substantiality.

The discovery of Beatrice's diabolic alliance, like the discovery of Duessa's true nature in *The Faerie Queene* (I.viii), dispels illusory appearances; unmasked, both witches are so ugly as to be unfit for heaven or earth. As Alsemero says of Beatrice's disguise, "there was a visor / O'er that cunning face, and that became you"

(V.iii.46-47). But when the "fair-fac'd saints" have been exposed as "cunning devils" (V.iii.108-109), the concealing beauty is itself recognized as ugliness:

> The black mask
> That so continually was worn upon't
> Condemns the face for ugly ere't be seen.
>
> (V.iii.3-5)[25]

Alsemero finally sees the full extent of her depravity— "Oh, thou art all deform'd!" (V.iii.77): the beautiful witch is now seen as the hag she is. These psychic demons have been made subjective and rationalized; but, although the playwrights have incorporated the objective evil into the poetic characterization, the alien substance is sufficiently activated for Beatrice to warn her father, echoing the caution that the *Malleus Maleficarum* gave to examiners of witches, "Oh come not near me, sir, I shall defile you" (V.iii.149).[26]

Beatrice's warning, along with the whole of the terrifying catastrophe, is universally attributed to Rowley. It is a scene far surpassing anything else he ever wrote. When we assert that **The Changeling** is also Middleton's masterpiece, we are clearly confronted with "the fact that the play's triumph is first and last a triumph of collaboration."[27] The aesthetic and the practical feat of such a partnership, I have tried to suggest, can best be comprehended if the essential aspects of the result—the psychosexual drama of the main plot and the reverberations between the subplot and the main tragic plot—are seen to arise from the sources of the play; and one must include among those sources a conceptual frame of reference for characterization to which the playwrights in their cooperative labor could appeal. Working from the hint in Reynolds, both Rowley and Middleton animated the broomstick figures in the source by internalizing and developing the demonic compulsion that didactically the prose work externalized. And the subplot, dissonantly counterpointing the tragic drama, offers supporting evidence that Rowley had studied Reynolds as respectfully as Middleton had and doubtlessly in close association with him.

No precise source for Rowley's subplot has been discovered,[28] but the situation of the jealous husband who confines his wife and sets a spy upon her occurs in a section of Reynolds's story which Middleton and Rowley discarded in fashioning the main plot. In the prose tale, after the murder of Alonzo permits the marriage, "*Alsemero,* like a fond husband, becomes ielous of his wife; so as hee curbes and restraynes her of her libertie, and would hardly permit her to see, yea, farre lesse to conferre or conuerse with any man" (p. 132). This jealous passion is entirely unmotivated; merely a "fearefull frensie." There is cause for jealousy in the play, because De Flores enforces the sexual alliance immediately following the death of Alonzo. In the tale,

however, the gallant murderer only receives "many kisses" for his reward and then disappears from the scene until he returns as a messenger to the guarded lady. Beatrice, now resentful of her husband's irrational passion, is at last eager to be unfaithful: "shee considering what [De Flores] hath done for her seruice, and ioyning therewith her husbands ielousie, not onely ingageth her selfe to him for the time present, but for the future" (p. 134). This incoherent turn of events, eliminated by the playwrights' alteration of De Flores, found its place with different characters in Rowley's subplot. For the name of this alter Alsemero, Rowley dipped into the next tale in Reynolds's collection and took the name of Alibius. As the playwrights discovered with Beatrice, De Flores, and Diaphanta, the name of Alibius—"being in another place"—was fortuitously a happy one. In the play Alibius, like Alsemero in Reynolds, "sets spies" upon the wife: Lollio in the play, Diaphanta in the source. In Reynolds, Diaphanta eventually discovers Beatrice and De Flores's "beastly pleasures" and betrays the lovers to the jealous husband; but of course Lollio, who yearns like De Flores in the main plot to take his "fool's share," oversees a wife who, although tempted, keeps her virtue intact.

Rowley and Middleton thus found leftover material in the primary source to cut a pattern in grotesque but ultimately happy contrast to the tragedy. Although Isabella feels the attraction of the changeling, she refuses to join the mad world of the black sabbath:

> Luna is now big-bellied, and there's room
> For both of us to ride with Hecate;
> I'll drag thee up into her silver sphere,
> And there we'll kick the dog, and beat the bush,
> That barks against the witches of the night.
>
> (III.iii.79-83)

The madmen who, as Isabella seems about to yield, cross the upper stage *some as birds, others as beasts,* conjure more fearful images than those of men descending the great chain of being. These illusory transformations, shaped by the malignant fantasies of sexual lunatics, suggest most compellingly the power of diabolic metamorphosis, the power of witches and demons to take any shape the depraved imagination can project. Those captivated by the flesh discover that, as Reynolds cautions in his preface to the reader, "the best of its beauty is but vanity and deformity" (sig. A4).

III

We must now consider the origin of another concatenation of events in the main plot of **The Changeling,** the substitution of Diaphanta for Beatrice-Joanna on her wedding night and the subsequent murder of the waiting-woman. In 1924 Bertram Lloyd identified the most immediate source for this episode as a novel by

Leonard Digges, *Gerardo the Unfortunate Spaniard,* translated from the Spanish of G. de Cespedes y Meneses.[29] Published in 1622, Digges's work was entered in the Stationers' Register on 11 March 1621/22; since ***The Changeling*** was licensed on 7 May 1622, the collaborators must have worked, as all the evidence indicates, with notable dispatch. I would like to suggest that something more urgent than a casual and random process of selection was involved. Middleton may have stumbled onto the Digges translation, but he selected the episode from the novel because of an impulse already disposing the plot in this direction. Before he discovered the events as ordered in the Spanish translation, Middleton was shaping the fable in response to yet another source. It can be identified if we isolate a crucial aspect of the plot not derived either from Digges or from Reynolds—the tripartite virginity test.

The climactic virginal trial is of course that of Beatrice on her wedding night, for which she substitutes Diaphanta. This test is similar to the one reported in Digges but there is an important difference: the husband in the source, unlike Alsemero, has no cause for suspicion; it is not, therefore, primarily and most immediately a judicial encounter, as metaphorically it is in the play:

> The more I think upon th'ensuing night,
> And whom I am to cope with in embraces,
> One that's ennobled both in blood and mind,
> So clear in understanding (that's my plague now),
> Before whose judgment will my fault appear
> Like malefactors' crimes before tribunals. . . .

> (IV.i.3-8)

But before "th'ensuing night" Beatrice-Joanna discovers Alsemero's fantastic "closet"; and with the plot's gratuitous disclosure that her new husband is a physician of the occult, she correctly fears that he will make a preliminary test of her virginity with "glass M." The following two examinations—first, of Diaphanta by Beatrice; second, of Beatrice by her husband—have no connection with Digges, where the "honesty" of neither woman is doubted.[30] These two comical tests, as they lead to the substitution of Diaphanta in Beatrice's wedding bed, are more important dramatically than the material in the Spanish novel, and Middleton indicates his inspiration with a topical allusion identified long ago but never investigated as, at the very least, a remarkable analogue to the events of the play: "She will not search me, will she," muses Diaphanta as Beatrice fetches the liquid, "Like the forewoman of a female jury?" (IV.i.100-101).[31] The complex of topical events to which Middleton alludes is much more relevant to ***The Changeling*** than is Digges: included among those events were a juridical examination for virginity and the substitution of a virgin for a wanton; the intrigue also involved the murder of one who stood in the way

of a lustful alliance. Finally, and most importantly for my purposes, the morbidity of these notorious crimes was attributed to the literal workings of witches and demons.

No ghost need come from the grave to tell us that Middleton was attuned to the life of his time, and in the London of 1613 only a ghost could have been deaf to the infamous divorce of the Countess of Essex and her marriage at the end of the year to the king's favorite, the newly created Earl of Somerset. Two years later the scandal deepened with the discovery that Sir Thomas Overbury, having stood in the way of Frances Howard's divorce from Essex and her remarriage to Somerset, had been secretly murdered in the Tower. These events, we can believe, touched Middleton intimately. Both Overbury and Middleton were of Queen's College, Oxford; Middleton matriculated in the university early in 1598, at the end of which year Overbury graduated B.A.[32] This collegial connection would urge at least a subsequent acquaintance, given their friends in common and their mutual participation in the literary life of London. As a part of the City's celebration of the Somerset marriage Middleton had written the *Masque of Cupid* for the scandalous lovers.[33] Unfortunately, this work, performed at the Guildhall on 4 January 1613/14, has not survived, but we can be certain that the masque idealized the marriage according to fashion. For such a master of dramatic irony as Middleton, the effect on him when the full corruption of the alliance became known must have been terrific. In ***The Changeling*** and ***Women Beware Women,*** when evil makes a mockery of the ideal, it was therefore not the first time that Middleton had celebrated corrupt nuptials with an ironic masque.

It has been suggested that Frances Howard was for Middleton a prototype of the evil but beautiful heroine of the later plays.[34] "Those that saw her Face," wrote one historian with an eye for drama, "might challenge Nature of too much Hypocrisy, for harbouring so wicked a Heart under so sweet and bewitching a Countenance."[35] But, as gossip would have it, the exhibition of her second wedding could not be so convincing as to disguise entirely the black truth: "She thinking all the World ignorant of her sly Practices, hath the Impudence to appear in the Habit of a Virgin, with her Hair pendant almost to her Feet; which Ornament of her Body (though a Fair one) could not cover the Deformities of her Soul."[36] Because white devils like Vittoria Corombona were already making such spectacles of themselves, we can see how, with all the world a stage, the most impudent lady of real life was viewed within the same moral and dramatic frame of vision: one pattern informs both the actual and the reflecting theater of God's judgment, as Sir Francis Bacon declared at Lady Frances's trial. In "the theatre of God's justice," he proclaimed histrionically, "Overbury's blood cried for revenge":

the great frame of justice, my lords, in this present action, hath a vault, and it hath a stage: a vault, wherein these works of darkness were contrived; and a stage with steps, by which they were brought to light.[37]

Bacon's metaphor imposes upon the playhouse its traditional metaphysical mysteries. The vault, of course, is Hell. The stage discloses those secret workings and the subsequent retribution that Heaven exacts. The Somerset tragedy of adultery and murder was viewed as the exemplary Jacobean tragedy of blood revenge, a tragedy which a contemporary pamphlet entitled *The Bloody downfall of Adultery, Murder, and Ambition, presented in a black seane of Gods iust Iudgements in reuenge of the Inocent blood lately shed in this Kingdome.*[38] This drama was also literally a tragedy of state, because James's part in the events implicated the monarchy.[39] His injudicious role in the nullity proceedings and his own part in the imprisonment of Overbury probably damaged his reputation, according to Samuel R. Gardiner, more than his rupture with the House of Commons.[40] William McElwee asserts that "It is doubtful if the popularity and prestige of the Stuart monarchy ever entirely recovered from the damage done by the Somerset case."[41]

In 1622 London witnessed an event that might well explain Middleton's recollecting the tragedy of the previous decade for transposition in *The Changeling.* Middleton, having celebrated their marriage with the *Masque of Cupid,* would not likely overlook the release of the Earl and Countess of Somerset from the Tower on 18 January 1621/22.[42] In 1615 both had been judged guilty of murder (though the earl almost certainly was innocent); but James, while committed to their prosecution and conviction, had never intended that the sentence of death be executed. Instead they were confined for nearly a decade, awaiting the royal pleasure. The release of the fallen great ones, with their retreat into obscurity, was nevertheless a fitting dramatic conclusion to a crime that confirmed the mysteries of God's justice. The stories in Reynolds, having at this same time caught Middleton's dramatic appreciation, are of course based upon the same mysterious structure; Reynolds in fact tells the reader in the preface that but for the author's discretion and compassion exemplary tales of God's triumphant revenge could be included from the English scene. Certainly the first such example to come to mind in the London of 1622 would be the Somerset story, the postscript to which had just been added:

> I haue purposely fetched these Tragicall Histories from forraine parts: because it grieues me to report and relate those that are too frequently committed in our owne country, in respect the misfortune of the dead may perchance either afflict, or scandalize their liuing friends; who rather want matter of new consolation, then cause of reuiuing old sorrowes, or because the iniquity of the times is such, that it is as easie to procure many enemies, as difficult to purchase one true friend: In which

respect, I know that diuers, both in matters of this, and of other natures, haue beene so cautious to disguise and maske their Actors, vnder the vayles of other names; and sometimes become inforced to lay their Scenes in strange and vnknowne Countries.

(sigs. B2ᵛ-B3)

Reynolds's testimony regarding the veiled transpositions of cautious dramatists is to the point. We are coming more and more to see the topical relevance of the Jacobean drama, disguised though the relevance might be by foreign settings and names.[43] The problems of censorship that arose in the first decade of the century made it clear that, for the deeper disillusionment of the time, some metaphoric mode would be required. "The Plays do not forbear to present upon their Stage the whole Course of this present Time," wrote Samuel Calvert to Winwood in March 1605; "not sparing either King, State or Religion, in so great Absurdity, and with such Liberty, that any would be afraid to hear them."[44] Such a state of affairs could not continue. A drama that truly gave the age its form and pressure would have to be a drama controlled by Reynolds's circumspection.[45]

The Somerset affair offered Middleton more than Diaphanta's comparison of her examination with one like that of Lady Essex, for Frances Howard like Beatrice had to pass her test—at least according to all accounts—well after she had lost her virginity. In 1606 she had been married to the Earl of Essex in an effort of the royal peacemaker to promote harmony between two powerful families. While the young earl was away in France for several years and before the immature couple had been permitted to cohabit, the Jacobean court thoroughly corrupted the young wife, and she became enamored of Robert Carr—Lord Rochester, favorite of the king and soon to become Earl of Somerset. Upon her husband's return she had no intention of giving up her romance and consummating a marriage with one she now loathed. All attempts by the earl at sexual intercourse were repelled; and finally, with the husband loathing his wife in return, both agreed to testify before an ecclesiastical commission set up by the king to nullify the union. In order to prove her virginity the commission appointed a jury of four noble ladies and two midwives to examine the countess. She was deemed *virgo intacta et incorrupta.* Had the judgment been made according to rumor, however, her divorce from Essex and her subsequent marriage to Somerset would have been aborted. Although Archbishop Abbot thought that the jury had probably been tampered with, rumor offered a more dramatic explanation, the substitution of a virgin for the adulterously deflowered woman:

> The Countess being ashamed, and bashful, to come to such a Tryal, would not expose her Face to the Light; but being to appear before the Matrons under a Veil, another young Gentlewoman, that had less offended, was fobbed into the Place; and she passed, in the Opinion, both of Jury and Judges, to be a Virgin.[46]

Like Lady Essex, Beatrice has to undergo a test of her virginity or else she will not succeed in her murderous plot to change lovers. Beatrice plans, like her topical counterpart, to fob a virgin into her place for that test; but first she must herself examine the substitute—who wittily evokes for the audience a gossipy recollection of the scandalous episode.

The lustful murder finally charged against Frances Howard was, like the evil in *The Changeling,* partially objectified as abetted by a literally demonic force. The prosecution was thereby able to present a coherent and satisfactory explanation for such sensational depravity, all without an extraordinary violation of judicial and rational experience and without compromising, despite their possession by an objective and alien evil, the moral culpability of the human agents. Even during the nullity trial, when Lady Essex was arranging the murder of Overbury and therefore before the facts of her evil proceedings transpired, demonology became a titillating part of the psychological and physiological explanation for the couple's sexual morbidity. Only evil could account for the abnormal situation, even if no human agent was available to indict.

The Earl of Essex was not willing to forgo the chance of a future marriage by confessing that he suffered a general condition of impotence; he only admitted that it was so with his wife, *impotentia versus hanc.* Archbishop Abbot, who had been led to believe that Essex simply had "no ink in his pen," was alarmed to hear his peculiar testimony and did not intend to establish a precedent that would encourage collusion between married partners who had merely ceased to care for each other.[47] Aware of the weakness of their case, the lawyers for the countess suggested that the earl had been bewitched. Later there would be evidence to support a charge of *maleficium,* but in 1613 the Archbishop was dubious of the supposition and argued that, even were it true, church law would not allow the devil to put asunder what God had joined together. King James, however, was entirely convinced: "if the Devil hath any power," he assured his prelate, "it is over the flesh, rather over the filthiest and most sinful part thereof, whereunto original sin is soldered." Had King James not existed, dramatists would have had to invent such a monarch to preside over the Jacobean fascination with phallic evil: "and if the power of witchcraft may reach to our life," the king told his archbishop, "much more to a member . . . wherein the Devil hath his principal operation."[48] James insisted that Abbot defer to the author of *Daemonologie*; and, when the archbishop showed no sign of doing so, the king packed the commission and suppressed the minority opinion.[49]

In 1613 the sober proceedings of Abbot's commission amused the public with its speculations; but, if these matters "were then smiled at, and since that time much sport had been made at the court and in London about them,"[50] the humor darkened in 1615 when the drama moved from the vault to the platform stage and revealed a true Jacobean tragedy of lust, murder, and revenge. Lust does indeed lead to murder, and neither is accomplished without demonological assistance. Murder, however, cannot be concealed, and God's vengeance will triumph at last. Real life is just as the didactic Reynolds and the dramatic structure would have it.

The lawyers for Lady Essex no doubt stumbled independently onto *maleficium* as a cause of her husband's impotence; but, when the prosecution tried Mistress Anne Turner as an accomplice in the murder of Sir Thomas Overbury, the evidence ironically supported the satanic speculations of the nullity trial. The agent of witchcraft and sorcery turned out to be the countess herself. As anyone could know from a glance at James's *Daemonologie,* the devil had the power "of weakening the nature of some men, to make them unable for women: and making it to abound in others, more then the ordinary course of nature would permit."[51] The frustrated Lady Essex, initiated by the unsavory Anne Turner, called upon those powers by consulting the notorious Dr. Simon Forman in his physician's closet in Lambeth.[52] Becoming disciples of the devil and Forman's "daughters," Lady Frances and Mistress Turner pursued their amorous strategies with forbidden secrets of nature, Mistress Turner to maintain Sir Arthur Mainwaring's love for her, Lady Frances to increase Robert Carr's passion for her with aphrodisiacs and to deter her husband's sexual advances with anaphrodisiacs. At Anne Turner's trial Sir Edward Coke exhibited a fascinating collection of obscene and phallic paraphernalia employed in Forman's devilish mischief, including "certain pictures of a man and woman in copulation, made in lead." At this moment in the crowded Guildhall, so charged was the pornographic atmosphere that an amazing phenomenon occurred: "there was heard a crack from the scaffolds, which caused great fear, tumult and confusion among the spectators, and throughout the hall, every one fearing hurt, as if the devil had been present, and grown angry to have his workmanship shewed, by such as were not his own scholars."[53] Perhaps vexed by the years of her husband's sexual activity with his fashionable clientele, Dr. Forman's widow testified about the strange events that took place behind closed doors:

> There was . . . enchantments shewed in court, written in parchment, wherein were contained all the names of the blessed Trinity, mentioned in the scriptures; and in another parchment, + B. + C. + D. + E. and in a third likewise in parchment, were written all the names of the Holy Trinity, as also a figure, in which was written this word Corpus; and upon the parchment was fastened a little piece of the skin of a man.—In some of these parchments, were the devils particular names, who were conjured to torment the lord Somerset and

sir Arthur Ma[i]nwaring, if their loves should not continue, the one to the countess, the other to Mrs. Turner.[54]

After Dr. Forman's sudden death on 8 September 1611, the two women procured the services of Dr. Savories, who "practised many sorceries upon the earl of Essex's person."[55] No doubt with the wily assistance of Lady Frances, the sorcery and witchcraft proved successful.

The prosecutors showed the pornographic objects again at the countess's trial, "which made them appear more odious as being known to converse with witches and wizards."[56] The strategy must also have been to render for the Jacobean jury a convincing psychological explanation for such impudent crimes. With a judicious use of demonology as a structural rationale, the prosecutors made a coherent and persuasive drama out of the case. The usual pattern of sexual and murderous intrigue had its inception and causality in an evil partially objectified but not entirely so: the devil, after all, merely comes to claim those already his own. In his closing speech at the earlier trial, Coke proclaimed Anne Turner "a whore, a bawd, a sorcerer, a witch, a papist, a felon, and a murderer, the daughter of the devil Forman," desiring her "to become a servant of Jesus Christ, and to pray to him to cast out of her those seven devils."[57] Objectifying the woman's psyche, these "devils" are all deviant oppositions to Jesus Christ in the service of whom are perfect freedom and mental health. If in moral terms of black and white the point of view is simple and absolute, Middleton and Rowley's *The Changeling* and Burton's *Anatomy of Melancholy* prove that the masterly tracing of the mind within that frame of reference can be satisfyingly subtle and variable to a modern vision. We can as easily be startled by the psychological disorder of evil as those witnesses in the Guildhall who felt the demon as a palpable thing.

Middleton and Rowley's fantasies of total sexual abandon, of possession by erotic desire, were almost inevitably projected, during the Jacobean period, with images of demonology. Even in his pagan world, King Lear perceives rapacious sexuality, the source of life itself, to be an inferno of devils:

> But to the girdle do the Gods inherit,
> Beneath is all the fiend's: there's hell, there's darkness,
> There is the sulphurous pit—burning, scalding,
> Stench, consumption. . . .
>
> (IV.vi.125-128)[58]

The only alternative lay in the virtue of chastity, as exemplified in the famous character of *A Wife* which Overbury had reputedly written to dissuade his friend from marrying Lady Frances:

> *One* is *loves number*: who from that doth fall,
> Hath lost his hold, and no *new rest* shall find.[59]

Beatrice falls; but, spreading and mounting to infinity, she gains a kind of peace in the assurance of the damned.

IV

"The essential critical point about a collaborative work is that it is the product not of one dramatic vision but of two or more; and the critic of a play like *The Changeling* who attempts seriously to account for its achievement must seek its roots not only in the Middleton canon but in the canon of William Rowley's plays as well."[60] Cyrus Hoy's challenge is a happy one, because for too long Rowley's contribution has received little more than apologetic justification. Although criticism from this negative stance has taught us much about the multiple plot in Renaissance drama,[61] we might still hesitate to address ourselves to a subject so humble as that of William Rowley's dramatic vision. It will always be an exceptional fact that this most successful of collaborations brought together two playwrights of such disparate abilities and achievements. No doubt one symptom of their congeniality is that each could adapt himself to different modes or genres so completely as almost to become anonymous. This negative capability certainly would contribute to a talent for collaboration, a method of creation that has itself been described as "the great Elizabethan disappearing act."[62] More positively, however, both Middleton and Rowley had evinced, before *The Changeling,* a notable interest in the dramatic possibilities of demonology, and this in an age when such an interest is not especially remarkable.

The most comprehensive book on the occult in Renaissance drama calls Middleton's *The Witch* (ca. 1615) "the most informative play of the period on the topic of contemporary witchcraft."[63] Almost all of that lore concerns the obscene sexuality of the diabolic world, a black sabbatism of incest, sodomy, and other uninhibited fantasies. "The man that I have lusted to enjoy," says Hecate of the approaching Almachildes; "I've had him thrice in incubus already."

ALMACHILDES:

> Is your name Goody Hag?

HECATE:

> 'Tis anything:
> Call me the horrid'st and unhallow'd things
> That life and nature trembles at, for thee
> I'll be the same.
>
> (I.ii.197-200)

The Witch does not go very far in suggesting the horror of the thing without a name, but the play is of considerable import in showing Middleton's more than common interest in the subject and in the moral permeation of the diabolical into the everyday world of evil. Furthermore, as R. C. Bald pointed out in a classic essay, *The Witch* appears to have been influenced by the diabolic nature of the Somerset scandal: "In Sebastian's scheme to prevent Antonio from consummating his marriage with Isabella, and in the charms he seeks from the witches to effect his purpose, there is a clear allusion to the notorious Essex divorce case of 1613."[64]

In addition to Sebastian's request for an anaphrodisiac, Bald might have observed Almachildes' visit to the witches for an aphrodisiac; and a third visitor, the Duchess, petitions Hecate to effect a "sudden and subtle" death (V.ii.4) for one who, because he thinks her an unchaste murderess, stands in the way of her marriage to the Lord Governor. All three interactions between the court and the witches thus reflect the evil meditations that led Frances Howard to consort with witches and demonologists. One might also consider, among the intricacies of bed tricks in the play, the instance in which the blindfolded Almachildes has been led to believe that he is deflowering Amoretta when actually "a hired strumpet" has been put in her place. This "examination" reveals to Almachildes what a true test of Frances Howard or Beatrice-Joanna would have exposed, a woman already possessed of sexual knowledge:

> This you that was a maid? how are you born
> To deceive men! I'd thought to have married you:
> I had been finely handled, had I not?
> I'll say that man is wise ever hereafter
> That tries his wife beforehand. 'Tis no marvel
> You should profess such bashfulness, to blind one,
> As if you durst not look a man i' th' face,
> Your modesty would blush so.
>
> (III.i.1-8)

Rowley's *The Birth of Merlin* (ca. 1608) has "the most decisive role assigned to an incubus or a succubus,"[65] although the demon who assumes the form of Helen for the damnation of Faustus is more famous. Both Middleton and Rowley were clearly fascinated by these sexual demons, and each playwright stumbled independently onto a highly ingenious theatrical doubling of such demons in their human form. In Middleton's *A Mad World, My Masters* (1606) the actor playing Mistress Harebrain is also required to play a succubus (IV.i) who tempts Penitent Brothel in the form of Mistress Harebrain. Critics have not stopped making faces over this impingement of the supernatural upon what they take to be the realism of the city comedy: does Middleton didactically bungle in this episode, or is the moral pattern of temptation, of sin and salvation, itself rendered with satiric irony? The questions so posed completely miss the real viability of the dramatic experience—that is, that the audience, not having the advantage of the stage direction (*Enter the devil* [*as* Succubus] *in her shape*), can no more know than Penitent Brothel that the form of Mistress Harebrain is not, strictly speaking, Mistress Harebrain. Penitent Brothel, in his

moral resolve, considers Mistress Harebrain metaphorically a bewitching devil whom he conjures away; but not until three scenes later—after he has questioned his servant, Harebrain's servant, and finally the woman herself—does he know literally that "Then was the devil in your likeness there":

> The very devil assum'd thee formally,
> That face, that voice, that gesture, that attire,
> E'en as it sits on thee, not a pleat alter'd,
> That beaver band, the color of that periwig,
> The farthingale above the navel, all,
> As if the fashion were his own invention.
>
> (IV.iv.28-33)[66]

With Penitent Brothel we experience in retrospect the *frisson* of the visitation—something like what Edward Alleyn felt, prompting his conversion, when he recognized that an unaccountable devil had joined in a performance of *Doctor Faustus*:

> What knows the lecher when he clips his whore
> Whether it be the devil his parts adore?
> They're both so like that, in our natural sense,
> I could discern no change nor difference.
>
> (IV.iv.55-58)

This blurring of the natural and the supernatural, indistinguishable to "our natural sense," suggests *mutatis mutandis* the metaphoric and psychological blurring of the supernatural into the natural conceptions of character. In the city comedy, written for a children's company, the blurring or doubling has no small effect on the characterization, for Mistress Harebrain is responsible for the demonic use of her form: "Be honest," Penitent advises her, "then the devil will ne'er assume thee" (IV.iv.44). For the greater verisimilitude of tragedy, written for adult actors, characters could be similarly developed according to the phenomenology of demons and witches, but with a subtlety more than satisfactory to our own popular conceptions of human nature.

The only other instance I have found of a doubling such as Middleton employed in 1606 is in *The Witch of Edmonton,* Rowley's collaboration just the year before *The Changeling.* There is general agreement on the division of labor among Rowley, Dekker, and Ford, and no one has questioned Rowley's responsibility for the comic Cuddy Banks scenes.[67] Parodying both serious plots, Rowley's clown engages Mother Sawyer's familiar spirit to make Katherine Carter return his love: "I am bewitched already. I would have thee so good as to unwitch me, or witch another with me for company" (II.i.251 ff.). The result is the brief appearance of a devil disguised as Katherine who leads Cuddy to a drenching. For a feeble joke the doubling of roles is a *coup de théâtre,* complicating the instance in *A Mad World.* In *The Witch of Edmonton* the actor playing

Katherine is also required to play a demon who, when he discards his "real" demonic face, has assumed the form of Katherine. Again the audience does not have the advantage of the stage direction: *Enter Spirit in shape of Katherine, vizarded, and takes it off*. The actor's speech accompanying this action, however, makes clear that the stage direction is wholly misleading as far as the conception of the bit part is concerned:

> Thus throw I off mine own essential horror,
> And take the shape of a sweet, lovely maid
> Whom this fool dotes on.
>
> (III.i.107-109)

The theatrical disguise of the horrible mask is not, conceptually, the disguise but the reality; the actor's own face—Katherine's own face—is the deceptive form. Something very close to this confused and confusing disguise informs the complex conception of Beatrice-Joanna's "mask." Her beauty at once hides her essential horror ("there was a visor / O'er that cunning face, and that became you") and at the same time reveals it:

> The black mask
> That so continually was worn upon't
> Condemns the face for ugly ere't be seen.
>
> (V.iii.3-5)

Rowley's part in *The Witch of Edmonton* may have been small, but I think he learned a great deal from the enterprise. With penetrating psychological realism, that remarkable play rationalizes the witch hysteria by showing the persecution of Mother Sawyer which drives her in revenge to call upon the powers of darkness: "'Tis all one / To be a witch as to be counted one" (II.i. 151-152). But when the fantastic Dog answers her call we see that the rationalization of evil does not mean that the supernatural power of evil is a delusion.[68] The Dog is rather, as Mark Stavig has shown, "an instructive illustration of the ways in which symbolism, realism, psychology, and morality are often linked in seventeenth-century plays."[69] The final emphasis, however, is upon the more than metaphoric applicability of witchcraft and demonology to the common experience of mankind as represented in the other two plots, from the farce of Cuddy Banks to the tragedy of Frank Thorney. Devils are everywhere, agrees Mother Sawyer, "But is every devil mine?" (V.iii.30). As for her being a witch, "Who is not?"

> Hold not that universal name in scorn, then.
> What are your painted things in princes' courts,
> Upon whose eyelids lust sits, blowing fires
> To burn men's souls in sensual hot desires,
> Upon whose naked paps a lecher's thought
> Acts sin in fouler shapes than can be wrought?
>
> (IV.i.131-137)

As the Dog explains to Cuddy Banks, the source of evil is both without and within the personality, both objective and subjective:

> I'll thus much tell thee: thou never art so distant
> From an evil spirit but that thy oaths,
> Curses, and blasphemies pull him to thine elbow.
> Thou never tell'st a lie but that a devil
> Is within hearing it; thy evil purposes
> Are ever haunted; but, when they come to act—
> As thy tongue slandering, bearing false witness,
> Thy hand stabbing, stealing, cozening, cheating—
> He's then within thee.
>
> (V.i.159-167)

And frequently the humanoids we see are, though imperceptible to our natural sense, devils in human form:

> An hot, luxurious lecher in his twines,
> When he has thought to clip his dalliance,
> There has provided been for his embrace
> A fine, hot, flaming devil in her place.
>
> (V.i.175-178)

In *The Changeling* Middleton and Rowley complete this process of diabolism in characterizing horrifically recognizable human beings: De Flores is the devil for Beatrice's lust (V.iii.53), the serpent that she strokes (V.iii.66). Once their covenant with death has been made, the most significant action in the tragedy takes place in the sealing of it, out of our tantalized view. It is entirely appropriate that the catastrophe occurs off-stage when Alsemero makes them enact one final time their "scene of lust" as a rehearsal for "the black audience" in hell. There, in that infernal playhouse, the characters will eternally exhibit themselves, for the "howls and gnashings" of their own kind, as literal demon lovers.

Notes

1. "Thomas Middleton," in *Selected Essays* (1932; rpt. London, 1951), pp. 161-170.

2. R. B. Parker, "Middleton's Experiments with Comedy and Judgement," in *Jacobean Theatre*, ed. John Russell Brown and Bernard Harris, Stratford-upon-Avon Studies, No. 1 (London, 1960), p. 179.

3. For the opposition see Helen Gardner, "Milton's 'Satan' and the Theme of Damnation in Elizabethan Tragedy," *ES*, N.S. I (1949), 46-66; and T. B. Tomlinson, "Poetic Naturalism—*The Changeling*," *JEGP*, LXIII (1964), 648-659, expanded in his *A Study of Elizabethan and Jacobean Tragedy* (Cambridge, Eng., 1964). Gardner acknowledges the psychological realism in the play but insists that "there is more than realism here" (p. 57). Tomlinson, however, is doggedly insensitive: "there is no mention in this play of 'damnation' (certainly not in the *Faustus* sense)"—*A Study*, p. 187, n. 1. The historical approach can also be needlessly limiting: Robert Jordan, in "Myth and Psychology in *The Changeling*," *RenD*, III (1970),

157-165, sees the play as based on the myth of beauty and the beast; what is apparent psychological subtlety is for him merely the by-blow of literary conventions at work.

4. Robert West, *The Invisible World: A Study of Pneumatology in Elizabethan Drama* (Athens, Ga., 1939), pp. 165-166.

5. *Artificial Persons: The Formation of Character in the Tragedies of Shakespeare* (Columbia, S.C., 1974), p. 21.

6. All references are to N. W. Bawcutt, ed., *The Changeling,* The Revels Plays (London, 1958).

7. S. Gorley Putt, "The Tormented World of Middleton," *TLS,* 2 August 1974, pp. 833-834.

8. Dorothy M. Farr, *Thomas Middleton and the Drama of Realism* (Edinburgh, 1973), p. 56.

9. The finger image is employed sexually in both plots (I.i.231-234; I.ii.27-31). In the Dumb Show preceding Act IV, "Alonzo's *ghost appears to* De Flores *in the midst of his smile, startles him, showing him the hand whose finger he had cut off.*" This obscene gesture manqué indicates not only the phallic obsession of the lovers but also the sexual nature of their nemesis.

10. For discussions of the parody of courtly love in the play see Robert Ornstein, *The Moral Vision of Jacobean Tragedy* (Madison, Wis., 1960), pp. 179-190; Thomas L. Berger, "The Petrarchan Fortress of *The Changeling,*" *RenP* (1969), pp. 37-46. For the importance of sexual innuendo in the language of the play—particularly in the word *service*—see Christopher Ricks, "The Moral and Poetic Structure of *The Changeling,*" *Essays in Criticism,* X (1960), 290-306.

11. In addition to Helen Gardner's important essay, see Penelope B. R. Doob, "A Reading of *The Changeling,*" *English Literary Renaissance,* III (1973), 183-206.

12. John Reynolds, *The Triumphs of Gods Revenge, Against the crying, and execrable Sinne of Murther* (London, 1621), sig. B2. Subsequent references are included in the text. Bawcutt reprints most of the relevant material.

13. The most authoritative work on English witchcraft in its social and intellectual setting is Keith Thomas, *Religion and the Decline of Magic* (New York, 1971), pp. 435-583. See also Alan Macfarlane, *Witchcraft in Tudor and Stuart England* (London, 1970); and Wallace Notestein, *A History of Witchcraft in England from 1558 to 1718* (Washington, D.C., 1911). Before the date of *The Changeling* the Continental ideas of erotic devil-worship were disseminated in England, with varying degrees of modesty and credulity, by the following: Reginald Scot, *The Discoverie of Witchcraft* (London, 1584); Henry Holland, *A Treatise Against Witchcraft* (Cambridge, Eng., 1590); George Gifford, *A Dialogue Concerning Witches and Witchcraftes* (London, 1593); King James, *Daemonologie* (Edinburgh, 1597); William Perkins, *A Discourse of the Damned Art of Witchcraft* (Cambridge, Eng., 1608); Alexander Roberts, *A Treatise of Witchcraft* (London, 1616); Thomas Cooper, *The Mystery of Witch-craft* (London, 1617). According to Keith Thomas, the Continental ideas of witchcraft were primarily adopted in England by intellectuals and theologians (p. 441).

14. Reginald Scot, *The Discoverie of Witchcraft* (1584), ed. Brinsley Nicholson (London, 1886), p. 56 (III.xix).

15. *Ibid.,* p. 67 (IV.x).

16. *The Mystery of Witch-craft* (London, 1617), p. 32.

17. Henry Charles Lea, comp., *Materials Toward a History of Witchcraft,* ed. Arthur C. Howland (1939; rpt. New York, 1957), II, 916-917. See Scot, p. 60 (IV.iii).

18. Cooper, pp. 92, 119.

19. *The Anatomy of Melancholy* (1621; rpt. London, 1932), III, 45-46 (III.2.i.1).

20. S. Gorley Putt observes "a degree of nymphomania in the heroine as marked as De Flores's resemblance to a satyr" (p. 834).

21. Edward Topsell, *The Historie of Foure-Footed Beastes* (London, 1607), pp. 14, 12, 13.

22. *The Works of Edmund Spenser,* A Variorum Edition, ed. Edwin Greenlaw et al. (Baltimore, Md., 1934), III, 150 (III.x.xlviii).

23. Topsell, pp. 452-454.

24. For the psychological analysis to which I refer, see Una Ellis-Fermor, *The Jacobean Drama* (London, 1936), pp. 146-149. The only critics to take seriously the fairylike nature of Beatrice-Joanna are William Empson, *Some Versions of Pastoral* (London, 1935), p. 50; and Richard Levin, *The Multiple Plot in English Renaissance Drama* (Chicago, 1971), p. 45.

25. See the perceptive discussion of this and related passages in George Walton Williams, ed., *The Changeling,* Regents Renaissance Drama Series (Lincoln, Nebr., 1966), pp. 92-93.

26. *Malleus Maleficarum,* trans. Montague Summers (1928; rpt. New York, 1970), pp. 227-230 (III. 15).

27. Cyrus Hoy, "Critical and Aesthetic Problems of Collaboration in Renaissance Drama," *RORD,* XIX (1976), 5.

28. See Bawcutt, p. xxxviii; and Williams, p. xiii.

29. Bertram Lloyd, "A Minor Source of *The Changeling,*" *MLR,* XIX (1924), 101-102.

30. See the reprinted selection from Digges in Bawcutt, pp. 127-129.

31. First noted by A. H. Bullen, *The Works of Thomas Middleton* (London, 1885), VI, 73.

32. See David George, "Thomas Middleton at Oxford," *MLR,* LXV (1970), 734-736; and "Overbury, Sir Thomas," *Dictionary of National Biography.*

33. R. C. Bald, "Middleton's Civic Employments," *MP,* XXXI (1933), 65.

34. William Power, "Middleton's Way with Names," *N&Q,* N.S. VII (1960), 96. Power does not, however, mention the topical reference to Frances Howard in *The Changeling.*

35. Arthur Wilson, *The History of Great Britain, being the Life and Reign of James I* (London, 1653). I have used the reprint in White Kennett, *A Complete History of England* (London, 1706), II, 687.

36. Kennett, II, 693.

37. Thomas B. Howell, ed., *Cobbett's Complete Collection of State Trials* (London, 1809-1826), II, 955, 958.

38. I.T. (London, [1616?]).

39. For the argument that the Jacobean drama topically reflected fatal symptoms in the Jacobean court, see J. W. Lever, *The Tragedy of State* (London, 1971).

40. *History of England, 1603-1642* (London, 1899), II, 174.

41. *The Murder of Sir Thomas Overbury* (London, 1952), p. 261. For the Somerset scandals, see also the account in Gardiner, vol. II, chaps. xvi, xx; and, for its excellent bibliography, Beatrice White, *Cast of Ravens: The Strange Case of Sir Thomas Overbury* (New York, 1965).

42. *State Trials,* II, 966. McElwee (p. 265) misleadingly gives the date as 1621.

43. See Lever; and G. K. Hunter, "English Folly and Italian Vice," in *Jacobean Theatre,* ed. John Russell Brown and Bernard Harris, Stratford-upon-Avon Studies, no. 1 (London, 1960), pp. 85-111.

44. Sir Ralph Winwood, *Memorials of Affairs of State in the Reigns of Queen Elizabeth and King James I,* ed. Edmund Sawyer (London, 1725), II.64. Cited in Daniel B. Dodson, "King James and *The Phoenix*—Again," *N&Q,* N.S.V (1958), 436.

45. It is a telling commentary that in 1661 an unidentifiable T. M., Esq., "digested" Reynolds's collection as *Blood for Blood: or Murthers Revenged* and added to the group an account of the murder of Sir Thomas Overbury, along with four other tales, to show "the sad Product of our own Times."

46. Kennett, II, 692.

47. *State Trials,* II, 806.

48. *Ibid.,* p. 801.

49. Thomas Cooper, in *The Mystery of Witch-craft* (1617), perhaps reflects the Essex nullity in discussing Satan's power to "hinder the operations of nature": "But *particularly* also, though the party may haue ability to others, yet to serue one, for the like reasons, he may be impotent, not able to performe the worke of Generation, and so deny that duety of marriage, and so happily produce a nullity thereof; vnlesse by *Phisicke,* or some spirituall means his power may be ouerruled, for which some time is to be graunted, and meanes vsed" (pp. 260-261). To the end Abbot protested that the Earl and Lady Essex had not resorted to prayer and fasting.

50. *State Trials,* II, 816.

51. *Daemonologie* (1597), ed. G. B. Harrison, The Bodley Head Quartos (London, 1924), p. xiii.

52. The fantastic dissonance of Alsemero's "physician's closet," along with the arcane virginity test, has disturbed many critics (see Bawcutt, p. lvii); I think that these original and somewhat extraneous details, whether successfully integrated with Reynolds or not, have their inspiration in the topical scandals.

53. *State Trials,* II, 932.

54. *Ibid.,* p. 933.

55. *Ibid.*

56. *Ibid.,* p. 951.

57. *Ibid.,* p. 935.

58. *King Lear,* ed. Kenneth Muir, The Arden Shakespeare (London, 1972).

59. *The Miscellaneous Works . . . of Sir Thomas Overbury,* ed. Edward F. Rimbault (London, 1856), p. 35.

60. Hoy, p. 6.

61. See Levin, pp. 34-48; and Empson, pp. 48-52; Muriel Bradbrook, *Themes and Conventions of Elizabethan Tragedy* (Cambridge, Eng., 1935), pp. 213-224; Karl Holzknecht, "The Dramatic Structure of *The Changeling,*" *RenP* (1954), pp. 77-87; Bawcutt, pp. lxii-lxviii; Williams, pp. xiii-xxiv.

62. Norman Rabkin, "Problems in the Study of Collaboration," *RORD*, XIX (1976), 12.

63. Robert R. Reed, Jr., *The Occult on the Tudor and Stuart Stage* (Boston, 1965), p. 171. I have cited the text of *The Witch* in Bullen, V, 351-453.

64. R. C. Bald, "The Chronology of Middleton's Plays," *MLR*, XXXII (1937), 41. The topicality of *The Witch* has not been given careful study, but scholars following Bald have been dubious: W. W. Greg and F. P. Wilson, eds., *The Witch,* Malone Society Reprints (London, 1948), p. vi; Power, pp. 96-97; David George, "The Problem of Middleton's *The Witch* and Its Sources," *N & Q,* N.S. XIV (1967), 210. Although I believe that Bald was correct, he perhaps overstated the case when he declared that "there is a clear allusion."

65. Reed, p. 229.

66. I have cited the text of Standish Henning, ed., *A Mad World, My Masters,* Regents Renaissance Drama Series (Lincoln, Nebr., 1965).

67. See H. Dugdale Sykes, "The Authorship of *The Witch of Edmonton,*" *N & Q,* CLI (1926), 435-438, 453-457; and Mark Stavig, *John Ford and the Traditional Moral Order* (Madison, Wis., 1968), p. 47. I have cited the text in *Stuart Plays,* ed. Arthur H. Nethercot et al. (New York, 1971), pp. 805-843.

68. See West, pp. 104-108, 144-154, and passim.

69. Stavig, p. 48.

A. L. Kistner and M. K. Kistner (essay date spring 1981)

SOURCE: Kistner, A. L., and M. K. Kistner. "The Five Structures of *The Changeling*." *Modern Language Studies* 11, no. 2 (spring 1981): 40-53.

[*In the following essay, Kistner and Kistner discuss what they view as the five structural frameworks of* The Changeling: *plot, subplot, verbal structure, organization of characters by motive and action, and hierarchy of moral responsibility.*]

The Changeling is probably unique among Jacobean plays in its number of internal structures and in the complexity of their interconnections. The structures are a means of organization which give the play its overall design and meaning. They are, in fact, indivisible from its meaning, for they exist to present, vary, develop and emphasize themes, and the complexity of the world and world-view that Middleton and Rowley have constructed in *The Changeling* could only be adequately presented by the intricacy of several interrelated structures.

The Changeling has five distinguishable frameworks that combine to form its whole. The first and most obvious organizational structure is the two plot levels, main plot and subplot, which are indicated by the division of the play's characters and action into two locales, castle and asylum. Each locale is nominally presided over by a ruler who has abandoned his authority to a subordinate: the asylum is headed by Alibius, the mental doctor who cannot cure, the castle by Vermandero, the governor who cannot rule. Alibius directly places Lollio in charge of his wife and his madmen and fools while he absents himself. Vermandero, indirectly and by default, places De Flores in command of the castle and its inhabitants and disappears, for all practical purposes, for the remainder of the play. Just as Lollio holds the keys to the fools' and madmen's wards and exhibits them to Isabella, De Flores keeps the keys to the castle and does the honors as host to the unsuspecting Alonzo.

The prized possession of both asylum and castle is a woman—Alibius' wife, Isabella, and Vermandero's daughter, Beatrice—yet the two men of authority also abandon these "jewels" to their lieutenants. Alibius' desertion puts Lollio in a position to help Isabella to her disguised lovers and to "put in for my thirds"; Vermandero's blindness permits De Flores, by assisting Beatrice in manipulating her suitors, to demand not just thirds, but her virginity.

In the scenes set in the asylum, there is frequent mention of the division of the madhouse into two wards—one for madmen, one for fools. At first these comments seem meaningless, but as reference piles upon reference it becomes apparent that the division is meant to extend to the world at large, which Middleton and Rowley maintain is also composed of fools and madmen.[1] This is the second structure, an outgrowth of the two plot locales, which bifurcates the world of the play like the world of the asylum (and by implication the macrocosm as well) into fools and madmen. This structure cuts across the castle-main plot/asylum-subplot division and supersedes that structure by uniting the two worlds, and as a result, the play.

The distinction between the two types of patients in the asylum is introduced by Lollio's comment that "we have but two sorts of people in the house . . . that's fools and madmen" (I.ii.45-55),[2] and it is quickly extended to the presumably sane inhabitants of the hospital when he assures Alibius that any gallants who come to view the insane need not think to look at his wife, for "if they come to see the fools and madmen, you and I may serve the turn" (I.ii.58-59).[3]

The fool/madman dichotomy is then carried yet another step—from the asylum's patients, to their keepers, to the world at large. Lollio explains to Isabella that her husband thinks she has no need to leave the hospital:

LOLLIO:

> He says you have company enough in the house, if you please to be sociable, of all sorts of people.

ISABELLA:

> Of all sorts? Why, here's none but fools and madmen.

LOLLIO:

> Very well; and where will you find any other, if you should go abroad? There's my master and I to boot too.

ISABELLA:

> Of either sort one, a madman and a fool.

>   (III.iii.12-17)

Moreover, the universality of the division is stressed again when Isabella sarcastically reminds her husband, "Y'ave a fine trade on't: / Madmen and fools are a staple commodity," and he replies, "Just at the lawyers' haven we arrive, / By madmen and by fools we both do thrive" (III,iii.270-74).

Thus, the microcosm of the asylum is separated into two wards, one housing fools, the other madmen, and the outside world is also divisible into these same two groups. But what is the difference between them? The asylum scenes point out that the fool is a harmless, curable fellow, whereas the madman is incurable and prone to violence. There is no hope of recovery for the Welsh lunatic who lost his cheese, but Lollio promises great improvement to Antonio; the distinction is between the "incurable mad of the one side and very fools on the other." Furthermore, the madmen continually raise a ruckus in their ward and must be subdued with whips; by contrast, the "fools' college" is seldom even locked, and one can walk among them without fear. The distinction is made most graphic in the characterizations of Antonio and Franciscus. When Lollio exhibits Tony to Isabella, he is harmless and amiable, but Franciscus, when displayed in his madman's role, grows violent and beats Lollio. In keeping with the love and transformation theme, however, Tony is altered into a madman when he believes he has lost all chance of possessing Isabella. Upon becoming mad, he also becomes violent (Iv.iii.129-42).

Finally, this bifurcation of the world is related to the theme of delegated authority when Lollio laments, "Would my master were come home! I am not able to govern both these wards together" (III.iii.163-65). Later Lollio again extends the specific to the general, paralleling his problems in governing his master's realm to a situation prevalent in the outside world:

> I would my master were come home; 'tis too much for one shepherd to govern two of these flocks, nor can I believe that one churchman can instruct two benefices at once; there will be some incurable mad of the one side and very fools on the other.

>   (III.iii.198-202)

It is not, then, only the unfortunate inmates of the asylum who can be so dichotomized. The world at large and particularly the world of the castle and its inhabitants are shown to be also divisible into two wards—in one, the curable fools, such as Alsemero and Tomazo, who, as we shall see, temporarily lose their reason and can be restored to sanity; in the other are De Flores and Beatrice who by completely submitting to their passions, take the irretrievable step into madness. They are so overwhelmed by their own wills that they become violent in the drive to satisfy them and finally transgress too far ever to return to sanity, thus reflecting the turbulent disorder and irreclaimable condition of Alibius' madmen. The madness of the asylum inmates serves to emphasize and define this metaphorical insanity of the main figures by reducing their condition to its lowest, most literal level of meaning.

The third organizational device is verbal structure, consisting of the repetition of words and concepts with various meanings to reflect and develop themes. We will not investigate each of these in this paper, but repetition of *blood, service, sweetness, act, deed, performance,* and images of food and hunger, the castle, the madhouse, sight rings, animals and jewels all cast shafts of light onto the meanings of the play. The multiplication of writers who have found the play's themes summarized in different images is an indication of the complexity of *The Changeling's* verbal structures.[4] One of the locales of the two plot levels, the castle, is part of this framework, as through an elaborate system of *double entendre,* it represents the "jewel" of the castle, Beatrice, as well as the physical setting.[5] The metaphor is first suggested when, after Alsemero has expressed his interest in Beatrice, she says to her father, "I find him much desirous / To see your castle" (I.i.154-55). Beatrice is dissembling to her parent in order to further her desire for Alsemero, but Vermandero's answer is true on both the literal and metaphorical level. "Our citadels," he explains to Alsemaro, "Are plac'd conspicuous to outward view / On promonts' tops, but within are secrets" (I.i.159-61). The secrets are, perhaps, most hidden from himself, for he insists that Alsemero, who wisely seeks to leave when hearing of Beatrice's bethrothal, visit them: "You must see my castle / And her best entertainment ere we part" (I.i.197-98). (The gender of the possessive pronoun selected for the castle also suggests its equivalence to Beatrice.) Alsemero accepts the invitation to see the castle, but queries, "How shall I dare to venture in his castle / When he discharges murderers [small cannon] at the gate?" (I.i.218-19). His aside is of particular thematic significance, for it emphasizes that Alsemero has been forewarned by the "murderers," the information that Beatrice is betrothed, and is well aware that he should broach neither the castle literal nor the castle metaphorical. The warning of her engagement discharged by the cannon should be sufficient to send him on his way had not his reason been overpowered by his passion. He knows what he should do but submits to the compulsion of his will: "But I must go on, for back I cannot go" (I.i.220).

Once inside the fortress, Alsemero becomes acquainted with some of its secrets as Diaphanta leads him along concealed corridors to and from a meeting with Beatrice, a rendezvous which, in view of her engagement, is as illicit as the routes used to arrive at it. And with smug satisfaction Beatrice reflects, "I have got him now the liberty of the house," that is, the liberty of its secret passages and freedom of access to herself (III.iv.12).

Like Alsemero, Alonzo too is lured by desire to see the building; he requests De Flores to show him "the full strength of the castle," which De Flores, who has already been commissioned by Beatrice to do away with her fiancé, is only too willing to do. When they meet for the tour, De Flores triumphantly announces that he now has all the keys to the fortress:

> Yes, here are all the keys; I was afraid, my lord,
> I'd wanted for the postern: this is it.
> I've all, I've all, my lord; this for the sconce.
>
> (III.i.1-3)

Through Vermandero's dereliction he already keeps the keys to the physical castle, and he now, with the upcoming murder of Alonzo, holds them to Beatrice as well. The postern, whose key he had been lacking, is "a back door; a private door; any door or gate distinct from the main entrance" and "an entrance other than the usual and honourable one" as well (*OED, postern,* 1 and 2b). In this context, in addition to its literal meaning, it has both a sexual connotation and a metaphoric significance—the dishonorable entrance into Beatrice to which Alonzo's death is the key. When Beatrice yields her virginity to De Flores in payment for the murder, "the master of the workings of the literal fortress becomes the master of the metaphorical one."[6]

After this climactic yielding of the castle, uses of the metaphor are less concentrated. Tomazo insists that the castle "is the place must yield account" for his missing brother (IV.ii.21), and it is true both that the murdered Alonzo is still hidden in the castle and that Beatrice must finally answer for his death. Revelation of her guilt comes about through Jasperino's and Alsemero's discovery of her in "a back part of the house" with De Flores, from which she takes "the back door" when leaving, the secret, non-public portions of the castle corresponding to the private part of Beatrice's life which must be hidden from even so "public" a gaze as her husband's. Finally, when the truth about De Flores and Beatrice is revealed, Vermandero exclaims, "An host of enemies enter'd my citadel / Could not amaze like this"

(V.iii.148-49). Vermandero's surprise is the amazement of Fabritio and the Duke of *Women Beware Women* when they view the final massacre of the masque; it is Middleton and Rowley's final irony that those whose business it is to rule and guide are the last to understand what has taken place in their demesnes. Vermandero is morally responsible for the defense and protection of the castle and Beatrice, yet the latter citadel was entered, taken and destroyed by the enemy without his knowledge.

The fourth structure is a person-by-person organization that compares the motives and actions of almost every character in the play, and then compares and contrasts the outcome of their actions. This structure develops the chief themes, the necessity for man's reason to curb passion and his transformation to madness when passion blinds his reason. In examining this structure, we still cannot abandon the dual plot structure because the subplot characters, while embodying thematic concepts in their own rights, frequently retain their subplot qualities as literal manifestations of perceptions largely metaphorical in the more realistic main plot. And even in the character-by-character approach, it is necessary to treat the two plot levels individually, considering first the themes as exposed by figures of the main plot before analyzing how the charades of the subplot characters recreate the themes.

Perhaps of all the characters, Alsemero exhibits the play's precepts most clearly and fully. As the play opens he is defying an omen and trying to convince himself that the sacrilege implicit in falling in love in church does not really exist (I.i.1-12). He knows, as he again acknowledges at the play's conclusion (V.iii.73-77), that lust which usurps the time set aside for holy worship is wrong, but he excuses himself with his "good intention" of marriage. The entry on the scene of his friend, Jasperino, reveals to the audience that Alsemero has undergone a transformation, that one who used to be impervious to women's charms has become a gallant lover. The symbol of change, the weathervane, is used to emphasize both Alsemero's alteration and the fact that he is proceeding in defiance of moral obstacles: Although the wind is right for the planned sea voyage, Alsemero claims that the temple's vane has turned against him, presumably indicating a change of direction corresponding to his own, but also symbolizing the immorality of the undertaking he is about to embark on.

Alsemero's second warning that he is proceeding amiss comes, ironically enough, from Beatrice herself, who explains to him that one's eyes can often blind one's judgment, and that it is the responsibility of judgment to overrule and correct the sight (I.i.68-73). In addition to these two warnings, Alsemero receives what should be another when he witnesses Beatrice's blatant lie to her father that Alsemero told her he wishes to see the castle. And finally, Vermandero's revelation of her engagement is such a deterrent that even the passion-blinded Alsemero realizes that he should leave; he makes his apologies to Vermandero and tries to depart, but then accedes to his will to see Beatrice and remains. The news of her engagement is a double warning, for it discloses both that she is legally and morally bound to another, thereby destroying his excuse that his intentions are honorable, and it reveals that Beatrice is not precisely honest in encouraging him under the circumstances. By the end of the first scene, then, Alsemero has allowed his reason to be blinded by his lust for Beatrice and has been transformed to one of love's tame madmen, a fool.

In the later acts, Alsemero is again warned—this time that something is afoot between Beatrice and De Flores. He tries Beatrice with his virginity test but is deceived by her response. He allows himself to be blinded to the truth by his faith in his medical tests just as he permits himself to be deceived by his faith in his eyesight and what he considers to be his judgment. He is ironically contrasted to De Flores, who is sure of her virginity without tests (III.iv.117-20), just as he is sure of her potential whoredom when he sees her leaning from Alonzo to Alsemero, a sight which Alsemero also observes but without drawing the logical conclusion.

Alsemero's judgment is finally restored by the sight of Beatrice and De Flores meeting together; this spectacle destroys his love and allows his reason to regain its ascendence. Learning that she is responsible for Alonzo's death, he realizes that he should have heeded the warning of the temple (V.iii.73-74). He at last understands that it was "blood," that is, lust, aroused by her physical beauty and not judgment that inspired his actions. And then with the final revelation of her unchastity, he recognizes his blindness that accepted her beautiful appearance for the hidden, hideous reality (V.iii.109-110). Thus, Alsemero is first transformed by love to a tame madman, an alteration which is reversed when his love ends and his reason is restored. His major transformation, however, is from a blind man who thinks he sees to a seeing man who knows he was blind.

In his brief appearance in the play, Alonzo shows himself to be like Alsemero—blinded by his passion and unwilling to heed the voice of reason, personified by his brother, Tomazo, who admonishes him that Beatrice no longer loves him (II.i.106 and 127-39). Alonzo refuses to listen; and displaying how thoroughly his reason has been overwhelmed by passion, he declares that he "should depart / An enemy, a dangerous, deadly one / To any but thyself that should but think / She knew the meaning of inconstancy" (II.i.144-47). Tomazo can only shake his head and summarize Alonzo's transformation: "Why here is love's tame madness; thus a man / Quickly steals into his vexation" (II.i.153-54). Unfor-

tunately, Alonzo's abrupt ending prevents his ever regaining his sanity.[7]

Tomazo's own grip on sanity and reason is weakened with the unexplained disappearance of his brother, and he grows obsessed with new passions, anger and desire for revenge. He first attacks Vermandero as the instigator of the crime and demands, "I claim a brother of you . . . [I seek him] 'mongst your dearest bloods" (IV.ii.18-19). He wrongly assumes that some of the young bloods of Vermandero's court must be responsible for carrying out the deed, but "your dearest bloods" has an ironic accuracy, for it is the dearest of Vermandero's blood, or family, that is guilty of the crime. Tomazo's passion has so overcome him that he refuses to listen to Vermandero's reasonable presentation of his side of the story; and gaining no satisfaction from Vermandero, he confronts Alsemero, quarrels, and threatens that they must settle the dispute on the field of honor.

At his next appearance, Tomazo has degenerated even further into insanity. He is obsessed by his wrongs and able to think of nothing else (V.ii.1-8). His sudden hatred for De Flores, whom he had previously regarded as "honest De Flores," "kind and true one," the possessor of "a wondrous honest heart," has even less reason than his outraged feelings for Vermandero, the supposed master of the castle and its inhabitants, and certainly less justification than his suspicion of Alsemero, who apparently gained most from Alonzo's disappearance. Tomazo wildly claims that De Flores "walks o' purpose by, sure, to choke me up, / To infect my blood" and insanely strikes De Flores when he approaches him (V.ii.24-25). Tomazo's reference to infecting his blood is a continuation of the imagery of venom and poison in association with De Flores that Tomazo, like other characters, has been using; in addition, it indicates that Tomazo's blood, his passionate anger, is aroused by the sight of De Flores and by nearly everyone else who comes near him. His abandonment of reason has reduced him to the condition of the springtime snake which, after losing its skin, strikes out in blindness at everything that approaches.

Immediately after Tomazo's assault on De Flores, Vermandero tells him that the murderers, Antonio and Franciscus, have been discovered. The madness displayed by Tomazo in his greed to learn whom to wreak his vengeance on is paralleled to that of De Flores when seeking his commission to murder Alonzo. De Flores exclaims, "Oh, blest occasion!" when presented with the opportunity to be of service to Beatrice and kneels before her, expressing a "reverence" to receive her orders. He insists, "I thirst for him," the yet unknown target, and upon hearing Alonzo's name declares, "His end's upon him; he shall be seen no more" (II.ii.113-35). In a graphic parallel expression of his desire,

Tomazo kneels to Vermandero, promising "reverence" to him for revealing the murderers, and hearing their names, exclaims, "Oh, blest revelation!" Echoing De Flores' eagerness to kill, he cries, "I thirst for 'em; / Like subtle lightning will I wind about 'em / and melt their marrow in 'em" (V.ii.63-87). The scene ends on these lines, with Tomazo prepared to take what Beatrice and De Flores already have taken, the final, violent step into irrecoverable madness and damnation—murder.

The revelation of the true murderers forestalls Tomazo's destruction; and when he sees his "injuries lie dead before" him, the satisfaction of his desire for justice restores his reason. In his relationship with Alsemero and Vermandero, he is altered "from an ignorant wrath / To knowing friendship" (V.iii.203-204). Like Alsemaro, his recovery from temporary madness has improved his sight and transformed him to a more rational man.

The person-by-person structure extends from these lesser figures to the two key characters as well. De Flores is another whose judgment has been overclouded by passion. When he is first introduced he has already succumbed to his lust for Beatrice, although he expects to gain nothing but abuse for his persistent efforts to see her (I.i.97-101 and later in the scene, II.231-33). He is a man who must have his will regardless of anyone's opposition, and so completely has he submitted to that will that he has become a wise madman who uses all of his many resources and experience only to feed his compulsion.

With his characteristic insight, De Flores is aware that his conduct is less than rational. He questions, "Whatever ails me?" that he should persist in seeing her only to be insulted and abused. And he asks,

> Why am not I an ass to devise ways
> Thus to be rail'd at? I must see her still;
> I shall have a mad qualm within this hour again,
> I know't, and like a common Garden bull
> I do but take breath to be lugg'd again.
>
> (II.i.77-81)

His "mad qualm" is an accurate description of the force that sends him to Beatrice's side despite her derision. It is knowledge of the irrational quality of his own passion that probably prompts his belief that he, too, may hope to be "belov'd beyond all reason."

When Beatrice finally calls him to her, he exults, "Ha, I shall run mad with joy" (II.ii.70); and the ease with which he convinces himself that he and she have in mind the same reward for Alonzo's murder is attributable to the abeyance of his reason before his passion. A person merely reading the text might subscribe to De Flores' superficial logic that concludes it is possible that a delicately-reared woman might chide herself to

bed with him. But faced on stage by the hideous malignity that De Flores is supposed to be, he might realize that only utter irrationality could expect such an outcome and only in madness could it come to pass. There is a tendency among critics to assume that part of De Flores' superior insight is his ability to realize, even before he sees Beatrice's affection shifting to Alsemero, that she may someday come to love him. His "realization" is, on the contrary, another indication of his complete lack of reason, and the fact that he is correct in his guess only an indication of her final madness as well.

Beatrice's ultimate madness and final damnation are not apparent at the start of the play; De Flores has already submitted to the passion which now controls him, but Beatrice is only at the beginning of the road which he has taken. Her difference from him is conveyed visually by her beauty contrasted to his ugliness, and at this time, her beauty is not a mask for her vice but a symbol of her innocence. Yet to be tried, she is still not guilty of sin.

Her first trial, Alsemero's advances, evokes a response which not only introduces the major theme (the need to curb passion with reason) but also gives evidence that Beatrice is aware, intellectually at least, of the need to rule physical urges with judgment. She cautions Alsemero:

> Our eyes are sentinels unto our judgments
> And should give certain judgment what they see,
> But they are rash sometimes and tells us wonders
> Of common things, which when our judgments find,
> They can then check the eyes and call them blind.
>
> (I.i.69-73)

It is typical of Middleton to put wise or moral messages on unlikely lips, perhaps for just this purpose—to show that the speaker knows right from wrong, but Beatrice does not convince us that she genuinely understands what she says. Her insight seems to be compartmentalized as an intellectual exercise, the sort of "a penny saved is a penny earned" adage that a child might be taught without ever grasping its significance. The impression that she knows not what she says is created in part by the glibness of her pronouncements and in part by her subsequent rationalizations that what she wants is truly the dictates of judgment. Only seven lines after she has lectured Alsemero on the need for judgment to rule the eyes she is arguing to herself that her eyes, which five days earlier told her Alonzo was her one and only, were wrong at that time and are now correct in assessing Alsemero as "the man meant for me" (I.i.80-82). She further rationalizes her switch in affections by the sophism that a man who chooses his associates well has good judgment, that Alsemero's own wisdom is proved by his choice of Jasperino as a friend, and that therefore she is wise in choosing Alsemero. "Methinks I love now with the eyes of judgment," she concludes this false syllogism (II.i.6-14). She knows that reason should rule emotions but hastily convinces herself that it is on the basis of reason that she prefers Alsemero to Alonzo.

Nevertheless, in a variety of ways, Beatrice is shown to be well aware that her conduct is wrong. For example, she feels it necessary to dissimulate to both Alsemero and her father. She conceals her engagement from Alsemero as long as she can and lies to her father about the tenor of her conversation with Alsemero. She meets her new lover in secret, an indirect confession of guilt, and when the idea of doing away with Alonzo arises, she knows that such an act becomes a foul visage, not a fair one. Her very concealment of the murder plans from Alsemero betrays her as knowing right from wrong and willfully electing the latter. Thus, Beatrice is conscious that her course of conduct is not moral. She herself is not amoral; she, like Alsemero, allows her passion, her will to have her new love, to rule her judgment.

A much more telling warning to Beatrice than her intellectual knowledge or even the feelings of guilt that prompt dissimulation is her instinctive reaction to De Flores. His physical appearance, for which she feels such repulsion, is a symbol of his submission to passion, or his madness. As Beatrice remarks when trying to cajole him, his ugliness is caused by the heat from his liver, the seat of passion. Her loathing is both a reaction to a person who is passion-dominated and a fear of her own pressuring emotions. Moreover, it is a warning to her to beware of this man and of the unruled passions that can dominate reason and control one's life. It is ironic that she apologizes for being unable to give any reason for her hatred, for her fear and loathing are based on an instinct stronger and truer than reason. When her end is upon her she admits her mistake in not heeding these warnings (V.iii.157-58), and she is indeed following her own better instincts when she plans to catch Vermandero in a good mood and plead for De Flores' dismissal.

Beatrice, then, stands in relation to her passions as she does in relation to their symbol, De Flores. They bother her, upset and irritate her, but she is still in control of them. She is the mistress; they (and he) the servants. Her downfall begins and she takes her first step down De Flores' own path of madness when she assumes that De Flores can be used to further her own ends (discarding Alonzo and marrying Alsemero). She is, at the same time that she approaches De Flores, submitting to her emotions, her will to have Alsemero. She believes that she can utilize De Flores and then dismiss him just as she believes that by following her will to marry Alsemero, she can make the course of passion

the course of judgment.[8] Beatrice momentarily reflects on the horror of employing De Flores but thrusts aside these feelings of foreboding:

> Why, put case I loath'd him
> As much as youth and beauty hates a sepulcher,
> Must I needs show it? Cannot I keep that secret
> And serve my turn upon him?
>
> (II.ii.66-69)

She is confident that she can control De Flores just as she believes her judgment controls her conduct.

When Beatrice makes this fatal error of yielding to her desire for Alsemero, she transforms her servant, who, like her emotions is supposedly beneath her and governed by her, into her master. In submitting to her unreasoning will, she also yields to the living symbol of the irrational. The reversal of Beatrice's and De Flores' relative positions is visually symbolized when, before the murder, De Flores kneels to her to beg for the opportunity to serve her and, after the deed, she kneels to him to beg to be spared the consequences of her crime. But as Middleton points out in this and other plays, the fatal step is irrevocable. The moment cannot be recovered, and the deed once done transforms the doer. De Flores makes plain to Beatrice (and to the audience) the fallacy of a woman dipped in blood talking of modesty, and when she appeals to "the distance that creation set 'twixt thy blood and mine," De Flores, now with the force of the inexorable destiny that Beatrice herself has set in motion, tells her of her transformation:

> Push, fly not to your birth, but settle you
> In what the act has made you; y'are no more now.
> You must forget your parentage to me;
> Y'are the deed's creature; by that name
> You lost your first condition, and I challenge you.
> As peace and innocency has turn'd you out
> And made you one with me.
>
> (III.iv.135-41)

The fate which Beatrice cannot weep from its determined purpose is that which she herself elected when she brushed aside the dictates of reason and of her own better nature and stepped into the irrational, chaotic world of De Flores.

In this mad and violent world, her better instincts are soon forgotten; lust and that which she once loathed become not only acceptable but loved. After their sexual and spiritual union, Beatrice exclaims of De Flores, "I am forc'd to love thee now" and "How heartily he serves me! His face loathes one, / But look upon his care, who would not love him? / The east is not more beauteous than his service" (V.i.47, 70-72). The sexual connotation of service places before the reader's mind how thoroughly Beatrice has surrendered to lust, and the extent of her transformation and madness is revealed by her belief that De Flores is "a man worth loving," "a wondrous necessary man" (V.i.76,91).

Beatrice's oneness with De Flores, the transformation which madness has wrought in her, is discovered by Alsemero, who finally penetrates the beauty which is now become a disguise for a reality as hideous as the appearance of De Flores. Alsemero reacts with the revulsion which earlier characterizes her attitude toward De Flores—"Oh, thou art all deform'd"—and locks up Beatrice, and then De Flores, like the madmen that they have become.[9] When he calls them from the closet, "Come forth, you twins of mischief," he emphasizes what De Flores has already proclaimed—their equivalence. Together they have been caught in irrecoverable madness and condemned to hell.

Beatrice at last realizes and admits that she has been transformed from her original identity. She tells Vermandero that she is "that of your blood was taken from you / For your better health . . . Let the common sewer take it from distinction" (V.iii.151-54). Moreover, she understands that the outcome of her life was not fated had she but heeded the warnings. Had she heeded rather than ignored her hatred of De Flores, she might have plucked her fate from him, since it was not the unchanging, all-governing stars that controlled her destiny, but only "yon meteor," whom she might have avoided (V.iii.155-59).

Repeating the diction of the subplot's madmen, De Flores summarizes the pair's punishment for their sins: "I coupled with your mate / At barley-break; now we are left in hell" (V.iii.63-64). Others have run through the circle of barley-break—Alsemero, Tomazo, Isabella, Antonio and Franciscus—but Beatrice and De Flores, through their complete submission to passion, their commission of irreversible acts of lust and violence, are caught in madness and in hell.[10] Thus, Beatrice's initial alteration in affection, her "giddy turning" from Alonzo to Alsemero, is only a prelude to her transformation from hatred of De Flores to love for him, from innocence to guilt, from master to servant, from the cossetted daughter of Vermandero to the vicious creature of the deed, from sanity to incurable madness.

As part of the person-by-person structure, even the least major figure of the main plot, Vermandero, is shown in his willful insistence on having his desires. He is not a particularly well-developed character, but there are indications that he is another whose will controls his reason in his own asseveration that "I'll want my will" if Beatrice does not marry Alonzo and in Beatrice's assurance,

> [My father's] blessing
> Is only mine as I regard his name;
> Else it goes from me and turns head against me,
> Transform'd into a curse.
>
> (II.i.20-23)

Vermandero, then, is like Fabritio in **Women Beware Women** in insisting that he have his "will" in regard to

his daughter's marriage despite warnings—Beatrice's marked coolness to Alonzo and her desire to postpone the wedding—that his desire is unreasonable and contrary to hers.

The characters of the subplot, like so many comic figures in Middleton's plays, are designed to restate in a simpler form the themes of the main plot. We have already seen that Alibius' actions caricature Vermandero's dereliction of authority, and in addition, the two would-be lovers, Antonio and Franciscus, approximate Alonzo, Alsemero and De Flores in being transformed by their lusts into fool and madman. Their alterations, in contrast to the mainplot figures' metamorphoses, are literal as well as metaphorical; they don the costumes of idiot and maniac in order to have access to Isabella, who contrasts not simply with Beatrice but with all the major characters as one whose judgment overrules her passion. Isabella mirrors the actions of other characters in being tempted to succumb to her interest in Antonio; but she ultimately sees through the love which he swears is based on an accurate judgment of her attributes to the underlying lust, and she is then able to check her own passion.

In addition, the turns of the subplot are couched in simpler, more direct phraseology than that used in the main, and this less metaphoric diction similarly helps to define the play's theses. When, for example, Antonio casts off his fool's disguise for Isabella, he tells her,

> Cast no amazing eye upon this change. . . .
> This shape of folly shrouds your dearest love,
> The truest servant to your powerful beauties,
> Whose magic had this force thus to transform me.
>
> (III.iii.116-20)

His lines, combined with his disguise, flatly state that he has been transformed to a fool by her "beauties." The same overt statement is made of Franciscus' transformation. Reading a love letter from Franciscus, Isabella describes his transformation by passion as well (IV.iii.1-4, 11-16, 21-24). She reads from the letter, "'Sweet lady, having now cast off this counterfeit cover of a madman, I appear to your best judgment a true and faithful lover of your beauty,'" and Lollio declares, "He is mad still," indicating that in or out of his disguise, Franciscus has been turned mad by love (IV.iii.11-16). Franciscus' letter goes on to say that Isabella's distance from him is the cause of his transformation to madness and her nearness could return his sanity. His passion has turned him mad, but its satisfaction can cure him. To Lollio he is a "mad rascal still." These exchanges, then, provide direct and obvious statements of theme.

Finally, the action surrounding Isabella's temptation and ultimate reassertion of judgment over lust is depicted as a farcical parody of the play's themes. When

Isabella is first fascinated by Antonio's revelation of his identity and resists Lollio's suggestion to return the fool to his ward, the offstage madmen chorus, "Catch there, catch the last couple in hell," defining the inevitable fate of those who yield to illicit lust. Similarly, when Antonio presents his Alsemero-like address to Isabella's perfection (III.iii.178-86), the madmen parade over the upper stage imitating birds and beasts and reflecting the irrational, bestial reality beneath Antonio's honeyed romanticism. Momentarily checked but not completely discouraged by this exhibition, which is "of fear enough to part us," Isabella disguises as a madwoman, which she is in danger of becoming, in order to escape Lollio and to see Antonio. He, however, rebuffs the misshapen hag, and Isabella recognizes the cruel reality beneath the romantic guise (IV.iii.129-33). Antonio is revealed to be once again like Alsemero, unable to see beyond surface appearances; he is not a quick-sighted lover but one whose eyes of judgment are blinded by those of lust. Isabella fortunately learns how shallow his love and her own attraction to him are, heeds the warning and departs. Like Beatrice, she has run through the circle of barley-break, but she has not allowed herself to be caught by her lust and passion in that hell.

The refusal of Vermandero, Beatrice, Alsemero, Antonio, Franciscus and the others to rule their wills with reason is a parallel to Vermandero's and Alibius' abdication of authority over their domains. Middleton repeats this theme of abandonment of one's moral responsibility on three levels: On one is Vermandero's and Alibius' turning over the government of their realms to their servants, De Flores and Lollio. On the second is the various characters' forsaking control of their conduct to their emotions. Instead of ruling their lives with judgment, they turn them over to their passions, who should be servants rather than masters. On the third level is Beatrice's specific yielding of her responsibilities, her chastity and ultimately her soul, to the servant, De Flores. (It is significant that De Flores' role as a servant is a change from Middleton and Rowley's sources, in which De Flores is a gentleman garrisoned in the castle.)¹¹

These three levels are the skeletal basis for the play's world-view. They are the fifth structure, a hierarchy of moral responsibility which is almost unstated verbally, but which is shown as essential to the play's highest meaning. This hierarchy organizes the world of *The Changeling* according to the moral obligations of its members. Like the bifurcation of madman and fool, this structure cuts across all others and encompasses them. It indicates that each person in the social order has a realm of moral responsibility. Each is charged (presumably by God) with the conduct and control of his person and with the preservation of his soul. To some is also given the higher responsibilities of the protection of other people and the government of groups of

people. Thus, in this system, Isabella, Franciscus, Antonio, Tomazo and Alsemero temporarily defect from their charges, some of them almost losing their souls and sanity in the process; Beatrice and De Flores completely fail to control their realms and must suffer damnation for their failure; Alibius fails in governing his realm and its inhabitants, but they take the responsibility for themselves; and Vermandero not only falls short of governing his own will, but also fails in his higher responsibilities for his daughter, his castle, and its inhabitants. His dereliction is brought home to him when he sees that his "citadel" has been breached, and it is appropriate that he whose lack of control over himself and his dependents has done so much to allow the tragedy to occur feels the confining circle of hell about him and echoes De Flores' words, "Now we are left in hell," with "We are all there, it circumscribes here" (V.iii.165).

These five structures—subplot/mainplot, madman-fool dichotomy, verbal, person-by-person, and moral hierarchy—organize, support and convey the meanings of the play. They divide the play into its components and reveal the relationships between the parts that create the whole. Without perception of the structures, it is nearly impossible to see the play in its masterful, complex entirety, but broken down to its structures, it displays the craftsmanship of its authors and illustrates several of the means of formal organization seen in other Tudor, Elizabethan and Jacobean plays as well.

Notes

1. Richard Levin comments on this division in the subplot but assumes that it "has no functional significance" (*The Multiple Plot in English Renaissance Drama* [Chicago: Univ. of Chicago Press, 1971], p. 46 n. 20); and Irving Ribner suggests that "there may be also in the division of Alibius' house into fools and madmen a suggestion that the entire world is so divided and that these are the elect and the damned of Calvinist theology" (*Jacobean Tragedy* [London: Methuen, 1962], p. 136).

2. Thomas Middleton and William Rowley, *The Changeling,* ed. George W. Williams (Lincoln: Univ. of Nebraska Press, 1972). All references to *The Changeling* are to this text.

3. It has sometimes been suggested that Lollio immediately penetrates Antonio's disguise because he responds to Pedro's assurance that Tony is a gentleman, "Nay, there's nobody doubted that; at first sight I knew him for a gentleman, he looks no other yet" (I.ii.113-14). It is more likely, however, that, first, Lollio's statement is intended as a joke at the expense of gentlemen, for Tony was doubtless dressed in a misshapen, clown-like costume and probably wandered about the stage dur-

ing the interview between Lollio and Pedro with his mouth hanging lax and engaging in a great deal of farcical, foolish behavior; and second, the statement has the more serious effect of reinforcing the idea that not all fools are locked up in wards, that sometimes the fool and the gentleman are indistinguishable.

4. See Christopher Ricks, "The Moral and Poetic Structure of *The Changeling*," *EIC,* X (1960), 290-306; Dorothea Kehler, "Rings and Jewels in *The Changeling*," *ELN,* 5 (1967), 15-17; Michael C. Andrews, "'Sweetness' in 'The Changeling,'" *Yearbook of English Studies,* 1 (1971), 63-67; Edward Engelberg, "Tragic Blindness in *The Changeling* and *Women Beware Women*," *MLQ,* 23 (1962), 20-28; and Normand Berlin, "The 'Finger' Image and Relationship of Character in *The Changeling*," *English Studies in Africa,* 12 (1969), 162-66.

5. See Thomas Berger's article, "The Petrarchan Fortress of *The Changeling*," which differs in detail from our explication of the castle imagery (*Renaissance Papers 1969*), 37-46.

6. Berger, p. 42.

7. M. C. Bradbrook notes that Alonzo "refuses to recognize her [Beatrice's] very plain dislike of him, since love has overpowered his judgment" (*Themes and Conventions of Elizabethan Tragedy* [Cambridge: Cambridge University Press, 1960], p. 215). Similarly, N. W. Bawcutt calls Alonzo "another of the play's self-willed, obstinate characters who refuse to recognize any obstacle to their desires" (*The Changeling,* ed. N. W. Bawcutt [London: Methuen, 1970], p. xlix).

8. Her shallowly rationalized desire is like that of *Women Beware Women's* Duke, who likewise tries to hallow his lust by marriage after an opposing person has been disposed of.

9. See Bawcutt, p. lxv.

10. See Ribner, p. 134, and Williams, editor, *The Changeling,* p. xxiv.

11. See Bawcutt, Appendix A, pp. 122-23.

Douglas Duncan (essay date March 1983)

SOURCE: Duncan, Douglas. "Virginity in *The Changeling*." *English Studies in Canada* 9, no. 1 (March 1983): 25-35.

[*In the following essay, Duncan explores the treatment of the theme of virginity in the main plot of* The Changeling *to illuminate questions about the work's realism and attitudes toward Christian moral values.*]

As a compact structure of related plots, a network of interlocking images and ironies, *The Changeling*[1] has benefited from critical studies of the objective, analytic type. Necessarily, however, such studies eschew the old and indeterminable questions of interpretation which continue to fascinate new readers. What, for example, is the ratio in DeFlores of complex individual and embodiment of evil? Is Beatrice only a wicked young woman whose pretences to the contrary are ironically flayed, or is she also in any sense tragic? And what is the real, as distinct from the symbolic, relationship between these two characters toward the end of the play? Such questions focus on that area of Middleton's art where his sleight of hand latterly became deft and hard to detect: the interweaving of his often conflicting interests in natural portraiture and schematic morality.[2] This essay reaches some views on those matters through examining the treatment in the main plot of the theme of virginity.

If one theme recurs more than others in Middleton's work it is the exploitation of woman's sexuality, and especially virginity, for the commercial and social advantage of herself or her family. The almost total absence of this theme from *The Changeling* is made the more remarkable by its prominence in Middleton's source.[3] Reynolds had stressed how both Beatrice's suitors, Piracquo and Alsemero, were superior to her family in rank and wealth; her father, Vermandero, gives encouragement to the former "as knowing it greatly for her preferment, & aduancement" and "because he perfectly knew that *Piracquo's* meanes farre exceed that of *Alsemero*." Middleton's Vermandero shows none of these normal concerns. He controls his daughter's choice, but chooses Piracquo as a "complete" gentleman to be preferred to "the proudest he" in Spain (I.i.212-17); he welcomes Alsemero first out of love for his father—a detail not in Reynolds—and second because of his "noble" reputation in Valencia (III.iv.1). Beatrice in the play is far from being Reynolds's "meane . . . gentlewoman" attracted to Alsemero by "the sumptuousnesse of his apparell." Instead, at some cost to credibility, she is shown as very rich, with unquestioned access to her riches. If the three thousand gold florins which she offers to DeFlores as blood-money is meant to sound like a large sum, the effect is to stress that, even when doubled (III.iv.73), it still falls far short of her entire wealth in gold and jewels which she is willing to stake against rape (157). So far from trading her virginity for worldly rewards, Beatrice offers vast wealth in order to protect it. Her lovers care about it too. Alsemero's concern, emphasized by his laboratory of testing equipment, is the reason for the drastic measures which Beatrice takes to conceal what she loses. Even DeFlores, obsessed with his "pleasure," insists at a moment of very high tension that half of his pleasure will depend on her virginity being "perfect" (III.iv.116-19).

It appears that Middleton, in making virginity central to his play, resisted opportunities afforded by his source of treating it in his favourite way as a marketed commodity. He treats it instead as a religious ideal. In related ways Alsemero and Beatrice venerate that ideal as inseparable from their concept of virtue and holy marriage, while for DeFlores too, on a different level, virginity is a religious emblem in the sense that his pursuit of Beatrice's body is seen as worship of a kind, a carnal travesty of chivalric devotion. Most plays of the period use the cheapening of virginity to stigmatize moral decadence. In **The Changeling** the blind over-valuing of it is both an object of ironic scrutiny and a factor contributing to tragedy.

Early remarks about Alsemero's indifference to women (I.i.36-39, 58-63) indicate, if not necessarily his virginity, at least a degree of sexual purity sufficient to authorize his concern for his wife's and to prepare us for the mistakes of an inexperienced lover. The strength and blindness of his religious idealism are most clearly epitomized in the test-scene (IV. ii). He starts by seeing "modesty's shrine" in the forehead of the guilty and scheming Beatrice and ends by hailing the virginity she has faked in images which make it sound like a sanction for holy procreation: "my Joanna! / Chaste as the breath of heaven, or morning's womb, / That brings the day forth." But it is in the speech with which he opens the play that Alsemero hints at his loftiest notion of chaste marriage. This measured soliloquy parallels that of Beatrice at the start of Act II in displaying the speaker's self-justifying efforts to rationalize sexual attraction. Alsemero lays claim to the highest reach of reason, theology. After dismissing "imaginary" omens, he draws from the coincidence of "holy place" (church) and "holy intent" (marriage) an intuition of God's purposes which causes a momentary tremor in his well-ordered syntax:

> And that, methinks, admits comparison
> With man's first creation, the place blest,
> And is his right home back, if he achieve it.

He ends more simply:

> The church hath first begun our interview,
> And that's the place must join us into one,
> So there's beginning and perfection too.

The primary point of the paradise analogy is that Alsemero's first glimpse of Beatrice in church has been like Adam's first sight of Eve; by leading her back to church to marry her he will "perfect" a circle, completing their union as that of Adam and Eve was completed by God through the marriage-bond. But by referring to paradise as "man's . . . right home back" he alludes to another circular movement, the return to Eden, and in the context is plainly contemplating marriage as the means of effecting it.[4]

This is a bold notion for which no support will be found in the Book of Common Prayer or by thumbing through contemporary sermons or manuals on marriage. It is more theologically specific than colloquial descriptions of good and bad unions as "heaven" and "hell"[5] and goes further than the common idea that a good choice of mate can help one on one's upward path.[6] A student of Milton's divorce-tracts comes close to it in his impression that "for Milton, marriage seems to be a corrective to the Fall, a condition in which it is possible to recover some of the happiness and freshness of the primitive world."[7] If this critic were right—but "seems" is his operative word—interesting connexions could be made between Milton and Alsemero as disappointed idealists in their sexual relations. The latter's remark must be explained as an expression of deluded optimism on the part of a man who knows nothing of his intended bride and forgets that both he and she are fallen beings. He instantly capitulates to an "imaginary omen" of the kind he claims to be avoiding, a mistake clearly planted in these opening lines to be recalled when his marriage has led him to the circumscribing hell of the final scene. We shall see, however, that Alsemero's religious image takes its place in a larger pattern.[8]

Beatrice's concern for her virginity is the object of the play's most trenchant irony but is less superficial than is usually thought. Somewhat misleadingly, her first and most effusive speech on the subject is patently disingenuous. Hoping to stall the marriage to Piracquo, she says to her father:

>   be not so violent, with speed
> I cannot render satisfaction
> Unto the dear companion of my soul,
> Virginity, whom I thus long have liv'd with,
> And part with it so rude and suddenly;
> Can such friends divide, never to meet again,
> Without a solemn farewell?
>
>   (I.i.191-97)

—to which he replies, "Tush, tush, there's a toy." Her speech is in character as a specious piece of wheedling to get what she wants but is deceptive in that she is later to be criticized, not for being coy or insincere about her virginity, but for relying on it to the exclusion of basic moral values. Vermandero's response, normal enough in marriage-making contexts, also misleads by momentarily detracting from the impression we are otherwise given that he guards her virginity like his castle. Earlier, when Beatrice introduces Alsemero to her father as "desirous / To see your castle" (159-60), the audience knows better what Alsemero wants, so that the conventional chastity-fortress analogy takes root from that point, to be developed on subsequent occasions. Not much is said in the play about Beatrice's upbringing, but most critics have felt licensed by Middleton's evident interest in the psychology of his heroine to accept Ellis-Fermor's description of her as a "spoilt child." Her wilful and selfish behaviour can be explained at least partly as the result of being raised by a father who has cared for one thing only and indulged her in all else. Her moral sense is undeveloped because she has not been taught to think morally. This diagnosis would have been confirmed for a Jacobean audience by what it knew, or thought it knew, about Catholic teaching on virginity.

Reynolds, who gave a long account of the amorous negotiations between Alsemero and Beatrice as they knelt side by side in church, denounced such behaviour as common "where the Romane religion reigneth." For theatre-goers a more subtle pointer, such as Beatrice's "I shall change my saint" (I.i.155), was enough to remind them of the alien religion which they associated with the southern societies depicted in tragedy. With regard to virginity, Protestant and Catholic teaching diverged in that the former stressed the exercise of moral self-discipline involved in resisting the flesh, while the latter laid its emphasis on the preservation of a spiritual state akin to innocence. Although the Protestant position has been obscured for posterity by such high-flown fancies as the cult of the Virgin Queen and the Platonic theories of Spenser and Milton, middle-class writers of instructional manuals gave no encouragement to a mystique of virginity, and in praising chaste marriage as the higher state were conscious of following reformed doctrine by reversing a Catholic emphasis. This is not to deny that, for moral and ethical as well as social reasons, Protestants could revere virginity as a woman's "treasure" or her "honour," and commiserate with her if she lost it under pressure, but they did not regard premarital chastity as of unique spiritual significance, to be valued above or in isolation from other standards of moral purity. Yet that was thought to be the Catholic position, the position which Shakespeare's Isabella, for example, had to learn to question. The statement of Catholic teaching best known in England was *The Instruction of a Christian Woman* by Juan Luis Vives, dedicated to Katharine of Aragon and still being printed at London in Richard Hyrde's translation as late as 1592. Vives subordinates every aspect of a girl's education to his theme

> that chastity is the principal vertue of a woman, & counterpeiseth with al the rest, if she have that, no man will looke for any other. . . . She that is chast is fair, well favored, rich, fruitfull, noble, and all best things that can be named: and contrary, she that is unchast, is a sea and treasure of all ilnesse.
>
> (Ch. 11, n.p.)

"Give her chastitie, and thou hast given her all things" (ch. 7). The potential for moral imbalance in such teaching is explored in Beatrice. When she makes her last and very moving plea to DeFlores—"Let me go poor

unto my bed with honour, / And I am rich in all things" (III.iv.158-59)—it is her tragedy that she believes what she says. The code she falls back on at this point is not, as some have thought, one of social respectability but a religious one which has relieved her of the necessity of learning how to think and act morally.

Scrutinizing the equation of virginity and innocence, Middleton is led to what he sees as its corollary, the notion of the sexual fall. This heresy, firmly rejected by Catholic and Protestant theologians alike, comes to the surface in any society where the phrase "fallen woman" is seriously used, and is one to which Beatrice's single-track creed makes her obviously prone. Originating in gnostic and rabbinical tradition, it was espoused by some patristic writers to extol the ideal of monastic celibacy. Though scotched by Augustine as an interpretation of Genesis, it survived in the Christian consciousness on the level of myth, serving to explain and indeed to encourage the phenomenon of sexual guilt.[9] Its variations are irrelevant here, but in essence it asserted that the original prohibition was sexual, that Adam and Eve in their perfect state were virginal, that Satan watched Eve with lustful intent and seduced her in the form of the serpent, so that lust (or in some versions the sex-act itself) was the original sin. As is well known, Milton, while discountenancing the myth, characteristically made room for it in *Paradise Lost*. Satan does experience "fierce desire" as he watches the lovers (IV.509), and Adam does consider the possibility that the enemy may be planning a sexual assault (IX.262-64).

The Changeling dramatizes this myth only in the limited sense that Beatrice and to a lesser extent Alsemero are shown to think in terms of it when their paradise is threatened. Middleton gives no sign that he himself conceived DeFlores as Satanic. He does, however, let his audience perceive and even share if it will the diabolic interpretation put on him by Beatrice.

Traditional associations of ugliness with evil and of sexual aggression with its destructive propensities form part of the background of ideas assumed in the play but are no more to be accepted than the corresponding associations of beauty with goodness and sexual purity with innocence. They are countered by the long series of authoritative asides in Act II which present DeFlores as a unique individual in the grip of an obsession, wryly puzzled by his "mad qualms," more baffled than threatening until he sees his opportunity. Even his sexual assurance, so violently suggested by the glove-episode in Act I, is called into question by his need to remind himself on three separate occasions that there are "precedents" for pretty women loving ugly men. Behind obvious contrasts between him and Alsemero as lovers of Beatrice lies the parallel of an implied inexperience of beauty which leads both to worship it blindly. At II.ii.50, after wallowing with masochistic relish in a description of physical ugliness ("swine-deformity"), DeFlores suddenly refers to Beatrice's "blessed eye." The context gives no suggestion that he resents or means to destroy this quality of blessedness, still less that he is abashed by it or wants it to convert him from his brutishness. The religious image prepares us rather for that sinister parody of chivalric courtship which Ornstein first noted;[10] but even without the literary referent it shows us on the psychological level how the ugly man's craving for the beautiful, his lust to possess it through the flesh, is as irrational and therefore as religious in its way as the emotion Alsemero lays claim to. Beatrice's virginity is "precious" to DeFlores (II.ii.129-32; III.iv.67, 114-19), not as a trophy for his *machismo,* but as a religious symbol of perfection, his religion being of the flesh and her perfection being of the body. The discovery of her moral imperfection, which abruptly terminates Alsemero's worship, has no effect on that of DeFlores—it merely gives him a handle. He gets what he wants—"her honour's prize was my reward"—but none of his words encourage us to see him as a devil who waits to be raised by Beatrice so that he can claim her soul. He remains to the end a complex, self-aware individual, a moral realist with an active conscience who sins knowingly in order to get and keep his woman and forces her to be as honest as he is in the acceptance of guilt.

But Beatrice never recognizes the real DeFlores. At first he is the "ominous ill-fac'd fellow" who "more disturbs me / Than all my other passions" (II.i.53-54). Whether this inner disturbance which she cannot explain is to be interpreted as moral or sexual, and whether the "harm" she anticipates from him (89-90) is spiritual or physical, are questions which need not be debated since the answer to each is both. She is herself very obviously both sexual and wicked, but has no understanding of sexuality or evil, and equates the two because lust is the only enemy she has been taught to fear. Her discussion with Alsemero about irrational aversions (I.i.109-28) contributes to the idea, widespread in the play, that where reason breaks down, "imaginary" religions take over. Alsemero has been trivially sententious on the subject: picking up her confession of "infirmity," he talks of "frailty," "imperfection," and "general fault," half-mocking the concept of the fall by proposing his aversion to cherries as a proof of it. But Beatrice's loathing of DeFlores, so far from being trivial, is a subconscious premonition of her fall as she thinks of it, so that the images she applies to him—"poison" and "serpent"—show her subconscious dread of him as the polluter of her (sexual) innocence, the destroyer of her (virginal) paradise. The fact that she brings herself to flirt with DeFlores in II.ii in no way contradicts that view. There we do see her using her sexuality for an evil purpose, but the point of the scene is that she is putting on an act, forcing herself to suppress her premonitions and behave pragmatically. The ironic result is

that, quite unwittingly, she tempts her devil to realize her subconscious fears.

In the great passage of dialogue which precedes her yielding, as her fears become reality, she gradually becomes conscious of the myth she is enacting. In her panic she shows little understanding of DeFlores's words, but "virginity" (III.iv.117) finally strikes home. The moral naiveté of her immediate response—"Why, 'tis impossible thou canst be so wicked / . . . To make his death the murderer of my honour!"—is exaggerated by Middleton's penchant for compressed irony ("his death" opposed to "my honour"; "murderer" recalling her own guilt). If Shakespeare's Isabella had said something similar—"To make his *life* the murderer of my honour"—she would have been less naive only by the accident of not being a murderess; what she does say— "More than our brother is our chastity"—shows the same instinctual refusal to weigh a spiritual state against the life and death of the body, an instinct nurtured in both women by the teaching of their church and the example of virgin martyrs. Beatrice then briefly seeks a refuge from reality by upbraiding DeFlores for his "language" and reminding him of his social position, but thereafter, as he turns his moral logic upon her, she utters nothing but incoherent cries until her final plea to go to bed with honour which shows that she hasn't understood it. We may even infer that she misinterprets what she half-hears in the light of her dominant idea. DeFlores's "I'll blast the hopes and joys of marriage" (148) sounds very like the policy attributed to Satan in the manuals. More certainly, his account of her moral fall—

> Y'are the deed's creature; by that name
> You lost your first condition, and I challenge you,
> As peace and innocency has turn'd you out,
> And made you one with me

—gets through to her only as it strengthens her awareness of the sexual fall which means more to her. Her last words in the scene—"Was my creation in the womb so curs'd, / It must engender with a viper first?"— clearly indicate that she sees herself as fated to act out Eve's role in the myth.

Adam's role in it is similarly suggested by the parallel question which Alsemero asks as he faces disillusionment in Act V: "Did my fate wait for this unhappy stroke / At my first sight of woman?" (iii.12-13). The reasoning behind his more hopeful reference to "man's first creation" at the start of the play is now less obscure. If virginity is a state of innocence, and the marriage of chaste partners is a higher state still, then how can it not be that such a marriage is "man's . . . right home back," his paradise regained? But the sexual fall destroys such reasoning and precipitates Adam into cuckoldom. Ribner used those parallel questions as evidence of "the power of a controlling destiny" in the play," but what they show is the fatalism of the speakers. Committed to a mythic ideal, they are trapped by its disastrous sequel. Beatrice's simple fatalism has been clear since she called Alsemero "the man was meant me" (I.i.85) and has been emphasized especially by her habit of referring to the way she was "created" (II.ii.107-08, III.iv.130, 165). DeFlores has criticized this by calling her "the deed's creature" and exploited it by posing as her fate when he closes for his kill ("Can you weep fate from its determin'd purpose? / So soon may you weep me"). When she calls him a "necessary man" (V.i.91) she means on one level her "fateful" man, and finally concludes, "upon yon meteor / Ever hung my fate . . . / I ne'er could pluck it from him" (V.iii.154-56). Alsemero on the other hand recants his fatalism. By admitting responsibility for his error in the church, "where blood and beauty first unlawfully / Fir'd their devotion, and quench'd the right one" (V.iii.74-75), he gains sufficient moral stature to preside with some authority over the end of the play.

"This fellow has undone me endlessly"—the words with which Beatrice opens Act IV give her own interpretation of her tragedy. They are ironic, however, in their immediate context, because she does not mean by them what she later will mean; she is thinking not of her soul's damnation, as the myth would lead us to expect, but of an instant, practical dilemma. Her loss of virginity is now a physical embarrassment to be concealed from her husband by the sacrifice of Diaphanta's, which Diaphanta is eager to trade for pleasure and a thousand ducats. The religious ideal is thus devalued twice over to the level more common in Middleton's plays. It is appropriate that the first sign of Beatrice's deterioration in the last acts should be shown through this cheapening of the one religious standard she has lived by. Flawed as it was, it had given her a naive kind of spiritual assurance, not far removed from innocence, of which no trace remains in later scenes. The extremes of shiftiness and nastiness she sinks to in her dealings with Alsemero—reaching a nadir in her "Is your witness dead then?" (V.iii.55)—result from her having lost her only spiritual bearings along with her virginity. She never realizes what is clear to DeFlores that she "fell" from the moment when she authorized murder. In her last speech to her father the defilement she speaks of is sexual-religious, not moral; she merely reiterates that DeFlores has undone her, though now meaning more than before. "My honour," she continues to believe, "fell with him." Vermandero's exclamation on first seeing her together with DeFlores—"An host of enemies enter'd my citadel / Could not amaze like this"—indicates the concern to which his daughter's whole speech is an answer. Of her guilt as a murderess she says nothing.

Since Eliot's essay it has been more usual to attribute Beatrice's deterioration to the evil influence of DeFlores, or at least to the habituation with her own evil which she finds reflected in him. Because she three times mentions loving him, it is also now common to suppose that he has succeeded in arousing her lust, as he foresaw, thereby coarsening her nature. That explanation is plausible but impossible to prove from the text. The mentions of love (V.i.47, 71, 76) all occur in a context where a panicking woman expresses her dependence on a man who is serving her efficiently; though the audience is reminded of the pun on "service," it is not allowed to think that she means it. As the victim of her own unconscious ironies she appears, after her "fall," to be not so much coarsened by evil as helplessly adrift in it, struggling to maintain the shadow of her honour when the substance is gone. Nothing can be said with certainty about her sexual feelings for DeFlores except that Middleton treats them with deliberate imprecision, so that in practice they are left for the actress or the reader to interpret. If we see them as intense, we could draw an analogy from the unexplained transformation of Bianca in **Women Beware Women** and suppose that the point of Middleton's reticence was to indicate the mysterious abruptness of woman's changes of appetite— "women are odd feeders." But where evidence is scanty the critic must be his own director. The present view of Beatrice is not inconsistent with supposing that from the start she has been sexually excited by DeFlores without knowing it; an actress could bring out the conflict within her between religious dread and half-recognized desire, even in those scenes where she pretends to herself that she is using DeFlores as her servant. But the climax of her last scene will be spoiled if at any time previously she has hinted at her complicity in an established sexual relationship. A better reason why she is seen so little with DeFlores in Acts IV and V is that Middleton wants to show her rebuilding her illusion of independence of him both before and after the dependence which she temporarily betrays in the emergency caused by Diaphanta. Even in that scene (V.i) DeFlores is irritated that she has gone her own way in choosing a substitute (20-22) and irritated that she thinks of Diaphanta's death as necessary for her honour, not the "pleasure and continuance" he hopes for (47-50). Earlier, in IV.ii, he has been overheard speaking words "which challenge interest in a woman," but it is not until he finally drags her from the closet that she acknowledges that interest to the full. What happens in the closet is notoriously ambiguous. Do the pair, as Alsemero luridly imagines, "rehearse again" their "scene of lust"? Are the "horrid sounds" of sex as well as murder? If so—and in drama a clearly-planted suspicion carries weight unless expressly contradicted— DeFlores through the sex-act reclaims Beatrice in the way that matters most to him, and she is brought savagely back to an awareness of her fall as it has meaning for her. His presentation of her as "that broken rib of mankind" (V.iii.145) is another fall-allusion interpreted morally by him and the audience and by Beatrice in terms of her myth.

This reading of the main plot of **The Changeling** has seen it less as an allegory of evil leading to damnation than as a study of religious delusions leading to tragedy. Such a reading does not whitewash the principal sinners: the souls of Beatrice and DeFlores, as murderers, may indeed fly to face the anger of heaven, as Tomazo envisages; the play's moral emphasis can still be located in the lust of the eye and spiritual blindness; its main dramatic interest continues to lie in the irony of Beatrice's self-ignorance. But to see her as misguided by a spiritual belief, one shared by Alsemero, makes more room for understanding and pity in our ironic view of her. And if we recognize that the whole aura of diabolism surrounding DeFlores emanates from Beatrice's deluded belief, the notion of evil embodied in ugliness is seen to be discredited as completely as the equation of virginity with goodness. The play shows what damage these false religious notions can wreak.[12] There is an appropriate shift of emphasis to reliance on human values in its final lines. Alsemero, now wiser, offers comfort and friendship to Tomazo and urges Vermandero to stop thinking of the mark against his name in the Book of Heaven, to avert the crippling impact of religious shame:

> Let it be blotted out, let your heart lose it,
> And it can never look you in the face,
> Nor tell a tale behind the back of life
> To your dishonour.

Only "life," the evidence of our actions, can determine "honour." We are the creatures of our deeds, not our beliefs.

Notes

1. Thomas Middleton and William Rowley, *The Changeling*, ed. N. W. Bawcutt, The Revels Plays (London: Methuen, 1958). References are to this edition. Since this essay deals only with the main plot, for which Middleton was largely responsible, authorship is ascribed to him, in spite of the fact that some passages discussed are thought to be by Rowley. Middleton's supervision of these can be assumed.

2. See R. B. Parker, "Middleton's Experiments with Comedy and Judgement," in *Jacobean Theatre,* ed. J. R. Brown and B. Harris, *Stratford-upon-Avon Studies,* I (London: Edward Arnold, 1960), pp. 179-99.

3. John Reynolds, *The Triumph of God's Revenge against . . . Murther* (1621). Subsequent quotations are from the text in Bawcutt, Appendix A.

4. Bawcutt (p. 4) quotes C. W. Dilke: "The meaning of Alsemero is, that a happy marriage is the most proper means for man to recover that paradise which Adam lost."

5. See dedicatory verses in A. Niccholes, *A Discourse of Marriage and Wiving* (1615), reprinted in *Harleian Miscellany,* II (London, 1809).

6. See R. Wilkinson, *The Merchant Royall* (1613), sig. c2[r]; S. Hieron, *Sermons* (1614), p. 648.

7. J. Halkett, *Milton and the Idea of Matrimony* (New Haven and London: Yale University Press, 1970), p. 92.

8. The pattern is outlined, with brief comments, by Bawcutt, p. lvi.

9. See John M. Bugge, *Virginitas: An Essay in the History of a Medieval Ideal* (The Hague: Martinus Nijhoff, 1975), especially chapter I.

10. R. Ornstein, *The Moral Vision of Jacobean Tragedy* (Madison: University of Wisconsin Press, 1965), pp. 179-90. See also R. Jordan, "Myth and Psychology in *The Changeling,*" *Renaissance Drama,* n.s. 3 (1970), 157-65.

11. I. Ribner, *Jacobean Tragedy: The Quest for Moral Order* (London: Methuen, 1952), p. 130.

12. Similarly criticized is the religious intensity of Tomazo's thirst for vengeance in Act V, Scene 2.

Lois E. Bueler (essay date winter 1984)

SOURCE: Bueler, Lois E. "The Rhetoric of Change in *The Changeling.*" *English Literary Renaissance* 14, no. 1 (winter 1984): 95-113.

[*In the following essay, Bueler investigates the "master metaphor" of metamorphosis in* The Changeling, *which, the critic maintains, is expressed chiefly through the play's language.*]

Who is The Changeling of Middleton and Rowley's wonderful play?[1] Antonio, of course, the counterfeit fool who invades Alibius' asylum to woo the keeper's wife.[2] And Beatrice Joanna, whose fatal change in sexual attachment creates the play's main plot. And De Flores, the "basilisk" who becomes Beatrice Joanna's "wondrous necessary" lover. Diaphanta, who takes her mistress' place in bed, and Alsemero, who exchanges embraces with wantonness; Alonzo, who is changed from a bridegroom to a corpse, and his brother Tomazo, who is changed from prospective kinsman to avenger and at last to sorrowing friend; Lollio, who plays both loyal keeper and would-be poacher; Alibius, who sees his folly and promises transformation; Isabella, who plays mad to disabuse a pretender to folly; the genuine madmen who are metamorphosed into beasts and birds. All are changelings. Disguisings and role-playings and changes of loyalty infuse both plots; metamorphosis, sometimes theatrically instantaneous and sometimes painstakingly incremental, is the master metaphor of the play.

The play's language is the chief, although of course not the only, vehicle through which change is expressed. Language, however, is also the object of change. Not only are the characters changelings; the words themselves, in their meanings and their constructions, are peculiarly subject to metamorphosis. Implicitly this is true of all language. By definition it is true of figurative language, which according to Quintilian's classic description, accepted by Tudor rhetoricians, is "a form of speech artfully varied from common usage."[3] The language of *The Changeling* is highly figurative. More to the point, it encourages the audience to be aware of that figurativeness in a manner especially appropriate to the notion of metamorphosis. Rather than discuss rhetorical effects directly, or appliqué the texture with heavily figured sententiousness, or ostentatiously multiply imagery—all techniques by which contemporary plays heighten the audience's rhetorical awareness—the play rings changes on the meaning and the structure of language. In the following pages I wish to trace three of the most consistent rhetorical figures of change in the play and to suggest ways in which these changes in language help reinforce the dramatic action.

Following the practice of most Tudor rhetoricians, who in turn follow the classical tradition, we may characterize artful variation in the common usage of language as either variation in meaning (tropes) or variation in construction (schemes).[4] Figured language usually combines tropes and schemes, as when metaphor is made more emphatic by repetition. In addition, as Tudor rhetoricians recognized, the manipulation of language is so intimately tied to the process of reasoning that to perform one operation is usually to perform the other. Hence the figures of language blend with the structures of logic; conversely, the process of reasoning has constant recourse to variations in language.[5] Exactly how figurative language expresses mental operations and how such expression affects an audience of readers or listeners could not be completely analyzed by Renaissance theoreticians any more than it can by us, although, thanks to the Aristotelian rhetorical categories of logos, ethos, and pathos, it could be argued, alluded to, to a degree schematized, and above all assumed to matter. Modern critics must decide how conscious of figurative language and rhetorical devices Middleton and Rowley's audience would have been. People of the Renaissance may have been better listeners, and the literate are known to have been more rhetorically educated, than we are. The question of awareness matters, for unlike

imagery, which may do its work without our conscious attention, the "artful variation" of figurative language seems fully powerful only when both the variation and the art are perceived.[6]

Unquestionably Middleton and Rowley of *The Changeling* are self-conscious and subtle manipulators of figures of language. By 1622 they had between them decades of theatrical experience, dozens of plays and other literary works, and much stylistic experimentation. Their first collaboration, *A Fair Quarrel* (1617), included a subplot attributed to Rowley[7] that contains, in its verbal spoofery of "roaring boys," word play as blatant as any the Jacobean stage produced. Middleton, for his part, had begun his literary career at sixteen with *The Wisdom of Solomon Paraphrased,* a long-winded verse amplification of the biblical text encrusted with the colors of rhetoric that displays both his school learning and his pleasure in verbal manipulation.[8] By *The Changeling,* however, Middleton had tempered and polished his ostentatious schoolboy's rhetoric to a sinewy straightforwardness capable of breathtaking dramatic effects. And Rowley, whose literary range was narrower, found in this pair of plots the kinds of verbal challenges that both exploited and sophisticated his technique. The scholarly consensus is that in *The Changeling* Middleton and Rowley divided the scenes between them, Rowley writing the subplot plus beginning and ending of the play, Middleton the bulk of the main plot.[9] There is unusual agreement about which author wrote what; it is also certain that the effect of the collaborators on each other was especially potent, and that stylistically the play works as a single piece, as I will treat it. Not only structural and thematic effects but also puns and other figurative verbal ploys from one plot occur in the other. Above all, each plot reinforces the audience's heightened consciousness of language itself and the manipulations it undergoes.

The Changeling does not have set pieces in which rhetoric is itself the subject of discussion. Such pieces, for instance the trial scene in Webster's *The White Devil,* lend themselves to a detailed application of contemporary rhetorical theory in which not only can grammar school exercises be directly equated to the playwright's work but contemporary audiences can be assumed to have followed and taken pleasure in the rhetorical demonstrations.[10] Instead *The Changeling* exploits the essence of figurative language: at once it reinforces the audience's expectations of the ordinary patterns and meanings of language and changes those patterns madly, foolishly, or glibly to express the madness, folly, or shallowness of the characters and their actions.

Christopher Ricks has elegantly taught us one aspect of the rhetorical logic of the word play. "The verbal basis of the play is a group of words each of which has two meanings, one of them sexual; by its end, they have become inextricable."[11] This series of related puns is literally created by the varied capacities of the characters to understand and act upon the varied meanings of words. The verbal structure "exactly provides the moral structure of the play" (Ricks, p. 303). For instance, *service,* the most important of the major words of Ricks' group (the others are *blood, will, act,* and *deed*), means to the playwrights and their audience both the duty of a servant, and copulation. Thus De Flores' service to Beatrice Joanna is the murder of Alonzo. In exchange, her service to him is copulation and "she cannot have the one kind of service without the other" (Ricks, p. 296). The intricate misunderstandings of the two negotiation scenes between De Flores and Beatrice Joanna result precisely from the negotiators' different interpretations of the sense of *service* and other equally weighted words. Moral fact forces the multiple meanings together; since one kind of service (murder) is performed, the other (copulation) will be also.

In following Ricks' analysis of the double sense of key words it is important to bear in mind both how the figures of speech we loosely call puns work and how drama may use them. Tudor rhetoricians distinguished three kinds of puns: paronomasia, in which one word sounds like another (Peacham: "I had rather lend him ten pound of his sword than of his word");[12] antanaclasis, in which a word is used in one sense and then repeated in another (Peacham, sig. Kii[v]: "Care for those things which shall discharge you of all care"); and syllepsis of the sense, in which a word, although stated only once, carries a double meaning (Puttenham: "One wrote thus of a young man, who slew a villain that had killed his father, and ravished his mother.

> Thus valiantly and with a manly mind,
> And by one feat of everlasting fame,
> This lusty lad fully requited kind,
> His father's death, and eke his mother's shame.

Where ye see this word *requite* serve a double sense: that is to say, to revenge, and to satisfy. For the parents' injury was revenged, and the duty of nature performed or satisfied by the child").[13]

In **The Changeling** the word play Ricks describes depends on both antanaclasis and syllepsis (paronomasia being little used).[14] These two kinds of puns have somewhat different dramatic uses. Syllepsis is the figure of speech that pre-eminently belongs to the sensitized audience, while antanaclasis is the figure that the characters use with each other. That is, at each use of the word susceptible to double meaning, the sensitized audience hears it as syllepsis and attempts to provide what Puttenham calls its "double supply" of meaning, thereby performing the integrative function appropriate to an auditor. The characters who use it while failing to hear it as anything but single thereby emphasize their failure

to understand or to communicate. When one or more of the characters *is* fully cognizant of multiple meanings of words, the figure of antanaclasis may be used to split the word play so that characters bandy words within or between speeches. Puttenham (p. 216) calls antanaclasis the "rebound"; in its use, the characters do not provide the double meaning until the rebound is complete. But even with antanaclasis, the sensitized member of the audience, hearing with a single, integrating mind, attempts at each use of the word to perform the integrating operation of syllepsis, and the dramatic effect of the author's word play is dependent on just that attempt.

The punning that Ricks isolates is only one of a number of major rhetorical patterns in which the play's dramatic action is reinforced or even realized by consistent types of verbal shifts. In the following pages, I will focus on three of these patterns whose artificiality, extension, and repetition draw particular attention to themselves. All of them share a high degree of rhetorical self-consciousness: they are deliberately used by both the dramatists and the speakers to create personalities for the speakers themselves and for other characters to whom they are applied. And all of them combine language and logic in variations so systematically repeated as to make both their relationships and their variations carry much of the meaning of the scenes where they occur. Their use helps emphasize the degree to which not just the characters but the very words and language patterns of the play are changelings.

Being exaggerated and localized, the verbal shifts of the subplot are therefore especially obvious; Ricks (p. 291) reminds us that the subplot is the sensitizing plot that alerts us to verbal innuendo in the main plot. The location of these blatant verbal manipulations is Alibius' asylum with its madmen and idiots. Although in the world of the asylum, costume and physical carriage are the first signs of madness or idiocy,[15] language is diagnostic. Madness and folly are exhibited through the abuse of language, and a specious wisdom is demonstrated by means of certain of its formal manipulations. By their words we shall know them. When we attend to the distinguishing features of the language of the mad and the foolish, we find a rhetorical consistency sufficiently strong eventually to breed in its hearers an automatic response: this is madness (one who talks like this is mad) or this is folly (one who talks like this is a fool).

Alibius and his lieutenant Lollio, the keepers of the asylum, divide their labors, Alibius taking charge of the madmen and Lollio of the fools. So closely are Alibius and Lollio tied to their respective charges that the dialogue repeatedly suggests how little there is to choose between officers and patients.[16] The connection of figures of language to the mental states of the mad and the foolish occurs first in the interview with the disguised

Antonio, in which Lollio, who classifies his patients by means of verbal catechisms and schools them by means of verbal play, gives Antonio his placement test: "I were best try his wit a little, that I may know what form to place him in" (1.2.142-43). Both here and in the second interview of 3.3, the test consists of a series of questions posed quantitatively: "How many true fingers has a tailor on his right hand?" (1.2.145-46); "How many fools goes to a wise man?" (150-51); "How many knaves make an honest man?" (157-58); "How many fools are here?" (170); "How many fools and knaves are here?" (172-73); and in the second interview, "How many is five times six?" and "How many is one hundred and seven?" (3.3.154-58). These questions have several attributes in common. They all pretend to be matters of arithmetic. They all seem to involve some sort of either specious or self-evident equivalency. They are all "solved" by means of verbal quibbles involving rhetorical figures of change. And their "solutions" raise issues of definition.

The aura of arithmetical legitimacy is the most immediately noticeable and unsettling thing about these questions. Their form (How many X = Y?) suggests that addition or multiplication will supply the answers. When Lollio asks, "How many fools are here?" Antonio answers handily, "Two, cousin, thou and I" (1.2.170-71). Even when the answer is not direct, it suggests an appropriate mathematical relationship. When asked, "How many is five times six?" Antonio responds as readily, "Five times six is six times five." As for the tailor's true fingers, he has as many on his right hand as on his left, because, it is clearly implied, he must have the usual number on each. In all cases the arithmetic seems flawless (although in none does Antonio quite get away with it). The only comic point seems to be the pointlessness of the exercise.

These relatively straightforward questions are followed, however, by others that, although seemingly couched in the same way ("How many fools and knaves are here?" "How many is one hundred and seven?" "How many [fingers] on both [hands]?"), turn out either to be or to become nonsense. The first is unsolvable because the terms *fools* and *knaves* are not mutually exclusive, the second because the term *one hundred and seven* is ambiguous. Other questions are worse. Although stated arithmetically, the question "How many knaves make an honest man?" cannot be solved arithmetically because an "honest man" is not composed of X parts of "knave." As for the follow-up question about the tailor's fingers—How many on both hands?—it just seems "stupid." Either the answer is self-evident, we think, or "there must be some trick." The idiocy of these questions by and for idiots seems to lie in either the inconsequentiality or the speciousness of their equivalencies.

But of course there is a trick. Antonio's responses, like Lollio's questions, yield only by means of verbal play.

Most of that play is based on the ambiguous trope of syllepsis. When Lollio asks, "How many true fingers has a tailor?" the question seems to use the word *true* in the sense of *actual* or *real*; Antonio's answer, however, uses it in the sense of *honest* or *truthful*. A tailor has no true fingers ("Two less than a deuce"—subtraction here) because tailors are notoriously dishonest. "How many fools goes to a wise man?" is couched as though *goes to* meant *goes to make up*, but the answer uses it to mean *goes to visit*. "How many knaves make an honest man?" seems to use *make* to mean *make up* or *comprise*, but the answer uses *make* to mean *manufacture* or *create*. The final question—"How many is one hundred and seven?"—is patently ambiguous: *one hundred and seven* may mean *107* or *100 + 7*; the connective *and* may merely link the three-digit number, or it may signal the mathematical operation of addition.[17]

A "double supply" of meaning is not the only kind of word play, as this last trick reminds us. Figures of change may involve structure as well as meaning. In the catechizing of 3.3, structure is the means to mindless, specious equivalency. Antonio has "solved" his first equation—"How many is five times six?"—by the scheme of antimetabole or, as Puttenham calls it, the "counterchange." Reversing the positions of his terms, he answers that "Five times six is six times five," and because *five* and *six* are single terms and because multiplication works with either term in either position, he is correct, although he hardly has an answer. (In fact, he has committed the logical fallacy of begging the question.) Faced with the second question—"How many is one hundred and seven?"—he counterchanges again, switching the last term with the first term: "One hundred and seven, is seven hundred and one." This switch is genuinely funny—probably the only funny joke of the lot—because the ear has been prepared to entertain the verbal pattern of antimetabole as a solution for mathematical equations. But of course the answer is nonsense, a mathematical version of the figure of disorder called hypallage. Even if one takes the question to involve a true equation ($100 + 7 = ?$), the fact that one of the terms (*one hundred*) consists of two words means that when Antonio mechanically shifts one of those words but not the other, he produces mathematical gibberish. Equivalency fails.

Finally, these fooling questions and their answers involve matters of definition. When Lollio asks, "How many fools are here?" and Tony answers, "Two, cousin, thou and I," Lollio's rebuke—"Nay, y'are too forward there, Tony" (1.2.170-72)—makes clear that the essential operation behind the answer is not one of arithmetic but one of definition. Before he can answer Lollio's question Antonio must decide who among the present company is a fool by deciding what constitutes a fool. Other questions force definitions of knaves, or wise men, or tailors, although the definitions are all implied rather than stated. Here is the most logically elaborate of these exchanges:

Lol.:

> How many fools goes to a wise man?

Ant.:

> Forty in a day sometimes.

Lol.:

> How prove you that?

Ant.:

> All that fall out among themselves and go to a law-
> yer to be made friends.

(1.2.150-55)

Clearly Lollio regards this as an exercise in formal logic, as his use of *prove* indicates. We have seen that Tony's answer depends first on syllepsis of the sense, taking *goes to* to mean *goes to visit* rather than *goes to make up*. It also depends on substituting the term *lawyer* for Lollio's term *wise man*; a lawyer then becomes a type of wise man. But Tony's "proof" consists of more than these two substitutions. It actually argues about the characteristics of both fools and lawyers, for what it means is "All that fall out among themselves and go to a lawyer to be made friends [are fools]." When expanded to the full implied syllogism, his enthymeme means this:

> All who go to strifemakers to patch up quarrels are
>   fools.
> Lawyers are strifemakers.
> All who go to lawyers to patch up quarrels are fools.

The point of the syllogism is to create a double definition of, and to link, lawyers and fools.

But nothing comes of this language or of the other patterns of portraying folly that appear in these testing exchanges: Antonio's idiotic laughter; the constant use of "cousin" as a term of address, with its insistence upon the kinship of fools; Lollio's fixation upon the hierarchical psychology of types making mankind a gallery of cartoon figures ranked by degrees of wit and guile. The combined effect is at once slippery and static. The far-fetched quibbles of tropes and schemes, the phony mathematics, the nonsensical questions all give us the feeling that nothing means what it seems to mean, even when it seems to mean nothing. On the other hand, the constant statements of definition and equivalency with their preponderance of static verbs—*be, make* (constitute), *have*—give us the sense of minds frozen at a level where the imagination functions, if at all, only to repeat itself. Change in people or in language seems mere pointless repetition.

People are born fools, the play tells us (see, for instance, Pedro's introduction of Antonio in 1.2), and despite Lollio's pedagogical pretensions stasis is their lot. But people become mad. The inmate Welshman "was undone by a mouse that spoil'd him a parmesan; lost his wits for't" (1.2.197-99). Lollio reports of Franciscus that he went mad "For love, mistress. He was a pretty poet too, and that set him forwards first; the muses then forsook him, he ran mad for a chambermaid" (3.3.45-47). When he realizes that the frantic woman who courted him is Isabella, Antonio begs her to "Stay, or I shall change condition / And become as you are"—mad (4.3.134-35). The richness and vigor of the language of the mad, as compared with the static language of the fools, is appropriate to this kind of sensitivity that responds to pressure by changes in personality. The cries of the madmen off-stage pulse with the repetition of active verbs and the hint of causes and transformations: "Fly, fly, and he catches the swallow" (1.2.190); "Give her more onion, or the devil put the rope around her crag" (1.2.191); "Bounce, bounce, he falls, he falls" (3.3.108); "Catch there, catch the last couple in hell" (3.3.162).

The most striking attribute of the mad is their supercharged imaginations. Unlike the sane, they do not control—that is, refuse to act upon—those imaginings. The madmen who pass across the upper stage in 3.3 shock Isabella into providing Antonio their "character":

> *Madmen above, some as birds, others as beasts*

Ant.:

> What are these?

Isa.:

> > Of fear enough to part us,
> > Yet are they but our schools of lunatics,
> > That act their fantasies in any shapes
> > Suiting their present thoughts; if sad, they cry;
> > If mirth be their conceit, they laugh again.
> > Sometimes they imitate the beasts and birds,
> > Singing or howling, braying, barking; all
> > As their wild fancies prompt 'em.

(3.3.188-95)

The essential feature of these people whose imaginings are expressed in sounds and actions—the feature that marks them as mad—is that they believe themselves to be the beasts they imitate. The play forces us to suspect that madness comes from believing oneself to be something other than what one is. The play's best expression of such a concept of madness is the perfectly ordinary but telling final phrase in Franciscus' love letter to Isabella. In a plethora of poetic images and antitheses in which poet, lunatic, and lover are neatly combined, Franciscus has explained that he has counterfeited madness to have access to her and that her favor will enable him to assume the proper shape of a lover. He ends with a figurative return to the notion of madness. "I remain, mad till I speak with you from whom I expect my cure, yours all, or one beside himself, Franciscus" (4.3.27-29). In this play, the madman is accompanied by the alter-ego, the "one beside himself," that his imagination creates.

The most extended mad scene occurs in 3.3 when Lollio brings Franciscus on to amuse Isabella. Franciscus launches into an extraordinary series of classical and mythical references that are not mere allusions but full-blown invitations to role-playing. These invitations address sometimes Lollio and sometimes Isabella by giving them specific characters or roles through which Franciscus' own roles are intermingled:

FRAN.:

> Anacreon, drink to my mistress' health, I'll pledge it.
>
> > (3.3.39-40)
>
> Hail, bright Titania,
> Why stand'st thou idle on these flowery banks?
>
> > (48-49)
>
> Oh, hold thy hand, great Diomede;
> Thou feed'st thy horses well, they shall obey thee.
> Get up, Bucephalus kneels.
>
> > (54-56)
>
> Come hither, Aesculapius, hide the poison.
>
> > (61)
>
> Did'st thou never hear of one Tiresias,
> A famous poet?

LOL.:

> Yes, that kept tame wild-geese.

FRAN.:

> That's he; I am the man.
>
> > (63-66)

And the list goes on: Juno struck him blind, Luna made him mad, he rides with Hecate.

The scene builds its pattern on the systematic use of a form of the rhetorical figure called antonomasia to provide Franciscus and his companions with these roles. Antonomasia is a figure of substitution, in Franciscus' use the substitution of a proper name for a quality associated with that name. Peachman notes that it is called antonomasia "When we give to one man the name of another for the affinity's sake of their manners or conditions. In praise thus, as when we call a grave man a *Cato*. . . . In dispraise, to call . . . a tyrant a *Nero*."[18] In Franciscus' use of antonomasia, Isabella is Titania, queen of the fairies, because she is queen of Franciscus' heart and recipient of the flowers of his rhetoric of love.[19] Lollio is Diomede because of his condition as

feeder and trainer of captive beasts, Aesculapius because of his role as physician, Anacreon because of his affinity with mad poets and his danger of being choked on the grapestone of Franciscus' guile. Franciscus himself is Bucephalus as fabulous but obedient beast of burden, and Tiresias because of his affinities with that blind and temporarily sexually transformed seer who angered Juno by knowing that women receive more pleasure from love than men. These figures are not mere verbal exercises; as a madman Franciscus "acts his fantasies," lifting his cup with Anacreon, kneeling as Bucephalus, cringing before Aesculapius' "poison," kicking and beating "The swift lycanthropi that walks the round" (3.3.83) in the guise of Lollio. Franciscus frightens Isabella: "I prithee hence with him, now he grows dangerous" (3.3.87). Yet he teaches her how to feign the language and actions of madness.

Antonomasia is a figure belonging to those rhetorical and logical topics of invention that are concerned with subjects and their adjuncts.[20] Subjects are things of whatever kind—people, places, ideas—that have attributes, qualities, or characteristics; adjuncts are those attributes, qualities, or characteristics. For instance, when Isabella says in explanation of Franciscus' madness that "His conscience is unquiet; sure that was / The cause of this" (3.3.59-60), *conscience* is the subject, *unquiet* is the adjunct. In *The Lawyer's Logic* (1588) Abraham Fraunce, who provides a particularly precise definition of the terms, notes that an adjunct may be either inherent or adherent in a subject. He mentions as an inherent adjunct the Aristotelian example of laughter inherent in man, the same example that Lollio uses to testify to Antonio's humanity in 1.2.101-02. Or, Fraunce says, an adjunct may be adherent: "The adherent adjunct doth either affect the subject: or is affected by it. So virtues, vices, learning, and all such qualities are adjuncts to man's mind."[21] But the most important thing about subjects and adjuncts is not their formal definitions but how they relate to each other. In ***The Changeling*** one of the key questions is what the attributes, qualities, and characteristics of events or people have to do with their essence.

Now the figure of antonomasia as Franciscus uses it works backwards, so to speak, from adjuncts to subjects. He starts with the "manners or conditions" of people and "for the affinity's sake" renames them. The man who is the animal keeper, the physician, and the conqueror becomes Diomede, Aesculapius, and by inference Alexander. The man who is the beast and the double-sighted seer becomes Bucephalus and Tiresias. The woman who is the queen of fantasies and the wife of the ruler becomes Titania. When it is Isabella's turn to play mad to disabuse the disguised Antonio, she uses language in just the same way. Antonio (4.3.82ff.) has been practicing his dancing, full of leaps and falls, in preparation for the masque at Vermandero's house.

When Isabella enters dressed as a madwoman, he is in full caper and she immediately takes her cue from his actions and from her knowledge of the illicit purpose for his presence:

> Hey, how he treads the air; shoo, shoo, t'other way, he
>   burns his wings else; here's wax enough below, Icarus,
>   more
> than will be canceled these eighteen moons.
> He's down, he's down; what a terrible fall he had.
> Stand up, thou son of Cretan Daedalus,
> And let us tread the lower labyrinth;
> I'll bring thee to the clue.
>
>   (4.3.100-06)

Using antonomasia, Isabella addresses him as Icarus because he rises and falls, because he risks burning his wings, and because as son of Cretan Daedalus he is being invited to penetrate this sexual labyrinth with the guidance of this Ariadne. A few lines later, inviting Antonio with another example of antonomasia—"Stay in the moon with me, Endymion" (119)—Isabella gives herself the character of Luna, because she is attracted to him and because she has the power to make him mad.

The naming operation of antonomasia carried out in Franciscus' and Isabella's mad scenes has a sort of sanity about it, for it suggests that fantastic actions bespeak fantastic beings. The minds that seek out this form of antonomasia understand the relationship between adjuncts and their subjects that Beatrice Joanna does not fully comprehend even when De Flores declares pointblank to her: "Y' are the deed's creature" (3.4.138). The illusion of madness lies not in the operation of naming itself but in the speed, multiplicity, and flux of the resulting roles. By this technique Franciscus and Isabella people the stage with a dizzying succession of "characters" serving as a vertiginous complement to the leaping and falling dances of the mad. Again the language pattern is a figure of change, and again its operation corresponds to and creates a logical pattern we are asked to construe as appropriate to the mental states of the characters who use it.

The characters of the main plot pretend to wisdom and judgment almost as strenuously as those of the subplot pretend to madness and folly. Beatrice Joanna prides herself on her reasoning capacity, and Alsemero both sees himself and is seen by Beatrice Joanna as a man of discretion, rationality, and scholarly attainments. Beatrice Joanna's conversation is from first almost to last an alternately self-congratulatory and frantic attempt to apply logic to her situation. In her first exchange with Alsemero she discusses the importance of judgment in correcting the evidence of the senses (1.1.69-73), she subsequently rationalizes her choice of Alsemero over Alonzo (2.1.6-19), and she attributes to her husband the most rigorous psychological and moral penetration (4.1.3-17). The characterization of Alsemero

as a wise man is visually confirmed by the most elaborate stage property of the play, his "physician's closet" in which he practices the medicine that Beatrice Joanna thinks "may be safely call'd your great man's wisdom" (4.1.23). Alsemero's reliance on the potion in the glass marked "M" to establish the chastity of his bride provides more than a quintly disruptive excursion into seventeenth-century sexual misinformation. The enormous amount of stage time devoted to this virginity test (the 127 lines of 4.1 and the final 45 lines of 4.2, with much stage business) allows the playing out in a set of formal variations of a rhetorical figure of logic comparable in importance and appropriateness to the rhetorical figures expressing folly and madness that we have seen in the subplot.

The virginity test is designed to answer the question "How to know whether a woman be a maid or not" (4.1.40). The instructions of "Antonius Mizaldus," Alsemero's authority, read, "'Give the party you suspect the quantity of a spoonful of the water in the glass M which upon her that is a maid makes three several effects: 'twill make her incontinently gape, then fall into a sudden sneezing, last into a violent laughing; else dull, heavy, and lumpish'" (4.1.46-50). This "proof" is a hypothetical proposition or hypothetical syllogism, the formula of the logic of cause and effect. Reduced to its starkest form, Mizaldus' proposition is this: If a woman is a virgin (upon drinking "M") she will gape, sneeze, and laugh. Modern readers or viewers must take care not to be distracted by the medical unlikelihood of this proposition. In the context of the play the truth of Mizaldus' proof is unquestioned; what is important is the validity or fallacy of the reasoning with which the characters apply it.[22] In the course of Act 4 the proposition is applied to both Beatrice Joanna and her maid Diaphanta so as to provide a complete demonstration of the formal tests for the validity of a hypothetical syllogism. The play, in effect, runs the proposition through all its logical forms, both valid and invalid, in such a way as to demonstrate and undercut the characters' pretensions to logic and wisdom. In 4.1 Beatrice Joanna administers the potion, and therefore the proposition, to both Diaphanta and herself to determine whether the glass marked "M" has the properties attributed to it. She applies the proposition validly, the potion turns out to work as advertised, and she is thus armed for her encounter with Alsemero. In 4.2 the potion is administered to her by Alsemero as a test of her virginity. She is able to counterfeit the desired results. Alsemero, however, misapplies the syllogism, draws a fallacious conclusion, and is tricked into believing her chaste.

The tests for the validity of a hypothetical proposition depend on the relationship between antecedent and consequent. The complete syllogism developed from this proposition involves a premise about a specific woman, in the play Beatrice Joanna or Diaphanta. In establishing logical proofs, if the second premise of a syllogism affirms the antecedent or denies the consequent, the syllogism is valid and the logic is sound. If the second premise affirms the consequent or denies the antecedent, the syllogism is invalid and the logic is faulty. In 4.1 where Beatrice Joanna discovers the potion and tries it out on herself and her maid, the two valid versions of the syllogism are used to prove that the potion "M" causes a virgin to respond in a given way. Although Beatrice Joanna pretends to use it to attest to Diaphanta's virginity, what she is really testing is the potion "M" itself. After both women drink, she watches the results with clinical attention, her vocabulary that of the field researcher:

BEA.:

> [*aside*] Now if the experiment be true, 'twill praise
>   itself
> And give me noble ease. Begins already.
> [*Diaphanta gapes*]
> There's the first symptom; and what haste it makes
> To fall into the second, there by this time.
> [*Diaphanta sneezes*]
> Most admirable secret. On the contrary,
> It stirs not me a whit, which most concerns it.

DIA.:

> Ha, ha, ha.

BEA.:

> [*aside*] Just in all things and in order
> As if 'twere circumscrib'd, one accident
> Gives way unto another.

(4.1.104-12)

Put schematically, Beatrice Joanna's syllogisms are structured thus:

> 1) If Diaphanta is a virgin, she will gape, sneeze, and laugh.
>
> Diaphanta is a virgin. (Second premise affirms the antecedent.)
>
> Therefore she will gape, sneeze, and laugh.

The syllogism is by definition a valid one. And Diaphanta does indeed gape, sneeze, and laugh.

> 2) If Beatrice Joanna is a virgin, she will gape, sneeze, and laugh.
>
> Beatrice Joanna does not gape, sneeze, and laugh. (Second premise denies the consequent.)
>
> Therefore she is not a virgin.

The syllogism is by definition valid. And Beatrice Joanna is indeed not a virgin. Given the assumption of the play, that Mizaldus' hypothetical proposition is absolutely true, the potion in the glass marked "M" must of necessity force a virgin who drinks it to gape, sneeze,

and laugh. And this is what 4.1 demonstrates, for Diaphanta is forced to these actions but Beatrice Joanna is stirred not a whit.

When Alsemero's turn comes to use the glass marked "M" in 4.2, his intention is the opposite of that of his bride. In 4.1 she knew her own condition and was reasonably sure of Diaphanta's; what she did not know, until it was demonstrated, was exactly how "M" worked. Alsemero, on the other hand, knows "M": "It has that secret virtue it ne'er miss'd, sir, / Upon a virgin" (4.2.140-41). What he does not know is Beatrice Joanna, who is furnished with the information she needs: "I'm put now to my cunning; th'effects I know, / If I can now but feign 'em handsomely" (4.2.138-39). So she performs her deception and her husband is overjoyed: "My Joanna, / Chaste as the breath of heaven or morning's womb, / That brings the day forth, thus my love encloses thee" (4.2.149-51). Put schematically, the syllogisms of this scene are structured thus:

> 3) If Beatrice Joanna is a virgin, she will gape, sneeze, and laugh.
>
> Beatrice Joanna gapes, sneezes, and laughs. (Second premise affirms the consequent.)
>
> Therefore she is a virgin.

This syllogism, which is what Alsemero assumes, is by definition invalid, for it refuses the possibility that the response is caused by something other than "M" (in this case Beatrice Joanna's ability to deceive).

> 4) If Beatrice Joanna is a virgin, she will gape, sneeze, and laugh.
>
> Beatrice Joanna is not a virgin. (Second premise denies the antecedent.)
>
> Therefore she will not gape, sneeze, and laugh.

This syllogism, the second premise of which is based on Beatrice Joanna's actual condition as we and she know it, is likewise invalid, again because it refuses to consider another cause of the response. So 4.2 shows us both of the invalid applications of Mizaldus' proposition.[23]

What happens with the proposition of the virginity test is analogous to what happens in the scenes of madness and folly in the subplot: a highly artificial rhetorical pattern built on verbal shifts or changes is extended and repeated as a means of creating and characterizing a crucial sequence in the plot. Here the figure, a set of implied syllogisms based on a logical proposition, is appropriate because one of the most important themes of the main plot is the pretensions of Beatrice Joanna and Alsemero to wisdom and rational analysis. Beatrice Joanna is shown using this pattern in her typical fashion: she thinks she has won her game of deception and death because with self-congratulatory cunning she has rung all the changes on Mizaldus' virginity-testing proposition to her temporary advantage. Actually she has lost, inasmuch as her resultant reliance on Diaphanta's cooperation and Alsemero's faith leads her to the deepening involvement with De Flores that ultimately exposes, disgraces, and kills her. Alsemero's mistake is more ironic but equally characteristic: his faith in appearances—Beatrice Joanna's beauty, modesty, air of sophistication, and hatred of De Flores; her father's solidly reassuring castle; the conveniently unexplained disappearance of the rival Alonzo—prepares us for his slightly pompous and self-congratulatory reliance on Antonius Mizaldus. As Beatrice Joanna's superficial cunning does her in, Alsemero's superficial wisdom nearly ruins him: he puts his faith in his scholarship but forgets one of the most elementary tests of the validity of his evidence.

The three rhetorical patterns we have followed are appropriate in part because they serve dramatic characterization and situation. More profoundly, they are appropriate because they are patterns of change, patterns in which change is itself the meaning. The play is full of such patterns. When Rowley's characters engage in what Dewar M. Robb calls "cue-catching" (p. 133), the point, as so often with Lollio's exercises, lies in its pointlessness, for Lollio's "changes" on language go nowhere and accomplish nothing:

ALIB.:

    I am old, Lollio.

LOL.:

    No, sir, *tis I am old Lollio.*

                         (1.2.19-20)

When Middleton uses the technique, again the meaning is found in the change itself, only this time the change carries the significance of mortally serious misunderstanding:

Bea.   *Take heed*, De Flores, of *forgetfulness:*
        'T will soon betray us.
De F.   *Take* you heed first;
    Faith, *y'are grown much forgetful; y'are too blame in't.*
Bea. [aside]   He's bold, and *I am blam'd for't.*   (3.4.95–98)

Here, as each character picks up the other's language, the referents shift, from Beatrice Joanna's insistence upon the inequality of sex and rank between mistress and manservant, to De Flores' insistence upon the moral equality of partners in murder, and back again. Such patterns seem to me so pointed, so extended and repeated, and so self-conscious as to justify the assumption that the audience is expected to notice the rhetorical effects. Chief among those effects is the sense that the grammatical, semantic, and logical ground is shifting beneath us. After Christopher Ricks' exposition of the double meaning of its key words, the play's rhetorical slipperiness and mutability comes as no surprise. Notable nevertheless is the persistence, almost the inexhaustibility, of Middleton and Rowley's capacity to build patterns of change into the play's language. "Changeling," which not coincidentally is Puttenham's English term for the rhetorical figure of disorder the Greeks called hypallage,[24] is the master metaphor not for the characters alone but for much of the text as well.

Notes

1. I began work on the rhetorical background for this essay during an NEH Summer Seminar in Humanist Rhetoric directed in 1979 by Thomas O. Sloane, University of California, Berkeley. Textual citations are from Thomas Middleton and William Rowley, *The Changeling* (1622), ed. George W. Williams (Lincoln, Neb., 1966).

2. The first quarto of 1653 identifies Antonio as "the changeling." Blessed with the interpretation of two popular comic actors, the role of Antonio was largely responsible for the success of the play into the Restoration. See N. W. Bawcutt's introduction to the Revels edition (London, 1958), pp. xxvi-xxx.

3. Quintilian, *Institutio oratoria,* 9.1.14 (Loeb Classical Library); quoted by Sister Miriam Joseph, *Shakespeare's Use of the Arts of Language* (New York, 1947), pp. 32-33, who cites evidence for the agreement of Tudor rhetoricians of all schools of thought.

4. Warren Taylor, *Tudor Figures of Rhetoric* (Whitewater, Wisc., 1972), pp. 135-42; Sister Miriam Joseph, pp. 33ff.

5. Sister Miriam Joseph's entire work argues for Tudor understanding of this relationship between the figures of language and the figures of logic; see pp. 34-37 and throughout.

6. This may be a minority opinion; no less a critic than Longinus, *On the Sublime,* trans. G. M. A. Grube (New York, 1957), insists upon the hidden figure as the greater art: "the best use of a figure is when the very fact that it is a figure goes unnoticed," p. 29; "For art at its best is mistaken for nature, and nature is successful when it contains hidden art," p. 33. Nevertheless, dramatists especially both need and count on the rhetorical mileage they get when the theater audience is alert to the artifice of the characters' speech, as Middleton and Rowley's repetitions in *The Changeling* make clear.

7. For the rationale of this generally accepted attribution, see Dewar M. Robb, "The Canon of William Rowley's Plays," *Modern Language Review,* 45 (April 1950), 129-41.

8. Norman A. Brittin, *Thomas Middleton* (New York, 1972), pp. 19-21, briefly analyzes the figures of rhetoric used by Middleton in *The Wisdom of Solomon.*

9. N. W. Bawcutt reviews the attribution of scenes in his introduction to the play, p. xxxix.

10. Such an application is thoroughly made by H. Bruce Franklin, "The Trial Scene of Webster's *The White Devil* Examined in Terms of Renaissance Rhetoric," *Studies in English Literature,* 1 (1961), 35-51.

11. Christopher Ricks, "The Moral and Poetic Structure of *The Changeling*," *Essays in Criticism,* 10 (1960), 291.

12. Henry Peacham, *The Garden of Eloquence* (1577), sig. Kii (rpt. Menston, Eng., 1971).

13. George Puttenham, *The Arte of English Poesie* (1589), ed. Edward Arber (London, 1906; facsimile Kent, Ohio, 1970), p. 177. This is syllepsis of the sense, not syllepsis of both sense and structure such as Pope performs in *The Rape of the Lock*—"Here thou, great Anna! whom three realms obey / Dost sometimes counsel *take*—and sometimes tea" or "*stain* her honour or her new brocade." In the Pope lines, syllepsis, as Edward P. J. Corbett, *Classical Rhetoric for the Modern Student,* 2nd ed. (New York, 1971), p. 483, defines it, is "a word understood differently in relation to two or more other words, which it modifies or governs." Puttenham's example does not do that, and further, he himself does not give his example its full explanation. His quote contains a "pun" on two words, *requited* and *kind,* and the real play is on *kind,* meaning on the one hand *kindred* and on the other *filial piety.* Puttenham has applied the term *syllepsis,* with its meaning of double supply, to the sense of double meaning pure and simple, not requiring any sort of syntactical repetition. This is how I am using the term here.

14. A punning exchange in which paronomasia *is* one of the effects occurs between Lollio and Isabella as they discuss how to handle the disguised gentlemen who have crept in among them:

Isa.:

But thy counsel now; how shall I deal with 'em?

Lol.:

Why, do you mean to deal with 'em?

Isa.:

Nay, the fair understanding; how to *use 'em*?

Lol.:

Abuse 'em; that's the way to mad the fool and make a fool of the madman, and then you *use 'em* kindly.

(4.3.42-46)

(Note also antanaclasis on *deal with 'em* and syllepsis on *kindly.*) *Use-abuse* is one of Peacham's examples of paronomasia: "he is better able to abuse himself than use himself" (sig. Kii^v).

15. Cf. Pedro's introduction of Antonio:

Enter Pedro and Antonio [dressed] like an Idiot.

Ped.:

Save you, sir, my business speaks itself;
This sight takes off the labor of my tongue.

(1.2.81-82)

16. The more conspicuous exchanges include Lollio's comments to Alibius: "if they come to see the fools and madmen, you and I may serve the turn" (1.2.58-59); "Go you to your madmen's ward, let me alone with your fools" (1.2.201); and Isabella's conversation with Lollio: "Why, here's none but fools and madmen." Lollio answers, "Very well: and where will you find any other, if you should go abroad? There's my master and I to boot too." Isabella retorts, "Of either sort one, a madman and a fool" (3.3.14-17).

17. Punning between the fools is not restricted to these questions and answers. When, after his catechizing, Antonio seeks other amusements, his exchange with Lollio is again based on the ambiguous use of a word, this time antanaclasis on the word *bite*:

Ant.:

I would see the madmen, cousin, if they would not bite.

Lol.:

No, they shall not bite thee, Tony.

Ant.:

They bite when they are at dinner, do they not, coz?

Lol.:

They bite at dinner, indeed, Tony.

(1.2.207-10)

18. Henry Peacham, *The Garden of Eloquence* (1593); cited by Sister Miriam Joseph, p. 320.

19. Franciscus' linking of rhetoric and flowers is both explicit and deliberately ambiguous: "I'll gather daisies, primrose, violets, / And bind them in a verse of poesie" (3.3.51-52).

20. Most Tudor rhetoricians do not attempt a strict distinction between logic and rhetoric. Even the Ramists, who do, must acknowledge the topics of

invention in their discussions of style; hence Abraham Fraunce, the English arch-Ramist, treats subjects and adjuncts in both his *Arcadian Rhetoric* and his *Lawyer's Logic*.

21. Abraham Fraunce, *The Lawyer's Logic* (1588) (Menston, Eng., 1969), fol. 41.

22. In short, in terms of the play, Mizaldus' proposition leads to a necessary conclusion based on infallible signs and stemming from universally true premises. Truth and necessity are coupled to result in "certain knowledge," as Fraunce terms it (*LL,* fol. 94), but only so long as the parts are coupled correctly.

23. It also shows us why Mizaldus' test, although it may be assumed to be medically accurate, can never be forensically accurate, for it cannot *prove* a woman a virgin. Through logic, although not through medicine, the dramatists undercut the whole notion of a virginity test.

24. As examples of the shifting or misapplication of words that constitutes hypallage, Puttenham cites extreme examples of what we would call inadvertent slips of the tongue: "as, he that should say, for *tell me troth and lie not, lie me troth and tell not. For come dine with me and stay not, come stay with me and dine not*" (p. 183). But hypallage need not be so extreme. John Smith, *Mystery of Rhetoric Unveil'd* (1657) (Menston, Eng., 1969), p. 200, citing many examples from Scripture, includes Job 17.4 "Thou hast hid their heart from understanding, (i.e.) thou hast hid understanding from their heart." Sister Miriam Joseph (p. 295) cites an example from the 1635 edition of Angel Day's *The English Secretary*: "the wicked wound thus given, for having thus wickedly wounded him." Interestingly, Puttenham's elaboration on his choice of the English word *changeling* to translate the Greek term hypallage links the rhetorical term to the character transformations that are the primary referents of the play's title:

> The Greeks call this figure *Hypallage,* the Latins *Submutatio,* we in our vulgar may call him the *Underchange,* but I had rather have him called the *Changeling,* nothing at all swerving from his original and much more aptly to the purpose and pleasanter to bear in memory: specially for your ladies and pretty mistresses in court for whose learning I write, because it is a term often in their mouths, and alluding to the opinion of nurses, who are wont to say that the fairies use to steal the fairest children out of their cradles and put other ill favoured in their places, which they called changelings or elves, so, if ye mark, doth our poet or maker play with his words, using a wrong construction for a right and an absurd for a sensible, by manner of exchange.

(pp. 183-84)

Dale B. J. Randall (essay date autumn 1984)

SOURCE: Randall, Dale B. J. "Some Observations on the Theme of Chastity in *The Changeling*." *English Literary Renaissance* 14, no. 3 (autumn 1984): 347-66.

[*In the following essay, Randall discusses some problematic implications of the theme of chastity or virginity in* The Changeling.]

Thomas Middleton's **More Dissemblers Besides Women** (1615) opens thus: "To be chaste, is Womans glory, / 'Tis her fame and honors story." Sung offstage in the theater, this value-laden declaration may be read in the study as both a literary *leitmotif* and a major social truism of the seventeenth century.

The jewel of woman's chastity was of great price partly because it was so susceptible to being lost or stolen. In fact, this essential truth underlies C. B. Watson's observation "that the theme of feminine infidelity was one of the most popular and yet most serious themes of Shakespeare's age."[1] Watson's statement, in turn, provides a good frame in which to view B. J. Baines' more specific reference to "The almost obsessive concern with some aspect of honor which dominates the Middleton canon"—honor for a female being "defined almost exclusively by her sexual behavior"[2] From his early poem on **"The Ghost of Lucrece"** (1600) through his **Mad World** (1606), in which a mother comments on the numerous times she has sold her daughter's virginity, through **Hengist** (1618), where a test for virginity is depicted onstage, Middleton continued to write on the subject. In **The Changeling,** his 1622 collaboration with William Rowley, however, he gives us his most important treatment of it.[3]

Throughout **The Changeling** the virginity of Beatrice-Joanna is a matter of concern—when the dazzled Alsemero sees her at church, when she requests the postponement of her marriage to Alonzo, when she first perceives and then gives in to the sexual threat posed by De Flores, when she discovers the bottle for testing virginity, when the various administrations of the virginity test are enacted, and even in the final scene when she attempts to defend herself to her disillusioned bridegroom. To the bridegroom himself, Alsemero, who is very much a man of his time, it is clear that "The honourablest piece 'bout man . . . [is] valour" (2.2.27), but for a woman the "honourablest piece" is assuredly chastity, and Alsemero wants Beatrice-Joanna only if she has never been "touch'd" (4.2.107).[4] As for De Flores, a gentleman servant who can scarcely wait to "touch" Beatrice-Joanna, money is acceptable only as partial payment for his criminal services. "And were I not resolv'd," he says, "in my belief / That thy virginity were perfect in thee, / I should but take my [monetary] recompense with grudging, / As if I had but half my hopes I agreed for" (3.4.116-19). Considering the emphasis and value placed on virginity by various characters in the play, it is painfully ironic to find Beatrice-Joanna working so hard to save the simulacrum of her honor in the later scenes. By that time even the shadow is fated to be short-lived.

Recognizing chastity's pervasiveness as a subject in *The Changeling* may enhance our understanding of the play. Equally important and a great deal more interesting and difficult is perceiving the variety of ways in which Middleton and Rowley set the subject forth. Hence the purpose of the present essay is to offer some new ideas on some of the more problematic manifestations of the theme of chastity in the play.

Many readers, for instance, have wondered why a work so thoroughly involved with chastity should be called *The Changeling.* Editors point out that the word "changeling" often refers to a child either taken or left by the fairies, the substituted child in the latter case being twisted mentally, deficient physically, or perhaps both. Yet scholars usually decline to relate this meaning to the play. George Walton Williams goes so far as to call it "the only meaning not relevant."[5] Setting aside, then, that De Flores is both mentally twisted and physically deficient, they move to a second meaning derived from the first: that "changeling" means half-wit or idiot. Pointing out that the *Dramatis Personae* specifically labels the counterfeit fool Antonio as *"the changeling,"* N. W. Bawcutt adds that much of the play's early success apparently derived "from the comic sub-plot centred on Antonio, the Changeling."[6] One might demur that Antonio is scarcely at stage-center in the subplot. For several reasons, in fact, he might be considered less important than Isabella, who speaks a good many more lines, has significant relationships with more characters, and is clearly the subplot's parallel to Beatrice-Joanna. Theatrical history does indicate much early interest in the role of Antonio, but that hardly helps to solve the problems at hand. As Williams points out, for example, within the subplot "Franciscus is as much of a changeling—an idiot—as Antonio" (p. xviii). Moreover, the play was called *The Changeling* long before anyone knew whether any of the characters, including Antonio, would have extended popularity on stage, and Middleton and Rowley themselves were in the end so uninterested in the rivalry between Antonio and Franciscus that they did not bother to stage or even allude to the confrontation which they had set up between them. Bawcutt contends, nonetheless, that the changeling of the title is clearly Antonio, and when other scholars move on to consider a third meaning of the term—that a changeling is one who changes, a waverer—he remarks, "There is some plausibility in this, though it does not seem very likely" (p. 3).

Most readers, however, include this third meaning in the range of implications suggested by the title, since one can thereby relate it to the main plot. In particular, one is able to relate it to Beatrice-Joanna, who is clearly the most important character in the play. Just as love causes Antonio's "change" to a "shape of folly" (3.3.117, 119), so Beatrice-Joanna's love-inspired action "blasts a beauty to deformity" (5.3.32). The playwrights make much of her change: she feels a "giddy turning" in herself (1.1.156), and from being her parents' daughter she comes to be "the deed's creature" (3.4.137). Most harshly put, her change is from maid to whore (3.4.142-44). Furthermore, the dramatists themselves, besides making considerable to-do about Beatrice-Joanna's change, take pains to depict other characters as changing also. They have De Flores say, for instance, that the murdered Alonzo is "chang'd now" (3.4.144). Most striking of all, however, the dramatists draw their play to a close with a sequence of speeches pointing to no fewer than seven changelings—the first three being, in order, Beatrice-Joanna, De Flores, and Alsemero (5.3.197-201). Plainly, then, Williams is correct to point to "changeableness" as a major theme in the play (p. xv). Although the references are worked in rather inconspicuously among the play's verbal details, one might add that in the world of *The Changeling* we have not only a predictably changeable moon (5.3.196), but a sun that "Shapes and transshapes" (4.3.21).

After having enjoyed the provocative abundance of changes here, nevertheless, we eventually must acknowledge that in the title the word "changeling" is singular. This brings us back either to Antonio, the subplot character who is called a changeling in the *Dramatis Personae,* or to Beatrice-Joanna, the changeling in the main plot who occupies most of our attention. But to which? While it is doubtless best to leave the question open so as to encourage continuing thought about the matter, there also remains a fourth meaning of "changeling" which offers the peculiar advantage of specific allusion both to the theme of chastity *and* to the chief character in the play. In his well-known *Arte of English Poesie* (1589) George Puttenham makes striking use of the word in a passage describing the ceremonies that take place after a wedding:

> In the morning when it was faire broad day, & that by liklyhood all tournes were sufficiently served, the last actes of the enterlude being ended, & that the bride must within few hours arise and apparrell her selfe, no more as a virgine, but as a wife, and about dinner time must by order come forth *Sicut sponsa de thalamo,* very demurely and stately to be sene and acknowledged of her parents and kinsfolkes whether she were the same woman or a changeling, or dead or alive, or maimed by any accident nocturnall.
>
> (p. 42)

In other words, "changeling" could be used to refer not merely to a woman who had changed the object of her affections, but to a woman who had had sexual intercourse. It would serve no purpose to argue here that the latter meaning is the sole meaning intended by Middleton and Rowley in their title. On the other hand, and especially considering the centrality of Beatrice-Joanna and chastity in their work, awareness of it should enrich for us the range of possible interpretations of the title and, at the same time, weaken any insistence that the play's title alludes only to a character in the comic subplot.

That Beatrice-Joanna is ultimately *the* changeling in a play that is full of changelings is further suggested by a definition in John Rider's *Dictionarie* (1640). Here under "Changeling children" (which returns us to the one meaning that is almost universally rejected by scholars of the play), we find "Lamiae" (sig. D3v). If we then turn to "Lamia" in the same work, we read that lamiae are "Women or devils in shape of women" (sig. 5H2v). Richard Perceval's dictionary gives corollary witness that a lamia is "*a witch or an hag.*"[7] And Edward Topsell tells us that these creatures are "wonderfull desirous of copulation with men."[8] Since Middleton and Rowley repeatedly encourage us to contemplate the contrast between Beatrice-Joanna's beautiful outside and ugly inside, the lamian connotations inherent in the word "changeling" should not be totally ignored. Nor should we underestimate the threat and potency they might have had for some of Middleton and Rowley's contemporaries. Here is Dr. Thomas Browne on the subject:

> Of all the delusions wherewith he [the devil] deceives mortalitie, there is not any that puzleth mee more than the Legerdemain of *Changelings*; I doe not credit those transformations of reasonable creatures into beasts, or that the Devill hath a power to transpeciate a man into a horse. . . . I could beleeve that Spirits use with man the act of carnality, and that in both sexes; I conceive they may assume, steale, or contrive a body, wherein there may be action enough to content decrepit lust, or passion to satisfie more active veneries.
>
> (*RM* [1643], p. 68)

Hence we probably should take seriously although not literally Alsemero's impassioned question when he discovers that Beatrice-Joanna has duped him. He exclaims, "oh cunning devils!" and asks, "How should blind men know you from fair-fac'd saints?" (5.3.108-09). J. L. Simmons, who has written recently of Beatrice-Joanna in terms of a lamia ("She is an alternate Eve, the Lilith who leaves her Eden to copulate with the serpent"), argues perhaps too forcefully for too narrow an interpretation and at the same time neglects the specific and necessary connection between lamia and changeling.[9] Nevertheless, a connection is there, and if one fuses it carefully with other interpretations, it is another means of enriching—and in this case darkening—the meaning of the play as a whole, and in particular the theme of chastity.

With the lamia-like duality of Beatrice-Joanna fresh in mind, one may be struck anew by the duality of her name. To be sure, it is borrowed directly from the source-story by John Reynolds. On the other hand, Middleton had long since proven himself alert to the possibility of communicating with names: Pursenet is a thief and Tailby a male prostitute in *Your Five Gallants* (1605), Shortyard in *Michaelmas Term* (1606) is impotent, and Sir Bounteous in *A Mad World* (1606) asks, "Is not my name Sir Bounteous? Am I not express'd there?" (4.3.100). Moreover, Middleton and Rowley seem to have been fortunate in the names Reynolds gave them to work with in *The Changeling*: De Flores becomes the deflowerer, Diaphanta's virtue is insubstantial, and Alibius (borrowed from Reynolds' next story) is too often in another place. Hence one is more likely to be struck by the unusual doubleness in the name of the play's chief changeling. "Beatrice," meaning she who makes happy or blessed, a blesser (the feminine of "beator"), suggests all that Beatrice-Joanna appears to be.[10] "Beatrice" is the name of the famed human embodiment of Dante's ideal. "Joanna," however, whatever its good connotations earlier, had by the sixteenth century become one of the commonest of English names and apparently fallen to the kitchen and the cottage.[11] Shakespeare writes that "greasy Joan doth keel the pot" (*LLL,* 5.2.929) and Herrick that

> *JONE* is a wench that's painted;
>   *Jone* is a Girle that's tainted;
>   Yet *Jone* she goes
>   Like one of those
> Whom purity had Sainted.
>
> (*Hesp.,* "Upon Jone and Jane," ll. 1-5)

And the misogynist Joseph Swetnam holds that "all women are alike: *Jone* is as good as my Lady, according to the Countrey mans Proverbe."[12] Undoubtedly some students of *The Changeling* will continue to regard the double name of Beatrice-Joanna as a merely borrowed label, but they should at least be aware of its possible relevance to her character. Certainly there is an unusually well-executed and provocative contrast between her façade and her interior, between her chaste, dutiful appearance and the terrible reality which, once she has "changed," finally leads to her coupling with De Flores in hell. This contrast may be reflected or partially conveyed in her name.

Imbued throughout with the theme of chastity, even in its title and perhaps in the name of its central character, *The Changeling* gives its most concentrated treatment to the subject in those scenes concerned with the virginity test. Near the beginning of Act 4, following the dumbshow in which Beatrice-Joanna marries Alsemero "*in great state,*" the player who takes her role must very soon re-enter to deliver a fifty-two-line soliloquy that conveys her discovery of the testing equipment in

Alsemero's closet. It seems reasonable to assume that even though Alsemero has presumably had time to go into the park, the player of Beatrice-Joanna is still arrayed at least partly in bridal trappings at the time of discovering the bottle marked "C" for testing pregnancy and the bottle marked "M" for testing virginity. In other words, the performer's very costuming itself almost inevitably emphasizes the threat faced by this bride who is no virgin.

Scholars, nevertheless, have had considerable trouble with the test, not only because of the nature of the potions involved but also because of the effects that bottle M brings about: a virgin is supposed to gape, sneeze, and laugh. Probably because they perceive themselves to be working with a play that is generally much closer to life than most, they have tended to disapprove of the virginity testing, describing it as "fantastic," "preposterous," "ridiculous," "absurd," "funny," and "comical."[13] Presumably they would not object to a potion in, say, *The Old Wives Tale,* but here, having been invited into a more "naturalistic" world, they feel that decorum is violated. For some, most notably Penelope B. R. Doob, the testing loses a little of its absurdity if viewed emblematically. For others, a minority led by M. C. Bradbrook, "The trick of the 'magic' glass . . . belongs with the 'omens' and other irrational elements rather than with the naturalism of character and speech."[14] Despite such rationalizations, however, the scenes which concern themselves most explicitly with the theme of chastity continue to be among the play's most problematic.

The importance of the issue is magnified because Middleton and Rowley not only troubled themselves to add the chastity test to what they had borrowed from elsewhere, but they then proceeded to spend a good deal of time developing it. After we first see Beatrice-Joanna discover the testing equipment, we see her try it on Diaphanta and herself, and subsequently we see Alsemero test Beatrice-Joanna. Furthermore, the dramatists do everything they can to make us take the test seriously. We are meant to believe that bottle M *works.* Although Jasperino initially thinks it "the strangest trick to know a maid by" (4.2.142), he is not the master of the closet, and both he and we together presently witness its efficacy. Moreover, Beatrice-Joanna's very first line in the play, addressed to Alsemero, is the suggestive question, "You are a scholar, sir?" (1.1.64). Now in the scene that follows her wedding, as she is pondering the danger of being a bride who is no virgin, she comes upon Alsemero's unlocked room with all its scholar's paraphernalia and makes the observation that "A right physician's closet 'tis" (4.1.20). And a right physician's closet it proves to be. Not only does bottle M produce accurate results if taken as directed, but with fitting irony this is the very chamber in which, with the key to the closet once more in his own hands, Alsemero in the

final scene confines his bride with her lover. The physician's closet becomes the place in which Beatrice-Joanna receives the death wound that sends her to hell.

In order to reach a fuller understanding of the virginity testing in **The Changeling** it might be well to remind ourselves that virginity tests have been known in virtually all times and places where marital fidelity has been valued. From earliest times it was realized that "*virginitatis probationem non minus difficilem quam obscuram esse,*"[15] yet tests of various sorts continued to be devised and administered. We ourselves may continue to chuckle at or scorn or regret the water-drinking test in Middleton and Rowley's play, but we should be advised, for example, that among the ancient Jews, according to Levitical law, a woman whose virginity was to be ascertained was made to drink water in the tabernacle.

Sifting through the scattered data on the subject, one gradually begins to perceive that all the old virginity tests, whether from literature or life, are variations on one of four basic kinds: tests by temptation, tests by magic, tests by science (or, from our perspective, pseudo-science), and tests by physical examination.[16] As with most such categorizing, the types sometimes shade into one another, but their basic natures are distinct enough to allow a few comments here.

Trial by temptation need concern us little. It appears in so many Fletcherian plays that N. C. Pearse has devoted much of a book to the subject.[17] Cervantes gave it definitive treatment in "El curioso impertinente," one of the stories from his *Novelas ejemplares* (1613), a collection to which Middleton and Rowley turned for *The Spanish Gypsy* in the year after **The Changeling.** And it is reported that actual English Gypsies at one time used such tests for women of their band who were about to become brides. Testing by temptation was probably always more common in literature than life, however, and need only be mentioned as a subject much in the air when Middleton and Rowley wrote.

The second type of test, using magic, need not detain us long either, although here we find the literary and the folkloric side by side and sometimes blended, and the folkloric, in turn, veering toward some of the more improbable tests recommended by the scholars. Clearly we are concerned with magic when we read of the little boy who gives King Arthur a mantle that may be worn only by a lady who is blameless, for when Guinevere puts it on, it shivers into shreds. Clearly we are again concerned with magic when the similar girdle that Spenser assigns to Florimell is said to loosen or break if any unchaste woman tries to wear it (*FQ,* 5.3.28) and when Fletcher's Clorin is given an herb which heals only if applied "With spotless hand on spotless breast" (*Faithful Shepherdess,* 5.1.70). On the other hand, we have moved into the realm of folklore when we read that in the Midlands in ages past a woman could prove her virginity by walking unstung through a swarm of bees.

Far more important to us here is a third type of testing, testing which has the earmarks of medical procedure. To put the salient details in perspective at the outset, we might recall that whereas Bradbrook apparently perceives a magician's closet in the play at hand, Beatrice-Joanna herself perceives "A right physician's closet." Why, then, should these last four words not be considered a straightforward line of scene-setting? Beatrice-Joanna goes on: "Sure he does practise physic" (4.1.22). That is, this place neither looks like nor is a magician's closet.[18] The playwrights even proceed through Beatrice-Joanna to rationalize why Alsemero would choose to move such equipment about with him from place to place: it is wise for a man of position and learning to "practise physic for his own use." When Beatrice-Joanna also perceives "white water in glass C," then, we may think of Dr. John Hall, Shakespeare's son-in-law, who recorded notes for a *"Terpintine potion, cal'd white potion"* and also *"Virgins milk,"* which was intended to make a maid's complexion clear.[19] Rather than turn to magic, it is more to the point for us to recall that realms of knowledge in Jacobean times were not yet thoroughly surveyed and separated, and that science and pseudo-science still interinanimated one another. When Samuel Boulton wrote of the virtues of weapon-salve, it was not because he believed in the powers of supra-real magic but because his assumptions about the physician's art were quite different from our own.[20]

Virginity testing of type three takes a variety of forms. Pliny (whose authority was available in Holland's 1601 translation) tells of a certain black stone called "geat" (the fossil wood we know as jet), which, when burned, gives off a smoke that will indicate whether a woman is a maid: "If she drinke it fasting, presently it provoketh urine, if she be a pure virgin."[21] Johannes de Ketham recommends putting purslane seeds on burning coals and then watching the results when a female's parts are exposed to the fumes; if the woman is not a virgin, one will see "mirabilia."[22] Caspar Wolff advises making a fume with sorrel flowers and charcoal; a true virgin will not pale. Since little distinction was made between authorities of different times, furthermore, any literate Englishman might have turned to *The Secrets of Albertus Magnus* (Alsemero's manuscript, it will be recalled, is headed "The Book of Experiment, / Call'd Secrets in Nature" [4.1.24-25]) in versions of either 1525 or, much closer to *The Changeling,* 1617. Saint Albert is credited with suggesting that one put a lodestone under the pillow of the woman to be tested (if she is unchaste, she will leap out of bed [sig. B6v]), or hand her a certain kind of stone that has been crushed and washed

("if she be not a virgin, she will shed her water" [sig. C7v]); or place on her breast while she sleeps some powder made from the heart of a dove and the head of a frog (she will show you all she has done [sigs. G5v-G6]). Perhaps helpful to those of us who wish to weigh contemporary attitudes toward such advice is the slightly equivocal view expressed by the 1617 English presenter of St. Albert: "I referre thee to the tryall of some of his secrets, which as thou shalt find true in part or all, I leave to thine owne report or commendation" (sig. A2v). The secrets are offered in good faith, but not guaranteed.

The following passage from Johann Jacob Wecker is especially instructive, for it tends toward inclusiveness, demonstrates the lingering habit of authorities to quote one another, has been available in various versions since the sixteenth century, and offers material significant enough to be augmented and re-presented in its present form by a physician almost forty years after the first appearance of the "absurd" chastity test in Middleton and Rowley's *Changeling.* Intended to explain *"How to know whether a woman be chast, and whether she ever lay with a Man or be with Child,"* it asserts that

> Antiquity affords us some experiments of this thing; and so doth this latter age, with things that are to be admired, and easie to be procured; that men seeing them, will sooner deny their sense, and confess themselves to be fools, than they will approve the truth; and those that are delighted with the desire of such a thing, go about to search for it, and greedily thirst to find it out. The Jet stone, (which is very frequent with us, wherewith we make Beads withall to pray, and to number and summe up our Prayers,) some scrapings of it, or the stone beaten in a Mortar, and sifted, so being brought into very fine pouder, and then drank with wine or water; if the woman do make water presently and cannot hold it, that is a sign she hath lost her Maiden-head; If she were never defloured, she will hold her water, and her retentive faculty is strengthned by it. White Amber is as good as the former (or Crystall,) which they call Electrum, if being poudred, it be drank with wine fasting, and so taken inwardly: for if she be polluted, this will make her make water. We may try it sooner by the fume of Purslane seed, or leaves of the great Burdock strewed upon burning coals, and put under her for a fume, and if that flie upward, it will discover the truth of the matter: let it be carried by a tunnel [i.e., funnel] or some small instrument into the mouth of the Matrix, it will cause her to Urine presently, nor can she forbear if she have made use of a man. But if she be chast, the smoke will do nothing, but she will hold her water, which signifies that she is a Maid.[23]

All four of these experiments, it will be noted, have to do with drinking or urinating or both.

Throughout the seventeenth century the testing of virginity continued to be taken seriously not merely by popularizers but also by scholars and physicians. One of the best treatises to discuss the matter, *De Relationibus Medicorum,* was published in 1602 by a Sicilian physician named Fortunato Fedeli (1550?-1630). To open his discussion, Fedeli cites instances in which it would be useful to know whether or not a woman is a virgin. In such cases, he says, it is customary to call in midwives as consultants, but the testimony of women is so uncertain and misleading that men have long felt moved to devise various kinds of virginity tests. At this point, protesting his dissatisfaction with all the old, popular procedures, he nonetheless mentions them—thereby recording them yet again. Thus we come to Pliny's powdered jet mixed with water or wine, to powdered amber (similarly prepared), to a drink made of powdered "xyloaloes," and to incense made from sorrel. But having attacked such tests, Fedeli has little to offer in their stead. He cannot believe, for example, in the claims of some that a woman who has given up her virginity will have more turbid urine, a deeper voice, or darker nipples. On the contrary, he concludes that there seem to be no sure indications of virginity at all—although against the various popular tests that men have passed around amongst themselves for centuries, he would willingly pit two simple, straightforward criteria: bleeding and lack of resistance.[24]

Yet to be considered is the one name that the play gives us to work with, that of Antoine Mizauld. In the manuscript that Beatrice-Joanna discovers Alsemero to have compiled she comes across "'A merry sleight, but true experiment, the author Antonius Mizaldus'" (4.1.45-46). "Merry" seems to convey the attitude of the young Alsemero at some former time when he was intrigued by thoughts of testing an as-yet-unknown girl friend. On the other hand, the adjective in the phrase "true experiment" suggests that, despite the tricksiness of any such experiment, the air of putting over something, and the cavalier attitude of the uncommitted bachelor tester, the experiment is supposed to work. Whether Alsemero himself is presumed to have added the word "true" or to have found it in his source, Mizauld's name is introduced into the play as that of an authority.

Born in Montluçon about 1520, Antoine Mizauld went to Paris to study medicine and received a doctorate there. During the same period in which he was acquiring a fundamental knowledge of the physician's art, he embarked also on a study of astrology with the mathematician Oronce Fine. (It is perhaps worth recalling that all early doctors were presumed to be knowledgeable about astrology.) Eventually Mizauld was to immerse himself in the study of a variety of interrelated subjects, the nature of which may be suggested best by the titles of some of his writing: *Cometographia* (1549), *Aesculapii et Uraniae Conjugium* (1550), *Planetologia* (1551), *De Mundi Sphaera* (1562), *Alexikepus, seu Auxiliaris hortus* (1565), *Memorabilium, utilium ac jucundorum Centuriae IX Arcanorum* (1566), and

Harmonia superioris Mundi et inferioris (1577). A respected and extremely industrious figure during his lifetime, Mizauld achieved a reputation which deflated rapidly in the century following his death in 1578—although *Mizaldus redivivus, sive Centuriae XII Arcanorum* was published as late as 1681. One can scarcely be precise in such a matter, but it would seem that at the time of **The Changeling** Mizauld's name still would have been useful for alluding to out-of-the-way learning on a wide variety of matters, learning that was authority-oriented and often concerned with topics appropriate to science, but, all in all, learning of the sort which Bacon and Browne (*Pseudodoxia Epidemica,* 1646) were to consider ripe for reappraisal.

Whether or not Robert G. Lawrence is right to suspect that "Middleton's lack of preciseness suggests that he had not read Mizaldus, but acquired information sufficient for his purpose at second hand,"[25] the play borrows Mizauld's general reputation, not some specific experiment. Mizauld's various *Centuriae* do yield some scattered virginity tests, of course. The old pulverized jet test from Pliny recurs in VII.12.[26] Both this test and the one at VII.64 (calling for the fumes of "portulaca" seeds—i.e., purslane seeds, as we have seen in Ketham and Wecker) are attributed by Mizauld himself to Giambattista della Porta (97v). A variation on the jet test calls for "*succinum album,*" white amber (VII.12 [89v]). And VI.54, a pregnancy test, advises thus:

> *Si experiri voles an mulier sit gravida, fac ut lotium reddat in vase aeneo, & noctem una acum ferream & perpolitam in illud demerge. Si praegnans erit, maculis rubris distinguetur: sin minus, nigrescet, vel ferruginea, aut aeruginosa evadet. Expertum fuisse intellexi.[27]*

The reader may decide whether Mizauld or the team of Middleton and Rowley is the more "fantastic." But a more important point to observe is that all of these men were very much of their time.

Our concern, then, is with a Mizauld-like experiment. The problem of Middleton and Rowley at this point in the play was neither to dream up a bit of magic to lengthen the action nor to lighten the atmosphere of verisimilitude that they had established in the main plot, nor to make us smile knowingly at Beatrice-Joanna's unwitting comedy in miming a virgin's response, but to heighten our sense of Beatrice-Joanna's peril by showing her discovery of a possible trap. Her position is something like that of a twentieth-century wrongdoer who suddenly learns of the existence and imminence of a polygraph test.

Furthermore and above all, the job of the dramatists was to maintain the tone and pace of the main plot by a device that was both convincingly threatening and also stageworthy. The threat of the "true experiment" to Beatrice-Joanna is intensified rather than lightened or diverted because, in keeping with various chastity tests that had been recommended for hundreds of years, it calls for the woman tested to drink a specially concocted liquid. Drinking a draft, fortunately, is simple to act onstage. But what about the effects which the drink is supposed to induce? One might observe that when Alsemero's manuscript (and hence Middleton and Rowley's text) calls for the tested virgin to gape, sneeze, and laugh "incontinently" (4.1.49), the adverb indicates action that is not only unrestrained but also immediate. For the test to be effective onstage it must cause symptoms that members of an audience can readily observe, and it must do so promptly so as to juxtapose unmistakably the drink and its effects, as well as keep the play moving. It cannot call for the player acting Beatrice-Joanna to urinate or fall asleep for twelve hours. And the three required actions in sequence—gaping, sneezing, and laughing—are in aggregate far more convincing than any single one of them would be alone. The test as we have it is very much in touch with tradition but modified to be stageworthy.

Even if it is inevitable that a certain amount of humor will be generated by nearly any modern staging of the test in *The Changeling* (and I am not persuaded it is), the players nevertheless can choose what sort of humor it will be. In *Jane Eyre* a prose of earnest confidentiality and obvious good sense is likely to forestall our chuckles at Charlotte Brontë's frequent reliance on phrenology. Just so, the players in *The Changeling* have the opportunity to show us by their manner that any humor lurking in the "true experiment" is deadly, a black and ironic humor consistent with the other horrid humor in the work—that is, with the display of Piracquo's betrothal ring on his severed finger, the ghost's display of a hand that lacks a finger, and the macabre dispatching of Diaphanta, whose defloration and death are promptly succeeded by musket fire up her chimney. Whatever humor is inherent in any of these moments, it should not be perceived as "comical." What could be more threatening to Beatrice-Joanna than exposure of the fact that she has lost her honor? She has proven herself willing to do anything, even forfeit honor itself, merely to retain the appearance of honor. What better way, then, to threaten her exposure than to set up a chastity test? The testing which ensues in *The Changeling* is not a blemish, not a strangely unaccountable lapse of taste or decorum on the playwrights' part, but an attempt to give serious, persuasive, interesting, and effective dramatic form—stageable form—to the theme of chastity.

One might point out also that the form chosen by the playwrights helps to integrate the chastity test with the physician theme. Alsemero, the physician of the main plot ("Sure he does practise physic"), has a counterpart in Alibius, the physician of the subplot ("My trade, my living 'tis" [1.2.50]). Each man develops doubts about

the faithfulness of his lady. And each lady in turn is a physician of sorts to a different man who would be her lover. Beatrice-Joanna is a mixer of waters for De Flores' face and will "trust no other" in her "work of cure" (2.2.85-86); and Isabella, who is expected to diagnose and cure Franciscus, is spoken of as casting his water (4.3.185-86). The right-hand men of both Alsemero and Alibius are also associated specifically with the physician theme. Jasperino says, "I know what physic is best" and "I'll ne'er profess physic again" (1.1.140, 145-46), and Lollio is addressed as "Esculapius" (3.3.61). The following chart may help to point up further the structural importance of presenting Alsemero as a figure of the physician:

Thus we may see why Alsemero's physicianly test in the serious plot is best regarded not as an excrescence but as a thoroughly integrated element in the play, not as a puzzlingly extended comic blot but as a major and serious part of the theme of chastity.

Having now noted chastity testing by temptation, by magic, and by various ostensibly scientific processes, let us note briefly a fourth and final type: testing by examination. This method had attracted considerable attention during the Essex divorce or nullity trial of 1613, to which the playwrights seem to refer in the lines of Diaphanta (4.1.100-01).[28] Among other matters of interest, Frances Howard, Lady Essex, who had insisted on wearing a veil during her examination, was said to have had a substitute (like Diaphanta). In the year of *The Changeling,* furthermore, the business would still have been remembered. For one thing, the Overbury scandal of which it was a part proved to be a very long-running affair, and for another, Frances Howard and Robert Carr (whom Frances took for her second husband and who became indirectly involved with her in Overbury's murder) were both released from the Tower in January of 1622—only about four months before *The Changeling* was licensed.[29]

On the other hand, examination of another sort, usually of a cloth which had been present at a bride's defloration, had been practiced since ancient times (Deut. 22.13-21) and certainly was still widely known in Renaissance Italy, France, Spain, and elsewhere.[30] The Gypsies were but one among many people who insisted on ocular proof of a bride's virginity, their test being conducted on the day of the wedding. A particularly striking form of this ceremony as it was practiced by the Scottish Gypsies is recorded by Walter Simson, an eminent nineteenth-century student of Gypsy lore of his own and earlier times.[31] Explaining that the ceremony in question was "undoubtedly of the highest antiquity," Simson writes,

> A marriage cup, or bowl, made out of solid wood, and of a capacity to contain about two Scotch pints, or about one gallon, is made use of at the ceremony. After the wedding-party is assembled, and everything prepared for the occasion, the priest takes the bowl and gives it to the bride, who passes urine into it; it is then handed, for a similar purpose, to the bridegroom. After this, the priest takes a quantity of earth from the ground, and throws it into the bowl, adding sometimes a quantity of brandy to the mixture. He then stirs the whole together, with a spoon made of a ram's horn, and sometimes with a large ram's horn itself, which he wears suspended from his neck by a string. He then presents the bowl . . . first to the bride, and then to the bridegroom; calling at the same time upon each to separate the mixture in the bowl, if they can. The young couple are then ordered to join hands over the bowl . . . ; when the priest, . . . in the Gipsy language, pronounces the parties to be husband and wife; and as none can separate the mixture in the bowl, so they, in their persons, cannot be separated till death dissolves their union.
>
> (pp. 260-61)

The use here of the bridal couple's "water" is put into perspective by the realization that the early Scots were accustomed to mingle the urine and dung of cattle with man's urine, and then to sprinkle the cattle with the mixture as an antidote against charms. For that matter, while we are trying to come to terms with what passed for physician's lore and what for folklore in the seventeenth century, we might recall Daniel Beckherus' *Medicus Microcosmus* (1660), which offers first-hand testimony that urine taken internally proved highly successful as a preservative against the plague between 1620 and 1630.[32] The use to which the Gypsy ceremony puts the ram's horn has been variously interpreted as symbolic of power and fertility, and the joining of the couple's hands over the inseparable ingredients in the bowl ("water," earth, spirits, and air) is an unmistakable symbol of union. Simson continues to write of the virginity test itself:

> As soon as that part of the ceremony [the business of the bowl] is performed, the couple undress, and repair to their nuptial couch. After remaining there for a considerable time, some of the most confidential relatives of the married couple are admitted to the apartment, as witnesses to the virginity of the bride; certain tokens being produced to the examining friends, at this stage of the ceremony. If all the parties concerned are satisfied, the bride receives a handsome present from the friends, as a mark of their respect for her remaining chaste till the hour of her marriage.
>
> (p. 261)

The bridal couple then arise, dress, and rejoin the festivities.

An important detail, however, has thus far been omitted, and at this point Simson explains what has happened to the mixture in the nuptial bowl. It has been

> carefully bottled up, and the bottle marked with the Roman character, M. In this state, it is buried in the earth, or kept in their houses or tents, and is carefully preserved, as evidence of the marriage of the parties. When it is buried in the fields, the husband and wife to whom it belongs frequently repair to the spot, and look at it, for the purpose of keeping them in remembrance of their nuptial vows. Small quantities of the compound are also given to individuals of the tribe, to be used for certain rare purposes.
>
> (p. 263)[33]

Initially symbolic of union, then, the bottle marked "M" in time becomes symbolic also of chaste fidelity.

Clearly it would be a mistake to attempt any direct linkage between the Gypsy bottle M and that in *The Changeling*. The *Changeling* water M tests virginity; the Gypsy M contains the bride's last water as a virgin, mingled now with that of the bridegroom. The *Changeling* M has the power to indicate virginity; the Gypsy M signifies union in which virginity is an essential ingredient. The *Changeling* M leads a virgin to laughter; the Gypsy M presumably leads to conjugal happiness based on enduring chastity in union. Whatever the differences and similarities, however, the point in citing them is not to imply anything specific about sources. (How far would one care to push the fact that the name of Shakespeare's Caliban is the same as the Gypsy name for darkness and blackness?) The aim here is to point out a striking and provocative addition to this fourth kind of virginity testing and to suggest yet again that we proceed thoughtfully before accepting such labels as "funny," "comic," and "absurd" for the testing in *The Changeling.*

Whether one is considering the theme of chastity generally in *The Changeling* or its particular manifestation in the virginity test, Middleton and Rowley are very much in touch with the beliefs of their time. And their time is not ours. Even if we are caught up in admiration for their rather spare but potent use of dialogue or their relatively close approach to psychological realism in the play, we would do well to bear in mind that they found the source of their main plot while reading Reynolds' moral-thumping *Triumphs of Gods Revenge* (1621). Lacking much sympathy for seventeenth-century fiction, most of us, unlike Middleton and Rowley, are not inclined to read what Reynolds wrote. We might assume correctly enough that he would inveigh against the "devillish and bloody murtherers" of his story (p.

146), but we are likely to overlook his assurance in the previous story that although his heroine "shooke hands with her mayden-hood . . . shee should have prized and esteemed [it] farre more precious then her life" (p. 81). We are also likely to miss the moral at the end: "May all maidens learne by her example, to preserve their chastities" (p. 103).

When it comes to testing maidenly chastity, of course, whether then or earlier or now, people have been quite aware of difficulties. Hence we find Robert Burton calling absurd the tests of men such as Wecker and Porta (*Anat.,* III.3.ii.1). Burton's bracing view is likely to produce within modern readers some of that narcissistic delight that we frequently are tempted to take whenever and wherever we come across an apparent modernity in seventeenth-century life or literature.[34] At the same time we point to Burton's intelligent skepticism about virginity tests, however, we might remind ourselves also of his claim that no physician can understand the cause or cure of a disease unless he has a knowledge of the stars. In fact, this is the same man who argues for the love-passion of male and female palm trees, and sends us to Antoine Mizauld to find more on the subject (*Anat.,* III.2.i.1).

Burton is very much a man of his time. When we consider William Harvey's extraordinarily important discovery of the circulation of blood (*De Motu Cordis* was first published in Frankfort six years after the composition of **The Changeling**), we should remember that Harvey believed in telegony; and at the same time we smile knowingly at Kenelm Digby's Powder of Sympathy, we would not do badly to remember that Digby was a pioneer student of the necessity of oxygen in the life cycle of plants. Although the seventeenth century was assuredly a golden age of scientific studies, and particularly a time of important new medical discoveries, the clouds from earlier days were a long time dispersing. In his *Novum Organum* of 1620 Bacon still found it essential to urge people to abandon their idols of accepted authority and popular opinion, and Galileo in 1633 was forced by the authorities to deny his own scientific discoveries. Even at mid-century, Noah Biggs, one of the more outspoken of English medical reformers, was complaining that physicians were still tied to Galen, Aristotle, and Avicenna.[35] Sir Theodore Turquet de Mayerne, reputedly the most fashionable physician in England at the time of **The Changeling,** dedicated to King James the pharmacopoeia of the College of Physicians (1618)—and still relied on such ingredients as powdered human skulls, balsam of bats, and earthworms.

While any reader of **The Changeling** is free to decide that the problematic chastity test is a comically unbelievable blot on the play, a fantastic breach of decorum,

such a decision does not square comfortably with all we know about the state of medical beliefs at the time. Such a decision, furthermore, leads to ahistorical criticism. In disregarding what one might call the relativity of absurdity, it precludes exploration of the possibility that Middleton and Rowley's chastity testing is a serious, explicable, and congruous element in the play.

Nowadays, when attitudes toward both chastity and medicine have proved constant only in their variety and change, we can produce serums to make a person tell the truth, we can administer gas to make a person laugh, and we can even take a human heart from one body and put it to work in another. Therefore, it is understandable if we are inclined to look back in puzzlement or amusement upon some of the claims of the physician's art in 1622. Like Middleton and Rowley, however, we should have learned never to abandon our sense of wonder and possibility. Even while we share with these playwrights a sober sense of lost values, our lingering sense of wonder and possibility, if combined with a greater awareness of some early beliefs about chastity, may help us view the various aspects of chastity in **The Changeling** with a greater sympathy and understanding. It may be that we will come to see **The Changeling** as an even better play than we thought.

Notes

1. *Shakespeare and the Renaissance Concept of Honor* (Princeton, N.J., 1960), p. 439.

2. *The Lust Motif in the Plays of Thomas Middleton,* Jacobean Drama Studies 29 (Salzburg, 1973), p. 4.

3. Mention should be made of Douglas Duncan, "Virginity in *The Changeling,*" *English Studies in Canada,* 9 (1983), 25-35, although Duncan's facts and goals are very different from those presented here.

4. All quotations from *The Changeling* are taken from N. W. Bawcutt's edition (Cambridge, Mass., 1961; 1st ed., 1958).

5. Ed., *The Changeling* (Lincoln, Neb., 1966), p. xv.

6. Bawcutt, p. xxvi.

7. *A Dictionarie in Spanish and English,* aug. by John Minsheu (1599), p. 156.

8. *The Historie of Foure-footed Beastes* (1607), p. 454. Topsell's discussion throws some light on Rider's definition, cited above: because Jove loved a beautiful paramour named Lamia, Juno had each of the many offspring of these lovers destroyed as it was born, "whereupon came the fable of changing of children" (p. 452).

9. "Diabolical Realism in Middleton and Rowley's *The Changeling,*" *Renaissance Drama,* N.S. 11 (1980), 148.

10. See William Power, "Middleton's Way with Names," *Notes and Queries,* 205 (1960), 176-77; and Charlotte M. Yonge, *History of Christian Names* (rev. ed., London, 1884) p. xxxiii.

11. E. G. Withycombe, *The Oxford Dictionary of English Christian Names* (Oxford, 3rd ed., 1977), pp. 176-77; and Yonge, p. 46.

12. *The Arraignment of Lewd, Idle, Froward, and Unconstant Women* (1622), p. 9.

13. Bawcutt, p. 69; Samuel Schoenbaum, *Middleton's Tragedies* (New York, 1955), pp. 145, 147; Baines, p. 113; Penelope B. R. Doob, "A Reading of *The Changeling,*" *English Literary Renaissance,* 3 (1973), 200; and Simmons, p. 154.

14. *Themes and Conventions of Elizabethan Tragedy* (Cambridge, 1964; 1st ed., 1935), p. 220.

15. See Adrian Beverland, *De Stolatae Virginitatis Jure Lucubratio Academica* (Leiden, 1680), p. 68.

16. The author wishes to point out that the following analysis is simply an informal attempt by a student of English to bring order to a subject where he has found none.

17. *John Fletcher's Chastity Plays* (Lewisburg, Pa., 1973).

18. The situation is complicated because a Renaissance physician often had something about him of the magus, but by and large people probably had a reasonably good working knowledge of which man of art was which.

19. *Select Observations on English Bodies: Or, Cures Both Empericall and Historicall,* tr. James Cooke (1657), sig. A11.

20. *Medicina Magica* (1665; preface dated 1656), pp. 4, 47, and esp. pp. 120-26.

21. *The Historie of the World,* II (1601), 589.

22. This example and the next (concerning Wolff) are cited by James V. Ricci in *The Genealogy of Gynaecology* (Philadelphia, 1943), pp. 288, 312.

23. *Eighteen Books of the Secrets of Art & Nature,* aug. by Dr. R. Read (1660), V, 104.

24. Fedeli, pp. 196-205. Other authors who manifest an interest in virginity from both a social and a medico-legal viewpoint include Heinrich Kornmann (fl. 1607); Melchior Sebische (1578-1674?); Lazare Riviere (1589-1655), whose lec-tures at Montpellier were attended by Thomas Browne in 1630; and Georg Franck von Franckenau (1643-1704). See Ricci, pp. 390-91.

25. "A Critical Edition of *The Changeling* by Thomas Middleton and William Rowley," unpub. Diss. Ph.D., Univ. of Wisconsin (1956), p. 162.

26. *Memorabilium . . .* (Paris, 1584), p. 89v.

27. *Memorabilium,* p. 80; available also in the English version of Thomas Lupton, *A Thousand Notable Things, of Sundry Sortes,* Bk. VI, no. 48 (1579), pp. 146-47.

28. Much is made of the relation between the trial and the play in Simmons's essay.

29. For a late example one might cite the examination of Dorothy Harvey of London in 1681. A thirteen-year-old widow who wished to marry her former husband's brother, Dorothy was permitted to do so after being inspected and attested a virgin by three experienced midwives ("Virginity Test," *Local Population Studies Magazine and Newsletter* [1969], no. 3, pp. 60-61).

30. See Louis de Gaya, *Cérémonies Nuptiales de Toutes les Nations* (Paris, 1680).

31. *A History of the Gipsies,* ed. James Simson (New York, 1866), pp. 260-63. Although early, Walter Simson's work has been highly regarded by later students. T. W. Thompson, for instance, accepts the present account of the virginity test as accurate, "unless Simson is mistaken for once, which is most unlikely" ("Gypsy Marriage in England," *Journal of The Gypsy Lore Society,* 6 [1927], 108).

32. This and further data are cited in John G. Bourke, *Scatalogic Rites of All Nations* (Washington, D.C., 1891), p. 302 and elsewhere.

33. Modern gypsiologists have thus far failed to explain the meaning of the "M" on the bottle (see my note in *Newsletter of the Gypsy Lore Society,* vol. 6, no. 1 [1983], p. 9).

34. Rather skeptical also, but perhaps more typically tolerant, is the attitude expressed in Shirley's *Hyde Park* (1632), which acknowledges folkloric testing and leaves the door open regarding the accuracy of a doctor's test by uroscopy, but lightly endorses a far pleasanter kind of diagnosis. When Mistress Bonavent asks Fairfield if he is skilled in determining a woman's virginity, he replies, "I'll know't by a kiss, / Better than any doctor by her urine" (4.3.182-83).

35. Biggs was the author of *Mataeotechnia Medicinae Praxews: The Vanity of the Craft of Physick* (1651); see Allen G. Debus, "Paracelsian Medicine: Noah Biggs and the Problem of Medical Reform," in *Medicine in Seventeenth Century England,* ed. Debus (Berkeley, Cal., 1974), pp. 33-48.

Sara Eaton (essay date October 1984)

SOURCE: Eaton, Sara. "Beatrice-Joanna and the Rhetoric of Love in *The Changeling*." *Theatre Journal* (October 1984): 371-82.

[*In the following essay, Eaton analyzes the language of courtly love and attitudes toward female impurity in* The Changeling.]

> Forsooth, if we are to hear of no wickedness, history must be done away with. So those comedies should be prized which condemn the vices which they bring to our ears, especially when the life of impure women ends in an unhappy death.
>
> —Scaliger

Scaliger's prized deaths of "impure women" suggest the seriousness of Renaissance attitudes toward femininity. Conventionalized in Courtly Love literature and under scrutiny in Puritan sermons and the popular press, femininity was considered especially in terms of modes of appearance, whether physical or theatrical. As Tuke explained in his *A Treatise against Painting,* "It is not enough to be good, but she that is good, must seem good: she that is chast, must seem chast."[1] This distinction between feminine being and seeming pervaded dominant Renaissance ideologies concerning and defining the wickedness of women. Implicit in the Courtly Love and edenic ideologies, for instance, is the assumption that women may be what they are, but that their gender does not allow them to seem so. Such logic allowed for a woman who failed to seem pure to be thought impure.

Complicating these Renaissance notions of feminine "seeming" is the fact that their source was male. Edenic and Courtly Love representations of women focus on female figures whose apparent purity is undercut by their failure to fulfill male expectations of their behavior. These notions of femininity subjected woman to a double-bind of either being pure but not seeming so or seeming so but not according to male conventions. Middleton and Rowley, I will suggest, locate the "frightful pleasure" of *The Changeling* in this double-bind. By linking the male problem of knowing women, the confusion of being and seeming, to the rhetoric of Courtly Love and edenic longing, the play displays its linguistic exchanges as a drama of sexual revenge leaving the deaths of impure women to be "prized."

Throughout *The Changeling,* Beatrice-Joanna succeeds all too well in her attempts to be as she is perceived. On one side of Courtly Love's polarities, she portrays Alsemero's idealization of her. On the other side, she personifies DeFlores's view of self-degradation. Her rhetoric merely reproducing theirs, Beatrice-Joanna becomes an apparently harmonious representation of their conflicting desires. As a woman capable of seeming to be as they perceive her, she comes to perceive herself as an image of both idealized and degraded femininity—as a fallen Eve. Not autonomous in her actions, Beatrice-Joanna internalizes and reflects the inherent contradictions in male perceptions of women, especially as couched in the rhetoric of Courtly Love. Through Beatrice-Joanna's representation of the effects of Courtly Love, *The Changeling* indicts courtly rhetoric in its historical personification as unhappy death.

If it is not surprising that Middleton and Rowley use Courtly Love rhetoric to expose its contradictions, it is surprising how many critics, like Scaliger, argue that Beatrice-Joanna is morally culpable in how she is perceived.[2] Such critical arguments repeat the characters' expectations for feminine behavior, that women should be as they seem. From this point of view, Alsemero or DeFlores is seen as the hero of the play, and Beatrice-Joanna, who has concealed her ethical vacuity and fooled the male characters into believing romantic notions about women, gets exactly what she deserves. This perspective does not account for the play's action, which forms in reaction to Beatrice-Joanna's attempts to be equal to the male characters' perceptions. If the critical endeavor accepts the notion that female characters should be merely the vehicles for other characters' moral and aesthetic "pleasures," Beatrice-Joanna's fate is trivialized, the male characters' views are valorized, and the main thrust of Middleton and Rowley's drama is lost.

The question the play asks, then, is what kind of pleasures women can offer. It shifts attention from the revenge tragedy motifs, heroic concerns, to psychological and linguistic ones that can reflect the mechanics of sexual revenge. Although one of *The Changeling*'s most obvious dramatic constructs is a tragic exploration of "the lunatic, the lover, and the poet," contemporary expectations for Senecan conventions are distinctive in this play's dramatic structure primarily because they matter so little. For example, Alonzo's ghost, instead of either terrorizing the guilty DeFlores and Beatrice-Joanna or urging his brother toward revenge, becomes "some ill thing that haunts the house."[3] His brother, the justified avenger, is frustrated; DeFlores enacts a sexual revenge. Traditional Senecan conventions are trivialized so that the audience must focus on characters who appear in a tragic "moonlight madness," slowly turning into a nightmare that explores the possession of women through the language of Courtly Love.

The dialogue in the first four acts presents polite, courtier-like statements, full of the customary wit and neoplatonic conceits common to wooing in Renaissance drama. But the characters puncture these dialogues with frequent asides that reveal to what extent the public, idealized language masks the characters' other assessments of situations. For example, in Act II, scene i, approximately two-thirds of the first ninety lines are spoken in either soliloquies or asides. Regardless of how this display of "private" language is staged, the audience is aware of these shifts in the play's language. Indeed, most of the dialogue between Beatrice-Joanna and DeFlores is directed toward the audience through asides:

BEA.:

> [*Aside*] Again!
> —This ominous ill-faced fellow more disturbs me
> Than all my other passions.

DEF.:

> [*Aside*] Now't begins again;
> I'll stand this storm of hail though the stones pelt
> me.

> [II. i. 52-54]

Her passionate revulsion and his physical determination are forcefully articulated—to the audience. The content and tone of the asides in themselves introduce a second level of signification in addition to that of the play's public language.[4]

The public and private languages demonstrate both sides of the rhetoric of Courtly Love, the idealized language appropriate to wooing, and the private language reflecting physical corruption. Beatrice-Joanna lives in a world where expectations of "transformations" in love are expressed in one version of Courtly Love rhetoric while the characters' private assessments of their world and each other are expressed in another. In a sense, then, the public dialogues, both in the plot and subplot, are merely a veneer covering other meanings in the play. By Act V, moreover, the asides of the first four acts disappear, as their reflections on the nature of love's transformations prevail and become the primary language. Although *The Changeling* here moves toward a rhetorical unity, I will suggest that this unity is essentially repressive: both the public and private languages hinge on the possession of females. In fact, Beatrice-Joanna's death at the end of the play means the end of her attempts to be rhetorically effective in her own world. The rhetorical unity of the play, then, amounts to the silencing of Beatrice-Joanna.[5]

Beatrice-Joanna's body is the referent of the play's rhetoric; the male characters discuss her as an object to be claimed and possessed. Alsemero views her as the ideal lady in a Courtly Love scheme in which he wants to believe; his language is the most obvious example of *The Changeling*'s public discourse. His talk of magic potions and his constant observations of omens reflect his doubts about love while reinforcing his idealized perceptions of Beatrice-Joanna as the perfect woman. His opening declaration, "With man's first creation, the place blest, / And is his right home back, if he achieve it" (I. i. 8-9), closes off Beatrice-Joanna's actual sexual identity by linking it to Eden and the temple where he first sees her. His perception of her sacred sexuality is verified and, from his point of view, realized, in his physician's closet. There he keeps his "Book of Experiments Call'd Secrets in Nature" (IV. i. 24-25), the "key that will lead to a pretty secret" (IV. ii. 111)—the secrets of chastity and feminine sexuality. Declaiming that she is "Chaste as the breath of heaven, or morning's womb, / That brings the day forth, thus my love encloses thee" (IV. ii. 149-150), he perceives Beatrice-Joanna as a way back to a sacred and enclosed world through his possession of her. His exalted perception is ironically revealed as an obsessive possessiveness when, in the last act, he forces her into the closet with the macabre threat, "enter my closet; / I'll be your keeper yet" (V. iii. 86-87).

But from the beginning of the play, when Alsemero tells her that "there is scarce a thing but is loved and loathed" (I. i. 126), we are aware that his view includes the underside of the Courtly Love tradition: the woman-as-monster, the Duessa. Alsemero "cannot be too sure" (IV. ii. 126) as he tests her virginity; he is disturbed and uncertain about his role as a courtly lover and distrusts his own judgment (an attitude that Jasperino, his man, aids and abets). Beatrice-Joanna argues that Alsemero is as implicated as she is in the murders, because she has become a "cruel murd'ress" (V. iii. 65) to insure their marriage. He is not affected by this reiteration of the argument used so successfully with Beatrice-Joanna by DeFlores. He ignores any logic or psychological truth in her argument, and instead pronounces his sense of her static, inherently flawed sexuality. Saying "Twas in my fears at first, 'twill have it now: / Oh, thou art all deformed" (V. iii. 76-77), he thinks of the marriage-bed in a crypt, "itself's a charnel, the sheets shrouds" (V. iii. 83), even though the marriage has not been consummated. Conflating sex and death, ignorant of how Beatrice-Joanna, DeFlores, and even Diaphanta have allied to insure his marriage, "this dangerous bridge of blood" (V. iii. 81), Alsemero expects Beatrice-Joanna to be a chimerical representation of female sexuality. She functions as a vaginal pathway back to an edenic world that he would also test in this one.

Alsemero begins the play as a frustrated revenger, and manages to continue in that role as he constantly suspects the "murderer" of his illusions to be one of the characters around him. Beatrice-Joanna becomes the vehicle for his return to a perfect world at the same time that she represents that impossibility. This dream requires a passive Beatrice-Joanna who does not murder, who will remain in the closet of "sweet secrets" as an imagined but frustrated version of female sexuality. When Alsemero forces her into the closet in Act V, his language again stresses love's dual nature: "I'll be your pander now; rehearse again / Your scene of lust, that you may be perfect" (V. iii. 114-115).

Alsemero's actions after this reveal the extent to which he has strengthened his allegiance to Vermandero, Beatrice-Joanna's father, in reaction to his own perceptions of love. His consolation to Vermandero as they view the bodies—"Sir, you have yet a son's duty living" (V. iii. 216)—suggests that "his right home back," the edenic world he has searched for since the opening of the play, is organized around a father who is still living. Alsemero sees himself as replacing Beatrice-Joanna in her father's eyes; he would maintain both his perception of female sexuality, and his identity as a would-be revenger, by acting in an essentially adolescent role that grants him the "father's son" position he has filled throughout the play. But, implicated by his marriage and Beatrice-Joanna's death, his place in this patrilineal system is based on ambivalence: his idealization and denial of Beatrice-Joanna's actions and what they mean.

Alsemero desperately needs to maintain the closet of "sweet secrets," although he never really recognizes the fears and desires projected on the "fallen Eve" locked up in it. He avoids meaningful action, when, for example, he thinks on his marriage: "The bed itself's a charnel, the sheets shrouds / For murdered carcasses; it must ask pause / What I must do in this" (V. iii. 83-85). And he counsels repression when he recommends to Vermandero: "Let it be blotted out; let your heart lose it, / And it can never look you in the face / Nor tell a tale behind the back of life" (V. iii. 182-184). Implied by his language, Alsemero's ambivalence is revealed in his actions—other than bedding Diaphanta and locking first Beatrice-Joanna and then DeFlores in the closet, he does nothing to initiate dramatic action. In the final analysis, Alsemero finds his "right home back" by locking his psyche in a closet of secrets.[6]

The other important male character, DeFlores, speaking in the corrupted private language of the asides, the underside of Courtly Love rhetoric, views Beatrice-Joanna as an "odd feeder" (II. ii. 153). His language and gestures characterize him as driven toward a violent, deadly possession of Beatrice-Joanna, and his view of her character, like Alsemero's, is a projection of his own desires. He would "thrust [his] fingers / Into her sockets" (I. i. 236-237), confusing a vaginal metaphor with, perhaps, a visual reference to her gloves. Anticipating fulfillment of *his* projected erotic intentions, he presents her dead Alonzo's finger, with her betrothal ring still on it. Representations of death and sexual possession are further conflated when, after killing the proxy-bride, Diaphanta, he brings her charred body back for Beatrice-Joanna to see. In these incidents, DeFlores im-

plicates Beatrice-Joanna in the murders through her perceptions. That is, he would have her see what he has seen and done for her favors. Description will not suffice. Distrusting the idealized metaphors of Courtly Love—the public language that Beatrice-Joanna espouses—he consistently produces the content, the bodies, that result from her usage of the play's public language. It is thus DeFlores who interprets and reproduces her metaphoric intentions in the flesh, enacting these connections between language and actions. When Beatrice-Joanna and DeFlores are locked into the closet together, Alsemero assumes fornication; instead, in an attempt at ultimate consummation, DeFlores stabs her with his penknife. Finally, stabbing himself and presenting his own body "as a token," he tells the dying Beatrice-Joanna to "make haste"; he would "not go to leave [her] far behind" (V. iii. 175, 177).

In his death speech, DeFlores tells Alsemero of his greedy obsession with Beatrice-Joanna; the taking of her virginity "was so sweet to me / That I have drunk up all, left none behind / For any man to pledge me" (V. iii. 169-171).[7] This is wishful thinking. DeFlores's actions can only be seen as an endless pursuit of absolute consummation, a continuous circling around a deflowered Beatrice-Joanna who by his own definition has been rendered nothing. For this reason, quite literally, he cannot get enough of her. Throughout the play, DeFlores signifies his intentions toward Beatrice-Joanna through violent oral and anal metaphors. He wants to "drink her up," and produces pieces of his murdered victims for her approval.[8] His metaphors indicate an intense egotism that he projects back on Beatrice-Joanna, anticipating that "peace and innocency has turned [her] out / And made [her] one with [him]" (III. iv. 139-140). To DeFlores, as with Alsemero, Beatrice-Joanna is still primarily the imagistic locus for an active psychological exchange of introjected and projected male sexual desires. But if Alsemero creates Courtly Love's version of idealized feminine sexuality, DeFlores designs one for his digestive tract. Beatrice-Joanna's identity remains elusive except in terms of the sexual excitement she generates, one that promises a reunion with Alsemero's and DeFlores's version of the "Other" that is "I."

What Alsemero locks away, DeFlores greedily drinks up. These two male characters would seem to be the play's actual "twins of mischief" (V. iii. 142). Their projections of desire onto Beatrice-Joanna seem to shape the play's rhetoric. Together Alsemero and DeFlores enact two psychological motions involved in the production of Courtly Love rhetoric. In a romance or a single poet's inspirational mode, Alsemero's idealization of Beatrice-Joanna would be complementary to DeFlores's ingestion or internalizing of what she represents as an idealized figure. Split, the two men act out variants of Courtly Love's tragic potential occurring when the source of poetic inspiration may not be as she appears. Frederick Goldin explains that in a harmonious Courtly Love relationship, the lover seeks the "guiding image of his completeness":

> first, that image coincides with the self-image of his class, so that the more he pursues his own desires, the more he is at one with his equal, the more he is part of a community; second, that personal image of his perfection, because it is embodied in the person of the lady, is now capable of responding to him, of loving him and making it possible for him to be at one with the image that guides him. This joy is worth the renunciation of every other joy, for it gives inner peace and certainty. Here now is the perfect dream of love: all the aspects of the Courtly man become harmonious and one.[9]

Alsemero constructs a "self-image of his class" which DeFlores would locate inside the psychological boundaries of his body. Like their characteristic languages, these men are psychological doubles, enacting the implications of their rhetoric.

Alsemero fears Beatrice-Joanna's unworthiness to the same degree that DeFlores defines her as such; conversely, DeFlores fears sharing Beatrice-Joanna with the "community" formed through her idealization to the same extent that Alsemero desires access to it. These characters could find completion in each other, and Beatrice-Joanna would still be the vehicle for expressing their desires. Instead, both characters act as though "knowing" Beatrice-Joanna as the "Other" includes seeing a corruption which must be enclosed, termed nothing, and rendered silent. The metaphors which reveal this knowledge deny her an autonomous identity while disclaiming any responsibility for her murder. What does she do to trigger the violent insistence that she has failed to reflect adequately their expectations of harmonious completeness?

In a play where the men see what they want to see, Beatrice-Joanna says: "Would creation— / . . . had formed me man . . . / Oh, tis the soul of freedom. / . . . I should have power / Then to oppose my loathings, nay, remove 'em / For ever from my sight" (II. ii. 107-109, 111-113). Beatrice-Joanna enlists DeFlores as her "man" primarily to dispose of Alonzo, upon whom her "eyes were mistaken" (I. i. 85). Her father is determined to see her married; whether to Alonzo or Alsemero seems to be of little importance so long as the marriage amounts to "the addition of a son" (II. i. 99). She would marry Alsemero, whom she sees "now with the eyes of judgment / And see the way to merit, clearly see it" (II. i. 13-14). In this world, it does not occur to her to act alone; she defines herself through others' perceptions of her, and she is, consequently, powerless "to oppose [her] loathings." She would "see" as the male characters do, but unlike them, she needs

an accomplice to turn her dreams into the play's "reality." Accordingly, she always assumes that DeFlores will respond as a courtier to her request for service. The "merit" she sees in Alsemero is his embodiment of the idealized Courtly Love rhetoric; ironically, he becomes her frustrated chivalric lover.

More importantly, she begins to perceive the world around her through male eyes. She becomes the Eve around whom Paradise will collapse. She is initially horrified at DeFlores's serpent-like interpretation of her complicity in Alonzo's murder—she says, "Thy language is so bold and vicious" (III. iv. 123)—but she finally is seduced by her own perceptions of what Alsemero and DeFlores represent. While before her defloration she asks, "Was my creation in the womb so cursed / It must engender with a viper first?" (III. iv. 165-166), she later declaims that "the east [the sunrise] is not more beauteous than [DeFlores's] service" (V. i. 72). She shares with Alsemero the public language that characterizes her perceptions of her world at the same time that she inures herself to the growing heap of bodies around her. Personifying Alsemero's ambivalence, she incorporates the debased concept of self that DeFlores offers.

Beatrice-Joanna's anger and disappointment with Diaphanta's lust in the marriage bed that should be hers, and her insistence to the end that she has been sexually honorable, do not necessarily indicate her villainy, or even her guilt. Rather, she refuses to relinquish what she perceives as her prerogative in the Courtly Love scenario. As DeFlores works out the details for Diaphanta's death, Beatrice-Joanna declares that she is "forced to love [him] now, / 'Cause [he] provid'st so carefully for my honor" (V. i. 47-48). Here, sex, death, love, and honor become equational terms, and the play's meanings behind the private and public languages converge. Still, she relies on DeFlores to implement those meanings, since she "must trust somebody" (V. i. 15) to sustain her power in a patriarchy. Beatrice-Joanna allows DeFlores to realize her dreams, to act on, and thereby define, her perceptions of what constitutes powerful behavior. For Beatrice-Joanna, DeFlores becomes the active equivalent of the asides in the first four acts; he is the agent of her desire to be as she appears.

Thus, Beatrice-Joanna accepts her role as the "fallen Eve" for the male characters. She voices, manipulates, and incorporates the public and private languages of the play, the languages of male projection that comprise the rhetoric of Courtly Love. Her allegiance to their rhetoric is evidenced not only by her refusal to admit adultery, but also by her insistence that DeFlores has done her only "service," as her "honor fell with him," and then her life (V. iii. 158). By perceiving her world as if, by extension, she could have been "formed a man," she has invested in her own destruction.

The transformation in love that Beatrice-Joanna accomplishes is, finally, one of reflection—she sees herself as a mirror reflecting male desires, as a vehicle for their pleasures. She reflects back upon Alsemero and DeFlores their language through her own; she adheres to the Courtly Love discourse whose underside is enacted for her by DeFlores. In this sense, she embodies the language that characterizes her world, and she unifies in one figure what in the previous acts has been rhetorically split. The asides of the first four acts disappear in the fifth because by then Beatrice-Joanna embodies all the possibilities of Courtly Love that the rhetoric of the play can offer.

Yet, we should not be too quick to argue only for patriarchal harmony in *The Changeling*. Beatrice-Joanna is perceived by the others as being "both of sport and wit, / Always a woman striving for the last hit" (V. i. 126-127). Her "sport" and "wit" are enough to reproduce the play's private and public languages, and to disturb the perfectly narcissistic image both Alsemero and DeFlores want to have mirrored back to them. Her dream of acquiring male prerogative is expressed, as Stilling suggests, in "the language of female rebellion, shown as an impulse toward evil."[10] Because she insists that she speaks the language of Courtly Love and that both Alsemero's and DeFlores's views of her are equivalent to her own perceptions (for which she has "kissed poison . . . stroked a serpent" [V. iii. 66]), her "sporting" discourse becomes the distorted reason for her destruction.

Beatrice-Joanna dies for the "truth within her," the power of the language she speaks and embodies. Even though she thinks her language includes her in the males' world, her rhetoric becomes the ultimate declaration of "Otherness" that DeFlores and Alsemero would close off in their possession of her. As a screen, as a vehicle of exchange in Courtly Love rhetoric, she actually reflects the opposite of what Alsemero and DeFlores *would* see. She personifies Alsemero's fears that her sexuality will disrupt his tenuous union with Vermandero, his community. To DeFlores she performs his inability to "fill himself up" with another human being, his sense of being alone in his physicality and not part of the male community he serves.[11] Both men define their community, then, in terms of other men: for Alsemero, it is Vermandero, for DeFlores, the men who cannot "pledge" him. Whereas Beatrice-Joanna mirrors what these characters would not see, she is like her counterpart in the subplot, Isabella, who reveals her suitors' folly in pursuing her love by reflecting back to them the roles they have presented to her. But Beatrice-Joanna assumes that her ability to mime, to speak the play's language of love, includes choosing how she will be perceived and possessed.

She does not "see," as Nancy Chodorow puts it, that

> feminine roles are less public or "social," that they exhibit less linguistic and institutional differentiation. . . . Women's roles are thus based on what are seen as personal rather than "social" or "cultural" ties. The corollary to this is that women's roles typically tend to involve the exercise of influence in face-to-face, personal contexts rather than legitimized power in contexts which are categorical and defined by authority. Finally, women's roles, and the biological symbolism attached to them, share a concern with the crossing of boundaries: Women mediate between the social and cultural concerns which men have defined; they bridge the gap and make transitions—especially in their role as socializer and mother—between nature and culture.[12]

Beatrice-Joanna mimes the rhetoric's failure to make the connection between "nature" and "culture," between DeFlores and Alsemero in these terms. But for the male characters, as an image of corrupted nature and failed culture, she also demonstrates the deadly possibilities of their conjunction that must be denied.

Such disintegration and disorder, moreover, threaten *The Changeling* from its first act; the characters are preoccupied with their world's outward symbols of stability—Vermandero's castle and Alibius's madhouse. Guarded against strangers, Vermandero explains that "our citadels / Are placed conspicuous to outward view, / On promonts' tops, but within are secrets" (I. i. 167-169). The bridegroom Alonzo's obvious curiosity and his pleasure at finally seeing the "most spacious and impregnable fort" (III. i. 4) the day before his wedding ironically leads him to his death. Nicholas Brooke comments that:

> The Castle and the House are derived from their medieval and renaissance significance as emblems of both the world and the human body. The peculiar imaginative power of DeFlores' leading Alonzo through the dark passages is that the suggestive language long established for him is sustained there; it is also a journey through the organs of a female body to an anal death, *and* a descent into hell.[13]

Vermandero supports this analysis when he says: "An host of enemies entered my citadel / Could not amaze like this: Joanna! Beatrice-Joanna!" (V. iii. 147-148), followed by "We are all there, [hell] circumscribes us here" (V. iii. 164). The analogies between Vermandero's castle and Beatrice-Joanna's body are further reinforced by Beatrice-Joanna's last assertion that her blood is Vermandero's, and that the "common sewer take it from distinction" (V. iii. 153), as though she is merely waste. Seen as the source of their language, Beatrice-Joanna has been kept "secret" as a body to be found out, defended against, and purged—in her father's castle, in Alsemero's physician's closet, and in DeFlores's body—just as Isabella has been locked in her husband's madhouse to save him from cuckoldry. But where

Isabella articulates the illusions in the male characters' perceptions ("I have no beauty now, / Nor never had, but what was in my garments" [IV. iii. 135-136]), Beatrice-Joanna is deluded into believing that her language, her garment of speech, corresponds to what the male characters perceive her to be in the flesh.

Beatrice-Joanna's persistent belief in the power of her rhetoric exposes Courtly Love as a linguistic system that must deny women a voice. When the play opens, Beatrice-Joanna's mother is already dead, in "heaven . . . married to joys eternal" (III. iv. 5), and Beatrice-Joanna and Diaphanta join her in deathly silence by the end of the play. In the comic subplot, Alibius, Isabella's husband, interprets Isabella's actions as a reason to "never keep / Scholars . . . wiser than myself" (V. iii. 214-215), not as reason enough to free her from the madhouse. The female characters are consistently forced to the boundaries of the dramatic action, and reduced to what is signified by the male characters. The male characters define the terms of what Chodorow calls social and cultural concerns—language, marriage, and the metaphors that connect them with sexual revenge and death. Beatrice-Joanna particularly disturbs these terms because she doubles, or reproduces and articulates, the pathological connections between Courtly Love and the action of the play. She mediates between those "secrets" of nature and culture which the male characters would not perceive as articulated in their linguistic community. She becomes what Caren Greenberg describes as "the point of intersection between masculine power and pleasure. . . . A sexual battleground important not because of her own intrinsic power, but rather as a mark of the father's power. In this sense, the wife/mother's body fulfills the first requirement of a language system: it marks something other than itself."[14] As the projection of the male characters' illusions, as the "mark" of a language system, Beatrice-Joanna is what she says—a "prophet to the rest" of her world in her destruction (V. iii. 157).

The last scene of the play reenacts a psychological stasis that characterizes the entire play and reveals the extent to which Beatrice-Joanna marks something other than herself. Alsemero pledges a "son's duty" to Vermandero, who has wanted all along "the addition of a son." Beatrice-Joanna, reinforcing this patriarchal system, tells her father that she "was blood taken from [him] / For [his] better health; look no more upon't, / But cast it to the ground regardlessly" (V. iii. 150-152). DeFlores presents her with a last dead "token"—himself. None of the characters change psychologically as a result of the dramatic action. The audience senses that this scene replicates previous ones—the death scenes of Beatrice-Joanna's mother before the play opens, and Diaphanta's during it—death scenes vigorously denied as meaningful to the participants. The male characters' language, shaped by the "truth" of Beatrice-Joanna's self-

affirmation as "Other" in her discourse, reveals the extent of their emotional investments in their perceptions, not only of her, but of their world. Their language, to quote D. W. Winnicott, is "organized to defend against a repetition of 'unthinkable anxiety' or a return to the acute confusional state that belongs to disintegration."[15] The characters employ Courtly Love as a language of power to defend against internal psychological disorder.

Beatrice-Joanna is as "blind" as the other characters. She becomes the "point of intersection" for locating meanings in the play because she represents a dramatic and rhetorical unity that is split in its practice. The asides, which originally were directed towards the audience, become lodged inside the dramatic action—inside Beatrice-Joanna, as her name implies. As Beatrice, she is Courtly Love's Lady; as Joanna, she is a pun, perhaps, on Gehenna, hell.[16] Her name symbolizes the play's rhetorical intentions to signify a spiritual hell. She becomes the focus of the dramatic action, organized to get her off the stage, because she is designated this hell's source.

The transformation in the language of love that does occur, the movement of the asides from the outside to the inside of the play's action, reveals the extent to which Beatrice-Joanna is both outside and inside of her own world. She marks the limits of the play's rhetoric as she embodies it. The tragedy occurs, not because Middleton and Rowley want to point out the depravity inherent in beautiful women, but because Beatrice-Joanna cannot successfully "mediate between the social and cultural categories which men have defined" as inward and outward symbolic experiences; she cannot "bridge the gap and make transitions" between being and seeming in relation to her appearance. Possessing no voice, she marks off the cultural boundaries. Her body is defined as a fortress and her language exposes the "gap," the locus of a societal "hell," that a cultural psychology has built upon the "secrets" of the female body, and then used as the referent for its language of love.

Middleton and Rowley point toward this interpretation through Alibius's description of the *danse macabre* his madmen will present to Beatrice-Joanna on her wedding night:

> Only an unexpected passage over
> To make a frightful pleasure, that is all,
> But not the all I aim at; could we so act it,
> To teach it in a wild distracted measure,
> Though out of form and figure, breaking time's head,
> It were no matter, 'twould be healed again
> In one age or other, if not in this.
>
> [III. iii. 270-276]

As a "frightful pleasure," Beatrice-Joanna (and Isabella to a greater extent than I have argued here) shapes the dramatic action of the play, and incorporates its meanings in her embodiment of its split rhetoric. Beatrice-Joanna's "unexpected passage" initiates Alsemero's and the other characters' movements toward a "right home back." They all participate in love's blind transformations. Beatrice-Joanna exposes to the audience the gaps in the drama's language even as she embodies its psychological coherence. She functions as an illusory body of text in which the male characters read the "wild distracted measure" of love's dreams turned nightmares, as though she were both the vehicle for dreaming and the origin of its hells.[17] For the audience, Beatrice-Joanna functions as an image which embodies in her designation as "Other" all the possibilities and limitations of the play's tragic language. She shapes everything and, finally, nothing, worth articulating about love's possessive power. Whether a "frightful pleasure" or an "impure woman," Beatrice-Joanna embodies the site of the interpretation of tragedy.

Notes

1. T. Tuke, *A Treatise Against Painting* (London, 1616), p. 10, as quoted by Sandra Clark, *The English Pamphleteers* (East Brunswick, N.J.: Farleigh Dickinson Press, 1983), p. 178.

2. Fredson Bowers, *Elizabethan Revenge Tragedy, 1587-1642* (Gloucester, Mass.: Princeton University Press, 1959), p. 204; Christopher Ricks's important study, "The Moral and Poetic Structure of *The Changeling*," *Essays in Criticism,* 10 (1960), 295; Roger Stilling, *Love and Death in Renaissance Tragedy* (Baton Rouge: Louisiana State University Press, 1976), p. 250-56; Lenora Leet Brodwin, *Elizabethan Love Tragedy* (New York: New York University Press, 1971); and Robert Jordan, "Myth and Psychology in *The Changeling*," *Renaissance Drama,* NS 3 (1970), p. 165.

3. Thomas Middleton and William Rowley, *The Changeling,* in *Drama of the English Renaissance,* Vol. II, ed. Russell A. Fraser and Norman Rabkin (New York: Macmillan, 1976), V. i. 62. All subsequent references from this edition are included in the text.

4. M. C. Bradbrook, *Themes and Conventions of Elizabethan Tragedy* (Cambridge: Cambridge University Press, 1952), p. 124.

5. The *OED* sheds light on both the title of the play and what I have been describing. Contemporary usages of "changeling" suggest: 1) One given to change, fickle or inconsistent person (the most cited explanation of the title); and 2) A person or thing (surreptitiously) put in exchange for another. Besides referring to the bed-switch and nearly every characters' shift in position in the play, the second meaning also would apply to a rhetorical exchange. The *OED* refers, moreover, to

Puttenham's description of the rhetorical figure, hypallage, as a "changeling." Etymology suggests, then, that the meanings of the word are variations on exchanges or what one might call metonymic transfers.

6. For further discussion, see Melanie Klein, *Envy and Gratitude and Other Works, 1946-1963* (New York: Dell, 1975), p. 217. Klein's description of the common male pre-Oedipal movement between the love-object and the authority figure (the mother and father) seems to provide an explanation for Alsemero's psychological realignment with Vermandero.

7. This assertion reflects ironically on Alsemero's assumptions that the potion Beatrice-Joanna drank was a "pledge" of her virginity. Alsemero's and DeFlores's perceptions converge metaphorically, leaving Beatrice-Joanna at their center.

8. Melanie Klein, "The Emotional Life of the Infant," *Envy and Gratitude.* Klein's description of the infant's libidinal responses, fixated on oral and anal functions, is useful in understanding DeFlores's preoccupation with drinking and dead bodies. The infant's sense of producing feces for the mother is both a pleasurable and a frequently conflicted psychological response. According to Klein, cathexis with a death-wish towards the self or mother often occurs.

9. Frederick Goldin, "The Array of Perspectives in the Early Courtly Love Lyric," *In Pursuit of Perfection: Courtly Love in Medieval Literature,* eds. Joan Farrante, George D. Economous, Frederick Goldin, Esther Quinn, Renata Karlin, Saul N. Brody (Port Washington, N.Y.: Kennikat Press, 1975), p. 56. For a discussion of narcissism in Courtly Love, see Goldin's *The Mirror of Narcissus in the Courtly Love Lyric* (Ithaca, N.Y.: Cornell University Press, 1967), pp. 50ff.

10. Stilling, p. 254.

11. Lacan's "Le Stade du miroir" underlies my discussion here. Without attempting to paraphrase the subtleties of his argument, I would expand it to include the psychodynamics of speech at work in the play. More suggestive, perhaps, is D. W. Winnicott's argument in "Mirror-role of Mother and Family in Child Development," *Playing and Reality* (New York: Basic Books, 1971). Responding to Lacan, Winnicott argues that "the precursor of the mirror is the mother's face" (p. 111), and expressions mediate "the discovery of meaning in a world of seen things" (p. 113). For Winnicott, as for Lacan, infants' assumptions of union with the mother are necessarily disrupted by their autonomous responses to beliefs that they are identical

to, and linked with, her. Healthy development depends on these autonomous disruptions of the sense of doubling. In a tragedy like *The Changeling,* where language, plots, and characters double, and "seeing" becomes problematic, the characters might be experiencing "unhealthy" disruptions of the sort Winnicott describes that result in pathological behavior. To the other characters, Beatrice-Joanna may represent the mother's face.

12. Nancy Chodorow, *The Reproduction of Mothering: Psychoanalysis and the Sociology of Gender* (Berkeley: University of California Press, 1978), p. 180.

13. Nicholas Brooke, *Horrid Laughter in Jacobean Tragedy* (London: Open Books, 1979), p. 85.

14. Caren Greenberg, "Reading Reading: Echo's Abduction of Language," *Women and Language in Literature and Society,* ed. Sally McConnell-Ginet, Ruth Borker, Nelly Furman (New York: Praeger, 1980), p. 302.

15. Winnicott, "The Location of Cultural Experience," *Playing and Reality,* p. 97. Winnicott's description of an infant's creation and use of a transitional object, and the emotional investment in it, has influenced my argument here; in the way Beatrice-Joanna mediates between language and culture, she seems to function as a transitional object for the other characters.

16. My thanks to Parker Johnson for suggesting this possibility.

17. Greenberg argues that a "mediating text is female—and dead" (p. 303).

Joost Daalder (essay date January 1988)

SOURCE: Daalder, Joost. "Folly and Madness in *The Changeling.*" *Essays in Criticism* 38, no. 1 (January 1988): 1-21.

[*In the following essay, Daalder contends that* The Changeling *is a dramatic study of idiocy and madness that seeks to point to what is abnormal in the human mind.*]

The challenge of *The Changeling* is, to put it bluntly, to discover what it is 'about', and if despite much recent activity critics have not been able to provide us with a satisfactory answer that is because they have failed to grasp how the sub-plot relates to the main plot.[1] It is certainly much harder than in most comparable instances of Renaissance plays to see what the two plots have to do with each other, and it is not surprising that earlier critics concentrated on the main plot,

in effect giving up the sub-plot in despair, and blaming its author Rowley, not only for writing less well than Middleton, but also for not relating his material to the main plot. Since William Empson made some comments on the play in *Some Versions of Pastoral,* it has been understood in a vague and general way that the plots must somehow be related, and that the relationship is one of irony, but nevertheless the sub-plot continues to be seen as some sort of adjunct to the play— possibly not irrelevant, but not essential. I believe that, on the contrary, we can only understand the main plot if we understand the sub-plot, and that the relationship is vital.

The Changeling is above all a study, in dramatic form, of folly and madness. It is interested in making us aware of what is 'abnormal' in the workings of the human mind. It is the sub-plot which sets up the most basic distinction between folly and madness, and develops the concept of madness which helps us to grasp its nature in the main plot.

Folly, or idiocy, is a good starting point from which to classify various kinds of mental abnormality, and so it is to the dramatists. The sub-plot first of all (I.ii) presents to us Alibius, 'a jealous doctor' according to the list of Dramatis Personae,[2] and Lollio, 'his man'. Alibius is in charge of a place (no doubt something like Bedlam) where 'brainsick patients' (l. 53) are kept. As Alibius cannot always be at home and is afraid that his wife may prove adulterous, he gives Lollio control over her, which means that she is to be kept as a prisoner in the asylum. Lollio cannot see whom his master might have cause to be jealous of, explaining:

> We have but two sorts of people in the house, and both under the whip, that's fools and madmen; the one has not wit enough to be knaves, and the other not knavery enough to be fools.

(44-47)

Fools, according to Lollio, are people lacking in 'wit' (intelligence, understanding). As they are intellectually deficient, they are incapable of being 'knaves' on that score. Madmen, however, cannot be knaves because they suffer from a different kind of brainsickness; therefore they would not be foolish enough to embark on a sexual relationship with Alibius's wife, Isabella.

The sub-plot offers us both a counterfeit fool and someone who pretends to be a madman. The fact that both characters put on roles gives us a clear notion of what the authors mean by 'fools' and 'madmen'. Antonio is the 'fool', Franciscus the 'madman'. Both are interested in Isabella (which implies, according to Lollio's concept of things, that neither is a real fool or madman); she, however, is neither foolish nor mad in any sense.

Antonio demonstrates to us, in his role as a fool, what such a person is like by answering certain questions correctly, on a simple principle, without realizing that the same simple principle cannot be applied to a somewhat different situation. Thus, in III.iii, Lollio ask him 'how many is five times six', to which he replies: 'six times five'. When he is to state 'how many is one hundred and seven', he logically but inadequately answers: 'seven hundred and one' (cf. ll. 155-61).

One reason why this answer must look like making some sort of sense is that it enables us to understand that madness is in all respects a much more serious condition than folly. Those who are mad, according to Lollio's understanding, may not be dangerous, but they disturb us by the illogicality—indeed, the incomprehensibility—of what they say. For example, Franciscus accosts Isabella thus:

> Hail, bright Titania!
> Why stand'st thou idle on these flow'ry banks?
> Oberon is dancing with his Dryades;
> I'll gather daisies, primrose, violets,
> And bind them in a verse of poesie.

(48-52)

As Bawcutt explains in his edition, this speech is no doubt intended by Franciscus as an invitation to Isabella (Titania) to solace herself with him in the absence of Alibius (Oberon), who, he insinuates, is enjoying himself with other women. At the same time, however, the speech is characteristic of the 'thinking' of a madman. The speech is mad, not because it is stupid (as Antonio was when he equated 'one hundred and seven' with 'seven hundred and one'), but because it shows—at least if we take his act at face value—that the speaker is out of touch with reality. The speaker, acting on his fantasy rather than on reason and observation of evidence, claims, and truly believes, that something is fact which we know not to exist. It is this propensity which enables us to distinguish between those whom the play sees as mad, and those who are merely foolish. In such individuals as Franciscus, society recognizes madness readily, and that is why they end up in lunatic asylums. Much of the play is dedicated to exploring more subtle, less immediately identifiable kinds of madness which are also, in the final analysis, the product of confusion between fantasy and an accurate grasp of reality.

In fact, the sub-plot gives us an excellent example of a superficially sane but actually mad person in the case of Alibius. In I.ii. Alibius explains to Lollio that because he is old while his wife is young, he fears the possibility of a rival's 'thrusting' (l. 31) into a ring which he would wear on his own finger.[3] This kind of sick fantasy—unjustified, indirect yet in a sense very detailed and precise—is similar to that of Iago and Othello when their minds dwell on sexual matters. As Lollio points out, Alibius in fact has nothing to fear from the inmates of Alibius's institution; but Alibius, who is intent on making his fantasy come true in reality, expresses his fear of those who come to visit his patients. Lollio answers this fear quite pertinently by saying that the visitors come to see the fools and madmen—not Isabella, who is 'of neither sort' (l. 60). Significantly, Lollio's healthy appreciation of Isabella's character is used to throw into relief the diseased nature of Alibius's mind, and the accuracy of Lollio's view is borne out by Isabella's behaviour throughout the play. In other words, Alibius is someone whom we should now normally call 'paranoid'.

That form of madness can certainly be recognized, but it is not of the gravest kind. It does lead to serious discomfort for Isabella, who is locked up as though she were insane while it is really the person who is in charge of the insane, Alibius himself, who should more appropriately take her place. She is subjected to a degree of sexual harassment from Antonio, Franciscus, and indeed Lollio, but Alibius's action, however misguided, does not place her in serious danger. In the main plot, his paranoia is matched by that of Alsemero, who, having just married Beatrice, at once wants to discover whether by some ill chance she is already pregnant, or no longer a virgin (see IV.i). The fact that we know that his wife deserves his suspicion, because of her intercourse with De Flores, does not diminish the irrationality of Alsemero's conduct. Unlike us, he has absolutely no ground for mistrusting her, and it is clear that his fear, like Alibius's, is merely the result of his own imagination. Both men, too, show their insanity in the extraordinary methods they choose for attempting to lay their fear at rest. A sane person would not entertain unjustified jealousy in the first place; but, if his fantasy did prompt him to be jealous, he would confront his wife about his feelings rather than engage in a further flight of fancy which, in the event, takes neither Alibius nor Alsemero any closer to reality.

The madness of Alibius and Alsemero may not be of the gravest kind but it is not harmless. For one thing, if Beatrice had not discovered her husband's plan to test her virginity, she would not have been tempted to ask her maid Diaphanta to take her place on her wedding night, and thus Diaphanta would have stayed alive instead of being killed by De Flores at the end of the play. For another, one reason why such seemingly normal people as these paranoid husbands are dangerous is that their madness is not readily apparent to others. The consequences of Alsemero's paranoia in the main plot are much more calamitous than those of Alibius in the sub-plot because in the madhouse little harm can be done; it is in the 'real' world of 'normal' people that even comparatively mild forms of madness lead to disaster.

The seriousness of madness in a person is not to be measured by the ease with which it can be identified. The play appears to suggest that most of us are too inclined to judge madness in shallow terms. We do not, to begin with, pay much attention to the distinction between folly and madness. Lollio recognizes that there is a difference between the two, but he does not consider lunatics more dangerous than fools—a point which has some validity in Alibius's institution. If someone thinks that Isabella is Titania, that person is obviously mad, and will be seen to be so by others. That means that he will be locked up and thus cannot do harm, and that in any case the nature of his delusion is probably such as will not hurt others. The mad, in Alibius's institution, are invariably innocuous: Lollio is right to think that they 'have not knavery enough to be fools'. But Lollio's concept of madness is too limited. Because the mad, in contrast to the foolish, confuse what is real and what is unreal, they can, in principle, be much more dangerous. If he showed any real understanding of the evidence in front of him, Lollio would thus have come to the conclusion that Alibius is not sane. But, although he fully realizes that Isabella is not mad (I.ii.65), and in general questions the wisdom of Alibius's judgement, he does not grasp that Alibius is paranoid. This indicates to us that those whose madness is not obvious, though it is at the same time potentially dangerous to others, are not likely to be prevented from doing harm. Yet, in their subtle way, the dramatists leave us in no doubt that *they* consider Alibius mad. We all know that it is common amongst the mad to think that they are normal while others are insane. Alibius significantly cannot or will not recognize his wife's sanity when he says that 'she's no fool' (I.ii.64); and it is equally significant that he, while crazy himself, is in charge of the 'madmen's ward'.

There is one other important fact about madness which the sub-plot enables us to see and which we must observe if we are to understand the play as a whole. Fools, clearly, are intellectually deficient from birth, while those who are mad become so at a later stage. The dramatists make a distinction which was officially accepted by their society:

> For the purposes of the Court of Wards and Liveries the difference between idiots (natural fools) and lunatics (*non compos mentis*) rested simply on the congenital nature of the condition; natural fools were those 'mentally subnormal from birth' and lunatics were those 'whose intellect and memory [failed] sometime after birth'.[4]

The legal distinction does not, however, concern itself with the way in which a person becomes a lunatic—a question that is naturally of paramount interest to the dramatists. The sub-plot gives us a hint:

> There's no hope of recovery of that Welsh madman, was undone by a mouse, that spoil'd him a permasant; lost his wits for't.

(I.ii.206-8)

The fondness of the Welsh for cheese was proverbial in Elizabethan England. However, the fact that the dramatists make a joke at the expense of the Welsh does not preclude their being serious at the same time. The Welshman referred to must obviously have had an inclination towards madness anyway, or else the incident in question would not have affected him so grievously. What we are to understand is that someone who has a propensity towards madness may remain sane under propitious circumstances, but will indeed become mad if some particular event brings on the condition. In that case, such a person loses his 'wits'; that is, he does not become stupid, but will no longer think rationally and coherently.

The sub-plot helps us to understand what madness in the world outside the lunatic asylum will be like, but, with the exception of the outsiders (Alibius, Lollio, Isabella, Antonio and Franciscus), the people who are presented to us are middle-of-the-road fools and madmen who are neither sane enough (like Isabella) to be kept outside, nor mentally deranged in a way which goes unrecognized by most people (as Alibius is). It is one of the major ironies of the play that the average mental patient is harmless. Although Alibius is wrong to lock up Isabella, she is in fact in a safe place so long as she is surrounded by those declared fools or madmen by society. Such danger as she is subjected to comes from outsiders: Alibius, Lollio, Antonio and Franciscus. Whether compared with the insiders or the outsiders, she is the picture of good mental health. One function of the sub-plot is to show to us how a woman pushed into a madhouse remains eminently sane despite her environment: contact with the supposedly foolish or mad inmates does not affect her. Furthermore, she is neither led astray by the real folly and madness of the keepers Lollio and Alibius, nor tempted by the counterfeits Antonio and Franciscus.

The relationship between the sub-plot and the main plot is one of carefully wrought irony. Compared with the people around her, Beatrice is mad. She stands out most against Isabella, however, not only because Isabella is the chief woman in the sub-plot as Beatrice is in the main plot, but also because if we compare Beatrice with other people in the main plot the contrast is not so glaring. Ostensibly, all those people are normal, and it would have been easy for the dramatists to give us a sub-plot with a sane woman surrounded by real idiots and lunatics which reverses a main plot containing an insane woman in a sane world. That comparatively simple model, however, is not that of *The Changeling*. It is certainly one which the dramatists have in mind, in that Isabella is sane and Beatrice insane, while each woman appears to inhabit a world contrasted with her. However, appearances are deceptive: although the people in Alibius's institution are indeed fools and madmen, they may in the end strike us as on a profound level less insane than the seemingly 'normal' people of Beatrice's Alicante.

The paranoia of the supposedly sane Alibius and Alsemero has already been discussed, but there is further evidence that Alsemero confuses fact and fantasy. Reflecting on the time he first saw Beatrice, he says:

> 'Twas in the temple where I first beheld her,
> And now again the same; what omen yet
> Follows of that? None but imaginary;
> Why should my hopes or fate be timorous?
>
> (I.i.1-4)

In modern terms, one would say that Alsemero's fear is instinctive, or in part produced by the unconscious. What the dramatists show, in the play as a whole, is that such fear is not to be dismissed. Alsemero calls it 'imaginary', but his foreboding of disaster is clearly based on something real. There is a frightening quality about Beatrice which those who trust the sane part of their mind can see. Later in the play, Tomazo De Piracquo, to whose brother Alonzo Beatrice is to be married, reacts to her in a way no one else does. While Alonzo himself dotes on Beatrice without question, and her father, Vermandero, has absolutely no sense of her true feelings, Tomazo warns his brother that he sees 'small welcome in her eye' (II.i.106), and expresses his conviction that she is in love with someone else. If we took the same view of things as Alsemero does, we should have to call Tomazo's feelings purely 'imaginary', but Alsemero (or for that matter Alonzo) is wrong. In his conscious mind, he suppresses his deeper sense of the truth: surely, thus he argues, he has no hard evidence for his fear. But it is the conscious part of his mind which is wrong in its rationalization, and the more grievously so because he allows himself to be guided by one sentiment in his unconscious, and not by another. That is, he rejects his fear but yields to his lust, which, in its turn, he rationalizes by converting it, consciously, into something far more noble (in his eye) than it is. Since he cannot admit to himself that he is propelled by sex, he has to convince himself that his devotion to Beatrice is religious and pure: 'The place is holy, so is my intent' (l. 5).

That Alsemero's response to Beatrice is indeed sexual, and that he is not aware of that fact, is shown by his own words towards the end of the play where he speaks of 'the temple / Where blood and beauty first unlawfully / Tir'd their devotion, and quench'd the right one' (V.iii.73-75). At the beginning, Alsemero is not conscious of the role of 'blood and beauty'; if he had been, no doubt lawful devotion would have been triumphant, or if not he would at least have acted on sexual impulse with some understanding of its nature.

What is harmful, the dramatists suggest, is not so much the sexual impulse in itself as our suppression of it, or allowing ourselves to be led by it without knowing that we are. Thus one important function of this first speech in a play which is intensely preoccupied with what people do *not* know about their deepest feelings is that it will help us to understand the workings of Beatrice's psyche.

At first Beatrice seems almost sensible. When Alsemero declares his love for her, she pontificates:

> 　　　　　　　　Be better advis'd, sir:
> Our eyes are sentinels unto our judgments,
> And should give certain judgment what they see;
> But they are rash sometimes, and tell us wonders
> Of common things, which when our judgments find,
> They can then check the eyes, and call them blind.
>
> (I.i.71-76)

Beatrice comes from 'a good family', and knows what sort of thing she ought to say. But her words are hollow in that they are at odds with her own inclination, which is to follow what her eyes tell her, and then to persuade herself that she is not led by them, but by sound judgement. Thus, in an aside a little later, she expresses regret about the fact that she allowed herself to be engaged to Alonzo five days before, saying: 'Sure mine eyes were mistaken, / This was the man was meant me' (ll. 84-85). But the thoughtful reader realizes that there is no reason for believing that her eyes have any more judgement this time than before. Beatrice is driven by a sexual impulse which she has even more trouble in recognizing than Alsemero, and which is stronger.

Having shifted from Alonzo to Alsemero, her impulse moves quite easily to the ugly De Flores, her father's servant. Most readers accept Beatrice's vehement criticism of him at face value. Yet De Flores undoubtedly has a good point when he thinks that 'She knows no cause for't' (l. 107). Beatrice indeed knows no cause for detesting De Flores, as (unbeknown to him and to herself) she is sexually attracted to him; her protestations of revulsion, in their very intensity, are actually manifestations of the emotion which she is dangerously unaware of. Her eroticism is obvious to us, though, when at the end of the scene she says to herself 'Not this serpent gone yet?' and then drops a glove (l. 225). The serpent, De Flores, is of course associated with the Garden of Eden (which Alsemero thinks of at the beginning). In her conscious mind, Beatrice rejects him as evil. Yet, unconsciously, she is drawn to him, and she shows this by taking off a piece of clothing which tempts him, just as, on an unconscious level, he tempts her. The image of the serpent is particularly appropriate because a serpent can lose its skin, and this process is matched by Beatrice when she peels off her glove. It is clear that she is not aware of what she has done because her father has to alert her to the fact that the glove has fallen. Significantly (to us, though not to him), Vermandero instructs De Flores to pick it up for her. This incites Beatrice to rail against De Flores, but she takes off her other glove as well, and throws that down too, urging him: 'Take'em and draw thine own skin off with'em' (l. 230). Having responded to the serpent by stripping, Beatrice now urges De Flores to engage in a similar act and thus to reinvigorate himself, to establish as a reality the potential to which she had reacted.

De Flores in part grasps what she is about:

> Here's a favour come, with a mischief! Now I know
> She had rather wear my pelt tann'd in a pair
> Of dancing pumps, than I should thrust my fingers
> Into her sockets here . . .
>
> (231-34)

Although he misinterprets Beatrice's unconscious attitude to him, he is right to see a relationship between the gloves and Beatrice's sexuality. He fails to understand that Beatrice actually does want him to thrust into her, but he nevertheless realizes that her actions are sexually symbolic. The word 'thrust' will be used in a similarly sexual sense later, when in the next scene (I.ii) Alibius and Lollio agree that it would be undesirable if another lover were to thrust into the ring which Alibius wears at present on his own finger (i.e. Isabella). Here, again, the image of the finger is phallic, as it will be later in the play (with the ring once again representing the vagina) when De Flores kills Alonzo, and gives Beatrice the finger which he has cut off, having the ring on it which she had sent to Alonzo as a first token (cf. III.iv).

In general, critics have by now come to see this network of symbolism for what it is, in sexual terms.[5] What they have not understood, however, is how the dramatists use this symbolism to bring out the fact that a person may feel and/or do something which he/she is not conscious of, and that that way madness lies. In this respect, De Flores is more aware than Beatrice, but certainly not completely so. Thus he sees his own fingers as phallic in relation to Beatrice's 'sockets', but later he does not comprehend that Alonzo's finger and the ring on it are also sexually symbolic, let alone work out the consequent implications. If he did, he would understand that he cuts off Alonzo's finger because the latter is his sexual rival, and that he offers the finger and the ring to Beatrice in order to assert his male supremacy over her as well as Alonzo. He would also see that in his own mind violence and sex are closely related. He is notably less mad than Beatrice because he knows better what drives him, but he does not know enough.

Still, it is Beatrice who is especially lacking in insight, who lives most in a fantasy world and who is thus, to use the modern word, more clearly 'psychotic'.

By the end of I.ii, Beatrice has revealed her unconscious sexual drive towards De Flores. In her conscious mind, however, she remains attracted to Alsemero, and

this leads her to invite De Flores to kill Alonzo—her official fiancé—on her behalf. We thus find her flattering De Flores in II.ii. This has an unfortunate effect upon De Flores of which she is totally unaware: De Flores understands that he himself is a sexual creature, but misinterprets Beatrice's attitude towards him as showing that she too is consciously aroused. It may well be, of course, that Beatrice genuinely finds it easier to flirt with De Flores because of the unconscious passion which she has been developing towards him. But such knowledge is not in her conscious mind, which still rejects De Flores, and the latter is dangerously deluded in supposing that she seeks his help in killing Alonzo because she wishes to seek a union with him. In fact, at the end of this scene, both characters are revealed as living in a fantasy world. Beatrice thinks that she will be able to rid herself of Alonzo and De Flores 'at one time'—the former by his death, the latter by being bribed to live elsewhere. De Flores imagines her in his arms already. Even so, this flight of fancy is more firmly rooted in reality than Beatrice's notion that she can expect him to kill Alonzo for her and that she can flatter him without intensifying his longing for her, which she had known of all along. De Flores engages in some wishful thinking when interpreting her actions, but it is understandable that he takes seriously such things as her statement that he looks much better than he used to, her touching him, her calling him 'my De Flores', and so on. Although his view of Beatrice is onesided, De Flores does make an effort to interpret her words and actions; Beatrice herself, by contrast, is so exclusively absorbed by her own preoccupations that she altogether fails to understand what goes on inside De Flores. She is more drastically divorced from the reality outside her than he.

To her, murder is merely something one thinks out in the abstract, not something which exists in reality, and when De Flores shows her the finger with the ring upon it in III.iv, she exclaims: 'Bless me! What hast thou done?', to which De Flores replies: 'Why, is that more / Than killing the whole man?' (ll. 29-30). Beatrice's conventional 'Bless me' is typical, not only in being ironically inappropriate but in being unconsciously so. Her sense of shock is not unfittingly dealt with by De Flores. He makes her aware, in this scene, that she cannot claim to be any less guilty of the murder than he is, though she would sooner forget the fact of her involvement. I do not mean, of course, that De Flores's line of reasoning towards her is altogether sound. Contrary to what he suggests, we may resist his implication that because she is 'dipp'd in blood' she should not 'talk of sexual modesty' (l. 126). Although he is right to insist that she has been a whore in her affection towards Alonzo (l. 142), it does not follow that she must now have intercourse with him. Even so, there is a more compelling kind of logic in these utterings than in Beatrice's feeble reactions to them. For example, there is—given the fact that she is an accomplice in the murder—very little sanity in her argument that De Flores should keep his distance because of the difference in class between them (cf. l. 130 ff.).

However, Beatrice's yielding to De Flores at the end of the scene comes easily less because of De Flores's arguments *per se* than because she had shared her sexual intensity and violence with him well before the scene, albeit unknowingly. Even if her sexual feeling had been only for Alsemero, the fact that she is prepared to engage in murder to satisfy it would have made her like De Flores, who kills Alonzo because he believes that that will enable him to satisfy his lust for her. But it is not only the similarity of sentiment which is important: De Flores and Beatrice have become obvious partners because, unconsciously, Beatrice has reciprocated his feeling for her when throwing down her gloves. If we insist on misreading the play as though Beatrice is conscious of what she is doing, her surrender to De Flores will continue to strike us as 'unrealistic'. The scene makes perfect sense, however, if we understand that De Flores's arguments merely bring into action a deep current of sexual feeling for him of which Beatrice had not been aware. At the end of this scene, her sexual enjoyment is obvious from De Flores's famous remark, ''Las, how the turtle pants!'.

All this does not mean that Beatrice has now reached an adequate understanding of herself. The fact that she engages in sexual action and enjoys it does not produce in her any greater consciousness of her psychological make-up. To protect her position she thinks up the absurd scheme of letting her maid Diaphanta substitute for her on her wedding night. Eventually, an action like this is of course certain to be unsuccessful because it is incompatible with what reality will normally allow to happen. As it is, the plan fails even if not in the way one expects: Alsemero does not recognize his 'bride', but Diaphanta is in her turn carried away by her lust, and stays with Alsemero beyond midnight, when she is meant to leave him so that Beatrice can replace her. What is more important than the potency of Diaphanta's sexuality, however, is the state of Beatrice's mind.

When Beatrice initially thought up this scheme, she did so because she did not want Alsemero to detect that she had lost her virginity. In her conscious mind, she continues yet more emphatically to do what she thinks society demands even now that she has followed the true inclination of her 'blood'. She is still not willing to admit that inclination to herself. What she makes herself believe is that she is an honest, respectable person, and this comes particularly to the fore in Act V which starts with the following speech by Beatrice:

> One struck, and yet she lies by't!—Oh my fears!
> This strumpet serves her own ends, 'tis apparent now,

> Devours the pleasure with a greedy appetite,
> And never minds my honour or my peace,
> Makes havoc of my right; but she pays dearly for't:
> No trusting of her life with such a secret,
> That cannot rule her blood to keep her promise.
> Beside, I have some suspicion of her faith to me
> Because I was suspected of my lord,
> And it must come from her,—hark, by my horrors,
> Another clock strikes two.

The measure of Beatrice's insanity here lies in the extent to which she deludes herself about feelings and actions which she imputes to Diaphanta when she should recognize them as her own. Diaphanta has no status as a 'strumpet', but Beatrice had shown herself a whore in her affection, as De Flores puts it (III.iv.142), by switching from Alonzo to Alsemero. Now that she has a sexual relationship with De Flores, begun even before her marriage to Alsemero, there can be no doubt that the word 'strumpet' is more applicable to her than to Diaphanta. She accuses Diaphanta of a 'greedy appetite' because that is what she has herself, though significantly she will not admit that to her conscious mind. Her talk about Diaphanta not minding her 'honour' shows just how confused she is about what she is doing. A 'normal' person might try to keep up appearances while aware of her own sin; Beatrice, by contrast, has persuaded herself that it is Diaphanta who is sinning while there is nothing wrong with her own actions. Again, it is Beatrice herself rather than Diaphanta who 'cannot rule her blood to keep her promise', first to Alonzo, then to Alsemero. She even appears to believe that Diaphanta may have had a prior sexual relationship with Alsemero because the latter tests her chastity in IV. ii. Her staggering ability to avoid seeing the truth about herself can only be explained on the assumption that she is insane. Indeed, she is insane exactly because she cannot see the truth about herself, and thus comes to invent a 'reality' which does not exist.

De Flores's grasp on reality is not perfect either. The lustful relationship between him and Beatrice has now become habitual, and, to protect what he calls 'Our pleasure and continuance' (l. 50), he proposes to set fire to part of Diaphanta's chamber, in order to wake up the household (which then presumably would create such chaos that none would realize that Diaphanta had been in Alsemero's bed). As even Beatrice realizes, this may 'endanger the whole house' (l. 33). It seems likely that the dramatists wish us to see the fire as symbolic of the sexual passion of the lovers, which De Flores is more dominated by than he knows. Although he does at least acknowledge that his relationship with Beatrice gives him 'pleasure', he appears to be unaware that it is clouding his judgement. In fact, he now appears to be influenced by Beatrice's psychology, for he counters her fear that he may endanger the whole house with the statement: 'You talk of danger when your fame's on fire?'.

The reference to her 'fame' immediately and tellingly distracts Beatrice's mind from the possibility that the whole house may get burnt, and her reaction is simply: 'That's true; do what thou wilt now'. De Flores explains to her that either the others will think that Diaphanta has escaped from her room because of the fire, or, if she hastens back towards her own lodging, he will shoot her there. This solicitude for her welfare prompts Beatrice to say:

> I'm forc'd to love thee now,
> 'Cause thou provid'st so carefully for my honour.
>
> (47-48)

Such a statement, in such a situation, does not proceed from a 'normal' person who is merely lying; it shows the confusion and self-deceit of a sick mind. One of the many interesting implications here is that Beatrice is now beginning to seek a rationalization for her love for De Flores rather than Alsemero. Similarly when the fire has been discovered, Beatrice exclaims:

> Already? How rare is that man's speed!
> How heartily he serves me! His face loathes one,
> But look upon his care, who would not love him?
> The east is not more beauteous than his service.
>
> (69-72)

And, in fact, De Flores's plot works, so that for the time being she can continue to live in her fantasy world. But Jasperino, Alsemero's servant who in IV.ii had already informed his master of the illicit relationship between De Flores and Beatrice, now produces the proof which had then been lacking. Thus V.iii opens with Jasperino's statement:

> Your confidence, I'm sure, is now of proof.
> The prospect from the garden has show'd
> Enough for deep suspicion.

When Alsemero, acting on what he has seen, accuses Beatrice of being a whore, she replies:

> What a horrid sound it hath!
> It blasts a beauty to deformity;
> Upon what face soever that breath falls,
> It strikes it ugly: oh, you have ruin'd
> What you can ne'er repair again.
>
> (31-35)

Typically, and madly, Beatrice is preoccupied with the 'sound' of the word 'whore', not with the content as it applies to her—indeed, she makes out that it is Alsemero who is doing her harm by using such an ugly word, and her words are those of a person who is lying to herself rather than to him. She tries to evade the reality which lies behind the word, as though the two can be separated.

Even when the truth comes closer to her, she still tries to turn it away and into something different. Amazingly, she comes to boast of the murder of Alonzo as some-thing caused by her love for Alsemero; and she sees similar virtue in her having 'kiss'd poison for't, strok'd a serpent' (l. 66). Strikingly, she now begins once again to deny her feelings for De Flores, and indeed it does not take her long to persuade herself that she has been loyal to Alsemero all along. In her conception of things, that loyalty is compatible with the sexual relationship which she has just confessed to having, and thus she no doubt believes her own falsehood when she says to Alsemero:

> Remember I am true unto your bed.
>
> (82)

Shortly afterwards, however, she experiences a rare moment of insight, and then admits:

> Alsemero, I am a stranger to your bed.
>
> (159)

By this time, De Flores has spoken openly about their misdeeds to Alsemero, who has locked up the pair in his closet. What happens here appears to be hinted at quite plainly in the text. Tomazo, Alonzo's brother, comes to seek recompense for 'murder and adultery' (l. 138). What he refers to, of course, is Alonzo's murder, and the adultery which he supposes Alsemero has committed by marrying Beatrice. But exactly as the words 'murder and adultery' are spoken, Beatrice, in the closet, is heard to utter 'Oh, oh, oh!', and Alsemero comments 'Hark, 'tis coming to you'. What he means, surely, is that at this very moment adultery is coming to Tomazo because De Flores and Beatrice are having intercourse, while at the same time De Flores is killing her. Again, sex and violence are combined.

Bizarre though the episode is, it shocks Beatrice into recognition of reality, and she is thus able to say to her father:

> Oh come not near me, sir, I shall defile you:
> I am that of your blood was taken from you
> For your better health . . .
>
> (149-51)

At last, Beatrice herself confirms to us what, at a deep level, has been plain throughout the play: that *she* is the changeling, not Antonio, to whom that role is assigned in the Dramatis Personae. Antonio is no more than a counterfeit fool, and that must mean that, as the sub-plot and the main plot are ironically related, the real changeling is a person who is genuinely mad. That person, as the text abundantly illustrates, is Beatrice. A changeling in the seventeenth century was an ugly or mentally deficient child which the fairies left in the place of a normal child which they stole, but this meaning is given an ironic twist by the dramatists. What the fairies had taken away from Beatrice's father when she was born was bad blood. If his daughter had not been born to become insane, no doubt he would have become so. Put differently: the price for his own normality is Beatrice's madness, with which he is now painfully confronted. His apparently angelic daughter turns out to be an ugly, insane changeling.

Is there some structure of contemporary thought—to be found in treatises on madness and the like—to which the play appears to correspond? Such an approach always has its dangers, since literature—particularly good literature—is a good deal more exploratory than any system which may be part of it, which it seeks to modify, or even to undermine. But an approach through 'background' is particularly unhelpful in the case of *The Changeling.* The more familiar medieval and Renaissance ways of thinking with respect to manifestations of abnormality are really not much to the point. The humoral theory is altogether too physical in its emphasis. According to this view, there would be an imbalance in the four humours (fluids) in Beatrice's body, and normality could be restored by the removal of the imbalance. While there is the odd reference to the humoral theory in the play, there is no indication that the dramatists believe that Beatrice could be successfully treated by this method. The dramatists clearly see the development of her madness in mental rather than physical terms.

The fascination with 'melancholy' as madness, best known to most of us through Robert Burton's *Anatomy of Melancholy* (which appeared in 1621, just before *The Changeling* was licensed in 1622), is not one which Middleton and Rowley seem to share. A study of that book, and of earlier ones dealing with melancholy, does not give us much insight into what these dramatists are doing. It does help us to understand certain characters in Renaissance literature, of course, such as Hamlet (partly) or those who adopted a melancholy pose as a matter of fashion, such as the melancholy Jaques. Admittedly the term 'melancholy' could be very far stretched by those who used it, and certain analysts saw a tendency to false imaginings as a characteristic of melancholy. Nevertheless, the typical melancholic is more conspicuously mad than Beatrice, and in quite a different way—her mood is not the sombre, despairing one of the melancholic.

Many writers saw madness of a fiercer and more passionate kind than melancholy (as well as melancholy itself) in religious terms: a mad person was 'possessed' by the devil. Although our dramatists certainly see madness as evil, and although the image of the serpent is of course associated with the devil, they obviously do not view Beatrice as just another witch.

The early seventeenth century was a time of great change, and many of the older beliefs were beginning to crack. The many contemporary tracts which deal in some way with madness do not offer any simple picture of what madness was held to be, how it was supposed to originate, or how it could be treated. A good comprehensive book on the subject still remains to be written, but it would certainly show that there were people who believed that madness could not be satisfactorily explained in terms of humoral theory, melancholy, or witchcraft. No treatise that I have seen, however, comes even remotely close to presenting a view so complex, coherent, profound and persuasive as that which is embodied in *The Changeling.* One must add that there were other literary writers, notably dramatists—Shakespeare, and particularly Webster and Ford come to mind—who appear to have made a remarkable contribution to the understanding of madness, well ahead of the 'professionals' such as members of the clergy and medical men. But *The Changeling,* in my view, is a more crucial play in this regard than any of the others, and this is one reason why it is so necessary for us to see clearly what it is about.

Notes

1. The following selection of recent discussions is particularly pertinent to my approach; Christopher Ricks, 'The Moral and Poetic Structure of *The Changeling*', *Essays in Criticism,* 10 (1960), 290-306; Normand Berlin, 'The "Finger" Image and Relationship of Character in *The Changeling*', *English Studies in Africa,* 12 (1969), 162-66; Robert Jordan, 'Myth and Psychology in *The Changeling*', *Renaissance Drama* n.s. III (1970), 157-65; S. Gorley Putt, 'The Tormented World of Middleton', *Times Literary Supplement* (August 2, 1974), 833-34; Penelope B. R. Doob, 'A Reading of *The Changeling*', *English Literary Renaissance* III (1973), 183-206; Joseph M. Duffy, 'Madhouse Optics: *The Changeling*', *Comparative Drama,* 8 (1974), 184-97; Emil Roy, 'Sexual Paradox in *The Changeling*', *Literature and Psychology,* XXX (1975), 124-32; J. L. Simmons, 'Diabolical Realism in Middleton and Rowley's *The Changeling*', *Renaissance Drama* n.s. XI (1980), 135-70; Peter Morrison, 'A Cangoun in Zombieland: Middleton's Tetralogical *Changeling*', in Kenneth Friedenreich ed., *'Accompaninge the players'—Essays Celebrating Thomas Middleton, 1580-1980* (New York, 1983), 219-41; Ann Pasternak Slater, 'Hypallage, Barley-Break, and *The Changeling*', *The Review of English Studies,* n.s. XXXIV (1983), 429-40; Charles W. Crupi, 'The Transformation of De Flores in *The Changeling*', *Neophilologus* 68 (1984), 142-49.

2. All references are to the edition of *The Changeling* by N. W. Bawcutt (1958), which from a scholarly point of view remains the best. Critically, Bawcutt is less satisfying. Thus he begins to move in the direction that he should when consid-

ering the relationship between the sub-plot and the main plot, but, like other critics, abandons his search exactly when he needs to press on with it (cf. particularly p. lxvii of his Introduction). Other editors fare no better—see e.g. Kenneth Muir in his Thomas Middleton, *Three Plays* (1975), p. xii.

3. 'Ring' in the sense of 'female pudenda' was common—see Eric Partridge, *A Dictionary of Slang and Unconventional English* 8th ed., rev. Paul Beale (1984).

4. Cf. the unpublished thesis by James Knight (supervised by Dr Francis Brooks), 'Images of Madness in England in the Late Sixteenth and Early Seventeenth Centuries' (Flinders University of South Australia, 1982), p. 34, with quotations from another thesis, by R. Neugebauer, 'Mental Illness and Government Policy in 16th Century and 17th Century England' (Columbia University, 1976), p. 13. The latter contains a detailed examination of the workings of the Court of Wards and Liveries. References to many of the tracts in the Renaissance which concerned themselves with questions of madness can be found in such books as R. Hunter and I. MacAlpine, *300 Years of Psychiatry 1535-1860: A History Presented in Selected English Texts* (1963); Bridget Lyons, *Voices of Melancholy: Studies in Literary Treatments of Melancholy in Renaissance England* (1971); Robert Shenk, *The Sinner's Progress: A Study of Madness in English Renaissance Drama* (1978); V. Skultans, *English Madness: Ideas on Insanity, 1580-1890* (1979).

5. See notably Berlin's excellent article, although some of his successors, too, comment on the issue here and there.

Cristina Malcolmson (essay date spring 1990)

SOURCE: Malcolmson, Cristina. "'As Tame as the Ladies': Politics and Gender in *The Changeling*." *English Literary Renaissance* 20, no. 2 (spring 1990): 320-39.

[In the following essay, Malcolmson argues that although in The Changeling *Middleton engaged in a critique of state policy and power, his work is still patriarchal in that it examines hierarchical relations in terms of male dominance and subjugation of the female.]*

In their recent books on seventeenth-century drama, Margot Heinemann and Jonathan Dollimore have characterized Thomas Middleton as a Puritan writing "opposition drama" and a playwright composing "radical tragedy." Heinemann sees Middleton appealing to and encouraging "'anti-establishment,' generally Parliamentary Puritan sympathies." Dollimore understands Jacobean dramatists to be engaged in the "demystification of state power and ideology," and a "contemporary critique of power relations." Both encourage critics to identify drama during this period as potentially subversive, and to recognize the extent to which plays by Middleton and others actively stimulated, as Dollimore puts it, "the crisis in confidence in the integrity of those in power."[1]

My argument will depend on these claims, but also qualify them. I hope to demonstrate that Thomas Middleton appealed to Parliamentary opposition to Stuart policy by objecting to James's plans for a Spanish marriage two years before *A Game at Chesse,* in fact in *The Changeling* in 1622.[2] But the strategy of *The Changeling* suggests that Middleton's work is far more patriarchal in a traditional sense than these characterizations would imply. *The Changeling* examines hierarchical relations in terms of male control over women and the institution of marriage, and in doing so subverts its own potential for a truly radical critique of "state power and ideology."

In January 1622, King James suspended Parliament and imprisoned several members because they advised him against planning a marriage for his son Charles to a Spanish Catholic princess. In May 1622, Middleton and Rowley presented *The Changeling,* a play which represents Spanish intrigue and villainy, as well as the repressive use of autocratic government. In the play's first scene the Spanish aristocrats Vermandero and Alsemero refer to their enemies as "those rebellious Hollanders," the Protestant Dutch who had in 1621 renewed their battle with Spain for religious and political independence.[3] The phrase "rebellious Hollanders" would remind a contemporary audience of the refusal by King James to create a strong Protestant coalition between the Netherlands, England, and Germany in order to fight Spain and the European Catholic powers, and it would also suggest that "rebellion" in this play is not necessarily wicked—that the language of authority could be used to justify religious and political repression. *The Changeling* was put on by the players patronized by Elizabeth of Bohemia, King James's daughter and the wife of Frederick of Bohemia. To English Protestants, Elizabeth and Frederick represented the European Protestant cause, and their position in Europe was felt to be severely jeopardized by a marriage between Prince Charles and the Spanish Infanta. Heinemann has shown that Middleton's city pageants and masques during this period made veiled references to the danger of a Catholic queen to the English church.[4] Middleton and Rowley do the same in *The Changeling,* not only in the play's portrait of Spanish degeneracy, but also in its questioning of those in power, whether master, father, husband, or king.

The play is made up of a series of rebellions: Beatrice-Joanna plots against her father's plans for her marriage, and de Flores plots against his master in order to sleep with Beatrice-Joanna; in the subplot Lollio plots against his master in order to sleep with his wife Isabella, and Isabella plots against her husband and his servant in order to maintain her freedom and integrity. In almost every case we are encouraged to see the justice of such rebellion since those in authority are abusing their responsibility. The play ruthlessly examines hierarchical relations and exposes them as relations of power; individuals are socially superior to others not because of their higher intelligence or morality, but because of the arbitrary factors of birth and gender and because of the use of force. At important moments in this play, women are morally and intellectually superior to men, servants to masters, and the members of the middle classes to the aristocracy. The play appears to be dismantling the principle of hierarchy.

The implications of this mode of gender and political analysis would be disastrous for Stuart theories of government. When Parliament petitioned James to stop negotiations for the Spanish match in December 1621, James's imprisonment of members of Parliament and his published declarations enforced the difference between king and subject, the ruler and the ruled. He defined the petition as an attack on his royal prerogative and an example of insolent disrespect for "what appertaineth to the height of a powerful Monarch." James accused Parliament of using "Anti-monarchical words," and invading his royal power: the petition was "an usurpation that the Majesty of a King can by no meanes endure." He insisted that his position of authority lifted him above the criticism or advice of those beneath him: "We needed not to bee measured by any other rule, but our own Princely will."[5] *The Changeling* suggests that such definitions of difference between higher and lower are often merely assertions of will, whether princely or otherwise. When the daughter Beatrice-Joanna and the servant de Flores begin their plotting at the end of the first scene of the play, they mark it by such an assertion: "I'll have my will" (1.1.216, 233). But the conventional association of willfulness with rebellion is undermined in this play by the fact that Vermandero, Beatrice-Joanna's father, has already expressed himself in these very words about his choice of a husband for his daughter: "I'll want / My will else" (1.1.215-16). The difference between ruler and ruled collapses here as the play reveals all individuals to be governed by an irrational willfulness; those in political or familial authority are simply more capable of enforcing it.

The play puts its dangerous political opinions in terms of sexual politics.[6] Instead of considering a repressive king who governs his country inadequately, *The Changeling* portrays repressive fathers and husbands who mistreat their daughters and wives. The play hides its political critique of the king's policy within the contemporary debate about the proper treatment of women by their male superiors. This controversy has recently been shown by many scholars to have been an exceptionally popular topic in pamphlets and on the stage, especially in the 1620s.[7] Middleton referred to this controversy in several of his plays, including *The Roaring Girl* and *Women Beware Women*.[8] In *The Changeling*, Middleton and Rowley use this controversy as a vehicle for the consideration of injustice and rebellion, but at a safe distance. In the analysis that follows I hope to show that by centering the play upon the debate about women, the writers not only protect themselves from political censure, they protect themselves and their audience from the implications of their own demystifications of power.

Middleton and Rowley use the contemporary debate about women to structure the play through their contrast between the main plot and the subplot, between the characters of Beatrice-Joanna and Isabella. The play considers the statement made by one of the participants in the debate, Joseph Swetnam, who wrote a pamphlet called *The Arraignment of Lewd, Idle, Froward, and Unconstant Women*, published in 1615: "Women are all necessary evils, . . . [Moses] also saith, That [women] were made of the Rib of a Man; and that their *froward nature* sheweth, for a Rib is a crooked thing, good for nothing else; and Women are crooked by Nature."[9] The defenders of women who answered Swetnam, like Rachel Speght in *A Mouzell for Melastomus, The Cynical Baytor of, and foule mouthed Barker against Evahs Sex* (1617) and Esther Sowernam in *Esther hath hanged Haman* (1617), argued that women were not pernicious by nature, but that, as Speght put it, "of men and women, there are two sorts, namely, good and bad.[10] *The Changeling* presents the good and the bad, not only in the contrast between Isabella and Beatrice-Joanna, but in the ethical differences in the men in the play. *The Changeling* in fact argues that women are not innately evil, that their moral character is as complex as a man's, and that, whereas a morally weak woman like Beatrice-Joanna can become a monster, a strong woman like Isabella can fully protect her integrity.

The play sets up the issue by putting its two female characters under the press of circumstances that are strikingly similar: both are imprisoned by the institution of marriage and the authority of their patriarchal guardians. This was a central question for the defenders of women in the controversy: to what extent is marriage a form of male tyranny? "Husbands should not consider their wives as their vassals," says Rachel Speght, "but as those that are heirs together of the grace of life."[11] Also central to the debate during this period was the problem of early or forced marriages, in which parents arranged their children's matches before they had come of age, or forced them to marry against their will. In Middleton's **Women Beware Women,** when Isabella's father compels her to marry a man unknown to her, she complains:

> Oh the heart-breakings
> Of miserable maids, where love's enforced!
> The best condition is but bad enough:
> When women have their choices, commonly
> They do but buy their thralldoms, and bring great portions
> To men to keep 'em in subjection . . .
> Men buy their slaves, but women buy their masters.[12]

The evidence that many considered forced and early marriages to be unjust comes not only from the drama of the period: Thomas Overbury attributes to King James the remark that "Parents may forbid their children an unfitt marriage, but they may not force their consciences to a fitt."[13]

The major cause for public concern about this problem was not so much a new sympathy for the plight of women, but the recent annulment of the early marriage between the Earl of Essex and Frances Howard (in 1613) followed in 1615 by the murder trial of Frances Howard and her new husband, the Earl of Somerset, for the poisoning of Thomas Overbury. Frances had been married to Essex when she was thirteen, and had later become involved with Robert Carr, the King's favorite, soon to be Earl of Somerset. Thomas Overbury, Carr's advisor and friend, was an outspoken critic against the match between Carr and Howard, and was found poisoned in the Tower just before the annulment of the Countess' first marriage. Somerset and the Countess were both found guilty of the murder, but it was clear from the trial that Frances herself had instigated the crime.[14] Much of the controversy about women was influenced by this scandal: Frances Howard lies behind the figure of the "masculine woman" in many of these tracts, including the famous *Hic Mulier, or the Man-Woman,* which condemned the masculine dress of the female aristocrat, as well as her desire to be a "man in action by pursuing revenge."[15] Swetnam models his image of the beautiful but villainous female on the Countess, and critics have argued that Frances Howard provided the model for Beatrice-Joanna in **The Changeling.**[16] The similarities between Beatrice-Joanna and Frances Howard are too striking to ignore: aside from the murder, the Countess had to undergo a chastity test to obtain her annulment, the positive results of which were widely distrusted. According to rumor, the Countess sent one of her cousins, veiled, to take the test for her. But even those who condemned women in general because of the Countess' murder recognized that her crime was in part the result of the injustice of an early marriage. The notorious Swetnam himself admits: "when Matches are made by the Parents, and the

Dowery told and paid before the young Couple have any knowledge of it, and so many times are forced against their Minds, fearing the Rigour and Displeasure of their Parents, they often promise with their Mouths, and they refuse with their Hearts."[17]

The Changeling itself is quite explicit in its depiction of this problem. In analyses of the opening scene critics have focused on Beatrice-Joanna's inconstancy of affection as she shifts her attentions from Piracquo to Alsemero, but they largely ignore her father's aggressive assertion of his control over her future. Vermandero speaks about Piracquo, his original choice for the marriage:

> I would not change him for a son-in-law
> For any he in Spain, the proudest he,
> And we have great ones, that you know . . .
> He shall be bound to me
> As fast as this tie can hold him; I'll want
> My will else.

> (1.1.211-16)

Beatrice-Joanna disappears in this formulation, except as a "tie," a symbol for the alliance between her father and her fiancé. The next scene makes visible the domineering willfulness of Vermandero through the explicitly coercive control of the old doctor Alibius, who imprisons his wife Isabella within his asylum to protect her chastity and puts her under the supervision of his servant Lollio. Both scenes unmask not only the authoritarian use of power by father and husband, they define this power as the capacity of men to control the sexuality of women. In graphic phallic imagery, Alibius defines his marriage ring and the finger that wears it in terms of his sexual possession of Isabella. The ringed finger becomes an image for sexual intercourse: "I would wear my ring on my own finger; / Whilst it is borrowed it is none of mine / But his that useth it" (1.2.27-29).[18] For another man to have intercourse with Isabella would signal Alibius' loss of ownership of her and her capacity for generation; Alibius understands marriage as the husband's ability to determine whose finger thrusts into the ring. This pattern of imagery in the subplot echoes that presented in the main plot, when de Flores finds Beatrice's glove and fantasizes that he could "Thrust my fingers into her sockets here" (1.1.230). The brutal nature of this imagery reveals the element of force that can structure a man's relationship to a woman, and reminds us of the assertion of will that has, thus far in the play, marked the social roles of husband and father.

In an undercurrent of jokes and repeated images, the play extends this critique of male authority to all forms of hierarchical government. It suggests that those who rule are superior not because of their innate worth but because they possess the power to imprison and control. Lollio, the asylum's caretaker and Alibius' servant, hints constantly that nothing differentiates his master from himself except Alibius' greater wealth and greater foolishness, and that nothing differentiates the two of them as supervisors of the asylum from the madmen and fools they govern except their position of authority and the whip they use to control the inmates. Lollio explodes the hierarchy of authority through his comment to Tony: "there is a knave, that's my master" (1.2.186), and through his question: "how many knaves make an honest man?" Lollio answers the question himself: "There's three knaves may make an honest man: a sergeant, a jailor, and a beadle: the sergeant catches him, the jailor holds him, and the beadle lashes him; and if he be not honest then, the hangman must cure him" (1.2.157-58, 161-64). Honesty here is simply the willingness to obey knaves in positions of authority: the process of teaching morality or healing fools is simply a matter of applying the lash. This lash becomes a visible prop in later scenes, when Lollio uses the whip to control the unruly madmen.[19] Lollio's whip and the confining walls of the asylum make visible the structure of relations that govern the main plot. Alsemero's desire to insure Beatrice-Joanna's virginity through his chastity test is shown to be just another strategy of control: when he thinks she has passed the test, he says: "My Joanna, / Chaste as the breath of heaven or morning's womb / That brings the day forth, thus my love encloses thee" (4.2.149-51). The stage direction in the Regents edition repeats this image visually: "He embraces her." The embrace signals affection according to the code of love and marriage, yet is revealed here to be invested with the same assertion of will that motivates Vermandero and Alibius. This pattern of imagery has been introduced already in the subplot, not only in the imprisonment of Isabella, but through her objection to it. She speaks sarcastically to her husband: "You were best lock me up." He answers, "In my arms and bosom, my sweet Isabella, / I'll lock thee up most nearly" (3.3.244-46).

Through this imagery of enclosure, the play reveals that gender relations are constituted through the use of force symbolized by Lollio's whip. In a grotesque echo of the mechanicals' play in *A Midsummer Night's Dream,* Alibius plans a dance of his madmen for the wedding night revels of Beatrice-Joanna and Alsemero. In *A Midsummer Night's Dream,* Snout comically worries if the actor playing the lion will be so lifelike that he will terrify the ladies present; in *The Changeling,* Alibius fears that his madmen will "Affright the ladies; they are nice things, you know" (4.3.59).[20] Lollio's response corrects his master's overly reverent sense of the delicate "court lady" by making explicit the analogy between the imprisoned madmen and the women of the play, whether from the professional or aristocratic classes: "You need not fear, sir; so long as we are there with our commanding pizzles, they'll be as tame as the la-

dies themselves" (4.3.60-61). Both inmates and women are governed by a force which is explicitly masculine and brutal: the phrase "commanding pizzles" associates Lollio's whip with the male genitals and links leadership and authority with sexual aggression. In this comment the play's own gender analysis emerges: masculine action is marked not by superior rationality or morality, but by the exertion of force. Women obey male authorities as madmen obey menacing guards. Sexual politics is defined in terms of attack here: women fear the violence of "commanding pizzles" whether in bed or out, and men only know themselves as "men," sexually and politically, through the subjugation of the women associated with them.

The subplot exposes the tyranny and injustice of gender relations in the main plot and in the Renaissance institution of marriage. The analysis of sexual politics threatens continually to spill over into a generalized critique of hierarchical social relations, and brings the play remarkably close to what Jonathan Dollimore calls "a demystification of state power and ideology."

Nevertheless, the play evades its own subversive critique of those in authority by representing the effects of rebellion as far worse than tyranny. Indeed, the play's implied solution to the problems it dramatizes is nothing like political or sexual equality, but rather a patriarchy which governs more wisely and sympathetically but far more powerfully than the government exercised by Alibius and Vermandero. The need for a benevolent but potent ruler is signaled by the play's recurring image of an invasion that threatens both the city's castle and the female body.[21] The play's husbands and fathers are inadequate because they cannot protect their domain from such penetration.

Vermandero's insistence on choosing Beatrice-Joanna's husband stems from his fear about the safety of his castle. When Vermandero meets Alsemero at the beginning of the play, he hesitates to show him his citadel, since such knowledge can be abused by his enemies:

> I must know
> Your country. We use not to give survey
> Of our chief strengths to strangers; our citadels
> Are plac'd conspicuous to outward view
> On promonts' tops, but within are secrets.
>
> (1.1.157-61)

Vermandero fears invasion, and the imagery of penetration and invasion continues throughout the play: in the courtiers' penetration into Alibius' asylum, in their desire to penetrate his wife, in the "private way" through which Diaphanta leads Alsemero to Beatrice-Joanna, and in the "back part of the house" where Jasperino overhears the secret meeting between Beatrice-Joanna and de Flores. When Beatrice-Joanna's assassin de

Flores kills Piracquo deep in the heart of the castle, the imagery of rings and fingers is given new meaning: whereas in the subplot, it suggested male possessiveness of the female body, here it represents castration (3.2.25). As de Flores cuts off the ringed finger that symbolizes Piracquo's intended marriage, he essentially castrates the father's plans for his daughter, destroys her fiancé's control over his potential wife's capacity for generation, and sets Beatrice-Joanna free to determine her own partner in marriage. When de Flores insists on Beatrice-Joanna's virginity as the reward for his services, the invasion is complete: Vermandero has fully lost control over his daughter. He understands the situation in just this way when he learns of the murder of Piracquo and the alliance between Beatrice-Joanna and de Flores: "An host of enemies enter'd my citadel / Could not amaze like this" (5.3.148-49). Vermandero's citadel is not only his castle, it is Beatrice-Joanna herself, and the threat of invasion figures the father's loss of control over the female body. Critics A. L. and M. K. Kistner point out the patriarchal implications of this pattern of imagery: "Vermandero is morally responsible for the defense and protection of the castle and Beatrice, yet the latter citadel was entered, taken, and destroyed by the enemy without his knowledge."[22]

The work of anthropologists and feminists who study the institution of marriage in pre-industrial societies can offer further insight into this association of the city's castle with the female body. In his discussion of the exchange of women, Levi-Strauss states that the primary relationship established by marriage in these societies is that between two groups of men, not between man and woman: marriage "provides the means of binding men together."[23] Feminist Patricia Klindienst Joplin argues that this system of exchange lies behind the social value of chastity: "Female chastity is not sacred out of the respect for the integrity of the woman as person. . . . The virgin's hymen must not be ruptured except in some manner that reflects and ensures the health of the existing political hierarchy. The father king regulates both the literal and metaphorical 'gates' to the city's power: the actual gates in the city wall or the hymen as the gateway to the daughter's body."[24] According to this analysis, a daughter's chastity preserves the father's right to determine who his allies will be, since it is through sexual intercourse with the daughter that a husband gains access to a larger intercourse with the father's family or city. Marriage creates alliances, and entrance into the female body represents entrance into the state.

In her book *Purity and Danger,* anthropologist Mary Douglas interprets the symbolic relationship between external boundaries of the body and the state: "The body is a model which can stand for any bounded system. Its boundaries can represent any boundaries which are threatened or precarious."[25] Douglas adds to this in

her book *Natural Symbols*: "The human body is always treated as an image of society. . . . Interest in its apertures depends on the preoccupation with social exits and entrances, escape routes and invasions."[26] In an article entitled "Patriarchal Territories," Peter Stallybrass describes how the surveillance of women during the Renaissance focused on the apertures of the body, particularly the mouth and the vagina, and how the chaste woman became not only an emblem of the perfect and impermeable container, but also "a map of the integrity of the state. The state, like a virgin, was a *hortus conclusus,* an enclosed garden walled off from enemies."[27] Queen Elizabeth's virginity signified not only her own purity, but the strength and impermeability of the boundaries of the nation, particularly during the attempted Spanish invasion of the country in 1588.

In the 1620s the pamphlets written against the Spanish marriage put their fears of invasion in terms of the female body and its sexual vulnerability. In the treatise called *The Foot out of the Snare,* John Gee describes Catholic attempts to proselytize English Protestants as a form of seduction: "yet some, like Dinah the daughter of Jacob, have lost their virginity, I meane *primam et puram fidem,* their first faith, by *going abroad, and have returned home impure.*"[28] Middleton's own *A Game at Chesse* represents the Spanish corruption of the English church through the plot of the Black King to seduce the White Queen. The same play figures the Catholic attack on the individual Protestant soul through the attempted rape of the White Queen's Pawn by the Black Bishop's Pawn.[29] In these cases the vulnerable female body symbolizes the weakness of the body of the state, disturbingly open to the infiltration of foreign Catholic powers who stand ready to enter England either through "open Invaders or secret underminers." A pamphlet called *Vox Populi* describes the Catholics in England: "Besides, in a small time they should work so farre into the Body of the State, *by buying offices and the like,* whether by *Sea* or *Land,* of Justice Civil or Ecclesiastical, in *Church* or *state,* that with the helpe of the Jesuits, they would undermine [the state] with meere wit."[30]

Fears about the seductive power of Catholic priests often became quite literal. Several pamphlets warned against priests and Jesuits who persuaded young English women to enter nunneries abroad. Such a process was described as being "Nunnified," and it was often directly linked with sexual misconduct. *The Anatomy of the English Nunnery at Lisbon in Portugal* (1622) claimed that the priests had regular sexual relations with the English nuns, and called on their families to save them from "such horrible and sacriligious rapine and spoile."[31] John Gee's treatises are filled with stories of young women led astray by Catholic priests, one of whom impregnated his follower, and therefore, according to Gee, was "a fitt man to be called a Father."[32] He sums up his attack on the Jesuits as follows: "Easily can they steal away *the hearts of the weaker sort*: and secretly do they creep into houses, *leading captive simple women loaden with sinnes and led away with divers lusts*."[33] Invasion into the female body, like invasion into "the house" of an Englishman, represents the permeability of the country's boundaries as well as its private spaces. Female sensuality represents that part of the country that Protestants cannot control, those consciences and households which elude state regulation.

A few treatises refer to unnamed but specific women in England who work as spies for the Catholic cause. As agents of Count Gondomar, the Spanish ambassador, these women are imagined as both vulnerable to Spanish manipulation and capable of extreme violence in carrying out Spanish plots. In *A Game at Chesse* the Black Knight is characterized as having "wrought / Women's soft soules e'en up to masculine Malice / To persue truth to death if the cause rowzed 'em."[34] *Vox Populi* refers to an unnamed Catholic priest in England who is particularly able to "serve himself into the closet of the heart, and to worke upon feminine levitie, who [that is, the women] in that Countrie have masculine Spirits to command and pursue their plots unto death."[35] Such references to "masculine malice" and "masculine spirits" recall the figure of Hic Mulier, the proud woman who dresses like a man, and who wishes to be a "man in action by pursuing revenge." Like the detractors of women in the current controversy, the writers of these pamphlets against the Spanish marriage measure the need for a strong patriarchal governor through the "unruliness" of women who move beyond the limits of conventional notions of gender. But the paradoxical association of vulnerability with aggressive and violent action in the masculine woman also suggests that the fear behind this gendered imagery is not only about the invasion of the country but about specific women as well.

It is not a coincidence that many observers at the time felt that France Howard's murder of Thomas Overbury was part of a complex plot initiated by her family, the Catholic Howards, to gain control over the King's favorite, Carr, and therefore, over the King. Frances' uncle, Henry Howard, the Earl of Northumberland, was known to be receiving a pension from the Spanish, and he had been actively working toward the success of the marriage between Prince Charles and the Infanta. Soon after Carr's marriage with Frances Howard, Carr made direct overtures to the Spanish ambassador on behalf of this marriage. Many Protestants felt that Overbury was sacrificed to insure that such negotiations could go forward. During the Overbury murder trial, Sir Edward Coke made it clear that he suspected a Catholic plot.[36]

The association of women with Spanish infiltration in the literature on the subject articulates a powerful fear about another specific woman: the Spanish princess, who as queen would be the mother to the future English king, and under whose Spanish Catholic influence the child would be reared.[37] Like Queen Mary, the Spanish Infanta was seen as the avenue through which the Catholic Church and the Spanish empire would enter the English state and rob it of its national strength. As the pamphlet put it, "If you can bring in the *Infanta,* doubt you not but she will usher in the Pope, and consequently hee the Catholic King."[38] Although explicit attacks on the Infanta are rare in this literature, the overwhelming disturbance about the infidelity of women to the English cause and their vulnerability to Spanish influence suggests a powerful suspicion that the Infanta would be politically and religiously, if not sexually, unfaithful to her husband. In 1645, William Prynne explicitly articulates what this literature implies. He speaks of Spanish hostility to England: "they fixed at last of latter times upon a more prevalent and successful meanes than any of the former; to wit, a project of *marrying us to the Whore of Rome* by matching the heire of the crowne of England to a *Romanist*."[39] Here the association of the Catholic Church with the Infanta almost becomes literal—like the Church, she is the whore of Rome, whose infidelity to the English cause is inevitable.

The proper response to the Spanish threat, according to these writers, was for King James to act like a man. Fearing the emasculation of the English nation through a Catholic queen, these pamphlets did not call for a curtailing of the King's power, nor for an increase in the capacity of his subjects or of Parliament to govern themselves, but for a more aggressive exercise and enforcement of male patriarchal authority. This meant war with Spain, and James was called on to give up his negotiations and strike first. One pamphlet states, "Tell [King James] that [which] Agesileus said, that words are feminine and deedes masculine, and that it is a great part of honour, discretion, and happiness for a Prince, to give the first blow to his Enemies. . . . King Phillip [of Spain] loves King James for his Gowne and Pen, yet no way feares his sword."[40] These pamphlets argue that the English upper classes had become effeminate through the long period of peace and the decadence of court life with its "Stage-Playes, Maskes, Revels and Carrowsing."[41] As the *Vox Populi* puts it, "Thus stands the state of that poore miserable Countrey, which had never *more people and fewer men*."[42]

In his works on kingship James regularly described himself as a father and a husband to his country. In one of his addresses to Parliament he said, "I am the Husband, and all the whole Isle is my lawfull Wife."[43] The literature against the Spanish marriage warned that this royal husband was neglecting his responsibilities, responsibilities which were imagined in a fully patriarchal way: the King must protect the purity of the country just as a husband and father must protect the chastity of a virgin daughter and a wife. Such protection requires the maintenance of one's "potency," and this included the capacity to defend the boundaries of the state: the English navy is defined in these pamphlets as the "Bulwarkes and walls of England," but also as having become "impotent" through the decay of its strength.[44] King James's status as a powerful and loving father is questioned because of his inability to protect his daughter, the Queen of Bohemia, and her husband, from the incursion of the European Catholic powers and from the loss of their patrimony, the Palatinate.[45] According to these Protestants, James was unaware and therefore vulnerable to the machinations of the Spanish, whose plots reached even into the private spaces of the country. The murder of Thomas Overbury, like the murder of Piracquo in *The Changeling,* took place in the city's fortified citadel, the Tower, and represented an invasion into the heart of English national strength. Many were shocked when King James pardoned the Countess and her husband, kept them in prison until January 1622, and then allowed them to retire to their country estate. Many had been shocked when King James failed to defend the Earl of Essex, Frances Howard's first husband, from the charge of impotency she leveled at him at the annulment trial. It could be argued that *The Changeling* attacks aristocratic degeneracy through its portrait of the corrupt Beatrice-Joanna, modeled on the figure of Frances Howard, especially in contrast to the virtuous, middle-class Isabella. But for the play, as for the opponents of the King's policy in Parliament, the point was not that members of the middle classes were more fit to rule than the aristocracy, but that King James, like Vermandero and Alibius, had become an ineffectual patriarch.

Through its questioning of hierarchical relations, *The Changeling* is both "opposition drama" and "radical tragedy." But the limits of its subversion are measured by its commitment to patriarchy and the male-governed institution of marriage. The play undermines its own status as "opposition" by displacing its dream of rebellion onto Isabella, who remains obedient, and Beatrice-Joanna and de Flores, who become horrifying.[46] This dream of rebellion becomes most titillating in the relationship between Beatrice-Joanna and de Flores, because in this alliance hierarchy is temporarily disrupted, and the aristocrat finds that her servant is her true equal. As rebel-hero, de Flores enacts the political science of the subplot because he treats the traditional order as empty convention. As he insists on his sexual reward from Beatrice-Joanna, he brushes aside her resistance as superficial morality:

> Look but into your conscience, read me there;
> 'Tis a true book; you'll find me there your equal.
> Push, fly not to your birth, but settle you
> In what the act has made you

                                                            (3.4.133-36)

Jonathan Dollimore argues that this episode discloses "'blood' and 'birth' to be myths in the service of historical and social forms of power."[47] But before we revel in this fantasy of equality, let us remember that at this, the play's most radical moment about the class hierarchy, it is also most traditional about the sexual hierarchy: the rising of the servant against his master is put in terms of the subordination of an upstart woman by her superior male counterpart. Beatrice-Joanna begins the scene by commanding, but ends by kneeling to her new master. This scene may be the most dramatic and erotic in the play, but we cannot afford to forget that it initiates a form of rape.[48] Middleton seemed to think of it as such, since immediately before de Flores carries Beatrice-Joanna off-stage, he describes her as panting like a turtle dove, an image that recurs precisely at the same moment in the explicit rape scene in Middleton's *Women Beware Women.*[49] De Flores' rape seals his rebellion against his master Vermandero, but it also insures that the play's most vivid imagination of equality will not go too far: de Flores simultaneously challenges the aristocracy and punishes those unruly women who would rebel against male authority.

It is possible to argue that, through her encounter with de Flores, the morally naïve Beatrice-Joanna comes to recognize her sexual nature, and deepens her understanding of herself. But such a process demands that de Flores seize control over her plot and her sexuality. An examination of the literary and historical sources for the character of Beatrice-Joanna reveals that in *The Changeling* she is far less capable and alert than her precursors. In Reynold's *The Triumph of God's Revenge* the character Beatrice-Joanna has de Flores kill Piracquo and then takes de Flores as her lover.[50] Isdaura in *The Unfortunate Spaniard* is raped by a servant who, like de Flores, demands her virginity as a fit reward for his service to her, but she then kills him in return.[51] Frances Howard was far more active than her lover Carr in planning the death of Overbury, and at the trial those who had served her in the murder were condemned to death, whereas she was pardoned. De Flores is the most original character in the play in part because he represents the playwrights' revenge against these masculine and deadly women, and the means by which the play reinstates the proper balance between female weakness and male rule. This reassertion of the conventional balance between male and female power occurs even on the most specific dramatic level: de Flores' lines are continually placed so as to deflect attention away from Beatrice-Joanna. In Act 2, scene 2, she reveals to him her desire to control her own destiny, to become the Hic Mulier, or the man-woman; yet de Flores steals the spotlight. He hears her sigh, and asks her to explain it, thinking she will declare her love for him:

BEATRICE:

              Would creation—

DE FLORES:

   Ay. Well said, that's it.

BEATRICE:

   Had form'd me man.

DE FLORES:

   Nay, that's not it.

                                        (2.2.107-09)

His comments deflate her potentially dramatic complaint and her following lines collapse a complex yearning to be free from the injustice of gender relations into what appears as a naïve desire simply to kill:

   Oh, 'tis the soul of freedom;
   I should not then be forc'd to marry one
   I hate beyond all depths; I should have power
   Then to oppose my loathings, nay, remove 'em
   Forever from my sight.

                                        (2.2.109-13)

By deflecting attention from Beatrice-Joanna to de Flores, the play reasserts the potency of masculine action, and insures that any consideration of the injustice of Beatrice-Joanna's marital situation will not go too far. We should wonder if the play has really offered us an alternative to the male authoritarianism that the subplot so effectively critiques. The gender issues in this relationship, like the play as a whole, circumscribe the authors' political thinking within the limits of patriarchy.

Because of its numerous references to *A Midsummer Night's Dream*, *The Changeling* should be read as rewriting Shakespeare's play, a revision which nostalgically laments a shift from what was considered the bright Elizabethan period to the disillusionment of the Stuart era. *A Midsummer Night's Dream* dramatizes the injustice of gender relations, as well as the madness and metamorphosis that occur in love and sexuality, but ends with a last act which commemorates a set of aristocratic marriages and attempts, however partially, to accommodate all orders of society, male and female, aristocrats and commoners.[52] *The Changeling* not only revises comedy into tragedy, it comments on Middleton's own *Masque of Cupid,* presented in honor of the marriage between Frances Howard and Robert Carr in 1614, at a time when their complicity in the murder of Thomas Overbury was not known.[53] Like *The Changeling*'s anti-masque of madmen and fools, the play satirizes the ability of such celebratory masques accurately to represent or prophesy the disruption and violence that these marriages can cause. It attempts to ward off the disorder that could result from such marriages as that between the Earl and Countess of Somerset, as well as between Prince Charles and the Infanta of Spain, marriages in which "the masculine woman" could challenge the foundation of English national strength.

Notes

1. Jonathan Dollimore, *Radical Tragedy: Religion, Ideology, and Power in the Drama of Shakespeare and His Contemporaries* (Chicago, 1984), pp. 4, 231; Margot Heinemann, *Puritanism and Theatre: Thomas Middleton and Opposition Drama under the Early Stuarts* (Cambridge, Eng., 1980), p. 16. I am indebted to the following colleagues who discussed these issues with me or reviewed earlier versions of this essay: Murray Biggs, Richard Burt, Jill Campbell, Richard Dutton, Patricia Klindienst Joplin, John Morrison, Peter Stallybrass, and Valerie Wayne.

2. For the circumstances surrounding *A Game at Chesse,* see the edition edited by R. C. Bald (Cambridge, Eng., 1929), pp. 1-25. Citations for the play will refer to this edition.

3. *The Changeling,* ed. George Walton Williams (Lincoln, Nebr., 1966), 1.1.178. All further citations from the play will refer to this edition.

4. Heinemann, pp. 126-41.

5. James I, *His Majesties Declaration Touching his proceedings in the Late Assemblie and Convention of Parliament* (1621/1622), sig. A$_3$; James I, *A Proclamation declaring His Majesties Pleasure Concerning the dissolving of the present Convention of Parliament* (1621), p. 18.

6. "Open political-religious allegory, similar to that in *A Game at Chess* later, would clearly have been too risky for the players in 1620-3, when Puritan preachers were being silenced and imprisoned for commenting on the marriage plan" (Heinemann, p. 141).

7. Sandra Clark, "*Hic Mulier, Haec Vir,* and the Controversy over Masculine Women," *Studies in Philology,* 82 (1985), 157-83; Katherine Usher Henderson and Barbara F. McManus, *Half Humankind: Contexts and Texts of the Controversy about Women in England, 1540-1640* (Urbana, Ill., 1985); Mary Beth Rose, "Women in Men's Clothing: Apparel and Social Stability in *The Roaring Girl,*" *English Literary Renaissance,* 14 (1984), 367-91; Linda Woodbridge, *Women and the English Renaissance: Literature and the Nature of Womankind, 1540-1620* (Urbana, Ill., 1984), pp. 139-51. See also Louis B. Wright, *Middle-Class Culture in Elizabethan England* (Chapel Hill, N.C., 1935), pp. 481-502.

8. See Rose, cited above, and *Women Beware Women,* ed. J. R. Mulryne (Manchester, Eng., 1975), pp. xxxv-xxxvi.

9. Swetnam, p. 1.

10. Speght, p. 18.

11. Speght, p. 15.

12. *Women Beware Women,* 1.2.166-71, 176.

13. *Crumms Fal'n From King James's Table, Or His Table Talk* in *The Miscellaneous Works . . . of Sir Thomas Overbury,* ed. Edward F. Rimbault (1856), p. 265.

14. G. P. V. Akrigg, *Jacobean Pageant* (Cambridge, Mass., 1962), pp. 180-204; William McElwee, *The Murder of Thomas Overbury* (New York, 1952); Beatrice White, *Cast of Ravens: The Strange Case of Sir Thomas Overbury* (London, 1965).

15. *Hic Mulier: Or, The Man-Woman: Being a Medicine to cure the Coltish Disease of the Staggers in the Masculine-Feminines of our Times* (1620), sig. B$_2$. The pamphlet refers directly but without name to the Countess and her accomplice, Mrs. Anne Turner, sig. A$_3$. (See *Half-Humankind,* p. 267.) "Hic Mulier" is a Latin joke, using the masculine form of the demonstrative adjective, "this," with the feminine word "woman" in order to satirize women who dress and act like men.

16. Swetnam, pp. 6, 16, 21, 29. For discussions of *The Changeling* and the Overbury murder, see Heinemann, pp. 178-79, and J. L. Simmons, "Diabolical Realism in Middleton and Rowley's *The Changeling,*" *Renaissance Drama,* N.S. 11 (1980), 290-306. The play refers explicitly to the Countess' chastity test in 4.1.99-100.

17. Swetnam, p. 71.

18. For other interpretations of this sexual imagery, see Barbara Joan Baines, *The Lust Motif in the Plays of Thomas Middleton* (Salzburg, 1973), pp. 114-15; A. L. and M. K. Kistner, *Middleton's Tragic Themes* (New York, 1984), p. 161; and Christopher Ricks, "The Moral and Poetic Structure of *The Changeling,*" *Essays in Criticism,* 10 (1960), 290-306.

19. See 3.3.53, 85 and 4.3.60-61.

20. *A Midsummer Night's Dream,* ed. Wolfgang Clemens (New York, 1963), 3.1.27. Further citations will refer to this edition.

21. For other interpretations of the image of the castle, see Thomas L. Berger, "The Petrarchan Fortress of *The Changeling,*" *Renaissance Papers* (1969), pp. 37-46; and G. R. Owst, *Literature and Pulpit in Medieval England* (Cambridge, Eng., 1933), pp. 77-83.

22. Kistners, p. 120. The Kistners present one of the most logical of the moral readings of the play, but they do not submit the play's patriarchal ideals to a feminist analysis.

23. *The Elementary Structures of Kinship,* trans. James Harle Bell, John Richard von Sturmer, and Rodney Needham; rev. ed. (Boston, 1969), p. 115, 480.

24. "The Voice of the Shuttle Is Ours," *Stanford Literature Review,* 1 (1984), 38. This article and my discussions with Patricia Joplin alerted me to the central role that the exchange of women plays in *The Changeling,* the public reaction to Frances Howard, and the Spanish marriage. For another reading of the significance of the body in *The Changeling,* see Frank Whigham, "Reading Social Conflict in the Alimentary Tract: More on the Body in Renaissance Drama," *ELH,* 55 (1988), 339-43.

25. *Purity and Danger* (1966; London, 1980), p. 115.

26. *Natural Symbols* (1970; New York, 1982), p. 70.

27. In *Rewriting the Renaissance,* ed. Margaret W. Ferguson, Maureen Quilligan, and Nancy Vickers (Chicago, 1986), p. 129.

28. *The Foot out of the Snare: With a Detection of Sundry late practices and Impostures of the Priests and Jesuites in England* (1624), p. 2. The story of Dinah is particularly appropriate, since her rape by Shechem the Hivite brings on the massacre of his tribe by the Israelites not because of the violence committed against Dinah, but because of Shechem's attempt to use the rape as an opportunity to intermarry with the Israelites and so pollute the purity of tribe. Thus Dinah is described as "defiled" (Genesis 34).

29. 2.1.15-26. See also Bald, pp. 11, 13.

30. Thomas Scot, *Vox Populi* (1620), p. 12.

31. Thomas Robinson (1622), p. 30.

32. Gee, *The Foot out of the Snare,* pp. 65-66. See also Gee, *New Shreds of the Old Snare* (1624).

33. Gee, *The Foot out of the Snare,* p. 2.

34. 4.2.27-29.

35. Scot, p. 20.

36. See Andrew Amos, *The Great Oyer of Poisoning* (1846), p. 371; McElwee, pp. 213-14; White, pp. 137-38.

37. The marriage negotiations largely focused on the number of Catholics that would be associated with the nursery, and the number of years that the prince would be under his mother's influence. See Samuel Rawson Gardiner, *Prince Charles and the Spanish Marriage,* 2 vols. (London, 1869), I, 26, 30, 33.

38. *Vox Coeli* (1624), p. 56.

39. *Hidden Workes of Darknes Brought to Publicke Light* (1645), p. 1.

40. *Vox Coeli*, sig. B₂.

41. *Vox Coeli*, p. 36.

42. *Vox Populi*, p. 21.

43. *The Political Works of James I,* ed. Charles H. McIlwain (Cambridge, Mass., 1918), p. 272.

44. *Vox Coeli*, p. 36; *Vox Populi*, p. 16.

45. *Vox Coeli*, sig. B₂; *The Honest Informer or Tom Tell-Truth's Observations upon Abuses of Government* (1642), sig. A₂. This pamphlet was passed around in manuscript in 1622, according to Gardiner, vol. 2, p. 183. See also S. R. Gardiner, *The Thirty Years' War, 1618-1648* (1919; New York, 1969). E. C. Morris argues, although few critics agree, that the gelding of the White Bishop's Pawn in *A Game at Chesse* represents Frederick's loss of the Palatinate. Most critics do agree that Catholic usurpation of the territory is defined as a rape in 2.2.128-30. In these cases, invasion is put in terms of male sexual weakness and female vulnerability.

46. As my colleague Murray Biggs pointed out to me, Isabella flirts with infidelity in her scene of disguise (4.3.100-33), but finally rejects Antonio as a superficial lover. The play thus permits us to believe that Isabella deserves a better mate than Alibius without actually allowing her to commit such a transgression. The play also pits Isabella against Beatrice-Joanna by showing that Isabella can use "masculine" qualities like wit, intelligence, and strategy without succumbing to vice. Yet her strength remains that chastity which insures her protection against Lollio (4.3.34-40), whereas Beatrice-Joanna becomes the victim of de Flores (2.2.57-65).

47. Dollimore, p. 178.

48. In her article, "Dissimulation Anatomized: *The Changeling*," *Philological Quarterly,* 56 (1977), 329-38, Paula Johnson defines this scene as "a rape-fantasy objectified" (p. 334), and argues that part of the emotional power of the scene stems from the fact that "the woman relinquishes her unnatural tyranny; the man escapes his unnatural servitude" (p. 336).

49. *Women Beware Women*, 2.2.320-21.

50. John Reynolds, *The Triumph of God's Revenge* (1621; 1640), pp. 41-56.

51. Leonard Digges, *Geraldo: The Unfortunate Spaniard* (1622), pp. 89-108.

52. See 3.3.48-52 and 4.3.1-4. The title of *The Changeling* itself suggests the thematic connections between the love metamorphoses dramatized in *A Midsummer Night's Dream* and their sinister counterpart in Beatrice-Joanna (1.1.150-51). But the playwrights may also be evoking the struggle between male and female modes of government figured in the quarrel between Titania and Oberon over the upbringing of the changeling boy and the gender metamorphosis that this will cause (2.1.20-31). Beatrice-Joanna undergoes a gender change as well as a change in love.

53. *The Works of Thomas Middleton,* 7 vols. ed. Rev. Alexander Dyce (1840), VII, xix. Dyce quotes from the City Records of January 1613/1614. The text of the masque has not survived.

Arthur L. Little, Jr. (essay date 1993)

SOURCE: Little, Arthur L., Jr. "'Transshaped' Women: Virginity and Hysteria in *The Changeling*." In *Madness in Drama*, pp. 19-42. Cambridge: Cambridge University Press, 1993.

[*In the following essay, Little investigates the "politics of corporeality" in* The Changeling, *pointing out that the physical female body is the site of the two main subjects of the play—virginity and the particular form of madness known as female hysteria.*]

> So Woman has not yet taken (a) place. The 'not yet' probably corresponds to a *system of hysterical fantasy* but/and it acknowledges a *historical condition* . . . She is never here and now because it is she who sets up that eternal elsewhere from which the 'subject' continues to draw his reserves . . . She is not uprooted from the earth, but yet, but still, she is already scattered into *x* number of places that are never gathered together into anything she knows of herself.[1]

Critics generally agree that virginity and madness are the two principal subjects of Middleton and Rowley's **The Changeling** (1622), but many of these critics disregard the physical body as the sight/site of these subjects and move instead to abstract the play's religious, moral, or topical meanings, transforming the play all too quickly from a dramatic piece of literature into an allegory about evil and damnation.[2] The play's vocabulary is unquestionably invested in religious terminology—note, for example, the frequent use of such words as 'creation', 'devotion', 'holy'. Several critics have taken the characters' use of religious terms as impetus for defining the play as a religious or allegorical exemplum. At least discursively, the characters seem to imagine that their lives are informed or structured by religious paradigms, the edenic story being the most pronounced. It does not necessarily follow, however, that the play itself is a grand religious allegory. Frequently, these interpretations end with the bodies onstage being almost if not entirely eradicated by the allegorical rubrics through which they are contemplated.[3]

Considering that virginity and madness are particularly relevant to cultural constructions of femininity, it perhaps would be more critically beneficial to investigate how the play succeeds finally in giving meaning to the physical, female body. This essay assumes more than it argues that women are allowed access to the patriarchal community through the transformation of themselves into physical or theatrical objects.[4] While readings of virginity as a 'religious ideal' or of madness as signifying sinfulness are not irrelevant, this essay is concerned more with virginity and madness as they contribute to our understanding of the politics of corporeality at work in Middleton and Rowley's play.

When critics do discuss the interconnectedness of virginity and madness, the propensity is towards an essentializing of them as binary opposites: virginity is good and madness is evil. Such oppositions allow the audience to become empathic participants and know all too well the cultural constructs that speak of sexuality itself as a kind of madness.[5] Instead of commenting further on this particular binarism, I wish to look more textually at the relationship between virginity and madness, and to argue that the patriarchal community in the play demands to see the virgin's madness as a way of either exorcising it from her or condemning (or sacrificing) the virgin because of its presence. This essay is most sympathetic towards those critics who at least hint at the political and gender dynamics of this play about madness.[6]

This essay argues that the investigated and textualized madness in *The Changeling* is hysteria, a madness which cultural thinkers from Plato through Robert Burton through Freud thought to be of an especially sexual and female kind. Hysteria, especially through the eighteenth century, has been defined as a disease caused by the woman's uterus which floats about her body attacking her; the wandering of the uterus usually signified some aberration in the woman's sexual constitution. This definition of hysteria is not dissociated from the more recent psychoanalytic and feminist readings of hysteria as a physical body at odds with its psychic self.[7] Hysteria—this disease of the free-floating uterus or of the woman divided against herself—often signified for the male voyeur the woman's sexual instability and was thought to be curable by the woman's proper initiation into the patriarchal community through marriage and family.[8] From division to cure, *The Changeling* makes a fetishistic investment in hysteria.

I

Both Beatrice in the main plot and Isabella in the sub-plot perform physical signs of madness during the play, Beatrice enacting the convulsive, symptomatic behavior called for by the virginity test and Isabella pretending to be a madwoman in order to protect the sanctity of her marriage. Isabella desires to teach Antonio a moral lesson about the relationship between one's inward character and one's outward appearance. Diaphanta, the only other named woman in the play, takes the virginity test and actually experiences the convulsive behavior that Beatrice will only mimic. The stories of virginity and madness come together in all three women.

Concerning the two most central women, we should not rush to differentiate between them simply because the first is condemned by her madness and the latter exorcised from it. This play is not merely interested in the patriarchal acceptance or rejection of these women but with how the masculinist community of the play demands their madness, irrespective of the individual woman's innocence or guilt in any essentialist sense. Whether one feigns madness to deceive one's lover/husband or to 'cure' him, the reconstruction of the community demands madness. Attempts to discern a polarity between the madnesses of these two women frequently result in the obliteration of Isabella's madness. Bawcutt argues, for example, that 'Beatrice becomes entangled in her own intrigues and is destroyed; Isabella retains her sanity and integrity through her own strength of character.'[9] Joost Daadler goes so far as to insist that Isabella 'is neither foolish nor mad in any sense'.[10] And Penelope Doob acknowledges some similarities between their madnesses, but her unguarded claim that 'one may justly laugh at the perpetrators of both human follies and crimes to the extent that the doer's own deeds reduce his stature and make him ridiculous' elides the fact that the virginity test (to which she most specifically refers) forces the virgin and not the sexually experienced woman to display physical signs of madness.[11] Even while insisting upon their opposition to each other, Doob herself parenthetically observes that 'the gaping and violent laughter [of Beatrice during the virginity test] are, after all, not far removed from the asylum'.[12] Hysteria emerges, as it so frequently does in masculinist literatures, as the always already present sign/symptom of a female self.

The Changeling works towards Beatrice's confession of her infirm (female) self. Hysteria demands this particular self-betrayal. Jacqueline Rose makes this point quite succinctly when she writes that

> [In] a case of hysteria, in which the symptom speaks across the body itself, the feminine is placed not only as source (origin and exclusion) but also as manifestation (the symptom). Within this definition, hysteria is assimilated to a body as site of the feminine, outside discourse, silent finally, or, at best, 'dancing'.[13]

From Beatrice's concern about her feminine body to her 'talk of modesty' being intercepted by DeFlores to her dance during the virginity test to her death, we find evidence of her hysterical disposition. Beatrice as origin, exclusion, and symptom is evident in the play and is repeated in the criticism, which so often, instead of attempting to contextualize Beatrice's evilness or madness in the social milieu of the play, castigates her for the play's shortcomings.[14]

Whether we wish in criticism to condemn or vindicate Beatrice, we should at least be cautious about the ease with which her every act seems ready to indict her. Lisa Jardine, who does not write about hysteria but about patriarchal assumptions in *The Changeling,* says about such women as Beatrice that

> in the eyes of the Jacobean audience they are above all *culpable,* and their *strength*—the ways in which they direct the action, scheme and orchestrate, evade the consequences of their impulsive decisions, and ultimately face resolutely the final outcome—need to be seen in this context.[15]

Jardine's argument attempts to resist blindly repeating those fictions perpetrated by the characters of Middleton and Rowley's drama. She questions the naturalness of patriarchy, unlike Christopher Ricks who argues that 'the morality against which Beatrice is broken is the morality of Nature',[16] suggesting that her 'broken' or hysterical disposition is apposite to some universal scheme. T. S. Eliot, who is frequently referenced by *Changeling* critics, also makes no such effort to resist. 'Beatrice is not a moral creature', Eliot writes. 'She becomes moral only by becoming damned. Our conventions are not the same as those which Middleton assumed for his play. But the possibility of that frightful discovery of morality remains permanent.'[17] The play is haunted throughout by a Beatrice who does not become a (subjective) self until she is damned. Eliot posits that within *The Changeling* Beatrice comes into her actualization as a moral self only through the damnation or destruction of that same self. By substituting the word 'patriarchy' for Eliot's 'morality', we begin to discern how patriarchy and morality are implicated the one in the other. What remains most frightful perhaps is the possibility of Beatrice's disclosure of patriarchy's own mythologized self.

Less in a moral sense than in a patriarchal sense, *The Changeling* is a 'tragedy of damnation'.[18] Beatrice is not so much the moral subject as she is the patriarchal object. In fact, her immorality is entangled in her desires for a male subjectivity (II, ii, 107-9). The court world of this play comes together to *return* Beatrice to her hysteria, her objectification. As Sara Eaton argues, Beatrice 'becomes the focus of the dramatic action, organized to get her off the stage, because she is designated this hell's source',[19] and the play effects her removal by transforming her body into something unhealthy and then turning that body against her more ideal feminine self. The play's repatriative objectives depend upon the on- and offstage audience's complicity and belief in the deformation of Beatrice. The play

'transshapes' her by dividing her body from her virginity.[20] Nicholas Brooke is right to argue that 'Beatrice's madness is built on a strange obsession, a total assumption of the twin values of her aristocratic world: Honour, and Love',[21] even though I would put it differently by speaking of virginity [honor] and the virgin's body [love] as the twin values of early seventeenth-century, patriarchal culture. The play also maintains that the woman's deformation is not explicitly related to her participation in illicit sexual activity; this is made apparent by the play's transshaping of Isabella.[22] Whatever else Middleton and Rowley's play is about, it is also about patriarchy's attempt to recover its idea of an original, paradisiacal order which necessitates the exorcism or condemnation of things feminine, and this includes Isabella.[23]

Her story of virginity and hysteria mimics and parodies Beatrice's story. Although *The Changeling* and several other plays of this period 'include contrasted female stereotypes, one saintly, submissive, faithful, forgiving and silent, and the other predatory, dominating, usually lustful, destructive and voluble',[24] the mere fact of this female pairing does not decide how the audience is supposed to read the relationship between them. Bawcutt's reading of the relationship between the main plot and the sub-plot may also be taken as paradigmatic of the relationship between Beatrice and Isabella: he observes that 'all the situations which parallel the main plot are turned to comic effect, and certain points in the sub-plot almost suggest a deliberate parody of the main plot'.[25] Because Isabella acts as Beatrice's parodic counterpart, however, we should not take this as a hint to set them in opposition and stop there.[26] The most telling difference between them is in their sexual choices. Beatrice consciously or romantically chooses Alsemero, and subconsciously or concupiscently DeFlores who is more interested in her body than in her disembodied self. Isabella has—if not before the play, certainly by the end of the play—made the choice of Alibius, a much older, dull-witted, and perhaps impotent man whose ownership of a madhouse only further underscores his buffoonery. He is the *senex iratus* of the fabliau displaced into seventeenth-century tragedy without much apology but with a lot of masculinist, sexual paranoia. He is never convincing as a concupiscent or romantic choice.

However, we do take seriously, and perhaps even more seriously because of Alibius, the effectiveness of Isabella's patriarchal inculcation.[27] Even though the fabliau tradition would allow her adultery, she refuses and chooses madness instead—a choice that has more to do with ideology than biology. Before the play ever begins, Isabella's sexual desires have already been subsumed by the *enclosure* of a mad, patriarchal ideology, an enclosure dramatized quite literally by Alibius' incarceration of her in his madhouse.[28] Isabella does not only mimic Beatrice's seriousness but is her parodic alternative. Isabella is the satirized good woman, a parodic Griselda. The characterization of Beatrice does not eminently depend, however, on the parodic caricature that is Isabella. In enacting her alternative role, Isabella signifies the parodic that is always already potentially present in a masculinist idealization of woman. Throughout, the men—Vermandero, DeFlores, Alsemero—along with Beatrice, transshape Beatrice's seriousness into parodic and grotesque representations. Beatrice's virginity (but not only hers) is subjected to this kind of transformation. Virginity, for Beatrice especially, is 'both an object of ironic scrutiny and a factor contributing to tragedy'.[29] Beatrice comes scripted with her own ironic reading; Isabella is her counterpart, not her opposite.

From one end to the other, the play advocates a thorough investigation of the woman's hymen, the original locus of her congenitally hysterical self. In any event, the woman's hysteria remains much less important than whether she evinces it through a closed or opened hymeneal self. Irrespective of her sexual experiences or lack thereof, as feminine body the woman is implicated in the drama of hysteria. The play progresses towards the sight/site of its hysterical origins; it moves from the secrets of the castle in the opening scene to the secrets of Beatrice's physical body, most aggressively from the fourth scene of act III to the end of the drama. The play continues to focus in until the audience on and off stage are not simply made privy to but become the speculum that stares into Beatrice's hymeneal self.

Alsemero begins this probing into Beatrice's secret self with his mythic reading of her virginal body. As Eaton says, 'Alsemero expects Beatrice-Joanna to be a chimerical representation of female sexuality. She functions as a vaginal pathway back to an edenic world that he would also test in this one.'[30] In the opening speech of the play, he soliloquizes about the first two times he sees her:

> 'Twas in the temple where I first beheld her,
> And now again the same; what omen yet
> Follows of that? None but imaginary;
> Why should my hopes or fate be timorous?
> The place is holy, so is my intent:
> I love her beauties to the holy purpose,
> And that, methinks, admits comparison
> With man's first creation, the place blest,
> And is his right home back, if he achieve it.
> The church hath first begun our interview,
> And that's the place must join us into one,
> So there's beginning and perfection too.
>
> (I, i, 1-12)[31]

As frequently noted, Alsemero's words allude to Adam's first sight of Eve and signify his belief that he can reclaim paradise through the bond of marriage.[32] He

does allude here to Eve but to Dante's Beatrice and Petrarch's Laura as well: Eve as *prototypical* woman, Beatrice as the woman who leads Dante *back* to paradise, and Laura (first seen by Petrarch in a church) as the woman through whom Petrarch *rediscovers* the original Platonic immortality of his soul. Here, Beatrice represents Alsemero's amalgam of these women: nonetheless, she unifies their prelapsarian, mythic identities more so than they are incorporated into her physical body.

Without teasing out these various intertextual presences in Middleton and Rowley's Beatrice, and whether seriously or parodically, her character evokes these women. By being drawn into a comparison by Alsemero, Beatrice's ontological status is posited somewhere among the biblical, the visionary, and the poetic. The woman Alsemero dreams of here is mythic. When we take into account the often disillusionary function of the *locus amoenus* (the lovely place) during the early modern period, it is perhaps all too easy to argue that instead of depicting Alsemero as a 'holy man' who dreams of the concomitant duo of marriage and paradise, the play sets him up first and foremost as one who is placed somewhere 'outside normal human experience'.[33] As a man ensconced in myths of perfection as opposed to the physical world of political bodies, Alsemero is counterpoised to and no less extreme than the quintessential world of imperfection represented by the madhouse community. The play submits Alsemero's vision to a disillusionment and replaces these more biblical, visionary, and poetic women with the tangible body of Beatrice who transshapes these mythic women into physical bodies.

DeFlores both impels Beatrice to and assists her in these transformations. When DeFlores enters the opening scene, for example, Beatrice and Alsemero's ethereal musings about eyes and judgment forcibly change to an exposition on physical ailments. His presence (with his diseased face) works instantly to recall Beatrice and Alsemero from their musings. DeFlores's message to announce the arrival of Beatrice's father is actually assisted by Beatrice who attempts to interrupt him:

DeFlores:

> Lady, your father—

Beatrice:

> Is in health, I hope.
>
> (line 93)

The completion of each other's lines becomes one of their dramatic signatures. Here also is Beatrice's own attention to the physical body, her thinking upon her father's health which stands in contradistinction to the sickness of DeFlores. Moreover, when DeFlores in an aside makes known his lust for Beatrice, the audience finds Beatrice dichotomized by two extreme responses to the female body. For Alsemero, she is something mythic; for DeFlores, she is so much a physical body that her mere physical presence amounts to a kind of orgasmic experience.

The woman's entrapment between these cross-purposed readings of her existence is not uncommon in sixteenth- and seventeenth-century tragedy. In Thomas Kyd's *The Spanish Tragedy* (1587), revenge tragedy's prototypical example, Bel-Imperia is caught in a similar dilemma with the more ethereal Balthazar and the more physical Horatio. This kind of division is especially prevalent in seventeenth-century tragedy, where these choices are inevitably made to collapse into each other. Othello exemplifies as much throughout *Othello* (1603/4) and especially in the murder scene in which he at one and the same time apotheosizes and demonizes Desdemona. Middleton dramatizes a similar breakdown in his **Women Beware Women** (1613): the adulation of Bianca's husband for her and the rapacious duke's lust for her become almost interchangeable. Like Eve, Dante's Beatrice, and Laura, these women—or at least the chimerical ideal of these women—figure also in the intertextual construction of Beatrice. The beginning of Middleton and Rowley's play positions Beatrice between the patriarchal ideals of virginity and whoredom but abruptly shifts attention from the mythic disembodiment of the first to the physical embodiment of the latter.

After the departure of DeFlores, the conversation between Beatrice and Alsemero changes into the subject of health and illness, and Beatrice speaks of DeFlores as her 'infirmity' and 'deadly poison' (lines 109, 112). And once Alsemero pontificates on the commonness of man and woman's allergic imperfections (lines 116-126), admitting to his own allergic reaction to cherries (line 128), he and Beatrice betray their entanglement in physical sexuality. Their dispositions are seemingly the same: both are allergic to sexual things. The sexual nature of Beatrice's allergy to DeFlores is scripted into DeFlores's name which refers either to 'defloration' or more pointedly to 'deflowerer'. Alsemero focuses his sexual infirmity on cherries.[34] His allergy to sexuality is further accentuated by his choosing aphrodisiac objects, when he casually and extemporaneously tries to name some of the allergic imperfections found in the population more generally: roses, oil, and wine (lines 118-23). His sexual subtext is The Song of Songs: 'O that you would kiss me with the kisses of your mouth! For your love is better than wine, your anointing oils are fragrant, your name is oil poured out; / therefore the maidens love you' and 'I am a rose of Sharon, a lily of the valleys. / As a lily among brambles so is my love among maidens' (1.1-2, 2.1-2). The Song (as subtext or intertext) betrays the sexual underpinnings of the conversation here between Beatrice and Alsemero.[35] The physical is also allowed to invade this scene through Diaphanta and Jasperino, Beatrice's waiting-woman and Alsemero's friend. They are engaged in a conversation about Jasperino's claim that he is a 'mad wag', and Diaphanta attempts to recommend him to a doctor whom she knows can 'cure' him (lines 137-51). Their seductive raillery foregrounds the easy conceptual commingling of madness, disease, and sexuality. In effect, their conversation repeats and perhaps parodies the dialogue between Beatrice and Alsemero who seem to stand in moral opposition to the physicality of the sexual body.

Notwithstanding the complicity of both Alsemero and Beatrice in this disembodied sexual fantasy, the ideology which will allow Alsemero to be rendered as something other to the physical and sexual will demand that Beatrice be seen as always already constructed as a physical and sexual subject. Alsemero evinces a patriarchal manliness throughout: he is husband, male gynecologist, and finally Tomazo's new brother and Vermandero's new son. His body comes into its birth, its newfound identities, in the closing moments of the play. Beatrice comes into her identity as a body whose death is demanded by the chief personages of the court. Her prizing of her virginal self is not the same as Alsemero's prizing of her virginal self; the play is about the difference, and the affecting of this difference through Beatrice being finally transshaped into the figure of Alsemero. In other words, Beatrice's wish that she had been formed a man comes true in a way that she herself had probably never suspected.

Like many women in seventeenth-century tragedy, Beatrice is not simply a virgin. She has a very defined and problematic relationship to her virginity. This also becomes clear in the opening scene of the play. Shortly after Vermandero enters, he announces that Beatrice must quickly prepare for her upcoming marriage to Alonzo. Beatrice responds,

> Nay, good sir, be not so violent, with speed
> I cannot render satisfaction
> Unto the dear companion of my soul,
> Virginity, whom I thus long have liv'd with
> And part with it so rude and suddenly;
> Can such friends divide, never to meet again,
> Without a solemn farewell?
>
> (lines 191-7)

And Vermandero dismissively protests this valuation of her virginity, 'Tush, tush, there's a toy' (lines 197). Beatrice makes this plea because she wishes, of course, to forestall her impending marriage to Alonzo so that she can be free to marry Alsemero. Nevertheless, she predicates her hesitancy on more than either of these marriages. Once she loses—or is divided from—her virginity, Beatrice realizes not only that her *enclosed* hymeneal self cannot be recovered but that she loses all power of sexual negotiation. Given the valuation placed on female, corporeal enclosure, the rude and sudden loss of her virginity would signify the first and last gesture of her patriarchally idealized self.

Moreover, instead of the terms 'part' and 'divide' being mere euphemisms, they connote what will literally happen to Beatrice's hymen. We may also compare her to Desdemona who speaks of her 'divided duty' (I, iii, 179),[36] and who remains essentially divided between her father's earlier reading of her as an enclosed patriarchal territory and Othello's knowledge or assumption of her body's penetrability. The division to which Beatrice refers is no less implicated in the story of father and husband. This patriarchal divide becomes, in effect, erased or normalized when the father transfers his daughter to her husband. The division from her virginity also replicates the parting from her father.[37] When the father does not give his real approval, as in *Othello,* or the father is, unbeknownst to him, duped into compliance with his daughter's will which would (if all were known) be in opposition to his own, then instead of the ideological erasure of this divide, the divide stands out in relief. True, Beatrice's concern for her virginity may be 'the object of the play's most trenchant irony', but we need not suspect Beatrice's seriousness about this virginity that becomes a primary object for DeFlores, Alsemero, and her father. And her father's response is in no way a momentary detraction from the significance he seems elsewhere to put on her virginity.[38] Vermandero can satirically dismiss Beatrice's virginity as a trifle for at least two related reasons. First, Beatrice's virginity is a 'toy', a thing that (for patriarchy) means everything and nothing—'nothing' also being another name in the sixteenth and seventeenth centuries for female genitalia. Her virginity stays secondary to the male power structure whose social interchange is guaranteed by its presence. Second, Vermandero evinces his confidence, his unshaken assurance in the inviolate and inviolable constitution of his daughter's virginity. His dismissal announces his patriarchal assuredness more than it acknowledges the actual presence of his daughter's virginity. In his remark, Beatrice's virginity exists as both a serious and parodic thing.

II

Female hysteria is also read as something serious and parodic. It represents both the seriously essentialized female body and the essential male body that her body seems constantly to parody. The emerging deformity of Beatrice's body is the result of her failure to recreate 'the unity which' Mary Jacobus argues, 'the hysteric yearns to recreate on the site of her body,'[39] or of what Eaton sees as the inability of Beatrice to resolve the

'inherent contradictions in male perceptions of women'[40] that she (Beatrice) has internalized. Beatrice is not enclosed or unified but divided; her body comes into its patriarchal identity through its being broken, made mad, silenced.

The opening scene prefaces the change (or easy slippage) of Beatrice from the mythic into the physically horrific. The scene begins with Alsemero seriously ruminating over his vision of Beatrice's perfect paradisiacal body and ends with DeFlores thrusting his fingers into the 'sockets' of her gloves (lines 233-4), quite sardonically mimicking the division or scattering of her hymeneal self.[41] While not as overt, the hymeneal story of the first act is part of the subtext of the second act. In the first scene of this two-scene act, Beatrice reasons that because any demonstration of nuptial improprieties would force her father's blessings to be 'transform'd into a curse[,] some speedy way / Must be remembered' (lines 20-5), meaning that she must find a way of changing her allegiance from Alonzo to Alsemero without offending her father. The language of transformation and the sense of expedience remind the audience of Beatrice's plea not to be parted so quickly from her virginity, but the transformation of her virginal self is inevitable once (in the next scene) she speaks of curing DeFlores by washing his face with her own hands (lines 83-7). By doing so, Beatrice takes the audience back to the opening scene, where DeFlores thrusts his hand into her glove. All of this culminates in act III, scene iv, when DeFlores brings Beatrice the dissevered finger of Alonzo still toting Beatrice's ring of which she says, ''Tis the first token my father made me send him' (line 33).

From DeFlores's hand to Alonzo's finger, Beatrice seems always represented as a penetrated self. This 'first token' also wittingly or unwittingly recalls those hymeneal first tokens in certain other choice late sixteenth- and early seventeenth-century texts, namely the handkerchief in *The Spanish Tragedy* and that in *Othello.*[42] In **The Changeling** Beatrice's 'first token', that is, the giving of her virginal self,[43] has all the makings of a scattered anatomy: Alonzo anticipates being first, DeFlores actually is, and Alsemero thought he was. Summarily, the instant she gives the ring to DeFlores as partial payment for his murdering Alonzo, she completes the exchange begun in the opening scene, where (presumably in disgust) she gives DeFlores not only the glove he touches when he stoops to retrieve it for her but the other one as well.

Beatrice's hymeneal story becomes salient in the fourth scene of the third act, where DeFlores demands her 'perfect' hymen as payment for his murdering of Alonzo. This episode is often noted for its strong allusions to edenic matters—Beatrice as Eve and DeFlores as the serpent[44]—its reenactment of the fall. As far as

Beatrice does represent Eve, this postlapsarian intrigue is, however, as much concerned about the birth as it is about the fall of Eve. In fact, through Beatrice the birth and fall of Eve become one and the same. This scene, in which Beatrice is made several times to 'remember' her origins, emerges as one of the misogynistic center-pieces of early modern drama: before the eyes of the audience, she comes into her birth as a fallen woman. When she attempts to speak to DeFlores about her modesty, her virginal self, he responds 'Push, you forget yourself! / A woman dipp'd in blood, and talk of modesty?' (lines 125-6). Beatrice represents the woman divided between paternal expectation, i.e., modesty, and the immodesty or excess that is signified by the existence of any female voice—*talk* of modesty? As Catherine Belsey argues,

> To speak is to possess meaning, to have access to the language which defines, delimits and locates power. To speak is to become a subject. But for women to speak is to threaten the system of differences which gives meaning to patriarchy.[45]

Belsey's observations are especially relevant here where DeFlores attempts to strip Beatrice of any vestiges of subjectivity (as Vermandero tries to do in his dismissive response to her plea for her virginity), and here where Beatrice is born as patriarchal difference. DeFlores demands an emblematic silence.[46] Here and elsewhere Beatrice is not a patriarchal ideal: she is not 'patient in her reserve, her modesty, her silence, even when the moment comes to endure violent consummation, to be torn apart, drawn and quartered'.[47] In DeFlores's undisguised and violent patriarchal reading of her body, the blood of which he speaks belongs not only to the murdered Alonzo. Beatrice's being dipped in blood amounts to her holy, moral, and patriarchal baptism into femininity—birth, menstruation, devirgination. Her immodesty is indubitably evinced by her willful complicity in the evocation of her feminine blood.

She tries also to insist on a social distinction between her blood and DeFlores's blood (lines 130-1), not realizing that in this scene blood is transformed from a code of social differentiation to a sign of physiology. The transformation becomes most apparent when DeFlores protests against Beatrice's evocation of their social differences:

> Push, fly not to your birth, but settle you
> In what the act has made you, y'are no more now;
> You must forget your parentage to me:
> Y'are the deed's creature; by that name
> You lost your first condition, and I challenge you,
> As peace and innocency has turn'd you out,
> And made you one with me.
>
> (lines 134-40)

Beatrice is figured not only as someone who has been turned out or expelled from an edenic world but as someone newly created apart from it. As the 'deed's creature', Beatrice is not simply expelled but created again. DeFlores challenges and rewrites her origins. Her last words in the scene affirm as much: 'Was my *creation* in the *womb* so curs'd, / It must *engender* with a viper *first*?' (lines 165-6).[48] Beatrice becomes in this scene newly engendered and newly gendered. The murdering of Alonzo allows Beatrice to reach her moment of patriarchal truth by pointing not, as she expects, towards her manly self who would presumably be capable of committing bloody deeds (II, ii, 107-9), but towards her womanly self whose blood is already understood to be about her—i.e. Eve's—original deed.

To the extent that Beatrice is surprised by this unwelcomed violation of her virginity, this scene also acts as a parodic moment. Her insistence upon her modesty and blood are used by DeFlores as invectives against her. We see this also when Beatrice urges DeFlores to take flight and he argues that it is not 'fit we two, engag'd so jointly, / Should part and live asunder' (lines 88-9). His words mock Beatrice's earlier insistence on not being so abruptly parted from her virginity. Instead of the momentous occasion being her departure from her virginity, it should be, DeFlores suggests, her departure from him. His suggestion or threat that they should 'stick together' (line 84) points to his desire not only to be beside but inside her. The playful way in which DeFlores mimics Beatrice's words exemplifies the parodic throughout this scene in which DeFlores mocks Beatrice's failure to grasp the violent sexual fantasies provoked by her 'perfect' virginity. It is not her sexual self but her virginal self that has aroused DeFlores. The mockery she endures from DeFlores resembles the suspicion she endures from critics. Bawcutt, for example, rebukes her for rebuking DeFlores 'as self-righteously as any blameless heroine'.[49] DeFlores's parody does not simply divide the virgin from her virginity but sets them in opposition.

This division found at the roots of hysteria receives its most elaborate pronouncement during the virginity test. The dramatic use of the test begins in the first scene of act IV, when Beatrice discovers Alsemero's physician's closet and finds inside a book supposedly by Antonius Mizaldus called, 'The Book of Experiment, / Call'd Secrets in Nature' (lines 24-5). Along with this she finds two glasses of liquid: one marked 'M' to test whether a woman is still a maiden, and the other marked 'C' to test whether a woman is with child. Shortly into this scene, Beatrice hires the virginal Diaphanta to take her place in bed on her wedding night and then gives her some liquid from glass 'M' to assure herself of the physical reactions the liquid promises to affect in a virginal woman. Diaphanta demonstrates the symptoms as scripted in the physician's text: ''Twill make her incontinently gape, then fall into a sudden sneezing, last into a violent laughing' (lines 48-50). On Beatrice and Alsemero's wedding night (in the next scene), Alsemero submits Beatrice to this test, and she, having learned the virgin's symptoms, performs them to Alsemero's satisfaction. The virginity test ends with Alsemero's patriarchal and territorial enclosure supposedly rewarding Beatrice for her virginal enclosure: 'Thus my love encloses thee' (IV, ii, 150).

The virginity test is somewhat more intricate to the construction of Beatrice's role in the drama than most critics allow. When dismissive, critics have read Beatrice's virginity test as 'preposterous'; when appreciative, as befitting the woman who has 'committed herself to evil'.[50] And while it is perhaps useful to explore the seriousness of virginity tests during the sixteenth and seventeenth centuries, as does Dale B. J. Randall, who argues (supported by numerous examples) that 'throughout the seventeenth century the testing of virginity continued to be taken seriously not merely by popularizers but also by scholars and physicians',[51] *The Changeling* is concerned not only with mimetic representation but with using the virginity test as a way of further delving into Beatrice's virginity which is always already a divided thing. Randall's argument is a very informative and convincing one for our understanding the unapologetic dramatization of the virginity test, but his claims are finally more interested in historically validating the scientific authenticity of the virginity test than studying its broader, interpretative implications in the play.

The virginity test literally forces the woman to display her madness; the woman's reactions during the test are easily recognizable as manifestations of hysteria. As Barbara Ehrenreich and Deirdre English note in their study of women's illnesses, 'Hysteria apeared, not only as fits and fainting, but in every other form: hysterical loss of voice, loss of appetite, hysterical coughing or sneezing, and, of course, hysterical screaming, laughing, and crying.'[52] In order to prove herself worthy of patriarchal enclosure, the woman must physically prove her hysterical disposition. The woman, in effect, confesses to being sexually experienced or impure, if her body remains unresponsive to the test—this test which supposedly exorcises (mad) sexuality from the virgin's body. Rather than simply evoke images of Beatrice as polluted, we need to think about the ways in which she comes into a pollution which her male audience knows to be ever present. The virginity test presents the woman with two choices: either she is mad in her purity or sane in her pollution, which amounts to one and the same thing. It should not be assumed, therefore, that Beatrice's being deflowered is in some way a necessary antecedent to her 'hysterical annihilation',[53] which begins (at the latest) the moment Alsemero first sees her in the temple. Before accepting Beatrice, Alsemero must first demand her madness as proof of her virginity. The other women must undergo a similar initiation into patriarchal enclosure: Diaphanta actually submits to the

test and Isabella (in the scene following Beatrice's) dons a mad disguise in order to prove the enclosure of her virginal and patriarchal self.

Rather than compare Beatrice's and Isabella's sexual statuses, we should, it seems, think more about their particular relationship to madness, since here they seem more alike than different. Beatrice, like Isabella, fakes her madness, but this does not distract from the seriousness of Beatrice's mad display during the virginity test. Doob, thinking about the difficulties many critics have with this scene, suggests that reading it emblematically removes many of the difficulties critics have with it. Doing so, she argues, 'Two aspects of the scene are striking: first, the actions that Beatrice must feign—gaping, sneezing, and violent laughter—are extremely grotesque and ugly; second, they are potentially quite comic.'[54] She goes on to say that even though Beatrice is a 'tragic and heroic figure' her physical 'deformity' attests to her sinful nature.[55] Arguably, Beatrice's symptoms are grotesque and potentially comic, but the transshaping of Beatrice's hymeneal self has been present since the opening scene. This scene pushes the transshaped Beatrice to the fore. The hysterical deformity that Beatrice exhibits in this scene is quite parodic, not only because of her exaggerated physical display but because she is pretending. It becomes difficult to decide, however, whether the reins of parody belong to Beatrice or to the onstage and offstage male audiences examining her.

Her madness acts as both her parody of Alsemero's science and that science's parody of woman. Perhaps the most exacting reading we can do here argues that the scene is both a serious and parodic display of female virginity. Beatrice's parody does have much comic potential, but such a reading does not work against her tragic or heroic status but seems doubly to emphasize it. Despite what some critics have argued, Beatrice performs this grotesque trick not because she is evil—indeed this grotesque display is the fate of every tested virgin—but because she wishes to protect the patriarchal validation of her virginal self. At least from the vantage of the twentieth century, this scene at best provides a comic pathos which works not to alienate our sympathies from Beatrice but to draw her firmly into them.[56] Instead of reading the scene emblematically, we need to focus more analytically on the harsh representation of corporeality. This scene repeats the voyeuristic and parodic attention to Beatrice's hymeneal self that begins in the opening scene. What we have here in the first scene of act 4 is a more climactic and demonstrative focus upon this self.

The mad or divided virgin receives her most destructive and inevitable reading in the last scene of the play. Several times during this scene, Alsemero speaks of Beatrice's 'deformity', this deformity which he finally admits has been in his fears ever since he first saw her in the temple (V, iii, 72-6). The body which is en/gendered in act III, scene iv, reaches its horrific and misogynistic pinnacle in this final scene. Alsemero's proclamation—about 'the temple / Where blood and beauty first unlawfully / Fir'd their devotion, and quench'd the right one' and 'the bed [which] itself's a charnel, [and] the sheets shrouds / For murdered carcasses' (lines 73-5, 83-4)—announces the destruction of Beatrice's hymeneal enclosure.[57] Sexual death is transshaped into mortal death.

As Alsemero begins his final exploration into his suspicions about Beatrice, he is told by his friend Jasperino, ''Tis not a shallow probe / Can search this ulcer soundly, I fear you'll find it / Full of corruption' (lines 7-9). Bawcutt compares Jasperino's words to *The Defence of Poesy* (1580), where Sir Philip Sidney writes that both 'the right use of comedy . . . [and] the high and excellent tragedy . . . openeth the greatest wounds, and showeth forth the ulcers that are covered with tissue'.[58] Beatrice seems both the embodiment of the 'high and excellent tragedy' and the tragedy's cathartic sacrifice. Because she figures as source and symptom (see the earlier quotation from Rose), her body also must consequently represent what such a tragedy finds necessary not simply to expurgate but obliterate. The probing of the corrupt ulcer in Middleton and Rowley's play indeed invites comparison to this ulcer in Sidney's *Defence*.

The relationship between the female anatomy and the wound is not a casual one. Culturally, this link is quite common. An affinity between the wound and womb is prevalent in the psychoanalytic studies of Freud and Luce Irigaray as well as in Hoffman R. Hays's anthropological work. Hays has observed, for example, that

> women by their recurring supernatural wound [i.e., their vulva] are set apart as aliens from the male norm. Sensitivity to contact and contagion is aroused and the symbol of the whole complex is blood, the powerful magic liquid on which life depends.[59]

The play has made its way to the sight/site of its contagion; it has moved from the mythic woman imagined in the temple in the first act to the woman's blood in the third act to the woman's wound here in the fifth act. The play finds its original pollution in the body of woman; its original health—*the* moment of cultural origin—in the body of man. A 'wounded' Beatrice speaks to this en/gendered difference when she says or perhaps rehearses what Bawcutt claims are the most famous lines in the play:[60] 'Oh come not near me, sir, I shall defile you: / I am that of your blood was taken from you / For your better health' (lines 149-51). Beatrice's *disclosure* of her supposedly self-fashioned and self-inflicted, wounded identity, resonates with a familiarity that resists reading her disclosure as being exclusively about her body. Among other cultural references, Beatrice is like the menstruating woman who must live in isolation and is obliged to cry out if approached, presumably to prevent the infection of others, 'I am unclean.'[61]

Despite and because of the simulated exorcism of Beatrice's (mad) sexuality in the third act, here she incarnates and is transformed into that pollution which her onstage audience thought had been eradicated. In her feminine contagion she stands in contradistinction to her father's healthy body. The purging of Beatrice's blood also rewrites the myth of Eve's being created from one of Adam's ribs. (This point is further underscored by DeFlores who immediately before Beatrice's speech refers to her as 'that broken rib of mankind', line 146.) Here woman is born as the physiological blood ejected from the male body. More than identifying Beatrice's blood as feminine, the play indicts femininity as being a disease, a contagion. It is an infirmity whose convulsive display and sexual conspicuity have transshaped the female body in all its original illness into both a tragical and theatrical spectacle.

As we muse over the dead and wounded body of Beatrice and the court's embracement of Isabella, perhaps the play asks the audience to inquire into the difference between deformity celebrated and then condemned and deformity celebrated and then exorcised. The court is secure with the death of Beatrice and with the presence of Isabella who is not only a woman from a parodic tradition but has in turn made mockery of that tradition. Whether condemned or exorcised, this putting of deformity *back* in its cultural place by licensing the play to return to its fantasy of its paradisiacal origins, ostensibly allows the patriarchal court to cure itself of its hysterical otherness. Bawcutt says as much when he argues that 'the normal tenor of life has been interrupted by a sudden crisis; at the end of the play the crisis is resolved and normality finally reasserts itself'.[62] The normality he speaks of is presumably that *reasserted* by Alsemero in the play's epilogue in which Alsemero responds to the forlorn brother of the murdered Alonzo as well as Alsemero and Vermandero and those in the audience: 'Your only smile have power to cause re-live / The dead again, or in their rooms to give / Brother a new brother, father a child; / If these appear, all griefs are reconcil'd' (lines 224-7). Alsemero's celebration of a homosocial enclosure presumably provides the on- and offstage male audience with the original, paradisiacal vision it has fantasized about all along. This dramatization of a sudden crisis, a presumed disruption of patriarchal normality, endeavors to prove, repeat, and mythologize the woman's hysterical or wounded virginity as the original sight/site of both her imperfect self and the imperfections of patriarchal culture.

Notes

1. Luce Irigaray, emphasis in text, *Speculum of the Other Woman,* trans. Gillian C. Gill (Ithaca: Cornell University Press, 1985), p. 227.

2. There are numerous examples of religious and moral readings of *The Changeling.* Two essays the reader may wish to consult for some sense of these are Penelope B. R. Doob's 'A Reading of *The Changeling*', *English Literary Renaissance* 3 (1973), 183-206, and Joost Daadler's 'Folly and Madness in *The Changeling*', *Essays in Criticism* 38 (1988), 1-21, respectively. These and other such critiques will occasionally be referenced in this essay. The topical story which sometimes figures into readings of the play involves the infamous divorce trial between the Count and Countess of Essex in 1613. Two years after the divorce, it was discovered that Sir Thomas Overbury, who attempted to bar the divorce, was clandestinely murdered. For an example, see J. L. Simmons, 'Diabolical Realism in *The Changeling*', *Renaissance Drama* 11 (1980), 135-70, esp. pp. 153-63.

3. For some examples, see N. W. Bawcutt's introduction to his edition of Thomas Middleton and William Rowley's *The Changeling,* The Revels Plays (London: Methuen & Co., Ltd.), pp. lvi-lvii. Also, Douglas Duncan, 'Virginity in *The Changeling*', *English Studies in Canada* 9 (1983), esp. pp. 26-7 and 33-4, and Doob, 'A Reading', esp. pp. 184-6.

4. See Sara Eaton, 'Beatrice-Joanna and the Rhetoric of Love in *The Changeling*', *Theatre Journal* 36 (1984), 371. Eaton pursues the physical and theatrical readings of women found in the courtly love tradition and argues that in this tradition women could be transgressive but they must not *seem* so. Her essay examines Beatrice's body through courtly love rhetoric. My essay agrees with the direction of Eaton's but assumes that the physical body is the most likely place to see such readings being put into cultural practice; also, Eaton's essay is not interested in madness in these physical and theatrical constructions. Madness, this essay argues, is *the* trope.

5. See Susan Mayberry, 'Cuckoos and Convention: Madness in Middleton and Rowley's *The Changeling*', *Mid-Hudson Language Studies* 8 (1985), 21-2.

6. See Mohammad Kowsar whose reading is interested in the presence of Kristevan abjection within institutional discourse. His essay is in sympathy with my argument, but he is more interested in discursive form as opposed to corporeal form even though these forms are ultimately inseparable: 'Middleton and Rowley's *The Changeling*: The Besieged Temple', *Criticism* 28 (1986), esp. pp. 145-7, where Kowsar most succinctly outlines his argument that 'the consecration of the undefiled female body has unavoidable juridico-political repercussions'. Also, Jonathan Dollimore, *Radical Tragedy: Religion, Ideology and Power in the Drama of Shakespeare and His Contemporaries* (Chicago: University of Chicago Press, 1984), where he discusses Beatrice's social fall and argues that blood and birth are 'myths in the service of historical and social forms of power, divested of which Beatrice becomes no more than what "the act" has made her', p. 178. And also, Lisa Jardine, who attempts to understand these 'strong' and 'manipulative' women of the Renaissance within their socio-historical context: '*The Duchess of Malfi*: A Case Study in the Literary Representation of Women', *Teaching the Text,* ed. Norman Bryson and Sussane Kappeler (London and Boston: Routledge & Kegan Paul, 1983), pp. 208-9.

7. Trying to determine the meanings of this division between the woman's physical and psychic selves often highlights the theoretical division between psychoanalysis and feminism. For an informative, brief discussion of femininity and hysteria consult Charles Bernheimer, 'Introduction Part One', *In Dora's Case: Freud—Hysteria—Feminism,* ed. Charles Bernheimer and Claire Kahane (New York: Columbia University Press, 1985), pp. 5-12. For an example more contemporaneous with the play, see Robert Burton, 'Symptoms of Maids', Nuns', and Widows' Melancholy' section in *The Anatomy of Melancholy,* ed. Floyd Dell and Paul Jordan-Smith (New York: Farrar & Rinehart Inc., 1927), 2.4, pp. 353-7; also Lawrence Babb's discussion of Burton in *Sanity in Bedlam: A Study of Robert Burton's 'Anatomy of Melancholy'* (New York: Greenwood, 1977), p. 11. For more attention to the socio-political dynamics, see Barbara Ehrenreich and Deirdre English, *Complaints and Disorders: The Sexual Politics of Sickness,* Glass Mountain Pamphlet, 2 (New York: The Feminist Press, 1973), pp. 14-44.

8. Bernheimer, 'Introduction', p. 5.

9. Bawcutt, 'Introduction', p. lxvii.

10. Daadler, 'Folly and Madness', p. 2.

11. Doob, 'A Reading', pp. 200-1. She also neglects to think through these seemingly effortless, cultural associations between madness and ridicule or between madness and punitive discourses. See, for example, Michel Foucault's chapter on incarceration in his *Madness and Civilization: A History of Insanity in the Age of Reason,* trans. Richard Howard (New York: Vintage Books, 1973), pp. 38-64.

12. Doob, 'A Reading', p. 201.

13. 'Dora—Fragment of an Analysis', *Sexuality in the Field of Vision* (London: Verso, 1986), p. 28.

14. The madness or 'evil' nature of the court is often made to belong most directly and innately to Beatrice. See, for some examples, Simons, 'Diabolical Realism', pp. 149-50; T. S. Eliot, 'Thomas Middleton', *Selected Essays, 1917-1932* (New York: Harcourt Brace & Co., 1932), pp. 142-3; Daadler, 'Folly and Madness', p. 7; and Doob, 'A Reading', pp. 187-8.

15. Emphases in the text, 'Case Study', p. 208.

16. Christopher Ricks, 'The Moral and Poetic Structure of *The Changeling*', *Essays in Criticism* 10 (1960), 303.

17. 'Thomas Middleton', p. 142.

18. Helen Gardner, 'The Tragedy of Damnation', *Elizabethan Drama: Modern Essays in Criticism,* ed. Ralph J. Kauffman (New York and Oxford: Oxford University Press, 1961), pp. 320-41.

19. 'Beatrice-Joanna', p. 381.

20. The term 'transshape' is from IV, iii, 21. My reading of Beatrice as a transshaped woman is further supported by Simmons who draws an association between Beatrice and certain demons from the Hebraic tradition who 'can transform themselves, like witches, into other shapes; or, more precisely, they can give the illusion of transformation', 'Diabolical Realism', pp. 148-9. Also see Dale B. J. Randall, 'Some Observations on the Theme of Chastity in *The Changeling*', *English Literary Renaissance* 14 (1984), 350-1, who quotes from John Rider's *Dictionarie* (1640) the definition of 'lamiae'—another meaning of 'changeling'—as 'Women or devils in shape of women'. More theoretically supportive is Iragaray who writes about patriarchy's reading of woman as 'deformed and formless', *Speculum*, p. 167.

21. *Horrid Laughter in Jacobean Tragedy* (London: Open Books, 1979), p. 79.

22. The mapping out of the relationship between madness and sexuality often leads to conclusions such as those made by Mayberry who argues that Isabella's self-preserving, mad performance is intended to exemplify 'the madness and ugliness of passion', 'Cuckoos and Convention', pp. 28-9.

23. There is a common agreement in criticism that the play moves towards some kind of paradisiacal vision. For some examples, see Bawcutt, 'Introduction', pp. lvi-lvii; Duncan, 'Virginity', pp. 26-7; and Doob, 'A Reading', pp. 187-94. In contradistinction to these critiques, this essay figures the 'paradise' of Middleton and Rowley's play not, most profoundly, as a biblical but a patriarchal construct—a world of innocence without the guilt presumably ushered in by femininity.

24. Catherine Belsey, *The Subject of Tragedy: Identity and Difference in Renaissance Drama* (London and New York: Methuen, 1985), p. 165.

25. Bawcutt, 'Introduction', p. lxv. For further demonstration of how critics have analyzed the relationship between the two plots, see Richard Levin who argues for 'a negative analogy built on direct moral contrast', *The Multiple Plot in English Renaissance Drama* (Chicago and London: University of Chicago Press, 1971), esp. pp. 34-8. Also consult William Empson, *Some Versions of Pastoral* (London: Chatto & Windus, 1950, first pub. 1935), pp. 48-52, and Bawcutt, 'Introduction', pp. lxiii-lxiv.

26. Doob's argument, for example, contrasting Beatrice's deception through madness to Isabella's cure through madness, takes the difference between their madnesses to signify the opposition between their moral dispositions, 'A Reading', p. 201.

27. We may relate Isabella's patriarchal inculcation to that of seventeenth-century women more generally. According to Peter Stallybrass's 'Patriarchal Territories: The Body Enclosed', William Whately in his conduct book, *A Bride-Bush* (1617), suggests a rigorous program of 'education' [Whately's word], supported by violence. Speaking of and quoting from Whately's text, Stallybrass writes, 'Woman is a horse to be broken in, only properly trained when "shee submits herself with quietness, cheerfully, even as a well-broken horse turnes at the least check of the riders bridle, readily going and standing as he wishes that sits upon his backe', *Rewriting the Renaissance: The Discourses of Sexual Difference in Early Modern Europe*, ed. Margaret W. Ferguson, Maureen Quilligan, and Nancy J. Vickers (Chicago and London: University of Chicago Press, 1986), p. 126. (See the discussion of the virginity test on pp. 32-3.) Understanding Whately's comment (as Stallybrass does) to be more typical than anomalous, we may read this *breaking* of woman through education and her subsequent quietness and cheerfulness as arguing that the gendered and manneristic 'education' of women refers predominantly to the hysterical transshaping of women.

28. The significance of this imprisonment is articulated quite well by Alibius and Lollio (I, ii, 69) and by Isabella herself (III, iii, 1-18). The fact that Isabella is not seen by the offstage audience until

the penultimate scene of the third act underscores the effectiveness and thoroughness of Alibius' enclosure of her. The term 'enclosure' here and elsewhere in this essay is indebted to Stallybrass who has said that 'the "unruly woman" presided over the destruction of literal and symbolic enclosures alike', 'Patriarchal Territories', p. 142. Throughout his essay Stallybrass discusses the valuation of the female body as a symbolic and political enclosure. He is especially interested in the ways the female body is made to signify a *hortus conclusus,* a garden fortified against intruders, ibid., pp. 123-42.

29. Duncan, 'Virginity', p. 26.

30. Eaton, 'Beatrice-Joanna', p. 374. To make a distinction that Eaton does not make, the imaginary representation of feminine sexuality includes the essential differentiation between the woman's virginal and vaginal selves. Also see Brooke's use of female genitalia imagery in his discussion of DeFlores and Alsemero's descent into the dark pathways of the castle, *Horrid Laughter,* p. 85.

31. All *Changeling* quotations are from Bawcutt's Revels Plays edition.

32. Duncan, 'Virginity', pp. 26-7.

33. A. Bartlett Giamatti, *The Earthly Paradise and the Renaissance Epic* (Princeton: Princeton University Press, 1966), p. 16. Giamatti attends to both the desire to 'return' to paradise and the inability of doing so. See esp. pp. 3-7, 15-16, 123-4, and 356-60.

34. On the subject of cherries, A. R. Braunmuller has referred me to Thomas Dekker, John Ford, Rowley et al., *The Witch of Edmonton* (1623): 'Well, I'll have a witch. I have loved a witch ever since I played at cherry-pit', *Three Jacobean Witchcraft Plays,* ed. Peter Corbin and Douglas Sedge (Manchester and New York: Manchester University Press, 1986), III, i, 18-19. It has been suggested that there is the possibility of a connection between 'cherry' and female genitalia, because in the child's game known as 'cherry-pit' the 'cherry-pit' was the name given to the hole in which the pits were tossed. See Thisbe's line to Pyramus in *A Midsummer Night's Dream,* 'My cherry lips have often kiss'd thy stones' (V, i, 192), which plays with images of sexual intercourse and oral sex—the former is relevant to my argument here: The Signet Classic Shakespeare edition, ed. Wolfgang Clemen (New York and London: New American Library, 1963). Also see 'cherry-pit' in *OED* and *Webster's Third New International Dictionary.* The latter defines 'cherry' as hymen and virginity, def. 5.

35. The New Oxford Annotated Bible, Revised Standard Version, 1973. The Song of Songs may also

be considered an appropriate choice for Alsemero, since the physical eroticism of the Song is often marginalized by or made secondary to more allegorical exegeses. Such allegorizing conveniently allows Alsemero to talk about/through sexuality without ever really naming the subject itself.

36. All *Othello* quotations are from the Signet Classic Shakespeare edition, ed. Alvin Kernan (New York and London: New American Library, 1963).

37. The play is replete with images of parting and dividing, with especial reference to Beatrice's self or to Beatrice's relationships with others.

38. Duncan, 'Virginity', pp. 27-8.

39. *Reading Woman: Essays in Feminist Criticism* (New York: Columbia University Press, 1986), p. 206.

40. Eaton, 'Beatrice-Joanna', p. 372.

41. On the subject of female scattering, see Nancy J. Vickers' study of the Diana/Acteon myth as it pertains to Petrarch's depictions of Laura in his *Rime Sparse* [*Scattered Rhymes*]: 'Diana Described: Scattered Woman and Scattered Rhyme', *Writing and Sexual Difference,* ed. Elizabeth Abel (Chicago and London: University of Chicago Press, 1982), pp. 95-109.

42. See both plays: I, iv, 47 and III, iii, 290, respectively.

43. Doob points out that whoever has Beatrice's ring is entitled to Beatrice's virginity, 'A Reading', p. 204; Doob insists on Beatrice's knowledge of this sexual propriety. This essay assumes that the audience is aware of the ring's significance but Beatrice is not.

44. For some examples of critics reading 3.4 in relation to the edenic fall, see Bawcutt, 'Introduction', p. lvi; pp. Duncan, 'Virginity', 31-2; and Doob, 'A Reading', pp. 191-2.

45. Belsey, 'Subject of Tragedy', p. 191. See chapter, 'Silence and Speech', pp. 149-91, esp. pp. 178ff.

46. Writing about what she understands to be Petrarch's (and Acteon's) linguistic power over Laura (and Diana), Vickers observes that 'silencing Diana is an emblematic gesture; it suppresses a voice, and it casts generations of would-be Lauras in a role predicated upon the muteness of its players', 'Diana Described', pp. 107-9.

47. Irigaray, *Speculum*, p. 227.

48. Emphases added.

49. Bawcutt, 'Introduction', p. lv. Also see Duncan, 'Virginity', pp. 26-7.

50. For a very good grasp and summary of critical responses, see Randall, p. 353; Doob, 'A Reading', p. 199; and Bawcutt, 'Introduction', p. lvii.

51. 'Some Observations', p. 357.

52. *Complaints and Disorders,* p. 40.

53. Simmons argues that Beatrice's hysteria is the consequence of her being deflowered, 'Diabolical Realism', p. 148.

54. Doob, 'A Reading', pp. 199-200.

55. Ibid., p. 200.

56. Doob argues that the virginity test gives the audience a 'comic detachment' from Beatrice and helps prepare the audience for Isabella's role in the 'moderately happy ending' of the play, 'A Reading', p. 201.

57. In a problematic marriage and consummation, Hymen, the god of marriage, seems to focus his energies on blood as opposed to the unity of disembodied souls. These problematic instances seem to expose the woman's hymeneal self. In a proper marriage and consummation, on the other hand, Hymen seems to deflect attention away from the hymen and towards the unity of souls. Alsemero's depiction of Hymen's marriage torches as being extinguished with blood is obviously a sign of an improper marriage and consummation: his marriage conjures up the image of the body not of the soul. For exemplification of these observations see Ben Jonson, *Hymenaei, or the Solemnities of Masque and Barriers at a Masque* (1606) in *Ben Jonson: The Complete Masques,* The Yale Ben Jonson, ed. Stephen Orgel (New Haven and London: Yale University Press, 1969), esp. lines 1-25. Also, Kyd's *The Spanish Tragedy,* ed. Philip Edwards, The Revels Plays (London: Methuen, 1959), where Revenge explains a dumbshow to the ghost of Andrea says: 'The two first, the nuptial torches bore, / As brightly burning as the midday's sun: / But after them doth Hymen hie as fast, / Clothed in sable, and a saffron robe, / And blows them out and quencheth them with blood, / As discontent that things continue so' (III, xv, 30-5).

58. *Selected Prose and Poetry,* ed. Robert Kimbrough (Madison: Madison University Press, 1983), p. 129. Also see Bawcutt's editorial gloss for V, iii, 7-9.

59. Hays, *The Dangerous Sex: The Myth of Feminine Evil* (New York: Pocket Books, 1964), p. 32. See especially Freud's 'Mourning and Melancholia' in the *Standard Edition of the Complete Psychological Works of Sigmund Freud,* ed. James Strachey et al. (London: Hogarth Press and the Institute of Psychoanalysis, 1957), 14, pp. 251-3, where he compares melancholia to an 'open wound', and then see Irigaray who discusses the relationship of Freud's 'wound' to the female body, this sick body whose lost, original health can be traced back to the little boy the little girl once was, *Speculum,* pp. 70-4.

60. Bawcutt, 'Introduction', p. xli.

61. Hays, *The Dangerous Sex,* pp. 39-48. Hays speaks here of Surinam women, but (as he himself argues and illustrates) such taboos are widespread, not exclusive to this part of South America. For some other examples, see Mary Douglas, *Purity and Danger: An Analysis of the Concepts of Pollution and Taboo* (London and New York: Routledge & Kegan Paul Inc., 1988, first pub. 1966), pp. 147, 151, 176-7. Especially see Janice Delaney et al., *The Curse: A Cultural History of Menstruation* (Urbana and Chicago: University of Chicago Press, 1988, rev. and expanded from 1974 edn), pp. 7-8, 13, 18-27. Both works may also be consulted more generally for further analysis of the cultural associations between women and pollution.

62. Bawcutt, 'Introduction', p. lxviii.

Deborah G. Burks (essay date 1995)

SOURCE: Burks, Deborah G. "'I'll Want My Will Else': *The Changeling* and Women's Complicity with their Rapists." *ELH* 62 (1995): 759-90.

[*In the following essay, Burks examines the sociocultural and historical background against which Beatrice-Joanna and her "crimes" are judged in* The Changeling.]

In the seventeenth century, marriage provided an important opportunity for propertied English families to form alliances, to build or repair their fortunes, to improve their social standing. When, in 1617, Sir Edward Coke began to negotiate a match between his youngest daughter, Frances, and Sir John Villiers, Coke's principal motive was to save his career as a Chief Justice, an appointment he had lost by angering James I.[1] Sir John Villiers was the older brother of James's powerful favorite, the Duke of Buckingham. That John Villiers's important family connections were Coke's principle consideration in the proposed match is clear; as a prospective bridegroom, Villiers lacked anything else to recommend him. In fact, he was reputed to suffer from a sometimes violent mental imbalance and from recurrent, incapacitating seizures.[2] Villiers's insufficiency as a mate may have struck the daughter more forcefully than it did the father. In any case, Frances Coke refused to cooperate with her father's plan for her marriage and became the center of a protracted dispute between her wealthy parents.

Coke's wife, Lady Elizabeth Hatton, was an extraordinarily powerful woman in her own right. The daughter of Thomas Cecil, the Earl of Exeter and granddaughter of William Cecil, Lord Burghley (Elizabeth I's leading minister), Lady Hatton was the widow of the extremely wealthy Sir Christopher Hatton when Coke married her for her money and connections.[3] In his negotiations with Villiers, Coke counted on using his wife's considerable resources to provide an enticing marriage settlement. However, Lady Hatton (who continued to use that name and title despite her remarriage) was unwilling that any of her property should enlarge the Villiers family coffers, so she took her daughter into hiding outside of London in order to evade Coke's plans for Frances's marriage.

As reported by John Chamberlain in a letter to Sir Dudley Carlton dated 19 July 1617,

> These eight or ten dayes here have ben great stirres twixt the Lord Cooke and his Lady about conveying away the younger daughter, which she will no wayes consent shold match with Sir John Villers . . . The daughter was first caried to the Lady Withipooles, from thence privilie to a house of the Lord Argiles by Hampton Court, whence her father with a warrant from Master Secretarie fetcht her; but indeed went further then his warrant and brake divers doores before he got her. His Lady was at his heeles and yf her coach had not tired in the pursuit after him there was like to be straunge tragedies. He delivered his daughter to the Lady Compton Sir Johns mother, but the next day Edmunds clarke of the counsaile was sent with a warrant to have the custodie of her at his owne house: the next day beeing all convented before the counsaile, she was sequestred to Master Atturny and yesterday upon a palliated agreement twixt Sir Ed: Cooke and his Lady she was sent home to Hatton House, with order that the Lady Compton and her sonne shold have accesse to win her and weare her.

> (*L*, 2:88-89)

In this letter, Chamberlain captures the dramatic potential of the Cokes' tug of war over their daughter. Contemporaries relished the idea of the notoriously curmudgeonly Sir Edward Coke being dragged before the same courts from which he had recently been expelled as a justice.[4] That he was brought to that pass and thus made a fool in public by his resourceful wife compounded his disgrace. Chamberlain's account of the mother's pursuit at breakneck speed in her coach, close "at his heeles," suggests not only the tragic potential of the situation, but its rich comic aspects as well. Sir Edward Coke, England's most formidable justice, was having his beard tweaked in public by an upstart wife and daughter.

However risible the proceedings may have seemed to others, Lady Hatton's revolt against her husband's authority was entirely in earnest. The conflict between the Cokes was a dispute over which of them would control and reap advantage from Frances's marriageability.[5] The Privy Council, which heard suits filed by each parent against the other, treated the matter with complete seriousness. If the matter had not eventually been settled out of court, the case would have forced a ruling about the rights of each parent to custody of the daughter and the limitations governing the exercise of those rights.

Chamberlain reports that "the Lord Cooke was in great daunger to be committed, for disobeying the counsailes order, for abusing his warrant, and for the violence used in breaking open doores, [and that] order be geven to prefer a bill against him in the Starchamber" (*L*, 2:89).[6] In other accounts, however, the emphasis is on the mother's usurpation of her husband's power and on her violence in stealing her daughter: "The yonge gentlewoman was stolen away by her mother; Sir Edward Cooke recovered her agayne . . . The Ladye Hatton, as is sayed, endeavoured to have taken the mayde by force frome her father, for the which she was committed prisoner to an alderman's house in London."[7]

Frances Coke's parents accused one another of "conveying away" or, more precisely, *ravishing* the young woman each from the other's custody.[8] Not only was the case sensational because of the prestige of the parties involved and because of the king's investment as a broker of the Coke-Villiers match, it was unprecedented for the vehemence and (initial) success with which mother and daughter opposed the father's will. Chamberlain wrote an epilogue to the scandal on 18 October 1617 in which he reads the affair precisely as Lady Hatton's insurrection against the proper authority of her husband:

> sure she hath don herself a great deale of wronge, in kicking against the pricke, and by indirect courses to hinder that which lay not in her power. Her daughter was maried to Sir John Villers at Hampton Court on Michaelmas day. The King himself gave the bride, and they were thrise publikely asked in the church. . . . Her mothers wilfulnes and animositie, together with the daunger of her continuall plottings made the busines go on the faster. She [Lady Hatton] lies still at Sir William Cravens, crasie in body and sicke in minde; there is a commission to the Lord Keper, the Lord Archbishop, Secretarie Winwod and I know not who els to examine her, of conspiracie, disobedience and many other misdemeanures.

> (*L*, 2:100)

Lady Hatton's insubordination against her husband proved impotent against the will of her husband and the will of the king. When the wedding took place, the mother was still under arrest. In her absence, the father's will was enforced and the king himself, a super-father figure, gave the bride in marriage to his favorite's brother. The bride appears entirely without will in this passage; the wilful mother seems to have been entirely subdued by the phallic authority of the "pricke" against which she had kicked. Chamberlain pictures her incapacitated physically and mentally, completely overwhelmed by the force that quelled her rebellion, still subject to examination and judgement at the hands of both civil and ecclesiastical authority for her transgression of the normative boundaries of gender and station.

The Coke-Villiers case clearly underscores the issues of property, status, and gender that were bound together in the marriage negotiations of the propertied classes—the same issues that made the crime of ravishment so threatening. Their case constituted a significant test of the patriarchalism of English law and demonstrated that in practice that system was not uniformly biased against women; there were individual cases in which women's rights were upheld against the claims of men.[9] Lady Hatton was a woman who held property in her own right, a right the courts did not deny, despite her husband's determination to wrest control of her lands, money, and goods away from her—even despite pressure from the king himself to resolve matters in favor of the Villiers (and against Lady Hatton). However, her ability to forestall her husband's claims on her separate property was more a result of her family connections and of the personal antagonism that Sir Edward Coke had provoked in his peers on the bench than an indication of the property rights of women generally.[10]

If Frances Coke Villiers's story had ended with her spectacular court wedding, most contemporary observers would have agreed that her adventure had worked itself through to a solid comic resolution. But, as Chamberlain sensed, the mother's and daughter's activities threatened to turn their drama from comedy to "straunge traged[y]" (*L,* 2:89). In fact, Frances Coke Villiers's marriage lasted only a few years before it fell apart in a public scandal over the groom's insane fits and ostensible impotence. For her part, the bride took a lover and became pregnant with a child the Villiers family refused to accept as a legitimate heir. Though her fate was less cataclysmic than the tragedies that befell so many stage heroines in her day, the comparison is tempting to draw.

Sixteenth- and seventeenth-century English dramatists linked women's sexual continence and their submission to the authority of their fathers and husbands not only to the well-ordering of family life, but to the preservation of social order.[11] The ideal woman could be relied upon absolutely to protect these boundaries, and the age did have a model of such feminine purity, however unrealistic she must have seemed. Lucrece, wife of Collatine, victim of Tarquin's lustful covetousness, was the English Renaissance's archetypal pattern of the violated, yet virtuous woman. Her rape, available in Ovid and Livy (and in translations of their works), was versified by Shakespeare and Middleton, dramatized by Heywood, and echoed in plays throughout the Elizabethan and Jacobean periods, including *Titus Andronicus, Valentinian,* and *Appius and Virginia.*[12] Lucrece was the model wife who took her own life rather than allow any doubt that her loyalty and her children belonged solely to her husband.

English custom, which did not valorize suicide, also did not provide any clear, reassuring measure of women's purity as an alternative. Instead, the culture fed its misogynist anxieties on a steady diet of sensational tales of unchaste, quite un-Lucrece-like women who deceived their parents, their suitors, and their husbands to indulge their desires. Thomas Middleton and William Rowley's play, *The Changeling* (1622), is just such a tale. Its depiction of Beatrice-Joanna's acceptance of her role as DeFlores's whore is symptomatic of a pervasive fear of women's desire.[13]

English law treated ravishment as a crime targeted at propertied men, through a piece of their property, women. The violation of the woman in this play is shown clearly and horribly to be an assault on a man. Alonzo de Piracquo's body first and most spectacularly bears the marks of DeFlores's violence, but the play multiplies the male victims of Beatrice-Joanna's ravishment. Her father is a victim, betrayed by a trusted servant, deceived by his daughter, cheated of his heirs and of the allegiances his daughter's marriage could have provided him. Her husband, Alsemero, (who marries her when her fiancé, Alonzo, disappears) is made a cuckold before he even sleeps with his bride. DeFlores cheats him of his wedding night and mates with Beatrice-Joanna while the serving woman, Diaphanta, supplies her place as virgin in the bridal chamber. Two other gentlemen of Vermandero's household (Francisco and Antonio) very nearly become victims of DeFlores's crime as well, when they are apprehended for Alonzo's supposed murder. In the nightmare world of the play, no man is safe from DeFlores's lust and Beatrice-Joanna's corruption.

Not only do the victims of the ravishment multiply, but the ravishment itself doubles and redoubles crazily. The subplot chronicles the efforts of Isabella, wife of an unjustifiably jealous husband, to avoid the would-be ravishers in the household to which her husband has confined her. In the main plot, the actual rape remains hidden, while Tomazo de Piracquo chases after an imagined conspiracy between Vermandero and Alsemero to deprive Alonzo of his right and perhaps his life. On the day Alsemero marries Beatrice-Joanna, Tomazo accuses Alsemero with having stolen her from Alonzo. At the end of the play, Tomazo makes his claims of ravishment explicit, demanding "a brother alive or dead: / Alive, a wife with him; if dead, for both / A recompense, for murder and adultery."[14] Vermandero and Alsemero are innocent of the crime Tomazo imagines; all three are lost in the funhouse-mirror effect of the play, in which victims and ravishers and crimes swirl and distort.

In a culture like England's, which linked social status to property holding, it is unsurprising to find that women's vulnerability to seduction or sexual assault was a recurrent, even an obsessive concern.[15] It is a concern that intensified in the second half of the sixteenth century, when the Parliament set about to stiffen the rape statutes and the courts followed with a series of precedent-setting opinions defining the limits of this new legislation. This concern with the social ramifications of rape intensified following the accession of James I. With the new monarch came opportunities for new fortunes to be made and for old ones to be lost. Furthermore, by the 1620's when Middleton and Rowley's play was performed, the nation was in the midst of an economic downturn that made property issues seem even more crucial than they had in earlier years.[16]

I. RAPE AS SOCIAL TRANSGRESSION

In Jacobean England, rape was a capital offense, "for the unlawfull and carnall knowledge and abuse of any woman above the age of ten years against her will."[17] This simple definition of the crime belies a history of contestation over the nature of the offense and its appropriate punishment. Beginning with the first statutes of Westminster issued early in the reign of Edward I, English law conflated two crimes: "stealing" women and forcing women to submit to sexual relations. The first crime might consist of taking poor women from their parents and pressing them into servitude against their wishes, but it also included kidnappings designed to extort money from wealthy families. An unmarried heiress might be kidnapped in order to force her parents to consent to a match between their child and a man they would not otherwise choose. Similarly, widows might be coerced into unfavorable matches under threat of violence or character assassination.[18]

This second kind of stealing was effective because a woman's marriageability could be compromised by any doubt cast on her chastity. Her parents were forced to consider whether they could make any match for their daughter other than the match proposed by the extortioner/kidnapper once the daughter's reputation had been tarnished by her captor. A widow, of course, had a similarly unhappy decision to make for herself:

> Women, aswel maydens as widdowes and wives, having substance, some in goods moveable, and some in landes and tenements, and some being heires apparant unto their ancesters, for the lucre of such substances beene oftentimes taken by misdoers, contrary to their will, and after marryed to such misdoers, or to other by their assent, or defiled, to the great displeasure of God, and contrary to the Kings Lawes, and dispergement of the said women, and utter heavinesse and discomfort of their friendes, and to the evill example of all other.[19]

Sexual violation was not necessary to this crime, because the possibility of its having occurred was sufficient to ruin a woman's value as a commodity in the marriage market.

The economic motive, "the lucre of such substances," was the principal concern of the statute-makers.[20] English law "from the beginning of Magna Charta" was interested primarily (almost exclusively) with property rights. In a society where status and access to legal rights depended on the ownership of property, the matter of law was the settlement of property disputes.[21] Rape was no exception. Each of the pertinent statutes identifies it as a crime against family property.

The language of the Henry VII statute quoted above is significant: the woman is subject to *disparagement*—the degradation and dishonor of marrying a social inferior. Her friends suffer "utter heavinesse and discomfort." Rape is not so much a physical as a social threat to women, and it is not awful because of the emotional devastation inflicted on *her*, but on account of the distress it causes her family and peers.[22] In general, the rape statutes are designed to redress a wrong committed against a woman's male relatives. These men, rather than the woman herself, are considered to be the victims of a rape.

Ravishment not only threatened the property of men of means, but also threatened to disrupt the divisions between different social strata. Ravishment was viewed by the law as a crime inspired by a desire to move up the social ladder. Whether many ravishers actually succeeded in accumulating money or position from such forced alliances, the strong fear behind the language of the law was that opportunistic men could exploit women sexually to infiltrate the higher classes.[23]

Social mobility was frightening not only because the upper classes sought to exclude outsiders from a closed circle, but also because an undesirable match could in reality lower the status of the woman's family, leaching away their resources and humiliating them before their peers. The costs of a successful ravishment might include a loss of liquid assets to the interloper, a loss of expected assets and alliances from an advantageous match for the ravished daughter, and a lessening of the likelihood of subsequent lucrative matches for the other children of the family.[24] A great deal of symbolic and real capital depended upon the chastity of women.

II. Complicity and Consent in Ravishment Law

Rape law encountered a tremendous difficulty in dealing with the fact that women, unlike other chattel, have wills of their own. A series of increasingly complicated supplemental statutes were passed in England to address the role of women within the crime of rape. What if a woman consented to be ravished? At what age could a woman be held responsible for her consent? What if a woman were forced through violence or threats, but then consented after the fact? Her family was no less damaged. There seems to have been a widespread and continuing sentiment that the common law allowed too many women to go unpunished for their part in crimes that wreaked havoc in their families' lives.

Though it finally climaxed with a flurry of legal maneuvering in the second half of the sixteenth century, the fervor to close the loopholes in rape law began very early in English juridical history. The Westminster II statutes (1285) suspected that some cases presented as ravishment were, in fact, adultery, and added a punishment for the woman to the judgement against the ravisher. If a wife can be shown to have consented either before or after the fact, Westminster II, cap. 34 states that she can be "barred forever of action to demand her dower, that she ought to have of her husbands lands." A 1383 law extended this provision to bar from their inheritance *any* "Ladies, daughters [of noble men], and other women," who "after such rape doe consent to such ravishers" (6 Richard II, cap. 6). It is not sufficient for a woman to have resisted a rape. These laws perceive a danger that she will be seduced by the rape, that her affection and loyalty to her husband or her duty to her father may be swayed by the man who raped her. The Richard II law states its perception that rapists in the fourteenth century were "offending more violently, and much more then they were wont," but its substance is not directed against the rapists at all. Apparently, what was of real concern was a perceived increase in the number of women who conspired with other men to deceive and defraud their husbands and families. What was violently offensive, then, was the sexual defection of women.

What we see in the statutes is a series of amendments to the common law meant to modify the sexual behavior of women. As the anonymous author of the sixteenth-century treatise, "A Discourse upon the Exposicion and Understandinge of Statutes," explained it, the function of the statutes with respect to the common law was understood to be a process of clarification and adjustment:

> The commen lawe then knowne, you shall fynde that the statute is either incresinge the commen lawe, or remedyenge a myschiefe at the commen lawe, or confyrminge the commen lawe, or making clere a doubte that was at the commen lawe, or abridginge the

commen lawe, or else quyte takinge yt awaye. As for those statutes that come in encrease of the commen lawe, they shall be taken by all equytye, for synce the commen lawe is grounded upon commen reason yt is good reason that that which augmenteth commen reason shulde be augmented.[25]

The rape statutes record an ongoing effort to make clear and eliminate the doubts left by common law with respect to women's sexuality and its consequences.

English law had two contradictory responses to women. On the one hand, as we have seen, it attempted to hold them ever more closely accountable for their actions. Simultaneously, however, it viewed them as incapable of managing their own affairs. For the most part, women were not treated as autonomous individuals in the eyes of the law. Young women and married women had limited access to the legal system except through their fathers or husbands, of whom they were merely extensions. While a woman could be brought to trial for committing a crime, she could not bring suit against another on her own behalf. Furthermore, the law tended to see women as having significant moral deficiencies that made them more susceptible to error and more likely to commit crimes than men whose moral sensibilities were more highly developed. This opinion of women creeps into the language of a statute passed in 1453 to address ravishers who trick women into becoming accessories to their own ravishment. The law singles out men who take advantage of the "innocencie and simplicitie" of women to get the women into their power and force them into marriage or into signing bonds that pay to the extortionist-ravisher (31 Henry VI, cap. 9). Women, though responsible for their actions, are strongly suspected of being incapable of acting responsibly.

From the earliest statute (Westminster I, passed in 1275), the law distinguished between a "damsell within age" and a woman (maid, wife, or widow) who had reached the age of consent (Westminster I, cap. 14). The age of consent traditionally had been twelve for women and fourteen for men, and indicated the age at which young people could officially be married. The age of consent was a legal interpretation of the age at which mind and body were fit to enter into marriage.[26] The law estimated that consummation and conception were possible for most adolescents at that age, and it was, therefore, also the age at which they were held accountable for their sexual behavior. A girl under twelve years old was assumed to be incapable of giving her consent even to relations she might think she desired, and she was believed to be too young to conceive a child even if her vagina proved large enough for penetration to be accomplished.[27] As there was no threat that she would conceive a bastard child, the culture could magnanimously consider a girl "within years" to be innocent whether she had consented to her ravisher or not. After turning twelve, however, she was held accountable for her sexual decisions because they could compromise her husband's or future husband's paternity and disrupt the primogenitural flow of wealth from father to child.

An act passed in 1558, the final year of Mary Tudor's reign, threw the ravishment statutes into confusion by identifying the crime as the illegal conveyance, marriage, or deflowering of "any maid or woman child unmarried, being *within age of sixteen yeeres,* out of, or from the possession, custodie, or gouernance, and against the will of the father" (4&5 Philip and Mary, cap. 8; emphasis added).[28] This statute targeted a lesser category of ravishment in which the taking away or seduction of the woman was effected without violence, a form of the crime that may have gone unpunished because the law's death penalty seemed inordinately harsh.[29] Although "4&5 Philip and Mary, cap. 8" was intended to facilitate the enforcement of rape law, its actual effect was to provide the grounds for disagreement about the age or ages that affected a girl's legal position in a ravishment case.

Sir Edward Coke, whose *Institutes of the Laws of England* were the definitive Jacobean interpretations of legal theory and precedent (and whose own daughter's marriage created such a stir), suggests that age became a key issue in the Elizabethan courts' consideration of rape cases.[30] According to Coke, "the doubt that was made in 14 Elizabeth at what age a woman child might be ravished was the cause of the making of the Act of 18 Elizabeth, cap. 6 for plain declaration of law."[31] The statute itself declares a need for clarity:

> And for plain declaration of law, be it enacted, that if any person shall unlawfully and carnally know and abuse any woman childe under the age of ten yeares, every such unlawful and carnall knowledge shall bee felony, and the offendor thereof being duely convicted, shall suffer as a felon, without allowance of Clergie.[32]

What this statute plainly declares is the sternest stand against rape in the history of the English state. Ravishers could no longer invoke their benefit of clergy to avoid the death sentence for their crime, and women were on notice that they were absolutely responsible for their sexual activity from a very early age.

Common law continued to insist that a woman be twelve for her consent to a parentally endorsed marriage to be binding, but statute law now held her responsible for her decision to go with an abductor, and to marry or have sex with him, two years earlier. England's justices had been forced to consider until what age a woman could still be said to be a child. They had decided, and the Parliament enacted their decision as law, that any woman "under the age of ten yeares" was still a child. Apparently they had serious doubts whether she remained so until age twelve.

Coke's *Institutes* suggest that the Elizabethan and Jacobean legal establishments tied themselves in knots with concern over the sexual conduct of ten and twelve year old women. In *Aristotle's Master-Piece,* a most popular text on reproductive biology, there is a caution to parents that attests to the age's concerns about female sexuality:

> 'Tis a duty incumbent upon Parents, to be careful in bringing up their Children in the ways of Vertue; and have ever a regard that they fully not[e] their Honour and Reputation, especially the Females, and most of all the Virgins, when they grow up to be marriagable, for if through the unnatural severity of rigid Parents they be crossed and frustrated in their love, many of them, out of a mad humour, if temptation lies in their way, throw themselves into the unchaste Arms of a subtle charming Tempter, being through the softness of good Nature, and strong Desire, to pursue their Appetites, easily induced to believe Men's Flatteries, and feigned Vows of promised Marriage, to cover the shame; and then too late the Parents find the effects of their rash Severity, which brought a lasting stain upon their Family.[33]

Rigid parents, of course, were not the only ones who feared the effects of desire on women's honor. If the prevalence of the theme in literature can be added to the great concern evidenced in these statutes, we might conclude that subtle charming Tempters lurked about the dark corners of many a father's and husband's nightmares. When *Aristotle's Master-Piece* describes "The softness of nature, and strong Desire," it pinpoints precisely the same traits that the law identified as the traits that left women vulnerable to rapists and made them apt to conspire in their own ravishment.

The dual nature of rape as violation and pleasure was embedded in the very terms used to identify the crime: rape and ravishment. Rape, which seems to be derived from the Latin, *rapere,* of which *raptus* is also a form, meant in English "the act of taking anything by force[, the] violent seizure (of goods), robbery" (*OED*). Ravishment, from the French *ravissement,* a form of the verb *ravir,* may derive from the same Latin root as rape. Drawing on the idea of transportation, both "rape" (rapture) and "ravishment" developed the additional meaning, "to transport with delight." The conjunction of meanings embedded in these words corresponds to an ambivalence about the crime: it was simultaneously understood to be a violent theft and a sexual dalliance. The first was certainly reprehensible; the second might be open to interpretation. In fact, both ravishment and rapture were terms that conspired to suggest that this kind of "stealing" might hold pleasures for the ravisher—and that the pleasure might even be experienced by the woman raped as well.

Kathryn Gravdal offers a history of the French legal and colloquial terminology for rape. She notes that in France (as in England) the legal definition of rape originally required an abduction to have taken place in order for a sexual assault to be chargeable. When, over time, the law changed to eliminate this requirement, it left the terms *ravir* and *ravissant* "free to become wholly figurative" in their popular use. It was at this point in England and in France that rapture and ravishment came to connote an emotional or sexual carrying-away. Gravdal points out that

> this transformation is inflected by a shift in gender coding: when *ravir* was literal, it was the male who ravished (carried away or abducted) the female. When the term soars off into the realm of the figurative, it is the female who is ravishing, who causes the male to be "carried away" and is responsible for any ensuing acts.[34]

What Gravdal notices in the language of rape was part of a larger inclination in the culture of both France and England to blame women for their own violation, which we have seen in the statutory history of English law.

Sixteenth- and seventeenth-century literature is full of women who have internalized this sense of their own culpability for men's assaults on them. At the end of Shakespeare's "Rape of Lucrece," that chaste woman blames her beauty for Tarquin's action:

> His scarlet Lust came euidence to sweare
>   That my poore beautie had purloin'd his eyes;
>   And when the Iudge is rob'd, the prisoner dies.[35]

The legal imagery of this line underscores the gender shift in the perception of rape. Lucrece is the guilty defendant, Tarquin the injured accuser. Her beauty is a thief, a ravisher. His lust stands as irrefutable truth. It is telling that in addition to being framed here as the injured party, Tarquin is also acknowledged to be the judge. He has the power of execution over Lucrece, a power these lines insist is just. Lucrece not only finds herself guilty as charged, but further condemns herself for having demonstrated poor judgement in choosing so powerful a man as her victim.

Ultimately, Shakespeare does not intend to lay blame on Lucrece for a crime perpetrated by so obviously villainous a man. However, the logic that inspires Lucrece to attribute Tarquin's lust to the action of female beauty is insidious. It lies beneath and eats away at the conscious attribution of responsibility for rape to the men who commit it. It says, "Yes, but had she not been beautiful, had she not been desirable . . . he would not have desired, he would not have raped." The suspicion of women's complicity is so deeply embedded in the culture's language of rape and desire that even the purest women fall under its shadow.

In ***The Changeling,*** DeFlores, like Tarquin, finds that the thought of a woman "ravishes" (***C,*** 2.2.132). He seeks out Beatrice-Joanna's company in order to "please

[him]self with the sight / Of her, at all opportunities" (***C,*** 1.1.104-5). His fantasy is that Beatrice-Joanna will be "ravished" when he rapes her, that she will find pleasure in what repulses her. "Methinks I feel . . . her wanton fingers combing out this beard, / And being pleasèd with, praising this bad face" (***C,*** 2.2.147-49). He imagines her an active participant in her rape. The play bears him out. Beatrice-Joanna, beautiful and desirable, is also desirous. She even comes to "love anon" what she initially "fear'st and faint'st to venture on"— DeFlores, the man she loaths (***C,*** 3.4.170-71). Middleton and Rowley created an archetype of the woman-driven-by-desire in the character of Beatrice-Joanna.

III. BEATRICE-JOANNA'S CRIME

The play opens at rape law's critical moment: it introduces Beatrice-Joanna at the precise moment of her sexual awakening. Beatrice-Joanna is a young woman who previously has seen no reason to contradict, or even involve herself in, her father's arrangements for her marriage. Unfortunately for all concerned, Beatrice-Joanna meets a man who creates "a giddy turning in [her]," which makes her realize that marriage could be a sexually fulfilling union (***C,*** 1.1.159). This new love, Alsemero, is suitable in all respects except for his arriving on the scene five days after Beatrice-Joanna's father has completed negotiations for her marriage to Alonzo de Piracquo. The daughter knows that her father cannot honorably withdraw from the match, and that he will not entertain her objections—so she circumvents his plan and follows her heart, allowing it to lead her into a disastrous spiral of crime and corruption.

The playwrights construct the conflict of interest between Beatrice-Joanna and her father as a contest of wills.[36] *Will* is a term whose significance is made much of by the play. At the close of the first scene there is an exchange that foregrounds this term in order to demonstrate what is at stake in the daughter's sexuality. Boasting to Alsemero of the fine match he has made with Alonzo de Piracquo, the father, Vermandero, vows,

> He shall be bound to me
> As fast as this tie can hold him; I'll want
> My will else.
>
> B-J:
>
>   (*aside*) I shall want mine if you do it.
>
>   (***C,*** 1.1.221-23)

Beatrice-Joanna completes and confutes her father's line with her aside. Her will, that is to say her desire and her intention, conflicts with his intent for her. This daughter asserts herself as having a will separate from her father's. In order to establish Beatrice-Joanna's responsibility for her subsequent actions, Middleton and

Rowley deliberately echo the language of ravishment law with its emphasis on the woman's will to have or avoid sexual activity ("with her will or against her will").

When the father speaks of his "will," the word invokes a second meaning. Here it not only refers to his immediate intentions for his daughter's marriage, but also reminds us that fathers have wills of another sort that concern their children. Her match, of course, has a material part in his will, his legal testament. Beatrice-Joanna is her father's sole heir, and her children will inherit his property. His will for the disposition of his estate requires her faithful participation, a condition with which Beatrice-Joanna willfully refuses to cooperate.

The term "will" had a further significance in the period that bears on this exchange in the play. "Will" also meant sexual desire, a connotation that resonates in Beatrice-Joanna's line.[37] The independence that she asserts is specifically framed in terms of her desire. Furthermore, when DeFlores closes the scene with the promise, "Though I get nothing else, I'll have my will" (C, 1.1.240), his use of the term evokes the contemporary slang in which "will" was a reference to the erect penis. The intertwined sexual and legal threads of this term underscore the fundamental interconnection of this family's sexual and social welfare, both of which are undermined by Beatrice-Joanna's corruption.

Beatrice-Joanna's discovery that she has a will contrary to her father's is her first step towards betraying his honor, a trespass she compounds with deceit. Beatrice-Joanna never makes her objections known, but undertakes secret steps to subvert her father's plan for her. In the moment of that first aside, her course takes shape.[38] We watch as a woman-child who once made her likes and dislikes painfully clear becomes a woman who disguises her intentions and falsifies her emotions. The aside and soliloquy become her characteristic modes of speech. Beatrice-Joanna's subsequent actions and conversations are marked increasingly by secrecy and disingenuousness.

Beatrice-Joanna has tremendous success with her program of deception, at least initially. She hides her disobedience from her father, gives Alsemero no reason to suspect her virtue, and even fools Alonzo into a false sense of her faithfulness. Tomazo de Piracquo is the first to see behind her mask. He notices her cool reception of his brother and tries to warn Alonzo to break off the match before he marries an unfaithful wife. Tomazo counsels his brother to:

> Think what a torment 'tis to marry one
> Whose heart is leaped into another's bosom:
> If ever pleasure she receive from thee,

> It comes not in thy name or of thy gift;
> She lies but with another in thine arms,
> He the half-father unto all thy children
> In the conception; if he get 'em not,
> She helps to get 'em for him; and how dangerous
> And shameful her restraint may go in time to,
> It is not to be thought on without sufferings.

(C, 2.1.131-40)

How accurate Tomazo's vision is, the play reveals quickly. Beatrice-Joanna's restraint gives way to danger and shame before Alonzo has a chance to marry her, but Alonzo cannot see his peril and ignores the warning. Alsemero, too, has no inkling that anything is amiss with Beatrice-Joanna until after he has married her, although he might have recognized her love for him— and her corresponding disregard for Alonzo—as an ominous sign if he had considered it carefully. The fact that neither lover picks up Beatrice-Joanna's dangerous signals is precisely the play's point. The danger of women's falseness is its subtlety, its secrecy, its ability to masquerade convincingly as virtue.

Like Tomazo, DeFlores can see what her noble lovers cannot, and he uses his knowledge to steal Beatrice-Joanna from the arms of these rivals. When he discovers Beatrice-Joanna in a secret tryst with Alsemero, DeFlores observes his advantage:

> . . . if a woman
> Fly from one point, from him she makes a husband,
> She spreads and mounts then like arithmetic,
> One, ten, a hundred, a thousand, ten thousand,
> Proves in time sutler to an army royal.

(C, 2.2.60-64)

This is the same logic applied by Brabantio and Iago to caution Othello against trusting Desdemona's chastity in Shakespeare's play. "She has deceived her father and may thee" (1.3.289). If Desdemona was an exception to this rule, Beatrice-Joanna is not.[39] Middleton and Rowley endorse DeFlores's analysis of her susceptibility to corruption, and the play confirms the underlying conventional wisdom that a woman false to one might be false to any.

When we consider Beatrice-Joanna, we can see what the law feared. She is willful and sexual; she is deceitful and unrepentant; she doesn't even recognize her error as she begins her course of immorality. We have seen that ravishment law was concerned that women might lack the moral sense to conduct themselves appropriately. Because their "innocencie and simplicitie" might be easily abused, women were subject to seduction and to moral error (31 Henry VI. cap. 9). Middleton and Rowley interpret women's willfulness in much the same way that the statute writers did.

As they have created her, Beatrice-Joanna is a young woman who understands her society's demand that women have sex only within marriage. Until she experiences sexual desire for the first time, she acquiesces to the match with Alonzo that her father designs for her. However, the playwrights place her in a moral dilemma when she meets and begins to desire Alsemero. When she sets about to subvert her father's plans for her marriage, Beatrice-Joanna may be attempting to find a culturally acceptable resolution to the problem she faces. If she could arrange to marry Alsemero, then she could also be an honorable wife. Then she would not desire anyone but her husband. She finds, however, that there is no social mechanism that will allow her to exercise her choice. She refuses to allow Alsemero to practice the one quasi-official means at his disposal to intervene in her marriage. She will not let him challenge Alonzo because she fears that the result will be either Alsemero's death or his imprisonment for murder. Finding no sanctioned means to escape a marriage she does not wish to make, Beatrice-Joanna slides easily into disreputable schemes. When DeFlores presents himself to her at the right moment, she leaps at the opportunity to allow him to kill her fiancé for her.

Beatrice-Joanna is both amoral and "simple." She does not hesitate to plot Alonzo's murder and apparently does not consider his death to have any moral significance. This ethical blindness also causes Beatrice-Joanna to fall prey to her own "innocencie and simplicitie" in her dealings with DeFlores. She has not the faintest inkling of the kind of obligation she incurs with DeFlores through her bargain with him. Beatrice-Joanna believes that DeFlores would do anything to serve her, when, in fact, his objective is sex not service. It is Beatrice-Joanna's plan to rid herself of DeFlores by getting him to commit murder, so he will have to flee her father's household. She assumes that DeFlores wants to earn a large reward for his task, but she cannot conceive of the reward he demands.

BEATRICE-JOANNA:

    Thy reward shall be precious.

DEFLORES:

    That I have thought on;
    I have assured myself of that beforehand,
    And know it will be precious; the thought *ravishes.*

          (*C*, 2.2.130-32; emphasis added)

Beatrice-Joanna assumes that the motive that drives men is desire for property; she overlooks DeFlores's sexual desires. Even the law, which assumes that covetousness is the principle motive for crime, does not make Beatrice-Joanna's mistake. In their anxiety over women's consent, the rape statutes always remember that sexual desire is a powerful motivator of men. Instead of taking her gold and running away, DeFlores exercises a power over Beatrice-Joanna that she neither realized she had given nor imagined he would take. She marvels that "He's bold, and I am blamed for it" (*C*, 3.4.97).

In fact, Beatrice-Joanna is so unaware of her position that DeFlores must explain her predicament to her quite bluntly:

    Though thou writ'st maid, thou whore in thy affection,
    'Twas changed from thy first love, and that's a kind
    Of whoredom in thy heart; and he's changed now,
    To bring thy second on, thy Alsemero,
    Whom by all sweets that darkness ever tasted,
    If I enjoy thee not, thou ne'er enjoy'st.

          (*C*, 3.4.142-47)

Beatrice-Joanna does not fathom her complicity in the murder, and, thus, cannot anticipate how DeFlores uses it to gain access to her. "Why, 'tis impossible thou canst be so wicked, / . . . / To make his death the murderer of my honor!" (*C*, 3.4.120, 122). She fails to recognize her responsibility for Alonzo's murder. It has not occurred to her that that act touched her honor in any way.

Middleton and Rowley have designed a heroine who confirms the law's paternalistic concern for women's moral weakness.[40] Beatrice-Joanna's moral compass is fundamentally skewed. In part, her behavior is guided by flawed interpretations of her culture's gender roles, but her most egregious acts are the product of a criminal disregard for human life. Beatrice-Joanna's assumption that desire might have a meaningful place within marriage or that women might under some circumstances be sanctioned to act on desire simply does not square with Jacobean notions of marriage and sexuality.

Beatrice-Joanna's project to marry the man she desires becomes a diabolic mirroring of Jacobean sexual mores. Her willfulness is seen to be an all-absorbing focus on herself that threatens everyone else. This self-absorption creates the cock-eyed view by which she sees herself as pursuing a logical course to an honorable marriage. "A woman dipped in blood," though she surely is, Beatrice-Joanna continues to "talk of modesty" (*C*, 3.4.126).

IV. CHANGELINGS

The law, with its straightforward statements about consent and age, its cold definitions of damage and disinheritance, is completely inadequate either to deter or address the crimes in Middleton and Rowley's play. The most frightening aspect of *The Changeling* is the success with which DeFlores and Beatrice-Joanna hide Alonzo's murder and the further betrayal of their sexual alliance. Once she succumbs to DeFlores's attack, Beatrice-Joanna actively covers up the crime, hiding her incontinence and counterfeiting chastity in order to proceed with her marriage to Alsemero. In *The Changeling*'s nightmare vision, women's desire is deadly and defiling. Middleton and Rowley play masterfully on all the legion fears about women and their traitorous sexuality to which the "consent and complicity" statutes were a reaction. With its powerful illustration of the corruptibility of women, the play confirms the validity of the statute-makers' concerns, but simultaneously undermines the comfort promised by their strict penalties.

Literature and law both expressed great concern that women might falsify their sexual activity. Rape law, which sought to fix blame and to redress wrong materially, was frustrated by the near impossibility of determining whether a woman had been forced or merely seduced by her ravisher. The maddening characteristic of most rapes, of course, was that they lacked witnesses, and their facts remained obscured in the irreconcilable difference between a woman's accusation and a man's defense.[41] This dilemma drove justices to search for a test that could determine the facts of a rape with certainty.

Michael Dalton, in *The Countrey Justice* (1618), claimed to have just such a test when he advised fellow magistrates that "if the woman at the time of the supposed rape do conceive with child, by the ravisher, this is no rape, for a woman cannot conceive with child except she do consent."[42] Dalton's understanding of biology was based in the Galenic medicine still much in use. The author of *Aristotle's Master-Piece* reports the view of this branch of medical wisdom that conception occurs when the male and female seed are released during copulation—a release that had to be accompanied in both sexes by orgasm. Dalton, then, based his legal test on the assumption that if a woman conceives, she must have experienced pleasure in the act of intercourse, which in turn signifies that she consented to the act, if not beforehand, then by virtue of having enjoyed it.

The test was necessary, of course, because women lack the obvious signifiers of desire with which men are equipped. Without penises, which offer visual confirmation of arousal and satisfaction, women could easily counterfeit their experience of the sexual act. Not only did this absence of ocular proof allow women to pretend pleasure when they felt none, it also made it possible for them to conceal their pleasure when it served them to do so.

Even as Dalton was circulating his consent test, however, the medical wisdom on which it was based was becoming obsolete. The *Master-Piece* reports Galenic opinion only to rebut it, proposing, instead, a biology of conception in which the active male seed searches out and fertilizes the passive ovum in the woman's body. Among the propositions it explicitly refutes is the Galenic belief that women's orgasm is produced by their ejaculation of seed.[43]

The *Master-Piece* also takes sides in another of the period's disputes over women's sexuality. It maintains that a ruptured hymen is not evidence of lack of virginity, claiming that "the Learned" affirm that

such fracture may happen divers ways by accidents, as well as Copulation with Man, *viz.* by extraordinary straining, violent coughing, immoderate sneezing, stopping of Urine, and violent motion of the Vessels, inforcibly sending down the humours, which pressing for passage break the Ligatures or Membrane, so that the intireness or fracture of this thing, commonly taken for the Virginity or Maidenhead, is no absolute sign of dishonesty.[44]

After taking away this absolute sign of a woman's falseness, the author of *The Master-Piece* offers a most interesting consolation to his readers. He will have it known that while a woman's sexual activity cannot be proved by her ruptured hymen, an intact hymen is a certain proof that she remains a virgin. He illustrates the importance of this truth with a legal case in which a woman was found to have falsely accused a man of raping her. Her deceit was discovered when a gynecological exam certified that she was still a virgin. Far from offering reassurance, this illustration demonstrates the dire need for discernible proof of women's sexual status. It cautions that even when women are chaste, they may perpetrate dangerous sexual falsehoods.

The Changeling exploits its culture's anxiety about the difficulty of ascertaining the facts of women's sexuality. Alibius, the subplot's jealous husband, fears that his wife will find opportunities to cuckold him if he allows her to leave his house, so he confines her indoors in the company of the madmen and fools he treats, and entrusts her to the oversight of his wily servant. Were she so inclined, Isabella could find plenty of opportunity to betray her husband without leaving home. Certainly his unreasonable confinement of her gives her ample motive for cuckolding him, but the playwrights maintain Isabella's chastity as a counterexample to Beatrice-Joanna's falseness. The lesson of the subplot is not so much that some women are capable of chastity, but that nothing men can do will guarantee women's honesty.

In the main plot, Tomazo de Piracquo spends the entire play suspecting Beatrice-Joanna of falseness he cannot prove. Alsemero becomes consumed by questions about his bride's chastity. The audience knows all of Beatrice-Joanna's secrets, and it waits for the other characters to realize the magnitude of her hidden sins. The plot is driven toward the moment when the truth will be revealed, but discovery is so slow in coming that it seems entirely possible that Beatrice-Joanna may get away with murder and adultery. The play, which makes its audience privy to all of the facts, builds suspense by postponing discovery until the last possible moment. It teases its audience with the specter of a woman's successful deception, withholding as long as practicable the reward of her violent punishment and her acceptance of guilt. The audience is as desperate that the truth be known as the characters are to discover that truth.

As soon as he has married her, Alsemero begins to be troubled by hints of Beatrice-Joanna's unfaithfulness. He has, however, come to marriage prepared to deal with such doubts. Alsemero owns a medical kit that contains special preparations with which he can discover whether Beatrice-Joanna is a virgin, and if not a virgin, whether she is pregnant. Such certain tests, if they had existed, would have been worth more to seventeenth-century husbands than possession of the philosopher's stone.[45] The liquid in Glass M, which would allow a man "to know whether a woman be a maid or not," would settle for once and all the uncertainty that even a woman's body could no longer be trusted to resolve (*C,* 4.1.41). Among its uses, Glass C, "to know whether a woman be with child," would have allowed Daltonite judges to resolve their cases much sooner, before a pregnancy could otherwise have been detected (*C,* 4.1.26). If Beatrice-Joanna were to fail the first test, but were then to claim that she had been raped by DeFlores, Glass C might have helped to establish her guilt.

But Alsemero's science is no more successful than Michael Dalton's. Beatrice-Joanna discovers his physician's closet and reads the secret of his procedures there. With this knowledge she is able to counterfeit the signs of chastity when she is put to the test. Alsemero's medicine fails because it relies on the female body to demonstrate symptoms that will indicate the woman's condition. The play asserts what its seventeenth-century audience already suspected, what the law tried so diligently to counteract: that women find it all too easy to counterfeit their reactions, to hide their deficiencies, to mask the signs that their bodies should offer as clear signals for men to read. When forced to swallow the contents of Glass M, Beatrice-Joanna gapes, sneezes, laughs and falls into melancholy just as Alsemero's text predicts a virgin will—but she is an actress, not a virgin. On her wedding night, Beatrice-Joanna supplies a body double to act her part in the darkened bridal chamber. Throughout her short marriage, Beatrice-Joanna plays the spotless bride; her act is a mask to cover the rottenness of her sin and the defilement of her body.

Women are changelings. They are changeable and interchangeable. Not only are women able to counterfeit their actions, they are able to disguise themselves and substitute themselves for one another. Beatrice-Joanna capitalizes on the fact that in the darkened bed chamber women's bodies were undetectably replaceable. Alsemero is able to search his bedmate's body for signs of virginity, but cannot discern that he has the wrong woman in his bed. Beatrice-Joanna's successful evasion of his investigations testifies that women's bodies, though fleshly and material, are elusive and undecipherable.

When Alsemero at last obtains ocular proof of Beatrice-Joanna's falseness (he sees Beatrice-Joanna and DeFlores in a private tryst in the garden), he realizes that instead of a wife he has married a player. He finally sees what lies behind the "visor" she has worn "O'er that cunning face" (*C,* 5.3.46, 47). Her infidelity and her deception and the false testimony of her body are the characteristic untruths of actors. Women's sexuality was, indeed, a puzzle akin to the destabilized image of the transvestite player. Insofar as it was noted, the appearance of the boy beneath the woman's clothes may have been taken as an image of the rotten core at the center of women, of the inauthenticity of the female sex.[46] Beatrice-Joanna is at last known to be "the changeling," a counterfeit daughter, a whore masquerading as a bride, an actor in women's clothes.

The play makes self-conscious use of this acting metaphor to call attention to what can be known and what eludes knowledge, what can be seen and what remains hidden. The final scene reenacts DeFlores's rape of Beatrice-Joanna and literalizes his "murder" of her honor, but stages this action where we cannot see it. Alsemero locks Beatrice-Joanna into a room with DeFlores, bidding them

> . . . rehearse again
> Your scene of lust, that you may be perfect
> When you shall come to act it to the black audience
> Where howls and gnashings shall be music to you.
>
> (*C,* 5.3.114-17)

From behind the closed door of the chamber come the sounds of that rehearsal, "horrid" sounds which are the climax of their relationship and of the play. This audible, but hidden, scene of lust supplies the moment of revelation for which Vermandero, Tomazo, Alsemero, and their audience have yearned. But even this revelation is unclear. Beatrice-Joanna can be heard uttering ambiguous sounds, perhaps of passion, perhaps of agony. DeFlores responds with equally suggestive words, as Alsemero interprets their performance for his father-in-law and Tomazo:

BEATRICE:

[*within*] Oh, oh, oh!

ALSEMERO:

Hark 'tis coming to you.

DEFLORES:

[*within*] Nay, I'll along for company.

BEATRICE:

Oh, oh!

(*C,* 5.3.139-40)

Alsemero's remark is as much a double-entendre as the rest of the exchange. It is both a bitter taunt directed at Beatrice-Joanna, and a response to Tomazo's demand for "a recompense, for murder and adultery" (*C*, 5.3.138).

Behind that closed door, DeFlores is stabbing Beatrice-Joanna, then turning the knife on himself. When he forced Beatrice-Joanna to sleep with him, DeFlores murdered her honor; now he finishes his crime with her actual murder. Her body, when DeFlores drags her out onto the stage, bears visible signs of his violation, signs which are a literalization of the violence their sexual union committed on her body and her honor and, by extension, on her family. Beatrice-Joanna makes this connection explicit when she warns her father not to touch her.

> Oh come not near me, sir; I shall defile you.
> I am that of your blood was taken from you
> For your better health; look no more upon't,
> But cast it to the ground regardlessly;
> Let the common sewer take it from distinction.

> (*C*, 5.3.149-53)

The daughter, of course, has already defiled her family by her actions. She understands that her body, which was vulnerable to DeFlores's assault, must be cut off from the family in order to restore it to honor. Her blood, the biological connection between father and daughter, must be shed to effect this social cure, even as seventeenth-century medicine would prescribe a therapeutic blood-letting in order to remove the defiling humour from a sick patient. In this final moment, Beatrice-Joanna acknowledges the duty accepted so much more gracefully by Lucrece. She realizes that, in order to erase the shame she has cast upon her father and her husband, she must die.

The ostracism demanded by the law of seventeenth-century women guilty of consenting to their ravishers' desires is pushed to an extreme on the stage in Middleton and Rowley's play. But Beatrice-Joanna's body—bloody, dead, and cast aside on the stage—is a literalization of the kind of cutting-off prescribed by the law to separate a family from the daughter whose body has betrayed them. In life as on stage, honor could only be salvaged through a ritual purging of the defiled part: the woman. Once that purge is complete, Alsemero can treat the matter as closed and can encourage his father-in-law to forget it entirely:

> Let it be blotted out; let your heart lose it,
> And it can never look you in the face
> Nor tell a tale behind the back of life
> To your dishonor; justice hath so right
> The guilty hit that innocence is quit
> By proclamation and may joy again.

> (*C*, 5.3.182-87)

When he declares, "I am satisfied, my injuries / Lie dead before me," Tomazo de Piracquo confirms the necessity and accepts the sufficiency of her death as a recompense. In this final scene, the playwrights render Beatrice-Joanna's body readable. While she lived, she was change-able and her body was a cipher. Once dead, her body's signs are clear, straightforward.

In deference to the demands of their genre for dramatic closure, or perhaps out of their own desire to reconcile the dangerous issues their play has addressed, Middleton and Rowley give their play a "happy" ending. What began as a nightmarish vision of the consequences of a woman's desire and her weakness in defence of her honor, ends like a fairy tale. In this fictional world, the truth finally comes to light and justice holds the guilty parties to account. Death compensates death, and the innocent survivors can see that they will "joy again." The family reconstitutes itself as a male circle, no longer vulnerable to the vagaries of women. Alsemero reminds Vermandero that he has "yet a son's duty living" (*C*, 5.3.216). The alliances Vermandero sought to forge with the Piracquo brothers and with Alsemero are realized despite Beatrice-Joanna's betrayal—and those bonds are more fast now that there is no further danger to be feared from her. Beatrice-Joanna's death is framed by these men, her survivors, as the necessary prerequisite to their formation of a more perfect family, an all male family.

The barrenness of this resolution is readily apparent. This "happy" ending betrays its own artificiality, with its rhymed couplets and self-referential theatricality—and, of course, it doesn't feel happy at all. It offers a manifestly fictional resolution to problems that defied such simplistic treatment. Only on stage could the fifth act be depended on to supply a full confession and a complete recompense to the victims of a ravishment. Of course, the law also sought to supply such a recompense. Ample evidence of the failure of the legal establishment to redress the damage of rape is available in the history of its perpetual tightening of the statutes and in the continued wrangling of judicial authorities over the interpretation and application of those laws. For all of its efforts to define women and to proscribe their sexual behavior, the law found them to be changelings, whose complicity eluded detection. Middleton and Rowley's play tries to manage what the law could not when it exposes the falseness of a woman for all to see, but it is ultimately no more successful than the law in allaying the fear that a woman might succeed in deceiving her family and friends. It was a fear fed rather than eased by stories like this one. This fear required, but could not be satisfied with, the bloodied bodies of women like Lucrece and Beatrice-Joanna. Its loathing of the vulnerability of the female body demanded scenes of retribution and blame like this one in *The Changeling*. But the self-condemning, willing death Beatrice-

Joanna dies could only increase the anxiety of a culture that set women as the sentinels to guard familial honor.

Notes

1. In a letter to Sir Dudley Carleton dated 6 July 1616, John Chamberlain wrote that "Lord Cooke (by the Kinges expresse order delivered by Secretarie Winwood) was sequestered from the counsaile table, from riding his circuit, . . . and willed to review and correct his reports as many wayes faulty and full of novelties in points of law. This was the summe of the censure for his corrupt dealing with Sir Robert Rich and Sir Christofer Hatton in the extent of theyre lands and instalment of the debt due to the King." Coke offended the king when he ruled against the king's interest in a case challenging the royal prerogative. When the king called Coke and the other justices of the King's Bench to his presence and demanded that they reconsider their decision, Coke offended James again with his "insolent behavior" and his refusal to reverse his decision in the case (*The Letters of John Chamberlain,* ed. Norman Egbert McClure, 2 vols. [Philadelphia: The American Philosophical Society, 1939], 2:14, 32-57, 64). Further references to these letters will be cited parenthetically in the text by volume and page, and abbreviated as *L*.

2. Modern accounts of the Coke-Villiers match can be found in Laura Norsworthy's biography of Lady Hatton, *The Lady of Bleeding Hart Yard. Lady Elizabeth Hatton 1578-1646* (London: Harcourt, Brace, 1935); Lawrence Stone's *Crisis of the Aristocracy, 1558-1641* (Oxford: Clarendon, 1965) and *The Family, Sex, and Marriage: 1500-1800* (New York: Harper and Row, 1977); in Antonia Fraser's *The Weaker Vessel* (New York: Vintage Books, 1985), and in Roger Lockyer's *The Political Career of George Villiers Duke of Buckingham* (London: Longman, 1981). With the exception of Lockyer, these writers make much of an apparently apocryphal story that Frances was "tied to the Bedposts [by her father] and whipped 'till she consented to the Match" (see for instance, Norsworthy [62]). This report does not seem to exist in any contemporary accounts of the event. The first reference to Coke's whipping of Frances (that I can discover) appears in the margins of an eighteenth-century manuscript in the British Library collection (Cole's MSS, vol. 33, 10).

3. Coke was one of the administrators of Hatton's estate, which he was accused of mismanaging in 1616.

4. Chamberlain reports the public's interest in Coke's fall from favor: "The common speach is that fowre Ps have overthrown and put him down, that is Pride, Prohibitions, Premunire, and Prerogative" (*L*, 2:34). Coke had made himself particularly unpopular for the vehemence and excessively personal tone of his questioning of Sir Walter Raleigh at the latter's trial for treason against James I.

5. Also in dispute was whether Lady Hatton could maintain independent control of property she brought to her second marriage or whether Coke could dispose of it according to his own will without her consent. This question was not brought before the courts.

6. The report of the Privy Councillors to Secretary Lake (who was at that time with the king in Scotland) indicates that Lady Hatton appeared before them on 13 July 1617, "complayning in somewhat a passionate and tragicall manner that . . . she was by vyolence dispossessed of her childe" by her husband, who had "with his sonne and 10 or 11 servantes weaponed in violent manner . . . with a piece of timber or forme broken open the doore and dragged [Frances] alonge to his coach." The Privy Council then preferred "an informacion into the courte of Starr Chamber against Sir Edward Coke for the force and ryott used by him" (*Acts of the Privy Council of England, 1542-1631,* 46 vols. [Nendeln/Lichtenstein: Kraus Reprint, 1974], 35:315-16).

7. September 1617, *Letters from George Lord Carew to Sir Thomas Roe, Ambassador to the Court of the Great Mogul 1615-1617,* ed. John Maclean (London: The Camden Society, 1860), 119. It should be noted that Carew was a member of the Privy Council to which Lady Hatton pleaded her cause. Carew was among the signers of the letter sent via Secretary Lake to inform the king of the Coke affair (*Acts of the Privy Council,* [note 6], 35:315-16).

8. Coke told the Privy Council that he suspected his wife of planning "to carry his daughter into Fraunce" in order to break the match with Villiers. The Council charged him with the burden of proving his charge against his wife for illegal "transporting," one of the legal terms for ravishment (*Acts of the Privy Council,* 35:316).

9. Steven Orgel called my attention to the success of the Countess of Shrewsbury in defending her estate against the claims of her husband and stepsons, as well as the courts' decisions favoring Lady Anne Clifford and Elizabeth Cary against their husbands' attempts to appropriate property.

10. Lady Hatton pressed her custody dispute in the Privy Council rather than in a formal court of law, and she was heard and humored by the Council so

long as it served their interests to favor her against her husband. When the king made it clear that he wanted the marriage to go forward, Lady Hatton found herself under arrest and in the end she was forced not only to reconcile herself to the fact of her daughter's marriage, but also to contribute the money and land that her husband had promised on her behalf.

11. In *Woman and Gender in Renaissance Tragedy* (Atlantic Highlands, NJ: Humanities Press International, 1989), Dympna Callaghan examines the Renaissance construction of gender and explores the construction of women and of female desire as socially disruptive and dangerous. Callaghan writes, "Desire is inscribed at at [sic] every level (social, economic, political, sexual) as the motivation for change, upheaval, disruption, and crucially, for female tragic transgression. It is a force of disorder in terms of both conceptual and social systems. Importantly, defining the category of woman in terms of desire is a Renaissance preoccupation, and yet, paradoxically, it is one which ultimately threatens to unfix the categories of gender difference because . . . this is precisely the point where differential markers themselves become problematic" (140). Susan Dwyer Amussen discusses the substantive as well as metaphorical connections between women's role in the family and social order or disorder in both her book length study, *An Ordered Society* (New York: Basil Blackwell, 1988) and her article, "Gender, Family and the Social Order, 1560-1725," in *Order and Disorder in Early Modern England,* ed. Anthony Fletcher and John Stevenson (Cambridge: Cambridge Univ. Press, 1985).

12. Middleton's poem, "The Ghost of Lucrece," was published in 1600. There were actually two dramatizations of *Appius and Virginia*. The first was an early Elizabethan interlude, the second is tentatively credited to John Webster and Thomas Heywood. See Leonard Tennenhouse, *Power on Display: the Politics of Shakespeare's Genres* (New York: Methuen, 1986), 111; Lee Bliss, *The World's Perspective: John Webster and the Jacobean Drama* (New Brunswick, NJ: Rutgers Univ. Press, 1983), 6.

13. The Jacobean public was treated to the scandalous tales of a number of real women of this stripe. The divorce and remarriage of Frances Howard in 1613 was perhaps the most publicized of these; she claimed incredibly to be a virgin after seven years of marriage in order to obtain the divorce and marry her reputed lover, Robert Carr, the Earl of Somerset. In 1615 it came to light that Howard had conspired to murder Carr's friend Sir Thomas Overbury for his opposition to her re-marraige.

She and Carr and a number of accessories were convicted of murder. In "Diabolical Realism in *The Changeling,*" *Renaissance Drama* n.s. 11 (1980): 135-170, J. L. Simmons makes a case for the importance of the Essex divorce as an inspiration for *The Changeling*. He particularly remarks the coincidence of the Earl and Countess of Somerset's release from the tower in January 1621/22 with the period at which Middleton and Rowley must have worked on the play which was licensed on 7 May 1622. Cristina Malcolmson, in "'As Tame as the Ladies': Politics and Gender in *The Changeling,*" *English Literary Renaissance* 20 (1990): 320-39, and Margot Heinemann, in *Puritanism and Theatre: Thomas Middleton and Opposition Drama Under the Early Stuarts* (Cambridge: Cambridge Univ. Press, 1980), also discuss the importance of the Howard scandal to Middleton and Rowley's portrait of Beatrice-Joanna.

14. Thomas Middleton and William Rowley, *The Changeling,* ed. Russell A. Fraser and Norman Rabkin (New York: Macmillan, 1976), 5.3.136-38. Further references are to this edition and will be cited in the text by act, scene and line, and abbreviated *C*.

15. See James Sharpe, "The People and the Law," in *Popular Culture in Seventeenth-Century England,* ed. Barry Reay (New York: St. Martin's, 1985). Sharpe discusses popular enthusiasm for litigation in the Jacobean period and the tendency of British subjects to define their legal rights in terms of property holding and in contrast to the prerogative rights asserted by the Stuart monarchs. The popular understanding of the law as the "cement" that held English society together is evident in this passage spoken at the 1620 York Assizes: "[Without justice] the land would be full of theeves, the sea full of pirates, the commons would ryse against the nobylytye, and the nobylytye against the Crowne, wee should not know what were our owne, what were another mans, what we should have from our auncestors, what wee should learn [sic] to our children. In a worde, there should be nothing certayne, nothing sure . . . all kingdomes and estates would be brought to confucyon, and all humane society would be dissolved" (qtd. Sharpe, 246-47).

16. Penelope Corfield discusses the economic pressures of the early seventeenth-century in her essay, "Economic Issues and Ideologies," in *The Origins of the English Civil War,* ed. Conrad Russell (New York: Barnes and Noble, 1973). Perez Zagorin sketches out the influence of these pressures on the English social hierarchy in his preliminary chapter on "Social Structure and the

Court and the Country," in *The Court and the Country: The Beginning of the English Revolution* (London: Routledge and Kegan Paul, 1969). Stone's *Crisis of the Aristocracy* (note 2) addresses these same issues. A number of historians expressly tie these economic stresses to pressures on the patriarchal family and the position of women within it. See, for instance, Keith Wrightson, *English Society: 1580-1680* (London: Hutchinson, 1982); David Underdown, *Revel, Riot and Rebellion: Popular Politics and Culture in England 1603-1660* (Oxford: Clarendon Press, 1985); Underdown, "The Taming of the Scold: The Enforcement of Patriarchal Authority in Early Modern England," *Order and Disorder in Early Modern England* (note 11); Gordon J. Schochet, *Patriarchalism in Political Thought: The Authoritarian Family and Political Speculation and Attitudes Especially in Seventeenth-Century England* (New York: Basic Books, 1975); Stephen Ozment, *When Fathers Ruled: Family Life in Reformation England* (Cambridge: Harvard Univ. Press, 1983). In her chapter on "Wealth, Inheritance and the Specter of Strong Women" in *Still Harping on Daughters* (New York: Barnes and Noble, 1983), Lisa Jardine addresses some of the demographic and economic factors which placed stress on English views of female heirs to substantial estates (68-98).

17. Edward Coke, *The Institutes of the Laws of England* (London: M. Flescher, 1644), cap. 11.

18. Even married women seem to have been vulnerable to this crime if they could be used to extort property from their husbands. They might be held for ransom, or in some cases, the ravishment might be part of a larger theft of a man's property.

19. "Anno 3, Henry VII, cap. 2," *A Collection in English, of the Statutes Now in Force, Continued from the Beginning of Magna Charta* (London: Thomas Wright, 1603), 170 c. Unless otherwise noted, all citations of statutes have been taken from this edition.

20. In her essay, "'The Blazon of Sweet Beauty's Best': Shakespeare's *Lucrece*," in *Shakespeare and the Question of Theory*, ed. Patricia Parker and Geoffry Hartman (New York: Methuen, 1985), 95-115, Nancy Vickers finds plentiful evidence in *The Rape of Lucrece* for the depiction of rape as covetousness in Renaissance England's conception of the crime. According to Vickers, "Shakespeare's narrator specifically casts Tarquin's desire for Lucrece as desire for lucre," and she cites the following passage from the poem:

> Those that much covet are with gain so fond
> That what they have not, that which they possess

> They scatter and unloose it from their bond;
> And so by hoping more they have but less,
> Of gaining more, the profit of excess
>   Is but to surfeit, and such griefs sustain,
>   That they prove bankrout in this poor rich gain.

(lines 134-40)

Vickers also notes Lucrece's statement after the rape that she has been "robb'd and ransack'd by injurious theft" (line 838; Vickers, 102).

21. Issues of physical assault and character defamation, though covered by statutes against mayhem (maiming) and murder, seem to have been settled out of court more often than in. Physical retribution continued to be a more direct way of dealing with such matters. The courts, which were slow and costly, were used to obtain monetary settlements in property disputes, but swifter and more personal retaliation was often sought in cases of physical affronts and assaults. Stone discusses the continuance of personal violence in the period in *The Crisis of the Aristocracy* (note 2).

22. It is worth noting, too, that ravishment was defined primarily as a crime committed against women of substance, though some of the laws do remember "others" (the most important of these others being servants who might be ravished away from their employers' service). There were other laws that concerned themselves with the sexual behavior of poor women: bastardy laws, including a very strict law passed early in James I's reign, punished indigent women for bearing children who would become a drain on their parish's charity. Ravishment statutes might be seen as rich women's bastardy laws. Martin Ingram discusses popular attitudes about fornication and bastardy in "The Reform of Popular Culture? Sex and Marriage in Early Modern England," in *Popular Culture in Seventeenth-Century England* (note 15), especially 151-56.

23. Coke (note 17) offers two examples from the Parliament Rolls of widows who were "shamefully" ravished, and forced by "dures and menace of imprisonment" to marry men they did not wish to marry (cap. 11).

24. In *Making A Match: Courtship in Shakespeare and His Society* (Princeton: Princeton Univ. Press, 1991), Ann Jennalie Cook discusses marriage negotiations and their financial importance to sixteenth- and seventeenth-century families. Cook quotes from the wedding sermon of Lord and Lady Hay (1607) to illustrate the economic and political importance of marriage between propertied families: "to marie ioynes sex and sex, to marie at home ioynes house and house, but your marriage ioyneth land and land, earth and earth" (239). In

"Rape in England between 1550 and 1700," *The Sexual Dynamics of History: Men's Power, Women's Resistance,* ed. The London Feminist History Group (London: Pluto Press, 1983), Nazife Bashar notes that cases which claimed a substantive economic damage to the family of a rape victim were more likely to be successfully prosecuted than claims made by working class families who could not claim much damage. She cites a case in which "Thomas Rockingham, an alehousekeeper, petitioned the King in the mid 16th century about the rape of his daughter Elizabeth, [complaining that] she 'haith lost hir maryag that she might have had and hir good name in that Contie'" (42). Other noteworthy work on property and alliance concerns in matchmaking includes Stone's *Crisis of the Aristocracy* (note 2); Ralph Houlbrooke, "The Making of Marriage in Mid-Tudor England," *Journal of Family History* 10 (1985): 339-52; David Cressy, "Kinship and Kin Interaction in Early Modern England," *Past and Present* 113 (1986): 38-69; Martin Ingram, "Spousals Litigation in the English Ecclesiastical Courts," in *Marriage and Society: Studies in the Social History of Marriage,* ed. R. B. Outhwaite (New York: St. Martin's, 1981); and Vivien Brodsky Elliott, "Single Women in the London Marriage Market: Age, Status and Mobility, 1598-1619," in *Marriage and Society,* ed. Outhwaite. Volume 40 of *Renaissance Quarterly,* which was devoted to "Recent Trends in Renaissance Studies: The Family, Marriage, and Sex," included two overviews of recent scholarship in the field: Barbara Diefendorf's "Family Culture, Renaissance Culture," and Linda Boose's "The Family in Shakespeare Studies."

25. *A Discourse Upon the Exposicion & Understandinge of Statutes with Sir Thomas Egerton's Additions,* ed. Samuel E. Thorne (San Marino, CA: Huntington Library, 1942), 143. The "Discourse," preserved among the Ellesmere papers in the Huntington Library, probably dates from the 1560s or '70s.

26. See William Blackstone, *Commentaries on the Lawes of England,* 4 vols. (New York: W. E. Dean, 1841). Blackstone notes that a girl within age "by reason of her tender years . . . is incapable of judgement and discretion," and that "a male infant, under the age of fourteen years, is presumed by law incapable to commit a rape, and therefore it seems cannot be found guilty of it. . . . As to this particular species of felony, the law supposes an imbecility of body as well as mind" (4:212). Cook (note 24) quotes Henry Swinburne who termed the ages of consent the "Ripe Age" at which "abilitie and fitnesse for procreation" begin (Cook, 20; Swinburne, 24). Swinburne's work, *A Treatise of Spousals, or Matrimonial Contracts,*

though published in 1686, must predate his death in 1624. See also Ian Maclean, *The Renaissance Notion of Women* (Cambridge: Cambridge Univ. Press, 1980); Stone, *The Family, Sex and Marriage* and *The Crisis of the Aristocracy* (note 2); and Ozment, *When Fathers Ruled* (note 16) for other discussions of the legal age of consent and its relation to physical maturity and sexual practices in the period.

27. Coke (note 17) affirms at numerous points in *The Institutes of the Laws of England* that penetration was necessary for a rape to have occurred. Ejaculation near but not within a woman's body did not constitute a crime. Similarly, sodomy was held to have occurred only in cases where anal penetration could be proven.

28. Under this act, girls between the ages of twelve and sixteen were still to be held accountable for their consent.

29. See Blackstone's interpretation of this statute in his *Commentaries* (note 26). For conveying a girl away from home, this statute prescribes either a fine or two years imprisonment. Deflowering her or marrying her against her parents' wishes carries the penalty of five years in prison or a (presumably stiffer) fine.

30. In *The Second Part of the Institutes,* cap. 7 (note 17), Coke chronicles another dispute that arose as a legacy of the Marian rape law that punished kidnapping separately from forced marriage or forced intercourse. Elizabethan courts were left to decide whether there was a felony offense of illegal transportation of women. They decided in 26 Elizabeth that without marriage or defilement, carrying away could not be judged a felony.

31. Coke, *The Third Part of the Institutes* (note 17), cap. 11. When Elizabeth Tudor came to the throne, there was much need for plain declaration with respect to laws passed or amended during her sister's reign: Elizabeth's first two Parliaments passed legislation revoking some Marian statutes, especially those concerning church governance and practice, and those giving Philip II of Spain power in the English state. At the same time, they also confirmed certain pre-Marian statutes, with the effect of turning back the legal clock on law and precedent. The rape statutes were among those to receive particular reconsideration, and in 5 Eliz., cap. 17, the statute of 3 Henry VII was reconfirmed.

32. 18 Elizabeth, cap. 7: "An act for the repressing of the most wicked and felonious Rapes or ravishments of women, maides, wives, and damsels" (*A Collection of Sundrie Statutes, Frequent in Use,* ed. Fardinando Pulton [London: M. Flesher, I. Hauiland, and R. Young, 1632]).

33. *Aristotle's Master-Piece* seems to have been hugely popular, although early editions of it are now extremely scarce. A Latin edition of 1583 and an English translation of 1595 are the earliest known printings of the work which ran through numerous editions and remained in print into the eighteenth century. I quote from the Garland press facsimile of the 1694 edition: *Aristotle's Master-Piece: Or, the Secrets of Generation,* ed. Randolph Trumbach (New York: Garland Publishing, 1986), 63.

34. Gravdal, *Ravishing Maidens: Writing Rape in Medieval French Literature and Law* (Philadelphia: Univ. of Pennsylvania Press, 1991), 5.

35. Citation from Shakespeare, "The Rape of Lucrece," in *The Complete Works: Original Spelling Edition,* ed. Stanley Wells and Gary Taylor (Oxford: Clarendon Press, 1986), lines 1650-52. Coppélia Kahn discusses Lucrece's complicity in two essays: "The Rape in Shakespeare's *Lucrece,*" in *Shakespeare Studies,* ed. J. Leeds Barroll III, Barry Gaines and Ann Jennalie Cook (New York: Burt Franklin, 1976) and "Lucrece: The Sexual Politics of Subjectivity," in *Rape and Representation,* ed. Lynn Higgins and Brenda Silver (New York: Columbia Univ. Press, 1992).

36. There seems to be almost uniform agreement among critics that Middleton was responsible for the main plot and that Rowley wrote the subplot. (See, for instance, Lois E. Bueler's discussion of attribution in "The Rhetoric of Change in *The Changeling,*" *English Literary Renaissance* 14 (1984): 95-113, and N. W. Bawcutt's consideration of the subject in his introduction to the 1958 Revels edition [London: Methuen].) The play's action, however, is so carefully integrated that it seems that this collaboration was a close one. For my purposes, I will treat the play as a joint effort, rather than attributing specific aspects to one of its authors or the other.

37. Christopher Ricks, in "The Moral and Poetic Structure of *The Changeling,*" *Essays in Criticism* 10 (1960): 290-306, discusses the sexual connotation of the word "will" in the play. He also calls attention to the double meanings of several other recurrent terms, particularly *service, blood, act,* and *deed,* and discusses their function within the play. Bueler (note 36) also discusses the rhetorical importance of these terms. The *OED* listings for "will" consume several pages and include most of the senses I have discussed. For the use of will as a reference to the penis (a pun that continues in current British usage), see Eric Partridge's discussion of Shakespeare's use of the term in *Shakespeare's Bawdy* (New York: Routledge, 1990).

38. Karen Newman observes that women's rebelliousness was often presented as a linguistic protest against patriarchal authority. Beatrice-Joanna's articulate, but secret, rebellion against her father's will might be seen as an alternative to Kate's shrewishness, which is Newman's subject in "Renaissance Family Politics and Shakespeare's *The Taming of the Shrew,*" *English Literary Renaissance* 16 (1986): 86-100.

39. Jardine (note 16) also notes the similar assumptions elicited from men by the behavior of Desdemona and Beatrice-Joanna. Jardine points out the undeniable sensuality of Desdemona's character, often forgotten or glossed over by modern critics (75).

40. It is significant that ravishment law does not punish ravished women as felons even when it finds them to be material accessories to the crime. Such women are to be ostracized rather than executed. In other words, the law seems to treat women as incapable of the felonious malice attributed to their ravishers. See Heinemann's discussion (note 13) of Beatrice-Joanna's moral deficiency (175-78).

41. In *Pleas of the Crown,* 2 vols. (London, 1678), Matthew Hale reflected on this unknowableness when he explained why juries should be reluctant to convict defendants in rape trials: "It is true rape is a most detestable crime, and therefore ought severely and impartially to be punished with death; but it must be remembered, that it is an accusation easy to be made and hard to be proved, and harder to be defended by the party accused tho' never so innocent" (1:634). If *men's* guilt was difficult to establish, *women's* complicity with their rapists, however it might be suspected, even more persistently eluded the kind of proof the law craved. It remained a mystery of the most unsettling kind.

42. G. R. Quaife quotes this statement as part of a larger passage from Dalton in his discussion of sexual violence in *Wanton Wenches and Wayward Wives: Peasants and Illicit Sex in Early Seventeenth Century England* (New Brunswick: Rutgers Univ. Press, 1979), 247. J. A. Sharpe also cites Dalton in the course of his helpful survey of rape cases prosecuted during the seventeenth century. See especially his *Crime in Seventeenth-Century England, 1550-1750* (New York: Longman, 1984), 63-65. Other legal texts promoted this "conception-equals-consent" rule, including Sir Henry Finch's *Law, or a Discourse Thereof* (1627), E. T.'s *The Lawes Resolution of Women's Rights* (1632), and William Lambarde's *Eirenarcha, or Of the Office of the Justices of the Peace* (1611).

43. *Aristotle's Master-Piece* (note 33), 22-25. The author of the *Master-Piece* disputes much of this Galenic biology, particularly the notion that women have seed (he believes the egg is materially different rather than strictly analogous to the male sperm). Although he does not specify whether orgasm is necessary to conception in his competing physiology, it seems likely that it is not, as it is his opinion that the woman's ovum is the passive recipient fertilized by the active male seed. In *Obstetrics and Gynaecology in Tudor and Stuart England* (Kent: Kent State Univ. Press, 1982), Audrey Eccles discusses at some length the transition from the Galenic theory of male and female seed to a theory of ovum and seed. Eccles demonstrates that even at the end of the seventeenth century the two theories still competed for popular acceptance, although the Galenic theory had been abandoned by most medical writers.

44. *Aristotle's Master-Piece*, 89.

45. Alsemero's medical guide seems to be a compilation of experiments selected out of other texts. Beatrice-Joanna mentions the name of one of the authors it cites, Antonius Mizaldus, a French physician whose works included precisely such potions and tests. Dale B. Randall has researched Renaissance metaphysical works for evidence that such tests were not uncommon, and reports a substantive tradition of virginity and pregnancy tests in "Some Observations on the Theme of Chastity in *The Changeling*," *English Literary Renaissance* 14 (1984): 347-66. Of particular note is the fact that Randall finds a waning of confidence in such tests by the seventeenth century. He mentions Fortunato Fedeli's *De Relationibus Medicorum* which concludes that there are no sure signs of virginity, and Robert Burton who dismisses virginity tests as cruel side effects of jealous melancholy (*The Anatomy of Melancholy* 3.3.2.1). In a paper delivered at the University of Pennsylvania conference, "Renaissance Subject/Early Modern Object," Marjorie Garber contextualized Alsemero's desire for proof of Beatrice-Joanna's sexual status as part of a larger desire on the part of sixteenth- and seventeenth-century English men to discover and demystify women's sexual pleasure ("Glass M and Glass C: The Art of Drug-Testing Women").

46. See, for example, Jardine's *Still Harping on Daughters* (note 16); Kathleen McLuskie's "The Act, The Role, and the Actor," *New Theatre Quarterly* 10 (1987): 120-30; Phyllis Rackin's "Androgyny, Mimesis, and the Marriage of the Boy Heroine on the English Renaissance Stage," *PMLA* 102 (1987): 29-41; Jean E. Howard's "Crossdressing, the Theatre, and Gender Struggle in Early Modern Europe," *Shakespeare Studies* 39 (1988): 418-40; Laura Levine's "Men in Women's Clothing," *Criticism* 28 (1986): 121-43; Stephen Orgel's "Nobody's Perfect; Or Why Did the English Stage Take Boys for Women?" *South Atlantic Quarterly* 88 (1989): 7-29; and J. W. Binns's "Women or transvestites on the Elizabethan stage?" *Sixteenth-Century Journal* 5 (1974): 95-120.

Lisa Hopkins (essay date 1997)

SOURCE: Hopkins, Lisa. "Beguiling the Master of the Mystery: Form and Power in *The Changeling*." In *Medieval and Renaissance Drama in England*, Volume 9, edited by John Pitcher, pp. 149-61. Cranbury, N.J.: Associated University Presses, Inc., 1997.

[*In the following essay, Hopkins explores gender and power relations in* The Changeling.]

When Beatrice-Joanna opens the closet of her new husband, Alsemero, she is appalled to discover that it contains a pregnancy test. She immediately plans her strategy for outwitting him:

> None of that water comes into my belly:
> I'll know you from a hundred. I could break you now,
> Or turn you into milk, and so beguile
> The master of the mystery, but I'll look to you.[1]

These lines perform a swift and probing exposure of the dynamics of gender and power relations in **The Changeling.** Alsemero presumably imagines that his scientific experiments will offer him full access to the hidden secrets of women's bodies. In terms of Renaissance fears about female sexuality, this would surely represent a powerfully attractive fantasy to the audience of the play.[2] All the men in this play seek, as Cristina Malcolmson among others has shown,[3] to exercise a highly repressive control over the actions of women; but while men like Alibius must suffer in a constant state of uncertainty about their wives' chastity, Alsemero believes himself to have to hand the infallible means of prying into the last secret of women and, consequently, exercising over them a control that is utterly unchallengeable. Ironically, he secretes the mechanism of this ostensible tool of control in his "closet," traditionally, as evidenced by the titles of such cookery books as *A Closet for Ladies and Gentlewomen* and *The Good Huswifes Closet,* a space demarcated for the exclusive use of women, and one, moreover, associated with the domestic skill of food preparation, to which Alsemero's own "concoctions" are thus paralleled, his invasion of the feminine space of the closet and his parody of the female-dominated process of cooking tellingly imaging his intended probing of the elusive internal secrets of the female body.

Beatrice's discovery of the closet, however, strikes a fundamental blow at the position of superiority into which Alsemero is confident that he has maneuvered himself. It is one of the scene's most telling structural ironies that before her discovery of the actual *means* of Alsemero's bid for omniscience, Beatrice was already firmly convinced that he *was* omniscient:

> Never was bride so fearfully distressed.
> The more I think upon th'ensuing night,
> And whom I am to cope with in embraces—
> One who's ennobled both in blood and mind,
> So clear in understanding (that's my plague now),
> Before whose judgement will my fault appear
> Like malefactors' crimes before tribunals
> (There is no hiding on't)—the more I dive
> Into my own distress.
>
> (4.2.1-10)

Beatrice's faith in Alsemero's "understanding" and "judgement" is absolute, leading her to subscribe to the myth that a man can detect the presence or absence of a hymen. But it is not in these physical terms that she envisages the processes of her detection: her language instead clusters round the metaphorical, the nonspecific, and the abstract—"ennobled," "clear in understanding," "judgement," "fault," "malefactors' crimes." Mechanics and specifics have no place here; within the transparency of the soliloquy, where Beatrice-Joanna's own mental processes are laid bare to us, she herself imagines a transparent world, where a phenomenology of "clarity" and "appearance" lays bare all crime to a detached surveillance. There is no personal dynamic encoded within her talk of "whom," "one who's ennobled," and "tribunals"; she figures instead an impersonal authority manifested in an appraising eye. She offers no theory of the mechanism of disclosure; although she is a daughter of the citadel, within which are "secrets" (1.1.164), it seems that she cannot, here, conceive of any process by which secrecy may be maintained.

All this changes when she herself performs precisely the act of laying bare that she imaginatively attributes to others, and when, in so doing, she becomes aware of the particular structures conditioning the epistemological power-relations that have been previously mystified for her. The rifling of Alsermero's closet becomes a means whereby she can read, preemptively, his own reading of her. Rather than relying on the innate and impersonal "judgement" with which she had so Foucauldianly credited him, Alsemero's superior knowledge and power need in fact to be maintained by the most artificial of helps. Moreover, the tools of his mastery are not exclusive to him. Much is made in this play of exclusivity of possession, particularly in Alibius's obsessive attitude to Isabella; what we see here is precisely that, as in the case of Alonzo de Piracquo's ringed finger, demarcators perceived as es-

sential to the maintenance of male identity can with the greatest of ease be transferred to others, whom they empower. Once she has understood this, Beatrice-Joanna can indeed proceed to "beguile / The master of the mystery" (4.1.37-38).

The means by which she does so are telling, for she has learned her lesson well. Her words chart a complete transformation from the abstractions that had earlier characterized her figuring of the processes of knowledge acquisition; she begins instead to pay precise attention to detail, having now understood that it is the medium of information transfer that conditions the message. The pregnancy test consists of "two spoonfuls of the white water in glass C." To forestall it, Beatrice-Joanna decides that she has essentially two options: "I could break you now, / Or turn you into milk" (4.1.36-37). The idea of turning the water into milk is presumably suggested to her by the fact that the water is white, but it is, in the context, in its turn suggestive of other aspects of the situation, and in particular the fundamental association of milk with pregnancy. The presence of milk in the breasts is at once often one of the early signs of pregnancy and also provided a standard test to which a woman suspected of having recently given birth could be subjected. Beatrice-Joanna's mention of milk in this connection, then, represents a deliberate subversion of the processes of gynecological inspection designed to ensure male control of female sexuality. She will deprive the master of the mystery by a mystery of her own, the inscrutable processes of pregnancy and lactation, and the female body will successfully mystify the scrutiny of the male eye. Interestingly, Cristina Malcolmson's account of the play links its fear of Spanish infiltration in general with a particular fear of a particular woman, the Spanish Infanta, as a mother, or at least as the mother of the future king of England: relating the play to the Puritan opposition to the proposed marriage of Prince Charles to the Infanta, she points out that "the marriage negotiations largely focused on the number of Catholics that would be associated with the nursery, and the number of years that the prince would be under his mother's influence."[4]

Ironically, of course, this particular plan of evasion is never put into action, for Beatrice-Joanna herself does not yet know whether or not she is pregnant, and so whether or not this is necessary; moreover, the rapidity of the play's narrative momentum means that even at the time of her death, the state of her womb will remain a mystery to herself and the audience alike. But what she discovers next makes the pregnancy test redundant:

> Ha! That which is next is ten times worse;
> "How to know whether a woman be a maid or not."
> If that should be applied, what would become of me?
>
> (4.1.39-41)

Here at least Beatrice-Joanna is sure of the truth, and she knows that Alsemero must not know it. This test, unlike the pregnancy one, comes equipped with a full scientific pedigree—"the author Antonius Mizaldus" (4.1.44-45)[5]—but, as Middleton surely knew and as Shakespeare certainly indicated in Hamlet's warnings to the players, the intentions of the *author* are always vulnerable to those of the *actor.* Beatrice-Joanna can frustrate Alsemero's processes of inquisition here too, but this time it will be through performance.

The notion of performance is one that often figures prominently in Middleton's tragic dramaturgy. *The Revenger's Tragedy* and *Women Beware Women* both culminate in elaborately ironic masques of death that, in the latter case at least, are pointedly at odds with the representational aesthetics prevalent in the bulk of the play: the "realist" setting of the widow's house forms an unlikely preparation for the spectacular court finale, with its mesh of tightly interlocking plot and counter-plot, while in *The Revenger's Tragedy* the theatricalization of the closing scene stylizes and attenuates the force of the moral point. In *The Changeling,* performance becomes openly equated with the immoral mendacity castigated by Puritan opposition to theater when Beatrice-Joanna first vicariously rehearses and then personally enacts a staging of virginity—in itself, ironically, a state guaranteed precisely by an *absence* of performance—which completely deceives her audience, Alsemero.

The performance of virginity here would, to a Jacobean audience, undoubtedly have been strongly reminiscent of the allegedly similar method employed in the divorce case of Frances Howard, daughter of the earl of Suffolk, and her first husband, Robert Devereux, second earl of Essex (son of Queen Elizabeth's favorite). Middleton's reworking of the story of Frances Howard both here and in his play *The Witch* has often been remarked;[6] I want to focus particularly, though, on his use not only of specific motifs and actions but on the processes of dramatization that he both employs and represents in relation to the Howard divorce case. (As the later trial of Frances and her second husband had revealed, the events surrounding the divorce had themselves been conceived of by those involved as highly theatrical in character, with correspondence using code names for the principal participants and with the Lieutenant of the Tower referring to Frances's lover as "so great an actor in this sta[g]e.")[7] Frances Howard's campaign to have her marriage annulled had in itself involved careful presenting and indeed staging of the evidence. Her initial petition was very anxious to represent her as frustrated by the impotence of her husband only because she wished to "be made a mother,"[8] rather than because of any specifically sexual desires; when it came to establishing her virginity, she set up an elaborate scene in which a heavily veiled woman who was widely be-

lieved to be a substitute was examined, as Diaphanta fears to be, by a female jury. Performing the self continued to feature strongly in Frances Howard's behavior when two years after her annulment had been granted and she had been married for a second time to Robert Carr, earl of Somerset, she was tried for the murder of Carr's friend, Sir Thomas Overbury. Decoratively dressed and weeping prettily, she succeeded in winning hearts at her trial in the most unpromising of circumstances: Lady Anne Clifford commented in her diary that "my Lady Somerset was arraigned & condemned at Westminster hall where she confessed her fault and asked the King's Mercy, & was much pitied by all beholders."[9] The king spared her life and indeed released her from the Tower shortly before Middleton and Rowley wrote their play.

That Diaphanta's reference to a female jury and the staging of the virginity test clearly allude to the Frances Howard story has, then, been established. There are, however, two other references to the history of Frances Howard in the play that both relate closely to the performative element of Beatrice-Joanna's response to the discovery of the virginity test. The first time that we see Beatrice-Joanna and De Flores together, she drops a glove, which De Flores retrieves for her. She rejects the returned glove angrily:

> Mischief on your officious forwardness!
> Who bade you stoop? They touch my hand no more:
> There, for t'other's sake I part with this—
> *(Takes off and throws down the other glove)*
> Take 'em and draw off thine own skin with 'em.
>
> (1.1.225-28)

The episode, apparently Middleton's invention,[10] seems to rework an occasion when Frances Howard, who may well have been angling to catch the attention of Prince Henry, is said to have dropped a glove, which the prince declined to take up on the crudely pointed grounds that it had been "stretcht by another."[11] The prince's use of sexual symbolism here is certainly similar to De Flores's suggestive delight at the thought that he "should thrust my fingers / Into her sockets here" (1.1.231-32); moreover, there is, arguably, a possible parallel with the celebrated episode of the countess of Salisbury's garter, and a telling contrast between the lubricity of the Jacobean interpretations and the pure-mindedness of Edward III's famous dictum "Honi soit qui mal y pense."[12] In Middleton's retelling, though, the roles of the participants are dramatically reversed to make the Frances Howard figure not the recipient but the inflicter of the insult. If we see this as an allusion to Prince Henry, in short, we must recognize that Beatrice-Joanna has here too beguiled the master of the mystery by using his own weapons against him.

The other occasion in which the past of the real Frances Howard becomes reworked in that of the fictional Beatrice-Joanna seems not to have been previously noticed,[13] but is even more pointedly, and literally, dramatic. Immediately before his defloration of Beatrice-Joanna, De Flores comments:

> 'Las, how the turtle pants! Thou'lt love anon
> What thou so fear'st and faint'st to venture on.
>
> (3.4.169-70)

Here he echoes very closely the Epithalamion of *Hymenaei,* the masque written by Jonson for Frances Howard's first marriage, to the earl of Essex:

> Shrink not, soft virgin, you will love
> Anon what you so fear to prove.[14]

Middleton is very likely to have been aware of Jonson's wedding poetry for Frances Howard, because he himself had been the author of the now lost **Masque of Cupid,** performed as part of the celebrations of Frances Howard's second marriage, to the earl of Somerset. Jonson too was involved once more: his *A Challenge at Tilt* and *The Irish Masque* formed part of the entertainment. Since *A Challenge at Tilt* was spoken by two Cupids, there may well have been enough thematic overlap between this and Middleton's Cupid-based masque to necessitate at least some degree of cooperation in ensuring programmatic continuity. Moreover, the passage in *Hymenaei* in which Truth and Opinion debate the relative merits of marriage and virginity may be seen as ironically paralleled in the exchange between the wife and supposed virgin, Beatrice-Joanna, and the maid, Diaphanta, who is so anxious to be rid of her virginity.

David Lindley has recently speculated at some length on the poets' feelings at discovering that they had, in effect, been inveigled into composing epithalamia for a wedding based on a web of deceit and murder. In Jonson's case, his situation may well have been particularly uncomfortable, since he had provided offerings for both the Countess's marriages; he would therefore surely have been struck even at the time of the second wedding by some element at least of incongruity in this second feting of a ritual that had proved so ill-fated the first time round. Nevertheless, Lindley has argued strongly that the writers of praise poems for the second marriage need not necessarily have had to grit their teeth quite so much as we, with the benefit of hindsight, might imagine:

> a lack of scrupulousness about the precise awareness that poets like Donne might be supposed to have had can fatally colour everything that follows. Since almost all critics also assume that an adulterous relationship between the couple was public knowledge in 1613, they are compelled to the position that the poets must have chosen to shut their ears and avert their moral gaze in order to praise Frances Howard. Since most critics have an investment in the defence of their authors' integrity they then search for the criticism that must, somehow, be present in the texts.[15]

He argues that the wedding was arranged in such haste that practical considerations would probably have been more pressing than ideological ones, particularly in the case of Middleton himself, "if Chamberlain's assertion that they only had 'fowre dayes warning' be credited. It must have been an 'off-the-peg' piece, and can scarcely have had much verbal material—one reason perhaps, why it has not survived."[16] Nevertheless, when the poets later came to hear all the sordid details of the Overbury murder, and to see that the Countess's demeanor in the witness stand apparently excused her from the penalties applied to her subordinates and assistants, they may well have felt that their services had been procured under false pretences, and that Frances Howard had, indeed, beguiled the masters of their mystery.

Middleton's rewriting of her story certainly seems to take a revenge on her, and, moreover, a peculiarly literary one. When Alsemero finally perceives her falsehood, he offers, at the same time, an ironic recognition of the cleverness with which she has deceived him: "You read me well enough. I am not well" (5.3.16). Beatrice at first attempts to face it out, and discovering that Alsermero suspects that Diaphanta was implicated, demands "Is your witness dead then?" (5.3.57) (interestingly, the Countess of Somerset's sorcerer, Simon Forman, had died before her case came to trial, but his name was nevertheless much used in the evidence against her, after searches of his house and interrogations of his widow). Finally, she attempts to clear herself by admitting what she clearly sees as the less damaging part of the truth: she confesses the murder of Piracquo, but continues to deny adultery, revealing the extent to which she has internalized her society's ideological fetishization of female chastity at the apparent expense of all else. In reply, Alsemero imprisons her, fittingly enough, in the very closet that she has violated; by the time she emerges from it, she is mortally wounded, and makes, finally, a full and free confession.

In this, she differs strikingly from the attitudes of many other Jacobean stage villains. Iago refuses explanation to the last:

> Demand me nothing; what you know, you know:
> From this time forth I never will speak word.[17]

Hieronimo in *The Spanish Tragedy,* despite having been already quite forthcoming, goes to the lengths of biting out his own tongue rather than provide further information, though what else remains him for him to tell is unclear; Vittoria in *The White Devil* offers splendid defiance to the tribunal of her accusers. Beatrice-Joanna, however, adopts a position of unmitigated repentance and self-abnegation, and, in what was presumably a pointed contrast with the behavior of the Countess of Someset, regards herself as unworthy of any mercy. Just as the outset of her closet scene soliloquy saw her fully interpellated into a position of ideological subjugation in which her image of herself was as a helpless and transparent prey of a culture of ceaseless surveillance, so she has now come again to internalize her husband's, her father's, and ever her lover's assumptions about her own status as whore and villainess. The brief moment of freedom in which *her* preemptive reading of *him* had rendered her opaque has been lost; she has resumed her designated position as the objectified other of demonization. Middleton, in short, has, by his staging of Beatrice-Joanna, returned the mystery to the master, reversing the perceived injustice of the Countess of Somerset's pardon by insisting on the full exaction of the processes of the law on her dramatic representative. Beatrice-Joanna and Frances Howard may each have been able to produce a substitute to beguile the master of the mystery of their own virginity tests, but Middleton regains the upper hand by his own dramatic substitution of the publicly chastised Beatrice-Joanna for the recently released Countess.

In doing so, the weapons he deploys against the figure of Frances Howard are derived precisely from the same species of theatricality as animated her own performances of herself (whether vicarious or personal) as virgin and as penitent. Had his *Masque of Cupid* survived, it would be fascinating to see whether he drew on its motifs, but the close parallel with the Jonson Epithalamion certainly suggests a reappropriation of dramatic material that had been previously "misused" in the service of the Howard/Somerset wedding. In many ways, *The Changeling* is in fact careful to present itself as a reworking of other plays. Cristina Malcolmson has remarked on its many affiliations with *Twelfth Night* (itself perhaps staged as a part of the celebration of a wedding),[18] and Joost Daalder points to Vermandero's echoing of *Doctor Faustus* when he says of Hell, "We are all there; it circumscribes [us] here."[19] Even more pointedly, *The Changeling* recasts many motifs and moments found in Middleton's own *Hengist, King of Kent,* written two or three years earlier.[20] Both plays are lavish in the use of the dumb show; both revolve round a licentious woman (Beatrice-Joanna, Roxena) believed to be virtuous, and a chaste one (Isabella, Castiza) mistreated by an unworthy husband; the role taken by Horsus, secret lover of Roxena, in planning villainies is not dissimilar to that of De Flores. Moreover, *Hengist* too has an overriding concern with chastity. The play opens in the reign of a king, Constantius, who has (most unusually for a male character in Jacobean drama) vowed perpetual chastity because of his strongly Catholic religious beliefs, and who persuades Castiza, the woman he is forced to marry, to take a similar resolve. Much is made of the religious angle—at one point Constantius wishes to fast because it is the eve of St. Agatha (1.2.216-20), and Vortiger resists the incoming

Saxons on the grounds that "y'are strangers in religion Cheifly" (2.3.34). At one point, chastity is associated both with Catholicism and with the image of the closet:

HERS.:

> Faire is shee and most fortunate may shee bee
> But in maide lost for ever, my desire
> Hath beene ye Close Confusion of that name
> A treasure tis, able to make more theeues
> Then Cabinetts set open to entice . . .
>
>   . . . . .

HENG.:

> Mary pray help my memory if I should
>
>   (2.3.160-68)

To prevent the detection of this loss of her chastity, Roxena spontaneously offers herself for an onstage virginity test: when Horsus falls down with grief at hearing that Vortiger desires her, she declares:

> Oh 'tis his Epilepsie, I know it well,
> I holp him once in Germany, Comst agen?
> A virgins right hand stroakt upon his heart
> Giues him ease streight But tmust be a pure virgin
> Or ells it brings no Comforth
>
>   (2.3.249-53)

At first Horsus threatens to shame her by refusing to cooperate; eventually, however, she persuades him that she has a plan, and he is duly "cured." Throughout this scene, it is Roxena who takes the lead, as is emphasized in the parodic visual image of the man, instead of the woman, "falling backwards." (There is also further ironic play on this motif when Castiza, who has been raped by her husband in disguise, refuses to swear onstage that she is chaste.) When Middleton reworks this scene in *The Changeling,* the comparison with *Hengist* works to ensure that although Beatrice too may seem, as Roxena was, in control, our awareness of the metatheatrical ancestry of the episode serves to stress that, however much greater her knowledge may be than that of Alsemero, she is merely a puppet of the omniscient author.

In making this play so pointedly and consistently a representation of events and speeches already alternatively presented, then, Middleton is doubly able to offer a reformation of homosocial bonding after disruption by threatening women, not only in the father-son and brother-brother relationship sealed between Alsemero and Vermandero and Alsemero and Tomazo over the dead body of Beatrice-Joanna, but also in the links that bind Middleton and Rowley themselves with Marlowe, Shakespeare, and Jonson in a controlled demonstration of mastery over the mysteries of performance that women's efforts at fallacious self-staging had attempted to beguile.[21] Metatheatricality is thus made the crucial tool for the undermining of Beatrice-Joanna's own too-potent theatricality.

For the Puritan in Middleton, the idea of performance securing and enacting its own punishment must have been an appealingly ironic one. His characteristic tragic strategy is indeed to involve his characters in fantastically complex self-staging situations in which their deaths are ironically brought about in ways that frustrate their performance intentions, as with the double masque of revengers at the end of **The Revenger's Tragedy** or the plotting and counterplotting of the closing scene of **Women Beware Women.** In each of these instances, those who attempt to wrest control of the script are brutally punished by the workings of a deeper plot of whose existence they have no inkling: the revenger's tragedy is in one sense at least precisely the revenge of the dramatist, and of metatheatrical conventions invisible to the intratheatrical character. The falsity that in Puritan ideology inheres in all acting is aptly countered by an aesthetic that punishes precisely the performative nature of the theatrical self, while at the same time ironically heightening the theatrical pleasure of the *audience* by its sophisticated self-referentiality. **The Changeling,** with its extravagantly theatrical deployment of a Webster-like antimasque of madmen and of the consciously archaic form of the dumb show,[22] partakes here of the same aesthetic of self-reflexivity as characterizes Middleton's habitual use of tragic form,[23] and makes his reinscription of Beatrice-Joanna into the cultural norms she has challenged so much the more overt an act of deployment of the most privileged forms of that culture. Ultimately, then, it is the mastery who retains the mystery.

Notes

1. Thomas Middleton and William Rowley, *The Changeling,* ed. Joost Daalder (London: A and C. Black, 1990), 4.1.35-38. All further quotations from the text will be taken from this edition.

2. Compare for instance Susan J. Wiseman, "*'Tis Pity She's a Whore*: Representing the Incestuous Body," in *Renaissance Bodies,* ed. Lucy Gent and Niegel Llewellyn (London: Reaktion Books, 1990), 180-97. For a powerfully developed argument that we should take the virginity test in *The Changeling* seriously, see Dale J. B. Randall, "Some Observations on the Theme of Chastity in *The Changeling*," *English Literary Renaissance* 14 (1984): 357-66, 355-60.

3. Cristina Malcolmson, "'As Tame as the Ladies': Politics and Gender in *The Changeling,*" *English Literary Renaissance* 20 (1990): 320-39, 326-27.

4. Ibid., 334, n. 37.

5. On the significance of Antoine Mizauld, see Randall, "Some Observations on the Theme of Chastity in *The Changeling,*" 358-59.

6. See Margot Heinemann, *Puritanism and Theatre: Thomas Middleton and Opposition Drama under the Early Stuarts* (Cambridge: Cambridge University Press, 1980), 178-79; Malcomson, "'As Tame as the Ladies'" 325-26 and 333-39; Thomas Middleton, *The Witch,* ed. Elizabeth Schafer (London: A. and C. Black, 1994), xv-xix, xxii; J. L. Simmons, "Diabolical Realism in Middleton and Rowley's *The Changeling,*" *Renaissance Drama* 11 (1980); 135-70, 155-65; David Lindley, *The Trials of Frances Howard* (London: Routledge, 1993), 67, 78-79, 114-15, and 120-21; Anne Lancashire, "*The Witch*: Stage Flop or Political Mistake?," in *"Accompaninge the Players": Essays Celebrating Thomas Middleton, 1580-1980,* ed. Kenneth Friendenreich (New York: AMS Press, 1983), 161-81, 163-69; and A. A. Bromham and Zara Bruzzi, *"The Changeling" and the Years of Crisis, 1619-1624* (London: Pinter, 1990). Douglas Duncan, in "Virginity in *The Changeling,*" *English Studies in Canada* 9 (1983), 25-35, 28, argues that Beatrice-Joanna's fetishization of her virginity aligns her very closely with the values attributed to Catholicism, which would work as a further connection between her and the world of the Howards.

7. Beatrice White, *Caste of Ravens: The Strange Case of Sir Thomas Overbury* (London: John Murray, 1965), 63-66.

8. Lindley, *The Trials of Frances Howard,* 81.

9. D. J. H. Clifford, ed., *The Diaries of Lady Anne Clifford* (Stroud: Alan Sutton, 1990), 35.

10. See Christopher Ricks, "The Moral and Poetic Structure of *The Changeling,*" *Essays in Criticism,* 10 (1960): 290-306, 301, for both the originality of the episode and comment on some of its possible significance. It should be noted that the stage direction cited here is a modern interpolation. The 1653 quarto has no directions for this crucial episode apart from an "Exeunt" after line 228, so it remains the decision of an editor (or director) as to whether this confrontation between Beatrice-Joanna and De Flores takes place in the sight and hearing of the Count or not.

11. Quoted in Lindley, *The Trials of Frances Howard,* 65. I am grateful to Zara Bruzzi for an illuminating conversation about the episode of the glove.

12. The story of Edward's picking up the Countess's garter and founding the chivalric Order of the Garter in response to the salacious jeers of his courtiers may be apocryphal, but although there is

no contemporary warrant for it, sixteenth-century chroniclers such as Vergil and Holinshed were defensive about its moral if not its historical rectitude.

13. See my forthcoming note, "An Echo of *Hymenaei* in *The Changeling*," *Notes and Queries* (June 1996).

14. Quoted in Lindley, *The Trials of Frances Howard*, 22. Malcolmson comments that the image is reused in *Women Beware Women* ("As Tame as the Ladies," 337).

15. Lindley, *The Trials of Frances Howard*, 126. Anne Lancashire interestingly suggests that one explanation for the failure of *The Witch* may have been that it worked, through the use of masque technique, to whitewash the Howards ("*The Witch*: Stage Flop or Political Mistake?" 171-72).

16. Lindley, *The Trials of Frances Howard*, 128.

17. William Shakespeare, *Othello*, ed. Kenneth Muir (Harmondsworth: Penguin, 1968), 5.2.300-301.

18. Malcolmson, "'As Tame as the Ladies,'" 338.

19. *The Changeling*, ed. Daalder, n. on 5.3.164.

20. See Thomas Middleton, *Hengist, King of Kent; or, The Mayor of Queenborough*, ed. R. C. Bald (New York: Charles Scribner's Sons, 1938), xiii, for the dating of the play. All quotations from *Hengist* will be taken from this edition.

21. Duncan ("Virginity in *The Changeling*," 28) compares Beatrice's attitude to her virginity with that of Isabella in *Measure for Measure*.

22. See my "Acting the Act in *The Changeling*," forthcoming in the *Revista Alicantina*.

23. For a very different view of the form of *The Changeling*, which sees it as deliberately unsatisfactory and "freakish," see Peter Morrison, "A Cangoun in Zombieland: Middleton's Teratological *Changeling*," in *Accompaninge the Players*," 219-41, 236; for an argument that its form is in fact mannerist, see Raymond J. Pentzell, "*The Changeling*: Notes on Mannerism in Dramatic Form," *Comparative Drama* 9 (1975): 3-28.

Richard L. Nochimson (essay date 2002)

SOURCE: Nochimson, Richard L. "'Sharing' *The Changeling* by Playwrights and Professors: The Certainty of Uncertain Knowledge about Collaboration." *Early Theatre* 5, no. 1 (2002): 37-57.

[*In the following essay, Nochimson expresses skepticism about the prevailing theory that Middleton wrote the main plot of* The Changeling *while Rowley composed the beginning, ending, and comic scenes, arguing that no external evidence exists to support this contention.*]

My purpose in this essay is to argue against the passive acceptance of received wisdom about collaborative authorship of plays in early modern England. I hope to demonstrate that carelessness in the application of attribution methodologies has led scholars astray in their consideration of various issues relating to multiple authorship. I focus on *The Changeling* because of the persistence with which students of that play have disregarded the implications of various thoughtful discussions of attribution methodologies and of dramatic collaboration for their practice of 'sharing' *The Changeling* between two playwrights. It is my basic contention that students of *The Changeling* are operating in an evidentiary vacuum. As I shall try to explain in the pages that follow, the evidence simply does not exist that would enable us to determine how much and which parts of *The Changeling* were 'written' (I will discuss that problematic word) by Thomas Middleton or by William Rowley.

The unusual degree to which scholars have agreed about details of the authorship of *The Changeling* did cause me to hesitate in forming my own skeptical conclusions. I was faced with a preponderance of critical opinion that Rowley wrote the beginning and the ending of the play, and the comic scenes throughout. This view was established by Fleay and Wiggin more than a century ago, and it has persisted up through the most recent edition of the play, Bawcutt's 1998 edition.[1] However, both the awkwardness and the neatness of the arrangement worried me. Would a playwright (Middleton, we are told) who had the role of creating the main plot of the play really be comfortable not having any role in the creation of the first and last acts? Does it make sense that each of two playwrights imaginatively immersed in the chaotic world described in Jacobean drama would abide by a neat, clearly arbitrary, obviously unnecessary arrangment to keep hands off the distinct portions of the play assigned to his collaborator? I was uncomfortable with the picture of the conditions of playwrighting that I was being asked to accept both as a fact for this play and as typical for collaborative playwrighting of the time.

My skeptical attitude (about the broader questions involved, although not about *The Changeling*) does have various kinds of honorable support. Although as far as I know Schoenbaum never questioned the received opinion about this particular play, some of his general warnings demand quotation here:[2]

> Many popular assumptions and facile generalizations about the nature of Elizabethan dramatic collaboration have no secure foundation in external fact, but rest instead on undemonstrated theories or on internal evidence garnered in cheerful violation of the elementary methods I have outlined.

(230)

External evidence cannot be ignored, no matter how inconvenient such evidence may be for the theories of the investigator.

(163)

[The use of internal evidence is problematic because] an author's individuality never exists as pure essence. . . . All plays, furthermore, are in a sense collaborations, shaped from conception to performance by the author's awareness of the resources of actors and theater, the wishes of impresario or shareholders, and the tastes and capacities of the audience.

(149-50)

It is risky to attempt the allocation of scenes in collaborations, even when all the partners are known . . . ; riskier still when not all the collaborators are specified.

(162)

External evidence about the authorship of *The Changeling* is extremely limited. The title page of the first edition attributes the work to 'Thomas Midleton, and William Rowley'. That edition, however, was not published until 1653. (Rowley died in 1626, Middleton in 1627.) The pertinent entry in the *Stationer's Register* is dated 19 October 1652; it refers to *The Changeling* as 'written by Rowley'. Clearly, one of these pieces of evidence is less than accurate. And the very fact of the discrepancy should call attention to the essential unreliability of both pieces of external evidence. In fact, as is well known, neither the *Stationer's Register* nor Renaissance title pages can be relied upon to be accurate. Bentley gives several examples of title pages that identify one author despite other evidence of collaborative authorship; he believes that 'the information on single author title pages is often incomplete'.[3] So, while the external evidence cannot be ignored, its very unreliability makes reliance upon internal evidence equally problematic. That is, if Middleton's name as an author of *The Changeling* could be omitted in the *Stationer's Register,* it is equally possible that the name of a third collaborator could have been omitted from both sources; and (as Schoenbaum has indicated) it is extremely risky to allocate parts in a case where not all the collaborators are known.

Also, as almost everyone notes—without accepting the consequences for study of the authorship of a particular play like *The Changeling*—attributing portions of a play to a particular playwright on the basis of internal evidence assumes that the text whose internal nature we are studying represents the actual intentions of the presumed playwright(s). In other words, we must be wary of textual interference by scribes, prompters, compositors, re-writers, or editors. In the case of a play first printed long after the deaths of its presumed authors, the assumption of a lack of editorial interference is extremely problematic. One twentieth-century editor of

The Changeling says, 'one may hazard the guess that the copy [of the 1653 quarto] was a fair scribal transcript . . . of the authors' foul papers, from which the promptbook would have been prepared'.[4] Bawcutt judges that the printed text was probably based on 'a transcript from theatrical prompt-copy'; he thinks that probably the transcript was made shortly before the actual printing—that is, in 1653, more than 25 years after the deaths of the presumed authors.[5]

Furthermore, distinguishing between the work of Middleton and the work of Rowley necessarily depends on our having knowledge of what their work was like when they worked alone. But do we really know what their unaided work was like? We have a better chance at such knowledge with Middleton. Despite the number of his collaborations with various collaborators, tradition assigns to Middleton approximately thirteen unaided plays. There are some reasons for caution about that figure. First, as already noted, title pages and other official records sometimes, at least, and possibly very often omitted collaborators' names. Moreover, for a majority of the thirteen presumably Middleton-only plays, what Lake calls the 'date of surname attribution' is years after (in two instances as many as 34 years) Middleton's death.[6]

With Middleton, however, I am willing to hold my skepticism at least to some degree in check; even if he had some or much help with many of those thirteen plays, a reasonable person could suppose that careful study of all the plays where there is no reference to a collaborator will give us at least some degree of legitimate information about Middleton's style.

About knowledge of Rowley's style, however, I do not believe we can be nearly so sanguine. Plays created by Rowley alone are usually identified as the following four: *A Shoemaker A Gentleman*; *A New Wonder, A Woman Never Vext*; *All's Lost by Lust*; *A Match at Midnight.* But the evidence for Rowley's singular authorship is merely the absence of any other name in the unreliable *Stationer's Register* or on the unreliable title pages. Such evidence, if we did not know (or think we know) better, could lead us to believe that *The Birth of Merlin* and *The Changeling* were written by Rowley alone.[7] It is noteworthy that we have no *Stationer's Register* reference to Rowley as sole author and no title page listing only Rowley as author until at least five years after his death. Moreover, the printed texts that we have of the four 'Rowley plays' are generally regarded as unreliable. The assumption that we know even one play that represents the unaided work of Rowley is an assumption that I am not prepared to make. As Schoenbaum points out with characteristic understatement: 'For any author proposed, a reasonable amount of unchallenged dramatic writing, apart from collaborations, must be extant. The more plays the better' (176). With Rowley, at most we have four unaided plays.

And even that number has been questioned. On the basis of stylistic discrepancies, Hoy doubts that *A Match at Midnight* was written by Rowley alone and also offers tentative support for the suggestion by Fleay that acts 4 and 5 of *A Woman Never Vext* were borrowed from an earlier play.[8] It is altogether possible that we do not have the text of even a single play by Rowley alone.

It is also important to note how the process of studying stylistic patterns and discrepancies seems to lead even very astute scholars astray. Jackson, careful in most respects, overlooks discrepancies when they are inconvenient for his conclusions. For instance, in studying what he regards as 'Middleton contractions', he argues that Rowley uses these contractions 'less frequently' than Middleton—without commenting on why *I'd* (to take just one example) appears only two times in *All's Lost* but as many as fifteen times in *A Woman Never Vext*. Similarly, he makes much of Rowley's greater use of *ye* compared with Middleton—but without commenting on the difference between the 34 instances in *A Shoemaker* and the four instances in *All's Lost*.[9]

Also, when Jackson does note a discrepancy, he tends to dismiss its significance. So, in analyzing the parts of *A Fair Quarrel* to be attributed to Middleton and Rowley, he says that 'The only real anomaly is that *on't* [one of those Middleton contractions] is more frequent in Rowley's share (17 instances) than in Middleton's (5 instances)' (123-4). Earlier, Jackson was pleased to find no instances of *on't* in Rowley's *All's Lost*. Rather than question his overall theory, Jackson is forced to conclude that 'Robb may be right in thinking that Middleton had a hand in the closing pages of *A Fair Quarrel*' (124). One more example of Jackson's tendency to occasionally disregard the inconvenient will suffice. He notes that Rowley was a greater parenthesizer than Middleton; parentheses appear 12 times in Rowley's approximately 1200 lines of *The Changeling,* only 2 times in Middleton's approximately 1000 lines of that play. And this pattern occurs in all their collaborations— except *A Fair Quarrel* (124). Of the significance of the exception, Jackson has nothing to say.

Like Jackson, Hoy is an ordinarily careful scholar who does not always take into account the possible implications of certain anomalies. For instance, he notes (79) the variation in the Middleton canon of the appearance of contractions with *y'* (such as *y'are*) from 51 instances in *Women Beware Women* to only one instance in *A Chaste Maid in Cheapside*; but he does not notice how such a variation in one aspect of style could cast any doubt on the conclusions that he draws from other pieces of stylistic evidence, where consistency within an author's work is assumed to be the norm. In his discussion of Rowley's use of the contraction *'em* (for *them*), he notes (without noting any possibility of a larger significance) a difference in the use of *'em* between *A Shoemaker* and Rowley's other unaided plays (83). But Hoy's real interest in this section of his work is in Rowley's use of the alternative contraction *'um*— because that form occurs less frequently in plays of the period and therefore may be more suggestive of Rowley's own hand, his own preference, his own distinct linguistic practice. He focuses on the Middleton-Rowley masque, *The World Tost at Tennis* (85-7), where he finds instances of *'um* to correspond to portions of the masque that are assigned to Rowley and instances of *'em* to correspond to portions assigned to Middleton.

By the time Hoy arrives at his discussion of *The Changeling,* Hoy's theory has become, for him, fact: *'um* demonstrates authorship by Rowley; *'em* demonstrates authorship by Middleton. He proceeds to find confirmation of his theory in the usual assignment of portions of the play. And where he comes upon discrepancies, he either dismisses them or changes the attribution of a portion of a scene:

> Here, as elsewhere, Rowley's *'um* first appears as *'em* (sig. B1ᵛ). [As I judge from an earlier part of his discussion, Hoy is postulating a printer's error.] *'Em* and *'um* appear together on sig. C3. [Apparently another printer's error.] But thereafter throughout act 1, which all students of the play agree is Rowley's, the pronominal form is *'um. 'Em,* on the other hand, is the form that prevails throughout act 2, and this, by general scholarly assent, is Middleton's. . . . Middleton's 3.4 displays a single occurrence of *'em*; his 4.1, two occurrences of the form. The extent to which this particular piece of linguistic evidence can point to two distinct authorial practices when it has been faithfully preserved in the printed text [why here does Hoy assume compositorial accuracy?] is shown in 4.2. Miss Wiggin, Robb, and Stork concur in giving the entire scene to Middleton, but the linguistic evidence displayed here makes possible a more precise attribution. Rowley opens the scene with the first five speeches that comprise the exchange between Vermandero and the servant; and *'um* occurs twice in Vermandero's speech beginning 'The time accuses *'um* (sig. F4). But immediately thereafter, with the entrance of Tomazo, Middleton's hand appears, and the Vermandero who has said *'um* a few lines earlier now says *'em* on the same quarto signature.

(87-8)

We may notice that Hoy assumes compositorial accuracy or inaccuracy according to his convenience, that he uses the attributions of earlier scholars when they support his theories and 'corrects' those earlier attributions when he comes upon a contradiction. Perhaps what is most striking in Hoy's analysis is his disregard (in this portion of his work) of the occurrences of *'em* that he has earlier noted in Rowley's unaided plays.

In the work of Jackson, Hoy, and other analysts of stylistic evidence, although occasional references to the complexities implicit to the task of making attributions do appear, there is an underlying tendency to disregard complexities. The possibility of scribal or compositorial intervention is mentioned only to be forgotten. The possibility that one playwright could consciously (or unconsciously) imitate (or be influenced by) another is just barely admitted. The possibility that there could be an additional collaborator, or significant changing by a later reviser or editor, does not get meaningful attention. Perhaps most important, there is a persistent, often unstated, assumption that collaboration always (or at least almost always) consisted of individual work on separable portions of a play. I believe that to a significant degree this probably misguided notion is attributable to the understandably major influence of Bentley, and particularly to what I believe to be Bentley's distortion of the evidence available in Henslowe's *Diary*.[10]

I am forced to note a striking inconsistency within Bentley's discussion of methods of collaboration (227-34). Bentley begins this seven-page section of his chapter on dramatic collaborations by admitting that there is little evidence and that such evidence as we do have suggests that various methods existed. Then, just one page into the section, without seeming to realize it, he takes an astonishing left turn against the oncoming traffic:

> But there is one method of collaboration used by the playwrights in these years which is most frequently referred to and which was evidently so much more generally practiced then than now that it deserves discussion. Separate composition of individual acts is a division of labor which was common from 1590 to 1642.
>
> (228)

Bentley says 'evidently' even though he had just said there is little evidence. As I am about to demonstrate, there is no evidence to support his assertion that following this method 'was common from 1590 to 1642'. And then Bentley devotes the remaining six pages of this section to this method only, a choice that I believe has contributed to misleading a whole generation of scholars influenced by Bentley's important work into believing they have seen evidence that 'separate composition of individual acts' by different playwrights was the normal method of collaboration by the professional dramatists of this period.

So what is the evidence that Bentley offers? His first example (228) is of a play that was published at the very beginning of Bentley's period, 1591, but actually was written for presentation at court in 1566 or 1567. It is important to note that while this play, *Tancred and Gismund*, probably was composed by the different writer for each act method, the writers involved were not professional dramatists but rather amateurs, 'the Gentlemen of the Inner Temple'. Second, Bentley provides three and a half pages of discussion of Henslowe materials. Bentley's exact wording seems important to quote:

> The many entries about payment for plays in Henslowe's diary are never explicit in assigning individual acts to the different collaborators [he's right, they are never explicit], but most of his serial payments are compatible with such composition, especially in the several instances where he pays one or two writers of a play in his early payments and adds others in his final payments.
>
> (228)

'Compatible with', yes. But Bentley is not even asserting here that he has found evidence that this method of composition was used by Henslowe's playwrights commonly—or even once.

The first specific example that Bentley gives in his pages devoted to the Henslowe materials is curious because the portion of the *Diary* that might provide the relevant evidence has not survived. The reference here is to the lost play, *The Isle of Dogs,* for which Thomas Nashe got into trouble. He quotes (229) from a later pamphlet by Nashe, in which Nashe says that he had begun the play, had written the induction and the first act, and then the company gave the play to others to finish. But there is no indication here of division by acts except in the sense that (if Nashe is telling the truth) Nashe wrote act 1 and not the other acts. The pamphlet provides no indication of what method of collaboration may have been used for the rest of the play.

Then Bentley returns to Henslowe's entries as follows:

> Three entries concerning the work of Ben Jonson and George Chapman certainly show composition by acts, but it is not clear that only one play is involved or that Jonson and Chapman worked together.
>
> (229)

The first of these entries, dated 3 December 1597, refers only to Jonson, whom Henslowe lends 20 shillings on the basis of a plot that Jonson has shown to the company. The second, dated 23 October 1598, more than ten months later, may or may not (as Bentley admits) refer to the same play. Here Chapman receives a loan of three pounds 'on his play book and two acts of a tragedy of Benjamin's plot' (229). Then we come to the third entry (229-30), which is dated 4 January 1598 (really 1599), that is, two months later, which Bentley admits may or may not refer to the same play. Here Chapman receives a loan—there is no reference at all to Ben Jonson—of three pounds 'upon three acts of a tragedy'.

At this point, Bentley seems to have almost forgotten that he is discussing collaboration. He concludes his discussion of these three entries as follows: 'In any event, whether these three entries represent one, two, or possibly even three different plays, the wording shows that composition was proceeding by acts' (230). What is important to note here is that, even if Bentley is right in guessing that these three entries form a unit and actually refer to a single play, there is no substantial collaboration involved: Chapman wrote all five acts, yes, possibly one act at a time, and was paid in two installments. There is no question here of two playwrights dividing up a play into separable parts.

Then Bentley leaves the *Diary,* turning for his final Henslowe example (230-1) to correspondence between Henslowe and Robert Daborne in 1613. Here again, Bentley seems to be forgetting that his subject is methods of collaboration. The correspondence refers to two plays, *Machiavelli and the Devil* and *The Owl.* In each case it is clear that Daborne is being paid in installments. In neither case, however, is there any indication at all that Daborne has a collaborator, so again there is no support for Bentley's belief that he is demonstrating that 'separate composition of individual acts' by different playwrights was the normal method of collaboration by the professional dramatists of this period.

Before leaving his curious analysis of the Henslowe-Daborne correspondence, Bentley seems to notice that so far he has not been very convincing; and curiously he attaches to this admission an interesting piece of information:

> In most of the correspondence of Robert Daborne making allusion to joint compositions in which he was engaged with Massinger, Field, or Fletcher he makes no mention [n.b.] of the method by which they collaborated. But in a letter concerning his work with Cyril Tourneur he does say how they were working.
>
> (231)

The letter indicates that to meet his deadline Daborne has 'given Cyril Tourneur an act of *The Arraignment of London* to write'. That's it. This is Bentley's only example so far of a professional dramatist's being assigned a separable piece of a play. And it is a stopgap measure, not a planned one. Confronted with several deadlines at once, Daborne sought help from Tourneur in this particular way so that he could satisfy the demands of the entrepreneur with the money.

At this point, Bentley interrupts his superficial consideration of historical evidence to refer, very briefly, to linguistic evidence, especially to the work of Hoy, whose conclusions he seems to accept uncritically. Then, having, he hopes, buttressed his 'argument', he devotes the final two pages of this section (232-4) to evidence from a lawsuit about a 1624 play that had the title *The Late Murder of the Son upon the Mother* and the subtitle, which apparently referred to the play's subplot, *Keep the Widow Waking.* Bentley refers to the testimony of Thomas Dekker, one of those accused of slandering the mother-in-law of Benjamin Garfield, noting Dekker's explanation that he wrote act 1 and a speech in the last scene of the last act. Bentley assumes, on the basis of what he regards as an 'equable division', that Ford, Webster, and William Rowley each contributed a whole act and 'a scene or a long speech in the last act' (234). Once again, it is clear that Bentley is offering speculation in place of evidence. That is, even if Dekker is telling the truth about the limits of his own contribution, we have no information at all about how the rest of the play was put together.

In short, the only real piece of evidence offered by Bentley that professional dramatists during his period ever collaborated by the method of assigning separate acts to different playwrights is the marginal case where Daborne gave Tourneur an act of *The Arraignment of London* under emergency conditions.

Now some of my readers may be asking themselves whether, having actually found good evidence in the Henslowe material, Bentley was merely careless in choosing his examples from the mass of material he had studied. I believe not. As I have already indicated, and as Bentley himself says, Henslowe never refers explcitly to paying someone for an act. I have looked carefully for wording that could be construed as suggestive of the possibility of a hint at such an arrangement. In the entire Foakes and Rickert volume, I find only two such passages. By my count, there are 160 other passages where arrangements for collaborative playwrighting are referred to; and so Henslowe had 160 other places where there was an an opportunity for wording that would hint at paying dramatists by the act. Let me say that again: out of 162 opportunities there are only two where Henslowe chose words that to me suggest some kind of possibility of reading into Henslowe's language a hint at dividing the work by acts.[11]

I don't want to be misunderstood. Nowhere does Henslowe's language deny the possibility of his paying playwrights by the act. But the belief of Bentley and others that such an arrangement was common certainly is not in any way supported by the evidence in the Foakes and Rickert volume. To demonstrate my point, I will now provide some representative samples.

First we have the entries regarding the *Funeral of Richard Coeur de Lion* by Robert Wilson, Henry Chettle, Anthony Munday, and Michael Drayton.

13 June 1598 5 shillings to Wilson

14 June 5 shillings to Chettle

15 June 5 shillings to Chettle

17 June 15 shillings to Chettle, Wilson, Munday

21 June 25 shillings to Chettle

23 June 20 shillings to Munday

24 June 30 shillings to Drayton

26 June 20 shillings to Wilson (*'for his parte'*)

TOTALS:

Chettle—40 shillings

Wilson—30 shillings

Drayton—30 shillings

Munday—25 shillings

We cannot, of course, be sure that money did not change hands in some way not recorded by Henslowe. All of the entries use the term 'lent', and most use the phrase 'in earneste'—which suggests that Henslowe was in this case giving his dramatists advances.

I call attention to the fact that this is one of the two instances that I counted as containing even the barest hint of paying a dramatist for a separable piece of a play.[12] That is, since Henslowe referred to lending Wilson 20 shillings for *his part* of the play, I decided to be cautious and admit that he could have been referring to a separable part of the play rather than just his part in a joint effort. Certainly I see nothing else in this set of entries that is even remotely suggestive of the arrangement that so many scholars have declared to be the norm.

Examples of more typical entries—in which there is no hint of paying different playwrights for separable pieces of a play—follow:

Black Bateman of the North (Part I and Part II)

Part I

undated 20 shillings to Chettle

22 May 1598 6 pounds to Wilson, Drayton, Dekker, Chettle

Part II

26 June 1598 20 shillings to Chettle

8 July 3 pounds to Chettle

13 July 10 shillings to Wilson

14 July 15 shillings to Wilson

14 July 15 shillings to Chettle

TOTALS FOR PART II:

Chettle—4 pounds, 15 shillings

Wilson—25 shillings

Madman's Morris

31 June 1598 3 pounds to Wilson, Drayton, Dekker

9 July 20 shillings to Drayton

40 shillings to Wilson & Dekker

TOTALS:

Wilson—2 pounds

Drayton—2 pounds

Dekker—2 pounds

The Stepmother's Tragedy

24 July 1599 10 shillings to Dekker

23 August 20 shillings to Chettle & Dekker

25 August 20 shillings to Chettle

14 October 4 pounds to Chettle

TOTALS:

Chettle—5 pounds, 10 shillings

Dekker—1 pound

Pierce of Winchester

undated 10 shillings to Dekker

8 August 1598 50 shillings to Drayton, Wilson, Dekker

10 August 50 shillings to Drayton, Wilson, Dekker

TOTALS:

5 pounds divided among Drayton, Wilson, & Dekker

+ an additional 10 shillings to Dekker

Seven Wise Masters

1 March 1599 40 shillings to Chettle, Dekker, Haughton, Day

8 March 50 shillings to Chettle & Day

2 March 30 shillings to Chettle

TOTALS:

Chettle—3 pounds, 5 shillings

Day—1 pound, 15 shillings

Dekker—10 shillings

Haughton—10 shillings

Six Yeomen of the West

20 May 1601 15 shillings to Haughton

21 May 20 shillings to Day

4 June 40 shillings to Day

6 June 15 shillings to Haughton

8 June 30 shillings to Haughton

TOTALS:

Haughton—3 pounds

Day—3 pounds

In none of these cases is the possibility of act-by-act division denied—but why should it be? Certainly in none of these instances can I find any hint of the act-by-act arrangement.

I now move back to *The Changeling* and the question of its joint authorship. As I have said, I find nothing in the historical record that has survived to indicate the likelihood of the conventional belief about the play's authorship, no external evidence at all to support that conventional belief, and, despite the amount of effort by reputable scholars over a long period of time, no rigorous, careful examination of the internal evidence that I can regard as convincing. In my view, emphasis on the spelling of individual words, even contractions, represents an extreme example of critical misdirection: such criticism is considering how a play is 'written'. I said at the beginning of this essay that I would return to that problematic word. I believe that many critics dealing with this play never really consider some fairly obvious aspects of the craft of play*wrighting*. I wish that they would remember that the root of the word deals not with writing but with making.

The students of the play who offer the least are those most fixed on assigning shares. Those who are most helpful are those who manage, even while persisting in the assignment of shares on the basis of insufficient evidence, to occasionally recognize a more meaningful kind of interaction between the two playwrights. Among these are Symons, Barber, and, especially, Mooney.

As I see it, the apparent consensus that has formed around the late nineteenth-century assignment of shares in *The Changeling* is actually less solid than it seems at first. I am not thinking merely of the one genuine iconoclast, W. D. Dunkel, who suggests that Rowley was the re-writer of Middleton's play, rather than an actual collaborator.[13] Symons divides the authorship of the play in something like the familiar way, but has also a vision of a unified play that is the work of two playwrights working together:

> The play is De Flores, and De Flores seems to grow greater as he passes from one to the other of the two playwrights, as they collaborate visibly at his creation. This great creation is the final result and justification of Middleton and Rowley's work in common; for it is certain that De Flores as he is would never have been possible either to Rowley or to Middleton alone.[14]

Even though Symons' overall inclination is to think of the composition of the play in terms of separable parts, he sees the parts coming together in a way that can illuminate the whole play for his readers.

A somewhat similar situation exists with C. L. Barber, who at first glance is merely quibbling about which of the two playwrights is responsible for a particular word in a particular scene. He argues that the use of 'honour' to mean 'a bow, obeisance, curtsey' is much more frequent in plays definitely by Middleton than elsewhere in English Renaissance drama and on that basis offers the tentative conclusion 'that Middleton had a hand in act 4 scene 3 of *The Changeling,* which is usually attributed to Rowley alone'.[15] Along the way, however, Barber considers Dunkel's theory of Rowley as mere reviser, and the tendency of Schoenbaum and other authorities to dismiss Dunkel's view as unsupported. Barber manages to find unity in diversity and harmony in disagreement:

> It seems to me, however, that Dunkel's evidence is of some value. . . . Evidence of this kind is cumulative. On the other hand, Dunkel's resemblances [between the comic scenes in *The Changeling* and comic scenes in earlier comedies by Middleton] do not necessarily seem to me to support his thesis that Rowley was merely a reviser: they suggest that Middleton had a hand in the planning of the whole play, even of the scenes mainly written by Rowley. This view, which enables Dunkel's evidence to be harmonized with that for the orthodox view, assumes an intimate collaboration between Middleton and Rowley in their joint plays.
>
> (163-64)

That Barber can manage to agree with both Dunkel and Schoenbaum is useful. Even more useful is what I regard as the best treatment of the dual authorship of *The Changeling,* that of Michael E. Mooney.[16]

As with Barber's evaluation of Dunkel, my view of Mooney's essay is only partially accepting. To me, Mooney seems totally uncritical of the attribution of shares of the play to the two playwrights. He does not notice the absence of real evidence, and starts with the assumption that the conventional division—with Hoy's (in my view) unconvincing 'correctin'—is accurate. Nevertheless, Mooney provides a sense of the whole play that is even more illuminating than that of Symons. And his sense of how the whole play was made by the playwrights is only incidentally dependent upon his faulty premise.

Mooney argues that, in their effort to elicit certain responses from the audience, Middleton and Rowley collaborated in a procedure of 'framing' the play. His effort is to show how the playwrights intertwine the tragic main plot and the comic subplot to enhance the effectiveness of both, how the madhouse scenes both contrast and echo the action of the tragic plot, how words and images of the two plots serve 'to recall and to mutually reinforce their separate actions' (305), how the playwright of act 1 (Mooney assumes it is Rowley) prepares the audience for the interweaving, how the playwright of act 5 (again, Rowley) fulfills the audience's complex anticipation through the use of language that brings together the concerns and the feelings of the tragic main plot and the comic subplot. Mooney really is attending not just to the writing down of words but to the craft of playwrighting.

Thus, more effectively than anyone else, Mooney accounts for the coherence and success of *The Changeling,* demonstrating how the play 'holds two modes in equipoise, the comic and the tragic, with the play's conclusion determined by the contrasting thrusts of comedy and tragedy' (311). Where Mooney goes wrong is not in his brilliant analysis of the structure of *The Changeling,* but in his assumption that that structure was created at least initially (he does speculate that Middleton and Rowley may have consulted together after the initial composition of the play) by two playwrights' writing their separate pieces. As I have suggested, the authorities upon whom Mooney depends for his assumption are involved in speculation—because of the absence of real evidence. In concluding, Mooney writes of 'a plan of operation that recognized the need for a unified tone at the beginning and at the end of a collaborative work'. He says that 'the interconnections among plots, characters, and concepts might then be initially sketched by one hand and finally reinforced, without a loss of consistency, by bringing main and subplots into harmonic conjunction' (312). For Mooney, it seems almost necessary—in order to maintain consistency—for the hand that is writing act 5 to be the same hand that wrote act 1; in this aspect of his essay he neglects the craft of playwrighting in favor of what must be speculation about the chronology of the act performed by two people in writing down a series of words that happen to constitute a play.

To be sure, Mooney and the others may be right in their speculative allocation of parts of *The Changeling* to two playwrights. It is not my intention to argue that they are wrong; rather, I contend that the evidence does not exist to support the assumption, the speculation, that Middleton wrote X and Rowley wrote Y and no third playwright was involved.

Since speculation seems so endemic in this particular aspect of the study of Renaissance drama, I should like to offer some speculation of my own. Recalling my very first quotation from Schoenbaum about 'popular assumptions and facile generalizations about the nature of Elizabethan dramatic collaboration', I wish to speculate about a possible alternative assumption: that Renaissance playwrights who were collaborating, at least some of the time, and probably often, actually worked together. I believe that our knowledge about the authorship of *The Booke of Sir Thomas Moore* supports my assumption.[17] Another instance of apparent working together is cited by Carson, who finds in Henslowe's papers (not the Diary) a statement by Daborne about his collaboration on a play with Massinger and Nathan Field; Daborne says that they spent 'a great deale of Time in conference about [the] plott'.[18]

In any case, I emphasize my awareness of my own assumptions and speculations. In the at least temporary, probably permanent, absence of evidence, why not? Specifically, I am speculating that the reason my students find *The Changeling* to be a unified and coherent play is that the two playwrights actually worked together. I will not go so far as to suggest which of the many possible models of collaboration they followed.[19] But I will suggest that they probably talked with each other while they were making their play, that some of the time they may have been in the same room while a part of the play was being made (or written), that they could have influenced each other in ways that Middleton and Rowley themselves might have had trouble describing to another person. I do not claim that Renaissance plays were never cut up into pieces, each piece to be written by a different author; but I can say that I have found no external evidence whatsoever that this strange event ever happened in the professional theatre of the time.

When my students and I read *The Changeling* together, we find a play marked by a thematic consistency that makes the concept of two playwrights working independently of each other on separate shares of the play seem highly improbable. The complex way in which act 2, scene 2, and act 3, scene 3, play off against each other, and then together lead to the climactic act 3, scene 4, provides a good example of dramaturgically successful interweaving. In the earlier (main plot) scene, the unnoticed De Flores observes the intimacy of an encounter between Beatrice and Alsemero. His mind jumps quickly to the possibility that Beatrice will be unfaithful to her intended husband, and concludes that such a lapse on her part would justify De Flores' attempting to have a sexual relationship with his master's wife. In the later (subplot) scene, Lollio's entry above enables him to observe Tony's attempt to seduce Isabella. Again we have a servant quickly assuming that his mistress may be unfaithful—again concluding that misbehavior with one man could lead to misbehavior with the observer.

Lollio's attempt in this scene to kiss Isabella serves as an interesting preparatory foil to the act 3, scene 4, attempt by De Flores to kiss Beatrice. In the literal madhouse, the vulnerable woman is allowed by the playwrights to avert the unwanted kiss and escape from disaster. In the madhouse that is the castle, averting the unwanted kiss provides only momentary escape—since the heroine has made her vulnerability absolute through the tragic error that she has already committed. While there is no way of proving that Middleton and Rowley worked together on these three scenes, in the total absence of evidence that Middleton created the two main plot scenes while Rowley was working independently on the subplot scene, I find the sitting-in-the-same-room-and-talking-together speculation much easier to accept than the assumption that the two playwrights worked separately and put the pieces together afterwards.

If I am right that we do not—and almost certainly will not ever—know details about the collaborative authorship of *The Changeling* and other Renaissance plays, what consequence does that lack of knowledge have for interpretation? Clearly there is great consequence for any critic who wishes to study the art and craft of a particular playwright. For such interpreters I can only recommend an attempt to avoid being captured by what Jack Stillinger calls 'the myth of solitary genius'.[20] For all kinds of interpretation, I do believe it to be very important for scholars to pay attention to the evidence, to avoid reaching definitive conclusions that the available evidence cannot support.[21] In other words, in the absence of surprising new information, I recommend that we learn to live with the certainty that our knowledge is uncertain.

As I review the state of published work in the area of attribution studies, I see bad news and good news. One aspect of bad news is that in this age of instant communication we do not seem to be very good at transmitting and receiving the news about what is being learned. For instance, most people who care about the drama of this period will never read this essay. Also, someone who does not read it but rather hears about it from someone else will retain his or her earlier opinion because received opinion has a way of staying with us—despite the evidence. This problem applies equally to me as someone who does not always learn about the useful material written by other scholars. When I was working on a much briefer version of this essay in 1996, I believed I was all alone in questioning the validity of Hoy's approach. When I read a 1997 article by Jeffrey Masten, an article that to my mind demolishes Hoy almost completely, I said to myself: good, someone agrees with me. It was only when I returned to this subject three years later that I discovered that Masten's 1997 attack on Hoy first appeared in 1992.[22] I had a respectable reason for not knowing, in 1996, about Masten's 1992 article. I was working on Middleton and Rowley. Masten was exposing the weakness of Hoy's work on the Beaumont and Fletcher canon. But the problem remains, partly because so much more is being published than anyone has the time to read. As I indicated at the very beginning, Bawcutt's 1998 edition of *The Changeling* is still totally accepting of the traditional attribu-

tion and of Hoy's work. So that's the bad news, that we don't learn about each other's work fast enough, and sometimes not at all.

The first aspect of good news is that so many people are doing so much work that they genuinely care about. The second aspect of good news is that, while continuing to seek for more information, while continuing to look for The Truth, we really can do without certain knowledge. There remains value in the process of seeking. In most respects, it seems to me we are not in such bad shape. In writing about Renaissance plays, or in talking about the plays with our students and colleagues, we can refer to what 'the playwright' is doing or to what 'the playwrights' are doing. We can even pick a name for the sake of convenience—just so long as we remember to tell *our* audience that when we say 'Middleton' or 'Rowley' or 'Gezinkus' we don't necessarily mean an actual person by that name who lived and worked at a certain time several centuries ago—but rather a single or double or triple or quadruple human entity that somehow bears the responsibility for the text of (in this case) *The Changeling* that we happen to be reading and discussing at the beginning of the twenty-first century.

The complexities here are potentially enormous. As D. C. Greetham explains in fascinating detail, defining 'a work', 'a text', 'an author' is no simple matter. For me, such decisions are often pragmatic ones determined by context. Greetham quotes Davison on pragmatic necessity: "'most of us, however assiduous we may be in leaving no stone unturned in checking the text with which we are concerned, must take on trust, to some extent at least, the work of others on other texts and problems'". (And notice that I am trusting Greetham to give me the quotation from Davison correctly, and not to distort it by taking it out of context.)[23] Recently, in teaching an undergraduate course in 'Tragedy', I included *The Changeling, Women Beware Women,* and *The Revenger's Tragedy* and used as a 'required text' for my students a Penguin edition that claims to contain five plays by Middleton. Because of the purposes of this particular course (my context), I was quite comfortable with this presentation of 'the texts' of these three plays to these students, most of whom were not majoring in English and none of whom had plans to study for a PhD in English. Of course, I did explain (very briefly) what we know and do not know about how these three plays were created. Presumably, however, my students' experience of the plays was affected by the particular nature of 'the text' that was presented to them—and by my explanation, which I suppose became part of 'the text' as they became engaged with it.

The point I am making here, which is that at least with *The Changeling* we should value textual authority rather than authorial authority, is, I think, identical to the main point of Stephen Orgel's essay, 'What Is a Text?', which was first published in 1981. Influenced by Bentley (but his point does not depend on the weakness I have identified in Bentley) and especially by Honigmann, Orgel argues against an emphasis on authorial authority, suggesting that we should take a Renaissance dramatic text on its own terms, without worrying, or at least without worrying in the wrong way, about the impossible task of finding out exactly how, by exactly whose agency, it got that way. That is, while of course we want to remove errors, the correct text that we will ultimately be dealing with ordinarily does not derive its authority from its author or authors; rather, it derives its authority from its existence as a performance text. Orgel, whose focus is primarily on the essentially collaborative nature of plays that have only one playwright, urges us to accept as a necessary fact 'that at the heart of our texts lies a hard core of uncertainty'.[24]

This kind of problem is addressed, in different ways, by Masten and by McMullan. Among other interesting points made by Masten is his warning (I like this point especially because we are always gratified to see in print ideas that we have been expressing in class) against 'the modern critical model of authorial development that dwells upon "date of composition"', a model that leads, for instance, to lists of Shakespeare's plays in chronological order ('Beaumont' 376). Masten, like Orgel, sees the text of a play in a performance context, emphasizing the various ways in which the text could, legitimately, change subsequent to its originally being put together by its original playwright(s).

McMullan, whose focus is on the plays of John Fletcher, and who in my judgment is too accepting of the methods of Hoy, takes Masten mildly to task for his Foucaultian rejection of the author—preferring to invoke Bakhtin:

> I prefer to argue, with Bakhtin, for the distinctiveness of the individual as an *orchestrator* of voices. In other words, while there is no such thing as original speech—all words have always already been previously voiced in some context or other . . .—there is nonetheless a role for the voice in organizing the innumerable discursive options available at a particular moment. This organization or orchestration can be distinctive without requiring belief in romantic notions of originality. And promoting collaboration is one way of demonstrating the profoundly social, dialogic nature of discourse, which does not deny (though it makes impossible, finally) the attempt to locate a working distinctiveness for the orchestrator of voices, influences, sources, and contexts known to literary history as Fletcher.[25]

In other words, because he is studying Fletcher, he necessarily, and rightly it seems to me, objects to Masten's implication that such a project is inappropriate. Nevertheless, he winds up admitting the impossibility of separating out 'Fletcher', or, to get back to the subject of this essay, 'Middleton' or 'Rowley', from the text of a play. McMullan's discussion of collaboration is complex. Ultimately he demonstrates the inevitability, and therefore the rightness, of the scholarly attempt to answer unanswerable questions. I will give the last word to Schoenbaum who asserts that 'we want to know', who playfully suggests that 'something there is that doesn't love an anonymous play' (218).

Notes

1. Frederick Gard Fleay, *A Biographical Chronicle of the English Drama, 1559-1642*, 2 vols. (London, 1891). Pauline Wiggin, *An Inquiry into the Authorship of the Middleton-Rowley Plays,* Radcliffe College Monographs 9 (Boston, 1897). N. W. Bawcutt (ed), *The Changeling,* by Thomas Middleton & William Rowley, Revels Student Editions (Manchester, 1998).

2. Samuel Schoenbaum, *Internal Evidence and Elizabethan Dramatic Authorship: An Essay in Literary History and Method* (Evanston, 1966).

3. Gerald Eades Bentley, *The Profession of Dramatist in Shakespeare's Time, 1590-1642* (Princeton, 1971) 210; see also 232-4.

4. George Walton Williams (ed), *The Changeling,* by Thomas Middleton and William Rowley (Lincoln, 1966), xi.

5. N. W. Bawcutt (ed), *The Changeling,* by Thomas Middleton & William Rowley, The Revels Plays (Cambridge, 1958), xvi.

6. David J. Lake, *The Canon of Thomas Middleton's Plays: Internal Evidence for the Major Problems of Authorship* (London, 1975), 20.

7. Those who have regarded *The Birth of Merlin* as the unaided work of Rowley presumably have assumed that the presence of Shakespeare's name as joint author is the only error on the 1662 title page.

8. Cyrus Hoy, 'The Shares of Fletcher and his Collaborators in the Beaumont and Fletcher Canon (V)', *Studies in Bibliography* 13 (1960), 82-3.

9. MacD. P. Jackson, *Studies in Attribution: Middleton and Shakespeare* (Salzburg, Austria, 1979), 119-20.

10. Kathleen E. McLuskie, for instance, appears to be following Bentley; see 'The Plays and the Playwrights: 1613-42', in *The Revels History of Drama in English* (London, 1981), vol. 4, 169-82.

11. Philip Henslowe, *Henslowe's Diary,* R. A. Foakes and R. T. Rickert (eds) (Cambridge, 1961).

12. For the other, see Henslowe's *Diary*, 135 and 294 (references to *Fair Constance of Rome, Part I* by Munday, Drayton, Hathaway, Dekker, and Wilson).

13. W. D. Dunkel, 'Did Not Rowley Merely Revise Middleton?', *PMLA* 48 (1933), 799-805.

14. Arthur Symons, 'Middleton and Rowley', *The Cambridge History of English Literature,* vol. 6, 87.

15. C. L. Barber, 'A Rare Use of "Honour" as a Criterion of Middleton's Authorship', *English Studies* 38 (1957), 168.

16. Michael E. Mooney, '"Framing" as Collaborative Technique: Two Middleton-Rowley Plays,' in *Drama in the Renaissance: Comparative and Critical Essays,* Clifford Davidson, C. J. Gianakaris, and John H. Stroupe (eds), (New York, 1986), 300-14.

17. See, for instance, Peter W. M. Blayney, '*The Booke of Sir Thomas Moore* Re-Examined', *Studies in Philology* 69 (1972), 167-91; and Carol A. Chillington, 'Playwrights at Work: Henslowe's, Not Shakespeare's, *Book of Sir Thomas More*', *English Literary Renaissance* 10 (1980), 439-79.

18. Neil Carson, *A Companion to Henslowe's Diary* (Cambridge, 1988), 55.

19. Sheldon P. Zitner gives an interesting list of possibilities for modes of collaboration: 'prior agreement on outline, vetting of successive drafts by a partner, composition in concert, brief and possibly infrequent intervention, and even a mutual contagion of style' in 'Introduction', *The Knight of the Burning Pestle* by Francis Beaumont, The Revels Plays (Manchester, 1984), 10.

20. Jack Stillinger, *Multiple Authorship and the Myth of Solitary Genius* (New York and Oxford, 1991).

21. The January 1996 issue of *PMLA* attempts to contextualize scholars' use of evidence, and their criticism of other scholars' misuse of evidence, in both theoretical and practical terms. Readers of Heather Dubrow's introductory essay to that issue will probably gather that I am a proponent of what she refers to as 'solid' criticism. I hope that I may be—at the same time—in favor of criticism that manages also to be 'fruitful', 'provocative', and, yes, even 'interesting'. See 'The Status of Evidence', *PMLA* 111 (1996), 16-17.

22. Jeffrey Masten, 'Playwrighting: Authorship and Collaboration', in *A New History of Early English Drama,* John D. Cox and David Scott Kastan (eds), (New York, 1997). 'Beaumont and/or Fletcher: Collaboration and the Interpretation of Renaissance Drama,' *ELH* 59 (1992), 337-56.

23. D. C. Greetham, 'Textual Forensics', *PMLA* 111 (1996), 42. See also Peter Davison, 'The Selection and Presentation of Bibliographical Evidence,' *Analytical and Enumerative Bibliography* 1 (1977), 101-36.

24. Stephen Orgel, 'What Is a Text?', in *Staging the Renaissance: Reinterpretations of Elizabethan and Jacobean Drama,* David Scott Kastan and Peter Stallybrass (eds) (New York, 1991), 83. For a more theoretical discussion of the issues addressed by Orgel, see Greetham, who points out that the various definitions of the word 'text' include two basically contradictory meanings: text as something woven, with texture, the 'style, tissue of a literary work'; and text as 'an orginal or authority' (Greetham 32-33). Orgel's view is that, at least for performance-based dramatic texts of the Renaissance, we need to reject the latter definition. See also E.A.J. Honigmann, *The Stability of Shakespeare's Text* (London, 1965).

25. Gordon McMullan, *The Politics of Unease in the Plays of John Fletcher* (Amherst, 1994), 155.

FURTHER READING

Criticism

Amster, Mary. "Frances Howard and Middleton and Rowley's *The Changeling*: Trials, Tests, and the Legibility of the Virgin Body." *Medieval and Renaissance Texts and Studies* 263 (2003): 211-32.
> Uses the case of Lady Frances Howard and the theme of chastity in *The Changeling* to explore the anxiety circulating around the legibility of the virginal body.

Andrews, Michael C. "'Sweetness' in *The Changeling*." *Yearbook of English Studies* 1 (1971): 61-67.
> Focuses on the image of sweetness as it functions in the plot and subplot of *The Changeling*.

Bawcutt, N. W. Introduction to *The Changeling,* by Thomas Middleton and William Rowley, edited by N. W. Bawcutt. Manchester, U.K.: Manchester University Press, 1991.
> General introduction to a 1958 edition of *The Changeling,* which is considered one of the best overviews in one of the finest modern editions of the play.

Black, Matthew W. Introduction to *The Changeling,* by Thomas Middleton and William Rowley, edited by Matthew W. Black, pp. 5-11. Philadelphia: University of Pennsylvania Press, 1966.

Introduction that focuses on the stage and textual history of *The Changeling.*

Bromham, A. A., and Zara Bruzzi. The Changeling *and the Years of Crisis, 1619-1624: A Hieroglyph of Britain.* London: Pinter Publications, 1990, 207 p.

In-depth study that covers the work's historical background and influences, political concerns, subplot, and religious imagery.

Daalder, Joost. "The Role of Diaphanta in *The Changeling.*" *AUMLA: The Journal of the Australasian Universities Language and Literature Association,* no. 76 (November 1991): 13-21.

Character study of Diaphanta that claims she helps the audience to better understand Beatrice-Joanna and Isabella.

———. "The Role of Isabella in *The Changeling.*" *English Studies* 73, no. 1 (February 1992): 22-9.

Character study of Isabella, pointing out that her sanity helps the audience to understand the nature of Beatrice's madness.

Dawson, Anthony B. "Giving the Finger: Puns and Transgressions in *The Changeling.*" In *The Elizabethan Theatre* XII, edited by A. L. Magnusson and C. E. McGee, pp. 93-112. Toronto: P. D. Meany, 1993.

Analyzes the rude word play and the instability of meaning in the language and action of *The Changeling.*

Duffy, Joseph M. "Madhouse Optics: *The Changeling.*" *Comparative Drama* 8, no. 2 (summer 1974): 184-98.

Discusses Beatrice-Joanna's failure of vision.

Eliot, T. S. "Thomas Middleton." In *Selected Essays 1919-1932,* pp. 148-69. London: Faber & Faber, 1932.

Important essay on Middleton, first published in the *Times Literary Supplement* in 1927, that praises Middleton as "a great comic writer and a great tragic writer" yet one who "has no point of view"; emphasizes *The Changeling*'s moral value and horror; and discusses the moral degeneration of Beatrice-Joanna.

Empson, William. "Double Plots." In *Some Versions of Pastoral,* pp. 27-88. London: Chatto & Windus, 1935.

Includes brief but important comments on *The Changeling* regarding the unity and meaning of the play.

Engelberg, Edward. "Tragic Blindness in *The Changeling* and *Women Beware Women.*" *MLQ,* 23 (1962), 20-8.

Describes the main action of *The Changeling* as one which stems from Beatrice-Joanna's faulty eyesight.

Farr, Dorothy M. "*The Changeling.*" *Modern Language Review* 62, no. 4 (October 1967): 586-97.

Argues that in *The Changeling* Middleton used the methods of comedy to transform and broaden the scope of tragedy.

Haber, Judith. "The Insincerity of Women." *Representations,* no. 81 (winter 2003): 79-98.

Explores how *The Changeling* anatomizes, criticizes, and participates in the assumptions about rape presented in Ben Jonson's *Hymenaei.*

Hébert, Catherine A. "A Note on the Significance on the Title of Middleton's *The Changeling.*" *CLA Journal* 12, no. 1 (September 1968): 66-9.

Analyzes the *The Changeling*'s title's proliferations of meaning, asserting that every one of the characters in the play is a changeling.

Jacobs, Henry E. "The Constancy of Change: Character and Perspective in *The Changeling.*" *Texas Studies in Literature and Language* 16, no. 4 (winter 1975): 651-74.

Discusses the critical controversy over the identification of the "changeling(s)" in the play and offers an analysis of what exactly Middleton and Rowley meant by the term.

Johnson, Paula. "Dissimulation Anatomized: *The Changeling.*" *Philological Quarterly* 56, no. 3 (summer 1977): 329-38.

Analyzes the use of "dissemblance and suspect," or deception and misunderstanding, in *The Changeling.*

Mayberry, Susan. "Cuckoos and Convention: Madness in Middleton and Rowley's *The Changeling.*" *Mid-Hudson Language Studies* 8 (1985): 21-9.

Discusses the theme of madness, focusing on its relationship with sexuality in the play.

Morrison, Peter. "A Cangoun in Zombieland: Middleton's Tetralogical *Changeling.*" In *"Accompanyinge the players": Essays Celebrating Thomas Middleton, 1580-1980,* edited by Kenneth Friedenreich, pp. 219-41. New York: AMS Press, 1983.

Reviews the major trends in criticism of *The Changeling,* arguing that most scholars have raised three main issues: the identification of the changeling(s), the relation of the plot and subplot, and the play's moral vision.

Ricks, Christopher. "The Moral and Poetic Structure of *The Changeling.*" *Essays in Criticism* 10 (1960): 290-306.

Seminal essay that analyzes the complex significance of important recurrent words in the play.

Roy, Emil. "Sexual Paradox in *The Changeling*." *Literature and Psychology* 25, no. 3 (1975): 124-32.

Discusses the complex interplay of sexual impulses and guilt in *The Changeling*.

Additional coverage of Middleton's life and career is contained in the following sources published by Thomson Gale: *British Writers,* **Vol. 2;** *Dictionary of Literary Biography,* **Vol. 58;** *DISCovering Authors Modules: Dramatists* **and** *Most-studied Authors*; *Drama Criticism,* **Vol. 5;** *Drama for Students,* **Vols. 18, 22;** *Literature Criticism from 1400 to 1800,* **Vol. 33;** *Literature Resource Center*; **and** *Reference Guide to English Literature,* **Ed. 2. Additional coverage of Rowley's life and career is contained in the following sources published by Thomson Gale:** *Dictionary of Literary Biography,* **Vol. 58;** *Drama for Students,* **Vol. 22;** *Literature Criticism from 1400 to 1800,* **Vol. 100;** *Literature Resource Center*; **and** *Reference Guide to English Literature,* **Ed. 2.**

How to Use This Index

The main references

> **Calvino, Italo**
> 1923-1985 .... **CLC 5, 8, 11, 22, 33, 39,**
> **73; SSC 3, 48**

list all author entries in the following Gale Literary Criticism series:

AAL = *Asian American Literature*
BG = *The Beat Generation: A Gale Critical Companion*
BLC = *Black Literature Criticism*
BLCS = *Black Literature Criticism Supplement*
CLC = *Contemporary Literary Criticism*
CLR = *Children's Literature Review*
CMLC = *Classical and Medieval Literature Criticism*
DC = *Drama Criticism*
HLC = *Hispanic Literature Criticism*
HLCS = *Hispanic Literature Criticism Supplement*
HR = *Harlem Renaissance: A Gale Critical Companion*
LC = *Literature Criticism from 1400 to 1800*
NCLC = *Nineteenth-Century Literature Criticism*
NNAL = *Native North American Literature*
PC = *Poetry Criticism*
SSC = *Short Story Criticism*
TCLC = *Twentieth-Century Literary Criticism*
WLC = *World Literature Criticism, 1500 to the Present*
WLCS = *World Literature Criticism Supplement*

The cross-references

> See also CA 85-88, 116; CANR 23, 61;
> DAM NOV; DLB 196; EW 13; MTCW 1, 2;
> RGSF 2; RGWL 2; SFW 4; SSFS 12

list all author entries in the following Gale biographical and literary sources:

AAYA = *Authors & Artists for Young Adults*
AFAW = *African American Writers*
AFW = *African Writers*
AITN = *Authors in the News*
AMW = *American Writers*
AMWR = *American Writers Retrospective Supplement*
AMWS = *American Writers Supplement*
ANW = *American Nature Writers*
AW = *Ancient Writers*
BEST = *Bestsellers*
BPFB = *Beacham's Encyclopedia of Popular Fiction: Biography and Resources*
BRW = *British Writers*
BRWS = *British Writers Supplement*
BW = *Black Writers*
BYA = *Beacham's Guide to Literature for Young Adults*
CA = *Contemporary Authors*
CAAS = *Contemporary Authors Autobiography Series*
CABS = *Contemporary Authors Bibliographical Series*
CAD = *Contemporary American Dramatists*
CANR = *Contemporary Authors New Revision Series*
CAP = *Contemporary Authors Permanent Series*
CBD = *Contemporary British Dramatists*
CCA = *Contemporary Canadian Authors*
CD = *Contemporary Dramatists*
CDALB = *Concise Dictionary of American Literary Biography*
CDALBS = *Concise Dictionary of American Literary Biography Supplement*
CDBLB = *Concise Dictionary of British Literary Biography*

CMW = *St. James Guide to Crime & Mystery Writers*
CN = *Contemporary Novelists*
CP = *Contemporary Poets*
CPW = *Contemporary Popular Writers*
CSW = *Contemporary Southern Writers*
CWD = *Contemporary Women Dramatists*
CWP = *Contemporary Women Poets*
CWRI = *St. James Guide to Children's Writers*
CWW = *Contemporary World Writers*
DA = *DISCovering Authors*
DA3 = *DISCovering Authors 3.0*
DAB = *DISCovering Authors: British Edition*
DAC = *DISCovering Authors: Canadian Edition*
DAM = *DISCovering Authors: Modules*
  DRAM: *Dramatists Module;* **MST:** *Most-studied Authors Module;*
  MULT: *Multicultural Authors Module;* **NOV:** *Novelists Module;*
  POET: *Poets Module;* **POP:** *Popular Fiction and Genre Authors Module*
DFS = *Drama for Students*
DLB = *Dictionary of Literary Biography*
DLBD = *Dictionary of Literary Biography Documentary Series*
DLBY = *Dictionary of Literary Biography Yearbook*
DNFS = *Literature of Developing Nations for Students*
EFS = *Epics for Students*
EXPN = *Exploring Novels*
EXPP = *Exploring Poetry*
EXPS = *Exploring Short Stories*
EW = *European Writers*
FANT = *St. James Guide to Fantasy Writers*
FW = *Feminist Writers*
GFL = *Guide to French Literature,* Beginnings to 1789, 1798 to the Present
GLL = *Gay and Lesbian Literature*
HGG = *St. James Guide to Horror, Ghost & Gothic Writers*
HW = *Hispanic Writers*
IDFW = *International Dictionary of Films and Filmmakers: Writers and Production Artists*
IDTP = *International Dictionary of Theatre: Playwrights*
LAIT = *Literature and Its Times*
LAW = *Latin American Writers*
JRDA = *Junior DISCovering Authors*
MAICYA = *Major Authors and Illustrators for Children and Young Adults*
MAICYAS = *Major Authors and Illustrators for Children and Young Adults Supplement*
MAWW = *Modern American Women Writers*
MJW = *Modern Japanese Writers*
MTCW = *Major 20th-Century Writers*
NCFS = *Nonfiction Classics for Students*
NFS = *Novels for Students*
PAB = *Poets: American and British*
PFS = *Poetry for Students*
RGAL = *Reference Guide to American Literature*
RGEL = *Reference Guide to English Literature*
RGSF = *Reference Guide to Short Fiction*
RGWL = *Reference Guide to World Literature*
RHW = *Twentieth-Century Romance and Historical Writers*
SAAS = *Something about the Author Autobiography Series*
SATA = *Something about the Author*
SFW = *St. James Guide to Science Fiction Writers*
SSFS = *Short Stories for Students*
TCWW = *Twentieth-Century Western Writers*
WLIT = *World Literature and Its Times*
WP = *World Poets*
YABC = *Yesterday's Authors of Books for Children*
YAW = *St. James Guide to Young Adult Writers*

Literary Criticism Series
Cumulative Author Index

20/1631
See Upward, Allen
A/C Cross
See Lawrence, T(homas) E(dward)
A. M.
See Megged, Aharon
Abasiyanik, Sait Faik 1906-1954
See Sait Faik
See also CA 123; 231
Abbey, Edward 1927-1989 .... **CLC 36, 59; TCLC 160**
See also AMWS 13; ANW; CA 45-48; 128; CANR 2, 41, 131; DA3; DLB 256, 275; LATS 1:2; MTCW 2; MTFW 2005; TCWW 1, 2
Abbott, Edwin A. 1838-1926 .... **TCLC 139**
See also DLB 178
Abbott, Lee K(ittredge) 1947- .... **CLC 48**
See also CA 124; CANR 51, 101; DLB 130
Abe, Kobo 1924-1993 ...... **CLC 8, 22, 53, 81; SSC 61; TCLC 131**
See also CA 65-68; 140; CANR 24, 60; DAM NOV; DFS 14; DLB 182; EWL 3; MJW; MTCW 1, 2; MTFW 2005; NFS 22; RGWL 3; SFW 4
Abe Kobo
See Abe, Kobo
Abelard, Peter c. 1079-c. 1142 ..... **CMLC 11, 77**
See also DLB 115, 208
Abell, Kjeld 1901-1961 .... **CLC 15**
See also CA 191; 111; DLB 214; EWL 3
Abercrombie, Lascelles
1881-1938 .... **TCLC 141**
See also CA 112; DLB 19; RGEL 2
Abish, Walter 1931- .... **CLC 22; SSC 44**
See also CA 101; CANR 37, 114; CN 3, 4, 5, 6; DLB 130, 227; MAL 5
Abrahams, Peter (Henry) 1919- .... **CLC 4**
See also AFW; BW 1; CA 57-60; CANR 26, 125; CDWLB 3; CN 1, 2, 3, 4, 5, 6; DLB 117, 225; EWL 3; MTCW 1, 2; RGEL 2; WLIT 2
Abrams, M(eyer) H(oward) 1912- ... **CLC 24**
See also CA 57-60; CANR 13, 33; DLB 67
Abse, Dannie 1923- .... **CLC 7, 29; PC 41**
See also CA 53-56; CAAS 1; CANR 4, 46, 74, 124; CBD; CN 1, 2, 3; CP 1, 2, 3, 4, 5, 6, 7; DAB; DAM POET; DLB 27, 245; MTCW 2
Abutsu 1222(?)-1283 .... **CMLC 46**
See Abutsu-ni
Abutsu-ni
See Abutsu
See also DLB 203

Achebe, (Albert) Chinua(lumogu)
1930- ..... **BLC 1; CLC 1, 3, 5, 7, 11, 26, 51, 75, 127, 152; WLC**
See also AAYA 15; AFW; BPFB 1; BRWC 2; BW 2, 3; CA 1-4R; CANR 6, 26, 47, 124; CDWLB 3; CLR 20; CN 1, 2, 3, 4, 5, 6, 7; CP 2, 3, 4, 5, 6, 7; CWRI 5; DA; DA3; DAB; DAC; DAM MST, MULT, NOV; DLB 117; DNFS 1; EWL 3; EXPN; EXPS; LAIT 2; LATS 1:2; MAICYA 1, 2; MTCW 1, 2; MTFW 2005; NFS 2; RGEL 2; RGSF 2; SATA 38, 40; SATA-Brief 38; SSFS 3, 13; TWA; WLIT 2; WWE 1
Acker, Kathy 1948-1997 .... **CLC 45, 111**
See also AMWS 12; CA 117; 122; 162; CANR 55; CN 5, 6; MAL 5
Ackroyd, Peter 1949- .... **CLC 34, 52, 140**
See also BRWS 6; CA 123; 127; CANR 51, 74, 99, 132; CN 4, 5, 6, 7; DLB 155, 231; HGG; INT CA-127; MTCW 2; MTFW 2005; RHW; SATA 153; SUFW 2
Acorn, Milton 1923-1986 .... **CLC 15**
See also CA 103; CCA 1; CP 1, 2, 3, 4; DAC; DLB 53; INT CA-103
Adam de la Halle c. 1250-c.
1285 .... **CMLC 80**
Adamov, Arthur 1908-1970 .... **CLC 4, 25**
See also CA 17-18; 25-28R; CAP 2; DAM DRAM; DLB 321; EWL 3; GFL 1789 to the Present; MTCW 1; RGWL 2, 3
Adams, Alice (Boyd) 1926-1999 .. **CLC 6, 13, 46; SSC 24**
See also CA 81-84; 179; CANR 26, 53, 75, 88, 136; CN 4, 5, 6; CSW; DLB 234; DLBY 1986; INT CANR-26; MTCW 1, 2; MTFW 2005; SSFS 14, 21
Adams, Andy 1859-1935 .... **TCLC 56**
See also TCWW 1, 2; YABC 1
Adams, (Henry) Brooks
1848-1927 .... **TCLC 80**
See also CA 123; 193; DLB 47
Adams, Douglas (Noel) 1952-2001 .. **CLC 27, 60**
See also AAYA 4, 33; BEST 89:3; BYA 14; CA 106; 197; CANR 34, 64, 124; CPW; DA3; DAM POP; DLB 261; DLBY 1983; JRDA; MTCW 2; MTFW 2005; NFS 7; SATA 116; SATA-Obit 128; SFW 4
Adams, Francis 1862-1893 .... **NCLC 33**
Adams, Henry (Brooks)
1838-1918 .... **TCLC 4, 52**
See also AMW; CA 104; 133; CANR 77; DA; DAB; DAC; DAM MST; DLB 12, 47, 189, 284; EWL 3; MAL 5; MTCW 1; NCFS 1; RGAL 4; TUS
Adams, John 1735-1826 .... **NCLC 106**
See also DLB 31, 183

Adams, Richard (George) 1920- ... **CLC 4, 5, 18**
See also AAYA 16; AITN 1, 2; BPFB 1; BYA 5; CA 49-52; CANR 3, 35, 128; CLR 20; CN 4, 5, 6, 7; DAM NOV; DLB 261; FANT; JRDA; LAIT 5; MAICYA 1, 2; MTCW 1, 2; NFS 11; SATA 7, 69; YAW
Adamson, Joy(-Friederike Victoria)
1910-1980 .... **CLC 17**
See also CA 69-72; 93-96; CANR 22; MTCW 1; SATA 11; SATA-Obit 22
Adcock, Fleur 1934- .... **CLC 41**
See also CA 25-28R, 182; CAAE 182; CAAS 23; CANR 11, 34, 69, 101; CP 1, 2, 3, 4, 5, 6, 7; CWP; DLB 40; FW; WWE 1
Addams, Charles (Samuel)
1912-1988 .... **CLC 30**
See also CA 61-64; 126; CANR 12, 79
Addams, (Laura) Jane 1860-1935 . **TCLC 76**
See also AMWS 1; CA 194; DLB 303; FW
Addison, Joseph 1672-1719 .... **LC 18**
See also BRW 3; CDBLB 1660-1789; DLB 101; RGEL 2; WLIT 3
Adler, Alfred (F.) 1870-1937 .... **TCLC 61**
See also CA 119; 159
Adler, C(arole) S(chwerdtfeger)
1932- .... **CLC 35**
See also AAYA 4, 41; CA 89-92; CANR 19, 40, 101; CLR 78; JRDA; MAICYA 1, 2; SAAS 15; SATA 26, 63, 102, 126; YAW
Adler, Renata 1938- .... **CLC 8, 31**
See also CA 49-52; CANR 95; CN 4, 5, 6; MTCW 1
Adorno, Theodor W(iesengrund)
1903-1969 .... **TCLC 111**
See also CA 89-92; 25-28R; CANR 89; DLB 242; EWL 3
Ady, Endre 1877-1919 .... **TCLC 11**
See also CA 107; CDWLB 4; DLB 215; EW 9; EWL 3
A.E. .... **TCLC 3, 10**
See Russell, George William
See also DLB 19
Aelfric c. 955-c. 1010 .... **CMLC 46**
See also DLB 146
Aeschines c. 390B.C.-c. 320B.C. .... **CMLC 47**
See also DLB 176
Aeschylus 525(?)B.C.-456(?)B.C. .. **CMLC 11, 51; DC 8; WLCS**
See also AW 1; CDWLB 1; DA; DAB; DAC; DAM DRAM, MST; DFS 5, 10; DLB 176; LMFS 1; RGWL 2, 3; TWA
Aesop 620(?)B.C.-560(?)B.C. .... **CMLC 24**
See also CLR 14; MAICYA 1, 2; SATA 64
Affable Hawk
See MacCarthy, Sir (Charles Otto) Desmond

Alexie, Sherman (Joseph, Jr.)
1966- .... **CLC 96, 154; NNAL; PC 53**
See also AAYA 28; BYA 15; CA 138;
CANR 65, 95, 133; CN 7; DA3; DAM
MULT; DLB 175, 206, 278; LATS 1:2;
MTCW 2; MTFW 2005; NFS 17; SSFS
18

al-Farabi 870(?)-950 .... **CMLC 58**
See also DLB 115

Alfau, Felipe 1902-1999 .... **CLC 66**
See also CA 137

Alfieri, Vittorio 1749-1803 .... **NCLC 101**
See also EW 4; RGWL 2, 3; WLIT 7

Alfonso X 1221-1284 .... **CMLC 78**

Alfred, Jean Gaston
See Ponge, Francis

Alger, Horatio, Jr. 1832-1899 .... **NCLC 8, 83**
See also CLR 87; DLB 42; LAIT 2; RGAL
4; SATA 16; TUS

Al-Ghazali, Muhammad ibn Muhammad
1058-1111 .... **CMLC 50**
See also DLB 115

Algren, Nelson 1909-1981 ..... **CLC 4, 10, 33;**
SSC 33
See also AMWS 9; BPFB 1; CA 13-16R;
103; CANR 20, 61; CDALB 1941-1968;
CN 1, 2; DLB 9; DLBY 1981, 1982,
2000; EWL 3; MAL 5; MTCW 1, 2;
MTFW 2005; RGAL 4; RGSF 2

al-Hariri, al-Qasim ibn 'Ali Abu
Muhammad al-Basri
1054-1122 .... **CMLC 63**
See also RGWL 3

Ali, Ahmed 1908-1998 .... **CLC 69**
See also CA 25-28R; CANR 15, 34; CN 1,
2, 3, 4, 5; EWL 3

Ali, Tariq 1943- .... **CLC 173**
See also CA 25-28R; CANR 10, 99

Alighieri, Dante
See Dante
See also WLIT 7

al-Kindi, Abu Yusuf Ya'qub ibn Ishaq c.
801-c. 873 .... **CMLC 80**

Allan, John B.
See Westlake, Donald E(dwin)

Allan, Sidney
See Hartmann, Sadakichi

Allan, Sydney
See Hartmann, Sadakichi

Allard, Janet .... **CLC 59**

Allen, Edward 1948- .... **CLC 59**

Allen, Fred 1894-1956 .... **TCLC 87**

Allen, Paula Gunn 1939- .... **CLC 84, 202;**
NNAL
See also AMWS 4; CA 112; 143; CANR
63, 130; CWP; DA3; DAM MULT; DLB
175; FW; MTCW 2; MTFW 2005; RGAL
4; TCWW 2

Allen, Roland
See Ayckbourn, Alan

Allen, Sarah A.
See Hopkins, Pauline Elizabeth

Allen, Sidney H.
See Hartmann, Sadakichi

Allen, Woody 1935- .... **CLC 16, 52, 195**
See also AAYA 10, 51; AMWS 15; CA 33-
36R; CANR 27, 38, 63, 128; DAM POP;
DLB 44; MTCW 1; SSFS 21

Allende, Isabel 1942- ... **CLC 39, 57, 97, 170;**
HLC 1; SSC 65; WLCS
See also AAYA 18; CA 125; 130; CANR
51, 74, 129; CDWLB 3; CLR 99; CWW
2; DA3; DAM MULT, NOV; DLB 145;
DNFS 1; EWL 3; FL 1:5; FW; HW 1, 2;
INT CA-130; LAIT 5; LAWS 1; LMFS 2;
MTCW 1, 2; MTFW 2005; NCFS 1; NFS
6, 18; RGSF 2; RGWL 3; SATA 163;
SSFS 11, 16; WLIT 1

Alleyn, Ellen
See Rossetti, Christina

Alleyne, Carla D. .... **CLC 65**

Allingham, Margery (Louise)
1904-1966 .... **CLC 19**
See also CA 5-8R; 25-28R; CANR 4, 58;
CMW 4; DLB 77; MSW; MTCW 1

Allingham, William 1824-1889 ...... **NCLC 25**
See also DLB 35; RGEL 2

Allison, Dorothy E. 1949- .... **CLC 78, 153**
See also AAYA 53; CA 140; CANR 66, 107;
CN 7; CSW; DA3; FW; MTCW 2; MTFW
2005; NFS 11; RGAL 4

Alloula, Malek .... **CLC 65**

Allston, Washington 1779-1843 .... **NCLC 2**
See also DLB 1, 235

Almedingen, E. M. .... **CLC 12**
See Almedingen, Martha Edith von
See also SATA 3

Almedingen, Martha Edith von 1898-1971
See Almedingen, E. M.
See also CA 1-4R; CANR 1

Almodovar, Pedro 1949(?)- .... **CLC 114;**
HLCS 1
See also CA 133; CANR 72; HW 2

Almqvist, Carl Jonas Love
1793-1866 .... **NCLC 42**

al-Mutanabbi, Ahmad ibn al-Husayn Abu
al-Tayyib al-Jufi al-Kindi
915-965 .... **CMLC 66**
See Mutanabbi, Al-
See also RGWL 3

Alonso, Damaso 1898-1990 .... **CLC 14**
See also CA 110; 131; 130; CANR 72; DLB
108; EWL 3; HW 1, 2

Alov
See Gogol, Nikolai (Vasilyevich)

al'Sadaawi, Nawal
See El Saadawi, Nawal
See also FW

Al-Shaykh 1945- .... **CLC 218**
See also CA 135; CANR 111; WLIT 6

Al Siddik
See Rolfe, Frederick (William Serafino
Austin Lewis Mary)
See also GLL 1; RGEL 2

Alta 1942- .... **CLC 19**
See also CA 57-60

Alter, Robert B(ernard) 1935- .... **CLC 34**
See also CA 49-52; CANR 1, 47, 100

Alther, Lisa 1944- .... **CLC 7, 41**
See also BPFB 1; CA 65-68; CAAS 30;
CANR 12, 30, 51; CN 4, 5, 6, 7; CSW;
GLL 2; MTCW 1

Althusser, L.
See Althusser, Louis

Althusser, Louis 1918-1990 .... **CLC 106**
See also CA 131; 132; CANR 102; DLB
242

Altman, Robert 1925- .... **CLC 16, 116**
See also CA 73-76; CANR 43

Alurista .... **HLCS 1; PC 34**
See Urista (Heredia), Alberto (Baltazar)
See also CA 45-48R; DLB 82; LLW

Alvarez, A(lfred) 1929- .... **CLC 5, 13**
See also CA 1-4R; CANR 3, 33, 63, 101,
134; CN 3, 4, 5, 6; CP 1, 2, 3, 4, 5, 6, 7;
DLB 14, 40; MTFW 2005

Alvarez, Alejandro Rodriguez 1903-1965
See Casona, Alejandro
See also CA 131; 93-96; HW 1

Alvarez, Julia 1950- .... **CLC 93; HLCS 1**
See also AAYA 25; AMWS 7; CA 147;
CANR 69, 101, 133; DA3; DLB 282;
LATS 1:2; LLW; MTCW 2; MTFW 2005;
NFS 5, 9; SATA 129; WLIT 1

Alvaro, Corrado 1896-1956 .... **TCLC 60**
See also CA 163; DLB 264; EWL 3

Amado, Jorge 1912-2001 ... **CLC 13, 40, 106;**
HLC 1
See also CA 77-80; 201; CANR 35, 74, 135;
CWW 2; DAM MULT, NOV; DLB 113,
307; EWL 3; HW 2; LAW; LAWS 1;
MTCW 1, 2; MTFW 2005; RGWL 2, 3;
TWA; WLIT 1

Ambler, Eric 1909-1998 .... **CLC 4, 6, 9**
See also BRWS 4; CA 9-12R; 171; CANR
7, 38, 74; CMW 4; CN 1, 2, 3, 4, 5, 6;
DLB 77; MSW; MTCW 1, 2; TEA

Ambrose, Stephen E(dward)
1936-2002 .... **CLC 145**
See also AAYA 44; CA 1-4R; 209; CANR
3, 43, 57, 83, 105; MTFW 2005; NCFS 2;
SATA 40, 138

Amichai, Yehuda 1924-2000 .. **CLC 9, 22, 57,**
116; PC 38
See also CA 85-88; 189; CANR 46, 60, 99,
132; CWW 2; EWL 3; MTCW 1, 2;
MTFW 2005; WLIT 6

Amichai, Yehudah
See Amichai, Yehuda

Amiel, Henri Frederic 1821-1881 .... **NCLC 4**
See also DLB 217

Amis, Kingsley (William)
1922-1995 ...... **CLC 1, 2, 3, 5, 8, 13, 40,**
44, 129
See also AITN 2; BPFB 1; BRWS 2; CA
9-12R; 150; CANR 8, 28, 54; CDBLB
1945-1960; CN 1, 2, 3, 4, 5, 6; CP 1, 2,
3, 4; DA; DA3; DAB; DAC; DAM MST,
NOV; DLB 15, 27, 100, 139; DLBY 1996;
EWL 3; HGG; INT CANR-8; MTCW 1,
2; MTFW 2005; RGEL 2; RGSF 2; SFW
4

Amis, Martin (Louis) 1949- .... **CLC 4, 9, 38,**
62, 101, 213
See also BEST 90:3; BRWS 4; CA 65-68;
CANR 8, 27, 54, 73, 95, 132; CN 5, 6, 7;
DA3; DLB 14, 194; EWL 3; INT CANR-
27; MTCW 2; MTFW 2005

Ammianus Marcellinus c. 330-c.
395 .... **CMLC 60**
See also AW 2; DLB 211

Ammons, A(rchie) R(andolph)
1926-2001 ... **CLC 2, 3, 5, 8, 9, 25, 57,**
108; PC 16
See also AITN 1; AMWS 7; CA 9-12R;
193; CANR 6, 36, 51, 73, 107; CP 1, 2,
3, 4, 5, 6, 7; CSW; DAM POET; DLB 5,
165; EWL 3; MAL 5; MTCW 1, 2; PFS
19; RGAL 4; TCLE 1:1

Amo, Tauraatua i
See Adams, Henry (Brooks)

Amory, Thomas 1691(?)-1788 .... **LC 48**
See also DLB 39

Anand, Mulk Raj 1905-2004 ...... **CLC 23, 93**
See also CA 65-68; 231; CANR 32, 64; CN
1, 2, 3, 4, 5, 6, 7; DAM NOV; EWL 3;
MTCW 1, 2; MTFW 2005; RGSF 2

Anatol
See Schnitzler, Arthur

Anaximander c. 611B.C.-c.
546B.C. .... **CMLC 22**

Anaya, Rudolfo A(lfonso) 1937- ...... **CLC 23,**
148; HLC 1
See also AAYA 20; BYA 13; CA 45-48;
CAAS 4; CANR 1, 32, 51, 124; CN 4, 5,
6, 7; DAM MULT, NOV; DLB 82, 206,
278; HW 1; LAIT 4; LLW; MAL 5;
MTCW 1, 2; MTFW 2005; NFS 12;
RGAL 4; RGSF 2; TCWW 2; WLIT 1

Andersen, Hans Christian
1805-1875 .... **NCLC 7, 79; SSC 6, 56;**
WLC
See also AAYA 57; CLR 6; DA; DA3;
DAB; DAC; DAM MST, POP; EW 6;
MAICYA 1, 2; RGSF 2; RGWL 2, 3;
SATA 100; TWA; WCH; YABC 1

Arden, John 1930- .... **CLC 6, 13, 15**
See also BRWS 2; CA 13-16R; CAAS 4; CANR 31, 65, 67, 124; CBD; CD 5, 6; DAM DRAM; DFS 9; DLB 13, 245; EWL 3; MTCW 1

Arenas, Reinaldo 1943-1990 .. **CLC 41; HLC 1**
See also CA 124; 128; 133; CANR 73, 106; DAM MULT; DLB 145; EWL 3; GLL 2; HW 1; LAW; LAWS 1; MTCW 2; MTFW 2005; RGSF 2; RGWL 3; WLIT 1

Arendt, Hannah 1906-1975 .... **CLC 66, 98**
See also CA 17-20R; 61-64; CANR 26, 60; DLB 242; MTCW 1, 2

Aretino, Pietro 1492-1556 .... **LC 12**
See also RGWL 2, 3

Arghezi, Tudor .... **CLC 80**
See Theodorescu, Ion N.
See also CA 167; CDWLB 4; DLB 220; EWL 3

Arguedas, Jose Maria 1911-1969 .... **CLC 10, 18; HLCS 1; TCLC 147**
See also CA 89-92; CANR 73; DLB 113; EWL 3; HW 1; LAW; RGWL 2, 3; WLIT 1

Argueta, Manlio 1936- .... **CLC 31**
See also CA 131; CANR 73; CWW 2; DLB 145; EWL 3; HW 1; RGWL 3

Arias, Ron(ald Francis) 1941- .... **HLC 1**
See also CA 131; CANR 81, 136; DAM MULT; DLB 82; HW 1, 2; MTCW 2; MTFW 2005

Ariosto, Lodovico
See Ariosto, Ludovico
See also WLIT 7

Ariosto, Ludovico 1474-1533 ... **LC 6, 87; PC 42**
See Ariosto, Lodovico
See also EW 2; RGWL 2, 3

Aristides
See Epstein, Joseph

Aristophanes 450B.C.-385B.C. .... **CMLC 4, 51; DC 2; WLCS**
See also AW 1; CDWLB 1; DA; DA3; DAB; DAC; DAM DRAM, MST; DFS 10; DLB 176; LMFS 1; RGWL 2, 3; TWA

Aristotle 384B.C.-322B.C. .... **CMLC 31; WLCS**
See also AW 1; CDWLB 1; DA; DA3; DAB; DAC; DAM MST; DLB 176; RGWL 2, 3; TWA

Arlt, Roberto (Godofredo Christophersen) 1900-1942 .... **HLC 1; TCLC 29**
See also CA 123; 131; CANR 67; DAM MULT; DLB 305; EWL 3; HW 1, 2; IDTP; LAW

Armah, Ayi Kwei 1939- . **BLC 1; CLC 5, 33, 136**
See also AFW; BRWS 10; BW 1; CA 61-64; CANR 21, 64; CDWLB 3; CN 1, 2, 3, 4, 5, 6, 7; DAM MULT, POET; DLB 117; EWL 3; MTCW 1; WLIT 2

Armatrading, Joan 1950- .... **CLC 17**
See also CA 114; 186

Armitage, Frank
See Carpenter, John (Howard)

Armstrong, Jeannette (C.) 1948- .... **NNAL**
See also CA 149; CCA 1; CN 6, 7; DAC; SATA 102

Arnette, Robert
See Silverberg, Robert

Arnim, Achim von (Ludwig Joachim von Arnim) 1781-1831 .. **NCLC 5, 159; SSC 29**
See also DLB 90

Arnim, Bettina von 1785-1859 ...... **NCLC 38, 123**
See also DLB 90; RGWL 2, 3

Arnold, Matthew 1822-1888 ..... **NCLC 6, 29, 89, 126; PC 5; WLC**
See also BRW 5; CDBLB 1832-1890; DA; DAB; DAC; DAM MST, POET; DLB 32, 57; EXPP; PAB; PFS 2; TEA; WP

Arnold, Thomas 1795-1842 .... **NCLC 18**
See also DLB 55

Arnow, Harriette (Louisa) Simpson 1908-1986 .... **CLC 2, 7, 18**
See also BPFB 1; CA 9-12R; 118; CANR 14; CN 2, 3, 4; DLB 6; FW; MTCW 1, 2; RHW; SATA 42; SATA-Obit 47

Arouet, Francois-Marie
See Voltaire

Arp, Hans
See Arp, Jean

Arp, Jean 1887-1966 .... **CLC 5; TCLC 115**
See also CA 81-84; 25-28R; CANR 42, 77; EW 10

Arrabal
See Arrabal, Fernando

Arrabal (Teran), Fernando
See Arrabal, Fernando
See also CWW 2

Arrabal, Fernando 1932- ... **CLC 2, 9, 18, 58**
See Arrabal (Teran), Fernando
See also CA 9-12R; CANR 15; DLB 321; EWL 3; LMFS 2

Arreola, Juan Jose 1918-2001 .... **CLC 147; HLC 1; SSC 38**
See also CA 113; 131; 200; CANR 81; CWW 2; DAM MULT; DLB 113; DNFS 2; EWL 3; HW 1, 2; LAW; RGSF 2

Arrian c. 89(?)-c. 155(?) .... **CMLC 43**
See also DLB 176

Arrick, Fran .... **CLC 30**
See Gaberman, Judie Angell
See also BYA 6

Arrley, Richmond
See Delany, Samuel R(ay), Jr.

Artaud, Antonin (Marie Joseph) 1896-1948 .... **DC 14; TCLC 3, 36**
See also CA 104; 149; DA3; DAM DRAM; DFS 22; DLB 258, 321; EW 11; EWL 3; GFL 1789 to the Present; MTCW 2; MTFW 2005; RGWL 2, 3

Arthur, Ruth M(abel) 1905-1979 ..... **CLC 12**
See also CA 9-12R; 85-88; CANR 4; CWRI 5; SATA 7, 26

Artsybashev, Mikhail (Petrovich) 1878-1927 .... **TCLC 31**
See also CA 170; DLB 295

Arundel, Honor (Morfydd) 1919-1973 .... **CLC 17**
See also CA 21-22; 41-44R; CAP 2; CLR 35; CWRI 5; SATA 4; SATA-Obit 24

Arzner, Dorothy 1900-1979 .... **CLC 98**

Asch, Sholem 1880-1957 .... **TCLC 3**
See also CA 105; EWL 3; GLL 2

Ascham, Roger 1516(?)-1568 .... **LC 101**
See also DLB 236

Ash, Shalom
See Asch, Sholem

Ashbery, John (Lawrence) 1927- .. **CLC 2, 3, 4, 6, 9, 13, 15, 25, 41, 77, 125; PC 26**
See Berry, Jonas
See also AMWS 3; CA 5-8R; CANR 9, 37, 66, 102, 132; CP 1, 2, 3, 4, 5, 6, 7; DA3; DAM POET; DLB 5, 165; DLBY 1981; EWL 3; INT CANR-9; MAL 5; MTCW 1, 2; MTFW 2005; PAB; PFS 11; RGAL 4; TCLE 1:1; WP

Ashdown, Clifford
See Freeman, R(ichard) Austin

Ashe, Gordon
See Creasey, John

Ashton-Warner, Sylvia (Constance) 1908-1984 .... **CLC 19**
See also CA 69-72; 112; CANR 29; CN 1, 2, 3; MTCW 1, 2

Asimov, Isaac 1920-1992 ..... **CLC 1, 3, 9, 19, 26, 76, 92**
See also AAYA 13; BEST 90:2; BPFB 1; BYA 4, 6, 7, 9; CA 1-4R; 137; CANR 2, 19, 36, 60, 125; CLR 12, 79; CMW 4; CN 1, 2, 3, 4, 5; CPW; DA3; DAM POP; DLB 8; DLBY 1992; INT CANR-19; JRDA; LAIT 5; LMFS 2; MAICYA 1, 2; MAL 5; MTCW 1, 2; MTFW 2005; RGAL 4; SATA 1, 26, 74; SCFW 1, 2; SFW 4; SSFS 17; TUS; YAW

Askew, Anne 1521(?)-1546 .... **LC 81**
See also DLB 136

Assis, Joaquim Maria Machado de
See Machado de Assis, Joaquim Maria

Astell, Mary 1666-1731 .... **LC 68**
See also DLB 252; FW

Astley, Thea (Beatrice May) 1925-2004 .... **CLC 41**
See also CA 65-68; 229; CANR 11, 43, 78; CN 1, 2, 3, 4, 5, 6, 7; DLB 289; EWL 3

Astley, William 1855-1911
See Warung, Price

Aston, James
See White, T(erence) H(anbury)

Asturias, Miguel Angel 1899-1974 .... **CLC 3, 8, 13; HLC 1**
See also CA 25-28; 49-52; CANR 32; CAP 2; CDWLB 3; DA3; DAM MULT, NOV; DLB 113, 290; EWL 3; HW 1; LAW; LMFS 2; MTCW 1, 2; RGWL 2, 3; WLIT 1

Atares, Carlos Saura
See Saura (Atares), Carlos

Athanasius c. 295-c. 373 .... **CMLC 48**

Atheling, William
See Pound, Ezra (Weston Loomis)

Atheling, William, Jr.
See Blish, James (Benjamin)

Atherton, Gertrude (Franklin Horn) 1857-1948 .... **TCLC 2**
See also CA 104; 155; DLB 9, 78, 186; HGG; RGAL 4; SUFW 1; TCWW 1, 2

Atherton, Lucius
See Masters, Edgar Lee

Atkins, Jack
See Harris, Mark

Atkinson, Kate 1951- .... **CLC 99**
See also CA 166; CANR 101; DLB 267

Attaway, William (Alexander) 1911-1986 .... **BLC 1; CLC 92**
See also BW 2, 3; CA 143; CANR 82; DAM MULT; DLB 76; MAL 5

Atticus
See Fleming, Ian (Lancaster); Wilson, (Thomas) Woodrow

Atwood, Margaret (Eleanor) 1939- ... **CLC 2, 3, 4, 8, 13, 15, 25, 44, 84, 135; PC 8; SSC 2, 46; WLC**
See also AAYA 12, 47; AMWS 13; BEST 89:2; BPFB 1; CA 49-52; CANR 3, 24, 33, 59, 95, 133; CN 2, 3, 4, 5, 6, 7; CP 1, 2, 3, 4, 5, 6, 7; CPW; CWP; DA; DA3; DAB; DAC; DAM MST, NOV, POET; DLB 53, 251; EWL 3; EXPN; FL 1:5; FW; GL 2; INT CANR-24; LAIT 5; MTCW 1, 2; MTFW 2005; NFS 4, 12, 13, 14, 19; PFS 7; RGSF 2; SATA 50; SSFS 3, 13; TCLE 1:1; TWA; WWE 1; YAW

Aubigny, Pierre d'
See Mencken, H(enry) L(ouis)

Aubin, Penelope 1685-1731(?) .... **LC 9**
See also DLB 39

EXPN; EXPS; HGG; LAIT 3, 5; LATS
1:2; LMFS 2; MAL 5; MTCW 1, 2;
MTFW 2005; NFS 1, 22; RGAL 4; RGSF
2; SATA 11, 64, 123; SCFW 1, 2; SFW 4;
SSFS 1, 20; SUFW 1, 2; TUS; YAW

Braddon, Mary Elizabeth
1837-1915 .... **TCLC 111**
See also BRWS 8; CA 108; 179; CMW 4;
DLB 18, 70, 156; HGG

Bradfield, Scott (Michael) 1955- .... **SSC 65**
See also CA 147; CANR 90; HGG; SUFW
2

Bradford, Gamaliel 1863-1932 .... **TCLC 36**
See also CA 160; DLB 17

Bradford, William 1590-1657 .... **LC 64**
See also DLB 24, 30; RGAL 4

Bradley, David (Henry), Jr. 1950- .... **BLC 1;
CLC 23, 118**
See also BW 1, 3; CA 104; CANR 26, 81;
CN 4, 5, 6, 7; DAM MULT; DLB 33

Bradley, John Ed(mund, Jr.) 1958- .. **CLC 55**
See also CA 139; CANR 99; CN 6, 7; CSW

Bradley, Marion Zimmer
1930-1999 .... **CLC 30**
See Chapman, Lee; Dexter, John; Gardner,
Miriam; Ives, Morgan; Rivers, Elfrida
See also AAYA 40; BPFB 1; CA 57-60; 185;
CAAS 10; CANR 7, 31, 51, 75, 107;
CPW; DA3; DAM POP; DLB 8; FANT;
FW; MTCW 1, 2; MTFW 2005; SATA 90,
139; SATA-Obit 116; SFW 4; SUFW 2;
YAW

Bradshaw, John 1933- .... **CLC 70**
See also CA 138; CANR 61

Bradstreet, Anne 1612(?)-1672 ...... **LC 4, 30;
PC 10**
See also AMWS 1; CDALB 1640-1865;
DA; DA3; DAC; DAM MST, POET; DLB
24; EXPP; FW; PFS 6; RGAL 4; TUS;
WP

Brady, Joan 1939- .... **CLC 86**
See also CA 141

Bragg, Melvyn 1939- .... **CLC 10**
See also BEST 89:3; CA 57-60; CANR 10,
48, 89; CN 1, 2, 3, 4, 5, 6, 7; DLB 14,
271; RHW

Brahe, Tycho 1546-1601 .... **LC 45**
See also DLB 300

Braine, John (Gerard) 1922-1986 . **CLC 1, 3,
41**
See also CA 1-4R; 120; CANR 1, 33; CD-
BLB 1945-1960; CN 1, 2, 3, 4; DLB 15;
DLBY 1986; EWL 3; MTCW 1

Braithwaite, William Stanley (Beaumont)
1878-1962 .... **BLC 1; HR 1:2; PC 52**
See also BW 1; CA 125; DAM MULT; DLB
50, 54; MAL 5

Bramah, Ernest 1868-1942 .... **TCLC 72**
See also CA 156; CMW 4; DLB 70; FANT

Brammer, Billy Lee
See Brammer, William

Brammer, William 1929-1978 .... **CLC 31**
See also CA 235; 77-80

Brancati, Vitaliano 1907-1954 .... **TCLC 12**
See also CA 109; DLB 264; EWL 3

Brancato, Robin F(idler) 1936- .... **CLC 35**
See also AAYA 9, 68; BYA 6; CA 69-72;
CANR 11, 45; CLR 32; JRDA; MAICYA
2; MAICYAS 1; SAAS 9; SATA 97;
WYA; YAW

Brand, Dionne 1953- .... **CLC 192**
See also BW 2; CA 143; CANR 143; CWP

Brand, Max
See Faust, Frederick (Schiller)
See also BPFB 1; TCWW 1, 2

Brand, Millen 1906-1980 .... **CLC 7**
See also CA 21-24R; 97-100; CANR 72

Branden, Barbara .... **CLC 44**
See also CA 148

Brandes, Georg (Morris Cohen)
1842-1927 .... **TCLC 10**
See also CA 105; 189; DLB 300

Brandys, Kazimierz 1916-2000 .... **CLC 62**
See also CA 239; EWL 3

Branley, Franklyn M(ansfield)
1915-2002 .... **CLC 21**
See also CA 33-36R; 207; CANR 14, 39;
CLR 13; MAICYA 1, 2; SAAS 16; SATA
4, 68, 136

Brant, Beth (E.) 1941- .... **NNAL**
See also CA 144; FW

Brant, Sebastian 1457-1521 .... **LC 112**
See also DLB 179; RGWL 2, 3

Brathwaite, Edward Kamau
1930- .... **BLCS; CLC 11; PC 56**
See also BW 2, 3; CA 25-28R; CANR 11,
26, 47, 107; CDWLB 3; CP 1, 2, 3, 4, 5,
6, 7; DAM POET; DLB 125; EWL 3

Brathwaite, Kamau
See Brathwaite, Edward Kamau

Brautigan, Richard (Gary)
1935-1984 .... **CLC 1, 3, 5, 9, 12, 34, 42;
TCLC 133**
See also BPFB 1; CA 53-56; 113; CANR
34; CN 1, 2, 3; CP 1, 2, 3, 4; DA3; DAM
NOV; DLB 2, 5, 206; DLBY 1980, 1984;
FANT; MAL 5; MTCW 1; RGAL 4;
SATA 56

Brave Bird, Mary .... **NNAL**
See Crow Dog, Mary (Ellen)

Braverman, Kate 1950- .... **CLC 67**
See also CA 89-92; CANR 141

Brecht, (Eugen) Bertolt (Friedrich)
1898-1956 ..... **DC 3; TCLC 1, 6, 13, 35,
169; WLC**
See also CA 104; 133; CANR 62; CDWLB
2; DA; DA3; DAB; DAC; DAM DRAM,
MST; DFS 4, 5, 9; DLB 56, 124; EW 11;
EWL 3; IDTP; MTCW 1, 2; MTFW 2005;
RGWL 2, 3; TWA

Brecht, Eugen Berthold Friedrich
See Brecht, (Eugen) Bertolt (Friedrich)

Bremer, Fredrika 1801-1865 .... **NCLC 11**
See also DLB 254

Brennan, Christopher John
1870-1932 .... **TCLC 17**
See also CA 117; 188; DLB 230; EWL 3

Brennan, Maeve 1917-1993 ... **CLC 5; TCLC
124**
See also CA 81-84; CANR 72, 100

Brenner, Jozef 1887-1919
See Csath, Geza
See also CA 240

Brent, Linda
See Jacobs, Harriet A(nn)

Brentano, Clemens (Maria)
1778-1842 .... **NCLC 1**
See also DLB 90; RGWL 2, 3

Brent of Bin Bin
See Franklin, (Stella Maria Sarah) Miles
(Lampe)

Brenton, Howard 1942- .... **CLC 31**
See also CA 69-72; CANR 33, 67; CBD;
CD 5, 6; DLB 13; MTCW 1

Breslin, James 1930-
See Breslin, Jimmy
See also CA 73-76; CANR 31, 75, 139;
DAM NOV; MTCW 1, 2; MTFW 2005

Breslin, Jimmy .... **CLC 4, 43**
See Breslin, James
See also AITN 1; DLB 185; MTCW 2

Bresson, Robert 1901(?)-1999 .... **CLC 16**
See also CA 110; 187; CANR 49

Breton, Andre 1896-1966 .. **CLC 2, 9, 15, 54;
PC 15**
See also CA 19-20; 25-28R; CANR 40, 60;
CAP 2; DLB 65, 258; EW 11; EWL 3;
GFL 1789 to the Present; LMFS 2;
MTCW 1, 2; MTFW 2005; RGWL 2, 3;
TWA; WP

Breytenbach, Breyten 1939(?)- .. **CLC 23, 37,
126**
See also CA 113; 129; CANR 61, 122;
CWW 2; DAM POET; DLB 225; EWL 3

Bridgers, Sue Ellen 1942- .... **CLC 26**
See also AAYA 8, 49; BYA 7, 8; CA 65-68;
CANR 11, 36; CLR 18; DLB 52; JRDA;
MAICYA 1, 2; SAAS 1; SATA 22, 90;
SATA-Essay 109; WYA; YAW

Bridges, Robert (Seymour)
1844-1930 .... **PC 28; TCLC 1**
See also BRW 6; CA 104; 152; CDBLB
1890-1914; DAM POET; DLB 19, 98

Bridie, James .... **TCLC 3**
See Mavor, Osborne Henry
See also DLB 10; EWL 3

Brin, David 1950- .... **CLC 34**
See also AAYA 21; CA 102; CANR 24, 70,
125, 127; INT CANR-24; SATA 65;
SCFW 2; SFW 4

Brink, Andre (Philippus) 1935- . **CLC 18, 36,
106**
See also AFW; BRWS 6; CA 104; CANR
39, 62, 109, 133; CN 4, 5, 6, 7; DLB 225;
EWL 3; INT CA-103; LATS 1:2; MTCW
1, 2; MTFW 2005; WLIT 2

Brinsmead, H. F(ay)
See Brinsmead, H(esba) F(ay)

Brinsmead, H. F.
See Brinsmead, H(esba) F(ay)

Brinsmead, H(esba) F(ay) 1922- ...... **CLC 21**
See also CA 21-24R; CANR 10; CLR 47;
CWRI 5; MAICYA 1, 2; SAAS 5; SATA
18, 78

Brittain, Vera (Mary) 1893(?)-1970 . **CLC 23**
See also BRWS 10; CA 13-16; 25-28R;
CANR 58; CAP 1; DLB 191; FW; MTCW
1, 2

Broch, Hermann 1886-1951 .... **TCLC 20**
See also CA 117; 211; CDWLB 2; DLB 85,
124; EW 10; EWL 3; RGWL 2, 3

Brock, Rose
See Hansen, Joseph
See also GLL 1

Brod, Max 1884-1968 .... **TCLC 115**
See also CA 5-8R; 25-28R; CANR 7; DLB
81; EWL 3

Brodkey, Harold (Roy) 1930-1996 .. **CLC 56;
TCLC 123**
See also CA 111; 151; CANR 71; CN 4, 5,
6; DLB 130

Brodsky, Iosif Alexandrovich 1940-1996
See Brodsky, Joseph
See also AITN 1; CA 41-44R; 151; CANR
37, 106; DA3; DAM POET; MTCW 1, 2;
MTFW 2005; RGWL 2, 3

Brodsky, Joseph . **CLC 4, 6, 13, 36, 100; PC
9**
See Brodsky, Iosif Alexandrovich
See also AMWS 8; CWW 2; DLB 285;
EWL 3; MTCW 1

Brodsky, Michael (Mark) 1948- .... **CLC 19**
See also CA 102; CANR 18, 41, 58; DLB
244

Brodzki, Bella ed. .... **CLC 65**

Brome, Richard 1590(?)-1652 .... **LC 61**
See also BRWS 10; DLB 58

Bromell, Henry 1947- .... **CLC 5**
See also CA 53-56; CANR 9, 115, 116

Clutha, Janet Paterson Frame 1924-2004
See Frame, Janet
See also CA 1-4R; 224; CANR 2, 36, 76, 135; MTCW 1, 2; SATA 119

Clyne, Terence
See Blatty, William Peter

Cobalt, Martin
See Mayne, William (James Carter)

Cobb, Irvin S(hrewsbury)
1876-1944 .... **TCLC 77**
See also CA 175; DLB 11, 25, 86

Cobbett, William 1763-1835 .... **NCLC 49**
See also DLB 43, 107, 158; RGEL 2

Coburn, D(onald) L(ee) 1938- .... **CLC 10**
See also CA 89-92

Cocteau, Jean (Maurice Eugene Clement)
1889-1963 ...... **CLC 1, 8, 15, 16, 43; DC 17; TCLC 119; WLC**
See also CA 25-28; CANR 40; CAP 2; DA; DA3; DAB; DAC; DAM DRAM, MST, NOV; DLB 65, 258, 321; EW 10; EWL 3; GFL 1789 to the Present; MTCW 1, 2; RGWL 2, 3; TWA

Codrescu, Andrei 1946- .... **CLC 46, 121**
See also CA 33-36R; CAAS 19; CANR 13, 34, 53, 76, 125; CN 7; DA3; DAM POET; MAL 5; MTCW 2; MTFW 2005

Coe, Max
See Bourne, Randolph S(illiman)

Coe, Tucker
See Westlake, Donald E(dwin)

Coen, Ethan 1958- .... **CLC 108**
See also AAYA 54; CA 126; CANR 85

Coen, Joel 1955- .... **CLC 108**
See also AAYA 54; CA 126; CANR 119

The Coen Brothers
See Coen, Ethan; Coen, Joel

Coetzee, J(ohn) M(axwell) 1940- ..... **CLC 23, 33, 66, 117, 161, 162**
See also AAYA 37; AFW; BRWS 6; CA 77-80; CANR 41, 54, 74, 114, 133; CN 4, 5, 6, 7; DA3; DAM NOV; DLB 225; EWL 3; LMFS 2; MTCW 1, 2; MTFW 2005; NFS 21; WLIT 2; WWE 1

Coffey, Brian
See Koontz, Dean R.

Coffin, Robert P(eter) Tristram
1892-1955 .... **TCLC 95**
See also CA 123; 169; DLB 45

Cohan, George M(ichael)
1878-1942 .... **TCLC 60**
See also CA 157; DLB 249; RGAL 4

Cohen, Arthur A(llen) 1928-1986 ...... **CLC 7, 31**
See also CA 1-4R; 120; CANR 1, 17, 42; DLB 28

Cohen, Leonard (Norman) 1934- ...... **CLC 3, 38**
See also CA 21-24R; CANR 14, 69; CN 1, 2, 3, 4, 5, 6; CP 1, 2, 3, 4, 5, 6, 7; DAC; DAM MST; DLB 53; EWL 3; MTCW 1

Cohen, Matt(hew) 1942-1999 .... **CLC 19**
See also CA 61-64; 187; CAAS 18; CANR 40; CN 1, 2, 3, 4, 5, 6; DAC; DLB 53

Cohen-Solal, Annie 1948- .... **CLC 50**
See also CA 239

Colegate, Isabel 1931- .... **CLC 36**
See also CA 17-20R; CANR 8, 22, 74; CN 4, 5, 6, 7; DLB 14, 231; INT CANR-22; MTCW 1

Coleman, Emmett
See Reed, Ishmael (Scott)

Coleridge, Hartley 1796-1849 .... **NCLC 90**
See also DLB 96

Coleridge, M. E.
See Coleridge, Mary E(lizabeth)

Coleridge, Mary E(lizabeth)
1861-1907 .... **TCLC 73**
See also CA 116; 166; DLB 19, 98

Coleridge, Samuel Taylor
1772-1834 ...... **NCLC 9, 54, 99, 111; PC 11, 39, 67; WLC**
See also AAYA 66; BRW 4; BRWR 2; BYA 4; CDBLB 1789-1832; DA; DA3; DAB; DAC; DAM MST, POET; DLB 93, 107; EXPP; LATS 1:1; LMFS 1; PAB; PFS 4, 5; RGEL 2; TEA; WLIT 3; WP

Coleridge, Sara 1802-1852 .... **NCLC 31**
See also DLB 199

Coles, Don 1928- .... **CLC 46**
See also CA 115; CANR 38; CP 7

Coles, Robert (Martin) 1929- .... **CLC 108**
See also CA 45-48; CANR 3, 32, 66, 70, 135; INT CANR-32; SATA 23

Colette, (Sidonie-Gabrielle)
1873-1954 .... **SSC 10; TCLC 1, 5, 16**
See Willy, Colette
See also CA 104; 131; DA3; DAM NOV; DLB 65; EW 9; EWL 3; GFL 1789 to the Present; MTCW 1, 2; MTFW 2005; RGWL 2, 3; TWA

Collett, (Jacobine) Camilla (Wergeland)
1813-1895 .... **NCLC 22**

Collier, Christopher 1930- .... **CLC 30**
See also AAYA 13; BYA 2; CA 33-36R; CANR 13, 33, 102; JRDA; MAICYA 1, 2; SATA 16, 70; WYA; YAW 1

Collier, James Lincoln 1928- .... **CLC 30**
See also AAYA 13; BYA 2; CA 9-12R; CANR 4, 33, 60, 102; CLR 3; DAM POP; JRDA; MAICYA 1, 2; SAAS 21; SATA 8, 70; WYA; YAW 1

Collier, Jeremy 1650-1726 .... **LC 6**

Collier, John 1901-1980 . **SSC 19; TCLC 127**
See also CA 65-68; 97-100; CANR 10; CN 1, 2; DLB 77, 255; FANT; SUFW 1

Collier, Mary 1690-1762 .... **LC 86**
See also DLB 95

Collingwood, R(obin) G(eorge)
1889(?)-1943 .... **TCLC 67**
See also CA 117; 155; DLB 262

Collins, Billy 1941- .... **PC 68**
See also AAYA 64; CA 151; CANR 92; MTFW 2005; PFS 18

Collins, Hunt
See Hunter, Evan

Collins, Linda 1931- .... **CLC 44**
See also CA 125

Collins, Tom
See Furphy, Joseph
See also RGEL 2

Collins, (William) Wilkie
1824-1889 .... **NCLC 1, 18, 93**
See also BRWS 6; CDBLB 1832-1890; CMW 4; DLB 18, 70, 159; GL 2; MSW; RGEL 2; RGSF 2; SUFW 1; WLIT 4

Collins, William 1721-1759 .... **LC 4, 40**
See also BRW 3; DAM POET; DLB 109; RGEL 2

Collodi, Carlo .... **NCLC 54**
See Lorenzini, Carlo
See also CLR 5; WCH; WLIT 7

Colman, George
See Glassco, John

Colman, George, the Elder
1732-1794 .... **LC 98**
See also RGEL 2

Colonna, Vittoria 1492-1547 .... **LC 71**
See also RGWL 2, 3

Colt, Winchester Remington
See Hubbard, L(afayette) Ron(ald)

Colter, Cyrus J. 1910-2002 .... **CLC 58**
See also BW 1; CA 65-68; 205; CANR 10, 66; CN 2, 3, 4, 5, 6; DLB 33

Colton, James
See Hansen, Joseph
See also GLL 1

Colum, Padraic 1881-1972 .... **CLC 28**
See also BYA 4; CA 73-76; 33-36R; CANR 35; CLR 36; CP 1; CWRI 5; DLB 19; MAICYA 1, 2; MTCW 1; RGEL 2; SATA 15; WCH

Colvin, James
See Moorcock, Michael (John)

Colwin, Laurie (E.) 1944-1992 .... **CLC 5, 13, 23, 84**
See also CA 89-92; 139; CANR 20, 46; DLB 218; DLBY 1980; MTCW 1

Comfort, Alex(ander) 1920-2000 .... **CLC 7**
See also CA 1-4R; 190; CANR 1, 45; CN 1, 2, 3, 4; CP 1, 2, 3, 4, 5, 6, 7; DAM POP; MTCW 2

Comfort, Montgomery
See Campbell, (John) Ramsey

Compton-Burnett, I(vy)
1892(?)-1969 .... **CLC 1, 3, 10, 15, 34**
See also BRW 7; CA 1-4R; 25-28R; CANR 4; DAM NOV; DLB 36; EWL 3; MTCW 1, 2; RGEL 2

Comstock, Anthony 1844-1915 ...... **TCLC 13**
See also CA 110; 169

Comte, Auguste 1798-1857 .... **NCLC 54**

Conan Doyle, Arthur
See Doyle, Sir Arthur Conan
See also BPFB 1; BYA 4, 5, 11

Conde (Abellan), Carmen
1901-1996 .... **HLCS 1**
See also CA 177; CWW 2; DLB 108; EWL 3; HW 2

Conde, Maryse 1937- ..... **BLCS; CLC 52, 92**
See also BW 2, 3; CA 110; 190; CAAE 190; CANR 30, 53, 76; CWW 2; DAM MULT; EWL 3; MTCW 2; MTFW 2005

Condillac, Etienne Bonnot de
1714-1780 .... **LC 26**
See also DLB 313

Condon, Richard (Thomas)
1915-1996 .... **CLC 4, 6, 8, 10, 45, 100**
See also BEST 90:3; BPFB 1; CA 1-4R; 151; CAAS 1; CANR 2, 23; CMW 4; CN 1, 2, 3, 4, 5, 6; DAM NOV; INT CANR-23; MAL 5; MTCW 1, 2

Condorcet .... **LC 104**
See Condorcet, marquis de Marie-Jean-Antoine-Nicolas Caritat
See also GFL Beginnings to 1789

**Condorcet, marquis de
Marie-Jean-Antoine-Nicolas Caritat**
1743-1794
See Condorcet
See also DLB 313

Confucius 551B.C.-479B.C. .... **CMLC 19, 65; WLCS**
See also DA; DA3; DAB; DAC; DAM MST

Congreve, William 1670-1729 ... **DC 2; LC 5, 21; WLC**
See also BRW 2; CDBLB 1660-1789; DA; DAB; DAC; DAM DRAM, MST, POET; DFS 15; DLB 39, 84; RGEL 2; WLIT 3

Conley, Robert J(ackson) 1940- .... **NNAL**
See also CA 41-44R; CANR 15, 34, 45, 96; DAM MULT; TCWW 2

Connell, Evan S(helby), Jr. 1924- . **CLC 4, 6, 45**
See also AAYA 7; AMWS 14; CA 1-4R; CAAS 2; CANR 2, 39, 76, 97, 140; CN 1, 2, 3, 4, 5, 6; DAM NOV; DLB 2; DLBY 1981; MAL 5; MTCW 1, 2; MTFW 2005

Connelly, Marc(us Cook) 1890-1980 . **CLC 7**
See also CA 85-88; 102; CAD; CANR 30; DFS 12; DLB 7; DLBY 1980; MAL 5; RGAL 4; SATA-Obit 25

Connor, Ralph .... **TCLC 31**
See Gordon, Charles William
See also DLB 92; TCWW 1, 2

Conrad, Joseph 1857-1924 ..... **SSC 9, 67, 69, 71; TCLC 1, 6, 13, 25, 43, 57; WLC**
See also AAYA 26; BPFB 1; BRW 6; BRWC 1; BRWR 2; BYA 2; CA 104; 131; CANR 60; CDBLB 1890-1914; DA; DA3; DAB; DAC; DAM MST, NOV; DLB 10, 34, 98, 156; EWL 3; EXPN; EXPS; LAIT 2; LATS 1:1; LMFS 1; MTCW 1, 2; MTFW 2005; NFS 2, 16; RGEL 2; RGSF 2; SATA 27; SSFS 1, 12; TEA; WLIT 4

Conrad, Robert Arnold
See Hart, Moss

Conroy, (Donald) Pat(rick) 1945- ... **CLC 30, 74**
See also AAYA 8, 52; AITN 1; BPFB 1; CA 85-88; CANR 24, 53, 129; CN 7; CPW; CSW; DA3; DAM NOV, POP; DLB 6; LAIT 5; MAL 5; MTCW 1, 2; MTFW 2005

Constant (de Rebecque), (Henri) Benjamin 1767-1830 .... **NCLC 6**
See also DLB 119; EW 4; GFL 1789 to the Present

Conway, Jill K(er) 1934- .... **CLC 152**
See also CA 130; CANR 94

Conybeare, Charles Augustus
See Eliot, T(homas) S(tearns)

Cook, Michael 1933-1994 .... **CLC 58**
See also CA 93-96; CANR 68; DLB 53

Cook, Robin 1940- .... **CLC 14**
See also AAYA 32; BEST 90:2; BPFB 1; CA 108; 111; CANR 41, 90, 109; CPW; DA3; DAM POP; HGG; INT CA-111

Cook, Roy
See Silverberg, Robert

Cooke, Elizabeth 1948- .... **CLC 55**
See also CA 129

Cooke, John Esten 1830-1886 .... **NCLC 5**
See also DLB 3, 248; RGAL 4

Cooke, John Estes
See Baum, L(yman) Frank

Cooke, M. E.
See Creasey, John

Cooke, Margaret
See Creasey, John

Cooke, Rose Terry 1827-1892 ...... **NCLC 110**
See also DLB 12, 74

Cook-Lynn, Elizabeth 1930- .... **CLC 93; NNAL**
See also CA 133; DAM MULT; DLB 175

Cooney, Ray .... **CLC 62**
See also CBD

Cooper, Anthony Ashley 1671-1713 .. **LC 107**
See also DLB 101

Cooper, Dennis 1953- .... **CLC 203**
See also CA 133; CANR 72, 86; GLL 1; HGG

Cooper, Douglas 1960- .... **CLC 86**

Cooper, Henry St. John
See Creasey, John

Cooper, J(oan) California (?)- .... **CLC 56**
See also AAYA 12; BW 1; CA 125; CANR 55; DAM MULT; DLB 212

Cooper, James Fenimore 1789-1851 .... **NCLC 1, 27, 54**
See also AAYA 22; AMW; BPFB 1; CDALB 1640-1865; DA3; DLB 3, 183, 250, 254; LAIT 1; NFS 9; RGAL 4; SATA 19; TUS; WCH

Cooper, Susan Fenimore 1813-1894 .... **NCLC 129**
See also ANW; DLB 239, 254

Coover, Robert (Lowell) 1932- ...... **CLC 3, 7, 15, 32, 46, 87, 161; SSC 15**
See also AMWS 5; BPFB 1; CA 45-48; CANR 3, 37, 58, 115; CN 1, 2, 3, 4, 5, 6, 7; DAM NOV; DLB 2, 227; DLBY 1981; EWL 3; MAL 5; MTCW 1, 2; MTFW 2005; RGAL 4; RGSF 2

Copeland, Stewart (Armstrong) 1952- .... **CLC 26**

Copernicus, Nicolaus 1473-1543 .... **LC 45**

Coppard, A(lfred) E(dgar) 1878-1957 .... **SSC 21; TCLC 5**
See also BRWS 8; CA 114; 167; DLB 162; EWL 3; HGG; RGEL 2; RGSF 2; SUFW 1; YABC 1

Coppee, Francois 1842-1908 .... **TCLC 25**
See also CA 170; DLB 217

Coppola, Francis Ford 1939- ... **CLC 16, 126**
See also AAYA 39; CA 77-80; CANR 40, 78; DLB 44

Copway, George 1818-1869 .... **NNAL**
See also DAM MULT; DLB 175, 183

Corbiere, Tristan 1845-1875 .... **NCLC 43**
See also DLB 217; GFL 1789 to the Present

Corcoran, Barbara (Asenath) 1911- .... **CLC 17**
See also AAYA 14; CA 21-24R, 191; CAAE 191; CAAS 2; CANR 11, 28, 48; CLR 50; DLB 52; JRDA; MAICYA 2; MAICYAS 1; RHW; SAAS 20; SATA 3, 77; SATA-Essay 125

Cordelier, Maurice
See Giraudoux, Jean(-Hippolyte)

Corelli, Marie .... **TCLC 51**
See Mackay, Mary
See also DLB 34, 156; RGEL 2; SUFW 1

Corinna c. 225B.C.-c. 305B.C. ...... **CMLC 72**

Corman, Cid .... **CLC 9**
See Corman, Sidney
See also CAAS 2; CP 1, 2, 3, 4, 5, 6, 7; DLB 5, 193

Corman, Sidney 1924-2004
See Corman, Cid
See also CA 85-88; 225; CANR 44; DAM POET

Cormier, Robert (Edmund) 1925-2000 .... **CLC 12, 30**
See also AAYA 3, 19; BYA 1, 2, 6, 8, 9; CA 1-4R; CANR 5, 23, 76, 93; CDALB 1968-1988; CLR 12, 55; DA; DAB; DAC; DAM MST, NOV; DLB 52; EXPN; INT CANR-23; JRDA; LAIT 5; MAICYA 1, 2; MTCW 1, 2; MTFW 2005; NFS 2, 18; SATA 10, 45, 83; SATA-Obit 122; WYA; YAW

Corn, Alfred (DeWitt III) 1943- .... **CLC 33**
See also CA 179; CAAE 179; CAAS 25; CANR 44; CP 3, 4, 5, 6, 7; CSW; DLB 120, 282; DLBY 1980

Corneille, Pierre 1606-1684 ... **DC 21; LC 28**
See also DAB; DAM MST; DFS 21; DLB 268; EW 3; GFL Beginnings to 1789; RGWL 2, 3; TWA

Cornwell, David (John Moore) 1931- .... **CLC 9, 15**
See le Carre, John
See also CA 5-8R; CANR 13, 33, 59, 107, 132; DA3; DAM POP; MTCW 1, 2; MTFW 2005

Cornwell, Patricia (Daniels) 1956- . **CLC 155**
See also AAYA 16, 56; BPFB 1; CA 134; CANR 53, 131; CMW 4; CPW; CSW; DAM POP; DLB 306; MSW; MTCW 2; MTFW 2005

Corso, (Nunzio) Gregory 1930-2001 . **CLC 1, 11; PC 33**
See also AMWS 12; BG 1:2; CA 5-8R; 193; CANR 41, 76, 132; CP 1, 2, 3, 4, 5, 6, 7; DA3; DLB 5, 16, 237; LMFS 2; MAL 5; MTCW 1, 2; MTFW 2005; WP

Cortazar, Julio 1914-1984 ... **CLC 2, 3, 5, 10, 13, 15, 33, 34, 92; HLC 1; SSC 7, 76**
See also BPFB 1; CA 21-24R; CANR 12, 32, 81; CDWLB 3; DA3; DAM MULT, NOV; DLB 113; EWL 3; EXPS; HW 1, 2; LAW; MTCW 1, 2; MTFW 2005; RGSF 2; RGWL 2, 3; SSFS 3, 20; TWA; WLIT 1

Cortes, Hernan 1485-1547 .... **LC 31**

Corvinus, Jakob
See Raabe, Wilhelm (Karl)

Corwin, Cecil
See Kornbluth, C(yril) M.

Cosic, Dobrica 1921- .... **CLC 14**
See also CA 122; 138; CDWLB 4; CWW 2; DLB 181; EWL 3

Costain, Thomas B(ertram) 1885-1965 .... **CLC 30**
See also BYA 3; CA 5-8R; 25-28R; DLB 9; RHW

Costantini, Humberto 1924(?)-1987 . **CLC 49**
See also CA 131; 122; EWL 3; HW 1

Costello, Elvis 1954- .... **CLC 21**
See also CA 204

Costenoble, Philostene
See Ghelderode, Michel de

Cotes, Cecil V.
See Duncan, Sara Jeannette

Cotter, Joseph Seamon Sr. 1861-1949 .... **BLC 1; TCLC 28**
See also BW 1; CA 124; DAM MULT; DLB 50

Couch, Arthur Thomas Quiller
See Quiller-Couch, Sir Arthur (Thomas)

Coulton, James
See Hansen, Joseph

Couperus, Louis (Marie Anne) 1863-1923 .... **TCLC 15**
See also CA 115; EWL 3; RGWL 2, 3

Coupland, Douglas 1961- .... **CLC 85, 133**
See also AAYA 34; CA 142; CANR 57, 90, 130; CCA 1; CN 7; CPW; DAC; DAM POP

Court, Wesli
See Turco, Lewis (Putnam)

Courtenay, Bryce 1933- .... **CLC 59**
See also CA 138; CPW

Courtney, Robert
See Ellison, Harlan (Jay)

Cousteau, Jacques-Yves 1910-1997 .. **CLC 30**
See also CA 65-68; 159; CANR 15, 67; MTCW 1; SATA 38, 98

Coventry, Francis 1725-1754 .... **LC 46**

Coverdale, Miles c. 1487-1569 .... **LC 77**
See also DLB 167

Cowan, Peter (Walkinshaw) 1914-2002 .... **SSC 28**
See also CA 21-24R; CANR 9, 25, 50, 83; CN 1, 2, 3, 4, 5, 6, 7; DLB 260; RGSF 2

Coward, Noel (Peirce) 1899-1973 . **CLC 1, 9, 29, 51**
See also AITN 1; BRWS 2; CA 17-18; 41-44R; CANR 35, 132; CAP 2; CBD; CDBLB 1914-1945; DA3; DAM DRAM; DFS 3, 6; DLB 10, 245; EWL 3; IDFW 3, 4; MTCW 1, 2; MTFW 2005; RGEL 2; TEA

Cowley, Abraham 1618-1667 .... **LC 43**
See also BRW 2; DLB 131, 151; PAB; RGEL 2

Cowley, Malcolm 1898-1989 .... **CLC 39**
See also AMWS 2; CA 5-8R; 128; CANR 3, 55; CP 1, 2, 3, 4; DLB 4, 48; DLBY 1981, 1989; EWL 3; MAL 5; MTCW 1, 2; MTFW 2005

Cowper, William 1731-1800 ..... **NCLC 8, 94; PC 40**
See also BRW 3; DA3; DAM POET; DLB 104, 109; RGEL 2

Cox, William Trevor 1928-
See Trevor, William
See also CA 9-12R; CANR 4, 37, 55, 76, 102, 139; DAM NOV; INT CANR-37; MTCW 1, 2; MTFW 2005; TEA

Coyne, P. J.
See Masters, Hilary

Cozzens, James Gould 1903-1978 . **CLC 1, 4, 11, 92**
See also AMW; BPFB 1; CA 9-12R; 81-84; CANR 19; CDALB 1941-1968; CN 1, 2; DLB 9, 294; DLBD 2; DLBY 1984, 1997; EWL 3; MAL 5; MTCW 1, 2; MTFW 2005; RGAL 4

Crabbe, George 1754-1832 .... **NCLC 26, 121**
See also BRW 3; DLB 93; RGEL 2

Crace, Jim 1946- .... **CLC 157; SSC 61**
See also CA 128; 135; CANR 55, 70, 123; CN 5, 6, 7; DLB 231; INT CA-135

Craddock, Charles Egbert
See Murfree, Mary Noailles

Craig, A. A.
See Anderson, Poul (William)

Craik, Mrs.
See Craik, Dinah Maria (Mulock)
See also RGEL 2

Craik, Dinah Maria (Mulock)
1826-1887 .... **NCLC 38**
See Craik, Mrs.; Mulock, Dinah Maria
See also DLB 35, 163; MAICYA 1, 2; SATA 34

Cram, Ralph Adams 1863-1942 ..... **TCLC 45**
See also CA 160

Cranch, Christopher Pearse
1813-1892 .... **NCLC 115**
See also DLB 1, 42, 243

Crane, (Harold) Hart 1899-1932 .... **PC 3; TCLC 2, 5, 80; WLC**
See also AMW; AMWR 2; CA 104; 127; CDALB 1917-1929; DA; DA3; DAB; DAC; DAM MST, POET; DLB 4, 48; EWL 3; MAL 5; MTCW 1, 2; MTFW 2005; RGAL 4; TUS

Crane, R(onald) S(almon)
1886-1967 .... **CLC 27**
See also CA 85-88; DLB 63

Crane, Stephen (Townley)
1871-1900 ...... **SSC 7, 56, 70; TCLC 11, 17, 32; WLC**
See also AAYA 21; AMW; AMWC 1; BPFB 1; BYA 3; CA 109; 140; CANR 84; CDALB 1865-1917; DA; DA3; DAB; DAC; DAM MST, NOV, POET; DLB 12, 54, 78; EXPN; EXPS; LAIT 2; LMFS 2; MAL 5; NFS 4, 20; PFS 9; RGAL 4; RGSF 2; SSFS 4; TUS; WYA; YABC 2

Cranmer, Thomas 1489-1556 .... **LC 95**
See also DLB 132, 213

Cranshaw, Stanley
See Fisher, Dorothy (Frances) Canfield

Crase, Douglas 1944- .... **CLC 58**
See also CA 106

Crashaw, Richard 1612(?)-1649 .... **LC 24**
See also BRW 2; DLB 126; PAB; RGEL 2

Cratinus c. 519B.C.-c. 422B.C. ..... **CMLC 54**
See also LMFS 1

Craven, Margaret 1901-1980 .... **CLC 17**
See also BYA 2; CA 103; CCA 1; DAC; LAIT 5

Crawford, F(rancis) Marion
1854-1909 .... **TCLC 10**
See also CA 107; 168; DLB 71; HGG; RGAL 4; SUFW 1

Crawford, Isabella Valancy
1850-1887 .... **NCLC 12, 127**
See also DLB 92; RGEL 2

Crayon, Geoffrey
See Irving, Washington

Creasey, John 1908-1973 .... **CLC 11**
See Marric, J. J.
See also CA 5-8R; 41-44R; CANR 8, 59; CMW 4; DLB 77; MTCW 1

Crebillon, Claude Prosper Jolyot de (fils)
1707-1777 .... **LC 1, 28**
See also DLB 313; GFL Beginnings to 1789

Credo
See Creasey, John

Credo, Alvaro J. de
See Prado (Calvo), Pedro

Creeley, Robert (White) 1926-2005 .. **CLC 1, 2, 4, 8, 11, 15, 36, 78**
See also AMWS 4; CA 1-4R; 237; CAAS 10; CANR 23, 43, 89, 137; CP 1, 2, 3, 4, 5, 6, 7; DA3; DAM POET; DLB 5, 16, 169; DLBD 17; EWL 3; MAL 5; MTCW 1, 2; MTFW 2005; PFS 21; RGAL 4; WP

Crenne, Helisenne de 1510-1560 .... **LC 113**

Crevecoeur, Hector St. John de
See Crevecoeur, Michel Guillaume Jean de
See also ANW

Crevecoeur, Michel Guillaume Jean de
1735-1813 .... **NCLC 105**
See Crevecoeur, Hector St. John de
See also AMWS 1; DLB 37

Crevel, Rene 1900-1935 .... **TCLC 112**
See also GLL 2

Crews, Harry (Eugene) 1935- ..... **CLC 6, 23, 49**
See also AITN 1; AMWS 11; BPFB 1; CA 25-28R; CANR 20, 57; CN 3, 4, 5, 6, 7; CSW; DA3; DLB 6, 143, 185; MTCW 1, 2; MTFW 2005; RGAL 4

Crichton, (John) Michael 1942- .... **CLC 2, 6, 54, 90**
See also AAYA 10, 49; AITN 2; BPFB 1; CA 25-28R; CANR 13, 40, 54, 76, 127; CMW 4; CN 2, 3, 6, 7; CPW; DA3; DAM NOV, POP; DLB 292; DLBY 1981; INT CANR-13; JRDA; MTCW 1, 2; MTFW 2005; SATA 9, 88; SFW 4; YAW

Crispin, Edmund .... **CLC 22**
See Montgomery, (Robert) Bruce
See also DLB 87; MSW

Cristofer, Michael 1945- .... **CLC 28**
See also CA 110; 152; CAD; CD 5, 6; DAM DRAM; DFS 15; DLB 7

Criton
See Alain

Croce, Benedetto 1866-1952 .... **TCLC 37**
See also CA 120; 155; EW 8; EWL 3; WLIT 7

Crockett, David 1786-1836 .... **NCLC 8**
See also DLB 3, 11, 183, 248

Crockett, Davy
See Crockett, David

Crofts, Freeman Wills 1879-1957 .. **TCLC 55**
See also CA 115; 195; CMW 4; DLB 77; MSW

Croker, John Wilson 1780-1857 .... **NCLC 10**
See also DLB 110

Crommelynck, Fernand 1885-1970 .. **CLC 75**
See also CA 189; 89-92; EWL 3

Cromwell, Oliver 1599-1658 .... **LC 43**

Cronenberg, David 1943- .... **CLC 143**
See also CA 138; CCA 1

Cronin, A(rchibald) J(oseph)
1896-1981 .... **CLC 32**
See also BPFB 1; CA 1-4R; 102; CANR 5; CN 2; DLB 191; SATA 47; SATA-Obit 25

Cross, Amanda
See Heilbrun, Carolyn G(old)
See also BPFB 1; CMW; CPW; DLB 306; MSW

Crothers, Rachel 1878-1958 .... **TCLC 19**
See also CA 113; 194; CAD; CWD; DLB 7, 266; RGAL 4

Croves, Hal
See Traven, B.

Crow Dog, Mary (Ellen) (?)- .... **CLC 93**
See Brave Bird, Mary
See also CA 154

Crowfield, Christopher
See Stowe, Harriet (Elizabeth) Beecher

Crowley, Aleister .... **TCLC 7**
See Crowley, Edward Alexander
See also GLL 1

Crowley, Edward Alexander 1875-1947
See Crowley, Aleister
See also CA 104; HGG

Crowley, John 1942- .... **CLC 57**
See also AAYA 57; BPFB 1; CA 61-64; CANR 43, 98, 138; DLBY 1982; FANT; MTFW 2005; SATA 65, 140; SFW 4; SUFW 2

Crowne, John 1641-1712 .... **LC 104**
See also DLB 80; RGEL 2

Crud
See Crumb, R(obert)

Crumarums
See Crumb, R(obert)

Crumb, R(obert) 1943- .... **CLC 17**
See also CA 106; CANR 107

Crumbum
See Crumb, R(obert)

Crumski
See Crumb, R(obert)

Crum the Bum
See Crumb, R(obert)

Crunk
See Crumb, R(obert)

Crustt
See Crumb, R(obert)

Crutchfield, Les
See Trumbo, Dalton

Cruz, Victor Hernandez 1949- ... **HLC 1; PC 37**
See also BW 2; CA 65-68; CAAS 17; CANR 14, 32, 74, 132; CP 1, 2, 3, 4, 5, 6, 7; DAM MULT, POET; DLB 41; DNFS 1; EXPP; HW 1, 2; LLW; MTCW 2; MTFW 2005; PFS 16; WP

Cryer, Gretchen (Kiger) 1935- .... **CLC 21**
See also CA 114; 123

Csath, Geza .... **TCLC 13**
See Brenner, Jozef
See also CA 111

Cudlip, David R(ockwell) 1933- .... **CLC 34**
See also CA 177

Cullen, Countee 1903-1946 . **BLC 1; HR 1:2; PC 20; TCLC 4, 37; WLCS**
See also AFAW 2; AMWS 4; BW 1; CA 108; 124; CDALB 1917-1929; DA; DA3; DAC; DAM MST, MULT, POET; DLB 4, 48, 51; EWL 3; EXPP; LMFS 2; MAL 5; MTCW 1, 2; MTFW 2005; PFS 3; RGAL 4; SATA 18; WP

Culleton, Beatrice 1949- .... **NNAL**
See also CA 120; CANR 83; DAC

Cum, R.
See Crumb, R(obert)

Cummings, Bruce F(rederick) 1889-1919
See Barbellion, W. N. P.
See also CA 123

Cummings, E(dward) E(stlin)
1894-1962 .. **CLC 1, 3, 8, 12, 15, 68; PC 5; TCLC 137; WLC**
See also AAYA 41; AMW; CA 73-76; CANR 31; CDALB 1929-1941; DA; DA3; DAB; DAC; DAM MST, POET; DLB 4, 48; EWL 3; EXPP; MAL 5; MTCW 1, 2; MTFW 2005; PAB; PFS 1, 3, 12, 13, 19; RGAL 4; TUS; WP

Cummins, Maria Susanna
1827-1866 .... **NCLC 139**
See also DLB 42; YABC 1

Cunha, Euclides (Rodrigues Pimenta) da
1866-1909 .... **TCLC 24**
See also CA 123; 219; DLB 307; LAW; WLIT 1

Cunningham, E. V.
See Fast, Howard (Melvin)

Dembry, R. Emmet
See Murfree, Mary Noailles

Demby, William 1922- .... **BLC 1; CLC 53**
See also BW 1, 3; CA 81-84; CANR 81;
DAM MULT; DLB 33

de Menton, Francisco
See Chin, Frank (Chew, Jr.)

Demetrius of Phalerum c.
307B.C.- .... **CMLC 34**

Demijohn, Thom
See Disch, Thomas M(ichael)

De Mille, James 1833-1880 .... **NCLC 123**
See also DLB 99, 251

Deming, Richard 1915-1983
See Queen, Ellery
See also CA 9-12R; CANR 3, 94; SATA 24

Democritus c. 460B.C.-c. 370B.C. . **CMLC 47**

de Montaigne, Michel (Eyquem)
See Montaigne, Michel (Eyquem) de

de Montherlant, Henry (Milon)
See Montherlant, Henry (Milon) de

Demosthenes 384B.C.-322B.C. ...... **CMLC 13**
See also AW 1; DLB 176; RGWL 2, 3

de Musset, (Louis Charles) Alfred
See Musset, (Louis Charles) Alfred de

de Natale, Francine
See Malzberg, Barry N(athaniel)

de Navarre, Marguerite 1492-1549 ... **LC 61;**
SSC 85
See Marguerite d'Angouleme; Marguerite
de Navarre

Denby, Edwin (Orr) 1903-1983 .... **CLC 48**
See also CA 138; 110; CP 1

de Nerval, Gerard
See Nerval, Gerard de

Denham, John 1615-1669 .... **LC 73**
See also DLB 58, 126; RGEL 2

Denis, Julio
See Cortazar, Julio

Denmark, Harrison
See Zelazny, Roger (Joseph)

Dennis, John 1658-1734 .... **LC 11**
See also DLB 101; RGEL 2

Dennis, Nigel (Forbes) 1912-1989 ...... **CLC 8**
See also CA 25-28R; 129; CN 1, 2, 3, 4;
DLB 13, 15, 233; EWL 3; MTCW 1

Dent, Lester 1904-1959 .... **TCLC 72**
See also CA 112; 161; CMW 4; DLB 306;
SFW 4

De Palma, Brian (Russell) 1940- ...... **CLC 20**
See also CA 109

De Quincey, Thomas 1785-1859 ..... **NCLC 4,**
87
See also BRW 4; CDBLB 1789-1832; DLB
110, 144; RGEL 2

Deren, Eleanora 1908(?)-1961
See Deren, Maya
See also CA 192; 111

Deren, Maya .... **CLC 16, 102**
See Deren, Eleanora

Derleth, August (William)
1909-1971 .... **CLC 31**
See also BPFB 1; BYA 9, 10; CA 1-4R; 29-
32R; CANR 4; CMW 4; CN 1; DLB 9;
DLBD 17; HGG; SATA 5; SUFW 1

Der Nister 1884-1950 .... **TCLC 56**
See Nister, Der

de Routisie, Albert
See Aragon, Louis

Derrida, Jacques 1930-2004 .... **CLC 24, 87**
See also CA 124; 127; 232; CANR 76, 98,
133; DLB 242; EWL 3; LMFS 2; MTCW
2; TWA

Derry Down Derry
See Lear, Edward

Dersonnes, Jacques
See Simenon, Georges (Jacques Christian)

Der Stricker c. 1190-c. 1250 .... **CMLC 75**
See also DLB 138

Desai, Anita 1937- .... **CLC 19, 37, 97, 175**
See also BRWS 5; CA 81-84; CANR 33,
53, 95, 133; CN 1, 2, 3, 4, 5, 6, 7; CWRI
5; DA3; DAB; DAM NOV; DLB 271;
DNFS 2; EWL 3; FW; MTCW 1, 2;
MTFW 2005; SATA 63, 126

Desai, Kiran 1971- .... **CLC 119**
See also BYA 16; CA 171; CANR 127

de Saint-Luc, Jean
See Glassco, John

de Saint Roman, Arnaud
See Aragon, Louis

Desbordes-Valmore, Marceline
1786-1859 .... **NCLC 97**
See also DLB 217

Descartes, Rene 1596-1650 .... **LC 20, 35**
See also DLB 268; EW 3; GFL Beginnings
to 1789

Deschamps, Eustache 1340(?)-1404 .. **LC 103**
See also DLB 208

De Sica, Vittorio 1901(?)-1974 .... **CLC 20**
See also CA 117

Desnos, Robert 1900-1945 .... **TCLC 22**
See also CA 121; 151; CANR 107; DLB
258; EWL 3; LMFS 2

Destouches, Louis-Ferdinand
1894-1961 .... **CLC 9, 15**
See Celine, Louis-Ferdinand
See also CA 85-88; CANR 28; MTCW 1

de Tolignac, Gaston
See Griffith, D(avid Lewelyn) W(ark)

Deutsch, Babette 1895-1982 .... **CLC 18**
See also BYA 3; CA 1-4R; 108; CANR 4,
79; CP 1, 2, 3; DLB 45; SATA 1; SATA-
Obit 33

Devenant, William 1606-1649 .... **LC 13**

Devkota, Laxmiprasad 1909-1959 . **TCLC 23**
See also CA 123

De Voto, Bernard (Augustine)
1897-1955 .... **TCLC 29**
See also CA 113; 160; DLB 9, 256; MAL
5; TCWW 1, 2

De Vries, Peter 1910-1993 ..... **CLC 1, 2, 3, 7,**
10, 28, 46
See also CA 17-20R; 142; CANR 41; CN
1, 2, 3, 4, 5; DAM NOV; DLB 6; DLBY
1982; MAL 5; MTCW 1, 2; MTFW 2005

Dewey, John 1859-1952 .... **TCLC 95**
See also CA 114; 170; CANR 144; DLB
246, 270; RGAL 4

Dexter, John
See Bradley, Marion Zimmer
See also GLL 1

Dexter, Martin
See Faust, Frederick (Schiller)

Dexter, Pete 1943- .... **CLC 34, 55**
See also BEST 89:2; CA 127; 131; CANR
129; CPW; DAM POP; INT CA-131;
MAL 5; MTCW 1; MTFW 2005

Diamano, Silmang
See Senghor, Leopold Sedar

Diamond, Neil 1941- .... **CLC 30**
See also CA 108

Diaz del Castillo, Bernal c.
1496-1584 .... **HLCS 1; LC 31**
See also DLB 318; LAW

di Bassetto, Corno
See Shaw, George Bernard

Dick, Philip K(indred) 1928-1982 ... **CLC 10,**
30, 72; SSC 57
See also AAYA 24; BPFB 1; BYA 11; CA
49-52; 106; CANR 2, 16, 132; CN 2, 3;
CPW; DA3; DAM NOV, POP; DLB 8;
MTCW 1, 2; MTFW 2005; NFS 5; SCFW
1, 2; SFW 4

Dickens, Charles (John Huffam)
1812-1870 .... **NCLC 3, 8, 18, 26, 37, 50,**
86, 105, 113, 161; SSC 17, 49, 88; WLC
See also AAYA 23; BRW 5; BRWC 1, 2;
BYA 1, 2, 3, 13, 14; CDBLB 1832-1890;
CLR 95; CMW 4; DA; DA3; DAB; DAC;
DAM MST, NOV; DLB 21, 55, 70, 159,
166; EXPN; GL 2; HGG; JRDA; LAIT 1,
2; LATS 1:1; LMFS 1; MAICYA 1, 2;
NFS 4, 5, 10, 14, 20; RGEL 2; RGSF 2;
SATA 15; SUFW 1; TEA; WCH; WLIT
4; WYA

Dickey, James (Lafayette)
1923-1997 .... **CLC 1, 2, 4, 7, 10, 15, 47,**
109; PC 40; TCLC 151
See also AAYA 50; AITN 1, 2; AMWS 4;
BPFB 1; CA 9-12R; 156; CABS 2; CANR
10, 48, 61, 105; CDALB 1968-1988; CP
1, 2, 3, 4; CPW; CSW; DA3; DAM NOV,
POET, POP; DLB 5, 193; DLBD 7;
DLBY 1982, 1993, 1996, 1997, 1998;
EWL 3; INT CANR-10; MAL 5; MTCW
1, 2; NFS 9; PFS 6, 11; RGAL 4; TUS

Dickey, William 1928-1994 .... **CLC 3, 28**
See also CA 9-12R; 145; CANR 24, 79; CP
1, 2, 3, 4; DLB 5

Dickinson, Charles 1951- .... **CLC 49**
See also CA 128; CANR 141

Dickinson, Emily (Elizabeth)
1830-1886 ... **NCLC 21, 77; PC 1; WLC**
See also AAYA 22; AMW; AMWR 1;
CDALB 1865-1917; DA; DA3; DAB;
DAC; DAM MST, POET; DLB 1, 243;
EXPP; FL 1:3; MAWW; PAB; PFS 1, 2,
3, 4, 5, 6, 8, 10, 11, 13, 16; RGAL 4;
SATA 29; TUS; WP; WYA

Dickinson, Mrs. Herbert Ward
See Phelps, Elizabeth Stuart

Dickinson, Peter (Malcolm de Brissac)
1927- .... **CLC 12, 35**
See also AAYA 9, 49; BYA 5; CA 41-44R;
CANR 31, 58, 88, 134; CLR 29; CMW 4;
DLB 87, 161, 276; JRDA; MAICYA 1, 2;
SATA 5, 62, 95, 150; SFW 4; WYA; YAW

Dickson, Carr
See Carr, John Dickson

Dickson, Carter
See Carr, John Dickson

Diderot, Denis 1713-1784 .... **LC 26**
See also DLB 313; EW 4; GFL Beginnings
to 1789; LMFS 1; RGWL 2, 3

Didion, Joan 1934- . **CLC 1, 3, 8, 14, 32, 129**
See also AITN 1; AMWS 4; CA 5-8R;
CANR 14, 52, 76, 125; CDALB 1968-
1988; CN 2, 3, 4, 5, 6, 7; DA3; DAM
NOV; DLB 2, 173, 185; DLBY 1981,
1986; EWL 3; MAL 5; MAWW; MTCW
1, 2; MTFW 2005; NFS 3; RGAL 4;
TCLE 1:1; TCWW 2; TUS

di Donato, Pietro 1911-1992 .... **TCLC 159**
See also CA 101; 136; DLB 9

Dietrich, Robert
See Hunt, E(verette) Howard, (Jr.)

Difusa, Pati
See Almodovar, Pedro

Dillard, Annie 1945- ...... **CLC 9, 60, 115, 216**
See also AAYA 6, 43; AMWS 6; ANW; CA
49-52; CANR 3, 43, 62, 90, 125; DA3;
DAM NOV; DLB 275, 278; DLBY 1980;
LAIT 4, 5; MAL 5; MTCW 1, 2; MTFW
2005; NCFS 1; RGAL 4; SATA 10, 140;
TCLE 1:1; TUS

Dillard, R(ichard) H(enry) W(ilde)
1937- .... **CLC 5**
See also CA 21-24R; CAAS 7; CANR 10;
CP 2, 3, 4, 5, 6, 7; CSW; DLB 5, 244

Dillon, Eilis 1920-1994 .... **CLC 17**
See also CA 9-12R; 182; 147; CAAE 182;
CAAS 3; CANR 4, 38, 78; CLR 26; MAI-
CYA 1, 2; MAICYAS 1; SATA 2, 74;
SATA-Essay 105; SATA-Obit 83; YAW

Dimont, Penelope
See Mortimer, Penelope (Ruth)

Dinesen, Isak ..... **CLC 10, 29, 95; SSC 7, 75**
See Blixen, Karen (Christentze Dinesen)
See also EW 10; EWL 3; EXPS; FW; GL
2; HGG; LAIT 3; MTCW 1; NCFS 2;
NFS 9; RGSF 2; RGWL 2, 3; SSFS 3, 6,
13; WLIT 2

Ding Ling .... **CLC 68**
See Chiang, Pin-chin
See also RGWL 3

Diphusa, Patty
See Almodovar, Pedro

Disch, Thomas M(ichael) 1940- ... **CLC 7, 36**
See Disch, Tom
See also AAYA 17; BPFB 1; CA 21-24R;
CAAS 4; CANR 17, 36, 54, 89; CLR 18;
CP 7; DA3; DLB 8; HGG; MAICYA 1, 2;
MTCW 1, 2; MTFW 2005; SAAS 15;
SATA 92; SCFW 1, 2; SFW 4; SUFW 2

Disch, Tom
See Disch, Thomas M(ichael)
See also DLB 282

d'Isly, Georges
See Simenon, Georges (Jacques Christian)

Disraeli, Benjamin 1804-1881 ... **NCLC 2, 39, 79**
See also BRW 4; DLB 21, 55; RGEL 2

Ditcum, Steve
See Crumb, R(obert)

Dixon, Paige
See Corcoran, Barbara (Asenath)

Dixon, Stephen 1936- .... **CLC 52; SSC 16**
See also AMWS 12; CA 89-92; CANR 17,
40, 54, 91; CN 4, 5, 6, 7; DLB 130; MAL
5

Dixon, Thomas, Jr. 1864-1946 ..... **TCLC 163**
See also RHW

Djebar, Assia 1936- .... **CLC 182**
See also CA 188; EWL 3; RGWL 3; WLIT
2

Doak, Annie
See Dillard, Annie

Dobell, Sydney Thompson
1824-1874 .... **NCLC 43**
See also DLB 32; RGEL 2

Doblin, Alfred .... **TCLC 13**
See Doeblin, Alfred
See also CDWLB 2; EWL 3; RGWL 2, 3

Dobroliubov, Nikolai Aleksandrovich
See Dobrolyubov, Nikolai Alexandrovich
See also DLB 277

Dobrolyubov, Nikolai Alexandrovich
1836-1861 .... **NCLC 5**
See Dobroliubov, Nikolai Aleksandrovich

Dobson, Austin 1840-1921 .... **TCLC 79**
See also DLB 35, 144

Dobyns, Stephen 1941- .... **CLC 37**
See also AMWS 13; CA 45-48; CANR 2,
18, 99; CMW 4; CP 4, 5, 6, 7; PFS 23

Doctorow, E(dgar) L(aurence)
1931- .... **CLC 6, 11, 15, 18, 37, 44, 65,
113, 214**
See also AAYA 22; AITN 2; AMWS 4;
BEST 89:3; BPFB 1; CA 45-48; CANR
2, 33, 51, 76, 97, 133; CDALB 1968-
1988; CN 3, 4, 5, 6, 7; CPW; DA3; DAM
NOV, POP; DLB 2, 28, 173; DLBY 1980;
EWL 3; LAIT 3; MAL 5; MTCW 1, 2;
MTFW 2005; NFS 6; RGAL 4; RHW;
TCLE 1:1; TCWW 1, 2; TUS

Dodgson, Charles L(utwidge) 1832-1898
See Carroll, Lewis
See also CLR 2; DA; DA3; DAB; DAC;
DAM MST, NOV, POET; MAICYA 1, 2;
SATA 100; YABC 2

Dodsley, Robert 1703-1764 .... **LC 97**
See also DLB 95; RGEL 2

Dodson, Owen (Vincent) 1914-1983 .. **BLC 1;
CLC 79**
See also BW 1; CA 65-68; 110; CANR 24;
DAM MULT; DLB 76

Doeblin, Alfred 1878-1957 .... **TCLC 13**
See Doblin, Alfred
See also CA 110; 141; DLB 66

Doerr, Harriet 1910-2002 .... **CLC 34**
See also CA 117; 122; 213; CANR 47; INT
CA-122; LATS 1:2

Domecq, H(onorio Bustos)
See Bioy Casares, Adolfo

Domecq, H(onorio) Bustos
See Bioy Casares, Adolfo; Borges, Jorge
Luis

Domini, Rey
See Lorde, Audre (Geraldine)
See also GLL 1

Dominique
See Proust, (Valentin-Louis-George-Eugene)
Marcel

Don, A
See Stephen, Sir Leslie

Donaldson, Stephen R(eeder)
1947- .... **CLC 46, 138**
See also AAYA 36; BPFB 1; CA 89-92;
CANR 13, 55, 99; CPW; DAM POP;
FANT; INT CANR-13; SATA 121; SFW
4; SUFW 1, 2

Donleavy, J(ames) P(atrick) 1926- .... **CLC 1,
4, 6, 10, 45**
See also AITN 2; BPFB 1; CA 9-12R;
CANR 24, 49, 62, 80, 124; CBD; CD 5,
6; CN 1, 2, 3, 4, 5, 6, 7; DLB 6, 173; INT
CANR-24; MAL 5; MTCW 1, 2; MTFW
2005; RGAL 4

Donnadieu, Marguerite
See Duras, Marguerite

Donne, John 1572-1631 ... **LC 10, 24, 91; PC
1, 43; WLC**
See also AAYA 67; BRW 1; BRWC 1;
BRWR 2; CDBLB Before 1660; DA;
DAB; DAC; DAM MST, POET; DLB
121, 151; EXPP; PAB; PFS 2, 11; RGEL
3; TEA; WLIT 3; WP

Donnell, David 1939(?)- .... **CLC 34**
See also CA 197

Donoghue, Denis 1928- .... **CLC 209**
See also CA 17-20R; CANR 16, 102

Donoghue, P. S.
See Hunt, E(verette) Howard, (Jr.)

Donoso (Yanez), Jose 1924-1996 ... **CLC 4, 8,
11, 32, 99; HLC 1; SSC 34; TCLC 133**
See also CA 81-84; 155; CANR 32, 73; CD-
WLB 3; CWW 2; DAM MULT; DLB 113;
EWL 3; HW 1, 2; LAW; LAWS 1; MTCW
1, 2; MTFW 2005; RGSF 2; WLIT 1

Donovan, John 1928-1992 .... **CLC 35**
See also AAYA 20; CA 97-100; 137; CLR
3; MAICYA 1, 2; SATA 72; SATA-Brief
29; YAW

Don Roberto
See Cunninghame Graham, Robert
(Gallnigad) Bontine

Doolittle, Hilda 1886-1961 . **CLC 3, 8, 14, 31,
34, 73; PC 5; WLC**
See H. D.
See also AAYA 66; AMWS 1; CA 97-100;
CANR 35, 131; DA; DAC; DAM MST,
POET; DLB 4, 45; EWL 3; FW; GLL 1;
LMFS 2; MAL 5; MAWW; MTCW 1, 2;
MTFW 2005; PFS 6; RGAL 4

Doppo, Kunikida .... **TCLC 99**
See Kunikida Doppo

Dorfman, Ariel 1942- .... **CLC 48, 77, 189;
HLC 1**
See also CA 124; 130; CANR 67, 70, 135;
CWW 2; DAM MULT; DFS 4; EWL 3;
HW 1, 2; INT CA-130; WLIT 1

Dorn, Edward (Merton)
1929-1999 .... **CLC 10, 18**
See also CA 93-96; 187; CANR 42, 79; CP
1, 2, 3, 4, 5, 6, 7; DLB 5; INT CA-93-96;
WP

Dor-Ner, Zvi .... **CLC 70**

Dorris, Michael (Anthony)
1945-1997 .... **CLC 109; NNAL**
See also AAYA 20; BEST 90:1; BYA 12;
CA 102; 157; CANR 19, 46, 75; CLR 58;
DA3; DAM MULT, NOV; DLB 175;
LAIT 5; MTCW 2; MTFW 2005; NFS 3;
RGAL 4; SATA 75; SATA-Obit 94;
TCWW 2; YAW

Dorris, Michael A.
See Dorris, Michael (Anthony)

Dorsan, Luc
See Simenon, Georges (Jacques Christian)

Dorsange, Jean
See Simenon, Georges (Jacques Christian)

Dorset
See Sackville, Thomas

Dos Passos, John (Roderigo)
1896-1970 ... **CLC 1, 4, 8, 11, 15, 25, 34,
82; WLC**
See also AMW; BPFB 1; CA 1-4R; 29-32R;
CANR 3; CDALB 1929-1941; DA; DA3;
DAB; DAC; DAM MST, NOV; DLB 4,
9, 274, 316; DLBD 1, 15; DLBY 1996;
EWL 3; MAL 5; MTCW 1, 2; MTFW
2005; NFS 14; RGAL 4; TUS

Dossage, Jean
See Simenon, Georges (Jacques Christian)

Dostoevsky, Fedor Mikhailovich
1821-1881 ... **NCLC 2, 7, 21, 33, 43, 119;
SSC 2, 33, 44; WLC**
See Dostoevsky, Fyodor
See also AAYA 40; DA; DA3; DAB; DAC;
DAM MST, NOV; EW 7; EXPN; NFS 3,
8; RGSF 2; RGWL 2, 3; SSFS 8; TWA

Dostoevsky, Fyodor
See Dostoevsky, Fedor Mikhailovich
See also DLB 238; LATS 1:1; LMFS 1, 2

Doty, M. R.
See Doty, Mark (Alan)

Doty, Mark
See Doty, Mark (Alan)

Doty, Mark (Alan) 1953(?)- .... **CLC 176; PC
53**
See also AMWS 11; CA 161, 183; CAAE
183; CANR 110

Doty, Mark A.
See Doty, Mark (Alan)

Doughty, Charles M(ontagu)
1843-1926 .... **TCLC 27**
See also CA 115; 178; DLB 19, 57, 174

Douglas, Ellen .... **CLC 73**
See Haxton, Josephine Ayres; Williamson,
Ellen Douglas
See also CN 5, 6, 7; CSW; DLB 292

Douglas, Gavin 1475(?)-1522 .... **LC 20**
See also DLB 132; RGEL 2

Douglas, George
See Brown, George Douglas
See also RGEL 2

Douglas, Keith (Castellain)
1920-1944 .... **TCLC 40**
See also BRW 7; CA 160; DLB 27; EWL
3; PAB; RGEL 2

Douglas, Leonard
See Bradbury, Ray (Douglas)

Douglas, Michael
See Crichton, (John) Michael

Douglas, (George) Norman
1868-1952 .... **TCLC 68**
See also BRW 6; CA 119; 157; DLB 34,
195; RGEL 2

Douglas, William
See Brown, George Douglas

Douglass, Frederick 1817(?)-1895 ..... **BLC 1; NCLC 7, 55, 141; WLC**
See also AAYA 48; AFAW 1, 2; AMWC 1; AMWS 3; CDALB 1640-1865; DA; DA3; DAC; DAM MST, MULT; DLB 1, 43, 50, 79, 243; FW; LAIT 2; NCFS 2; RGAL 4; SATA 29

Dourado, (Waldomiro Freitas) Autran 1926- .... **CLC 23, 60**
See also CA 25-28R, 179; CANR 34, 81; DLB 145, 307; HW 2

Dourado, Waldomiro Freitas Autran
See Dourado, (Waldomiro Freitas) Autran

Dove, Rita (Frances) 1952- . **BLCS; CLC 50, 81; PC 6**
See also AAYA 46; AMWS 4; BW 2; CA 109; CAAS 19; CANR 27, 42, 68, 76, 97, 132; CDALBS; CP 7; CSW; CWP; DA3; DAM MULT, POET; DLB 120; EWL 3; EXPP; MAL 5; MTCW 2; MTFW 2005; PFS 1, 15; RGAL 4

Doveglion
See Villa, Jose Garcia

Dowell, Coleman 1925-1985 .... **CLC 60**
See also CA 25-28R; 117; CANR 10; DLB 130; GLL 2

Dowson, Ernest (Christopher) 1867-1900 .... **TCLC 4**
See also CA 105; 150; DLB 19, 135; RGEL 2

Doyle, A. Conan
See Doyle, Sir Arthur Conan

Doyle, Sir Arthur Conan 1859-1930 . **SSC 12, 83; TCLC 7; WLC**
See Conan Doyle, Arthur
See also AAYA 14; BRWS 2; CA 104; 122; CANR 131; CDBLB 1890-1914; CMW 4; DA; DA3; DAB; DAC; DAM MST, NOV; DLB 18, 70, 156, 178; EXPS; HGG; LAIT 2; MSW; MTCW 1, 2; MTFW 2005; RGEL 2; RGSF 2; RHW; SATA 24; SCFW 1, 2; SFW 4; SSFS 2; TEA; WCH; WLIT 4; WYA; YAW

Doyle, Conan
See Doyle, Sir Arthur Conan

Doyle, John
See Graves, Robert (von Ranke)

Doyle, Roddy 1958- .... **CLC 81, 178**
See also AAYA 14; BRWS 5; CA 143; CANR 73, 128; CN 6, 7; DA3; DLB 194; MTCW 2; MTFW 2005

Doyle, Sir A. Conan
See Doyle, Sir Arthur Conan

Dr. A
See Asimov, Isaac; Silverstein, Alvin; Silverstein, Virginia B(arbara Opshelor)

Drabble, Margaret 1939- ...... **CLC 2, 3, 5, 8, 10, 22, 53, 129**
See also BRWS 4; CA 13-16R; CANR 18, 35, 63, 112, 131; CDBLB 1960 to Present; CN 1, 2, 3, 4, 5, 6, 7; CPW; DA3; DAB; DAC; DAM MST, NOV, POP; DLB 14, 155, 231; EWL 3; FW; MTCW 1, 2; MTFW 2005; RGEL 2; SATA 48; TEA

Drakulic, Slavenka 1949- .... **CLC 173**
See also CA 144; CANR 92

Drakulic-Ilic, Slavenka
See Drakulic, Slavenka

Drapier, M. B.
See Swift, Jonathan

Drayham, James
See Mencken, H(enry) L(ouis)

Drayton, Michael 1563-1631 .... **LC 8**
See also DAM POET; DLB 121; RGEL 2

Dreadstone, Carl
See Campbell, (John) Ramsey

Dreiser, Theodore (Herman Albert) 1871-1945 .... **SSC 30; TCLC 10, 18, 35, 83; WLC**
See also AMW; AMWC 2; AMWR 2; BYA 15, 16; CA 106; 132; CDALB 1865-1917; DA; DA3; DAC; DAM MST, NOV; DLB 9, 12, 102, 137; DLBD 1; EWL 3; LAIT 2; LMFS 2; MAL 5; MTCW 1, 2; MTFW 2005; NFS 8, 17; RGAL 4; TUS

Drexler, Rosalyn 1926- .... **CLC 2, 6**
See also CA 81-84; CAD; CANR 68, 124; CD 5, 6; CWD; MAL 5

Dreyer, Carl Theodor 1889-1968 ...... **CLC 16**
See also CA 116

Drieu la Rochelle, Pierre(-Eugene) 1893-1945 .... **TCLC 21**
See also CA 117; DLB 72; EWL 3; GFL 1789 to the Present

Drinkwater, John 1882-1937 .... **TCLC 57**
See also CA 109; 149; DLB 10, 19, 149; RGEL 2

Drop Shot
See Cable, George Washington

Droste-Hulshoff, Annette Freiin von 1797-1848 .... **NCLC 3, 133**
See also CDWLB 2; DLB 133; RGSF 2; RGWL 2, 3

Drummond, Walter
See Silverberg, Robert

Drummond, William Henry 1854-1907 .... **TCLC 25**
See also CA 160; DLB 92

Drummond de Andrade, Carlos 1902-1987 .... **CLC 18; TCLC 139**
See Andrade, Carlos Drummond de
See also CA 132; 123; DLB 307; LAW

Drummond of Hawthornden, William 1585-1649 .... **LC 83**
See also DLB 121, 213; RGEL 2

Drury, Allen (Stuart) 1918-1998 .... **CLC 37**
See also CA 57-60; 170; CANR 18, 52; CN 1, 2, 3, 4, 5, 6; INT CANR-18

Druse, Eleanor
See King, Stephen

Dryden, John 1631-1700 ..... **DC 3; LC 3, 21, 115; PC 25; WLC**
See also BRW 2; CDBLB 1660-1789; DA; DAB; DAC; DAM DRAM, MST, POET; DLB 80, 101, 131; EXPP; IDTP; LMFS 1; RGEL 2; TEA; WLIT 3

du Bellay, Joachim 1524-1560 .... **LC 92**
See also GFL Beginnings to 1789; RGWL 2, 3

Duberman, Martin (Bauml) 1930- ..... **CLC 8**
See also CA 1-4R; CAD; CANR 2, 63, 137; CD 5, 6

Dubie, Norman (Evans) 1945- .... **CLC 36**
See also CA 69-72; CANR 12, 115; CP 3, 4, 5, 6, 7; DLB 120; PFS 12

Du Bois, W(illiam) E(dward) B(urghardt) 1868-1963 ..... **BLC 1; CLC 1, 2, 13, 64, 96; HR 1:2; TCLC 169; WLC**
See also AAYA 40; AFAW 1, 2; AMWC 1; AMWS 2; BW 1, 3; CA 85-88; CANR 34, 82, 132; CDALB 1865-1917; DA; DA3; DAC; DAM MST, MULT, NOV; DLB 47, 50, 91, 246, 284; EWL 3; EXPP; LAIT 2; LMFS 2; MAL 5; MTCW 1, 2; MTFW 2005; NCFS 1; PFS 13; RGAL 4; SATA 42

Dubus, Andre 1936-1999 ..... **CLC 13, 36, 97; SSC 15**
See also AMWS 7; CA 21-24R; 177; CANR 17; CN 5, 6; CSW; DLB 130; INT CANR-17; RGAL 4; SSFS 10; TCLE 1:1

Duca Minimo
See D'Annunzio, Gabriele

Ducharme, Rejean 1941- .... **CLC 74**
See also CA 165; DLB 60

du Chatelet, Emilie 1706-1749 .... **LC 96**
See Chatelet, Gabrielle-Emilie Du

Duchen, Claire .... **CLC 65**

Duclos, Charles Pinot- 1704-1772 .... **LC 1**
See also GFL Beginnings to 1789

Dudek, Louis 1918-2001 .... **CLC 11, 19**
See also CA 45-48; 215; CAAS 14; CANR 1; CP 1, 2, 3, 4, 5, 6, 7; DLB 88

Duerrenmatt, Friedrich 1921-1990 ... **CLC 1, 4, 8, 11, 15, 43, 102**
See Durrenmatt, Friedrich
See also CA 17-20R; CANR 33; CMW 4; DAM DRAM; DLB 69, 124; MTCW 1, 2

Duffy, Bruce 1953(?)- .... **CLC 50**
See also CA 172

Duffy, Maureen (Patricia) 1933- ...... **CLC 37**
See also CA 25-28R; CANR 33, 68; CBD; CN 1, 2, 3, 4, 5, 6, 7; CP 7; CWD; CWP; DFS 15; DLB 14, 310; FW; MTCW 1

Du Fu
See Tu Fu
See also RGWL 2, 3

Dugan, Alan 1923-2003 .... **CLC 2, 6**
See also CA 81-84; 220; CANR 119; CP 1, 2, 3, 4, 5, 6, 7; DLB 5; MAL 5; PFS 10

du Gard, Roger Martin
See Martin du Gard, Roger

Duhamel, Georges 1884-1966 .... **CLC 8**
See also CA 81-84; 25-28R; CANR 35; DLB 65; EWL 3; GFL 1789 to the Present; MTCW 1

Dujardin, Edouard (Emile Louis) 1861-1949 .... **TCLC 13**
See also CA 109; DLB 123

Duke, Raoul
See Thompson, Hunter S(tockton)

Dulles, John Foster 1888-1959 .... **TCLC 72**
See also CA 115; 149

Dumas, Alexandre (pere) 1802-1870 .... **NCLC 11, 71; WLC**
See also AAYA 22; BYA 3; DA; DA3; DAB; DAC; DAM MST, NOV; DLB 119, 192; EW 6; GFL 1789 to the Present; LAIT 1, 2; NFS 14, 19; RGWL 2, 3; SATA 18; TWA; WCH

Dumas, Alexandre (fils) 1824-1895 ...... **DC 1; NCLC 9**
See also DLB 192; GFL 1789 to the Present; RGWL 2, 3

Dumas, Claudine
See Malzberg, Barry N(athaniel)

Dumas, Henry L. 1934-1968 .... **CLC 6, 62**
See also BW 1; CA 85-88; DLB 41; RGAL 4

du Maurier, Daphne 1907-1989 .. **CLC 6, 11, 59; SSC 18**
See also AAYA 37; BPFB 1; BRWS 3; CA 5-8R; 128; CANR 6, 55; CMW 4; CN 1, 2, 3, 4; CPW; DA3; DAB; DAC; DAM MST, POP; DLB 191; GL 2; HGG; LAIT 3; MSW; MTCW 1, 2; NFS 12; RGEL 2; RGSF 2; RHW; SATA 27; SATA-Obit 60; SSFS 14, 16; TEA

Du Maurier, George 1834-1896 ..... **NCLC 86**
See also DLB 153, 178; RGEL 2

Dunbar, Paul Laurence 1872-1906 ... **BLC 1; PC 5; SSC 8; TCLC 2, 12; WLC**
See also AFAW 1, 2; AMWS 2; BW 1, 3; CA 104; 124; CANR 79; CDALB 1865-1917; DA; DA3; DAC; DAM MST, MULT, POET; DLB 50, 54, 78; EXPP; MAL 5; RGAL 4; SATA 34

Dunbar, William 1460(?)-1520(?) .... **LC 20; PC 67**
See also BRWS 8; DLB 132, 146; RGEL 2

Dunbar-Nelson, Alice .... **HR 1:2**
See Nelson, Alice Ruth Moore Dunbar

Duncan, Dora Angela
See Duncan, Isadora

French, Albert 1943- .... **CLC 86**
  See also BW 3; CA 167
French, Antonia
  See Kureishi, Hanif
French, Marilyn 1929- .. **CLC 10, 18, 60, 177**
  See also BPFB 1; CA 69-72; CANR 3, 31,
  134; CN 5, 6, 7; CPW; DAM DRAM,
  NOV, POP; FL 1:5; FW; INT CANR-31;
  MTCW 1, 2; MTFW 2005
French, Paul
  See Asimov, Isaac
Freneau, Philip Morin 1752-1832 .. **NCLC 1,
  111**
  See also AMWS 2; DLB 37, 43; RGAL 4
Freud, Sigmund 1856-1939 .... **TCLC 52**
  See also CA 115; 133; CANR 69; DLB 296;
  EW 8; EWL 3; LATS 1:1; MTCW 1, 2;
  MTFW 2005; NCFS 3; TWA
Freytag, Gustav 1816-1895 .... **NCLC 109**
  See also DLB 129
Friedan, Betty (Naomi) 1921- .... **CLC 74**
  See also CA 65-68; CANR 18, 45, 74; DLB
  246; FW; MTCW 1, 2; MTFW 2005;
  NCFS 5
Friedlander, Saul 1932- .... **CLC 90**
  See also CA 117; 130; CANR 72
Friedman, B(ernard) H(arper)
  1926- .... **CLC 7**
  See also CA 1-4R; CANR 3, 48
Friedman, Bruce Jay 1930- ...... **CLC 3, 5, 56**
  See also CA 9-12R; CAD; CANR 25, 52,
  101; CD 5, 6; CN 1, 2, 3, 4, 5, 6, 7; DLB
  2, 28, 244; INT CANR-25; MAL 5; SSFS
  18
Friel, Brian 1929- .... **CLC 5, 42, 59, 115; DC
  8; SSC 76**
  See also BRWS 5; CA 21-24R; CANR 33,
  69, 131; CBD; CD 5, 6; DFS 11; DLB
  13, 319; EWL 3; MTCW 1; RGEL 2; TEA
Friis-Baastad, Babbis Ellinor
  1921-1970 .... **CLC 12**
  See also CA 17-20R; 134; SATA 7
Frisch, Max (Rudolf) 1911-1991 ... **CLC 3, 9,
  14, 18, 32, 44; TCLC 121**
  See also CA 85-88; 134; CANR 32, 74; CD-
  WLB 2; DAM DRAM, NOV; DLB 69,
  124; EW 13; EWL 3; MTCW 1, 2; MTFW
  2005; RGWL 2, 3
Fromentin, Eugene (Samuel Auguste)
  1820-1876 .... **NCLC 10, 125**
  See also DLB 123; GFL 1789 to the Present
Frost, Frederick
  See Faust, Frederick (Schiller)
Frost, Robert (Lee) 1874-1963 .. **CLC 1, 3, 4,
  9, 10, 13, 15, 26, 34, 44; PC 1, 39;
  WLC**
  See also AAYA 21; AMW; AMWR 1; CA
  89-92; CANR 33; CDALB 1917-1929;
  CLR 67; DA; DA3; DAB; DAC; DAM
  MST, POET; DLB 54, 284; DLBD 7;
  EWL 3; EXPP; MAL 5; MTCW 1, 2;
  MTFW 2005; PAB; PFS 1, 2, 3, 4, 5, 6,
  7, 10, 13; RGAL 4; SATA 14; TUS; WP;
  WYA
Froude, James Anthony
  1818-1894 .... **NCLC 43**
  See also DLB 18, 57, 144
Froy, Herald
  See Waterhouse, Keith (Spencer)
Fry, Christopher 1907-2005 ... **CLC 2, 10, 14**
  See also BRWS 3; CA 17-20R; 240; CAAS
  23; CANR 9, 30, 74, 132; CBD; CD 5, 6;
  CP 1, 2, 3, 4, 5, 6, 7; DAM DRAM; DLB
  13; EWL 3; MTCW 1, 2; MTFW 2005;
  RGEL 2; SATA 66; TEA
Frye, (Herman) Northrop
  1912-1991 .... **CLC 24, 70; TCLC 165**
  See also CA 5-8R; 133; CANR 8, 37; DLB
  67, 68, 246; EWL 3; MTCW 1, 2; MTFW
  2005; RGAL 4; TWA

Fuchs, Daniel 1909-1993 .... **CLC 8, 22**
  See also CA 81-84; 142; CAAS 5; CANR
  40; CN 1, 2, 3, 4, 5; DLB 9, 26, 28;
  DLBY 1993; MAL 5
Fuchs, Daniel 1934- .... **CLC 34**
  See also CA 37-40R; CANR 14, 48
Fuentes, Carlos 1928- .. **CLC 3, 8, 10, 13, 22,
  41, 60, 113; HLC 1; SSC 24; WLC**
  See also AAYA 4, 45; AITN 2; BPFB 1;
  CA 69-72; CANR 10, 32, 68, 104, 138;
  CDWLB 3; CWW 2; DA; DA3; DAB;
  DAC; DAM MST, MULT, NOV; DLB
  113; DNFS 2; EWL 3; HW 1, 2; LAIT 3;
  LATS 1:2; LAW; LAWS 1; LMFS 2;
  MTCW 1, 2; MTFW 2005; NFS 8; RGSF
  2; RGWL 2, 3; TWA; WLIT 1
Fuentes, Gregorio Lopez y
  See Lopez y Fuentes, Gregorio
Fuertes, Gloria 1918-1998 .... **PC 27**
  See also CA 178; 180; DLB 108; HW 2;
  SATA 115
Fugard, (Harold) Athol 1932- . **CLC 5, 9, 14,
  25, 40, 80, 211; DC 3**
  See also AAYA 17; AFW; CA 85-88; CANR
  32, 54, 118; CD 5, 6; DAM DRAM; DFS
  3, 6, 10; DLB 225; DNFS 1, 2; EWL 3;
  LATS 1:2; MTCW 1; MTFW 2005; RGEL
  2; WLIT 2
Fugard, Sheila 1932- .... **CLC 48**
  See also CA 125
Fujiwara no Teika 1162-1241 .... **CMLC 73**
  See also DLB 203
Fukuyama, Francis 1952- .... **CLC 131**
  See also CA 140; CANR 72, 125
Fuller, Charles (H.), (Jr.) 1939- .... **BLC 2;
  CLC 25; DC 1**
  See also BW 2; CA 108; 112; CAD; CANR
  87; CD 5, 6; DAM DRAM, MULT; DFS
  8; DLB 38, 266; EWL 3; INT CA-112;
  MAL 5; MTCW 1
Fuller, Henry Blake 1857-1929 .... **TCLC 103**
  See also CA 108; 177; DLB 12; RGAL 4
Fuller, John (Leopold) 1937- .... **CLC 62**
  See also CA 21-24R; CANR 9, 44; CP 1, 2,
  3, 4, 5, 6, 7; DLB 40
Fuller, Margaret
  See Ossoli, Sarah Margaret (Fuller)
  See also AMWS 2; DLB 183, 223, 239; FL
  1:3
Fuller, Roy (Broadbent) 1912-1991 ... **CLC 4,
  28**
  See also BRWS 7; CA 5-8R; 135; CAAS
  10; CANR 53, 83; CN 1, 2, 3, 4, 5; CP 1,
  2, 3, 4; CWRI 5; DLB 15, 20; EWL 3;
  RGEL 2; SATA 87
Fuller, Sarah Margaret
  See Ossoli, Sarah Margaret (Fuller)
Fuller, Sarah Margaret
  See Ossoli, Sarah Margaret (Fuller)
  See also DLB 1, 59, 73
Fuller, Thomas 1608-1661 .... **LC 111**
  See also DLB 151
Fulton, Alice 1952- .... **CLC 52**
  See also CA 116; CANR 57, 88; CP 7;
  CWP; DLB 193
Furphy, Joseph 1843-1912 .... **TCLC 25**
  See Collins, Tom
  See also CA 163; DLB 230; EWL 3; RGEL
  2
Fuson, Robert H(enderson) 1927- .... **CLC 70**
  See also CA 89-92; CANR 103
Fussell, Paul 1924- .... **CLC 74**
  See also BEST 90:1; CA 17-20R; CANR 8,
  21, 35, 69, 135; INT CANR-21; MTCW
  1, 2; MTFW 2005
Futabatei, Shimei 1864-1909 .... **TCLC 44**
  See Futabatei Shimei
  See also CA 162; MJW

Futabatei Shimei
  See Futabatei, Shimei
  See also DLB 180; EWL 3
Futrelle, Jacques 1875-1912 .... **TCLC 19**
  See also CA 113; 155; CMW 4
Gaboriau, Emile 1835-1873 .... **NCLC 14**
  See also CMW 4; MSW
Gadda, Carlo Emilio 1893-1973 ...... **CLC 11;
  TCLC 144**
  See also CA 89-92; DLB 177; EWL 3;
  WLIT 7
Gaddis, William 1922-1998 ... **CLC 1, 3, 6, 8,
  10, 19, 43, 86**
  See also AMWS 4; BPFB 1; CA 17-20R;
  172; CANR 21, 48; CN 1, 2, 3, 4, 5, 6;
  DLB 2, 278; EWL 3; MAL 5; MTCW 1,
  2; MTFW 2005; RGAL 4
Gaelique, Moruen le
  See Jacob, (Cyprien-)Max
Gage, Walter
  See Inge, William (Motter)
Gaiman, Neil (Richard) 1960- .... **CLC 195**
  See also AAYA 19, 42; CA 133; CANR 81,
  129; DLB 261; HGG; MTFW 2005; SATA
  85, 146; SFW 4; SUFW 2
Gaines, Ernest J(ames) 1933- .. **BLC 2; CLC
  3, 11, 18, 86, 181; SSC 68**
  See also AAYA 18; AFAW 1, 2; AITN 1;
  BPFB 1; BW 2, 3; BYA 6; CA 9-12R;
  CANR 6, 24, 42, 75, 126; CDALB 1968-
  1988; CLR 62; CN 1, 2, 3, 4, 5, 6, 7;
  CSW; DA3; DAM MULT; DLB 2, 33,
  152; DLBY 1980; EWL 3; EXPN; LAIT
  5; LATS 1:2; MAL 5; MTCW 1, 2;
  MTFW 2005; NFS 5, 7, 16; RGAL 4;
  RGSF 2; RHW; SATA 86; SSFS 5; YAW
Gaitskill, Mary (Lawrence) 1954- .... **CLC 69**
  See also CA 128; CANR 61; DLB 244;
  TCLE 1:1
Gaius Suetonius Tranquillus
  See Suetonius
Galdos, Benito Perez
  See Perez Galdos, Benito
  See also EW 7
Gale, Zona 1874-1938 .... **TCLC 7**
  See also CA 105; 153; CANR 84; DAM
  DRAM; DFS 17; DLB 9, 78, 228; RGAL
  4
Galeano, Eduardo (Hughes) 1940- . **CLC 72;
  HLCS 1**
  See also CA 29-32R; CANR 13, 32, 100;
  HW 1
Galiano, Juan Valera y Alcala
  See Valera y Alcala-Galiano, Juan
Galilei, Galileo 1564-1642 .... **LC 45**
Gallagher, Tess 1943- .... **CLC 18, 63; PC 9**
  See also CA 106; CP 3, 4, 5, 6, 7; CWP;
  DAM POET; DLB 120, 212, 244; PFS 16
Gallant, Mavis 1922- ..... **CLC 7, 18, 38, 172;
  SSC 5, 78**
  See also CA 69-72; CANR 29, 69, 117;
  CCA 1; CN 1, 2, 3, 4, 5, 6, 7; DAC; DAM
  MST; DLB 53; EWL 3; MTCW 1, 2;
  MTFW 2005; RGEL 2; RGSF 2
Gallant, Roy A(rthur) 1924- .... **CLC 17**
  See also CA 5-8R; CANR 4, 29, 54, 117;
  CLR 30; MAICYA 1, 2; SATA 4, 68, 110
Gallico, Paul (William) 1897-1976 ...... **CLC 2**
  See also AITN 1; CA 5-8R; 69-72; CANR
  23; CN 1, 2; DLB 9, 171; FANT; MAI-
  CYA 1, 2; SATA 13
Gallo, Max Louis 1932- .... **CLC 95**
  See also CA 85-88
Gallois, Lucien
  See Desnos, Robert
Gallup, Ralph
  See Whitemore, Hugh (John)

Guillen, Nicolas (Cristobal)
1902-1989 .... **BLC 2; CLC 48, 79; HLC 1; PC 23**
See also BW 2; CA 116; 125; 129; CANR 84; DAM MST, MULT, POET; DLB 283; EWL 3; HW 1; LAW; RGWL 2, 3; WP

Guillen y Alvarez, Jorge
See Guillen, Jorge

Guillevic, (Eugene) 1907-1997 .... **CLC 33**
See also CA 93-96; CWW 2

Guillois
See Desnos, Robert

Guillois, Valentin
See Desnos, Robert

Guimaraes Rosa, Joao 1908-1967 .... **HLCS 2**
See Rosa, Joao Guimaraes
See also CA 175; LAW; RGSF 2; RGWL 2, 3

Guiney, Louise Imogen
1861-1920 .... **TCLC 41**
See also CA 160; DLB 54; RGAL 4

Guinizelli, Guido c. 1230-1276 ...... **CMLC 49**
See Guinizzelli, Guido

Guinizzelli, Guido
See Guinizelli, Guido
See also WLIT 7

Guiraldes, Ricardo (Guillermo)
1886-1927 .... **TCLC 39**
See also CA 131; EWL 3; HW 1; LAW; MTCW 1

Gumilev, Nikolai (Stepanovich)
1886-1921 .... **TCLC 60**
See Gumilyov, Nikolay Stepanovich
See also CA 165; DLB 295

Gumilyov, Nikolay Stepanovich
See Gumilev, Nikolai (Stepanovich)
See also EWL 3

Gump, P. Q.
See Card, Orson Scott

Gunesekera, Romesh 1954- .... **CLC 91**
See also BRWS 10; CA 159; CANR 140; CN 6, 7; DLB 267

Gunn, Bill .... **CLC 5**
See Gunn, William Harrison
See also DLB 38

Gunn, Thom(son William)
1929-2004 . **CLC 3, 6, 18, 32, 81; PC 26**
See also BRWS 4; CA 17-20R; 227; CANR 9, 33, 116; CDBLB 1960 to Present; CP 1, 2, 3, 4, 5, 6, 7; DAM POET; DLB 27; INT CANR-33; MTCW 1; PFS 9; RGEL 2

Gunn, William Harrison 1934(?)-1989
See Gunn, Bill
See also AITN 1; BW 1, 3; CA 13-16R; 128; CANR 12, 25, 76

Gunn Allen, Paula
See Allen, Paula Gunn

Gunnars, Kristjana 1948- .... **CLC 69**
See also CA 113; CCA 1; CP 7; CWP; DLB 60

Gunter, Erich
See Eich, Gunter

Gurdjieff, G(eorgei) I(vanovich)
1877(?)-1949 .... **TCLC 71**
See also CA 157

Gurganus, Allan 1947- .... **CLC 70**
See also BEST 90:1; CA 135; CANR 114; CN 6, 7; CPW; CSW; DAM POP; GLL 1

Gurney, A. R.
See Gurney, A(lbert) R(amsdell), Jr.
See also DLB 266

Gurney, A(lbert) R(amsdell), Jr.
1930- .... **CLC 32, 50, 54**
See Gurney, A. R.
See also AMWS 5; CA 77-80; CAD; CANR 32, 64, 121; CD 5, 6; DAM DRAM; EWL 3

Gurney, Ivor (Bertie) 1890-1937 ... **TCLC 33**
See also BRW 6; CA 167; DLBY 2002; PAB; RGEL 2

Gurney, Peter
See Gurney, A(lbert) R(amsdell), Jr.

Guro, Elena (Genrikhovna)
1877-1913 .... **TCLC 56**
See also DLB 295

Gustafson, James M(oody) 1925- ... **CLC 100**
See also CA 25-28R; CANR 37

Gustafson, Ralph (Barker)
1909-1995 .... **CLC 36**
See also CA 21-24R; CANR 8, 45, 84; CP 1, 2, 3, 4; DLB 88; RGEL 2

Gut, Gom
See Simenon, Georges (Jacques Christian)

Guterson, David 1956- .... **CLC 91**
See also CA 132; CANR 73, 126; CN 7; DLB 292; MTCW 2; MTFW 2005; NFS 13

Guthrie, A(lfred) B(ertram), Jr.
1901-1991 .... **CLC 23**
See also CA 57-60; 134; CANR 24; CN 1, 2, 3; DLB 6, 212; MAL 5; SATA 62; SATA-Obit 67; TCWW 1, 2

Guthrie, Isobel
See Grieve, C(hristopher) M(urray)

Guthrie, Woodrow Wilson 1912-1967
See Guthrie, Woody
See also CA 113; 93-96

Guthrie, Woody .... **CLC 35**
See Guthrie, Woodrow Wilson
See also DLB 303; LAIT 3

Gutierrez Najera, Manuel
1859-1895 .... **HLCS 2; NCLC 133**
See also DLB 290; LAW

Guy, Rosa (Cuthbert) 1925- .... **CLC 26**
See also AAYA 4, 37; BW 2; CA 17-20R; CANR 14, 34, 83; CLR 13; DLB 33; DNFS 1; JRDA; MAICYA 1, 2; SATA 14, 62, 122; YAW

Gwendolyn
See Bennett, (Enoch) Arnold

H. D. .... **CLC 3, 8, 14, 31, 34, 73; PC 5**
See Doolittle, Hilda
See also FL 1:5

H. de V.
See Buchan, John

Haavikko, Paavo Juhani 1931- .. **CLC 18, 34**
See also CA 106; CWW 2; EWL 3

Habbema, Koos
See Heijermans, Herman

Habermas, Juergen 1929- .... **CLC 104**
See also CA 109; CANR 85; DLB 242

Habermas, Jurgen
See Habermas, Juergen

Hacker, Marilyn 1942- ...... **CLC 5, 9, 23, 72, 91; PC 47**
See also CA 77-80; CANR 68, 129; CP 3, 4, 5, 6, 7; CWP; DAM POET; DLB 120, 282; FW; GLL 2; MAL 5; PFS 19

Hadewijch of Antwerp fl. 1250- ... **CMLC 61**
See also RGWL 3

Hadrian 76-138 .... **CMLC 52**

Haeckel, Ernst Heinrich (Philipp August)
1834-1919 .... **TCLC 83**
See also CA 157

Hafiz c. 1326-1389(?) .... **CMLC 34**
See also RGWL 2, 3; WLIT 6

Hagedorn, Jessica T(arahata)
1949- .... **CLC 185**
See also CA 139; CANR 69; CWP; DLB 312; RGAL 4

Haggard, H(enry) Rider
1856-1925 .... **TCLC 11**
See also BRWS 3; BYA 4, 5; CA 108; 148; CANR 112; DLB 70, 156, 174, 178; FANT; LMFS 1; MTCW 2; RGEL 2; RHW; SATA 16; SCFW 1, 2; SFW 4; SUFW 1; WLIT 4

Hagiosy, L.
See Larbaud, Valery (Nicolas)

Hagiwara, Sakutaro 1886-1942 .... **PC 18; TCLC 60**
See Hagiwara Sakutaro
See also CA 154; RGWL 3

Hagiwara Sakutaro
See Hagiwara, Sakutaro
See also EWL 3

Haig, Fenil
See Ford, Ford Madox

Haig-Brown, Roderick (Langmere)
1908-1976 .... **CLC 21**
See also CA 5-8R; 69-72; CANR 4, 38, 83; CLR 31; CWRI 5; DLB 88; MAICYA 1, 2; SATA 12; TCWW 2

Haight, Rip
See Carpenter, John (Howard)

Hailey, Arthur 1920-2004 .... **CLC 5**
See also AITN 2; BEST 90:3; BPFB 2; CA 1-4R; 233; CANR 2, 36, 75; CCA 1; CN 1, 2, 3, 4, 5, 6, 7; CPW; DAM NOV, POP; DLB 88; DLBY 1982; MTCW 1, 2; MTFW 2005

Hailey, Elizabeth Forsythe 1938- ..... **CLC 40**
See also CA 93-96, 188; CAAE 188; CAAS 1; CANR 15, 48; INT CANR-15

Haines, John (Meade) 1924- .... **CLC 58**
See also AMWS 12; CA 17-20R; CANR 13, 34; CP 1, 2, 3, 4; CSW; DLB 5, 212; TCLE 1:1

Hakluyt, Richard 1552-1616 .... **LC 31**
See also DLB 136; RGEL 2

Haldeman, Joe (William) 1943- .... **CLC 61**
See Graham, Robert
See also AAYA 38; CA 53-56, 179; CAAE 179; CAAS 25; CANR 6, 70, 72, 130; DLB 8; INT CANR-6; SCFW 2; SFW 4

Hale, Janet Campbell 1947- .... **NNAL**
See also CA 49-52; CANR 45, 75; DAM MULT; DLB 175; MTCW 2; MTFW 2005

Hale, Sarah Josepha (Buell)
1788-1879 .... **NCLC 75**
See also DLB 1, 42, 73, 243

Halevy, Elie 1870-1937 .... **TCLC 104**

Haley, Alex(ander Murray Palmer)
1921-1992 .... **BLC 2; CLC 8, 12, 76; TCLC 147**
See also AAYA 26; BPFB 2; BW 2, 3; CA 77-80; 136; CANR 61; CDALBS; CPW; CSW; DA; DA3; DAB; DAC; DAM MST, MULT, POP; DLB 38; LAIT 5; MTCW 1, 2; NFS 9

Haliburton, Thomas Chandler
1796-1865 .... **NCLC 15, 149**
See also DLB 11, 99; RGEL 2; RGSF 2

Hall, Donald (Andrew, Jr.) 1928- ...... **CLC 1, 13, 37, 59, 151**
See also AAYA 63; CA 5-8R; CAAS 7; CANR 2, 44, 64, 106, 133; CP 1, 2, 3, 4, 5, 6, 7; DAM POET; DLB 5; MAL 5; MTCW 2; MTFW 2005; RGAL 4; SATA 23, 97

Hall, Frederic Sauser
See Sauser-Hall, Frederic

Hall, James
See Kuttner, Henry

Hall, James Norman 1887-1951 ..... **TCLC 23**
See also CA 123; 173; LAIT 1; RHW 1; SATA 21

Hall, Joseph 1574-1656 .... **LC 91**
See also DLB 121, 151; RGEL 2

Harrison, Elizabeth (Allen) Cavanna
 1909-2001
 See Cavanna, Betty
 See also CA 9-12R; 200; CANR 6, 27, 85,
 104, 121; MAICYA 2; SATA 142; YAW

Harrison, Harry (Max) 1925- .... **CLC 42**
 See also CA 1-4R; CANR 5, 21, 84; DLB
 8; SATA 4; SCFW 2; SFW 4

Harrison, James (Thomas) 1937- ...... **CLC 6,
 14, 33, 66, 143; SSC 19**
 See Harrison, Jim
 See also CA 13-16R; CANR 8, 51, 79, 142;
 DLBY 1982; INT CANR-8

Harrison, Jim
 See Harrison, James (Thomas)
 See also AMWS 8; CN 5, 6; CP 1, 2, 3, 4,
 5, 6, 7; RGAL 4; TCWW 2; TUS

Harrison, Kathryn 1961- .... **CLC 70, 151**
 See also CA 144; CANR 68, 122

Harrison, Tony 1937- .... **CLC 43, 129**
 See also BRWS 5; CA 65-68; CANR 44,
 98; CBD; CD 5, 6; CP 2, 3, 4, 5, 6, 7;
 DLB 40, 245; MTCW 1; RGEL 2

Harriss, Will(ard Irvin) 1922- .... **CLC 34**
 See also CA 111

Hart, Ellis
 See Ellison, Harlan (Jay)

Hart, Josephine 1942(?)- .... **CLC 70**
 See also CA 138; CANR 70; CPW; DAM
 POP

Hart, Moss 1904-1961 .... **CLC 66**
 See also CA 109; 89-92; CANR 84; DAM
 DRAM; DFS 1; DLB 7, 266; RGAL 4

Harte, (Francis) Bret(t)
 1836(?)-1902 ... **SSC 8, 59; TCLC 1, 25;
 WLC**
 See also AMWS 2; CA 104; 140; CANR
 80; CDALB 1865-1917; DA; DA3; DAC;
 DAM MST; DLB 12, 64, 74, 79, 186;
 EXPS; LAIT 2; RGAL 4; RGSF 2; SATA
 26; SSFS 3; TUS

Hartley, L(eslie) P(oles) 1895-1972 ... **CLC 2,
 22**
 See also BRWS 7; CA 45-48; 37-40R;
 CANR 33; CN 1; DLB 15, 139; EWL 3;
 HGG; MTCW 1, 2; MTFW 2005; RGEL
 2; RGSF 2; SUFW 1

Hartman, Geoffrey H. 1929- .... **CLC 27**
 See also CA 117; 125; CANR 79; DLB 67

Hartmann, Sadakichi 1869-1944 ... **TCLC 73**
 See also CA 157; DLB 54

Hartmann von Aue c. 1170-c.
 1210 .... **CMLC 15**
 See also CDWLB 2; DLB 138; RGWL 2, 3

Hartog, Jan de
 See de Hartog, Jan

Haruf, Kent 1943- .... **CLC 34**
 See also AAYA 44; CA 149; CANR 91, 131

Harvey, Caroline
 See Trollope, Joanna

Harvey, Gabriel 1550(?)-1631 .... **LC 88**
 See also DLB 167, 213, 281

Harwood, Ronald 1934- .... **CLC 32**
 See also CA 1-4R; CANR 4, 55; CBD; CD
 5, 6; DAM DRAM, MST; DLB 13

Hasegawa Tatsunosuke
 See Futabatei, Shimei

Hasek, Jaroslav (Matej Frantisek)
 1883-1923 .... **SSC 69; TCLC 4**
 See also CA 104; 129; CDWLB 4; DLB
 215; EW 9; EWL 3; MTCW 1, 2; RGSF
 2; RGWL 2, 3

Hass, Robert 1941- ... **CLC 18, 39, 99; PC 16**
 See also AMWS 6; CA 111; CANR 30, 50,
 71; CP 1, 3, 4, 5, 6, 7; DLB 105, 206; EWL
 3; MAL 5; MTFW 2005; RGAL 4; SATA
 94; TCLE 1:1

Hastings, Hudson
 See Kuttner, Henry

Hastings, Selina .... **CLC 44**

Hathorne, John 1641-1717 .... **LC 38**

Hatteras, Amelia
 See Mencken, H(enry) L(ouis)

Hatteras, Owen .... **TCLC 18**
 See Mencken, H(enry) L(ouis); Nathan,
 George Jean

Hauptmann, Gerhart (Johann Robert)
 1862-1946 .... **SSC 37; TCLC 4**
 See also CA 104; 153; CDWLB 2; DAM
 DRAM; DLB 66, 118; EW 8; EWL 3;
 RGSF 2; RGWL 2, 3; TWA

Havel, Vaclav 1936- ..... **CLC 25, 58, 65, 123;
 DC 6**
 See also CA 104; CANR 36, 63, 124; CD-
 WLB 4; CWW 2; DA3; DAM DRAM;
 DFS 10; DLB 232; EWL 3; LMFS 2;
 MTCW 1, 2; MTFW 2005; RGWL 3

Haviaras, Stratis .... **CLC 33**
 See Chaviaras, Strates

Hawes, Stephen 1475(?)-1529(?) .... **LC 17**
 See also DLB 132; RGEL 2

Hawkes, John (Clendennin Burne, Jr.)
 1925-1998 .. **CLC 1, 2, 3, 4, 7, 9, 14, 15,
 27, 49**
 See also BPFB 2; CA 1-4R; 167; CANR 2,
 47, 64; CN 1, 2, 3, 4, 5, 6; DLB 2, 7, 227;
 DLBY 1980, 1998; EWL 3; MAL 5;
 MTCW 1, 2; MTFW 2005; RGAL 4

Hawking, S. W.
 See Hawking, Stephen W(illiam)

Hawking, Stephen W(illiam) 1942- . **CLC 63,
 105**
 See also AAYA 13; BEST 89:1; CA 126;
 129; CANR 48, 115; CPW; DA3; MTCW
 2; MTFW 2005

Hawkins, Anthony Hope
 See Hope, Anthony

Hawthorne, Julian 1846-1934 .... **TCLC 25**
 See also CA 165; HGG

Hawthorne, Nathaniel 1804-1864 ... **NCLC 2,
 10, 17, 23, 39, 79, 95, 158; SSC 3, 29,
 39, 89; WLC**
 See also AAYA 18; AMW; AMWC 1;
 AMWR 1; BPFB 2; BYA 3; CDALB
 1640-1865; CLR 103; DA; DA3; DAB;
 DAC; DAM MST, NOV; DLB 1, 74, 183,
 223, 269; EXPN; EXPS; GL 2; HGG;
 LAIT 1; NFS 1, 20; RGAL 4; RGSF 2;
 SSFS 1, 7, 11, 15; SUFW 1; TUS; WCH;
 YABC 2

Hawthorne, Sophia Peabody
 1809-1871 .... **NCLC 150**
 See also DLB 183, 239

Haxton, Josephine Ayres 1921-
 See Douglas, Ellen
 See also CA 115; CANR 41, 83

Hayaseca y Eizaguirre, Jorge
 See Echegaray (y Eizaguirre), Jose (Maria
 Waldo)

Hayashi, Fumiko 1904-1951 .... **TCLC 27**
 See Hayashi Fumiko
 See also CA 161

Hayashi Fumiko
 See Hayashi, Fumiko
 See also DLB 180; EWL 3

Haycraft, Anna (Margaret) 1932-2005
 See Ellis, Alice Thomas
 See also CA 122; 237; CANR 90, 141;
 MTCW 2; MTFW 2005

Hayden, Robert E(arl) 1913-1980 ..... **BLC 2;
 CLC 5, 9, 14, 37; PC 6**
 See also AFAW 1, 2; AMWS 2; BW 1, 3;
 CA 69-72; 97-100; CABS 2; CANR 24,
 75, 82; CDALB 1941-1968; CP 1, 2; DA;
 DAC; DAM MST, MULT, POET;
 DLB 5, 76; EWL 3; EXPP; MAL 5;
 MTCW 1, 2; PFS 1; RGAL 4; SATA 19;
 SATA-Obit 26; WP

Haydon, Benjamin Robert
 1786-1846 .... **NCLC 146**
 See also DLB 110

Hayek, F(riedrich) A(ugust von)
 1899-1992 .... **TCLC 109**
 See also CA 93-96; 137; CANR 20; MTCW
 1, 2

Hayford, J(oseph) E(phraim) Casely
 See Casely-Hayford, J(oseph) E(phraim)

Hayman, Ronald 1932- .... **CLC 44**
 See also CA 25-28R; CANR 18, 50, 88; CD
 5, 6; DLB 155

Hayne, Paul Hamilton 1830-1886 . **NCLC 94**
 See also DLB 3, 64, 79, 248; RGAL 4

Hays, Mary 1760-1843 .... **NCLC 114**
 See also DLB 142, 158; RGEL 2

Haywood, Eliza (Fowler)
 1693(?)-1756 .... **LC 1, 44**
 See also DLB 39; RGEL 2

Hazlitt, William 1778-1830 ...... **NCLC 29, 82**
 See also BRW 4; DLB 110, 158; RGEL 2;
 TEA

Hazzard, Shirley 1931- .... **CLC 18, 218**
 See also CA 9-12R; CANR 4, 70, 127; CN
 1, 2, 3, 4, 5, 6, 7; DLB 289; DLBY 1982;
 MTCW 1

Head, Bessie 1937-1986 ...... **BLC 2; CLC 25,
 67; SSC 52**
 See also AFW; BW 2, 3; CA 29-32R; 119;
 CANR 25, 82; CDWLB 3; CN 1, 2, 3, 4;
 DA3; DAM MULT; DLB 117, 225; EWL
 3; EXPS; FL 1:6; FW; MTCW 1, 2;
 MTFW 2005; RGSF 2; SSFS 5, 13; WLIT
 2; WWE 1

Headon, (Nicky) Topper 1956(?)- ..... **CLC 30**

Heaney, Seamus (Justin) 1939- ..... **CLC 5, 7,
 14, 25, 37, 74, 91, 171; PC 18; WLCS**
 See also AAYA 61; BRWR 1; BRWS 2; CA
 85-88; CANR 25, 48, 75, 91, 128; CD-
 BLB 1960 to Present; CP 1, 2, 3, 4, 5, 6,
 7; DA3; DAB; DAM POET; DLB 40;
 DLBY 1995; EWL 3; EXPP; MTCW 1,
 2; MTFW 2005; PAB; PFS 2, 5, 8, 17;
 RGEL 2; TEA; WLIT 4

Hearn, (Patricio) Lafcadio (Tessima Carlos)
 1850-1904 .... **TCLC 9**
 See also CA 105; 166; DLB 12, 78, 189;
 HGG; MAL 5; RGAL 4

Hearne, Samuel 1745-1792 .... **LC 95**
 See also DLB 99

Hearne, Vicki 1946-2001 .... **CLC 56**
 See also CA 139; 201

Hearon, Shelby 1931- .... **CLC 63**
 See also AITN 2; AMWS 8; CA 25-28R;
 CANR 18, 48, 103, 146; CSW

Heat-Moon, William Least .... **CLC 29**
 See Trogdon, William (Lewis)
 See also AAYA 9

Hebbel, Friedrich 1813-1863 . **DC 21; NCLC
 43**
 See also CDWLB 2; DAM DRAM; DLB
 129; EW 6; RGWL 2, 3

Hebert, Anne 1916-2000 .... **CLC 4, 13, 29**
 See also CA 85-88; 187; CANR 69, 126;
 CCA 1; CWP; CWW 2; DA3; DAC;
 DAM MST, POET; DLB 68; EWL 3; GFL
 1789 to the Present; MTCW 1, 2; MTFW
 2005; PFS 20

Hecht, Anthony (Evan) 1923-2004 .... **CLC 8,
 13, 19**
 See also AMWS 10; CA 9-12R; 232; CANR
 6, 108; CP 1, 2, 3, 4, 5, 6, 7; DAM POET;
 DLB 5, 169; EWL 3; PFS 6; WP

Hecht, Ben 1894-1964 ..... **CLC 8; TCLC 101**
 See also CA 85-88; DFS 9; DLB 7, 9, 25,
 26, 28, 86; FANT; IDFW 3, 4; RGAL 4

Hedayat, Sadeq 1903-1951 .... **TCLC 21**
 See also CA 120; EWL 3; RGSF 2

Hewes, Cady
See De Voto, Bernard (Augustine)

Heyen, William 1940- .... **CLC 13, 18**
See also CA 33-36R, 220; CAAE 220; CAAS 9; CANR 98; CP 3, 4, 5, 6, 7; DLB 5

Heyerdahl, Thor 1914-2002 .... **CLC 26**
See also CA 5-8R; 207; CANR 5, 22, 66, 73; LAIT 4; MTCW 1, 2; MTFW 2005; SATA 2, 52

Heym, Georg (Theodor Franz Arthur)
1887-1912 .... **TCLC 9**
See also CA 106; 181

Heym, Stefan 1913-2001 .... **CLC 41**
See also CA 9-12R; 203; CANR 4; CWW 2; DLB 69; EWL 3

Heyse, Paul (Johann Ludwig von)
1830-1914 .... **TCLC 8**
See also CA 104; 209; DLB 129

Heyward, (Edwin) DuBose
1885-1940 .... **HR 1:2; TCLC 59**
See also CA 108; 157; DLB 7, 9, 45, 249; MAL 5; SATA 21

Heywood, John 1497(?)-1580(?) .... **LC 65**
See also DLB 136; RGEL 2

Heywood, Thomas 1573(?)-1641 .... **LC 111**
See also DAM DRAM; DLB 62; LMFS 1; RGEL 2; TEA

Hibbert, Eleanor Alice Burford
1906-1993 .... **CLC 7**
See Holt, Victoria
See also BEST 90:4; CA 17-20R; 140; CANR 9, 28, 59; CMW 4; CPW; DAM POP; MTCW 2; MTFW 2005; RHW; SATA 2; SATA-Obit 74

Hichens, Robert (Smythe)
1864-1950 .... **TCLC 64**
See also CA 162; DLB 153; HGG; RHW; SUFW

Higgins, Aidan 1927- .... **SSC 68**
See also CA 9-12R; CANR 70, 115; CN 1, 2, 3, 4, 5, 6, 7; DLB 14

Higgins, George V(incent)
1939-1999 .... **CLC 4, 7, 10, 18**
See also BPFB 2; CA 77-80; 186; CAAS 5; CANR 17, 51, 89, 96; CMW 4; CN 2, 3, 4, 5, 6; DLB 2; DLBY 1981, 1998; INT CANR-17; MSW; MTCW 1

Higginson, Thomas Wentworth
1823-1911 .... **TCLC 36**
See also CA 162; DLB 1, 64, 243

Higgonet, Margaret ed. .... **CLC 65**

Highet, Helen
See MacInnes, Helen (Clark)

Highsmith, (Mary) Patricia
1921-1995 .... **CLC 2, 4, 14, 42, 102**
See Morgan, Claire
See also AAYA 48; BRWS 5; CA 1-4R; 147; CANR 1, 20, 48, 62, 108; CMW 4; CN 1, 2, 3, 4, 5; CPW; DA3; DAM NOV, POP; DLB 306; MSW; MTCW 1, 2; MTFW 2005

Highwater, Jamake (Mamake)
1942(?)-2001 .... **CLC 12**
See also AAYA 7; BPFB 2; BYA 4; CA 65-68; 199; CAAS 7; CANR 10, 34, 84; CLR 17; CWRI 5; DLB 52; DLBY 1985; JRDA; MAICYA 1, 2; SATA 32, 69; SATA-Brief 30

Highway, Tomson 1951- ...... **CLC 92; NNAL**
See also CA 151; CANR 75; CCA 1; CD 5, 6; CN 7; DAC; DAM MULT; DFS 2; MTCW 2

Hijuelos, Oscar 1951- .... **CLC 65; HLC 1**
See also AAYA 25; AMWS 8; BEST 90:1; CA 123; CANR 50, 75, 125; CPW; DA3; DAM MULT, POP; DLB 145; HW 1, 2; LLW; MAL 5; MTCW 2; MTFW 2005; NFS 17; RGAL 4; WLIT 1

Hikmet, Nazim 1902-1963 .... **CLC 40**
See Nizami of Ganja
See also CA 141; 93-96; EWL 3; WLIT 6

Hildegard von Bingen 1098-1179 . **CMLC 20**
See also DLB 148

Hildesheimer, Wolfgang 1916-1991 .. **CLC 49**
See also CA 101; 135; DLB 69, 124; EWL 3

Hill, Geoffrey (William) 1932- ...... **CLC 5, 8, 18, 45**
See also BRWS 5; CA 81-84; CANR 21, 89; CDBLB 1960 to Present; CP 1, 2, 3, 4, 5, 6, 7; DAM POET; DLB 40; EWL 3; MTCW 1; RGEL 2

Hill, George Roy 1921-2002 .... **CLC 26**
See also CA 110; 122; 213

Hill, John
See Koontz, Dean R.

Hill, Susan (Elizabeth) 1942- ...... **CLC 4, 113**
See also CA 33-36R; CANR 29, 69, 129; CN 2, 3, 4, 5, 6, 7; DAB; DAM MST, NOV; DLB 14, 139; HGG; MTCW 1; RHW

Hillard, Asa G. III .... **CLC 70**

Hillerman, Tony 1925- .... **CLC 62, 170**
See also AAYA 40; BEST 89:1; BPFB 2; CA 29-32R; CANR 21, 42, 65, 97, 134; CMW 4; CPW; DA3; DAM POP; DLB 206, 306; MAL 5; MSW; MTCW 2; MTFW 2005; RGAL 4; SATA 6; TCWW 2; YAW

Hillesum, Etty 1914-1943 .... **TCLC 49**
See also CA 137

Hilliard, Noel (Harvey) 1929-1996 ... **CLC 15**
See also CA 9-12R; CANR 7, 69; CN 1, 2, 3, 4, 5, 6

Hillis, Rick 1956- .... **CLC 66**
See also CA 134

Hilton, James 1900-1954 .... **TCLC 21**
See also CA 108; 169; DLB 34, 77; FANT; SATA 34

Hilton, Walter (?)-1396 .... **CMLC 58**
See also DLB 146; RGEL 2

Himes, Chester (Bomar) 1909-1984 .. **BLC 2; CLC 2, 4, 7, 18, 58, 108; TCLC 139**
See also AFAW 2; BPFB 2; BW 2; CA 25-28R; 114; CANR 22, 89; CMW 4; CN 1, 2, 3; DAM MULT; DLB 2, 76, 143, 226; EWL 3; MAL 5; MSW; MTCW 1, 2; MTFW 2005; RGAL 4

Himmelfarb, Gertrude 1922- .... **CLC 202**
See also CA 49-52; CANR 28, 66, 102

Hinde, Thomas .... **CLC 6, 11**
See Chitty, Thomas Willes
See also CN 1, 2, 3, 4, 5, 6; EWL 3

Hine, (William) Daryl 1936- .... **CLC 15**
See also CA 1-4R; CAAS 15; CANR 1, 20; CP 1, 2, 3, 4, 5, 6, 7; DLB 60

Hinkson, Katharine Tynan
See Tynan, Katharine

Hinojosa(-Smith), Rolando (R.)
1929- .... **HLC 1**
See Hinojosa-Smith, Rolando
See also CA 131; CAAS 16; CANR 62; DAM MULT; DLB 82; HW 1, 2; LLW; MTCW 2; MTFW 2005; RGAL 4

Hinton, S(usan) E(loise) 1950- .. **CLC 30, 111**
See also AAYA 2, 33; BPFB 2; BYA 2, 3; CA 81-84; CANR 32, 62, 92, 133; CDALBS; CLR 3, 23; CPW; DA; DA3; DAB; DAC; DAM MST, NOV; JRDA; LAIT 5; MAICYA 1, 2; MTCW 1, 2; MTFW 2005 !**; NFS 5, 9, 15, 16; SATA 19, 58, 115, 160; WYA; YAW

Hippius, Zinaida (Nikolaevna) .... **TCLC 9**
See Gippius, Zinaida (Nikolaevna)
See also DLB 295; EWL 3

Hiraoka, Kimitake 1925-1970
See Mishima, Yukio
See also CA 97-100; 29-32R; DA3; DAM DRAM; GLL 1; MTCW 1, 2

Hirsch, E(ric) D(onald), Jr. 1928- .... **CLC 79**
See also CA 25-28R; CANR 27, 51; DLB 67; INT CANR-27; MTCW 1

Hirsch, Edward 1950- .... **CLC 31, 50**
See also CA 104; CANR 20, 42, 102; CP 7; DLB 120; PFS 22

Hitchcock, Alfred (Joseph)
1899-1980 .... **CLC 16**
See also AAYA 22; CA 159; 97-100; SATA 27; SATA-Obit 24

Hitchens, Christopher (Eric)
1949- .... **CLC 157**
See also CA 152; CANR 89

Hitler, Adolf 1889-1945 .... **TCLC 53**
See also CA 117; 147

Hoagland, Edward (Morley) 1932- .. **CLC 28**
See also ANW; CA 1-4R; CANR 2, 31, 57, 107; CN 1, 2, 3, 4, 5, 6, 7; DLB 6; SATA 51; TCWW 2

Hoban, Russell (Conwell) 1925- ... **CLC 7, 25**
See also BPFB 2; CA 5-8R; CANR 23, 37, 66, 114, 138; CLR 3, 69; CN 4, 5, 6, 7; CWRI 5; DAM NOV; DLB 52; FANT; MAICYA 1, 2; MTCW 1, 2; MTFW 2005; SATA 1, 40, 78, 136; SFW 4; SUFW 2; TCLE 1:1

Hobbes, Thomas 1588-1679 .... **LC 36**
See also DLB 151, 252, 281; RGEL 2

Hobbs, Perry
See Blackmur, R(ichard) P(almer)

Hobson, Laura Z(ametkin)
1900-1986 .... **CLC 7, 25**
See also BPFB 2; CA 17-20R; 118; CANR 55; CN 1, 2, 3, 4; DLB 28; SATA 52

Hoccleve, Thomas c. 1368-c. 1437 ...... **LC 75**
See also DLB 146; RGEL 2

Hoch, Edward D(entinger) 1930-
See Queen, Ellery
See also CA 29-32R; CANR 11, 27, 51, 97; CMW 4; DLB 306; SFW 4

Hochhuth, Rolf 1931- .... **CLC 4, 11, 18**
See also CA 5-8R; CANR 33, 75, 136; CWW 2; DAM DRAM; DLB 124; EWL 3; MTCW 1, 2; MTFW 2005

Hochman, Sandra 1936- .... **CLC 3, 8**
See also CA 5-8R; CP 1, 2, 3, 4; DLB 5

Hochwaelder, Fritz 1911-1986 .... **CLC 36**
See Hochwalder, Fritz
See also CA 29-32R; 120; CANR 42; DAM DRAM; MTCW 1; RGWL 3

Hochwalder, Fritz
See Hochwaelder, Fritz
See also EWL 3; RGWL 2

Hocking, Mary (Eunice) 1921- .... **CLC 13**
See also CA 101; CANR 18, 40

Hodgins, Jack 1938- .... **CLC 23**
See also CA 93-96; CN 4, 5, 6, 7; DLB 60

Hodgson, William Hope
1877(?)-1918 .... **TCLC 13**
See also CA 111; 164; CMW 4; DLB 70, 153, 156, 178; HGG; MTCW 2; SFW 4; SUFW 1

Hoeg, Peter 1957- .... **CLC 95, 156**
See also CA 151; CANR 75; CMW 4; DA3; DLB 214; EWL 3; MTCW 2; MTFW 2005; NFS 17; RGWL 3; SSFS 18

Hoffman, Alice 1952- .... **CLC 51**
See also AAYA 37; AMWS 10; CA 77-80; CANR 34, 66, 100, 138; CN 4, 5, 6, 7; CPW; DAM NOV; DLB 292; MAL 5; MTCW 1, 2; MTFW 2005; TCLE 1:1

Hoffman, Daniel (Gerard) 1923- . **CLC 6, 13, 23**
See also CA 1-4R; CANR 4, 142; CP 1, 2, 3, 4, 5, 6, 7; DLB 5; TCLE 1:1

Hougan, Carolyn 1943- .... **CLC 34**
See also CA 139

Household, Geoffrey (Edward West)
1900-1988 .... **CLC 11**
See also CA 77-80; 126; CANR 58; CMW
4; CN 1, 2, 3, 4; DLB 87; SATA 14;
SATA-Obit 59

Housman, A(lfred) E(dward)
1859-1936 .... **PC 2, 43; TCLC 1, 10;**
WLCS
See also AAYA 66; BRW 6; CA 104; 125;
DA; DA3; DAB; DAC; DAM MST,
POET; DLB 19, 284; EWL 3; EXPP;
MTCW 1, 2; MTFW 2005; PAB; PFS 4,
7; RGEL 2; TEA; WP

Housman, Laurence 1865-1959 .... **TCLC 7**
See also CA 106; 155; DLB 10; FANT;
RGEL 2; SATA 25

Houston, Jeanne (Toyo) Wakatsuki
1934- .... **AAL**
See also AAYA 49; CA 103, 232; CAAE
232; CAAS 16; CANR 29, 123; LAIT 4;
SATA 78

Howard, Elizabeth Jane 1923- ..... **CLC 7, 29**
See also BRWS 11; CA 5-8R; CANR 8, 62,
146; CN 1, 2, 3, 4, 5, 6, 7

Howard, Maureen 1930- .... **CLC 5, 14, 46,**
151
See also CA 53-56; CANR 31, 75, 140; CN
4, 5, 6, 7; DLBY 1983; INT CANR-31;
MTCW 1, 2; MTFW 2005

Howard, Richard 1929- .... **CLC 7, 10, 47**
See also AITN 1; CA 85-88; CANR 25, 80;
CP 1, 2, 3, 4, 5, 6, 7; DLB 5; INT CANR-
25; MAL 5

Howard, Robert E(rvin)
1906-1936 .... **TCLC 8**
See also BPFB 2; BYA 5; CA 105; 157;
FANT; SUFW 1; TCWW 1, 2

Howard, Warren F.
See Pohl, Frederik

Howe, Fanny (Quincy) 1940- .... **CLC 47**
See also CA 117, 187; CAAE 187; CAAS
27; CANR 70, 116; CP 7; CWP; SATA-
Brief 52

Howe, Irving 1920-1993 .... **CLC 85**
See also AMWS 6; CA 9-12R; 141; CANR
21, 50; DLB 67; EWL 3; MAL 5; MTCW
1, 2; MTFW 2005

Howe, Julia Ward 1819-1910 .... **TCLC 21**
See also CA 117; 191; DLB 1, 189, 235;
FW

Howe, Susan 1937- .... **CLC 72, 152; PC 54**
See also AMWS 4; CA 160; CP 7; CWP;
DLB 120; FW; RGAL 4

Howe, Tina 1937- .... **CLC 48**
See also CA 109; CAD; CANR 125; CD 5,
6; CWD

Howell, James 1594(?)-1666 .... **LC 13**
See also DLB 151

Howells, W. D.
See Howells, William Dean

Howells, William D.
See Howells, William Dean

Howells, William Dean 1837-1920 ... **SSC 36;**
TCLC 7, 17, 41
See also AMW; CA 104; 134; CDALB
1865-1917; DLB 12, 64, 74, 79, 189;
LMFS 1; MAL 5; MTCW 2; RGAL 4;
TUS

Howes, Barbara 1914-1996 .... **CLC 15**
See also CA 9-12R; 151; CAAS 3; CANR
53; CP 1, 2, 3, 4; SATA 5; TCLE 1:1

Hrabal, Bohumil 1914-1997 ...... **CLC 13, 67;**
TCLC 155
See also CA 106; 156; CAAS 12; CANR
57; CWW 2; DLB 232; EWL 3; RGSF 2

Hrabanus Maurus 776(?)-856 .... **CMLC 78**
See also DLB 148

Hrotsvit of Gandersheim c. 935-c.
1000 .... **CMLC 29**
See also DLB 148

Hsi, Chu 1130-1200 .... **CMLC 42**

Hsun, Lu
See Lu Hsun

Hubbard, L(afayette) Ron(ald)
1911-1986 .... **CLC 43**
See also AAYA 64; CA 77-80; 118; CANR
52; CPW; DA3; DAM POP; FANT;
MTCW 2; MTFW 2005; SFW 4

Huch, Ricarda (Octavia)
1864-1947 .... **TCLC 13**
See Hugo, Richard
See also CA 111; 189; DLB 66; EWL 3

Huddle, David 1942- .... **CLC 49**
See also CA 57-60; CAAS 20; CANR 89;
DLB 130

Hudson, Jeffrey
See Crichton, (John) Michael

Hudson, W(illiam) H(enry)
1841-1922 .... **TCLC 29**
See also CA 115; 190; DLB 98, 153, 174;
RGEL 2; SATA 35

Hueffer, Ford Madox
See Ford, Ford Madox

Hughart, Barry 1934- .... **CLC 39**
See also CA 137; FANT; SFW 4; SUFW 2

Hughes, Colin
See Creasey, John

Hughes, David (John) 1930-2005 ..... **CLC 48**
See also CA 116; 129; 238; CN 4, 5, 6, 7;
DLB 14

Hughes, Edward James
See Hughes, Ted
See also DA3; DAM MST, POET

Hughes, (James Mercer) Langston
1902-1967 ..... **BLC 2; CLC 1, 5, 10, 15,**
35, 44, 108; DC 3; HR 1:2; PC 1, 53;
SSC 6; WLC
See also AAYA 12; AFAW 1, 2; AMWR 1;
AMWS 1; BW 1, 3; CA 1-4R; 25-28R;
CANR 1, 34, 82; CDALB 1929-1941;
CLR 17; DA; DA3; DAB; DAC; DAM
DRAM, MST, MULT, POET; DFS 6, 18;
DLB 4, 7, 48, 51, 86, 228, 315; EWL 3;
EXPP; EXPS; JRDA; LAIT 3; LMFS 2;
MAICYA 1, 2; MAL 5; MTCW 1, 2;
MTFW 2005; NFS 21; PAB; PFS 1, 3, 6,
10, 15; RGAL 4; RGSF 2; SATA 4, 33;
SSFS 4, 7; TUS; WCH; WP; YAW

Hughes, Richard (Arthur Warren)
1900-1976 .... **CLC 1, 11**
See also CA 5-8R; 65-68; CANR 4; CN 1,
2; DAM NOV; DLB 15, 161; EWL 3;
MTCW 1; RGEL 2; SATA 8; SATA-Obit
25

Hughes, Ted 1930-1998 . **CLC 2, 4, 9, 14, 37,**
119; PC 7
See Hughes, Edward James
See also BRWC 2; BRWR 2; BRWS 1; CA
1-4R; CANR 1, 33, 66, 108; CLR 3;
CP 1, 2, 3, 4, 5, 6; DAB; DAC; DLB 40,
161; EWL 3; EXPP; MAICYA 1, 2;
MTCW 1, 2; MTFW 2005; PAB; PFS 4,
19; RGEL 2; SATA 49; SATA-Brief 27;
SATA-Obit 107; TEA; YAW

Hugo, Richard
See Huch, Ricarda (Octavia)
See also MAL 5

Hugo, Richard F(ranklin)
1923-1982 .... **CLC 6, 18, 32; PC 68**
See also AMWS 6; CA 49-52; 108; CANR
3; CP 1, 2, 3; DAM POET; DLB 5, 206;
EWL 3; PFS 17; RGAL 4

Hugo, Victor (Marie) 1802-1885 .... **NCLC 3,**
10, 21, 161; PC 17; WLC
See also AAYA 28; DA; DA3; DAB; DAC;
DAM DRAM, MST, NOV, POET; DLB
119, 192, 217; EFS 2; EW 6; EXPN; GFL

1789 to the Present; LAIT 1, 2; NFS 5,
20; RGWL 2, 3; SATA 47; TWA

Huidobro, Vicente
See Huidobro Fernandez, Vicente Garcia
See also DLB 283; EWL 3; LAW

Huidobro Fernandez, Vicente Garcia
1893-1948 .... **TCLC 31**
See Huidobro, Vicente
See also CA 131; HW 1

Hulme, Keri 1947- .... **CLC 39, 130**
See also CA 125; CANR 69; CN 4, 5, 6, 7;
CP 7; CWP; EWL 3; FW; INT CA-125

Hulme, T(homas) E(rnest)
1883-1917 .... **TCLC 21**
See also CA 117; 203; DLB 19

Humboldt, Wilhelm von
1767-1835 .... **NCLC 134**
See also DLB 90

Hume, David 1711-1776 .... **LC 7, 56**
See also BRWS 3; DLB 104, 252; LMFS 1;
TEA

Humphrey, William 1924-1997 .... **CLC 45**
See also AMWS 9; CA 77-80; 160; CANR
68; CN 1, 2, 3, 4, 5, 6; CSW; DLB 6, 212,
234, 278; TCWW 1, 2

Humphreys, Emyr Owen 1919- .... **CLC 47**
See also CA 5-8R; CANR 3, 24; CN 1, 2,
3, 4, 5, 6, 7; DLB 15

Humphreys, Josephine 1945- ..... **CLC 34, 57**
See also CA 121; 127; CANR 97; CSW;
DLB 292; INT CA-127

Huneker, James Gibbons
1860-1921 .... **TCLC 65**
See also CA 193; DLB 71; RGAL 4

Hungerford, Hesba Fay
See Brinsmead, H(esba) F(ay)

Hungerford, Pixie
See Brinsmead, H(esba) F(ay)

Hunt, E(verette) Howard, (Jr.)
1918- .... **CLC 3**
See also AITN 1; CA 45-48; CANR 2, 47,
103; CMW 4

Hunt, Francesca
See Holland, Isabelle (Christian)

Hunt, Howard
See Hunt, E(verette) Howard, (Jr.)

Hunt, Kyle
See Creasey, John

Hunt, (James Henry) Leigh
1784-1859 .... **NCLC 1, 70**
See also DAM POET; DLB 96, 110, 144;
RGEL 2; TEA

Hunt, Marsha 1946- .... **CLC 70**
See also BW 2, 3; CA 143; CANR 79

Hunt, Violet 1866(?)-1942 .... **TCLC 53**
See also CA 184; DLB 162, 197

Hunter, E. Waldo
See Sturgeon, Theodore (Hamilton)

Hunter, Evan 1926-2005 .... **CLC 11, 31**
See McBain, Ed
See also AAYA 39; BPFB 2; CA 5-8R; 241;
CANR 5, 38, 62, 97; CMW 4; CN 1, 2, 3,
4, 5, 6, 7; CPW; DAM POP; DLB 306;
DLBY 1982; INT CANR-5; MSW;
MTCW 1; SATA 25; SFW 4

Hunter, Kristin
See Lattany, Kristin (Elaine Eggleston)
Hunter
See also CN 1, 2, 3, 4, 5, 6

Hunter, Mary
See Austin, Mary (Hunter)

Hunter, Mollie 1922- .... **CLC 21**
See McIlwraith, Maureen Mollie Hunter
See also AAYA 13; BYA 6; CANR 37, 78;
CLR 25; DLB 161; JRDA; MAICYA 1,
2; SAAS 7; SATA 54, 106, 139; SATA-
Essay 139; WYA; YAW

Ivask, Ivar Vidrik 1927-1992 .... **CLC 14**
See also CA 37-40R; 139; CANR 24
Ives, Morgan
See Bradley, Marion Zimmer
See also GLL 1
Izumi Shikibu c. 973-c. 1034 .... **CMLC 33**
J. R. S.
See Gogarty, Oliver St. John
Jabran, Kahlil
See Gibran, Kahlil
Jabran, Khalil
See Gibran, Kahlil
Jackson, Daniel
See Wingrove, David (John)
Jackson, Helen Hunt 1830-1885 .... **NCLC 90**
See also DLB 42, 47, 186, 189; RGAL 4
Jackson, Jesse 1908-1983 .... **CLC 12**
See also BW 1; CA 25-28R; 109; CANR
27; CLR 28; CWRI 5; MAICYA 1, 2;
SATA 2, 29; SATA-Obit 48
Jackson, Laura (Riding) 1901-1991 .... **PC 44**
See Riding, Laura
See also CA 65-68; 135; CANR 28, 89;
DLB 48
Jackson, Sam
See Trumbo, Dalton
Jackson, Sara
See Wingrove, David (John)
Jackson, Shirley 1919-1965 . **CLC 11, 60, 87;
SSC 9, 39; WLC**
See also AAYA 9; AMWS 9; BPFB 2; CA
1-4R; 25-28R; CANR 4, 52; CDALB
1941-1968; DA; DA3; DAC; DAM MST;
DLB 6, 234; EXPS; HGG; LAIT 4; MAL
5; MTCW 2; MTFW 2005; RGAL 4;
RGSF 2; SATA 2; SSFS 1; SUFW 1, 2
Jacob, (Cyprien-)Max 1876-1944 .... **TCLC 6**
See also CA 104; 193; DLB 258; EWL 3;
GFL 1789 to the Present; GLL 2; RGWL
2, 3
Jacobs, Harriet A(nn)
1813(?)-1897 .... **NCLC 67, 162**
See also AFAW 1, 2; DLB 239; FL 1:3; FW;
LAIT 2; RGAL 4
Jacobs, Jim 1942- .... **CLC 12**
See also CA 97-100; INT CA-97-100
Jacobs, W(illiam) W(ymark)
1863-1943 .... **SSC 73; TCLC 22**
See also CA 121; 167; DLB 135; EXPS;
HGG; RGEL 2; RGSF 2; SSFS 2; SUFW
1
Jacobsen, Jens Peter 1847-1885 .... **NCLC 34**
Jacobsen, Josephine (Winder)
1908-2003 .... **CLC 48, 102; PC 62**
See also CA 33-36R; 218; CAAS 18; CANR
23, 48; CCA 1; CP 2, 3, 4, 5, 6, 7; DLB
244; PFS 23; TCLE 1:1
Jacobson, Dan 1929- .... **CLC 4, 14**
See also AFW; CA 1-4R; CANR 2, 25, 66;
CN 1, 2, 3, 4, 5, 6, 7; DLB 14, 207, 225,
319; EWL 3; MTCW 1; RGSF 2
Jacqueline
See Carpentier (y Valmont), Alejo
Jacques de Vitry c. 1160-1240 ...... **CMLC 63**
See also DLB 208
Jagger, Michael Philip
See Jagger, Mick
Jagger, Mick 1943- .... **CLC 17**
See also CA 239
Jahiz, al- c. 780-c. 869 .... **CMLC 25**
See also DLB 311
Jakes, John (William) 1932- .... **CLC 29**
See also AAYA 32; BEST 89:4; BPFB 2;
CA 57-60, 214; CAAE 214; CANR 10,
43, 66, 111, 142; CPW; CSW; DA3; DAM
NOV, POP; DLB 278; DLBY 1983;
FANT; INT CANR-10; MTCW 1, 2;
MTFW 2005; RHW; SATA 62; SFW 4;
TCWW 1, 2

James I 1394-1437 .... **LC 20**
See also RGEL 2
James, Andrew
See Kirkup, James
James, C(yril) L(ionel) R(obert)
1901-1989 .... **BLCS; CLC 33**
See also BW 2; CA 117; 125; 128; CANR
62; CN 1, 2, 3, 4; DLB 125; MTCW 1
James, Daniel (Lewis) 1911-1988
See Santiago, Danny
See also CA 174; 125
James, Dynely
See Mayne, William (James Carter)
James, Henry Sr. 1811-1882 .... **NCLC 53**
James, Henry 1843-1916 .... **SSC 8, 32, 47;
TCLC 2, 11, 24, 40, 47, 64, 171; WLC**
See also AMW; AMWC 1; AMWR 1; BPFB
2; BRW 6; CA 104; 132; CDALB 1865-
1917; DA; DA3; DAB; DAC; DAM MST,
NOV; DLB 12, 71, 74, 189; DLBD 13;
EWL 3; EXPS; GL 2; HGG; LAIT 2;
MAL 5; MTCW 1, 2; MTFW 2005; NFS
12, 16, 19; RGAL 4; RGEL 2; RGSF 2;
SSFS 9; SUFW 1; TUS
James, M. R.
See James, Montague (Rhodes)
See also DLB 156, 201
James, Montague (Rhodes)
1862-1936 .... **SSC 16; TCLC 6**
See James, M. R.
See also CA 104; 203; HGG; RGEL 2;
RGSF 2; SUFW 1
James, P. D. .... **CLC 18, 46, 122**
See White, Phyllis Dorothy James
See also BEST 90:2; BPFB 2; BRWS 4;
CDBLB 1960 to Present; CN 4, 5, 6; DLB
87, 276; DLBD 17; MSW
James, Philip
See Moorcock, Michael (John)
James, Samuel
See Stephens, James
James, Seumas
See Stephens, James
James, Stephen
See Stephens, James
James, William 1842-1910 .... **TCLC 15, 32**
See also AMW; CA 109; 193; DLB 270,
284; MAL 5; NCFS 5; RGAL 4
Jameson, Anna 1794-1860 .... **NCLC 43**
See also DLB 99, 166
Jameson, Fredric (R.) 1934- .... **CLC 142**
See also CA 196; DLB 67; LMFS 2
James VI of Scotland 1566-1625 .... **LC 109**
See also DLB 151, 172
Jami, Nur al-Din 'Abd al-Rahman
1414-1492 .... **LC 9**
Jammes, Francis 1868-1938 .... **TCLC 75**
See also CA 198; EWL 3; GFL 1789 to the
Present
Jandl, Ernst 1925-2000 .... **CLC 34**
See also CA 200; EWL 3
Janowitz, Tama 1957- .... **CLC 43, 145**
See also CA 106; CANR 52, 89, 129; CN
5, 6, 7; CPW; DAM POP; DLB 292;
MTFW 2005
Japrisot, Sebastien 1931- .... **CLC 90**
See Rossi, Jean-Baptiste
See also CMW 4; NFS 18
Jarrell, Randall 1914-1965 .... **CLC 1, 2, 6, 9,
13, 49; PC 41**
See also AMW; BYA 5; CA 5-8R; 25-28R;
CABS 2; CANR 6, 34; CDALB 1941-
1968; CLR 6; CWRI 5; DAM POET;
DLB 48, 52; EWL 3; EXPP; MAICYA 1,
2; MAL 5; MTCW 1, 2; PAB; PFS 2;
RGAL 4; SATA 7

Jarry, Alfred 1873-1907 .... **SSC 20; TCLC 2,
14, 147**
See also CA 104; 153; DA3; DAM DRAM;
DFS 8; DLB 192, 258; EW 9; EWL 3;
GFL 1789 to the Present; RGWL 2, 3;
TWA
Jarvis, E. K.
See Ellison, Harlan (Jay)
Jawien, Andrzej
See John Paul II, Pope
Jaynes, Roderick
See Coen, Ethan
Jeake, Samuel, Jr.
See Aiken, Conrad (Potter)
Jean Paul 1763-1825 .... **NCLC 7**
Jefferies, (John) Richard
1848-1887 .... **NCLC 47**
See also DLB 98, 141; RGEL 2; SATA 16;
SFW 4
Jeffers, (John) Robinson 1887-1962 .. **CLC 2,
3, 11, 15, 54; PC 17; WLC**
See also AMWS 2; CA 85-88; CANR 35;
CDALB 1917-1929; DA; DAC; DAM
MST, POET; DLB 45, 212; EWL 3; MAL
5; MTCW 1, 2; MTFW 2005; PAB; PFS
3, 4; RGAL 4
Jefferson, Janet
See Mencken, H(enry) L(ouis)
Jefferson, Thomas 1743-1826 . **NCLC 11, 103**
See also AAYA 54; ANW; CDALB 1640-
1865; DA3; DLB 31, 183; LAIT 1; RGAL
4
Jeffrey, Francis 1773-1850 .... **NCLC 33**
See Francis, Lord Jeffrey
Jelakowitch, Ivan
See Heijermans, Herman
Jelinek, Elfriede 1946- .... **CLC 169**
See also AAYA 68; CA 154; DLB 85; FW
Jellicoe, (Patricia) Ann 1927- .... **CLC 27**
See also CA 85-88; CBD; CD 5, 6; CWD;
CWRI 5; DLB 13, 233; FW
Jelloun, Tahar ben 1944- .... **CLC 180**
See Ben Jelloun, Tahar
See also CA 162; CANR 100
Jemyma
See Holley, Marietta
Jen, Gish .... **AAL; CLC 70, 198**
See Jen, Lillian
See also AMWC 2; CN 7; DLB 312
Jen, Lillian 1955-
See Jen, Gish
See also CA 135; CANR 89, 130
Jenkins, (John) Robin 1912- .... **CLC 52**
See also CA 1-4R; CANR 1, 135; CN 1, 2,
3, 4, 5, 6, 7; DLB 14, 271
Jennings, Elizabeth (Joan)
1926-2001 .... **CLC 5, 14, 131**
See also BRWS 5; CA 61-64; 200; CAAS
5; CANR 8, 39, 66, 127; CP 1, 2, 3, 4, 5,
6, 7; CWP; DLB 27; EWL 3; MTCW 1;
SATA 66
Jennings, Waylon 1937-2002 .... **CLC 21**
Jensen, Johannes V(ilhelm)
1873-1950 .... **TCLC 41**
See also CA 170; DLB 214; EWL 3; RGWL
3
Jensen, Laura (Linnea) 1948- .... **CLC 37**
See also CA 103
Jerome, Saint 345-420 .... **CMLC 30**
See also RGWL 3
Jerome, Jerome K(lapka)
1859-1927 .... **TCLC 23**
See also CA 119; 177; DLB 10, 34, 135;
RGEL 2
Jerrold, Douglas William
1803-1857 .... **NCLC 2**
See also DLB 158, 159; RGEL 2

Jordan, June (Meyer)
1936-2002 .. **BLCS; CLC 5, 11, 23, 114; PC 38**
See also AAYA 2, 66; AFAW 1, 2; BW 2, 3; CA 33-36R; 206; CANR 25, 70, 114; CLR 10; CP 3, 4, 5, 6, 7; CWP; DAM MULT, POET; DLB 38; GLL 2; LAIT 5; MAICYA 1, 2; MTCW 1; SATA 4, 136; YAW

Jordan, Neil (Patrick) 1950- .... **CLC 110**
See also CA 124; 130; CANR 54; CN 4, 5, 6, 7; GLL 2; INT CA-130

Jordan, Pat(rick M.) 1941- .... **CLC 37**
See also CA 33-36R; CANR 121

Jorgensen, Ivar
See Ellison, Harlan (Jay)

Jorgenson, Ivar
See Silverberg, Robert

Joseph, George Ghevarughese .... **CLC 70**

Josephson, Mary
See O'Doherty, Brian

Josephus, Flavius c. 37-100 .... **CMLC 13**
See also AW 2; DLB 176

Josiah Allen's Wife
See Holley, Marietta

Josipovici, Gabriel (David) 1940- ...... **CLC 6, 43, 153**
See also CA 37-40R, 224; CAAE 224; CAAS 8; CANR 47, 84; CN 3, 4, 5, 6, 7; DLB 14, 319

Joubert, Joseph 1754-1824 .... **NCLC 9**

Jouve, Pierre Jean 1887-1976 .... **CLC 47**
See also CA 65-68; DLB 258; EWL 3

Jovine, Francesco 1902-1950 .... **TCLC 79**
See also DLB 264; EWL 3

Joyce, James (Augustine Aloysius)
1882-1941 .... **DC 16; PC 22; SSC 3, 26, 44, 64; TCLC 3, 8, 16, 35, 52, 159; WLC**
See also AAYA 42; BRW 7; BRWC 1; BRWR 1; BYA 11, 13; CA 104; 126; CD-BLB 1914-1945; DA; DA3; DAB; DAC; DAM MST, NOV, POET; DLB 10, 19, 36, 162, 247; EWL 3; EXPN; EXPS; LAIT 3; LMFS 1, 2; MTCW 1, 2; MTFW 2005; NFS 7; RGSF 2; SSFS 1, 19; TEA; WLIT 4

Jozsef, Attila 1905-1937 .... **TCLC 22**
See also CA 116; 230; CDWLB 4; DLB 215; EWL 3

Juana Ines de la Cruz, Sor
1651(?)-1695 ...... **HLCS 1; LC 5; PC 24**
See also DLB 305; FW; LAW; RGWL 2, 3; WLIT 1

Juana Inez de La Cruz, Sor
See Juana Ines de la Cruz, Sor

Judd, Cyril
See Kornbluth, C(yril) M.; Pohl, Frederik

Juenger, Ernst 1895-1998 .... **CLC 125**
See Junger, Ernst
See also CA 101; 167; CANR 21, 47, 106; DLB 56

Julian of Norwich 1342(?)-1416(?) . **LC 6, 52**
See also DLB 146; LMFS 1

Julius Caesar 100B.C.-44B.C.
See Caesar, Julius
See also CDWLB 1; DLB 211

Junger, Ernst
See Juenger, Ernst
See also CDWLB 2; EWL 3; RGWL 2, 3

Junger, Sebastian 1962- .... **CLC 109**
See also AAYA 28; CA 165; CANR 130; MTFW 2005

Juniper, Alex
See Hospital, Janette Turner

Junius
See Luxemburg, Rosa

Junzaburo, Nishiwaki
See Nishiwaki, Junzaburo
See also EWL 3

Just, Ward (Swift) 1935- .... **CLC 4, 27**
See also CA 25-28R; CANR 32, 87; CN 6, 7; INT CANR-32

Justice, Donald (Rodney)
1925-2004 .... **CLC 6, 19, 102; PC 64**
See also AMWS 7; CA 5-8R; 230; CANR 26, 54, 74, 121, 122; CP 1, 2, 3, 4, 5, 6, 7; CSW; DAM POET; DLBY 1983; EWL 3; INT CANR-26; MAL 5; MTCW 2; PFS 14; TCLE 1:1

Juvenal c. 60-c. 130 .... **CMLC 8**
See also AW 2; CDWLB 1; DLB 211; RGWL 2, 3

Juvenis
See Bourne, Randolph S(illiman)

K., Alice
See Knapp, Caroline

Kabakov, Sasha .... **CLC 59**

Kabir 1398(?)-1448(?) .... **LC 109; PC 56**
See also RGWL 2, 3

Kacew, Romain 1914-1980
See Gary, Romain
See also CA 108; 102

Kadare, Ismail 1936- .... **CLC 52, 190**
See also CA 161; EWL 3; RGWL 3

Kadohata, Cynthia (Lynn)
1956(?)- .... **CLC 59, 122**
See also CA 140; CANR 124; SATA 155

Kafka, Franz 1883-1924 ... **SSC 5, 29, 35, 60; TCLC 2, 6, 13, 29, 47, 53, 112; WLC**
See also AAYA 31; BPFB 2; CA 105; 126; CDWLB 2; DA; DA3; DAB; DAC; DAM MST, NOV; DLB 81; EW 9; EWL 3; EXPS; LATS 1:1; LMFS 2; MTCW 1, 2; MTFW 2005; NFS 7; RGSF 2; RGWL 2, 3; SFW 4; SSFS 3, 7, 12; TWA

Kahanovitsch, Pinkhes
See Der Nister

Kahn, Roger 1927- .... **CLC 30**
See also CA 25-28R; CANR 44, 69; DLB 171; SATA 37

Kain, Saul
See Sassoon, Siegfried (Lorraine)

Kaiser, Georg 1878-1945 .... **TCLC 9**
See also CA 106; 190; CDWLB 2; DLB 124; EWL 3; LMFS 2; RGWL 2, 3

Kaledin, Sergei .... **CLC 59**

Kaletski, Alexander 1946- .... **CLC 39**
See also CA 118; 143

Kalidasa fl. c. 400-455 .... **CMLC 9; PC 22**
See also RGWL 2, 3

Kallman, Chester (Simon)
1921-1975 .... **CLC 2**
See also CA 45-48; 53-56; CANR 3; CP 1, 2

Kaminsky, Melvin 1926-
See Brooks, Mel
See also CA 65-68; CANR 16; DFS 21

Kaminsky, Stuart M(elvin) 1934- ..... **CLC 59**
See also CA 73-76; CANR 29, 53, 89; CMW 4

Kamo no Chomei 1153(?)-1216 .... **CMLC 66**
See also DLB 203

Kamo no Nagaakira
See Kamo no Chomei

Kandinsky, Wassily 1866-1944 .... **TCLC 92**
See also AAYA 64; CA 118; 155

Kane, Francis
See Robbins, Harold

Kane, Henry 1918-
See Queen, Ellery
See also CA 156; CMW 4

Kane, Paul
See Simon, Paul (Frederick)

Kanin, Garson 1912-1999 .... **CLC 22**
See also AITN 1; CA 5-8R; 177; CAD; CANR 7, 78; DLB 7; IDFW 3, 4

Kaniuk, Yoram 1930- .... **CLC 19**
See also CA 134; DLB 299

Kant, Immanuel 1724-1804 ..... **NCLC 27, 67**
See also DLB 94

Kantor, MacKinlay 1904-1977 .... **CLC 7**
See also CA 61-64; 73-76; CANR 60, 63; CN 1, 2; DLB 9, 102; MAL 5; MTCW 2; RHW; TCWW 1, 2

Kanze Motokiyo
See Zeami

Kaplan, David Michael 1946- .... **CLC 50**
See also CA 187

Kaplan, James 1951- .... **CLC 59**
See also CA 135; CANR 121

Karadzic, Vuk Stefanovic
1787-1864 .... **NCLC 115**
See also CDWLB 4; DLB 147

Karageorge, Michael
See Anderson, Poul (William)

Karamzin, Nikolai Mikhailovich
1766-1826 .... **NCLC 3**
See also DLB 150; RGSF 2

Karapanou, Margarita 1946- .... **CLC 13**
See also CA 101

Karinthy, Frigyes 1887-1938 .... **TCLC 47**
See also CA 170; DLB 215; EWL 3

Karl, Frederick R(obert)
1927-2004 .... **CLC 34**
See also CA 5-8R; 226; CANR 3, 44, 143

Karr, Mary 1955- .... **CLC 188**
See also AMWS 11; CA 151; CANR 100; MTFW 2005; NCFS 5

Kastel, Warren
See Silverberg, Robert

Kataev, Evgeny Petrovich 1903-1942
See Petrov, Evgeny
See also CA 120

Kataphusin
See Ruskin, John

Katz, Steve 1935- .... **CLC 47**
See also CA 25-28R; CAAS 14, 64; CANR 12; CN 4, 5, 6, 7; DLBY 1983

Kauffman, Janet 1945- .... **CLC 42**
See also CA 117; CANR 43, 84; DLB 218; DLBY 1986

Kaufman, Bob (Garnell) 1925-1986 . **CLC 49**
See also BG 1:3; BW 1; CA 41-44R; 118; CANR 22; CP 1; DLB 16, 41

Kaufman, George S. 1889-1961 ...... **CLC 38; DC 17**
See also CA 108; 93-96; DAM DRAM; DFS 1, 10; DLB 7; INT CA-108; MTCW 2; MTFW 2005; RGAL 4; TUS

Kaufman, Moises 1964- .... **DC 26**
See also CA 211; DFS 22; MTFW 2005

Kaufman, Sue .... **CLC 3, 8**
See Barondess, Sue K(aufman)

Kavafis, Konstantinos Petrou 1863-1933
See Cavafy, C(onstantine) P(eter)
See also CA 104

Kavan, Anna 1901-1968 .... **CLC 5, 13, 82**
See also BRWS 7; CA 5-8R; CANR 6, 57; DLB 255; MTCW 1; RGEL 2; SFW 4

Kavanagh, Dan
See Barnes, Julian (Patrick)

Kavanagh, Julie 1952- .... **CLC 119**
See also CA 163

Kavanagh, Patrick (Joseph)
1904-1967 .... **CLC 22; PC 33**
See also BRWS 7; CA 123; 25-28R; DLB 15, 20; EWL 3; MTCW 1; RGEL 2

Keynes, John Maynard
1883-1946 .... **TCLC 64**
See also CA 114; 162, 163; DLBD 10;
MTCW 2; MTFW 2005

Khanshendel, Chiron
See Rose, Wendy

Khayyam, Omar 1048-1131 ... **CMLC 11; PC 8**
See Omar Khayyam
See also DA3; DAM POET; WLIT 6

Kherdian, David 1931- .... **CLC 6, 9**
See also AAYA 42; CA 21-24R, 192; CAAE 192; CAAS 2; CANR 39, 78; CLR 24; JRDA; LAIT 3; MAICYA 1, 2; SATA 16, 74; SATA-Essay 125

Khlebnikov, Velimir .... **TCLC 20**
See Khlebnikov, Viktor Vladimirovich
See also DLB 295; EW 10; EWL 3; RGWL 2, 3

Khlebnikov, Viktor Vladimirovich 1885-1922
See Khlebnikov, Velimir
See also CA 117; 217

Khodasevich, Vladislav (Felitsianovich)
1886-1939 .... **TCLC 15**
See also CA 115; DLB 317; EWL 3

Kielland, Alexander Lange
1849-1906 .... **TCLC 5**
See also CA 104

Kiely, Benedict 1919- ... **CLC 23, 43; SSC 58**
See also CA 1-4R; CANR 2, 84; CN 1, 2, 3, 4, 5, 6, 7; DLB 15, 319; TCLE 1:1

Kienzle, William X(avier)
1928-2001 .... **CLC 25**
See also CA 93-96; 203; CAAS 1; CANR 9, 31, 59, 111; CMW 4; DA3; DAM POP; INT CANR-31; MSW; MTCW 1, 2; MTFW 2005

Kierkegaard, Soren 1813-1855 ..... **NCLC 34, 78, 125**
See also DLB 300; EW 6; LMFS 2; RGWL 3; TWA

Kieslowski, Krzysztof 1941-1996 .... **CLC 120**
See also CA 147; 151

Killens, John Oliver 1916-1987 .... **CLC 10**
See also BW 2; CA 77-80; 123; CAAS 2; CANR 26; CN 1, 2, 3, 4; DLB 33; EWL 3

Killigrew, Anne 1660-1685 .... **LC 4, 73**
See also DLB 131

Killigrew, Thomas 1612-1683 .... **LC 57**
See also DLB 58; RGEL 2

Kim
See Simenon, Georges (Jacques Christian)

Kincaid, Jamaica 1949- ...... **BLC 2; CLC 43, 68, 137; SSC 72**
See also AAYA 13, 56; AFAW 2; AMWS 7; BRWS 7; BW 2, 3; CA 125; CANR 47, 59, 95, 133; CDALBS; CDWLB 3; CLR 63; CN 4, 5, 6, 7; DA3; DAM MULT, NOV; DLB 157, 227; DNFS 1; EWL 3; EXPS; FW; LATS 1:2; LMFS 2; MAL 5; MTCW 2; MTFW 2005; NCFS 1; NFS 3; SSFS 5, 7; TUS; WWE 1; YAW

King, Francis (Henry) 1923- .... **CLC 8, 53, 145**
See also CA 1-4R; CANR 1, 33, 86; CN 1, 2, 3, 4, 5, 6, 7; DAM NOV; DLB 15, 139; MTCW 1

King, Kennedy
See Brown, George Douglas

King, Martin Luther, Jr. 1929-1968 . **BLC 2; CLC 83; WLCS**
See also BW 2, 3; CA 25-28; CANR 27, 44; CAP 2; DA; DA3; DAB; DAC; DAM MST, MULT; LAIT 5; LATS 1:2; MTCW 1, 2; MTFW 2005; SATA 14

King, Stephen 1947- .... **CLC 12, 26, 37, 61, 113; SSC 17, 55**
See also AAYA 1, 17; AMWS 5; BEST 90:1; BPFB 2; CA 61-64; CANR 1, 30, 52, 76, 119, 134; CN 7; CPW; DA3; DAM NOV, POP; DLB 143; HGG; JRDA; LAIT 5; MTCW 1, 2; MTFW 2005; RGAL 4; SATA 9, 55, 161; SUFW 1, 2; WYAS 1; YAW

King, Stephen Edwin
See King, Stephen

King, Steve
See King, Stephen

King, Thomas 1943- .... **CLC 89, 171; NNAL**
See also CA 144; CANR 95; CCA 1; CN 6, 7; DAC; DAM MULT; DLB 175; SATA 96

Kingman, Lee .... **CLC 17**
See Natti, (Mary) Lee
See also CWRI 5; SAAS 3; SATA 1, 67

Kingsley, Charles 1819-1875 .... **NCLC 35**
See also CLR 77; DLB 21, 32, 163, 178, 190; FANT; MAICYA 2; MAICYAS 1; RGEL 2; WCH; YABC 2

Kingsley, Henry 1830-1876 .... **NCLC 107**
See also DLB 21, 230; RGEL 2

Kingsley, Sidney 1906-1995 .... **CLC 44**
See also CA 85-88; 147; CAD; DFS 14, 19; DLB 7; MAL 5; RGAL 4

Kingsolver, Barbara 1955- .... **CLC 55, 81, 130, 216**
See also AAYA 15; AMWS 7; CA 129; 134; CANR 60, 96, 133; CDALBS; CN 7; CPW; CSW; DA3; DAM POP; DLB 206; INT CA-134; LAIT 5; MTCW 2; MTFW 2005; NFS 5, 10, 12; RGAL 4; TCLE 1:1

Kingston, Maxine (Ting Ting) Hong
1940- .... **AAL; CLC 12, 19, 58, 121; WLCS**
See also AAYA 8, 55; AMWS 5; BPFB 2; CA 69-72; CANR 13, 38, 74, 87, 128; CDALBS; CN 6, 7; DA3; DAM MULT, NOV; DLB 173, 212, 312; DLBY 1980; EWL 3; FL 1:6; FW; INT CANR-13; LAIT 5; MAL 5; MAWW; MTCW 1, 2; MTFW 2005; NFS 6; RGAL 4; SATA 53; SSFS 3; TCWW 2

Kinnell, Galway 1927- ..... **CLC 1, 2, 3, 5, 13, 29, 129; PC 26**
See also AMWS 3; CA 9-12R; CANR 10, 34, 66, 116, 138; CP 1, 2, 3, 4, 5, 6, 7; DLB 5; DLBY 1987; EWL 3; INT CANR-34; MAL 5; MTCW 1, 2; MTFW 2005; PAB; PFS 9; RGAL 4; TCLE 1:1; WP

Kinsella, Thomas 1928- .... **CLC 4, 19, 138; PC 69**
See also BRWS 5; CA 17-20R; CANR 15, 122; CP 1, 2, 3, 4, 5, 6, 7; DLB 27; EWL 3; MTCW 1, 2; MTFW 2005; RGEL 2; TEA

Kinsella, W(illiam) P(atrick) 1935- . **CLC 27, 43, 166**
See also AAYA 7, 60; BPFB 2; CA 97-100; 222; CAAE 222; CAAS 7; CANR 21, 35, 66, 75, 129; CN 4, 5, 6, 7; CPW; DAC; DAM NOV, POP; FANT; INT CANR-21; LAIT 5; MTCW 1, 2; MTFW 2005; NFS 15; RGSF 2

Kinsey, Alfred C(harles)
1894-1956 .... **TCLC 91**
See also CA 115; 170; MTCW 2

Kipling, (Joseph) Rudyard 1865-1936 . **PC 3; SSC 5, 54; TCLC 8, 17, 167; WLC**
See also AAYA 32; BRW 6; BRWC 1, 2; BYA 4; CA 105; 120; CANR 33; CDBLB 1890-1914; CLR 39, 65; CWRI 5; DA; DA3; DAB; DAC; DAM MST, POET; DLB 19, 34, 141, 156; EWL 3; EXPS; FANT; LAIT 3; LMFS 1; MAICYA 1, 2;

MTCW 1, 2; MTFW 2005; NFS 21; PFS 22; RGEL 2; RGSF 2; SATA 100; SFW 4; SSFS 8, 21; SUFW 1; TEA; WCH; WLIT 4; YABC 2

Kircher, Athanasius 1602-1680 .... **LC 121**
See also DLB 164

Kirk, Russell (Amos) 1918-1994 .. **TCLC 119**
See also AITN 1; CA 1-4R; 145; CAAS 9; CANR 1, 20, 60; HGG; INT CANR-20; MTCW 1, 2

Kirkham, Dinah
See Card, Orson Scott

Kirkland, Caroline M. 1801-1864 . **NCLC 85**
See also DLB 3, 73, 74, 250, 254; DLBD 13

Kirkup, James 1918- .... **CLC 1**
See also CA 1-4R; CAAS 4; CANR 2; CP 1, 2, 3, 4, 5, 6, 7; DLB 27; SATA 12

Kirkwood, James 1930(?)-1989 .... **CLC 9**
See also AITN 2; CA 1-4R; 128; CANR 6, 40; GLL 2

Kirsch, Sarah 1935- .... **CLC 176**
See also CA 178; CWW 2; DLB 75; EWL 3

Kirshner, Sidney
See Kingsley, Sidney

Kis, Danilo 1935-1989 .... **CLC 57**
See also CA 109; 118; 129; CANR 61; CDWLB 4; DLB 181; EWL 3; MTCW 1; RGSF 2; RGWL 2, 3

Kissinger, Henry A(lfred) 1923- ..... **CLC 137**
See also CA 1-4R; CANR 2, 33, 66, 109; MTCW 1

Kivi, Aleksis 1834-1872 .... **NCLC 30**

Kizer, Carolyn (Ashley) 1925- ... **CLC 15, 39, 80; PC 66**
See also CA 65-68; CAAS 5; CANR 24, 70, 134; CP 1, 2, 3, 4, 5, 6, 7; CWP; DAM POET; DLB 5, 169; EWL 3; MAL 5; MTCW 2; MTFW 2005; PFS 18; TCLE 1:1

Klabund 1890-1928 .... **TCLC 44**
See also CA 162; DLB 66

Klappert, Peter 1942- .... **CLC 57**
See also CA 33-36R; CSW; DLB 5

Klein, A(braham) M(oses)
1909-1972 .... **CLC 19**
See also CA 101; 37-40R; CP 1; DAB; DAC; DAM MST; DLB 68; EWL 3; RGEL 2

Klein, Joe
See Klein, Joseph

Klein, Joseph 1946- .... **CLC 154**
See also CA 85-88; CANR 55

Klein, Norma 1938-1989 .... **CLC 30**
See also AAYA 2, 35; BPFB 2; BYA 6, 7, 8; CA 41-44R; 128; CANR 15, 37; CLR 2, 19; INT CANR-15; JRDA; MAICYA 1, 2; SAAS 1; SATA 7, 57; WYA; YAW

Klein, T(heodore) E(ibon) D(onald)
1947- .... **CLC 34**
See also CA 119; CANR 44, 75; HGG

Kleist, Heinrich von 1777-1811 ...... **NCLC 2, 37; SSC 22**
See also CDWLB 2; DAM DRAM; DLB 90; EW 5; RGSF 2; RGWL 2, 3

Klima, Ivan 1931- .... **CLC 56, 172**
See also CA 25-28R; CANR 17, 50, 91; CDWLB 4; CWW 2; DAM NOV; DLB 232; EWL 3; RGWL 3

Klimentev, Andrei Platonovich
See Klimentov, Andrei Platonovich

Klimentov, Andrei Platonovich
1899-1951 .... **SSC 42; TCLC 14**
See Platonov, Andrei Platonovich; Platonov, Andrey Platonovich
See also CA 108; 232

Kubrick, Stanley 1928-1999 .... **CLC 16;**
TCLC 112
See also AAYA 30; CA 81-84; 177; CANR
33; DLB 26

Kumin, Maxine (Winokur) 1925- ..... **CLC 5,**
13, 28, 164; PC 15
See also AITN 2; AMWS 4; ANW; CA
1-4R; CAAS 8; CANR 1, 21, 69, 115,
140; CP 2, 3, 4, 5, 6, 7; CWP; DA3; DAM
POET; DLB 5; EWL 3; EXPP; MTCW 1,
2; MTFW 2005; PAB; PFS 18; SATA 12

Kundera, Milan 1929- . **CLC 4, 9, 19, 32, 68,**
115, 135; SSC 24
See also AAYA 2, 62; BPFB 2; CA 85-88;
CANR 19, 52, 74, 144; CDWLB 4; CWW
2; DA3; DAM NOV; DLB 232; EW 13;
EWL 3; MTCW 1, 2; MTFW 2005; NFS
18; RGSF 2; RGWL 3; SSFS 10

Kunene, Mazisi (Raymond) 1930- ... **CLC 85**
See also BW 1, 3; CA 125; CANR 81; CP
1, 7; DLB 117

Kung, Hans .... **CLC 130**
See Kung, Hans

Kung, Hans 1928-
See Kung, Hans
See also CA 53-56; CANR 66, 134; MTCW
1, 2; MTFW 2005

Kunikida Doppo 1869(?)-1908
See Doppo, Kunikida
See also DLB 180; EWL 3

Kunitz, Stanley (Jasspon) 1905- .. **CLC 6, 11,**
14, 148; PC 19
See also AMWS 3; CA 41-44R; CANR 26,
57, 98; CP 1, 2, 3, 4, 5, 6, 7; DA3; DLB
48; INT CANR-26; MAL 5; MTCW 1, 2;
MTFW 2005; PFS 11; RGAL 4

Kunze, Reiner 1933- .... **CLC 10**
See also CA 93-96; CWW 2; DLB 75; EWL
3

Kuprin, Aleksander Ivanovich
1870-1938 .... **TCLC 5**
See Kuprin, Aleksandr Ivanovich; Kuprin,
Alexandr Ivanovich
See also CA 104; 182

Kuprin, Aleksandr Ivanovich
See Kuprin, Aleksander Ivanovich
See also DLB 295

Kuprin, Alexandr Ivanovich
See Kuprin, Aleksander Ivanovich
See also EWL 3

Kureishi, Hanif 1954- .. **CLC 64, 135; DC 26**
See also BRWS 11; CA 139; CANR 113;
CBD; CD 5, 6; CN 6, 7; DLB 194, 245;
GLL 2; IDFW 4; WLIT 4; WWE 1

Kurosawa, Akira 1910-1998 ..... **CLC 16, 119**
See also AAYA 11, 64; CA 101; 170; CANR
46; DAM MULT

Kushner, Tony 1956- .... **CLC 81, 203; DC 10**
See also AAYA 61; AMWS 9; CA 144;
CAD; CANR 74, 130; CD 5, 6; DA3;
DAM DRAM; DFS 5; DLB 228; EWL 3;
GLL 1; LAIT 5; MAL 5; MTCW 2;
MTFW 2005; RGAL 4; SATA 160

Kuttner, Henry 1915-1958 .... **TCLC 10**
See also CA 107; 157; DLB 8; FANT;
SCFW 1, 2; SFW 4

Kutty, Madhavi
See Das, Kamala

Kuzma, Greg 1944- .... **CLC 7**
See also CA 33-36R; CANR 70

Kuzmin, Mikhail (Alekseevich)
1872(?)-1936 .... **TCLC 40**
See also CA 170; DLB 295; EWL 3

Kyd, Thomas 1558-1594 .... **DC 3; LC 22**
See also BRW 1; DAM DRAM; DFS 21;
DLB 62; IDTP; LMFS 1; RGEL 2; TEA;
WLIT 3

Kyprianos, Iossif
See Samarakis, Antonis

L. S.
See Stephen, Sir Leslie

La₃amon
See Layamon
See also DLB 146

Labe, Louise 1521-1566 .... **LC 120**

Labrunie, Gerard
See Nerval, Gerard de

La Bruyere, Jean de 1645-1696 .... **LC 17**
See also DLB 268; EW 3; GFL Beginnings
to 1789

Lacan, Jacques (Marie Emile)
1901-1981 .... **CLC 75**
See also CA 121; 104; DLB 296; EWL 3;
TWA

Laclos, Pierre-Ambroise Francois
1741-1803 .... **NCLC 4, 87**
See also DLB 313; EW 4; GFL Beginnings
to 1789; RGWL 2, 3

Lacolere, Francois
See Aragon, Louis

La Colere, Francois
See Aragon, Louis

La Deshabilleuse
See Simenon, Georges (Jacques Christian)

Lady Gregory
See Gregory, Lady Isabella Augusta (Persse)

Lady of Quality, A
See Bagnold, Enid

La Fayette, Marie-(Madelaine Pioche de la
Vergne) 1634-1693 .... **LC 2**
See Lafayette, Marie-Madeleine
See also GFL Beginnings to 1789; RGWL
2, 3

Lafayette, Marie-Madeleine
See La Fayette, Marie-(Madelaine Pioche
de la Vergne)
See also DLB 268

Lafayette, Rene
See Hubbard, L(afayette) Ron(ald)

La Flesche, Francis 1857(?)-1932 ...... **NNAL**
See also CA 144; CANR 83; DLB 175

La Fontaine, Jean de 1621-1695 .... **LC 50**
See also DLB 268; EW 3; GFL Beginnings
to 1789; MAICYA 1, 2; RGWL 2, 3;
SATA 18

Laforgue, Jules 1860-1887 . **NCLC 5, 53; PC**
14; SSC 20
See also DLB 217; EW 7; GFL 1789 to the
Present; RGWL 2, 3

Lagerkvist, Paer (Fabian)
1891-1974 ..... **CLC 7, 10, 13, 54; TCLC**
144
See Lagerkvist, Par
See also CA 85-88; 49-52; DA3; DAM
DRAM, NOV; MTCW 1, 2; MTFW 2005;
TWA

Lagerkvist, Par .... **SSC 12**
See Lagerkvist, Paer (Fabian)
See also DLB 259; EW 10; EWL 3; RGSF
2; RGWL 2, 3

Lagerloef, Selma (Ottiliana Lovisa)
.... **TCLC 4, 36**
See Lagerlof, Selma (Ottiliana Lovisa)
See also CA 108; MTCW 2

Lagerlof, Selma (Ottiliana Lovisa)
1858-1940
See Lagerloef, Selma (Ottiliana Lovisa)
See also CA 188; CLR 7; DLB 259; RGWL
2, 3; SATA 15; SSFS 18

La Guma, (Justin) Alex(ander)
1925-1985 . **BLCS; CLC 19; TCLC 140**
See also AFW; BW 1, 3; CA 49-52; 118;
CANR 25, 81; CDWLB 3; CN 1, 2, 3;
CP 1; DAM NOV; DLB 117, 225; EWL
3; MTCW 1, 2; MTFW 2005; WLIT 2;
WWE 1

Laidlaw, A. K.
See Grieve, C(hristopher) M(urray)

Lainez, Manuel Mujica
See Mujica Lainez, Manuel
See also HW 1

Laing, R(onald) D(avid) 1927-1989 . **CLC 95**
See also CA 107; 129; CANR 34; MTCW 1

Laishley, Alex
See Booth, Martin

Lamartine, Alphonse (Marie Louis Prat) de
1790-1869 .... **NCLC 11; PC 16**
See also DAM POET; DLB 217; GFL 1789
to the Present; RGWL 2, 3

Lamb, Charles 1775-1834 ..... **NCLC 10, 113;**
WLC
See also BRW 4; CDBLB 1789-1832; DA;
DAB; DAC; DAM MST; DLB 93, 107,
163; RGEL 2; SATA 17; TEA

Lamb, Lady Caroline 1785-1828 ... **NCLC 38**
See also DLB 116

Lamb, Mary Ann 1764-1847 .... **NCLC 125**
See also DLB 163; SATA 17

Lame Deer 1903(?)-1976 .... **NNAL**
See also CA 69-72

Lamming, George (William) 1927- ... **BLC 2;**
CLC 2, 4, 66, 144
See also BW 2, 3; CA 85-88; CANR 26,
76; CDWLB 3; CN 1, 2, 3, 4, 5, 6, 7; CP
1; DAM MULT; DLB 125; EWL 3;
MTCW 1, 2; MTFW 2005; NFS 15;
RGEL 2

L'Amour, Louis (Dearborn)
1908-1988 .... **CLC 25, 55**
See also AAYA 16; AITN 2; BEST 89:2;
BPFB 2; CA 1-4R; 125; CANR 3, 25, 40;
CPW; DA3; DAM NOV, POP; DLB 206;
DLBY 1980; MTCW 1, 2; MTFW 2005;
RGAL 4; TCWW 1, 2

Lampedusa, Giuseppe (Tomasi) di
.... **TCLC 13**
See Tomasi di Lampedusa, Giuseppe
See also CA 164; EW 11; MTCW 2; MTFW
2005; RGWL 2, 3

Lampman, Archibald 1861-1899 ... **NCLC 25**
See also DLB 92; RGEL 2; TWA

Lancaster, Bruce 1896-1963 .... **CLC 36**
See also CA 9-10; CANR 70; CAP 1; SATA
9

Lanchester, John 1962- .... **CLC 99**
See also CA 194; DLB 267

Landau, Mark Alexandrovich
See Aldanov, Mark (Alexandrovich)

Landau-Aldanov, Mark Alexandrovich
See Aldanov, Mark (Alexandrovich)

Landis, Jerry
See Simon, Paul (Frederick)

Landis, John 1950- .... **CLC 26**
See also CA 112; 122; CANR 128

Landolfi, Tommaso 1908-1979 .... **CLC 11, 49**
See also CA 127; 117; DLB 177; EWL 3

Landon, Letitia Elizabeth
1802-1838 .... **NCLC 15**
See also DLB 96

Landor, Walter Savage
1775-1864 .... **NCLC 14**
See also BRW 4; DLB 93, 107; RGEL 2

Landwirth, Heinz 1927-
See Lind, Jakov
See also CA 9-12R; CANR 7

Lane, Patrick 1939- .... **CLC 25**
See also CA 97-100; CANR 54; CP 3, 4, 5,
6, 7; DAM POET; DLB 53; INT CA-97-
100

Lang, Andrew 1844-1912 .... **TCLC 16**
See also CA 114; 137; CANR 85; CLR 101;
DLB 98, 141, 184; FANT; MAICYA 1, 2;
RGEL 2; SATA 16; WCH

Lang, Fritz 1890-1976 .... **CLC 20, 103**
See also AAYA 65; CA 77-80; 69-72;
CANR 30

Leblanc, Maurice (Marie Emile)
1864-1941 .... **TCLC 49**
See also CA 110; CMW 4

Lebowitz, Fran(ces Ann) 1951(?)- ... **CLC 11, 36**
See also CA 81-84; CANR 14, 60, 70; INT CANR-14; MTCW 1

Lebrecht, Peter
See Tieck, (Johann) Ludwig

le Carre, John .... **CLC 3, 5, 9, 15, 28**
See Cornwell, David (John Moore)
See also AAYA 42; BEST 89:4; BPFB 2; BRWS 2; CDBLB 1960 to Present; CMW 4; CN 1, 2, 3, 4, 5, 6, 7; CPW; DLB 87; EWL 3; MSW; MTCW 2; RGEL 2; TEA

Le Clezio, J(ean) M(arie) G(ustave)
1940- .... **CLC 31, 155**
See also CA 116; 128; CWW 2; DLB 83; EWL 3; GFL 1789 to the Present; RGSF 2

Leconte de Lisle, Charles-Marie-Rene
1818-1894 .... **NCLC 29**
See also DLB 217; EW 6; GFL 1789 to the Present

Le Coq, Monsieur
See Simenon, Georges (Jacques Christian)

Leduc, Violette 1907-1972 .... **CLC 22**
See also CA 13-14; 33-36R; CANR 69; CAP 1; EWL 3; GFL 1789 to the Present; GLL 1

Ledwidge, Francis 1887(?)-1917 .... **TCLC 23**
See also CA 123; 203; DLB 20

Lee, Andrea 1953- .... **BLC 2; CLC 36**
See also BW 1, 3; CA 125; CANR 82; DAM MULT

Lee, Andrew
See Auchincloss, Louis (Stanton)

Lee, Chang-rae 1965- .... **CLC 91**
See also CA 148; CANR 89; CN 7; DLB 312; LATS 1:2

Lee, Don L. .... **CLC 2**
See Madhubuti, Haki R.
See also CP 2, 3, 4

Lee, George W(ashington)
1894-1976 .... **BLC 2; CLC 52**
See also BW 1; CA 125; CANR 83; DAM MULT; DLB 51

Lee, (Nelle) Harper 1926- . **CLC 12, 60, 194; WLC**
See also AAYA 13; AMWS 8; BPFB 2; BYA 3; CA 13-16R; CANR 51, 128; CDALB 1941-1968; CSW; DA; DA3; DAB; DAC; DAM MST, NOV; DLB 6; EXPN; LAIT 3; MAL 5; MTCW 1, 2; MTFW 2005; NFS 2; SATA 11; WYA; YAW

Lee, Helen Elaine 1959(?)- .... **CLC 86**
See also CA 148

Lee, John .... **CLC 70**

Lee, Julian
See Latham, Jean Lee

Lee, Larry
See Lee, Lawrence

Lee, Laurie 1914-1997 .... **CLC 90**
See also CA 77-80; 158; CANR 33, 73; CP 1, 2, 3, 4; CPW; DAB; DAM POP; DLB 27; MTCW 1; RGEL 2

Lee, Lawrence 1941-1990 .... **CLC 34**
See also CA 131; CANR 43

Lee, Li-Young 1957- .... **CLC 164; PC 24**
See also AMWS 15; CA 153; CANR 118; CP 7; DLB 165, 312; LMFS 2; PFS 11, 15, 17

Lee, Manfred B(ennington)
1905-1971 .... **CLC 11**
See Queen, Ellery
See also CA 1-4R; 29-32R; CANR 2; CMW 4; DLB 137

Lee, Nathaniel 1645(?)-1692 .... **LC 103**
See also DLB 80; RGEL 2

Lee, Shelton Jackson 1957(?)- .. **BLCS; CLC 105**
See Lee, Spike
See also BW 2, 3; CA 125; CANR 42; DAM MULT

Lee, Spike
See Lee, Shelton Jackson
See also AAYA 4, 29

Lee, Stan 1922- .... **CLC 17**
See also AAYA 5, 49; CA 108; 111; CANR 129; INT CA-111; MTFW 2005

Lee, Tanith 1947- .... **CLC 46**
See also AAYA 15; CA 37-40R; CANR 53, 102, 145; DLB 261; FANT; SATA 8, 88, 134; SFW 4; SUFW 1, 2; YAW

Lee, Vernon .... **SSC 33; TCLC 5**
See Paget, Violet
See also DLB 57, 153, 156, 174, 178; GLL 1; SUFW 1

Lee, William
See Burroughs, William S(eward)
See also GLL 1

Lee, Willy
See Burroughs, William S(eward)
See also GLL 1

Lee-Hamilton, Eugene (Jacob)
1845-1907 .... **TCLC 22**
See also CA 117; 234

Leet, Judith 1935- .... **CLC 11**
See also CA 187

Le Fanu, Joseph Sheridan
1814-1873 .... **NCLC 9, 58; SSC 14, 84**
See also CMW 4; DA3; DAM POP; DLB 21, 70, 159, 178; GL 3; HGG; RGEL 2; RGSF 2; SUFW 1

Leffland, Ella 1931- .... **CLC 19**
See also CA 29-32R; CANR 35, 78, 82; DLBY 1984; INT CANR-35; SATA 65

Leger, Alexis
See Leger, (Marie-Rene Auguste) Alexis Saint-Leger

Leger, (Marie-Rene Auguste) Alexis
Saint-Leger 1887-1975 .. **CLC 4, 11, 46; PC 23**
See Perse, Saint-John; Saint-John Perse
See also CA 13-16R; 61-64; CANR 43; DAM POET; MTCW 1

Leger, Saintleger
See Leger, (Marie-Rene Auguste) Alexis Saint-Leger

Le Guin, Ursula K(roeber) 1929- ..... **CLC 8, 13, 22, 45, 71, 136; SSC 12, 69**
See also AAYA 9, 27; AITN 1; BPFB 2; BYA 5, 8, 11, 14; CA 21-24R; CANR 9, 32, 52, 74, 132; CDALB 1968-1988; CLR 3, 28, 91; CN 2, 3, 4, 5, 6, 7; CPW; DA3; DAB; DAC; DAM MST, POP; DLB 8, 52, 256, 275; EXPS; FANT; FW; INT CANR-32; JRDA; LAIT 5; MAICYA 1, 2; MAL 5; MTCW 1, 2; MTFW 2005; NFS 6, 9; SATA 4, 52, 99, 149; SCFW 1, 2; SFW 4; SSFS; SUFW 1, 2; WYA; YAW

Lehmann, Rosamond (Nina)
1901-1990 .... **CLC 5**
See also CA 77-80; 131; CANR 8, 73; CN 1, 2, 3, 4; DLB 15; MTCW 2; RGEL 2; RHW

Leiber, Fritz (Reuter, Jr.)
1910-1992 .... **CLC 25**
See also AAYA 65; BPFB 2; CA 45-48; 139; CANR 2, 40, 86; CN 2, 3, 4, 5; DLB 8; FANT; HGG; MTCW 1, 2; MTFW 2005; SATA 45; SATA-Obit 73; SCFW 1, 2; SFW 4; SUFW 1, 2

Leibniz, Gottfried Wilhelm von
1646-1716 .... **LC 35**
See also DLB 168

Leimbach, Martha 1963-
See Leimbach, Marti
See also CA 130

Leimbach, Marti .... **CLC 65**
See Leimbach, Martha

Leino, Eino .... **TCLC 24**
See Lonnbohm, Armas Eino Leopold
See also EWL 3

Leiris, Michel (Julien) 1901-1990 ..... **CLC 61**
See also CA 119; 128; 132; EWL 3; GFL 1789 to the Present

Leithauser, Brad 1953- .... **CLC 27**
See also CA 107; CANR 27, 81; CP 7; DLB 120, 282

le Jars de Gournay, Marie
See de Gournay, Marie le Jars

Lelchuk, Alan 1938- .... **CLC 5**
See also CA 45-48; CAAS 20; CANR 1, 70; CN 3, 4, 5, 6, 7

Lem, Stanislaw 1921- ...... **CLC 8, 15, 40, 149**
See also CA 105; CAAS 1; CANR 32; CWW 2; MTCW 1; SCFW 1, 2; SFW 4

Lemann, Nancy (Elise) 1956- .... **CLC 39**
See also CA 118; 136; CANR 121

Lemonnier, (Antoine Louis) Camille
1844-1913 .... **TCLC 22**
See also CA 121

Lenau, Nikolaus 1802-1850 .... **NCLC 16**

L'Engle, Madeleine (Camp Franklin)
1918- .... **CLC 12**
See also AAYA 28; AITN 2; BPFB 2; BYA 2, 4, 5, 7; CA 1-4R; CANR 3, 21, 39, 66, 107; CLR 1, 14, 57; CPW; CWRI 5; DA3; DAM POP; DLB 52; JRDA; MAICYA 1, 2; MTCW 1, 2; MTFW 2005; SAAS 15; SATA 1, 27, 75, 128; SFW 4; WYA; YAW

Lengyel, Jozsef 1896-1975 .... **CLC 7**
See also CA 85-88; 57-60; CANR 71; RGSF 2

Lenin 1870-1924
See Lenin, V. I.
See also CA 121; 168

Lenin, V. I. .... **TCLC 67**
See Lenin

Lennon, John (Ono) 1940-1980 .. **CLC 12, 35**
See also CA 102; SATA 114

Lennox, Charlotte Ramsay
1729(?)-1804 .... **NCLC 23, 134**
See also DLB 39; RGEL 2

Lentricchia, Frank, (Jr.) 1940- .... **CLC 34**
See also CA 25-28R; CANR 19, 106; DLB 246

Lenz, Gunter .... **CLC 65**

Lenz, Jakob Michael Reinhold
1751-1792 .... **LC 100**
See also DLB 94; RGWL 2, 3

Lenz, Siegfried 1926- .... **CLC 27; SSC 33**
See also CA 89-92; CANR 80; CWW 2; DLB 75; EWL 3; RGSF 2; RGWL 2, 3

Leon, David
See Jacob, (Cyprien-)Max

Leonard, Elmore (John, Jr.) 1925- . **CLC 28, 34, 71, 120**
See also AAYA 22, 59; AITN 1; BEST 89:1, 90:4; BPFB 2; CA 81-84; CANR 12, 28, 53, 76, 96, 133; CMW 4; CN 5, 6, 7; CPW; DA3; DAM POP; DLB 173, 226; INT CANR-28; MSW; MTCW 1, 2; MTFW 2005; RGAL 4; SATA 163; TCWW 1, 2

Leonard, Hugh .... **CLC 19**
See Byrne, John Keyes
See also CBD; CD 5, 6; DFS 13; DLB 13

Leonov, Leonid (Maximovich)
1899-1994 .... **CLC 92**
See Leonov, Leonid Maksimovich
See also CA 129; CANR 76; DAM NOV; EWL 3; MTCW 1, 2; MTFW 2005

MacDonald, John D(ann)
1916-1986 .... **CLC 3, 27, 44**
See also BPFB 2; CA 1-4R; 121; CANR 1, 19, 60; CMW 4; CPW; DAM NOV, POP; DLB 8, 306; DLBY 1986; MSW; MTCW 1, 2; MTFW 2005; SFW 4

Macdonald, John Ross
See Millar, Kenneth

Macdonald, Ross ..... **CLC 1, 2, 3, 14, 34, 41**
See Millar, Kenneth
See also AMWS 4; BPFB 2; CN 1, 2, 3; DLBD 6; MSW; RGAL 4

MacDougal, John
See Blish, James (Benjamin)

MacDougal, John
See Blish, James (Benjamin)

MacDowell, John
See Parks, Tim(othy Harold)

MacEwen, Gwendolyn (Margaret)
1941-1987 .... **CLC 13, 55**
See also CA 9-12R; 124; CANR 7, 22; CP 1, 2, 3, 4; DLB 53, 251; SATA 50; SATA-Obit 55

Macha, Karel Hynek 1810-1846 .... **NCLC 46**

Machado (y Ruiz), Antonio
1875-1939 .... **TCLC 3**
See also CA 104; 174; DLB 108; EW 9; EWL 3; HW 2; PFS 23; RGWL 2, 3

Machado de Assis, Joaquim Maria
1839-1908 .... **BLC 2; HLCS 2; SSC 24; TCLC 10**
See also CA 107; 153; CANR 91; DLB 307; LAW; RGSF 2; RGWL 2, 3; TWA; WLIT 1

Machaut, Guillaume de c.
1300-1377 .... **CMLC 64**
See also DLB 208

Machen, Arthur .... **SSC 20; TCLC 4**
See Jones, Arthur Llewellyn
See also CA 179; DLB 156, 178; RGEL 2; SUFW 1

Machiavelli, Niccolo 1469-1527 ... **DC 16; LC 8, 36; WLCS**
See also AAYA 58; DA; DAB; DAC; DAM MST; EW 2; LAIT 1; LMFS 1; NFS 9; RGWL 2, 3; TWA; WLIT 7

MacInnes, Colin 1914-1976 .... **CLC 4, 23**
See also CA 69-72; 65-68; CANR 21; CN 1, 2; DLB 14; MTCW 1, 2; RGEL 2; RHW

MacInnes, Helen (Clark)
1907-1985 .... **CLC 27, 39**
See also BPFB 2; CA 1-4R; 117; CANR 1, 28, 58; CMW 4; CN 1, 2; CPW; DAM POP; DLB 87; MSW; MTCW 1, 2; MTFW 2005; SATA 22; SATA-Obit 44

Mackay, Mary 1855-1924
See Corelli, Marie
See also CA 118; 177; FANT; RHW

Mackay, Shena 1944- .... **CLC 195**
See also CA 104; CANR 88, 139; DLB 231, 319; MTFW 2005

Mackenzie, Compton (Edward Montague)
1883-1972 .... **CLC 18; TCLC 116**
See also CA 21-22; 37-40R; CAP 2; CN 1; DLB 34, 100; RGEL 2

Mackenzie, Henry 1745-1831 .... **NCLC 41**
See also DLB 39; RGEL 2

Mackey, Nathaniel (Ernest) 1947- .... **PC 49**
See also CA 153; CANR 114; CP 7; DLB 169

MacKinnon, Catharine A. 1946- .... **CLC 181**
See also CA 128; 132; CANR 73, 140; FW; MTCW 2; MTFW 2005

Mackintosh, Elizabeth 1896(?)-1952
See Tey, Josephine
See also CA 110; CMW 4

MacLaren, James
See Grieve, C(hristopher) M(urray)

MacLaverty, Bernard 1942- .... **CLC 31**
See also CA 116; 118; CANR 43, 88; CN 5, 6, 7; DLB 267; INT CA-118; RGSF 2

MacLean, Alistair (Stuart)
1922(?)-1987 .... **CLC 3, 13, 50, 63**
See also CA 57-60; 121; CANR 28, 61; CMW 4; CP 2, 3, 4, 5, 6, 7; CPW; DAM POP; DLB 276; MTCW 1; SATA 23; SATA-Obit 50; TCWW 2

Maclean, Norman (Fitzroy)
1902-1990 .... **CLC 78; SSC 13**
See also AMWS 14; CA 102; 132; CANR 49; CPW; DAM POP; DLB 206; TCWW 2

MacLeish, Archibald 1892-1982 ... **CLC 3, 8, 14, 68; PC 47**
See also AMW; CA 9-12R; 106; CAD; CANR 33, 63; CDALBS; CP 1, 2; DAM POET; DFS 15; DLB 4, 7, 45; DLBY 1982; EWL 3; EXPP; MAL 5; MTCW 1, 2; MTFW 2005; PAB; PFS 5; RGAL 4; TUS

MacLennan, (John) Hugh
1907-1990 .... **CLC 2, 14, 92**
See also CA 5-8R; 142; CANR 33; CN 1, 2, 3, 4; DAC; DAM MST; DLB 68; EWL 3; MTCW 1, 2; MTFW 2005; RGEL 2; TWA

MacLeod, Alistair 1936- .... **CLC 56, 165**
See also CA 123; CCA 1; DAC; DAM MST; DLB 60; MTCW 2; MTFW 2005; RGSF 2; TCLE 1:2

Macleod, Fiona
See Sharp, William
See also RGEL 2; SUFW

MacNeice, (Frederick) Louis
1907-1963 .... **CLC 1, 4, 10, 53; PC 61**
See also BRW 7; CA 85-88; CANR 61; DAB; DAM POET; DLB 10, 20; EWL 3; MTCW 1, 2; MTFW 2005; RGEL 2

MacNeill, Dand
See Fraser, George MacDonald

Macpherson, James 1736-1796 .... **LC 29**
See Ossian
See also BRWS 8; DLB 109; RGEL 2

Macpherson, (Jean) Jay 1931- .... **CLC 14**
See also CA 5-8R; CANR 90; CP 1, 2, 3, 4, 5, 6, 7; CWP; DLB 53

Macrobius fl. 430- .... **CMLC 48**

MacShane, Frank 1927-1999 .... **CLC 39**
See also CA 9-12R; 186; CANR 3, 33; DLB 111

Macumber, Mari
See Sandoz, Mari(e Susette)

Madach, Imre 1823-1864 .... **NCLC 19**

Madden, (Jerry) David 1933- .... **CLC 5, 15**
See also CA 1-4R; CAAS 3; CANR 4, 45; CN 3, 4, 5, 6, 7; CSW; DLB 6; MTCW 1

Maddern, Al(an)
See Ellison, Harlan (Jay)

Madhubuti, Haki R. 1942- ... **BLC 2; CLC 6, 73; PC 5**
See Lee, Don L.
See also BW 2, 3; CA 73-76; CANR 24, 51, 73, 139; CP 5, 6, 7; CSW; DAM MULT, POET; DLB 5, 41; DLBD 8; EWL 3; MAL 5; MTCW 2; MTFW 2005; RGAL 4

Madison, James 1751-1836 .... **NCLC 126**
See also DLB 37

Maepenn, Hugh
See Kuttner, Henry

Maepenn, K. H.
See Kuttner, Henry

Maeterlinck, Maurice 1862-1949 ..... **TCLC 3**
See also CA 104; 136; CANR 80; DAM DRAM; DLB 192; EW 8; EWL 3; GFL 1789 to the Present; LMFS 2; RGWL 2, 3; SATA 66; TWA

Maginn, William 1794-1842 .... **NCLC 8**
See also DLB 110, 159

Mahapatra, Jayanta 1928- .... **CLC 33**
See also CA 73-76; CAAS 9; CANR 15, 33, 66, 87; CP 4, 5, 6, 7; DAM MULT

Mahfouz, Naguib (Abdel Aziz Al-Sabilgi)
1911(?)- .... **CLC 153; SSC 66**
See Mahfuz, Najib (Abdel Aziz al-Sabilgi)
See also AAYA 49; BEST 89:2; CA 128; CANR 55, 101; DA3; DAM NOV; MTCW 1, 2; MTFW 2005; RGWL 2, 3; SSFS 9

Mahfuz, Najib (Abdel Aziz al-Sabilgi)
.... **CLC 52, 55**
See Mahfouz, Naguib (Abdel Aziz Al-Sabilgi)
See also AFW; CWW 2; DLBY 1988; EWL 3; RGSF 2; WLIT 6

Mahon, Derek 1941- .... **CLC 27; PC 60**
See also BRWS 6; CA 113; 128; CANR 88; CP 1, 2, 3, 4, 5, 6, 7; DLB 40; EWL 3

Maiakovskii, Vladimir
See Mayakovski, Vladimir (Vladimirovich)
See also IDTP; RGWL 2, 3

Mailer, Norman (Kingsley) 1923- . **CLC 1, 2, 3, 4, 5, 8, 11, 14, 28, 39, 74, 111**
See also AAYA 31; AITN 2; AMW; AMWC 2; AMWR 2; BPFB 2; CA 9-12R; CABS 1; CANR 28, 74, 77, 130; CDALB 1968-1988; CN 1, 2, 3, 4, 5, 6, 7; CPW; DA; DA3; DAB; DAC; DAM MST, NOV, POP; DLB 2, 16, 28, 185, 278; DLBD 3; DLBY 1980, 1983; EWL 3; MAL 5; MTCW 1, 2; MTFW 2005; NFS 10; RGAL 4; TUS

Maillet, Antonine 1929- .... **CLC 54, 118**
See also CA 115; 120; CANR 46, 74, 77, 134; CCA 1; CWW 2; DAC; DLB 60; INT CA-120; MTCW 2; MTFW 2005

Maimonides, Moses 1135-1204 ..... **CMLC 76**
See also DLB 115

Mais, Roger 1905-1955 .... **TCLC 8**
See also BW 1, 3; CA 105; 124; CANR 82; CDWLB 3; DLB 125; EWL 3; MTCW 1; RGEL 2

Maistre, Joseph 1753-1821 .... **NCLC 37**
See also GFL 1789 to the Present

Maitland, Frederic William
1850-1906 .... **TCLC 65**

Maitland, Sara (Louise) 1950- .... **CLC 49**
See also BRWS 11; CA 69-72; CANR 13, 59; DLB 271; FW

Major, Clarence 1936- ... **BLC 2; CLC 3, 19, 48**
See also AFAW 2; BW 2, 3; CA 21-24R; CAAS 6; CANR 13, 25, 53, 82; CN 3, 4, 5, 6, 7; CP 2, 3, 4, 5, 6, 7; CSW; DAM MULT; DLB 33; EWL 3; MAL 5; MSW

Major, Kevin (Gerald) 1949- .... **CLC 26**
See also AAYA 16; CA 97-100; CANR 21, 38, 112; CLR 11; DAC; DLB 60; INT CANR-21; JRDA; MAICYA 1, 2; MAIC-YAS 1; SATA 32, 82, 134; WYA; YAW

Maki, James
See Ozu, Yasujiro

Makine, Andrei 1957- .... **CLC 198**
See also CA 176; CANR 103; MTFW 2005

Malabaila, Damiano
See Levi, Primo

Malamud, Bernard 1914-1986 .. **CLC 1, 2, 3, 5, 8, 9, 11, 18, 27, 44, 78, 85; SSC 15; TCLC 129; WLC**
See also AAYA 16; AMWS 1; BPFB 2; BYA 15; CA 5-8R; 118; CABS 1; CANR 28, 62, 114; CDALB 1941-1968; CN 1, 2, 3, 4; CPW; DA; DA3; DAB; DAC; DAM MST, NOV, POP; DLB 2, 28, 152; DLBY

McGinley, Patrick (Anthony) 1937- . **CLC 41**
  See also CA 120; 127; CANR 56; INT CA-127

McGinley, Phyllis 1905-1978 .... **CLC 14**
  See also CA 9-12R; 77-80; CANR 19; CP 1, 2; CWRI 5; DLB 11, 48; MAL 5; PFS 9, 13; SATA 2, 44; SATA-Obit 24

McGinniss, Joe 1942- .... **CLC 32**
  See also AITN 2; BEST 89:2; CA 25-28R; CANR 26, 70; CPW; DLB 185; INT CANR-26

McGivern, Maureen Daly
  See Daly, Maureen

McGrath, Patrick 1950- .... **CLC 55**
  See also CA 136; CANR 65; CN 5, 6, 7; DLB 231; HGG; SUFW 2

McGrath, Thomas (Matthew)
  1916-1990 .... **CLC 28, 59**
  See also AMWS 10; CA 9-12R; 132; CANR 6, 33, 95; CP 1, 2, 3, 4; DAM POET; MAL 5; MTCW 1; SATA 41; SATA-Obit 66

McGuane, Thomas (Francis III)
  1939- .... **CLC 3, 7, 18, 45, 127**
  See also AITN 2; BPFB 2; CA 49-52; CANR 5, 24, 49, 94; CN 2, 3, 4, 5, 6, 7; DLB 2, 212; DLBY 1980; EWL 3; INT CANR-24; MAL 5; MTCW 1; MTFW 2005; TCWW 1, 2

McGuckian, Medbh 1950- .... **CLC 48, 174; PC 27**
  See also BRWS 5; CA 143; CP 4, 5, 6, 7; CWP; DAM POET; DLB 40

McHale, Tom 1942(?)-1982 .... **CLC 3, 5**
  See also AITN 1; CA 77-80; 106; CN 1, 2, 3

McHugh, Heather 1948- .... **PC 61**
  See also CA 69-72; CANR 11, 28, 55, 92; CP 4, 5, 6, 7; CWP

McIlvanney, William 1936- .... **CLC 42**
  See also CA 25-28R; CANR 61; CMW 4; DLB 14, 207

McIlwraith, Maureen Mollie Hunter
  See Hunter, Mollie
  See also SATA 2

McInerney, Jay 1955- .... **CLC 34, 112**
  See also AAYA 18; BPFB 2; CA 116; 123; CANR 45, 68, 116; CN 5, 6, 7; CPW; DA3; DAM POP; DLB 292; INT CA-123; MAL 5; MTCW 2; MTFW 2005

McIntyre, Vonda N(eel) 1948- .... **CLC 18**
  See also CA 81-84; CANR 17, 34, 69; MTCW 1; SFW 4; YAW

McKay, Claude .... **BLC 3; HR 1:3; PC 2; TCLC 7, 41; WLC**
  See McKay, Festus Claudius
  See also AFAW 1, 2; AMWS 10; DAB; DLB 4, 45, 51, 117; EWL 3; EXPP; GLL 2; LAIT 3; LMFS 2; MAL 5; PAB; PFS 4; RGAL 4; WP

McKay, Festus Claudius 1889-1948
  See McKay, Claude
  See also BW 1, 3; CA 104; 124; CANR 73; DA; DAC; DAM MST, MULT, NOV, POET; MTCW 1, 2; MTFW 2005; TUS

McKuen, Rod 1933- .... **CLC 1, 3**
  See also AITN 1; CA 41-44R; CANR 40; CP 1

McLoughlin, R. B.
  See Mencken, H(enry) L(ouis)

McLuhan, (Herbert) Marshall
  1911-1980 .... **CLC 37, 83**
  See also CA 9-12R; 102; CANR 12, 34, 61; DLB 88; INT CANR-12; MTCW 1, 2; MTFW 2005

McManus, Declan Patrick Aloysius
  See Costello, Elvis

McMillan, Terry (L.) 1951- . **BLCS; CLC 50, 61, 112**
  See also AAYA 21; AMWS 13; BPFB 2; BW 2, 3; CA 140; CANR 60, 104, 131; CN 7; CPW; DA3; DAM MULT, NOV, POP; MAL 5; MTCW 2; MTFW 2005; RGAL 4; YAW

McMurtry, Larry 1936- .... **CLC 2, 3, 7, 11, 27, 44, 127**
  See also AAYA 15; AITN 2; AMWS 5; BEST 89:2; BPFB 2; CA 5-8R; CANR 19, 43, 64, 103; CDALB 1968-1988; CN 2, 3, 4, 5, 6, 7; CPW; CSW; DA3; DAM NOV, POP; DLB 2, 143, 256; DLBY 1980, 1987; EWL 3; MAL 5; MTCW 1, 2; MTFW 2005; RGAL 4; TCWW 1, 2

McNally, T. M. 1961- .... **CLC 82**

McNally, Terrence 1939- ... **CLC 4, 7, 41, 91; DC 27**
  See also AAYA 62; AMWS 13; CA 45-48; CAD; CANR 2, 56, 116; CD 5, 6; DA3; DAM DRAM; DFS 16, 19; DLB 7, 249; EWL 3; GLL 1; MTCW 2; MTFW 2005

McNamer, Deirdre 1950- .... **CLC 70**

McNeal, Tom .... **CLC 119**

McNeile, Herman Cyril 1888-1937
  See Sapper
  See also CA 184; CMW 4; DLB 77

McNickle, (William) D'Arcy
  1904-1977 .... **CLC 89; NNAL**
  See also CA 9-12R; 85-88; CANR 5, 45; DAM MULT; DLB 175, 212; RGAL 4; SATA-Obit 22; TCWW 1, 2

McPhee, John (Angus) 1931- .... **CLC 36**
  See also AAYA 61; AMWS 3; ANW; BEST 90:1; CA 65-68; CANR 20, 46, 64, 69, 121; CPW; DLB 185, 275; MTCW 1, 2; MTFW 2005; TUS

McPherson, James Alan 1943- . **BLCS; CLC 19, 77**
  See also BW 1, 3; CA 25-28R; CAAS 17; CANR 24, 74, 140; CN 3, 4, 5, 6; CSW; DLB 38, 244; EWL 3; MTCW 1, 2; MTFW 2005; RGAL 4; RGSF 2

McPherson, William (Alexander)
  1933- .... **CLC 34**
  See also CA 69-72; CANR 28; INT CANR-28

McTaggart, J. McT. Ellis
  See McTaggart, John McTaggart Ellis

McTaggart, John McTaggart Ellis
  1866-1925 .... **TCLC 105**
  See also CA 120; DLB 262

Mead, George Herbert 1863-1931 . **TCLC 89**
  See also CA 212; DLB 270

Mead, Margaret 1901-1978 .... **CLC 37**
  See also AITN 1; CA 1-4R; 81-84; CANR 4; DA3; FW; MTCW 1, 2; SATA-Obit 20

Meaker, Marijane (Agnes) 1927-
  See Kerr, M. E.
  See also CA 107; CANR 37, 63, 145; INT CA-107; JRDA; MAICYA 1, 2; MAIC-YAS 1; MTCW 1; SATA 20, 61, 99, 160; SATA-Essay 111; YAW

Medoff, Mark (Howard) 1940- .... **CLC 6, 23**
  See also AITN 1; CA 53-56; CAD; CANR 5; CD 5, 6; DAM DRAM; DFS 4; DLB 7; INT CANR-5

Medvedev, P. N.
  See Bakhtin, Mikhail Mikhailovich

Meged, Aharon
  See Megged, Aharon

Meged, Aron
  See Megged, Aharon

Megged, Aharon 1920- .... **CLC 9**
  See also CA 49-52; CAAS 13; CANR 1, 140; EWL 3

Mehta, Deepa 1950- .... **CLC 208**

Mehta, Gita 1943- .... **CLC 179**
  See also CA 225; CN 7; DNFS 2

Mehta, Ved (Parkash) 1934- .... **CLC 37**
  See also CA 1-4R, 212; CAAE 212; CANR 2, 23, 69; MTCW 1; MTFW 2005

Melanchthon, Philipp 1497-1560 .... **LC 90**
  See also DLB 179

Melanter
  See Blackmore, R(ichard) D(oddridge)

Meleager c. 140B.C.-c. 70B.C. ...... **CMLC 53**

Melies, Georges 1861-1938 .... **TCLC 81**

Melikow, Loris
  See Hofmannsthal, Hugo von

Melmoth, Sebastian
  See Wilde, Oscar (Fingal O'Flahertie Wills)

Melo Neto, Joao Cabral de
  See Cabral de Melo Neto, Joao
  See also CWW 2; EWL 3

Meltzer, Milton 1915- .... **CLC 26**
  See also AAYA 8, 45; BYA 2, 6; CA 13-16R; CANR 38, 92, 107; CLR 13; DLB 61; JRDA; MAICYA 1, 2; SAAS 1; SATA 1, 50, 80, 128; SATA-Essay 124; WYA; YAW

Melville, Herman 1819-1891 ..... **NCLC 3, 12, 29, 45, 49, 91, 93, 123, 157; SSC 1, 17, 46; WLC**
  See also AAYA 25; AMW; AMWR 1; CDALB 1640-1865; DA; DA3; DAB; DAC; DAM MST, NOV; DLB 3, 74, 250, 254; EXPN; EXPS; GL 3; LAIT 1, 2; NFS 7, 9; RGAL 4; RGSF 2; SATA 59; SSFS 3; TUS

Members, Mark
  See Powell, Anthony (Dymoke)

Membreno, Alejandro .... **CLC 59**

Menand, Louis 1952- .... **CLC 208**
  See also CA 200

Menander c. 342B.C.-c. 293B.C. .... **CMLC 9, 51; DC 3**
  See also AW 1; CDWLB 1; DAM DRAM; DLB 176; LMFS 1; RGWL 2, 3

Menchu, Rigoberta 1959- .. **CLC 160; HLCS 2**
  See also CA 175; CANR 135; DNFS 1; WLIT 1

Mencken, H(enry) L(ouis)
  1880-1956 .... **TCLC 13**
  See also AMW; CA 105; 125; CDALB 1917-1929; DLB 11, 29, 63, 137, 222; EWL 3; MAL 5; MTCW 1, 2; MTFW 2005; NCFS 4; RGAL 4; TUS

Mendelsohn, Jane 1965- .... **CLC 99**
  See also CA 154; CANR 94

Mendoza, Inigo Lopez de
  See Santillana, Inigo Lopez de Mendoza, Marques de

Menton, Francisco de
  See Chin, Frank (Chew, Jr.)

Mercer, David 1928-1980 .... **CLC 5**
  See also CA 9-12R; 102; CANR 23; CBD; DAM DRAM; DLB 13, 310; MTCW 1; RGEL 2

Merchant, Paul
  See Ellison, Harlan (Jay)

Meredith, George 1828-1909 .. **PC 60; TCLC 17, 43**
  See also CA 117; 153; CANR 80; CDBLB 1832-1890; DAM POET; DLB 18, 35, 57, 159; RGEL 2; TEA

Meredith, William (Morris) 1919- .... **CLC 4, 13, 22, 55; PC 28**
  See also CA 9-12R; CAAS 14; CANR 6, 40, 129; CP 1, 2, 3, 4, 5, 6, 7; DAM POET; DLB 5; MAL 5

Merezhkovsky, Dmitrii Sergeevich
  See Merezhkovsky, Dmitry Sergeyevich
  See also DLB 295

Merezhkovsky, Dmitry Sergeevich
See Merezhkovsky, Dmitry Sergeyevich
See also EWL 3

Merezhkovsky, Dmitry Sergeyevich
1865-1941 .... **TCLC 29**
See Merezhkovsky, Dmitrii Sergeevich;
Merezhkovsky, Dmitry Sergeevich
See also CA 169

Merimee, Prosper 1803-1870 ... **NCLC 6, 65;**
SSC 7, 77
See also DLB 119, 192; EW 6; EXPS; GFL
1789 to the Present; RGSF 2; RGWL 2,
3; SSFS 8; SUFW

Merkin, Daphne 1954- .... **CLC 44**
See also CA 123

Merleau-Ponty, Maurice
1908-1961 .... **TCLC 156**
See also CA 114; 89-92; DLB 296; GFL
1789 to the Present

Merlin, Arthur
See Blish, James (Benjamin)

Mernissi, Fatima 1940- .... **CLC 171**
See also CA 152; FW

Merrill, James (Ingram) 1926-1995 .. **CLC 2,**
3, 6, 8, 13, 18, 34, 91; PC 28; TCLC
173
See also AMWS 3; CA 13-16R; 147; CANR
10, 49, 63, 108; CP 1, 2, 3, 4; DA3; DAM
POET; DLB 5, 165; DLBY 1985; EWL 3;
INT CANR-10; MAL 5; MTCW 1, 2;
MTFW 2005; PAB; PFS 23; RGAL 4

Merriman, Alex
See Silverberg, Robert

Merriman, Brian 1747-1805 .... **NCLC 70**

Merritt, E. B.
See Waddington, Miriam

Merton, Thomas (James)
1915-1968 . **CLC 1, 3, 11, 34, 83; PC 10**
See also AAYA 61; AMWS 8; CA 5-8R;
25-28R; CANR 22, 53, 111, 131; DA3;
DLB 48; DLBY 1981; MAL 5; MTCW 1,
2; MTFW 2005

Merwin, W(illiam) S(tanley) 1927- ... **CLC 1,**
2, 3, 5, 8, 13, 18, 45, 88; PC 45
See also AMWS 3; CA 13-16R; CANR 15,
51, 112, 140; CP 1, 2, 3, 4, 5, 6, 7; DA3;
DAM POET; DLB 5, 169; EWL 3; INT
CANR-15; MAL 5; MTCW 1, 2; MTFW
2005; PAB; PFS 5, 15; RGAL 4

Metastasio, Pietro 1698-1782 .... **LC 115**
See also RGWL 2, 3

Metcalf, John 1938- .... **CLC 37; SSC 43**
See also CA 113; CN 4, 5, 6, 7; DLB 60;
RGSF 2; TWA

Metcalf, Suzanne
See Baum, L(yman) Frank

Mew, Charlotte (Mary) 1870-1928 .. **TCLC 8**
See also CA 105; 189; DLB 19, 135; RGEL
2

Mewshaw, Michael 1943- .... **CLC 9**
See also CA 53-56; CANR 7, 47; DLBY
1980

Meyer, Conrad Ferdinand
1825-1898 .... **NCLC 81; SSC 30**
See also DLB 129; EW; RGWL 2, 3

Meyer, Gustav 1868-1932
See Meyrink, Gustav
See also CA 117; 190

Meyer, June
See Jordan, June (Meyer)

Meyer, Lynn
See Slavitt, David R(ytman)

Meyers, Jeffrey 1939- .... **CLC 39**
See also CA 73-76; 186; CAAE 186; CANR
54, 102; DLB 111

Meynell, Alice (Christina Gertrude
Thompson) 1847-1922 .... **TCLC 6**
See also CA 104; 177; DLB 19, 98; RGEL
2

Meyrink, Gustav .... **TCLC 21**
See Meyer, Gustav
See also DLB 81; EWL 3

Michaels, Leonard 1933-2003 ..... **CLC 6, 25;**
SSC 16
See also CA 61-64; 216; CANR 21, 62, 119;
CN 3, 45, 6, 7; DLB 130; MTCW 1;
TCLE 1:2

Michaux, Henri 1899-1984 .... **CLC 8, 19**
See also CA 85-88; 114; DLB 258; EWL 3;
GFL 1789 to the Present; RGWL 2, 3

Micheaux, Oscar (Devereaux)
1884-1951 .... **TCLC 76**
See also BW 3; CA 174; DLB 50; TCWW
2

Michelangelo 1475-1564 .... **LC 12**
See also AAYA 43

Michelet, Jules 1798-1874 .... **NCLC 31**
See also EW 5; GFL 1789 to the Present

Michels, Robert 1876-1936 .... **TCLC 88**
See also CA 212

Michener, James A(lbert)
1907(?)-1997 .. **CLC 1, 5, 11, 29, 60, 109**
See also AAYA 27; AITN 1; BEST 90:1;
BPFB 2; CA 5-8R; 161; CANR 21, 45,
68; CN 1, 2, 3, 4, 5, 6; CPW; DA3; DAM
NOV, POP; DLB 6; MAL 5; MTCW 1, 2;
MTFW 2005; RHW; TCWW 1, 2

Mickiewicz, Adam 1798-1855 . **NCLC 3, 101;**
PC 38
See also EW 5; RGWL 2, 3

Middleton, (John) Christopher
1926- .... **CLC 13**
See also CA 13-16R; CANR 29, 54, 117;
CP 1, 2, 3, 4, 5, 6, 7; DLB 40

Middleton, Richard (Barham)
1882-1911 .... **TCLC 56**
See also CA 187; DLB 156; HGG

Middleton, Stanley 1919- .... **CLC 7, 38**
See also CA 25-28R; CAAS 23; CANR 21,
46, 81; CN 1, 2, 3, 4, 5, 6, 7; DLB 14

Middleton, Thomas 1580-1627 ...... **DC 5; LC**
33, 123
See also BRW 2; DAM DRAM, MST; DFS
18, 22; DLB 58; RGEL 2

Migueis, Jose Rodrigues 1901-1980 . **CLC 10**
See also DLB 287

Mikszath, Kalman 1847-1910 .... **TCLC 31**
See also CA 170

Miles, Jack .... **CLC 100**
See also CA 200

Miles, John Russiano
See Miles, Jack

Miles, Josephine (Louise)
1911-1985 .... **CLC 1, 2, 14, 34, 39**
See also CA 1-4R; 116; CANR 2, 55; CP 1,
2, 3, 4; DAM POET; DLB 48; MAL 5;
TCLE 1:2

Militant
See Sandburg, Carl (August)

Mill, Harriet (Hardy) Taylor
1807-1858 .... **NCLC 102**
See also FW

Mill, John Stuart 1806-1873 .... **NCLC 11, 58**
See also CDBLB 1832-1890; DLB 55, 190,
262; FW 1; RGEL 2; TEA

Millar, Kenneth 1915-1983 .... **CLC 14**
See Macdonald, Ross
See also CA 9-12R; 110; CANR 16, 63,
107; CMW 4; CPW; DA3; DAM POP;
DLB 2, 226; DLBD 6; DLBY 1983;
MTCW 1, 2; MTFW 2005

Millay, E. Vincent
See Millay, Edna St. Vincent

Millay, Edna St. Vincent 1892-1950 ..... **PC 6,**
61; TCLC 4, 49, 169; WLCS
See Boyd, Nancy
See also AMW; CA 104; 130; CDALB
1917-1929; DA; DA3; DAB; DAC; DAM
MST, POET; DLB 45, 249; EWL 3;
EXPP; FL 1:6; MAL 5; MAWW; MTCW
1, 2; MTFW 2005; PAB; PFS 3, 17;
RGAL 4; TUS; WP

Miller, Arthur 1915-2005 ..... **CLC 1, 2, 6, 10,**
15, 26, 47, 78, 179; DC 1; WLC
See also AAYA 15; AITN 1; AMW; AMWC
1; CA 1-4R; 236; CABS 3; CAD; CANR
2, 30, 54, 76, 132; CD 5, 6; CDALB
1941-1968; DA; DA3; DAB; DAC; DAM
DRAM, MST; DFS 1, 3, 8; DLB 7, 266;
EWL 3; LAIT 1, 4; LATS 1:2; MAL 5;
MTCW 1, 2; MTFW 2005; RGAL 4;
TUS; WYAS 1

Miller, Henry (Valentine)
1891-1980 .... **CLC 1, 2, 4, 9, 14, 43, 84;**
WLC
See also AMW; BPFB 2; CA 9-12R; 97-
100; CANR 33, 64; CDALB 1929-1941;
CN 1, 2; DA; DA3; DAB; DAC; DAM
MST, NOV; DLB 4, 9; DLBY 1980; EWL
3; MAL 5; MTCW 1, 2; MTFW 2005;
RGAL 4; TUS

Miller, Hugh 1802-1856 .... **NCLC 143**
See also DLB 190

Miller, Jason 1939(?)-2001 .... **CLC 2**
See also AITN 1; CA 73-76; 197; CAD;
CANR 130; DFS 12; DLB 7

Miller, Sue 1943- .... **CLC 44**
See also AMWS 12; BEST 90:3; CA 139;
CANR 59, 91, 128; DA3; DAM POP;
DLB 143

Miller, Walter M(ichael, Jr.)
1923-1996 .... **CLC 4, 30**
See also BPFB 2; CA 85-88; CANR 108;
DLB 8; SCFW 1, 2; SFW 4

Millett, Kate 1934- .... **CLC 67**
See also AITN 1; CA 73-76; CANR 32, 53,
76, 110; DA3; DLB 246; FW; GLL 1;
MTCW 1, 2; MTFW 2005

Millhauser, Steven (Lewis) 1943- .... **CLC 21,**
54, 109; SSC 57
See also CA 110; 111; CANR 63, 114, 133;
CN 6, 7; DA3; DLB 2; FANT; INT CA-
111; MAL 5; MTCW 2; MTFW 2005

Millin, Sarah Gertrude 1889-1968 ... **CLC 49**
See also CA 102; 93-96; DLB 225; EWL 3

Milne, A(lan) A(lexander)
1882-1956 .... **TCLC 6, 88**
See also BRWS 5; CA 104; 133; CLR 1,
26; CMW 4; CWRI 5; DA3; DAB; DAC;
DAM MST; DLB 10, 77, 100, 160; FANT;
MAICYA 1, 2; MTCW 1, 2; MTFW 2005;
RGEL 2; SATA 100; WCH; YABC 1

Milner, Ron(ald) 1938-2004 ..... **BLC 3; CLC**
56
See also AITN 1; BW 1; CA 73-76; 230;
CAD; CANR 24, 81; CD 5, 6; DAM
MULT; DLB 38; MAL 5; MTCW 1

Milnes, Richard Monckton
1809-1885 .... **NCLC 61**
See also DLB 32, 184

Milosz, Czeslaw 1911-2004 .... **CLC 5, 11, 22,**
31, 56, 82; PC 8; WLCS
See also AAYA 62; CA 81-84; 230; CANR
23, 51, 91, 126; CDWLB 4; CWW 2;
DA3; DAM MST, POET; DLB 215; EW
13; EWL 3; MTCW 1, 2; MTFW 2005;
PFS 16; RGWL 2, 3

Milton, John 1608-1674 ..... **LC 9, 43, 92; PC**
19, 29; WLC
See also AAYA 65; BRW 2; BRWR 2; CD-
BLB 1660-1789; DA; DA3; DAB; DAC;
DAM MST, POET; DLB 131, 151, 281;
EFS 1; EXPP; LAIT 1; PAB; PFS 3, 17;
RGEL 2; TEA; WLIT 3; WP

Min, Anchee 1957- .... **CLC 86**
 See also CA 146; CANR 94, 137; MTFW
 2005
Minehaha, Cornelius
 See Wedekind, (Benjamin) Frank(lin)
Miner, Valerie 1947- .... **CLC 40**
 See also CA 97-100; CANR 59; FW; GLL
 2
Minimo, Duca
 See D'Annunzio, Gabriele
Minot, Susan (Anderson) 1956- ...... **CLC 44,
 159**
 See also AMWS 6; CA 134; CANR 118;
 CN 6, 7
Minus, Ed 1938- .... **CLC 39**
 See also CA 185
Mirabai 1498(?)-1550(?) .... **PC 48**
Miranda, Javier
 See Bioy Casares, Adolfo
 See also CWW 2
Mirbeau, Octave 1848-1917 .... **TCLC 55**
 See also CA 216; DLB 123, 192; GFL 1789
 to the Present
Mirikitani, Janice 1942- .... **AAL**
 See also CA 211; DLB 312; RGAL 4
Mirk, John (?)-c. 1414 .... **LC 105**
 See also DLB 146
Miro (Ferrer), Gabriel (Francisco Victor)
 1879-1930 .... **TCLC 5**
 See also CA 104; 185; DLB 322; EWL 3
Misharin, Alexandr .... **CLC 59**
Mishima, Yukio ... **CLC 2, 4, 6, 9, 27; DC 1;
 SSC 4; TCLC 161**
 See Hiraoka, Kimitake
 See also AAYA 50; BPFB 2; GLL 1; MJW;
 RGSF 2; RGWL 2, 3; SSFS 5, 12
Mistral, Frederic 1830-1914 .... **TCLC 51**
 See also CA 122; 213; GFL 1789 to the
 Present
Mistral, Gabriela
 See Godoy Alcayaga, Lucila
 See also DLB 283; DNFS 1; EWL 3; LAW;
 RGWL 2, 3; WP
Mistry, Rohinton 1952- ... **CLC 71, 196; SSC
 73**
 See also BRWS 10; CA 141; CANR 86,
 114; CCA 1; CN 6, 7; DAC; SSFS 6
Mitchell, Clyde
 See Ellison, Harlan (Jay)
Mitchell, Emerson Blackhorse Barney
 1945- .... **NNAL**
 See also CA 45-48
Mitchell, James Leslie 1901-1935
 See Gibbon, Lewis Grassic
 See also CA 104; 188; DLB 15
Mitchell, Joni 1943- .... **CLC 12**
 See also CA 112; CCA 1
Mitchell, Joseph (Quincy)
 1908-1996 .... **CLC 98**
 See also CA 77-80; 152; CANR 69; CN 1,
 2, 3, 4, 5, 6; CSW; DLB 185; DLBY 1996
Mitchell, Margaret (Munnerlyn)
 1900-1949 .... **TCLC 11, 170**
 See also AAYA 23; BPFB 2; BYA 1; CA
 109; 125; CANR 55, 94; CDALBS; DA3;
 DAM NOV, POP; DLB 9; LAIT 2; MAL
 5; MTCW 1, 2; MTFW 2005; NFS 9;
 RGAL 4; RHW; TUS; WYAS 1; YAW
Mitchell, Peggy
 See Mitchell, Margaret (Munnerlyn)
Mitchell, S(ilas) Weir 1829-1914 .... **TCLC 36**
 See also CA 165; DLB 202; RGAL 4
Mitchell, W(illiam) O(rmond)
 1914-1998 .... **CLC 25**
 See also CA 77-80; 165; CANR 15, 43; CN
 1, 2, 3, 4, 5, 6; DAC; DAM MST; DLB
 88; TCLE 1:2

Mitchell, William (Lendrum)
 1879-1936 .... **TCLC 81**
 See also CA 213
Mitford, Mary Russell 1787-1855 ... **NCLC 4**
 See also DLB 110, 116; RGEL 2
Mitford, Nancy 1904-1973 .... **CLC 44**
 See also BRWS 10; CA 9-12R; CN 1; DLB
 191; RGEL 2
Miyamoto, (Chujo) Yuriko
 1899-1951 .... **TCLC 37**
 See Miyamoto Yuriko
 See also CA 170, 174
Miyamoto Yuriko
 See Miyamoto, (Chujo) Yuriko
 See also DLB 180
Miyazawa, Kenji 1896-1933 .... **TCLC 76**
 See Miyazawa Kenji
 See also CA 157; RGWL 3
Miyazawa Kenji
 See Miyazawa, Kenji
 See also EWL 3
Mizoguchi, Kenji 1898-1956 .... **TCLC 72**
 See also CA 167
Mo, Timothy (Peter) 1950- .... **CLC 46, 134**
 See also CA 117; CANR 128; CN 5, 6, 7;
 DLB 194; MTCW 1; WLIT 4; WWE 1
Modarressi, Taghi (M.) 1931-1997 .... **CLC 44**
 See also CA 121; 134; INT CA-134
Modiano, Patrick (Jean) 1945- .... **CLC 18,
 218**
 See also CA 85-88; CANR 17, 40, 115;
 CWW 2; DLB 83, 299; EWL 3
Mofolo, Thomas (Mokopu)
 1875(?)-1948 .... **BLC 3; TCLC 22**
 See also AFW; CA 121; 153; CANR 83;
 DAM MULT; DLB 225; EWL 3; MTCW
 2; MTFW 2005; WLIT 2
Mohr, Nicholasa 1938- .... **CLC 12; HLC 2**
 See also AAYA 8, 46; CA 49-52; CANR 1,
 32, 64; CLR 22; DAM MULT; DLB 145;
 HW 1, 2; JRDA; LAIT 5; LLW; MAICYA
 2; MAICYAS 1; RGAL 4; SAAS 8; SATA
 8, 97; SATA-Essay 113; WYA; YAW
Moi, Toril 1953- .... **CLC 172**
 See also CA 154; CANR 102; FW
Mojtabai, A(nn) G(race) 1938- ..... **CLC 5, 9,
 15, 29**
 See also CA 85-88; CANR 88
Moliere 1622-1673 ..... **DC 13; LC 10, 28, 64;
 WLC**
 See also DA; DA3; DAB; DAC; DAM
 DRAM, MST; DFS 13, 18, 20; DLB 268;
 EW 3; GFL Beginnings to 1789; LATS
 1:1; RGWL 2, 3; TWA
Molin, Charles
 See Mayne, William (James Carter)
Molnar, Ferenc 1878-1952 .... **TCLC 20**
 See also CA 109; 153; CANR 83; CDWLB
 4; DAM DRAM; DLB 215; EWL 3;
 RGWL 2, 3
Momaday, N(avarre) Scott 1934- ...... **CLC 2,
 19, 85, 95, 160; NNAL; PC 25; WLCS**
 See also AAYA 11, 64; AMWS 4; ANW;
 BPFB 2; BYA 12; CA 25-28R; CANR 14,
 34, 68, 134; CDALBS; CN 2, 3, 4, 5, 6,
 7; CPW; DA; DA3; DAB; DAC; DAM
 MST, MULT, NOV, POP; DLB 143, 175,
 256; EWL 3; EXPP; INT CANR-14;
 LAIT 4; LATS 1:2; MAL 5; MTCW 1, 2;
 MTFW 2005; NFS 10; PFS 2, 11; RGAL
 4; SATA 48; SATA-Brief 30; TCWW 1,
 2; WP; YAW
Monette, Paul 1945-1995 .... **CLC 82**
 See also AMWS 10; CA 139; 147; CN 6;
 GLL 1
Monroe, Harriet 1860-1936 .... **TCLC 12**
 See also CA 109; 204; DLB 54, 91
Monroe, Lyle
 See Heinlein, Robert A(nson)

Montagu, Elizabeth 1720-1800 .... **NCLC 7,
 117**
 See also FW
Montagu, Mary (Pierrepont) Wortley
 1689-1762 .... **LC 9, 57; PC 16**
 See also DLB 95, 101; FL 1:1; RGEL 2
Montagu, W. H.
 See Coleridge, Samuel Taylor
Montague, John (Patrick) 1929- ..... **CLC 13,
 46**
 See also CA 9-12R; CANR 9, 69, 121; CP
 1, 2, 3, 4, 5, 6, 7; DLB 40; EWL 3;
 MTCW 1; PFS 12; RGEL 2; TCLE 1:2
Montaigne, Michel (Eyquem) de
 1533-1592 .... **LC 8, 105; WLC**
 See also DA; DAB; DAC; DAM MST; EW
 2; GFL Beginnings to 1789; LMFS 1;
 RGWL 2, 3; TWA
Montale, Eugenio 1896-1981 ... **CLC 7, 9, 18;
 PC 13**
 See also CA 17-20R; 104; CANR 30; DLB
 114; EW 11; EWL 3; MTCW 1; PFS 22;
 RGWL 2, 3; TWA; WLIT 7
Montesquieu, Charles-Louis de Secondat
 1689-1755 .... **LC 7, 69**
 See also DLB 314; EW 3; GFL Beginnings
 to 1789; TWA
Montessori, Maria 1870-1952 ...... **TCLC 103**
 See also CA 115; 147
Montgomery, (Robert) Bruce 1921(?)-1978
 See Crispin, Edmund
 See also CA 179; 104; CMW 4
Montgomery, L(ucy) M(aud)
 1874-1942 .... **TCLC 51, 140**
 See also AAYA 12; BYA 1; CA 108; 137;
 CLR 8, 91; DA3; DAC; DAM MST; DLB
 92; DLBD 14; JRDA; MAICYA 1, 2;
 MTCW 2; MTFW 2005; RGEL 2; SATA
 100; TWA; WCH; WYA; YABC 1
Montgomery, Marion H., Jr. 1925- .... **CLC 7**
 See also AITN 1; CA 1-4R; CANR 3, 48;
 CSW; DLB 6
Montgomery, Max
 See Davenport, Guy (Mattison, Jr.)
Montherlant, Henry (Milon) de
 1896-1972 .... **CLC 8, 19**
 See also CA 85-88; 37-40R; DAM DRAM;
 DLB 72, 321; EW 11; EWL 3; GFL 1789
 to the Present; MTCW 1
Monty Python
 See Chapman, Graham; Cleese, John
 (Marwood); Gilliam, Terry (Vance); Idle,
 Eric; Jones, Terence Graham Parry; Palin,
 Michael (Edward)
 See also AAYA 7
Moodie, Susanna (Strickland)
 1803-1885 .... **NCLC 14, 113**
 See also DLB 99
Moody, Hiram (F. III) 1961-
 See Moody, Rick
 See also CA 138; CANR 64, 112; MTFW
 2005
Moody, Minerva
 See Alcott, Louisa May
Moody, Rick .... **CLC 147**
 See Moody, Hiram (F. III)
Moody, William Vaughan
 1869-1910 .... **TCLC 105**
 See also CA 110; 178; DLB 7, 54; MAL 5;
 RGAL 4
Mooney, Edward 1951-
 See Mooney, Ted
 See also CA 130
Mooney, Ted .... **CLC 25**
 See Mooney, Edward

Moorcock, Michael (John) 1939- ...... **CLC 5, 27, 58**
See Bradbury, Edward P.
See also AAYA 26; CA 45-48; CAAS 5; CANR 2, 17, 38, 64, 122; CN 5, 6, 7; DLB 14, 231, 261, 319; FANT; MTCW 1, 2; MTFW 2005; SATA 93; SCFW 1, 2; SFW 4; SUFW 1, 2

Moore, Brian 1921-1999 ... **CLC 1, 3, 5, 7, 8, 19, 32, 90**
See Bryan, Michael
See also BRWS 9; CA 1-4R; 174; CANR 1, 25, 42, 63; CCA 1; CN 1, 2, 3, 4, 5, 6; DAB; DAC; DAM MST; DLB 251; EWL 3; FANT; MTCW 1, 2; MTFW 2005; RGEL 2

Moore, Edward
See Muir, Edwin
See also RGEL 2

Moore, G. E. 1873-1958 .... **TCLC 89**
See also DLB 262

Moore, George Augustus
1852-1933 .... **SSC 19; TCLC 7**
See also BRW 6; CA 104; 177; DLB 10, 18, 57, 135; EWL 3; RGEL 2; RGSF 2

Moore, Lorrie .... **CLC 39, 45, 68**
See Moore, Marie Lorena
See also AMWS 10; CN 5, 6, 7; DLB 234; SSFS 19

Moore, Marianne (Craig)
1887-1972 .... **CLC 1, 2, 4, 8, 10, 13, 19, 47; PC 4, 49; WLCS**
See also AMW; CA 1-4R; 33-36R; CANR 3, 61; CDALB 1929-1941; CP 1; DA; DA3; DAB; DAC; DAM MST, POET; DLB 45; DLBD 7; EWL 3; EXPP; FL 1:6; MAL 5; MAWW; MTCW 1, 2; MTFW 2005; PAB; PFS 14, 17; RGAL 4; SATA 20; TUS; WP

Moore, Marie Lorena 1957- .... **CLC 165**
See Moore, Lorrie
See also CA 116; CANR 39, 83, 139; DLB 234; MTFW 2005

Moore, Michael 1954- .... **CLC 218**
See also AAYA 53; CA 166

Moore, Thomas 1779-1852 .... **NCLC 6, 110**
See also DLB 96, 144; RGEL 2

Moorhouse, Frank 1938- .... **SSC 40**
See also CA 118; CANR 92; CN 3, 4, 5, 6, 7; DLB 289; RGSF 2

Mora, Pat(ricia) 1942- .... **HLC 2**
See also AMWS 13; CA 129; CANR 57, 81, 112; CLR 58; DAM MULT; DLB 209; HW 1, 2; LLW; MAICYA 2; MTFW 2005; SATA 92, 134

Moraga, Cherrie 1952- ...... **CLC 126; DC 22**
See also CA 131; CANR 66; DAM MULT; DLB 82, 249; FW; GLL 1; HW 1, 2; LLW

Morand, Paul 1888-1976 .... **CLC 41; SSC 22**
See also CA 184; 69-72; DLB 65; EWL 3

Morante, Elsa 1918-1985 .... **CLC 8, 47**
See also CA 85-88; 117; CANR 35; DLB 177; EWL 3; MTCW 1, 2; MTFW 2005; RGWL 2, 3; WLIT 7

Moravia, Alberto .... **CLC 2, 7, 11, 27, 46; SSC 26**
See Pincherle, Alberto
See also DLB 177; EW 12; EWL 3; MTCW 2; RGSF 2; RGWL 2, 3; WLIT 7

More, Hannah 1745-1833 ...... **NCLC 27, 141**
See also DLB 107, 109, 116, 158; RGEL 2

More, Henry 1614-1687 .... **LC 9**
See also DLB 126, 252

More, Sir Thomas 1478(?)-1535 .... **LC 10, 32**
See also BRWC 1; BRWS 7; DLB 136, 281; LMFS 1; RGEL 2; TEA

Moreas, Jean .... **TCLC 18**
See Papadiamantopoulos, Johannes
See also GFL 1789 to the Present

Moreton, Andrew Esq.
See Defoe, Daniel

Morgan, Berry 1919-2002 .... **CLC 6**
See also CA 49-52; 208; DLB 6

Morgan, Claire
See Highsmith, (Mary) Patricia
See also GLL 1

Morgan, Edwin (George) 1920- .... **CLC 31**
See also BRWS 9; CA 5-8R; CANR 3, 43, 90; CP 1, 2, 3, 4, 5, 6, 7; DLB 27

Morgan, (George) Frederick
1922-2004 .... **CLC 23**
See also CA 17-20R; 224; CANR 21, 144; CP 2, 3, 4, 5, 6, 7

Morgan, Harriet
See Mencken, H(enry) L(ouis)

Morgan, Jane
See Cooper, James Fenimore

Morgan, Janet 1945- .... **CLC 39**
See also CA 65-68

Morgan, Lady 1776(?)-1859 .... **NCLC 29**
See also DLB 116, 158; RGEL 2

Morgan, Robin (Evonne) 1941- .... **CLC 2**
See also CA 69-72; CANR 29, 68; FW; GLL 2; MTCW 1; SATA 80

Morgan, Scott
See Kuttner, Henry

Morgan, Seth 1949(?)-1990 .... **CLC 65**
See also CA 185; 132

Morgenstern, Christian (Otto Josef Wolfgang) 1871-1914 .... **TCLC 8**
See also CA 105; 191; EWL 3

Morgenstern, S.
See Goldman, William (W.)

Mori, Rintaro
See Mori Ogai
See also CA 110

Mori, Toshio 1910-1980 .... **SSC 83**
See also CA 116; DLB 312; RGSF 2

Moricz, Zsigmond 1879-1942 .... **TCLC 33**
See also CA 165; DLB 215; EWL 3

Morike, Eduard (Friedrich)
1804-1875 .... **NCLC 10**
See also DLB 133; RGWL 2, 3

Mori Ogai 1862-1922 .... **TCLC 14**
See Ogai
See also CA 164; DLB 180; EWL 3; RGWL 3; TWA

Moritz, Karl Philipp 1756-1793 .... **LC 2**
See also DLB 94

Morland, Peter Henry
See Faust, Frederick (Schiller)

Morley, Christopher (Darlington)
1890-1957 .... **TCLC 87**
See also CA 112; 213; DLB 9; MAL 5; RGAL 4

Morren, Theophil
See Hofmannsthal, Hugo von

Morris, Bill 1952- .... **CLC 76**
See also CA 225

Morris, Julian
See West, Morris L(anglo)

Morris, Steveland Judkins 1950(?)-
See Wonder, Stevie
See also CA 111

Morris, William 1834-1896 . **NCLC 4; PC 55**
See also BRW 5; CDBLB 1832-1890; DLB 18, 35, 57, 156, 178, 184; FANT; RGEL 2; SFW 4; SUFW

Morris, Wright (Marion) 1910-1998 . **CLC 1, 3, 7, 18, 37; TCLC 107**
See also AMW; CA 9-12R; 167; CANR 21, 81; CN 1, 2, 3, 4, 5, 6; DLB 2, 206, 218; DLBY 1981; EWL 3; MAL 5; MTCW 1, 2; MTFW 2005; RGAL 4; TCWW 1, 2

Morrison, Arthur 1863-1945 .... **SSC 40; TCLC 72**
See also CA 120; 157; CMW 4; DLB 70, 135, 197; RGEL 2

Morrison, Chloe Anthony Wofford
See Morrison, Toni

Morrison, James Douglas 1943-1971
See Morrison, Jim
See also CA 73-76; CANR 40

Morrison, Jim .... **CLC 17**
See Morrison, James Douglas

Morrison, Toni 1931- ..... **BLC 3; CLC 4, 10, 22, 55, 81, 87, 173, 194**
See also AAYA 1, 22, 61; AFAW 1, 2; AMWC 1; AMWS 3; BPFB 2; BW 2, 3; CA 29-32R; CANR 27, 42, 67, 113, 124; CDALB 1968-1988; CLR 99; CN 3, 4, 5, 6, 7; CPW; DA; DA3; DAB; DAC; DAM MST, MULT, NOV, POP; DLB 6, 33, 143; DLBY 1981; EWL 3; EXPN; FL 1:6; FW; GL 3; LAIT 2, 4; LATS 1:2; LMFS 2; MAL 5; MAWW; MTCW 1, 2; MTFW 2005; NFS 1, 6, 8, 14; RGAL 4; RHW; SATA 57, 144; SSFS 5; TCLE 1:2; TUS; YAW

Morrison, Van 1945- .... **CLC 21**
See also CA 116; 168

Morrissy, Mary 1957- .... **CLC 99**
See also CA 205; DLB 267

Mortimer, John (Clifford) 1923- ..... **CLC 28, 43**
See also CA 13-16R; CANR 21, 69, 109; CBD; CD 5, 6; CDBLB 1960 to Present; CMW 4; CN 5, 6, 7; CPW; DA3; DAM DRAM, POP; DLB 13, 245, 271; INT CANR-21; MSW; MTCW 1, 2; MTFW 2005; RGEL 2

Mortimer, Penelope (Ruth)
1918-1999 .... **CLC 5**
See also CA 57-60; 187; CANR 45, 88; CN 1, 2, 3, 4, 5, 6

Mortimer, Sir John
See Mortimer, John (Clifford)

Morton, Anthony
See Creasey, John

Morton, Thomas 1579(?)-1647(?) .... **LC 72**
See also DLB 24; RGEL 2

Mosca, Gaetano 1858-1941 .... **TCLC 75**

Moses, Daniel David 1952- .... **NNAL**
See also CA 186

Mosher, Howard Frank 1943- .... **CLC 62**
See also CA 139; CANR 65, 115

Mosley, Nicholas 1923- .... **CLC 43, 70**
See also CA 69-72; CANR 41, 60, 108; CN 1, 2, 3, 4, 5, 6, 7; DLB 14, 207

Mosley, Walter 1952- .... **BLCS; CLC 97, 184**
See also AAYA 57; AMWS 13; BPFB 2; BW 2; CA 142; CANR 57, 92, 136; CMW 4; CN 7; CPW; DA3; DAM MULT, POP; DLB 306; MSW; MTCW 2; MTFW 2005

Moss, Howard 1922-1987 . **CLC 7, 14, 45, 50**
See also CA 1-4R; 123; CANR 1, 44; CP 1, 2, 3, 4; DAM POET; DLB 5

Mossgiel, Rab
See Burns, Robert

Motion, Andrew (Peter) 1952- .... **CLC 47**
See also BRWS 7; CA 146; CANR 90, 142; CP 4, 5, 6, 7; DLB 40; MTFW 2005

Motley, Willard (Francis)
1909-1965 .... **CLC 18**
See also BW 1; CA 117; 106; CANR 88; DLB 76, 143

Motoori, Norinaga 1730-1801 .... **NCLC 45**

Mott, Michael (Charles Alston)
1930- .... **CLC 15, 34**
See also CA 5-8R; CAAS 7; CANR 7, 29

Mountain Wolf Woman 1884-1960 . **CLC 92; NNAL**
See also CA 144; CANR 90

Moure, Erin 1955- .... **CLC 88**
See also CA 113; CP 7; CWP; DLB 60

Oskison, John Milton
1874-1947 .... **NNAL; TCLC 35**
See also CA 144; CANR 84; DAM MULT;
DLB 175

Ossian c. 3rd cent. - .... **CMLC 28**
See Macpherson, James

Ossoli, Sarah Margaret (Fuller)
1810-1850 .... **NCLC 5, 50**
See Fuller, Margaret; Fuller, Sarah Margaret
See also CDALB 1640-1865; FW; LMFS 1;
SATA 25

Ostriker, Alicia (Suskin) 1937- .... **CLC 132**
See also CA 25-28R; CAAS 24; CANR 10,
30, 62, 99; CWP; DLB 120; EXPP; PFS
19

Ostrovsky, Aleksandr Nikolaevich
See Ostrovsky, Alexander
See also DLB 277

Ostrovsky, Alexander 1823-1886 .. **NCLC 30,
57**
See Ostrovsky, Aleksandr Nikolaevich

Otero, Blas de 1916-1979 .... **CLC 11**
See also CA 89-92; DLB 134; EWL 3

O'Trigger, Sir Lucius
See Horne, Richard Henry Hengist

Otto, Rudolf 1869-1937 .... **TCLC 85**

Otto, Whitney 1955- .... **CLC 70**
See also CA 140; CANR 120

Otway, Thomas 1652-1685 ... **DC 24; LC 106**
See also DAM DRAM; DLB 80; RGEL 2

Ouida .... **TCLC 43**
See De la Ramee, Marie Louise (Ouida)
See also DLB 18, 156; RGEL 2

Ouologuem, Yambo 1940- .... **CLC 146**
See also CA 111; 176

Ousmane, Sembene 1923- ... **BLC 3; CLC 66**
See Sembene, Ousmane
See also BW 1, 3; CA 117; 125; CANR 81;
CWW 2; MTCW 1

Ovid 43B.C.-17 .... **CMLC 7; PC 2**
See also AW 2; CDWLB 1; DA3; DAM
POET; DLB 211; PFS 22; RGWL 2, 3;
WP

Owen, Hugh
See Faust, Frederick (Schiller)

Owen, Wilfred (Edward Salter)
1893-1918 ... **PC 19; TCLC 5, 27; WLC**
See also BRW 6; CA 104; 141; CDBLB
1914-1945; DA; DAB; DAC; DAM MST,
POET; DLB 20; EWL 3; EXPP; MTCW
2; MTFW 2005; PFS 10; RGEL 2; WLIT
4

Owens, Louis (Dean) 1948-2002 .... **NNAL**
See also CA 137, 179; 207; CAAE 179;
CAAS 24; CANR 71

Owens, Rochelle 1936- .... **CLC 8**
See also CA 17-20R; CAAS 2; CAD;
CANR 39; CD 5, 6; CP 1, 2, 3, 4, 5, 6, 7;
CWD; CWP

Oz, Amos 1939- ...... **CLC 5, 8, 11, 27, 33, 54;
SSC 66**
See also CA 53-56; CANR 27, 47, 65, 113,
138; CWW 2; DAM NOV; EWL 3;
MTCW 1, 2; MTFW 2005; RGSF 2;
RGWL 3; WLIT 6

Ozick, Cynthia 1928- .... **CLC 3, 7, 28, 62,
155; SSC 15, 60**
See also AMWS 5; BEST 90:1; CA 17-20R;
CANR 23, 58, 116; CN 3, 4, 5, 6, 7;
CPW; DA3; DAM NOV, POP; DLB 28,
152, 299; DLBY 1982; EWL 3; EXPS;
INT CANR-23; MAL 5; MTCW 1, 2;
MTFW 2005; RGAL 4; RGSF 2; SSFS 3,
12

Ozu, Yasujiro 1903-1963 .... **CLC 16**
See also CA 112

Pabst, G. W. 1885-1967 .... **TCLC 127**

Pacheco, C.
See Pessoa, Fernando (Antonio Nogueira)

Pacheco, Jose Emilio 1939- .... **HLC 2**
See also CA 111; 131; CANR 65; CWW 2;
DAM MULT; DLB 290; EWL 3; HW 1,
2; RGSF 2

Pa Chin .... **CLC 18**
See Li Fei-kan
See also EWL 3

Pack, Robert 1929- .... **CLC 13**
See also CA 1-4R; CANR 3, 44, 82; CP 1,
2, 3, 4, 5, 6, 7; DLB 5; SATA 118

Padgett, Lewis
See Kuttner, Henry

Padilla (Lorenzo), Heberto
1932-2000 .... **CLC 38**
See also AITN 1; CA 123; 131; 189; CWW
2; EWL 3; HW 1

Page, James Patrick 1944-
See Page, Jimmy
See also CA 204

Page, Jimmy 1944- .... **CLC 12**
See Page, James Patrick

Page, Louise 1955- .... **CLC 40**
See also CA 140; CANR 76; CBD; CD 5,
6; CWD; DLB 233

Page, P(atricia) K(athleen) 1916- ...... **CLC 7,
18; PC 12**
See Cape, Judith
See also CA 53-56; CANR 4, 22, 65; CP 1,
2, 3, 4, 5, 6, 7; DAC; DAM MST; DLB
68; MTCW 1; RGEL 2

Page, Stanton
See Fuller, Henry Blake

Page, Stanton
See Fuller, Henry Blake

Page, Thomas Nelson 1853-1922 .... **SSC 23**
See also CA 118; 177; DLB 12, 78; DLBD
13; RGAL 4

Pagels, Elaine Hiesey 1943- .... **CLC 104**
See also CA 45-48; CANR 2, 24, 51; FW;
NCFS 4

Paget, Violet 1856-1935
See Lee, Vernon
See also CA 104; 166; GLL 1; HGG

Paget-Lowe, Henry
See Lovecraft, H(oward) P(hillips)

Paglia, Camille (Anna) 1947- .... **CLC 68**
See also CA 140; CANR 72, 139; CPW;
FW; GLL 2; MTCW 2; MTFW 2005

Paige, Richard
See Koontz, Dean R.

Paine, Thomas 1737-1809 .... **NCLC 62**
See also AMWS 1; CDALB 1640-1865;
DLB 31, 43, 73, 158; LAIT 1; RGAL 4;
RGEL 2; TUS

Pakenham, Antonia
See Fraser, Antonia (Pakenham)

Palamas, Costis
See Palamas, Kostes

Palamas, Kostes 1859-1943 .... **TCLC 5**
See Palamas, Kostis
See also CA 105; 190; RGWL 2, 3

Palamas, Kostis
See Palamas, Kostes
See also EWL 3

Palazzeschi, Aldo 1885-1974 .... **CLC 11**
See also CA 89-92; 53-56; DLB 114, 264;
EWL 3

Pales Matos, Luis 1898-1959 .... **HLCS 2**
See Pales Matos, Luis
See also DLB 290; HW 1; LAW

Paley, Grace 1922- .. **CLC 4, 6, 37, 140; SSC
8**
See also AMWS 6; CA 25-28R; CANR 13,
46, 74, 118; CN 2, 3, 4, 5, 6, 7; CPW;
DA3; DAM POP; DLB 28, 218; EWL 3;
EXPS; FW; INT CANR-13; MAL 5;
MAWW; MTCW 1, 2; MTFW 2005;
RGAL 4; RGSF 2; SSFS 3, 20

Palin, Michael (Edward) 1943- .... **CLC 21**
See Monty Python
See also CA 107; CANR 35, 109; SATA 67

Palliser, Charles 1947- .... **CLC 65**
See also CA 136; CANR 76; CN 5, 6, 7

Palma, Ricardo 1833-1919 .... **TCLC 29**
See also CA 168; LAW

Pamuk, Orhan 1952- .... **CLC 185**
See also CA 142; CANR 75, 127; CWW 2;
WLIT 6

Pancake, Breece Dexter 1952-1979
See Pancake, Breece D'J
See also CA 123; 109

Pancake, Breece D'J .... **CLC 29; SSC 61**
See Pancake, Breece Dexter
See also DLB 130

Panchenko, Nikolai .... **CLC 59**

Pankhurst, Emmeline (Goulden)
1858-1928 .... **TCLC 100**
See also CA 116; FW

Panko, Rudy
See Gogol, Nikolai (Vasilyevich)

Papadiamantis, Alexandros
1851-1911 .... **TCLC 29**
See also CA 168; EWL 3

Papadiamantopoulos, Johannes 1856-1910
See Moreas, Jean
See also CA 117

Papini, Giovanni 1881-1956 .... **TCLC 22**
See also CA 121; 180; DLB 264

Paracelsus 1493-1541 .... **LC 14**
See also DLB 179

Parasol, Peter
See Stevens, Wallace

Pardo Bazan, Emilia 1851-1921 .... **SSC 30**
See also EWL 3; FW; RGSF 2; RGWL 2, 3

Pareto, Vilfredo 1848-1923 .... **TCLC 69**
See also CA 175

Paretsky, Sara 1947- .... **CLC 135**
See also AAYA 30; BEST 90:3; CA 125;
129; CANR 59, 95; CMW 4; CPW; DA3;
DAM POP; DLB 306; INT CA-129;
MSW; RGAL 4

Parfenie, Maria
See Codrescu, Andrei

Parini, Jay (Lee) 1948- .... **CLC 54, 133**
See also CA 97-100, 229; CAAE 229;
CAAS 16; CANR 32, 87

Park, Jordan
See Kornbluth, C(yril) M.; Pohl, Frederik

Park, Robert E(zra) 1864-1944 ..... **TCLC 73**
See also CA 122; 165

Parker, Bert
See Ellison, Harlan (Jay)

Parker, Dorothy (Rothschild)
1893-1967 . **CLC 15, 68; PC 28; SSC 2;
TCLC 143**
See also AMWS 9; CA 19-20; 25-28R; CAP
2; DA3; DAM POET; DLB 11, 45, 86;
EXPP; FW; MAL 5; MAWW; MTCW 1,
2; MTFW 2005; PFS 18; RGAL 4; RGSF
2; TUS

Parker, Robert B(rown) 1932- .... **CLC 27**
See also AAYA 28; BEST 89:4; BPFB 3;
CA 49-52; CANR 1, 26, 52, 89, 128;
CMW 4; CPW; DAM NOV, POP; DLB
306; INT CANR-26; MSW; MTCW 1;
MTFW 2005

Parkin, Frank 1940- .... **CLC 43**
See also CA 147

Parkman, Francis, Jr. 1823-1893 .. **NCLC 12**
See also AMWS 2; DLB 1, 30, 183, 186,
235; RGAL 4

Parks, Gordon (Alexander Buchanan)
1912- .... **BLC 3; CLC 1, 16**
See also AAYA 36; AITN 2; BW 2, 3; CA
41-44R; CANR 26, 66, 145; DA3; DAM
MULT; DLB 33; MTCW 2; MTFW 2005;
SATA 8, 108

Reyes y Basoalto, Ricardo Eliecer Neftali
See Neruda, Pablo
Reymont, Wladyslaw (Stanislaw)
1868(?)-1925 .... **TCLC 5**
See also CA 104; EWL 3
Reynolds, John Hamilton
1794-1852 .... **NCLC 146**
See also DLB 96
Reynolds, Jonathan 1942- .... **CLC 6, 38**
See also CA 65-68; CANR 28
Reynolds, Joshua 1723-1792 .... **LC 15**
See also DLB 104
Reynolds, Michael S(hane)
1937-2000 .... **CLC 44**
See also CA 65-68; 189; CANR 9, 89, 97
Reznikoff, Charles 1894-1976 .... **CLC 9**
See also AMWS 14; CA 33-36; 61-64; CAP 2; CP 1, 2; DLB 28, 45; WP
Rezzori (d'Arezzo), Gregor von
1914-1998 .... **CLC 25**
See also CA 122; 136; 167
Rhine, Richard
See Silverstein, Alvin; Silverstein, Virginia B(arbara Opshelor)
Rhodes, Eugene Manlove
1869-1934 .... **TCLC 53**
See also CA 198; DLB 256; TCWW 1, 2
R'hoone, Lord
See Balzac, Honore de
Rhys, Jean 1890-1979 .... **CLC 2, 4, 6, 14, 19, 51, 124; SSC 21, 76**
See also BRWS 2; CA 25-28R; 85-88; CANR 35, 62; CDBLB 1945-1960; CD-WLB 3; CN 1, 2; DA3; DAM NOV; DLB 36, 117, 162; DNFS 2; EWL 3; LATS 1:1; MTCW 1, 2; MTFW 2005; NFS 19; RGEL 2; RGSF 2; RHW; TEA; WWE 1
Ribeiro, Darcy 1922-1997 .... **CLC 34**
See also CA 33-36R; 156; EWL 3
Ribeiro, Joao Ubaldo (Osorio Pimentel)
1941- .... **CLC 10, 67**
See also CA 81-84; CWW 2; EWL 3
Ribman, Ronald (Burt) 1932- .... **CLC 7**
See also CA 21-24R; CAD; CANR 46, 80; CD 5, 6
Ricci, Nino (Pio) 1959- .... **CLC 70**
See also CA 137; CANR 130; CCA 1
Rice, Anne 1941- .... **CLC 41, 128**
See Rampling, Anne
See also AAYA 9, 53; AMWS 7; BEST 89:2; BPFB 3; CA 65-68; CANR 12, 36, 53, 74, 100, 133; CN 6, 7; CPW; CSW; DA3; DAM POP; DLB 292; GL 3; GLL 2; HGG; MTCW 2; MTFW 2005; SUFW 2; YAW
Rice, Elmer (Leopold) 1892-1967 ...... **CLC 7, 49**
See Reizenstein, Elmer Leopold
See also CA 21-22; 25-28R; CAP 2; DAM DRAM; DFS 12; DLB 4, 7; IDTP; MAL 5; MTCW 1, 2; RGAL 4
Rice, Tim(othy Miles Bindon)
1944- .... **CLC 21**
See also CA 103; CANR 46; DFS 7
Rich, Adrienne (Cecile) 1929- ... **CLC 3, 6, 7, 11, 18, 36, 73, 76, 125; PC 5**
See also AMWR 2; AMWS 1; CA 9-12R; CANR 20, 53, 74, 128; CDALBS; CP 1, 2, 3, 4, 5, 6, 7; CSW; CWP; DA3; DAM POET; DLB 5, 67; EWL 3; EXPP; FL 1:6; FW; MAL 5; MAWW; MTCW 1, 2; MTFW 2005; PAB; PFS 15; RGAL 4; WP
Rich, Barbara
See Graves, Robert (von Ranke)
Rich, Robert
See Trumbo, Dalton
Richard, Keith .... **CLC 17**
See Richards, Keith

Richards, David Adams 1950- .... **CLC 59**
See also CA 93-96; CANR 60, 110; CN 7; DAC; DLB 53; TCLE 1:2
Richards, I(vor) A(rmstrong)
1893-1979 .... **CLC 14, 24**
See also BRWS 2; CA 41-44R; 89-92; CANR 34, 74; CP 1, 2; DLB 27; EWL 3; MTCW 2; RGEL 2
Richards, Keith 1943-
See Richard, Keith
See also CA 107; CANR 77
Richardson, Anne
See Roiphe, Anne (Richardson)
Richardson, Dorothy Miller
1873-1957 .... **TCLC 3**
See also CA 104; 192; DLB 36; EWL 3; FW; RGEL 2
Richardson (Robertson), Ethel Florence Lindesay 1870-1946
See Richardson, Henry Handel
See also CA 105; 190; DLB 230; RHW
Richardson, Henry Handel .... **TCLC 4**
See Richardson (Robertson), Ethel Florence Lindesay
See also DLB 197; EWL 3; RGEL 2; RGSF 2
Richardson, John 1796-1852 .... **NCLC 55**
See also CCA 1; DAC; DLB 99
Richardson, Samuel 1689-1761 ...... **LC 1, 44; WLC**
See also BRW 3; CDBLB 1660-1789; DA; DAB; DAC; DAM MST, NOV; DLB 39; RGEL 2; TEA; WLIT 3
Richardson, Willis 1889-1977 .... **HR 1:3**
See also BW 1; CA 124; DLB 51; SATA 60
Richler, Mordecai 1931-2001 .... **CLC 3, 5, 9, 13, 18, 46, 70, 185**
See also AITN 1; CA 65-68; 201; CANR 31, 62, 111; CCA 1; CLR 17; CN 1, 2, 3, 4, 5, 7; CWRI 5; DAC; DAM MST, NOV; DLB 53; EWL 3; MAICYA 1, 2; MTCW 1, 2; MTFW 2005; RGEL 2; SATA 44, 98; SATA-Brief 27; TWA
Richter, Conrad (Michael)
1890-1968 .... **CLC 30**
See also AAYA 21; BYA 2; CA 5-8R; 25-28R; CANR 23; DLB 9, 212; LAIT 1; MAL 5; MTCW 1, 2; MTFW 2005; RGAL 4; SATA 3; TCWW 1, 2; TUS; YAW
Ricostranza, Tom
See Ellis, Trey
Riddell, Charlotte 1832-1906 .... **TCLC 40**
See Riddell, Mrs. J. H.
See also CA 165; DLB 156
Riddell, Mrs. J. H.
See Riddell, Charlotte
See also HGG; SUFW
Ridge, John Rollin 1827-1867 ...... **NCLC 82; NNAL**
See also CA 144; DAM MULT; DLB 175
Ridgeway, Jason
See Marlowe, Stephen
Ridgway, Keith 1965- .... **CLC 119**
See also CA 172; CANR 144
Riding, Laura .... **CLC 3, 7**
See Jackson, Laura (Riding)
See also CP 1, 2, 3, 4; RGAL 4
Riefenstahl, Berta Helene Amalia 1902-2003
See Riefenstahl, Leni
See also CA 108; 220
Riefenstahl, Leni .... **CLC 16, 190**
See Riefenstahl, Berta Helene Amalia
Riffe, Ernest
See Bergman, (Ernst) Ingmar
Riggs, (Rolla) Lynn
1899-1954 .... **NNAL; TCLC 56**
See also CA 144; DAM MULT; DLB 175

Riis, Jacob A(ugust) 1849-1914 ..... **TCLC 80**
See also CA 113; 168; DLB 23
Riley, James Whitcomb 1849-1916 .... **PC 48; TCLC 51**
See also CA 118; 137; DAM POET; MAI-CYA 1, 2; RGAL 4; SATA 17
Riley, Tex
See Creasey, John
Rilke, Rainer Maria 1875-1926 .... **PC 2; TCLC 1, 6, 19**
See also CA 104; 132; CANR 62, 99; CD-WLB 2; DA3; DAM POET; DLB 81; EW 9; EWL 3; MTCW 1, 2; MTFW 2005; PFS 19; RGWL 2, 3; TWA; WP
Rimbaud, (Jean Nicolas) Arthur
1854-1891 ... **NCLC 4, 35, 82; PC 3, 57; WLC**
See also DA; DA3; DAB; DAC; DAM MST, POET; DLB 217; EW 7; GFL 1789 to the Present; LMFS 2; RGWL 2, 3; TWA; WP
Rinehart, Mary Roberts
1876-1958 .... **TCLC 52**
See also BPFB 3; CA 108; 166; RGAL 4; RHW
Ringmaster, The
See Mencken, H(enry) L(ouis)
Ringwood, Gwen(dolyn Margaret) Pharis
1910-1984 .... **CLC 48**
See also CA 148; 112; DLB 88
Rio, Michel 1945(?)- .... **CLC 43**
See also CA 201
Rios, Alberto (Alvaro) 1952- .... **PC 57**
See also AAYA 66; AMWS 4; CA 113; CANR 34, 79, 137; CP 7; DLB 122; HW 2; MTFW 2005; PFS 11
Ritsos, Giannes
See Ritsos, Yannis
Ritsos, Yannis 1909-1990 .... **CLC 6, 13, 31**
See also CA 77-80; 133; CANR 39, 61; EW 12; EWL 3; MTCW 1; RGWL 2, 3
Ritter, Erika 1948(?)- .... **CLC 52**
See also CD 5, 6; CWD
Rivera, Jose Eustasio 1889-1928 ... **TCLC 35**
See also CA 162; EWL 3; HW 1, 2; LAW
Rivera, Tomas 1935-1984 .... **HLCS 2**
See also CA 49-52; CANR 32; DLB 82; HW 1; LLW; RGAL 4; SSFS 15; TCWW 2; WLIT 1
Rivers, Conrad Kent 1933-1968 .... **CLC 1**
See also BW 1; CA 85-88; DLB 41
Rivers, Elfrida
See Bradley, Marion Zimmer
See also GLL 1
Riverside, John
See Heinlein, Robert A(nson)
Rizal, Jose 1861-1896 .... **NCLC 27**
Roa Bastos, Augusto (Jose Antonio)
1917-2005 .... **CLC 45; HLC 2**
See also CA 131; 238; CWW 2; DAM MULT; DLB 113; EWL 3; HW 1; LAW; RGSF 2; WLIT 1
Robbe-Grillet, Alain 1922- .... **CLC 1, 2, 4, 6, 8, 10, 14, 43, 128**
See also BPFB 3; CA 9-12R; CANR 33, 65, 115; CWW 2; DLB 83; EW 13; EWL 3; GFL 1789 to the Present; IDFW 3, 4; MTCW 1, 2; MTFW 2005; RGWL 2, 3; SSFS 15
Robbins, Harold 1916-1997 .... **CLC 5**
See also BPFB 3; CA 73-76; 162; CANR 26, 54, 112; DA3; DAM NOV; MTCW 1, 2
Robbins, Thomas Eugene 1936-
See Robbins, Tom
See also CA 81-84; CANR 29, 59, 95, 139; CN 7; CPW; CSW; DA3; DAM NOV, POP; MTCW 1, 2; MTFW 2005

Robbins, Tom .... **CLC 9, 32, 64**
See Robbins, Thomas Eugene
See also AAYA 32; AMWS 10; BEST 90:3;
BPFB 3; CN 3, 4, 5, 6, 7; DLBY 1980

Robbins, Trina 1938- .... **CLC 21**
See also AAYA 61; CA 128

Roberts, Charles G(eorge) D(ouglas)
1860-1943 .... **TCLC 8**
See also CA 105; 188; CLR 33; CWRI 5;
DLB 92; RGEL 2; RGSF 2; SATA 88;
SATA-Brief 29

Roberts, Elizabeth Madox
1886-1941 .... **TCLC 68**
See also CA 111; 166; CLR 100; CWRI 5;
DLB 9, 54, 102; RGAL 4; RHW; SATA
33; SATA-Brief 27; TCWW 2; WCH

Roberts, Kate 1891-1985 .... **CLC 15**
See also CA 107; 116; DLB 319

Roberts, Keith (John Kingston)
1935-2000 .... **CLC 14**
See also BRWS 10; CA 25-28R; CANR 46;
DLB 261; SFW 4

Roberts, Kenneth (Lewis)
1885-1957 .... **TCLC 23**
See also CA 109; 199; DLB 9; MAL 5;
RGAL 4; RHW

Roberts, Michele (Brigitte) 1949- .... **CLC 48, 178**
See also CA 115; CANR 58, 120; CN 6, 7;
DLB 231; FW

Robertson, Ellis
See Ellison, Harlan (Jay); Silverberg, Robert

Robertson, Thomas William
1829-1871 .... **NCLC 35**
See Robertson, Tom
See also DAM DRAM

Robertson, Tom
See Robertson, Thomas William
See also RGEL 2

Robeson, Kenneth
See Dent, Lester

Robinson, Edwin Arlington
1869-1935 .... **PC 1, 35; TCLC 5, 101**
See also AMW; CA 104; 133; CDALB
1865-1917; DA; DAC; DAM MST,
POET; DLB 54; EWL 3; EXPP; MAL 5;
MTCW 1, 2; MTFW 2005; PAB; PFS 4;
RGAL 4; WP

Robinson, Henry Crabb
1775-1867 .... **NCLC 15**
See also DLB 107

Robinson, Jill 1936- .... **CLC 10**
See also CA 102; CANR 120; INT CA-102

Robinson, Kim Stanley 1952- .... **CLC 34**
See also AAYA 26; CA 126; CANR 113,
139; CN 6, 7; MTFW 2005; SATA 109;
SCFW 2; SFW 4

Robinson, Lloyd
See Silverberg, Robert

Robinson, Marilynne 1944- ...... **CLC 25, 180**
See also CA 116; CANR 80, 140; CN 4, 5,
6, 7; DLB 206; MTFW 2005

Robinson, Mary 1758-1800 .... **NCLC 142**
See also DLB 158; FW

Robinson, Smokey .... **CLC 21**
See Robinson, William, Jr.

Robinson, William, Jr. 1940-
See Robinson, Smokey
See also CA 116

Robison, Mary 1949- .... **CLC 42, 98**
See also CA 113; 116; CANR 87; CN 4, 5,
6, 7; DLB 130; INT CA-116; RGSF 2

Roches, Catherine des 1542-1587 ...... **LC 117**

Rochester
See Wilmot, John
See also RGEL 2

Rod, Edouard 1857-1910 .... **TCLC 52**

Roddenberry, Eugene Wesley 1921-1991
See Roddenberry, Gene
See also CA 110; 135; CANR 37; SATA 45;
SATA-Obit 69

Roddenberry, Gene .... **CLC 17**
See Roddenberry, Eugene Wesley
See also AAYA 5; SATA-Obit 69

Rodgers, Mary 1931- .... **CLC 12**
See also BYA 5; CA 49-52; CANR 8, 55,
90; CLR 20; CWRI 5; INT CANR-8;
JRDA; MAICYA 1, 2; SATA 8, 130

Rodgers, W(illiam) R(obert)
1909-1969 .... **CLC 7**
See also CA 85-88; DLB 20; RGEL 2

Rodman, Eric
See Silverberg, Robert

Rodman, Howard 1920(?)-1985 .... **CLC 65**
See also CA 118

Rodman, Maia
See Wojciechowska, Maia (Teresa)

Rodo, Jose Enrique 1871(?)-1917 .... **HLCS 2**
See also CA 178; EWL 3; HW 2; LAW

Rodolph, Utto
See Ouologuem, Yambo

Rodriguez, Claudio 1934-1999 .... **CLC 10**
See also CA 188; DLB 134

Rodriguez, Richard 1944- .... **CLC 155; HLC 2**
See also AMWS 14; CA 110; CANR 66,
116; DAM MULT; DLB 82, 256; HW 1,
2; LAIT 5; LLW; MTFW 2005; NCFS 3;
WLIT 1

Roelvaag, O(le) E(dvart) 1876-1931
See Rolvaag, O(le) E(dvart)
See also CA 117; 171

Roethke, Theodore (Huebner)
1908-1963 .... **CLC 1, 3, 8, 11, 19, 46, 101; PC 15**
See also AMW; CA 81-84; CABS 2;
CDALB 1941-1968; DA3; DAM POET;
DLB 5, 206; EWL 3; EXPP; MAL 5;
MTCW 1, 2; PAB; PFS 3; RGAL 4; WP

Rogers, Carl R(ansom)
1902-1987 .... **TCLC 125**
See also CA 1-4R; 121; CANR 1, 18;
MTCW 1

Rogers, Samuel 1763-1855 .... **NCLC 69**
See also DLB 93; RGEL 2

Rogers, Thomas Hunton 1927- .... **CLC 57**
See also CA 89-92; INT CA-89-92

Rogers, Will(iam Penn Adair)
1879-1935 .... **NNAL; TCLC 8, 71**
See also CA 105; 144; DA3; DAM MULT;
DLB 11; MTCW 1

Rogin, Gilbert 1929- .... **CLC 18**
See also CA 65-68; CANR 15

Rohan, Koda
See Koda Shigeyuki

Rohlfs, Anna Katharine Green
See Green, Anna Katharine

Rohmer, Eric .... **CLC 16**
See Scherer, Jean-Marie Maurice

Rohmer, Sax .... **TCLC 28**
See Ward, Arthur Henry Sarsfield
See also DLB 70; MSW; SUFW

Roiphe, Anne (Richardson) 1935- .. **CLC 3, 9**
See also CA 89-92; CANR 45, 73, 138;
DLBY 1980; INT CA-89-92

Rojas, Fernando de 1475-1541 ... **HLCS 1, 2; LC 23**
See also DLB 286; RGWL 2, 3

Rojas, Gonzalo 1917- .... **HLCS 2**
See also CA 178; HW 2; LAWS 1

Roland (de la Platiere), Marie-Jeanne
1754-1793 .... **LC 98**
See also DLB 314

Rolfe, Frederick (William Serafino Austin Lewis Mary) 1860-1913 .... **TCLC 12**
See Al Siddik
See also CA 107; 210; DLB 34, 156; RGEL 2

Rolland, Romain 1866-1944 .... **TCLC 23**
See also CA 118; 197; DLB 65, 284; EWL
3; GFL 1789 to the Present; RGWL 2, 3

Rolle, Richard c. 1300-c. 1349 ...... **CMLC 21**
See also DLB 146; LMFS 1; RGEL 2

Rolvaag, O(le) E(dvart) .... **TCLC 17**
See Roelvaag, O(le) E(dvart)
See also DLB 9, 212; MAL 5; NFS 5;
RGAL 4

Romain Arnaud, Saint
See Aragon, Louis

Romains, Jules 1885-1972 .... **CLC 7**
See also CA 85-88; CANR 34; DLB 65,
321; EWL 3; GFL 1789 to the Present;
MTCW 1

Romero, Jose Ruben 1890-1952 .... **TCLC 14**
See also CA 114; 131; EWL 3; HW 1; LAW

Ronsard, Pierre de 1524-1585 . **LC 6, 54; PC 11**
See also EW 2; GFL Beginnings to 1789;
RGWL 2, 3; TWA

Rooke, Leon 1934- .... **CLC 25, 34**
See also CA 25-28R; CANR 23, 53; CCA
1; CPW; DAM POP

Roosevelt, Franklin Delano
1882-1945 .... **TCLC 93**
See also CA 116; 173; LAIT 3

Roosevelt, Theodore 1858-1919 ..... **TCLC 69**
See also CA 115; 170; DLB 47, 186, 275

Roper, William 1498-1578 .... **LC 10**

Roquelaure, A. N.
See Rice, Anne

Rosa, Joao Guimaraes 1908-1967 ... **CLC 23; HLCS 1**
See Guimaraes Rosa, Joao
See also CA 89-92; DLB 113, 307; EWL 3;
WLIT 1

Rose, Wendy 1948- . **CLC 85; NNAL; PC 13**
See also CA 53-56; CANR 5, 51; CWP;
DAM MULT; DLB 175; PFS 13; RGAL
4; SATA 12

Rosen, R. D.
See Rosen, Richard (Dean)

Rosen, Richard (Dean) 1949- .... **CLC 39**
See also CA 77-80; CANR 62, 120; CMW
4; INT CANR-30

Rosenberg, Isaac 1890-1918 .... **TCLC 12**
See also BRW 6; CA 107; 188; DLB 20,
216; EWL 3; PAB; RGEL 2

Rosenblatt, Joe .... **CLC 15**
See Rosenblatt, Joseph
See also CP 3, 4, 5, 6, 7

Rosenblatt, Joseph 1933-
See Rosenblatt, Joe
See also CA 89-92; CP 1, 2; INT CA-89-92

Rosenfeld, Samuel
See Tzara, Tristan

Rosenstock, Sami
See Tzara, Tristan

Rosenstock, Samuel
See Tzara, Tristan

Rosenthal, M(acha) L(ouis)
1917-1996 .... **CLC 28**
See also CA 1-4R; 152; CAAS 6; CANR 4,
51; CP 1, 2, 3, 4; DLB 5; SATA 59

Ross, Barnaby
See Dannay, Frederic

Ross, Bernard L.
See Follett, Ken(neth Martin)

Ross, J. H.
See Lawrence, T(homas) E(dward)

Ross, John Hume
See Lawrence, T(homas) E(dward)

Ross, Martin 1862-1915
See Martin, Violet Florence
See also DLB 135; GLL 2; RGEL 2; RGSF 2

Ross, (James) Sinclair 1908-1996 ... **CLC 13; SSC 24**
See also CA 73-76; CANR 81; CN 1, 2, 3, 4, 5, 6; DAC; DAM MST; DLB 88; RGEL 2; RGSF 2; TCWW 1, 2

Rossetti, Christina 1830-1894 ... **NCLC 2, 50, 66; PC 7; WLC**
See also AAYA 51; BRW 5; BYA 4; DA; DA3; DAB; DAC; DAM MST, POET; DLB 35, 163, 240; EXPP; FL 1:3; LATS 1:1; MAICYA 1, 2; PFS 10, 14; RGEL 2; SATA 20; TEA; WCH

Rossetti, Christina Georgina
See Rossetti, Christina

Rossetti, Dante Gabriel 1828-1882 . **NCLC 4, 77; PC 44; WLC**
See also AAYA 51; BRW 5; CDBLB 1832-1890; DA; DAB; DAC; DAM MST, POET; DLB 35; EXPP; RGEL 2; TEA

Rossi, Cristina Peri
See Peri Rossi, Cristina

Rossi, Jean-Baptiste 1931-2003
See Japrisot, Sebastien
See also CA 201; 215

Rossner, Judith (Perelman) 1935- . **CLC 6, 9, 29**
See also AITN 2; BEST 90:3; BPFB 3; CA 17-20R; CANR 18, 51, 73; CN 4, 5, 6, 7; DLB 6; INT CANR-18; MAL 5; MTCW 1, 2; MTFW 2005

Rostand, Edmond (Eugene Alexis)
1868-1918 .... **DC 10; TCLC 6, 37**
See also CA 104; 126; DA; DA3; DAB; DAC; DAM DRAM, MST; DFS 1; DLB 192; LAIT 1; MTCW 1; RGWL 2, 3; TWA

Roth, Henry 1906-1995 ..... **CLC 2, 6, 11, 104**
See also AMWS 9; CA 11-12; 149; CANR 38, 63; CAP 1; CN 1, 2, 3, 4, 5, 6; DA3; DLB 28; EWL 3; MAL 5; MTCW 1, 2; MTFW 2005; RGAL 4

Roth, (Moses) Joseph 1894-1939 ... **TCLC 33**
See also CA 160; DLB 85; EWL 3; RGWL 2, 3

Roth, Philip (Milton) 1933- ... **CLC 1, 2, 3, 4, 6, 9, 15, 22, 31, 47, 66, 86, 119, 201; SSC 26; WLC**
See also AAYA 67; AMWR 2; AMWS 3; BEST 90:3; BPFB 3; CA 1-4R; CANR 1, 22, 36, 55, 89, 132; CDALB 1968-1988; CN 3, 4, 5, 6, 7; CPW 1; DA; DA3; DAB; DAC; DAM MST, NOV, POP; DLB 2, 28, 173; DLBY 1982; EWL 3; MAL 5; MTCW 1, 2; MTFW 2005; RGAL 4; RGSF 2; SSFS 12, 18; TUS

Rothenberg, Jerome 1931- .... **CLC 6, 57**
See also CA 45-48; CANR 1, 106; CP 1, 2, 3, 4, 5, 6, 7; DLB 5, 193

Rotter, Pat ed. .... **CLC 65**

Roumain, Jacques (Jean Baptiste)
1907-1944 .... **BLC 3; TCLC 19**
See also BW 1; CA 117; 125; DAM MULT; EWL 3

Rourke, Constance Mayfield
1885-1941 .... **TCLC 12**
See also CA 107; 200; MAL 5; YABC 1

Rousseau, Jean-Baptiste 1671-1741 ...... **LC 9**

Rousseau, Jean-Jacques 1712-1778 .... **LC 14, 36, 122; WLC**
See also DA; DA3; DAB; DAC; DAM MST; DLB 314; EW 4; GFL Beginnings to 1789; LMFS 1; RGWL 2, 3; TWA

Roussel, Raymond 1877-1933 .... **TCLC 20**
See also CA 117; 201; EWL 3; GFL 1789 to the Present

Rovit, Earl (Herbert) 1927- .... **CLC 7**
See also CA 5-8R; CANR 12

Rowe, Elizabeth Singer 1674-1737 ..... **LC 44**
See also DLB 39, 95

Rowe, Nicholas 1674-1718 .... **LC 8**
See also DLB 84; RGEL 2

Rowlandson, Mary 1637(?)-1678 .... **LC 66**
See also DLB 24, 200; RGAL 4

Rowley, Ames Dorrance
See Lovecraft, H(oward) P(hillips)

Rowley, William 1585(?)-1626 ... **LC 100, 123**
See also DFS 22; DLB 58; RGEL 2

Rowling, J. K. 1966- .... **CLC 137, 217**
See also AAYA 34; BYA 11, 13, 14; CA 173; CANR 128; CLR 66, 80; MAICYA 2; MTFW 2005; SATA 109; SUFW 2

Rowling, Joanne Kathleen
See Rowling, J.K.

Rowson, Susanna Haswell
1762(?)-1824 .... **NCLC 5, 69**
See also AMWS 15; DLB 37, 200; RGAL 4

Roy, Arundhati 1960(?)- .... **CLC 109, 210**
See also CA 163; CANR 90, 126; CN 7; DLBY 1997; EWL 3; LATS 1:2; MTFW 2005; NFS 22; WWE 1

Roy, Gabrielle 1909-1983 .... **CLC 10, 14**
See also CA 53-56; 110; CANR 5, 61; CCA 1; DAB; DAC; DAM MST; DLB 68; EWL 3; MTCW 1; RGWL 2, 3; SATA 104; TCLE 1:2

Royko, Mike 1932-1997 .... **CLC 109**
See also CA 89-92; 157; CANR 26, 111; CPW

Rozanov, Vasilii Vasil'evich
See Rozanov, Vassili
See also DLB 295

Rozanov, Vasily Vasilyevich
See Rozanov, Vassili
See also EWL 3

Rozanov, Vassili 1856-1919 .... **TCLC 104**
See Rozanov, Vasilii Vasil'evich; Rozanov, Vasily Vasilyevich

Rozewicz, Tadeusz 1921- ...... **CLC 9, 23, 139**
See also CA 108; CANR 36, 66; CWW 2; DA3; DAM POET; DLB 232; EWL 3; MTCW 1, 2; MTFW 2005; RGWL 3

Ruark, Gibbons 1941- .... **CLC 3**
See also CA 33-36R; CAAS 23; CANR 14, 31, 57; DLB 120

Rubens, Bernice (Ruth) 1923-2004 . **CLC 19, 31**
See also CA 25-28R; 232; CANR 33, 65, 128; CN 1, 2, 3, 4, 5, 6, 7; DLB 14, 207; MTCW 1

Rubin, Harold
See Robbins, Harold

Rudkin, (James) David 1936- .... **CLC 14**
See also CA 89-92; CBD; CD 5, 6; DLB 13

Rudnik, Raphael 1933- .... **CLC 7**
See also CA 29-32R

Ruffian, M.
See Hasek, Jaroslav (Matej Frantisek)

Ruiz, Jose Martinez .... **CLC 11**
See Martinez Ruiz, Jose

Ruiz, Juan c. 1283-c. 1350 .... **CMLC 66**

Rukeyser, Muriel 1913-1980 . **CLC 6, 10, 15, 27; PC 12**
See also AMWS 6; CA 5-8R; 93-96; CANR 26, 60; CP 1, 2, 3; DA3; DAM POET; DLB 48; EWL 3; FW; GLL 2; MAL 5; MTCW 1, 2; PFS 10; RGAL 4; SATA-Obit 22

Rule, Jane (Vance) 1931- .... **CLC 27**
See also CA 25-28R; CAAS 18; CANR 12, 87; CN 4, 5, 6, 7; DLB 60; FW

Rulfo, Juan 1918-1986 .. **CLC 8, 80; HLC 2; SSC 25**
See also CA 85-88; 118; CANR 26; CD-WLB 3; DAM MULT; DLB 113; EWL 3; HW 1, 2; LAW; MTCW 1, 2; RGSF 2; RGWL 2, 3; WLIT 1

Rumi, Jalal al-Din 1207-1273 ...... **CMLC 20; PC 45**
See also AAYA 64; RGWL 2, 3; WLIT 6; WP

Runeberg, Johan 1804-1877 .... **NCLC 41**

Runyon, (Alfred) Damon
1884(?)-1946 .... **TCLC 10**
See also CA 107; 165; DLB 11, 86, 171; MAL 5; MTCW 2; RGAL 4

Rush, Norman 1933- .... **CLC 44**
See also CA 121; 126; CANR 130; INT CA-126

Rushdie, (Ahmed) Salman 1947- .... **CLC 23, 31, 55, 100, 191; SSC 83; WLCS**
See also AAYA 65; BEST 89:3; BPFB 3; BRWS 4; CA 108; 111; CANR 33, 56, 108, 133; CN 4, 5, 6, 7; CPW 1; DA3; DAB; DAC; DAM MST, NOV, POP; DLB 194; EWL 3; FANT; INT CA-111; LATS 1:2; LMFS 2; MTCW 1, 2; MTFW 2005; NFS 22; RGEL 2; RGSF 2; TEA; WLIT 4

Rushforth, Peter (Scott) 1945- .... **CLC 19**
See also CA 101

Ruskin, John 1819-1900 .... **TCLC 63**
See also BRW 5; BYA 5; CA 114; 129; CD-BLB 1832-1890; DLB 55, 163, 190; RGEL 2; SATA 24; TEA; WCH

Russ, Joanna 1937- .... **CLC 15**
See also BPFB 3; CA 25-28; CANR 11, 31, 65; CN 4, 5, 6, 7; DLB 8; FW; GLL 1; MTCW 1; SCFW 1, 2; SFW 4

Russ, Richard Patrick
See O'Brian, Patrick

Russell, George William 1867-1935
See A.E.; Baker, Jean H.
See also BRWS 8; CA 104; 153; CDBLB 1890-1914; DAM POET; EWL 3; RGEL 2

Russell, Jeffrey Burton 1934- .... **CLC 70**
See also CA 25-28R; CANR 11, 28, 52

Russell, (Henry) Ken(neth Alfred)
1927- .... **CLC 16**
See also CA 105

Russell, William Martin 1947-
See Russell, Willy
See also CA 164; CANR 107

Russell, Willy .... **CLC 60**
See Russell, William Martin
See also CBD; CD 5, 6; DLB 233

Russo, Richard 1949- .... **CLC 181**
See also AMWS 12; CA 127; 133; CANR 87, 114

Rutherford, Mark .... **TCLC 25**
See White, William Hale
See also DLB 18; RGEL 2

Ruyslinck, Ward .... **CLC 14**
See Belser, Reimond Karel Maria de

Ryan, Cornelius (John) 1920-1974 ..... **CLC 7**
See also CA 69-72; 53-56; CANR 38

Ryan, Michael 1946- .... **CLC 65**
See also CA 49-52; CANR 109; DLBY 1982

Ryan, Tim
See Dent, Lester

Rybakov, Anatoli (Naumovich)
1911-1998 .... **CLC 23, 53**
See Rybakov, Anatolii (Naumovich)
See also CA 126; 135; 172; SATA 79; SATA-Obit 108

Rybakov, Anatolii (Naumovich)
See Rybakov, Anatoli (Naumovich)
See also DLB 302

Sanders, Noah
See Blount, Roy (Alton), Jr.
Sanders, Winston P.
See Anderson, Poul (William)
Sandoz, Mari(e Susette) 1900-1966 .. **CLC 28**
See also CA 1-4R; 25-28R; CANR 17, 64;
DLB 9, 212; LAIT 2; MTCW 1, 2; SATA
5; TCWW 1, 2
Sandys, George 1578-1644 .... **LC 80**
See also DLB 24, 121
Saner, Reg(inald Anthony) 1931- .... **CLC 9**
See also CA 65-68; CP 3, 4, 5, 6, 7
Sankara 788-820 .... **CMLC 32**
Sannazaro, Jacopo 1456(?)-1530 .... **LC 8**
See also RGWL 2, 3; WLIT 7
Sansom, William 1912-1976 . **CLC 2, 6; SSC 21**
See also CA 5-8R; 65-68; CANR 42; CN 1,
2; DAM NOV; DLB 139; EWL 3; MTCW
1; RGEL 2; RGSF 2
Santayana, George 1863-1952 .... **TCLC 40**
See also AMW; CA 115; 194; DLB 54, 71,
246, 270; DLBD 13; EWL 3; MAL 5;
RGAL 4; TUS
Santiago, Danny .... **CLC 33**
See James, Daniel (Lewis)
See also DLB 122
**Santillana, Inigo Lopez de Mendoza,
Marques de** 1398-1458 .... **LC 111**
See also DLB 286
Santmyer, Helen Hooven
1895-1986 .... **CLC 33; TCLC 133**
See also CA 1-4R; 118; CANR 15, 33;
DLBY 1984; MTCW 1; RHW
Santoka, Taneda 1882-1940 .... **TCLC 72**
Santos, Bienvenido N(uqui)
1911-1996 ... **AAL; CLC 22; TCLC 156**
See also CA 101; 151; CANR 19, 46; CP 1;
DAM MULT; DLB 312; EWL; RGAL 4;
SSFS 19
Sapir, Edward 1884-1939 .... **TCLC 108**
See also CA 211; DLB 92
Sapper .... **TCLC 44**
See McNeile, Herman Cyril
Sapphire
See Sapphire, Brenda
Sapphire, Brenda 1950- .... **CLC 99**
Sappho fl. 6th cent. B.C.- ... **CMLC 3, 67; PC 5**
See also CDWLB 1; DA3; DAM POET;
DLB 176; FL 1:1; PFS 20; RGWL 2, 3;
WP
Saramago, Jose 1922- ..... **CLC 119; HLCS 1**
See also CA 153; CANR 96; CWW 2; DLB
287; EWL 3; LATS 1:2
Sarduy, Severo 1937-1993 .... **CLC 6, 97;
HLCS 2; TCLC 167**
See also CA 89-92; 142; CANR 58, 81;
CWW 2; DLB 113; EWL 3; HW 1, 2;
LAW
Sargeson, Frank 1903-1982 .... **CLC 31**
See also CA 25-28R; 106; CANR 38, 79;
CN 1, 2, 3; EWL 3; GLL 2; RGEL 2;
RGSF 2; SSFS 20
Sarmiento, Domingo Faustino
1811-1888 .... **HLCS 2**
See also LAW; WLIT 1
Sarmiento, Felix Ruben Garcia
See Dario, Ruben
Saro-Wiwa, Ken(ule Beeson)
1941-1995 .... **CLC 114**
See also BW 2; CA 142; 150; CANR 60;
DLB 157
Saroyan, William 1908-1981 ... **CLC 1, 8, 10,
29, 34, 56; SSC 21; TCLC 137; WLC**
See also AAYA 66; CA 5-8R; 103; CAD;
CANR 30; CDALBS; CN 1, 2; DA; DA3;
DAB; DAC; DAM DRAM, MST, NOV;
DFS 17; DLB 7, 9, 86; DLBY 1981; EWL

3; LAIT 4; MAL 5; MTCW 1, 2; MTFW
2005; RGAL 4; RGSF 2; SATA 23; SATA-
Obit 24; SSFS 14; TUS
Sarraute, Nathalie 1900-1999 .... **CLC 1, 2, 4,
8, 10, 31, 80; TCLC 145**
See also BPFB 3; CA 9-12R; 187; CANR
23, 66, 134; CWW 2; DLB 83, 321; EW
12; EWL 3; GFL 1789 to the Present;
MTCW 1, 2; MTFW 2005; RGWL 2, 3
Sarton, (Eleanor) May 1912-1995 ..... **CLC 4,
14, 49, 91; PC 39; TCLC 120**
See also AMWS 8; CA 1-4R; 149; CANR
1, 34, 55, 116; CN 1, 2, 3, 4, 5, 6; CP 1,
2, 3, 4; DAM POET; DLB 48; DLBY
1981; EWL 3; FW; INT CANR-34; MAL
5; MTCW 1, 2; MTFW 2005; RGAL 4;
SATA 36; SATA-Obit 86; TUS
Sartre, Jean-Paul 1905-1980 . **CLC 1, 4, 7, 9,
13, 18, 24, 44, 50, 52; DC 3; SSC 32;
WLC**
See also AAYA 62; CA 9-12R; 97-100;
CANR 21; DA; DA3; DAB; DAC; DAM
DRAM, MST, NOV; DFS 5; DLB 72,
296, 321; EW 12; EWL 3; GFL 1789 to
the Present; LMFS 2; MTCW 1, 2; MTFW
2005; NFS 21; RGSF 2; RGWL 2, 3;
SSFS 9; TWA
Sassoon, Siegfried (Lorraine)
1886-1967 .... **CLC 36, 130; PC 12**
See also BRW 6; CA 104; 25-28R; CANR
36; DAB; DAM MST, NOV, POET; DLB
20, 191; DLBD 18; EWL 3; MTCW 1, 2;
MTFW 2005; PAB; RGEL 2; TEA
Satterfield, Charles
See Pohl, Frederik
Satyremont
See Peret, Benjamin
Saul, John (W. III) 1942- .... **CLC 46**
See also AAYA 10, 62; BEST 90:4; CA 81-
84; CANR 16, 40, 81; CPW; DAM NOV,
POP; HGG; SATA 98
Saunders, Caleb
See Heinlein, Robert A(nson)
Saura (Atares), Carlos 1932-1998 .... **CLC 20**
See also CA 114; 131; CANR 79; HW 1
Sauser, Frederic Louis
See Sauser-Hall, Frederic
Sauser-Hall, Frederic 1887-1961 ...... **CLC 18**
See Cendrars, Blaise
See also CA 102; 93-96; CANR 36, 62;
MTCW 1
Saussure, Ferdinand de
1857-1913 .... **TCLC 49**
See also DLB 242
Savage, Catharine
See Brosman, Catharine Savage
Savage, Richard 1697(?)-1743 .... **LC 96**
See also DLB 95; RGEL 2
Savage, Thomas 1915-2003 .... **CLC 40**
See also CA 126; 132; 218; CAAS 15; CN
6, 7; INT CA-132; SATA-Obit 147;
TCWW 2
Savan, Glenn 1953-2003 .... **CLC 50**
See also CA 225
Sax, Robert
See Johnson, Robert
Saxo Grammaticus c. 1150-c.
1222 .... **CMLC 58**
Saxton, Robert
See Johnson, Robert
Sayers, Dorothy L(eigh) 1893-1957 . **SSC 71;
TCLC 2, 15**
See also BPFB 3; BRWS 3; CA 104; 119;
CANR 60; CDBLB 1914-1945; CMW 4;
DAM POP; DLB 10, 36, 77, 100; MSW;
MTCW 1, 2; MTFW 2005; RGEL 2;
SSFS 12; TEA
Sayers, Valerie 1952- .... **CLC 50, 122**
See also CA 134; CANR 61; CSW

Sayles, John (Thomas) 1950- .... **CLC 7, 10,
14, 198**
See also CA 57-60; CANR 41, 84; DLB 44
Scammell, Michael 1935- .... **CLC 34**
See also CA 156
Scannell, Vernon 1922- .... **CLC 49**
See also CA 5-8R; CANR 8, 24, 57, 143;
CN 1, 2; CP 1, 2, 3, 4, 5, 6, 7; CWRI 5;
DLB 27; SATA 59
Scarlett, Susan
See Streatfeild, (Mary) Noel
Scarron 1847-1910
See Mikszath, Kalman
Scarron, Paul 1610-1660 .... **LC 116**
See also GFL Beginnings to 1789; RGWL
2, 3
Schaeffer, Susan Fromberg 1941- ..... **CLC 6,
11, 22**
See also CA 49-52; CANR 18, 65; CN 4, 5,
6, 7; DLB 28, 299; MTCW 1, 2; MTFW
2005; SATA 22
Schama, Simon (Michael) 1945- ..... **CLC 150**
See also BEST 89:4; CA 105; CANR 39,
91
Schary, Jill
See Robinson, Jill
Schell, Jonathan 1943- .... **CLC 35**
See also CA 73-76; CANR 12, 117
Schelling, Friedrich Wilhelm Joseph von
1775-1854 .... **NCLC 30**
See also DLB 90
Scherer, Jean-Marie Maurice 1920-
See Rohmer, Eric
See also CA 110
Schevill, James (Erwin) 1920- .... **CLC 7**
See also CA 5-8R; CAAS 12; CAD; CD 5,
6; CP 1, 2, 3, 4
Schiller, Friedrich von 1759-1805 ...... **DC 12;
NCLC 39, 69**
See also CDWLB 2; DAM DRAM; DLB
94; EW 5; RGWL 2, 3; TWA
Schisgal, Murray (Joseph) 1926- .... **CLC 6**
See also CA 21-24R; CAD; CANR 48, 86;
CD 5, 6; MAL 5
Schlee, Ann 1934- .... **CLC 35**
See also CA 101; CANR 29, 88; SATA 44;
SATA-Brief 36
Schlegel, August Wilhelm von
1767-1845 .... **NCLC 15, 142**
See also DLB 94; RGWL 2, 3
Schlegel, Friedrich 1772-1829 .... **NCLC 45**
See also DLB 90; EW 5; RGWL 2, 3; TWA
Schlegel, Johann Elias (von)
1719(?)-1749 .... **LC 5**
Schleiermacher, Friedrich
1768-1834 .... **NCLC 107**
See also DLB 90
Schlesinger, Arthur M(eier), Jr.
1917- .... **CLC 84**
See also AITN 1; CA 1-4R; CANR 1, 28,
58, 105; DLB 17; INT CANR-28; MTCW
1, 2; SATA 61
Schlink, Bernhard 1944- .... **CLC 174**
See also CA 163; CANR 116
Schmidt, Arno (Otto) 1914-1979 ...... **CLC 56**
See also CA 128; 109; DLB 69; EWL 3
Schmitz, Aron Hector 1861-1928
See Svevo, Italo
See also CA 104; 122; MTCW 1
Schnackenberg, Gjertrud (Cecelia)
1953- .... **CLC 40; PC 45**
See also AMWS 15; CA 116; CANR 100;
CP 7; CWP; DLB 120, 282; PFS 20
Schneider, Leonard Alfred 1925-1966
See Bruce, Lenny
See also CA 89-92

Shepherd, Michael
See Ludlum, Robert

Sherburne, Zoa (Lillian Morin)
1912-1995 .... **CLC 30**
See also AAYA 13; CA 1-4R; 176; CANR
3, 37; MAICYA 1, 2; SAAS 18; SATA 3;
YAW

Sheridan, Frances 1724-1766 .... **LC 7**
See also DLB 39, 84

Sheridan, Richard Brinsley
1751-1816 .... **DC 1; NCLC 5, 91; WLC**
See also BRW 3; CDBLB 1660-1789; DA;
DAB; DAC; DAM DRAM, MST; DFS
15; DLB 89; WLIT 3

Sherman, Jonathan Marc 1968- .... **CLC 55**
See also CA 230

Sherman, Martin 1941(?)- .... **CLC 19**
See also CA 116; 123; CAD; CANR 86;
CD 5, 6; DFS 20; DLB 228; GLL 1; IDTP

Sherwin, Judith Johnson
See Johnson, Judith (Emlyn)
See also CANR 85; CP 2, 3, 4; CWP

Sherwood, Frances 1940- .... **CLC 81**
See also CA 146, 220; CAAE 220

Sherwood, Robert E(mmet)
1896-1955 .... **TCLC 3**
See also CA 104; 153; CANR 86; DAM
DRAM; DFS 11, 15, 17; DLB 7, 26, 249;
IDFW 3, 4; MAL 5; RGAL 4

Shestov, Lev 1866-1938 .... **TCLC 56**

Shevchenko, Taras 1814-1861 .... **NCLC 54**

Shiel, M(atthew) P(hipps)
1865-1947 .... **TCLC 8**
See Holmes, Gordon
See also CA 106; 160; DLB 153; HGG;
MTCW 2; MTFW 2005; SCFW 1, 2;
SFW 4; SUFW

Shields, Carol (Ann) 1935-2003 ...... **CLC 91,
113, 193**
See also AMWS 7; CA 81-84; 218; CANR
51, 74, 98, 133; CCA 1; CN 6, 7; CPW;
DA3; DAC; MTCW 2; MTFW 2005

Shields, David (Jonathan) 1956- ...... **CLC 97**
See also CA 124; CANR 48, 99, 112

Shiga, Naoya 1883-1971 .... **CLC 33; SSC 23;
TCLC 172**
See Shiga Naoya
See also CA 101; 33-36R; MJW; RGWL 3

Shiga Naoya
See Shiga, Naoya
See also DLB 180; EWL 3; RGWL 3

Shilts, Randy 1951-1994 .... **CLC 85**
See also AAYA 19; CA 115; 127; 144;
CANR 45; DA3; GLL 1; INT CA-127;
MTCW 2; MTFW 2005

Shimazaki, Haruki 1872-1943
See Shimazaki Toson
See also CA 105; 134; CANR 84; RGWL 3

Shimazaki Toson .... **TCLC 5**
See Shimazaki, Haruki
See also DLB 180; EWL 3

Shirley, James 1596-1666 .... **DC 25; LC 96**
See also DLB 58; RGEL 2

Sholokhov, Mikhail (Aleksandrovich)
1905-1984 .... **CLC 7, 15**
See also CA 101; 112; DLB 272; EWL 3;
MTCW 1, 2; MTFW 2005; RGWL 2, 3;
SATA-Obit 36

Shone, Patric
See Hanley, James

Showalter, Elaine 1941- .... **CLC 169**
See also CA 57-60; CANR 58, 106; DLB
67; FW; GLL 2

Shreve, Susan
See Shreve, Susan Richards

Shreve, Susan Richards 1939- .... **CLC 23**
See also CA 49-52; CAAS 5; CANR 5, 38,
69, 100; MAICYA 1, 2; SATA 46, 95, 152;
SATA-Brief 41

Shue, Larry 1946-1985 .... **CLC 52**
See also CA 145; 117; DAM DRAM; DFS
7

Shu-Jen, Chou 1881-1936
See Lu Hsun
See also CA 104

Shulman, Alix Kates 1932- .... **CLC 2, 10**
See also CA 29-32R; CANR 43; FW; SATA
7

Shuster, Joe 1914-1992 .... **CLC 21**
See also AAYA 50

Shute, Nevil .... **CLC 30**
See Norway, Nevil Shute
See also BPFB 3; DLB 255; NFS 9; RHW;
SFW 4

Shuttle, Penelope (Diane) 1947- .... **CLC 7**
See also CA 93-96; CANR 39, 84, 92, 108;
CP 3, 4, 5, 6, 7; CWP; DLB 14, 40

Shvarts, Elena 1948- .... **PC 50**
See also CA 147

Sidhwa, Bapsi
See Sidhwa, Bapsy (N.)
See also CN 6, 7

Sidhwa, Bapsy (N.) 1938- .... **CLC 168**
See Sidhwa, Bapsi
See also CA 108; CANR 25, 57; FW

Sidney, Mary 1561-1621 .... **LC 19, 39**
See Sidney Herbert, Mary

Sidney, Sir Philip 1554-1586 . **LC 19, 39; PC
32**
See also BRW 1; BRWR 2; CDBLB Before
1660; DA; DA3; DAB; DAC; DAM MST,
POET; DLB 167; EXPP; PAB; RGEL 2;
TEA; WP

Sidney Herbert, Mary
See Sidney, Mary
See also DLB 167

Siegel, Jerome 1914-1996 .... **CLC 21**
See Siegel, Jerry
See also CA 116; 169; 151

Siegel, Jerry
See Siegel, Jerome
See also AAYA 50

Sienkiewicz, Henryk (Adam Alexander Pius)
1846-1916 .... **TCLC 3**
See also CA 104; 134; CANR 84; EWL 3;
RGSF 2; RGWL 2, 3

Sierra, Gregorio Martinez
See Martinez Sierra, Gregorio

Sierra, Maria (de la O'LeJarraga) Martinez
See Martinez Sierra, Maria (de la
O'LeJarraga)

Sigal, Clancy 1926- .... **CLC 7**
See also CA 1-4R; CANR 85; CN 1, 2, 3,
4, 5, 6, 7

Siger of Brabant 1240(?)-1284(?) . **CMLC 69**
See also DLB 115

Sigourney, Lydia H.
See Sigourney, Lydia Howard (Huntley)
See also DLB 73, 183

Sigourney, Lydia Howard (Huntley)
1791-1865 .... **NCLC 21, 87**
See Sigourney, Lydia H.; Sigourney, Lydia
Huntley
See also DLB 1

Sigourney, Lydia Huntley
See Sigourney, Lydia Howard (Huntley)
See also DLB 42, 239, 243

Siguenza y Gongora, Carlos de
1645-1700 .... **HLCS 2; LC 8**
See also LAW

Sigurjonsson, Johann
See Sigurjonsson, Johann

Sigurjonsson, Johann 1880-1919 ... **TCLC 27**
See also CA 170; DLB 293; EWL 3

Sikelianos, Angelos 1884-1951 .... **PC 29;
TCLC 39**
See also EWL 3; RGWL 2, 3

Silkin, Jon 1930-1997 .... **CLC 2, 6, 43**
See also CA 5-8R; CANR 89; CP
1, 2, 3, 4, 5, 6; DLB 27

Silko, Leslie (Marmon) 1948- .... **CLC 23, 74,
114, 211; NNAL; SSC 37, 66; WLCS**
See also AAYA 14; AMWS 4; ANW; BYA
12; CA 115; 122; CANR 45, 65, 118; CN
4, 5, 6, 7; CP 4, 5, 6, 7; CPW 1; CWP;
DA; DA3; DAC; DAM MST, MULT,
POP; DLB 143, 175, 256, 275; EWL 3;
EXPP; EXPS; LAIT 4; MAL 5; MTCW
2; MTFW 2005; NFS 4; PFS 9, 16; RGAL
4; RGSF 2; SSFS 4, 8, 10, 11; TCWW 1,
2

Sillanpaa, Frans Eemil 1888-1964 ... **CLC 19**
See also CA 129; 93-96; EWL 3; MTCW 1

Sillitoe, Alan 1928- .. **CLC 1, 3, 6, 10, 19, 57,
148**
See also AITN 1; BRWS 5; CA 9-12R, 191;
CAAE 191; CAAS 2; CANR 8, 26, 55,
139; CDBLB 1960 to Present; CN 1, 2, 3,
4, 5, 6; CP 1, 2, 3, 4; DLB 14, 139; EWL
3; MTCW 1, 2; MTFW 2005; RGEL 2;
RGSF 2; SATA 61

Silone, Ignazio 1900-1978 .... **CLC 4**
See also CA 25-28; 81-84; CANR 34; CAP
2; DLB 264; EW 12; EWL 3; MTCW 1;
RGSF 2; RGWL 2, 3

Silone, Ignazione
See Silone, Ignazio

Silver, Joan Micklin 1935- .... **CLC 20**
See also CA 114; 121; INT CA-121

Silver, Nicholas
See Faust, Frederick (Schiller)

Silverberg, Robert 1935- .... **CLC 7, 140**
See also AAYA 24; BPFB 3; BYA 7, 9; CA
1-4R, 186; CAAE 186; CAAS 3; CANR
1, 20, 36, 85, 140; CLR 59; CN 6, 7;
CPW; DAM POP; DLB 8; INT CANR-
20; MAICYA 1, 2; MTCW 1, 2; MTFW
2005; SATA 13, 91; SATA-Essay 104;
SCFW 1, 2; SFW 4; SUFW 2

Silverstein, Alvin 1933- .... **CLC 17**
See also CA 49-52; CANR 2; CLR 25;
JRDA; MAICYA 1, 2; SATA 8, 69, 124

Silverstein, Shel(don Allan)
1932-1999 .... **PC 49**
See also AAYA 40; BW 3; CA 107; 179;
CANR 47, 74, 81; CLR 5, 96; CWRI 5;
JRDA; MAICYA 1, 2; MTCW 2; MTFW
2005; SATA 33, 92; SATA-Brief 27;
SATA-Obit 116

Silverstein, Virginia B(arbara Opshelor)
1937- .... **CLC 17**
See also CA 49-52; CANR 2; CLR 25;
JRDA; MAICYA 1, 2; SATA 8, 69, 124

Sim, Georges
See Simenon, Georges (Jacques Christian)

Simak, Clifford D(onald) 1904-1988 . **CLC 1,
55**
See also CA 1-4R; 125; CANR 1, 35; DLB
8; MTCW 1; SATA-Obit 56; SCFW 1, 2;
SFW 4

Simenon, Georges (Jacques Christian)
1903-1989 .... **CLC 1, 2, 3, 8, 18, 47**
See also BPFB 3; CA 85-88; 129; CANR
35; CMW 4; DA3; DAM POP; DLB 72;
DLBY 1989; EW 12; EWL 3; GFL 1789
to the Present; MSW; MTCW 1, 2; MTFW
2005; RGWL 2, 3

Simic, Charles 1938- .... **CLC 6, 9, 22, 49, 68,
130; PC 69**
See also AMWS 8; CA 29-32R; CAAS 4;
CANR 12, 33, 52, 61, 96, 140; CP 2, 3, 4,
5, 6, 7; DA3; DAM POET; DLB 105;
MAL 5; MTCW 2; MTFW 2005; PFS 7;
RGAL 4; WP

Simmel, Georg 1858-1918 .... **TCLC 64**
See also CA 157; DLB 296

Smith, Iain Crichton 1928-1998 .... **CLC 64**
See also BRWS 9; CA 21-24R; 171; CN 1, 2, 3, 4, 5, 6; CP 1, 2, 3, 4; DLB 40, 139, 319; RGSF 2

Smith, John 1580(?)-1631 .... **LC 9**
See also DLB 24, 30; TUS

Smith, Johnston
See Crane, Stephen (Townley)

Smith, Joseph, Jr. 1805-1844 .... **NCLC 53**

Smith, Lee 1944- .... **CLC 25, 73**
See also CA 114; 119; CANR 46, 118; CN 7; CSW; DLB 143; DLBY 1983; EWL 3; INT CA-119; RGAL 4

Smith, Martin
See Smith, Martin Cruz

Smith, Martin Cruz 1942- .. **CLC 25; NNAL**
See also BEST 89:4; BPFB 3; CA 85-88; CANR 6, 23, 43, 65, 119; CMW 4; CPW; DAM MULT, POP; HGG; INT CANR-23; MTCW 2; MTFW 2005; RGAL 4

Smith, Patti 1946- .... **CLC 12**
See also CA 93-96; CANR 63

Smith, Pauline (Urmson)
1882-1959 .... **TCLC 25**
See also DLB 225; EWL 3

Smith, Rosamond
See Oates, Joyce Carol

Smith, Sheila Kaye
See Kaye-Smith, Sheila

Smith, Stevie .... **CLC 3, 8, 25, 44; PC 12**
See Smith, Florence Margaret
See also BRWS 2; CP 1; DLB 20; EWL 3; PAB; PFS 3; RGEL 2

Smith, Wilbur (Addison) 1933- .... **CLC 33**
See also CA 13-16R; CANR 7, 46, 66, 134; CPW; MTCW 1, 2; MTFW 2005

Smith, William Jay 1918- .... **CLC 6**
See also AMWS 13; CA 5-8R; CANR 44, 106; CP 1, 2, 3, 4, 5, 6, 7; CSW; CWRI 5; DLB 5; MAICYA 1, 2; SAAS 22; SATA 2, 68, 154; SATA-Essay 154; TCLE 1:2

Smith, Woodrow Wilson
See Kuttner, Henry

Smith, Zadie 1976- .... **CLC 158**
See also AAYA 50; CA 193; MTFW 2005

Smolenskin, Peretz 1842-1885 .... **NCLC 30**

Smollett, Tobias (George) 1721-1771 ... **LC 2, 46**
See also BRW 3; CDBLB 1660-1789; DLB 39, 104; RGEL 2; TEA

Snodgrass, W(illiam) D(e Witt)
1926- .... **CLC 2, 6, 10, 18, 68**
See also AMWS 6; CA 1-4R; CANR 6, 36, 65, 85; CP 1, 2, 3, 4, 5, 6, 7; DAM POET; DLB 5; MAL 5; MTCW 1, 2; MTFW 2005; RGAL 4; TCLE 1:2

Snorri Sturluson 1179-1241 .... **CMLC 56**
See also RGWL 2, 3

Snow, C(harles) P(ercy) 1905-1980 ... **CLC 1, 4, 6, 9, 13, 19**
See also BRW 7; CA 5-8R; 101; CANR 28; CDBLB 1945-1960; CN 1, 2; DAM NOV; DLB 15, 77; DLBD 17; EWL 3; MTCW 1, 2; MTFW 2005; RGEL 2; TEA

Snow, Frances Compton
See Adams, Henry (Brooks)

Snyder, Gary (Sherman) 1930- . **CLC 1, 2, 5, 9, 32, 120; PC 21**
See also AMWS 8; ANW; BG 1:3; CA 17-20R; CANR 30, 60, 125; CP 1, 2, 3, 4, 5, 6, 7; DA3; DAM POET; DLB 5, 16, 165, 212, 237, 275; EWL 3; MAL 5; MTCW 2; MTFW 2005; PFS 9, 19; RGAL 4; WP

Snyder, Zilpha Keatley 1927- .... **CLC 17**
See also AAYA 15; BYA 1; CA 9-12R; CANR 38; CLR 31; JRDA; MAICYA 1, 2; SAAS 2; SATA 1, 28, 75, 110, 163; SATA-Essay 112, 163; YAW

Soares, Bernardo
See Pessoa, Fernando (Antonio Nogueira)

Sobh, A.
See Shamlu, Ahmad

Sobh, Alef
See Shamlu, Ahmad

Sobol, Joshua 1939- .... **CLC 60**
See Sobol, Yehoshua
See also CA 200

Sobol, Yehoshua 1939-
See Sobol, Joshua
See also CWW 2

Socrates 470B.C.-399B.C. .... **CMLC 27**

Soderberg, Hjalmar 1869-1941 ...... **TCLC 39**
See also DLB 259; EWL 3; RGSF 2

Soderbergh, Steven 1963- .... **CLC 154**
See also AAYA 43

Sodergran, Edith (Irene) 1892-1923
See Soedergran, Edith (Irene)
See also CA 202; DLB 259; EW 11; EWL 3; RGWL 2, 3

Soedergran, Edith (Irene)
1892-1923 .... **TCLC 31**
See Sodergran, Edith (Irene)

Softly, Edgar
See Lovecraft, H(oward) P(hillips)

Softly, Edward
See Lovecraft, H(oward) P(hillips)

Sokolov, Alexander V(sevolodovich) 1943-
See Sokolov, Sasha
See also CA 73-76

Sokolov, Raymond 1941- .... **CLC 7**
See also CA 85-88

Sokolov, Sasha .... **CLC 59**
See Sokolov, Alexander V(sevolodovich)
See also CWW 2; DLB 285; EWL 3; RGWL 2, 3

Solo, Jay
See Ellison, Harlan (Jay)

Sologub, Fyodor .... **TCLC 9**
See Teternikov, Fyodor Kuzmich
See also EWL 3

Solomons, Ikey Esquir
See Thackeray, William Makepeace

Solomos, Dionysios 1798-1857 .... **NCLC 15**

Solwoska, Mara
See French, Marilyn

Solzhenitsyn, Aleksandr I(sayevich)
1918- .. **CLC 1, 2, 4, 7, 9, 10, 18, 26, 34, 78, 134; SSC 32; WLC**
See Solzhenitsyn, Aleksandr Isaevich
See also AAYA 49; AITN 1; BPFB 3; CA 69-72; CANR 40, 65, 116; DA; DA3; DAB; DAC; DAM MST, NOV; DLB 302; EW 13; EXPS; LAIT 4; MTCW 1, 2; MTFW 2005; NFS 6; RGSF 2; RGWL 2, 3; SSFS 9; TWA

Solzhenitsyn, Aleksandr Isaevich
See Solzhenitsyn, Aleksandr I(sayevich)
See also CWW 2; EWL 3

Somers, Jane
See Lessing, Doris (May)

Somerville, Edith Oenone
1858-1949 .... **SSC 56; TCLC 51**
See also CA 196; DLB 135; RGEL 2; RGSF 2

Somerville & Ross
See Martin, Violet Florence; Somerville, Edith Oenone

Sommer, Scott 1951- .... **CLC 25**
See also CA 106

Sommers, Christina Hoff 1950- ...... **CLC 197**
See also CA 153; CANR 95

Sondheim, Stephen (Joshua) 1930- . **CLC 30, 39, 147; DC 22**
See also AAYA 11, 66; CA 103; CANR 47, 67, 125; DAM DRAM; LAIT 4

Sone, Monica 1919- .... **AAL**
See also DLB 312

Song, Cathy 1955- .... **AAL; PC 21**
See also CA 154; CANR 118; CWP; DLB 169, 312; EXPP; FW; PFS 5

Sontag, Susan 1933-2004 ... **CLC 1, 2, 10, 13, 31, 105, 195**
See also AMWS 3; CA 17-20R; 234; CANR 25, 51, 74, 97; CN 1, 2, 3, 4, 5, 6, 7; CPW; DA3; DAM POP; DLB 2, 67; EWL 3; MAL 5; MAWW; MTCW 1, 2; MTFW 2005; RGAL 4; RHW; SSFS 10

Sophocles 496(?)B.C.-406(?)B.C. .... **CMLC 2, 47, 51; DC 1; WLCS**
See also AW 1; CDWLB 1; DA; DA3; DAB; DAC; DAM DRAM, MST; DFS 1, 4, 8; DLB 176; LAIT 1; LATS 1:1; LMFS 1; RGWL 2, 3; TWA

Sordello 1189-1269 .... **CMLC 15**

Sorel, Georges 1847-1922 .... **TCLC 91**
See also CA 118; 188

Sorel, Julia
See Drexler, Rosalyn

Sorokin, Vladimir .... **CLC 59**
See Sorokin, Vladimir Georgievich

Sorokin, Vladimir Georgievich
See Sorokin, Vladimir
See also DLB 285

Sorrentino, Gilbert 1929- .. **CLC 3, 7, 14, 22, 40**
See also CA 77-80; CANR 14, 33, 115; CN 3, 4, 5, 6, 7; CP 1, 2, 3, 4, 5, 6, 7; DLB 5, 173; DLBY 1980; INT CANR-14

Soseki
See Natsume, Soseki
See also MJW

Soto, Gary 1952- ... **CLC 32, 80; HLC 2; PC 28**
See also AAYA 10, 37; BYA 11; CA 119; 125; CANR 50, 74, 107; CLR 38; CP 4, 5, 6, 7; DAM MULT; DLB 82; EWL 3; EXPP; HW 1, 2; INT CA-125; JRDA; LLW; MAICYA 2; MAICYAS 1; MAL 5; MTCW 2; MTFW 2005; PFS 7; RGAL 4; SATA 80, 120; WYA; YAW

Soupault, Philippe 1897-1990 .... **CLC 68**
See also CA 116; 147; 131; EWL 3; GFL 1789 to the Present; LMFS 2

Souster, (Holmes) Raymond 1921- .... **CLC 5, 14**
See also CA 13-16R; CAAS 14; CANR 13, 29, 53; CP 1, 2, 3, 4, 5, 6, 7; DA3; DAC; DAM POET; DLB 88; RGEL 2; SATA 63

Southern, Terry 1924(?)-1995 .... **CLC 7**
See also AMWS 11; BPFB 3; CA 1-4R; 150; CANR 1, 55, 107; CN 1, 2, 3, 4, 5, 6; DLB 2; IDFW 3, 4

Southerne, Thomas 1660-1746 .... **LC 99**
See also DLB 80; RGEL 2

Southey, Robert 1774-1843 .... **NCLC 8, 97**
See also BRW 4; DLB 93, 107, 142; RGEL 2; SATA 54

Southwell, Robert 1561(?)-1595 .... **LC 108**
See also DLB 167; RGEL 2; TEA

Southworth, Emma Dorothy Eliza Nevitte
1819-1899 .... **NCLC 26**
See also DLB 239

Souza, Ernest
See Scott, Evelyn

Soyinka, Wole 1934- .. **BLC 3; CLC 3, 5, 14, 36, 44, 179; DC 2; WLC**
See also AFW; BW 2, 3; CA 13-16R; CANR 27, 39, 82, 136; CD 5, 6; CDWLB 3; CN 6, 7; CP 1, 2, 3, 4, 5, 6 ,7; DA; DA3; DAB; DAC; DAM DRAM, MST, MULT; DFS 10; DLB 125; EWL 3; MTCW 1, 2; MTFW 2005; RGEL 2; TWA; WLIT 2; WWE 1

Spackman, W(illiam) M(ode)
1905-1990 .... **CLC 46**
See also CA 81-84; 132

Stephen, Adeline Virginia
See Woolf, (Adeline) Virginia
Stephen, Sir Leslie 1832-1904 .... **TCLC 23**
See also BRW 5; CA 123; DLB 57, 144, 190
Stephen, Sir Leslie
See Stephen, Sir Leslie
Stephen, Virginia
See Woolf, (Adeline) Virginia
Stephens, James 1882(?)-1950 .... **SSC 50; TCLC 4**
See also CA 104; 192; DLB 19, 153, 162; EWL 3; FANT; RGEL 2; SUFW
Stephens, Reed
See Donaldson, Stephen R(eeder)
Steptoe, Lydia
See Barnes, Djuna
See also GLL 1
Sterchi, Beat 1949- .... **CLC 65**
See also CA 203
Sterling, Brett
See Bradbury, Ray (Douglas); Hamilton, Edmond
Sterling, Bruce 1954- .... **CLC 72**
See also CA 119; CANR 44, 135; CN 7; MTFW 2005; SCFW 2; SFW 4
Sterling, George 1869-1926 .... **TCLC 20**
See also CA 117; 165; DLB 54
Stern, Gerald 1925- .... **CLC 40, 100**
See also AMWS 9; CA 81-84; CANR 28, 94; CP 3, 4, 5, 6, 7; DLB 105; RGAL 4
Stern, Richard (Gustave) 1928- ... **CLC 4, 39**
See also CA 1-4R; CANR 1, 25, 52, 120; CN 1, 2, 3, 4, 5, 6, 7; DLB 218; DLBY 1987; INT CANR-25
Sternberg, Josef von 1894-1969 .... **CLC 20**
See also CA 81-84
Sterne, Laurence 1713-1768 .... **LC 2, 48; WLC**
See also BRW 3; BRWC 1; CDBLB 1660-1789; DA; DAB; DAC; DAM MST, NOV; DLB 39; RGEL 2; TEA
Sternheim, (William Adolf) Carl 1878-1942 .... **TCLC 8**
See also CA 105; 193; DLB 56, 118; EWL 3; IDTP; RGWL 2, 3
Stevens, Margaret Dean
See Aldrich, Bess Streeter
Stevens, Mark 1951- .... **CLC 34**
See also CA 122
Stevens, Wallace 1879-1955 . **PC 6; TCLC 3, 12, 45; WLC**
See also AMW; AMWR 1; CA 104; 124; CDALB 1929-1941; DA; DA3; DAB; DAC; DAM MST, POET; DLB 54; EWL 3; EXPP; MAL 5; MTCW 1, 2; PAB; PFS 13, 16; RGAL 4; TUS; WP
Stevenson, Anne (Katharine) 1933- .. **CLC 7, 33**
See also BRWS 6; CA 17-20R; CAAS 9; CANR 9, 33, 123; CP 3, 4, 5, 6, 7; CWP; DLB 40; MTCW 1; RHW
Stevenson, Robert Louis (Balfour) 1850-1894 ...... **NCLC 5, 14, 63; SSC 11, 51; WLC**
See also AAYA 24; BPFB 3; BRW 5; BRWC 1; BRWR 1; BYA 1, 2, 4, 13; CDBLB 1890-1914; CLR 10, 11; DA; DA3; DAB; DAC; DAM MST, NOV; DLB 18, 57, 141, 156, 174; DLBD 13; GL 3; HGG; JRDA; LAIT 1, 3; MAICYA 1, 2; NFS 11, 20; RGEL 2; RGSF 2; SATA 100; SUFW; TEA; WCH; WLIT 4; WYA; YABC 2; YAW
Stewart, J(ohn) I(nnes) M(ackintosh) 1906-1994 .... **CLC 7, 14, 32**
See Innes, Michael
See also CA 85-88; 147; CAAS 3; CANR 47; CMW 4; CN 1, 2, 3, 4, 5; MTCW 1, 2

Stewart, Mary (Florence Elinor) 1916- .... **CLC 7, 35, 117**
See also AAYA 29; BPFB 3; CA 1-4R; CANR 1, 59, 130; CMW 4; CPW; DAB; FANT; RHW; SATA 12; YAW
Stewart, Mary Rainbow
See Stewart, Mary (Florence Elinor)
Stifle, June
See Campbell, Maria
Stifter, Adalbert 1805-1868 .. **NCLC 41; SSC 28**
See also CDWLB 2; DLB 133; RGSF 2; RGWL 2, 3
Still, James 1906-2001 .... **CLC 49**
See also CA 65-68; 195; CAAS 17; CANR 10, 26; CSW; DLB 9; DLBY 01; SATA 29; SATA-Obit 127
Sting 1951-
See Sumner, Gordon Matthew
See also CA 167
Stirling, Arthur
See Sinclair, Upton (Beall)
Stitt, Milan 1941- .... **CLC 29**
See also CA 69-72
Stockton, Francis Richard 1834-1902
See Stockton, Frank R.
See also AAYA 68; CA 108; 137; MAICYA 1, 2; SATA 44; SFW 4
Stockton, Frank R. .... **TCLC 47**
See Stockton, Francis Richard
See also BYA 4, 13; DLB 42, 74; DLBD 13; EXPS; SATA-Brief 32; SSFS 3; SUFW; WCH
Stoddard, Charles
See Kuttner, Henry
Stoker, Abraham 1847-1912
See Stoker, Bram
See also CA 105; 150; DA; DA3; DAC; DAM MST, NOV; HGG; MTFW 2005; SATA 29
Stoker, Bram . **SSC 62; TCLC 8, 144; WLC**
See Stoker, Abraham
See also CA 23; BPFB 3; BRWS 3; BYA 5; CDBLB 1890-1914; DAB; DLB 304; GL 3; LATS 1:1; NFS 18; RGEL 2; SUFW; TEA; WLIT 4
Stolz, Mary (Slattery) 1920- .... **CLC 12**
See also AAYA 8; AITN 1; CA 5-8R; CANR 13, 41, 112; JRDA; MAICYA 1, 2; SAAS 3; SATA 10, 71, 133; YAW
Stone, Irving 1903-1989 .... **CLC 7**
See also AITN 1; BPFB 3; CA 1-4R; 129; CAAS 3; CANR 1, 23; CN 1, 2, 3, 4; CPW; DA3; DAM POP; INT CANR-23; MTCW 1, 2; MTFW 2005; RHW; SATA 3; SATA-Obit 64
Stone, Oliver (William) 1946- .... **CLC 73**
See also AAYA 15, 64; CA 110; CANR 55, 125
Stone, Robert (Anthony) 1937- ... **CLC 5, 23, 42, 175**
See also AMWS 5; BPFB 3; CA 85-88; CANR 23, 66, 95; CN 4, 5, 6, 7; DLB 152; EWL 3; INT CANR-23; MAL 5; MTCW 1; MTFW 2005
Stone, Ruth 1915- .... **PC 53**
See also CA 45-48; CANR 2, 91; CP 7; CSW; DLB 105; PFS 19
Stone, Zachary
See Follett, Ken(neth Martin)
Stoppard, Tom 1937- ... **CLC 1, 3, 4, 5, 8, 15, 29, 34, 63, 91; DC 6; WLC**
See also AAYA 63; BRWC 1; BRWR 2; BRWS 1; CA 81-84; CANR 39, 67, 125; CBD; CD 5, 6; CDBLB 1960 to Present; DA; DA3; DAB; DAC; DAM DRAM, MST; DFS 2, 5, 8, 11, 13, 16; DLB 13, 233; DLBY 1985; EWL 3; LATS 1:2; MTCW 1, 2; MTFW 2005; RGEL 2; TEA; WLIT 4

Storey, David (Malcolm) 1933- . **CLC 2, 4, 5, 8**
See also BRWS 1; CA 81-84; CANR 36; CBD; CD 5, 6; CN 1, 2, 3, 4, 5, 6; DAM DRAM; DLB 13, 14, 207, 245; EWL 3; MTCW 1; RGEL 2
Storm, Hyemeyohsts 1935- ... **CLC 3; NNAL**
See also CA 81-84; CANR 45; DAM MULT
Storm, (Hans) Theodor (Woldsen) 1817-1888 .... **NCLC 1; SSC 27**
See also CDWLB 2; DLB 129; EW; RGSF 2; RGWL 2, 3
Storni, Alfonsina 1892-1938 . **HLC 2; PC 33; TCLC 5**
See also CA 104; 131; DAM MULT; DLB 283; HW 1; LAW
Stoughton, William 1631-1701 .... **LC 38**
See also DLB 24
Stout, Rex (Todhunter) 1886-1975 ..... **CLC 3**
See also AITN 2; BPFB 3; CA 61-64; CANR 71; CMW 4; CN 2; DLB 306; MSW; RGAL 4
Stow, (Julian) Randolph 1935- ... **CLC 23, 48**
See also CA 13-16R; CANR 33; CN 1, 2, 3, 4, 5, 6, 7; CP 1, 2, 3, 4; DLB 260; MTCW 1; RGEL 2
Stowe, Harriet (Elizabeth) Beecher 1811-1896 .... **NCLC 3, 50, 133; WLC**
See also AAYA 53; AMWS 1; CDALB 1865-1917; DA; DA3; DAB; DAC; DAM MST, NOV; DLB 1, 12, 42, 74, 189, 239, 243; EXPN; FL 1:3; JRDA; LAIT 2; MAICYA 1, 2; NFS 6; RGAL 4; TUS; YABC 1
Strabo c. 64B.C.-c. 25 .... **CMLC 37**
See also DLB 176
Strachey, (Giles) Lytton 1880-1932 .... **TCLC 12**
See also BRWS 2; CA 110; 178; DLB 149; DLBD 10; EWL 3; MTCW 2; NCFS 4
Stramm, August 1874-1915 .... **PC 50**
See also CA 195; EWL 3
Strand, Mark 1934- .. **CLC 6, 18, 41, 71; PC 63**
See also AMWS 4; CA 21-24R; CANR 40, 65, 100; CP 1, 2, 3, 4, 5, 6, 7; DAM POET; DLB 5; EWL 3; MAL 5; PAB; PFS 9, 18; RGAL 4; SATA 41; TCLE 1:2
Stratton-Porter, Gene(va Grace) 1863-1924
See Porter, Gene(va Grace) Stratton
See also ANW; CA 137; CLR 87; DLB 221; DLBD 14; MAICYA 1, 2; SATA 15
Straub, Peter (Francis) 1943- ... **CLC 28, 107**
See also BEST 89:1; BPFB 3; CA 85-88; CANR 28, 65, 109; CPW; DAM POP; DLBY 1984; HGG; MTCW 1, 2; MTFW 2005; SUFW 2
Strauss, Botho 1944- .... **CLC 22**
See also CA 157; CWW 2; DLB 124
Strauss, Leo 1899-1973 .... **TCLC 141**
See also CA 101; 45-48; CANR 122
Streatfeild, (Mary) Noel 1897(?)-1986 .... **CLC 21**
See also CA 81-84; 120; CANR 31; CLR 17, 83; CWRI 5; DLB 160; MAICYA 1, 2; SATA 20; SATA-Obit 48
Stribling, T(homas) S(igismund) 1881-1965 .... **CLC 23**
See also CA 189; 107; CMW 4; DLB 9; RGAL 4
Strindberg, (Johan) August 1849-1912 ... **DC 18; TCLC 1, 8, 21, 47; WLC**
See also CA 104; 135; DA; DA3; DAB; DAC; DAM DRAM, MST; DFS 4, 9; DLB 259; EW 7; EWL 3; IDTP; LMFS 2; MTCW 2; MTFW 2005; RGWL 2, 3; TWA
Stringer, Arthur 1874-1950 .... **TCLC 37**
See also CA 161; DLB 92

Szirtes, George 1948- .... **CLC 46; PC 51**
See also CA 109; CANR 27, 61, 117; CP 4,
5, 6, 7

Szymborska, Wislawa 1923- ... **CLC 99, 190;
PC 44**
See also CA 154; CANR 91, 133; CDWLB
4; CWP; CWW 2; DA3; DLB 232; DLBY
1996; EWL 3; MTCW 2; MTFW 2005;
PFS 15; RGWL 3

T. O., Nik
See Annensky, Innokenty (Fyodorovich)

Tabori, George 1914- .... **CLC 19**
See also CA 49-52; CANR 4, 69; CBD; CD
5, 6; DLB 245

Tacitus c. 55-c. 117 .... **CMLC 56**
See also AW 2; CDWLB 1; DLB 211;
RGWL 2, 3

Tagore, Rabindranath 1861-1941 .... **PC 8;
SSC 48; TCLC 3, 53**
See also CA 104; 120; DA3; DAM DRAM,
POET; EWL 3; MTCW 1, 2; MTFW
2005; PFS 18; RGEL 2; RGSF 2; RGWL
2, 3; TWA

Taine, Hippolyte Adolphe
1828-1893 .... **NCLC 15**
See also EW 7; GFL 1789 to the Present

Talayesva, Don C. 1890-(?) .... **NNAL**

Talese, Gay 1932- .... **CLC 37**
See also AITN 1; CA 1-4R; CANR 9, 58,
137; DLB 185; INT CANR-9; MTCW 1,
2; MTFW 2005

Tallent, Elizabeth (Ann) 1954- .... **CLC 45**
See also CA 117; CANR 72; DLB 130

Tallmountain, Mary 1918-1997 .... **NNAL**
See also CA 146; 161; DLB 193

Tally, Ted 1952- .... **CLC 42**
See also CA 120; 124; CAD; CANR 125;
CD 5, 6; INT CA-124

Talvik, Heiti 1904-1947 .... **TCLC 87**
See also EWL 3

Tamayo y Baus, Manuel
1829-1898 .... **NCLC 1**

Tammsaare, A(nton) H(ansen)
1878-1940 .... **TCLC 27**
See also CA 164; CDWLB 4; DLB 220;
EWL 3

Tam'si, Tchicaya U
See Tchicaya, Gerald Felix

Tan, Amy (Ruth) 1952- . **AAL; CLC 59, 120,
151**
See also AAYA 9, 48; AMWS 10; BEST
89:3; BPFB 3; BYA 3; CA 136; CANR 54,
105, 132; CDALBS; CN 6, 7; CPW 1; DA3;
DAM MULT, NOV, POP; DLB 173, 312;
EXPN; FL 1:6; FW; LAIT 3, 5; MAL 5;
MTCW 2; MTFW 2005; NFS 1, 13, 16;
RGAL 4; SATA 75; SSFS 9; YAW

Tandem, Felix
See Spitteler, Carl (Friedrich Georg)

Tanizaki, Jun'ichiro 1886-1965 ... **CLC 8, 14,
28; SSC 21**
See Tanizaki Jun'ichiro
See also CA 93-96; 25-28R; MJW; MTCW
2; MTFW 2005; RGSF 2; RGWL 2

Tanizaki Jun'ichiro
See Tanizaki, Jun'ichiro
See also DLB 180; EWL 3

Tannen, Deborah F(rances) 1945- .. **CLC 206**
See also CA 118; CANR 95

Tanner, William
See Amis, Kingsley (William)

Tao Lao
See Storni, Alfonsina

Tapahonso, Luci 1953- .... **NNAL; PC 65**
See also CA 145; CANR 72, 127; DLB 175

Tarantino, Quentin (Jerome)
1963- .... **CLC 125**
See also AAYA 58; CA 171; CANR 125

Tarassoff, Lev
See Troyat, Henri

Tarbell, Ida M(inerva) 1857-1944 . **TCLC 40**
See also CA 122; 181; DLB 47

Tarkington, (Newton) Booth
1869-1946 .... **TCLC 9**
See also BPFB 3; BYA 3; CA 110; 143;
CWRI 5; DLB 9, 102; MAL 5; MTCW 2;
RGAL 4; SATA 17

Tarkovskii, Andrei Arsen'evich
See Tarkovsky, Andrei (Arsenyevich)

Tarkovsky, Andrei (Arsenyevich)
1932-1986 .... **CLC 75**
See also CA 127

Tartt, Donna 1964(?)- .... **CLC 76**
See also AAYA 56; CA 142; CANR 135;
MTFW 2005

Tasso, Torquato 1544-1595 .... **LC 5, 94**
See also EFS 2; EW 2; RGWL 2, 3; WLIT
7

Tate, (John Orley) Allen 1899-1979 .. **CLC 2,
4, 6, 9, 11, 14, 24; PC 50**
See also AMW; CA 5-8R; 85-88; CANR
32, 108; CN 1, 2; CP 1, 2; DLB 4, 45, 63;
DLBD 17; EWL 3; MAL 5; MTCW 1, 2;
MTFW 2005; RGAL 4; RHW

Tate, Ellalice
See Hibbert, Eleanor Alice Burford

Tate, James (Vincent) 1943- ..... **CLC 2, 6, 25**
See also CA 21-24R; CANR 29, 57, 114;
CP 1, 2, 3, 4, 5, 6, 7; DLB 5, 169; EWL
3; PFS 10, 15; RGAL 4; WP

Tate, Nahum 1652(?)-1715 .... **LC 109**
See also DLB 80; RGEL 2

Tauler, Johannes c. 1300-1361 ...... **CMLC 37**
See also DLB 179; LMFS 1

Tavel, Ronald 1940- .... **CLC 6**
See also CA 21-24R; CAD; CANR 33; CD
5, 6

Taviani, Paolo 1931- .... **CLC 70**
See also CA 153

Taylor, Bayard 1825-1878 .... **NCLC 89**
See also DLB 3, 189, 250, 254; RGAL 4

Taylor, C(ecil) P(hilip) 1929-1981 .... **CLC 27**
See also CA 25-28R; 105; CANR 47; CBD

Taylor, Edward 1642(?)-1729 . **LC 11; PC 63**
See also AMW; DA; DAB; DAC; DAM
MST, POET; DLB 24; EXPP; RGAL 4;
TUS

Taylor, Eleanor Ross 1920- .... **CLC 5**
See also CA 81-84; CANR 70

Taylor, Elizabeth 1912-1975 ..... **CLC 2, 4, 29**
See also CA 13-16R; CANR 9, 70; CN 1,
2; DLB 139; MTCW 1; RGEL 2; SATA
13

Taylor, Frederick Winslow
1856-1915 .... **TCLC 76**
See also CA 188

Taylor, Henry (Splawn) 1942- .... **CLC 44**
See also CA 33-36R; CAAS 7; CANR 31;
CP 7; DLB 5; PFS 10

Taylor, Kamala (Purnaiya) 1924-2004
See Markandaya, Kamala
See also CA 77-80; 227; MTFW 2005; NFS
13

Taylor, Mildred D(elois) 1943- .... **CLC 21**
See also AAYA 10, 47; BW 1; BYA 3, 8;
CA 85-88; CANR 25, 115, 136; CLR 9,
59, 90; CSW; DLB 52; JRDA; LAIT 3;
MAICYA 1, 2; MTFW 2005; SAAS 5;
SATA 135; WYA; YAW

Taylor, Peter (Hillsman) 1917-1994 .. **CLC 1,
4, 18, 37, 44, 50, 71; SSC 10, 84**
See also AMWS 5; BPFB 3; CA 13-16R;
147; CANR 9, 50; CN 1, 2, 3, 4, 5; CSW;
DLB 218, 278; DLBY 1981, 1994; EWL
3; EXPS; INT CANR-9; MAL 5; MTCW
1, 2; MTFW 2005; RGSF 2; SSFS 9; TUS

Taylor, Robert Lewis 1912-1998 .... **CLC 14**
See also CA 1-4R; 170; CANR 3, 64; CN
1, 2; SATA 10; TCWW 1, 2

Tchekhov, Anton
See Chekhov, Anton (Pavlovich)

Tchicaya, Gerald Felix 1931-1988 .. **CLC 101**
See Tchicaya U Tam'si
See also CA 129; 125; CANR 81

Tchicaya U Tam'si
See Tchicaya, Gerald Felix
See also EWL 3

Teasdale, Sara 1884-1933 .... **PC 31; TCLC 4**
See also CA 104; 163; DLB 45; GLL 1;
PFS 14; RGAL 4; SATA 32; TUS

Tecumseh 1768-1813 .... **NNAL**
See also DAM MULT

Tegner, Esaias 1782-1846 .... **NCLC 2**

Teilhard de Chardin, (Marie Joseph) Pierre
1881-1955 .... **TCLC 9**
See also CA 105; 210; GFL 1789 to the
Present

Temple, Ann
See Mortimer, Penelope (Ruth)

Tennant, Emma (Christina) 1937- .. **CLC 13,
52**
See also BRWS 9; CA 65-68; CAAS 9;
CANR 10, 38, 59, 88; CN 3, 4, 5, 6, 7;
DLB 14; EWL 3; SFW 4

Tenneshaw, S. M.
See Silverberg, Robert

Tenney, Tabitha Gilman
1762-1837 .... **NCLC 122**
See also DLB 37, 200

Tennyson, Alfred 1809-1892 ... **NCLC 30, 65,
115; PC 6; WLC**
See also AAYA 50; BRW 4; CDBLB 1832-
1890; DA; DA3; DAB; DAC; DAM MST,
POET; DLB 32; EXPP; PAB; PFS 1, 2, 4,
11, 15, 19; RGEL 2; TEA; WLIT 4; WP

Teran, Lisa St. Aubin de .... **CLC 36**
See St. Aubin de Teran, Lisa

Terence c. 184B.C.-c. 159B.C. ...... **CMLC 14;
DC 7**
See also AW 1; CDWLB 1; DLB 211;
RGWL 2, 3; TWA

Teresa de Jesus, St. 1515-1582 .... **LC 18**

Teresa of Avila, St.
See Teresa de Jesus, St.

Terkel, Louis 1912-
See Terkel, Studs
See also CA 57-60; CANR 18, 45, 67, 132;
DA3; MTCW 1, 2; MTFW 2005

Terkel, Studs .... **CLC 38**
See Terkel, Louis
See also AAYA 32; AITN 1; MTCW 2; TUS

Terry, C. V.
See Slaughter, Frank G(ill)

Terry, Megan 1932- .... **CLC 19; DC 13**
See also CA 77-80; CABS 3; CAD; CANR
43; CD 5, 6; CWD; DFS 18; DLB 7, 249;
GLL 2

Tertullian c. 155-c. 245 .... **CMLC 29**

Tertz, Abram
See Sinyavsky, Andrei (Donatevich)
See also RGSF 2

Tesich, Steve 1943(?)-1996 .... **CLC 40, 69**
See also CA 105; 152; CAD; DLBY 1983

Tesla, Nikola 1856-1943 .... **TCLC 88**

Teternikov, Fyodor Kuzmich 1863-1927
See Sologub, Fyodor
See also CA 104

Tevis, Walter 1928-1984 .... **CLC 42**
See also CA 113; SFW 4

Tey, Josephine .... **TCLC 14**
See Mackintosh, Elizabeth
See also DLB 77; MSW

Ustinov, Peter (Alexander)
1921-2004 .... **CLC 1**
See also AITN 1; CA 13-16R; 225; CANR
25, 51; CBD; CD 5, 6; DLB 13; MTCW
2

U Tam'si, Gerald Felix Tchicaya
See Tchicaya, Gerald Felix

U Tam'si, Tchicaya
See Tchicaya, Gerald Felix

Vachss, Andrew (Henry) 1942- .... **CLC 106**
See also CA 118, 214; CAAE 214; CANR
44, 95; CMW 4

Vachss, Andrew H.
See Vachss, Andrew (Henry)

Vaculik, Ludvik 1926- .... **CLC 7**
See also CA 53-56; CANR 72; CWW 2;
DLB 232; EWL 3

Vaihinger, Hans 1852-1933 .... **TCLC 71**
See also CA 116; 166

Valdez, Luis (Miguel) 1940- ..... **CLC 84; DC
10; HLC 2**
See also CA 101; CAD; CANR 32, 81; CD
5, 6; DAM MULT; DFS 5; DLB 122;
EWL 3; HW 1; LAIT 4; LLW

Valenzuela, Luisa 1938- .... **CLC 31, 104;
HLCS 2; SSC 14, 82**
See also CA 101; CANR 32, 65, 123; CD-
WLB 3; CWW 2; DAM MULT; DLB 113;
EWL 3; FW; HW 1, 2; LAW; RGSF 2;
RGWL 3

Valera y Alcala-Galiano, Juan
1824-1905 .... **TCLC 10**
See also CA 106

Valerius Maximus fl. 20- .... **CMLC 64**
See also DLB 211

Valery, (Ambroise) Paul (Toussaint Jules)
1871-1945 .... **PC 9; TCLC 4, 15**
See also CA 104; 122; DA3; DAM POET;
DLB 258; EW 8; EWL 3; GFL 1789 to
the Present; MTCW 1, 2; MTFW 2005;
RGWL 2, 3; TWA

Valle-Inclan, Ramon (Maria) del
1866-1936 .... **HLC 2; TCLC 5**
See del Valle-Inclan, Ramon (Maria)
See also CA 106; 153; CANR 80; DAM
MULT; DLB 134; EW 8; EWL 3; HW 2;
RGSF 2; RGWL 2, 3

Vallejo, Antonio Buero
See Buero Vallejo, Antonio

Vallejo, Cesar (Abraham)
1892-1938 .... **HLC 2; TCLC 3, 56**
See also CA 105; 153; DAM MULT; DLB
290; EWL 3; HW 1; LAW; RGWL 2, 3

Valles, Jules 1832-1885 .... **NCLC 71**
See also DLB 123; GFL 1789 to the Present

Vallette, Marguerite Eymery
1860-1953 .... **TCLC 67**
See Rachilde
See also CA 182; DLB 123, 192

Valle Y Pena, Ramon del
See Valle-Inclan, Ramon (Maria) del

Van Ash, Cay 1918-1994 .... **CLC 34**
See also CA 220

Vanbrugh, Sir John 1664-1726 .... **LC 21**
See also BRW 2; DAM DRAM; DLB 80;
IDTP; RGEL 2

Van Campen, Karl
See Campbell, John W(ood, Jr.)

Vance, Gerald
See Silverberg, Robert

Vance, Jack .... **CLC 35**
See Vance, John Holbrook
See also DLB 8; FANT; SCFW 1, 2; SFW
4; SUFW 1, 2

Vance, John Holbrook 1916-
See Queen, Ellery; Vance, Jack
See also CA 29-32R; CANR 17, 65; CMW
4; MTCW 1

Van Den Bogarde, Derek Jules Gaspard
Ulric Niven 1921-1999 .... **CLC 14**
See Bogarde, Dirk
See also CA 77-80; 179

Vandenburgh, Jane .... **CLC 59**
See also CA 168

Vanderhaeghe, Guy 1951- .... **CLC 41**
See also BPFB 3; CA 113; CANR 72, 145;
CN 7

van der Post, Laurens (Jan)
1906-1996 .... **CLC 5**
See also AFW; CA 5-8R; 155; CANR 35;
CN 1, 2, 3, 4, 5, 6; DLB 204; RGEL 2

van de Wetering, Janwillem 1931- ... **CLC 47**
See also CA 49-52; CANR 4, 62, 90; CMW
4

Van Dine, S. S. .... **TCLC 23**
See Wright, Willard Huntington
See also DLB 306; MSW

Van Doren, Carl (Clinton)
1885-1950 .... **TCLC 18**
See also CA 111; 168

Van Doren, Mark 1894-1972 .... **CLC 6, 10**
See also CA 1-4R; 37-40R; CANR 3; CN
1; CP 1; DLB 45, 284; MAL 5; MTCW
1, 2; RGAL 4

Van Druten, John (William)
1901-1957 .... **TCLC 2**
See also CA 104; 161; DLB 10; MAL 5;
RGAL 4

Van Duyn, Mona (Jane) 1921-2004 .. **CLC 3,
7, 63, 116**
See also CA 9-12R; 234; CANR 7, 38, 60,
116; CP 1, 2, 3, 4, 5, 6, 7; CWP; DAM
POET; DLB 5; MAL 5; MTFW 2005;
PFS 20

Van Dyne, Edith
See Baum, L(yman) Frank

van Itallie, Jean-Claude 1936- .... **CLC 3**
See also CA 45-48; CAAS 2; CAD; CANR
1, 48; CD 5, 6; DLB 7

Van Loot, Cornelius Obenchain
See Roberts, Kenneth (Lewis)

van Ostaijen, Paul 1896-1928 .... **TCLC 33**
See also CA 163

Van Peebles, Melvin 1932- .... **CLC 2, 20**
See also BW 2, 3; CA 85-88; CANR 27,
67, 82; DAM MULT

van Schendel, Arthur(-Francois-Emile)
1874-1946 .... **TCLC 56**
See also EWL 3

Vansittart, Peter 1920- .... **CLC 42**
See also CA 1-4R; CANR 3, 49, 90; CN 4,
5, 6, 7; RHW

Van Vechten, Carl 1880-1964 ... **CLC 33; HR
1:3**
See also AMWS 2; CA 183; 89-92; DLB 4,
9, 51; RGAL 4

van Vogt, A(lfred) E(lton) 1912-2000 . **CLC 1**
See also BPFB 3; BYA 13, 14; CA 21-24R;
190; CANR 28; DLB 8, 251; SATA 14;
SATA-Obit 124; SCFW 1, 2; SFW 4

Vara, Madeleine
See Jackson, Laura (Riding)

Varda, Agnes 1928- .... **CLC 16**
See also CA 116; 122

Vargas Llosa, (Jorge) Mario (Pedro)
1936- .... **CLC 3, 6, 9, 10, 15, 31, 42, 85,
181; HLC 2**
See Llosa, (Jorge) Mario (Pedro) Vargas
See also BPFB 3; CA 73-76; CANR 18, 32,
42, 67, 116, 140; CDWLB 3; CWW 2;
DA; DA3; DAB; DAC; DAM MST,
MULT, NOV; DLB 145; DNFS 2; EWL
3; HW 1, 2; LAIT 5; LATS 1:2; LAW;
LAWS 1; MTCW 1, 2; MTFW 2005;
RGWL 2; SSFS 14; TWA; WLIT 1

Varnhagen von Ense, Rahel
1771-1833 .... **NCLC 130**
See also DLB 90

Vasari, Giorgio 1511-1574 .... **LC 114**

Vasiliu, George
See Bacovia, George

Vasiliu, Gheorghe
See Bacovia, George
See also CA 123; 189

Vassa, Gustavus
See Equiano, Olaudah

Vassilikos, Vassilis 1933- .... **CLC 4, 8**
See also CA 81-84; CANR 75; EWL 3

Vaughan, Henry 1621-1695 .... **LC 27**
See also BRW 2; DLB 131; PAB; RGEL 2

Vaughn, Stephanie .... **CLC 62**

Vazov, Ivan (Minchov) 1850-1921 . **TCLC 25**
See also CA 121; 167; CDWLB 4; DLB
147

Veblen, Thorstein B(unde)
1857-1929 .... **TCLC 31**
See also AMWS 1; CA 115; 165; DLB 246;
MAL 5

Vega, Lope de 1562-1635 ... **HLCS 2; LC 23,
119**
See also EW 2; RGWL 2, 3

Vendler, Helen (Hennessy) 1933- ... **CLC 138**
See also CA 41-44R; CANR 25, 72, 136;
MTCW 1, 2; MTFW 2005

Venison, Alfred
See Pound, Ezra (Weston Loomis)

Ventsel, Elena Sergeevna 1907-2002
See Grekova, I.
See also CA 154

Verdi, Marie de
See Mencken, H(enry) L(ouis)

Verdu, Matilde
See Cela, Camilo Jose

Verga, Giovanni (Carmelo)
1840-1922 .... **SSC 21, 87; TCLC 3**
See also CA 104; 123; CANR 101; EW 7;
EWL 3; RGSF 2; RGWL 2, 3; WLIT 7

Vergil 70B.C.-19B.C. ... **CMLC 9, 40; PC 12;
WLCS**
See Virgil
See also AW 2; DA; DA3; DAB; DAC;
DAM MST, POET; EFS 1; LMFS 1

Vergil, Polydore c. 1470-1555 .... **LC 108**
See also DLB 132

Verhaeren, Emile (Adolphe Gustave)
1855-1916 .... **TCLC 12**
See also CA 109; EWL 3; GFL 1789 to the
Present

Verlaine, Paul (Marie) 1844-1896 .. **NCLC 2,
51; PC 2, 32**
See also DAM POET; DLB 217; EW 7;
GFL 1789 to the Present; LMFS 2; RGWL
2, 3; TWA

Verne, Jules (Gabriel) 1828-1905 ... **TCLC 6,
52**
See also AAYA 16; BYA 4; CA 110; 131;
CLR 88; DA3; DLB 123; GFL 1789 to
the Present; JRDA; LAIT 2; LMFS 2;
MAICYA 1, 2; MTFW 2005; RGWL 2, 3;
SATA 21; SCFW 1, 2; SFW 4; TWA;
WCH

Verus, Marcus Annius
See Aurelius, Marcus

Very, Jones 1813-1880 .... **NCLC 9**
See also DLB 1, 243; RGAL 4

Vesaas, Tarjei 1897-1970 .... **CLC 48**
See also CA 190; 29-32R; DLB 297; EW
11; EWL 3; RGWL 3

Vialis, Gaston
See Simenon, Georges (Jacques Christian)

Vian, Boris 1920-1959(?) .... **TCLC 9**
See also CA 106; 164; CANR 111; DLB
72, 321; EWL 3; GFL 1789 to the Present;
MTCW 2; RGWL 2, 3

Viaud, (Louis Marie) Julien 1850-1923
See Loti, Pierre
See also CA 107

Vicar, Henry
See Felsen, Henry Gregor

Vicente, Gil 1465-c. 1536 .... **LC 99**
See also DLB 318; IDTP; RGWL 2, 3

Vicker, Angus
See Felsen, Henry Gregor

Vidal, (Eugene Luther) Gore 1925- .. **CLC 2, 4, 6, 8, 10, 22, 33, 72, 142**
See Box, Edgar
See also AAYA 64; AITN 1; AMWS 4; BEST 90:2; BPFB 3; CA 5-8R; CAD; CANR 13, 45, 65, 100, 132; CD 5, 6; CDALBS; CN 1, 2, 3, 4, 5, 6, 7; CPW; DA3; DAM NOV, POP; DFS 2; DLB 6, 152; EWL 3; INT CANR-13; MAL 5; MTCW 1, 2; MTFW 2005; RGAL 4; RHW; TUS

Viereck, Peter (Robert Edwin)
1916- .... **CLC 4; PC 27**
See also CA 1-4R; CANR 1, 47; CP 1, 2, 3, 4, 5, 6, 7; DLB 5; MAL 5; PFS 9, 14

Vigny, Alfred (Victor) de
1797-1863 .... **NCLC 7, 102; PC 26**
See also DAM POET; DLB 119, 192, 217; EW 5; GFL 1789 to the Present; RGWL 2, 3

Vilakazi, Benedict Wallet
1906-1947 .... **TCLC 37**
See also CA 168

Villa, Jose Garcia 1908-1997 ... **AAL; PC 22, TCLC 176**
See also CA 25-28R; CANR 12, 118; CP 1, 2, 3, 4; DLB 312; EWL 3; EXPP

Villard, Oswald Garrison
1872-1949 .... **TCLC 160**
See also CA 113; 162; DLB 25, 91

Villarreal, Jose Antonio 1924- .... **HLC 2**
See also CA 133; CANR 93; DAM MULT; DLB 82; HW 1; LAIT 4; RGAL 4

Villaurrutia, Xavier 1903-1950 ...... **TCLC 80**
See also CA 192; EWL 3; HW 1; LAW

Villaverde, Cirilo 1812-1894 .... **NCLC 121**
See also LAW

Villehardouin, Geoffroi de
1150(?)-1218(?) .... **CMLC 38**

Villiers, George 1628-1687 .... **LC 107**
See also DLB 80; RGEL 2

Villiers de l'Isle Adam, Jean Marie Mathias Philippe Auguste 1838-1889 ... **NCLC 3; SSC 14**
See also DLB 123, 192; GFL 1789 to the Present; RGSF 2

Villon, Francois 1431-1463(?) . **LC 62; PC 13**
See also DLB 208; EW 2; RGWL 2, 3; TWA

Vine, Barbara .... **CLC 50**
See Rendell, Ruth (Barbara)
See also BEST 90:4

Vinge, Joan (Carol) D(ennison)
1948- .... **CLC 30; SSC 24**
See also AAYA 32; BPFB 3; CA 93-96; CANR 72; SATA 36, 113; SFW 4; YAW

Viola, Herman J(oseph) 1938- .... **CLC 70**
See also CA 61-64; CANR 8, 23, 48, 91; SATA 126

Violis, G.
See Simenon, Georges (Jacques Christian)

Viramontes, Helena Maria 1954- .... **HLCS 2**
See also CA 159; DLB 122; HW 2; LLW

Virgil
See Vergil
See also CDWLB 1; DLB 211; LAIT 1; RGWL 2, 3; WP

Visconti, Luchino 1906-1976 .... **CLC 16**
See also CA 81-84; 65-68; CANR 39

Vitry, Jacques de
See Jacques de Vitry

Vittorini, Elio 1908-1966 .... **CLC 6, 9, 14**
See also CA 133; 25-28R; DLB 264; EW 12; EWL 3; RGWL 2, 3

Vivekananda, Swami 1863-1902 .... **TCLC 88**

Vizenor, Gerald Robert 1934- .... **CLC 103; NNAL**
See also CA 13-16R, 205; CAAE 205; CAAS 22; CANR 5, 21, 44, 67; DAM MULT; DLB 175, 227; MTCW 2; MTFW 2005; TCWW 2

Vizinczey, Stephen 1933- .... **CLC 40**
See also CA 128; CCA 1; INT CA-128

Vliet, R(ussell) G(ordon)
1929-1984 .... **CLC 22**
See also CA 37-40R; 112; CANR 18; CP 2, 3

Vogau, Boris Andreyevich 1894-1938
See Pilnyak, Boris
See also CA 123; 218

Vogel, Paula A(nne) 1951- ... **CLC 76; DC 19**
See also CA 108; CAD; CANR 119, 140; CD 5, 6; CWD; DFS 14; MTFW 2005; RGAL 4

Voigt, Cynthia 1942- .... **CLC 30**
See also AAYA 3, 30; BYA 1, 3, 6, 7, 8; CA 106; CANR 18, 37, 40, 94, 145; CLR 13, 48; INT CANR-18; JRDA; LAIT 5; MAICYA 1, 2; MAICYAS 1; MTFW 2005; SATA 48, 79, 116, 160; SATA-Brief 33; WYA; YAW

Voigt, Ellen Bryant 1943- .... **CLC 54**
See also CA 69-72; CANR 11, 29, 55, 115; CP 7; CSW; CWP; DLB 120; PFS 23

Voinovich, Vladimir (Nikolaevich)
1932- .... **CLC 10, 49, 147**
See also CA 81-84; CAAS 12; CANR 33, 67; CWW 2; DLB 302; MTCW 1

Vollmann, William T. 1959- .... **CLC 89**
See also CA 134; CANR 67, 116; CN 7; CPW; DA3; DAM NOV, POP; MTCW 2; MTFW 2005

Voloshinov, V. N.
See Bakhtin, Mikhail Mikhailovich

Voltaire 1694-1778 . **LC 14, 79, 110; SSC 12; WLC**
See also BYA 13; DA; DA3; DAB; DAC; DAM DRAM, MST; DLB 314; EW 4; GFL Beginnings to 1789; LATS 1:1; LMFS 1; NFS 7; RGWL 2, 3; TWA

von Aschendrof, Baron Ignatz
See Ford, Ford Madox

von Chamisso, Adelbert
See Chamisso, Adelbert von

von Daeniken, Erich 1935- .... **CLC 30**
See also AITN 1; CA 37-40R; CANR 17, 44

von Daniken, Erich
See von Daeniken, Erich

von Hartmann, Eduard
1842-1906 .... **TCLC 96**

von Hayek, Friedrich August
See Hayek, F(riedrich) A(ugust von)

von Heidenstam, (Carl Gustaf) Verner
See Heidenstam, (Carl Gustaf) Verner von

von Heyse, Paul (Johann Ludwig)
See Heyse, Paul (Johann Ludwig von)

von Hofmannsthal, Hugo
See Hofmannsthal, Hugo von

von Horvath, Odon
See von Horvath, Odon

von Horvath, Odon
See von Horvath, Odon

von Horvath, Odon 1901-1938 .... **TCLC 45**
See von Horvath, Oedoen
See also CA 118; 194; DLB 85, 124; RGWL 2, 3

von Horvath, Oedoen
See von Horvath, Odon
See also CA 184

von Kleist, Heinrich
See Kleist, Heinrich von

von Liliencron, (Friedrich Adolf Axel) Detlev
See Liliencron, (Friedrich Adolf Axel) Detlev von

Vonnegut, Kurt, Jr. 1922- . **CLC 1, 2, 3, 4, 5, 8, 12, 22, 40, 60, 111, 212; SSC 8; WLC**
See also AAYA 6, 44; AITN 1; AMWS 2; BEST 90:4; BPFB 3; BYA 3, 14; CA 1-4R; CANR 1, 25, 49, 75, 92; CDALB 1968-1988; CN 1, 2, 3, 4, 5, 6, 7; CPW 1; DA; DA3; DAB; DAC; DAM MST, NOV, POP; DLB 2, 8, 152; DLBD 3; DLBY 1980; EWL 3; EXPN; EXPS; LAIT 4; LMFS 2; MAL 5; MTCW 1, 2; MTFW 2005; NFS 3; RGAL 4; SCFW; SFW 4; SSFS 5; TUS; YAW

Von Rachen, Kurt
See Hubbard, L(afayette) Ron(ald)

von Rezzori (d'Arezzo), Gregor
See Rezzori (d'Arezzo), Gregor von

von Sternberg, Josef
See Sternberg, Josef von

Vorster, Gordon 1924- .... **CLC 34**
See also CA 133

Vosce, Trudie
See Ozick, Cynthia

Voznesensky, Andrei (Andreievich)
1933- .... **CLC 1, 15, 57**
See Voznesensky, Andrey
See also CA 89-92; CANR 37; CWW 2; DAM POET; MTCW 1

Voznesensky, Andrey
See Voznesensky, Andrei (Andreievich)
See also EWL 3

Wace, Robert c. 1100-c. 1175 .... **CMLC 55**
See also DLB 146

Waddington, Miriam 1917-2004 .... **CLC 28**
See also CA 21-24R; 225; CANR 12, 30; CCA 1; CP 1, 2, 3, 4, 5, 6, 7; DLB 68

Wagman, Fredrica 1937- .... **CLC 7**
See also CA 97-100; INT CA-97-100

Wagner, Linda W.
See Wagner-Martin, Linda (C.)

Wagner, Linda Welshimer
See Wagner-Martin, Linda (C.)

Wagner, Richard 1813-1883 ..... **NCLC 9, 119**
See also DLB 129; EW 6

Wagner-Martin, Linda (C.) 1936- .... **CLC 50**
See also CA 159; CANR 135

Wagoner, David (Russell) 1926- .... **CLC 3, 5, 15; PC 33**
See also AMWS 9; CA 1-4R; CAAS 3; CANR 2, 71; CN 1, 2, 3, 4, 5, 6, 7; CP 1, 2, 3, 4, 5, 6, 7; DLB 5, 256; SATA 14; TCWW 1, 2

Wah, Fred(erick James) 1939- .... **CLC 44**
See also CA 107; 141; CP 1, 7; DLB 60

Wahloo, Per 1926-1975 .... **CLC 7**
See also BPFB 3; CA 61-64; CANR 73; CMW 4; MSW

Wahloo, Peter
See Wahloo, Per

Wain, John (Barrington) 1925-1994 . **CLC 2, 11, 15, 46**
See also CA 5-8R; 145; CAAS 4; CANR 23, 54; CDBLB 1960 to Present; CN 1, 2, 3, 4, 5; CP 1, 2, 3, 4; DLB 15, 27, 139, 155; EWL 3; MTCW 1, 2; MTFW 2005

Wajda, Andrzej 1926- .... **CLC 16, 219**
See also CA 102

Wakefield, Dan 1932- .... **CLC 7**
See also CA 21-24R, 211; CAAE 211; CAAS 7; CN 4, 5, 6, 7

Wakefield, Herbert Russell
1888-1965 .... **TCLC 120**
See also CA 5-8R; CANR 77; HGG; SUFW

Wakoski, Diane 1937- ...... **CLC 2, 4, 7, 9, 11, 40; PC 15**
See also CA 13-16R, 216; CAAE 216; CAAS 1; CANR 9, 60, 106; CP 1, 2, 3, 4, 5, 6, 7; CWP; DAM POET; DLB 5; INT CANR-9; MAL 5; MTCW 2; MTFW 2005

Wakoski-Sherbell, Diane
See Wakoski, Diane

Walcott, Derek (Alton) 1930- ... **BLC 3; CLC 2, 4, 9, 14, 25, 42, 67, 76, 160; DC 7; PC 46**
See also BW 2; CA 89-92; CANR 26, 47, 75, 80, 130; CBD; CD 5, 6; CDWLB 3; CP 1, 2, 3, 4, 5, 6, 7; DA3; DAB; DAC; DAM MST, MULT, POET; DLB 117; DLBY 1981; DNFS 1; EFS 1; EWL 3; LMFS 2; MTCW 1, 2; MTFW 2005; PFS 6; RGEL 2; TWA; WWE 1

Waldman, Anne (Lesley) 1945- .... **CLC 7**
See also BG 1:3; CA 37-40R; CAAS 17; CANR 34, 69, 116; CP 1, 2, 3, 4, 5, 6, 7; CWP; DLB 16

Waldo, E. Hunter
See Sturgeon, Theodore (Hamilton)

Waldo, Edward Hamilton
See Sturgeon, Theodore (Hamilton)

Walker, Alice (Malsenior) 1944- .... **BLC 3; CLC 5, 6, 9, 19, 27, 46, 58, 103, 167; PC 30; SSC 5; WLCS**
See also AAYA 3, 33; AFAW 1, 2; AMWS 3; BEST 89:4; BPFB 3; BW 2, 3; CA 37-40R; CANR 9, 27, 49, 66, 82, 131; CDALB 1968-1988; CN 4, 5, 6, 7; CPW; CSW; DA; DA3; DAB; DAC; DAM MST, MULT, NOV, POET, POP; DLB 6, 33, 143; EWL 3; EXPN; EXPS; FL 1:6; FW; INT CANR-27; LAIT 3; MAL 5; MAWW; MTCW 1, 2; MTFW 2005; NFS 5; RGAL 4; RGSF 2; SATA 31; SSFS 2, 11; TUS; YAW

Walker, David Harry 1911-1992 ...... **CLC 14**
See also CA 1-4R; 137; CANR 1; CN 1, 2; CWRI 5; SATA 8; SATA-Obit 71

Walker, Edward Joseph 1934-2004
See Walker, Ted
See also CA 21-24R; 226; CANR 12, 28, 53

Walker, George F(rederick) 1947- .. **CLC 44, 61**
See also CA 103; CANR 21, 43, 59; CD 5, 6; DAB; DAC; DAM MST; DLB 60

Walker, Joseph A. 1935-2003 .... **CLC 19**
See also BW 1, 3; CA 89-92; CAD; CANR 26, 143; CD 5, 6; DAM DRAM, MST; DFS 12; DLB 38

Walker, Margaret (Abigail)
1915-1998 .... **BLC; CLC 1, 6; PC 20; TCLC 129**
See also AFAW 1, 2; BW 2, 3; CA 73-76; 172; CANR 26, 54, 76, 136; CN 1, 2, 3, 4, 5, 6; CP 1, 2, 3, 4; CSW; DAM MULT; DLB 76, 152; EXPP; FW; MAL 5; MTCW 1, 2; MTFW 2005; RGAL 4; RHW

Walker, Ted .... **CLC 13**
See Walker, Edward Joseph
See also CP 1, 2, 3, 4, 5, 6, 7; DLB 40

Wallace, David Foster 1962- ... **CLC 50, 114; SSC 68**
See also AAYA 50; AMWS 10; CA 132; CANR 59, 133; CN 7; DA3; MTCW 2; MTFW 2005

Wallace, Dexter
See Masters, Edgar Lee

Wallace, (Richard Horatio) Edgar
1875-1932 .... **TCLC 57**
See also CA 115; 218; CMW 4; DLB 70; MSW; RGEL 2

Wallace, Irving 1916-1990 .... **CLC 7, 13**
See also AITN 1; BPFB 3; CA 1-4R; 132; CAAS 1; CANR 1, 27; CPW; DAM NOV, POP; INT CANR-27; MTCW 1, 2

Wallant, Edward Lewis 1926-1962 ... **CLC 5, 10**
See also CA 1-4R; CANR 22; DLB 2, 28, 143, 299; EWL 3; MAL 5; MTCW 1, 2; RGAL 4

Wallas, Graham 1858-1932 .... **TCLC 91**

Waller, Edmund 1606-1687 .... **LC 86**
See also BRW 2; DAM POET; DLB 126; PAB; RGEL 2

Walley, Byron
See Card, Orson Scott

Walpole, Horace 1717-1797 .... **LC 2, 49**
See also BRW 3; DLB 39, 104, 213; GL 3; HGG; LMFS 1; RGEL 2; SUFW 1; TEA

Walpole, Hugh (Seymour)
1884-1941 .... **TCLC 5**
See also CA 104; 165; DLB 34; HGG; MTCW 2; RGEL 2; RHW

Walrond, Eric (Derwent) 1898-1966 . **HR 1:3**
See also BW 1; CA 125; DLB 51

Walser, Martin 1927- .... **CLC 27, 183**
See also CA 57-60; CANR 8, 46, 145; CWW 2; DLB 75, 124; EWL 3

Walser, Robert 1878-1956 ..... **SSC 20; TCLC 18**
See also CA 118; 165; CANR 100; DLB 66; EWL 3

Walsh, Gillian Paton
See Paton Walsh, Gillian

Walsh, Jill Paton .... **CLC 35**
See Paton Walsh, Gillian
See also CLR 2, 65; WYA

Walter, Villiam Christian
See Andersen, Hans Christian

Walters, Anna L(ee) 1946- .... **NNAL**
See also CA 73-76

Walther von der Vogelweide c.
1170-1228 .... **CMLC 56**

Walton, Izaak 1593-1683 .... **LC 72**
See also BRW 2; CDBLB Before 1660; DLB 151, 213; RGEL 2

Wambaugh, Joseph (Aloysius), Jr.
1937- .... **CLC 3, 18**
See also AITN 1; BEST 89:3; BPFB 3; CA 33-36R; CANR 42, 65, 115; CMW 4; CPW 1; DA3; DAM NOV, POP; DLB 6; DLBY 1983; MSW; MTCW 1, 2

Wang Wei 699(?)-761(?) .... **PC 18**
See also TWA

Warburton, William 1698-1779 .... **LC 97**
See also DLB 104

Ward, Arthur Henry Sarsfield 1883-1959
See Rohmer, Sax
See also CA 108; 173; CMW 4; HGG

Ward, Douglas Turner 1930- .... **CLC 19**
See also BW 1; CA 81-84; CAD; CANR 27; CD 5, 6; DLB 7, 38

Ward, E. D.
See Lucas, E(dward) V(errall)

Ward, Mrs. Humphry 1851-1920
See Ward, Mary Augusta
See also RGEL 2

Ward, Mary Augusta 1851-1920 ... **TCLC 55**
See Ward, Mrs. Humphry
See also DLB 18

Ward, Nathaniel 1578(?)-1652 .... **LC 114**
See also DLB 24

Ward, Peter
See Faust, Frederick (Schiller)

Warhol, Andy 1928(?)-1987 .... **CLC 20**
See also AAYA 12; BEST 89:4; CA 89-92; 121; CANR 34

Warner, Francis (Robert le Plastrier)
1937- .... **CLC 14**
See also CA 53-56; CANR 11; CP 1, 2, 3, 4

Warner, Marina 1946- .... **CLC 59**
See also CA 65-68; CANR 21, 55, 118; CN 5, 6, 7; DLB 194; MTFW 2005

Warner, Rex (Ernest) 1905-1986 ...... **CLC 45**
See also CA 89-92; 119; CN 1, 2, 3, 4; CP 1, 2, 3, 4; DLB 15; RGEL 2; RHW

Warner, Susan (Bogert)
1819-1885 .... **NCLC 31, 146**
See also DLB 3, 42, 239, 250, 254

Warner, Sylvia (Constance) Ashton
See Ashton-Warner, Sylvia (Constance)

Warner, Sylvia Townsend
1893-1978 .. **CLC 7, 19; SSC 23; TCLC 131**
See also BRWS 7; CA 61-64; 77-80; CANR 16, 60, 104; CN 1, 2; DLB 34, 139; EWL 3; FANT; FW; MTCW 1, 2; RGEL 2; RGSF 2; RHW

Warren, Mercy Otis 1728-1814 ..... **NCLC 13**
See also DLB 31, 200; RGAL 4; TUS

Warren, Robert Penn 1905-1989 .. **CLC 1, 4, 6, 8, 10, 13, 18, 39, 53, 59; PC 37; SSC 4, 58; WLC**
See also AITN 1; AMW; AMWC 2; BPFB 3; BYA 1; CA 13-16R; 129; CANR 10, 47; CDALB 1968-1988; CN 1, 2, 3, 4; CP 1, 2, 3, 4; DA; DA3; DAB; DAC; DAM MST, NOV, POET; DLB 2, 48, 152, 320; DLBY 1980, 1989; EWL 3; INT CANR-10; MAL 5; MTCW 1, 2; MTFW 2005; NFS 13; RGAL 4; RGSF 2; RHW; SATA 46; SATA-Obit 63; SSFS 8; TUS

Warrigal, Jack
See Furphy, Joseph

Warshofsky, Isaac
See Singer, Isaac Bashevis

Warton, Joseph 1722-1800 .... **NCLC 118**
See also DLB 104, 109; RGEL 2

Warton, Thomas 1728-1790 .... **LC 15, 82**
See also DAM POET; DLB 104, 109; RGEL 2

Waruk, Kona
See Harris, (Theodore) Wilson

Warung, Price .... **TCLC 45**
See Astley, William
See also DLB 230; RGEL 2

Warwick, Jarvis
See Garner, Hugh
See also CCA 1

Washington, Alex
See Harris, Mark

Washington, Booker T(aliaferro)
1856-1915 .... **BLC 3; TCLC 10**
See also BW 1; CA 114; 125; DA3; DAM MULT; LAIT 2; RGAL 4; SATA 28

Washington, George 1732-1799 .... **LC 25**
See also DLB 31

Wassermann, (Karl) Jakob
1873-1934 .... **TCLC 6**
See also CA 104; 163; DLB 66; EWL 3

Wasserstein, Wendy 1950-2006 . **CLC 32, 59, 90, 183; DC 4**
See also AMWS 15; CA 121; 129; CABS 3; CAD; CANR 53, 75, 128; CD 5, 6; CWD; DA3; DAM DRAM; DFS 5, 17; DLB 228; EWL 3; FW; INT CA-129; MAL 5; MTCW 2; MTFW 2005; SATA 94

Waterhouse, Keith (Spencer) 1929- . **CLC 47**
See also CA 5-8R; CANR 38, 67, 109; CBD; CD 6; CN 1, 2, 3, 4, 5, 6, 7; DLB 13, 15; MTCW 1, 2; MTFW 2005

West, Dorothy 1907-1998 ...... **HR 1:3; TCLC 108**
See also BW 2; CA 143; 169; DLB 76

West, (Mary) Jessamyn 1902-1984 ... **CLC 7, 17**
See also CA 9-12R; 112; CANR 27; CN 1, 2, 3; DLB 6; DLBY 1984; MTCW 1, 2; RGAL 4; RHW; SATA-Obit 37; TCWW 2; TUS; YAW

West, Morris L(anglo) 1916-1999 ..... **CLC 6, 33**
See also BPFB 3; CA 5-8R; 187; CANR 24, 49, 64; CN 1, 2, 3, 4, 5, 6; CPW; DLB 289; MTCW 1, 2; MTFW 2005

West, Nathanael 1903-1940 .. **SSC 16; TCLC 1, 14, 44**
See also AMW; AMWR 2; BPFB 3; CA 104; 125; CDALB 1929-1941; DA3; DLB 4, 9, 28; EWL 3; MAL 5; MTCW 1, 2; MTFW 2005; NFS 16; RGAL 4; TUS

West, Owen
See Koontz, Dean R.

West, Paul 1930- .... **CLC 7, 14, 96**
See also CA 13-16R; CAAS 7; CANR 22, 53, 76, 89, 136; CN 1, 2, 3, 4, 5, 6, 7; DLB 14; INT CANR-22; MTCW 2; MTFW 2005

West, Rebecca 1892-1983 ... **CLC 7, 9, 31, 50**
See also BPFB 3; BRWS 3; CA 5-8R; 109; CANR 19; CN 1, 2, 3; DLB 36; DLBY 1983; EWL 3; FW; MTCW 1, 2; MTFW 2005; NCFS 4; RGEL 2; TEA

Westall, Robert (Atkinson) 1929-1993 .... **CLC 17**
See also AAYA 12; BYA 2, 6, 7, 8, 9, 15; CA 69-72; 141; CANR 18, 68; CLR 13; FANT; JRDA; MAICYA 1, 2; MAICYAS 1; SAAS 2; SATA 23, 69; SATA-Obit 75; WYA; YAW

Westermarck, Edward 1862-1939 . **TCLC 87**

Westlake, Donald E(dwin) 1933- . **CLC 7, 33**
See also BPFB 3; CA 17-20R; CAAS 13; CANR 16, 44, 65, 94, 137; CMW 4; CPW; DAM POP; INT CANR-16; MSW; MTCW 2; MTFW 2005

Westmacott, Mary
See Christie, Agatha (Mary Clarissa)

Weston, Allen
See Norton, Andre

Wetcheek, J. L.
See Feuchtwanger, Lion

Wetering, Janwillem van de
See van de Wetering, Janwillem

Wetherald, Agnes Ethelwyn 1857-1940 .... **TCLC 81**
See also CA 202; DLB 99

Wetherell, Elizabeth
See Warner, Susan (Bogert)

Whale, James 1889-1957 .... **TCLC 63**

Whalen, Philip (Glenn) 1923-2002 .... **CLC 6, 29**
See also BG 1:3; CA 9-12R; 209; CANR 5, 39; CP 1, 2, 3, 4, 5, 6, 7; DLB 16; WP

Wharton, Edith (Newbold Jones) 1862-1937 ... **SSC 6, 84; TCLC 3, 9, 27, 53, 129, 149; WLC**
See also AAYA 25; AMW; AMWC 2; AMWR 1; BPFB 3; CA 104; 132; CDALB 1865-1917; DA; DA3; DAB; DAC; DAM MST, NOV; DLB 4, 9, 12, 78, 189; DLBD 13; EWL 3; EXPS; FL 1:6; GL 3; HGG; LAIT 2, 3; LATS 1:1; MAL 5; MAWW; MTCW 1, 2; MTFW 2005; NFS 5, 11, 15, 20; RGAL 4; RGSF 2; RHW; SSFS 6, 7; SUFW; TUS

Wharton, James
See Mencken, H(enry) L(ouis)

Wharton, William (a pseudonym) 1925- .... **CLC 18, 37**
See also CA 93-96; CN 4, 5, 6, 7; DLBY 1980; INT CA-93-96

Wheatley (Peters), Phillis 1753(?)-1784 ... **BLC 3; LC 3, 50; PC 3; WLC**
See also AFAW 1, 2; CDALB 1640-1865; DA; DA3; DAC; DAM MST, MULT, POET; DLB 31, 50; EXPP; FL 1:1; PFS 13; RGAL 4

Wheelock, John Hall 1886-1978 .... **CLC 14**
See also CA 13-16R; 77-80; CANR 14; CP 1, 2; DLB 45; MAL 5

Whim-Wham
See Curnow, (Thomas) Allen (Monro)

White, Babington
See Braddon, Mary Elizabeth

White, E(lwyn) B(rooks) 1899-1985 .... **CLC 10, 34, 39**
See also AAYA 62; AITN 2; AMWS 1; CA 13-16R; 116; CANR 16, 37; CDALBS; CLR 1, 21; CPW; DA3; DAM POP; DLB 11, 22; EWL 3; FANT; MAICYA 1, 2; MAL 5; MTCW 1, 2; MTFW 2005; NCFS 5; RGAL 4; SATA 2, 29, 100; SATA-Obit 44; TUS

White, Edmund (Valentine III) 1940- .... **CLC 27, 110**
See also AAYA 7; CA 45-48; CANR 3, 19, 36, 62, 107, 133; CN 5, 6, 7; DA3; DAM POP; DLB 227; MTCW 1, 2; MTFW 2005

White, Hayden V. 1928- .... **CLC 148**
See also CA 128; CANR 135; DLB 246

White, Patrick (Victor Martindale) 1912-1990 ...... **CLC 3, 4, 5, 7, 9, 18, 65, 69; SSC 39, TCLC 176**
See also BRWS 1; CA 81-84; 132; CANR 43; CN 1, 2, 3, 4; DLB 260; EWL 3; MTCW 1; RGEL 2; RGSF 2; RHW; TWA; WWE 1

White, Phyllis Dorothy James 1920-
See James, P. D.
See also CA 21-24R; CANR 17, 43, 65, 112; CMW 4; CN 7; CPW; DA3; DAM POP; MTCW 1, 2; MTFW 2005; TEA

White, T(erence) H(anbury) 1906-1964 .... **CLC 30**
See also AAYA 22; BPFB 3; BYA 4, 5; CA 73-76; CANR 37; DLB 160; FANT; JRDA; LAIT 1; MAICYA 1, 2; RGEL 2; SATA 12; SUFW 1; YAW

White, Terence de Vere 1912-1994 ... **CLC 49**
See also CA 49-52; 145; CANR 3

White, Walter
See White, Walter F(rancis)

White, Walter F(rancis) 1893-1955 ... **BLC 3; HR 1:3; TCLC 15**
See also BW 1; CA 115; 124; DAM MULT; DLB 51

White, William Hale 1831-1913
See Rutherford, Mark
See also CA 121; 189

Whitehead, Alfred North 1861-1947 .... **TCLC 97**
See also CA 117; 165; DLB 100, 262

Whitehead, E(dward) A(nthony) 1933- .... **CLC 5**
See Whitehead, Ted
See also CA 65-68; CANR 58, 118; CBD; CD 5; DLB 310

Whitehead, Ted
See Whitehead, E(dward) A(nthony)
See also CD 6

Whiteman, Roberta J. Hill 1947- ...... **NNAL**
See also CA 146

Whitemore, Hugh (John) 1936- .... **CLC 37**
See also CA 132; CANR 77; CBD; CD 5, 6; INT CA-132

Whitman, Sarah Helen (Power) 1803-1878 .... **NCLC 19**
See also DLB 1, 243

Whitman, Walt(er) 1819-1892 .. **NCLC 4, 31, 81; PC 3; WLC**
See also AAYA 42; AMW; AMWR 1; CDALB 1640-1865; DA; DA3; DAB; DAC; DAM MST, POET; DLB 3, 64, 224, 250; EXPP; LAIT 2; LMFS 1; PAB; PFS 2, 3, 13, 22; RGAL 4; SATA 20; TUS; WP; WYAS 1

Whitney, Phyllis A(yame) 1903- .... **CLC 42**
See also AAYA 36; AITN 2; BEST 90:3; CA 1-4R; CANR 3, 25, 38, 60; CLR 59; CMW 4; CPW; DA3; DAM POP; JRDA; MAICYA 1, 2; MTCW 2; RHW; SATA 1, 30; YAW

Whittemore, (Edward) Reed, Jr. 1919- .... **CLC 4**
See also CA 9-12R; 219; CAAE 219; CAAS 8; CANR 4, 119; CP 1, 2, 3, 4, 5, 6, 7; DLB 5; MAL 5

Whittier, John Greenleaf 1807-1892 .... **NCLC 8, 59**
See also AMWS 1; DLB 1, 243; RGAL 4

Whittlebot, Hernia
See Coward, Noel (Peirce)

Wicker, Thomas Grey 1926-
See Wicker, Tom
See also CA 65-68; CANR 21, 46, 141

Wicker, Tom .... **CLC 7**
See Wicker, Thomas Grey

Wideman, John Edgar 1941- ... **BLC 3; CLC 5, 34, 36, 67, 122; SSC 62**
See also AFAW 1, 2; AMWS 10; BPFB 4; BW 2, 3; CA 85-88; CANR 14, 42, 67, 109, 140; CN 4, 5, 6, 7; DAM MULT; DLB 33, 143; MAL 5; MTCW 2; MTFW 2005; RGAL 4; RGSF 2; SSFS 6, 12; TCLE 1:2

Wiebe, Rudy (Henry) 1934- .. **CLC 6, 11, 14, 138**
See also CA 37-40R; CANR 42, 67, 123; CN 1, 2, 3, 4, 5, 6, 7; DAC; DAM MST; DLB 60; RHW; SATA 156

Wieland, Christoph Martin 1733-1813 .... **NCLC 17**
See also DLB 97; EW 4; LMFS 1; RGWL 2, 3

Wiene, Robert 1881-1938 .... **TCLC 56**

Wieners, John 1934- .... **CLC 7**
See also BG 1:3; CA 13-16R; CP 1, 2, 3, 4, 5, 6, 7; DLB 16; WP

Wiesel, Elie(zer) 1928- .... **CLC 3, 5, 11, 37, 165; WLCS**
See also AAYA 7, 54; AITN 1; CA 5-8R; CAAS 4; CANR 8, 40, 65, 125; CDALBS; CWW 2; DA; DA3; DAB; DAC; DAM MST, NOV; DLB 83, 299; DLBY 1987; EWL 3; INT CANR-8; LAIT 4; MTCW 1, 2; MTFW 2005; NCFS 4; NFS 4; RGWL 3; SATA 56; YAW

Wiggins, Marianne 1947- .... **CLC 57**
See also BEST 89:3; CA 130; CANR 60, 139; CN 7

Wigglesworth, Michael 1631-1705 .... **LC 106**
See also DLB 24; RGAL 4

Wiggs, Susan .... **CLC 70**
See also CA 201

Wight, James Alfred 1916-1995
See Herriot, James
See also CA 77-80; SATA 55; SATA-Brief 44

Wilbur, Richard (Purdy) 1921- ..... **CLC 3, 6, 9, 14, 53, 110; PC 51**
See also AMWS 3; CA 1-4R; CABS 2; CANR 2, 29, 76, 93, 139; CDALBS; CP 1, 2, 3, 4, 5, 6, 7; DA; DAB; DAC; DAM MST, POET; DLB 5, 169; EWL 3; EXPP;

Wilson, Snoo 1948- .... **CLC 33**
  See also CA 69-72; CBD; CD 5, 6
Wilson, William S(mith) 1932- .... **CLC 49**
  See also CA 81-84
Wilson, (Thomas) Woodrow
    1856-1924 .... **TCLC 79**
  See also CA 166; DLB 47
Wilson and Warnke eds. .... **CLC 65**
Winchilsea, Anne (Kingsmill) Finch
    1661-1720
  See Finch, Anne
  See also RGEL 2
Windham, Basil
  See Wodehouse, P(elham) G(renville)
Wingrove, David (John) 1954- .... **CLC 68**
  See also CA 133; SFW 4
Winnemucca, Sarah 1844-1891 .... **NCLC 79; NNAL**
  See also DAM MULT; DLB 175; RGAL 4
Winstanley, Gerrard 1609-1676 .... **LC 52**
Wintergreen, Jane
  See Duncan, Sara Jeannette
Winters, Arthur Yvor
  See Winters, Yvor
Winters, Janet Lewis .... **CLC 41**
  See Lewis, Janet
  See also DLBY 1987
Winters, Yvor 1900-1968 .... **CLC 4, 8, 32**
  See also AMWS 2; CA 11-12; 25-28R; CAP 1; DLB 48; EWL 3; MAL 5; MTCW 1; RGAL 4
Winterson, Jeanette 1959- .... **CLC 64, 158**
  See also BRWS 4; CA 136; CANR 58, 116; CN 5, 6, 7; CPW; DA3; DAM POP; DLB 207, 261; FANT; FW; GLL 1; MTCW 2; MTFW 2005; RHW
Winthrop, John 1588-1649 .... **LC 31, 107**
  See also DLB 24, 30
Wirth, Louis 1897-1952 .... **TCLC 92**
  See also CA 210
Wiseman, Frederick 1930- .... **CLC 20**
  See also CA 159
Wister, Owen 1860-1938 .... **TCLC 21**
  See also BPFB 3; CA 108; 162; DLB 9, 78, 186; RGAL 4; SATA 62; TCWW 1, 2
Wither, George 1588-1667 .... **LC 96**
  See also DLB 121; RGEL 2
Witkacy
  See Witkiewicz, Stanislaw Ignacy
Witkiewicz, Stanislaw Ignacy
    1885-1939 .... **TCLC 8**
  See also CA 105; 162; CDWLB 4; DLB 215; EW 10; EWL 3; RGWL 2, 3; SFW 4
Wittgenstein, Ludwig (Josef Johann)
    1889-1951 .... **TCLC 59**
  See also CA 113; 164; DLB 262; MTCW 2
Wittig, Monique 1935-2003 .... **CLC 22**
  See also CA 116; 135; 212; CANR 143; CWW 2; DLB 83; EWL 3; FW; GLL 1
Wittlin, Jozef 1896-1976 .... **CLC 25**
  See also CA 49-52; 65-68; CANR 3; EWL 3
Wodehouse, P(elham) G(renville)
    1881-1975 . **CLC 1, 2, 5, 10, 22; SSC 2; TCLC 108**
  See also AAYA 65; AITN 2; BRWS 3; CA 45-48; 57-60; CANR 3, 33; CDBLB 1914-1945; DAC; DAM NOV; DLB 34, 162; EWL 3; MTCW 1, 2; MTFW 2005; RGEL 2; RGSF 2; SATA 22; SSFS 10
Woiwode, L.
  See Woiwode, Larry (Alfred)
Woiwode, Larry (Alfred) 1941- ... **CLC 6, 10**
  See also CA 73-76; CANR 16, 94; CN 3, 4, 5, 6, 7; DLB 6; INT CANR-16

Wojciechowska, Maia (Teresa)
    1927-2002 .... **CLC 26**
  See also AAYA 8, 46; BYA 3; CA 9-12R, 183; 209; CAAE 183; CANR 4, 41; CLR 1; JRDA; MAICYA 1, 2; SAAS 1; SATA 1, 28, 83; SATA-Essay 104; SATA-Obit 134; YAW
Wojtyla, Karol (Jozef)
  See John Paul II, Pope
Wojtyla, Karol (Josef)
  See John Paul II, Pope
Wolf, Christa 1929- .... **CLC 14, 29, 58, 150**
  See also CA 85-88; CANR 45, 123; CD-WLB 2; CWW 2; DLB 75; EWL 3; FW; MTCW 1; RGWL 2, 3; SSFS 14
Wolf, Naomi 1962- .... **CLC 157**
  See also CA 141; CANR 110; FW; MTFW 2005
Wolfe, Gene 1931- .... **CLC 25**
  See also AAYA 35; CA 57-60; CAAS 9; CANR 6, 32, 60; CPW; DAM POP; DLB 8; FANT; MTCW 2; MTFW 2005; SATA 118, 165; SCFW 2; SFW 4; SUFW 2
Wolfe, Gene Rodman
  See Wolfe, Gene
Wolfe, George C. 1954- .... **BLCS; CLC 49**
  See also CA 149; CAD; CD 5, 6
Wolfe, Thomas (Clayton)
    1900-1938 ...... **SSC 33; TCLC 4, 13, 29, 61; WLC**
  See also AMW; BPFB 3; CA 104; 132; CANR 102; CDALB 1929-1941; DA; DA3; DAB; DAC; DAM MST, NOV; DLB 9, 102, 229; DLBD 2, 16; DLBY 1985, 1997; EWL 3; MAL 5; MTCW 1, 2; NFS 18; RGAL 4; SSFS 18; TUS
Wolfe, Thomas Kennerly, Jr.
    1931- .... **CLC 147**
  See Wolfe, Tom
  See also CA 13-16R; CANR 9, 33, 70, 104; DA3; DAM POP; DLB 185; EWL 3; INT CANR-9; MTCW 1, 2; MTFW 2005; TUS
Wolfe, Tom .... **CLC 1, 2, 9, 15, 35, 51**
  See Wolfe, Thomas Kennerly, Jr.
  See also AAYA 8, 67; AITN 2; AMWS 3; BEST 89:1; BPFB 3; CN 5, 6, 7; CPW; CSW; DLB 152; LAIT 5; RGAL 4
Wolff, Geoffrey (Ansell) 1937- .... **CLC 41**
  See also CA 29-32R; CANR 29, 43, 78
Wolff, Sonia
  See Levitin, Sonia (Wolff)
Wolff, Tobias (Jonathan Ansell)
    1945- .... **CLC 39, 64, 172; SSC 63**
  See also AAYA 16; AMWS 7; BEST 90:2; BYA 12; CA 114; 117; CAAS 22; CANR 54, 76, 96; CN 5, 6, 7; CSW; DA3; DLB 130; EWL 3; INT CA-117; MTCW 2; MTFW 2005; RGAL 4; RGSF 2; SSFS 4, 11
Wolfram von Eschenbach c. 1170-c.
    1220 .... **CMLC 5**
  See Eschenbach, Wolfram von
  See also CDWLB 2; DLB 138; EW 1; RGWL 2
Wolitzer, Hilma 1930- .... **CLC 17**
  See also CA 65-68; CANR 18, 40; INT CANR-18; SATA 31; YAW
Wollstonecraft, Mary 1759-1797 .... **LC 5, 50, 90**
  See also BRWS 3; CDBLB 1789-1832; DLB 39, 104, 158, 252; FL 1:1; FW; LAIT 1; RGEL 2; TEA; WLIT 3
Wonder, Stevie .... **CLC 12**
  See Morris, Steveland Judkins
Wong, Jade Snow 1922- .... **CLC 17**
  See also CA 109; CANR 91; SATA 112
Woodberry, George Edward
    1855-1930 .... **TCLC 73**
  See also CA 165; DLB 71, 103

Woodcott, Keith
  See Brunner, John (Kilian Houston)
Woodruff, Robert W.
  See Mencken, H(enry) L(ouis)
Woolf, (Adeline) Virginia 1882-1941 .. **SSC 7, 79; TCLC 1, 5, 20, 43, 56, 101, 123, 128; WLC**
  See also AAYA 44; BPFB 3; BRW 7; BRWC 2; BRWR 1; CA 104; 130; CANR 64, 132; CDBLB 1914-1945; DA; DA3; DAB; DAC; DAM MST, NOV; DLB 36, 100, 162; DLBD 10; EWL 3; EXPS; FL 1:6; FW; LAIT 3; LATS 1:1; LMFS 2; MTCW 1, 2; MTFW 2005; NCFS 2; NFS 8, 12; RGEL 2; RGSF 2; SSFS 4, 12; TEA; WLIT 4
Woollcott, Alexander (Humphreys)
    1887-1943 .... **TCLC 5**
  See also CA 105; 161; DLB 29
Woolrich, Cornell .... **CLC 77**
  See Hopley-Woolrich, Cornell George
  See also MSW
Woolson, Constance Fenimore
    1840-1894 .... **NCLC 82**
  See also DLB 12, 74, 189, 221; RGAL 4
Wordsworth, Dorothy 1771-1855 . **NCLC 25, 138**
  See also DLB 107
Wordsworth, William 1770-1850 .. **NCLC 12, 38, 111; PC 4, 67; WLC**
  See also BRW 4; BRWC 1; CDBLB 1789-1832; DA; DA3; DAB; DAC; DAM MST, POET; DLB 93, 107; EXPP; LATS 1:1; LMFS 1; PAB; PFS 2; RGEL 2; TEA; WLIT 3; WP
Wotton, Sir Henry 1568-1639 .... **LC 68**
  See also DLB 121; RGEL 2
Wouk, Herman 1915- .... **CLC 1, 9, 38**
  See also BPFB 2, 3; CA 5-8R; CANR 6, 33, 67, 146; CDALBS; CN 1, 2, 3, 4, 5, 6; CPW; DA3; DAM NOV, POP; DLBY 1982; INT CANR-6; LAIT 4; MAL 5; MTCW 1, 2; MTFW 2005; NFS 7; TUS
Wright, Charles (Penzel, Jr.) 1935- .. **CLC 6, 13, 28, 119, 146**
  See also AMWS 5; CA 29-32R; CAAS 7; CANR 23, 36, 62, 88, 135; CP 3, 4, 5, 6, 7; DLB 165; DLBY 1982; EWL 3; MTCW 1, 2; MTFW 2005; PFS 10
Wright, Charles Stevenson 1932- ..... **BLC 3; CLC 49**
  See also BW 1; CA 9-12R; CANR 26; CN 1, 2, 3, 4, 5, 6, 7; DAM MULT, POET; DLB 33
Wright, Frances 1795-1852 .... **NCLC 74**
  See also DLB 73
Wright, Frank Lloyd 1867-1959 .... **TCLC 95**
  See also AAYA 33; CA 174
Wright, Jack R.
  See Harris, Mark
Wright, James (Arlington)
    1927-1980 .... **CLC 3, 5, 10, 28; PC 36**
  See also AITN 2; AMWS 3; CA 49-52; 97-100; CANR 4, 34, 64; CDALBS; CP 1, 2; DAM POET; DLB 5, 169; EWL 3; EXPP; MAL 5; MTCW 1, 2; MTFW 2005; PFS 7, 8; RGAL 4; TUS; WP
Wright, Judith (Arundell)
    1915-2000 .... **CLC 11, 53; PC 14**
  See also CA 13-16R; 188; CANR 31, 76, 93; CP 1, 2, 3, 4, 5, 6, 7; CWP; DLB 260; EWL 3; MTCW 1, 2; MTFW 2005; PFS 8; RGEL 2; SATA 14; SATA-Obit 121
Wright, L(aurali) R. 1939- .... **CLC 44**
  See also CA 138; CMW 4
Wright, Richard (Nathaniel)
    1908-1960 ... **BLC 3; CLC 1, 3, 4, 9, 14, 21, 48, 74; SSC 2; TCLC 136; WLC**
  See also AAYA 5, 42; AFAW 1, 2; AMW; BPFB 3; BW 1; BYA 2; CA 108; CANR 64; CDALB 1929-1941; DA; DA3; DAB;

Zelazny, Roger (Joseph) 1937-1995 . **CLC 21**
　　See also AAYA 7, 68; BPFB 3; CA 21-24R;
　　148; CANR 26, 60; CN 6; DLB 8; FANT;
　　MTCW 1, 2; MTFW 2005; SATA 57;
　　SATA-Brief 39; SCFW 1, 2; SFW 4;
　　SUFW 1, 2
Zhang Ailing
　　See Chang, Eileen
　　See also CWW 2; RGSF 2
Zhdanov, Andrei Alexandrovich
　　1896-1948 .... **TCLC 18**
　　See also CA 117; 167
Zhukovsky, Vasilii Andreevich
　　See Zhukovsky, Vasily (Andreevich)
　　See also DLB 205
Zhukovsky, Vasily (Andreevich)
　　1783-1852 .... **NCLC 35**
　　See Zhukovsky, Vasilii Andreevich
Ziegenhagen, Eric .... **CLC 55**
Zimmer, Jill Schary
　　See Robinson, Jill
Zimmerman, Robert
　　See Dylan, Bob
Zindel, Paul 1936-2003 ...... **CLC 6, 26; DC 5**
　　See also AAYA 2, 37; BYA 2, 3, 8, 11, 14;
　　CA 73-76; 213; CAD; CANR 31, 65, 108;
　　CD 5, 6; CDALBS; CLR 3, 45, 85; DA;

DA3; DAB; DAC; DAM DRAM, MST,
NOV; DFS 12; DLB 7, 52; JRDA; LAIT
5; MAICYA 1, 2; MTCW 1, 2; MTFW
2005; NFS 14; SATA 16, 58, 102; SATA-
Obit 142; WYA; YAW
Zinn, Howard 1922- .... **CLC 199**
　　See also CA 1-4R; CANR 2, 33, 90
Zinov'Ev, A. A.
　　See Zinoviev, Alexander (Aleksandrovich)
Zinov'ev, Aleksandr (Aleksandrovich)
　　See Zinoviev, Alexander (Aleksandrovich)
　　See also DLB 302
Zinoviev, Alexander (Aleksandrovich)
　　1922- .... **CLC 19**
　　See Zinov'ev, Aleksandr (Aleksandrovich)
　　See also CA 116; 133; CAAS 10
Zizek, Slavoj 1949- .... **CLC 188**
　　See also CA 201; MTFW 2005
Zoilus
　　See Lovecraft, H(oward) P(hillips)
Zola, Emile (Edouard Charles Antoine)
　　1840-1902 ...... **TCLC 1, 6, 21, 41; WLC**
　　See also CA 104; 138; DA; DA3; DAB;
　　DAC; DAM MST, NOV; DLB 123; EW
　　7; GFL 1789 to the Present; IDTP; LMFS
　　1, 2; RGWL 2; TWA

Zoline, Pamela 1941- .... **CLC 62**
　　See also CA 161; SFW 4
Zoroaster 628(?)B.C.-551(?)B.C. ... **CMLC 40**
Zorrilla y Moral, Jose 1817-1893 .... **NCLC 6**
Zoshchenko, Mikhail (Mikhailovich)
　　1895-1958 .... **SSC 15; TCLC 15**
　　See also CA 115; 160; EWL 3; RGSF 2;
　　RGWL 3
Zuckmayer, Carl 1896-1977 .... **CLC 18**
　　See also CA 69-72; DLB 56, 124; EWL 3;
　　RGWL 2, 3
Zuk, Georges
　　See Skelton, Robin
　　See also CCA 1
Zukofsky, Louis 1904-1978 ... **CLC 1, 2, 4, 7,
　　11, 18; PC 11**
　　See also AMWS 3; CA 9-12R; 77-80;
　　CANR 39; CP 1, 2; DAM POET; DLB 5,
　　165; EWL 3; MAL 5; MTCW 1; RGAL 4
Zweig, Paul 1935-1984 .... **CLC 34, 42**
　　See also CA 85-88; 113
Zweig, Stefan 1881-1942 .... **TCLC 17**
　　See also CA 112; 170; DLB 81, 118; EWL
　　3
Zwingli, Huldreich 1484-1531 .... **LC 37**
　　See also DLB 179

Literary Criticism Series
Cumulative Topic Index

This index lists all topic entries in Gale's *Children's Literature Review* (CLR), *Classical and Medieval Literature Criticism* (CMLC), *Contemporary Literary Criticism* (CLC), *Drama Criticism* (DC), *Literature Criticism from 1400 to 1800* (LC), *Nineteenth-Century Literature Criticism* (NCLC), *Short Story Criticism* (SSC), and *Twentieth-Century Literary Criticism* (TCLC). The index also lists topic entries in the Gale Critical Companion Collection, which includes the following publications: *The Beat Generation* (BG), and *Harlem Renaissance* (HR).

Topic Index

Topic Index

LC Cumulative Nationality Index

Nationality Index

LC-123 Title Index

ISBN 0-7876-8740-5

9 780787 687403

90000